Freedom in the World
2013

The findings of *Freedom in the World 2013* include events from January 1, 2012, through December 31, 2012.

Freedom in the World 2013
The Annual Survey of
Political Rights & Civil Liberties

Arch Puddington
General Editor

Aili Piano
Managing Editor

Jennifer Dunham, Bret Nelson, Tyler Roylance
Associate Editors

Freedom House • New York, NY and Washington, DC
Rowman & Littlefield Publishers, Inc. • Lanham, Boulder,
New York, Toronto, Oxford

ROWMAN & LITTLEFIELD PUBLISHERS, INC.

Published in the United States of America
by Rowman & Littlefield Publishers, Inc.
A wholly owned subsidary of The Rowman & Littlefield Publishing Group, Inc.
4501 Forbes Boulevard, Suite 200, Lanham, Maryland 20706
www.rowmanlittlefield.com

Estover Road, Plymouth PL6 7PY, United Kingdom

British Library Cataloguing in Publication Information Available

Library of Congress Cataloging-in-Publication Data

Freedom in the world / —1978–
New York : Freedom House, 1978–
v. : map; 25 cm.—(Freedom House Book)
Annual.
ISSN 0732-6610=Freedom in the World.
1. Civil rights—Periodicals. I. R. Adrian Karatnycky, et al. I. Series.
JC571 .F66 323.4'05—dc 19 82-642048
AACR 2   MARC-S
Library of Congress [84101]

ISBN: 978-1-4422-0121-7 (cloth : alk. paper)
ISBN: 978-1-4422-0122-4 (pbk : alk. paper)
ISBN: 978-1-4422-0123-1 (electronic)
ISSN: 0732-6610

Printed in the United States of America

The paper used in this publication meets the minimum requirements of American National Standard for Information Sciences—Permanence of Paper for Printed Library Materials, ANSI/NISO Z39.48-1992.

Contents

Acknowledgments

Freedom in the World 2013 could not have been completed without the contributions of numerous Freedom House staff members and consultants. The section titled "The Survey Team" contains a detailed list of the writers and advisers without whose efforts this project would not have been possible.

Aili Piano served as the project director for this year's survey. Jennifer Dunham, Morgan Huston, Bret Nelson, and Tyler Roylance provided extensive research, analytical, editorial, and administrative assistance, and Zselyke Csaky, Rafaela Fischman, Mark Keller, Marissa Miller, and Andrew Rizzardi provided additional research and administrative support. Ronald Eniclerico, Alexandra Kendall, Lynn Messina, and Shannon O'Toole served as additional country report editors. Overall guidance for the project was provided by David J. Kramer, president of Freedom House, and Arch Puddington, vice president for research. A number of Freedom House staff offered valuable additional input on the country reports and/or ratings process

Freedom House would like to acknowledge the generous financial support for *Freedom in the World* by The Lynde and Harry Bradley Foundation, Smith Richardson Foundation, Lilly Endowment, F. M. Kirby Foundation, and the Freedom House Board of Trustees.

Freedom in the World 2013
Democratic Breakthroughs in the Balance

Arch Puddington

As the year 2012 drew to a close, events in the Middle East dramatized two competing trends: demands for change pushed forward by popular democratic movements, and an authoritarian response that combines intransigence with strategic adaptability.

The ambiguous nature of these developments, combined with either instability or authoritarian retrenchment in other regions, had a significant impact on the state of global freedom. The findings of *Freedom in the World 2013*, the latest edition of Freedom House's annual report on political rights and civil liberties, showed that more countries registered declines than exhibited gains over the course of 2012. This marks the seventh consecutive year in which countries with declines outnumbered those with improvements. Yet the number of countries ranked as Free increased by three, and now stands at 90, suggesting that the overall ferment includes a potential for progress as well as deterioration.

Developments in Egypt in particular encapsulated a pattern in which gains for freedom in the Middle East and North Africa (MENA) were threatened by opposition from governments, security forces, ruling families, or religiously based political factions. In Egypt, the year was notable for a flawed but competitive presidential election, the withdrawal of the military from its self-appointed political supremacy, and a continued assertiveness by popular movements in the face of antidemocratic threats. Despite the energy of civil society and the shift to civilian rule, however, the country was confronted by daunting problems, experiencing at various times a campaign to hobble foreign and local nongovernmental organizations (NGOs), the dissolution of an elected parliament by the judiciary, a faulty process to draft a new constitution, resistance to change by entrenched elites, and a power grab by newly elected president Mohamed Morsi that was only partially thwarted by mass protests. Finally, at year's end, the state prosecutor announced plans to investigate leading opposition figures on charges of treason, and political commentators for alleged defamation.

As in the world at large, more countries in the MENA region endured declines than made gains in their drive toward freedom in 2012. Aspirations for elections and accountable government were often fiercely suppressed through arrests, imprisonment, police violence, and in Syria, a murderous war waged by the state against its own people. However, there is reason to remain cautiously optimistic about the region's future. Events in Tunisia and Libya, where popular uprisings before and after Egypt's had also expelled longtime dictators in early 2011, were generally positive in 2012, even if each encountered challenges and setbacks. Moreover, the societal impulse to shake off autocratic rule, pervasive injustice, and rampant corruption has clearly spread from Tunisia, Libya, and Egypt to neighboring countries.

Much will depend on the commitment to democracy of the Muslim Brotherhood and other Islamist groups that now or may soon find themselves in positions of power. But the past year has provided more evidence that Middle Eastern countries long subject to the dictator's heel are quickly developing resilient and informed civil societies willing to push back against attempts to curb freedom of expression and thought, distort the electoral process, or concentrate power in the hands of military or religious authorities. In this context, factions or governments that seek to reduce freedom could find it increasingly difficult to do so.

Meanwhile, the world's most powerful authoritarian leaders have watched events in the Middle East with concern. The findings of *Freedom in the World* point to a stepped-up drive by authoritarian governments in other regions to weaken precisely the elements of democratic governance that pose the most serious threats to repressive and corrupt rule: independent civil society groups, a free press, and the rule of law. Indeed, a five-year set of comparative data show that while the indicators related to competitive elections and political pluralism declined slightly or actually improved on a global scale between 2008 and 2012, there were notable declines for freedom of the press and expression, freedom of assembly and the rights of NGOs, an independent judiciary, and equal protection under the law. Of particular concern is the ongoing campaign in Russia, Venezuela, Iran, and elsewhere to thwart those NGOs whose work is deemed to be political in nature. This can include activism in a wide range of fields, including opposing censorship, environmental protection, women's rights, gay rights, anticorruption efforts, and fair treatment for minorities.

Such repressive campaigns were especially apparent in Eurasia, where a number of already grim settings grew even more constrained. Russia took a decided turn for the worse after Vladimir Putin's return to the presidency. Having already marginalized the formal political opposition, he pushed through a series of laws meant to squelch a burgeoning societal opposition. The measures imposed severe new penalties on unauthorized political demonstrations, restricted the ability of NGOs to raise funds and conduct their work, and placed new controls on the internet.

Among other Eurasian countries, Kazakhstan, Tajikistan, and Ukraine were evaluated as less free than in the previous year, while Azerbaijan, Uzbekistan, Turkmenistan, and Belarus remained some of the world's most repressive states. This dismal record was partially offset by peaceful, competitive elections in Armenia and Georgia. Yet even Georgia, which experienced its first orderly transfer of power to the opposition through democratic elections, finished the year on a less than satisfying note after the new government quickly arrested some 30 officials of the previous government, raising concerns about politically motivated prosecutions.

In China, hopes for meaningful political reform were dealt a serious blow with the selection of a new Communist Party leadership team, whose members have generally built their careers on hard-line policies. As if to emphasize the point that the new leaders are unlikely to usher in an era of political liberalization, the government has taken steps in the last two months to reinforce internet censorship and surveillance. As in the Middle East, developments in Africa reflected a combination of gains and declines, a great deal of volatility, and a disturbing escalation in armed

Freedom in the World—2013 Survey

The population of the world as estimated in mid-2012 was 7,036.9 million persons, who reside in 195 sovereign states. The level of political rights and civil liberties as shown comparatively by the *Freedom House* survey is:

Free: 3,046.2 million (43 percent of the world's population) live in 90 of the states.

Partly Free: 1,613.9 million (23 percent of the world's population) live in 58 of the states.

Not Free: 2,376.8 million (34 percent of the world's population) live in 47 of the states.

A Record of the Survey (population in millions)

Year under Review	FREE	PARTLY FREE	NOT FREE	WORLD POPULATION
Mid-1992	1,352.2 (24.83%)	2,403.3 (44.11%)	1,690.4 (31.06%)	5,446.0
Mid-1993	1,046.2 (19.00%)	2,224.4 (40.41%)	2,234.6 (40.59%)	5,505.2
Mid-1994	1,119.7 (19.97%)	2,243.4 (40.01%)	2,243.9 (40.02%)	5,607.0
Mid-1995	1,114.5 (19.55%)	2,365.8 (41.49%)	2,221.2 (38.96%)	5,701.5
Mid-1996	1,250.3 (21.67%)	2,260.1 (39.16%)	2,260.6 (39.17%)	5,771.0
Mid-1997	1,266.0 (21.71%)	2,281.9 (39.12%)	2,284.6 (39.17%)	5,832.5
Mid-1998	2,354.0 (39.84%)	1,570.6 (26.59%)	1,984.1 (33.58%)	5,908.7
Mid-1999	2,324.9 (38.90%)	1,529.0 (25.58%)	2,122.4 (35.51%)	5,976.3
Mid-2000	2,465.2 (40.69%)	1,435.8 (23.70%)	2,157.5 (35.61%)	6,058.5
Mid-2001	2,500.7 (40.79%)	1,462.9 (23.86%)	2,167.1 (35.35%)	6,130.7
Mid-2002	2,717.6 (43.85%)	1,293.1 (20.87%)	2,186.3 (35.28%)	6,197.0
Mid-2003	2,780.1 (44.03%)	1,324.0 (20.97%)	2,209.9 (35.00%)	6,314.0
Mid-2004	2,819.1 (44.08%)	1,189.0 (18.59%)	2,387.3 (37.33%)	6,395.4
Mid-2005	2,968.8 (45.97%)	1,157.7 (17.93%)	2,331.2 (36.10%)	6,457.7
Mid-2006	3,005.0 (46.00%)	1,083.2 (17.00%)	2,448.6 (37.00%)	6,536.8
Mid-2007	3,028.2 (45.85%)	1,185.3 (17.94%)	2,391.4 (36.21%)	6,604.9
Mid-2008	3,055.9 (45.73%)	1,351.0 (20.21%)	2,276.3 (34.06%)	6,683.2
Mid-2009	3,088.7 (45.49%)	1,367.4 (20.14%)	2,333.9 (34.37%)	6,790.0
Mid-2010	2,952.0 (42.95%)	1,487.0 (21.63%)	2,434.3 (35.42%)	6,873.3
Mid-2011	3,016.6 (43.30%)	1,497.4 (21.49%)	2,453.2 (35.21%)	6,967.2
Mid-2012	3,046.2 (43.29%)	1,613.9 (22.93%)	2,376.8 (33.78%)	7,039.9

* The large shift in the population figure between 1997 and 1998 is due to India's change in status from Partly Free to Free.

conflicts. Rebel groups threatened to overrun government forces in the Democratic Republic of the Congo and the Central African Republic. Mali, a country with a reputation as a model African democracy, was battered by a reinvigorated Tuareg rebellion, a military coup that overthrew the elected government, and the seizure of its northern provinces by Islamist militants whose crude imitation of Islamic law helped to drive hundreds of thousands of inhabitants into neighboring countries. And in northern Nigeria, the Boko Haram sect has prosecuted a reign of terror that targets Christians, government officials, and security forces. Nevertheless, Africa also accounted for three of the four countries that moved from Partly Free to Free in 2012, highlighting the continent's remarkable diversity of political environments.

FREEDOM'S TRAJECTORY IN 2012

The number of countries exhibiting gains for the past year, 16, lagged behind the number with declines, 28. The most noteworthy gains were in Egypt, Libya, Burma, and Côte d'Ivoire. While the Middle East experienced some of the most significant improvements, it also registered major declines, with a list of worsening countries that includes Iraq, Jordan, Kuwait, Lebanon, Oman, Syria, and the United Arab Emirates. Declines were also noted in a number of countries in Eurasia and sub-Saharan Africa.

An assessment of the *Freedom in the World* indicators over the past five years shows the greatest gains in the Asia-Pacific and MENA regions, and the most pronounced declines in sub-Saharan Africa. The Eurasia subregion registered the lowest scores for political rights, while MENA had the worst scores for civil liberties categories. The Hispanic America subregion also saw declines in most indicators, especially in the civil liberties categories.

MAJOR DEVELOPMENTS AND TRENDS INCLUDE:

- **Volatility in West Africa:** This section of Africa saw major declines in Mali, which experienced both a military coup and the takeover of its northern section by Islamist militants, and Guinea-Bissau, which has increasingly come to resemble a military narcostate. At the same time, there were important gains. Côte d'Ivoire, which was only recently riven by internal conflict, moved from Not Free to Partly Free due to the peaceful inauguration of a new parliament and the adoption of laws on transparency and corruption. Guinea showed steady improvements in freedom of belief, freedom of association, and the right to own property or engage in private business. Senegal moved from Partly Free to Free owing to free and fair presidential and parliamentary elections that resulted in a peaceful rotation of power, as well as nascent efforts by the president to increase government accountability and transparency. Sierra Leone moved from Partly Free to Free as a result of a free, fair, and peaceful presidential election in November.

- **Gulf States Retreat:** The past several years, and the past year in particular, have featured a steady decline in democratic institutions and in some cases an increase in repressive policies among the Persian Gulf states. Kuwait's political rights rating declined due to a parliamentary crisis and the government's attempts to undermine the political opposition by revising the electoral law. Oman lost ground due to the ongoing arrests of human rights and reform activists, and the increased suppression of free expression in online forums. The United Arab Emirates was downgraded due to stepped-up arrests of activists, lawyers, and judges calling for political reform; the passage of a highly restrictive internet law that punishes online activism and free expression; and the dismissal and deportation of academics who were critical of government policies. For a second year, Bahrain systematically persecuted opposition activists, handing out extremely lengthy prison sentences in some instances. In addition to continuing its domestic repression, Saudi Arabia has sent security forces to help quell protests in Bahrain and provided assistance to other governments and parties in the region to counter the influence of democratic countries.

- **Civil Liberties at Risk in Turkey:** During his early years in power, Prime Minister Recep Tayyip Erdogan pushed through important reforms that enshrined civilian rule, enhanced fairness at the polls, and made halting steps toward greater minority rights. More recently, however, his government has jailed hundreds of journalists, academics, opposition party officials, and military officers in a series of prosecutions aimed at alleged conspiracies against the state and Kurdish organizations. Turkey currently leads the world in the number of journalists behind bars, and democracy advocates are expressing deep concern for the state of press freedom and the rule of law.

• **Muslim-on-Muslim Violence:** The persecution and killing of Muslims by other Muslims on supposed religious grounds reached horrifying levels in Pakistan, and remained a serious problem in Iraq and elsewhere. Sufis and Shiites were the most frequent victims, but members of other sects, local medical workers, advocates for women and girls, and human rights defenders were also targeted. The growing presence in the Syrian opposition of fighters from radical Sunni groups may pose a serious obstacle to the creation of a democratic and pluralistic society after the end of the current conflict.

RESULTS FOR 2012

The number of countries designated by *Freedom in the World* as Free in 2012 stood at 90, representing 46 percent of the world's 195 polities and 3,046,158,000 people—43 percent of the global population. The number of Free countries increased by three from the previous year's survey.

The number of countries qualifying as Partly Free stood at 58, or 30 percent of all countries assessed by the survey, and they were home to 1,613,858,500 people, or 23 percent of the world's total. The number of Partly Free countries declined by two from the previous year.

A total of 47 countries were deemed Not Free, representing 24 percent of the world's polities. The number of people living under Not Free conditions stood at 2,376,822,100, or 34 percent of the global population, though it is important to note that more than half of this number lives in just one country: China. The number of Not Free countries declined by one from 2011.

The number of electoral democracies stood at 118, the same as for 2011. Two countries, Georgia and Libya, achieved electoral democracy status, while two were dropped from the category, Mali and the Maldives.

Four countries moved from Partly Free to Free: Lesotho, Senegal, Sierra Leone, and Tonga. Three countries rose

The Global Trend

Year Under Review	Free	Partly Free	Not Free
1982	52	56	58
1992	75	73	38
2002	89	55	48
2012	90	58	47

Tracking Electoral Democracy

Year Under Review	Number of Electoral Democracies
2002	121
2007	121
2012	118

from Not Free to Partly Free: Côte d'Ivoire, Egypt, and Libya. Mali fell two tiers, from Free to Not Free, and Guinea-Bissau dropped from Partly Free to Not Free.

MIDDLE EAST AND NORTH AFRICA: DEMOCRATIC GAINS AMID INTENSIFIED REPRESSION

In a region notable for sectarian polarization, civil strife, and repressive autocracies, freedom scored some grudging but nonetheless impressive gains in 2012. Indeed, despite predictions that the initial accomplishments of the Arab Spring would fall victim to the Middle East's perennial antidemocratic currents, Tunisia retained the gains of the previous year, which had transformed the country from a showcase for Arab autocracy into an electoral democracy, whose leaders have pledged themselves to moderation, civil liberties, and the rule of law. There were, of course, challenges to the new order. The constitutional drafting process was delayed amid disagreement, a faltering economy and high unemployment threatened to undermine popular support for elected government, and Salafi Muslim forces demanded adherence to their beliefs, sometimes using violence to punish perceived vices. Nevertheless, the advances of the previous year by and large held firm.

Another relative success story in the MENA region is Libya. Having ranked among the world's worst tyrannies for decades, the country scored major gains in 2012, especially in the political rights categories, and is now ranked as Partly Free. Libya continues to suffer from a lack of clear government control over many parts of its territory, a problem that is compounded by the actions of autonomous local militias and radical Islamists. But in defiance of forecasts of chaos and failure, the country held successful elections for a General National Congress that included candidates from a range of regional and political backgrounds, while free expression and civic activity continued to grow.

Egypt also moved from Not Free to Partly Free, though it experienced jarring setbacks at different points during the year. Thus, while the presidential election was regarded as having met most international standards, it took place after a number of leading contenders had been disqualified. In November, President Morsi proclaimed his right to rule without judicial oversight as part of a bid to push through a new constitution, only to step back incrementally in the face of street protests. Critics warned that the constitution, which was ultimately approved in a flawed referendum process, included provisions that could be interpreted to justify restrictions on freedom of expression and other fundamental rights. While the media featured criticism of government policies that would have been unthinkable during the Mubarak period, there were efforts to prosecute journalists and commentators for insulting the president or other authorities. Clearly, the future of the Middle East will depend in significant ways on the success of Egypt's democratic experiment, which in turn rests at least in part on the ruling Islamists' commitment to democratic norms. In light of the past year's developments, the outcome remains very much an open question.

Syria has suffered by far the worst repercussions from the Arab Spring. In 2011, the regime of President Bashar al-Assad responded to peaceful demands for political change by waging war against his own people. In 2012, amid inaction by the international community, the bloody conflict developed starker sectarian overtones and drew in fighters affiliated with al-Qaeda and other terrorist groups.

Sectarian conflict also plagued Lebanon and Iraq during the year. Lebanon faced a deterioration in the security environment and increasing attacks and restrictions on journalists, activists, and refugees as different groups took sides in the Syrian conflict. Iraq's political rights rating declined due to the concentration of power in the hands of Prime Minister Nouri al-Maliki and growing pressure on the opposition, as exemplified by the arrest and death sentence in absentia of Vice President Tariq al-Hashimi, the country's most senior Sunni Arab politician. Separately, Jordan registered a decline in freedom of assembly due to the repression of protests against a new electoral law and the lack of meaningful political reform.

Iran's government stepped up its repression of journalists and bloggers, civil society activists, academics, and minorities in 2012, including through extrajudicial detentions. The number of executions continued to be among the highest in the world, with the death penalty applied for a range of political and social offenses. Among the most egregious cases, four Iranian Arab prisoners accused of terrorist activity were executed in June following a closed-door trial, and critical blogger Sattar Beheshti died in police custody in November. Parliamentary elections held in March, which fell far short of international standards, further entrenched supporters of supreme leader Ayatollah Ali Khamenei and ushered in a new generation of hardliners, all of whom were considered opponents of President Mahmoud Ahmadinejad.

Israel remains the region's only Free country. In recent years, controversies have surrounded proposed laws that threatened freedom of expression and the rights of civil society organizations. In most cases, however, these measures have either been quashed by the government or parliament, or struck down by the Supreme Court. Israeli politics have also been roiled by an escalating controversy over the role of ultra-Orthodox Jews and their positions on issues such as military service and gender equality.

SUB-SAHARAN AFRICA: COUPS AND CONFLICT OVERSHADOW ELECTORAL SUCCESSES

In recent years, sub-Saharan Africa has ranked as the world's most politically volatile region, with major democratic breakthroughs in some countries and coups, civil strife, and authoritarian crackdowns in others. Over the past five years, scores for all seven topical categories measured in *Freedom in the World* showed decline, with substantial downgrades for those that fall under the umbrella of civil liberties. This pattern continued in 2012. While the region saw several significant gains, especially in West Africa, civil conflicts and the emergence in some countries of violent Islamist groups prevented an overall upgrade for political freedom.

Three countries moved from Partly Free to Free: Lesotho, Sierra Leone, and Senegal. Lesotho's political rights indicators improved, because despite preelection violence, it held free and fair parliamentary elections that resulted in a peaceful rotation of power. Senegal, after political tension and uncertainty in 2011, also experienced a peaceful power transfer through presidential and parliamentary elections, and benefited from nascent efforts by the new president to increase government accountability and transparency. Sierra Leone, 10 years after the end of a brutal civil war, successfully completed its own free and fair national elections, during which reformed electoral institutions operated with transparency and demonstrated the ability to function without undue influence from the international community.

Côte d'Ivoire showed substantial improvement just a year after a violent civil conflict, moving from Not Free to Partly Free. Two other countries, Guinea and Malawi, also showed gains. In Guinea there was evidence of steady improvements in religious freedom, the rights of local and international NGOs, and the climate for small businesses and private enterprise. Malawi underwent a peaceful power transfer to new president Joyce Banda, which was followed by an easing of repression, including improvements in academic freedom and freedom of assembly.

Unfortunately, these impressive advances were more than offset by a series of declines, several of which derived from civil conflict. Mali suffered one of the greatest single-year declines in the history of *Freedom in the World*, dropping precipitously from Free to Not Free. Nigeria, another country plagued by Islamist militants, suffered a less dramatic decline, as did the Central African Republic, which at year's end risked being conquered by a rebel group. Guinea-Bissau's status declined from Partly Free to Not Free due to an April military coup, which entailed the removal of the interim president, the suspension of the national legislature, the halting of the electoral process, and increased repression of civil liberties. The Gambia's civil liberties rating declined due to the absence of due process for defendants, as exhibited by the execution of nine prisoners who had no access to lawyers and without notification of their families.

In East and Southern Africa, notable declines were seen in Kenya, Uganda, and Madagascar. Kenya's civil liberties rating dropped as a result of increased ethnic and religious tensions and incidents of violence throughout the country in advance of the 2013 elections. These problems were driven in part by the heavy-handed counterterrorism efforts of the domestic security forces since Kenya's incursion into neighboring Somalia in late 2010. Uganda continued its recent downward trend, with increased harassment of the opposition and a campaign to obstruct and shut down NGOs that focus on sensitive issues such as gay rights, corruption, term limits, and land rights. Madagascar registered a decline due to increasing repression and both physical and economic insecurity caused by ongoing political instability that began with a 2009 coup. South Africa suffered a decline in freedom of association, stemming from deadly police confrontations with striking mine workers, and the advancement of the Protection of State Information Bill through the parliament raised concerns about media freedom and access to information.

CENTRAL AND EASTERN EUROPE/EURASIA: RETURN OF THE IRON FIST IN RUSSIA

The return of Vladimir Putin to the Russian presidency ushered in a new period of accelerated repression. Since his inauguration in May, Putin has moved in a calculated way to stifle independent political and civic activity, pushing through a series of laws meant to restrict public protest, limit the work of NGOs, and inhibit free expression on the internet. The regime also forced the U.S. Agency for International Development (USAID) to end its work in Russia, and has severely hampered the ability of foreign broadcasters to reach the Russian audience. At year's end, in retaliation for a U.S. law imposing visa and asset restrictions on Russian human rights abusers, Putin signed a ban on the adoption of Russian orphans by families in the United States.

With Russia setting the tone, Eurasia (consisting of the countries of the former Soviet Union minus the Baltic states) now rivals the Middle East as one of the most repressive areas on the globe. Indeed, Eurasia is in many respects the world's least free subregion, given the entrenchment of autocrats in most of its 12 countries.

The authoritarian temptation poses a threat even in Eurasian countries with recent histories of dynamic, if erratic, democratic governance. Thus Ukraine suffered a decline for a second year due to the politically motivated imprisonment of opposition leaders, flawed legislative elections, and a new law favoring the Russian-speaking portion of the population. In Central Asia, Tajikistan's civil liberties rating declined due to a military operation in Gorno-Badakhshan, which resulted in scores of deaths, extrajudicial killings, and a media crackdown. Kazakhstan's media environment deteriorated in the wake of a crackdown on labor unrest in late 2011, with authorities banning opposition newspapers and blocking opposition websites and social media.

There were some positive developments in Eurasia. The most notable was in Georgia, which saw an improvement in its political rights rating after the opposition Georgian Dream party won competitive parliamentary elections. The vote led to an orderly and democratic transfer of power, the first in the nation's history, and the campaign featured more pluralistic media coverage. In the elections' aftermath, however, the new government detained some 30 officials from its predecessor, prompting claims of a political witch hunt. Armenia's political rights rating rose due to peaceful parliamentary elections in May, which rebalanced the decline stemming from the violent aftermath of the 2008 presidential vote.

Two of the region's breakaway territories also made gains. Abkhazia's political rights rating improved due to the competiveness of parliamentary elections held in March, which allowed a shift toward independent candidates and away from either government or traditional opposition parties. Nagorno-Karabakh's status improved from Not Free to Partly Free due to a competitive presidential vote in July.

For Central and Eastern Europe, the year brought few major political changes. Still, a number of countries in the subregion remained highly vulnerable to economic difficulties, the corrupt merging of business and political interests, and government intolerance of checks and balances. Romania, for instance, was rocked by the prime minister's politicized but ultimately unsuccessful attempt to impeach the president. However, the only significant change was a gain in political rights for Bosnia and Herzegovina, due to the long-delayed formation of a central government and the gradual reduction of international supervision.

ASIA-PACIFIC: WITH GUARDED GAINS, BURMA LEAVES CHINA BEHIND

For years ranked among the world's most repressive regimes, Burma continued to push ahead with a process of democratic reform that was launched in 2010. While it remains a Not Free country, it registered improvements in both its political rights and civil liberties ratings. Of particular importance in 2012 was the successful participation of the main opposition party, the National League for Democracy, in parliamentary by-elections. The party was allowed to campaign with considerable freedom, and won nearly all of the seats at stake. Nevertheless, the ruling Union Solidarity and Development Party retains an overwhelming majority in the legislature, and the military's outsized power is still entrenched in the constitution and in practice. Freedoms of expression and association have improved markedly in the last two years, but they depend more on current government policy than on deep institutional changes, and the authorities continue to employ repressive crowd-control measures at demonstrations, violate workers' rights, restrict the operations of NGOs, tolerate land-grabbing, and hinder judicial independence.

Moreover, Burma is still plagued by conflicts between the military and ethnic minority guerrilla forces. And in 2012, communal violence flared between the Rohingya minority, which is largely Muslim, and the majority Buddhist population of Rakhine State.

For all its lingering problems, Burma has now surpassed China on both political rights and civil liberties. Facing a sensitive leadership transition in November, an increasingly vocal citizenry, and political scandals that revealed high-level infighting and corruption, China's Communist Party rulers renewed their commitment in 2012 to censorship, suppression of minorities, and grassroots surveillance. Legal amendments reinforced the ability of security forces to arbitrarily detain activists, Tibetan regions were subjected to repeated communications blackouts, and almost daily censorship directives sought to restrict Chinese citizens' ability to circulate information on corruption, police brutality, and threats to public health. In the run-up to the 18th Party Congress, dozens of dissidents, activists, and religious believers were harassed, detained, or given long prison terms, and Beijing residents endured onerous restrictions on movement and expression. While some of these measures eased after the congress, it remains to be seen whether the new leadership will take meaningful steps to dismantle the world's most complex and sophisticated apparatus for political control. Indeed, despite prominent rhetoric about fighting corruption, the last weeks of the year were marked by official speeches, state media pronouncements, and practical measures designed to justify or implement increased control over online communications.

The bright spot in China was the determination of not only high-profile dissidents but also large numbers of ordinary citizens to assert their rights and challenge injustice. Public protests, online campaigns, and underground networks of activists scored many small victories during the year, ranging from the firing of corrupt officials and the abandonment of unpopular industrial projects to the daring escape of blind activist Chen Guangcheng from extralegal house arrest.

The most serious declines in the Asia-Pacific region for 2012 took place in the Maldives and Sri Lanka. The Maldives suffered a decline in its political rights rating due to the forcible removal of democratically elected president Mohamed Nasheed, the violence perpetrated against him and his party, the suspension of the parliament's summer session, and the role the military played in facilitating these events. Sri Lanka's scores deteriorated because of increasing corruption and an attempt to impeach the chief justice of the Supreme Court.

Among the region's notable improvements, Mongolia conducted parliamentary elections that were deemed more competitive and fair than in the past. Bhutan's political rights scores similarly rose due to the improved conduct of by-elections. Civil liberties advanced in Indian Kashmir after detention laws were relaxed. And Tonga's status was upgraded from Partly Free to Free due to expanded media freedom and the increased ability of NGOs to form and function without interference by ruling elites.

AMERICAS: LOOKING TOWARD A POST-CHÁVEZ ERA

As the year ended, Venezuelan strongman Hugo Chávez was in a Cuban hospital, attempting to recover from surgery for an undisclosed form of cancer. The apparent gravity of his condition led him to name his vice president, Nicolás Maduro, as his successor should he be unable to serve the new presidential term he won in October.

For over a decade, Chávez has been a significant figure in regional politics and has aspired, with less success, to a leading role on the global stage. He spent his country's oil revenues lavishly at home and abroad, seeking to propagate a form of "21st-century socialism." Other left-populist governments emerged in Bolivia, Ecuador, and Nicaragua, but most countries in the region opted for social democratic models that included adherence to democratic norms, broad civil liberties, and market-based economies.

Chávez's reelection in 2012 typified the state of politics during his 12 years in power. On one hand, the opposition candidate, Henrique Capriles Radonski, was able to hold rallies and engage in traditional forms of campaigning. On the other hand, Chávez benefited from massive use of state resources that enabled him to dominate media time by a margin of 25-to-1, distribute household goods to constituents, and convince many voters that the state could punish them for casting a ballot for the opposition. In other words, the electoral playing field was badly skewed in Chávez's direction.

Three other countries in the region suffered notable declines in their democratic performance. Ecuador lost ground due to widespread irregularities in the constitutionally mandated registration process for political organizations, and a change to the seat-allocation formula for the national legislature that favors the ruling party. Paraguay experienced a setback due to the impeachment of President Fernando Lugo in a hurried process that deprived Paraguayans of any serious opportunity for debate. And Suriname declined because of a legal amendment that granted immunity to President Desiré Bouterse and 24 other suspects on trial for the 1982 murder of 15 political opponents. As a result, the trial was adjourned in May and had yet to reconvene by year's end.

WESTERN EUROPE AND NORTH AMERICA: BEARING THE STRAINS OF ECONOMIC WEAKNESS

With the rise of the Golden Dawn party, Greece has become the latest country in Western Europe to face a surge in nationalist sentiment in response to an influx of immigrants and the impact of the financial crisis. The Greek party stands out in the region for its propensity to street violence and its disturbingly high level of support, including among police, who have failed to provide adequate protection to immigrants and those advocating for their rights. But there is evidence that the popularity of nationalist political movements may have reached its peak in much of Europe. Thus the Party for Freedom, the anti-immigrant group led by Geert Wilders, fared rather poorly in parliamentary elections in the Netherlands in 2012. Likewise, the National Front party of Marine Le Pen failed to increase its share of the vote in France's presidential election, which was won by the Socialist candidate, François Hollande.

In general, the countries of the European Union (EU) have so far weathered the most serious economic downturn of the postwar period without a serious weakening of their traditionally high level of respect for democratic standards and civil liberties. The past year was marked by demonstrations against austerity measures, but most were peaceful, and the authorities by and large avoided heavy-handed responses. Greece was an exception; yet again, anarchist elements set fires and attacked police, and the authorities in turn used batons and tear gas to restore order.

While Europeans have shown a reluctance to elevate anti-immigrant parties to national leadership roles, most have evaded the responsibility to implement rational and humane policies to integrate newcomers from foreign cultures into their societies. Hostility to migrants is reflected in actions by parties of both right and left. While Hollande had criticized then president Nicolas Sarkozy for his abrupt expulsion of foreign Roma from France, his own Socialist government took similar measures once in power. These problems are likely to worsen in coming years given dislocations abroad and economic woes at home, the continued ambivalence of European societies toward ethnic minorities, and the unwillingness of European political leaders to advance policies that might meet the challenge.

Great Britain continued to grapple with the fallout from the "phone-hacking" scandal, in which journalists stand accused of colluding with police and others to abuse privacy rights in pursuit of sensationalistic stories. The case has led to the arrest of a number of high-ranking editors from the newspaper empire owned by Rupert Murdoch, and a commission of inquiry has recommended the creation of a new, independent body to deal with allegations of press abuse. The plan, which would replace the current system of self-regulation, is sharply opposed by the press and media freedom organizations.

In the United States, President Barack Obama won a second term in elections that also saw gains for his Democratic Party in both houses of Congress. While the Republican Party still controls the lower chamber, its majority has shrunk, enhancing the prospects for Obama to overcome the legislative gridlock of recent years. The president won despite a disappointing economy, persistent unemployment, and a massive budget deficit. His calls for higher taxes on the rich and the protection of social programs, among other policies, garnered strong support from the country's growing ethnic minority populations, while his opponent, former Massachusetts governor Mitt Romney, drew mostly white male voters with his program of tax and spending cuts. Romney was notably the first Mormon to win a major party's presidential nomination. The election was by far the most expensive in American history, with both sides spending billions of dollars raised largely through special committees designed to circumvent political contribution limits for candidates and political parties.

While the Obama administration has instituted changes in the country's antiterrorism effort, a number of controversial policies are still in place. The president has been criticized by civil libertarians for the United States's expansive use of unmanned aircraft to kill suspected terrorists and allied militants—including U.S. citizens—in Pakistan, Afghanistan, and Yemen. Nevertheless, Obama's approach to the war on terrorism generally enjoys bipartisan support from the American people and members of Congress.

The president endorsed the concept of same-sex marriage during the year, becoming the first in his position to do so. And referendum voters in three more states approved equal marriage rights for gay men and lesbians in November. Nevertheless, most states continue to ban such rights, including a number that have enshrined a limited definition of marriage in their constitutions. The Supreme Court is scheduled to issue important rulings on gay marriage in the coming months.

CONCLUSION
BRINGING LIGHT TO THE DARK CORNERS OF THE WORLD

Among the findings of this report, none is more surprising than the fact that Libya registered by far the most impressive gains in its level of freedom for 2012. Each spring, Freedom House publishes a supplemental report that shines a spotlight on the world's most repressive regimes—the worst of the worst. And until the uprising in 2011, Libya was a perennial member of that appalling group. Now, after months of civil war and over a year of tenuous nation building, Libya has an elected government, comparatively wide-ranging freedoms, and a leadership that seems committed to accountable rule and openness. Other postrevolutionary governments have begun well and ended poorly, and the Libyan experience with freedom could go awry. Clearly there are forces, both in Libya and in its neighborhood, that are hoping for failure. But for the time being, the country qualifies as a success story that deserves the support of freedom's advocates everywhere.

Overwhelming credit for Libya's achievements must go to those who risked and in many cases lost their lives by rebelling against the brutal rule of Mu'ammar al-Qadhafi. That the democratic world, including the United States, played a critical role in the country's liberation should also be recognized. Notwithstanding Libya's ongoing problems and events like the deadly assault on the U.S. consulate in Benghazi in September, the overall outcome ranks among Obama's most notable foreign policy accomplishments. Yet the United States seems uncomfortable with acknowledging its contribution to this important step forward for democratic values and the transformation of politics in the Middle East.

Such apparent ambivalence about vigorously supporting democratic change bodes ill for the region, which, as this report makes clear, remains very much in transition and turmoil. The old order of ossified dictatorships is giving way to something else, hopefully to governments based on humane principles and free institutions. But there are many other options available. Although the future of the Middle East will be determined by the people who live there, the United States and other established democracies have some part to play, as they had in major openings elsewhere in the world.

For example, the subregion consisting of Central Europe, the Baltics, and the Balkans now enjoys a level of political rights and civil liberties second only to that of Western Europe. These countries endured decades of communist domination, often preceded by some other variant of authoritarianism. Their free status today owes a great deal to the EU's embrace of democratic standards, and its imposition of those standards as a requirement for good relations and eventual accession.

To be sure, Egypt is no Poland, and there is no regional equivalent of the EU to provide aid and encouragement to changing Arab societies. But in its time, the democratization of the postcommunist world was understood to be critical to a peaceful and cooperative global environment, and the same can certainly be said of the Middle East today.

Moreover, the Middle East is not the only part of the world where freedom is in the balance. In Russia, Putin has launched a new round of repression and heaped contempt on the values of open societies. He sets a disturbing example for other Eurasian autocrats, and provides diplomatic backing for dictators confronted by calls for reform. In China, the new leadership includes figures who have been instrumental in building the world's most sophisticated system of political control, and no one should expect them to suddenly change course and disavow a lifetime of commitment to one-party rule. These countries—Russia and China—have consistently worked together to block international action that could, for example, help free the Syrian people. But even where such authoritarian powers do not throw up obstacles, the international community seems unable or unwilling to intervene in support of democracy. While there is general consensus that an international, principally African, coalition is needed in Mali, the political will to plan and carry out such a mission has been seriously wanting.

There is thus a critical need for leadership from the United States and other democracies. In the United States, the reluctance to provide that leadership represents a rare case of bipartisan agreement. President Obama has made clear his desire to focus on domestic concerns; the Tea Party wing of the Republican Party has fixated on across-the-board reductions in spending, including on foreign assistance; libertarians, also a growing influence in the GOP, are hostile to the very idea of American global leadership; even the party's leaders now seem ambivalent about America's role in the world. In Europe, the leading states are weighed down by the financial crisis. Meanwhile, rising democratic powers like Brazil, South Africa, and India have shown a profound aversion to condemning governments in other developing countries, including those that routinely commit atrocities against their own people.

The retreat of the leading democracies is taking place, ironically, at a time of unprecedented popular resistance to oppression around the world. The dissidents who labored for human rights during the Cold War—isolated and often anonymous— have been replaced by movements that command the support of sizable constituencies. Some are focused on single issues; others seek broad democratic reform. Most are pragmatic and skilled in maneuvering in repressive settings.

The data from this report tell us that civil society is under duress in the countries where it could do the most good. Though disturbing, this is in fact a tribute to the potency of civic movements. Many autocrats over the last few decades have offered a tacit social contract whereby they preserve political monopolies but abandon totalitarian control of society and promise economic development. As a result, these leaders often have little to fear from their battered formal opposition parties, but are hard-pressed to staunch the energy and independence of citizen activists.

If the United States and other democracies are seeking strategies to foster reform in the world's despotisms, one place to start would be a commitment to bolster and protect thinkers and activists who are the likely agents for change in their societies. Among other things, this project would require the development of methods to provide assistance in settings where the leadership has sought to snuff out foreign aid, as Putin has done in Russia.

Furthermore, our leaders, including the president, should confer with leading regime critics and activists, and speak out on behalf of those who are the targets of persecution.

But by far the most important point is for our leaders, and President Obama in particular, to declare their determination to support people who aspire to democracy anywhere in the world. The administration has built an uneven record on support for freedom to date. There have been some positive initiatives, but there have also been occasions when the United States stood by while those who put their lives on the line for political change were crushed, as with Iran in 2009. More recently, the administration utterly failed to offer a credible response when the USAID mission in Russia was abruptly shuttered by the Putin regime, a step that will further weaken a civil society sector that is already under serious state pressure.

A program of support for civic movements would be just one aspect of a truly comprehensive effort by the major democracies to reassert global leadership. But even by itself, support for civil society would have the practical benefit of directing attention to those who are committed to making freedom a reality in the world's dark corners. And it would send a critical message to the agents of repression that, no matter what our various domestic woes may be, the spread of freedom is still very much on the global agenda.

This report was prepared with the assistance of Jennifer Dunham, Bret Nelson, Aili Piano, and Tyler Roylance.

Introduction

The *Freedom in the World 2013* survey contains reports on 195 countries and 14 related and disputed territories. Each country report begins with a section containing the following information: **population, capital, political rights** (numerical rating), **civil liberties** (numerical rating), **status** (Free, Partly Free, or Not Free), and a **10-year ratings timeline**. Each territory report begins with a section containing the same information, except for capital. The population figures are drawn primarily from the *2012 World Population Data Sheet* of the Population Reference Bureau.

The **political rights** and **civil liberties** categories contain numerical ratings between 1 and 7 for each country or territory, with 1 representing the most free and 7 the least free. The **status** designation of Free, Partly Free, or Not Free, which is determined by the combination of the political rights and civil liberties ratings, indicates the general state of freedom in a country or territory. The ratings of countries or territories that have improved or declined since the previous survey are indicated by notations next to the ratings. Positive or negative trends that do not warrant a ratings change since the previous year may be indicated by upward or downward trend arrows, which are located next to the name of the country or territory. A brief explanation of ratings changes or trend arrows is provided for each country or territory as required. For a full description of the methods used to determine the survey's ratings, please see the chapter on the survey's methodology.

The **10-year ratings timeline** lists the political rights and civil liberties ratings and status for each of the last 10 years. Each year that is included in the timeline refers to the year under review, *not* the edition of the survey. Thus, the ratings and status from the *Freedom in the World 2013* edition are listed under "2012" (the year that was under review for the 2013 survey edition).

Following the section described above, each country and territory report is divided into two parts: an **overview** and an analysis of **political rights and civil liberties**. The overview provides a brief historical background and a description of major recent events. The political rights and civil liberties section summarizes each country's or territory's degree of respect for the rights and liberties that Freedom House uses to evaluate freedom in the world.

Afghanistan

Political Rights: 6
Civil Liberties: 6
Status: Not Free

Population: 33,397,000
Capital: Kabul

Ten-Year Ratings Timeline For Year Under Review (Political Rights, Civil Liberties, Status)

2003	2004	2005	2006	2007	2008	2009	2010	2011	2012
6,6NF	5,6NF	5,5PF	5,5PF	5,5PF	5,6NF	6,6NF	6,6NF	6,6NF	6,6NF

Overview: U.S. troops continued to depart from Afghanistan in 2012, and detention facilities were handed over in line with the ongoing transition of control over security from coalition forces to the Afghan government. Though a decline in civilian casualties in the first half of the year reversed a five-year trend, it was coupled with a series of attacks on foreign troops by members of the Afghan army and police, raising doubts about the government's capacity to maintain order after the final withdrawal of foreign combat forces in 2014. Such doubts were also fueled by uncertainty over the 2014 electoral process and an anticipated decline in foreign aid.

After decades of intermittent attempts to assert control and ward off Russian influence in the country, Britain recognized Afghanistan as a fully independent monarchy in 1921. Muhammad Zahir Shah ruled from 1933 until he was deposed in a 1973 coup and a republic was declared. Afghanistan entered a period of continuous civil conflict in 1978, when a Marxist faction staged a coup and set out to transform the country's highly traditional society. The Soviet Union invaded to support its allies in 1979 but was defeated by U.S.-backed guerrillas and forced to withdraw in 1989.

The mujahideen guerrilla factions finally overthrew the Marxist government in 1992 and then battled one another for control of Kabul, killing more than 25,000 civilians in the capital by 1995. The Islamist Taliban movement entered the fray, seizing Kabul in 1996 and quickly established control over most of the country, the rest of which remained in the hands of other factions. In response to the terrorist attacks of September 11, 2001, the United States launched a military campaign to topple the Taliban regime and eliminate Saudi militant Osama bin Laden's terrorist network, al-Qaeda.

As a result of the December 2001 Bonn Agreement, an interim administration took office to replace the ousted Taliban. In June 2002, the United Nations oversaw an emergency *loya jirga* (gathering of representatives) that appointed a Transitional Administration (TA) to rule Afghanistan for another two years. Interim leader Hamid Karzai won the votes of more than 80 percent of the delegates to become president and head of the TA.

In 2004, Karzai won a presidential election under the country's new constitution, taking 55 percent of the vote and forming a cabinet that was a mix of technocrats and regional power-brokers. Relatively peaceful elections for a National Assembly and 34 provincial councils were held in September 2005. However, a large number of warlords and others involved in organized crime and human rights abuses were elected.

The new parliament made little progress over the next several years on addressing political and economic reforms or passing key legislation. While some analysts had expressed concern that the legislative branch would be largely subservient to the executive, it was often at odds with the president, making it difficult for him to advance the government's agenda.

The UN-mandated International Security Assistance Force (ISAF), which had been managed by NATO since August 2003, completed the expansion of its security and reconstruction mission from Kabul to the rest of the country in 2006. Despite tens of thousands of additional U.S. and allied troops, and the ongoing development of the Afghan army, Afghanistan largely remained under the sway of local military commanders, tribal leaders, warlords, drug traffickers, and petty bandits. Meanwhile, the resurgent Taliban increased their attacks on the government and international forces, and steadily extended their influence over vast swaths of territory, particularly in the southern provinces of Kandahar and Helmand, but also in previously quiet areas of the north and west.

The constitution called for the 2009 presidential election to be held by April, but it was delayed until August and conducted amid reports of fraud, low turnout, and insecurity. Karzai initially emerged as the outright winner with more than 50 percent of the vote, but the confirmation of large-scale fraud significantly reduced his total, necessitating a November runoff against his main opponent, former foreign minister Abdullah Abdullah. However, Abdullah withdrew before the vote, arguing that the flaws in the electoral system had not been adequately addressed, and Karzai was declared the winner.

Lingering doubts about the Karzai administration's legitimacy, combined with the continued deterioration in security, posed a major challenge to the central and provincial governments as they struggled to control areas under their jurisdiction, deliver basic services, and engage in vital reconstruction efforts.

The country's institutional integrity was dealt another blow when the September 2010 parliamentary elections also proved to be deeply flawed, with low voter turnout and widespread fraud. Karzai did not inaugurate the new parliament until January 2011, ruling by decree in the interim, and it was not until August 2011 that disagreements over 62 candidates for the 249-seat lower house were resolved, with the Independent Election Commission (IEC) agreeing to replace only 9 of the seated lawmakers. In October 2012, the IEC announced that the next presidential and provincial elections would be held in April 2014, dispelling fears that Karzai would try to delay the voting in an effort to retain power beyond his constitutionally sanctioned two terms.

Also during 2012, there was a decline in violence against civilians, with the United Nations reporting 1,145 civilians killed and 1,954 injured between January 1 and June 30, a 15 percent decrease compared with the same period in 2011 and a reversal of a five-year trend of increasing civilian deaths; some 80 percent of these casualties were attributed to insurgents. However, local discontent with ISAF rose during the year after a video released in January showed U.S. troops urinating on dead Taliban fighters, U.S. personnel inadvertently burned copies of the Koran at the Bagram detention facility in February, and an American soldier allegedly went on a rampage and killed 17 civilians near a base in Kandahar Province. In a sign of friction between ISAF and Afghan personnel, members of the Afghan army and police attacked foreign troops with increasing frequency, killing some 60 people. These so-called insider, or green-on-blue, attacks raised serious concerns about the competence of Afghan forces to maintain order and defend the government after the departure of international combat troops. This concern was further reinforced in a December report by the U.S. Department of Defense, stating that only 1 out of 23 Afghan National Army brigades can operate effectively without NATO assistance.

Despite such concerns, ISAF continued with its scheduled troop withdrawals during the year, leaving the United States with roughly 68,000 military personnel in the country as of September. The United States also reached an agreement in March on the transfer of detention facilities to the Afghan government. The overwhelming majority of detainees, numbering in the thousands, were handed over to Afghan authorities by September. However, disagreements between the two sides over newly captured detainees prompted Karzai to order the takeover of Bagram detention facility in November, an order that was only partially implemented.

Political Rights and Civil Liberties: Afghanistan is not an electoral democracy. The overall results of the 2004 presidential election and delayed 2005 parliamentary elections were broadly accepted by Afghans and the international community, despite allegations of intimidation by militias and insurgent groups, partisanship within the electoral administration, and other irregularities. However, the 2009 presidential and 2010 parliamentary elections were critically undermined by fraud and other problems, and state institutions have failed to provide effective governance or transparency. Afghanistan's district council elections, which were scheduled to take place in 2010, were canceled.

The directly elected president serves five-year terms and has the power to appoint ministers, subject to parliamentary approval. In the directly elected lower house of the National Assembly, the 249-seat Wolesi Jirga (House of the People), members stand for five-year terms. In the 102-seat Meshrano Jirga (House of Elders), the upper house, two-thirds of members are indirectly elected by the provincial councils for three- or four-year terms, and one-third are appointed by the president for five-year terms. Ten of the Wolesi Jirga seats are reserved from the nomadic Kuchi community, including at least three women, and another 65 seats are reserved for women. Provisions for women's representation have also been implemented for the Meshrano Jirga and provincial councils.

Violence, insecurity, and repression continue to restrict political activity nationwide, particularly outside urban areas. Critics have warned that vague language in the 2003 Political Parties Law could be exploited to deny registration to parties on flimsy grounds. In addition, analysts viewed the adoption of the single-nontransferable-vote system ahead of the 2005 legislative elections as a disadvantage for new political parties. Parties lack a formal role within the legislature, which further weakens their ability to contribute to stable political, policymaking, and legislative processes. There have been regular violent and often deadly attacks against government officials at all levels, including assassination attempts aimed at the president. In the first half of 2012, there were more than 155 attacks aimed at government officials, an increase of more than 50 percent over the same period in 2011.

Corruption, nepotism, and cronyism are rampant at all levels of government, and woefully inadequate salaries encourage corrupt behavior by public employees. The international community, concerned that government corruption is crippling the counterinsurgency campaign, has pressed the administration of President Hamid Karzai to make the issue its top priority. To that end, the government released a detailed 33-chapter anticorruption decree in July 2012, which includes provisions against political nepotism, cronyism, and land grabs. To signal the decree's implementation, Karzai dismissed five governors and made changes to leading positions in almost a third of the country's 34 provinces in late September. Also during the year, defendants went on trial for their alleged roles in a massive fraud scandal at Kabul Bank that emerged in 2010 and undermined confidence in Afghan financial institutions. Afghanistan was ranked 174 of 176 countries surveyed in Transparency International's 2012 Corruption Perceptions Index.

Afghan media continue to grow and diversify, but they face major challenges, including physical attacks and intimidation. Though a 2007 media law was intended to clarify press freedoms and limit government interference, a growing number of journalists have been arrested, threatened, or harassed by politicians, security services, and others in positions of power as a result of their coverage. Media diversity and freedom are markedly higher in Kabul than elsewhere in the country, but some local warlords display a limited tolerance for independent media in their areas. Dozens of private radio stations and several private television channels currently operate, conveying a range of viewpoints to much of the population and often carrying criticism of the government. Some independent outlets and publications have been denounced by conservative clerics for content that "opposes Islam and national values," or fined by the authorities for similar reasons. Rapidly expanding use of the internet and mobile telephones has broadened the flow of news and other information, particularly for urban residents, but Taliban attacks on mobile-phone infrastructure has worked against this trend. In February 2012 a radio reporter was murdered in Paktika Province; the circumstances of his death were unclear.

Religious freedom has improved since the fall of the Taliban government in late 2001, but is still hampered by violence and harassment aimed at religious minorities and reformist Muslims. The constitution establishes Islam as the official religion. Blasphemy and apostasy by Muslims are considered capital crimes. While faiths other than Islam are permitted, non-Muslim proselytizing is strongly discouraged. A 2007 court ruling found the minority Baha'i faith to be a form of blasphemy, jeopardizing the legal status of that community. Hindus, Sikhs, and Shiite Muslims—particularly those from the Hazara ethnic group—have also faced official obstacles and discrimination by the Sunni Muslim majority. Militant groups have targeted mosques and clerics as part of the larger civil conflict. An October 2012 attack at a mosque in Maimana Province killed over 45 worshippers.

Aside from constitutional provisions regarding the role of Islam in education, academic freedom is not officially restricted, but insurgents have attacked or destroyed schools associated with the government or foreign donors, particularly girls' schools. There were 185 documented attacks on educational and health facilities in 2011. In two notable incidents in 2012 in Takhar Province, over 150 schoolgirls were hospitalized in April as a result of contaminated water, and another 120 were hospitalized in May after a toxic agent was sprayed in their classrooms. The quality of school instruction and resources remains poor. Higher education is subject to bribery and prohibitively expensive for most Afghans.

The constitution guarantees the rights to assembly and association, subject to some restrictions, but they are upheld erratically from region to region. Police and other security personnel have occasionally used excessive force when confronted with demonstrations or protests.

The work of hundreds of international and Afghan nongovernmental organizations (NGOs)—the latter numbered over 1,700 in 2012—is not formally constrained by the authorities, but their ability to operate freely and effectively is impeded by the security situation. Both foreign and Afghan NGO staff members have been targeted in kidnappings and violent attacks by criminals and insurgents. Civil society activists, particularly those who focus on human rights or accountability issues, continue to face threats and harassment. Despite broad constitutional protections for workers, labor rights are not well defined, and there are currently no enforcement or dispute-resolution mechanisms. Child labor is reportedly common.

The judicial system operates haphazardly, and justice in many places is administered on the basis of a mixture of legal codes by inadequately trained judges. Corruption in the judiciary is extensive, and judges and lawyers are often subject to threats from local leaders or armed groups. Traditional justice is the main recourse for the population, especially in rural areas. The Supreme Court, composed of religious scholars who have little knowledge of civil jurisprudence, is particularly in need of reform. The president created an unconstitutional Special Election Court at the end of 2010 to adjudicate disputes from that year's parliamentary elections, but it was dissolved under international pressure in August 2011.

Prison conditions are extremely poor, with many detainees held illegally. The national intelligence agency as well as some warlords and political leaders maintain their own prisons and do not allow access to detainees. A March 2012 report by the Afghanistan Independent Human Rights Commission (AIHRC) documented incidents of torture and other violations of detainee rights perpetrated by the Afghan intelligence service. U.S. forces have reportedly made some improvements to their detention practices in recent years, but Afghan detainees handed over to local authorities continue to suffer abuses.

In a prevailing climate of impunity, government officials as well as warlords in some provinces sanction widespread abuses by the police, military, local militias, and intelligence forces under their command, including arbitrary arrest and detention, torture, extortion, and extrajudicial killings. The AIHRC receives hundreds of complaints of rights violations each year. In addition to the abuses by security forces, the reported violations have involved land theft, displacement, kidnapping, child trafficking, domestic violence, and forced marriage.

The Afghan military and police continued to be plagued in 2012 by inadequate training, illiteracy, corruption, involvement in drug trafficking, and high rates of desertion. Hundreds of recruits were fired, and joint patrols and training with foreign personnel were temporarily suspended in September 2012 in response to an increase in "insider" attacks that led to roughly 60 coalition deaths.

Disarmament programs have stalled, and foreign military programs to rearm informal militias as a counterinsurgency force are undermining efforts to curtail and regulate the distribution of weaponry. Ongoing programs aimed at reintegrating former insurgents have failed to ensure that they disarm.

Over 447,000 civilians were displaced within the country as of January 2012, according to the Office of the UN High Commissioner for Refugees. Humanitarian agencies and Afghan authorities are ill-equipped to deal with the displaced. Factors like the poor security situation and widespread land-grabbing have prevented refugees from returning to their homes, and many congregate instead around major urban centers. In the absence of a properly functioning legal system, the state remains unable to protect property rights.

Women's formal rights to education and employment have been restored, and in some areas, women are once again participating in public life. They accounted for about 16 percent of the candidates in the 2010 parliamentary elections, and roughly 41 percent of registered voters were women; 69 female candidates were elected. There were two women among the 41 candidates for the 2009 presidential election. On the whole, female electoral participation has been limited by threats, harassment, and social restrictions on traveling alone and appearing in public. Adult female literacy remains at a strikingly low 13 percent. Legislation passed in 2009 derogated many constitutional rights for women belonging to the Shiite Muslim minority, leaving questions of inheritance, marriage, and personal freedoms to be determined by conservative Shiite religious authorities.

Societal discrimination and domestic violence against women remain pervasive, with the latter often going unreported because of social acceptance of the practice. Women's choices regarding marriage and divorce remain circumscribed by custom and discriminatory laws, and the forced marriage of young girls to older men or widows to their husbands' male relations is a problem, with the UN Children's Fund (UNICEF) reporting that nearly 40 percent of Afghan girls are married before the legal age of 16. In one high-profile case in January 2012, Sarah Gul, a 14-year-old who was married off to a man by her stepbrother, was rescued after six months of detention in a basement toilet, where she was abused after refusing to be forced into prostitution. In June UNICEF reported sizable improvements in terms of women and children's access to drinking water and education as well as child mortality, though it also noted increased risk of child death due to security incidents. Human Rights Watch has expressed concerns about the potential deterioration of women's rights after foreign troops withdraw, despite a May strategic partnership agreement between the Afghan government and the United States that underlines Afghanistan's commitment to respect and promote women's rights. In October, at a conference in Kabul that was seen as an encouraging sign by women's rights activists, religious leaders openly opposed violence against women.

Albania

Political Rights: 3
Civil Liberties: 3
Status: Partly Free

Population: 2,832,500
Capital: Tirana

Ten-Year Ratings Timeline For Year Under Review (Political Rights, Civil Liberties, Status)

2003	2004	2005	2006	2007	2008	2009	2010	2011	2012
3,3PF	3,3PF	3,3PF	3,3PF	3,3PF	3,3PF	3,3PF	3,3PF	3,3PF	3,3PF

Overview: Prime Minister Sali Berisha installed his interior minister, Bujar Nishani, as president in June 2012. Nishani subsequently named allies of the ruling Democratic Party to lead the intelligence service and the High Council of Justice, prompting complaints from the opposition Socialist Party that Berisha was taking over all key institutions in the country. In December, Nishani also replaced Prosecutor General Ina Rama, who had brought a number of corruption cases against senior government officials.

Ruling from World War II until his death in 1985, communist dictator Enver Hoxha turned Albania into the most isolated country in Europe. The regime began to adopt more liberal policies in the late 1980s, and multiparty elections in 1992 brought the Democratic Party (PD), led by Sali Berisha, to power. Continuing poverty and corruption, along with unrest after the collapse of large-scale investment scams, resulted in the election of a new government led by the Socialist Party (PS) in 1997. The PS led the government until 2005, when the PD won parliamentary elections, and Berisha became prime minister. In 2007, the parliament elected PD candidate Bamir Topi as the country's president.

Berisha's government was plagued by allegations of corruption and abuse of office in 2008. Nevertheless, in the 2009 parliamentary elections, the PD took 68 of 140 seats and eventually formed a coalition government with three smaller parties that collectively held 6 seats. A Greek minority party took one seat. The PS, in opposition with 65 seats, claimed fraud and boycotted the new parliament. Although the PS finally named a deputy parliament speaker and committee members in June 2010, it continued to mount protests and for a time blocked key legislative votes that required a three-fifths majority.

In January 2011, after the Albanian media publicized a video recording that showed Deputy Prime Minister Ilir Meta apparently discussing corrupt dealings, the PS led a large protest against Berisha's government in Tirana. Four demonstrators were shot and killed, allegedly by Republican Guards protecting the prime minister's office, and dozens of protesters and police were injured in related clashes. Prosecutor General Ina Rama launched an investigation into the deaths, but Berisha set up a rival parliamentary inquiry and accused Rama, Topi, the PS, the State Intelligence Service (SHISH), and leading journalists of orchestrating an attempted coup.

As both inquiries stalled, PD candidate Lulzim Basha won the Tirana mayoralty in May municipal elections, narrowly defeating PS leader and three-term incumbent Edi Rama (no relation to the prosecutor general) after PD-dominated electoral bodies decided a protracted legal battle over miscast ballots.

In April 2012, Ina Rama filed indictments charging four people in the January 2011 violence: two former Republican Guard commanders were accused of murder, one of their drivers was charged with obstructing justice, and a computer expert with the prime minister's office was accused of deleting video evidence. The computer expert was acquitted in July, and the trial of the others was ongoing at year's end. Berisha continued to voice his coup claims during 2012, and threatened to have Rama arrested once she left office.

Meanwhile, in June the parliament elected Bujar Nishani, Berisha's interior minister, to succeed Topi as president. Nishani subsequently nominated a Berisha ally as administrative head of the High Council of Justice, which oversees the judiciary, and replaced the head of the SHISH with a deputy cabinet minister. All three outgoing officials had come under intense political pressure from the government. Finally, in December, Nishani named Adriatik Llalla, a former prosecutor and head of an asset auditing body, to replace Ina Rama as her term drew to a close. Llalla was confirmed by the parliament, though most PS lawmakers abstained from the vote.

Also in December, the European Council declined for the third consecutive year to grant Albania European Union (EU) candidate status, citing insufficient progress on a series of reform priorities.

Political Rights and Civil Liberties: Albania is an electoral democracy. International observers of the 2009 parliamentary elections hailed improvements in a number of areas, but also cited problems including media bias, abuse of state resources, political pressure on public employees, and flaws in the tabulation process. The unicameral, 140-member Kuvendi (Assembly) is elected through proportional representation in 12 regional districts of varying size. All members serve four-year terms. The prime minister is designated by the majority party or coalition, and the president—who does not hold executive powers but heads the military and plays an important role in selecting senior judges—is chosen by the parliament for a maximum of two five-year terms.

The sharp, personality-driven rivalry between the two main political parties, the PD and the PS, escalated significantly in 2011. The campaign for the May municipal elections featured interparty violence as well as party-line decisions, boycotts, acrimony within the Central Election Commission, and political pressure on public employees. Nevertheless, observers noted improvements on some issues, including abuse of administrative resources and voter list accuracy. Bipartisan cooperation appeared to improve somewhat in 2012, with the PD and PS agreeing on legislation governing the 2013 parliamentary elections, though smaller parties complained that they were shut out of the process.

Corruption is pervasive, and the European Union (EU) has repeatedly called for rigorous implementation of antigraft measures. Until she was replaced in December 2012, Prosecutor General Ina Rama had worked to pursue high-level cases with support from U.S. and EU officials, while simultaneously facing regular accusations of political bias by Prime Minister Sali Berisha. Many of her prosecutions were thwarted by parliamentary immunity and unfavorable court rulings. In January 2012, citing a lack of evidence, the Supreme Court dismissed charges against Ilir Meta, who had resigned as deputy prime minister in 2011, after a video showed him apparently discussing acts of corruption. In a parallel case against former economy minister Dritan Prifti, the court ruled in September 2012 that another incriminating video was inadmissible, leading prosecutors to drop the charges. Also that month, under international pressure, the parliament approved constitutional amendments that would limit the immunity from prosecution of lawmakers, judges, and other senior officials, allowing investigations to begin without prior authorization. Albania was ranked 113 out of 176 countries surveyed in Transparency International's 2012 Corruption Perceptions Index.

While the constitution guarantees freedom of expression, the intermingling of powerful business, political, and media interests inhibits the development of independent media outlets; most are seen as biased toward either the PS or the PD. Reporters have little job security and remain subject to lawsuits, intimidation, and in some cases, physical attacks by those facing media scrutiny. Berisha's government has placed financial pressure on critical outlets, and an opposition lawmaker in September 2012 provided evidence that state advertising purchases had been funneled to PD-friendly media over the past five years. The parliament reformed the civil and penal codes in February and March, limiting the fines in civil defamation cases and eliminating imprisonment as a punishment for criminal defamation. The government does not limit internet access.

The constitution provides for freedom of religion, and it is generally upheld in practice. The government typically does not limit academic freedom, though students and teachers have faced political pressure ahead of elections.

Freedoms of association and assembly are generally respected. Although the deaths and injuries suffered during the January 2011 opposition protests went unpunished in 2012, subsequent demonstrations by both major parties have been relatively peaceful. A gay pride march set for May 2012 in Tirana was canceled amid threats of violence, including from a deputy defense minister, though Berisha had expressed support for the event. Nongovernmental organizations function without restrictions but have limited funding and policy influence.

The constitution guarantees workers the rights to organize and bargain collectively, and most have the right to strike. However, effective collective bargaining remains limited, and union members have little protection against discrimination by employers. Child labor is a problem, and informal child workers sometimes face hazardous conditions.

The constitution provides for an independent judiciary, but the underfunded courts are subject to political pressure. The replacement of President Bamir Topi with a Berisha ally in June 2012 eased a lengthy standoff between the parliamentary majority and the presidency over senior judicial appointments, but it also increased the threat of political influence over the courts. Judicial immunity has obstructed investigations of corruption among the country's poorly paid judges, who also face threats of violence. Before her replacement as prosecutor general, Rama had complained that court officials effectively protected one another when accused of wrongdoing. In December 2012, a judge in Durres was dismissed for deliberately stalling an appeal in a murder case, allowing the release of an organized crime figure who was then arrested for a new murder. High court fees allegedly limit access to justice for ordinary Albanians.

Police reportedly engage in abuse of suspects during arrest and interrogation, and such ill-treatment is lightly if ever punished. Prison inmates suffer from poor living conditions and lack of adequate medical treatment.

Weak state institutions have augmented the power of crime syndicates. Albania is known as a transshipment point for heroin smugglers and a key site for cannabis production. Traditional tribal law and revenge killings are practiced in parts of the north, leading to dozens of deaths each year, by some estimates.

Roma face significant discrimination in education, health care, employment, and housing. A 2010 law bars discrimination based on several categories, including sexual orientation and gender identity, but bias against gay and transgender people remains strong in practice.

Women are underrepresented in most governmental institutions, and a quota for women in party candidate lists is not well enforced. Domestic violence is believed to be widespread, though the parliament in March 2012 passed legislation imposing up to five years in prison for the specific offense of domestic violence, and reporting of the crime has increased. Albania is a source country for trafficking in women and children.

Algeria

Political Rights: 6
Civil Liberties: 5
Status: Not Free

Population: 37,402,000
Capital: Algiers

Ten-Year Ratings Timeline For Year Under Review (Political Rights, Civil Liberties, Status)

2003	2004	2005	2006	2007	2008	2009	2010	2011	2012
6,5NF	6,5NF	6,5NF	6,5NF	6,5NF	6,5NF	6,5NF	6,5NF	6,5NF	6,5NF

Overview: Protests against economic and political conditions in Algeria continued throughout 2012. New laws relating to political and civil liberties were criticized for failing to protect basic rights, and harassment of the political opposition and civil society were ongoing. Parliamentary elections in May were judged to be largely free by international monitors, though local groups alleged fraud and irregularities.

Algeria secured independence from France after a guerrilla war that lasted from 1954 to 1962. The military overthrew the country's first president in 1965 and dominated Algerian politics for the next four decades, backing the National Liberation Front (FLN) for most of that time. President Chadli Benjedid permitted the establishment of legal opposition parties in 1989, and an Islamist movement quickly gained popularity in the face of the government's failures; the Islamic Salvation Front (FIS) became the main opposition faction. With the FIS poised to win parliamentary elections in 1992, the army canceled the elections, forced Benjedid from office, and imprisoned thousands of FIS supporters under a declared state of emergency.

Over the next decade, the military government and various Islamist groups engaged in a bloody civil conflict. All sides targeted civilians and perpetrated large-scale human rights abuses, causing an estimated 200,000 deaths and the disappearance of at least 7,000 people.

A military-backed candidate, former foreign minister Abdelaziz Bouteflika, easily won the 1999 presidential election after his opponents withdrew to protest alleged fraud. Bouteflika's first attempt at resolving the civil war was the Civil Concord Law, which granted partial amnesty to combatants who renounced violence. Bouteflika began to distance himself from the military and won a second term in 2004. In 2005, a referendum approved the Charter for Peace and National Reconciliation, which offered amnesty to most militants and government agents for crimes committed during the civil war. However, human rights organizations criticized the charter for not addressing the issue of the disappeared and for allowing perpetrators to escape justice. The FLN, which had gained ground in the 2002 and 2003 elections, remained the largest party in both houses of Parliament in elections held in 2007 for the lower house and 2009 for the upper house.

Bouteflika won a third term in an April 2009 election, taking about 90 percent of the vote amid widespread accusations of fraud. A power struggle developed between the ailing Bouteflika and General Mohamed "Toufik" Mediène, the powerful head of the Department of Intelligence and Security, over rumors that Bouteflika's younger brother would succeed him.

In early 2011, the Algerian government remained firmly in control as political change gripped its Arab neighbors. Protests over high unemployment, rising prices, and the lack of political freedoms were violently subdued by the police. The government quickly introduced new subsidies and wage increases to head off a more widespread uprising and lifted the country's long-standing emergency law in February 2011. It passed new laws in December 2011 and January 2012 that revised regulations on political parties, associations, the media, access to information, and electoral list quotas for female candidates. The new laws on associations and the media, in particular, were criticized for continuing to restrict the activities of civil society, freedom of the press, and access to information.

In advance of the May 2012 elections for the lower house of Parliament, protests criticizing the government and calling on Algerians to boycott the elections were suppressed, on some occasions violently. In the elections, the FLN won 221 seats, the military-backed National Democratic Rally (RND), 70, and the Green Algeria Alliance—comprised of multiple Islamist parties—47. The government estimated participation in the elections at approximately 42 percent. Foreign observers from the European Union, United Nations, the Arab League, and other institutions declared the elections largely free and fair, and praised the new law mandating one-third representation of women on electoral lists, which led to 146 women being elected to Parliament. Opposition candidates and some human rights groups, however, asserted that the elections were fraudulent and that participation rates were much lower than the government stated. Fifteen parties that won a combined 29 seats announced that they would boycott the new Parliament. The election commission set up by the Algerian government itself condemned the elections as "not credible," although FLN and RND members on the commission refused to sign the final report. Political gridlock prevented the formation of a new cabinet until early September. In September, Bouteflika appointed former water resources minister Abdelmalek Sellal the new prime minister. Sellal presented a reform plan to the Parliament in October which stressed the need to continue with political reforms, enhance security, boost the economy, and fight corruption.

In municipal elections held in late November, the FLN and RND dominated seats won in the People's Communal Assemblies and People's Provincial Assemblies. The government estimated voter participation at 44 percent, though the opposition alleged fraud and inflated estimates of turnout.

Attacks on Algerian police officers and political officials by al-Qaeda in the Islamic Maghreb (AQIM), a militant Islamist group affiliated with al-Qaeda, continued throughout the year. The army killed several suspected AQIM leaders in the last few months of 2012, while the lead-up to an anticipated foreign intervention in neighboring Mali against Islamist extremists kept security concerns at the forefront of political debate.

Political Rights and Civil Liberties: Algeria is not an electoral democracy. The military and intelligence services still play an important role in politics despite their ongoing rivalries with the political establishment. The size of the People's National Assembly, the lower house of Parliament, was increased from 389 to 462 members directly elected for five-year terms in advance of the May 2012 elections. The upper house, the National Council, has 144 members serving six-year terms; 96 members are chosen by local assemblies, and the president appoints the remaining 48. The president is directly elected for five-year terms, and constitutional amendments passed in 2008 abolished the two-term limit, allowing President Abdelaziz Bouteflika to run for a third term in 2009. The amendments also increased the president's powers relative to the premiership and other entities.

The Ministry of the Interior must approve political parties before they can operate legally. The 2012 elections were also supervised by a judicial body, the National Election Observation Commission. A January 2012 law liberalized the party registration process, and 23 new political parties were allowed to register for the first time since 1999. The FLN, RND, Green Algeria Alliance (comprised of the Movement for the Society of Peace [MSP], Ennahda, and Islah parties), the Front of Socialist Forces, the Workers Party, and a number of parties with fewer than 10 seats each sit in the current Parliament.

High levels of corruption plague Algeria's business and public sectors, especially the energy sector. In 2012, Algerian courts sentenced Mohamed Boukhari, the former executive officer of state-owned Algeria Telecom, to 18 years in prison for accepting bribes from two Chinese firms over a period of three years. Algeria was ranked 105 out of 174 countries surveyed in Transparency International's 2012 Corruption Perceptions Index.

There are an array of restrictions on press freedom, but the situation has improved since the peak of the civil war in the mid-1990s. Privately owned newspapers have been published for nearly two decades, and journalists have been aggressive in their coverage of government affairs. However, most newspapers rely on the central government for printing, and the state-owned advertising agency favors progovernment newspapers, encouraging self-censorship. A new press law adopted in December 2011 was criticized by journalists and human rights activists for containing vague language that reinforces the government's ability to block reporting on certain sensitive topics, including those deemed to undermine the country's security or economic interests. Both government officials and private entities use criminal defamation laws to pressure independent newspapers. In 2012, several journalists and human rights activists were arrested on charges of libel. A number of journalists and human rights defenders were also the target of assaults by police officers.

A July 2009 cybercrime law gives authorities the right to block websites "contrary to the public order or decency," and a centralized system monitors internet traffic. In February 2011, amid protests against the regime, activists in Algiers and the northwestern city of Annaba accused the government of shutting down the internet and disrupting social-networking activities. In May 2012, a blogger who posted videos to the internet calling for Algerians to boycott the parliamentary elections was arrested and given an eight-month suspended jail sentence.

Algeria's population is overwhelmingly Sunni Muslim, and small non-Muslim communities do not face systematic harassment. However, non-Muslims may gather to worship only at state-approved locations, proselytizing by non-Muslims is illegal, and the government in 2008 began enforcing an ordinance that tightened restrictions on minority faiths. In 2012, some Christians faced harassment at their places of worship. Security services monitor mosques for radical Islamist activity, but Muslims are also sometimes harassed for a perceived lack of piety. Academic freedom is largely respected, though debate is somewhat circumscribed.

The government continued to forcibly disrupt and discourage public gatherings and protests in 2012, despite the repeal of the emergency law in February 2011. International human rights groups criticized the suppression of demonstrations in advance of the May 2012 elections. During the year, activists protesting government policies also faced arrest, often on vague charges, and others were apprehended when they protested the detention of their colleagues. According to government estimates, there were more than 4,500 protests in the first nine months of 2012 alone, more than 3,000 of which turned violent.

The January 2012 law on associations was criticized for continuing to restrict the formation, funding, and operations of civil society. Permits are required to establish nongovernmental organizations, and those with Islamist leanings are regarded with suspicion by the government. Workers can establish independent trade unions, but the main labor federation, the General Union of Algerian Workers, has been criticized for being too close to the government and failing to advocate aggressively for workers' interests. In 2012, numerous union leaders and activists advocating for the rights of the unemployed were subject to harassment and arrest for organizing demonstrations.

The judiciary is susceptible to government pressure. International human rights activists have accused the security forces of practicing torture, and have also highlighted lengthy delays in bringing cases to trial. Prison conditions in Algeria generally do not meet international standards due to overcrowding and poor nutrition and hygiene.

Algeria's ethnic composition is a mixture of Arabs and Berbers, with Arabs traditionally forming the country's elite. In recent years, following outbreaks of antigovernment violence in the Berber community, officials have made more of an effort to recognize Berber cultural demands. Tamazight, the Berber language, is now a national language. The Berber-dominated Rally for Culture and Democracy (RCD) party was one of the few parties to boycott the May 2012 elections entirely.

While most citizens are free to move throughout the country and travel abroad, the authorities closely monitor and limit the movement of suspected terrorists. Access to visas for non-Algerians is carefully controlled. Men of military draft age are not allowed to leave the country without government consent.

Women continue to face discrimination at both the legal and societal levels, but 2012 saw their access to elected office expand. A November 2011 law required that female candidates comprise one-third of any candidate list for legislative elections. As a result, women occupy more than a third of seats in the newly elected Parliament, a higher percentage than in any other Arab country. Women's rights groups praised the outcome, but some questioned whether the women in Parliament would be able to have an impact on the overall political system. Under the family code, which is based on Islamic law, women do not enjoy equal rights in marriage, divorce, and inheritance. Algeria is one of the few countries in the region to allow women to transfer their nationality to their children, regardless of the father's nationality. A law adopted in January 2009 criminalized all forms of trafficking in persons, but the government has made little effort to enforce it, according to the U.S. State Department's 2012 Trafficking in Persons Report.

Andorra

Political Rights: 1
Civil Liberties: 1
Status: Free

Population: 71,800
Capital: Andorra la Vella

Ten-Year Ratings Timeline For Year Under Review (Political Rights, Civil Liberties, Status)

2003	2004	2005	2006	2007	2008	2009	2010	2011	2012
1,1F	1,1F	1,1F	1,1F	1,1F	1,1F	1,1F	1,1F	1,1F	1,1F

Overview: Andorra continued updating its financial laws throughout 2012 in order to meet international standards. In April, a survey distributed by the Union of Workers of Andorra la Vella showed widespread concern for corruption and abuse in the workplace. Meanwhile, a new law was implemented in June to reform the application process for residency permits.

As a co-principality, Andorra was ruled for centuries by the French head of state and the bishop of Seu d'Urgel, Spain. The 1993 constitution retained these titular co-princes but transformed the government into a parliamentary democracy. Andorra joined the United Nations that year and the Council of Europe in 1994. While Andorra is not a member of the European Union (EU), the country began using the euro in 2002 as its sole circulating currency.

The April 2009 national elections brought the Social Democratic Party to power with 14 of the 28 seats in the Consell General, or parliament. Jaume Bartumeu replaced Albert Pintat Santolària as the cap de govern (head of government) in June.

After two years of government deadlock, including the failure to pass a national budget, Bartumeu on February 15, 2011, requested that Andorra's two co-princes dissolve parliament and hold early elections. In the April 3 polls, the Democrats for Andorra won a decisive victory, securing 20 parliamentary seats. Antoni Martí became the new head of government.

The Andorran government has worked in recent years to address the country's reputation as a tax haven and bring its financial laws into compliance with the standards of the Organization for Economic Co-Operation and Development, including a plan to introduce a value-added tax with a rate of 4.5 percent by the start of 2013. The Foreign Direct Investment Law of July 2012 newly allows foreign individuals and companies, including both residents and nonresidents, to own 100 percent of an Andorran company. In October 2012, after years of political impasse, Andorra announced its 2013 budget, including the continued gradual implementation of corporate and income taxes for nonresidents.

Political Rights and Civil Liberties: Andorra is an electoral democracy. Popular elections are held every four years to the 28-member Consell General, which selects the executive council president, or head of government. Half of the members are chosen in two-seat constituencies known as parishes, and the other half are chosen through a national system of proportional representation.

The people have the right to establish and join different political parties. However, more than 60 percent of the population consists of noncitizens, who do not have the right to vote.

In June 2011, the Council of Europe's Group of States against Corruption (GRECO) released a report finding some "shortcomings" in Andorra's bribery laws, and calling for tougher penalties for bribery and influence peddling. GRECO also highlighted the fact that there are still no adequate campaign finance transparency laws. GRECO is set to release a follow-up report in 2013.

Freedom of speech is respected across the country. There are two independent daily newspapers, *Diari d'Andorra* and *El Periòdic d'Andorra*, and two free weekday papers, *Bon Dia* and *Diari Més*. There is only one Andorran television station, operated by the public broadcaster Ràdio I Televisió d'Andorra, though residents have access to broadcasts from neighboring France and Spain. Internet access is unrestricted.

Although the constitution recognizes the state's special relationship with the Roman Catholic Church, the government no longer subsidizes it. Religious minorities like Mormons and Jehovah's Witnesses are free to seek converts. Despite years of negotiations between the Muslim community and the government, a proper mosque for the country's roughly 2,000 Muslims still has not been built. While requests to convert public buildings or former churches for this purpose have been denied, the government does provide the Muslim community with public facilities for various religious functions. Academic freedom is respected.

Freedoms of assembly and association are generally respected, and domestic and international human rights organizations operate freely. While the government recognizes that both workers and employers have the right to defend their interests, the right to strike is not legally guaranteed. There are also no laws in place to penalize antiunion discrimination or regulate collective bargaining, though the government passed a law in 2009 that guarantees unions the right to operate. In March 2012, results of a survey by the Union of Workers of Andorra la Vella showed widespread concern for workplace corruption, as well as physical and psychological abuse of workers. Although the government showed concern over the report, no specific steps have been taken to investigate the issue. In October and November 2012, police unions organized a strike to protest unkept promises, especially in the area of pension reform. Reportedly constructive meetings were held in November between the two leading police unions and the minister of the interior, though no official decisions were announced by year's end.

The government generally respects the independence of the judiciary. Defendants enjoy the presumption of innocence and the right to a fair trial. Police can detain suspects for up to 48 hours without charge. Prison conditions meet international standards.

Under Andorra's restrictive naturalization criteria, one must marry a resident Andorran or live in the country for more than 20 years to qualify for citizenship. Prospective citizens are also required to learn Catalan, the national language. Although they do not have the right to vote, noncitizen residents receive most of the social and economic benefits of citizenship. In 2012, Andorra introduced a new law on residency, which applies to all those seeking non-work residency permits and affects applicants as of June 27, 2012. Applications are assessed under three categories of residency, including a passive residency for individuals who can show they are financially self-sufficient, business residency for individuals who own foreign companies, and a cultural residency for renowned artists and other public figures.

Immigrant workers, primarily from North Africa, complain that they lack the rights of citizens. Nearly 7,000 such immigrants have legal status, but many hold only "temporary work authorizations." Temporary workers are in a precarious position, as they must leave the country when their job contract expires.

Citizens have the right to own property. Legislation passed in 2008 fully opened 200 key economic sectors to foreign investment. This law also gives noncitizens the right to hold up to 49 percent capital in other established sectors.

Women enjoy the same legal rights as men. Fifteen seats were captured by women in the 2011 parliamentary elections, making Andorra the first European country to elect a majority female legislature, and the second globally, after Rwanda. However, there are no specific laws addressing the problem of violence against women, nor are there any government departments for women's issues or government-run shelters for battered women. Abortion is illegal, except to save the life of the mother.

Angola

Political Rights: 6
Civil Liberties: 5
Status: Not Free

Population: 20,945,000
Capital: Luanda

Ten-Year Ratings Timeline For Year Under Review (Political Rights, Civil Liberties, Status)

2003	2004	2005	2006	2007	2008	2009	2010	2011	2012
6,5NF	6,5NF	6,5NF	6,5NF	6,5NF	6,5NF	6,5NF	6,5NF	6,5NF	6,5NF

Overview:
The ruling Popular Movement for the Liberation of Angola dominated August 2012 parliamentary elections, taking more than 70 percent of the vote. While the polls suffered from serious flaws, including outdated and inaccurate voter rolls, the results were endorsed by the African Union. A spate of urban-based antigovernment protests that had begun in 2011 continued in 2012, leading to state-backed intimidation of protest leaders, scores of arrests, and the violent dispersal of demonstrations.

Angola was racked by civil war for nearly three decades following independence from Portugal in 1975. José Eduardo dos Santos took over as president in 1979, after the death of Angola's first postindependence leader, Agostinho Neto. Peace accords in 1991 and 1994 failed to end fighting between the rebel National Union for the Total Independence of Angola (UNITA) and the government, controlled by dos Santos's Popular Movement for the Liberation of Angola (MPLA). The death of UNITA leader Jonas Savimbi in 2002 helped to spur a successful ceasefire deal later that year, and UNITA subsequently transformed itself into Angola's largest opposition party.

The conflict claimed an estimated one million lives, displaced more than four million people, and forced over half a million to flee to neighboring countries. Many resettled people have remained without land, basic resources, or even identification documents.

Legislative elections, delayed repeatedly since 1997, were finally held in September 2008. The ruling MPLA took the vast majority of seats, with UNITA placing second among 14 parties. While domestic and international observers found that the results reflected the people's will, the campaign was marred by political violence and pro-MPLA bias by both the state media and the National Electoral Commission (CNE), which denied the opposition access to the voter registry and obstructed the accreditation of domestic monitors who were not aligned with the government.

In 2010, the MPLA-dominated parliament approved a new constitution that abolished direct presidential elections, stipulating instead that the leader of the largest party in the parliament would become the president. After a number of delays, parliamentary elections were held in August 2012. The MPLA's 72 percent of the vote marked a notable decline from its 82 percent showing in 2008, though the party still maintained its overwhelming dominance of the National Assembly, garnering 175 of 220 seats. UNITA took 32 seats, while the newly formed Salvation-Electoral Coalition won 8 seats. The Social Renewal Party (SRP) won 3 seats, and the Angolan National Liberation Front (FNLA) took the remaining 2. Dos Santos was easily reelected by the MPLA-dominated National Assembly in September.

While the African Union deemed the elections "free, fair, transparent and credible," the polls were deeply flawed. Voter rolls were outdated and inaccurate, and many registered voters were not listed or told to vote at distant polling stations. Additionally, the election commission failed to provide accreditation for many opposition party delegates and domestic observers to monitor the vote and ballot count. Media coverage, especially by the state-dominated broadcast sector, was biased toward the MPLA. Voter turnout dropped from 80 percent in 2008 to 60 percent countrywide and to 50 percent in the most populous province, Luanda.

The spate of small, sporadic antigovernment demonstrations in urban areas that had begun in 2011 continued throughout 2012, as did authorities' efforts to crack down on dissent. Security forces used tear gas—and in some cases live ammunition—to break up a number of antigovernment rallies by youth groups in Luanda, as well as protests in Benhuela and Cabinda City. Scores were arrested, about a dozen jailed, and protest leaders were assaulted, intimidated, and allegedly threatened with death by nonstate actors aligned with the government.

Political Rights and Civil Liberties: Angola is not an electoral democracy. The August 2012 legislative elections, while largely reflective of the people's will and an improvement over the 2008 polls, were not free and fair. The 220-seat National Assembly, whose members serve four-year terms, has little power, and 90 percent of legislation originates in the executive branch. Under the 2010 constitution, the largest party in the National Assembly selects the head of state. The constitution also mandates that, as of 2012, the president may serve a maximum of two five-year terms, and directly appoints the vice president, cabinet, and provincial governors. The last direct presidential election was held in 1992. Vice President Manuel Vicente, the former chairman of the national oil company Sonangol, is rumored to be the most likely successor to dos Santos as MPLA head and thus state president when dos Santos retires (although he can technically serve until 2022).

While five political parties are represented in the National Assembly, the ruling MPLA dominates Angola's party system. UNITA is the largest opposition party. Nine parties and coalitions participated in the 2012 elections. In a victory for political pluralism, in May the Angolan Supreme Court blocked the appointment of MPLA-favored CNE head Susana Ingles, which had been opposed by UNITA and other opposition parties; they argued that Ingles's status as a lawyer, rather than a judge, disqualified her from the position. André da Silva Neto was appointed to the post in June. In July, the CNE disallowed diaspora Angolans from voting in elections.

Corruption and patronage are endemic in the government, and bribery often underpins business activity. While President José Eduardo dos Santos has criticized MPLA members for misallocating significant portions of the country's oil revenues, the president himself is alleged to be one of the country's richest men. A December 2011 International Monetary Fund (IMF) report stated that $32 billion in government funds from 2007 to 2010, believed to be linked to Sonangol, could not be accounted for. In May, the IMF reported that the government attributed about $18.2 billion of that money to infrastructure projects, and about another $14 billion to overseas financial transactions. Angola was ranked 157 out of 174 countries surveyed in Transparency International's 2012 Corruption Perceptions Index.

Despite constitutional guarantees of freedom of expression, journalists are driven to self-censorship by the threat of dismissal, detention, and prosecution. The state owns the only daily newspaper and national radio station, as well as the main television stations, and private media are often denied access to official information and events. Libel and defamation are punishable by imprisonment and fines. Journalists, particularly those covering antigovernment protests and reporting on corruption, endured harassment, attacks, and detentions by security forces in 2012. According to Human Rights Watch (HRW), state media incited progovernment vigilantes to violence against antigovernment protesters. In March, security forces raided the offices of the independent weekly *Folha 8* and confiscated its computers, alleging that the newspaper had committed "crimes of outrage" against the state and the president. Editor William Tonet—who in 2011 was convicted of libel and fined 10 million kwanza ($105,000) for reporting allegations of corruption by close dos Santos associates—said the raid was connected to the paper's re-publication of photos satirizing dos Santos and other top officials, which had also spurred a criminal investigation of the paper in 2001. In July, two Angolan journalists working for the Portuguese state broadcaster and Voice of America were arrested and briefly detained while covering a demonstration in Luanda. Authorities have consistently prevented the outspoken Roman Catholic radio station Radio Ecclesia from broadcasting outside the capital.

In recent years, the government has tried to restrict electronic communication; many of the antigovernment protests in 2011 and 2012 were organized over social networks and SMS. Although opposition from civic organizations and local media played a role in the government's 2011 decision to scrap legislation that would have criminalized the electronic publication or distribution of what authorities deemed to be sensitive or subversive information, the government announced that same year that it would incorporate clauses from the law into an ongoing reform of the penal code.

Religious freedom is widely respected, despite colonial-era statutes that ban non-Christian religious groups. The educational system barely functions, suffering from underpaid and often corrupt teachers and severely damaged infrastructure.

The constitution guarantees freedoms of assembly and association, although these rights are not respected in practice. In 2012, authorities continued to violently disperse sporadic demonstrations by mostly young antigovernment protesters, and to arrest and intimidate protest leaders. According to HRW, between January and April 2012, security forces banned and/or dispersed at least five demonstrations and arrested at least 46 protesters, 11 of whom were sentenced to up to 90 days in prison; another 10 were arrested in July. In March, progovernment vigilantes raided the home of rap artist and protest leader Dionísio Casimiro "Carbono," beating him and three associates. In May and June, MPLA-affiliated war veterans staged a number of large protests calling for higher benefits from the government, under the auspices of an ad hoc grouping, the United Patriotic Movement. The government cracked down severely: 50 protesters were detained—some for weeks—and 3 were killed in June, while a number of protest leaders were allegedly assaulted. In October, the government agreed to dispense more generous pensions for the veterans.

Hundreds of nongovernmental organizations (NGOs) operate in Angola, many of them advocating for political reform, government accountability, and human rights protections. However, the government has occasionally threatened such organizations with closure. In 2011 authorities restricted the activities of a number of local and international NGOs relating to a Southern African Development Community summit. The right to strike and form unions is provided by the constitution, but the MPLA dominates the labor movement, and only a few independent unions exist. Some 85 percent of the population engages in subsistence agriculture.

The judiciary is subject to extensive political influence, particularly from the executive, though courts occasionally rule against the government. The president appoints Supreme Court judges to life terms without legislative input; the May 2012 decision disapproving the government's candidate for CNE head was a rare sign of independence. The courts in general are hampered by a lack of training and infrastructure, a large backlog of cases, corruption, and conflicts of interest. While the government has sought to train more municipal magistrates, municipal courts are rarely operational, leading to the use of traditional or informal courts.

Lengthy pretrial detention is common, and prisoners are subject to torture, severe overcrowding, sexual abuse, extortion, and a lack of basic services, including food and water. The government is building five new prisons in order to reduce overcrowding by 2013. According to Amnesty International, Angolan jails contain a number of political prisoners, mostly members of peaceful activist groups and advocates of regional autonomy. An estimated four million weapons in civilian hands threaten to contribute to lawlessness, and both government and private security personnel have committed murders and other abuses in connection with the diamond-mining industry.

In 2006, the government signed a peace agreement with secessionists in the oil-rich northern exclave of Cabinda, hoping to end a conflict that had continued intermittently since 1975. While between 80 and 90 percent of the rebel fighters have reportedly joined the army or demobilized, some violence has continued. The military continues to arrest Cabindans for alleged state security crimes. Most of these detainees are allegedly denied basic due process rights and subjected to inhumane treatment. Citing continued attacks by rebels—primarily from the FLEC-FAC group, a splinter from the main FLEC movement—the military restarted a counterinsurgency campaign in Cabinda in 2011, which continued in 2012. In August, the rebels called for talks with the government, which did not take place by year's end.

Minefields from the civil war continue to restrict freedom of movement, as does the country's rigid system of entry and exit visas. Tension involving refugees and migrants along the Angolan-Congolese border has led to a series of tit-for-tat expulsions affecting tens of thousands of people. In 2011, about 100,000 Democratic Republic of Congo nationals were deported from Angola. In May 2012, HRW reported that deportees are commonly subjected to sexual assault, beatings, arbitrary arrests, and denial of due process before their deportation.

Since 2001, security forces have evicted thousands of people from informal settlements in and around Luanda without adequate notice, compensation, or resettlement provisions, ostensibly for development purposes.

Women enjoy legal protections, and occupy cabinet positions and 75 seats in the National Assembly. However, de facto discrimination and violence against women remain common, particularly in rural areas. A new law on domestic violence, which included a broader definition of sexual violence, took effect in 2011. According to the government, the law significantly increased the frequency of reports of domestic violence in 2012, particularly in rural areas. Child labor is a major problem, and there have been reports of trafficking in women and children for prostitution or forced labor. A recent study by Angola's National Children's Institute and the UN Children's Fund found "a significant and growing" trend of abuse and abandonment of children who are accused of witchcraft after the death of a family member, usually from AIDS.

Antigua and Barbuda

Political Rights: 2*　　　　　　　　　　　　　**Population:** 87,000
Civil Liberties: 2　　　　　　　　　　　　　　**Capital:** St. John's
Status: Free

Ratings Change: Antigua and Barbuda's political rights rating improved from 3 to 2 due to a decline in corrupt foreign business influence over the government.

Ten-Year Ratings Timeline For Year Under Review (Political Rights, Civil Liberties, Status)

2003	2004	2005	2006	2007	2008	2009	2010	2011	2012
4,2PF	2,2F	2,2F	2,2F	2,2F	2,2F	3,2F	3,2F	3,2F	2,2F

Overview:　　　　The government of Antigua and Barbuda took steps in 2012 to reform the country's financial regulatory environment in the aftermath of the discovery of a $7 billion dollar Ponzi scheme, which had exposed deep ties between foreign businesses and the government. In June, bank executive R. Allen Stanford, who had orchestrated the scheme, was found guilty of fraud in a U.S. court and sentenced to 110 years in prison. Meanwhile, the opposition Antigua Labour Party (ALP) and its leader, Lester Bird, accused the government of lacking transparency and making unlawful changes to the procedures and composition of the country's electoral commission. In November, Gaston Browne defeated Bird to become ALP leader.

Antigua and Barbuda, a member of the Commonwealth, gained its independence from Britain in 1981. In the 2004 elections, the opposition United Progressive Party (UPP), led by Baldwin Spencer, defeated Prime Minister Lester Bird and the ruling Antigua Labour Party (ALP), ending the Bird political dynasty that had governed the country since 1976.

The 2009 parliamentary elections returned Spencer and the UPP to power with 9 seats in the 17-seat lower house; the ALP took 7 seats, while the Barbuda People's Movement (BPM) retained the single seat representing Barbuda. While elections were deemed fair and competitive by the Organization of American States, a High Court ruling in March 2010 invalidated the election of Spencer and others due to electoral irregularities, though the Eastern Caribbean Court of Appeals overturned the verdict in October 2010.

The 2009 collapse of the Stanford Financial Group, run by U.S. financier R. Allen Stanford, exposed deep ties between Stanford and the government of Antigua and Barbuda. A consortium of defrauded investors sued the government, claiming that top officials had been aware of and benefited from Stanford's $7 billion Ponzi scheme, in which clients were encouraged to invest in certificates of deposit from the Stanford International Bank of Antigua with false promises of security and high returns.

Although no Antiguan officials connected to the Stanford case have been brought to trial in Antigua and Barbuda, Stanford himself was found guilty by a U.S. court in March 2012 of 13 counts of conspiracy, fraud, and money laundering. He was sentenced to 110 years in prison in June. The U.S. government has also requested the extradition of Leroy King, former chief executive of Antigua's Financial Services Regulatory Commission (FSRC), who faces multiple charges of fraud, conspiracy, and money laundering related to his alleged involvement in Stanford's scheme. In April, Prime Minister Spencer issued a warrant for King's arrest. King remained under house arrest in Antigua at year's end, awaiting extradition to the United States.

Fallout from the collapse of the Stanford Financial Group's companies, which had been one of the main providers of jobs in the country, as well as the global economic downturn and the consequent decline in tourism, continued to impact Antigua and Barbuda's economy in 2012. Many former Stanford employees are still waiting for severance and pension payments.

Meanwhile, Bird and his ALP challenged the legitimacy and transparency of numerous government actions throughout 2012, including what they deemed to be unconstitutional changes made in December 2011 to the procedures and composition of the Antigua and Barbuda Electoral Commission, as well as the unlawful removal of some of its members. Bird also challenged the prime minister on his failure to request Parliament's approval on a series of loan agreements dating back to 2004, as well as a controversial purchase by the Antigua Public Utilities Authority. However, Bird himself lost his position as ALP leader to Gaston Browne in November party elections, representing the first time in 66 years that the party will not be led by a member of the Bird family.

Political Rights and Civil Liberties: Antigua and Barbuda is an electoral democracy. The 1981 constitution establishes a parliamentary system, with a governor general representing the British monarch as ceremonial head of state. The bicameral Parliament is composed of the 17-seat House of Representatives (16 seats for Antigua, 1 for Barbuda), to which members are elected for five-year terms, and an appointed 17-seat Senate. Antigua and Barbuda's prime minister is typically the leader of the majority party or coalition that emerges from the legislative elections. Political parties can organize freely.

The government has overseen the enactment of anticorruption and transparency legislation in recent years, but implementation has been slow. In 2012, Lester Bird and the opposition ALP accused the UPP government and Prime Minister Baldwin Spencer of not meeting the requirements of the country's anticorruption and freedom of information legislation. Nevertheless, the government did take positive steps during the year to reform the country's FSRC as well as regulations for the offshore financial and insurance sectors in order to combat corruption and restore confidence in the marketplace.

Antigua and Barbuda generally respects freedom of the press. However, defamation remains a criminal offense punishable by up to three years in prison, and politicians often file libel suits against opposing party members. Media outlets are concentrated among a small number of firms affiliated with either the current government or its predecessor. In October 2012, radio journalist Percival Simon was banned from ZDK Radio, which is owned by Bird, for openly supporting Gaston Browne, Bird's political opponent for leadership of the ALP. The government owns one of three radio stations and the public television station. There are no restrictions on access to the internet.

The government generally respects religious and academic freedoms.

Nongovernmental organizations are active but inadequately funded and often influenced by the government. Demonstrators are occasionally subject to police harassment. Labor unions can organize freely and bargain collectively. The Industrial Court mediates labor disputes.

The country's legal system is based on English common law. During the Bird years, the ALP government manipulated the nominally independent judicial system, which was powerless to address corruption in the executive branch. However, in recent years, the courts have increasingly asserted independence through controversial decisions against the government.

Crime continues to be a problem in Antigua and Barbuda, and the government has responded with increased community policing, the reintroduction of roadblocks, and stiffer fines for firearms violations. The United Nations Development Programme's 2012 Caribbean Human Development Report reported that Antigua and Barbuda suffers from a high rate of property crimes, such as robberies, with a lower violent crime rate. The country's prison is overcrowded, and conditions are very poor. The abuse of inmates has been reported, though visits by independent human rights groups are permitted

The 2005 Equal Opportunity Act bars discrimination on the basis of race, gender, class, political affinity, or place of origin. However, societal discrimination and violence against women remain problems. Women hold only 10 percent of the elected seats of the House of Representatives. Male and female same-sex sexual activity also remains criminalized under a 1995 law, and there have been cases of excessive force and discrimination of people based on sexual orientation at the hands of the police. Antigua and Barbuda serves as both a destination and transit country for the trafficking of men, women, and children for the purposes of forced labor and prostitution.

Argentina

Political Rights: 2
Civil Liberties: 2
Status: Free

Population: 40,829,000
Capital: Buenos Aires

Ten-Year Ratings Timeline For Year Under Review (Political Rights, Civil Liberties, Status)

2003	2004	2005	2006	2007	2008	2009	2010	2011	2012
2,2F	2,2F	2,2F	2,2F	2,2F	2,2F	2,2F	2,2F	2,2F	2,2F

Overview: The government of President Cristina Fernández de Kirchner in 2012 continued indirect government censorship through the discriminatory allocation of official advertising and increased unfair tax treatment of political opponents. Official corruption remained a problem, with Vice President Amado Boudou becoming the latest government official to face allegations of illegal enrichment. Meanwhile, Argentina also continued to try and convict perpetrators of human rights violations committed during the "dirty war."

Argentina gained independence from Spain in 1816. Democratic rule was often interrupted by war and military coups over the following century. The end of former president Juan Perón's populist and authoritarian regime in 1955 led to a series of right-wing military dictatorships that lasted until 1983. The beginning of civilian rule brought an end to Argentina's "dirty war," which was waged against real or suspected dissidents by the far-right military regime.

Carlos Menem, a populist of the Justicialist Party (PJ, commonly known as the Peronist Party) who ran on a platform of nationalism and state intervention in the economy, was elected president in 1989 amid hyperinflation and food riots. As president, he implemented an economic liberalization program and unconditionally allied the country with the United States. His convertibility plan, which pegged the peso to the U.S. dollar through a currency board, ended the country's chronic bouts of hyperinflation.

Buenos Aires mayor Fernando de la Rúa, of the center-left Alianza coalition, was elected president in 1999. Record unemployment and reduced government wages spurred demonstrations and unprecedented economic insecurity. Government efforts to stop a run on Argentina's banking system sparked violent protests in December 2001, forcing de la Rúa to resign. He was replaced by interim president Adolfo Rodríguez Saá, who resigned less than a week later. On December 31, Congress selected Menem's former vice president, Eduardo Duhalde, as Argentina's new president. A steep devaluation of the peso and a debilitating default on its foreign debt left Argentina teetering on the brink of political and economic collapse throughout 2002.

Néstor Kirchner of the Front for Victory (FPV) coalition, a faction of the Peronists, was elected president in 2003. While working to stabilize the economy, Kirchner moved to purge the country's military and police leadership of authoritarian elements. He took steps to remove justices from the highly politicized Supreme

Court—considered the country's most corrupt institution—and signed a decree that permitted the extradition of former military officials accused of human rights abuses. In 2006, Kirchner implemented a series of measures to centralize power in the executive branch. He also changed the tax system to limit the influence of historically powerful provincial governors and created new state-owned enterprises while nationalizing privatized ones.

Kirchner successfully passed power on to his wife, Senator Cristina Fernández de Kirchner, when she was elected president in October 2007. In practice, she began to govern in tandem with her husband, and the Argentine media commonly referred to their rule as a dual presidency, or "Los K," leading to confusion as to who exactly was in charge.

Fernández's once-strong political alliance and majority in Congress fractured following a standoff with Argentina's agricultural sector in 2008 over her administration's failed attempt to increase export taxes on certain farm products. Midterm legislative elections held in June 2009 in the midst of an economic downturn brought significant losses for Fernández and her party.

Beginning in mid-2010, the economy began to recover, fueled by a more benign international economic environment and rising agricultural prices. To finance increased spending, including on social welfare programs, Fernández pushed a law through Congress in February 2010 allowing the government to tap into Argentina's foreign currency reserves. The nationalization of $30 billion in private pension funds in December 2008 provided additional financial support. Fernández continued to centralize power around the executive even after Néstor Kirchner's sudden death in October 2010.

Fernández was reelected on October 23, 2011, garnering 54 percent of the vote, the largest margin of victory in the first round of an Argentine presidential election since the return of democracy in 1983. Fernández's FPV, with its allies, also won eight of the nine governors' races, reclaimed the lower house of Congress, and increased their majority in the Senate. A fragmented opposition contributed to Fernández's reelection, as did strong economic growth fueled by government spending and high commodity prices. Ongoing sympathy for the death of Néstor Kirchner, still wildly popular, also contributed to her landslide election.

Capital flight, unofficial annual inflation of 20-30 percent, a growing fiscal deficit, and a debilitating drought hurt the Argentine economy in 2012. The Fernández administration's expropriation of Spanish oil company YPF in April 2012 also contributed to economic uncertainty. Declining public services and public safety prompted "anti-Cristina" pot-banging demonstrations in September. Contributing to frustration was a commuter train wreck in February that killed 51 people and revealed the government's neglect of the country's transportation network. Meanwhile, the administration continued to crack down on its opponents, including economic firms publishing independent inflation statistics, through the government's tax agency.

Political Rights and Civil Liberties: Argentina is an electoral democracy. As amended in 1994, the constitution provides for a president elected for four years, with the option of reelection for one additional term. Presidential candidates must win 45 percent of the vote to avoid a runoff. The National Congress consists of the 257-member Chamber of Deputies, whose members are directly elected for four-year terms, with half of the seats up for election every two years; and the 72-member Senate, whose members are directly elected for six-year terms, with one-third of the seats up for election every two years.

The right to organize political parties is generally respected. Major parties include the Justicialist Party (also known as the Peronist Party), which holds two opposing factions: the center-left FPV faction, and the center-right Federal Peronism faction. Other parties include the centrist Radical Civic Union, the center-right Republican Proposal, and the socialist Broad Progressive Front. The Peronists have been a dominant force in politics since 1946.

Recent corruption scandals revealed the degree to which entrenched corruption plagues Argentine society. Former president and current senator Carlos Menem was charged in 2008 with illegally supplying weapons to Ecuador and Croatia, but was acquitted in September 2011. Former secretary of transportation Ricardo Jaime was indicted twice in 2010 on separate charges of embezzlement that reportedly occurred during his tenure from 2003 to 2009; a trial had not yet begun by the end of 2012. The trial of former president Fernando de la Rúa on charges of bribing senators to approve labor reform during his presidency in 2000 began in August 2012 and was ongoing at year's end. Vice President Amado Boudou is also subject to an ongoing investigation for embezzlement and influence peddling. Meanwhile, the government's censorship and manipulation of INDEC, the national statistics agency, in recent years has resulted in distorted economic figures, as well as the agency's loss of domestic and international credibility. Argentina was ranked 102 out of 176 countries surveyed in Transparency International's 2012 Corruption Perceptions Index.

Freedom of expression is guaranteed by law. However, while Congress decriminalized libel and slander in 2009, the government of Cristina Fernández de Kirchner has consistently limited press freedom in practice. The press environment as a whole worsened in 2012, as the administration carried out smear campaigns against critical journalists, usually through public media. Although a 2011 Supreme Court ruling urged the government to apply more balance in the distribution of state advertising, there are currently no laws that regulate government discretion in allocating state advertising. In 2012, the government continued to manipulate the distribution of official advertising and granting of operational licenses to reward supportive media and to damage critical media such as Grupo Clarín, Argentina's largest media conglomerate. While the Senate passed a freedom of information bill in 2010 that would apply to all branches of the government, the bill had yet to pass the Chamber of Deputies by the end of 2012. Several Argentine provinces passed their own freedom of information laws, though enforcement and funding undermined their impact. Journalists in Argentina traditionally face less risk than in neighboring countries, but attacks were on the rise in 2012; two separate attacks on journalists occurred in August, likely in connection with their reporting on local corruption.

The constitution guarantees freedom of religion, and anti-Semitism is reportedly on the decline. In June 2010, Fernández appointed the first Jewish foreign minister in Argentine history. Nevertheless, the country's Jewish community, the largest in Latin America, remains a target of discrimination and vandalism. The 1994 bombing of a Jewish cultural center continues to play a role in Argentine politics, as no convictions have been made. Academic freedom is a cherished Argentine tradition and is largely observed in practice.

The rights of freedom of assembly and association are generally respected. Civic organizations are robust and play a major role in society, although some fall victim to Argentina's pervasive corruption. Labor is dominated by Peronist unions, though union influence has diminished dramatically in recent years due to internal divisions.

The justice system remains plagued by scores of incompetent and corrupt judges who retain their positions through tenure. The lower courts are highly politicized, and the relatively independent Supreme Court received heightened pressure from the government in 2012 surrounding the Grupo Clarín case. A 2012 report published by the World Economic Forum ranked Argentina 133 out of 144 countries in judicial independence. Police misconduct, including torture and brutality of suspects in custody, is endemic. Arbitrary arrests and abuse by police are rarely punished in the courts, owing to intimidation of witnesses and judges, particularly in Buenos Aires province. Prisons are overcrowded, and conditions remain substandard throughout the country.

In 2005, the Supreme Court ruled that laws passed in the 1980s to protect the military from prosecution were unconstitutional. The decision laid the foundation for the prosecution of past military crimes, leading Néstor Kirchner to initiate prosecution proceedings against former officials involved in Argentina's dirty war. Prosecutions of perpetrators of human rights violations committed during that period have continued under the Fernández administration. Twelve military and police officers, including Ricardo Cavallo and Alfredo Astiz, were convicted with torture, murder, and forced disappearance in October 2011 and sentenced to life in prison. In July 2012, former military dictator and principal architect of the dirty war, Jorge Videla, was convicted and sentenced to fifty years in prison for his plan to systemically steal the children of kidnapped prisoners. The 85-year-old Videla already had a life sentence for other crimes against humanity, and has been imprisoned since 2010.

Argentina's indigenous peoples, who represent between 1.5 and 3.5 percent of the population, are largely neglected by the government. Approximately 70 percent of the country's rural indigenous communities lack title to their lands. While the Kirchner administration returned lands to several communities, most disputes remain unresolved. Forced evictions of indigenous communities still occur, despite laws prohibiting this practice.

Women actively participate in politics in Argentina. In addition to the 2011 reelection of Fernández as president, women were elected to 38 percent of the seats in the Chamber of Deputies in October and 39 percent of seats in the Senate. Decrees mandate that one-third of Congress members be women. Argentina's Supreme Court ruled in March 2012 that women who have an abortion after being raped can no longer be prosecuted; an estimated 500,000 illegal abortions are performed in Argentina each year. Domestic abuse remains a serious problem, and women also face economic discrimination and gender wage gaps. In 2002, Buenos Aires became the first South American city to pass a domestic partnership law, and Argentina became the second country in the Americas—after Canada—to legalize same-sex marriage nationwide in July 2010.

Armenia

Political Rights: 5*
Civil Liberties: 4
Status: Partly Free

Population: 3,282,300
Capital: Yerevan

Ratings Change: Armenia's political rights rating improved from 6 to 5 due to the absence of postelection violence following parliamentary balloting in May and the entry of an authentic opposition party into the legislature.

Note: The numerical ratings and status listed above do not reflect conditions in Nagorno-Karabakh, which is examined in a separate report.

Ten-Year Ratings Timeline For Year Under Review (Political Rights, Civil Liberties, Status)

2003	2004	2005	2006	2007	2008	2009	2010	2011	2012
4,4PF	5,4PF	5,4PF	5,4PF	5,4PF	6,4PF	6,4PF	6,4PF	6,4PF	5,4PF

Overview: A new electoral code adopted in 2011 provided a basic democratic framework for the May 2012 parliamentary elections, which were praised for their competitive and peaceful character despite the reporting of certain electoral irregularities. While the ruling Republican Party retained power, the opposition Armenian National Congress captured seats for the first time. Meanwhile, border clashes and the controversial extradition of convicted murderer Ramil Safarov threatened to halt peace talks with Azerbaijan over Nagorno-Karabakh, though Armenia pledged not to withdraw from the negotiations.

Following a short period of independence amid the turmoil at the end of World War I, Armenia was divided between Turkey and the Soviet Union by 1922. Most Armenians in the Turkish portion were killed or driven abroad during the war and its aftermath, but those in the east survived Soviet rule. The Soviet republic of Armenia declared its independence in 1991, propelled by a nationalist movement that had initially focused on demands to transfer the substantially ethnic Armenian region of Nagorno-Karabakh from Azerbaijan to Armenia. Nagorno-Karabakh was recognized internationally as part of Azerbaijan, but by the late 1990s it was held by ethnic Armenian forces who claimed independence. Prime Minister Robert Kocharian, a former president of Nagorno-Karabakh, was elected president of Armenia in March 1998.

On October 27, 1999, five gunmen assassinated Prime Minister Vazgen Sarkisian, assembly speaker Karen Demirchian, and several other senior officials. Allegations that Kocharian or members of his inner circle had orchestrated the shootings prompted opposition calls for the president to resign. Citing a lack of evidence, however, prosecutors did not press charges against Kocharian, who gradually consolidated his power during the following year.

Kocharian was reelected in a 2003 presidential election that was marred by fraud. During the runoff vote, authorities detained more than 200 opposition supporters for over 15 days. Opposition parties boycotted subsequent sessions of the National Assembly, and police violently dispersed protests mounted in the spring of 2004 over the government's failure to redress the problems of the 2003 vote.

The Republican Party of Armenia (HHK)—the party of Prime Minister Serzh Sarkisian, a close Kocharian ally—won a dominant majority of seats along with two other major propresidential parties in the 2007 legislative elections. Opposition parties suffered from disadvantages regarding media coverage and the abuse of state resources ahead of the vote.

In the 2008 presidential election, Sarkisian defeated the main opposition candidate, former president Levon Ter-Petrosian. The opposition, which alleged that the vote had been falsified, led peaceful demonstrations on February 21 that turned violent a week later; 10 people were killed and more than 200 were injured during clashes with police, and more than 100 people were arrested.

Inspired by ongoing uprisings in Arab countries, tens of thousands of opposition protesters took to the streets in spring 2011. Combined with increased international pressure, the demonstrations convinced the Armenian authorities to release all political prisoners still held from the 2008 crackdown, remove a ban on rallies in Yerevan's Freedom Square that also dated to 2008, reopen the investigation into the 10 deaths during the crackdown, and begin a dialogue with opposition parties. However, the dialogue was suspended in September 2011 without any tangible results, and no substantial progress had been made on the investigation into the 2008 deaths by the end of 2012.

As a result of the negative assessments by international observers of the 2008 election, as well as of the 2009 municipal elections won by the HHK, the government adopted a new electoral code in 2011. While the Council of Europe regarded it as an improvement over the previous code, it did not incorporate any of the suggestions made by opposition parties.

The integrity of the new code was put to the test during the May 6, 2012, parliamentary vote. Many observers praised the elections as being noticeably more competitive and peaceful than in previous years, with a marked improvement in free expression and assembly during the campaign period, as well as an absence of postelection violence. International observers found that the new electoral code provided a solid framework for free and fair elections, though a number of issues were raised regarding its content and implementation, including recommendations for measures to ensure greater voter secrecy and eliminate vote buying and selling. Other criticisms included the misuse of administrative resources and irregularities in the tabulation process.

The outgoing ruling coalition captured a total of 118 seats in the elections: the HHK won 69, Prosperous Armenia secured 37 seats, and the Armenian Revolutionary Federation and Rule of Law each took 6 seats. The Armenian National Congress, the formerly anti-institution opposition coalition led by Ter-Petrosian, made a historic entry into the parliament with seven seats. After the elections, HHK was unable to reestablish its coalition with any of its former partners except Rule of Law. Many ministers retained their posts following the elections, including Prime Minister Tigran Sarkisyan, though members of Prosperous Armenia in the outgoing cabinet were replaced by appointees from HHK.

Stagnating peace negotiations with Azerbaijan over the contested Nagorno-Karabakh territory faced new challenges in June 2012, as an outbreak of border clashes led to casualties on both sides. Tensions further intensified in August, when the Hungarian government extradited Ramil Safarov, an Azerbaijani soldier convicted of killing an Armenian soldier with an axe in 2004, to a hero's welcome in the Azerbaijani capital, Baku. Despite its outrage, the Armenian government pledged not to withdraw from peace talks over Nagorno-Karabakh, though no progress was made in the talks by year's end.

Political Rights and Civil Liberties: Armenia is not an electoral democracy. The unicameral National Assembly is elected for five-year terms, with 90 seats chosen by proportional representation and 41 through races in single-member districts. The president is elected by popular vote for up to two five-year terms. However, elections since the 1990s have been marred by major irregularities. The 2008 presidential election was seriously undermined by problems with the vote count, a biased and restricted media environment, and the abuse of administrative resources in favor of ruling party candidate Serzh Sarkisian. The Yerevan municipal elections held in May 2009 also suffered from significant violations, though international observers claimed that the fraud did not jeopardize the overall legitimacy of the results. In 2011 local elections were held in several districts, but the polls were boycotted by the opposition and not observed by international monitors. In addition to parliamentary elections, local polls in larger cities (excluding Yerevan) and several regions were also monitored by international observers without incident in September 2012.

Corruption is pervasive, and bribery and nepotism are reportedly common among government officials, who are rarely prosecuted or removed for abuse of office. Corruption is also believed to be a serious problem in law enforcement. A five-year initiative to combat graft, announced in 2008, has not made meaningful headway against the country's entrenched culture of corruption.

There are limits on press freedom. The authorities use informal pressure to maintain control over broadcast outlets, the chief source of news for most Armenians. State-run Armenian Public Television is the only station with nationwide coverage, and the owners of most private channels have close government ties. In June 2010, the National Assembly enacted legislation related to a switch to digital broadcasting that reduced the maximum number of television stations to 18 in the capital—down from at least 22 operating at the time—and 9 in other regions. The new law also obliged a number of the new total to focus on content other than domestic news and political affairs. In 2011, the legislation contributed to the denial of a digital license to GALA TV, the sole remaining station that regularly criticized the government. The station is almost certain to leave the airwaves when the country completes the switchover to digital broadcasting in 2015. The government also continued to deny a license to the independent television station A1+, despite a 2008 ruling in the network's favor by the European Court of Human Rights. The station's battle for licensing remained unresolved in 2012, though it returned to the airwaves as of September, via ArmNews TV, which has granted A1+ a one-year renewable contract to broadcast a news bulletin over its frequency. Although libel was decriminalized in May 2010, journalists face high fines under the civil code for defamation and insult, though there were fewer cases in the first half of 2012 than during the same period in 2011. Violence against journalists remains a problem, particularly during election periods. The authorities do not interfere with internet access.

Freedom of religion is generally respected, though the dominant Armenian Apostolic Church enjoys certain exclusive privileges, and members of minority faiths sometimes face societal discrimination. Jehovah's Witnesses are forced to serve prison terms for refusing to participate in either military service or the military-administered alternative service for conscientious objectors.

The government generally does not restrict academic freedom. Public schools are required to display portraits of the president and the head of the Armenian Apostolic Church, and to teach the church's history.

In the aftermath of the 2008 postelection violence, the government imposed restrictions on freedom of assembly. Under pressure from major opposition rallies in the spring of 2011 as well as criticism from the Council of Europe, the authorities ended the practice of forbidding demonstrations in the capital's Freedom Square, the traditional venue for political gatherings since the late 1980s. However, authorities have been known to create artificial obstacles for people attempting to travel from the provinces to participate in such rallies.

Registration requirements for nongovernmental organizations (NGOs) are cumbersome and time consuming. Some 3,000 NGOs are registered with the Ministry of Justice, though many are not active in a meaningful way. While the constitution provides for the right to form and join trade unions, labor organizations are weak and relatively inactive in practice.

The judiciary is subject to political pressure from the executive branch and suffers from considerable corruption. Police make arbitrary arrests without warrants, beat detainees during arrest and interrogation, and use torture to extract confessions. Prison conditions in Armenia are poor, and threats to prisoner health are significant. Although members of the country's tiny ethnic minority population rarely report cases of overt discrimination, they have complained about difficulties in receiving education in their native languages. Members of the Yezidi community have sometimes reported discrimination by police and local authorities.

Citizens have the right to own private property and establish businesses, but an inefficient and often corrupt court system and unfair business competition hinder such activities. Key industries remain in the hands of so-called oligarchs and influential cliques who received preferential treatment in the early stages of privatization. Illegal expropriation of private property by the state is a problem; in 2012, the European Convention on Human Rights found the government guilty of violating property rights in two separate cases, each with multiple plaintiffs; the state was fined a total of 131,000 euros ($170,000) in damages for both cases.

According to the new electoral code, women must occupy every 6th position—20 percent—on a party's candidate list for the parliament's proportional-representation seats. Although this quota was met in the registrations for the May 2012 elections, women make up only 11 percent of the new parliament, since many female candidates were withdrawn after the lists were registered. Domestic violence and trafficking in women and girls for the purpose of prostitution are believed to be serious problems. Though homosexuality was decriminalized in 2003, gay men and lesbians still face violence and persecution. In May 2012, a gay-friendly bar in Yerevan was fire-bombed in what is believed to be a hate crime. Two parliamentarians from the nationalist Armenian Revolutionary Federation posted bail for the assailants and publicly defended their actions.

Australia

Political Rights: 1
Civil Liberties: 1
Status: Free

Population: 22,035,000
Capital: Canberra

Ten-Year Ratings Timeline For Year Under Review (Political Rights, Civil Liberties, Status)

2003	2004	2005	2006	2007	2008	2009	2010	2011	2012
1,1F	1,1F	1,1F	1,1F	1,1F	1,1F	1,1F	1,1F	1,1F	1,1F

Overview:
Australia's Labor-led government in 2012 readopted the Pacific Solution plan for asylum seekers that it once rejected, signing new agreements with Nauru and Papua New Guinea to re-open detention and processing centers on those islands. Australia's controversial new tax on carbon dioxide went into effect in July. In September, a bill to legalize same-sex marriage was defeated after heated debate.

The British colonies in Australia, first settled in 1788, were organized as a federative commonwealth in 1901, and gradually gained full independence from Britain. Since World War II, political power has alternated between the center-left Labor Party and a conservative coalition of the Liberal Party and the smaller National Party.

The Labor Party was successful in 2007 elections, with Labor's Kevin Rudd replacing the Liberal Party's John Howard as prime minister. The Rudd government reversed several of its predecessor's positions, including issuing a formal apology for past laws and policies that had "inflicted profound grief, suffering, and loss" on the country's Aborigines. It also closed the detention centers in Nauru and Papua New Guinea that the Howard government had created as part of its Pacific Solution plan to deal with the massive influx of asylum seekers from South Asia. By the end of 2008, however, the Rudd government was forced to open a new detention center on Christmas Island to receive an increasing number of migrants. Public sentiment on both sides of the issue intensified as asylum seekers set fire to their boats, went on hunger strikes, committed suicide, or took other extreme measures to demand entry into Australia.

Rudd resigned as party leader and prime minister in June 2010 in the face of multiple difficulties, including the asylum crisis, a national home-insulation scheme that was linked to four deaths and many fires, a controversial proposal for a "super tax" on the coal and iron-ore industries, and parliamentary rejection of a carbon-emissions trading scheme. Labor chose Deputy Prime Minister Julia Gillard to replace Rudd, making her Australia's first female prime minister. She called snap elections in August 2010. Although Labor won only 72 seats compared to 73 for the conservative parties, Labor secured support from the Green Party and three independents.

Escalating violence, suicides, hunger strikes, and arson at the Christmas Island detention center ultimately forced the Gillard government to readopt the Pacific Solution. In 2012, the government signed new agreements with Nauru and Papua New Guinea to reopen the refugee centers on those islands; the Nauru center alone was expected to cost almost $2 billion to maintain over four years. Gillard's decision to reopen the overseas centers was strongly criticized by human rights groups. By year's end, 386 and 50 asylum seekers were, respectively, sent to Nauru and Papua New Guinea.

Australia's controversial tax on carbon dioxide emissions went into effect in July; the law places a tax on the country's top 500 carbon emitters, which is scheduled to be replaced with an emissions permit trading system in 2015. Although the plan's supporters say it is necessary to combat global warming, opponents claim the tax could devastate the Australian economy.

Political Rights and Civil Liberties: Australia is an electoral democracy. A governor general, who is appointed on the recommendation of the prime minister, represents the British monarch as head of state. The prime minister is the leader of the majority party or coalition in Parliament.

Voting is compulsory, and citizens participate in free and fair multiparty elections to choose representatives for the bicameral Parliament. The Senate, the upper house, has 76 seats, with 12 senators from each of the six states and two from each of the two mainland territories. Half of the state members, who serve six-year terms, are up for election every three years; all territory members are elected every three years. The House of Representatives, the lower house, has 150 seats. All members are elected by popular preferential voting to serve three-year terms, and no state can have fewer than five representatives.

The Labor and Liberal parties are the two major parties. Minor parties represented in Parliament are the left-leaning Green Party and three right-leaning factions (the Liberal National Party of Queensland, the National Party, and the Country Liberal Party).

Australia is regarded as one of the least corrupt societies in the world, ranking 7 out of 176 countries surveyed in Transparency International's 2012 Corruption Perceptions Index.

There are no constitutional protections for freedoms of speech and the press, but citizens and the media freely criticize the government without reprisal. Some laws restrict publication and dissemination of material that promotes or incites terrorist acts. There are numerous public and private television and radio broadcasters, but ownership of private print media is highly concentrated.

Freedom of religion is respected, as is academic freedom. Under antiterrorism laws, mosques and Islamic schools are barred from disseminating anti-Australian messages.

Freedoms of assembly and association are not codified in law, but the government respects these rights in practice. Workers can organize and bargain collectively.

The judiciary is independent, and prison conditions generally meet international standards. Antiterrorism legislation enacted in 2005, with a 10-year sunset clause, includes police powers to detain suspects without charge, "shoot to kill" provisions, the criminalization of violence against the public and Australian troops overseas, and authorization for the limited use of soldiers to meet terrorist threats on domestic soil.

Some 40 people have been arrested on terrorism charges since 2000. Five men of Libyan, Bangladeshi, and Lebanese origin arrested in 2005 were sentenced in February 2010 to prison terms ranging from 23 to 28 years for conspiracy to commit acts of terrorism. Australian immigration has been expanding the use of electronic biometric captures of fingerprints and facial images for visitors since 2011, with emphasis on those from countries deemed a high risk for Islamic extremism, such as Yemen and Somalia.

In 2011 the military was embroiled in a series of scandals involving rape, homophobia, bullying, and sexual predation. In September 2011, a navy male cadet was found guilty of raping a female cadet, and in December, a navy commander was found guilty of abusing a female subordinate by spanking her. In November 2012, the government officially apologized to victims after a government-commissioned study found more than 1,000 claims of abuse from the 1950s to the present.

Racial tensions involving South Asian and other immigrant groups have grown in recent years, especially in Melbourne, where the bulk of interracial violence has occurred. The number of South Asian applications to universities in Australia fell for two consecutive years in the 2010 and 2011 academic years. Foreign student enrollment dropped by 8.4 percent in the first half of 2012, and the number of new Indian students—the largest group from South Asia—dropped by 24 percent during the same period. With tuition from foreign students an important source of income for universities, the government decided in October 2012 to reduce the cost of applying for a student visa.

Aborigines, who comprise about 2 percent of the population, are underrepresented at all levels of political leadership and lag far behind other groups in key social and economic indicators, including life expectancy and employment. Aborigines are reportedly routinely mistreated by police and prison officials, and they experience higher rates of incarceration and levels of violence, including homicide and child abuse.

Women enjoy equal rights and have attained greater parity in pay and promotion in public and private sector jobs. A new law allowing women in the military to serve in combat positions went into effect in 2012. Violence against women remains a serious problem, particularly within the Aboriginal population. In 2011, New South Wales gave new powers to the police to order women to remove burqas and other face coverings if they are suspected of a crime. Those who refuse to remove the coverings could face one year in jail or be fined around A$5,500 (US$5,384).

Gay men and lesbians can serve in the military, and federal law grants legal residence to foreign same-sex partners of Australian citizens. However, there is no federal ban on discrimination based on sexual orientation, and a 2004 amendment to the Federal Marriage Act defines marriage as a union between a man and a woman. In September 2012, after days of heated debate, lawmakers voted to reject a bill to legalize gay marriage. Both Prime Minister Julia Gillard—whose party backed the bill—and opposition leader Tony Abbott voted against the proposal.

Austria

Political Rights: 1
Civil Liberties: 1
Status: Free

Population: 8,485,200
Capital: Vienna

Ten-Year Ratings Timeline For Year Under Review (Political Rights, Civil Liberties, Status)

2003	2004	2005	2006	2007	2008	2009	2010	2011	2012
1,1F	1,1F	1,1F	1,1F	1,1F	1,1F	1,1F	1,1F	1,1F	1,1F

Overview:
Political corruption scandals continued in Austria in 2012, tainting both the conservative government of the previous decade and the current Social Democratic chancellor, Werner Faymann. A new ethics law was passed in June, but the major parties sought to limit a parliamentary investigation of Faymann on corruption charges. Meanwhile, Austro-Canadian car parts magnate Frank Stronach announced that he was founding a new party and would run for chancellor in the 2013 election.

Modern Austria, which emerged from the collapse of the Austro-Hungarian Empire in World War I, was annexed to Nazi Germany in 1938 before being restored to independence after World War II. The country remained neutral during the Cold War and joined the European Union (EU) in 1995.

From 1986 until 2000, the two largest political parties—the center-left Social Democratic Party of Austria (SPÖ) and the center-right People's Party of Austria (ÖVP)—governed together in a grand coalition. The 1999 elections produced the first government since 1970 that did not include the SPÖ. Instead, the ÖVP formed a coalition with the Freedom Party of Austria (FPÖ), a far-right nationalist party that won 27 percent of the popular vote. In 2000, the European Union (EU) briefly suspended ties with Austria, imposing diplomatic sanctions in response to the FPÖ's inclusion in the government. In 2005 most of the FPÖ's members of the parliament, including its controversial leader, Jörg Haider, left the party to form the Alliance for the Future of Austria (BZÖ).

In October 2006, the SPÖ won parliamentary elections by a small margin and formed another grand coalition with the ÖVP. Alfred Gusenbauer of the SPÖ served as chancellor from 2007 through 2008. In the summer of 2008, the ÖVP announced its exit from the coalition amid political battles over health, tax, and pension reforms.

In the September 2008 elections, the SPÖ and ÖVP lost ground to the BZÖ and FPÖ, which were buoyed by xenophobic sentiment and deep skepticism toward the EU. However, both the SPÖ and the ÖVP refused to form a coalition with the far right, and in late 2008, they agreed to revive their alliance. Werner Faymann of the SPÖ became chancellor.

February 2009 state elections suggested a continued movement toward the right, with the SPÖ suffering dramatic losses. However, the ÖVP again ruled out a coalition with the FPÖ.

In October 2010 state elections in Vienna, the SPÖ lost its absolute majority in the legislature for only the second time since World War II, though it still led with 44.2 percent of the vote. The FPÖ placed second with 27 percent, while the ÖVP logged its worst-ever result in Vienna with only 13.2 percent.

In September 2012, Austrian-born Canadian car parts magnate Frank Stronach, an 80-year-old billionaire, announced that he was forming an Austrian political party, called Team Stronach, and would be a candidate for chancellor in the 2013 general election. In November, Team Stronach was allowed to take its first seats in the parliament when five sitting members of a small right-wing opposition party defected to join the new party.

Political Rights and Civil Liberties: Austria is an electoral democracy. The lower house of the Federal Assembly, the Nationalrat (National Council), has 183 members chosen through proportional representation at the district, state, and federal levels. Members serve five-year terms, extended from four in 2008. The president, who is elected for a six-year term, appoints the chancellor, who needs the support of the legislature to govern. The 62 members of the upper house, the Bundesrat (Federal Council), are chosen by state legislatures for five- or six-year terms.

Though Austria has competitive political parties and free and fair elections, the traditional practice of grand coalitions has fostered disillusionment with the political process. The participation of Slovene, Hungarian, and Roma minorities in local government remains limited despite governmental efforts to provide bilingual education, media, and access to federal funds.

Recent corruption scandals have damaged the reputation of Austria's political class. According to a Eurobarometer poll conducted in September 2011 and released in February 2012, 80 percent of Austrians said they believed corruption was a major problem, up from 61 percent in 2009—the largest such increase for any European country. The scandals led the parliament to pass an ethics reform bill in June 2012, tightening disclosure rules for political contributions and gifts. Prosecutors in August indicted former interior minister Ernst Strasser on corruption charges. Strasser had resigned his seat in the European Parliament in 2011 after accepting a bribe offered by British reporters posing as lobbyists. Gabriela Moser, the head of a parliamentary committee investigating alleged corruption involving Chancellor Werner Faymann, resigned in September 2012, asserting that opposition from the SPÖ and ÖVP was limiting her effectiveness. According to the allegations, Faymann, in his previous post as transportation minister, pressured the state railroad and highway agency to pay for advertisements favorable to him. Prosecutors in October brought the first indictments in a wide-ranging fraud and corruption case concerning Telekom Austria, which included the alleged bribery of lobbyists and politicians such as former vice chancellor Hubert Gorbach. Austria was ranked 25 out of 176 countries surveyed in Transparency International's 2012 Corruption Perceptions Index

The federal constitution and the Media Law of 1981 provide the basis for free media in Austria, and the government generally respects these provisions in practice. However, libel and slander laws protect politicians and government officials, and a large number of defamation cases have been brought by public officials, particularly from the FPÖ, in recent years. Despite a 2003 law to promote media diversity, media ownership remains highly concentrated. There are no restrictions on internet access.

While there is no official censorship, Austrian law prohibits any form of neo-Nazism or anti-Semitism, as well as the public denial, approval, or justification of Nazi crimes, including the Holocaust. However, the far-right FPÖ has been accused of anti-Semitic rhetoric in recent years. Additionally, the FPÖ has been criticized for fueling anti-Muslim feelings in Austria through controversial ad campaigns. A number of recent high-profile court cases have centered on the balance between freedom of speech and hate speech, including the February 2011 conviction of lecturer Elisabeth Sabaditsch-Wolff for denigrating Islamic teachings during an FPÖ-sanctioned seminar.

Religious freedom is constitutionally guaranteed. Austrian law divides religious organizations into three legal categories: officially recognized religious societies, religious confessional communities, and associations. Many religious minority groups have complained that the law impedes their legitimate claims for recognition and demotes them to second- or third-class status. However, in July 2012, the government and Muslim groups celebrated the centenary of Austria's Law on Islam, which assured Muslims of "the same legal protection as is granted to other legally recognized religious communities." There are no government restrictions on academic freedom. Freedoms of assembly and association are protected in the constitution and in practice. Nongovernmental organizations operate without restrictions. Trade unions are free to organize and to strike, and they are considered an essential partner in national policymaking.

The judiciary is independent, and the Constitutional Court examines the compatibility of legislation with the constitution. The quality of prisons generally meets high European standards.

Residents are usually afforded equal protection under the law. However, immigration has fueled some resentment toward minorities and foreigners. Austria has one of the world's highest numbers of asylum seekers per capita, and the Office of the UN High Commissioner for Refugees has criticized Austria's strict asylum law. Some asylum seekers can be deported while appeals are pending, and new arrivals are asked for full statements within 72 hours. In addition, the number of people who have been naturalized has fallen dramatically since the establishment of a more restrictive national integration policy in 2009.

A 1979 law guarantees women's freedom from discrimination in various areas, including the workplace. However, the income gap between men and women remains significant. The 2009 Second Protection Against Violence Act increased penalties for perpetrators of domestic violence and authorized further measures against chronic offenders. A 2009 law permits civil partnerships for same-sex couples, giving them equal rights to pension benefits and alimony. However, it does not provide same-sex couples with the same adoption rights as heterosexual couples or equal access to assisted reproductive technologies.

Azerbaijan

Political Rights: 6
Civil Liberties: 5
Status: Not Free

Population: 9,284,000
Capital: Baku

Note: The numerical ratings and status listed above do not reflect conditions in Nagorno-Karabakh, which is examined in a separate report.

Ten-Year Ratings Timeline For Year Under Review (Political Rights, Civil Liberties, Status)

2003	2004	2005	2006	2007	2008	2009	2010	2011	2012
6,5NF	6,5NF	6,5NF	6,5NF	6,5NF	6,5NF	6,5NF	6,5NF	6,5NF	6,5NF

Overview: **The authorities in 2012 used violent tactics to disperse antigovernment rallies, detained more than 70 demonstrators and journalists, and filed dubious criminal charges against government critics. Also during the year, investigative reports by foreign media exposed the outsized wealth of the ruling Aliyev family, leading the president to sign legal amendments aimed at protecting the confidentiality of corporate structures and ownership. In August, the government pardoned a former soldier convicted of murdering an Armenian officer at a NATO training camp in Hungary in 2004, igniting anger in Armenia and nearly ending negations over the disputed territory of Nagorno-Karabakh. Separately, ahead of the Eurovision song contest in May, the government continued to forcibly evict Baku residents to make way for the construction of the contest venue.**

After a short period of independence from 1918 to 1920, Azerbaijan was occupied by Soviet forces and formally entered the Soviet Union in 1922. Following a referendum in 1991, Azerbaijan declared independence from the disintegrating union.

In 1992, Abulfaz Elchibey, leader of the nationalist opposition Azerbaijan Popular Front, was elected president in a generally free and fair vote. A military coup one year later ousted him from power and installed the former first secretary of the Azerbaijan Communist Party, Heydar Aliyev, in his place. In the 1993 presidential election, Aliyev was credited with receiving nearly 99 percent of the vote. Five leading opposition parties and some 600 independent candidates were barred from the first post-Soviet parliamentary elections in 1995, allowing Aliyev's New Azerbaijan Party (YAP) to win the most seats. In 1998, Aliyev was reelected with more than 70 percent of the vote in balloting that was marred by irregularities, and the YAP won fraudulent parliamentary polls in 2000.

Prime Minister Ilham Aliyev, Heydar Aliyev's son, became a candidate in the October 2003 presidential election after his father fell ill in April. Final election results showed Ilham Aliyev defeating seven challengers with nearly 77 percent of the ballots. His closest rival, opposition Musavat Party leader Isa Gambar, received 14 percent. According to Organization for Security and Cooperation in Europe (OSCE) observers, the vote was again tainted by widespread fraud. After violent clashes between security forces and demonstrators in Baku in October, the authorities unleashed a crackdown in which more than 600 people were detained, including election officials who refused to certify fraudulent results. Heydar Aliyev died in December 2003.

The opposition captured just 10 of 125 seats amid low turnout in the 2005 parliamentary elections, with a substantial majority going to the ruling YAP and its allies. The results were contested by the opposition, which organized a number of rallies in the capital.

Aliyev easily won a second term in the 2008 presidential election, taking 89 percent of the vote amid 75 percent turnout, according to official results. Most of the opposition boycotted the poll, citing barriers to media access and the overwhelming administrative resources deployed by the YAP. In 2009, a constitutional amendment that removed presidential term limits reportedly passed a referendum with more than 90 percent of the vote, allowing Aliyev to run again in 2013.

The November 2010 parliamentary elections followed the established trend of increasing manipulation, and the YAP emerged with 71 seats, up from 61 in the 2005 polls. The remainder went to 41 independents and 10 minor parties, none of which garnered more than three seats.

In March and April 2011, a series of antigovernment protests calling for democratic reforms were violently dispersed by authorities, and dozens of people—including well-known journalists, youth activists, and opposition members—were arrested on dubious charges. In 2012, authorities used similar tactics to suppress renewed protests and restrict freedom of expression. Two international events hosted in Baku, the Eurovision song contest in May and the Internet Governance Forum (IGF) in November, provided an opportunity for the state to bolster its international image without making any progress on reform.

No progress was made in 2012 toward a resolution of the dispute over Nagorno-Karabakh, a region of Azerbaijan that has been ruled by ethnic Armenian separatists since the early 1990s. Border skirmishes in June and the Azeri government's pardoning of convicted murderer Ramil Safarov in August nearly derailed negotiations with Armenia. Safarov had killed an Armenian officer with an ax in 2004 while receiving training at a NATO camp in Hungary, and Hungarian authorities agreed to extradite him to Azerbaijan in 2012, whereupon he was pardoned and given a hero's welcome. No country or international organization recognizes Nagorno-Karabakh's self-proclaimed independence.

Political Rights and Civil Liberties: Azerbaijan is not an electoral democracy. The constitution provides for a strong presidency, and the 125-member Milli Majlis (National Assembly) exercises little or no independence from the executive branch. The president and members of parliament serve five-year terms, and a 2009 referendum eliminated presidential term limits.

Elections since the early 1990s have been considered neither free nor fair by international observers. As with previous votes, the 2010 parliamentary balloting featured the abuse of state administrative resources, including news media, to ensure the dominance of the YAP. The OSCE also cited voter intimidation and the improper disqualification of some opposition candidates.

Corruption is widespread, and wealth from the country's massive oil exports creates ever greater opportunities for graft. Because critical institutions, including the media and judiciary, are largely subservient to the president and ruling party, government officials are rarely held accountable for corruption. Several investigative reports published by foreign media in early 2012 revealed evidence that President Ilham Aliyev and his immediate family control prodigious private assets, including monopolies in the economy's most lucrative sectors. In response, the president in July signed a series of legal amendments that allow companies' organizational structures and ownership to remain secret, significantly limiting journalists' ability to uncover corruption.

While the constitution guarantees freedom of the press, the authorities severely restrict the media in practice. Broadcast media generally reflect progovernment views. Most television stations are controlled by the government, which also controls approval of broadcast licenses. While there is more pluralism in the print media, circulation and readership are relatively small. Some 80 percent of newspapers are owned by the state. Independent and opposition papers struggle financially and have faced heavy fines and imprisonment of their staff. State-owned companies rarely if ever advertise in such papers. Those who supply information to opposition newspapers have at times been subject to threats and arrest. In early 2012, the state replaced kiosks owned by the private companies Qasid and Qaya, which distribute the independent newspapers *Yeni Musavat* and *Azadliq*, making it easier for authorities to block the dissemination of such media. Local radio broadcasts of key international news services, including the British Broadcasting Corporation (BBC), Radio Free Europe/Radio Liberty (RFE/RL), and Voice of America, were banned in 2009.

Despite the government's pledge to decriminalize defamation in 2012, it remains a criminal offense punishable by exorbitant fines and imprisonment. Journalists are threatened and assaulted with impunity, and several have been jailed on fabricated charges of drug trafficking, ethnic hatred, high treason, and hooliganism, among other offenses. Executive director Vugar Gonagov and editor-in-chief Zaur Guliyev, both at Khayal TV, were arrested in March 2012 and faced up to 3 and 10 years in prison, respectively, on charges of inciting mass disorder and abuse of office, having uploaded a video to YouTube that depicted the governor of Quba district insulting local residents. Newspaper editor Avaz Zeynalli has been in detention since October 2011 and could be sentenced to 10 years in prison if convicted of extortion and failure to implement a court decision. Journalists were among the more than 70 people detained during antigovernment protests surrounding the Eurovision song contest in May 2012, and they, too, risked lengthy prison sentences. Website editor Nijat Aliyev and youth activist Anar Aliyev were arrested that month after criticizing government abuses; the former was charged with drug possession and faced up to three years in prison if convicted.

Internet-based reporting and social networking have increased significantly in recent years as a means of sidestepping government censorship and mobilizing protesters. The government has repeatedly blocked some websites that feature opposition views and intimidated the online community through harsh treatment of critical bloggers. Authorities monitor the internet use of protest leaders, and online surveillance reportedly increased in 2012.

The government restricts the practice of "nontraditional" minority religions—

those other than Islam, Orthodox Christianity, and Judaism—through burdensome registration requirements and interference with the importation and distribution of printed religious materials. A 2009 law required religious groups to reregister with the authorities and religious figures to be recertified. It also barred foreign citizens from leading prayers. A 2011 amendment to the law significantly increased fines for distribution of unapproved religious material and prescribed multiyear prison sentences for leaders of unsanctioned religious services. In Baku in October 2012, police arrested 72 people who were participating in a demonstration against the country's ban on headscarves in secondary schools.

The authorities have linked academic freedom to political activity in recent years. Some professors and teachers have reported being dismissed for links to opposition groups, and students have faced expulsion and other punishments for similar reasons.

The government restricts freedom of assembly, especially for opposition parties. The authorities unlawfully denied registration for public protests in March and April 2011 and May 2012, a number of which were violently dispersed. Dozens of protesters were arrested, many on false or trumped-up charges. Among them were several well-known youth activists and opposition figures. The president denounced such activists as "traitors" during a July 2012 cabinet meeting.

Legal amendments enacted in 2009 require nongovernmental organizations (NGOs) to register their grants with the authorities and foreign NGOs to reach agreements with the government before opening offices in the country. The rules have been used to put pressure on both local and foreign organizations. In 2012, NGOs were harassed by authorities for releasing reports that revealed human rights abuses. Some local freedom of expression groups were barred from the IGF and prohibited from distributing their materials. The U.S.-based National Democratic Institute was shut down in March 2011 but allowed to reopen the following September.

Although the law permits the formation of trade unions and the right to strike, the majority of trade unions remain closely affiliated with the government, and most major industries are state owned.

The judiciary is corrupt, inefficient, and subservient to the executive branch. Arbitrary arrest and detention are common, particularly for members of the political opposition. Detainees are often held for long periods before trial, and their access to lawyers is restricted. Police abuse of suspects during arrest and interrogation reportedly remains common; torture is sometimes used to extract confessions. Prison conditions are severe, with many inmates suffering from overcrowding and inadequate medical care. Protesters detained in 2012 reported ill-treatment in custody. Most were arrested arbitrarily and denied legal counsel in closed pretrial hearings.

Some members of ethnic minority groups, including the small ethnic Armenian population, have complained of discrimination in areas including education, employment, and housing. Hundreds of thousands of ethnic Azeris who were displaced by the war in Nagorno-Karabakh in the early 1990s remain subject to restrictions on their place of residence and often live in dreadful conditions.

As part of a citywide redevelopment project, the government evicted many Baku residents in the summer of 2011, forcibly removing and illegally demolishing the homes of those who refused to be resettled. Evictions continued in 2012 to make way for the construction of Crystal Hall, the venue for the Eurovision contest. Significant parts of the economy are controlled by a corrupt elite, which severely limits equality of opportunity. Supporters of the political opposition face job discrimination, demotion, and dismissal.

Traditional societal norms and poor economic conditions restrict women's professional roles, and they remain underrepresented in government. Women hold 20 seats in the parliament. Domestic violence is a problem, and the country is believed to be a source, transit point, and destination for the trafficking of women for prostitution. A 2005 law criminalized human trafficking, but the U.S. State Department's 2012 Trafficking in Persons Report placed Azerbaijan on its Tier 2 Watch List for the fifth consecutive year.

Bahamas

Political Rights: 1
Civil Liberties: 1
Status: Free

Population: 362,000
Capital: Nassau

Ten-Year Ratings Timeline For Year Under Review (Political Rights, Civil Liberties, Status)

2003	2004	2005	2006	2007	2008	2009	2010	2011	2012
1,1F	1,1F	1,1F	1,1F	1,1F	1,1F	1,1F	1,1F	1,1F	1,1F

Overview: The Progressive Liberal Party (PLP) was victorious in the May 2012 general elections, holding a commanding lead over the opposition Free National Movement in the new Parliament. PLP leader Perry Christie once again became prime minister.

The Bahamas, a former British colony, became an independent state within the Commonwealth in 1973. Lynden Pindling served as the country's first prime minister and head of the Progressive Liberal Party (PLP) for a quarter-century. After years of allegations of corruption and involvement by high-ranking officials in narcotics trafficking, Pindling and the PLP were defeated by the Free National Movement (FNM) party in 1992 elections.

The FNM ruled the Bahamas for 10 years under Prime Minister Hubert Ingraham, until the 2002 elections brought the PLP, led by Perry Christie, back to power. The FNM regained its parliamentary majority in May 2007, restoring Ingraham to the premiership.

The PLP was victorious in general elections held in May 2012, winning 29 seats, while the FNM took 9 seats. As a result of the elections, Christie once again became prime minister; Ingraham resigned from Parliament in July.

The Bahamas has established a model service economy based on an impressive tourism sector—which accounts for a large share of national income—and offshore financial services. However, the Bahamian tourism industry continues to suffer from the global economic crisis that struck in late 2008, posing challenges for the Ingraham government. Marijuana cultivation and trafficking by foreign nationals residing in the country have led the United States to keep the Bahamas on the list of major drug-producing or drug-transit countries.

Crime rates fell somewhat in 2012, indicating that anticrime measures taken by the government had achieved some success. After a dramatic rise in the rates of murder, rape, and robbery in 2011, the government amended existing laws and introduced new legislation related to the functioning of the criminal justice system, including amendments to the Penal Code, the Dangerous Drugs Act, the Firearms Act, the Bail Act, the Sexual Offences Bill, and the Court of Appeal Act. The measures appeared to be successful in 2012; the government reported that in the period between January 1 and July 24, the murder rate fell 14 percent compared to the same period in the previous year. Rapes fell by 11 percent, and attempted rapes by 65 percent. However, armed robberies increased by 21 percent, with 617 incidents in this period, demonstrating that the crime problem is far from resolved.

Political Rights and Civil Liberties: The Bahamas is an electoral democracy. The lower house of the bicameral Parliament, the 38-member House of Assembly, is directly elected for five-year terms. The 16 members of the upper house, the Senate, are appointed for five-year terms by the governor general based on recommendations made by the prime minister and the opposition leader. The governor general represents the British monarch as head of state. The head of the majority party or coalition in Parliament typically serves as prime minister. Political parties can organize freely.

Corruption remains a problem at all levels of government. Top officials frequently face allegations of administrative graft, domestically and from abroad. A freedom of information bill was passed by Parliament in February 2012; the government has pledged to enforce the law, but has not specified when it would come into effect.

The Bahamas has a well-developed tradition of respecting press freedom. The privately owned daily and weekly newspapers express a variety of views, as do the government-run radio station and four privately-owned radio broadcasters. Strict and antiquated libel laws dating to British legal codes are seldom invoked. Access to the internet is unrestricted.

Religious and academic freedoms are respected.

Freedoms of assembly and association are protected. Constitutional guarantees of the right to form nongovernmental organizations (NGOs) are generally respected, and human rights organizations have broad access to institutions and individuals. Labor, business, and professional organizations are also generally free from government interference. Unions have the right to strike, and collective bargaining is prevalent.

The judicial system is headed by the Supreme Court and a court of appeals, with the additional right of appeal to the Privy Council in London under certain circumstances. In 2006, the Privy Council ruled that mandatory death sentences for individuals convicted of murder in the Bahamas are unconstitutional. In practice, the death penalty was last carried out in 2000. However, in light of the rising crime rate, calls for resuming capital punishment have been issued recently by government representatives.

NGOs have occasionally documented cases of prisoner abuse and arbitrary arrest. Overcrowding in the country's prison remains a major problem, and juveniles are often housed with adults, increasing the risk of sexual abuse. The correctional training institute established in 2005 has worked to segregate violent and nonviolent offenders. However, the institute continues to face problems of limited capacity, including inadequate space to segregate offenders and insufficient numbers of trained personnel.

The Bahamas remains a major transit point for migrants coming from other Caribbean islands, especially Cuba and Haiti, who are trying to reach the United States. Discrimination against Haitian immigrants persists, and at least 30,000 undocumented Haitians reside in the Bahamas. Strict citizenship requirements and a stringent work-permit system leave Haitians with few rights. While the government halted the deportation of Haitians for a short period following the Haitian earthquake in January 2010, the financial crisis and its effects on the country's tourism sector—which is a main employer of undocumented workers—led the government to resume repatriation of undocumented migrants to Haiti later that year.

Although gender discrimination is not legally protected, criminal "quid pro quo" sexual harassment is prohibited. Violence against women, including domestic violence, is a serious problem. Despite laws against domestic violence, police are often reportedly reluctant to intervene in domestic disputes. Only 12 percent of the seats in Parliament are held by women. Discrimination against same-sex relationships is not prohibited by the constitution, and efforts have been promoted to weave antigay clauses into existing marriage acts.

Bahrain

Political Rights: 6
Civil Liberties: 6
Status: Not Free

Population: 1,336,000
Capital: Manama

Ten-Year Ratings Timeline For Year Under Review (Political Rights, Civil Liberties, Status)

2003	2004	2005	2006	2007	2008	2009	2010	2011	2012
5,5PF	5,5PF	5,5PF	5,5PF	5,5PF	5,5PF	6,5NF	6,5NF	6,6NF	6,6NF

Overview: Despite an ongoing security crackdown, prodemocracy protests continued throughout 2012. While most remained peaceful, there were signs that the opposition was becoming more radicalized. Bahraini courts upheld life sentences for opposition leaders, and the year featured new rounds of arrests and incarcerations of human rights activists, including Nabeel Rajab and Zaynab al-Khawaja. The government promised to meet international human rights standards and implement the recommendations of an official 2011 inquiry, but it failed to enact substantive reforms in practice. Although several police officers were put on trial for abuses carried out in 2011, the details of the proceedings and sentences remained unclear. No high-level officials had been held accountable for torture or police brutality by year's end, and the government refused to engage in meaningful discussions with the opposition.

The al-Khalifa family, which belongs to Bahrain's Sunni Muslim minority, has ruled the Shiite-majority country for more than two centuries. Bahrain gained independence in 1971 after more than a hundred years as a British protectorate. The first constitution provided for a legislative assembly, with both elected and appointed members, but the monarch dissolved the body in 1975 for attempting to end al-Khalifa rule.

In 1994, prominent individuals who had petitioned for the reestablishment of democratic institutions were detained, sparking unrest that left more than 40 people dead, thousands arrested, and hundreds either imprisoned or exiled.

After Sheikh Hamad bin Isa al-Khalifa ascended to the throne in 1999, he released political prisoners, permitted the return of exiles, and eliminated emergency laws and courts. He also introduced the National Charter, which aimed to create a constitutional monarchy with an elected parliament, an independent judicial branch, and rights guaranteeing women's political participation.

Voters approved the National Charter in 2001, and the country was proclaimed a constitutional kingdom the following year. However, leading Shiite groups and leftists boycotted local and parliamentary elections in 2002 to protest campaigning restrictions and gerrymandering aimed at diminishing the power of the Shiite majority. The government barred international monitors, and Sunni groups won most seats in the new National Assembly.

Shiite groups that boycotted the 2002 voting took part in the next elections in 2006. Al-Wefaq, a Shiite political society, won 42 percent of the vote and 17 of the 40 seats in the Council of Representatives, the lower house of the National Assembly.

In 2007, security forces began an escalating crackdown on the government's critics. Tensions increased after the 2009 arrest of Hassan Mushaima, Abduljalil al-Singace, and Mohammed Habib al-Muqdad, three leaders of the opposition political association Haq. Protests and arrests grew more frequent in 2010, and torture of detainees was reported.

In elections for the Council of Representatives in October 2010, Al-Wefaq won 18 seats. A combination of 17 independents and 5 Islamists—all Sunnis and supporters of the ruling family—captured the remainder. As in 2002 and 2006, critics accused the government of granting citizenship to foreigners to boost the number of Sunni voters.

In February 2011, Bahraini activists, mostly from economically depressed Shiite communities, organized small demonstrations to call for political reform and an end to sectarian discrimination. The brutal police response galvanized support for the protest movement, and tens of thousands of demonstrators converged on central Manama. Military and security forces dispersed the crowd in a violent nighttime raid on February 17, but hundreds of thousands of Bahrainis continued to demonstrate in various parts of the capital. In March, the government declared martial law and summoned troops from regional allies, including Saudi Arabia, to backstop a prolonged crackdown.

In the subsequent months, the authorities arrested hundreds of activists and prodemocracy demonstrators. Many were tortured and tried by military courts. Leaders including Mushaima, Singace, Ibrahim Sharif, and human rights activist Abd al-Hadi al-Khawaja were sentenced to life in prison. The arrests also extended to journalists and bloggers who reported on the crackdown, and medical personnel who treated injured protesters. Thousands of people were fired from their jobs for supporting the uprising.

The government lifted martial law in June 2011 but maintained a heavy security presence in primarily Shiite villages. Security forces restricted the movements of

Shiite citizens, periodically destroyed property, and continued to arrest regime critics and activists. In June, King Hamad appointed a Bahrain Independent Commission of Inquiry (BICI) to investigate allegations of human rights abuses during the crackdown. In late November, the panel concluded that security personnel had used excessive force. The BICI found no evidence that Iran or other foreign elements were behind the uprising, contradicting a key government claim. The report recommended that the government reinstate fired workers, release political prisoners, and punish members of the security forces who broke the law.

Widespread protests and the systematic security crackdown continued throughout 2012, and several protesters were killed during the year. The regime also continued to abuse suspected dissidents. In one prominent case, 16-year-old Ali al-Singace was allegedly arrested, tortured, sexually assaulted, stabbed, bound in handcuffs, and dumped on the street. The protest movement was most visible in April, when the country hosted an international Formula One race despite activists' objections that the government was using it to paper over ongoing political unrest. Protesters remained mostly peaceful, although younger activists grew more confrontational with police, in some cases throwing Molotov cocktails.

In September, the government pledged to honor over 120 UN recommendations on improving human rights conditions, but the year featured targeted arrests of human rights activists who had communicated effectively with international audiences. The country's best-known activist, Nabeel Rajab, was arrested in June and subsequently sentenced to two years in prison for allegedly organizing demonstrations. In August, authorities arrested Zaynab al-Khawaja, daughter of Abd al-Hadi al-Khawaja, for tearing up a picture of the king; she was sentenced to two months in jail. Her father, who had staged a lengthy hunger strike, was again sentenced to life in prison in September after securing a retrial in a civilian court. Other retrials during the year upheld convictions for nine medical personnel who treated wounded protesters in 2011. In October, police arrested Mohammed al-Maskati, head of the Bahrain Human Rights Youth Society, for organizing demonstrations.

Even as the crackdown continued, Bahraini authorities took small steps to account for the abuses of 2011. Several police officers were reportedly tried during 2012 for mistreating activists. The government claimed that a number were convicted, but it withheld their identities and closed the court proceedings to the public, making it difficult to verify any actual punishments. In June, the government announced that it would distribute $2.6 million in compensation to the families of 17 people who were killed in 2011, addressing one of the BICI recommendations.

Political Rights and Civil Liberties: Bahrain is not an electoral democracy. The 2002 constitution gives the king power over the executive, legislative, and judicial authorities. He appoints cabinet ministers and members of the 40-seat Consultative Council, the upper house of the National Assembly. The lower house, or Council of Representatives, consists of 40 elected members serving four-year terms. The National Assembly may propose legislation, but the cabinet must draft the laws. Bahrain's main opposition group, Al-Wefaq, withdrew its 18 members from the Council of Representatives in February 2011 to protest the government's crackdown. The opposition then boycotted interim elections held that September to fill the seats, with the result that all 40 seats are now held by government supporters.

While formal political parties are illegal, the government has generally allowed political societies or groupings to operate. A 2005 law makes it illegal to form political associations based on class, profession, or religion, and requires all political associations to register with the Ministry of Justice. While the government claimed that political societies remained free to operate in 2011, it imprisoned key opposition leaders, including Hassan Mushaima (Haq), Ibrahim Sharif (Democratic Action Society), Abd al-Jalil Singace (Haq), Matar Ibrahim Matar (Al-Wefaq), and Jawad Fairuz (Al-Wefaq). Mushaima, Sharif, and Singace were sentenced to life in prison for their activism. After a lengthy appeals process, Bahrain's courts upheld their sentences in September 2012.

Bahrain has some anticorruption laws, but enforcement is weak, and high-ranking officials suspected of corruption are rarely punished. A source of frustration for many citizens is the perception that Khalifa bin Salman al-Khalifa, the king's uncle and Bahrain's prime minister since 1971, is both corrupt and a key opponent of reform. Bahrain was ranked 53 out of 176 countries surveyed in Transparency International's 2012 Corruption Perceptions Index.

Restrictions on freedom of expression continued in 2012. The government owns all broadcast media outlets, and the private owners of the three main newspapers have close ties to the state. The government and its supporters have used the press to smear human rights and opposition activists. In May, state television engaged in one such campaign against the independent newspaper *Al-Wasat*, repeating a pattern of harassment that began in 2011. Self-censorship is encouraged by the vaguely worded 2002 Press Law, which allows the state to imprison journalists for criticizing the king or Islam, or for threatening "national security." Human rights activist Nabeel Rajab was arrested in May and June 2012 for criticizing the government on the Twitter microblogging service, though his three-month jail sentence was later overturned. He remained behind bars due to an August sentence of three years in prison for organizing protests, reduced to two years on appeal in December. The prominent blogger Ali Abdulemam, a regular contributor to the popular opposition web forum *Bahrain Online*, was sentenced in absentia to 15 years in prison by a military court in 2011, and he remained missing in 2012. The government continued to block a number of opposition websites during the year, including those that broadcast live events, such as protests. The authorities also obstructed foreign journalists' attempts to operate in the country. Jonathan Miller, a foreign correspondent for Britain's Channel 4, was arrested and deported along with his crew in April after covering demonstrations.

Islam is the state religion. However, non-Muslim minorities are generally free to practice their faiths. All religious groups must obtain a permit from the Ministry of Justice and Islamic Affairs to operate legally, though the government has not punished groups that operate without a permit. In 2010, the government stripped Ayatollah Hussein Mirza Najati, one of the country's top Shiite clerics, of his Bahraini nationality. Police and military forces destroyed over 40 Shiite places of worship during the spring 2011 crackdown. The government has promised to rebuild at least 12 of the mosques, but had not begun widespread efforts to do so in 2012.

Academic freedom is not formally restricted, but scholars who criticize the government are subject to dismissal. In 2011, a number of faculty and administrators were fired for supporting the call for democracy, and hundreds of students and some faculty were expelled. Those who remained were forced to sign loyalty pledges.

Citizens must obtain a license to hold demonstrations, which are banned from sunrise to sunset in any public arena. Police regularly use violence to break up political protests, most of which occur in Shiite villages. The 1989 Societies Law prohibits any nongovernmental organization (NGO) from operating without a permit. In 2010, the government dissolved the board of directors of the Bahrain Human Rights Society, an independent NGO, and assigned a government-appointed director to run the organization. The authorities blocked visits by foreign NGOs during 2012. Among others, Richard Sollom of Physicians for Human Rights was denied entry in January, and a delegation from the International Trade Union Confederation and the International Labour Organization were denied entry in September.

Bahrainis have the right to establish independent labor unions, but workers must give two weeks' notice before a strike, and strikes are banned in a variety of economic sectors. Private sector employees cannot be dismissed for union activities, but harassment of unionist workers occurs in practice. Foreign workers lack the right to organize and seek help from Bahraini unions. A 2009 decision that shifted responsibility for sponsoring foreign workers from private employers to the Labor Market Regulatory Authority did not apply to household servants, who remain particularly vulnerable to exploitation. Among the several thousand people known to have been fired in 2011 for allegedly supporting the prodemocracy protests were key officials in the General Federation of Bahraini Trade Unions. In September 2012, the government prevented a delegation from the International Trade Union Confederation and the United Nation's International Labour Organization from entering the country to participate in the annual congress of the General Federation of Bahrain Trade Unions.

The king appoints all judges, and courts have been subject to government pressure. Members of the royal family hold all senior security-related offices. Bahrain's antiterrorism law prescribes the death penalty for members of terrorist groups and prison terms for those who use religion to spread extremism. Critics have argued that the law's definition of terrorist crimes is too broad and that it has encouraged the use of torture and arbitrary detention.

Shiites are underrepresented in government and face various forms of discrimination. Fears of Shiite power and suspicions about their loyalties have limited employment opportunities for young Shiite men and fueled government attempts to erode the Shiite majority, mostly by granting citizenship to foreign-born Sunnis. In 2012 the regime continued its systematic sectarian discrimination and recruited over 5,000 foreign Sunnis to take up Bahraini citizenship.

The government continued to obstruct foreign travel by key opposition figures and activists in 2012. Authorities also restricted movement inside the country, particularly for residents of largely Shiite villages outside Manama. A tight security cordon blocked easy access to the capital.

Although women have the right to vote and participate in elections, they are underrepresented politically. Women are generally not afforded equal protection under the law. The government drafted a personal status law in 2008 but withdrew it in 2009 under pressure from Shiite clergy; the Sunni portion was later passed by the parliament. Personal status and family law issues for Shiite Bahrainis are consequently still governed by Sharia (Islamic law) court rulings based on the interpretations of predominantly male religious scholars, rather than by any formal statute.

Bangladesh

Political Rights: 3
Civil Liberties: 4
Status: Partly Free

Population: 152,875,000
Capital: Dhaka

Ten-Year Ratings Timeline For Year Under Review (Political Rights, Civil Liberties, Status)

2003	2004	2005	2006	2007	2008	2009	2010	2011	2012
4,4PF	4,4PF	4,4PF	4,4PF	5,4PF	4,4PF	3,4PF	3,4PF	3,4PF	3,4PF

Overview:
Political polarization and dysfunction continued to worsen during 2012, as the opposition held numerous street protests and threatened to boycott elections that must be held by early 2014. The government failed to address the problem of extrajudicial executions, and other human rights abuses, including forced disappearances and discrimination against women, remained concerns. Critical nongovernmental organizations faced increased pressure and restrictions on their activities, as did labor activists fighting to improve dangerous conditions for factory workers.

Bangladesh gained independence from Britain in 1947 as part of the newly formed state of Pakistan, and successfully split from Pakistan in December 1971, after a nine-month war. The 1975 assassination of independence leader and prime minister Sheikh Mujibur Rahman by soldiers precipitated 15 years of military rule. The last military ruler resigned in 1990 after weeks of prodemocracy demonstrations. Elections in 1991 brought the Bangladesh Nationalist Party (BNP) to power under Prime Minister Khaleda Zia.

However, the ensuing decade featured increasing political deadlock as the opposition center-left Awami League (AL) party, led by Sheikh Hasina Wajed, began boycotting Parliament. After the AL won the 1996 elections, the BNP also marked its time in opposition by boycotting Parliament and organizing periodic nationwide strikes, or hartals. The pattern continued when a new BNP-led coalition that included two Islamist parties took power in 2001. Much of the partisan tension reflected the personal animosity between Hasina, the daughter of Rahman, and Zia, the widow of a military ruler who was allegedly complicit in his assassination.

As planned 2007 elections approached, the AL demanded reform of Bangladesh's caretaker government (CG) system, in which a theoretically nonpartisan government takes power temporarily to oversee parliamentary voting. The AL also questioned the conduct and impartiality of the Election Commission (EC) and its preparation of a new voter list. Faced with the possibility of balloting that lacked credibility, in January 2007, the army pressured the president to declare a state of emergency, cancel the elections, and install a new, military-backed CG, headed by technocrat Fakhruddin Ahmed. This "soft coup" was carried out partly within the constitutional framework, stopping short of martial law and leaving a civilian CG in nominal control. A new Anti-Corruption Commission (ACC) investigated high-level politicians and their business allies, arresting dozens. However, after both main parties decided to boycott preelection talks with the EC unless their leaders were released, the CG capitulated, weakening its anticorruption campaign.

In elections held in December 2008, turnout was extremely high, at 87 percent, and included a large proportion of first-time, women, and minority voters. An electoral alliance led by the AL won an overwhelming 263 seats (230 for the AL). The BNP took 30 seats, and its ally, the Jamaat-e-Islami (Islamic Party, or JI), took only 2. Independents and minor parties captured the remainder. Zia accepted the results, and Hasina took office as prime minister, returning Bangladesh to elected civilian rule.

In keeping with its campaign promises, the new government established a tribunal to try suspected war criminals in 2010. The tribunal indicted and arrested several key members of the JI, whose leaders and student wing played a role in atrocities against civilians during the 1971 war of independence. However, experts remained concerned that the process would not adhere to international standards.

Another important part of the AL's agenda was the restoration of the 1972 constitution, which would reestablish Bangladesh's character as a secular republic. In a key step toward that end, a February 2010 Supreme Court decision nullified elements of the fifth amendment to the constitution, effectively paving the way for a reinstatement of the principle of secularism and a ban on religiously based political parties. Meanwhile, the government took a harder line on Islamist extremism, arresting dozens of activists and those suspected of links to terrorist groups. The first 1971 war crimes trial began in late 2011, and a crackdown in September—in the wake of violent JI protests regarding the war crimes issue—led to the arrest of several party leaders and hundreds of activists.

In June 2011, following a Supreme Court decision on the validity of interim administrations, the AL-dominated Parliament passed the 15th amendment to the constitution, which scrapped the CG system and replaced it with a nominally independent electoral commission. Other articles of the amendment termed any criticism of the constitution an act of sedition, instituted the death penalty for those convicted of plotting to overthrow the government, guaranteed secularism and freedom of religion, and effectively forbade further amendments to large parts of the constitution.

The BNP-led opposition continued to intermittently boycott Parliament and rigidly oppose the AL government's initiatives in 2012, resorting once again to the use of hartals and mass protests. More than 100,000 people participated in one rally in March. A key goal of BNP activism during the year was the reinstatement of the CG system for the next elections, which must be held by early 2014. Following a rally in April that turned violent, 33 senior party leaders were arrested and charged with vandalism and arson. Separately, in another sign of instability, the army alleged in January that it had foiled an attempted coup by mid-ranking officers with Islamist leanings, aided by retired officers and expatriate Bangladeshis. In November 2012, the war crimes trial of JI member Abul Kalam Azad began in absentia.

Political Rights and Civil Liberties: Bangladesh is an electoral democracy. The December 2008 parliamentary elections were deemed free and fair by European Union observers and other monitoring groups. Terms for both the unicameral National Parliament and the largely ceremonial presidency are five years. Under provisions contained in the 15th amendment to the constitution, Parliament is composed of 350 members, of whom 300 are directly elected, and 50 are women nominated by political parties—based on their share of the elected seats—and then voted on by their fellow lawmakers. The president is elected by Parliament.

A new, considerably more accurate voter registry and a series of other electoral reforms enacted in 2008 were designed to curtail the widespread bribery, rigging, and violence that had characterized past elections. While the December 2008 national voting was relatively clean, more recent local government polls have been marred by more extensive violence and intimidation, as well as suspected rigging. The level of political violence remains relatively high; the human rights group Odhikar registered 169 deaths and more than 17,000 people injured as a result of inter- or intraparty clashes during 2012, an increase from the previous year. Harassment of the opposition became more widespread in 2012, ranging from charges filed against senior BNP members to limitations placed on political activities, particularly rallies and processions. A number of party activists have also disappeared; BNP politician Ilias Ali went missing in April, with some alleging an abduction by security forces and others attributing the case to intraparty politics.

Endemic corruption and criminality, weak rule of law, limited bureaucratic transparency, and political polarization have long undermined government accountability. Moreover, regular opposition boycotts of Parliament have significantly hampered the legislature's role in providing thorough scrutiny of government policies, budgets, and proposed legislation. The 2009 Right to Information Act mandates public access to all information held by public bodies and overrides secrecy legislation. Bangladesh was ranked 144 out of 176 countries surveyed by Transparency International (TI) in its 2012 Corruption Perceptions Index. Under the present government, anticorruption efforts have been weakened by patchy or biased enforcement and subversion of the judicial process, according to TI–Bangladesh. Dozens of pre-2009 cases against Prime Minister Sheikh Hasina Wajed and other AL politicians have been withdrawn, while those against BNP politicians, including party leader Khaleda Zia and her family, have remained open, and additional charges have been filed by the AL government. In April 2012, newly appointed railway minister Suranjit Sengupta was implicated in a corruption scandal, when his personal secretary and two other railway officials were caught traveling with roughly $90,000 in cash in a minibus. Sengupta denied any link to the money, which allegedly consisted of bribes from railway job applicants, but he nevertheless resigned.

Bangladesh's media environment remained relatively unfettered in 2012, though the legal and regulatory framework allows for some restrictions, and the government showed signs of intolerance during the year. Print media are generally given more leeway when covering sensitive topics than broadcasters. In March 2012, the transmissions of several television stations were suspended shortly before a planned opposition rally.

Journalists continue to be threatened and attacked with impunity by organized crime groups, party activists, and Islamist factions, which sometimes leads to self-censorship on sensitive topics. After seven years without a murder of a journalist, three were killed in 2012, according to the Committee to Protect Journalists. While the motive for the February murder of a husband-and-wife team of broadcast journalists remained unclear, the June killing of newspaper reporter Jamal Uddin was linked to his coverage of local drug traffickers. There also appeared to be an increase in other types of physical harassment against the press. In May, nine journalists were injured when armed men attacked the newsroom of the bdnews24.com website. In a separate incident that month, three photojournalists from the daily *Prothom Alo* were badly beaten by police while attempting to cover a story. Some journalists received threatening telephone calls from intelligence agencies seeking to prevent negative coverage.

Attempts to censor internet-based content occasionally occur. In January 2012, a university teacher was given a six-month jail sentence for comments he made about Prime Minister Hasina on the social-networking site Facebook in 2011. In September 2012, the government blocked the video-sharing site YouTube following a global uproar over an anti-Islam video produced in the United States. Various forms of artistic expression, including books and films, are occasionally banned or censored.

A June 2011 amendment to the constitution confirmed Islam as the official religion but also reaffirmed the secular nature of the state. Muslims form an overwhelming majority; about 10 percent of the population is Hindu, and there are smaller numbers of Buddhists and Christians. Although religious minorities have the right to worship freely, they face societal discrimination as well as harassment and legal repercussions for proselytizing. In September 2012, more than 20 mostly Buddhist temples, along with homes and shops in ethnic minority villages, were attacked and set on fire by Muslim protesters in southeastern Bangladesh following the posting of a photograph of a burned Koran on Facebook. Members of the Ahmadiyya sect are considered heretical by some Muslims, and despite increased state protection since 2009, they have encountered physical attacks, boycotts, and demands that the state declare them non-Muslims. They are also occasionally denied permission to hold religious events. In November 2012, Islamist extremists attacked an Ahmadi mosque and several homes of Ahmadis in the village of Taraganj in Rangpur; some 15 people were injured and two homes destroyed in the attack. Religious minorities remain underrepresented in politics and state employment, but the secularist AL government has appointed several members of minority groups to leadership positions. It has also initiated curriculum reform in Islamic schools.

While authorities largely respect academic freedom, research on sensitive political and religious topics is reportedly discouraged. Political polarization at many universities, including occasional clashes involving the armed student wings of the three main parties, inhibits education and access to services.

The rights of assembly and association were restored in late 2008 with the lifting of emergency regulations. The authorities have sometimes tried to prevent rallies by arresting party activists, and protesters are frequently injured and occasionally killed during clashes with police. Nevertheless, demonstrations took place regularly in 2012, including a growing number of nationwide strikes and rallies called by the BNP.

Numerous nongovernmental organizations (NGOs) operate in Bangladesh. While most are able to function without onerous restrictions, they must obtain clearance from the NGO Affairs Bureau (NAB)—which reports to the prime minister's office—to use foreign funds. The bureau is also empowered to approve or reject individual projects after a review period of 45 days. In September 2012, Human

Rights Watch criticized the formation of a new commission designed to provide further regulation and scrutiny of NGOs. Authorities also canceled the registration of several thousand NGOs during the year and announced draft legislation to further restrict foreign donations. Groups such as Odhikar that are seen as overly critical of the government, particularly on human rights issues, have been subject to increasing harassment and surveillance and are regularly denied permission for proposed projects. Grameen Bank, one of the country's largest and most influential microfinance institutions, remained without a managing director in 2012 after Nobel laureate Muhammad Yunus was ousted in an allegedly politicized proceeding in 2011. The government was reportedly mulling new rules that would increase the level of political control over the appointment of the bank's board of directors.

Labor union formation is hampered by a 30 percent employee-approval requirement, restrictions on organizing by unregistered unions, and rules against unionization by certain categories of civil servants. Worker grievances fuel unrest at factories, particularly in the rapidly expanding and lucrative garment industry, where strikes and protests against low wages and unsafe working conditions are common. In November 2012, a fire at a garment factory in Dhaka killed more than 100 people, and many more were hospitalized due to burns and smoke inhalation. According to Clean Clothes Campaign, an antisweatshop advocacy organization, more than 500 workers have died in factory fires since 2006. Child labor is widespread. Reforms of the system are hampered by the fact that a growing number of factory owners are also members of Parliament or owners of influential media outlets.

Organizations and individuals that advocate for labor rights have faced increased harassment over the past several years. The Bangladesh Center for Workers' Solidarity (BCWS) was stripped of its legal status by the NAB in 2010 for allegedly inciting labor unrest. Its leaders face pending criminal cases and have reportedly suffered abuse in custody. A prominent organizer for BCWS, Aminul Islam, went missing in April 2012 and was later found dead with marks of torture on his body. According to Amnesty International, his family suspected that he was abducted by security forces as a result of his activism.

Politicization of the judiciary remains an issue, despite a 1999 Supreme Court directive ordering the separation of the judiciary from the executive and efforts by the military-backed CG to implement it. Political authorities have continued to make appointments to the higher judiciary, in some cases demonstrating an overt political bias, leading to protests from the Supreme Court Bar Association. Harassment of witnesses and the dismissal of cases following political pressure are also growing issues of concern.

The court system is prone to corruption and severely backlogged with an estimated two million pending cases. Pretrial detention is often lengthy, and many defendants lack counsel. The indigent have little access to justice through the courts. Prison conditions are extremely poor, severe overcrowding is common, and juveniles are often incarcerated with adults. Suspects are routinely subject to arbitrary arrest and detention, demands for bribes, and physical abuse by police. Torture is often used to extract confessions and intimidate political detainees. Criminal cases against ruling-party activists are regularly withdrawn on the grounds of "political consideration," which has undermined the judicial process and entrenched a culture of impunity.

Security forces including the Rapid Action Battalion (RAB), a paramilitary unit composed of military and police personnel, have been criticized for excesses like extrajudicial executions. According to Odhikar, there were 70 extrajudicial killings by law enforcement agencies in 2012, and it is estimated that more than 800 people have been killed by the RAB since its formation in 2004. The Directorate General–Forces Intelligence (DGFI), a military intelligence unit, has been responsible for a number of cases of abuse during interrogations. Although the AL government initially promised a "zero-tolerance" approach on torture and extrajudicial executions, high-level officials routinely excuse or deny the practices, and the rate of custodial deaths has increased since the AL took office. Abductions and disappearances are also a growing concern, according to the International Crisis Group and other organizations, with dozens recorded in 2012.

Law enforcement abuses are facilitated by legislation such as the 1974 Special Powers Act, which permits arbitrary detention without charge, and Section 54 of the criminal procedure code, which allows detention without a warrant. A 2009 counterterrorism law includes an overly broad definition of terrorism and generally does not meet international standards. In February 2012, Parliament passed an amendment to this law that instated the death penalty as the maximum punishment for funding terrorist activity. The National Human Rights Commission (NHRC), reestablished in 2010, is empowered to investigate and rule on complaints against the armed forces and security services, and it can request reports from the government at its own discretion.

Following a February 2009 mutiny by the paramilitary Bangladesh Rifles (BDR) force—in which some 70 officers and family members were killed—more than 6,000 BDR members have been arrested, and at least 60 have died in custody under suspicious circumstances, with some bodies bearing marks of torture and other abuse. The suspects' trials have been marred by problems, including limited access to defense counsel, lack of individualized incriminating evidence, and the alleged use of torture to extract confessions. In June 2012, one of several mass trials of BDR members before a military court ended in the conviction of 611 of 621 accused, while a court in July sentenced 253 of 256 soldiers to various terms of imprisonment. Overall, more than 4,000 have been found guilty, and hundreds also face charges under the criminal code that could result in the death penalty.

Revisions in 2009 and 2011 to the International War Crimes Tribunal Act of 1973 and the current tribunal's procedural rules were intended to help meet international standards on issues such as victim and witness protection, the presumption of innocence, defendant access to counsel, and the right to bail. However, observers in 2012 continued to raise concerns about due process shortcomings as well as threats and harassment against witnesses and defense lawyers. As of July, the tribunal had indicted eight prominent political leaders, including six leaders of the JI and two from the BNP. Although some trials had started, none were concluded by year's end. In October, the tribunal commenced trial proceedings against six more former JI leaders, bringing the total number of defendants to 14. Also that month, armed police raided the offices of the war crimes defense counsel and recorded all the names and addresses of the employees present. On November 5, a defense witness was allegedly abducted by plainclothes officers while standing in front of the tribunal building in Dhaka.

Islamist militant groups continue to operate and maintain contact with regional allies, but Islamist violence has been negligible since a 2006 crackdown on the groups. The AL government has been aggressive in arresting cadres and closely monitoring their activities. Separately, casualties from clashes involving Maoist militants have declined somewhat in the past several years; according to the South Asia Terrorism Portal, just 15 people, all of them militants, were killed in 2012.

Land rights for the Hindu minority remain tenuous. The 2011 Vested Properties Return Act allows Hindus to reclaim land that was seized from them by the government or other individuals. However, human rights groups have critiqued the government for its slow implementation of the law. Tribal minorities have little control over land decisions affecting them, and Bengali-speaking settlers continue to illegally encroach on tribal lands in the Chittagong Hill Tracts (CHT), with the reported connivance of government officials and the army. A 1997 accord ended a 24-year insurgency by indigenous groups in the CHT, but implementation of the accord has been lacking. Security forces in the area are occasionally implicated in the suppression of protests, the arrest of political activists, and extrajudicial killings. Moreover, indigenous people remain subject to physical attacks and property destruction by Bengali settlers. In 2009 the AL government announced a military drawdown in the area and plans to set up a commission that would allocate land to indigenous tribes, but the panel's activities have suffered from delays and interruptions, and it has not addressed land disputes effectively.

Roughly 230,000 ethnic Rohingyas who fled forced labor, discrimination, and other abuses in Burma in the early 1990s remain in Bangladesh and are subject to some harassment. Starting in June 2012, authorities began turning away Rohingya and other refugees seeking to escape new outbreaks of ethnic and sectarian violence in Burma, and in August officials suspended the activities of international aid organizations providing humanitarian assistance to the refugees, claiming that such aid was encouraging further influxes. Bangladesh also hosts camp-like settlements of some 300,000 non-Bengali Muslims, often called Biharis, who had emigrated from India in 1947 and were rendered stateless at independence in 1971, as many had sided with and initially sought repatriation to Pakistan. A landmark 2008 court ruling granted citizenship rights to this group.

Under the personal status laws affecting all religious communities, women have fewer marriage, divorce, and inheritance rights than men, which increases their socioeconomic insecurity, according to a September 2012 report by Human Rights Watch. However, Parliament that month passed the Hindu Marriage Bill, which aims to grant legal and social protection to members of the Hindu community, particularly women. In rural areas, religious leaders sometimes impose flogging and other extrajudicial punishments on women accused of violating strict moral codes, despite Supreme Court orders calling on the government to stop such practices. Women also face some discrimination in health care, education, and employment. In 2012, Islamic clergy and women's groups remained at loggerheads over implementation of the National Women Development Policy, which holds that women and men should have equal political, social, and economic rights.

Rape, dowry-related assaults, acid throwing, and other forms of violence against women occur regularly. A law requiring rape victims to file police reports and obtain medical certificates within 24 hours of the crime in order to press charges prevents most cases from reaching the courts. Police also accept bribes to quash rape cases and rarely enforce existing laws protecting women. The Acid Survivors Foundation (ASF), a local NGO, recorded 71 acid attacks during 2012; they affected 98 victims, most of them women. While attacks have declined since the passage of the Acid Crime Prevention Act in 2002, investigations remain inadequate. A 2010 law offers greater protection to women and children from domestic violence, including both physical and mental abuse. Giving or receiving dowry is a criminal offense, but coercive requests remain a problem, as does the country's high rate of early marriage. Odhikar noted an increase in dowry-related violence against women in 2012, with more than 250 murders recorded during the year.

Women and children are trafficked both overseas and within the country for the purposes of domestic servitude or sexual exploitation, while men are trafficked primarily for labor abroad. The government has taken steps to raise awareness and prosecute sex traffickers somewhat more vigorously, with dozens convicted each year and some sentenced to life in prison. In February 2012, Parliament passed a comprehensive anti-trafficking law that provided further protection to male as well as female victims.

A criminal ban on homosexual acts is rarely enforced, but societal discrimination remains the norm. Transgender people also face persecution, though a government-sponsored rally in the capital in October 2011 urged greater recognition for the group.

Barbados

Political Rights: 1
Civil Liberties: 1
Status: Free

Population: 277,000
Capital: Bridgetown

Ten-Year Ratings Timeline For Year Under Review (Political Rights, Civil Liberties, Status)

2003	2004	2005	2006	2007	2008	2009	2010	2011	2012
1,1F	1,1F	1,1F	1,1F	1,1F	1,1F	1,1F	1,1F	1,1F	1,1F

Overview:

Barbados continued in 2012 to grapple with the impact of the global recession as Prime Minister Freundel Stuart faced a sluggish economy and rising crime rate. Meanwhile, the year saw a number of highly publicized sexual abuse allegations involving Barbadian customs officers.

Barbados gained its independence from Britain in 1966 but remained a member of the Commonwealth. The Barbados Labour Party (BLP), under Prime Minister Owen Arthur, governed from 1994 to January 2008, when the opposition Democratic Labour Party (DLP) won a clear majority of 20 seats in the lower house of Parliament, leaving the BLP with the remaining 10 seats. However, the new government led by David Thompson of the DLP did not break markedly from the policies pursued by the Arthur government.

During much of the summer of 2010, Thompson remained out of office due to an undisclosed ailment, and DLP member Freundel Stuart took over as acting prime minister. While Thompson returned to office in late August, many important economic decisions, including the new budget and several proposed judicial and other reforms, were delayed. Thompson died on October 23, 2010, of pancreatic cancer and was replaced by Stuart.

As Barbados struggled to emerge from the economic recession, the government was forced to cut expenditures, freeze public wages, and shore up the country's foreign reserves. According to the International Monetary Fund (IMF), Barbados experienced only 1 percent economic growth in 2011, with the unemployment rate reaching more than 12 percent. According to a 2012 report by the Caribbean Development Bank, almost 10 percent of Barbadians are without an adequate supply of food, and close to 20 percent lack other basic necessities. Barbados is particularly weighed down by its debt-to-GDP ratio, and the IMF recommended that the country lower spending on its social partnership scheme of entitlements. In 2012, Barbados applied for a BD$66 (US$33 million) loan from the Inter-American Development Bank, but the bank has expressed concern about the country's fiscal situation, in particular its ability to collect enough funds through taxes.

Political Rights and Civil Liberties: Barbados is an electoral democracy. Members of the 30-member House of Assembly, the lower house of the bicameral Parliament, are directly elected for five-year terms. The governor-general, who represents the British monarch as head of state, appoints the 21 members of the Senate: 12 on the advice of the prime minister, 2 on the advice of the leader of the opposition, and the remaining 7 at his own discretion. The prime minister is appointed by the governor-general and is usually the leader of the political party with a majority in the House.

Political parties are free to organize. Historically, power has alternated between two centrist parties—the DLP and the BLP. Other political organizations without representation in Parliament include the small, left-wing Workers Party of Barbados and the People's Empowerment Party, an opposition force favoring trade union rights and greater state intervention in the economy.

Barbados was ranked 15 out of 176 countries surveyed in Transparency International's 2012 Corruption Perceptions Index, the second-best ranking in the Americas after Canada.

Freedom of expression is respected. Public opinion expressed through the news media, which are free of censorship and government control, has a powerful influence on policy. Newspapers, including the two major dailies, are privately owned. Four private and two government-run radio stations operate. The single television station, operated by the government-owned Caribbean Broadcasting Corporation, presents a wide range of political viewpoints. The DLP has so far failed to make good on its promise to introduce a new Freedom of Information Act. Access to the internet is not restricted.

The constitution guarantees freedom of religion, which is widely respected for mainstream religious groups. However, members of Barbados's small Rastafarian community have protested prison regulations that require inmates to have their long dreadlocks cut off while in detention, and have also reported discrimination in the areas of education and employment. Academic freedom is fully respected.

Barbados's legal framework provides important guarantees for freedom of assembly, which are upheld in practice. The right to form civic organizations and labor unions is respected. Two major labor unions, as well as various smaller ones, are active.

The judicial system is independent, and the Supreme Court includes a high court and a court of appeals. Barbados has ratified the Caribbean Court of Justice as its highest appellate court. There are occasional reports and complaints of the use of excessive force by the Royal Barbados Police Force to extract confessions, along with reports that police do not always seek warrants before searching homes.

Barbados has been more successful than other Caribbean countries in combating violent crime, though the crime rate in 2012 remained at high levels. The drug trade continues to be an important problem for Barbados, as the island has become a transshipment point for cocaine originating from Venezuela.

The government has taken some positive steps to address overcrowding in the prison system and to discharge prison personnel accused of beating inmates, but there has not been substantial progress in their prosecution. The death penalty remains mandatory for certain capital crimes, though it has not been implemented since 1984. In October 2011, the government announced plans to update the Corporal Punishment Act, the Juvenile Offenders Act, and the Prevention of Cruelty Act, in response to rulings by the Inter-American Court of Human Rights that found Barbados in violation of certain protections that are enshrined in the American Convention on Human Rights; however, no steps had been taken by the end of 2012.

Barbadian authorities have been criticized for excessively restrictive migration policies, including the treatment of foreign nationals at airports. In several separate cases, visitors from Jamaica claim to have been sexually abused and even raped by Barbadian immigration officers. In one case, the Caribbean Court of Justice in September 2012 accepted a lawsuit by Jamaican Shanique Myrie and the Jamaican government, and invited other interested regional states to join the suit. Barbados is a source and destination for human trafficking.

Women comprise roughly half of the country's workforce, although the World Economic Forum reported that in 2010 women earned 26 percent less than men for comparable work. Women are underrepresented in the political sphere, comprising only 10 percent of the elected House. Violence against women and children remains a serious problem.

Belarus

Political Rights: 7
Civil Liberties: 6
Status: Not Free

Population: 9,457,000
Capital: Minsk

Ten-Year Ratings Timeline For Year Under Review (Political Rights, Civil Liberties, Status)

2003	2004	2005	2006	2007	2008	2009	2010	2011	2012
6,6NF	7,6NF	7,6NF	7,6NF	7,6NF	7,6NF	7,6NF	7,6NF	7,6NF	7,6NF

Overview: The September 2012 parliamentary elections were neither free nor fair and once again resulted in a legislature that lacked any opposition representation. Although Belarus released two political prisoners in the spring, the authorities held at least a dozen more. The regime of President Alyaksandr Lukashenka continued to crack down on all forms of protest, further concentrate power in the hands of Lukashenka's sons, maintain tight control over the media, and harass leaders of internet news sites.

Belarus declared independence in 1991, ending centuries of rule by Poland, Russia, and the Soviet Union. In 1994, voters made Alyaksandr Lukashenka, a member of parliament with close links to the security services, Belarus's first post-Soviet president. He pursued reunification with Russia and subordinated the government, legislature, and courts to his political whims while denying citizens basic rights and liberties. A widely criticized 1996 referendum approved constitutional amendments that extended Lukashenka's term through 2001, broadened presidential powers, and created a new bicameral parliament, the National Assembly.

Lukashenka won a second term through disputed elections in September 2001, amid accusations by former security officials that the president was directing a death squad aimed at silencing his opponents. Four politicians and journalists who had been critical of the regime disappeared during 1999 and 2000. Not a single opposition candidate won a seat in the 2004 parliamentary elections (three had been elected in 2000), and voters ostensibly endorsed a parallel referendum proposal to allow Lukashenka to run again in 2006.

The March 2006 presidential election, in which Lukashenka won a third term, did not meet democratic standards. The poll brought 10,000 to 15,000 protesters to Minsk's October Square on election day. The authorities detained and beat many activists, and opposition activity dwindled after the protests as the government jailed opposition leaders and intimidated their supporters with fees and warnings. Alyaksandr Kazulin, one of three opposition candidates, was sentenced to five and a half years in prison for protesting the flawed election and the subsequent crackdown.

To bolster his international standing, Lukashenka released all political prisoners identified by the European Union (EU) and the United States by August 2008, including Kazulin. However, no opposition candidates won seats in the September 2008 parliamentary elections, and the authorities arrested a new batch of political prisoners in a February 2009 crackdown.

On December 19, 2010, Lukashenka won a fourth term as president in a deeply flawed election, though some opposition candidates were allowed to run. When approximately 15,000 protesters turned out to question the legitimacy of the vote, the authorities arrested more than 700 individuals, including seven of the nine opposition presidential candidates, and many of them remained in jail for long periods. The regime later sentenced three of the former candidates to prison: Andrei Sannikau (five years), Dzmitry Uss (five and a half years, released in October 2011), and Mikalay Statkevich (six years). In August 2011, the authorities arrested Viasna Human Rights Center leader Ales Byalyatski after he circulated reports about the regime's crackdown on freedom of assembly; he was sentenced to four and a half years in jail for tax evasion. In 2012, despite releasing Sannikau and his colleague Dzmitry Bandarenka in the spring, the authorities continued to hold at least 12 political prisoners, including Byalyatski, Statkevich, and Dzmitry Dashkevich, leader of the Young Front political movement, who had a third year added to his original two-year sentence in August for disobedience in prison.

Parliamentary elections held on September 23, 2012, once again failed to elect a single member of the opposition. The Organization for Security and Co-operation in Europe declared that the elections were "not competitive from the start." The outcome in 1 of the 110 races remained undecided when the only candidate running failed to win the necessary number of votes to validate his election. Official voter participation was 74.6 percent, though observers claimed that the turnout was inflated through ballot stuffing. More than a quarter of the voters cast early ballots, often an indicator of fraud. The authorities blocked key opposition figures from running for office, harassed critics of the regime, failed to administer the elections fairly, and prevented observers from independently verifying the vote count. The opposition was divided over whether to boycott the elections or to participate, with two major parties—the United Civic Party and the Belarussian Peoples Front—pulling out of the elections just before the balloting. In contrast to previous elections, no protests followed the blatantly rigged voting, suggesting that the authorities had improved the effectiveness of their repressive techniques. In October, the EU extended its sanctions against 243 officials in the Belarusan regime and 32 state-controlled entities for another year.

Amid the ongoing crackdown, Lukashenka appeared increasingly interested in concentrating power in the hands of his family. During a trip to Venezuela, the president hinted that he was grooming his seven-year-old son, Mikalay, to be his successor. Lukashenko subsequently denied such an intention, but the child frequently accompanies him as he performs his official duties. Another son, Viktar, 36, is officially the president's adviser on national security issues and reportedly controls the KGB; within the past year, he has subordinated the police to the organization, making him the second-most powerful man in the country. However, following the dismissal of KGB chairman Vladimir Zaitsev in November 2012, some analysts have argued that Viktar's influence is weakening, and the president remains the only key player.

Political Rights and Civil Liberties: Belarus is not an electoral democracy. Serious and widespread irregularities have marred all recent elections, including the December 2010 presidential poll and the September 2012 parliamentary elections. The 110 members of the Chamber of Representatives, the lower house of the rubber-stamp National Assembly, are popularly elected for four years from single-mandate constituencies. The upper house, the Council of the Republic, consists of 64 members serving four-year terms; 56 are elected by regional councils and 8 are appointed by the president. The constitution vests most power in the president, giving him control over the government, courts, and even the legislative process by stating that presidential decrees have a higher legal force than ordinary legislation. The president is elected for five-year terms, and there are no term limits.

There is no official progovernment political party. Opposition parties have no representation in the National Assembly, while most members of the parliament are unaffiliated with any party. Young members of opposition parties report being deliberately drafted into the military; soldiers are banned from party membership. Amendments to the electoral law adopted in 2009 give parties more opportunities to campaign but do not provide for a transparent vote count. Groups that advocate election boycotts, such as Tell the Truth, face prison terms and other harassment.

The state controls 70 percent of the Belarusian economy, feeding widespread corruption. Graft is also encouraged by an overall lack of transparency and accountability in government. Belarus was ranked 123 out of 176 countries surveyed in the 2012 Transparency International Corruption Perceptions Index.

President Alyaksandr Lukashenka systematically curtails press freedom. Libel is both a civil and a criminal offense, and a 2008 media law gives the state a monopoly over information about political, social, and economic affairs. Belarusian national television is completely under the control of the state and does not present alternative or opposition views. The state-run press distribution monopoly limits the availability of private newspapers. The authorities routinely harass and censor the remaining independent media outlets, including by using physical force, confiscating equipment, and revoking journalists' credentials. The authorities do allow two independent newspapers to publish: *Nasha Niva* and *Narodnaya Volya*.

Internet penetration has doubled from a quarter to nearly half of the population over the last five years. Every day, more than 400,000 Belarusians—the audience size for state television—visit news websites. To deal with this shift, the government is seeking greater control over the internet, through legal and technical means. The 2008 media law subjects internet outlets to the same restrictions as traditional media, and the government owns the country's sole internet-service provider. A presidential decree that took effect in June 2010 requires internet café owners to identify users and track their activities. At the beginning of 2012, a law codified the provisions of the decree. The authorities have repeatedly blocked access to social-networking sites, such as the Russian VKontakte and U.S.-based Facebook and Twitter, while the KGB harasses online opposition activists. The opposition website Charter97.org frequently experiences denial-of-service attacks, and its staff members have been threatened and arrested; its editors now work from Poland and Lithuania. Web sites that claimed the parliamentary election turnout figures were exaggerated were blocked from the view of Belarusan internet users. In July 2012, photojournalist blogger Anton Suryapin was arrested for posting images of a Swedish plane dropping teddy bears into Belarus to support local dissidents; he faces a potential prison term of seven years.

Despite constitutional guarantees of religious equality, government decrees and registration requirements have increasingly restricted religious activity. Legal amendments in 2002 provided for government censorship of religious publications and barred foreigners from leading religious groups. The amendments also placed strict limitations on religious groups that have been active in Belarus for fewer than 20 years. The government in 2003 signed a concordat with the Belarusian Orthodox Church, which enjoys a privileged position. The authorities have discriminated against Protestant clergy and ignored anti-Semitic attacks.

Academic freedom is subject to intense state ideological pressures, and institutions that use a liberal curriculum or are suspected of disloyalty face harassment and liquidation. Regulations stipulate immediate dismissal and revocation of degrees for students and professors who join opposition protests. Wiretapping by state security agencies limits the right to privacy.

The government restricts freedom of assembly for critical independent groups. Protests and rallies require authorization from local authorities, who can arbitrarily deny permission. When public demonstrations do occur, police frequently break them up and arrest participants.

Freedom of association is severely restricted. More than a hundred of the most active nongovernmental organizations (NGOs) were forced to close down between 2003 and 2005, and participation in an unregistered or liquidated political party or organization was criminalized in 2005. Registration of groups remains selective. As a result, most human rights activists operating in the country face potential jail terms ranging from six months to two years. Regulations introduced in 2005 ban foreign assistance to NGOs, parties, and individuals deemed to have promoted "meddling in the internal affairs" of Belarus from abroad.

Independent trade unions face harassment, and their leaders are frequently fired and prosecuted for peaceful protests. No independent trade unions have been registered since 1999. Over 90 percent of workers have fixed-term contracts, meaning that they can be arbitrarily dismissed when the contract expires.

Although the constitution calls for judicial independence, courts are subject to significant executive influence. The right to a fair trial is often not respected in cases with political overtones. Observers raised questions about the fairness of a trial that sentenced two men to death for a 2011 train bombing that killed 15; the men were executed in a hasty manner in March 2012 by being shot in the back of the head. Human rights groups continue to document instances of beatings, torture, and psychological pressure during detention in cases involving leaders of the democratic opposition. An October 2012 report from Human Rights Watch documented cases of abuse against political prisoners such as Ales Byalyatski and Dzmitry Dashkevich and warned that the situation was getting worse. Several lawyers for the political opposition have been disbarred. The power to extend pretrial detention lies with a prosecutor rather than a judge, in violation of international norms. Ethnic Poles and Roma often face discrimination.

An internal passport system limits freedom of movement and choice of residence. Some opposition activists have been turned back at the border or detained for lengthy searches. On December 7, 2012, Lukashenka signed a decree preventing wood-processing plant employees from quitting without their superior's permission, effectively blocking labor migration to Russia. The state has also nationalized companies that had earlier been privatized. Belarus's command economy severely limits economic freedom.

Women are not specifically targeted for discrimination, but there are significant discrepancies in income between men and women, and women are poorly represented in leading government positions. As a result of extreme poverty, many women have become victims of the international sex trade. In May 2012, the government denied gay activists a permit to protest discrimination.

Belgium

Political Rights: 1
Civil Liberties: 1
Status: Free

Population: 11,120,500
Capital: Brussels

Ten-Year Ratings Timeline For Year Under Review (Political Rights, Civil Liberties, Status)

2003	2004	2005	2006	2007	2008	2009	2010	2011	2012
1,1F	1,1F	1,1F	1,1F	1,1F	1,1F	1,1F	1,1F	1,1F	1,1F

Overview: Flemish nationalism was resurgent in 2012 as the separatist New Flemish Alliance, led by Bart de Wever, made strong gains in October local elections across Flanders, emboldening the party in its demands for greater autonomy from Brussels. Belgium's 2011 ban on face coverings continued to cause controversy, as a riot broke out in Brussels when a women was arrested after refusing to take off her veil, and the far-right Vlaams Belang offered bounties to anyone who reported violators of the ban to police.

Modern Belgium dates to 1830, when the largely Roman Catholic territory broke away from the mostly Protestant Netherlands and formed an independent constitutional monarchy. In the 20th century, Belgium became one of the founding members of the European Union (EU) and hosts the organization's central administration in Brussels.

Ethnic and linguistic conflicts prompted a series of constitutional amendments in 1970, 1971, and 1993 that devolved considerable power from the central government to the three regions in the federation: French-speaking Wallonia in the south; Flemish-speaking Flanders in the north; and Brussels, the capital, where French and Flemish share the same official status. Cultural and economic differences between the regions have contributed to political rifts between Flemish and Francophone parties across the ideological spectrum, with the wealthier Flemish north seeking increased self-rule and reduced taxpayer support for the less prosperous Wallonia. Voting takes place along strict linguistic lines; with the exception of the bilingual district encompassing Brussels, parties are only permitted to run in their respective linguistic regions.

Parliamentary elections held in June 2007 ended with Flemish and Walloon parties unable to agree on terms to form a coalition; after 196 days of negotiations, the king finally asked outgoing prime minister Guy Verhofstadt to form an interim government with the authority to act on pressing economic and other concerns.

In February 2008, a majority of political parties agreed on an outline for limited constitutional reform, which cleared the way for Flanders premier Yves Leterme of the centrist Christian Democratic and Flemish (CD&V) party to become prime minister the following month. Leterme's government was brought down at the end of the year, after being accused of interfering in a court case concerning the failed bank Fortis. The prime minister offered his resignation, and on December 30, the king swore in Herman Van Rompuy, also of the CD&V, to replace him.

In November 2009, Van Rompuy was appointed as the first permanent president of the European Council, the EU's intergovernmental decision-making body, and Leterme again became prime minister. However, his government fell in April 2010, when its coalition partner, the Flemish Liberals and Democrats (VLD), withdrew over disagreements over proposed changes to voting rules in the district encompassing Brussels.

The separatist New Flemish Alliance (N-VA) led June 2010 national elections with 27 seats in the Chamber of Deputies, while the Francophone Socialist Party (PS) placed second with 26 seats. Coalition negotiations again stalled over a series of issues linked to the balance of power between Flanders and Wallonia. The Leterme government remained in place for most of 2011 in a caretaker capacity. In September, the Dutch and Francophone parties reached a compromise on the separation of the contentious Brussels-area electoral district, and a final agreement was reached at the end of November. The new government, which notably did not include the N-VA, was led by Elio Di Rupo of the PS, the first French-speaking prime minister in more than 30 years; it took over from the caretaker government in December 2011.

N-VA leader Bart de Wever was victorious in Antwerp's October 2012 mayoral election, becoming the city's first non-Socialist mayor since World War II. The N-VA was successful in local elections across Flanders, winning about 30 percent of the total vote and taking 38 percent in Antwerp, compared to 28 percent for the Socialists. De Wever said the results signaled that Flanders wanted more independence, and he demanded that Di Rupo agree to further concessions. The victories were expected to provide the N-VA with momentum ahead of the 2014 parliamentary elections. In December, King Albert II in his annual Christmas speech warned Belgians to beware of populism, invoking the rise of fascism in the 1930s; de Wever alleged that the king had violated the impartiality of his role as head of state.

Political Rights and Civil Liberties: Belgium is an electoral democracy. Parliament consists of two houses: the Chamber of Deputies and the Senate. The 150 members of the Chamber of Deputies are elected directly by proportional representation. There are 71 seats in the Senate, with 40 filled by direct popular vote and 31 by indirect vote. Members serve four-year terms in both houses. The prime minister, who is the leader of the majority party or coalition, is appointed by the monarch and approved by Parliament. The party system is highly fragmented, with separate Flemish and Walloon parties representing all traditional parties of the left and right.

The xenophobic Vlaams Blok party was banned in 2004 for violating the country's antiracism laws. It changed its name to Vlaams Belang (Flemish Interest) and removed some of the more overtly racist elements from its platform. However, the party maintains its opposition to immigration and its commitment to an independent Flanders.

Corruption is relatively rare in Belgium, which was ranked 16 out of 176 countries surveyed in Transparency International's 2012 Corruption Perceptions Index.

Freedoms of speech and the press are guaranteed by the constitution and generally respected by the government. Belgians have access to numerous private media outlets. However, concentration of newspaper ownership has progressed in recent decades, leaving most of the country's papers in the hands of a few corporations. Internet access is unrestricted.

Freedom of religion is protected. About half of the country's population identifies itself as Roman Catholic. However, members of a number of minority religions have complained of discrimination by the government, which has been criticized for its characterization of some non-Catholic groups as "sects." In April 2010, the Chamber of Deputies approved a ban on the partial or total covering of the face in public locations; although it did not specifically mention the veils worn by some Muslim women, these were widely seen as the target. The ban took effect in July 2011. Offenders face a fine of up to 137.50 euros (US$183) or a week in jail. Two women who were fined 50 euros (US$66) in July for wearing full veils challenged the law in court, but the Constitutional Court in October 2011 refused to suspend the ban, ruling that the two women had not proved that they had been discriminated against. Protesters rioted outside a Brussels police station in May 2012, after a woman was arrested for refusing to remove her veil. In response to the incident, Filip Dewinter, a leader of the Vlaams Belang, in June offered a bounty of 250 euros (US$310) to anyone who reported a woman wearing a headscarf to police. The government does not restrict academic freedom.

Freedom of assembly is respected. Freedom of association is guaranteed by law, except for groups that practice discrimination "overtly and repeatedly." Employers found guilty of firing workers because of union activities are required to reinstate the workers or pay an indemnity.

The judiciary is independent, and the rule of law generally prevails in civil and criminal matters. Although conditions in prisons and detention centers meet most international standards, many continue to suffer from overcrowding.

Specific antiracism laws penalize the incitement of discrimination, acts of hatred, and violence based on race, ethnicity, or nationality. An imam was killed in an arson attack on a Shiite Muslim mosque in a Brussels suburb in March 2012; police arrested a Sunni Muslim man who Mosque officials said was motivated by sectarian hatred. While a 2009 government decision regularized 25,000 illegal immigrants, there have been complaints about the treatment of rejected asylum seekers and illegal immigrants awaiting deportation, who can sometimes be held in unsanitary conditions in the Brussels airport for several months.

The law provides for the free movement of citizens at home and abroad, and the government does not interfere with these rights. However, individual communities may expel Roma from city limits at the discretion of the local government.

The government actively promotes equality for women. The state Institute for the Equality of Men and Women is empowered to initiate sex-discrimination lawsuits. In the 2010 elections, women won about 40 percent of the seats in the Chamber of Deputies, and 37 percent of the seats in the Senate. Belgium legalized same-sex marriage in 2003, and in 2006 it gave gay and lesbian couples the right to adopt children. In 2011, Di Rupo became the country's first openly gay prime minister. Belgium is a source, destination, and transit point for trafficked persons. However, according to the U.S. State Department's 2012 Trafficking in Persons Report, the country complies fully with the minimum standards for eliminating trafficking.

Belize

Political Rights: 1
Civil Liberties: 2
Status: Free

Population: 326,000
Capital: Belmopan

Ten-Year Ratings Timeline For Year Under Review (Political Rights, Civil Liberties, Status)

2003	2004	2005	2006	2007	2008	2009	2010	2011	2012
1,2F	1,2F	1,2F	1,2F	1,2F	1,2F	1,2F	1,2F	1,2F	1,2F

Overview: **The ruling United Democratic Party (UDP) won a slight majority of seats in the March 2012 general elections, allowing UDP leader Dean Barrow to remain prime minister. Meanwhile, violent crime and trafficking in drugs, arms, and humans remained serious concerns in Belize throughout the year.**

Belize achieved independence from Britain in 1981 but has remained a member of the British Commonwealth. Control of the government has since alternated between the center-right United Democratic Party (UDP) and the center-left People's United Party (PUP).

Said Wilbert Musa of the PUP was elected prime minister in 1998, replacing George Cadle Prince, the cofounder of the PUP and Belize's first prime minister. Musa became the country's first prime minister to secure a second consecutive term after the PUP won again in 2003. However, the opposition UDP swept the 2008 national elections, amid public dissatisfaction with corruption, increased taxation, and rising crime rates. The UDP's Dean Barrow became prime minister.

The Barrow government proposed controversial amendments to the constitution in 2008 that would allow wiretapping, preventative detention, and the right to seize land where mineral resources were discovered. Opponents argued that this latter measure could easily be abused and did not respect the land rights of Mayan minority groups. The Barrow government also faced criticism for its 2009 takeover of Belize Telemedia Limited, the country's largest telecommunications company. Although the Supreme Court upheld the nationalization in 2010, the Belizean Court of Appeals ruled in June 2011 that the move was unconstitutional. The Belizean government nationalized Telemedia a second time in July 2011, believing that it had addressed the issues that the court had found to be illegal; in June 2012, however, the Court of Appeals once again found the nationalization unconstitutional. The government has appealed the court's decision.

In general elections held on March 7, 2012, the UDP captured 50.4 percent of the national vote and 17 seats—8 fewer than in the previous legislative election—and the PUP took 47.5 percent and 14 seats—8 more seats than previously; turnout was 73.2 percent. However, the PUP alleged that the elections were not free and fair, claiming that there were credible, documented reports of abuse and illegality in the electoral process. The Organization of American States' first ever Electoral Observation Mission (EOM) to Belize noted similar problems, including complaints of voter list irregularities. The observer mission also voiced concerns that party activists were electioneering outside of polling centers, with many of them wearing T-shirts that supported specific candidates; it also alleged that in at least one case, a party activist was paying voters as they left a polling center. Although the EOM still characterized the elections as free and fair, it did call on the government to pass campaign finance legislation, noting that political financing is unregulated in Belize; there are no limits on campaign spending and no disclosure requirement of campaign contributions or expenditures.

Political Rights and Civil Liberties: Belize is an electoral democracy. The head of state is the British monarch, who is represented by a governor general. Members of the 31-seat House of Representatives, the lower house of the bicameral National Assembly, are directly elected for five-year terms. The 12 members of the Senate are currently appointed to five-year terms, though Belizeans voted in a 2008 referendum to change to an elected Senate following the 2012 general elections.

There are no restrictions on the right to organize political parties, and the interests of Mestizo, Creole, Mayan, and Garifuna ethnic groups are represented in the National Assembly.

Government corruption remains a serious problem. Belize is the only country in Central America that is not a party to the UN Convention against Corruption. After running on an anticorruption platform and winning the 2008 election, Dean Barrow's popularity suffered in the last term as the result of several corruption scandals involving members of his administration. Barrow fired or demoted several ministers accused of wrongdoing. In January 2012, Merlene Bailey-Martinez resigned from Belize's Social Security Board amid allegations that she and other state workers had used funds from a government mortgage program to enrich themselves. Later in the year, however, Baily-Martinez became head of the country's Transport Board.

Belize has a generally open media environment. The constitution guarantees freedom of the press, but there are exceptions in the interest of national security, public order, and morality. Journalists or others who question the financial disclosures of government officials may face up to three years in prison or up to US$2,500 in fines, but this law has not been applied in recent years. The Belize Broadcasting Authority has the right to prior restraint of all broadcasts for national security or emergency reasons, though this, too, is rarely invoked. Despite the availability of diverse sources of media, including privately owned weekly newspapers, and radio and television stations, concerns over government control of the broadcast industry remain after the attempted nationalization of Telemedia. While the government does not restrict internet access or use, internet penetration is low due to lack of infrastructure and high costs.

Residents of Belize enjoy full freedom of religion, and academic freedom is respected.

Freedoms of assembly and association are generally upheld, and demonstrations are usually peaceful. A large number of nongovernmental organizations are active, and labor unions remain politically influential despite their shrinking ranks. Official boards of inquiry adjudicate labor disputes, and businesses are penalized for labor-code violations. However, the government has done little to combat antiunion discrimination, and workers who are fired for organizing rarely receive compensation.

The judiciary is independent, and the rule of law is generally respected. However, concerns remain that the judicial system is vulnerable to political interference. A 2011 report by the American Bar Association scored Belize poorly on 16 out of 28 factors in evaluating its prosecutorial and criminal justice system, and it found that only 1 in 10 murders leads to a conviction. Defendants can remain free on bail or in pretrial detention for years amid a heavy case backlog; about one-fifth of the country's detainees are awaiting trial.

Violent crime, money laundering, gang violence, and drug trafficking continued to be serious concerns in 2012; the country saw more than 100 murders for the third year in a row. Extrajudicial killings and the use of excessive force by police remain concerns, and Belizeans lack confidence in a police force they perceive as highly corrupt. Belize was added to the U.S. list of "major" drug-producing and transit countries in 2011 because of large numbers of drugs and weapons seized along its border with Mexico and weak anticorruption measures; it was added again to the list in September 2012. The U.S. government listed John Zabaneh, a well-known businessman who owns one of Belize's largest banana farms, as a "drug kingpin" in August 2012. The classification prevents any individual or entity from the United States from doing business with Zabaneh or his companies. The government established a committee in July 2012 to investigate decriminalizing marijuana. According to the International Center for Prison Studies, Belize has the world's 9th-highest prisoner-to-public ratio, with about 439 inmates per 100,000 inhabitants. Prisons do not meet minimum international standards, although there are some indications that they are improving.

While the government actively discourages ethnic discrimination, most Spanish-speaking immigrants in the country lack legal status and face discrimination.

Violence against women and children remains a serious concern, as does the prevalence of child labor in agriculture. Gender disparities are profound; Belize ranks 102 out of 132 countries on the World Economic Forum's 2012 Global Gender Gap Report. One female candidate won office in the March 2012 elections; Belize had previously been the only country in the Americas where no woman served in its elected lower house of government. Only 3 out of 74 candidates who competed in the elections were women. Belize is a source, transit, and destination country for women and children trafficked for prostitution and forced labor. The majority of trafficked women are from Guatemala, Honduras, and El Salvador, and there is concern that Belize is emerging as a sex tourism destination.

There have been reports of discrimination against people living with HIV/AIDS, despite the government's efforts to educate the public about the illness. LGBT (lesbian, gay, bisexual, and transgender) persons face legal and societal discrimination. While female same-sex sexual activity is legal, male same-sex sexual activity is illegal and can result in 10 years imprisonment. The Supreme Court is set to rule on the constitutionality of this law beginning in May 2013.

Benin

Political Rights: 2
Civil Liberties: 2
Status: Free

Population: 9,374,000
Capital: Porto-Novo

Ten-Year Ratings Timeline For Year Under Review (Political Rights, Civil Liberties, Status)

2003	2004	2005	2006	2007	2008	2009	2010	2011	2012
2,2F	2,2F	2,2F	2,2F	2,2F	2,2F	2,2F	2,2F	2,2F	2,2F

Overview: Tensions between the government and the opposition remained high in 2012 due to perceived irregularities in the 2011 presidential poll, in which President Boni Yayi won reelection. In October, the country was stunned by the arrest of three people for an alleged assassination attempt on the president. More promisingly, the National Assembly passed legislation abolishing the death penalty and banning torture.

Six decades of French rule in Benin lasted until 1960. Twelve years later, Mathieu Kérékou took power, ending a series of coups and countercoups and imposing a one-party Marxist-Leninist government. By 1990, economic hardship and rising internal unrest forced Kérékou to hold a national conference that eventually ushered in a peaceful democratic transition. Following his defeat by Nicéphore Soglo in the 1991 presidential election, the country's human rights record improved. Kérékou returned to power in 1996 through a democratic election, and he secured another term in 2001. The 2003 legislative elections gave the ruling coalition a majority in the National Assembly.

The 2006 presidential election—for which both Kérékou and Soglo were ineligible due to their ages—was won by Boni Yayi, an independent and former president of the regional development bank. A pro-Yayi coalition, led by the Cowrie Forces for an Emerging Benin (FCBE), won 35 of 83 seats in generally free and fair 2007 legislative elections. In 2009, this loose alliance began to break apart, posing a challenge to Yayi's efforts to enact electoral and economic reforms. By 2010, several FCBE members had defected to the opposition, causing the alliance to lose its majority and effectively blocking any new legislation. In August 2010, more than half of the National Assembly's members called for Yayi's impeachment, accusing him of involvement in a high-profile Ponzi scheme. Although parliament was unable to secure the necessary two-thirds majority to impeach Yayi, the president's reputation suffered greatly.

The scandal unified the five major opposition parties of the south for the first time since independence to form Build the Nation Union (UN), which fielded former prime minister Adrien Houngbédji as its candidate in the 2011 presidential election. Nonetheless, in March 2011, Yayi was reelected with 53 percent of the vote. The election had been delayed by nearly a month due to alleged irregularities, including problems with a new electronic voting system, but was eventually deemed free and fair by international observers. Houngbédji, who received 36 percent, refused to accept the results and appealed to the Constitutional Court. The court confirmed

Yayi's victory, leading to mass opposition demonstrations that were dispersed with tear gas and other police violence.

Houngbédji's refusal to accept the results undermined the opposition's campaign for the April legislative polls. Yayi's coalition gained a majority, winning 49 of 83 National Assembly seats, with 41 going to his core party, FCBE, in an election that international observers believed to be fair. This majority is enough to push through legislation but not constitutional reform, assuaging concerns that Yayi would seek to amend the constitution to allow for a third term. At the end of 2011, the position of prime minister, abolished since 1998, was reinstated, with the intention of preventing the centralization of power in the presidency that many feared. The new prime minister, Pascal Koupaki, had been serving in Yayi's administration and already effectively held many responsibilities of the post.

In October 2012, Yayi's niece, his doctor, and a former commerce minister were arrested for allegedly trying to poison the president. Patrice Talon, a wealthy businessman, is believed by the administration to have coordinated the assassination attempt. Talon, formerly a staunch Yayi supporter and funder of his campaigns, had recently become a vocal opponent of the president. All three remained in prison at year's end.

Tens of thousands of people were displaced by floods in Benin's south in June, and more than 35,000 refugees fled over the border escaping the violence in Mali, straining already limited resources in the north.

Political Rights and Civil Liberties: Benin is an electoral democracy. Despite delays, serious problems with the new electronic voting system, and doubts about the performance of the Autonomous National Electoral Commission, the 2011 presidential and legislative polls were considered largely free and fair by international observers. The president is elected by popular vote for up to two five-year terms and serves as both the chief of state and head of government. Delegates to the 83-member, unicameral National Assembly and the prime minister all serve four-year terms.

Historically, Benin has been divided between northern and southern ethnic groups. President Boni Yayi's support comes primarily from the north, while the main opposition parties hail primarily from the south. All political parties, regardless of ethnic or regional affiliation, normally operate freely throughout the country, and small ethnic groups are well represented in government bodies.

Yayi came to power in 2006 on an anticorruption platform and subsequently enacted a number of measures to combat corruption, including an internationally praised audit of 60 state-run companies. In August 2011, the National Assembly voted unanimously to pass an antigraft law, initially proposed by Yayi in 2006, which requires government employees to declare their assets when they enter and leave office. Despite frequent accusations from opposition politicians that Yayi has himself been involved in corruption, he has managed to maintain a reputation, both domestically and abroad, for being tough on corruption.

Constitutional guarantees of freedom of expression are largely respected in practice, though they were more at risk around the 2011 elections as the High Authority of Broadcasting (HAAC) handed out sanctions and suspensions with particular ease. Domestic respect for the HAAC has declined since 2011, when the president appointed a new chairman, who many considered to be a Yayi partisan, in a process that lacked transparency. The HAAC suspended one station, the private television station Canal 3, in 2012 at the request of the president for "undermining national unity." Libel and defamation remain criminalized in Benin, though they are rarely used. A pluralistic press publishes articles that are highly critical of both government and opposition leaders, though most media outlets receive direct financial support from politicians and few are considered genuinely independent.

The government actively seeks to ensure religious and academic freedoms. While the majority of Beninese identify themselves as either Muslim or Christian, many also practice some form of voodoo. Confrontations between religious groups are rare. Benin reportedly has the world's fastest growing Roman Catholic population, and the president is frequently criticized by the opposition for favoring the evangelical Christian population, though these criticisms are generally thought to be unfounded.

Freedom of assembly is respected, and requirements for permits and registration have often been ignored. Nonetheless, demonstrators encountered more problems than usual surrounding the 2011 elections, as widespread opposition demonstrations were at times violently suppressed by the police. Police also arrested a number of the protesters, including opposition officials, citing a directive from the security ministry banning such demonstrations. No such events were reported in 2012.

Nongovernmental organizations and human rights groups operated freely in 2012. The right to organize and join labor unions is constitutionally guaranteed, even for government employees and civil servants. The right to strike, however, is more limited; in October 2011, a new law extended a ban on the right to strike for military personnel and police officers to include customs officers and water and forestry workers. Unions played a central role in the country's democratization and were a vocal force supporting Houngbédji in 2011. Civil servant unions went on strike in June 2011, demanding a 25 percent pay increase, halting the strike when the government agreed to the increase a month later. In February 2012, the teachers' union went on strike for two months, complaining that they had been omitted from the deal, before returning to work without an immediate pay raise in response to the government's assertion that they had indeed received the 2011 increase.

The judiciary's independence is generally respected by the executive branch, but the courts are highly inefficient and susceptible to corruption, largely due to their serious and persistent lack of funding. Nevertheless, the constitutional court demonstrated remarkable independence in 2010, when it ruled on a number of complex issues regarding electoral reform, and in 2011, during the election controversy. Prisons are harsh and overcrowded, and criminal cases are rarely processed on time. In March 2012, the National Assembly unanimously passed a law in keeping with the recommendations of the UN Committee Against Torture. There have been no executions in Benin for 25 years, and in July, the country ratified a UN treaty abolishing the death penalty.

Relations among Benin's ethnic groups are generally amicable, although regional divisions occasionally flare up, particularly between the north and south. Minority ethnic groups are well represented in government agencies, the civil service, and the armed forces.

Although the constitution provides for gender equality and a national gender promotion policy aims to achieve gender equality by 2025, women enjoy fewer educational and employment opportunities than men, particularly in rural areas. A family code promulgated in 2004 improved women's inheritance, property, and marriage rights, and prohibited forced marriage and female genital mutilation, but these laws have not yet been well enforced.

Human trafficking is widespread in Benin; the vast majority of victims are girls trafficked inside the country from rural to urban areas. A law formally outlawing the trafficking of children was passed in 2006, but there is no legislation specifically addressing the trafficking of adults.

↑ Bhutan

Political Rights: 4
Civil Liberties: 5
Status: Partly Free

Population: 708,300
Capital: Thimphu

Trend Arrow: Bhutan received an upward trend arrow due to by-elections that were judged free and fair by international observers.

Ten-Year Ratings Timeline For Year Under Review (Political Rights, Civil Liberties, Status)

2003	2004	2005	2006	2007	2008	2009	2010	2011	2012
6,5NF	6,5NF	6,5NF	6,5NF	6,5NF	4,5PF	4,5PF	4,5PF	4,5PF	4,5PF

Overview: By-elections for vacant positions not filled by 2011's local elections were held in 2012 in a free and peaceful
manner. While tens of thousands of Nepali-speaking Bhutanese refugees who
were displaced in the 1990s have been resettled in other countries in recent
years, thousands of people remained in camps in Nepal by year's end. Bhutan
increasingly worked to end its international isolation in 2012, trying to take an
Asian seat at the UN Security Council.

Britain helped to install the Wangchuck dynasty as Bhutan's ruling family in 1907, and a 1949 treaty allowed newly independent India to assume Britain's role in conducting the kingdom's foreign and defense policies. In 1971, Jigme Singye Wangchuck succeeded his father as king.

The government in the 1980s imposed restrictions on Nepali speakers, also known as Southern Bhutanese, to protect the culture of the ruling Ngalong Drukpa ethnic group. The newly formed Bhutanese People's Party (BPP) responded in 1990 with violent demonstrations, prompting a government crackdown. Tens of thousands of Southern Bhutanese fled or were expelled to Nepal in the early 1990s, and soldiers raped and beat many villagers and detained thousands as "antinationals."

The king launched a gradual transition to democracy in 1998. Political parties were legalized in June 2007, and elections for an upper house of Parliament were held in two rounds in December 2007 and January 2008. Elections for the lower house, the National Assembly, took place in March 2008. The Bhutan Peace and Prosperity Party won 45 of the 47 seats, while the People's Democratic Party took the remainder; voter turnout was nearly 80 percent. A new constitution promulgated in July provided for some fundamental rights, but it upheld the primacy of the monarchy and did not adequately protect the rights of Nepali speakers.

Jigme Khesar Namgyel Wangchuck succeeded his father as king in November 2008, though he had been in power since the outgoing king's abdication in 2006. The monarchy remained highly popular with the public, and many Bhutanese expressed reservations about the shift toward democracy, excacerbated by the lack of qualified politicians in the country.

Local elections that had been postponed since late 2008 were finally held across the country in early 2011. Officials experienced difficulty recruiting qualified candidates to stand in the elections in a country with a small population, voter apathy, and high education requirements. All candidates were officially required to be nonpartisan and to prove that they had no party affiliations. Several candidates in the local elections ultimately were disqualified, because they did not meet the age or professional requirements. Some polls took long to open due to logistical difficulties, and turnout was relatively low, reportedly due in part to the remoteness of certain areas of the country and to voter apathy and distrust that the polls would result in concrete change.

By-elections for vacant positions not filled by the previous year's elections were held in 2012 and were more successful than those from 2011, with a better-funded election commission able to issue audits, hold the elections, and commission outside analyses of its results. The government also helped aspiring Bhutanese politicians learn more about democracy by organizing seminars and sending them for training in India.

Political Rights and Civil Liberties: Bhutan is an electoral democracy. Despite concerns about problems that kept some Nepalese from voting during the 2012 by-elections, international monitors deemed the elections to have been free and fair.

The constitution provides for a bicameral Parliament, with a 25-seat upper house, the nonpartisan National Council, and a 47-seat lower house, the National Assembly, both serving five-year terms. The king appoints 5 members of the National Council, and the remaining 20 are elected; the lower house is entirely elected, and the head of the majority party is nominated by the king to serve as prime minister. The cabinet previously was nominated by the king and approved by the National Assembly, but in 2012 there were many disputes among cabinet members about whether these positions should be chosen by Parliament. The cabinet has increasingly taken on the role of governing, and not just deferred to the monarch for guidance. The king remains the head of state and appoints members of the Supreme Court, the attorney general, and the heads of national commissions. He can return legislation with objections or amendments, but once it has been reconsidered and resubmitted, the king must sign it into law.

Political parties, previously illegal, were allowed to begin registering in 2007; four new political parties were registered in 2012.

The government operates with limited transparency and accountability, but steps have been taken in recent years to improve both. The 2006 Anti-Corruption Act established whistle-blower protections, and the Anti-Corruption Commission (ACC) is tasked with investigating and preventing graft. In 2011, the National Assembly passed an anticorruption law that strengthened and expanded the ACC's mandate. Bhutan was ranked 33 out of 176 countries surveyed in Transparency International's 2012 Corruption Perceptions Index.

The authorities restrict freedom of expression, and a 1992 law prohibits criticism of the king and the political system. A 2006 media law led to the establishment of two independent radio stations, but it did not provide specific protections for journalists or guarantee freedom of information. Since then, the government has liberalized the issuing of media licenses, allowing more outlets to emerge, particularly in the past two years. The state-owned *Kuensel* and two independent weeklies, the *Bhutan Times* and the *Daily Observer*, generally publish progovernment articles but occasionally cover criticism of the government. In February 2012, The *Bhutanese*, the country's first national broadsheet newspaper, launched with a plan to become the first daily paper in the country. The internet is accessed by about 15 percent of Bhutan's population. The government monitors online content and blocks material that is seen as pornographic, but rarely blocks political content.

The constitution protects freedom of religion, and a 2007 election law bars any ordained religious figure or "religious personality" from voting or running for office. In 2010, the election commission maintained that even lay members of religious organizations would be prevented from voting, but in 2011 and 2012, monks and other members of religious groups participated heavily in the local elections. While Bhutanese of all faiths can worship relatively freely, the Drukpa Kagyupa school of Mahayana Buddhism is the official religion and reportedly receives various subsidies. The Christian minority is allegedly subject to harassment by the authorities, and permits for the construction of Hindu temples are apparently difficult to obtain. Few restrictions on academic freedom have been reported, though nongovernmental organizations (NGOs) claim that the teaching of Nepali and Sanskrit is banned. The government requires that Bhutanese wear traditional dress on certain occasions and at certain times.

The constitution guarantees freedom of assembly, but the government must approve the purpose of any protests. In recent years, security forces have arrested Southern Bhutanese refugees based in Nepal who entered Bhutan to demonstrate for the right to return home.

The constitution guarantees freedom of association, but only for groups "not harmful to the peace and unity of the country." NGOs that work on human rights, the refugee issue, or other sensitive matters are not legally allowed to operate. Under the 2007 Civil Society Organization Act, all new NGOs must register with the government. The government prohibits independent trade unions and strikes, though most of the country's workforce is engaged in subsistence agriculture.

An independent Judicial Service Council created in 2007 controls judicial appointments and promotions. However, critics have alleged that the judiciary is not fully independent. Until a new Supreme Court was finally seated in early 2010, the king served as the final arbiter of appeals. Concerns were raised in 2012 by the press and the public over the quality of the justices and their lack of training for their jobs.

Arbitrary arrest, detention, and torture remain areas of concern, and dozens of political prisoners continue to serve lengthy sentences.

Prior to the mass expulsions of Nepali speakers in the early 1990s, the government had stripped thousands of their citizenship under a 1985 law that required both parents to be Bhutanese citizens. While the Office of the UN High Commissioner for Refugees (UNHCR) asserts that the overwhelming majority of refugees have proof of Bhutanese nationality, the government maintains that many left voluntarily or had been illegal immigrants. Some 55,000 refugees live in extremely poor conditions in Nepal and have been denied reentry to Bhutan, and the Bhutanese government continues to harshly criticize the UNHCR. A resettlement effort aimed at transferring the refugees to third countries began in 2007. According to the Office of the United Nations High Commissioner for Refugees, "more than 69,000 of an original total of 108,000 refugees from Bhutan have found a durable solution in third countries," including the United States.

Women participate freely in social and economic life but continue to be underrepresented in government and politics, though they participated heavily in the 2011 elections. They also comprise nearly 50 percent of the workforce.

Bolivia

Political Rights: 3
Civil Liberties: 3
Status: Partly Free

Population: 10,836,000
Capital: La Paz (administrative), Sucre (judicial)

Ten-Year Ratings Timeline For Year Under Review (Political Rights, Civil Liberties, Status)

2003	2004	2005	2006	2007	2008	2009	2010	2011	2012
3,3PF	3,3PF	3,3PF	3,3PF	3,3PF	3,3PF	3,3PF	3,3PF	3,3PF	3,3PF

Overview: In 2012, President Evo Morales faced social unrest on issues including indigenous land rights and disputes over natural resources. In January, 56 newly elected high court justices were sworn in following elections held in 2011 that were marred by procedural problems and voter discontent. Meanwhile, attacks against journalists and media outlets critical of the government continued during the year.

After achieving independence from Spain in 1925 and enduring years of military rule and 180 coups in 157 years, Bolivia has enjoyed relative stability and a succession of civilian presidents since 1982. In 2002, Gonzalo Sánchez de Lozada, who had held the presidency in the 1990s, was returned to office on the basis of a narrow first-round victory and a subsequent vote in Congress. The 2002 election also saw the emergence of Evo Morales of the Movement Toward Socialism (MAS) party as a national political leader. In 2003, widespread protests over the government's plan to export natural gas to the United States via Chile resulted in dozens of deaths; Sánchez de Lozada was forced to resign and fled the country for the United States.

Vice President Carlos Mesa assumed the presidency. Despite successfully increasing state control over natural resources, he failed to quell mounting protests over gas revenues, regional autonomy, and other issues, and he ultimately resigned in June 2005. The chief justice of the Supreme Court temporarily served as president to oversee new elections. Morales won the December presidential election with 54 percent of the popular vote—the first outright electoral majority since the return to democracy—and the MAS became the largest party in Congress.

In 2006, the MAS and allied parties won a majority of delegates for a constituent assembly charged with writing a new constitution. From 2006 to 2009, recurring conflicts erupted over voting procedures in the constituent assembly and the substance of the draft constitution, pitting the government and its supporters against congressional and regionally based political opponents, especially from Bolivia's eastern departments.

Morales won a recall referendum in August 2008 with 67 percent of the vote. Political confrontations during this period sometimes turned violent; a September 2008 clash between pro-Morales peasants and followers of opposition prefect Leopoldo Fernández in Pando left at least 14 people dead and triggered a criminal indictment for Fernández.

By October 2008, opposing sides reached compromise on the draft constitution that retained most of the administration's proposals, though notable changes included an easing of potentially restrictive media language, a higher bar for future constitutional amendments, expansion of the electoral commission, and the limitation of consecutive presidential terms to two. In a January 2009 referendum, the new constitution was approved by over 61 percent of voters, with a turnout of over 90 percent.

In 2009 national elections, Morales was reelected with 64 percent of the vote amid a record 95 percent turnout. Monitors from the European Union characterized the elections as generally free and fair, but reported some misuse of state resources, a complaint echoed by opposition leaders. Some opposition members also claimed they were targeted with criminal investigations, causing them to flee the country.

The MAS also dominated the 2009 legislative elections, winning majorities in the lower chamber and the Senate. Meanwhile, the remainder of Bolivia's nine departments approved regional autonomy statutes, joining four that had already done so in 2006. In April 2010 regional elections, MAS candidates won governorships in six of the nine departments, but opposition candidates from the left and right became mayors in 7 of the 10 principal cities. The MAS used its legislative majority to pass new laws during 2010, including anticorruption and antiracism laws.

While regional opposition from the political right dominated Morales's first term as president, his second term has been marked by challenges from unions and social movements on the left. The December 2010 announcement of plans to remove state gasoline subsidies, which would lead to sharp price increases, triggered street protests. Bolivia's largest trade union organization, the Bolivian Workers' Center, scheduled a mass demonstration for January 2011, forcing Morales to rescind his proposal.

In 2011, indigenous groups from the Indigenous Territory and National Park of Isiboro Sécure (TIPNIS) joined with other social organizations and opposition groups to block a planned $415 million highway through the territory that would link the cities of Trinidad and Cochabamba. Indigenous leaders argued that the Brazilian-financed highway would cause environmental damage and increase encroachment by coca growers, loggers, and migrants. The movement began by invoking the community's right to a prior consultation (*consulta previa*) as stipulated in the 2010 constitution. In August 2011, TIPNIS residents and supporters staged a march to La Paz to demand that the government scrap the highway plan. After the protesters detained Foreign Minister David Choquehuanca and forced him to march with them, police beat and tear-gassed the marchers, leaving 70 people injured. Human rights groups called for an investigation; Morales condemned the violence and accepted the resignations of his defense and interior ministers. TIPNIS protesters resumed their march and were welcomed by La Paz residents. Indigenous leaders secured promises from Morales and other government officials to protect their territory. Legislation passed in October banned highway construction across the designated areas, prohibited illegal settlements, and authorized the use of force to remove squatters, until the consultation process was completed.

Progress ground to a halt in 2012, however, as the consultation process ran into administrative hurdles, opposition from indigenous communities, and the practical difficulties of navigating lowland rivers during the dry season. In late December, a commission representing the Catholic Church, the Permanent Assembly of Human Rights in Bolivia, and the Inter-American Federation of Human Rights reported that 30 of the 36 communities they visited rejected the proposed road; three communities favored road construction, and three indicated that they would accept the road if its route were changed. These findings contradicted the government's earlier assertions that 80 percent of the communities included in the official consultation process supported the road. The commission also found that the government's consultation process did not meet international or even national legal standards for prior and informed consent.

Political Rights and Civil Liberties: Bolivia is an electoral democracy. Elections and referendums since 2005 have been deemed free and fair by international observers. Under the new constitution, presidential and legislative terms are both five years, with up to two consecutive terms permitted. The Plurinational Legislative Assembly consists of a 130-member Chamber of Deputies and a 36-member Senate, in which all senators and 53 deputies are elected by proportional representation, and 70 deputies are elected in individual districts. Seven seats in the Chamber of Deputies are reserved for indigenous representatives. The 2009 constitution includes a presidential runoff provision to replace the previous system, in which the legislature had decided elections when no candidate won an outright majority.

Citizens have the right to organize political parties. President Evo Morales's MAS draws support from a diverse range of social movements, unions, and civil society actors. With the election of Morales, the traditional political parties have all but collapsed. Following the 2010 local and regional elections, the Movement Without Fear party—a group previously allied with the MAS, and led by former La Paz mayor Juan del Granado—emerged as a centrist alternative to the ruling party.

Corruption remains a problem in Bolivia, affecting a range of government entities and economic sectors, including extractive industries. Anticorruption legislation enacted in 2010 has been criticized for permitting retroactive enforcement. The government has established an Anti-Corruption Ministry, outlined policies to combat corruption, and opened investigations into official corruption cases. In 2011, legislators voted to prosecute former presidents Gonzalo Sánchez de Lozada and Jorge Quiroga for approving hydrocarbon contracts that are alleged to have contravened national interests. Three former ministers were also included in the indictment. In September 2012, the U.S. government announced that it would not extradite Sánchez de Lozada. Separately, there have been concerns about the long-standing problem of corruption of law enforcement bodies in connection with the illegal drug trade. In 2012, Bolivia was ranked 105 out of 176 countries surveyed in Transparency International's Corruption Perceptions Index.

Although the constitution guarantees freedom of expression, the media are subject to some limitations in practice. Press associations have complained that the language of a 2010 antiracism law is vague and contributes to a climate of self-censorship. In particularly serious cases, the law allows publication of racist or discriminatory ideas to be punished with fines, the loss of broadcast licenses, and prison sentences of up to five years. In many cases, a public apology can result in the waiver of such sanctions. In February 2011, the government created a Ministry of Communications, raising hopes that the "right to communication," established in the new constitution would be enforced. Since the ministry's establishment, however, two successive ministers have failed to promote the passage of such a law, leaving in question the constitution's guarantee of freedom of expression.

Most media outlets are privately owned, and radio is the leading source of information. Print media has seen a wave of consolidation and the closing of some newspapers. Electronic media is growing in importance as a source of news. Many newspapers and television stations feature opposition rather than progovernment opinion pieces; the opposite holds true in state media. The 2011 telecommunications law would allocate 33 percent of all broadcast licenses to state-run media, another 33 percent to commercial broadcasters, and 17 percent each to local communities and indigenous groups.

Attacks against journalists and independent media continued in 2012. In October, a radio journalist in the southern city of Yacuiba, near the Argentine border, was severely injured by attackers who broke into his studio and set him on fire. The journalist had reported on cross-border smuggling, and had spoken out against local authorities during his radio broadcasts. In June, attacks against radio stations—including at least three dynamite attacks—and individual journalists occurred in Oruro and elsewhere, during a strike of the national police force. In November, Ghilka Sanabria, the editor of the newspaper *El Diario* and a freedom of expression advocate, suffered serious injuries following a beating she received while on her way home.

In October 2012, the Plurinational Constitutional Court declared unconstitutional Article 162 of the penal code, which made it a crime to criticize a government official in the exercise of his or her office. This decision brings Bolivia into accordance with three international conventions ratified by the Bolivian government: the Universal Declaration on Human Rights, the Inter-American Convention on Human Rights, and the International Pact on Civil and Political Rights.

Freedom of religion is guaranteed by the constitution. The new constitution ended the Roman Catholic Church's official status and created a secular state. The government does not restrict academic freedom.

Bolivian law provides for the rights of peaceful assembly and freedom of association, though protests sometimes turn violent. The Morales government has been highly critical of nongovernmental organizations, especially those that supported the TIPNIS protest. The right to form labor unions is guaranteed by the constitution. Labor and peasant unions are an active force in society and have significant political influence.

In 2012, the judicial system faced ongoing systemic challenges. Judicial elections were held in 2011 to remedy a crisis in the judicial branch, which had been rocked by resignations, charges of corruption, and a backlog of cases. The elections were marred by procedural problems and voter discontent. Candidates for the Supreme Court, the Constitutional Tribunal, and other entities were nominated through a two-thirds vote in the legislature, which allowed the MAS to dominate the selection process. Election officials ruled that candidates were not permitted to campaign openly, and that information about the candidates would be disseminated through official channels. In results that were interpreted as a defeat for the government, voters cast null ballots in numbers that exceeded the overall valid vote. Nevertheless, 56 new high court judges were sworn in in January 2012, and Bolivia became the first country in Latin America to swear in elected judges to its highest courts, including the Constitutional Tribunal, the Supreme Court, and the newly created Agroenvironmental Tribunal.

The new justices face a daunting caseload. In 2011, the Bolivian Supreme Court ruled on 2,206 cases, leaving approximately 29,000 pending. Prosecutorial independence is viewed as weak, and enforcement at times focuses on opposition members and sympathizers, with former presidents and many opposition politicians facing charges ranging from graft to treason.

Bolivian prisons are overcrowded, and conditions for prisoners are extremely poor. In June 2012, the National Prison Administrator reported that 84 percent of inmates were in pretrial detention. Trial dates are frequently postponed. A 1988 law passed at the urging of the United States that substantially lengthened prison sentences for drug-related crimes has contributed to prison overcrowding, as has an increase in urban crime rates. In response to overcrowding, the government approved a pardon in 2012 that stands to benefit some 5,000 prisoners, granting some immediate release. Government officials in the United States have denounced the pretrial detention of Brooklyn businessman Jacob Ostreicher, who has been imprisoned in Bolivia for more than a year. A representative of the UN High Commission on Human Rights concluded in July that Ostreicher's case is not unusual in Bolivia's extremely slow and underresourced judicial system.

While the 2009 constitution and jurisdictional law recognize indigenous customary law regarding conflict resolution, jurisdictional reform efforts have not fully resolved questions pertaining to indigenous customary law. This lack of clarity has allowed some perpetrators of vigilante crimes, including lynching, to misrepresent their actions as a form of indigenous justice. A February 2012 report by the United Nations Office of the High Commissioner for Human Rights stated that lynchings had substantially decreased during the previous two years, though violent extrajudicial punishment remains a problem in many parts of Bolivia.

Bolivia is the world's third-largest producer of the coca leaf, after Colombia and Peru. By law, 12,000 hectares of land are designated for the legal cultivation of the crop. The United Nations estimates that another 27,200 hectares are used for unregulated coca production destined for the illegal cocaine trade. The Bolivian government has expressed concern about increased cocaine production in the country, as well as the increasing flow of Peruvian cocaine through Bolivian territory. In September 2012, the United States government sharply criticized Bolivian counter-narcotics efforts, asserting that cocaine production in Bolivia had exceeded that of Colombia. However, in a separate report also released in September, the United Nations Office on Drugs and Crime (UNDOC) indicated that coca cultivation in Bolivia had decreased by 12 percent during the previous year; UNDOC attributed the decrease to the Morales government's policies of control and eradication. Notably, UNDOC and the United States differed by only a single percentage point in their estimates of the area dedicated to coca cultivation, though they differed sharply in their interpretations of this figure. While UNDOC praised the reduction in coca cultivation, a representative of the U.S. Embassy in La Paz argued that, in spite of the reduction, Bolivia had failed to meet its obligations under international narcotics agreements.

The 2009 constitution recognizes 36 indigenous nationalities, declares Bolivia a "plurinational" state—changing the official name of the country from the Republic of Bolivia to the Plurinational State of Bolivia—and formalizes local political and judicial control within indigenous territories. In general, racism is rife in the country, especially against indigenous groups. Indigenous people from the country's Andean west who move to Santa Cruz de la Sierra and some other areas in the eastern lowlands for economic reasons are subject to considerable racism and occasional violence, some of which involves organized armed gangs. The 2010 antira-cism contains measures to combat discrimination and impose criminal penalties for discriminatory acts.

While the law protects freedom of movement, protesters often block highways and city streets.

The constitution prohibits discrimination based on gender and sexual orientation, but it reserves marriage only for opposite-sex couples, and there is no provision for same-sex civil unions. Women enjoy the same formal rights to property ownership as men, but discrimination is pervasive, leading to disparities in property ownership and access to resources. Women's political representation has increased in recent years. Ballot-alternation requirements resulted in women winning 44 percent of the seats in the current Senate, but only 28 percent of the seats in the Chamber of Deputies. Gender parity election rules were also applied to the 2011 judicial elections, resulting in gender parity in elected judges. Violence against women is pervasive, and the justice system is ineffective at safeguarding women's broader legal rights. The penal code does not recognize spousal rape and permits a rapist to escape punishment if he marries his victim. More than half of Bolivian women are believed to suffer domestic violence at some point during their lives.

Child labor, forced labor, and human trafficking are ongoing problems. Child labor in cooperatively run mines and in agriculture is common, and a 2012 study by the United Nations reported instances of forced child labor in mining, agriculture, and the drug trade. Forced labor has also been reported on agricultural estates in the Chaco region. In 2012, authorities achieved their first forced-labor conviction. Human trafficking continues to be a problem in Bolivia, although the government is making progress in addressing the problem, including the establishment of an office to coordinate human trafficking prosecution efforts.

Bosnia and Herzegovina

Political Rights: 3*
Civil Liberties: 3
Status: Partly Free

Population: 3,843,000
Capital: Sarajevo

Ratings Change: Bosnia and Herzegovina's political rights rating improved from 4 to 3 due to the formation of a central government and the declining role of the international community in domestic affairs.

Ten-Year Ratings Timeline For Year Under Review (Political Rights, Civil Liberties, Status)

2003	2004	2005	2006	2007	2008	2009	2010	2011	2012
4,4PF	4,3PF	4,3PF	3,3PF	4,3PF	4,3PF	4,3PF	4,3PF	4,3PF	3,3PF

Overview: After a 16-month deadlock following the October 2010 elections, a new government was confirmed in February 2012. Despite initial optimism about the country's progress toward passing key reforms, the ruling coalition proved highly unstable, leading to another political crisis and cabinet reshuffling. Local elections took place in October 2012, with the nationalist parties securing most votes.

Formerly a constituent republic within socialist Yugoslavia, Bosnia and Herzegovina (BiH) is among the most ethnically diverse countries in the region. The bulk of the population consists of three ethnic groups: Bosniaks, who are mainly Muslim; Serbs, who are generally Orthodox Christian; and Croats, who are mainly Roman Catholic. As Yugoslavia began to disintegrate in the early 1990s, BiH was recognized as an independent state in April 1992. A 43-month-long civil war ensued, resulting in the deaths of tens of thousands of people and the forced resettlement of approximately half of BiH's population.

The 1995 Dayton Peace Accords brought an end to the war by creating a loosely knit state composed of the Bosniak-Croat Federation of Bosnia and Herzegovina (the Federation) and the largely Serb Republika Srpska. The final status of the Brcko district was decided in 1999 by a special arbitration council, which defined it as a self-governing administrative unit that is formally part of both the Federation and the Republika Srpska. The Dayton Accords gave significant authority to international civilian agencies such as the Office of the High Representative (OHR). However, despite years of considerable efforts by the international community to aid the country's integration, most aspects of political, social, and economic life remained divided along ethnic lines.

A coalition government formed in early 2007, following October 2006 elections, proved to be highly unstable, particularly due to a thorny working relationship between Serb leader Milorad Dodik of the Alliance of Independent Social Democrats (SNSD), who was determined to maintain the Republika Srpska's autonomy, and Bosniak leader Haris Silajdžic of the Party for BiH (SzBiH), who sought to create a unitary BiH. Meanwhile, most Croat officials advocated further decentralization and the creation of a third constituent entity for Croat-majority areas. Despite these tensions, in June 2008, the European Union (EU) and BiH signed a Stabilization and Association Agreement, a key step toward EU membership.

In March 2009, Austrian diplomat Valentin Inzko was appointed as the new high representative. Long-standing tensions between the OHR and the Bosnian Serb leadership continued, with the latter challenging several of Inzko's decisions. In a step condemned by the OHR, the parliament of the Republika Srpska adopted a law in February 2010 that made it easier for the Republika Srpska authorities to call referendums in the Republika Srpska on national issues, raising the possibility of a vote on secession.

Parliamentary and presidential elections on the national and entity levels took place in October 2010, bringing a power shift to several government bodies. The SNSD remained the dominant party in the Republika Srpska, and Dodik, who had served as prime minister since 2006 and had stepped up his nationalist rhetoric ahead of the vote, was elected president of the Serb entity. The more moderate and largely Bosniak Social Democratic Party (SDP) secured a plurality of seats in the Federation at the expense of the Party of Democratic Action (SDA) and the SzBiH, with the latter seeing a major defeat. The Croat Democratic Union of BiH (HDZ BiH) remained the most popular party among Bosnian Croats, while Zivko Budimir of the Croatian Party of Rights BiH became president of the Federation.

In the tripartite presidential election, incumbent Željko Komšic of the SDP was reelected as the Croat member of the presidency. In a surprise victory, Bakir Izetbegovic of the SDA, the son of the late president Alija Izetbegovic, defeated the incumbent Silajdžic in the race for the Bosniak seat. SNSD incumbent Nebojša Radmanovic was reelected as the Serb member of the presidency.

In the months following the elections, prolonged political wrangling over the formation of ruling coalitions—both on the national and the Federation levels— paralyzed the country. An agreement on a new central government was not reached until late December 2011, in large part due to disagreements over which party should receive the premiership and other key cabinet positions. The SDP argued that it should name the prime minister, as it won a plurality of votes in the elections, but the HDZ BiH and HDZ 1990 claimed the right to choose the key officeholders, citing the informal system of rotating core posts among the three main ethnic groups. The December compromise agreement permitted the HDZ BiH to nominate candidates for only three out of four key ministry positions allocated to Croats, though HDZ BiH's Vjekoslav Bevanda was confirmed as prime minister in January 2012.

The new government received a parliamentary vote of confidence in February 2012, ending the 16-month crisis and spurring hopes that the country would start tackling key reforms necessary for BiH to formally apply for EU membership. In February, the national parliament adopted a law on the census and another law on state aid, both of which were preconditions for EU integration. In March, the central government agreed on the process for the allocation of military and state property, which was one of the key requirements for future membership in NATO.

A fresh government crisis, however, emerged in May over proposed cuts in the state budget, this time between the SDP and the SDA. After five months of political maneuvering, the parliament in October voted to dismiss two SDA cabinet ministers, handing a victory to the SDP. In order to achieve this, the SDP had allegedly stricken a compromise with the SNSD and Croatian parties; in exchange for their support in removing the SDA ministers, the SDP supposedly promised to somewhat dilute its strong position toward further centralization of the state. Meanwhile, in the Federation, the SDA and smaller Croatian parties were struggling at year's end to remain in the ruling coalition.

Local elections took place in October, with the long-established nationalist parties—the SDA, the HDZ BiH, and the Serb Democratic Party (SDS)—coming out as the overall winners. Dodik's SNSD won only 18 municipalities, down from 41. The SDP received fewer votes than the SDA, prompting speculation about whether its power would continue to erode in the lead-up to the 2014 national elections.

At the end of August, the international supervisor of the Brcko district suspended his authority, although he will still theoretically keep some powers in case of a future crisis. Additionally, the EU Police Mission, which focused on fighting corruption and organized crime in Bosnia, closed down in June. These closures were generally seen as steps toward the international community's gradual withdrawal from the country, and as potentially paving the way for the eventual closure of the OHR.

Political Rights and Civil Liberties: The Republic of Bosnia and Herzegovina (BiH) is an electoral democracy. In general, voters can freely elect their representatives, although the OHR has the authority to remove elected officials if they are deemed to be obstructing the peace process. The state-level government is led by a prime minister, and the role of head of state is performed by a three-member presidency composed of one Bosniak, one Serb, and one Croat. The Parliamentary Assembly is a bicameral body. The 15-seat upper house, the House of Peoples, consists of five members from each of the three main ethnic groups, elected by the Federation and Republika Srpska legislatures for four-year terms. The lower house, the House of Representatives, has 42 popularly elected members serving four-year terms, with 28 seats assigned to representatives from the Federation and 14 to representatives from the Republika Srpska. Both the Federation and the Republika Srpska have their own presidents, parliaments, and other governing bodies, which are responsible for policymaking on the entity level.

Corruption remains a serious problem. Enforcement of legislation designed to combat it has been weak, due in part to the lack of strong and independent anticorruption agencies and a dearth of political will to seriously address the issue. In its annual report on Bosnia's progress toward EU membership, the European Commission in 2012 identified serious flaws in the fight against corruption and noted a shortage of effective investigations, prosecutions, and convictions in corruption cases. BiH was ranked 72 among 176 countries surveyed in Transparency International's 2012 Corruption Perceptions Index.

The constitution and the human rights annex to the Dayton Peace Accords provide for freedom of the press, but this right is not always respected in practice.

While a large number of independent broadcast and print outlets operate, they tend to appeal to narrow ethnic audiences, and most neglect substantive or investigative reporting. This was evident during campaigning for local elections in 2012, during which many media outlets revealed a clearly partisan point of view. The public broadcaster BiH Radio Television (BHRT), which is designed to cater to multiethnic audiences, has faced growing political pressure in recent years.

Attacks on journalists take place occasionally, and reporters have faced pressure from government officials. In July, several people physically attacked Štefica Galic, a local filmmaker and the chief editor of the web portal *tacno.net*, two days after the screening of her documentary about her late husband's efforts to help Bosnian Muslims during the 1990s conflict. At a June press conference, Dodik called journalist Ljiljana Kovacevic of the Belgrade-based news agency Beta a liar, and demanded that she leave Republika Srpska's Presidential Palace and never return.

Citizens enjoy full freedom of religion, but only in areas where their particular group represents a majority. Acts of vandalism against holy sites of all three major faiths continue to occur, although they appear to have decreased. According to the Inter-Religious Council of Bosnia, 27 attacks on religious sites, objects, and officials took place between November 2011 and October 2012, with 9 attacks recorded in Republika Srpska and 18 in the Federation.

While the authorities do not restrict academic freedom at institutions of higher education, academic appointments are heavily politicized, with ethnic favoritism playing a significant role. Primary and secondary school curriculums are also politicized. Depending on their ethnicity, children use textbooks printed in Croatia, Serbia, or Sarajevo. In parts of the region of Herzegovina, students are often divided by ethnicity, with separate classrooms, entrances, textbooks, and class times. The educational sector is among the most corrupt in BiH, with studies showing that bribery and inappropriate expenditures are pervasive.

The constitution provides for freedoms of assembly and association, and the various levels of government generally respect these rights in practice. Nonetheless, nongovernmental organizations (NGOs)—particularly those that are critical of the authorities—have faced some intimidation. Authorities in Banja Luka fined the local NGO Oštra Nula 1,400 convertible marks ($900) in September 2011 for placing a banner in the city's main square that aimed to draw attention to the fact that a new central government had yet to be formed, despite growing economic challenges facing the country. A series of high-profile public demonstrations against cuts in public administration and in benefits for former military personnel took place in 2012. Although there are no legal restrictions on the right of workers to form and join labor unions, discrimination against union members persists. Unemployment in BiH is among the highest in Europe, and many workers have reportedly declined to file antiunion-related complaints with labor inspectors for fear of losing their jobs. However, courts in both entities frequently rule in favor of workers when faced with such cases.

Despite evidence of growing independence, the judiciary remains susceptible to influence by nationalist political parties, and faces pressure from the executive branch. The lack of a single, supreme judicial body and the existence of four separate court systems—for the central state, Republika Srpska, the Federation, and the Brcko district—contributes to overall inefficiency. The country has made some efforts to reduce its case backlog, but the number of pending cases remains high. As of April 2012, there were over 400,000 unresolved cases across all jurisdictions, in addition to about 1.5 million pending cases related to unpaid utility bills.

The state court—established in 2002 to handle organized crime, war crimes, corruption, and terrorism cases—has made progress on adjudicating cases of organized crime and war crimes. In April 2011, the Republika Srpska's parliament voted in favor of holding a referendum that would have disputed the jurisdiction of the state court and the state prosecutor's office on the territory of Republika Srpska. The parliament rescinded its decision in late May, after the Office of the EU Representative offered to initiate a "structured dialogue" on judicial reform in BiH. Meanwhile, witness protection programs are not always available to those who need them, though in March, media outlets reported that efforts were being undertaken to train staff at entity-level courts to better work with protected witnesses.

Individuals face discrimination in employment, housing, and social services in regions that are not dominated by their own ethnic group. In December 2009, the European Court of Human Rights (ECHR) ruled that the constitution was discriminatory for allowing only Bosniaks, Croats, and Serbs to run for the presidency or serve in the upper house of parliament, excluding candidates from the Jewish, Romany, and other smaller minorities. However, no remedies have been implemented to date. Implementation of the ECHR decision is viewed as one of the priorities for the country's application for EU membership.

Women are legally entitled to full equality with men. However, they are underrepresented in politics and government and face discrimination in the workplace. The issue of sexual harassment is poorly understood, and improper behavior frequently goes unpunished. The police are still largely unresponsive to violent domestic disputes, particularly in rural areas. According to the U.S. State Department, BiH is considered a source, destination and transit country for men, women, and children trafficked for the purpose of prostitution and forced labor. The government has failed to meet the minimum international standards for the elimination of trafficking, in part due to insufficient political support.

Botswana

Political Rights: 3
Civil Liberties: 2
Status: Free

Population: 1,850,000
Capital: Gaborone

Ten-Year Ratings Timeline For Year Under Review (Political Rights, Civil Liberties, Status)

2003	2004	2005	2006	2007	2008	2009	2010	2011	2012
2,2F	2,2F	2,2F	2,2F	2,2F	2,2F	3,2F	3,2F	3,2F	3,2F

Overview: A landmark High Court ruling in October 2012 held that customary law could no longer be used to deny a woman's right to inheritance, setting a critical legal precedent. In June, President Ian Khama controversially pardoned three policemen convicted of the 2009 politically motivated killing of alleged criminal John Kalafatis.

Elected governments, all led by the Botswana Democratic Party (BDP), have ruled the country since it gained independence from Britain in 1966. Vice President Festus Mogae rose to the presidency when longtime president Ketumile Masire retired in 1998, and he was confirmed as the country's leader after the BDP easily won legislative elections in 1999. The BDP took 44 of the 57 contested seats in the 2004 elections, securing a second presidential term for Mogae.

In 2008 Mogae—like Masire before him—retired before the end of his term, leaving Vice President Seretse Khama Ian Khama to assume the presidency. Khama, the son of independence leader and first president Seretse Khama, had been appointed vice president by Mogae in 1998 and was elected chairman of the BDP in 2003. He quickly shuffled the cabinet and appointed former foreign minister Mompati Merafhe as vice president. Critics have accused the BDP of subverting democratic institutions through this "automatic succession" process.

Significant rifts within the ruling party emerged before legislative elections in October 2009. Most notably, Khama suspended his rival, BDP secretary general Gomolemo Motswaledi, preventing him from competing in parliamentary elections. In September, the High Court rejected Motswaledi's related lawsuit against Khama, citing the head of state's constitutional immunity from civil suits.

The BDP won 45 of the 57 National Assembly seats in the 2009 elections with 53.3 percent of the vote. The Botswana National Front (BNF) won six seats, while the Botswana Congress Party (BCP) took four. Parliament confirmed Khama for a full presidential term later that month, and observers declared the elections free and fair.

In March 2010, leaders of the so-called Barata-Pathi faction of the BDP—including Motswaledi and fellow suspended BDP parliamentarian Botsalo Ntuane—officially withdrew from the BDP and declared their intention to form a new opposition party, the Botswana Movement for Democracy (BMD). Accusing Khama of violating the party's constitution by concentrating power in the presidency and among his "A-Team" faction, the BMD party was officially registered in June, led by Ntuane and including some 20 former BDP legislators. However, shuffling of legislators between the BMD and BDP has subsequently diminished the former's representation in parliament.

In June 2012, Khama issued a "conditional" pardon to three members of the Botswana Defence Force—Gotshosamang Sechele, Ronny Matako, and Boitshoko Maifala—who had been convicted in 2011 of murdering alleged organized crime suspect John Kalafatis in 2009. The murder, which occurred amid a spate of extrajudicial killings by security forces in 2009, was reportedly ordered by the president's Directorate of Intelligence and Security (DIS). Khama has denied any involvement in ordering Kalafatis's execution, although the pardon revived the accusation by media outlets, civic groups, and opposition parties. The three policemen had been sentenced to 11 years imprisonment; the conditions of their pardon remained unclear at year's end.

Political Rights and Civil Liberties: Botswana is an electoral democracy. The 63-seat National Assembly, the lower house, is elected for five years, and chooses the president to serve a five-year term. Of the body's 63 members, 57 are directly elected, 4 are nominated by the president and approved by the assembly, and 2—the president and the attorney general—are ex-officio members. Despite being elected indirectly, the president holds significant power. While the president can prolong or dismiss the legislature, the legislature is not empowered to impeach the president.

Democracy advocates have alleged that power has become increasingly centralized around President Seretse Khama Ian Khama, with many top jobs going to military officers and family members. The 2007 Intelligence and Security Services Act created the DIS within the Ministry of Justice, Defense and Security with substantial powers (for example, the director can authorize arrests without warrants) and without strong parliamentary oversight mechanisms. Director Issac Ksogi is a close confidant of Khama from the military, though relations between the two were becoming strained by the end of 2012.

A House of Chiefs, which serves primarily as an advisory body, represents the country's eight major Setswana-speaking tribes and some smaller ones. Groups other than the eight major tribes tend to be left out of the political process; under the Territories Act, land in ethnic territory is distributed under the jurisdiction of majority groups. Due in part to their lack of representation in the House of Chiefs, minority groups are subject to patriarchal Tswana customary law despite having their own traditional rules for inheritance, marriage, and succession.

Botswana's anticorruption body has special powers of investigation, arrest, and search and seizure, and the body generally boasts a high conviction rate. Nevertheless, there are almost no restrictions on the private business activities of public servants, and a number of high-profile officials have been cleared of corruption charges in recent years. Most notably, in 2011, Minister of Justice, Defense and Security (and cousin of Khama) Ramadeluka Seretse—who had been charged with corruption in 2010 for failing to disclose his position as a shareholder in a company, owned by his wife, that won a massive defense contract in 2009—was acquitted of all charges. Seretse, who had relinquished his post as a result of the charges, was reinstated the next day by Khama. In April 2012, the Directorate of Public Prosecution's appeal of the acquittal was dismissed by the Court of Appeals. Minister of Finance and Development Planning Kenneth Matambo was also cleared of corruption charges in November 2011 for allegedly having indirect interests in contracting the Botswana Development Corporation.

Botswana has a free and vigorous press, with several independent newspapers and magazines. The private Gaborone Broadcasting Corporation television system and two private radio stations have limited reach, though Botswana easily receives broadcasts from neighboring South Africa. State-owned outlets dominate the local broadcast media, which reach far more residents than the print media, yet provide inadequate access to the opposition and government critics. In addition, the government sometimes censors or otherwise restricts news sources or stories that it finds undesirable. The 2008 Media Practitioners Act established a media regulatory body and mandated the registration of all media workers and outlets; a 2010 lawsuit by 32 representatives of media, trade, and civil society groups did not succeed in altering or overturning the law. Botswana does not have a freedom of information law, and critics accuse the government of excessive secrecy. Khama had yet to hold a domestic press conference by the end of 2012. The government does not restrict internet access, though such access is rare outside cities.

Freedom of religion is guaranteed, but all religious organizations must register with the government. There are over 1,000 church groups in Botswana. Academic freedom is generally respected.

The government generally respects the constitutional rights of assembly and association. Nongovernmental organizations, including human rights groups, operate openly without harassment. However, the government has barred organizations supporting the rights of the San (an indigenous tribal population) from entering the Central Kgalagadi Game Reserve (CKGR), the subject of a long-running land dispute, and demonstrations at the reserve have been forcibly dispersed. While independent labor unions are permitted, workers' rights to strike and bargain collectively are sometimes restricted. In 2011 almost 100,000 public sector workers—including "essential" workers in the health sector—staged an eight-week strike, leading to the closure of all public schools, while many clinics and hospitals were forced to close or partially shut down. Unions demanded a 16 percent wage increase but eventually settled for only 3 percent. The government fired nearly 2,600 striking health workers and demanded that they reapply for their jobs following the settlement. In July 2012, the Gaborone High Court ordered the government to reinstate 556 fired workers, though the decision was later overturned by the Court of Appeals.

The courts are generally considered to be fair and free of direct political interference, although the legal system is affected by staffing shortages and a large backlog of cases. Trials are usually public, and those accused of the most serious violent crimes are provided with attorneys. Civil cases, however, are sometimes tried in customary courts, where defendants have no legal counsel. The 2007 Intelligence and Security Services Act created the DIS in the office of the president. Critics charged that it vested too much power in the agency's director—including allowing him to authorize arrests without warrants—and lacked parliamentary oversight mechanisms.

Occasional police abuse to obtain evidence or confessions has been reported, and Botswana has been criticized by rights groups for continuing to use corporal and capital punishment. Prisons are overcrowded and suffer from poor health conditions, though the government has responded by building new facilities and providing HIV testing to inmates.

Since 1985, authorities have relocated about 5,000 San, who tend to be marginalized in education and employment opportunities, to settlements outside the CKGR. Almost all of the remaining San fled in 2002, when the government cut off water, food, health, and social services in the area. In 2006, a three-judge panel of the Lobatse High Court ordered the government to allow the San to return to the CKGR. Several hundred San have since gone back, though disagreement remains as to how many will be allowed to live in the reserve. By court order, the issue is being mediated by the Botswana Centre for Human Rights. In July 2010, those San who had returned to CKGR lost a court battle with the government to reopen a water hole on the reserve. In April 2011, an appeals court overturned the decision, ruling that the San have rights to subsurface water, which led to the reopening of the Mothomelo borehole in September and the return of many San to the area. The government insists that the San have been relocated to give them access to modern education and health facilities and have been adequately compensated, and it rejects claims that it simply wanted unrestricted access to diamond reserves in the region. In May 2012, the government began establishing police camps in the CKGR to combat poaching. The rights group Survival International claimed the camps were also intended to intimidate local San.

Undocumented immigrants from Zimbabwe face increasing xenophobia and are subject to exploitation in the labor market. Botswana has built a fence along its border with Zimbabwe, ostensibly to control foot-and-mouth disease among livestock, but the barrier is popularly supported as a means of halting illegal immigration; thousands of Zimbabweans have are deported from Botswana every month. In 2010, the government announced a set of new immigration policies to halt the flow of undocumented immigrants into the country, mostly from Zimbabwe. The new policies introduced an online passport system, mandated electronic permits for visitors and immigrants, and increased the number of official workplace inspections.

Women enjoy the same rights as men under the constitution, though customary laws limit their property rights, and women married under traditional laws have the same legal status as minors. The 2004 Abolition of Marital Powers Act established equal control of marriage estates and equal custody of children, removed restrictive domicile rules, and set the minimum marriage age at 18. However, enforcement of the act is not uniform and generally requires the cooperation of traditional authorities, which is not always forthcoming. In October 2012, the Gaborone High Court ruled that a customary law that favors a youngest-born son over older sisters in awarding inheritance was unconstitutional and could not be enforced, setting a precedent for the supremacy of civil over customary law in Botswana. Three sisters who brought the suit had lost their original case and appeal before applying to the civil court system. The government contested the case but vowed to respect the ruling.

Women are underrepresented in the government, comprising less than 8 percent of the National Assembly seats following the 2009 elections. Domestic violence and trafficking for the purposes of prostitution and labor remain significant problems. Same-sex sexual relations are illegal and can carry a prison sentence of up to seven years. A 2010 amendment to the Employment Act outlaws workplace dismissal based on an individual's sexual orientation or HIV status.

Brazil

Political Rights: 2　　　　　　　　　　　　**Population:** 194,334,000
Civil Liberties: 2　　　　　　　　　　　　　　　**Capital:** Brasilia
Status: Free

Ten-Year Ratings Timeline For Year Under Review (Political Rights, Civil Liberties, Status)

2003	2004	2005	2006	2007	2008	2009	2010	2011	2012
2,3F	2,3F	2,2F	2,2F	2,2F	2,2F	2,2F	2,2F	2,2F	2,2F

Overview:　　　　　**President Dilma Rousseff's tough stance toward corruption helped bolster her approval rating throughout 2012. In May, Brazil's Truth Commission began investigating human rights violations committed by the country's military regime, and a racial equality act was enacted in August to widen access to education for minorities and the poor. Approximately half of Brazil's federal workforce went on strike between May and August, demanding increased pay and improved working conditions.**

After gaining independence from Portugal in 1822, Brazil retained a monarchical system until a republic was established in 1889. Democratic governance was interrupted by long periods of authoritarian rule, and the last military regime gave way to an elected civilian government in 1985. However, Brazil's democracy has been marred by frequent corruption scandals. One scandal eventually led Congress to impeach President Fernando Collor de Mello in 1992.

Brazilian Social Democracy Party (PSDB) leader Fernando Henrique Cardoso—a market-oriented, centrist finance minister—was elected president in 1994, and he subsequently oversaw a highly successful currency-stabilization program that included fiscal reform, privatization of state enterprises, and a new currency pegged to the U.S. dollar. He also ushered in a new era of dialogue with international human rights and good-governance groups. In 1998, Cardoso handily won a second term in a rematch against his 1994 opponent, former labor leader and political prisoner Luiz Inácio Lula da Silva of the left-leaning Workers' Party (PT).

Lula won the presidency in 2002, promising to maintain orthodox economic policies while initiating meaningful social-welfare programs. These included "Bolsa Família," a cash-transfer program that benefited approximately one-fourth of the population, and "ProUni," a fund providing low-income students with scholarships to private colleges.

Lula was reelected by a comfortable margin in the October 2006 presidential runoff, drawing on his popularity among working-class voters. Despite the fact that the legislature was widely seen as the most corrupt in the country's history, the PT did not suffer losses in the concurrent congressional elections.

In August 2007, the government released a report outlining the fate of political dissidents who were "disappeared" by the military between 1961 and 1988. Unlike in other Latin American countries with recent histories of military rule, former officials in Brazil remain protected by a 1979 amnesty law, and none have faced charges for human rights violations. Brazil's Supreme Court upheld the constitutionality of the amnesty in April 2010. A December 2010 Inter-American Court of Human Rights ruling deemed the law invalid, and served as a catalyst for the creation of Brazil's Truth Commission in November 2011. In May 2012, the commission began investigating human rights abuses committed during the rule of the military regime; it has a two-year mandate.

Dilma Rousseff, Lula's chosen successor, was elected president in October 2010 with 56 percent of the vote, defeating rival PSDB candidate José Serra. The PT and its coalition partners also strengthened their majorities in both the Senate and Chamber of Deputies in concurrent legislative elections. As president, Rousseff has taken a strong stance against corruption, removing six cabinet-level officials from office for corruption during her first year in office. Thirty-eight prominent members of the ruling party were put on trial in August 2012 before Brazil's Supreme Court for their involvement in the 2005 mensalao (big monthly allowance) vote-buying scandal. By the end of 2012, 25 of the 37 were found guilty, including the former PT president and party treasurer. The trials were historic in that the accused were leading members of Rousseff's own party. Meanwhile, the "clean record" law banning individuals who have been found guilty of a crime from taking office was determined to be constitutional by the Supreme Court in February. Rousseff's "ethical cleansing" campaign has earned her respect from many for taking a hard line against corruption, and by the end of the year, her popular support levels remained above 70 percent.

Despite the high-profile corruption trial and conviction of PT party leaders, the PT captured a total of 635 mayoral races, up 14 percent from 2008, in the October 2012 municipal elections.

In June 2011, Rousseff launched an antipoverty program known as Brasil Sem Miseria (Brazil without Poverty)—an initiative intended to fully eliminate the extreme poverty that afflicts an estimated 16.2 million Brazilians. The program increases the transfer payments already provided by Bolsa Familia, adding a monthly $35 to each household member facing extreme poverty.

Political Rights and Civil Liberties: Brazil is an electoral democracy. The 2010 national and 2012 municipal elections were free and fair. The constitution provides for a president, to be elected for up to two four-year terms, and a bicameral National Congress. The Senate's 81 members serve eight-year terms, with a portion coming up for election every four years, and the 513-member Chamber of Deputies is elected for four-year terms.

The four largest political parties, accounting for more than half of the seats in the Chamber of Deputies and the Senate, are the centrist Brazilian Democratic Movement Party, the leftist PT, the conservative Democratic Party, and the center-left PSDB. Seventeen other parties are also represented in Congress. The electoral system encourages the proliferation of parties, a number of which are based in a single state. A 2007 Supreme Court decision outlawed party switching after elections, though lawmakers have continued to switch parties on occasion for financial and other inducements.

In spite of the Dilma Rousseff administration's public intolerance of corruption, official corruption still remains an endemic problem in Brazil. In 2012, some two dozen prominent PT members were found guilty of corruption in a vote-buying scandal. The country was ranked 69 out of 176 countries surveyed in Transparency International's 2012 Corruption Perceptions Index.

The constitution guarantees freedom of expression, and both libel and slander were decriminalized in 2009. A long-awaited freedom of information bill, which covers all branches of government at all levels, went into effect in May 2012. The press is privately owned, and there are dozens of daily newspapers and a variety of television and radio stations across the country. The print media have played a central role in exposing official corruption. However, journalists—especially those who focus on organized crime, corruption, or military-era human rights violations—are frequently the targets of violence. According to the International Press Institute, four journalists were killed in 2012 in probable connection to their work. The judicial branch—particularly judges outside large urban centers—remained active in 2012 in preventing media outlets from covering numerous stories, often involving politicians. The government does not impose restrictions on access to the internet. However, local and regional courts posed an increased threat to internet freedom in 2012. In September, the Brazil director of Google was arrested for refusing to remove videos that attacked a mayoral candidate. Further, a proposed "internet bill of rights," guaranteeing basic rights for internet users and intermediaries, was postponed in Congress in November 2012, with no immediate prospect for a vote.

The constitution guarantees freedom of religion, and the government generally respects this right in practice. The government does not restrict academic freedom.

Freedoms of association and assembly are generally respected, as is the right to strike. Industrial labor unions are well organized; organized labor represents 17 percent of the Brazilian work force. Although they are politically connected, Brazilian unions tend to be freer from political party control than their counterparts in most other Latin American countries. Labor issues are adjudicated in a system of special labor courts. In 2012, a three-month strike by teachers at federal universities attracted almost half of the federal workforce, including the police and judiciary. Strikes by construction workers in the Amazon region also delayed the construction of several hydroelectric dams—a key part of the administration's plan to meet Brazil's growing demand for electricity. The strikers, led by a powerful group of unions with strong ties to the ruling PT party, were able to negotiate a settlement with the Rousseff administration without undermining the government's goals of fiscal balance.

Brazil's largely independent judiciary is overburdened and plagued by corruption. The judiciary is often subject to intimidation and other external influences, especially in rural areas, and public complaints over its inefficiency are frequent. Access to justice also varies greatly due to Brazil's income inequality.

Brazil has maintained an average homicide rate of 26 per 100,000 residents (compared to a global average of approximately 7 per 100,000). Most violent crime in the country is related to the illegal drug trade. Highly organized and well-armed drug gangs frequently fight against the military police as well as private militias comprising off-duty police officers, prison guards, and firefighters. However, the homicide rate for the state of Rio has fallen in the last decade; the government's aggressive counterinsurgency against drug-related violence ahead of the 2016 Summer Olympic Games has likely contributed to that reduction. Most notably, the longer-term presence of "peace police" forces successfully pacified several of the city's dangerous favelas, or slums; however, the sustainability of this peace remains in question, as does the government's ability to successfully expand the program to other impoverished areas. In September 2012, Brazil's special forces began using unmanned drone aircraft to monitor the drug trade in Rio's large favelas. In Rio de Janeiro, 1.2 million citizens—20 percent of the population—live in favelas.

Corruption and violence remain entrenched in Brazil's police forces. Torture is used systematically to extract confessions from suspects, and extrajudicial killings are portrayed as shootouts with dangerous criminals. Police officers are rarely prosecuted for abuses, and those charged are almost never convicted. Police investigator Tapajos Macedo, who had been investigating an illegal gambling cartel, was shot and killed in July 2012 while watering the flowers on his parents' grave. No one had been arrested by the end of 2012, but military police were known for obstructing Macedo's work.

The prison system is anarchic, overcrowded, and largely unfit for human habitation. Brazil's prisons held 550,000 inmates in 2012, representing the world's fourth-largest prison population—three-quarters more than the system's intended capacity. Overcrowding sometimes results in men and women being held in the same facilities.

Racial discrimination, long officially denied as a problem in Brazil, began to receive both recognition and remediation during Luiz Inácio Lula da Silva's first term. Afro-Brazilians earn less than 50 percent of the average earnings of other citizens, and they suffer from the highest homicide, poverty, and illiteracy rates. The

2010 Statute of Racial Equality recognized the right of quilombos—communities of descendants of escaped slaves—to receive title to their land. It also called for the establishment of non-quota affirmative action policies in education and employment, as well as programs to improve Afro-Brazilians' access to health care. Accordingly, in August 2012, the government enacted a broad affirmative action law requiring public universities to reserve half of their admission spots to the mostly poor students attending public schools, as well as to increase the number of students from African descent in accordance with the racial composition of each state.

The owners of large estates control nearly 60 percent of the country's arable land, while the poorest 30 percent of the population hold less than 2 percent. Land invasions are organized by the grassroots Landless Workers' Movement, which claims that the seized land is unused or illegally held. Progress on land reform has been slow, due in part to a strong farm caucus and the economic importance of large-scale agriculture.

Although Brazil abolished slavery in 1888, thousands of rural laborers still work under slavery-like conditions. Landowners who enslave workers face two to eight years in prison, in addition to fines. Mobile inspection groups established under Lula's presidency have been effective in the fight to end slave labor; they have rescued an estimated 41,500 workers since the creation of the program in 1995. Measures to fight the impunity of employers, such as a public "black list" of offending companies and landowners, have also proven effective in reducing slave labor in rural Brazil. In May 2012, Brazil's Congress passed a constitutional amendment that will allow the government to confiscate all property of landholders found to be using slave labor, among other penalties.

Brazil's indigenous population numbers less than 1 percent of the country's total population. Violence and discrimination against indigenous people continues; 51 were killed in Brazil in 2011, with close to half of the murders related to land battles, according to the Indigenous Missionary Council. An indigenous leader was shot to death in November 2011, after returning to the land from which ranchers had evicted him; 18 individuals were arrested in July 2012 for the murder. Half of the indigenous population lives in poverty in Brazil, and most indigenous communities lack adequate sanitation and education services. The government promised in 2003 to demarcate large swaths of ancestral lands as the first step in creating indigenous reserves. A 2009 Supreme Court ruling defended the creation of one of the largest protected indigenous areas in the world, and the nonindigenous farmers living there peacefully left the 1.7 million hectare reservation that year.

Brazil's Supreme Court ruled in May 2011 that gays and lesbians have the right to form civil unions, and that couples in civil unions have the same rights as heterosexual married couples in regards to alimony, health, and retirement benefits, as well as adoption rights. While discrimination based on sexual orientation is prohibited by law, violence against members of the LGBT (gay, lesbian, bisexual, and transgender) community remains a problem.

A 2003 legal code made women equal to men under the law for the first time in the country's history. Upon entering office, President Rousseff vowed to push women's rights onto the national and international agenda, and women make up almost a third of Rousseff's cabinet. Nevertheless, violence against women and children is commonplace, and protective laws are rarely enforced. More than one million children between the ages of 10 and 14 worked in 2010. The government has sought to address the problem by cooperating with various nongovernmental organizations, increasing inspections, and offering cash incentives to keep children in school. Human trafficking continues from and within Brazil for the purpose of forced labor and commercial sexual exploitation.

Brunei

Political Rights: 6
Civil Liberties: 5
Status: Not Free

Population: 412,900
Capital: Bandar Seri Begawan

Ten-Year Ratings Timeline For Year Under Review (Political Rights, Civil Liberties, Status)

2003	2004	2005	2006	2007	2008	2009	2010	2011	2012
6,5NF	6,5NF	6,5NF	6,5NF	6,5NF	6,5NF	6,5NF	6,5NF	6,5NF	6,5NF

Overview: **Brunei, which has been ruled continuously by Sultan Hassanal Bolkiah Mu'izzaddin Waddaulah since 1967, experienced little political change in 2012. There were, however, several incidents of increased religious restrictions, as seen in the arrests of over 40 individuals for eating in public during Ramadan.**

The oil-rich sultanate of Brunei became a British protectorate in 1888. The 1959 constitution vested full executive powers in the sultan while providing for five advisory councils, including a Legislative Council. In 1962, Sultan Omar Ali Saifuddien annulled legislative election results after the leftist and antimonarchist Brunei People's Party (BPP) won all 10 elected seats in the 21-member council. British troops put down an insurrection mounted by the BPP, and Omar declared a state of emergency, which remains in force. Continuing his father's absolute rule, Hassanal Bolkiah Mu'izzaddin Waddaulah became Brunei's 29th sultan in 1967. The British granted Brunei full independence in 1984.

In 2004, Hassanal reconvened the Legislative Council, which had been suspended since 1984. The Council passed a constitutional amendment to expand its size to 45 seats, 15 of which would be elected. However, in 2005 Hassanal appointed a new, 29-member Legislative Council, including 5 indirectly elected members representing village councils; most of the members of this body were either relatives or loyalists. Following the completion of its five-year term, the Legislative Council was disbanded in March 2011 and replaced with a newly appointed and expanded 33-member council in June.

Hassanal instituted a significant reshuffle of the Cabinet of Ministers in May 2010. While many ministers retained their positions, and the sultan continued to hold the posts of prime minister, minister of defense, and minister of finance, the changes that were instituted signified a small step toward improving governance. The new cabinet included the country's first woman cabinet member as deputy minister for culture, youth, and sports.

Energy wealth has long allowed the government to stave off demands for political reform by employing much of the population, providing citizens with extensive benefits, and sparing them an income tax. Despite a declining gross domestic product growth rate, Brunei remains the fourth-largest oil producer in Southeast Asia and the ninth-largest exporter of liquefied natural gas in the world. In December 2010, Brunei and Malaysia moved forward with a "milestone" offshore oil exploration deal in which both countries agreed to a 50-50 sharing partnership for a period of 40 years.

Political Rights and Civil Liberties: Brunei is not an electoral democracy. The sultan continues to wield broad powers under a long-standing state of emergency, and no direct legislative elections have been held since 1962. Citizens convey concerns to their leaders through government-vetted councils of elected village chiefs.

The reform efforts of Sultan Hassanal Bolkiah Mu'izzaddin Waddaulah have been largely superficial and are designed to attract foreign investment. The unicameral Legislative Council has no political standing independent of the sultan. However, the council's mounting oversight activity and queries aimed at the government reflect a growing demand for accountability and responsible spending. These tentative reforms were considered preparations for an eventual succession and the expected depletion of the country's oil and gas reserves, which account for about 90 percent of state revenues.

Genuine political activity remains extremely limited. In 2007, the Registrar of Societies disbanded the People's Awareness Party and forced the president of the Brunei National Solidarity Party (PPKB) to resign. The PPKB was then deregistered without explanation in 2008, leaving the National Development Party as Brunei's sole remaining political party.

The government claims to have a zero-tolerance policy on corruption, and its Anti-Corruption Bureau has successfully prosecuted a number of lower-level officials in recent years. The sultan's brother and former finance minister, Prince Jefri Bolkiah, has faced a number of legal challenges, including a 2008 arrest warrant, over accusations that he misappropriated state funds, and he was ordered to return personal assets to the state. In 2012, Hassanal's nephew, Prince Abdul Hakeem Jefri, was sued for a breach of agreement over shares of the Singaporean company Elektromotive Group Ltd. Brunei was ranked 46 out of 176 countries surveyed in Transparency International's 2012 Corruption Perceptions Index.

Journalists in Brunei face considerable restrictions. Officials may close newspapers without cause, and fine and imprison journalists for up to three years for reporting deemed "false and malicious." The national sedition law was amended in 2005 to strengthen prohibitions on criticizing the sultan and the national "Malay Muslim Monarchy" ideology. The country's main English-language daily newspaper, the *Borneo Bulletin*, is controlled by the sultan's family and often practices self-censorship. A second English-language daily, the *Brunei Times*, was launched by prominent businessmen in 2006 to attract foreign investors. A smaller, Malay-language newspaper and several Chinese-language papers are also published. Brunei's only television station is state run, but residents can receive Malaysian broadcasts and satellite channels. The country's internet practice code stipulates that content must not be subversive or encourage illegitimate reform efforts.

The constitution allows for the practice of religions other than the official Shafeite school of Sunni Islam, but proselytizing by non-Muslims is prohibited. Non-Shafeite forms of Islam are actively discouraged, in part due to concerns about security and foreign investment. Christianity is the most common target of censorship, and the Baha'i faith is banned. Marriage between Muslims and non-Muslims is not allowed. Muslims require permission from the Ministry of Religious Affairs to convert to other faiths, though official and societal pressures make conversion nearly impossible. In 2012, 41 people were arrested for eating in public during Ramadan, which is illegal under the Qadi Courts Act and carries a penalty of up to $1,000 in fines.

The study of Islam, Malay Muslim Monarchy ideology, and the Jawi (Arabic script used for writing the Malay language) is mandatory in all schools, public or private. The teaching of all other religions is prohibited.

Emergency laws continue to restrict freedoms of assembly and association. Most nongovernmental organizations are professional or business groups. All groups must register and name their members, and registration can be refused for any reason. No more than 10 people can assemble for any purpose without a permit. Brunei only has three, largely inactive, trade unions, all of which are in the oil sector and represent only about 5 percent of the industry's labor force. Strikes are illegal, and collective bargaining is not recognized.

The constitution does not provide for an independent judiciary. Although the courts generally appear to act independently, they have yet to be tested in political cases. Final recourse for civil cases is managed by the Privy Council in the United Kingdom. Sharia (Islamic law) takes precedence in areas including divorce, inheritance, and some sex crimes, though it does not apply to non-Muslims. A backlog of capital cases results in lengthy pretrial detention for those accused of serious crimes. Caning is mandatory for 42 criminal offenses, including immigration violations, and is commonly carried out, though an attending doctor can interrupt the punishment for medical reasons.

Religious enforcement officers raid homes to arrest people for khalwat, the mingling of unrelated Muslim men and women. However, most first offenders are fined or released due to a lack of evidence. The authorities also detain suspected antigovernment activists under the Internal Security Act, which permits detention without trial for renewable two-year periods. Prison conditions generally meet international standards.

Brunei's many "stateless" people, mostly longtime ethnic Chinese residents, are denied the full rights and benefits of citizens, while migrant workers, who comprise approximately one quarter of the workforce, are largely unprotected by labor laws and vulnerable to exploitation. Workers who overstay visas are regularly imprisoned and, in some cases, caned or whipped.

Islamic law generally places women at a disadvantage in cases of divorce and inheritance. All women in government-run institutions and schools are required or pressured to wear traditional Muslim head coverings. An increasing number of women have entered the workforce in recent years, comprising 50.4 percent of the civil service in 2010. Brunei appointed its first female attorney general, Hayati Salleh, in 2009; she was formerly the first female High Court judge. Brunei serves as a destination, transit, and source country for the trafficking of men and women for forced labor and prostitution.

Bulgaria

Political Rights: 2
Civil Liberties: 2
Status: Free

Population: 7,240,000
Capital: Sofia

Ten-Year Ratings Timeline For Year Under Review (Political Rights, Civil Liberties, Status)

2003	2004	2005	2006	2007	2008	2009	2010	2011	2012
1,2F	1,2F	1,2F	1,2F	1,2F	2,2F	2,2F	2,2F	2,2F	2,2F

Overview: In July 2012, a suicide bomber attacked a bus at an air-port in the coastal city of Burgas, killing the driver and five Israeli tourists. A European Union progress report released the same day found continued shortcomings in Bulgaria's attempts to fight corruption and organized crime and implement judicial reforms. The center-right government of Prime Minister Boyko Borisov nevertheless survived a confidence motion in the parliament later that month.

Bulgaria gained autonomy within the Ottoman Empire in 1878 and full independence in 1908. Its monarchy was replaced by communist rule after Soviet forces occupied the country during World War II. Communist leader Todor Zhivkov governed Bulgaria from 1954 until 1989, when the broader political changes sweeping the region inspired a massive prodemocracy rally in Sofia.

Over the next 12 years, power alternated between the Bulgarian Socialist Party (BSP)—the successor to the Communist Party—and the center-right Union of Democratic Forces (UDF). In 2001, the National Movement for Simeon II, led by the former monarch, won national elections and formed a governing coalition with the Movement for Rights and Freedoms (DPS), a party representing Bulgaria's ethnic Turkish minority. However, both parties became junior partners in a BSP-led coalition government after the 2005 elections.

Bulgaria formally joined the European Union (EU) in January 2007, and its first elections for the European Parliament in May featured the emergence of a new right-leaning opposition party, Citizens for the European Development of Bulgaria (GERB), led by Sofia mayor Boyko Borisov. The party gained popularity as the BSP and its allies were blamed for unchecked corruption, particularly after the EU suspended hundreds of millions of dollars in aid funds over the issue in July 2008.

GERB captured 117 of 240 seats in the July 2009 parliamentary elections. Borisov took office as prime minister with the support of the ultranationalist Ataka party (21 seats), the center-right Blue Coalition (15 seats), and the new right-wing Order, Law, and Justice (RZS) party (10 seats). The BSP-led Coalition for Bulgaria was left in opposition with 40 seats, as was the DPS, with 37.

The new GERB government pledged to tackle corruption and organized crime, and oversaw a series of high-profile reforms, police raids, and prosecutions that lasted through 2010. However, according to EU progress reports, flawed investigations and deep-seated problems with the judiciary meant that few major cases resulted in convictions.

In the October 2011 presidential election, GERB candidate Rosen Plevneliev, a businessman who had served as regional development and public-works minister in Borisov's government, led the first round with 40 percent of the vote, followed by Ivailo Kalfin of the BSP with 29 percent. Meglena Kuneva, a former member of the European Commission and head of the Bulgaria for Citizens party, took 14 percent of the vote, and Ataka leader Volen Siderov won 3.6 percent; more than a dozen other candidates took smaller shares of the vote. Plevneliev went on to win the run-off with about 53 percent and formally replaced the term-limited Georgi Parvanov of the BSP in January 2012. GERB also performed well in concurrent municipal elections, winning in most large cities.

A suicide bombing at the Burgas airport in July 2012 killed five Israeli tourists and a Bulgarian bus driver. The attack, which Israel and other observers attributed to the Lebanese Islamist militant group Hezbollah, raised questions about the effectiveness of Bulgaria's security services. Later that month, the government survived a parliamentary confidence vote that was triggered by the airport bombing and a negative EU progress report on Bulgaria's efforts to reform its judiciary and fight corruption and organized crime.

Political Rights and Civil Liberties: Bulgaria is an electoral democracy. The unicameral National Assembly, composed of 240 members, is elected every four years. The president, elected for up to two five-year terms, is the head of state, but his powers are limited. The legislature chooses the prime minister, who serves as head of government. International observers generally praised the 2011 presidential and municipal elections, but found flaws in the Central Election Commission's performance, adherence to vote counting procedures, and accuracy of the voter list. There were widespread claims of vote-buying.

Bulgaria's multiparty system includes a variety of left- and right-leaning factions, and the ethnic Turkish minority is represented by the DPS. Roma are not as well represented, with just one Romany candidate winning a National Assembly seat in 2009. However, a number of small Romany parties are active, and many Roma reportedly vote for the DPS.

Corruption is a serious concern in Bulgaria. The European Commission's July 2012 progress report found that acquittal rates were disproportionately high in corruption cases against senior government officials, and that the number of cases in the courts declined sharply in 2011, after increases in 2009 and 2010. The director of a new commission for the identification and seizure of criminal assets resigned in early 2012, citing insufficient political support. A new law passed in May allowed assets to be seized through the civil courts rather than requiring a criminal conviction, though the EU report warned that further improvements were needed for the commission to be effective. The informal, untaxed "shadow economy" accounts for an estimated one-third of Bulgaria's gross domestic product, and the Sofia-based Center for the Study of Democracy estimated in June 2012 that an average of 150,000 bribes were paid each month in 2011. Bulgaria was ranked 75 out of 176 countries surveyed in Transparency International's 2012 Corruption Perceptions Index.

Bulgarian media have become more vulnerable to political and economic pressures as some foreign media firms withdraw from the struggling market and domestic ownership becomes more concentrated. Although the state-owned media generally provide balanced coverage, ineffective legislation leaves them exposed to political influence. Journalists continued to face the threat of violence during 2012. The car of veteran organized crime reporter Lidia Pavlova, who had endured multiple threats and attacks in the past, was set on fire in May. In July, Varna-based newspaper correspondent Spas Spasov received a threatening message that appeared related to his investigation of a construction project. The government does not place restrictions on internet access.

Members of minority faiths report occasional instances of harassment and discrimination despite constitutional guarantees of religious freedom, and some local authorities have blocked proselytizing or the construction of minority religious buildings. In September 2012, a group of 13 Muslims, most of them imams, went on trial for allegedly distributing extremist literature and conspiring to undermine democracy and the constitution. The case was ongoing at year's end. The government does not restrict academic freedom.

The authorities generally respect freedoms of assembly and association. A gay pride parade in Sofia proceeded without incident in June 2012, despite condemnations from the Orthodox Church and past violence at a 2008 gay rights march. Workers have the right to join trade unions, but public employees cannot strike or bargain collectively, and private employers often discriminate against union members without facing serious repercussions. A week-long strike by coal miners in January ended after their state-owned mining company agreed to concessions on issues including bonuses and working conditions.

Bulgaria's judiciary has benefited from reforms associated with EU accession, but the 2012 European Commission report found that institutional and legal improvements have not led to practical gains in efficiency or accountability. The EU has noted ongoing flaws in the judicial appointment and disciplinary processes. In November 2012, a judge resigned from the Constitutional Court just weeks after her appointment due to allegations of abuse of office in a prior judicial posting.

Organized crime remains a serious problem, and scores of suspected contract killings over the past decade have gone unsolved. A number of fresh murders with organized crime connections occurred during 2012. The GERB government has overseen the arrest and prosecution of many alleged mob figures, but there have been few major convictions to date; the EU has cited weaknesses in investigations, evidence collection, and witness protection for the lack of convictions. Prosecutors in 2012 declined to investigate evidence of past links between Borisov and organized crime. Incidents of mistreatment by police have been reported, and prison conditions remain inadequate in many places.

Ethnic minorities, particularly Roma, continue to face discrimination in employment, health care, education, and housing. The murder of an ethnic Bulgarian youth by men linked to reputed local Romany crime boss Kiril Rashkov set off sometimes violent nationwide anti-Roma protests in the fall of 2011. Rashkov was sentenced to three and a half years in prison in January 2012, after being convicted of making death threats against two villagers.

Discrimination based on sexual orientation is illegal, but societal bias reportedly persists.

Women remain underrepresented in political life, accounting for 21 percent of the National Assembly seats after the 2009 elections. Also that year, however, the chamber elected Bulgaria's first female Speaker, and Sofia elected its first female mayor. Domestic violence is an ongoing concern. The country is a source of human-trafficking victims, of whom Roma make up a disproportionately large share.

Burkina Faso

Political Rights: 5
Civil Liberties: 3
Status: Partly Free

Population: 17,482,000
Capital: Ouagadougou

Ten-Year Ratings Timeline For Year Under Review (Political Rights, Civil Liberties, Status)

2003	2004	2005	2006	2007	2008	2009	2010	2011	2012
4,4PF	5,4PF	5,3PF	5,3PF	5,3PF	5,3PF	5,3PF	5,3PF	5,3PF	5,3PF

Overview: Burkina Faso stabilized in 2012 following mass protests and army mutinies the previous year, though some small-scale demonstrations continued. In December, President Blaise Campaoré's Congress for Democracy and Progress party won a majority in concurrent parliamentary and municipal elections that were considered largely free and fair.

Burkina Faso experienced a series of military coups after gaining independence from France in 1960. In 1987, army captain Blaise Compaoré ousted Thomas Sankara, a populist president who had risen to power through a 1983 coup. In 1991, a democratic constitution was approved in a referendum, and Compaoré won that year's presidential election due to an opposition boycott. Compaoré secured another seven-year term in the 1998 election.

The government undertook a series of political reforms after 1998. The 2002 National Assembly elections were the first conducted without a significant opposition boycott, and Compaoré's Congress for Democracy and Progress (CDP) party won only half of the assembly seats.

Two-term presidential limits were reintroduced in 2000, but the law was not retroactive, allowing for Compaoré's reelection to a third term in 2005. The country's first municipal elections were held in 2006, with the CDP capturing nearly two-thirds of the local council seats; the CDP was also victorious in the 2007 National Assembly elections.

In the November 2010 presidential election, six opposition candidates ran against Compaoré, who won with over 80 percent of the vote. Although opposition candidates challenged Compaoré's victory, the Constitutional Council upheld the results. The 2010 election was the last in which Compaoré was eligible to run under the current constitution. However, in 2012 the CDP stated that it would revise Article 37 of the charter in order to allow Compaoré to run again.

In February 2011, student riots broke out in many major cities in reaction to the death of a student, Justin Zongo, in police custody. The government closed the nation's universities and cut off funding for student services. Starting in March, army soldiers mutinied over unpaid wages, beginning a period of general violence and unrest nationwide. In April, police officers and teachers joined the protests. Compaoré responded in mid-April by replacing the prime minister and the security chiefs, and naming himself minister of defense. In June, Compaoré replaced all 13 of the country's regional governors. In July, 217 leaders of the mutiny were arrested and 566 soldiers who took part were dismissed. In August, three policemen were sentenced for Zongo's death.

Minor protests continued throughout 2012, despite steps taken by the government to increase the wages of civil servants and reduce corruption. Separately, the 2012 crisis in neighboring Mali resulted in almost 36,000 refugees fleeing to Burkina Faso, including many into the country's already drought-ridden Sahel region. Clashes between ethnic groups along the border of Mali and Burkina Faso left 25 people dead in May.

The CDP won a comfortable majority in concurrent parliamentary and municipal elections in December. In the 127-seat National Assembly, the CDP took 70 seats; along with its allies, pro-Compaoré parties control 97 seats. The next two largest parties—the Alliance for Democracy and Federation-African Democratic Rally and the new Union for Progress and Change—won 19 seats each.

According to the International Monetary Fund, Burkina Faso's economy grew significantly in 2012 compared with 2011, largely as a result of gold mining and good rainfall.

Political Rights and Civil Liberties: Burkina Faso is not an electoral democracy. International monitors have judged recent elections to be generally free but not entirely fair, due to the ruling CDP's privileged access to state resources and the media. Some reported problems with the 2010 presidential election included traditional leaders mobilizing voters for the incumbent, inadequate numbers of voting cards and ballots at the polls, incorrect electoral lists, and the use of state resources for President Blaise Compaoré's campaign. The 2012 parliamentary and municipal elections were run more efficiently and were generally considered free by domestic and international observers, even though the opposition claimed similar privileged access to state resources by the ruling party. The newly expanded 127-seat National Assembly is unicameral, and members serve five-year terms. The legislature is independent, but subject to executive influence. In July 2011, the National Assembly dissolved the National Electoral Commission at the request of the opposition, and a new commission was formed prior to the December 2012 elections.

The constitution guarantees the right to form political parties, and 13 parties are currently represented in the legislature. Electoral reforms in 2009 extended the right to vote in presidential elections and referendums to Burkinabè living abroad, but not until the 2015 presidential election. Reforms also included an injunction against the practice of switching parties after elections. In January 2010, the National Assembly passed a law requiring that all voters show picture identification when arriving at the polls. In June 2012, the parliament voted to give all presidents since Burkina Faso's 1960 independence immunity from prosecution, despite an opposition boycott of the vote.

Corruption remains widespread, despite a number of public and private anticorruption initiatives. The courts have been unwilling or unable to adequately prosecute many senior officials charged with corruption. The government stepped up anticorruption efforts in 2012, firing the head of the country's notoriously corrupt customs office in January. Burkina Faso was ranked 83 out of 176 countries surveyed in Transparency International's 2012 Corruption Perceptions Index.

Although freedom of expression is constitutionally guaranteed and generally respected, many media outlets practice self-censorship. Journalists occasionally face criminal libel prosecutions, death threats, and other forms of harassment and intimidation. In October 2012, two journalists at the private weekly *L'Ouragan* were sentenced to 12 months in prison for defamation, and their paper was suspended for six months, for publishing allegations of corruption against the state prosecutor's office. In December, the Higher Council for Communication suspended the daily *Le Quotidien* for one week for breach of journalistic ethics, an act criticized by advocacy groups as a restriction on freedom of information. Along with the state-owned outlets, there are over 50 private radio stations, three private television stations, and several independent newspapers. The government does not restrict internet access.

Burkina Faso is a secular state, and freedom of religion is respected. Academic freedom is also unrestricted.

The constitution provides for the right to assemble, though demonstrations are sometimes suppressed or banned. While many nongovernmental organizations operate openly and freely, human rights groups have reported abuses by security forces. After violent demonstrations in 2011, continuing protests in 2012 have been peaceful. The constitution guarantees the right to strike, and unions are able to engage freely in strikes and collective bargaining, although only a minority of the workforce is unionized.

The judicial system is formally independent, but it is subject to executive influence and corruption. The courts are further weakened by a lack of resources and citizens' poor knowledge of their rights.

Human rights advocates in Burkina Faso have repeatedly criticized the military and police for committing abuses with impunity. Police often use excessive force and disregard pretrial detention limits. The sentencing in August 2011 of three police officers charged with the torture and death of Zongo was seen as a positive step.

Discrimination against various ethnic minorities occurs but is not widespread. However, gay men and lesbians, as well as those infected with HIV, routinely experience discrimination. In an effort to address discrimination against the disabled, Burkina Faso ratified the Convention on the Rights of Persons with Disabilities in 2009 and adopted a new law on the protection and promotion of the rights of the disabled in April 2010. Civil society actors also noted increased government efforts in 2010 to provide access to health care and a decrease in costs for maternal health services.

The constitution provides for freedom of movement within the country, although security checks on travelers are common. Equality of opportunity is hampered in part by the advantages conferred on CDP members, who receive preferential treatment in securing public contracts.

While illegal, gender discrimination remains common in employment, education, property, and family rights, particularly in rural areas. There are 20 women in the 127-seat National Assembly. Reforms in 2009 established a 30 percent quota for women on all party candidate lists in municipal and legislative elections, but the law is vague regarding implementation. In the north, early marriage contributes to lower female school enrollment and a heightened incidence of obstetric fistula. Human rights groups have recorded a significant drop in the prevalence of female genital mutilation since its criminalization in 1996.

Burkina Faso is a source, transit, and destination country for trafficking in women and children, who are subject to forced labor and sexual exploitation. According to the U.S. State Department's 2012 Trafficking in Persons Report, Burkina Faso does not comply with the minimum standards for eliminating human trafficking and it is placed in Tier 2. However, the report also noted the government's reform efforts as evidenced by a larger number of children—1,112—intercepted from traffickers in 2011.

Burma (Myanmar)

Political Rights: 6*
Civil Liberties: 5*
Status: Not Free

Population: 54,584,700
Capital: Nay Pyi Taw

Ratings Change: Burma's political rights rating improved from 7 to 6, and its civil liberties rating improved from 6 to 5, due to the successful participation of opposition parties in legislative by-elections and the continued easing of long-standing restrictions on the media, private discussion, public assembly, civil society, private enterprise, and other activities.

Ten-Year Ratings Timeline For Year Under Review (Political Rights, Civil Liberties, Status)

2003	2004	2005	2006	2007	2008	2009	2010	2011	2012
7,7NF	7,7NF	7,7NF	7,7NF	7,7NF	7,7NF	7,7NF	7,7NF	7,6NF	6,5NF

Overview: In April 2012, opposition leader Aung San Suu Kyi and her National League for Democracy (NLD) swept parliamentary by-elections, having boycotted the main elections in 2010. The NLD's inclusion in the political process was accompanied by the continued liberalization of the media, internet, and economy, and by the sporadic release of political prisoners. Burma's relations with foreign democracies also improved during the year, with several significant visits by international leaders. Despite this progress, ethnic and sectarian violence flared in parts of the country, and armed conflicts between the government and some of the country's ethnic minority militias remained unresolved.

Burma gained independence from Britain in 1948 after a long anticolonial struggle. In 1962, following a period of unruly parliamentary politics, General Ne Win led a coup that toppled the civilian government. The ruling Revolutionary Council subsequently consolidated all legislative, executive, and judicial power and pursued radical socialist and isolationist policies. As a result of decades of mismanagement by unelected regimes, Burma, once one of the wealthiest countries in Southeast Asia, eventually became one of the most impoverished in the region.

A new military junta, eventually led by Senior General Than Shwe, dramatically asserted its power in 1988, when the army opened fire on peaceful, student-led, prodemocracy protesters, killing an estimated 3,000 people. In the aftermath of this violence, a younger generation of army commanders created the State Law and Order Restoration Council (SLORC) to rule the country. The SLORC refused to cede power in 1990 after the National League for Democracy (NLD) won 392 of 485 parliament seats in Burma's first free elections in three decades. Instead, the junta nullified the results and jailed dozens of NLD members, including party leader Aung San Suu Kyi, who spent most of the next two decades in detention.

In late 2000, the military leadership, who renamed themselves the State Peace and Development Council (SPDC), began holding talks with Aung San Suu Kyi, leading to an easing of restrictions on the NLD by mid-2002. However, the party's revitalization apparently rattled hard-liners within the regime during the first half of 2003. On May 30 of that year, scores of NLD leaders and supporters were killed when SPDC thugs ambushed an NLD motorcade. Arrests and detentions of political activists, journalists, and students followed the attack.

The largest demonstrations in nearly 20 years erupted in cities across the country in August and September 2007, triggered by a sharp fuel-price increase. The 88 Generation Students, a group composed of dissidents active in the 1988 protests, formed the vanguard of many demonstrations. The protest movement expanded to include thousands of Buddhist monks and nuns, who were encouraged by the general populace. Soldiers, riot police, and members of the paramilitary Union Solidarity and Development Association (USDA) and the Swan Arr Shin militia group responded brutally, killing at least 31 people. The crackdown targeted important religious sites and included the public beating, shooting, and arrest of monks, further delegitimizing the regime in the eyes of many Burmese.

In May 2008, the government pushed through a constitutional referendum despite the devastation caused by Cyclone Nargis, which had struck just a week earlier, killing over 150,000 people. Burmese political opposition and international human rights groups denounced the new charter, which was approved by an implausibly high margin and would ensure military control of the political system even after elections. In an apparent bid to remove potential obstacles prior to the voting, the authorities continued to arrest and imprison dissidents throughout 2009. More than 300 activists, ranging from political and labor figures to artists and bloggers, received harsh sentences after closed trials, with some prison terms exceeding 100 years.

The national elections held in November 2010 were neither free nor fair, as the SPDC had handpicked the election commission and wrote election laws designed to favor military-backed parties, leading the NLD to boycott the polls. There were many allegations of rigged "advanced voting" and other irregularities. Ultimately, the Union Solidarity and Development Party (USDP), the political reincarnation of the USDA, captured 129 of the 168 elected seats in the Nationalities Assembly, or upper house, and 259 of 330 elected seats in the People's Assembly, or lower house. The USDP also secured 75 percent of the seats in the 14 state and regional assemblies. The Rakhine Nationalities Development Party and the Shan National Democracy Party (SNDP) earned the second-highest percentage of seats in the Nationalities Assembly and People's Assembly, respectively. However, the vote for ethnic minority parties would likely have been higher had balloting not been canceled in several minority-dominated areas. The National Democratic Force (NDF), a breakaway faction of the NLD that decided to contest the elections, won just four seats in the upper house and eight in the lower.

Outgoing prime minister Thein Sein, who had retired from the military to register as a civilian candidate, was chosen as president by the new parliament, and took office in March 2011. SPDC leader Than Shwe officially retired, but he reportedly retained influence through his allies in the new government.

Thein Sein took a number of steps toward reform in 2011, easing controls on the media, releasing scores of political prisoners, urging the return of political exiles, and legalizing peaceful demonstrations. He also launched a dialogue with Aung San Suu Kyi, who had been released from house arrest shortly after the elections, allowing her to travel the country and meet with members of her party.

In April 2012, the NLD participated in by-elections for both chambers of the national parliament. The party won all 37 seats at stake in the lower house, with 1 seat going to Aung San Suu Kyi. In the upper house, the NLD captured four of the six seats that were contested, with the other two going to the USDP and the SNDP. However, voting was postponed in three constituencies in the war-torn Kachin State.

Also during 2012, the authorities continued to liberalize the environment for foreign media operating in Burma, further eased constraints on internet access, and all but eliminated censorship of the domestic press. Aung San Suu Kyi became a regular fixture in the national media, and her image was widely visible in Burmese towns and cities, including in private homes and taxis. Meanwhile, diplomats from democratic countries were allowed to travel within Burma far more freely than at any time in the past, and a series of high-profile visits by international leaders included one by U.S. president Barack Obama in November.

The government met with some success in 2012, especially with the Karen National Union, in its long-standing effort to convince ethnic minority militias to give up their claims to autonomy. However, the Kachin Independence Army, one of the largest groups, had resumed fighting with the government in June 2011, and the conflict continued to intensify throughout 2012, with major battles occurring on a weekly basis.

Perhaps the most significant challenge for Thein Sein's government that emerged in 2012 was an outbreak of violence between the Rohingya minority—Muslims who the government asserts are illegal migrants from Bangladesh—and the Buddhist populations of Rakhine State. Long-simmering animosity between the communities was stoked by allegations of criminal attacks and reprisals. More than 100 people were reportedly killed, tens of thousands more were displaced, and mobilizations of government security forces led to allegations of human rights abuses. The situation in Rakhine State remained tense at year's end.

Political Rights and Civil Liberties: Burma is not an electoral democracy. The military, which has long controlled all executive, legislative, and judicial powers, carefully rigged the electoral framework for the 2010 national elections, which were neither free nor fair. The process of drafting the 2008 constitution, which the elections put into effect, was closely controlled by the military and excluded key stakeholders such as the NLD. Although the charter establishes a parliament and a civilian president, it also entrenches military dominance, and allows the military to dissolve the civilian government if it determines that the "disintegration of the Union or national solidarity" is at stake.

The bicameral legislature consists of the 440-seat People's Assembly, or lower house, and the 224-seat Nationalities Assembly, or upper house. A quarter of the seats in both houses are reserved for the military and filled through appointment by the commander in chief, an officer who has broad powers and is selected by the military-dominated National Defense and Security Council. The legislature elects the president, though the military members have the right to nominate one of the three candidates, with the other two nominated by the elected members of each chamber. The charter's rights guarantees are limited by existing laws and may be suspended in a state of emergency. The military retains the right to administer its own affairs, and members of the outgoing military government received blanket immunity for all official acts. The military budget is still not publicly available, although some parliamentary scrutiny of military affairs has recently become possible.

In 2011 and 2012, the government allowed members of the parliament to speak about democratic rights. The legislators' time to speak was severely limited, but many of their speeches received coverage in the domestic media, and they were not harassed for their remarks.

In 2010, the Political Party Registration Law gave new political parties only 60 days to register, mandated that existing parties reregister, and required parties to expel members currently serving prison terms. However, during the 2012 by-elections, there were fewer restrictions on party organization and mobilization, with only sporadic reports of mild interference, and many parties, including the NLD, convened meetings and rallies throughout the country.

In a system that lacks transparency and accountability, corruption and economic mismanagement are rampant at both the national and local levels. Burma was ranked 172 out of 176 countries surveyed in Transparency International's 2012 Corruption Perceptions Index. The government in 2012 continued to pursue economic reforms that had begun under the military regime, including the privatization of many state assets. However, the process has been marred by accusations that it primarily benefited family members and associates of senior government officials. While the space for public debate of these sensitive economic issues is still limited, there is a growing consensus that the country's future development will require more transparency.

The government has relaxed some restrictions on the free operation of the press. Private publications and blogs are proliferating, and the state has gradually removed prepublication censorship protocols. Previous restrictions on internet access have been largely unraveled, and the primary limitations are now bandwidth and access to inexpensive connections. Efforts to attack opposition media and internet operations have sharply diminished. Nonetheless, the violence in Rakhine State in 2012 generated unprecedented online vitriol, especially against those perceived to harbor pro-Rohingya sympathies.

The 2008 constitution provides for freedom of religion. It distinguishes Buddhism as the majority religion, but also recognizes Christianity, Islam, Hinduism, and animism. At times the government interferes with religious assemblies and attempts to control the Buddhist clergy. Buddhist temples and monasteries have been kept under close surveillance since the 2007 protests and crackdown. The authorities have also discriminated against minority religious groups, refusing to grant them permission to celebrate holidays and hold gatherings, and restricting educational activities, proselytizing, and construction of houses of worship.

Academic freedom has been severely limited. Under the military junta, teachers enjoyed no freedom of expression and were often held accountable for the political activities of their students. Universities were sporadically closed, and many campuses were relocated to relatively isolated areas to disperse the student population. However, there have been signs of more open academic discussion since 2011, as well as eased restrictions on private education, and there are growing efforts to reform the University of Rangoon, with significant support from foreign backers.

Freedoms of association and assembly are better respected than under the military regime, though there have been unsystematic efforts to rescind laws restricting freedom of assembly and public expression. Authorities reportedly remain concerned about the destabilizing potential of large-scale demonstrations, and continue to rely on repressive crowd-control tactics. In November 2012, security forces violently dispersed a protest by monks and villagers against the expansion of the Letpadaung copper mine in upper Burma. The assault, which caused significant injuries among the protesters, drew a public outcry and an unusual apology from a senior police representative. Other public gatherings during the year, including some that were technically illegal, proceeded largely without incident.

Nongovernmental organizations (NGOs) providing social services in remote areas, especially those where ethnic conflict continues, regularly face threats to their activities. International humanitarian organizations have expanded their work in the country but continue to encounter severe restrictions and monitoring, again most notably in ethnic minority areas. In 2012, international organizations met with fewer obstacles in acquiring visas for their members to visit the country, and a growing number of domestic NGOs sought to influence the government's reform efforts.

The government violates workers' rights and represses union activity. Some public sector employees and ordinary citizens were compelled to join the USDA during the years of military rule. Independent trade unions, collective bargaining, and strikes are illegal. However, garment workers have held strikes in Rangoon in recent years, with fewer repercussions than in the past. Various commercial and other interests continue to use forced labor despite a formal ban on the practice in 2000.

The judiciary is not independent. Judges are appointed or approved by the government and adjudicate cases according to its decrees. Administrative detention laws allow individuals to be held without charge, trial, or access to legal counsel for up to five years if the government concludes that they have threatened the state's security or sovereignty. Political prisoners have often been held incommunicado in pretrial detention, facilitating torture, but it is unclear exactly how widespread such practices were in 2012. The government allowed several large-scale prisoner releases in 2011 and 2012, and the freed inmates included some political prisoners. However, the release of political prisoners often coincides with trips abroad by Burmese officials or visits to Burma by high-profile delegations, and conditions are often placed on the release of political prisoners, who can be arbitrarily returned to prison. Impunity for crimes and human rights violations committed by state security forces remains deeply entrenched.

Some of the worst human rights abuses take place in border regions populated by ethnic minorities, who comprise roughly 35 percent of Burma's population. In these areas the military kills, beats, rapes, and arbitrarily detains civilians, according to human rights groups. The Kachin, Chin, Karen, and Rohingya minorities are frequent victims. In 2012, renewed fighting in Kachin areas resulted in some 100,000 people being displaced from their homes. Tens of thousands of ethnic minorities in Shan, Karenni, Karen, and Mon states still live in squalid relocation centers as a legacy of previous military campaigns.

China's sizable investments in various extractive industries in Burma, in addition to the migration of hundreds of thousands of Chinese workers and businesspeople, have led to rising anti-China sentiment in recent years.

Burmese women have traditionally enjoyed high social and economic status, but women remain underrepresented in the government and civil service. Notwithstanding the prominence of Aung San Suu Kyi, few women have achieved public recognition during the current political opening. Domestic violence and human trafficking are concerns, and women and girls in refugee camps are at an increased risk of sexual violence and exploitation by traffickers. In the past, the Women's League of Burma has accused the military of systematically using rape and forced marriage as weapons against ethnic minorities during counterinsurgency campaigns.

Burundi

Political Rights: 5
Civil Liberties: 5
Status: Partly Free

Population: 10,557,000
Capital: Bujumbura

Ten-Year Ratings Timeline For Year Under Review (Political Rights, Civil Liberties, Status)

2003	2004	2005	2006	2007	2008	2009	2010	2011	2012
5,5NF	5,5PF	3,5PF	4,5PF	4,5PF	4,5PF	4,5PF	5,5PF	5,5PF	5,5PF

Overview: Violence between supporters of the ruling party and opposition groups decreased in 2012, though most cases of extrajudicial killings remained uninvestigated. Corruption has become a deepening problem, and Burundi is considered by advocacy groups to be the most corrupt in east Africa. In 2012 a prominent antigraft activist and a radio host were sentenced in separate cases to long prison terms.

The minority Tutsi ethnic group governed Burundi for most of the period since independence from Belgium in 1962. The military, judiciary, education system, business sector, and news media were also traditionally dominated by the Tutsi. Violence between them and the majority Hutu has broken out repeatedly since independence. A 1992 constitution introduced multiparty politics, but the 1993 assassination of the newly elected Hutu president, Melchior Ndadaye of the Front for Democracy in Burundi (FRODEBU) party, led to sustained and widespread ethnic violence. The resulting 12-year civil war killed more than 300,000 people.

Ndadaye's successor was killed in 1994, along with Rwandan president Juvénal Habyarimana, when their plane was shot down as it approached Kigali airport in Rwanda. This event triggered the Rwandan genocide and intensified the fighting in Burundi.

A 1994 power-sharing arrangement between FRODEBU and the mainly Tutsi-led Unity for National Progress (UPRONA) party installed Hutu politician Sylvestre Ntibantunganya as Burundi's new president, but he was ousted in a 1996 military coup led by former president Pierre Buyoya, a Tutsi whom Ndadaye had defeated in the 1993 election. Peace and political stability remained elusive, as insurgents sporadically staged attacks and government forces pursued a campaign of intimidation. In 2000, 19 groups from across the political spectrum agreed to form a transitional government. The new government was installed in 2001, with Buyoya temporarily remaining chief of state and FRODEBU's Domitien Ndayizeye serving as vice president. Key elements of two Hutu rebel groups, the Forces for the Defense of Democracy (FDD) and the National Liberation Forces (FNL), failed to participate in the transition, resulting in both continued negotiations and additional violence.

By the end of 2002, most factions had agreed to stop the fighting and participate in transitional arrangements leading to national elections. In April 2003, Buyoya stepped down and was replaced as president by Ndayizeye, and the FDD subsequently reached an agreement with the government in October. An August 2004 agreement outlined the shape of new democratic institutions—designed to balance the interests of the Hutu and Tutsi populations—and the holding of elections.

In 2005 Burundi held its first local and national elections since 1993. The largely Hutu National Council for the Defense of Democracy (CNDD), the political wing of the FDD, emerged as the country's largest party, and Parliament chose Pierre Nkurunziza as president. Domestic and international observers generally regarded the voting as legitimate and reflective of the people's will.

A tentative ceasefire agreement was reached with the last significant FNL faction in 2007, but violence involving the group flared again in 2008. Nonetheless, FNL leader Agathon Rwasa soon returned to participate in negotiations on the demobilization of his guerrillas and the transformation of the FNL into a political party. These discussions were complicated by complaints regarding repressive actions taken by the CNDD and counterclaims that the FNL was continuing to recruit military cadres.

The talks finally led the FNL to lay down its arms in 2009, leading to its recognition as a legal political party. In April of that year, an independent election commission was sworn in to prepare for elections due in 2010, and a new electoral code was adopted. However, political uncertainty and tension remained, as opposition parties accused the government of trying to manipulate the electoral process.

Local elections took place in May 2010, which the CNDD won with almost two-thirds of the vote. Following increasing efforts by the CNDD to close political space, opposition candidates boycotted both the June presidential election and July parliamentary polls. Prior to the presidential poll, the government placed serious restrictions on freedom of movement for opposition leaders, arrested dozens of opposition activists, and banned all opposition party meetings. According to opposition parties and human rights organizations, the ostensibly independent election commission failed to adequately investigate allegations of preelectoral violence and make public some individual polling place results. In the legislative poll, the CNDD captured 81 percent of the vote, followed by UPRONA with almost 12 percent and FRODEBU with nearly 6 percent, while Nkurunziza was reelected president with some 92 percent of the vote. Observers viewed the elections as a missed opportunity for strengthening Burundi's democratic culture, as political polarization increased, and several leading opposition figures—including Rwasa—fled the country fearing for their safety. Political rifts and violence were mainly between rival Hutu groups, and not between Hutus and Tutsis as in the past.

Incidents of political violence between the CNDD and opposition parties decreased in 2012 compared to 2011, though justice has not been pursued in the majority of cases of violence and killings in recent years. In January 2012, however, 16 people were found guilty of the September 2011 massacre of at least 30 people in a bar in Gatumba on the Congolese border. Intelligence services attributed the attack to the FNL, allegedly as retribution for government violence against its members. The trial was seen as seriously flawed by both local and international observers, with defendants alleging that they had been tortured and forced either to confess or to implicate the FNL in the attack.

Political Rights and Civil Liberties: Burundi is not an electoral democracy. The country lacks representative institutions at the national level, in both the legislative and executive branches of government. Despite citizens' ability to change their government democratically in 2005, serious electoral irregularities and repression during the May 2010 local elections led most opposition parties to boycott subsequent presidential and parliamentary polls. The 2010 presidential election was the first by direct vote, but without meaningful competition, the results lacked legitimacy. The president, who is elected to a five-year term, appoints two vice presidents, one Tutsi and one Hutu, and they must be approved separately by a two-thirds majority in both the lower and upper houses.

While the lower house of Parliament—the 100-seat National Assembly—is directly elected for a five-year term, locally elected officials choose members of the Senate, also for five-year terms. Each of Burundi's 17 provinces chooses two senators—one Tutsi and one Hutu. Carefully crafted constitutional arrangements require the National Assembly to be no more than 60 percent Hutu and no less than 40 percent Tutsi, with three additional deputies from the Twa ethnic minority, who are also allocated three senators. In both houses, a minimum of 30 percent of the legislators must be women.

There are more than two dozen active political parties in the country, ranging from those that champion radical Tutsi positions to those that hold extremist Hutu views. Most are small in terms of membership, and many Tutsi have now joined formerly Hutu-dominated parties. The government appointed in September 2010 consists of members from the three political parties represented in Parliament: the CNDD, UPRONA, and FRODEBU. Many political parties include youth groups that intimidate and attack opponents.

Corruption remains a significant problem. Burundi was ranked 165 out of 176 countries surveyed in Transparency International's 2012 Corruption Perceptions Index, making it the most corrupt country in east Africa. In February 2012, prominent antigraft activist Faustin Ndikumana was arrested after he reported on alleged bribes that judges were forced to pay for their appointments. Ndikumana was convicted in July and sentenced to five years in prison for making "false declarations" under an anticorruption law. In May, 14 people were convicted for the April 2009 assassination of the deputy head of Burundi's largest anticorruption organization, the Anticorruption and Economic Malpractice Observatory, despite concerns that the investigation had targeted the wrong suspects and exonerated police and military officers who were known to have been involved. The jail sentences ranged from 10 years to life imprisonment.

Freedom of speech is legally guaranteed, but press laws restrict journalists in broad, imprecise ways, and sanctions for defamation and insult include harsh fines and imprisonment. Several draft laws were introduced in the National Assembly in 2012 that would further restrict freedoms of expression and assembly. While journalists continue to engage in self-censorship and are sometimes censored by authorities, they have been increasingly willing to express opinions critical of the government. Radio is the primary source of information for the majority of the population. The media is dominated by the government, which owns the public television and radio stations; it also runs *Le Renouveau*, the only daily newspaper. Several private broadcast media outlets also operate, though most have a limited broadcast range. The British Broadcasting Corporation, Radio France Internationale, and Voice of America are available on FM radio in the capital. Print runs of most newspapers remain small, and readership is limited by low literacy levels. Access to the internet remains largely confined to urban areas.

Despite the recent emergence of a more pluralistic press, journalists have been arbitrarily arrested, harassed, or threatened on numerous occasions. Following the Gatumba attack in September 2011, the government imposed a 30-day media blackout regarding the massacre, issuing a statement banning "publishing, commenting or doing analyses in connection with the ongoing investigations into the carnage in Gatumba." After the 30-day period expired, the government harassed and intimidated journalists who attempted to report on or investigate the attack or the other murders that had occurred throughout the year. In June 2012, Hassan Ruvakuki, a reporter for Radio France Internationale in Burundi, was sentenced to life in prison, along with 13 others, for purportedly participating in the Gatumba attack. The charges were levied against Ruvakuki primarily on the basis that he had conducted an interview in Tanzania with the leader of a new rebel group, the Front for the Restoration of Democracy-Abanyagihugu.

Freedom of religion is generally observed. For many years, the ongoing civil strife and the Tutsi social and institutional dominance had impeded academic freedom by limiting educational opportunities for the Hutu, but this situation has improved in recent years.

The constitution provides for freedoms of assembly and association, although members of human rights groups that criticize the government have been threatened with or subjected to surveillance. There is modest but important civil society activity with a focus on human rights. In June 2011, members of the newly created National Independent Human Rights Commission were sworn in, and a 2012 assessment by Human Rights Watch of the commission's work found that it has thus far been able to investigate politically sensitive cases and operate independently.

Constitutional protections for organized labor are in place, and the right to strike is guaranteed by the labor code. The Confederation of Burundi Trade Unions has been independent since its establishment in 1995. Most union members are civil servants and have bargained collectively with the government.

Burundi's judiciary is hindered by corruption, a lack of resources and training, and executive interference in legal matters. Crimes, especially those related to political violence, often go unreported or uninvestigated. An unusually high number of extrajudicial executions have been reported in recent years, though there were fewer in 2012. The current judicial system struggles to function effectively or independently and cannot handle the large number of pending cases, many of which are politically sensitive. Prisons are overcrowded, unhygienic, and at times life threatening. In June 2012, President Pierre Nkurunziza pardoned several thousand prisoners—including those serving terms of five years or less, pregnant or breast-feeding women, prisoners over 60 and under 18 years of age, and the terminally ill—in order to alleviate prison overcrowding and celebrate Burundi's 50th anniversary. In July 2011, the president had announced the creation of a truth and reconciliation commission designed to provide accountability for past abuses, but the commission had yet to begin work by the end of 2012.

Women have limited opportunities for advancement in the economic and political spheres, especially in rural areas. Burundi continues to have a serious problem with sexual and domestic violence, and these crimes are rarely reported. The 2009 penal code criminalizes same-sex relationships. Albinos face a particular threat from discrimination and violence; an albino girl was kidnapped and killed in May 2012.

Cambodia

Political Rights: 6
Civil Liberties: 5
Status: Not Free

Population: 14,952,700
Capital: Phnom Penh

Ten-Year Ratings Timeline For Year Under Review (Political Rights, Civil Liberties, Status)

2003	2004	2005	2006	2007	2008	2009	2010	2011	2012
6,5NF	6,5NF	6,5NF	6,5NF	6,5NF	6,5NF	6,5NF	6,5NF	6,5NF	6,5NF

Overview: The UN-backed tribunal trying former leaders of the Khmer Rouge experienced severe problems in 2012, with several foreign judges resigning amid allegations of government meddling and public outrage after a former high-ranking official was declared mentally unfit to stand trial. Violent crackdowns on journalists and protesters occurred throughout the year, including against those attempting to organize around meetings of the Association of Southeast Asian Nations, which Cambodia hosted in 2012.

Cambodia won independence from France in 1953. King Norodom Sihanouk ruled until he was ousted in 1970 by U.S.-backed military commander Lon Nol, and the communist Khmer Rouge (KR) seized power in 1975. Approximately two million of Cambodia's seven million people died from disease, overwork, starvation, or execution under the KR before Vietnamese forces toppled the regime and installed a new communist government in 1979. Fighting continued in the 1980s between the Hanoi-backed government and the allied armies of Sihanouk, the KR, and other political contenders. The 1991 Paris Peace Accords halted open warfare, but the KR continued to wage a low-grade insurgency until its disintegration in the late 1990s.

Since entering government as part of the Vietnamese-backed regime in 1979, Prime Minister Hun Sen and his Cambodian People's Party (CPP) have played a leading role in the country's politics, generally controlling the National Assembly, military, courts, and police. In the early 1990s, Hun Sen used his control of the security forces to coerce the royalist party, known as Funcinpec, into sharing power, even though Funcinpec won the largest number of seats in the first parliamentary elections after the peace accords, held in 1993. Hun Sen later ousted the prime minister, Prince Norodom Ranariddh of Funcinpec, in a 1997 coup, and the CPP won a majority of seats in the 1998 parliamentary elections, which were held under restrictive conditions.

The deeply flawed parliamentary elections in 2003 featured violence and voter intimidation by the CPP. Nevertheless, the party failed to obtain the two-thirds majority required to form a government. Following the formation of a CPP-Funcinpec coalition, Hun Sen turned to silencing opposition leader Sam Rainsy's attacks on government corruption and abuse. After fleeing the country, Rainsy was convicted in absentia of defaming Prince Ranariddh and Hun Sen in 2005. However, under pressure from international donors, Hun Sen negotiated a settlement in 2006 that allowed Rainsy to receive a royal pardon and return to Cambodia in exchange for a public apology and a withdrawal of his allegations.

In the 2008 elections, the CPP took 90 of 123 parliamentary seats, and Hun Sen was reelected as prime minister. Opposition parties rejected the results, citing political intimidation and violence. However, with the opposition divided and unproven in the eyes of voters, and the country enjoying relative political stability and sustained economic growth, the CPP had started to command a measure of popular credibility. Meanwhile, Rainsy returned to exile ahead of a 2010 conviction on charges related to his claims that the government had ceded territory along the border to Vietnam, and he remained outside the country at the end of 2012.

Local elections were held at the commune level in 2012, with the CPP winning nearly every commune. International observers found widespread electoral irregularities; Reporters Without Borders noted that the Cambodian information ministry had banned foreign broadcasters such as Radio Free Asia from reporting on the elections and from transmitting their broadcasts throughout Cambodia. Participation in the elections fell to 54 percent of eligible voters, down from 87 percent 10 years prior.

There remains a great deal of controversy surrounding attempts to try the accused perpetrators of atrocities committed under the Khmer Rouge regime. In July 2010, the former chief of the Tuol Sleng prison, Kang Kek Ieu (also known as Duch), was found guilty of war crimes and sentenced to 35 years in prison, reduced to 19 years given time served. In June 2011, the Extraordinary Chambers in the Courts of Cambodia began trial proceedings against four high-ranking former KR officials on charges of genocide and other crimes against humanity. One of the four defendants,

Ieng Thirith, was declared mentally unfit to stand trial, a verdict that sparked widespread public protest; she was released in 2012. Meanwhile, several foreign judges quit the tribunal in 2011 and 2012 after having their attempts to charge and try additional suspects rebuffed by their Cambodian colleagues. Hun Sen has publicly called for the tribunal not to investigate any other former KR officials, and allegedly does not want the tribunal to delve too deeply into the past or weaken the prevailing climate of impunity for the powerful.

In 2012, the government eased its dispute with Thailand over a shared border temple, in part because the new Thai government, elected in 2011, was led by Yingluck Shinawatra, sister of former Cambodian prime minister Thaksin Shinawatra and a friend of Hun Sen. The government had been using the conflict to boost nationalism and place more power in the hands of Hun Sen's son, who oversaw Cambodian forces on the border.

In 2012, Cambodia served as the host of meetings of the Association of Southeast Asian Nations (ASEAN), a task that rotates among members of the 10-country organization. At the organization's July meeting for foreign ministers, several ASEAN members alleged that Cambodian officials had been leaking information about internal ASEAN deliberations to China, which is Cambodia's largest donor and investor. Also at the meeting, the organization was unable to come to a consensus on a statement regarding territorial disputes in the South China Sea, and some members accused Cambodia of purposely blocking consensus on behalf of China. Meanwhile, violence against activists and journalists intensified in 2012, including against those attempting to organize around the ASEAN meetings.

Political Rights and Civil Liberties: Cambodia is not an electoral democracy. Elections are conducted under often repressive conditions, and the opposition is hampered by serious legal and physical harassment. The current constitution was promulgated in 1993 by the king, who serves as head of state. The monarchy remains highly revered as a symbol of national unity, but has little political power. Prince Norodom Sihamoni, who lived abroad for much of his life, succeeded his father, King Norodom Sihanouk, in 2004, after the latter abdicated for health reasons. Some palace experts charge that Sihamoni is a virtual prisoner of the government, with no control over his own activities.

The prime minister and cabinet must be approved by a majority vote in the 123-seat National Assembly, whose members are elected by party-list voting to serve five-year terms. The upper house of the bicameral parliament, the Senate, has 61 members, of whom 2 are appointed by the king, 2 are elected by the National Assembly, and 57 are chosen by local legislators. Senators serve six-year terms. Voting is tied to a citizen's permanent resident status in a village, township, or urban district, and this status cannot be changed easily. The CPP's strong influence in rural areas, with its presence of party members and control of local and provincial government officials, gives it an advantage over the opposition Sam Rainsy Party, which finds support mainly in urban centers.

Corruption is a serious problem that hinders economic development and social stability. Many in the ruling elite abuse their positions for private gain. While economic growth in recent years has been sustained by increased investment in mining, forestry, agriculture, textile manufacturing, tourism, hydropower, and real estate, these enterprises frequently involve land grabs by powerful politicians, bureaucrats, and military officers. Repeated efforts by international donors to promote tough anticorruption laws have been stalled and watered down by the government.

The government does not fully respect freedom of speech. Media controls are largely focused on local broadcast outlets. Print journalists are somewhat freer to criticize the government, but the print media reach only about 10 percent of the population. There are many privately owned print and broadcast outlets, including several owned and operated by the CPP and opposition parties, though broadcast licensing processes remain opaque. There are no restrictions on access to foreign broadcasts via satellite. The government has increasingly used lawsuits and criminal prosecution as a means of media intimidation over the past three years. A 2010 penal code drew criticism for several vague provisions relating to freedom of expression, including one that criminalizes any action that "affects the dignity" of a public official. In September 2012, journalist Hang Serei Odom, who had focused on illegal logging and its link to wealthy politicians, was killed, allegedly by a military policeman. His colleagues urged a more thorough investigation into the murder, but none was forthcoming. In April, writer and environmentalist Chut Watty, who focused on logging in protected forests, also was murdered, allegedly by police. The internet is fairly free of government control, though access is largely limited to urban centers. In November 2012, the Ministry of Communications issued a decree prohibiting internet cafes from being located within 500 meters of a school or allowing access to websites with pornographic content or those used for playing games, such as betting on football. Critics of the decree, including Reporters Without Borders, charge that the provisions can be widely interpreted by the authorities and represent a step toward tighter government control over the internet.

The majority of Cambodians are Theravada Buddhists and can generally practice their faith freely, but societal discrimination against ethnic Cham Muslims remains a problem. Terrorist attacks by Islamist militants elsewhere in Southeast Asia in recent years have raised new suspicions about Muslims. The government generally respects academic freedom, though criticism of the prime minister and his family is often punished.

The authorities' tolerance for freedoms of association and assembly has declined over the past few years, with violence against activists increasing in 2012. Authorities jailed at least thirteen women during the year, plus one activist monk, for protesting the forced resettlement of families at Boeung Kak Lake in Phnom Penh; in several instances, demonstrators also used violence, including throwing Molotov cocktails at police and smashing officers with bricks. In January, authorities opened fire on demonstrators in a land dispute in Kratie Province, and in February, local authorities shot three protestors in Bavet during a labor rally. A few weeks later, a girl was killed by authorities while protesting a forced eviction.

Civil society groups work on a broad spectrum of issues and offer social services, frequently with funding from overseas. Those that work on social or health issues, as opposed to justice and human rights, generally face less harassment from the state. Civil society activists who attempted to organize during the 2012 ASEAN meetings hosted by Cambodia were detained and kept out of meeting spaces, allegedly had electricity to their gatherings cut, and were arrested for trying to bring the issue of land evictions to members of the media present at the ASEAN events.

Cambodia has a small number of independent unions. Workers have the right to strike, and many have done so to protest low wages and poor or dangerous working conditions. Lack of resources and experience limits union success in collective bargaining, and union leaders report harassment and physical threats. The garment industry has made several compacts with international companies to ensure the fair treatment of workers, but these have not prevented the harassment of union leaders in the industry.

The judiciary is marred by inefficiency, corruption, and a lack of independence. There is a severe shortage of lawyers, and the system's poorly trained judges are subject to political pressure from the CPP, which has also undermined the Khmer Rouge tribunal. Abuse by law enforcement officers, including illegal detention and the torture of suspects, is common. Jails are seriously overcrowded, and inmates often lack sufficient food, water, and health care. Police, soldiers, and government officials are widely believed to tolerate, or be involved in, the trafficking of guns, drugs, and people, as well as other crimes.

The constitution guarantees the right to freedom of travel and movement, and the government generally respects this right. However, there have been reports of authorities restricting travel for opposition politicians, particularly during election campaigns. The Cambodian government closed the UN refugee center in Phnom Penh in early 2011, making it more difficult for Uighurs from China, Montagnards from Vietnam, and other people fleeing persecution to gain refugee status in Cambodia.

Land and property rights are regularly abused for the sake of private development projects. Over the past several years, tens of thousands of people have been forcibly removed—from both rural and urban areas, and with little or no compensation or relocation assistance—to make room for commercial plantations, mine operations, factories, and high-end office and residential developments. High-ranking officials and their family members are frequently involved in these ventures, alongside international investors.

Women suffer widespread economic and social discrimination, lagging behind men in secondary and higher education. Rape and domestic violence are common and are often tied to alcohol and drug abuse by men. Women and girls are trafficked to and from Cambodia for prostitution.

Cameroon

Political Rights: 6
Civil Liberties: 6
Status: Not Free

Population: 20,919,000
Capital: Yaoundé

Ten-Year Ratings Timeline For Year Under Review (Political Rights, Civil Liberties, Status)

2003	2004	2005	2006	2007	2008	2009	2010	2011	2012
6,6NF	6,6NF	6,6NF	6,6NF	6,6NF	6,6NF	6,6NF	6,6NF	6,6NF	6,6NF

Overview: In the spring of 2012, legislative elections scheduled for July were postponed until 2013 in order to address procedural concerns raised by the opposition. Writer and activist Enoh Meyomesse remained imprisoned throughout 2012, and in December received a seven-year sentence for complicity in the theft and illegal sale of gold. Also during the year, the government continued to aggressively prosecute those suspected of homosexual activity, which is outlawed.

Colonized by Germany in the late 19th century, Cameroon was later administered by Britain and France, first through League of Nations mandates and then as a UN trust territory after World War II. Independence for French Cameroon in 1960 was followed a year later by independence for Anglophone Cameroon, part of which opted for union with Nigeria. The rest joined Francophone Cameroon in a federation, which became a unitary state in 1972.

The country's first president, Ahmadou Ahidjo, oversaw a repressive, one-party system until his resignation in 1982. He was succeeded by Paul Biya, whose Cameroon People's Democratic Movement (CPDM) did not face multiparty legislative elections until 1992. It failed to win an absolute majority, despite a boycott by the main opposition party, the Anglophone-led Social Democratic Front (SDF).

In 1992, Biya was reelected in a vote that was condemned by international observers. A 1996 constitutional revision extended the presidential term from five to seven years, and Biya has won every election since amid numerous irregularities. The CPDM's victories in legislative and municipal elections have been similarly tainted. Electoral gerrymandering provided the CPDM with significant inroads into the SDF support base in the 2007 legislative and municipal polls, and SDF parliamentary representation decreased to 16 of 180 total seats. In 2008, Biya secured a constitutional amendment to remove the two-term presidential limit, allowing him to stand for reelection in 2011. Approximately 100 people were killed in clashes with police during subsequent antigovernment riots.

In the 2011 presidential election, Biya easily defeated his 22 rivals, claiming 78 percent of the vote. His closest challenger, SDF leader John Fru Ndi, received just 11 percent. Foreign diplomats and members of the opposition protested the results, citing irregularities. The 79-year-old president's advancing age and rumored failing health have fueled concerns that he could become incapacitated while in office, potentially sparking a political crisis, as Biya has not officially anointed a successor.

In the spring of 2012, legislative elections scheduled for July were postponed until 2013 in accordance with opposition demands. The delay will allow the electoral commission, Elections Cameroon (ELECAM), to update the voter registration list using biometric verification, which is intended to reduce fraud.

Political Rights and Civil Liberties: Cameroon is not an electoral democracy. Although the 1996 constitutional revisions created an upper chamber for the legislature, a decentralized system of regional government, and a Constitutional Court, none of these provisions have been implemented. The president is not required to consult the National Assembly, and the Supreme Court may review the constitutionality of a law only at the president's request. Since 1992, the executive has initiated every bill passed by the legislature. The unicameral National Assembly has 180 seats and is dominated by President Paul Biya's CPDM. Members are elected by direct popular vote for five-year terms.

ELECAM was created in 2006 to address concerns about the fair management of previous elections, but CPDM partisans dominate the body. In March 2010, an amendment was passed requiring ELECAM to collaborate with the Ministry of Territorial Administration and Decentralization; the move was widely criticized for placing election management into the hands of a ministry loyal to Biya. In February 2012, civil society groups and the opposition called for ELECAM to be replaced with a new body, citing its lack of independence from the executive. In April, amendments to the electoral law took effect that introduced biometric registration and were intended to enhance ELECAM's independence.

There are more than 250 recognized political parties, but Biya's CPDM, with its access to state patronage, dominates. Continued marginalization of the Anglophone community has fueled a nonviolent campaign for independence by the Southern Cameroons National Council (SCNC), which has been declared an illegal organization. Throughout 2012, several SCNC members were arrested and charged with secession, participating in illegal meetings, or attempting to destabilize the state. Meanwhile, the northern-based Fulani, who once enjoyed political prominence under former president Ahmadou Ahidjo, still resent Biya for a bloody 1984 crackdown on northerners in the armed forces. The Cameroon Renaissance Movement, a new coalition made up of several opposition parties and led by former justice minister Maurice Kamto, was introduced in August 2012.

Corruption remains endemic in Cameroon. Biya's administration has encouraged cronyism, with members of the president's Beti ethnic group dominating many key positions. Revenues from the oil, gas, and mining sectors are not openly reported. The National Anticorruption Commission, created in 2006, is the country's principal independent anticorruption agency, though its subservience to the president undermines its effectiveness. The National Financial Investigations Unit is a separate intelligence unit that tracks money laundering. In recent years, Biya has resumed an anticorruption initiative, Opération Épervier, but critics argue that it has been used to eliminate political opponents and enemies. In September 2012, Marafa Hamidou Yaya, a former minister and presidential hopeful, was sentenced to 25 years in prison for embezzlement. Biya had fired Yaya in 2011. Cameroon was ranked 144 out of 176 countries surveyed in Transparency International's 2012 Corruption Perceptions Index.

The constitution guarantees free speech, but genuine freedom of expression remains elusive. Although the 1996 constitution ended prepublication censorship, the charter's Article 17 gives officials the power to ban newspapers based on a claimed threat to public order. Libel and defamation remain criminal offenses, and judicial harassment and arrests of journalists and writers have engendered self-censorship. In one high-profile case, author and founding member of the Cameroon Writers Association Enoh Meyomesse—who had run as an opposition candidate in the 2011 presidential election—was arrested in November 2011 and charged with attempting to organize a coup, possessing a firearm, and aggravated theft, though he maintained that the arrest was politically motivated. Those charges were dropped in June 2012, but he remained in custody and was later charged with complicity in stealing and illegally trafficking in gold. He was found guilty in December, and sentenced to seven years in prison. There is no systematic internet censorship in Cameroon.

Freedom of religion is generally respected. There are no legal restrictions on academic freedom, but state security informants operate on university campuses, many professors exercise self-censorship, and some argue that entrance into university requires bribery or the support of a powerful patron.

The requisite administrative authorization for public meetings is often used to restrict freedoms of assembly and association. Meetings of the SCNC, banned in 2001, are routinely disrupted. In February 2012, former opposition presidential candidate Vincent-Sosthène Fouda and several others were arrested in connection with a demonstration held after a newborn baby was stolen from a hospital in the capital; Fouda was charged with holding an unlawful demonstration. In March, police disrupted a peaceful rally in the northern city of Maroua organized by the Movement for the Defense of Human Rights and Fundamental Freedoms and arrested the organization's president and 14 other members; they were released the same day. In November, security forces used tear gas to disperse a crowd of a 1,000 gathered to protest Biya's extended time in power. Trade union formation is permitted, but subject to numerous restrictions.

The judiciary is subordinate to the Ministry of Justice, and courts are weakened by political influence and corruption. Military tribunals exercise jurisdiction over civilians in cases involving civil unrest or organized armed violence. Acts of brutality against civilians by Cameroon's elite security unit, the Bataillon d'Intervention Rapide, are increasing, although some troops have been dismissed for unnecessary use of force. Prison conditions are poor and sometimes life threatening, with overcrowding, poorly maintained facilities, and widespread violence by guards and among inmates. Torture and ill-treatment of detainees are routine. A 2010 report by the UN Committee Against Torture found that over half of Cameroon's prisoners were in provisional detention, and that many remained in jail much longer than the maximum time for pretrial detention. The absence of habeas corpus provisions in Francophone civil law further undermines due process. In the north, traditional rulers (lamibe) operate private militias, courts, and prisons, which are used against political opponents.

Slavery reportedly persists in parts of the north, and indigenous groups and ethnic minorities, particularly the Baka, face discrimination.

Despite legal protections, there is widespread violence and discrimination against women, and female genital mutilation is practiced in the Southwest and Far North regions. Cameroon is a child labor market and a transit center for child trafficking.

Prejudice and discrimination against the LGBT (lesbian, gay, bisexual, and transgender) community is pervasive. The law forbids homosexual activity, and stipulates prison terms of six months to five years. At least 28 people have been prosecuted under the penal code's Article 347 since 2010. Cases of alleged homosexuality are often fraught with violations of due process rights and based on weak evidence. Further, convictions for homosexual acts often rely on perceived sexual orientation, despite the fact that the law requires an individual be caught engaging in a sexual act. In February, police arrested a man for alleged homosexuality, and released him on the condition that he publicly denounce the work of Alternatives-Cameroun, an organization that provides HIV/AIDS services to the community; the organization suspended its activities as a result. Authorities in the capital shut down a workshop on the rights of sexual and gender minorities in March. In December, an appeals court upheld a conviction and three-year prison sentence for a university student accused of homosexuality, though he had no legal representation at his original trial. Lawyers representing clients of accused homosexuality were subjected to threats of violence throughout 2012 due to their work.

Canada

Political Rights: 1
Civil Liberties: 1
Status: Free

Population: 34,860,000
Capital: Ottawa

Ten-Year Ratings Timeline For Year Under Review (Political Rights, Civil Liberties, Status)

2003	2004	2005	2006	2007	2008	2009	2010	2011	2012
1,1F	1,1F	1,1F	1,1F	1,1F	1,1F	1,1F	1,1F	1,1F	1,1F

Overview: Prime Minister Stephen Harper's Conservative government passed controversial crime and immigration laws in 2012, though it failed to pass a bill that would have allowed police to monitor private information on the internet. Student-led protests in Québec in May over proposed tuition hikes led to a controversial emergency law that limited free expression and assembly. General elections in Québec in September resulted in the election of the province's first female premier.

Colonized by French and British settlers in the 17th and 18th centuries, Canada was secured by the British Crown under the terms of the Treaty of Paris in 1763. After granting home rule in 1867, Britain retained a theoretical right to override the Canadian Parliament until 1982, when Canadians established complete control over their own constitution.

After a dozen years of center-left Liberal Party rule, the Conservative Party emerged from the 2006 parliamentary elections with a plurality and established a fragile minority government with Stephen Harper as prime minister. While the Conservatives expanded their position in the 2008 national elections, they failed to attain a majority. The Liberals, the principal opposition party, formed an alliance with the social democratic New Democratic Party (NDP) and the Québec-based Bloc Québécois, which favors Québec separatism.

Early elections were called in May 2011, after the parliamentary opposition voted in March to hold the government in contempt for allegedly failing to disclose accurate costs for key programs. However, the Conservative government triumphed in the election as a result of Canada's success in largely avoiding the economic turmoil that had engulfed much of the global economy since 2008, securing 166 seats, well over the 155 necessary to form a majority government. Placing second with 103 seats was the NDP, which for the first time became the leading opposition party. The Liberals finished in third place with 34 seats, while the Bloc Québécois, suffered a devastating defeat, with just 4 members elected to Parliament. The Green Party captured one seat.

In May 2012, the provincial government of Québec passed an emergency law to stifle student-led demonstrations against tuition increases that had been taking place since February. The emergency law—Bill 78—provided for fines of up to C$125,000 (about US$125,000) for groups failing to obtain police permission to hold a demonstration or for deviating from an agreed upon route or time limit. In response to the new law, thousands from the general public joined the demonstrations, known as "casseroles," in which protestors banged pots and pans, a tactic used in Chilean student protests. The police response to the months-long demonstrations occasionally turned violent and included mass arrests of up to 2,500 people, the use of tear gas, and the tactic of kettling. On May 23, over 500 people were arrested in a single demonstration in Montreal.

Pauline Marois of the separatist Parti Québécois (PQ) defeated Jean Charest to become Québec's first female premier on September 4, 2012. In her first day on the job, Marois dissolved Bill 78 and canceled the tuition increase. The victory of Marois, however, was marred by tragedy when Richard Henry Bain, an English-speaking businessman and advocate for the separation of Montreal from Québec for linguistic purposes, opened fire outside of the PQ victory party, killing one bystander and wounding another. Bain was awaiting trial at year's end. In provincial elections in Alberta, Alison Redford and the Progressive Conservatives won their 12th consecutive majority on April 23, 2012.

Political Rights and Civil Liberties: Canada is an electoral democracy. The country is governed by a prime minister, a cabinet, and Parliament, which consists of an elected 308-member House of Commons and an appointed 105-member Senate. Senators may serve until age 75, while lower-house elections are to be held every four years, with early elections called only if the government loses a parliamentary no-confidence vote. The British monarch remains head of state, represented by a ceremonial governor-general who is appointed on the advice of the prime minister.

Civil liberties have been protected since 1982 by the federal Charter of Rights and Freedoms, but they are limited by the constitutional "notwithstanding" clause, which permits provincial governments to exempt themselves with respect to individual provisions in their jurisdictions. Québec has used the clause to retain its provincial language law, which restricts the use of languages other than French on signs.

Canada has a reputation for clean government and has a record of vigorous prosecution of corruption cases. However, the Organisation for Economic Co-operation and Development has criticized Canada for failing to effectively combat bribery of foreign public officials in international business transactions. In 2011, the government attempted to address these complaints by imposing a C$9.5 million (US$9.5 million) fine on Calgary-based oil company Niko Resources for bribing a Bangladeshi energy minister. In 2012, the Royal Canadian Mounted Police was in the process of investigating around 35 additional cases of foreign bribery. Canada was ranked 9 out of 176 countries surveyed in Transparency International's 2012 Corruption Perceptions Index.

Canada's media are generally free, and journalists are mostly free from violence and harassment and are able to express diverse views. However, defamation remains a criminal offense, punishable by up to five years in prison. There are no statutory laws to protect confidential sources, and the courts often decide whether or not to respect source confidentiality on a case-by-case basis. A 2007 policy prohibits federally funded scientists from speaking to the media about their research, even after it has been published. Despite the existence of Canada's Access to Information Act, there are many challenges to obtaining information, including lengthy delays and excessive costs. Media ownership continued to become more concentrated in 2012.

While there are no restrictions on internet access, the government introduced a controversial bill in February 2012 that would have permitted police to monitor online subscriber information from internet service providers without a warrant. After heavy criticism, the bill appeared to be permanently shelved at year's end.

Religious freedom is protected by the constitution and other legislation. However, there have been cases of societal discrimination based on religious affiliation, including numerous acts of violence and vandalism against Canada's Jewish and Muslim communities in 2012. There has also been debate surrounding the legality of wearing religious clothing and face coverings, such as the niqab or burqa, in public. On December 20, 2012, the Supreme Court ruled in a split decision that women have the right to wear the niqab while testifying in court in certain circumstances. Academic freedom is respected.

Freedoms of association and assembly are generally respected. However, the right to assemble was restricted in May 2012 by the Québec government with the passing of its emergency law. Police conduct during the protests surrounding the 2010 meeting of the Group of 20 in Toronto, including the use of excessive force and illegal imprisonment, was heavily criticized in a report released by the Office of the Independent Police Review in May 2012.

Trade unions and business associations enjoy high levels of membership and are well organized. In 2012, however, the government continued to adopt a tough line with unions representing public workers and to interfere in the rights of workers to organize, strike, and bargain collectively. It also introduced legislation to impose binding arbitration in numerous labor disputes, including between Air Canada and the unions representing its pilots and machinists in March.

The judiciary is independent. Canada's criminal law is based on legislation enacted by Parliament; its tort and contract law is based on English common law, with the exception of Québec, where it is based on the French civil code. The federal government passed an anticrime law in March 2012, which increased mandatory minimum sentences and harsher sentences for young offenders, and eliminated conditional sentences such as house arrest or community service for some crimes. Critics argued that the new law would increase the number of people in prison and detention costs, and inflict unconstitutional punishments on people.

Canada maintains relatively liberal immigration policies. However, concern has mounted over a June 2012 immigration law that, according to Amnesty International and the Canadian Council for Refugees, creates an unfair system by increasing detention time for refugees and granting sole discretion to the Minister of Citizenship and Immigration to designate certain countries of origin as "safe." The new law also imposes a waiting period of five years before refugees can apply for permanent residence.

While authorities have taken important steps to protect the rights of the country's indigenous population, they remain subject to multiple forms of discrimination and have unequal access to education, health care, and employment. There are frequent controversies over control of land in various provinces, including the building of gas and oil wells on traditional territories.

The country boasts a generous welfare system, including national health care, which supplements the largely open, competitive economy.

Women's rights are protected in law and in practice. Women hold about 25 percent of the seats in the lower house of Parliament and about 37 percent of Senate seats. Women have made major gains in the economy, and are well represented in the labor force, though they still earned 28 percent less than men for the same work in Ontario in 2012. Indigenous women face racial and economic discrimination, as well as extreme gender-based violence. Canada legalized same-sex marriage in 2005.

Cape Verde

Political Rights: 1
Civil Liberties: 1
Status: Free

Population: 510,000
Capital: Praia

Ten-Year Ratings Timeline For Year Under Review (Political Rights, Civil Liberties, Status)

2003	2004	2005	2006	2007	2008	2009	2010	2011	2012
1,1F	1,1F	1,1F	1,1F	1,1F	1,1F	1,1F	1,1F	1,1F	1,1F

Overview: Cape Verde continued to serve as a model for political rights and civil liberties in Africa in 2012. In January 2012 municipal elections, the Movement for Democracy (MDP) won the majority of city councils. The African Party for Independence of Cape Verde has continued to decline in popularity since its candidate was defeated by the MDP in the 2011 presidential election. Both elections were considered credible and fair by international observers.

After achieving independence from Portugal in 1975, Cape Verde was governed for 16 years as a Marxist, one-party state under the African Party for the Independence of Guinea and Cape Verde, later renamed the African Party for Independence of Cape Verde (PAICV). The establishment of the opposition Movement for Democracy (MPD) in 1990 helped to bring one-party rule to an end, and in 1991 the country became the first former Portuguese colony in Africa to abandon Marxist political and economic systems and hold democratic elections. The MPD won both the legislative and presidential elections, with candidate António Mascarenhas Monteiro elected president by a landslide victory. In 1995 legislative elections, the MPD increased its majority in the National Assembly, and Monteiro was reelected in 1996.

The 2001 presidential election was more competitive, with PAICV candidate Pedro Verona Rodrigues Pires narrowly defeating Carlos Alberto Wahnon de Carvalho Veiga of the MPD in the second round. The PAICV also captured a majority in the legislative elections that had been held a month earlier. The January 2006 legislative elections had a similar outcome, with the PAICV taking 41 of the 72 seats, and the MPD placing second with 29. Pires won a new five-year mandate in the February presidential election. While Veiga claimed that the results were fraudulent, they were endorsed by international observers.

In June 2007, the legislature unanimously passed new electoral code provisions aimed at strengthening the National Electoral Commission's transparency and independence.

In the February 2011 legislative elections, the PAICV secured 38 seats, while the MPD garnered 32, and the Democratic and Independent Cape Verdean Union (UCID)—a smaller opposition party—took 2. However, in the August presidential election, former foreign minister Jose Carlos Fonseca of the MPD defeated Manuel Sousa of the PAICV, claiming 54 percent of the vote in a second-round runoff. International observers declared both elections to be free and fair. Subsequently, Fonseca and Prime Minister José Maria das Neves of the PAICV promised to put aside their political differences and work together to ensure Cape Verde's stability and increased prosperity.

In January 2012, Cape Verde held its second municipal elections since the new electoral code was instituted. The MPD won 14 of 22 municipalities, 2 more than in 2008; the PAICV in turn lost 2 city councils and had to settle for a total of 8. An independent movement supported by the MPD won the remaining city council. The MPD's strong performance confirmed the PAICV's decline in popularity.

Services, particularly tourism, dominate the economy, representing nearly 80 percent of the gross domestic product. As a result of persistent droughts, the country experienced heavy emigration in the second half of the 20th century, and Cape Verde's expatriate population is greater than its domestic population; remittances therefore continue to be a major source of wealth. While the United Nations raised Cape Verde out of the least developed countries category in 2008, the country's official unemployment rate is still around 11 percent, and there is significant income inequality.

Political Rights and Civil Liberties: Cape Verde is an electoral democracy. The president and members of the 72-seat National Assembly are elected by universal suffrage for five-year terms. The prime minister is nominated by the National Assembly and appointed by the president.

Cape Verde received the second-highest ranking for governance performance in the 2012 Ibrahim Index of African Governance. However, in a recent survey of Cape

Verdeans, the police and city council members were deemed to be corrupt by 17 and 85 percent of those interviewed, respectively. Cape Verde was ranked 39 out of 176 countries in Transparency International's 2012 Corruption Perceptions Index.

While government authorization is needed to publish newspapers and other periodicals, freedom of the press is guaranteed in law and generally respected in practice. The independent press is small but vigorous, and there are several private and community-run radio stations. State-run media include radio and television stations. The government does not impede or monitor internet access.

According to the 2011 U.S. Department of State's International Religious Freedom Report, there were no societal or governmental incidents of religious intolerance, and the constitution requires the separation of church and state. However, the vast majority of Cape Verdeans belong to the Roman Catholic Church, which enjoys a somewhat privileged status. Academic freedom is respected.

Freedoms of assembly and association are legally guaranteed and observed in practice. Nongovernmental organizations operate freely. The constitution also protects the right to unionize, and workers may form and join unions without restriction. Approximately a quarter of the workforce is unionized, but collective bargaining is reportedly rare.

Cape Verde's judiciary is independent. However, the capacity and efficiency of the courts are limited, and lengthy pretrial detention remains a problem. In 2010, Cape Verde signed the Dakar Initiative to fight trafficking by strengthening judicial systems, improving security forces, and increasing international cooperation. In 2011, Interpol agreed to work on a permanent basis with Cape Verdean authorities. In June 2012, Cape Verde's attorney general declared that "money laundering" was on the rise, along with an increase in drug trafficking.

Ethnic divisions are not a salient problem in Cape Verde, although there are tensions between the authorities and West African immigrants. Work conditions for undocumented migrants in the country are often dire.

While discrimination based on gender is legally prohibited, problems such as violence against women and inequalities in the areas of education and employment persist. To address these issues, the government has adopted a series of legislative reforms, including a 2010 law criminalizing gender violence and a National Action Plan to fight gender violence (2009–11). The gender issue was declared to be one of the four main elements of the government program for 2011–16.

Central African Republic

Political Rights: 5
Civil Liberties: 5
Status: Partly Free

Population: 4,576,000
Capital: Bangui

Trend Arrow: The Central African Republic received a downward trend arrow due to the takeover of more than half of the country by rebel forces and curtailed freedoms of expression and assembly in rebel-held areas.

Ten-Year Ratings Timeline For Year Under Review (Political Rights, Civil Liberties, Status)

2003	2004	2005	2006	2007	2008	2009	2010	2011	2012
7,5NF	6,5NF	5,5NF	5,4PF	5,5PF	5,5PF	5,5PF	5,5PF	5,5PF	5,5PF

Overview: Insecurity continued to plague much of the country during 2012. After the last major rebel group, the Convention of Patriots for Justice and Peace, signed a peace treaty with the government in August, efforts were made toward rehabilitating and disarming all rebel groups. However, on December 10 a coalition of rebel factions launched an offensive and took control of large areas of the country. As of December 31, rebel attacks and advances toward the capital continued.

The Central African Republic (CAR) gained independence from France in 1960 after a period of brutal colonial exploitation. General André Kolingba deposed President David Dacko in 1981. Mounting political pressure led Kolingba to introduce a multiparty system in 1991, and Ange-Félix Patassé was elected president in 1993. With French assistance, he survived three attempted coups between 1996 and 1997. French forces were replaced by African peacekeepers in 1997, and the United Nations took over peacekeeping duties in 1998. Patassé won a second six-year term in 1999, and UN peacekeepers withdrew in 1999. Patassé was ousted by General François Bozizé in 2003, allegedly with backing from President Idriss Déby of Chad.

Bozizé initiated a transition to civilian rule, and voters approved a new constitution in 2004. With the backing of the National Convergence Kwa Na Kwa (KNK) coalition, Bozizé won a May 2005 presidential runoff. The KNK and its allies won a majority in the National Assembly.

Between 2005 and 2007, several major rebellions were launched by groups such as the Popular Army for the Restoration of the Republic and Democracy (APRD), the Union of Democratic Forces for Unity (UFDR), and the Central African People's Democratic Front (FDPC). An estimated 200,000 Central Africans were internally displaced or fled to neighboring countries due to the fighting.

After a series of failed attempts, a Comprehensive Peace Agreement was signed between the government, the UFDR, and the APRD in June 2008. The National Assembly passed a law in September providing government and rebel forces with immunity for abuses committed after March 15, 2003. The Inclusive Political Dialogue, which was held between the government, the opposition, and rebel groups in December, established an interim government until 2010 elections, and outlined a disarmament, demobilization, and reintegration (DDR) program. By December 2009, all rebel groups except the Convention of Patriots for Justice and Peace (CPJP) were participating in the peace process, but the demobilization of these groups has been slow and partial.

Presidential and legislative elections were held in January 2011 after being delayed twice the previous year. Bozizé, with the backing of the KNK, won the presidential poll, defeating four candidates with 66 percent of the vote. His closest challenger, Patassé, captured 20 percent. Opposition leaders and candidates challenged the result, which were upheld by the Constitutional Court, but revised down to 64 percent. The KNK won 63 out of the 105 seats in concurrent National Assembly elections. The polls were considered free, and security officers did not intimidate voters as they had in previous elections. However, the opposition criticized both elections as unfair, citing fictitious and displaced polling stations, problematic electoral rolls, and numbers on voting cards not matching those in voting station rolls.

In June 2011, the CPJP signed a ceasefire with the government, although it engaged in clashes with UFDR rebels over control of the diamond trade. The two rebel groups agreed to a ceasefire in October. The CPJP and the government signed a peace deal in August 2012. During 2012, the government increased its efforts to disarm rebel groups as part of the DDR program, with about half of the APRD rebels participating in a program that gave them the option of joining the military or special civilian programs; the CPJP also agreed to participate as part of the peace accord. Separately, a Chadian rebel group operating in northern CAR surrendered and began to return to Chad in October, signaling an important step toward security in the area. However, the Lord's Resistance Army, a Ugandan rebel group, continued to carry out attacks in the CAR in 2012, including a September assault on an army convoy that killed one soldier and a raid on a village in which 55 people—including at least 25 girls—were abducted.

An offshoot of the CPJP formed its own rebel group—the Fundamental CPJP—and attacked three cities in September. While those attacks were repelled, a new rebel alliance, called Seleka, seized three towns in the north on December 10. Seleka had been created in August and was made up of a faction of the UFDR; the Fundamental CPJP; and a lesser-known group, the Convention of Patriots for Salvation and Kodro. The alliance demanded the proper implementation of the 2007 accords, including payments for demobilized rebels fighters and releases of prisoners. The group advanced quickly toward Bangui, and by December 31, only the town of Damara stood between the rebels and the capital.

In response to the swift rebel advance and lack of government control over large areas of the country, representatives from the Economic Community of Central African States (ECCAS) agreed at a meeting in Gabon on December 28 to send a multinational force to the CAR, in addition to the 560 troops already in the country. The size and timing of this force had yet to be specified as of the end of 2012. Meanwhile, the Chadian government pledged a force of 2,000 soldiers; an unknown number were already in the CAR. However, they have not engaged with the rebels, and withdrew with the CAR army as the rebels advanced toward Bangui.

Decades of conflict and poor governance have led to economic and social collapse in the CAR. The country was ranked 180 out of 186 countries in the UN

Development Programme's 2012 Human Development Index. However, according to the International Monetary Fund, the economy recovered slightly in 2012.

Political Rights and Civil Liberties: The CAR is not an electoral democracy. The 2011 presidential and parliamentary elections were marked by irregularities and criticized by opposition candidates as unfair. The president, who is elected for a five-year term and eligible for a second term, appoints the cabinet and dominates the legislative and judicial branches. However, with the December 2012 rebel offensive, the government of President François Bozizé effectively lost control over much of the country. Members of the unicameral, 105-seat National Assembly are elected by popular vote for five-year terms.

Though the KNK coalition is the country's leading political force, other parties operate freely. However, the government sometimes withheld approval for meetings of political opposition groups in 2012.

Corruption remains pervasive, despite some steps toward reform in recent years. Diamonds account for about half of the country's export earnings, but a large percentage circumvent official channels. The CAR was ranked 144 of 176 countries surveyed in Transparency International's 2012 Corruption Perceptions Index.

The government generally respects the right to free speech, but many journalists practice self-censorship. It is illegal to broadcast information that is "false" or that could incite ethnic or religious tension. The state dominates the broadcast media, but private radio stations exist. Several private newspapers offer competing views, though they have limited influence due to low literacy levels and high poverty rates. There are no government restrictions on the internet, but the vast majority of the population is unable to access it. However, with the security situation declining as a result of the rebel advance in December, the movement of journalists and their ability to report was severely limited.

The constitution guarantees religious freedom. However, the government prohibits activities that it considers subversive or fundamentalist, and the constitution bans the formation of religious-based parties. Academic freedom is generally respected.

Freedoms of assembly and association are constitutionally protected and generally upheld in practice. However, permission is required to hold public meetings and demonstrations, and authorities sometimes deny such requests on the grounds that they could stoke ethnic or religious tensions. Due to the rebel attacks in December, freedom of assembly was effectively curtailed as a result of the security situation. The rights to unionize and strike are constitutionally protected and generally respected, though only a small percentage of workers are unionized.

Corruption, political interference, and lack of training undermine the judiciary. The president appoints judges and proceedings are prone to executive influence. Limitations on police searches and detention are often ignored. While the penal code prohibits torture, police brutality remains a serious problem. The military and members of the presidential guard continue to commit human rights abuses, including extrajudicial killings, with impunity. Prison conditions are poor.

Insecurity restricts the movement of citizens and greatly undermines the protection of private property. The Office of the UN High Commissioner for Refugees estimated the number of internally displaced persons at 105,200, the number of refugees in the CAR at 16,730, and the number of Central African refugees abroad at 162,800.

Constitutional guarantees for women's rights are not enforced, especially in rural areas. There is no specific law criminalizing domestic abuse, which is widespread, and there is a high incidence of sexual violence against women by state and nonstate actors. Abortion is prohibited in all circumstances. Women were elected to only 13 percent of the seats in the National Assembly in 2011. The U.S. State Department's 2012 Trafficking in Persons Report put the CAR in Tier 3 for the second year in a row, as a result of the ongoing trafficking of children for forced labor and sexual exploitation, as well as their use in armed conflict.

Chad

Political Rights: 7
Civil Liberties: 6
Status: Not Free

Population: 11,831,000
Capital: N'Djamena

Ten-Year Ratings Timeline For Year Under Review (Political Rights, Civil Liberties, Status)

2003	2004	2005	2006	2007	2008	2009	2010	2011	2012
6,5NF	6,5NF	6,5NF	6,6NF	7,6NF	7,6NF	7,6NF	7,6NF	7,6NF	7,6NF

Overview: **The security situation in Chad continued to improve in 2012, although bandit and rebel attacks persisted. In September, leader of the Popular Front for Recovery rebel group surrendered to the government. Judicial harassment of political opponents and inhumane prison conditions remain rampant. A drought and rising global food prices have left Chad facing a severe food crisis.**

Since gaining independence from France in 1960, Chad has been beset by civil conflict and rebellions. Hissène Habré seized control in 1982 and led a one-party dictatorship characterized by widespread atrocities against individuals and ethnic groups seen as threats to the regime. In 1989, Idriss Déby, a military commander, launched a rebellion against Habré, ousting him in 1990 with support from Libya and no opposition from French troops stationed in Chad.

Déby won a presidential election held under a new constitution in 1996 despite the ongoing threat of rebel violence. In 1997 legislative elections, his Patriotic Salvation Movement (MPS) party won 65 of the 125 seats. International observers charged that both elections were marred by irregularities.

Déby was reelected in 2001, and the six opposition candidates were briefly detained for alleging that the election results were fraudulent. The MPS secured 113 seats in the enlarged, 155-seat National Assembly during the 2002 legislative elections, which were boycotted by several opposition parties. Voters approved the elimination of presidential term limits in a 2005 constitutional referendum, though the balloting was marred by irregularities and the government cracked down on the media during the campaign.

Security forces, assisted by French intelligence and air support, repelled an April 2006 attack on N'Djamena by the United Front for Change (FUC) rebel group. The

May presidential election was held on schedule despite an opposition boycott, and Déby secured a third term. The military launched a new assault on eastern-based rebel forces in September, and in November the government declared a six-month state of emergency, including a ban on media coverage of sensitive issues. In February 2008, some 2,000 rebel fighters attacked the capital. Although the two sides soon agreed on a ceasefire and the rebels withdrew, Déby declared another state of emergency, suspending due process rights and tightening already harsh media restrictions. Human rights groups accused the regime of extrajudicial detention and killing of suspected rebels, their supporters, and members of the Goran ethnic group, some of whom had been involved in the rebel assault. The state of emergency was lifted on March 15, but fighting continued in the east during the year.

Déby and Sudanese president Omar al-Bashir had long traded accusations over support for rebels in each other's territory. In May 2009, the Chadian and Sudanese governments signed the latest of several accords aimed at normalizing relations. However, shortly thereafter, the Union of Resistance Forces (UFR)—an alliance of eight rebel groups—launched an attack on Chad from its base in Sudan's war-torn western Darfur region. Violence along the border increased over the subsequent months, and in July Chadian planes bombed targets in Darfur.

In April 2010, government forces clashed with the rebel Popular Front for National Resistance near Tissi, reportedly killing more than 100 fighters. In May, former defense minister Mahamat Nouri announced the formation of the rebel the National Alliance for Democratic Change.

Relations between Sudan and Chad improved significantly in 2010, starting with a January agreement that led to a series of presidential visits. In February, the governments established a joint patrol of 3,000 troops along the border. Authorities reopened the border to civilian traffic in April after it had been closed for seven years. In May, Chad prohibited the head of a leading Darfur rebel group, the Justice and Equality Movement, from returning to Sudan. Meanwhile, the Sudanese authorities pressured Chadian rebel groups to leave Sudan. In October 2011, a reported 171 UFR fighters returned to Chad from Darfur.

In February 2011, after years of delay, parliamentary elections were held, the first in which opposition parties participated. In the enlarged, 188-seat National Assembly, Déby's MPS party won 117 seats, and 14 more went to Déby's allies, securing an absolute majority for the president. The most successful opposition party won only 10 seats. Citing irregularities before and during the parliamentary elections, the three main opposition candidates boycotted the presidential poll in April, which Déby won with 89 percent of the vote. The Independent Electoral Commission (CENI) reported voter participation at 64 percent, though African Union observers said the turnout was much lower.

The security situation in Chad improved significantly in 2012, despite bandit attacks across the country. In September 2012, Abdel Kader Baba-Laddé, the leader of the Popular Front for Recovery (FPR) rebel group, surrendered from his base in Central African Republic and returned to Chad; the two countries had launched an offensive against the group in January. In October, 150 FPR rebels surrendered to the government, part of a plan to repatriate about 3,000 followers of Baba-Laddé.

After years of regular fighting in the region, by the end of 2012 Chad had become home to some 90,000 internally displaced persons (IDPs), 91,000 returned

IDPs, and an estimated 345,000 refugees from Darfur and the Central African Republic, according to the Office of the UN High Commissioner for Refugees. After the return of 91,000 IDPs to their areas of origin, further returns stalled in 2012 due to instabilities in Sudan and the Central African Republic.

The United Nations has warned of an impending famine in Chad due to a drought and rising global food prices; the situation is expected to worsen as thousands of migrant workers return from Libya and overseas remittances decrease.

Political Rights and Civil Liberties: Chad is not an electoral democracy. The country has never experienced a free and fair transfer of power through elections. The president is elected for five-year terms, and a 2005 constitutional amendment abolished term limits. The executive branch dominates the judicial and legislative branches, and the president appoints the prime minister. The unicameral National Assembly consists of 188 members elected for four-year terms.

Legislative elections due in 2006 were repeatedly postponed due to insufficient equipment and staffing, as well as delays in voter registration, but finally took place in February 2011. The European Union praised the peaceful and fair conduct of the elections, despite some logistical problems. However, the opposition claimed that irregularities occurred both before the vote—due to the government's media dominance and the use of state resources to benefit the ruling party—and during the elections, including issues with electoral rolls and voter registration cards. They also pointed to CENI's official results page, which showed irregularities. A request by opposition parties to reprint voter registration cards was rejected.

There are more than 70 political parties operating in Chad, although a number of them were created by the government to divide the opposition. Only the ruling MPS has significant influence. Despite rivalries within Déby's northeastern Zaghawa ethnic group, members of that and other northern ethnic groups continue to control Chad's political and economic systems, causing resentment among the country's more than 200 other ethnic groups.

Corruption is rampant within Déby's inner circle. Despite becoming an oil producer in 2003, Chad remains one of the world's poorest nations. Weaknesses in revenue management and oversight facilitate the diversion of oil revenues from national development projects to private interests and growing military expenditures. Chad was ranked 165 out of 176 countries surveyed in Transparency International's 2012 Corruption Perceptions Index.

The constitution provides for freedom of the press and expression. However, both are severely restricted, and self-censorship is common. Broadcast media are controlled by the state. The High Council of Communication (HCC) exerts control over most content on the radio—the most important means of mass communication—and while there are roughly a dozen private stations, they face high licensing fees and the threat of closure for critical coverage. In 2008, the HCC banned reporting on the activities of rebels or any other information that could harm national unity. A small number of private newspapers circulate in the capital, and internet access is not restricted, but the reach of both is limited by poverty, illiteracy, and inadequate infrastructure. In August 2010, the National Assembly passed a media bill that eliminated imprisonment as a punishment for libel, slander, or insulting the president, but created sentences of heavy fines or prison time for inciting racial and ethnic hatred and "condoning violence." However, in September 2012, Jean-Claude Nekim, editor of the biweekly *N'Djamena Bi-Hebdo*, was convicted of criminal defamation for publishing parts of a trade union's petition that was critical of the government. Nekim received a 12-month suspended prison sentence and a fine of 1 million CFA francs (US$2,000), and *N'Djamena Bi-Hebdo* was banned for three months.

Although Chad is a secular state, religion is a divisive force. Muslims, who make up slightly more than half of the population, hold a disproportionately large number of senior government posts, and some policies favor Islam in practice. At the same time, the authorities have banned Muslim groups that are seen as promoting violence. The government does not restrict academic freedom, but funds meant for the education system have reportedly been lost to corruption. In November 2011, University of N'Djamena students protesting failed payment of their grants clashed with police in the capital, resulting in 150 arrests and injuries to 9 officers.

Despite the constitutional guarantee of free assembly, the authorities ban demonstrations by groups thought to be critical of the government. In September 2011, Amnesty International issued a report condemning the arrest of two students for allegedly planning proreform protests and demanding investigation into allegations of torture during their time in custody. The constitution guarantees the rights to strike and unionize, but a 2007 law imposed new limits on public sector workers' right to strike. Despite those limits, public sector workers went on strike for three weeks in the fall of 2011 and in July 2012, demanding promised wage increases. Both protests ended with deals with the government.

The rule of law and the judicial system remain weak, and the courts are heavily influenced by the political leadership. According to Amnesty International, judicial harassment of political opponents was frequent throughout 2012. Civilian leaders do not maintain control of the security forces, which routinely ignore constitutional protections regarding search, seizure, and detention. Human rights groups credibly accuse the security forces and rebel groups of killing and torturing with impunity. Prison conditions are inhumane, and many inmates are held for years without charge. In July 2012, the Senegalese government agreed to establish a special court to try former Chadian president Hissène Habré—who has been living in exile in Senegal—for political killings and torture committed during his rule. Senegal's long-awaited decision came after an International Court of Justice ruling earlier that month that it either try Habré or extradite him to Belgium.

Clashes are common between Christian farmers of the various southern ethnic groups and Muslim Arab groups living largely in the north. Turmoil linked to ethnic and religious differences is exacerbated by clan rivalries and external interference along the insecure borders. Communal tensions in eastern Chad have worsened due to the proliferation of small arms and ongoing disputes over the use of land and water resources.

The government restricts the movement of citizens within the country. Insecurity has severely hindered the activities of humanitarian organizations in recent years. Despite relative stability during 2011 and 2012, recurrent bandit attacks on humanitarian workers make access to the population difficult.

Chadian women face widespread discrimination and violence. Twelve of the

188 National Assembly members, or about 12 percent, are women. Female genital mutilation is illegal, but routinely practiced by several ethnic groups. Chad is a source, transit, and destination country for child trafficking, and the government has not made significant efforts to eliminate the problem. The U.S. State Department again placed Chad on the Tier 2 Watch List in its 2012 Trafficking in Persons Report.

Chile

Political Rights: 1
Civil Liberties: 1
Status: Free

Population: 17,403,000
Capital: Santiago

Ten-Year Ratings Timeline For Year Under Review (Political Rights, Civil Liberties, Status)

2003	2004	2005	2006	2007	2008	2009	2010	2011	2012
1,1F	2,1F	1,1F	1,1F	1,1F	1,1F	1,1F	1,1F	1,1F	1,1F

Overview: **President Sebastián Piñera of the center-right Coalition for Change continued in 2012 to struggle with student demonstrations that brought much of the country to a halt the previous summer. Student demands for universal free higher education were not placated by the administration's moderate policy response. Tensions between Chile's Mapuche Indians and the government escalated in response to a series of devastating forest fires in January. In May, Congress passed a landmark antidiscrimination law.**

The Republic of Chile was founded after independence from Spain in 1818. Democratic rule predominated in the 20th century until 1973, when General Augusto Pinochet led a military coup against President Salvador Allende. An estimated 3,000 people were killed or "disappeared" under Pinochet's regime. The 1980 constitution provided for a plebiscite in which voters could bar another presidential term for the general. When the poll was held in 1988, some 55 percent of voters rejected eight more years of military rule, and competitive presidential and legislative elections were scheduled for the following year. Christian Democrat Patricio Aylwin of the center-left bloc Concertación (Coalition of Parties for Democracy) won the presidential vote, ushering in an era of regular democratic power transfers as well as two decades of Concertación rule.

In the first step in what would become a years-long effort to hold Pinochet responsible for his regime's human rights atrocities, the former leader was detained in London in 1998 under an extradition order from Spain. After being released for health reasons in 2000, he returned to Chile, where he was eventually indicted in 2004 for tax evasion and two outstanding human rights cases. A September 2006 Supreme Court decision cleared the way for his trial, but Pinochet died in December of that year.

Michelle Bachelet, who served as health and defense minister under the outgoing Concertación president, won the 2006 presidential election. Bachelet presided over popular spending projects, including the construction of new hospitals, homes, and nursery schools.

Sebastián Piñera of the center-right Coalition for Change was elected president in January 2010. The new administration was challenged by a massive earthquake that struck Chile in late February, but Piñera was able to carry out effective reconstruction due to the nation's sound public finances. The government also assumed full control over the rescue of 33 miners who were trapped by accident in a gold and copper mine in northern Chile in August. Their successful rescue 69 days later boosted Piñera's popularity as well as Chile's international image. In response to the incident, Chile ratified an International Labour Organization convention in April 2011 on occupational safety and health.

Piñera's popularity was short lived; massive student protests and strikes began in April 2011, developing into one of Chile's most intractable political problems in decades, with hundreds of thousands of students taking to the streets. The students demanded a major overhaul of the country's largely privatized education system, including free public college education. Although the Piñera administration responded by replacing the education minister in 2011 and promising increased spending on education, demonstrations continued into 2012. Tax reforms adopted in September 2012 raised corporate tax levels and closed loopholes in order to finance increased education funding; education spending will increase to $12.8 billion in 2013, up from $7.9 billion in 2009. The plan will also finance increased scholarships for higher education and reduce the annual interest rate on all student loans from 6 percent to 2 percent. Meanwhile, the government was criticized for its handling of the protests, including claims of illegal detention and torture of student protestors and journalists, and Piñera's approval rating hovered between 25 percent and 30 percent for much of the year.

Political Rights and Civil Liberties: Chile is an electoral democracy. The president is elected for a single four-year term. The Senate's 38 members serve eight-year terms, with half up for election every four years, and the 120-member Chamber of Deputies is elected for four years. In 2005, the Senate passed reforms that repealed some of the last vestiges of military rule, ending authoritarian curbs on the legislative branch and restoring the president's right to remove top military commanders. Municipal elections held in October 2012 were considered free and fair.

The major political groupings in Chile include the center-left Concertación, composed of the Christian Democratic Party, the Socialist Party, the Party for Democracy, and the Social Democratic Radical Party; the center-right Alliance coalition, consisting of the Independent Democratic Union and the National Renewal party; and the Communist Party. The Coalition for Change, encompassing the Alliance coalition, independents, and some Concertación defectors, was formed in 2009. Congress passed significant transparency and campaign finance laws in 2003 that contributed to Chile's reputation for good governance. A 2007 law further improved transparency by offering protections for public employees who expose corruption. Chile was ranked 20 out of 176 countries surveyed in Transparency International's 2012 Corruption Perceptions Index.

Guarantees of free speech are generally respected, though some laws barring defamation of state institutions remain on the books. The print media are dominated by two right-leaning companies, but the television market is considered highly diverse. A freedom of information law enacted in 2008 was praised by civil society groups. However, in 2012, many members of the press were detained and harassed by the police while covering student protests. There are no government restrictions on the internet.

The constitution provides for freedom of religion, and the government generally upholds this right in practice. The government does not restrict academic freedom.

The rights to form nongovernmental organizations and to assemble peacefully are largely respected. Although the government regularly granted permits for the student demonstrations beginning in 2011, police allegedly used excessive force against protesters. Despite laws protecting worker and union rights, antiunion practices by private employers are reportedly common.

The constitution provides for an independent judiciary, and the courts are generally free from political interference. The right to legal counsel is constitutionally guaranteed, but indigent defendants have not always received effective representation. Over 75 percent of the some 3,000 documented "disappearances" under military rule have been heard by courts or were under court jurisdiction by the end of 2012. Further, Chilean courts have convicted hundreds of military officers of committing heinous crimes during military rule, though sentences have tended to be lenient.

The government has developed effective mechanisms to investigate and punish police abuse and corruption. However, excessive force and human rights abuses committed by the Carabineros—a national police element of the armed forces—still occur. In August 2012, the Carabineros allegedly used excessive force against members of the Mapuche indigenous community when breaking up a land occupation. Chile's prisons are overcrowded and increasingly violent. Inmates suffer from physical abuse as well as substandard medical and food services.

A bill that would remove a relic of the former regime—the Copper Reserve Law—which obliged the state-owned copper producer Codelco to transfer 10 percent of its earnings to the military was introduced in early 2010. Public support for stopping the automatic military transfer increased after the massive reconstruction costs resulting from the February 2010 earthquake. The lower house unanimously voted to end the copper law in July 2012; it awaited Senate approval at year's end.

Approximately 1 million Chileans identify themselves with indigenous ethnic groups. While they still experience societal discrimination, their poverty levels are declining, aided by government scholarships, land transfers, and social spending. A 1993 law officially recognized the Mapuche and paved the way for the return of their land, but rather than appeasing the Mapuche, it prompted additional land claims, land seizures, and violence. Over 30 Mapuche accused of such attacks participated in an extended hunger strike in 2010, which prompted a change to Chile's antiterrorism law. The law, which dated to the Augusto Pinochet era, had allowed for secret witnesses, pretrial detention, and the use of military courts in trying Mapuches accused of employing arson and other violent means to reclaim ancestral lands. As amended by Congress in September 2010, the new law presumes innocence and carries a reduced sentence for arson. However, in a worrisome development, President Sebastián Piñera invoked the old antiterrorism laws to pursue the perpetrator of a spate of forest fires allegedly started by Mapuche activists in January 2012.

The "Plan Araucanía"—a development plan for the southern Araucanía area, one of Chile's poorest regions and the homeland of the Mapuche—was implemented in August 2012. The plan financed construction of new schools and hospitals, funded the building of new roads, and provided financial support to victims of violence.

President Michelle Bachelet made great strides to reduce gender discrimination, including appointing women to half of the positions in her cabinet. She also enacted new laws to increase women's labor rights and to eliminate the gender pay gap. However, violence against women and children remains a problem. The Piñera administration passed landmark legislation in 2011 banning all types of human trafficking for the purpose of labor or sexual exploitation. Congress passed an antidiscrimination law in May 2012 that had been stalled in the legislature for seven years; its swift approval was prompted by the brutal beating and subsequent death of a gay man in Santiago in March 2012. The new law allows people to file antidiscrimination lawsuits, and includes hate crime sentences for violent crimes.

China

Political Rights: 7
Civil Liberties: 6
Status: Not Free

Population: 1,350,378,000
Capital: Beijing

Note: The numerical ratings and status listed above do not reflect conditions in Hong Kong or Tibet, which are examined in separate reports.

Ten-Year Ratings Timeline For Year Under Review (Political Rights, Civil Liberties, Status)

2003	2004	2005	2006	2007	2008	2009	2010	2011	2012
7,6NF	7,6NF	7,6NF	7,6NF	7,6NF	7,6NF	7,6NF	7,6NF	7,6NF	7,6NF

Overview: At its 18th Congress in November 2012, the Chinese Communist Party announced a new slate of leaders for the next five years. Conservative figures made up a majority of the new Politburo Standing Committee, which would be headed by general secretary Xi Jinping. The delicate leadership transition had been disrupted in February, when a subordinate of Politburo member Bo Xilai fled to a U.S. consulate, setting off China's biggest political scandal in years. The subsequent months were marked by intense political wrangling, Bo's expulsion from the party, his wife's conviction for the murder of a British businessman, and a nationwide clampdown on activists. After the party congress, the new leadership pledged to strengthen anticorruption efforts, but also imposed tighter internet censorship and surveillance. Despite the regime's hostility toward organized dissent, however, a growing number of Chinese asserted basic rights, shared uncensored information online, and challenged perceived injustice, sometimes forcing government concessions. Key dissidents who had been silenced for much of 2011 as part of a crackdown in the wake of the Arab Spring were more vocal during 2012, adding to society's pushback against official repression.

The Chinese Communist Party (CCP) took power in mainland China in 1949. Party leader Mao Zedong subsequently oversaw devastating collectivist and ideological-purification campaigns, such as the Great Leap Forward (1958–61) and the Cultural Revolution (1966–76), which resulted in tens of millions of deaths.

Following Mao's death in 1976, Deng Xiaoping emerged as paramount leader. Over the next two decades, he maintained the CCP's absolute rule in the political sphere while relaxing ideological controls and launching widespread economic and social reforms.

The CCP signaled its resolve to avoid democratization with the deadly 1989 military assault on prodemocracy protesters in Beijing's Tiananmen Square and surrounding areas. Jiang Zemin was named CCP general secretary later in 1989 and state president in 1993. He became China's top leader following Deng's death in 1997. Jiang continued Deng's policy of rapid economic growth, but maintained a hard line in the political sphere.

Hu Jintao succeeded Jiang as CCP general secretary in 2002, state president in 2003, and head of the military in 2004. Many observers expected Hu and Premier Wen Jiabao to implement modest political reforms to address pressing socioeconomic problems. However, particularly during their second term, the CCP intensified repressive measures in response to citizen activism and perceived threats to its authority. In March 2008, Shanghai party chief Xi Jinping was appointed vice president, setting the stage for him to succeed Hu.

The CCP's next leadership transition, set to be finalized at the 18th party congress in late 2012, was unexpectedly upset in February of that year, when Chongqing police chief Wang Lijun fled to the U.S. consulate in Chengdu, setting off China's biggest political scandal in years. Wang, who left the consulate after 24 hours and was taken into custody by central authorities, reportedly made a number of criminal allegations against Chongqing party secretary Bo Xilai, a contender for a seat on the Politburo Standing Committee (PSC). Over the following months, Bo was expelled from the party, and his allies in the CCP's neo-Maoist wing fell out of favor amid intense political wrangling. At the party congress in November, conservative figures emerged with a majority on the new PSC. Xi became CCP general secretary, and Li Keqiang was named as his deputy; in March 2013, the pair will become state president and premier, respectively.

Despite CCP hostility toward organized dissent, a growing number of Chinese took steps to assert basic rights and combat perceived injustice. Millions of people joined public protests, online campaigns, and collective petitions to challenge local-level abuses of power, arbitrary detention of fellow citizens, corruption, and pollution, sometimes forcing government concessions.

In response, the party committed more resources to internal security forces and intelligence agencies, enhanced controls over online social media, and increased societal surveillance. Some observers expressed concerns about the destabilizing effect of the CCP's reluctance to end repressive policies and institute reforms that would fundamentally address citizen grievances. Conditions in Tibet and Xinjiang, both home to restive ethnic and religious minorities, remained highly repressive in 2012.

China's economy grew at the slowest rate since 1999, though it appeared to be rebounding at year's end. Also during 2012, China asserted its territorial claims over islands in the South and East China Seas more aggressively, souring relations with several neighboring countries. Meanwhile, the regime's mistreatment of human rights defenders drew international attention in April, when blind activist Chen Guangcheng made a daring escape from extralegal house arrest to the U.S. embassy in Beijing. Following negotiations, Chen was permitted to travel to New York for legal studies.

Political Rights and Civil Liberties: China is not an electoral democracy. The CCP has a monopoly on political power, and its Politburo Standing Committee (PSC) sets government and party policy. In November 2012, a new PSC was announced following an opaque, internal selection process. The committee shrank from nine to seven members, only two of whom—new CCP general secretary Xi Jinping and his deputy, Li Keqiang—had served on the previous panel. Party members—who number over 80 million—hold almost all top posts in the government, military, and internal security services, as well as in many economic entities and social organizations. The country's legislature, the 3,000-member National People's Congress (NPC), is elected for five-year terms by subnational congresses, formally elects the state president for up to two five-year terms, and confirms the premier after he is nominated by the president. However, the NPC is a largely symbolic body. Only its standing committee meets regularly, while the full congress convenes for just two weeks a year to approve proposed legislation.

Citizens who attempt to form opposition parties or advocate for democratic reforms have been sentenced to long prison terms in recent years. In January 2012, Li Tie of Hubei Province was sentenced to 10 years in prison for being a member of the China Social Democracy Party and for his online writings. In October, Cao Haibo of Yunnan Province was sentenced to eight years for starting online discussion groups about a possible political party. Democracy advocate and 2010 Nobel Peace Prize winner Liu Xiaobo remained behind bars in 2012, having been sentenced in 2009 to 11 years in prison. His wife, Liu Xia, was under strict house arrest throughout the year. In addition to democracy advocates, tens of thousands of grassroots activists, petitioners, Falun Gong practitioners, Christians, Tibetans, and Uighurs are believed to be in prison or extrajudicial forms of detention for their political or religious views, although complete figures are unavailable. In October, the U.S. Congressional-Executive Commission on China published a partial list of over 1,400 political prisoners. The rights group Chinese Human Rights Defenders documented 3,833 cases of arbitrary detention of human rights defenders during 2011, of which some 86 percent apparently had no basis in Chinese law.

Corruption remains endemic despite increased government antigraft efforts, and top party leaders acknowledged growing public resentment over the issue in 2012. Thousands of officials are investigated and punished each year by government or CCP entities, but prosecution is selective and highly opaque, with informal personal networks and internal CCP power struggles influencing both the choice of targets and the outcomes. During 2012, dozens of lower- and mid-level officials were disciplined, demoted, dismissed, or prosecuted after bloggers and journalists exposed evidence of corruption online. The highest-level targets in 2012 were former Chongqing party chief Bo Xilai, charged with bribery in September, and Sichuan Province deputy party secretary Li Chuncheng, who was dismissed in December for influence peddling and questionable real-estate deals. Investigations by Bloomberg News and the *New York Times* found that the family members of Xi Jinping and outgoing premier Wen Jiabao held assets worth $376 million and $2.7 billion, respectively, raising questions about corruption and conflict of interest. However, the reports were suppressed in China, and both outlets' websites were blocked shortly after the articles' publication.

CCP officials increasingly seek input from academics and civic groups, though without relinquishing control over the decision-making process. Since open-government regulations took effect in 2008, many agencies have become more forthcoming in publishing official documents. However, implementation has been incomplete, and government bodies retain wide discretion to classify or withhold information, including on vital public matters such as food safety, home demolitions, and environmental disasters. Courts have largely hesitated to enforce information requests, while the poor quality of official responses dampens citizens' initial enthusiasm to lodge complaints. China was ranked 80 out of 176 countries surveyed in Transparency International's 2012 Corruption Perceptions Index.

Despite relative freedom in private discussion and citizen efforts to push the limits of permissible speech, China's media environment remains extremely restrictive. All media are owned, though not always directly operated, by the CCP or the state. Moreover, all news outlets are required to follow regularly issued CCP directives to avoid certain topics or publish content from party mouthpieces. Routinely censored topics include calls for greater autonomy in Tibet and Xinjiang, independence for Taiwan, the 1989 Tiananmen Square crackdown, the persecuted Falun Gong spiritual group, the writings of prominent activists, and critical commentary regarding CCP leaders. Other directives issued in 2012 barred, or "guided," reporting on Chen Guangcheng's escape, certain cases of police brutality and official corruption, and deadly floods in Beijing. Outlets that disobey official guidance risk closure, and journalists face dismissal and sometimes imprisonment. Censorship decisions during the year were often uneven or arbitrary, resulting in information vacuums on major events, fleeting openings on sensitive topics, and intrusive propaganda campaigns surrounding the Bo Xilai scandal and internal CCP power struggles. This uncertainty fueled speculation, online rumors, and increased use of circumvention tools by internet users seeking independent reporting from foreign media. Neo-Maoist programming initiatives piloted in Chongqing under Bo, such as the wholesale replacement of commercial advertisements with propaganda spots on television, were reversed after his ouster, but national media regulators continued to impose new restrictions on television entertainment programs and online video. Pressure on investigative journalism also intensified, as several periodicals and journalists known for their muckraking faced suspension, dismissals, or tighter supervision.

According to international watchdog groups, at least 67 journalists and online activists were behind bars in China in 2012, including many Uighurs and Tibetans, though the actual number was likely much higher. In the latter half of the year, human rights groups recorded dozens of cases of bloggers, petitioners, and free expression activists being displaced or detained in the run-up to the 18th party congress. Nevertheless, the harshness of the crackdown was not as severe as in 2011 in the wake of the Arab Spring, and key activists were more vocal in 2012 than the previous year. Authorities continued to harass prominent artist and blogger Ai Weiwei, who was abducted and held incommunicado for 81 days in 2011. During 2012, he was barred from traveling abroad, his appeal in a politically fraught tax case was rejected, and the license of his art company was revoked.

Harassment and violent assaults against foreign reporters escalated during the year, and their Chinese sources and assistants were intimidated. Two foreign correspondents—Melissa Chan of Al-Jazeera English and Chris Buckley of the *New York Times*—were forced to leave the country after the government refused to renew their visas, while others had difficulty obtaining visas to enter the country. Some international radio and television broadcasts, including the U.S. government–funded Radio Free Asia, remain jammed.

China's population of internet users, estimated at over 530 million in 2012, remained the world's largest. According to official figures, mobile-telephone users exceeded one billion, with approximately one-third accessing the internet via their devices. Alongside growing access, the government maintains an elaborate apparatus for censoring and monitoring internet and mobile-phone communications. The authorities block websites or force the deletion of content they deem politically threatening, and sometimes detain those who post such information. The U.S.-based social media platforms Twitter and Facebook remain blocked. Domestic microblogging services—with over 300 million users in 2012—have grown rapidly in influence as a source of news, an outlet for public opinion, and a tool for mobilization, though the companies in question are obliged to adhere to official censorship directives. Several public outcries and online campaigns in 2012 were credited with forcing government concessions, such as the release of a petitioner from a labor camp, an investigation into a labor activist's death in custody, and upgrades to air quality monitoring in Shanghai. In response to such netizen activity, authorities stepped up pressure on microblogging services to tighten existing controls, and arrests for spreading "rumors" online reportedly increased. The two leading services—Sina Weibo and Tencent—shut down their commenting functions for three days in April, Sina launched a new points-based system to encourage users to self-censor in May, and in December the NPC passed regulations requiring real-name registration for users after implementation of previous rules on the issue proved inadequate.

Religious freedom is sharply curtailed. Religious and ethnic minorities remained a key target of repression in 2012, with several deaths in custody reported. All religious groups must register with the government, which regulates their activities, makes personnel decisions, and guides their theology. Some groups, including certain Buddhist and Christian sects, are forbidden, and their members face harassment, imprisonment, and torture. The CCP continues to devote considerable resources to suppressing the Falun Gong spiritual group and coercing adherents to renounce their beliefs. During the year, authorities abducted practitioners in home raids, sentenced them to labor camps and long prison terms, and punished those who appealed on their behalf. Other unregistered groups, including unofficial Protestant and Roman Catholic congregations, operate in a legal gray zone. State tolerance of them varies from place to place. In April 2012, authorities in Hebei Province raided a house church meeting and detained over 50 people. Most were released, but seven, including the church's preacher, were awaiting criminal sentencing at year's end.

In the Xinjiang Uighur Autonomous Region, an increased security presence that followed ethnic clashes in 2009 remained in place for much of 2012, and many of the hundreds of people detained in 2009 remained imprisoned or unaccounted for. Authorities intensified curbs on Islam in the region, raiding private study sessions and destroying thousands of publications, including copies of the Koran. In May, a court in Kashgar sentenced nine people to between 6 and 15 years in prison for participating in "illegal" religious activities. Policies marginalizing use of the Uighur language in education, government efforts to alter the region's demography through resettlement and work-transfer programs, and displacement linked to destructive "urban renewal" projects in the ancient city of Kashgar continued throughout 2012.

Academic freedom remains restricted with respect to politically sensitive issues. The CCP controls the appointment of university officials, and many scholars practice self-censorship to preserve their positions and personal safety. Political indoctrination is a required component of the curriculum at all levels of education.

Freedoms of assembly and association are severely restricted. Citizens risk punishment for organizing demonstrations without prior government approval, which is rarely granted. Nevertheless, workers, farmers, and urban residents held tens of thousands of protests during 2012, reflecting growing public anger over wrongdoing by officials, especially land confiscation, corruption, pollution, and fatal police beatings. In some cases, officials tolerated demonstrations or agreed to protesters' demands. In July, for example, thousands of people peacefully protested against the construction of a copper plant in Shifang, Sichuan Province. Police responded with tear gas, stun grenades, and beatings. After photographs spread via social media, the authorities announced that they would cancel the project and release detained protesters, though residents expressed fears that the project would resume once attention died down. Local officials face penalties if they fail to limit the flow of petitioners traveling to Beijing to report injustices to the central government. As a result, petitioners are routinely intercepted, harassed, detained in illegal "black jails," or sent to labor camps without trial. Detained petitioners are reportedly subject to beatings, psychological abuse, and sexual violence.

Nongovernmental organizations (NGOs) are required to register, obtain a government sponsoring entity, and follow strict regulations, including vague prohibitions on advocating non-CCP rule, "damaging national unity," or "upsetting ethnic harmony." Hundreds of thousands of charitable organizations operate with government supervision to provide social and educational services. Groups seeking more independence organize informally or register as businesses, though they are vulnerable to closure at any time. While the number of organizations whose work is not politically sensitive continues to expand, restrictions have tightened on human rights advocacy and even previously tolerated activism on issues like public health. At least 10 NGOs assisting migrant workers in Shenzhen, Guangdong Province, were evicted from their offices or forced to close in 2012, despite eased provincial registration rules that took effect in July. Regulations from 2010 that increased obstacles to foreign donations for grassroots NGOs remain in effect.

The only legal labor union is the government-controlled All-China Federation of Trade Unions, and independent labor leaders are harassed and jailed. Collective bargaining is legal but does not occur in practice. Nevertheless, workers have increasingly asserted themselves informally via strikes, collective petitioning, and selection of negotiating representatives. Three 2008 labor laws were designed to protect workers, counter discrimination, and facilitate complaints against employers, while also empowering CCP-controlled unions. However, implementation has been undermined by the lack of independent arbitration bodies, a growing backlog of complaints, and companies' exploitation of loopholes, such as the use of middleman employment agencies, to evade certain safeguards. In December 2012, amendments to the 2008 Labor Contract Law were passed to restrict the use of such agencies. Separately, new regulations that took effect in January required the establishment of mediation committees at all large companies to handle disputes internally, easing pressure on labor tribunals but strengthening the government's role in dispute resolution. Dangerous workplace conditions continue to claim lives, with many tens of thousands of deaths reported each year. Forced labor, including by inmates in "reeducation through labor" camps and juveniles in government-sanctioned "work-study" programs, remains a serious problem.

The CCP controls the judiciary and directs verdicts and sentences, especially in politically sensitive cases. In 2012, this was particularly evident in the opaque proceedings involving Bo Xilai, his wife, and their associates. Bo was held incommunicado after his detention in March, and his case was transferred to prosecutors in October, with charges of abuse of power, bribery, and sexual misconduct. His trial was pending at year's end. His wife, Gu Kailai, received a suspended death sentence for the murder of a British businessman following a one-day show trial in August. In September, former police chief Wang Lijun—whose flight to the U.S. consulate in Chengdu sparked the scandal—was sentenced to 15 years in prison for abuse of power, defection, and corruption. The cases featured blatant disregard for due process, use of the extralegal shuanggui detention system for interrogating party officials in isolation, and other violations of fundamental rights. Prosecutors also failed to pursue Bo and Wang for severe human rights abuses they reportedly oversaw in office, focusing instead on personal misconduct.

Adjudication in minor civil and administrative disputes is fairer than in politically sensitive or criminal cases, but even in commercial litigation and civil suits involving private individuals, previous limited progress toward the rule of law has stalled or been reversed, particularly since the appointment of a CCP veteran with no formal legal training as chief justice in 2008. Judges have increasingly been pressured to resolve civil disputes through mediation, sometimes forced, rather than actual adjudication. The downgrading of the CCP portfolio overseeing the legal system in November 2012, and more progressive wording in an October white paper on judicial reform, sparked speculation on a possible reduction of political control over the judiciary in the coming years.

Civil rights lawyers continued to face restrictions in 2012. Lawyers were prevented from seeing their clients, disbarred, harassed during sensitive times like the 18th party congress, and in some cases imprisoned. In March, relatives confirmed that prominent lawyer Gao Zhisheng was alive after two years of incommunicado detention by security forces, though he remained imprisoned and at severe risk of torture at year's end. In April, self-trained, blind lawyer Chen Guangcheng escaped from extralegal house arrest imposed after he completed a four-year prison term in 2010, having helped victims of forced abortions to file a class-action suit.

Criminal trials in China, which often amount to mere sentencing announcements, are frequently closed to the public, and the conviction rate is estimated at 98 percent. In March 2012, the NPC enacted amendments to the Criminal Procedure Law that will take effect in January 2013. They include improvements for ordinary criminal defendants, including exclusion of evidence obtained through torture, access for lawyers to their clients, and the possibility of witnesses being cross-examined. However, legal experts raised concerns that the revised law features exceptions for cases of "endangering state security," "terrorism," and "major bribery"—categories often employed to punish nonviolent activism and political expression. The amendments allow such suspects to be secretly detained for up to six months, essentially legalizing the practice of enforced disappearances.

Torture remains widespread, security agents routinely flout legal protections, and impunity is the norm for police brutality and suspicious deaths in custody. Many citizens—including a large contingent of political and religious prisoners—are detained by bureaucratic fiat in "reeducation through labor" camps, which permit individuals to be held for up to four years without a judicial hearing. Overall, detention facilities are estimated to hold three to five million people. Conditions are generally harsh, with reports of inadequate food, regular beatings, and deprivation of medical care; the government generally does not permit visits by independent monitoring groups. New forms of extralegal detention have multiplied in recent years, including the "black jails" for petitioners, psychiatric confinement of citizen activists, and disappearances of political dissidents for weeks or months at a time.

Fifty-five crimes, including nonviolent offenses, carry the death penalty. The number of executions each year is a state secret, but an estimate by the San Francisco–based Duihua Foundation put the number of executions in 2011 at 4,000, which would be the world's largest. Executed prisoners continue to be the primary source of organs for transplant operations, though the government announced plans in March 2012 to end the practice in the next three to five years. Some experts continued to raise concerns that those imprisoned for their religious beliefs or ethnic identity have also been used as sources for organs.

Security forces work closely with the CCP at all levels. During 2012, the party continued to expand its apparatus for "stability maintenance," a term that encompasses maintaining law and order, suppressing peaceful dissent, and closely monitoring the populace. Key components include state intelligence agencies, such as the Public Security Bureau; paramilitary forces like the People's Armed Police; and extralegal CCP-based entities like the 610 Office, stability-maintenance units, and administrative enforcers called chengguan who routinely engage in abusive conduct at the grassroots level. In March, the government announced that it would allocate 702 billion yuan (US$111 billion) that year for internal security forces, an increase of over 12 percent from 2011. The new total surpassed the military budget for the second consecutive year. The massive spending has fueled a lucrative market for outsourcing surveillance to civilians and private companies. As the CCP leadership transition proceeded during the year, analysts said some party chiefs were pushing to curb the growing power of the security apparatus.

Minorities, the disabled, and people with HIV/AIDS or hepatitis B face widespread societal and official discrimination, including in access to employment and education. The hukou (household registration) system remains in place, mostly affecting China's 200 million internal migrants and rural residents. Some local governments have experimented with reforms, but citizens continue to face restrictions on changing employers or residence, and many migrants are unable to fully access social services, such as education for their children. Among other restrictions on freedom of movement, dissidents, human rights defenders, and certain scholars are prevented from traveling abroad or placed under house arrest, particularly during politically sensitive periods. In the run-up to the 18th party congress in 2012, a series of restrictions on commerce, travel, and expression were imposed on Beijing residents. Law enforcement agencies continue to seek out and repatriate North Korean refugees, who face imprisonment or execution upon return. In August 2012, Chinese authorities repatriated at least 1,000 ethnic Kachin refugees from Burma who had fled violent conflict in their region.

Property rights protection remains weak in practice. Urban land is formally owned by the state, while rural land is collectively owned by villages. Tens of thousands of forced evictions and illegal land confiscations occurred in 2012. Residents who resist eviction, seek legal redress, or organize protests often face violence at the hands of local police or hired thugs. Regulations adopted in 2011 offered greater protections against expropriation in urban areas by defining "public interest," requiring compensation at market value, and allowing for administrative review. However, implementation has been undermined by the lack of independent courts and local governments' reliance on land development as a key source of operating revenue and a driver of economic growth statistics. The regulations do not apply to rural land, which lies at the center of most land conflicts.

Despite increasing discussion of potential reforms, China's population controls remain in place, and couples are required to obtain government permission before conceiving. In urban areas, only one child per couple is permitted, while many rural families are limited to two children. Compulsory abortion and sterilization, though less common than in the past, still occur fairly frequently, and high-profile cases sparked public outrage during 2012. According to the Congressional-Executive Commission on China, regulations in 18 of 31 provincial-level administrative units explicitly endorse mandatory abortions as an enforcement tool. Officials who fail to meet birth and sterilization quotas risk disciplinary action, and relatives of unsterilized women or couples with unapproved pregnancies were subjected to high fines, job dismissal, and detention in 2012. These controls, combined with commercial ultrasound technology and cultural and economic pressures favoring boys, have led to sex-selective abortion and a general shortage of females, exacerbating the problem of human trafficking.

Domestic violence affects one-quarter of Chinese women, according to statistics published in 2011 by the CCP-controlled All-China Women's Federation. In 2012, the NPC placed a draft law identifying domestic violence as a crime on its legislative agenda, but no decision had been made by year's end; the problem is currently addressed inadequately via scattered provisions in other laws. Several laws bar gender discrimination in the workplace, and gender equality has reportedly improved over the past decade, but China's score and relative ranking have dropped since 2009 on the Global Gender Gap Report. Women remain underrepresented in consequential CCP and government positions.

Colombia

Political Rights: 3
Civil Liberties: 4
Status: Partly Free

Population: 47,415,000
Capital: Bogotá

Ten-Year Ratings Timeline For Year Under Review (Political Rights, Civil Liberties, Status)

2003	2004	2005	2006	2007	2008	2009	2010	2011	2012
4,4PF	4,4PF	3,3PF	3,3PF	3,3PF	3,4PF	3,4PF	3,4PF	3,4PF	3,4PF

Overview: Talks between the Colombian government and the Revolutionary Armed Forces of Colombia (FARC) rebel group were announced in August 2012 and began in Norway in October. The FARC declared a unilateral 60-day ceasefire in November, though some fighting continued between the revolutionary group and the government. The talks were opposed by some Colombian politicians, including former president Álvaro Uribe.

Following independence from Spain in 1819, Gran Colombia broke into what became Venezuela, Ecuador, and modern Colombia. The 1903 secession of Panama, engineered by the United States, left Colombia with its present borders. A civil war between Liberals and Conservatives erupted in 1948 and resulted in some 200,000 deaths before subsiding after 1953. From 1958 to 1974, the two parties alternated in the presidency under the terms of a 1957 coalition pact aimed at ending civil strife. Colombia has since been marked by corrupt politics as well as left-wing guerrilla insurgencies, right-wing paramilitary violence, the emergence of vicious drug cartels, and human rights abuses committed by all sides.

A peace process between the government and the leftist Revolutionary Armed Forces of Colombia (FARC) rebel group unraveled in 2001, and Álvaro Uribe, a former provincial governor, won the 2002 presidential election after pledging to crush the rebels by military means. Right-wing paramilitary death squads, grouped together as the United Self-Defense Forces of Colombia (AUC), also battled the guerrillas, sometimes with the tolerance or covert complicity of government forces. By 2005, the leftist guerrillas had largely ceded control of major cities to the paramilitaries, though they held out in remote areas, using the narcotics trade and extortion for financial support.

The 2005 Justice and Peace Law was designed to demobilize and grant a partial amnesty to the paramilitaries, but human rights groups said it failed to ensure the permanent dismantling of the groups and encouraged impunity. In May 2006, the Constitutional Court struck down certain elements of the law and mandated full confessions, asset seizures, and the provision of reparations to victims. Meanwhile, bolstered by a growing economy and the perception of improved security, Uribe won a second term in that month's presidential election by an overwhelming margin. By late 2006, more than 30,000 paramilitaries had formally demobilized, though human rights groups reported problems with the disarmament, including the formation of fragmented "successor groups" created in part by recalcitrant or recidivist paramilitaries that continued to engage in drug trafficking, land theft, and assassinations of human rights activists.

In April 2008, 14 paramilitary chiefs were extradited to the United States to face long prison sentences for drug trafficking, though they ceased cooperation with Colombia's confessions process. Meanwhile, the "parapolitics" scandal, which linked scores of politicians to paramilitaries, resulted in the investigation, arrest, or conviction of over 90 legislators by the close of the 2006–2010 Congress.

In 2011, Colombia's intelligence agency, the Administrative Security Department (DAS), was dissolved after the conviction of former officials, including former chief Jorge Noguera, on murder and conspiracy charges following revelations that the office had been spying extensively on various targets, including Supreme Court justices, journalists, activists, and politicians, since 2003. The DAS scandal added to friction between Uribe and the Supreme Court, which had opposed various means used by the president to consolidate power. In March 2010, just weeks before congressional elections, the Constitutional Court ruled that Uribe could not stand for a third consecutive term as president.

In the March 2010 congressional elections, Uribe's allies won a substantial majority in both chambers. Former defense minister Juan Manuel Santos, who benefited from his association with the Uribe administration's security achievements, overcame an ideologically diverse array of opponents in the first round of the presidential poll in May and ultimately defeated Green Party member and former Bogotá mayor Antanas Mockus in a June runoff with 69 percent of the vote.

In regional and local elections held in October 2011, Santos's Partido de la U, the Liberal Party, and independents won the greatest share of governorships and mayoralties. In Bogotá, left-wing independent Gustavo Petro became mayor after running on an anticorruption platform. Although the elections were generally viewed as an improvement over those of 2007, 41 candidates were killed, and interference by armed actors, particularly paramilitary successor groups, skewed the results in many rural municipalities.

The Santos administration adopted a far more conciliatory approach than the previous government, and by mid-2011, Santos had expanded his National Unity coalition to include most parties in Congress. He used this control to enact a series of far-reaching laws, the most ambitious and widely lauded of which was the Victims and Land Restitution Law, enacted in June over the vigorous opposition of Uribe and his staunchest supporters. The law recognized the legitimacy of claims by victims of conflict-related abuses, including those committed by government forces. It also established a framework for reparations and resettlement of displaced people who had lost their land during the conflict. Analysts and rights groups predicted implementation would be difficult given the sheer scale of the undertaking, as well as ongoing collaboration between rural landholders and armed groups. The government made some progress in 2012 in preparing to implement the reform, and began the process of indemnifying victims. It was less effective, however, in protecting victims' advocates, accelerating the pace of formal title transfers, and formulating comprehensive rural development programs.

In November 2011, the Santos administration registered a dramatic military success when a bombing raid killed the FARC's leader, Alfonso Cano. After increasing its attacks each year between 2005 and 2011, FARC entered secret preliminary discussions with the government in Havana, Cuba, in early 2012. The discussions became public in August, and Santos formally announced the initiation of a peace process in early September. Despite vocal opposition from Uribe and his supporters, who considered the process a negotiation with terrorists, formal contact began in Oslo, Norway, in October, with the first round of official negotiations starting in Havana in November. The talks centered on rural development, one of five main issues on the agenda, along with ending the conflict, political rights for demobilized guerrillas, drug trafficking, and victims' rights.

Opinion polls showed Colombians resoundingly backing the process, though they were skeptical of its prospects for success. The government called for the talks to last no longer than one year, while the FARC sought a less-defined period. Although the government refused to consider a ceasefire, FARC imposed one for 60 days, starting in November. By Christmas, two rounds of talks had yielded guardedly optimistic statements from both parties, and a process was launched for civil society groups within Colombia to submit ideas to the negotiators.

The Santos administration continued a détente in 2012 with Ecuador and Venezuela, both of which had cut off diplomatic ties after Colombian forces attacked a FARC camp in Ecuador in 2008. In November 2012, the International Court of Justice awarded Nicaragua nearly 40,000 square miles of maritime territory previously controlled by Colombia, prompting a nationalistic reaction throughout Colombian society. At the end of the year, Santos, whose approval ratings had slipped after the decision, requested clarification of the ruling from the court and had not explicitly stated whether Colombia would comply.

Political Rights and Civil Liberties: Colombia is an electoral democracy. The 2010 legislative elections, while less violent than previous campaigns, were marred by vote-buying, murky campaign finance practices, and intimidation in some areas, particularly former paramilitary strongholds. The 2010 presidential election was relatively peaceful.

Congress is composed of the Senate and the Chamber of Representatives, with all seats up for election every four years. Of the Senate's 102 members, 2 are chosen by indigenous communities and 100 by the nation at large, using a closed-list system. The Chamber of Representatives consists of 166 members elected by closed-list proportional representation in multimember districts.

The traditional Liberal-Conservative partisan duopoly in Congress has in recent years been supplanted by a rough division between urban, modernizing forces, and more conservative, often rural sectors aligned with former president Álvaro Uribe. Factional divides within both right- and left-wing parties in 2012 exacerbated the ongoing problem of party fragmentation.

Corruption occurs at multiple levels of public administration. Scandals have emerged in recent years within an array of federal government agencies. In addition, contracting abuses in Bogotá led to the May 2011 removal of Mayor Samuel Moreno from office and the arrests of both him and his brother, Senator Iván Moreno; their cases continued throughout 2012. The national health system was revealed in 2012 to have suffered more than $2 billion in embezzlement over a decade-long period. Colombia was ranked 94 out of 176 countries surveyed in Transparency International's 2012 Corruption Perceptions Index.

The constitution guarantees freedom of expression, and opposition views are commonly expressed in the media. However, dozens of journalists have been murdered since the mid-1990s, many for reporting on drug trafficking and corruption. Most of the cases remain unsolved, and although violence has declined in recent years, a local press watchdog recorded at least 123 threats and other abuses against the press in 2012. Self-censorship is common, and slander and defamation remain criminal offenses. The government does not restrict access to the internet or censor websites, and Twitter and other social media platforms have become important arenas of political discourse.

The constitution provides for freedom of religion, and the government generally respects this right in practice. The authorities also uphold academic freedom, and university debates are often vigorous, though armed groups maintain a presence on many campuses to generate political support and intimidate opponents.

Constitutional rights regarding freedoms of assembly and association are restricted in practice by violence. Although the government provides extensive protection to hundreds of threatened human rights workers, trust in the program varies widely, and scores of activists have been murdered in recent years, mostly by paramilitary groups and their successors. Between 2010 and September 2012, 33 human rights defenders were killed in the department of Antioquia alone. Although the Santos administration has reiterated respect for nongovernmental organizations (NGOs), violations against activists have risen since Santos took office. Victims' and land rights' campaigners are especially threatened by former paramilitaries seeking to smother criticism of their ill-gotten assets. In early 2012, a group calling itself the Anti-Restitution Army began a campaign of threats and harassment against land rights' advocates in northern Colombia; one of the group's alleged founders was arrested in October.

More than 2,600 labor union activists and leaders have been killed over the last two decades, with attacks coming from all of Colombia's illegally armed groups. Killings have declined substantially from their early-2000s peak, and fell from 29 in 2011 to 15 through November 2012. Although a special prosecutorial unit has substantially increased prosecutions for such assassinations since 2007, most have avoided those who ordered the killings. The Labor Action Plan, linked to the 2011 U.S. free-trade agreement, which calls for enhanced investigation of rights violations and stepped-up enforcement regarding abusive labor practices, resulted in only minor improvements in 2012.

The justice system remains compromised by corruption and extortion. Although the Constitutional Court and Supreme Court have demonstrated independence from the executive in recent years, revelations of questionable behavior involving Supreme Court justices in 2012 resulted in diminished support for the court in opinion polls. A long-debated justice reform bill failed in July 2012, when President Santos returned the bill to Congress after an outcry over multiple provisions, particularly one that would have stripped the Supreme Court of jurisdiction over criminal allegations against parliamentarians. Congress subsequently revoked the new law, and Minister of Justice Juan Carlos Esguerra resigned his position.

Many soldiers work under limited civilian oversight, though the government has in recent years increased human rights training and investigated a greater number of military personnel for human rights abuses. Collaboration between security forces and illegally armed groups declined following AUC demobilization, but rights groups report toleration of the roughly 8,000-strong paramilitary successor groups in some regions. Primary responsibility for combating them rests with the police, who lack the resources of the military, are frequently accused of colluding with criminal groups, and are largely absent from many rural areas where the groups are active. However, several of the paramilitary groups' key leaders were killed or arrested in 2012, as were several of Colombia's most wanted drug traffickers.

The systematic killing of civilians to fraudulently inflate guerrilla death tolls has declined substantially since a 2008 scandal over the practice led to the firing of dozens of senior army officers. More than 2,000 people may have been killed in this fashion, and thousands of security personnel remained under investigation at the end of 2012. Dozens of convictions were obtained in cases transferred to civilian courts, but far more cases proceeded slowly due to a shortage of prosecutors and delaying tactics by defense lawyers.

Jurisdiction over human rights violations is a sensitive issue. Several convictions of high-ranking officers for forced disappearances in 2010 and 2011 added to already rising tensions between military and civilian justice institutions and prompted a government-sponsored constitutional amendment that would have made crimes committed by security forces subject to military, rather than civilian, justice. Following enormous domestic and international outcry, extrajudicial executions and several other crimes were excluded from military jurisdiction, and the bill was passed in December 2012. Despite the exceptions, human rights groups warned that the law would weaken efforts to hold soldiers accountable for rights abuses.

While violence has declined since the early 2000s and homicides reached a 27-year low in 2012, some areas, particularly resource-rich zones and drug-trafficking corridors, remain besieged by violence. FARC guerrillas and paramilitary successor groups regularly extort payments from businesspeople and engage in forced recruitment, including of minors. The use of land mines has added to casualties among both civilians and the military. Impunity for crime in general is rampant. Rights groups cautioned that provisions contained within the Legal Framework for Peace, a constitutional reform enacted in July, could allow near-complete impunity for all armed actors accused of atrocities during the conflict between guerillas and paramilitary groups.

Colombia's more than 1.7 million indigenous inhabitants live on over 34 million hectares granted to them by the government, often in resource-rich, strategic regions that are increasingly contested by the various armed groups. Indigenous people are frequently targeted by all sides. The Office of the UN High Commissioner for Refugees and the Constitutional Court have warned in recent years that many groups face extinction, often after being displaced by the conflict. In July 2012, an indigenous group in Cauca expelled a Colombian army unit from its territory after complaining that clashes between the army and guerrillas had resulted in civilian deaths.

Afro-Colombians, who account for as much as 25 percent of the population, make up the largest sector of Colombia's over 4 million displaced people, and 80 percent of Afro-Colombians fall below the poverty line. Consultation with Afro-Colombians is constitutionally mandated on issues affecting their communities, but activists expressed dismay over shortcomings in the government's consultation process for the Victims and Land Restitution Law in 2011. In December 2012, a prominent advocate for Afro-Colombians, Miller Angulo, was murdered in Nariño.

Child labor is a serious problem in Colombia, as are child recruitment into illegal armed groups and related sexual abuse. Sexual harassment, violence against women, and the trafficking of women for sexual exploitation remain major concerns. Thousands of rapes have occurred as part of the conflict, generally with impunity. The country's abortion-rights movement has challenged restrictive laws, and a 2006 Constitutional Court ruling allowed abortion in cases of rape or incest, or to protect the mother's life. In December 2012, a bill to legalize same-sex marriage passed an initial hurdle in hurdle in Congress despite staunch opposition from conservatives.

Comoros

Political Rights: 3
Civil Liberties: 4
Status: Partly Free

Population: 773,000
Capital: Moroni

Ten-Year Ratings Timeline For Year Under Review (Political Rights, Civil Liberties, Status)

2003	2004	2005	2006	2007	2008	2009	2010	2011	2012
5,4PF	4,4PF	4,4PF	3,4PF	4,4PF	3,4PF	3,4PF	3,4PF	3,4PF	3,4PF

Overview: In 2012, President Ikililou Dhoinine continued to push aggressive fiscal management and governance reforms in response to stagnant economic growth, rampant corruption, and high unemployment. The first sign of success came in December, when the International Monetary Fund and World Bank's International Development Association announced a $76 million debt relief plan for Comoros. Corruption remained a serious problem, and a case against former president Ahmed Abdallah Sambi remained pending at year's end.

The Union of the Comoros comprises three islands: Grande Comore, Anjouan, and Mohéli. Mayotte, the fourth island of the archipelago, voted to remain under French rule in 1974. Two mercenary invasions and at least 18 other coups have shaken Comoros since it gained independence from France in 1975. The 1996 presidential election was considered free and fair by international monitors, but Anjouan and Mohéli fell under the control of separatists the following year. A 1999 coup restored order, installing Colonel Azali Assoumani as leader of the country, and led to the signing of a reconciliation agreement. A 2001 referendum approved a new constitution that increased autonomy for the three islands. Azali took the federal presidency in the 2002 election, after his two opponents claimed fraud and withdrew. Ahmed Abdallah Sambi—a moderate Islamist preacher and businessman—won the federal presidency in May 2006.

Mohamed Bacar, the present of Anjouan, organized unauthorized elections in 2007 to extend his rule and claimed to have won with 90 percent of the vote. In March 2008, an African Union military force removed him from power, and Moussa Toybou, a Sambi supporter, was elected in June 2008.

In a May 2009 referendum, voters approved constitutional reforms that increased the powers of the federal government at the expense of the individual island governments. The reforms instituted a rotation of the federal presidency among the islands every five (previously four) years, downgraded island presidents to the status of governors, limited the size of cabinets, empowered the president to dissolve the federal parliament, and allowed the president to rule by decree with parliament's approval.

In December 2009 legislative elections, the president's supporters won 19 of the 24 directly elected seats. Sambi's term of office expired in May 2010, but an election to choose his successor was postponed due to political disputes. This delay provoked tension, especially among residents of Mohéli, which was the next island scheduled to hold the office of federal president.

In December 2010, Sambi's protégé, Vice President Ikililou Dhoinine, won the presidential election with 61 percent of the vote. He became the first president of Comoros from Mohéli. His main rival, Mohamed Said Fazul, claimed fraud. However, the national election monitoring group upheld the legitimacy of the election, and Dhoinine was sworn in on May 26, 2011. Opponents alleged that the long transition period, combined with the delayed election, effectively extended Sambi's term by one year.

Large numbers of Comorans illegally immigrate to Mayotte to settle or to seek entry into metropolitan France, and the economy depends heavily on remittances and foreign aid. In 2009, the global economic downturn contributed to delays and suspensions of public sector salary payments and a decline in public services. Under Dhoinine's leadership, the Comorian government in 2012 made noteworthy progress in its fiscal consolidation through an aggressive structural reform agenda that included government-wide spending controls and a decision to privatize Comores Télécom in an effort to overhaul management of the water and electricity utility.

While the country's unemployment rate continues to hover around 15 percent, and unemployment among young adults at about 45 percent, the government has declared this issue a priority and promised to improve economic conditions through the continued implementation of reforms. After determining that Comoros had fulfilled its requirements to reach the completion point under the Heavily Indebted Poor Countries Initiative, the IMF and the World Bank's International Development Association decided in December 2012 to support $176 million in debt relief for Comoros, representing a 59 percent reduction of its future external debt service over a period of 40 years.

Political Rights and Civil Liberties: Comoros is an electoral democracy. Since 1996, Comorans have voted freely in several parliamentary and presidential elections. The unicameral Assembly of the Union consists of 33 members, with 9 selected by the assemblies of the three islands and 24 by direct popular vote; all members serve five-year terms. Each of the three islands also has an individual parliament, which is directly elected. Political parties are mainly defined by their positions regarding the division of power between the federal and local governments.

Corruption remains a major problem. There are reports of corruption at all levels of the government, judiciary, and civil service, as well as among the police and security forces. In September 2011, the opposition Convention for the Renewal of the Comoros (CRC), led by former president Azali Assoumani, filed a complaint in a Moroni court against former president Ahmed Abdallah Sambi for alleged misuse of public funds while in office. The allegations concern the sale of Comoros nationality to citizens of Gulf countries, which supposedly generated $200 million, although this money was never accounted for during financial reconciliations. The case was still pending at the end of 2012 while the courts determined if Sambi holds presidential immunity, which would prevent him from appearing before the courts. Comoros was ranked 133 out of 176 countries surveyed in Transparency International's 2012 Corruption Perceptions Index.

The constitution and laws provide for freedoms of speech and the press, though self-censorship is reportedly widespread. In April 2012, Interior Minister Hamada Abdallah withdrew the state daily *Al-Watan*'s monthly supplement from distribution and issued a decree suspending the outlet's managing editor, Pétan Mouignihazi. The insert featured a special report on corruption and waste in the state sector.

Islam is the state religion, and 98 percent of the population is Sunni Muslim. Tensions have occasionally arisen between Sunni and Shiite Muslims, and non-Muslims are reportedly subject to restrictions, detentions, and harassment. Conversion from Islam and non-Muslim proselytizing are illegal. Academic freedom is generally respected.

The government typically upholds freedoms of assembly and association. A few human rights and other nongovernmental organizations operate in the country. Workers have the right to bargain collectively and to strike, but collective bargaining is rare.

The judicial system is based on both Sharia (Islamic law) and the French legal code, and is subject to influence by the executive branch and other elites. Minor disputes are often settled informally by village elders. Harsh prison conditions include severe overcrowding and inadequate sanitation, medical care, and nutrition.

The law prohibits discrimination based on gender. However, in practice, women are still underrepresented at the political level. Economic equality also remains a key challenge, as women have far fewer opportunities for education and salaried employment than men, especially in rural areas. Sexual violence is believed to be widespread, but is rarely reported to authorities.

Congo, Democratic Republic of (Kinshasa)

Political Rights: 6
Civil Liberties: 6
Status: Not Free

Population: 69,117,000
Capital: Kinshasa

Ten-Year Ratings Timeline For Year Under Review (Political Rights, Civil Liberties, Status)

2003	2004	2005	2006	2007	2008	2009	2010	2011	2012
6,6NF	6,6NF	6,6NF	5,6NF	5,6NF	6,6NF	6,6NF	6,6NF	6,6NF	6,6NF

Overview: Instability and insecurity persisted in 2012, as a nascent rebel movement briefly occupied Goma, eastern Congo's most important city. The combination of entrenched corruption, foreign interference, and mismanaged mineral resources contributed to the lack of progress in ameliorating the country's extreme poverty. Meanwhile, the government continued to suppress civil society and independent media, with security forces threatening and attacking journalists critical of government officials.

In the late 19th century, the king of Belgium claimed a vast area of Central Africa as his private property, and the territory was exploited with extreme brutality. After achieving independence from Belgium in 1960, Colonel Joseph Mobutu seized power of the then Republic of Congo with backing from the United States in 1965. Mobutu changed the country's name to Zaire in 1971, renamed himself Mobutu Sese Seko, and assumed dictatorial powers.

Mobutu was formally stripped of most of his powers in 1992 in a national convention, and a transitional government was formed with a new prime minister, longtime Mobutu opponent Étienne Tshisekedi. However, Mobutu created a rival government, leading to a political standoff. In a compromise that marginalized Tshisekedi, the two governments merged in 1994, with Mobutu remaining head of state. Presidential and legislative elections were scheduled repeatedly but never took place.

After the 1994 genocide in neighboring Rwanda, the Rwandan and Ugandan governments turned their cross-border pursuit of Rwandan Hutu militia members into an advance on Kinshasa. Rwandan troops and the Alliance of Democratic Forces for the Liberation of Congo-Zaire (ADFL)—a coalition led by former Zairian rebel leader Laurent-Désiré Kabila—took Kinshasa in May 1997. Kabila declared himself president after Mobutu fled, and changed the country's name to the Democratic Republic of Congo (DRC).

Relations between Kabila and his Rwandan and Ugandan backers deteriorated after he ordered all foreign forces to leave the DRC in 1998. Rwanda and Uganda each backed rebel groups, and other regional powers became involved on the side of the Congolese government. These rebel groups established control over large swathes of the DRC, and the country's vast mineral wealth spurred the involvement of multinational companies, criminal networks, and other foreign governments.

Military stalemate led to the signing of the Lusaka Peace Agreement in 1999, which included a ceasefire. Kabila was assassinated in 2001 and succeeded by his son Joseph, who revived the peace process. The 2002 Sun City Agreement led to the creation of a transitional government in 2003 and a formal end to the war.

In 2006, the DRC held its first multiparty polls since independence, and promulgated a new constitution. Kabila's People's Party for Reconstruction and Democracy (PPRD) gained a plurality of seats in the National Assembly, and Kabila defeated Jean-Pierre Bemba in the concurrent presidential poll that was fraught with irregularities.

In January 2008, a peace agreement was signed between the government and 22 armed groups, though it did not include the Rwandan government or the Democratic Forces for the Liberation of Rwanda (FDLR), an ethnic Hutu–dominated militia led by perpetrators of the Rwandan genocide who had fled to the DRC. Fighting broke out in August 2008 between government troops and rebel leader Laurent Nkunda's National Congress for the Defense of the People (CNDP), which allegedly received backing from Rwanda.

In late 2008, the DRC and Rwanda signed an agreement to begin a joint military operation against the FDLR and negotiations with the CNDP. The early 2009 operation coincided with the surprise arrest of Nkunda in Rwanda and a settlement with the CNDP, transforming the group into a political party and integrating its leadership into the DRC armed forces (FARDC). In March, Congolese and UN forces began a new military operation against the FDLR. Separately, the FARDC embarked on a joint military operation with Uganda from December 2008 to March 2009 to pursue the Lord's Resistance Army (LRA), a Ugandan rebel group then operating in northeastern Congo.

The impact of years of fighting on civilians is catastrophic, with over five million conflict-related deaths since 1998. The DRC was ranked lowest in the world on the UN Development Program's 2012 Human Development Index. The Senate in 2011 rejected a bill establishing a specialized mixed court to prosecute serious crimes, and by the end of 2012 had not reintroduced it.

In advance of the November 2011 presidential and National Assembly elections, a number of changes to the electoral law were enacted despite opposition protests, including eliminating the requirement for a runoff if no presidential candidate wins more than 50 percent of the vote in the first round. The amendment was seen by opposition parties as an intentional manipulation to secure Kabila's reelection.

Opposition politicians and their supporters faced violence and harassment by police in the run-up to the polls. Kabila was declared the winner on December 9 and was sworn in on December 20, despite widespread criticism of the election by international observers. National Assembly elections suffered from similar problems. Kabila's PPRD won 61 seats, down from the 111 seats it held prior to November 2011, while the opposition Union for Democracy and Social Progress (UDPS) took 41. Kabila's overall coalition won 260 of the 500 seats. Tshisekedi supporters protested the results, and numerous civil society groups called for new elections.

In March 2012, former CNDP rebels who had joined the FARDC mutinied, claiming that the government had failed to fully implement the March 23, 2009, agreement that had integrated them into government forces. Several of the leaders of the March 23 Movement (M23) have been accused of committing human rights violations while serving with previous rebel movements. Most notably, General Bosco Ntaganda is wanted by the International Criminal Court (ICC) for alleged war crimes and crimes against humanity, and Sultani Makenga was allegedly involved in the recruitment of children and several massacres in the east. The M23, supplemented by subsequent defections from the FARDC, also reportedly recruited child soldiers and conducted summary executions. The M23—which consisted of 1,500 to 2,500 men—created a political wing in July, established an alternative government, and began collecting taxes in areas in eastern Congo under its control. Also in July, rebels killed a UN peacekeeper and fired on a UN base. On November 15, after Kabila's government refused to enter into negotiations with the group, the M23 rebels broke the de facto ceasefire with the FARDC and advanced on Goma. In response, UN forces engaged in heavy bombardment of rebel positions. Nonetheless, the rebel forces occupied Goma on November 20 as UN forces stood by and the FARDC presence dissolved. Tens of thousands of civilians fled the area, bringing the rebels to the Rwandan border. The M23 withdrew from Goma on December 1 after the diplomatic intervention of East African nations, and peace talks began on December 9, though nothing substantive was agreed upon before the end of the year.

According to an October UN Security Council's Group of Experts report, Rwanda and Uganda were actively involved in providing material and command support to the M23 movement in the DRC in 2012, thereby violating the UN arms embargo. This support reportedly included direct troop reinforcements, and the provision of arms, ammunition, intelligence, and political advice. In November, Kabila met with Rwandan president Paul Kagame to pursue a diplomatic solution to the situation. The Security Council also placed global travel bans and asset freezes on three top military leaders of the M23.

Following the fall of Goma, antigovernment protests around the country severely weakened Kabila's already shaky credibility with the majority of Congolese. The upheaval caused by the M23 movement in the east also occupied national resources and attention, allowing various rebel groups to remain active in other parts of the country.

Political Rights and Civil Liberties: The DRC is not an electoral democracy. The 2011 elections were marked by a lack of preparation, changes in the structure and function of the electoral commission, limited international logistical support, and inadequate accountability and follow-through on irregularities. The legitimacy of the Independent Electoral Commission (CENI) is questionable, as four of its seven members are appointed by the presidential coalition, and it does not include members of civil society. CENI has not yet been revised, despite calls for reform. The electoral calendar was postponed in June, and donors have made any future electoral financing conditional upon significant electoral reforms. Local and provincial elections originally to be held in early 2012 were not rescheduled during the year.

The president is elected for up to two five-year terms. The president nominates a prime minister from the leading party or coalition in the 500-seat National Assembly, whose members are popularly elected to serve five-year terms. Provincial assemblies elect the 108-seat Senate, as well as the provincial governors, for five-year terms.

According to CENI, there are 445 political parties in the country. Political parties are often divided along ethnic, communal, or regional lines, and usually lack national reach. President Joseph Kabila's coalition, the Presidential Majority (PM), requires members to have national representation, ensuring that the PPRD remains in the majority within the coalition. Other major parties include the opposition UDPS and Movement for the Liberation of Congo (MLC). Nearly 100 different parties and many independents are represented in the parliament.

Corruption and impunity continue to be serious problems in the DRC. The clandestine trade in mineral resources by rebel groups and elements of the FARDC help finance the violence and deplete government revenues from the sector. Recruitment for government posts is often determined by nepotism, and political interference is rampant. Despite incremental improvements in revenue reporting due to the Extractive Industries Transparency Initiative and International Monetary Fund requirements, there is little transparency in the state's financial affairs. The complicated system of taxation and regulation has made bribery and corruption a regular aspect of business dealings. Hundreds of millions of dollars are embezzled every year. Beginning in 2012, civil servants and members of the military were paid electronically, with the aim of curbing corruption and ensuring regular, accurate payments. The country was ranked 180 out of 185 countries in the World Bank's 2012 Doing Business survey, and 160 out of 176 countries surveyed in Transparency International's 2012 Corruption Perceptions Index.

Although guaranteed by the constitution, freedoms of speech and the press are limited. Radio is the dominant medium in the country. Newspapers are limited mostly to large cities. The content of private television and radio stations is occasionally restricted, but lively political debate is growing in urban areas. The government does not monitor online communications or restrict access to the internet, but use is limited by lack of infrastructure. In November, China and the DRC agreed to have China launch a communications satellite within the next three years, making the DRC the second African country after Nigeria to acquire this technology.

Throughout 2012, there were multiple reports of security forces threatening, detaining, and attacking journalists critical of government officials. A total of 6 journalists were beaten and 23 threatened or harassed during the year, though no journalists were reported killed or disappeared. In June, the communications minister indefinitely banned the private daily *Le Journal* for an editorial accusing DRC-based Rwandans of promoting Rwandan interests, which he argued incited racism and tribalism. Radio Television Autonome du Sud Kasaii was forced off the air in August after its owner was arrested over alleged links with a rebel leader; by December, the owner remained in custody. The Higher Council for Broadcasting and Communication (CSAC), the state media regulatory agency, announced its intention to indefinitely suspend broadcasters that aired content about the conflict between rebel groups and the government in the east; by November, three stations had been ordered off the air. Nonstate armed groups have also targeted journalists. In July, the M23 took over community radio stations in Rutshuru territory, threatening staff and confiscating equipment. Local leaders, chiefs, journalists, and activists who denounced the abuses of the M23 rebels were also targeted and threatened. In December, UN-sponsored Radio Okapi's signal was jammed for four days for failing to submit a programming schedule to CSAC, and Radio France

Internationale was suspended for broadcasting Étienne Tshisekedi's New Year's address.

Freedom of religion is guaranteed by the constitution and generally respected in practice. Although religious groups must register with the government in order to be recognized, unregistered groups operate unhindered. There are no formal government restrictions on academic freedom.

The constitution guarantees freedoms of assembly and association, though these are limited in practice. The government has restricted the activities of opposition groups, particularly the UDPS. In February, the secretary general of the UDPS was arrested by immigration officials and held for 22 hours before release. Police prevented UDPS members from entering their local headquarters in April. In July, police arrested the deputy secretary general of the UDPS on what officials and supporters claim were politically motivated and arbitrary charges; he was released after two days.

Groups holding public events must register with local authorities in advance, and security forces occasionally act against unregistered demonstrations and marches. There are about 5,000 registered nongovernmental organizations (NGOs) in the country, though they often have narrow scopes devoted to ethnic and local concerns. NGOs are generally able to operate, though domestic human rights advocates are subject to harassment, arbitrary arrest, and detention. In January 2012, the home of a human rights defender was burned down under suspicious circumstances after he publicly criticized the recent election results; no charges were filed by the end of 2012. Dr. Denis Mukwege, a noted human rights activist and the director of a hospital that treats victims of sexual violence, narrowly escaped an assassination attempt in September and fled the country. In 2011, eight national police officers were sentenced for the June 2010 murder of prominent human rights activist Floribert Chebeya Bahizire. The eight were back on trial in 2012 when the plaintiffs demanded that former police chief John Numbi be considered the prime suspect in the murder. In October, the military court trying the police officers determined that Numbi would not be required to appear in court, and several plaintiffs withdrew from the case in protest.

Congolese who fulfill a residency requirement of 20 years can form and join trade unions, though government employees and members of state security forces are not permitted to unionize. It is against the law for employers to retaliate against strikers. Unions organize strikes regularly. In May 2012, Kinshasa's largest private transportation syndicate organized a citywide strike for two days, after which the government announced measures to improve public transportation. Some labor leaders and activists face harassment.

Kabila appoints members of the judiciary, which remains subject to corruption and political manipulation. The courts, which lack both trained personnel and resources and reportedly often grant favorable verdicts for the highest bribe, are concentrated in urban areas, leaving the majority of the country reliant on customary courts. Military courts are often used, even in civilian cases, and are subject to interference by high-ranking military personnel. Prison conditions are life threatening, and long periods of pretrial detention are common.

Civilian authorities do not maintain effective control of the security forces. The FARDC are largely undisciplined, and soldiers and police regularly commit serious human rights abuses, including rape and torture. Low pay and inadequate provisions commonly lead soldiers to seize goods from civilians, and demobilized combatants who were not successfully integrated into the civilian economy have again taken up arms as part of the M23. Most government and government-allied forces enjoy apparent impunity for even the most heinous crimes. There are notable exceptions; in March 2012, 4 soldiers were sentenced to death, and 10 others to various prison sentences by a military tribunal for rape and sexual violence. In September, National Deputy Adolphe Onusumba was convicted of rape and sentenced to one year in prison and a $100,000 fine.

The UN extended its peacekeeping operations mandate for 12 months in June 2012. By the end of the year, there were 19,000 peacekeepers, military observers, and police in the country under the mandate.

The ICC continues to pursue cases in the DRC, including against rebel leader Germain Katanga, who was awaiting a verdict at the end of 2012, as well as the ongoing trial against MLC leader Jean-Pierre Bemba. Mathieu Ngudjolo Chui, a rebel leader accused of war crimes, was acquitted in December. In the court's first verdict, General Thomas Lubanga was convicted in March of recruiting child soldiers. In 2008, the ICC issued a warrant for the arrest of General Bosco Ntaganda, who allegedly committed war crimes and crimes against humanity while serving under Lubanga. Despite the warrant, Ntaganda, formerly of the CNDP, openly served as a general in the FARDC after the 2009 integration of the CNDP and through March 2012. The ICC issued another warrant for his arrest and expanded the charges against him in July.

Ethnic discrimination, including against indigenous populations, is a major problem. There are reports of indigenous people being kidnapped and forced into slavery. Rwandophone minorities in the Kivus have been the victims of violence and hate speech for decades.

Although the law provides for freedom of movement, security forces seeking bribes or travel permits restrict this right in practice, and foreigners must regularly submit to immigration controls when traveling internally. In conflict zones, various armed groups and soldiers have seized private property and destroyed homes, as well as stolen crops and livestock. By the end of 2012, 2.4 million Congolese were internally displaced due to violence in the east. Human Rights Watch documented the forced recruitment of young men and boys by M23 forces, as well as by Rwandan military officials on behalf of the M23. The M23 also reportedly forced civilians to work for them, and at times imposed tolls on vehicles passing through their territory. Congolese armed forces have also been implicated in human rights abuses in eastern DRC, including arbitrary arrests, the mistreatment of detainees, and widespread looting. The LRA was responsible for theft and looting in Orientale Province in 2012, contributing significantly to the displacement of local populations.

Property rights are recognized in the constitution, but the expropriation of private property is common. The majority of land in the DRC is held through customary tenure, and this lack of legal title to the land leads to regular confiscation of property.

Despite constitutional guarantees, women face discrimination in nearly every aspect of their lives, especially in rural areas. Violence against women and girls, including sexual and gender-based violence, has soared since fighting began in

1994, though sex crimes often affect men and boys as well. The M23 rebels and FARDC soldiers have been implicated in kidnappings, killings, and rape. Mass rapes continued in 2012, and convictions remain rare. Abortion is prohibited, and women's access to contraception is extremely low. Women are also greatly underrepresented in government, making up only 9 percent of the National Assembly and 5 percent of the Senate, and 16 percent of government and vice ministers are women. In 2012, the government entered a UN-backed plan to end the use of child soldiers in the FARDC, and the government made significant progress towards reducing their numbers in the military. The DRC is both a source and destination country for the trafficking of men, women, and children for the purposes of labor and sexual exploitation.

Congo, Republic of (Brazzaville)

Political Rights: 6
Civil Liberties: 5
Status: Not Free

Population: 4,247,000
Capital: Brazzaville

Ten-Year Ratings Timeline For Year Under Review (Political Rights, Civil Liberties, Status)

2003	2004	2005	2006	2007	2008	2009	2010	2011	2012
5,4PF	5,4PF	5,5PF	6,5NF	6,5NF	6,5NF	6,5NF	6,5NF	6,5NF	6,5NF

Overview: **President Denis Sassou-Nguesso's ruling Congolese Labor Party won the majority of seats in the July 2012 legislative elections, which were marred by fraud, low voter turnout, and postelection violence. In March, an explosion in a munitions depot in a densely populated area caused hundreds of deaths and displaced tens of thousands. Entrenched corruption, especially in the oil industry, continued to stymie the country's economic growth.**

Since gaining independence from France in 1960, the Republic of Congo has been marked by conflict and military coups. Current president Denis Sassou-Nguesso first came to power in 1979 with military support. Domestic and international pressure finally forced him to hold multiparty presidential elections in 1992, in which he was defeated by Pascal Lissouba.

In 1993, disputed parliamentary elections triggered violent clashes between rival militia groups. The fighting ended in 1997, when Sassou-Nguesso ousted Lissouba with the help of Angolan troops and French political support. In 2002, voters adopted a new constitution by referendum, which extended the presidential term from five to seven years. Sassou-Nguesso and his Congolese Labor Party (PCT) and its allies captured the presidency and most legislative seats in 2002 elections. Although the polls failed to foster genuine reconciliation, most of the country's rebel factions signed a peace agreement in 2003.

The PCT and its allies won a majority again in 2007 legislative elections, which were boycotted by the opposition. Following his electoral victory in July 2009,

Sassou-Nguesso eliminated the post of prime minister, becoming both head of state and head of government.

Further efforts were made by Sassou-Nguesso in 2011 to strengthen his grip on power. During the PCT's congress in July, his son, Denis Christel Sassou-Nguesso, became a member of both the party's newly elected 471-member Central Committee and the 51-member Political Bureau, fueling rumors that he was being groomed for succession. Sassou-Nguesso's allies won yet another overwhelming victory in October 2011 indirect elections for half of the 72 Senate seats.

Amid allegations that the PCT was considering constitutional amendments to remove presidential term limits, the party took 89 of the 139 available seats in the July 2012 National Assembly elections. The PCT and its allies now control 117 of the body's seats. The elections were marred by accusations of fraud, low voter turnout, and postelection violence.

On March 4, 2012, an arms depot exploded in a residential neighborhood of Brazzaville, killing at least 240 people, seriously injuring 2,300, and displacing tens of thousands of families. The emergency response was largely ineffectual and hampered by subsequent, smaller explosions. After a similar disaster in 2009, the government had pledged to remove arms depots from heavily populated areas, but Brazzaville still has at least five repositories for aging munitions. Defense Minister Charles Zacharie Bowao was dismissed for refusing to resign after the explosion, and was charged with criminal negligence in October. He joined 23 others, mainly military personnel, being detained awaiting a January 2013 trial in connection to the blast.

Congo is one of sub-Saharan Africa's major oil producers, though corruption and decades of instability have contributed to poor humanitarian conditions. Congo was ranked 137 out of 187 countries on the 2011 UN Human Development Index.

Political Rights and Civil Liberties: The Republic of Congo is not an electoral democracy. Irregularities, opposition boycotts and disqualifications, and the absence of an independent electoral commission consistently tarnish elections. The 2002 constitution limits the president to two seven-year terms. However, President Denis Sassou-Nguesso has held office continuously since seizing power in 1997. The Senate consists of 72 members, with councilors from each department electing six senators for five-year terms. Half of them come up for election every three years. Members of the 139-seat National Assembly are directly elected for five-year terms. Most of the over 100 registered political parties are personality-driven and ethnically based. Members of Sassou-Nguesso's northern Mbochi ethnic group dominate key government posts, while the opposition remains weak and fragmented.

As a result of the Congo's oil wealth, economic growth has stabilized, though it has not sufficiently diversified, and the ruling party's hold on the political system is largely consolidated. The percentage of Congolese living in extreme poverty has increased despite the mineral wealth of the country, and the oil export market is dependent on Chinese demand. Congo is implementing the steps outlined in the Extractive Industries Transparency Initiative (EITI), though it has not yet fulfilled all of the requirements necessary to become fully compliant. It also cooperates with the African Peer Mechanism Review, and a national Anti-Corruption Commission was created in September 2009. However, corruption, especially in the extractive industries, remains pervasive. The government will not release oil revenue data, and the state oil company is directly under the control of the president's family and advisers. French authorities are investigating Sassou-Nguesso and his family for the alleged embezzlement of public funds to acquire assets in France, including real estate and bank accounts. Domestic prosecutions for corruption have been limited and are often politically motivated when they do occur. Congo was ranked 144 out of 176 countries surveyed in Transparency International's 2012 Corruption Perceptions Index.

While the constitution provides for freedom of speech and of the press, the government's respect for press freedom is limited. Speech that is perceived as inciting ethnic hatred, violence, or civil war is illegal, and the government can impose fines for defamation and incitement to violence. During the election campaign period, opposition parties reported a lack of access to state media. With no nationwide radio or television stations, most citizens get their news from local broadcast sources, and the state publishes the only daily newspaper. The government systematically censors journalists, and uses government-owned media to counter critical reports in the independent media. However, most of the newspapers published in Brazzaville are privately owned, and some print articles and editorials critical of the government. There are no government restrictions on internet access, though sites that "radically criticize" the government are only permitted to operate outside of the country.

Religious and academic freedoms are guaranteed and respected.

Freedoms of assembly and association are provided for in the constitution, though security forces have shown little tolerance for political demonstrations. Groups must receive official authorization to hold public assemblies. Nongovernmental organizations generally operate without interference, so long as they do not challenge the ruling elite. Workers' rights to join trade unions and to strike are protected, and collective bargaining is practiced freely, though rarely. Most workers in the formal business sector, including the oil industry, belong to unions, which have also made efforts to organize informal sectors, such as agriculture and retail trade. Members of the security forces and other essential services are not allowed to form unions.

Congo's underfunded judiciary is subject to corruption and political influence, and crippled by institutional weakness and a lack of technical capability. Traditional courts are the dominant judicial system in rural Congo, presiding over local property, inheritance, and domestic cases. The Human Rights Commission, charged with addressing complaints about abuses committed by security forces, is largely ineffectual and does not enjoy the trust of the people, as most of its members are presidential appointees. Members of the security forces act with impunity, and there have been reports of arbitrary arrests and suspects being tortured and dying during apprehension or in custody. Prison conditions are life threatening. The death penalty is still on the books, though executions are not carried out.

Indigenous groups are often concentrated in isolated rural areas, are not registered to vote, and are actively discriminated against, leaving them politically marginalized. In particular, native Mbendjele Yaka suffer discrimination, with many held in lifetime servitude. Ethnic discrimination is common in hiring practices, and urban neighborhoods tend to be segregated. An indigenous rights law, the first of its kind in Africa, was promulgated in 2011 with the goal of addressing systematic discrimination against indigenous minorities. The National Action Plan on the Improvement of Quality of Life of Indigenous Peoples, introduced in 2009 and set to end in 2013, establishes benchmarks for measures that would improve the lives of the Congolese indigenous population. This was followed by the adoption of Africa's first law on indigenous rights in February 2011. The Promotion and Protection of Indigenous Populations Act contains provisions on cultural rights, education, and land rights, explicitly prohibiting forced assimilation and discrimination; the enforcement of this law continues to be a challenge.

Harassment by military personnel and militia groups inhibits travel, though such practices have declined. The judicial system offers few protections for business and property rights.

Homosexual acts are punishable by up to two years in prison, though this is rarely enforced. Congo is a destination for and source of human trafficking, and substantial improvements to the prevention and prosecution of the practice have not occurred. Despite constitutional safeguards, legal and societal discrimination against women persists. Equal access to education and employment is limited, and civil codes regarding marriage formalize women's inferior status. Most women work in the informal sector, and do not receive employment benefits or protection from abusive employers. Violence against women is reportedly widespread. Rape, including marital rape, is illegal, but this common crime is rarely reported or prosecuted. Abortion is prohibited in all cases except to save the life of the mother. Women are underrepresented in government and decision-making positions, holding just 7 percent of seats in the National Assembly and 14 percent of Senate seats.

Costa Rica

Political Rights: 1
Civil Liberties: 1
Status: Free

Population: 4,481,000
Capital: San José

Ten-Year Ratings Timeline For Year Under Review (Political Rights, Civil Liberties, Status)

2003	2004	2005	2006	2007	2008	2009	2010	2011	2012
1,2F	1,1F	1,1F	1,1F	1,1F	1,1F	1,1F	1,1F	1,1F	1,1F

Overview: Public confidence in President Laura Chinchilla continued to decline in 2012 as resignations and corruption scandals plagued her administration. While the homicide rate decreased in 2012 for the first time in years, crime rates rose and drug-related violence remained a significant threat. Gains from increased economic growth and foreign investment were undermined by rising poverty and unemployment.

Costa Rica achieved independence from Spain in 1821 and gained full sovereignty in 1838. The country enjoyed relative political stability until 1948, when

José "Pepe" Figueres launched a brief civil war to restore power to the rightful winner of that year's presidential election and successfully pushed to disband Costa Rica's military. In 1949, the country adopted a new constitution that ultimately strengthened democratic rule. Figueres later served as president for two separate terms under the National Liberation Party (PLN). Since 1949, power has alternated between the PLN and the Social Christian Unity Party (PUSC).

PLN candidate Óscar Arias, who had served as Costa Rica's president from 1986-1990, was reelected in 2006. In that year's parliamentary elections, the PLN captured the largest number of seats.

In February 2010, former vice president Laura Chinchilla of the PLN became Costa Rica's first female president, capturing nearly 47 percent of the vote in the first round and defeating Ottón Solís of the Citizens' Action Party (PAC) and Otto Guevara of the Libertarian Movement Party (PML). In concurrent legislative elections, the PLN captured 24 seats, the PAC won 11, the PML took 9, the PUSC won 6, and the Accessibility without Exclusion Party (PASE) captured 4, with the remaining 3 seats going to other smaller parties. In April 2011, the PAC's Juan Carlos Mendoza was elected president of the Assembly; Mendoza's election marked the first time in 46 years that the president of the Assembly was not a member of the ruling party.

Chinchilla began her presidency in May 2010 with a strong mandate and clear policy priorities to strengthen environmental protections, security, and family welfare. While she initially enjoyed strong public approval, by July 2011, public confidence in her administration eventually fell due to corruption scandals and the faltering economy. By September 2012, one poll revealed that Chinchilla had the lowest approval rating in the hemisphere—13 percent. Routine cabinet changes during Chinchilla's term reinforced the lack of confidence in her administration; 13 cabinet ministers resigned for various reasons during her first two years in office. In February 2011, Chinchilla introduced a 10-year crime reduction plan, which aims to promote interagency coordination to combat growing public insecurity, crime, and narcotics trafficking. Improved surveillance and coordination of security agencies were credited with a slight decrease in crime levels in 2011. The country's homicide rate fell to an estimated 10 murders for every 100,000 people in 2012, the first drop since 2004.

While the quality of life in Costa Rica is relatively high for the region, economic growth is hampered by the national debt, inflation, and cost-of-living increases. Though foreign direct investment in the economy reached record levels in 2011 and the economy grew at a faster than expected rate in 2012, poverty rates and unemployment increased.

Following the failure of proposed tax reform legislation in 2011, Chinchilla introduced a new tax plan in 2012 to address the growing budget deficit. The draft bill—which included the elimination of the national sales tax, the introduction of a new value-added tax, and a 15 percent withholding tax on new companies in the free trade zones—was found unconstitutional by a Supreme Court ruling in April for violating constitutional procedure. Chinchilla ultimately settled for a less ambitious reform plan that included mechanisms to improve tax collection and fiscal transparency.

Political Rights and Civil Liberties: Costa Rica is an electoral democracy. The 2010 legislative and presidential elections were considered free and fair. The president and members of the 57-seat, unicameral Legislative Assembly are elected for single four-year terms and can seek a nonconsecutive second term. A special chamber of the Supreme Court chooses an independent national election commission. Ahead of the 2010 elections, Costa Rica approved reforms to its electoral law, including revised regulations on political party and campaign financing, and new quotas for women's participation in political parties. The main political parties are the PLN, the PAC, the PML, and the PUSC.

Every president since 1990 has been accused of corruption after leaving office, with the exception of Óscar Arias. In December 2012, the appeals court overturned the corruption conviction of former president Miguel Ángel Rodríguez. Rodríguez was convicted in 2011 on corruption charges related to a business deal between the Costa Rican Electricity Institute and Alcatel, a French telecommunications company.

Like her predecessors, Chinchilla's government has been plagued by corruption scandals. In March 2012, Finance Minister Fernando Herrero; his wife, presidential consultant Floriasbel Rodriguez; and Tax Administrator Francisco Villalobos were accused of tax evasion by undervaluing their property. It was later revealed that Herrero and Rodriguez benefited from irregular bidding on a state-owned oil refinery project, which led to an investigation of Vice President Luis Lieberman and Minister of Education Leonardo Garnier for influence peddling. Chinchilla's refusal to dismiss them resulted in a standoff with the Legislative Assembly. Minister of Public Works Francisco Jimenez resigned in May amid allegations of corruption surrounding a road project along the San Juan River. Costa Rica was ranked 48 out of 176 countries surveyed in Transparency International's 2012 Corruption Perception Index.

The Costa Rican media are generally free from state interference. A February 2010 Supreme Court ruling removed prison terms for defamation. There are six privately owned dailies, and both public and commercial broadcast outlets are available, including at least four private television stations and more than 100 private radio stations. There have been reports of abuse of government advertising and direct pressure from senior officials to influence media content. Internet access is unrestricted.

The government recognizes freedom of religion. President Arias backed a 2009 bill that sought to declare Costa Rica a "secular state" rather than a Roman Catholic state. However, the bill, which was not supported by current president Laura Chinchilla, had not been adopted by the end of 2012. Academic freedom is respected.

The constitution provides for freedoms of assembly and association, and numerous nongovernmental organizations (NGOs) are active. Although labor unions organize and mount frequent protests with minimal governmental interference, employers often ignore minimum wage and social security laws, and the resulting fines are insignificant.

The judicial branch is independent, with members elected by the legislature. However, there are often substantial delays in the judicial process resulting in lengthy pretrial detention. There have been complaints of police brutality, and organized criminal networks are suspected of having infiltrated law enforcement institutions. An attempted prison break at a maximum-security facility in May 2011 led to an investigation of prison conditions, which revealed corruption, overcrowding, guard shortages, and guard-initiated abuse. Deadly prison riots in January and October 2012 underscored the severity of overcrowding in prisons, which has more than quintupled since 2009.

The country's Pacific Coast serves as a major drug transshipment route. During her first year in office, President Laura Chinchilla created a national antidrug commission, hired 1,000 new police officers, earmarked additional funds for the country's judicial investigation agency, and made plans to expand prison capacity. As Costa Rica has no standing army, Chinchilla also agreed in 2010 to station more than 13,000 U.S. military personnel on Costa Rican territory to lead regional antidrug efforts.

A 2006 law permits security forces to raid any home, business, or vehicle where they suspect undocumented immigrants, who can then be detained indefinitely. Abuse and extortion of migrants by the border guard have also been reported. Legislation governing migration issues imposes fines for employers who hire undocumented immigrants and stricter controls over marriages between Costa Ricans and foreigners.

Indigenous rights are not a government priority, and NGOs estimate that about 73 percent of the country's 70,000 indigenous people have little access to health and education services, electricity, or potable water. Costa Ricans of African descent have also faced racial and economic discrimination.

Women face discrimination in the economic realm. Female domestic workers are subject to exploitation and lack legal protections. Despite the existence of domestic violence legislation, violence against women and children is a major problem. Women were elected to 39 percent of the Legislative Assembly seats in the 2010 elections. Costa Rica has failed to enforce antitrafficking legislation and remains a transit and destination country for trafficked persons.

Chinchilla faced criticism from civil society organizations and LGBT (lesbian, gay, bisexual, and transgender) rights advocates when she supported a referendum put forth by conservative groups against same-sex unions. However, the Constitutional Court ruled in 2010 that holding a referendum on this issue was unconstitutional. In October 2011, the Supreme Court ruled against sexual orientation as grounds for discrimination by overturning a regulation that had prohibited conjugal visits for same-sex prisoners. In May 2012, PLN legislator Justo Orozco, known for his antigay views, was elected president of the Legislative Assembly's Human Rights Committee. His election was criticized by the LGBT community, which called on Chinchilla to speak out in support of LGBT rights.

Côte d'Ivoire

Political Rights: 5*
Civil Liberties: 5*
Status: Partly Free

Population: 20,646,000
Capital: Yamoussoukro (official); Abidjan (de facto)

Status Change: Côte d'Ivoire's political rights rating improved from 6 to 5, its civil liberties rating improved from 6 to 5, and its status improved from Not Free to Partly Free due to the peaceful inauguration of a new parliament; the adoption of several important laws on transparency and corruption; the reopening of opposition newspapers, public universities, and courts; renewed if halting attempts to curb abuses by the military; and a general improvement in the security situation.

Ten-Year Ratings Timeline For Year Under Review (Political Rights, Civil Liberties, Status)

2003	2004	2005	2006	2007	2008	2009	2010	2011	2012
6,5NF	6,6NF	6,6NF	7,6NF	7,5NF	6,5NF	6,5NF	7,6NF	6,6NF	5,5PF

Overview: In 2012, Côte d'Ivoire continued to recover from an early 2011 conflict—sparked by a disputed presidential election—that left about 3,000 dead and an estimated one million displaced. A new parliament was successfully seated, and the government of President Alassane Outtara made halting progress in reforming the judiciary and curbing abuses by the national army. Likewise, several important laws were adopted on transparency and corruption. However, despite some improvements to the security situation, lawlessness and impunity continued in many parts of the country.

Côte d'Ivoire gained independence from France in 1960, and its first president, Félix Houphouët-Boigny, presided over a period of economic prosperity until his death in 1993. Henri Konan Bédié, the speaker of the National Assembly, assumed power and, in the absence of any significant challenger, and won the 1995 presidential election. The main opposition parties had boycotted the election, alleging that the conditions for free and democratic elections did not exist. Bédié popularized the concept of Ivoirité, claiming that only ethnic groups from the country's south were "true" Ivoirians. Bédié used the concept to discredit his opponent, northerner Alassane Ouattara, due to his alleged Burkinabè origins.

General Robert Guéï seized power in 1999 and declared himself the winner of an October 2000 presidential election after initial results showed he was losing to opposition politician Laurent Gbagbo. Ouattara and Bédié, candidates to the presidential election, had been declared ineligible to run by the Supreme Court; Ouattara was disqualified on the grounds he did not meet citizenship requirements, and Bédié because he did not file the proper documents. Guéï was soon toppled by a popular uprising, and Gbagbo, who had assumed the presidency, refused to call new polls. Postelection violence cost hundreds of lives and deepened divisions between the north and south, as well as between Muslims and Christians. In December 2000 legislative elections, Gbagbo's Ivorian Popular Front (FPI) won a small majority of seats over Bédié's Democratic Party of Côte d'Ivoire–African

Democratic Rally (PDCI-RDA). Ouattara was again declared ineligible to run, and his Rally of the Republicans (RDR) party boycotted the polls.

Civil war erupted in September 2002 when soldiers mounted a coup attempt and government forces killed Guéï under unclear circumstances. Rebel forces quickly took control of the north and called for Gbagbo to step down and organize inclusive elections. By December 2002, various rebel factions had united to form the New Forces (FN), led by Guillaume Soro.

Gbagbo's government and the FN, as well as the main political parties, signed a French-brokered comprehensive peace agreement in 2003, but it soon broke down. In April 2005, South African president Thabo Mbeki brokered a new peace accord that addressed more closely issues related to a presidential election set to be held in October. However, the country remained divided in two; disarmament, demobilization, and reintegration (DDR) stalled; and election preparations were behind schedule. In October, the African Union and the UN Security Council postponed the presidential poll and extended Gbagbo's term, and a Security Council resolution appointed an interim prime minister, economist Charles Konan Banny. Similar delays prevented elections from taking place in 2006. With the expiration of Gbagbo's extended mandate in October 2006, the Security Council passed a resolution transferring all political and military power to the prime minister until elections. Gbagbo refused to accept the move, calling for a direct dialogue with the FN and the withdrawal of all foreign troops.

In March 2007, Gbagbo and Soro signed a new peace deal brokered by Burkinabé president Blaise Compaoré, the Ouagadougou Political Accord (APO), under which Soro was appointeed interim prime minister until elections could be held. The situation began to slowly improve, and the "confidence zone" separating north and south was officially dismantled.

The elections envisioned in the APO were postponed five times over the next three years. Less than 12,000 of the more than 30,000 FN troops and almost none of the pro-Gbagbo militia groups slated for disarmament actually went through the process. Some progress was made on voter registration, particularly among previously disenfranchised groups in the north, widely perceived as foreigners by southern ethnic groups. Nonetheless, the registration effort was badly organized and frequently contested by all sides.

The first round of the presidential election was finally held on October 31, 2010, and was deemed relatively free and fair by domestic and international observers. The runoff was relatively peaceful, and domestic and international observers generally approved of the polling. However, violence increased considerably during the period before the results were announced.

On December 2, the Independent Electoral Commission (IEC) announced that Ouattara had won with 54 percent of the vote. The Constitutional Council, filled with Gbagbo loyalists, quickly annulled results from largely pro-Ouattara northern districts, alleging widespread fraud, and announced that Gbagbo had won with 51 percent. The United Nations, tasked by Ivoirian leaders to certify that the electoral process abided by international standards, confirmed that the results announced by the IEC were credible. By December 4, both Gbagbo and Ouattara had been sworn in as president in separate ceremonies.

This standoff led to a protracted conflict with former FN rebels and other pro-

Ouattara fighters pitted against Gbagbo's security forces and militia groups. The fighting resulted in the death of approximately 3,000 civilians and the displacement of up to one million between December 2010 and April 2011. Ouattara's forces launched a nationwide military offensive in March, with the support of French and UN troops backed by a Security Council resolution, ending in the seizure of the presidential palace and the arrest of Gbagbo.

Forces on both sides were guilty of committing atrocities during the conflict. However, it is widely believed that pro-Ouattara forces were responsible for the single largest massacre of the period, in which up to 1,000 people were murdered in a single day in March 2011 in the western town of Duékoué.

In September 2011, Ouattara's government launched a Truth and Reconciliation Commission, and in October a prosecutor from the International Criminal Court (ICC) was given permission to investigate those most responsible for the violence. In November, Gbagbo was handed over to the ICC to face four charges of crimes against humanity; the scope of the inquiry was expanded in February 2012 to include crimes committed during and after the 2002 crisis. Gbagbo appeared before the ICC for an initial hearing in December 2011—the first former head of state to face prosecution by the ICC. By the end of 2012, the court had yet to rule on whether he would face a full trial. The national courts have been more aggressive in prosecuting forces loyal to Gbagbo than those affiliated with Ouattara, though in March 2012 a military tribunal began hearings against nine members of the pro-Ouattara Republican Forces of Côte d'Ivoire (FRCI). By the end of the year, Abidjan's military prosecutor had opened a total of 77 cases against FRCI soldiers, though most were related to minor offenses.

Parliamentary elections in December 2011 were deemed largely peaceful and fair, with Ouattara's RDR party taking just over 42 percent of the 255 available seats and the PDCI-RDA capturing nearly 29 percent. Gbagbo's party, the FPI, boycotted the vote, accusing the electoral commission of bias and the security forces of intimidation. The first meeting of the new assembly was held in March 2012, and Soro, the outgoing prime minister and an RDR member, was elected speaker. Despite disruptions caused by Oauttara's dissolution of the government ahead of a cabinet reshuffling in November, the year witnessed an increase in legislative activity, including the adoption of state-imposed minimum prices for cocoa—the country's most important export—and controversial legislation adopted in November guaranteeing equal rights for legally married couples, overturning a previous law that designated the husband as the sole head of the family.

While the security situation slowly stabilized in 2012, some serious problems remain. Ouattara's government has made progress in purging the FRCI—now reconstituted as the national army—of irregulars who had joined during the crisis, returning soldiers to their barracks, and prosecuting indiscipline in the ranks. Nevertheless, the FRCI remains corrupt, and soldiers are frequently implicated in human rights violations. Meanwhile, the presence of dozos, traditional hunters who helped secure the country in the aftermath of the 2011 crisis, has strained access to land and fomented tensions with civilians, especially in the west. A Disarmament, Demobilization and Reintegration Authority (ADDR) responsible for supervising all DDR operations was created in August, but implementation had barely begun by year's end.

Although the level of violence has declined from 2011 levels, there were several high-profile incidents in 2012 that drew international condemnation. In June, 16 people, including 7 UN peacekeepers, were killed in an apparent militia attack in the western border region of Tai; despite multiple UN inquiries, the circumstances surrounding the killings remain unclear. In July, a mob of around 1,000 descended upon a camp for internally displaced persons in Duékoué, killing 6, in what was described as an attack rooted in tensions over ethnicity and land rights. The next month, assailants attacked police stations and an army camp in Abidjan, the most serious attack in the city since Gbagbo's ouster. New mass graves were discovered in October near the site of the Duékoué massacre, prompting allegations that the government had intentionally downplayed its casualty estimates in order to protect the FRCI from accusations of complicity in the attack.

Political Rights and Civil Liberties: Côte d'Ivoire is not an electoral democracy. December 2011 saw the first largely peaceful and fair parliamentary elections in over a decade. The constitution provides for the popular election of a president and a unicameral National Assembly—currently comprising 255 members—for five-year terms. In 2011, Ouattara reappointed ally and former rebel leader Guillaume Soro as prime minister, and in 2012 Soro was named Speaker of the National Assembly. Soro and other former rebel leaders, to whom Ouattara is greatly indebted, appear to have significant influence over his policy decisions.

Ouattara's RDR party dominates the political scene, followed by the PDCI-RDA. Former president Laurent Gbagbo's FPI party remains disorganized and has conditioned its participation in the political process on demands—such as Gbagbo's release—that are unlikely to be met in the near future.

Corruption is a serious problem, and perpetrators rarely face prosecution or public exposure. Ouattara instructed his ministers to sign an antigraft code of ethics in 2011, and his administration has drafted legislation that would establish more robust penalties for corruption. He has enforced new rules against tardiness and absenteeism for civil servants, and has dismissed or threatened dismissal for ministers charged with corruption. Progress in public sector reform has been slow, however, with laws enforced inconsistently and often ineffectively. Côte d'Ivoire was ranked 130 out of 176 countries surveyed in Transparency International's 2012 Corruption Perceptions Index.

Freedom of speech and of the press is protected by the constitution and in the country's laws, although there are prohibitions on speech that incites violence, ethnic hatred, or rebellion. Ouattara's first year in power witnessed several high-profile detentions and legal cases targeting pro-Gbagbo journalists and media outlets. While this lessened in 2012, some intimidation of opposition reporters persisted. The National Press Council, the regulatory body, briefly suspended several pro-Gbagbo newspapers in September for publishing photos of individuals close to the former president with captions indicating their government titles during the postelectoral crisis.

Legal guarantees of religious freedom are typically upheld, though the political divide between north and south often overlaps with a religious divide between Muslims and Christians. Religious and traditional organizations have been instrumental in leading the postcrisis reconciliation process at the local level.

Academic freedom was severely limited under Gbagbo, with progovernment student organizations engaging in systematic intimidation on campuses. In 2011, universities throughout the country were closed, occupied by military forces from both sides, and used as military bases and training grounds. While the militias were eventually expelled, the country's five public universities remained closed for the remainder of the 2011–12 academic year but reopened in September 2012.

The constitution protects the right to free assembly, but it is often denied in practice. During an FPI meeting in Abidjan in January, clashes erupted when members of the ruling coalition attempted to disrupt the proceedings, resulting in one death and several injuries. Under Ouattara, the security forces have targeted Gbagbo's former supporters and co-ethnics, including the high profile arrest in June of opposition leader Martial Yavo, interim president of the Pan African Congress of Youth and Patriots—an arrest that was publicly condemned by the Dialogue, Truth and Reconciliation Commission. Nevertheless, freedom of association improved in 2012, and both domestic and international nongovernmental organizations generally operated freely.

The right to organize and join labor unions is constitutionally guaranteed, and workers have the right to bargain collectively. Unions suffered greatly during the 2011 crisis, becoming disorganized and largely ineffectual. While they have enjoyed moments of resurgence in 2012, the country's 44 percent unemployment rate continues to stifle labor's political efficacy.

The judiciary is not independent, and judges are highly susceptible to external interference and bribes. Some progress has been made under Ouattara; in April, the country adopted a national justice sector strategy, which is beginning to reinvigorate the long-stalled judicial reform process. All of the country's 37 courts and 22 prisons have reopened since the end of the 2011 crisis.

The security situation remained tenuous in 2012, with improvements in Abidjan but deterioration in other parts of the country. Crime is rampant, and small arms remain ubiquitous; a national commission has been created to recover illegal firearms, but progress has been slow. The United Nations has extended the mandate of its approximately 10,000 uniformed personnel through July 2013.

Conflicts between immigrant groups and longer-term residents played a significant part in the recent conflict, and progress on reconciliation has been slow. On a more positive note, in 2012, the government granted citizenship to more than 100,000 long-time residents who had previously lacked documentation—a significant milestone in a country where questions of national identity have been recurrent causes of violence.

Economic freedom and employment suffered as a result of the conflict, with businesses across the country forced to close. Many have since reopened, and the economy grew at a rate of more than 8.5 percent in 2012, after a contraction of 4.7 percent in 2011. Corruption and the weakness of the judiciary, however, continue to be impediments to investment, and many of the procedures essential to starting and running a business—including registering property—remain laborious and slow.

Tens of thousands of children from the region are believed to be working on Ivoirian plantations. Some progress was made on the issue of child trafficking in 2012, including the conviction of a suspected trafficker, the rescue of three victims, and the establishment of a Joint Ministerial Committee and national action plan to combat trafficking.

Despite constitutional protections, women suffer widespread legal and economic discrimination. Rape was common during the 2011 conflict, and remains pervasive. State law mandates onerously high standards of evidence to prosecute domestic violence, and perpetrators are often released if victims fail to provide costly medical certificates. Women are heavily underrepresented in government and decision-making positions.

Croatia

Political Rights: 1
Civil Liberties: 2
Status: Free

Population: 4,273,000
Capital: Zagreb

Ten-Year Ratings Timeline For Year Under Review (Political Rights, Civil Liberties, Status)

2003	2004	2005	2006	2007	2008	2009	2010	2011	2012
2,2F	2,2F	2,2F	2,2F	2,2F	2,2F	1,2F	1,2F	1,2F	1,2F

Overview: Croatia ratified its European Union (EU) accession treaty in March 2012 and was expected to join the EU in 2013. The government continued with key EU reforms, though Brussels urged Croatia to redress a culture of impunity for war crimes. Croatia continued its anticorruption drive in 2012; in November, former prime minister Ivo Sanader was convicted of corruption charges and sentenced to 10 years in prison.

Formerly a constituent republic within socialist Yugoslavia, Croatia held its first multiparty elections in 1990, won by the former communist general and dissident Franjo Tudman and his Croatian Democratic Union (HDZ). Independence was subsequently declared in June 1991. From 1991 to 1995, Croatia was consumed by the wars accompanying Yugoslavia's disintegration, both on its own territory, where the indigenous Serb population attempted to secede, and in neighboring Bosnia and Herzegovina.

Tudman's HDZ continued to rule Croatia until his death in December 1999. An erstwhile Tudman ally, Stjepan Mesic, was elected president in January 2000, and parliamentary elections held later that month resulted in a victory for a center-left coalition led by the Social Democratic Party (SDP). Ivica Racan, leader of the SDP, became prime minister.

The HDZ returned to power in 2003 under the leadership of Prime Minister Ivo Sanader and refashioned itself as a conventional European center-right party. The Sanader government's policies focused on gaining Croatian membership to both NATO and the European Union (EU). Croatia formally joined NATO in April 2009.

The HDZ won the November 2007 parliamentary elections and formed a governing coalition with the Croatian Peasant Party, the Croatian Social Liberal Party, and all eight of the country's ethnic minority parliamentary representatives. In July 2009, Sanader unexpectedly resigned, and was replaced by Jadranka Kosor, a deputy prime minister of the HDZ. Ivo Josipovic, the SDP candidate, was elected president in January 2010.

In the December 2011 parliamentary elections, the center-left opposition Kukuriku coalition, comprising the SDP and three other parties, placed first with 80 seats. The HDZ and its coalition partners, the Croatian Civic Party and the Democratic Centre, followed with 47 seats. Zoran Milanovic of the SDP succeeded Kosor as prime minister.

Croatia continued to cooperate with the International Criminal Tribunal for the former Yugoslavia (ICTY) at The Hague, the Netherlands, a pre-condition for EU membership. In April 2011, the court convicted Croatian army generals Ante Gotovina and Mladen Markac of crimes against humanity for participating in Operation Storm, a 1995 campaign to remove ethnic Serbs from the Krajina, a self-proclaimed Serb republic within Croatia that existed from 1991 to 1995. In November 2012, an appeals court at the ICTY, in a controversial split decision, overturned their convictions, and Gotovina and Markac were immediately released from detention facilities at The Hague. The decision was hailed across Croatia, but drew condemnations from Serbia and Russia.

In March 2012, Croatian lawmakers ratified the EU accession treaty following a successful membership referendum. Croatia's EU bid had stalled in recent years over concerns about insufficient cooperation with the ICTY, mixed results at reducing corruption, and a territorial dispute with Slovenia. In 2011, the EU had cleared the country for membership after noting increased anticorruption efforts and reforms in the judiciary. Josipovic and Kosor signed the Accession Treaty that December. Assuming all 27 EU countries ratify the treaty, Croatia should become the 28th member in July 2013.

Political Rights and Civil Liberties: Croatia is an electoral democracy. The 151-member unicameral parliament (Sabor) comprises 140 members from 10 geographical districts; in addition, 8 members represent ethnic minorities, and 3 represent Croatians abroad. Members are elected to four-year terms. The president, who serves as head of state, is elected by popular vote for a maximum of two five-year terms. The prime minister is appointed by the president and requires parliamentary approval.

The largest political parties are the center-right HDZ and center-left SDP. Several smaller parties have also won representation in the parliament.

In 2012, the European Commission (EC) noted progress on Croatia's anticorruption efforts, singling out law enforcement for taking a proactive approach, especially on high-profile cases. However, most of these cases remain unresolved. In January, the government passed legislation to increase transparency in public procurement; the EC urged its effective implementation and also called for the overdue appointment of a commission to monitor conflicts of interest among public officials. In 2011, authorities expanded their investigation into the so-called Fimi media case, which includes indictments of Ivo Sanader and other HDZ officials. In Croatia's first legal case against a political party, the HDZ is accused of funneling money from public companies to a slush fund from 2003 to 2009. In April 2012, the HDZ and Sanader pleaded not guilty in the Fimi case. By September 2012, Sanader had been indicted in five corruption cases. In November, he was convicted of taking a 5 million euro ($6.5 million) bribe from a Hungarian energy company in 2008, and of taking another 545,000 euros ($695,000) in bribes from an Austrian bank in 1995 during his tenure as deputy foreign minister. Sanader, who was sentenced to 10 years in prison, called the trial politically motivated. In December, he was indicted on corruption charges alongside a former HDZ agriculture minister over a 2009 real estate deal. Croatia was ranked 62 out of 176 countries surveyed in Transparency International's 2012 Corruption Perceptions Index.

The constitution guarantees freedoms of expression and the press, and these rights are generally respected. However, journalists—particularly those covering organized crime and corruption—face political pressure, intimidation, and attacks. In July 2012, a Croatian daily reported that at least seven key editors at the HRT public broadcaster had been replaced in what the HDZ called a political purge following Kukuriku's December election win. Internet access is unrestricted.

The constitution guarantees freedom of religion. A group needs at least 500 members and five years of registered operation to be recognized as a religious organization. Members of the Serbian Orthodox Church continue to report cases of intimidation and vandalism, although such incidents are declining. In June 2012, the Serbian Orthodox Patriarch met with Croatian religious and political leaders in what many called an historic three-day visit to heal lingering wounds between the two countries, as well as between the Orthodox and Catholic churches. Little progress has been made in restoring property nationalized by the communists to non-Roman Catholic groups. Academic freedom is guaranteed by law.

The constitution provides for freedoms of association and assembly. After attacks at a June 2011 gay pride parade in Split, police stepped up security at the 2012 event. Amnesty International (AI) criticized police for failing to investigate an attack a few days after the festival by a group of men of six young women in Split for their perceived sexual orientation. A variety of nongovernmental organizations operate in Croatia without governmental interference or harassment. The constitution allows workers to form and join trade unions, though unlawful dismissals of union members have been reported.

Croatia continued in 2012 to implement reforms to improve the independence and efficiency of the judiciary. The EC urged further reforms, especially regarding the selection procedures for judges and prosecutors. The recently reformed State Judicial and Prosecutorial Councils function independently and began establishing a track record of merit-based appointments. In February, a new council was created to focus on courts' efficiency, a noted area of improvement with the backlog of criminal cases down 12 percent in the first half of 2012. Prison conditions do not meet international standards due to overcrowding and poor medical care.

The legacy of the 1991–95 war in Croatia remains a sensitive issue. AI has criticized Croatia for failing to identify the total number of war crimes cases and prosecute them expeditiously. In 2012, the government continued to cooperate with the ICTY and implemented a strategy to tackle impunity. There were also some high-profile domestic cases, including against a former Interior Ministry official for the alleged killing of Serbian civilians during the conflict. However, most war crimes have not been resolved or even investigated, according to the EC, which urged Croatia to address impunity, train judges to specifically handle war crimes cases, and improve witness protection.

Respect for minority rights has improved over the past decade. Although returning Serbs face harassment by local populations, such incidents have declined in recent years. Some 70,000 Croatian Serbs are registered refugees. The 2011 Housing Care Program to aid returning refugees has been fully implemented, though conditions for returnees remain inadequate. Roma face widespread discrimination. In May 2012, a parliamentary committee condemned a recent outpouring of anti-Roma rhetoric and discrimination, including threats by a mayor in Dalmatia against a local Roma family.

The constitution prohibits gender discrimination, but women have a higher unemployment rate and earn less than men for comparable work. Domestic violence against women is believed to be widespread and underreported, though law enforcement is strengthening its capacity to combat such crimes. Croatia remains a transit country for women trafficked to Western Europe for prostitution.

Cuba

Political Rights: 7
Civil Liberties: 6
Status: Not Free

Population: 11,219,000
Capital: Havana

Ten-Year Ratings Timeline For Year Under Review (Political Rights, Civil Liberties, Status)

2003	2004	2005	2006	2007	2008	2009	2010	2011	2012
7,7NF	7,7NF	7,7NF	7,7NF	7,7NF	7,6NF	7,6NF	7,6NF	7,6NF	7,6NF

Overview: **The Cuban government oversaw a systematic increase in short-term "preventative" detentions of dissidents in 2012, in addition to harassment, beatings, acts of repudiation, and restrictions on foreign and domestic travel. Such repressive actions intensified surrounding politically sensitive dates throughout the year. A Communist Party conference in January imposed the regime's first-ever term limits for top party and government officials. The government continued with its program of limited economic reforms, and the number of legally self-employed Cubans reached 400,000. A new migration law published in October promised to eliminate the exit-visa requirement for the first time in 50 years beginning in January 2013.**

Cuba achieved independence from Spain in 1898 at the end of the Spanish-American War, which capped a longer struggle against colonial rule. The Republic of Cuba was established in 1902 but remained a U.S. protectorate until 1934. On January 1, 1959, the dictatorship of Fulgencio Batista was overthrown, and Fidel Castro's rebel July 26th Movement took power. Castro quickly eliminated civil society, and tensions between his radical nationalist revolution and the United States soon emerged. The United States sponsored a failed 1961 invasion by Cuban exiles and imposed a trade embargo on the island, while the new socialist regime turned to the Soviet Union during the early 1960s. In late 1961, Castro declared his affiliation with communism, and the country has since been governed by a one-party state.

Following the 1991 collapse of the Soviet Union and the end of Soviet subsidies, Cuba suffered an economic depression. In response, Castro opened some sectors of the economy to direct foreign investment, legalized use of the U.S. dollar, and allowed limited self-employment. Inequality increased as access to dollars from remittances or through the tourist industry enriched some, while the majority continued to live on peso wages averaging less than $10 a month. Meanwhile, the authorities remained highly intolerant of political dissent, enacting harsh sedition legislation in 1999 and mounting defamation campaigns against dissidents that portrayed them as U.S. agents.

In 1999, Cuba and Venezuela began an economic partnership whereby Cuba received subsidized oil and provided Venezuela with technical and intelligence assistance. The arrangement helped to alleviate the economic pressures of the 1990s; however, the incapacitation of Venezuelan president Hugo Chávez since beginning a third round of cancer surgeries in December 2012 does not bode well for the future stability of the relationship.

In 2002, the Varela Project, championed by the dissident Oswaldo Payá and his Christian Liberation Movement, petitioned for a referendum on political reforms. The project obtained the 10,000 signatures required by the 1976 constitution, but the National Assembly rejected the proposal, instead holding a referendum that declared the socialist system "irrevocable." The government cracked down on the prodemocracy opposition in March 2003, with 75 people sentenced to long prison terms after summary trials.

In July 2006, a gravely ill Fidel Castro transferred provisional power to his younger brother, defense minister and first vice president Raúl Castro. The octogenarian Fidel resigned as president in February 2008, and Raúl, 76, formally replaced him.

Beginning in 2008, the government approved a series of unprecedented economic reforms. These included allowing Cubans to buy consumer electronic goods and stay in tourist hotels, eliminating salary caps, and raising pensions for retirees. In 2009, the government began to distribute land leases to agricultural workers. In late 2010, it was announced that more than a million state sector workers would be laid off over the next 18 months, while 178 economic activities would be opened up to self-employment. However, layoffs were soon scaled back, since continued restrictions on microenterprises made rapid job creation untenable. Eased rules on private home and car sales were announced in late 2011; home sales were growing rapidly in 2012.

From July 2010 to March 2011, through negotiations with the Roman Catholic Church and the Spanish government, Cuban authorities released 166 political prisoners, including the 52 remaining from the 2003 crackdown. While most were forced into exile, 12 remained in Cuba under a form of parole. Meanwhile, the authorities ramped up short-term detentions of dissidents, making them the preferred form of repression. The Damas de Blanco (Ladies in White), a group of relatives of the 2003 political prisoners, continued their protests into 2012, despite repeated episodes of harassment and the late 2011 death of their leader, Laura Pollán. They joined forces with a related group, the Damas de Apoyo (Ladies in Support), to pursue the release of all political prisoners and demand the restoration of fundamental civil and political freedoms. They also spread across the country, gaining adherents in eastern Cuba.

In July 2012, Payá and fellow dissident Harold Cepero were killed when a car driven by Spanish political activist Ángel Carromero struck a tree. While Payá's family maintains that the car was deliberately forced off the road, Carromero was convicted of manslaughter for the crash and sentenced to four years in prison in October. In December he was allowed to return to Spain to serve out his sentence. Short-term political detentions continued to rise in 2012, intensifying around major events like the March visit of Pope Benedict XVI, the Payá car crash in July, the first anniversary of Pollán's death, and International Human Rights Day on December 10. Among other repressive tactics, the mobile telephones of scores of dissidents were cut off during the pope's visit. Cuba's leading blogger and citizen journalist, Yoani Sánchez, was prevented from traveling abroad for the 19th consecutive time in late January and was detained twice in the fall, once while trying to cover the Carromero trial.

U.S. government contractor Alan Gross remained in prison in 2012, having been arrested in December 2009 for distributing communications equipment to Jewish groups in Cuba and sentenced to 15 years in prison in March 2011 for engaging in "subversive" activities aimed at undermining Cuban sovereignty; a United Nations panel concluded in late 2012 that his detention was arbitrary and violated international human rights standards. The U.S. government has eased some travel restrictions in recent years but maintains its economic sanctions on the island.

Political Rights and Civil Liberties: Cuba is not an electoral democracy. Longtime president Fidel Castro and his brother, current president Raúl Castro, dominate the one-party political system, in which the Communist Party of Cuba (PCC) controls all government and most civil institutions. The 1976 constitution provides for a National Assembly, which designates the Council of State. This body in turn appoints the Council of Ministers in consultation with its president, who serves as chief of state and head of government. Raúl Castro is now president of the Council of Ministers and the Council of State, commander in chief of the armed forces, and first secretary of the PCC. In April 2011, the PCC held its sixth congress. In addition to electing Raúl Castro as head of the party, delegates appointed a greater number of high-level military officials to the PCC Politburo and Central Committee, but they made little progress in adding younger party members. A PCC national conference in January 2012 imposed a limit of two five-year terms on elected officials, but no senior officials were immediately retired or replaced.

In the January 2008 National Assembly elections, as in previous elections, voters were asked to either support or reject a single PCC-approved candidate for each of the 614 seats. All candidates received the requisite 50 percent approval, with Raúl Castro winning support from over 99 percent of voters. In April 2010, Cuba held elections for the roughly 15,000 delegates to the country's 169 municipal councils, which are elected every two and a half years.

All political organizing outside the PCC is illegal. Political dissent, whether spoken or written, is a punishable offense, and dissidents frequently receive years of imprisonment for seemingly minor infractions. The regime has called on its neighborhood-watch groups, known as Committees for the Defense of the Revolution, to strengthen vigilance against "antisocial behavior," a euphemism for opposition activity.

In recent years, dissident leaders have reported an increase in intimidation and harassment by state-sponsored groups as well as short-term detentions by state security forces. The independent Cuban Commission of Human Rights and National Reconciliation reported 6,602 short-term detentions in 2012, a 60 percent increase over 2011. In November 2012, a group of independent lawyers, journalists, and activists were briefly and violently detained for promoting the "Citizen Demand for Another Cuba" petition, which calls on the government to ratify the International Covenant on Civil and Political Rights (ICCPR) and the International Covenant on Economic, Social, and Cultural Rights (ICESCR). Antonio Rodiles, a leader of the petition drive, was charged with resisting arrest and held for 19 days before being released amid mounting international pressure.

Official corruption remains a serious problem, with a culture of illegality shrouding the mixture of limited private enterprise and a vast state-controlled economy. The Raúl Castro government has made the fight against corruption a central priority, with long sentences for both high-placed Cuban nationals and foreign businessmen who are convicted of economic crimes. Cuba was ranked 58 out of 176 countries surveyed in Transparency International's 2012 Corruption Perceptions Index.

The news media are owned and controlled by the state, and private bookstores remain banned. The government considers the independent press to be illegal and uses agents to infiltrate and report on unauthorized outlets. Independent journalists, particularly those associated with the dozen small news agencies that have been established outside state control, are subject to harassment. Nevertheless, some state media have begun to cover previously taboo topics, such as corruption in the health and education sectors. The national newspaper *Granma* has begun to publish letters to the editor complaining about economic issues. Some publications of the Catholic Church have emerged as key players in debates over the country's future.

Access to the internet remains tightly controlled, and it is difficult for most Cubans to connect from their homes. The estimated effective internet penetration rate is less than 3 percent, one of the lowest in the world, while a higher percentage have access to e-mail and a limited, domestic intranet. While there are state-owned internet cafés in major cities, the costs are prohibitively high for most residents. Only selected state employees have workplace access to e-mail, and access to websites deemed inappropriate by superiors is restricted.

There are an estimated 70 independent, journalistic bloggers working on the island. While some have kept their distance from the political opposition and restricted their activities to the internet, others have faced harassment and detention for supporting dissidents. A growing group of cyberactivists, led by pioneering blogger Yoani Sánchez, have recently begun to hold public gatherings and link up with other independent civil society groups.

In 1991, Roman Catholics and other believers were granted permission to join the PCC, and the constitutional reference to official atheism was dropped the following year. The Catholic Church has been playing an increasingly important role in civil society, enabling discussion of topics of public concern and offering material assistance to the population. Nevertheless, official obstacles to religious freedom remain substantial. Churches are not allowed to conduct ordinary educational activities, and many church-based publications are subject to censorship. While Roman Catholicism is the traditionally dominant faith, an estimated 70 percent of the population practices some form of Afro-Cuban religion, and as in the rest of Latin America, Protestantism is making rapid gains.

The government restricts academic freedom. Teaching materials for subjects including mathematics and literature must contain ideological content. Affiliation with PCC structures is generally needed to gain access to educational institutions, and students' report cards carry information regarding their parents' involvement with the party.

According to the constitution, limited rights of assembly and association may not be "exercised against the existence and objectives of the Socialist State." Recent initiatives by emergent nongovernmental organizations, such as the independent Cuban Legal Association and its consulting services, have been forcefully rebuffed by the state. Workers do not have the right to strike or bargain collectively, and independent labor unions are illegal.

The Council of State controls the courts and the judicial process as a whole. From 1991 to 2007, the United Nations voted annually to assign a special investigator on human rights to Cuba, which consistently denied the appointee a visa. The investigator position was terminated in 2007. Cuban government representatives signed two UN human rights treaties, the ICCPR and ICESCR, in 2008, but the agreements have not been ratified or implemented on the island. Cuba does not grant international humanitarian organizations access to its prisons.

Afro-Cubans have reported widespread discrimination by government and law enforcement officials. Many Afro-Cubans have only limited access to the dollar-earning sectors of the economy. Autonomous racial advocacy or civil rights organizations are illegal. Berta Soler, the current leader of the dissident group Ladies in White, is an Afro-Cuban woman.

Since 2008, Cuba has made important strides to redress discrimination against the LGBT (lesbian, gay, bisexual, and transgender) community, thanks in part to the advocacy work of Mariela Castro, director of the National Center for Sexual Education (CENESEX) and Raúl Castro's daughter. The government has helped to sponsor an annual International Day Against Homophobia, and the Ministry of Public Health has authorized government-provided sex-reassignment surgeries for transgender people. In 2010, Fidel Castro issued an apology for the regime's past persecution of LGBT individuals. Nonetheless, a bill proposing the legalization of same-sex marriages has been stalled in the National Assembly since 2008. Moreover, the authorities do not recognize the work of independent, grassroots LGBT rights groups, and their efforts have often been attacked by CENESEX.

Freedom of movement and the right to choose one's residence and place of employment are severely restricted. Cubans working abroad are not paid directly by their employers, but rather through the Cuban state, in violation of International Labour Organization statutes.

In October 2012, the government published a new migration law that rescinded the exit visa and letter of invitation that were previously required to travel abroad. While the measure, to take effect in early 2013, represented a potentially dramatic step forward in restoring fundamental rights, it did little to restore the rights of exiles. Moreover, the new law gives the Interior Ministry broad discretion in its implementation.

Only state enterprises can enter into economic agreements with foreigners as minority partners; ordinary citizens cannot participate. There are very few fully private foreign businesses in Cuba. PCC membership is still required to obtain good jobs, suitable housing, and real access to social services, including medical care and educational opportunities.

The number of self-employment licenses has grown from 157,000 in October

2010 to 400,000 by the end of 2012. As many as 67 percent of these licenses have gone to people who were previously unemployed, suggesting a limited benefit for those laid off from the state sector. A new income tax law and new cooperative regulations were issued in late 2012, but it remained unclear whether these would help jump-start the economic modernization process, which seemed to stall during the year. Private credit remains mostly nonexistent, severely curtailing any expansion of the private sector beyond small businesses.

The Cuban constitution establishes the full equality of women. About 40 percent of all women work in the official labor force, and they are well represented in most professions. However, the ongoing economic reforms have begun to widen the gender gap in the labor force.

Cyprus

Political Rights: 1
Civil Liberties: 1
Status: Free

Population: 1,172,000
Capital: Nicosia

Note: The numerical ratings and status listed above do not reflect conditions in Northern Cyprus, which is examined in a separate report.

Ten-Year Ratings Timeline For Year Under Review (Political Rights, Civil Liberties, Status)

2003	2004	2005	2006	2007	2008	2009	2010	2011	2012
1,1F	1,1F	1,1F	1,1F	1,1F	1,1F	1,1F	1,1F	1,1F	1,1F

Overview: Cyprus's recession intensified in 2012 as the country's debt crisis led to bailout negotiations with the European Union. Faced with these financial troubles, Cyprus continued to aggressively exploit natural gas reserves in its territorial waters, a move that further increased tensions with Turkey and Northern Cyprus.

Cyprus gained independence from Britain in 1960 after a five-year guerrilla campaign by partisans demanding union with Greece. In July 1974, Greek Cypriot National Guard members, backed by Greece's military junta, staged an unsuccessful coup aimed at such unification. Five days later, Turkey invaded from the north, seizing control of 37 percent of the island. Since then, a buffer zone known as the Green Line has divided Cyprus; the Greek and Turkish communities remain almost completely separated in the south and north, respectively. In 1983, Turkish-controlled Cyprus declared its independence, a move recognized only by Turkey. UN resolutions stipulate that Cyprus is a single country of which the northern third is illegally occupied.

In 2004, both parts of the island voted simultaneously on a unification plan prepared by then UN secretary general Kofi Annan. Ultimately, 76 percent of Greek Cypriots voted against the plan, while 65 percent of Turkish Cypriots voted in favor. With the island still divided, only Greek Cyprus joined the European Union as scheduled in May 2004.

In the 2008 presidential election, Demetris Christofias of the Progressive Party of the Working Republic (AKEL), a communist party, won 53 percent of a runoff vote, making him the only communist head of state in Europe. His cabinet included ministers from the Democratic Party (DIKO), as well as the Movement for Social Democrats. Christofias had voiced a commitment toward unification but has made only symbolic progress. Tripartite talks in January, March, and July 2011 between UN secretary general Ban Ki-moon and representatives of Cyprus and Northern Cyprus failed to bring the two sides substantially closer to unification.

In parliamentary elections held in May 2011, the Democratic Rally (DISY) party took 20 seats, AKEL won 19 seats, and DIKO took 9 seats; three small parties captured the remaining 8 seats. In July, a massive explosion of confiscated weaponry occurred on a naval base, killing 13 and causing billions in economic damage. Following the incident, DIKO withdrew from the coalition government.

The weakening of Christofias's coalition, which was amenable to unification, negatively affected negotiations with Northern Cyprus. In September 2012, DIKO voted to support DISY's Nicos Anastasiadis for president in parliamentary elections scheduled for February 2013. Anastasiadis has promised to repudiate the Christofias administration's concessions to Northern Cyprus.

A recession that had begun in 2011 intensified in 2012. Cyprus's bond rating was downgraded, and the banking sector, heavily invested in Greek bonds, required a bailout following the 53.5 percent write-down on Greek debt that occurred in February 2012. Cyprus received a 2.5 billion euro ($3.34 billion) loan from Russia in late 2011 to cover shortfalls and is currently negotiating with both Russia and its European partners for additional funds and debt modifications. The country hopes to avoid the type of austerity program that has crippled other countries in the region.

Tensions continued to escalate over natural gas exploration in the eastern Mediterranean Sea. Due to its economic problems, Cyprus is moving aggressively with its Israeli and American partners to exploit natural gas reserves in its territorial waters. The Northern Cypriots have designated this activity illegal and have called on energy companies to halt activities in the region. Turkey, too, has voiced its disapproval and threatened to deploy its navy. The emerging contest over resources threatens to delay a return to serious unification negotiations.

Political Rights and Civil Liberties: Cyprus is an electoral democracy. The president is elected by popular vote to serve a five-year term. The unicameral House of Representatives has 80 seats filled through proportional representation for five-year terms; 24 seats are reserved for the Turkish Cypriot community, but they have not been occupied since Turkish Cypriot representatives withdrew from the chamber in 1964.

Following a 2004 ruling against Cyprus by the European Court of Human Rights (ECHR), a law was passed allowing Turkish Cypriots living in the south to vote and run for office in Greek Cypriot elections. Turkish Cypriots cannot run for president, as the constitution states that a Greek Cypriot should hold that post, and a Turkish Cypriot should be vice president. The Maronites (Levantine Catholics), Armenians, and Latins (Roman Catholics) elect special nonvoting representatives.

Corruption is not a major problem in Cyprus. Laws passed in 2008 aimed to prevent conflicts of interest for government officials and criminalized the with-holding of information on bribery in defense procurement. Parliamentary hearings on freedom of information in May 2009 indicated that many legal requests for information are not fulfilled, mostly due to lack of resources. Cyprus was ranked 29 out of 176 countries surveyed in Transparency International's 2012 Corruption Perceptions Index.

Freedom of speech is constitutionally guaranteed and generally respected. A vibrant independent press frequently criticizes the authorities, and several private television and radio stations compete effectively with public stations. Although Turkish Cypriot journalists can enter the south, Turkish journalists based in the north have reported difficulties crossing the border. Access to the internet is unrestricted.

Freedom of religion is guaranteed by the constitution and protected in practice. Nearly all inhabitants of the south are Orthodox Christians, and some discrimination against other religions has been alleged. State schools use textbooks containing negative language about Turkish Cypriots and Turkey.

Freedoms of association and assembly are generally respected, though Cyprus received international criticism in 2011 for putting Doros Polycarpou, director of the local human rights group KISA, on trial for illegal assembly. Polycarpou had organized a multicultural unity festival in December 2010 that was attacked by members of the far-right nationalist group ELAM. Polycarpou was acquitted of all charges in June 2012. Nongovernmental organizations generally operate without government interference. Workers have the right to strike and to form trade unions without employer authorization.

The independent judiciary operates according to the British tradition, upholding due process rights. However, the ECHR ruled against Cyprus in 2009 for failure to provide a timely trial in a case that lasted nearly six years. The problem of indefinite detentions of asylum seekers has improved somewhat since the country's ombudsperson filed complaints on the matter in 2008, but long-term detention of migrants continues. The Council of Europe and other groups have noted cases of police brutality, including targeted beatings of minorities. Prison overcrowding has decreased but remains a problem.

A 1975 agreement between the two sides of the island governs treatment of minorities. Turkish Cypriots are now entitled to Republic of Cyprus passports, and thousands have obtained them. However, Turkish Cypriots in the south have reported difficulty obtaining identity cards and other documents, as well as harassment and discrimination. Asylum seekers face regular discrimination, especially in employment, and KISA has warned of racially motivated attacks.

Since 2004, all citizens have been able to move freely throughout the island using a growing number of border crossings. While the Greek Cypriots have thwarted attempts to lift international trade and travel bans on the north, trade has increased between the two sides.

The status of property abandoned by those moving across the Green Line after the 1974 invasion is a point of contention in reunification talks. A 1991 law states that property left by Turkish Cypriots belongs to the state. Under the law in the north, Greek Cypriots can appeal to the Immovable Property Commission, which in March 2010 was recognized by the ECHR as an adequate local authority for the resolution of property disputes. As of December 2012, a total of 4,224 applications have been lodged with the commission and 295 have been settled, and approximately $133 million has been dispersed.

Gender discrimination in the workplace, sexual harassment, and violence against women are problems in Cyprus. Women are underrepresented in government, with only four women in the cabinet and six in the parliament. While the government has made genuine progress in preventing human trafficking and launched a new antitrafficking plan in 2010, Cyprus remains a transit and destination country, and prosecution is weak.

Czech Republic

Political Rights: 1
Civil Liberties: 1
Status: Free

Population: 10,546,000
Capital: Prague

Ten-Year Ratings Timeline For Year Under Review (Political Rights, Civil Liberties, Status)

2003	2004	2005	2006	2007	2008	2009	2010	2011	2012
1,2F	1,1F	1,1F	1,1F	1,1F	1,1F	1,1F	1,1F	1,1F	1,1F

Overview: The government of Petr Necas faced a significant decline in popularity in 2012 in the face of criticism over multiple corruption scandals and unpopular austerity measures. The three-party government terminated its coalition agreement in April, though Necas subsequently survived a no-confidence vote that same month; Necas's cabinet survived another confidence vote in November. In the spring, the European Commission suspended European Union funding for development projects due to suspected fund mismanagement and misallocation.

Czechoslovakia was created in 1918 amid the collapse of the Austro-Hungarian Empire. Soviet forces helped establish a communist government after World War II, and in 1968 they crushed the so-called Prague Spring, a period of liberalization under reformist leader Alexander Dubcek.

In December 1989, a series of peaceful anticommunist demonstrations led by dissident Václav Havel and the Civic Forum opposition group resulted in the resignation of the government, in what became known as the Velvet Revolution. Open elections were held the following year. A new constitution was adopted in 1992, and the country began an ambitious program of political and economic reform under Václav Klaus of the center-right Civic Democratic Party (ODS), who became prime minister that year. In 1993, the state dissolved peacefully into separate Czech and Slovak republics.

Close parliamentary elections in 1998 brought the center-left Czech Social Democratic Party (CSSD) to power. Klaus was elected president by Parliament in 2003. The Czech Republic joined NATO in 1999 and the European Union (EU) in 2004.

The 2006 legislative elections divided the Chamber of Deputies, the country's lower house, evenly between left- and right-leaning parties, leading to a series of short-lived, ODS-led coalitions and caretaker governments. Independent Jan Fischer took over as prime minister in 2009 and led a caretaker government until May 2010, when parliamentary elections resulted in 56 and 53 seats in the lower house for CSSD and ODS, respectively. The center-right, free-market Tradition Responsibility Prosperity 09 (TOP 09) party placed third with 41 seats, the Communist Party of Bohemia and Moravia (KSCM) took 26 seats, and the right-leaning Public Affairs (VV) party captured 24. In June, Klaus appointed ODS leader Petr Ne as to serve as prime minister; Necas formed a center-right coalition government with TOP 09 and VV.

In response to a 2009 recession, Necas's government pledged to implement an unpopular austerity package in 2011. The move helped the opposition gain control of the Senate in October 2010 elections, giving the CSSD and other opposition parties the power to obstruct legislation passed by the Chamber of Deputies. In October 2010, the lower house declared a legislative state of emergency, allowing it to bypass the opposition and expedite the passage of several controversial austerity bills. In 2011 the Constitutional Court rejected the government's austerity package and declared the fast-tracked legislation procedures unconstitutional. After months of infighting and a veto by the CSSD-controlled Senate, the lower house pushed through health-care and welfare reforms in June. In November, Klaus signed the health-care reforms into law, as well as amendments to unemployment and welfare benefits. After a long battle against the opposition, the lower house passed major pension reforms in November that would partially privatize the pension system.

Necas's government faced a significant decline in popularity in 2012 due to continued criticism over austerity measures, as well as a series of corruption scandals. In April, the country's deputy prime minister, Karolina Peake of VV, and several other VV ministers quit the junior coalition party after its unofficial leader, Vit Barta, received an 18-month suspended prison sentence for paying off party members in exchange for their support. The ODS and TOP 09 then agreed to terminate their coalition agreement with the remaining members of VV on April 22. Without VV, the coalition was left with only 92 of the 200 seats in the Chamber of Deputies, but Peake pledged to maintain support for the prime minister. On April 27, Necas's government narrowly survived a parliamentary confidence vote. Peake subsequently formed a new faction—LIDEM, meaning "for the people"—which became a coalition partner. However, Peake threatened that LIDEM would leave the coalition after she was fired from her position as defense minister in December, leaving the government at risk of collapse at year's end.

Meanwhile, in Senate elections held in late October, the CSSD increased its representation to 46 seats in the 81-seat chamber, while the ODS captured only 15 seats. Necas's cabinet survived another vote of confidence in November, avoiding early elections that would likely result in a leftist cabinet.

Ratings agencies and investors have commended Ne as for pension reforms and other spending cuts that have moved the country toward full compliance with EU deficit limits. After initially being vetoed by the upper and lower houses of Parliament, a bill to increase the value-added tax and income taxes for top earners was eventually adopted in December; the hikes will take place beginning in 2013. In September, Klaus vetoed the 2011 pension reforms, but Ne as was able to cobble together enough support to overturn Klaus's move in a November 7 vote. The Czech Republic joined the United Kingdom in January in opting out of an EU fiscal compact that limits the borrowing and spending of EU member states. Necas, who said the treaty was not in the country's best interest, subsequently faced criticism from his coalition partners and others, who accused him of failing to stand up to euroskeptics within the ODS.

Political Rights and Civil Liberties: The Czech Republic is an electoral democracy. The 200 members of the Chamber of Deputies, the lower house of Parliament, are elected to four-year terms by proportional representation. The Senate has 81 members elected for six-year terms, with one-third up for election every two years. Under a 2012 constitutional amendment, the president will be elected directly by Czech citizens, instead of by Parliament, beginning with the presidential elections scheduled for January 2013. The president can veto legislation, and appoints judges and central bank officials as well as the prime minister and other cabinet members, but the post holds few other formal powers. The two main political parties are the center-left CSSD and the center-right ODS. Two other right-leaning parties, TOP 09 and VV, entered Parliament for the first time in 2010, though VV splintered in 2012 following the conviction of one its de facto leaders, Vit Barta, on bribery charges.

Corruption and lack of transparency remained serious problem in 2012. In October, the labor and social affairs minister, Jaromír Drábek of TOP 09, resigned after police accused his first deputy of bribery. In the spring, the EU suspended funding for development projects due to suspected fund mismanagement and misallocation. For example, in May, David Rath, a CSSD member of Parliament and the governor of the Central Bohemia Region, was arrested on suspicion of corruption related to the diversion of EU funds meant for the renovation of a hospital and manor house. While some payments were resumed in July after Czech authorities agreed to implement reforms in the administration of EU subsidies, as of December, the European Commission had cut around 500 million euros ($650 million) of EU aid to the Czech Republic.

Freedom of expression is respected, though the constitution-based Charter of Fundamental Rights and Freedoms prohibits threats against individual rights, state and public security, public health, and morality. Most media outlets are owned by private foreign companies and do not appear to be influenced by the state. Journalists have complained that the 2009 "muzzle law"—which prohibits the press from identifying victims of serious crimes and publishing information obtained through police wiretaps—prevents them from effectively reporting on corruption. An amendment to the law that took effect in August 2011 allows for exceptions in cases where it is deemed in the public interest.

The government generally upholds freedom of religion. Promoting denial of the Holocaust or past communist crimes is illegal, as is inciting religious hatred. In July 2012, the lower house passed legislation under which the state would return some of the church land confiscated under the 1948–89 communist regime and pay compensation for the rest. While the Senate vetoed the bill in August, the lower house approved the legislation in November. Academic freedom is respected.

Czechs may assemble peacefully, form associations, and petition the government. Trade unions and professional associations function freely but are weak in practice. There were a number of anti-austerity protests in 2011 and 2012. In April 2012, some 90,000 Czechs demonstrated against austerity measures and government corruption in Prague's Wenceslas Square, in what observers called the largest antigovernment demonstration since 1989.

The independence of the judiciary is largely respected, though its complexity and multilayered composition has led to the slow delivery of judgments. A 2010 report produced by the country's counterintelligence agency found that corruption within the Czech Republic's judicial system was "very sophisticated," making detection difficult. The rule of law generally prevails in civil and criminal matters, though corruption also remains a problem within law enforcement agencies. Prisons suffer from overcrowding and poor sanitation.

The 2009 Antidiscrimination Act provides for equal treatment regardless of sex, race, age, or sexual orientation. However, members of the small Roma community sometimes face threats and violence from right-wing groups, and Romany children continue to face discrimination in the country's public school system.

New legislation came into force in January 2011 that increased the possible time for immigration detention to a maximum of 18 months, raising concerns that foreign nationals could remain in custody for extended periods of time solely for immigration reasons. Asylum seekers are routinely detained in the Czech Republic. Conditions in detention centers are generally poor. The remote location of detention and reception centers limits the ability of nongovernmental organizations to visit them.

Gender discrimination is legally prohibited. However, sexual harassment in the workplace appears to be fairly common, and women are underrepresented at the highest levels of government and business. Women nevertheless increased their parliamentary presence in the 2010 elections, capturing 44 seats in the 200-member Chamber of Deputies; there were 14 women in the Senate following the 2012 elections. Trafficking of women and girls for the purpose of prostitution remains a problem.

Denmark

Political Rights: 1
Civil Liberties: 1
Status: Free

Population: 5,590,500
Capital: Copenhagen

Ten-Year Ratings Timeline For Year Under Review (Political Rights, Civil Liberties, Status)

2003	2004	2005	2006	2007	2008	2009	2010	2011	2012
1,1F	1,1F	1,1F	1,1F	1,1F	1,1F	1,1F	1,1F	1,1F	1,1F

Overview: A scandal involving a leak to the press in 2011 of Prime Minister Helle Thorning-Schmidt's personal tax audit made headlines throughout 2012. Meanwhile, reforms to Denmark's strict immigration laws in May and June were praised by human rights groups, though critics charged that the changes were not far-reaching enough.

Denmark has been a monarchy since the Middle Ages, though the monarch's role became largely ceremonial after the promulgation of the first democratic constitution in 1849. The country was occupied by Nazi Germany during World War II, despite its attempts to maintain neutrality, and in 1949, it joined NATO. In 1973, Denmark became a member of the European Economic Community, forerunner of the European Union (EU).

Postwar Danish politics have been dominated by the Social Democratic Party. However, in the 2001 elections, a right-wing coalition led by Anders Fogh Rasmussen's Liberal Party won control by pledging to reduce immigration and lower taxes. The coalition, which also included the Conservative People's Party, was supported by the anti-immigrant and Euroskeptic Danish People's Party. Denmark has had a conflicted relationship with the EU, securing opt-outs from the bloc's 1992 Maastricht Treaty on justice, foreign, and monetary policy, and opting not to adopt the euro in 2000.

The Liberal Party won reelection in 2005, maintaining its coalition with the Conservative People's Party and receiving external support from the Danish People's Party. Prime Minister Rasmussen was returned to office in the 2007 elections, but resigned in April 2009, after being named NATO secretary general; he was replaced by finance minister Lars Løkke Rasmussen (no relation).

Parliamentary elections in September 2011 led to a change of government, with Helle Thorning-Schmidt leading the Social Democratic Party to power after forming a coalition with the Social Liberal Party, the Socialist People's Party, and the Red-Green Party. Although Thorning-Schmidt's coalition was able to narrowly defeat Rasmussen's center-right coalition, the Social Democratic Party itself suffered its worst electoral result since 1903 and won fewer seats in parliament than Rasmussen's Liberal Party. As a result of the election, Thorning-Schmidt became Denmark's first female prime minister.

Since taking office, the new government has faced internal divisions on issues including unpopular welfare reforms and changes in May and June 2012 to the country's strict immigration laws. Several ministers were replaced, and the government saw its popularity decline.

Since the September 2005 publications of the controversial cartoons by the Danish newspaper *Jyllands-Posten* depicting the prophet Muhammad, Denmark has been hit with a string of attempted terrorist attacks. In 2009, two men were arrested in Chicago in connection with a plot to bomb the offices of *Jyllands-Posten*. One of those arrested, Pakistani-American David Headley, pleaded guilty in 2010 to planning the attack, as well as participating in the planning of the 2008 terrorist attack in Mumbai, India. In September 2011, his accomplice, Tahawur Rana, was found guilty of planning to attack *Jyllands-Posten* but had not been sentenced by year's end.

The cartoonist Kurt Westergaard, who had drawn the most contentious of the Muhammad cartoons, was attacked in his home in January 2010 by a Somali assailant wielding an axe and a knife. Westergaard escaped unharmed, and the intruder, Mohamed Geele, was apprehended by police. Geele, who was believed to have ties to the Shabaab, an Islamist militant group based in Somalia, was sentenced in June 2011 to nine years in prison.

In September 2010, a small bomb exploded in a hotel in central Copenhagen, causing little material damage but injuring the bomber. The bomber was apprehended and found guilty of carrying out a terrorist attack and sentenced to 12 years in prison in May 2011. The intended target was *Jyllands-Posten*, particularly its former editor, Flemming Rose, who commissioned the cartoons.

Political Rights and Civil Liberties: Denmark is an electoral democracy. The current constitution, adopted in 1953, established a single-chamber parliament (the Folketing) and retained a monarch, currently Queen Margrethe II, with mostly ceremonial duties. The parliament's 179 representatives are elected at least once every four years through a system of modified proportional representation. The leader of the majority party or government coalition is usually chosen to be prime minister by the monarch. Danish governments most often control a minority of seats in the parliament, ruling with the aid of one or more supporting parties. Since 1909, no single party has held a majority of seats, helping to create a tradition of compromise.

The territories of Greenland and the Faroe Islands each have two representatives in the Folketing. They also have their own elected institutions, which have power over almost all areas of governance, except foreign and financial policy.

Levels of corruption are generally very low in Denmark, which was tied with Finland and New Zealand for first place out of 176 countries surveyed in Transparency International's 2012 Corruption Perceptions Index. However, the so-called Taxgate scandal involving a leak to the press of then opposition leader Helle Thorning-Schmidt's tax audit unfolded throughout 2012. The leak had occurred just one week before the 2011 general election, while Thorning-Schmidt was in the political opposition. Fallout from the high-profile scandal included the dismissal of a top official in the tax ministry in March 2012. In September, police formally charged Peter Arnfeldt, special counsel to then tax minister Troels Lund Poulsen, with unlawfully leaking confidential information. As of the end of 2012, an independent commission was investigating whether Poulsen had abused his power by improperly interfering in the tax ministry's handling of Thorning-Schmidt's audit.

The constitution guarantees freedom of expression. The media reflect a wide variety of political opinions and are frequently critical of the government. The state finances radio and television broadcasting, but state-owned television companies have independent editorial boards. Independent radio stations are permitted but tightly regulated. After complaints from the Turkish Ambassador to Denmark in March 2010, the Danish attorney-general charged the Danish-based, Kurdish-language satellite television station Roj-TV with promoting the Kurdistan Workers' Party, which the EU and the United States consider a terrorist organization. In January 2012, the Copenhagen City Court fined Roj-TV 5.2 million kroner (US$885,000) for promoting a terrorist group. An appeal to a higher court was pending at year's end. The station was the first Danish media organization to face prosecution for promoting terrorism, and the trial has been criticized across the political spectrum for harming freedom of speech and being unduly influenced by Turkish political pressure on the Danish government. Access to the internet is not restricted, and Denmark's internet penetration rate is among the highest in the world.

Freedom of worship is legally protected. However, the Evangelical Lutheran Church is subsidized by the government as the official state religion. The faith is taught in public schools, though students may withdraw from religious classes with parental consent. At present, about half of all schoolchildren are exempted from the catechism taught in public schools. In 2009, religious and political symbols were banned from judicial attire. Denmark denies religious worker visas, thereby restricting access to missionaries entering the country from abroad.

The constitution provides for freedoms of assembly and association. Demonstrations during 2012 were peaceful. Civil society is vibrant, and workers are free to organize. The labor market is mainly regulated by agreements between employers' and employees' organizations.

The judiciary is independent, and citizens enjoy full due process rights. The court system consists of 100 local courts, two high courts, and the 15-member Supreme Court, with judges appointed by the monarch on the government's recommendation. Prisons generally meet international standards.

Discrimination is prohibited under the law. However, strict immigration laws introduced in 2002 were tightened further in 2010 and 2011, including those adding more obstacles for citizens attempting to bring foreign spouses into the country. Denmark has closed many of its asylum centers since the introduction of the restrictive 2002 immigration laws. The European Court of Human Rights in 2010 called on Denmark to stop deporting asylum seekers to Greece, their point of entry to the EU; a binding decision from the Strasbourg court was pronounced in January 2011, compelling Denmark to stop the practice. The new socialist government honored one of its campaign pledges when new, less restrictive, immigration laws regarding family reunification cases and permanent residency came into effect in May and June 2012, respectively. The reforms included the elimination of a fee to apply for family reunification and the replacement of an immigration test with a Danish language exam. While human rights groups praised the reforms, some critics argued that the country's immigration policies remain too stringent; Denmark continues to have some of the harshest immigration laws in Europe.

Women enjoy equal rights in Denmark and represent half of the workforce. However, disparities have been reported in the Faroe Islands and Greenland. Denmark is a destination and transit point for women and children trafficked for the purpose of sexual exploitation. Following the 2003 adoption of legislation that defined and criminalized such trafficking, the government began working regularly with nongovernmental organizations in their trafficking-prevention campaigns.

Djibouti

Political Rights: 6
Civil Liberties: 5
Status: Not Free

Population: 923,000
Capital: Djibouti

Ten-Year Ratings Timeline For Year Under Review (Political Rights, Civil Liberties, Status)

2003	2004	2005	2006	2007	2008	2009	2010	2011	2012
5,5PF	5,5PF	5,5PF	5,5PF	5,5PF	5,5PF	5,5PF	6,5NF	6,5NF	6,5NF

Overview: Djibouti's president, Ismail Omar Guelleh, has continued to stifle political rights and civil liberties since his reelection in April 2011. In 2012 the government suppressed freedom of expression, including through regular arrests of independent journalists and union workers. The death of Djiboutian League of Human Rights chairman Jean-Paul Noël Abdi, the country's leading rights activist, was a significant loss for the advocacy community.

Djibouti gained independence from France in 1977. Its people are divided along ethnic and clan lines, with the majority Issa (Somali) and minority Afar peoples traditionally falling into opposing political camps. An Afar rebel group, the Front for the Restoration of Unity and Democracy (FRUD), launched a guerrilla war against Issa domination in 1991. In 1994 the largest FRUD faction agreed to end its insurgency in exchange for inclusion in the government and electoral reforms. President Hassan Gouled Aptidon controlled a one-party system until 1992, when a new constitution authorized four political parties. In 1993, Gouled won a fourth six-year term in Djibouti's first contested presidential election, which was considered fraudulent by international observers.

Gouled stepped down in 1999, but his nephew, Ismail Omar Guelleh, won the 1999 presidential poll with 74 percent of the vote. It was regarded as Djibouti's first fair election since independence. In 2001 a peace accord was signed with the remaining Afar rebel groups. A four-party coalition, the Union for the Presidential Majority (UMP), ran against a four-party opposition bloc, the Union for a Democratic Alternative (UAD), in the 2003 parliamentary elections, and won all 65 seats.

In 2005, Guelleh won a second six-year term. The only challenger withdrew from the election, citing government control of the media and repression of the opposition. Legislative elections in 2008 were also boycotted by the main opposition parties.

Unresolved grievances among the Afar led to a revival of the FRUD insurgency, with sporadic violence in 2010. In April 2010, Guelleh, a member of the Issa majority, pressured the parliament into passing a constitutional amendment that overturned the two-term limit for presidents; the change cleared the way for him to run for a third term in 2011.

In early 2011, a series of protests by university students against failures in the education system quickly broadened into antigovernment demonstrations. In the largest rally, several thousand people gathered outside Djibouti's national stadium to protest Guelleh's decision to stand for another term. At least two people were killed, and another 100 were arrested, including the leaders of three political parties.

The 2011 presidential election campaign was marred by the harassment of opposition leaders and a clampdown on public gatherings. Soon after the ban on demonstrations, Democracy International, a U.S.-funded international electoral observation organization, was expelled from the country. Opposition parties argued that the restrictions made it impossible to fairly contest the election and chose not to select candidates for the presidential race. As a result, Guelleh faced only one challenger in the April election, independent candidate Mohammed Warsama, and won with 81 percent of the vote. An African Union observer mission declared the election process peaceful, fair, and transparent.

Guelleh has used Djibouti's strategic location on the Gulf of Aden to generate millions of dollars in state revenue by renting military bases to his allies. Since 2001, Djibouti has been home to large U.S. and French bases, and Japan opened a naval facility in 2011.

Although food insecurity in some regions of the country remains at crisis levels following a severe drought in 2011, conditions began to stabilize in July 2012. In February 2012, the International Monetary Fund agreed to loan Djibouti $14 million to help counter the effects of the drought. However, certain regions of the country remained in a food crisis during the year due to ongoing rainfall deficits.

Political Rights and Civil Liberties: Djibouti is not an electoral democracy. The ruling UMP coalition party has effectively usurped the state. The constitutional amendment passed by the parliament in 2010, in addition to removing the two-term limit for presidents, reduced presidential terms from six years to five, and specified that candidates must be between the ages of 40 and 75. The changes allowed President Ismail Omar Guelleh to stand for a third term in 2011.

The 65 members of the unicameral parliament, the National Assembly, are directly elected for five-year terms. The 2010 constitutional changes provide for the formation of a bicameral parliament comprising the existing National Assembly and a newly created Senate, though steps to establish one have yet to be taken. Opposition parties are disadvantaged by the country's first-past-the-post electoral system, as well as the government's abuse of the administrative apparatus. In the last legislative elections contested by the opposition, in 2003, the UMP won 62 percent of the vote but captured all the seats in the National Assembly, because the election law stipulates that the winner of the majority in each of the country's five electoral constituencies is awarded all seats in that district.

Political parties are required to register with the government. In 2008, Guelleh issued a decree that dissolved the opposition Movement for Democratic Renewal and Development party, whose leader had reportedly voiced support for that year's Eritrean military incursion.

Efforts to curb corruption have met with little success. Government corruption is a serious problem and public officials are not required to disclose their assets.

Despite constitutional protections, freedom of speech is not upheld in practice. There are no privately owned or independent media, though political parties are allowed to publish a journal or newspaper. The government dominates the domestic media sector and monopolized the airwaves during the 2011 election. The government owns the principal newspaper, *La Nation*, as well as Radio-Television Djibouti, which operates the national radio and television stations. Strict libel laws lead journalists to practice self-censorship. While the government places few restrictions on internet access, opposition internet radio station and critical news website *La Voix de Djibouti*, run by Djiboutian exiles in Europe, is regularly blocked. In February 2012, *La Voix de Djibouti* journalist Farah Abadid Hildid was detained for 24 hours and was reported to have been subjected to physical and psychological torture. Hildid had been arrested and held twice in 2011 after participating in antigovernment protests. Another *La Voix de Djibouti* journalist, Houssein Ahmed Farah, was arrested in August 2012 and charged with forgery and evasion of judicial supervision. Farah was conditionally released in November after being held for three months.

Islam is the state religion, and 99 percent of the population is Sunni Muslim. Freedom of worship is respected. While academic freedom is generally upheld, higher educational opportunities are limited.

Freedoms of assembly and association are nominally protected under the constitution, but are not respected in practice. The interior minister placed a ban on public assembly during the during the 2011 election season. Local human rights groups do not operate freely. Djiboutian League of Human Rights chairman Jean-Paul Noël Abdi, the country's leading human rights activist, died of natural causes in April 2012. Prior to his death, Abdi had been arrested several times, including at least three times since 2007.

Workers may join unions and strike. However, the government discourages truly independent unions and has been accused of meddling in their internal elections and harassing union representatives. There were at least 117 arrests of strikers seeking unpaid wages in 2011, including the arrest and detention of 62 dock workers for two weeks in January as well as arrests against nurses and 55 railroad workers in April.

The judicial system is based on the French civil code, though Sharia (Islamic law) prevails in family matters. The courts are not independent of the government. A lack of resources often delays legal proceedings. Security forces frequently make arrests without a proper decree from a judicial magistrate, in violation of constitutional requirements. Allegations of politically motivated prosecutions surfaced in 2010, following the conviction in absentia of Djiboutian businessman Abdourahman Boreh on charges of terrorism. Boreh, who received a 15-year sentence, had been planning to stand against Guelleh in 2011 but withdrew his bid after the demonstrations turned violent. Though in exile, he continues to publically condemn Guelleh's administration; in October 2012, Boreh gave an interview to the BBC in which he accused the government of failing Djiboutians.

Following the arrests of more than 100 antigovernment protesters in February 2011, about 80 suspects were brought to court and charged with assault and demonstrating without a permit. According to Human Rights Watch, a judge dismissed 40 of these cases and was promptly removed by the justice minister. His replacement then proceeded to convict and imprison 25 defendants. Prison conditions are harsh, but have improved in recent years. The 2010 constitutional amendments abolished the death penalty.

Minority groups including the Afar people, Yemeni Arabs, and non-Issa Somalis suffer social and economic marginalization.

Women face discrimination under customary practices related to inheritance and other property matters, divorce, and the right to travel. The law prohibits female genital mutilation, but more than 90 percent of women are believed to have undergone the procedure. An estimated 50 percent of girls are now receiving primary education following efforts to increase female enrollment. While the law requires at least 20 percent of upper-level public service positions to be held by women, women still hold just close to 14 percent of legislative seats.

Dominica

Political Rights: 1
Civil Liberties: 1
Status: Free

Population: 71,000
Capital: Roseau

Ten-Year Ratings Timeline For Year Under Review (Political Rights, Civil Liberties, Status)

2003	2004	2005	2006	2007	2008	2009	2010	2011	2012
1,1F	1,1F	1,1F	1,1F	1,1F	1,1F	1,1F	1,1F	1,1F	1,1F

Overview: **Dominica's High Court in January 2012 ruled in favor of Prime Minister Roosevelt Skerrit and Education Minister Petter Saint Jean, who had been accused by the opposition United Workers Party of holding dual citizenship at the time of their elections to the parliament in 2009. Eliud Williams was elected by the House of Assembly in September to replace former president Nicholas Liverpool, who resigned for health reasons.**

Dominica gained independence from Britain in 1978. The centrist Dominica Labour Party (DLP) swept to victory in the January 2000 parliamentary elections, and formed a coalition with the right-wing Dominica Freedom Party (DFP). DLP leader Roosevelt "Rosie" Douglas was named prime minister, but died of a heart attack in October 2000. His replacement, Pierre Charles, died of heart failure in January 2004, and was succeeded by DLP member Roosevelt Skerrit. After the DLP won a majority of seats in the following year's parliamentary elections, the DFP struggled to remain relevant and was not represented in the parliament.

In the December 2009 legislative elections, the DLP captured 18 seats, while the United Workers Party (UWP) took only 3. The elections were deemed generally fair by regional observer teams. However, opposition members accused the DLP of misconduct during the campaign and filed complaints of electoral irregularities, including having been denied equal access to state media during the campaign period. They also accused Skerrit and Education Minister Petter Saint Jean of holding dual citizenship at the time of the elections, which under Dominican law would have made them ineligible to hold office. The courts rejected all of the complaints in 2010, except for the dual citizenship case, which was brought to trial in September

2011. In January 2012, a High Court judge ruled that the 2009 elections of Skerrit and St. Jean had been constitutional and that they should retain their posts. The UWP filed an appeal with the Eastern Caribbean Supreme Court, which the court heard in November; however, the court had yet to issue a ruling at year's end.

Following the resignation of President Nicholas Liverpool for health reasons, the House of Assembly was called to session on September 17, 2012, to elect a new president. DLP candidate Eliud Williams was sworn in that day, with approval from the prime minister, though the UWP protested and boycotted the election, arguing that the process leading to his nomination was unconstitutional. Williams will hold office until general elections in October 2013.

Economic growth continued to be slow in 2012. The International Monetary Fund reported that weak demand and an outbreak of banana leaf disease—which has negatively impacted the nation's important banana industry—have affected Dominica's attempts to recover from the global economic crisis.

Political Rights and Civil Liberties: Dominica is an electoral democracy. The unicameral House of Assembly consists of 30 members who serve five-year terms; 21 members are directly elected and 9 senators are appointed—5 by the prime minister and 4 by the opposition leader. The president, who is the ceremonial head of state, is elected by the House of Assembly for a five-year term, and the prime minister is appointed by the president. The three main political parties are the ruling DLP, the opposition UWP, and the DFP.

The government generally implements anticorruption laws effectively. As an offshore financial center with a significant international business company presence, Dominica passed a series of laws in November 2011 to combat money laundering and the financing of terrorism. Dominica was ranked 41 out of 176 countries surveyed in Transparency International's 2012 Corruption Perceptions Index.

Freedom of expression is constitutionally guaranteed, and the press is generally free in practice. However, the country lacks access to information legislation, and defamation remains a criminal offense punishable by imprisonment or fines. Libel lawsuits and threats are commonly used by the Skerrit government against members of the media, which has resulted in the practice of self-censorship. In late December 2011, Prime Minister Roosevelt Skerrit filed a libel lawsuit against economist Thomson Fontaine over allegations Fontaine had made on his popular blog that the government was abusing its economic citizenship program that sells passports to foreigners. The case was ongoing at the end of 2012. Broadcaster Lennox Linton, who was found guilty in 2011 of defamation and sentenced to pay EC$50,000 (about US$18,500) in damages to accountant Keiron Pinard-Byrne, appealed his case before the Eastern Caribbean Supreme Court in April 2012; the court reserved its judgment in May, and had yet to pass a judgment at year's end. Four private weekly newspapers are published without interference, and there are both public and private radio stations. Citizens have unimpeded access to cable television and the internet.

Freedom of religion is protected under the constitution and other laws. While the majority of the population is Roman Catholic, there are some Protestant churches. Academic freedom is respected.

The authorities uphold freedoms of assembly and association, and advocacy groups operate freely. Workers have the right to organize, strike, and bargain collectively, and laws prohibit antiunion discrimination by employers. Nevertheless, there is little union organizing in the informal sector, and less than 30 percent of the private sector is unionized.

The judiciary is independent, and the rule of law is enhanced by the courts' subordination to the inter-island Eastern Caribbean Supreme Court. Efforts to establish the Caribbean Court of Justice as its final court of appeal, instead of the Privy Council in London, continued in 2012 with no resolution by year's end. The judicial system generally operates with efficiency, though staffing shortfalls remain a problem.

The Dominica police force, which became responsible for security after the military was disbanded in 1981, operates professionally and with few human rights complaints.

Dominica's small indigenous population, the Carib-Kalingo, face a variety of challenges, including a higher poverty rate than the rest of the country, encroachment on their territory by farmers, and difficulties in obtaining loans from banks. Rastafarians in Dominica also report discrimination and profiling by the police.

Women are underrepresented in government and hold just four seats in the House of Assembly. There are no laws mandating equal pay for equal work in private sector jobs or criminalizing domestic abuse. Same-sex relations are criminalized for both men and women with punishments of imprisonment, and gay men and lesbians face significant social discrimination.

Dominican Republic

Political Rights: 2
Civil Liberties: 2
Status: Free

Population: 10,135,000
Capital: Santo Domingo

Ten-Year Ratings Timeline For Year Under Review (Political Rights, Civil Liberties, Status)

2003	2004	2005	2006	2007	2008	2009	2010	2011	2012
3,2F	2,2F	2,2F	2,2F	2,2F	2,2F	2,2F	2,2F	2,2F	2,2F

Overview: The Dominican Liberation Party's Danilo Medina defeated Dominican Revolutionary Party candidate Hipólito Mejía in the May 2012 presidential election. Meanwhile, the country's economy grew slower in 2012 than in previous years; in November, the government passed a fiscal reform package that raised some taxes and slashed spending.

After achieving independence from Spain in 1821 and from Haiti in 1844, the Dominican Republic endured recurrent domestic conflict, foreign occupation, and authoritarian rule. The assassination of General Rafael Trujillo in 1961 ended 30 years of dictatorship, but a 1963 military coup led to civil war and U.S. intervention. Under a new constitution, civilian rule was restored in 1966 with the election of conservative president Joaquín Balaguer. His ouster in the 1978 election marked the first time an incumbent president peacefully handed power to an elected opponent.

Since the mid-1990s, Dominican politics have been defined by competition between the Dominican Liberation Party (PLD) and the Dominican Revolutionary Party (PRD), although Balaguer's Social Christian Reformist Party (PRSC) remained an important factor. The PLD's Leonel Fernández, who was first elected president in 1996, was reelected in 2004. While his 1996–2000 presidential term had featured substantial economic growth, Fernández returned to face serious financial difficulties, including a ballooning foreign debt, high unemployment and inflation rates, and a deep energy crisis. Nonetheless, the country's economy improved dramatically, posting a 9 percent growth rate in 2005. In return for International Monetary Fund (IMF) financing, the government agreed to cut subsidies on fuel and electricity and reduce the bloated government payroll. The PLD captured a majority in both houses of Congress in the 2006 legislative elections, and Fernández secured a third term in the 2008 presidential election.

Capitalizing on the president's continued successful economic management, the PLD captured 31 of 32 Senate seats in the May 2010 legislative elections, while the PRSC took the remaining seat. In the Chamber of Deputies, the PLD secured 105 seats, the PRD won 75, and the PRSC took only 3. The PLD also won a majority of the municipal elections. The opposition subsequently presented allegations of electoral fraud to the Organization of American States (OAS), and international observers noted that campaigning resources were not equally distributed between government and opposition candidates. The OAS also noted certain irregularities, including vote-buying, though it certified the results.

The PLD's Danilo Medina was victorious in the presidential election held on May 20, 2012, winning 51 percent of the vote and defeating PRD candidate Hipólito Mejia; Fernández was barred by the constitution from seeking another consecutive term. Medina took office in August, pledging to reduce poverty, improve the country's educational system, and expand infrastructure projects.

The Dominican Republic has faced various economic challenges over the past few years. The country became a conduit for relief and reconstruction efforts in the wake of the 2010 earthquake that devastated neighboring Haiti; the resulting influx of refugees, combined with emergency financial assistance to Haiti, strained the Dominican Republic's economy. In July 2011, demonstrations against fiscal and economic measures, including increases on income tax and electricity tariffs, paralyzed transportation and trade, and three protesters were killed in clashes with police. Although experiencing higher growth than most Latin American countries, the Dominican Republic's economic growth rate in 2012 was estimated to have slowed to less than 4 percent. In November, the parliament approved a fiscal reform package that will increase sales taxes, place taxes on tobacco products and alcoholic beverages, and institute an array of spending cuts.

Political Rights and Civil Liberties: The Dominican Republic is an electoral democracy. The 2008 presidential election and the 2010 legislative elections were deemed free and fair, though the OAS did note several electoral violations in the 2010 polls, including vote-buying. The bicameral National Congress consists of the 32-member Senate and the 183-member Chamber of Deputies, with members of both chambers elected to four-year terms. The country's 38th constitution, which was promulgated in January 2010, removed restrictions on nonconsecutive presidential reelection, which would allow Leonel Fernández to run for president again in 2016.

The three main political parties are the ruling PLD, the opposition PRD, and the smaller PRSC.

Official corruption remains a serious problem. In December 2012, protestors in Santo Domingo demanded an end to government corruption and imprisonment for most of the officials in the administration of former president Leonel Fernandez. The Dominican Republic was ranked 118 out of 176 countries surveyed in Transparency International's 2012 Corruption Perceptions Index.

The law provides for freedoms of speech and the press, and the government generally respects these rights. There are five national daily newspapers and a large number of local publications. The state-owned Radio Television Dominicana operates radio and television services. Private owners operate more than 300 radio stations and over 40 television stations, most of which are small, regional broadcasters. Journalists reporting on possible collusion between drug traffickers and state officials have faced intimidation, and some have been killed. Internet access is unrestricted but not widely available outside of large urban areas.

Constitutional guarantees regarding religious and academic freedom are generally observed.

Freedom of assembly is generally respected. Freedom of association is constitutionally guaranteed, but is limited for public servants. The government upholds the right to form civic groups, and civil society organizations in the Dominican Republic are some of the best organized and most effective in Latin America. Labor unions are similarly well organized. Although legally permitted to strike, they are often subject to government crackdowns. In November 2012, police used tear gas and fired guns on union-led demonstrators protesting tax reforms deemed to be unfavorable to the working class; several protestors were wounded.

The judiciary is politicized and riddled with corruption, and the legal system offers little recourse to those without money or influence. However, reforms implemented in recent years have included measures aimed at promoting greater efficiency and due process. The 2010 constitution seeks to further modernize the judiciary, with measures such as the creation of a Constitutional Court and Judiciary Branch Council, as well as mandating retirement for Supreme Court magistrates over the age of 75 years. Extrajudicial killings by police remain a problem, and low salaries encourage endemic corruption in law enforcement institutions. According to the Dominican Republic's Office of the Prosecutor General, at least 154 people were killed by police from January to July 2011, compared to 125 people during the same period in 2010. According to the country's National Human Rights Commission, at least 290 people were killed by police in 2012. In November 2012, Amnesty International called for a reform to the nation's police services following the shooting by police of a university student during a demonstration against tax increases in Santo Domingo. Prisons suffer from severe overcrowding, poor sanitation, and routine violence.

The Dominican Republic is a major transit hub for South American drugs, mostly cocaine, en route to the United States. Local, Puerto Rican, and Colombian drug smugglers use the country as both a command-and-control center and a transshipment point. The connection between drug smuggling and involvement by elements in the Dominican Republic's police and army remains a major concern. In September 2011, prosecutors from U.S. federal courts indicated that Colombian drug smugglers had in at least three cases even been able to use Dominican military facilities to transfer narcotics. In October 2012, Francisco Hiraldo Guerrero, the former chief operating officer of the National Drug Control Directorate, was arrested and extradited to the United States for allegedly trafficking cocaine.

The mistreatment of Haitian migrants continues to mar the Dominican Republic's international reputation, but no strategy has been adopted to handle this growing problem. The 2010 constitution removed the possibility of Dominican citizenship for children born of illegal Haitian migrants. Despite important advances in relations with Haiti, especially after the January 2010 earthquake, Dominican authorities continued to illegally deprive Dominicans of Haitian descent of their nationality, leaving them without access to health care, education, employment, or the right to vote. This virtual statelessness increases their chance of being subjected to arbitrary detentions and mass expulsion, without judicial review, and in violation of bilateral agreements with Haiti. Mass deportations of Haitians illegally in the Dominican Republic continued in 2012.

Recent proposals to reduce the recommended prison time for some acts of domestic violence and sexual abuse, such as sexual abuse of a minor, has led to an outpouring of protest from human rights and women groups. The trafficking in women and girls, child prostitution, and child abuse are major concerns. The new Dominican constitution includes one of the most restrictive abortion laws in the world, making the practice illegal even in cases of rape, incest, or to protect the life of the mother. The new constitution also defines marriage as solely between a man and a woman, making the country one of the few in the world to ban same-sex marriage at the constitutional level.

East Timor

Political Rights: 3
Civil Liberties: 4
Status: Partly Free

Population: 1,125,800
Capital: Dili

Ten-Year Ratings Timeline For Year Under Review (Political Rights, Civil Liberties, Status)

2003	2004	2005	2006	2007	2008	2009	2010	2011	2012
3,3PF	3,3PF	3,3PF	3,4PF	3,4PF	3,4PF	3,4PF	3,4PF	3,4PF	3,4PF

Overview: In 2012, Timor-Leste successfully held presidential and parliamentary elections, which were deemed largely free and fair by observers. Former head of the National Defense Force Major General José Maria Vasconcelos, popularly known as Taur Matan Ruak, became the country's new president. The National Congress for Timorese Reconstruction, in coalition with the Democratic Party and the new Frenti-Mudanca, formed a government in August, led again by Kay Rala Xanana Gusmão. The UN Integrated Mission in Timor-Leste departed in December.

Portugal abandoned its colony of East Timor in 1975, and Indonesia invaded within days of the declaration of independence by the leftist Revolutionary Front for an Independent East Timor (Fretilin). Over the next two decades, Fretilin's armed wing, Falintil, waged a low-grade insurgency against the Indonesian army, which committed widespread human rights abuses as it consolidated control. Civil conflict and famine reportedly killed between 100,000 and 250,000 Timorese during Indonesian rule.

International pressure on Indonesia mounted following the 1991 Dili massacre, in which Indonesian soldiers were captured on film killing more than 200 people. In 1999, 78.5 percent of the East Timorese electorate voted for independence in a referendum approved by Indonesian president B. J. Habibie. The Indonesian army's scorched-earth response to the vote killed roughly 1,000 civilians, produced more than 250,000 refugees, and destroyed approximately 80 percent of East Timor's buildings and infrastructure before an Australian-led multinational force restored order.

In 2001 East Timor elected a Constituent Assembly to draft a constitution. Kay Rala Xanana Gusmão—former commander in chief of Falintil and leader of Fretilin until he broke from the party in 1988 to form a wider resistance coalition—won the presidency the following year. Independence was officially granted in May 2002. The Fretilin party, led by Prime Minister Mari Alkatiri, won the country's first local elections in 2004 and 2005.

A political crisis in 2006 erupted into widespread rioting and armed clashes with the police, leading to numerous deaths and the displacement of an estimated 150,000 people. Alkatiri was forced to resign as prime minister in June 2006, and a United Nations Integrated Mission in Timor-Leste (UNMIT) was established to help restore peace and increase police presence. José Ramos-Horta, who was appointed to replace Alkatiri, won the May 2007 presidential runoff election. Outgoing president Gusmão launched a new party, the National Congress for Timorese Reconstruction (CNRT), to compete in the June 2007 parliamentary elections. With no party gaining sufficient seats to form a government, the CNRT joined smaller parties to form the Alliance of the Parliamentary Majority, and it was invited by Ramos-Horta to form a government, with Gusmão as prime minister.

Timor-Leste successfully completed presidential and parliamentary elections in 2012, which, despite some minor technical problems, were deemed largely free and fair by observers. Fretilin party chair Francisco Guterres, known as Lú-Olo, and former head of the National Defense Force (F-FDTL) Major General José Maria Vasconcelos, better known as Taur Matan Ruak, emerged as contenders after the first round of the presidential election on March 17. Ruak, who ran as an independent but received last-minute support from the CNRT, won in the second round on April 16 with 61 percent of the vote.

Due to the 3 percent electoral threshold to enter Parliament, only 4 out of 21 competing parties garnered seats in the July 7 legislative elections. Gusmão secured a second term as prime minister after the CNRT captured 30 seats, just short of the number needed to form a government. The CNRT entered into a coalition with the Democratic Party, which won eight seats, and the new Frenti-Mudanca—which had broken from Fretilin in 2011—which took two seats; the new government took office in August. Fretilin, which secured 25 seats, remained in opposition.

UNMIT formally departed Timor in December after transferring full responsibility to Timor's National Police in October. The security operations of the Australian-led International Stabilization Force (ISF) concluded in November 2012, and the ISF will withdraw by April 2013. Various UN agencies will maintain offices in the country.

East Timor's weak economy is fueled primarily by oil and gas revenues. Despite an oil fund balance valued at over $11.7 billion at the end of the year, East Timor remained the poorest country in Southeast Asia, with more than 40 percent of the population living below the national poverty line.

Political Rights and Civil Liberties: East Timor is an electoral democracy. The 2012 presidential and parliamentary elections were deemed generally free and fair. The directly elected president is a largely symbolic figure, with formal powers limited to the right to veto legislation and make certain appointments. The leader of the majority party or coalition in the 65-seat, unicameral Parliament becomes prime minister. The president and members of Parliament serve five-year terms, with the president eligible for a maximum of two terms.

Voter frustration with corruption and nepotism has plagued both Fretilin and CNRT-led governments. An anticorruption commission was created in 2009 with a broad mandate, except for powers of prosecution. In June 2012, former justice minister Lucia Lobato was found guilty of corruption on a government procurement project and sentenced to five years in prison; her appeal was rejected in December. The country was ranked 113 out of 176 countries surveyed in Transparency International's 2012 Corruption Perceptions Index.

Journalists often practice self-censorship, and authorities regularly deny access to government information. The 2009 penal code decriminalized defamation, but it remains part of the civil code. Two journalists were placed under house arrest in October 2012 by the Public Prosecutor's office after allegedly writing false accounts of a 2011 traffic accident; they were awaiting trial at years end. The free flow of information remains hampered primarily by poor infrastructure and scarce resources. Radio has the greatest reach, with 63 percent of people listening on a monthly basis. The country has three major daily newspapers, some of which are loosely aligned with the ruling or opposition parties. Printing costs and illiteracy rates generally prevent the expansion of print media. In 2012, an estimated 0.9 percent of the population had access to the internet.

East Timor is a secular state, though 98 percent of the population is Roman Catholic. There are no significant threats to religious freedom or clashes between religious groups. Academic freedom is generally respected, though religious education is compulsory in schools.

Freedoms of association and assembly are constitutionally guaranteed. However, a 2004 law regulates political gatherings and prohibits demonstrations aimed at "questioning constitutional order" or disparaging the reputations of the head of state and other government officials. The law requires that demonstrations and public protests be authorized in advance.

Workers, other than police and military personnel, are permitted to form and join labor organizations, bargain collectively, and strike. In 2011, the government approved a law governing the right of workers to strike, which reduced the time required for written notification prior to a strike from 10 days to 5 days. In June 2012, a new labor law was implemented that, among other things, established a minimum wage of $115 per month. Unionization rates are low due to high levels of unemployment and informal economic activity.

The country suffers from weak rule of law and a prevailing culture of impunity. There is a considerable backlog in the understaffed court system, with approximately 4,700 criminal cases pending at the Office of the Prosecutor General as of September 2012. Due process rights are often restricted or denied, owing largely to a lack of resources and personnel. Alternative methods of dispute resolution and customary law are widely used, though they lack enforcement mechanisms and have other significant shortcomings, including unequal treatment of women. UNMIT passed all casework related to serious crimes committed during the Indonesian withdrawal between January and October 1999, to Timor; as of September 2012, 79 percent of the 396 cases had been concluded. In December, three defendants were convicted for crimes against humanity committed in 1999, and sentenced to between 6 and 16 years in prison.

Internal security continued to improve in 2012, though the postelection period was marred by brief conflict resulting in one death after it was announced that Fretilin was excluded from the CNRT's ruling coalition. Gang violence—sometimes directed by rival elites or fueled by land disputes—continued sporadically. Police officers and F-FDTL soldiers are regularly accused of excessive force and abuse of power—60 cases were reported between January and September 2012—though the courts have had success prosecuting them. A police officer was sentenced to 10 years in prison in February for homicide, and another was sentenced to 4 years in August for negligent homicide. Six F-FDTL soldiers stood trial for assault and homicide in September; the case was ongoing at year's end.

The status and reintegration of the thousands of Timorese refugees who still remain in the Indonesian province of West Timor after fleeing the 1999 violence remained unresolved in 2012. The Timorese government has long encouraged the return of the refugees, but concerns over access to property and other rights, as well as the status of former militia members, continues to hinder their return.

Community property comprises approximately 90 percent of the land in East Timor; land reform remains an unresolved and contentious issue. In February 2012, Parliament passed three land laws that facilitated grant titles for plots with uncontested ownership, created a legal category for communal land, and established a system to resolve land disputes outside of the court system.

Equal rights for women are constitutionally guaranteed, but discrimination and gender inequality persist in practice and in customary law. Women hold 25 of the 65 seats in Parliament. Amendments to the election laws in 2011 increased the quota requiring one-third of candidates on party lists for parliamentary elections to be women. Despite a 2010 law against domestic violence, gender-based and domestic violence remain widespread. East Timor is a source and destination country for human trafficking into forced labor and prostitution.

⬇ Ecuador

Political Rights: 3
Civil Liberties: 3
Status: Partly Free

Population: 14,865,000
Capital: Quito

Trend Arrow: Ecuador received a downward trend arrow due to widespread irregularities in the constitutionally mandated reregistration process for political organizations and a change to the parliamentary seat allocation formula that favors the ruling party.

Ten-Year Ratings Timeline For Year Under Review (Political Rights, Civil Liberties, Status)

2003	2004	2005	2006	2007	2008	2009	2010	2011	2012
3,3PF	3,3PF	3,3PF	3,3PF	3,3PF	3,3PF	3,3PF	3,3PF	3,3PF	3,3PF

Overview: In preparation for the 2013 general elections, and in compliance with a constitutional mandate, political organizations reregistered with the electoral authority in 2012 through a process that was marred by irregularities. Also during the year, President Rafael Correa used his line item veto powers to reform the electoral law, changing the parliamentary seat allocation formula to favor the ruling party and limiting media coverage during the electoral campaign. Correa's plan to restructure the judicial branch was implemented amid controversy over a lack of transparency in the appointment of judges and key court rulings that sided with the government.

Established in 1830 after the region achieved independence from Spain in 1822, the Republic of Ecuador has endured many interrupted presidencies and military governments. The last military regime gave way to civilian rule after a new constitution was approved by referendum in 1978. However, since 1998, three presidents have been forced from office before the conclusion of their terms as a result of popular protests and congressional action.

Indicating their frustration with political instability and the traditional parties, voters endorsed change in the 2006 presidential election. The winning candidate was Rafael Correa, a charismatic young economist who had served briefly as finance minister. A fiery critic of neoliberal economic policies, Correa promised to spearhead a transformative "Citizens' Revolution" that would include a new constitution. In the election's second round, Correa won with 57 percent of the vote.

After taking office in early 2007, Correa eliminated the legal barriers to a constitutional referendum, using questionable maneuvers to remove opposition legislators and members of the Constitutional Court. In April 2007, 82 percent of the electorate approved the creation of a constituent assembly in a national referendum. Correa's Proud and Sovereign Homeland (PAIS) party then captured 80 of the assembly's 130 seats in September elections. A year later, the newly written constitution won popular approval with 64 percent of the vote.

The 2008 constitution stipulated an array of new rights for groups including women, indigenous people, and the disabled. It also created a new branch of government called Transparency and Social Control, organized around the Council of

Popular Participation and Social Control. The council was endowed with important powers in organizing the appointment processes for the attorney general, the human rights ombudsman, and the Judicial Council charged with selecting National Court of Justice members. Executive power was enhanced by a constitutional provision allowing presidents to serve up to two consecutive terms and the creation of a line item veto.

Correa won a new four-year term in the April 2009 general elections, taking 52 percent of the vote in the first round. PAIS captured 59 of 124 seats in the new National Assembly. Smaller parties allied with PAIS garnered over a dozen seats, giving it a working majority. However, subsequent defections from PAIS and diminished support from other small parties made it difficult for the government to maintain its majority.

On September 30, 2010, a date known as 30-S, police and a few military regiments staged a one-day rebellion, protesting a new public service law that altered salaries and benefits. After an angry confrontation with the protesters, Correa was forced to take refuge in a nearby hospital and declared a state of emergency. By the end of the day, he had been rescued in a military operation that left five people dead. The government alleged that the events constituted an attempted coup by Correa opponents.

In February 2011, Guayaquil's leading newspaper, *El Universo*, published an opinion column suggesting that Correa could be held accountable in the future for the use of lethal force during the 30-S episode. In response, Correa lodged a lawsuit against the author, Emilio Palacio, and the owners of the newspaper. All four defendants were found guilty of aggravated defamation and sentenced to three years in prison and an unprecedented fine of $40 million. International human rights and press freedom organizations, the Organization of American States (OAS), and the United Nations denounced the court decision as a clear effort to intimidate the press.

In May 2011, Correa promoted and won a national referendum that included controversial reforms to the judiciary and the media. One provision that created a government-controlled media oversight body was a particular source of concern. Critics also argued that the judicial overhaul was unconstitutional because it violated the system prescribed in 2008. The government justified the measure as the only way to address the acute problem of corruption and the backlog in the courts, which was estimated at 1.2 million cases. A Transitional Judicial Council was established in July 2011 to implement the judicial reform, with the power to fire, hire, or reappoint judges and prosecutors at all levels. It oversaw the appointment of the National Court of Justice in January 2012, appointed hundreds of judges to lower courts, and reviewed other appointments in the judicial branch.

After the Transitional Judicial Council's creation, the government won a number of key cases in the courts, including the aforementioned El Universo case. Although those sentences were appealed, in February 2012 the Constitutional Court ruled in favour of Correa, who subsequently pardoned the defendants. In August 2012, Palacio was granted asylum in the United States. The courts in 2011 ruled against the government in the high-profile case of César Carrión, a colonel whom the government accused of attempting to assassinate the president during the 30-S incident. However, the Transitional Judicial Council later fired the judges who acquitted Carrión. The council's tenure was due to end in January 2013, with the appointment of the permanent Judicial Council. Commentators expressed fears that the nominees to the permanent body, who included a former private secretary and cabinet member in the Correa administration, would lack independence from the executive.

Separately, in January 2012, Correa used his line item veto power to make a series of revisions to the electoral law ahead of the 2013 general elections. Among other changes, he altered the parliamentary seat allocation formula in a way that appeared to benefit the ruling party and restricted media coverage during the campaign period. In response to several lawsuits, the Constitutional Court ruled in October that the revisions were largely constitutional, though it eased the restrictions on media coverage. The National Union of Journalists requested a clarification of the vaguely worded prohibition on media outlets indirectly promoting a particular candidate or view during the campaign. In December, the Constitutional Court responded by requiring the media to give equal space or air time to candidates. It also tasked the electoral authority with drafting specific guidelines for implementing these provisions, which were not done by year's end.

Political Rights and Civil Liberties: Ecuador is an electoral democracy. The 2009 elections, the first under the 2008 constitution, were deemed generally free and fair by international observers, although the European Union monitoring team noted some problems with vote-tabulation procedures and the abuse of state resources on behalf of progovernment candidates.

The 2011 referendum was monitored by an OAS observer mission. While it found no major irregularities in the voting process itself, the mission recommended enhanced monitoring and legislation to control campaign spending and the unfettered use of public resources. Unregulated campaign spending by the government has also been a focal point of concern among domestic observers.

The new constitution provides for a president elected to serve up to two four-year terms. The unicameral, 124-seat National Assembly is elected via open-list proportional representation for four-year terms. The president has the authority to dissolve the legislature once in his term, which triggers new elections for both the assembly and the presidency. The assembly can likewise dismiss the president, though under more stringent rules. The president enjoys line item veto power over legislation.

For decades, Ecuador's political parties have been largely personality based, clientelist, and fragile. President Rafael Correa's PAIS party remains by far the largest in the legislature, though it has suffered defections. The opposition includes the center-right Institutional Renewal Party of National Action (PRIAN), the Social Christian Party–Madera de Guerrero, and the Patriotic Society Party. Pachakutik, a party with four seats in the legislature, is loosely affiliated with the Confederation of Indigenous Nationalities (CONAIE), the leading national organization representing indigenous groups.

The 2008 constitution mandated the reregistration of political organizations as a requirement for eligibility to participate in the 2013 general elections. The process drew controversy as it unfolded during 2012, with reports that voters were signed up to support parties without their knowledge, among other irregularities. As of December, there were 42 legally recognized political organizations—11 at the national level and 31 at the provincial level—including PAIS, PRIAN, and the Social Christian Party. The parliamentary seat allocation changes enacted by Correa in January 2012 favored larger parties, prompting critics to warn that they would benefit PAIS. A government-sponsored revision of the electoral law removed language that would have forced Correa to take a leave of absence during the presidential race, though he ultimately requested voluntary leave in late December in order to campaign full time. The National Electoral Council that will supervise the 2013 elections was appointed in 2011, and the Council of Popular Participation was criticized for a lack of transparency in its selection of the body's members.

Ecuador has long been wracked by corruption. The weak judiciary and lack of investigative capacity in government oversight agencies contribute to an atmosphere of impunity. Corruption investigations fall under the jurisdiction of the Council of Popular Participation, which has an estimated backlog of over 3,000 unresolved cases. Ecuador was ranked 118 out of 176 countries surveyed in Transparency International's 2012 Corruption Perceptions Index.

The environment for freedom of expression did not improve in 2012. Correa continued his use of national broadcasts to castigate opposition and indigenous leaders, and his January reforms of the electoral law barred the media from influencing the electoral campaign. In addition to Correa's regular verbal attacks on the press, the government uses its unlimited access to public service airtime to interrupt news programming on privately owned stations and discredit journalists. During the UN Human Rights Council's 2012 Universal Periodic Review process for Ecuador, the government denied the existence of laws criminalizing opinion and rejected the standards recommended by the Inter-American Commission on Human Rights, alleging that only the Inter-American Court on Human Rights had jurisdiction over the matter.

The press watchdog Fundamedios reported 173 cases of verbal, physical, or legal harassment against journalists during the year. In June, Correa prohibited his ministers from giving interviews to privately owned media, and a judge upheld the decision in September after a nongovernmental organization (NGO) challenged its legality. Also in September, Correa's communications secretary warned the newspaper *El Comercio* that some reader comments on its website were offensive to the president and others and could be considered criminal offenses. In response, the newspaper temporarily suspended online comments. Separately, in compliance with a court order, the newspaper *La Hora* printed a front-page apology to the government in November for having published inaccurate information about government spending on publicity.

Freedom of religion is constitutionally guaranteed and generally respected in practice. Academic freedom is not restricted.

The right to organize political parties, civic groups, and unions is unabridged in law. However, domestic and international NGOs have come under increasing government scrutiny and regulation. A July 2011 presidential decree outlined broadly framed regulations for foreign-sponsored NGOs, forbidding activities that are "incompatible with public security and peace." Correa has accused many NGOs of forming part of a right-wing conspiracy to bring down his government.

Numerous protests occur peacefully. However, national security legislation that predates the Correa administration provides a broad definition of sabotage and terrorism, which includes acts against persons and property by unarmed individuals. The use of such charges, along with other criminal and civil laws, against protesters has increased under Correa. Indigenous organizations in particular complain that the government is criminalizing protest by targeting leaders for legal harassment and using more aggressive police tactics against demonstrators. The Ecumenical Commission for Human Rights reported that 15 people were charged with sabotage and 10 others were accused of terrorism during 2012. In August 2012, three community leaders were sentenced to eight days in jail for blocking a road during a 2010 protest in Azuay Province.

The country's labor unions have the right to strike, though the labor code limits public sector strikes. Only 1 percent of the workforce is unionized, partly because most people work in the informal sector.

The highest judicial bodies under the new constitution are the nine-member Constitutional Court, whose members were appointed in January 2012, and the 21-member National Court of Justice, whose members were appointed in November. Opposition members and a panel of foreign experts cited problems in the appointment process to the National Court of Justice, including a lack of transparency in hiring decisions. The primary criticism regarding the selection of justices for the Constitutional Court was that the members of the selection committee were too closely aligned with the government. A new attorney general was appointed in April 2011, and the system used by the Council of Popular Participation to vet candidates was similarly criticized for a lack of transparency.

Judicial processes remain slow, and many inmates reach the time limit for pretrial detention while their cases are still under investigation. Prisons are seriously overcrowded, and torture and ill-treatment of detainees and prisoners are widespread. Various projects to reform the penal and criminal procedure codes in order to improve efficiency and fairness were undertaken in 2009 and 2010, but rising crime—partly blamed on prisoners who were released to relieve overcrowding—pushed the focus of debate away from comprehensive reform. A government-sponsored bill proposing a comprehensive reform of the criminal code had not been approved by the legislature by the end of 2012. Voters endorsed more restrictive rules on pretrial detention in the 2011 referendum.

As of December 2012, Ecuador had granted 55,323 refugee visas out of 162,687 requests, many of them to Colombians fleeing violence in their country. This makes Ecuador the largest recipient of refugees in Latin America. The government provides refugees with access to health facilities, schools, and small-business loans.

Indigenous people continue to suffer discrimination at many levels of society. In the Amazon region, indigenous groups have attempted to win a share of oil revenues and a voice in decisions on natural resources and development. The government has maintained that it will not hand indigenous groups a veto on core matters of national interest.

Women took 40 of 124 assembly seats in the 2009 elections, and the new constitution calls for a significant female presence in public office. The election law requires that women account for 50 percent of the party lists in national legislative elections. Violence against women is common, as is employment discrimination. The 2008 constitution does not provide for same-sex marriage, but civil unions are recognized. Trafficking in persons, generally women and children, remains a problem.

Egypt

Political Rights: 5*
Civil Liberties: 5
Status: Partly Free

Population: 82,283,000
Capital: Cairo

Status Change: Egypt's political rights rating improved from 6 to 5, and its status improved from Not Free to Partly Free, due to the holding of a presidential election that, although imperfect, was close to international standards, and the removal from power of the Supreme Council of the Armed Forces (SCAF).

Ten-Year Ratings Timeline For Year Under Review (Political Rights, Civil Liberties, Status)

2003	2004	2005	2006	2007	2008	2009	2010	2011	2012
6,6NF	6,5NF	6,5NF	6,5NF	6,5NF	6,5NF	6,5NF	6,5NF	6,5NF	5,5PF

Overview: Political instability and protests continued throughout 2012, as a contentious transition from military to civilian rule was followed by heated debate over the unilateral actions of the new Islamist-dominated government. Elections for the People's Assembly, Egypt's lower house of parliament, were completed in January 2012, with nearly 70 percent of the new chamber held by Islamist parties that were illegal before the ouster of authoritarian president Hosni Mubarak in early 2011. However, the People's Assembly was dismissed in mid-June, after various electoral laws were ruled unconstitutional in what many described as a power struggle between the judiciary and the political establishment. Mohamed Morsi of the Muslim Brotherhood won a presidential runoff later in June, and in November, he claimed extensive executive powers in a decree that he defended as necessary to ensure the adoption of a new constitution in a chaotic political environment. The resulting constitution, which opponents criticized as a highly problematic document written by an unrepresentative and overwhelmingly Islamist constituent assembly, was approved in a mid-December referendum, but its passage failed to quell deep mistrust and tensions between liberal and Islamist political factions at year's end.

Egypt formally gained independence from Britain in 1922 and acquired full sovereignty in 1952. After leading a coup that overthrew the monarchy, Colonel Gamal Abdel Nasser ruled until his death in 1970. The constitution adopted in 1971 under his successor, Anwar al-Sadat, established a strong presidential system with nominal guarantees for political and civil rights that were not respected in practice. Sadat signed a peace treaty with Israel in 1979 and built an alliance with the United States, which subsequently provided the Egyptian government with substantial military and other aid payments on an annual basis.

Following Sadat's 1981 assassination, then vice president Hosni Mubarak became president and declared a state of emergency, which remained in force until 2012. Amid an Islamist insurgency in the 1990s, authorities jailed thousands of suspected militants without charge and cracked down on dissent. Although the armed infrastructure of Islamist groups was largely eradicated by 1998, the government continued to restrict political and civil liberties.

Economic growth in the late 1990s temporarily alleviated dire socioeconomic problems, until a 2001 downturn. Disaffection with the government then spread, and antigovernment demonstrations were harshly suppressed.

Mubarak sought to recast himself as a reformer in 2004, with a new cabinet of young technocrats and market-friendly economic changes. However, associates of the president's son Gamal, a rising star in the ruling National Democratic Party (NDP), received key portfolios, stoking suspicions of an impending hereditary succession.

In December 2004, Kifaya (Enough), an informal movement encompassing a broad spectrum of secular and Islamist activists, held the first-ever demonstration calling for Mubarak to step down. Similar protests in 2005 were met with official brutality.

A Mubarak-initiated constitutional amendment allowing Egypt's first multicandidate presidential election required candidates to be nominated by licensed parties or a substantial bloc of elected officials. All major opposition groups denounced the measure and boycotted the May 2005 referendum that approved it. Mubarak subsequently won 88 percent of the vote in the September presidential election. His main opponent, Al-Ghad (Tomorrow) Party leader Ayman Nour, took just 8 percent and was later sentenced to five years in prison on fraud charges.

The banned Muslim Brotherhood, whose candidates ran as independents, increased its representation in the NDP-dominated lower house sixfold in the 2005 parliamentary elections, securing 88 of 454 seats. However, judges criticized the government's intimidation of opposition voters and refused to certify the results, prompting the authorities to suppress judicial independence in 2006.

In 2007, constitutional amendments passed in an opposition-boycotted referendum limited judicial election monitoring and prohibited the formation of religious political parties. The referendum and upper-house elections held that June were marred by irregularities and tighter restrictions on the Muslim Brotherhood.

Political tension rose in 2010, amid rumors of Mubarak's failing health and growing uncertainty over his successor. Popular dissatisfaction with the regime swelled after parliamentary elections in November, in which almost no opposition representatives were elected. The campaign period featured an array of state abuses, and the results were seen as blatantly rigged. Increases in state violence, including the police murder of Alexandria-based blogger Khaled Said in June, exacerbated animosity between the population and the authorities.

This tension erupted into protests in January 2011, shortly after longtime Tunisian president Zine el-Abidine Ben Ali was popularly deposed. An 18-day protest against Mubarak and the NDP began on January 25, as demonstrators occupied Cairo's Tahrir Square and other public spaces across the country. The Mubarak regime responded with brute force, assaulting protesters and shutting down the internet to prevent organizers from communicating. However, the protests continued. Mubarak stepped down on February 11, and the Supreme Council of the Armed Forces (SCAF), a group of senior army officers, took over, dissolving the NDP-controlled legislature and promising an orderly transition to civilian rule.

The months after Mubarak's ouster were marked by rising sectarian tensions and periodic protests demanding an end to military rule. The military leadership faced criticism for ongoing human rights abuses and the trials of thousands of civilians in military courts. In October, security forces killed 28 civilians while crushing a largely Coptic Christian protest near the state television building in Cairo.

Delayed elections for the People's Assembly, the lower house of parliament, were held in three rounds between November 28, 2011, and January 11, 2012. The Democratic Alliance, led by the Muslim Brotherhood's Freedom and Justice Party (FJP), won 235 of the 498 elected seats, and a bloc led by the Salafist party Al-Nour won 123 seats. A coalition of liberal parties, the Egyptian Bloc, won 34 seats, and the center-right Wafd party won 38. Several smaller groups took the remainder. Including the 10 members nominated by the SCAF in its role as de facto executive, there were just 10 women and 13 Coptic Christians in the new assembly.

Elections for the 270-seat upper house, the Consultative Council (Majlis al-Shura), were held on January 29 and February 7. The FJP's Democratic Alliance won about 60 percent of the elected seats, with a total of 105 seats. Al-Nour's bloc placed second with 45 seats, or 25.5 percent of elected spots, followed by Wafd with 14, the Egyptian Bloc with 8, and small parties and independents with the remainder.

Ongoing judicial interventions in the political process started in January, when the Supreme Constitutional Court (SCC) declared unconstitutional a SCAF-initiated draft law for presidential elections. Over the next several months, the SCC disqualified three presidential candidates on questionable grounds, disbanded a constituent assembly appointed by the parliament to draft a new constitution, and dismissed the People's Assembly in June after finding legal flaws in its election. Critics charged that these moves were orchestrated by sympathizers of the Mubarak regime in reaction to the positive electoral performance of Islamist parties.

Nevertheless, amid rising public demands for a transition to civilian rule, a two-round presidential election was held in May and June. FJP candidate Mohamed Morsi led the first round on May 23–24, taking over 24 percent of the vote. Mubarak-era prime minister Ahmed Shafik placed second with roughly 23 percent. In the June 16–17 runoff, Morsi won the presidency with 51.7 percent of the vote.

The transition to civilian rule continued on August 12, when Morsi fired the head of the SCAF, Defense Minister Mohamed Tantawi, in addition to the acting chiefs of the branches of the Egyptian military. Morsi also annulled SCAF-issued decrees that reduced executive power, in a move toward greater civilian authority over the military.

Following indications that the judiciary would disband the second constituent assembly, and capitalizing on international and domestic praise after helping to broker a ceasefire between Israel and Hamas, Morsi issued a presidential decree on November 22 that declared his decisions to be above judicial review and immunized the constituent assembly and Consultative Council from judicial dismissal. Morsi defended the decree as necessary to protect the constitutional drafting process, but it was widely criticized as a power grab.

Mass demonstrations, both for and against Morsi's action, ensued immediately and continued for weeks. Morsi attempted to clarify the broadly worded decree's implications and thereby quell the negative response, but antigovernment protesters were undeterred. A coalition of opposition parties demanded the reversal of the presidential decree and the replacement of the constituent assembly with a more representative group.

The protests peaked in early December, when the opposing sides converged at the presidential palace. Members of the Muslim Brotherhood allegedly detained and beat at least 49 antigovernment protesters. Another 10 demonstrators, most of them Muslim Brotherhood members, were killed in the clashes, and more than 700 were injured.

Morsi eventually agreed to rescind his decree, but pushed ahead with a December 15 vote on the draft constitution, which the constituent assembly had rushed to complete. While the document contained some welcome provisions limiting executive powers, detractors argued that it was drafted by an unrepresentative, Islamist-dominated group, and that its vague language and lack of protections for women and minorities, press freedom, and other civil liberties constituted grave flaws.

Amid ongoing protests and declarations by many judges that they would not supervise the voting, the constitutional referendum was held on December 15 and 22. Observers criticized the polls as hasty and marred by irregularities and insufficient judicial oversight, which is required by Egyptian law. The constitution ultimately passed with 64 percent approval among the 33 percent of eligible voters who turned out.

Political Rights and Civil Liberties: Egypt is not an electoral democracy. The SCAF exercised executive powers through the first half of 2012, and the newly elected lower house of parliament, dissolved by the judiciary in June, had not been replaced by year's end.

The 508-seat People's Assembly (Majlis al-Sha'b), the parliament's lower house, consists of 166 members who are elected through individual candidacy, 332 elected through a party-list system, and 10 appointed by the executive. All members serve five-year terms. Observers of the elections held from November 2011 through January 2012 indicated that they broadly met international standards regarding election-day conduct, with some complaints of campaigning violations and polling difficulties. However, the chamber was disbanded when the SCC ruled that members of political parties had improperly been allowed to run for the individual-candidacy seats, which were meant for independents.

The 270-seat upper house, the Consultative Council, has traditionally functioned solely in an advisory capacity. The president appoints 90 of its members, and 180 are directly elected. Elections for the council in early 2012 were marred by problems including low turnout, with less than 15 percent of eligible voters participating. President Mohamed Morsi chose the chamber's 90 appointed members in December. They included members of 17 political parties; representatives of three churches; a representative from the country's leading Islamic institution, Al-Azhar; and various artists, athletes, and judicial representatives.

Observers of the May and June 2012 presidential election, the first genuinely competitive presidential contest in Egypt's history, reported that election-day conduct was generally consistent with international standards, but criticized a number of factors in the electoral process. In April, the SCC disqualified three leading presidential candidates on what some considered to be political grounds, though the judges defended the decisions as consistent with electoral law. Significant restrictions were placed on election observers, including long delays in granting accreditation and time limits on observers' presence in polling stations. Excessive powers were vested in the Presidential Election Commission, the decisions of which were final and not subject to appeal. Other problems included violations of ballot secrecy, polling stations opening late, and additional basic procedural irregularities.

The 2012 electoral victories of Islamist groups like the previously banned Muslim Brotherhood, and the formation of several new parties from across the political spectrum, represented a clear departure from the Mubarak era, in which the legal and electoral framework was designed to ensure solid majorities for the ruling NDP at all levels of government. An April 2011 court ruling had dissolved the NDP, though many figures affiliated with the party remained active in politics. A law on political corruption, designed to ban the participation of such individuals, was issued by the SCAF in November 2011 but declared unconstitutional by the SCC on June 14, 2012, in the same ruling that disbanded the People's Assembly.

Corruption remains pervasive at all levels of government. Egypt was ranked 118 out of 176 countries surveyed in Transparency International's 2012 Corruption Perceptions Index. Deposed president Hosni Mubarak and his former interior minister, Habib el-Adly, were sentenced to life in prison in June 2012 for their roles in the deaths of unarmed protesters during the February 2011 uprising. However, judges in the same trial dismissed corruption charges against Mubarak and his sons, Gamal and Alaa, citing technicalities.

Freedom of the press improved slightly after Mubarak's ouster, particularly through an increase in independent television stations and other media. President Morsi banned the pretrial detention of journalists in August 2012, but media workers faced significant restrictions during the year, and they argued that the draft constitution lacked sufficient protections for a free press. Media advocacy groups reported attacks on journalists covering the December protests against the draft constitution, including targeted assaults on several reporters.

Censorship, both official and self-imposed, is widespread. The Consultative Council reportedly appointed the editors of several prominent state-run newspapers in 2012. A number of independent dailies, criticizing the move as an attempt to restrict negative coverage of the Morsi administration, ran blank columns on August 9 in protest.

Defamation remains a criminal offense. In October 2012, media owner and talk-show host Tawfik Okasha was sentenced in absentia to four months in prison on charges of defaming Morsi. A number of other media figures, including Islam Afifi, editor in chief of *Al-Dustour*, and Hanan Youssef, deputy editor in chief of *Al-Messa*, also faced defamation charges following negative coverage of Morsi and his allies.

Islam is the state religion. Some reforms were initiated in 2012 to decrease state involvement in religious institutions, including a bill that would allow a group of senior scholars at Al-Azhar, rather than the president, to elect their grand sheikh. While most Egyptians are Sunni Muslims, Coptic Christians form a substantial minority, and there are a very small number of Jews, Shiite Muslims, and Baha'is. The Baha'i faith is not recognized, though a 2009 decree allowed adherents to obtain identification papers without claiming to be Muslims or Christians. Separately, a 2008 court ruling found that Christian converts to Islam were free to return to Christianity. Anti-Christian employment discrimination is evident in the public sector, especially the security services and military, and the government frequently denies or delays permission to build and repair churches.

Sectarian bloodshed has increased in recent years, with Christians suffering the brunt of the violence. In February 2012, eight families were evicted from their homes in the village of Sharbat after violent skirmishes over a rumored affair between a Christian man and a Muslim woman. In September, several Christian families fled their homes in Sinai following threats from suspected Islamist militants and a shooting at a Christian-owned shop. Throughout 2012, minority religious communities expressed concern that Islamist political power would render them more vulnerable to abuse. Coptic members of the constituent assembly resigned, claiming that their interests were not represented in the process. The referendum results reflected a sectarian divide, with very few Copts voting in favor of the charter.

Academic freedom improved somewhat after the fall of Mubarak. University leaders are no longer appointed by the government, and a series of Mubarak-era education officials have resigned.

Freedoms of assembly and association are restricted, but Egyptians continued to actively participate in large-scale demonstrations throughout 2012. Protests repeatedly turned violent or prompted police crackdowns, with many demonstrators suffering abuses and injuries.

Numerous civil society activists were harassed by the authorities during 2012, particularly before the transition to civilian rule. In March, complaints against 12 prominent activists for slandering and "inciting hate against" the SCAF were referred for military prosecution; the cases were pending at year's end.

The Law of Associations prohibits the establishment of groups "threatening national unity [or] violating public morals," bars nongovernmental organizations (NGOs) from receiving foreign grants without the approval of the Social Affairs Ministry, and allows the ministry to dissolve NGOs without a judicial order. Government officials continued to harass NGOs after Mubarak's fall. In December 2011, security forces raided the offices of 17 domestic and international civil society groups, confiscating equipment and temporarily detaining some staff. In January 2012, 43 NGO workers were indicted on charges of operating an organization and receiving funds from a foreign government without a license. Representatives of the NGOs argued that the charges were political and that they had been operating transparently. The case was ongoing at the end of 2012.

The labor movement made important advances during and after the 2011 uprising, as strikes played a significant role in increasing pressure on Mubarak to step down. Workers were granted the right to establish independent trade unions and formed an independent union federation, ending the long-standing monopoly of the state-allied federation. Labor activists criticized the November 2012 adoption of Decree No. 97, an amendment to the 1976 labor law that increased government control over unions. Such control is most evident in a provision setting a maximum age of 60 for board members of the historically state-dominated Egyptian Trade Union Federation, which would lead to the dismissal of more than 160 of 524 members and allow the Morsi government to fill any vacancy for which there was no runner-up in the most recent election. The provision had yet to be implemented at year's end.

The Supreme Judicial Council, a supervisory body of senior judges, nominates and assigns most members of the judiciary. However, the Justice Ministry controls promotions and compensation, giving it undue influence over the courts. The judiciary was at the center of political tensions in 2012, as judges disbanded the first constituent assembly and the People's Assembly elected in early 2012. Representatives of the judiciary defended these rulings as indications of judicial independence and the rule of law, but detractors argued that Mubarak-era judges were making politicized decisions that undermined the will of the electorate.

The state of emergency that had been in place since 1981 was lifted by the SCAF on May 31, 2012. Under the Emergency Law, "security" cases were usually referred to executive-controlled exceptional courts that denied defendants many constitutional protections. The Emergency Law empowered the government to tap telephones, intercept mail, conduct warrantless searches, and indefinitely detain suspects without charge if they were deemed a threat to national security.

Because military judges are appointed by the executive branch to renewable two-year terms, military tribunals lack independence. Verdicts are based on little more than the testimony of security officers and informers, and are reviewed only by a body of military judges and the president. Charges brought in military courts are often vague and trumped up, according to human rights organizations. They can include property damage, insulting the army, and general vandalism. Throughout 2012, human rights groups urged the SCAF and later President Morsi to release the more than 150 people held in military detention and to end military trials for civilians. Human rights advocates expressed concern that a law issued by the president on December 9—granting the military the authority to arrest and try civilians in the period before the constitutional referendum—would result in further abuses, though Morsi's office denied that the law would be used to try civilians. Furthermore, critics warned that vague wording in the new constitution would allow for military trials of civilians in cases where the government felt that military interests were harmed.

General prison conditions are very poor; inmates are subject to torture and other abuse, overcrowding, and a lack of sanitation and medical care. Thousands of inmates escaped amid the disorder surrounding Mubarak's resignation, and many avoided recapture. This led to a decrease in security following the revolution.

Some aspects of the law and many traditional practices discriminate against women. Job discrimination is evident in the civil service. Muslim women are placed at a disadvantage by laws on divorce and other personal status issues. However, Christians are not subject to such provisions of Islamic law. Domestic violence is common, as is sexual harassment on the street. Spousal rape is not illegal, and the penal code allows for leniency in so-called honor killings. Female genital mutilation is widely practiced.

The new constitution limits women's rights to those compatible with Islamic law. Women's rights advocates cautioned that the document's vague wording and lack of specific protections put women at risk, particularly in light of the political dominance of conservative Islamist leaders.

In March 2011, soldiers subjected women arrested at the Tahrir Square protests to "virginity checks," in addition to beating them and photographing them after they were strip-searched. Cairo's administrative court eventually banned the checks in a December ruling. In March 2012, a doctor accused of forcing female protesters to undergo these examinations in 2011 was acquitted. No other suspects were charged. In August, General Abdul Fattah al-Sisi, who had been criticized for defending the checks, was appointed defense minister and commander of Egypt's armed forces.

El Salvador

Political Rights: 2
Civil Liberties: 3
Status: Free

Population: 6,264,000
Capital: San Salvador

Ten-Year Ratings Timeline For Year Under Review (Political Rights, Civil Liberties, Status)

2003	2004	2005	2006	2007	2008	2009	2010	2011	2012
2,3F	2,3F	2,3F	2,3F	2,3F	2,3F	2,3F	2,3F	2,3F	2,3F

Overview:
In legislative and municipal elections held in March 2012, the Nationalist Republican Alliance regained political ground that it had lost to the Farabundo Martí National Liberation Front in 2009. Also in March, the Mara Salvatrucha and 18th Street gangs agreed to a truce that cut the country's murder rate by more than 40 percent. The Constitutional Court in June rejected a second set of appointments to the Supreme Court, which led to a showdown with the legislative branch.

El Salvador gained independence from Spain in 1821 and broke away from the Central American Federation in 1841. A republican political system dominated by an oligarchy of landowning elite, and subject to foreign interference, gave way to military rule in the mid-20th century. A 1979-92 civil war pitted El Salvador's Christian Democratic Party (PDC) government, the right-wing oligarchy, and the military, with support from the United States, against the Marxist-Leninist Farabundo Martí National Liberation Front (FMLN) and other leftist groups. The war left more than 75,000 dead and 500,000 displaced. In 1989, the conservative Nationalist Republican Alliance (ARENA) captured the presidency, and the civil war ended in 1992 with the signing of a peace treaty. ARENA held the presidency for two decades, with ongoing competition from the FMLN party.

In the March 2009 presidential election, Mauricio Funes became the first president from the FMLN. While the FMLN has supported Funes on several issues since taking office, important disagreements have complicated their relationship, causing a rift between the president and his party. Funes was accused by some on the left of moving towards the center after taking office and deviating from the FMLN's original program. Contentious issues included Funes' replacement of FMLN members from his cabinet, allegedly under pressure from the U.S. government; in November 2011, for example, Funes replaced Minister of Justice and Public Security Manuel Melgar, an FMLN militant, with former general David Munguía Payés.

El Salvador held legislative and local elections in March 2012, with a turnout of 51 percent of registered voters. The elections returned ARENA to power, with the party winning 33 seats. The FMLN followed with 31 seats, the Grand Alliance for National Unity (GANA) with 11, the National Conciliation (CN) with 7, and the Party of Hope (PES) and the Democratic Change Party (PDC) with 1 seat each. The elections marked the first time that candidates could run for office independently of parties, though independents won less than 1 percent of the national vote. In municipal elections, ARENA captured 116 out of 262 mayorships. The FMLN won 95 mayoral races, including 8 in a coalition with the PDC and 2 with the PES; the CN won 26 races, including 3 in coalition with the PES; and GANA won 18, including 1 in coalition with the PES. The PES won 4 mayorships, and the PDC won 3. An electoral observer mission from the Organization of American States (OAS) made a number of recommendations to improve the legitimacy of El Salvador's electoral process, including the passage of campaign finance and accountability laws, as well as measures to increase female representation in the national- and municipal-level governments.

In March 2012, online investigative journal *El Faro* uncovered a truce between the Mara Salvatrucha (MS-13) and the 18th Street gangs, facilitated by former guerrilla and member of congress Raul Mijango, along with the military bishop Fabio Colindres. The gang leaders agreed to the ceasefire in return for improved prison conditions. After initially denying involvement with the truce, the government eventually acknowledged it and held several meetings with representatives of civil society, political parties, the business community, and the OAS in order to devise a long-term plan to sustain the peace. While the country's murder rate dropped by more than 40 percent in 2012 compared to 2011, the public remained skeptical that overall violence had decreased and that the truce could be sustained. In December, the two mediators of the truce requested that the Legislative Assembly adopt new laws that would offer a legal framework for the continuation of the truce. Among the proposed measures was one for the creation of jobs for at-risk youths. All political parties were open to these suggestions.

After overcoming a constitutional crisis with the passage of Decree 743 in 2011—which required the Constitutional Chamber of the Supreme Court to reach unanimous decisions before rulings could take effect—the independence of the country's judiciary was tested once again in 2012. The constitutional crisis was triggered when FMLN deputies elected a new attorney general during the legislature's April lame duck session. The Supreme Court declared the election unconstitutional, and the legislators retaliated by trying to change the composition of the Supreme Court. On June 5, the Constitutional Chamber ruled that the those judicial appointments, as well as appointments that had been made in 2006, were unconstitutional on the grounds that legislators voted twice to elect judges in each year despite being authorized by the constitution to vote only once during each term. President Funes helped the political parties broker an agreement in August, whereby the legislature re-elected, the 2006 and 2012 Supreme Court judges, four judges elected to the Constitutional Chamber in 2009 remained in their positions, and José Salomón Padilla was elected president of the Supreme Court and the Constitutional Chamber.

The global economic crisis continued to have a significant effect on the country, as the economy is closely linked to that of the United States through trade and remittances. Analysts estimate that economic growth will remain low for the next several years. It is estimated that 41 percent of all Salvadoran live in poverty, which has fueled social alienation, as well as organized crime and violence.

Political Rights and Civil Liberties: El Salvador is an electoral democracy. The president is elected for a five-year term, and the 84-member, unicameral Legislative Assembly is elected for three years. The two largest political parties are the conservative ARENA and the leftist FMLN.

Corruption remains a serious problem in El Salvador, and few high-level public officials have ever been charged or convicted. In March 2011, the Legislative Assembly passed a law requiring public entities to provide information in order to promote accountability and to encourage participation and public oversight; the reforms went into effect in 2012. Zaira Navas resigned as inspector general of the National Civil Police (PNC) in January 2012, claiming that the military had gained too much influence over the nation's security institutions, including the PNC and the State Intelligence Agency, and that further investigations into corruption would be blocked. Shortly after Navas's resignation, several officers who had been under investigation were promoted. In October, President Mauricio Funes announced that his administration had investigated 307 cases of anomalies in governance, including 172 from his term. While 111 cases were sufficiently documented to be taken to the prosecutor, only 3 were in judicial proceedings as of October. El Salvador was ranked 83 out of 176 countries surveyed in Transparency International's 2012 Corruption Perceptions Index.

The constitution provides for freedom of the press, and this right is generally respected in practice. In September 2011, the Legislative Assembly approved reforms to the penal code that would replace jail time with fines in cases involving crimes against public image and privacy. A member of MS-13 accused of murdering Canal 33 cameraman Alfredo Antonio Hurtado in April 2011 was convicted in May 2012. The staff of the newspaper *El Faro* have received threats and reported being followed after reporting in May 2011 about connections between gang leaders, politicians, and businessmen, as well as the March 2012 gang truce. The media are privately owned, but ownership is confined to a small group of powerful businesspeople who often impose controls on journalists to protect their political or economic interests. ARENA-aligned Telecorporación Salvadoreña owns three of the five private television networks and dominates the market. There is unrestricted access to the internet, and the government and private organizations have worked to extend internet access to the poor.

The government does not encroach on religious freedom, and academic freedom is respected.

Freedoms of assembly and association are generally upheld. The Legislative Assembly passed a controversial law in 2010 criminalizing gang membership. Critics argued that the law threatened freedom of association and would not succeed in addressing gang-related crime. El Salvador's nongovernmental organizations (NGOs) generally operate freely, but some have reported registration difficulties. Labor unions have long faced obstacles in a legal environment that has traditionally favored business interests.

The judicial system continued to demonstrate its independence in a number of important cases in 2012, including corruption investigations against former political officials. However, judges and others continue to speak out against the corruption and obstructionism that still permeates the Supreme Court and the entire judiciary. While very few complaints against judges ever move forward, the Supreme Court investigation unit dismissed two judges and suspended six others in 2011. In December 2012, the Constitutional Chamber demonstrated its independence once again when it ruled that elements of the regulations issued by the Funes administration to implement the Access to Information Law were unconstitutional.

Law enforcement officials continue to be criticized for brutality, corruption, arbitrary arrest, and lengthy pretrial detention. In September 2012, Colonel Alberto Gonzalez Quezada, who had served as head of the military's Logistics Division in 2010 and 2011, was arrested and charged with illegal arms sales. There are an estimated 20,000 gang members in the country; nearly 10,000 were in detention centers in 2011. The U.S. Treasury Department named MS-13 a transnational criminal organization in October 2012. Primarily as a result of the March 2012 gang truce, El Salvador ended the year with a homicide rate of approximately 42 per 100,000 compared to 70 per 100,000 in 2011. El Salvador was added to the U.S. list of "major" drug producing and transit countries in 2011. The Legislative Assembly elects a human rights ombudsman for a three-year term. According to the country's Prison Directorate, as of June 2012, the prison system was operating at over 300 percent of its capacity, and nearly 30 percent of inmates had not been convicted of a crime. After having increased military authority over the country's prison system in recent years, the Funes government began to demilitarize prisons in April 2012.

Salvadoran law, including a 1993 general amnesty, bars prosecution of crimes and human rights violations committed during the civil war, but the authorities have faced criticism from NGOs and the Inter-American Court of Human Rights (IACHR) for failing to adequately investigate such crimes. In November 2011, the Spanish government formally requested the extradition of 15 military officers for their involvement in the murders of six Jesuit priests—five of whom were Spanish—and their housekeeper and her daughter in 1989. The Supreme Court denied the request in May 2012. In December, the IACHR ruled that that the 1993 amnesty law was invalid and that the government must investigate a 1981 massacre in and around the village of El Mozote, in which the armed forces killed more than 800 civilians as part of an antiguerilla campaign.

There are no national laws regarding indigenous rights. Access to land and credit remain a problem for indigenous people, along with poverty, unemployment, and labor discrimination.

Businesses are subject to regular extortion by organized criminal groups. While the murder rate decreased in 2012, there are concerns that extortion by gangs increased.

While women are granted equal rights under the constitution, they are often discriminated against in practice, including in employment. Violence against women, including domestic violence, is a serious problem. Despite governmental efforts, El Salvador remains a source, transit, and destination country for the trafficking of women and children for the purposes of prostitution and forced labor.

Equatorial Guinea

Political Rights: 7
Civil Liberties: 7
Status: Not Free

Population: 740,000
Capital: Malabo

Ten-Year Ratings Timeline For Year Under Review (Political Rights, Civil Liberties, Status)

2003	2004	2005	2006	2007	2008	2009	2010	2011	2012
7,6NF	7,6NF	7,6NF	7,6NF	7,6NF	7,7NF	7,7NF	7,7NF	7,7NF	7,7NF

Overview: President Teodoro Obiang Nguema Mbasogo appointed his eldest son as second vice president in May 2012, putting him second in line for the presidency. Equatorial Guinea hosted the Africa Cup of Nations in January, which led to crackdowns on press freedom and other civil liberties. Several human rights activists were detained on questionable charges and then released during the year, while the head of the country's press association died under suspicious circumstances in November.

Equatorial Guinea achieved independence from Spain in 1968. Current president Teodoro Obiang Nguema Mbasogo seized power in 1979 after deposing and executing his uncle, the country's first president, Francisco Macías Nguema. While international pressure compelled Obiang to establish a multiparty system in 1991, Equatorial Guinea has yet to hold credible elections. The discovery and exploitation of offshore hydrocarbon resources has allowed Obiang to amass a vast personal fortune, bolstering his domestic position and making him largely impervious to calls from abroad to implement meaningful political reforms.

Obiang dissolved the parliament in February 2008 and called legislative and municipal elections for May, which where swept by his Democratic Party of Equatorial Guinea (PDGE) and its coalition partners amid allegations of widespread irregularities. The Convergence for Social Democracy (CPDS), the sole opposition party, was reduced from two seats to one.

In February 2009, a group of unidentified gunmen attacked the presidential palace in Malabo. The government asserted that the assailants were Niger Delta militants working with members of the Equatoguinean opposition-in-exile. In the ensuing months, security forces rounded up and expelled hundreds of foreign residents. Seven Nigerian suspects were convicted and sentenced in April on charges related to the attack. In August 2010, four former military and government officials were executed within an hour of being sentenced to death by a military court for attempting to assassinate the president during the attacks. According to Amnesty International, Equatoguinean operatives abducted the four individuals in Benin, where they had been living as refugees, and proceeded to hold them incommunicado in Black Beach Prison, where the suspects were reportedly tortured before confessing to the attack.

Obiang swept the November 2009 presidential elections with 95.4 percent of the vote, although the election reportedly featured intimidation and harassment of the opposition by security forces and was widely regarded as rigged. The president's main opponent, CPDS leader Plácido Micó Abogo, received less than 4 percent of the vote.

There was a dramatic increase in arbitrary arrests and police raids in the months leading up to the country's hosting of the June 2011 meeting of the 17th African Union summit. Some observers attributed the crackdown to preemptive government efforts to prevent any manifestations of political unrest during the summit.

On November 13, 2011, a constitutional referendum was approved by 97.7 percent of voters, though organizations such as Human Rights Watch reported voting fraud. While the reforms imposed a limit of two consecutive terms for the presidency, the age limit for eligibility was lifted, which would allow Obiang to run for a third term in the future. The referendum also allowed the president to appoint a vice president who would assume the presidency should Obiang retire or die in office. In May 2012, Obiang appointed a new cabinet, including several of his close relatives, along with a new first vice president; many of those in powerful positions in the previous cabinet were merely moved into other powerful positions. Obiang also appointed his eldest son, Teodoro Nguema Obiang Mangue, as second vice president in May. The move, which would make Mangue second in line to succeed the president after the first vice president, was seen as a step toward grooming Mangue to succeed his father.

Equatorial Guinea's abundant oil revenues do not reach the majority of its citizens, with 77 percent of the population living on less than $2 a day. According to Human Rights Watch, the government spent four times as much money building facilities to host the African Union summit in 2011 as it did on education in 2008. The government built or expanded several stadiums to host the Africa Cup of Nations soccer competition in January 2012, but has not made the cost public.

Political Rights and Civil Liberties: Equatorial Guinea is not an electoral democracy. Power rests firmly in the hands of Teodoro Obiang Nguema Mbasogo and his supporters, the overwhelming majority of whom hail from the Esangui clan, part of the Fang ethnic group. The 100 members of the unicameral House of People's Representatives are elected to five-year terms, but wield little power; all but one of the chamber's seats are held by members of the propresidential coalition. The November 2011 referendum approved the creation of a new bicameral parliament to consist of a 100-member Chamber of Deputies and a 70-member Senate. Each body is to be directly elected for five-year terms, but the law will determine how many senators the president may nominate. Elections for this new parliament are scheduled for 2013.

Obiang's regime has little tolerance for political dissent. Equatoguinean security agents closely monitor suspected Obiang opponents, including members of the CPDS. PDGE party membership is essentially a prerequisite for government employment, and civil servants are reluctant to criticize the authorities for fear that their family members will be blacklisted from securing public employment.

Obiang and his inner circle dominate Equatorial Guinea's economic landscape, and graft is rampant. Most major business transactions cannot transpire without involving an individual connected to the regime. In June 2012, the U.S. Department of Justice filed a complaint alleging that the president's son, Teodoro Nguema Obiang Mangue, had used money obtained through corruption to purchase a California mansion and private jet. In July, French authorities issued an arrest warrant for Mangue on money-laundering charges. In August, authorities in Paris, where Mangue had been living, seized much of his property as a result of outstanding charges of corruption against Obiang. Equatorial Guinea was ranked 163 out of 176 countries surveyed in Transparency International's 2012 Corruption Index.

Although the constitution guarantees media freedom, a 1992 press law authorizes government censorship. Libel remains a criminal offense, and the government requires all journalists to register with state officials. A few private newspapers are published irregularly but face intense financial and political pressure. The government holds a monopoly on broadcast media, with the exception of RTV-Asonga, a private radio and television outlet owned by Obiang's son. The government harassed foreign reporters covering the Africa Cup of Nations in 2012, especially those who tried to report on more than the tournament. In November, Manuel Nzé Nsongo, the president of the Equatorial Guinea Press Association, died under suspicious circumstances after attending a working lunch with Agustín Nzé Nfumu, the Minister of Information, Press, and Radio; his relatives suspected that he had been poisoned.

The constitution protects religious freedom, though in practice it is sometimes affected by the country's broader political repression. Official preference is given to the Roman Catholic Church and the Reform Church of Equatorial Guinea. Academic freedom is also politically constrained, and self-censorship among faculty is common.

Freedom of assembly is severely restricted, and political gatherings must have official authorization to proceed. The government also uses more indirect means to restrict meetings, including organizing parallel competing meetings and raising the price of renting meeting facilities. The few international nongovernmental organizations that operate in the country promote social and economic improvements rather than political and civil rights. The few local groups that do exist are underfunded, relying on small grants from foreign embassies as virtually no international grant-giving organizations work in Equatorial Guinea. In February 2012, Dr. Wenceslao Mansogo Alo, an outspoken human rights activist, was arrested on trumped-up charges of medical negligence. He was convicted in May, though Obiang pardoned him in June, in line with his history of arresting and then pardoning his opponents. On October 22, Fabian Nsue Nguema, a human rights lawyer, was arrested without a warrant while visiting a client at the Black Beach prison, and was illegally held at a police station without being charged until his release on October 30.

The constitution provides for the right to organize unions, but there are many legal barriers to collective bargaining. While it has ratified key International Labour Organization conventions, the government has refused to register a number of trade unions. The country's only legal labor union is the Unionized Organization of Small Farmers.

The judiciary is not independent. Judges in sensitive cases reportedly need to consult with the president's office before making decisions. Civil cases rarely go to trial, and military tribunals handle national security cases. Equatorial Guinea has been condemned internationally for holding detainees in secret, denying them access to lawyers, and jailing them for long periods without charge, in violation of domestic law. UN investigators have also reported systematic torture in the penal system. Prison conditions are deplorable.

Immigrants from neighboring African states and the ethnic Bubi are frequent targets of government harassment. Foreign workers have frequently been expelled or jailed. The Bubi have seen their economic rights undermined by successive Fang-dominated regimes. Harassment of immigrants tends to increase after international events. Following the Africa Cup of Nations in January 2012, the government increased harassment of African immigrants to prevent them from using the games to obtain entry visas and stay in the country illegally.

The authorities frequently harass activists attempting to travel abroad, often confiscating passports long enough to cause them to miss international conferences or meetings.

Constitutional and legal guarantees of equality for women are largely ignored. Women hold just 8 percent of the seats in the House of People's Representatives. Violence against women is reportedly widespread.

Eritrea

Political Rights: 7
Civil Liberties: 7
Status: Not Free

Population: 5,581,000
Capital: Asmara

Ten-Year Ratings Timeline For Year Under Review (Political Rights, Civil Liberties, Status)

2003	2004	2005	2006	2007	2008	2009	2010	2011	2012
7,6NF	7,6NF	7,6NF	7,6NF	7,6NF	7,6NF	7,7NF	7,7NF	7,7NF	7,7NF

Overview:

Eritrea made tentative efforts to end its international isolation in 2012, but at home, the government continued to deny its citizens basic political rights and civil liberties. Four journalists, part of a group held without trial for up to 11 years, were confirmed to have died in detention.

Britain ended Italian colonial rule in Eritrea during World War II, and the country was formally incorporated into Ethiopia in 1952. Its independence struggle began in 1962 as a nationalist and Marxist guerrilla war against the Ethiopian government of Emperor Haile Selassie. The seizure of power in Ethiopia by a Marxist junta in 1974 removed the ideological basis of the conflict, and by the time Eritrea defeated Ethiopia's northern armies in 1991, the Eritrean People's Liberation Front (EPLF) had discarded Marxism. Formal independence was achieved in May 1993 after a referendum supervised by the United Nations produced a landslide vote for statehood. EPLF leader Isaias Afwerki was chosen by the Transitional National Assembly to fill the position of president until elections could be held; these elections were eventually scheduled for 2001 but were postponed and have yet to take place.

A territorial dispute with Ethiopia led to a war from 1998 to 2000, which killed tens of thousands of people. Under the terms of a peace treaty signed in December 2000, both countries accepted an independent ruling that set the common border, but Ethiopia later reneged on the agreement. The war and unresolved grievances stemming from the broken peace deal have driven the Eritrean government's fixation with national security and perpetuated the militarization of the state.

In May 2001, a group of 15 senior ruling-party members publicly criticized President Isaias and called for "the rule of law and for justice, through peaceful and legal ways and means." Eleven members of the group were arrested for treason, the small independent media was shut down, and a number of journalists were imprisoned. Many of the jailed dissidents and journalists were subsequently reported to have died in custody, but the government steadfastly refuses to divulge information about them.

The government clamped down on nongovernmental organizations (NGOs) in 2005, and ordered the U.S. Agency for International Development to end its operations in the country. In 2006 reports emerged that hundreds of followers of various unregistered churches were being detained, harassed, and abused. The government has continued suppressing civil society, religious practice, and political dissent. Arbitrary detention remains the authorities' most common method of stifling independent action by citizens.

A border dispute with Djibouti that led to a military confrontation in 2008 was resolved in 2010 when both sides agreed to a negotiated settlement. Tensions with Ethiopia escalated once more in 2011 when the United Nations accused Eritrean officials of masterminding a failed plot to bomb the African Union (AU) headquarters in Addis Ababa. In March 2012, Ethiopian troops carried out a series of military incursions into Eritrea, the first since the end of the war. Ethiopia claimed that the attacks were aimed at camps used by Ethiopian rebels responsible for kidnapping a group of foreign tourists inside Ethiopia in January. In April, Isaias appeared on national television to dispel long-running rumors of ill health. Instead, it was his archrival, Ethiopian prime minister Meles Zenawi, who succumbed to illness. His death in August raised hopes of a rapprochement between the two countries, although there was no immediate improvement in relations.

Eritrea made tentative moves to improve relations with other neighbors in the region in 2012 by trying to reengage with the AU and the regional Intergovernmental Authority on Development. In July, a UN report found that Eritrea had scaled back direct support of Islamist militant groups in Somalia, including the Shabaab. However, it also found that Eritrea continued to violate UN Security Council resolutions and recommended that an arms embargo remain in place. In July, the United States imposed sanctions on Eritrea's spy chief and a senior military official, accusing them of providing financial and logistical support to the Shabaab.

Political Rights and Civil Liberties: Eritrea is not an electoral democracy. Created in 1994 as a successor to the EPLF, the People's Front for Democracy and Justice (PFDJ) is the only legal political party. Instead of moving toward a democratic system, the PFDJ government has become harshly authoritarian since the end of the war with Ethiopia.

A new constitution was ratified in 1997, calling for "conditional" political pluralism and an elected 150-seat National Assembly, which would choose the president from among its members by a majority vote. However, this system has never been implemented, as national elections planned for 2001 have been postponed indefinitely. The Transitional National Assembly is comprised of 75 PFDJ members and 75 elected members. In 2004, regional assembly elections were conducted, but they were carefully orchestrated by the PFDJ and offered no real choice to voters.

The PFDJ and the military, both strictly subordinate to President Isaias Afwerki, are in practice the only institutions of political significance in Eritrea.

Corruption is a major problem. The government's control over foreign exchange effectively gives it sole authority over imports. At the same time, those in favor with the regime are allowed to profit from the smuggling and sale of scarce goods such as building materials, food, and alcohol. According to the International Crisis Group, senior military officials are the chief culprits in this trade. They have also been accused of enriching themselves by charging fees to assist some of the approximately 900 Eritreans who try to flee the country each month, using conscripts for private building projects, and seizing private property for their own use.

The law does not allow independent media to operate in Eritrea, and the government controls all broadcasting outlets. A group of journalists arrested in 2001 remained imprisoned without charge, and the government refuses to provide any information on their status. Reporters Without Borders said in August that it had received confirmation of the deaths of three of the journalists detained in 2001 as well as a fourth, held since 2009. Eleven members of the Asmara-based broadcaster Radio Bana, who were detained in 2009 on suspicion of collaborating with exiled opposition groups, remained in custody without charge. According to the Committee to Protect Journalists, at least 28 journalists were in prison in Eritrea as of December 2012. The government controls the internet infrastructure and is thought to monitor online communications. Foreign media are available to those few who can afford a satellite dish.

The government places significant limitations on the exercise of religion. Since 2002 it has officially recognized only four faiths: Islam, Orthodox Christianity, Roman Catholicism, and Lutheranism as practiced by the Evangelical Church of Eritrea. Members of Evangelical and Pentecostal churches face persecution, but the most severe treatment is reserved for Jehovah's Witnesses, who are barred from government jobs and refused business permits or identity cards. Abune Antonios, patriarch of the Eritrean Orthodox Church, has been under house arrest since speaking out against state interference in religion in 2006. The Ecumenical Canonical Orthodox Church Worldwide said in March 2012 that it had received reports that the patriarch was in poor health and was being denied adequate treatment. According to Amnesty International, members of other churches have been jailed and tortured or otherwise ill-treated to make them abandon their faith. As many as 3,000 people from unregistered religious groups are currently in prison because of their beliefs. Three Christians incarcerated at a military detention center died from mistreatment in 2011. A Jehovah's Witness also died in prison in 2011, following an extended period of solitary confinement. In October 2012, 17 Christians were arrested near Asmara while holding a prayer meeting. Witnesses say they were beaten by security officials and taken away on military trucks.

Academic freedom is constrained. Students in their last year of secondary school are subject to obligatory military service. Academics practice self-censorship, and the government interferes with their course content and limits their ability to conduct research abroad. Eritrea's university system has been effectively closed, replaced by regional colleges whose main purposes are military training and political indoctrination. Freedom of expression in private discussions is limited. People are guarded in voicing their opinions for fear of being overheard by government informants.

Freedoms of assembly and association are not recognized. The government maintains a hostile attitude toward civil society, and independent NGOs are not tolerated. A 2005 law requires NGOs to pay taxes on imported materials, submit project reports every three months, renew their licenses annually, and meet government-established target levels of financial resources. The six remaining international NGOs that had been working in Eritrea were forced to leave in 2011. The government placed strict controls on UN operations in the country, preventing staff from leaving the capital.

The government controls all union activity. The National Confederation of Eritrean Workers is the country's main union body and has affiliated unions for women, teachers, young people, and general workers.

The judiciary, which was formed by decree in 1993, is understaffed, unprofessional, and has never issued rulings at odds with government positions. Constitutional due process guarantees are often ignored in cases related to state security. The International Crisis Group has described Eritrea as a "prison state" for its flagrant disregard of the rule of law and its willingness to detain anyone suspected of opposing the regime, usually without charge. Torture, arbitrary detentions, and political arrests are common. In February 2012, an Eritrean opposition group accused the government of kidnapping one of its officials who had been living in eastern Sudan. In June, the UN High Commissioner for Human Rights reported that there were between 5,000 and 10,000 political prisoners in Eritrea. The police are poorly paid and prone to corruption. Prison conditions are harsh, and outside monitors such as the International Committee of the Red Cross are denied access to detainees. Juvenile prisoners are often incarcerated alongside adults. In some facilities, inmates are held in metal shipping containers or underground cells in extreme temperatures. Prisoners are often denied medical treatment. The government maintains a network of secret detention facilities.

The Kunama people, one of Eritrea's nine ethnic groups, face severe discrimination. Members of the Afar ethnic group have also been targeted, and several hundred Afars were arrested in 2010, according to Human Rights Watch. In October 2012, members of the Afar diaspora condemned plans by the authorities in Yemen to deport 300 Afar asylum seekers back to Eritrea, claiming they would be persecuted upon return. LGBT (lesbian, gay, bisexual, and transgender) individuals face legal and social discrimination due to the criminalization of homosexual conduct.

Freedom of movement, both inside and outside the country, is heavily restricted. Eritreans under the age of 50 are rarely given permission to go abroad, and those who try to travel without the correct documents face imprisonment. The authorities adopt a shoot-on-sight policy toward people found in locations deemed off-limits, such as mining facilities and areas close to the border. Eritrean refugees and asylum seekers who are repatriated from other countries are also detained. These strict penalties fail to deter thousands of people from risking their lives to escape the country each year.

Government policy is officially supportive of free enterprise, and citizens are in theory able to choose their employment, establish private businesses, and operate them without government harassment. However, few private businesses remain in Eritrea, and the country is ranked 182 out of 185 in the World Bank's October 2012 Doing Business report. Successful private businesses have been expropriated by government officials, without compensation. A conscription system ties most able-bodied men and women to an indefinite period of obligatory military service and can also entail compulsory labor for enterprises controlled by the political elite. The official 18-month service period is frequently open-ended in practice, and conscientious-objector status is not recognized. The government imposes collective punishment on the families of deserters, forcing them to pay heavy fines or putting them in prison. The enforced contraction of the labor pool, combined with a lack of investment and rigid state control of private enterprise, has crippled the national economy. The government levies a compulsory 2 percent tax on income earned by citizens living overseas, and those who do not pay place their relatives back home at risk of arrest.

The U.S. State Department 2012 Trafficking in Persons Report ranks Eritrea at Tier 3, describing it as a source country for individuals subjected to forced labor and sexual exploitation. The report found that the government had taken no known measures to address this problem.

Women hold some senior government positions, including four ministerial posts. The government has made attempts to promote women's rights, with laws mandating equal educational opportunity, equal pay for equal work, and penalties for domestic violence. However, traditional societal discrimination against women persists in the countryside. While female genital mutilation was banned by the government in 2007, the practice remains widespread in rural areas.

Estonia

Political Rights: 1
Civil Liberties: 1
Status: Free

Population: 1,339,400
Capital: Tallinn

Ten-Year Ratings Timeline For Year Under Review (Political Rights, Civil Liberties, Status)

2003	2004	2005	2006	2007	2008	2009	2010	2011	2012
1,2F	1,1F	1,1F	1,1F	1,1F	1,1F	1,1F	1,1F	1,1F	1,1F

Overview: In 2012, Estonia adopted new anticorruption legislation and became the last European Union member to criminalize human trafficking. In August, the parliament voted to ratify the European Stability Mechanism, Europe's new bailout fund for heavily indebted members of the eurozone. Also in August, the Justice Department released a draft of a new law that would allow same-sex couples some protections already granted to married couples.

Estonia gained independence from Russia in 1918, but was captured—along with Latvia and Lithuania—by Soviet troops during World War II. Under Soviet rule, approximately one-tenth of Estonia's population was deported, executed, or forced to flee abroad. Subsequent Russian immigration reduced ethnic Estonians to just over 60 percent of the population by 1989. Estonia regained its independence with the disintegration of the Soviet Union in 1991. It adopted a new constitution in July 1992 and held its first legislative elections in September of that year.

Estonia joined both NATO and the European Union (EU) in 2004. Prime Minister Andrus Ansip's center-right Reform Party won parliamentary elections in 2007 and formed a coalition with the Union of Pro Patria and Res Publica (IRL) and Social Democratic Party (SDE).

In parliamentary elections held in March 2011, the Reform Party won 33 seats, with its coalition partner, IRL, capturing 23 seats. The opposition Center Party, which drew much of its support from Estonia's Russian-speaking population, took 26 seats, and the SDE, which had broken with the ruling coalition, won 19 seats. In August of that year, the parliament reelected President Toomas Hendrik Ilves to a second five-year term.

Estonia in 2012 continued its recovery from the global economic crisis of 2008. In 2009, the country had implemented an austerity program, increasing taxes and reducing public sector salaries, among other measures, which caused a dramatic spike in the unemployment rate in 2010. However, the country's gross domestic product (GDP) began growing again in 2010, and in 2011, GDP grew by more than 7 percent. Economic growth has since slowed, with GDP growing by 3.2 percent in 2012. Unemployment for 2012 stood at 10.2 percent.

Estonia adopted the euro currency in 2011. In August 2012, the parliament voted to ratify the 500 billion euros ($666 billion) European Stability Mechanism, a new, permanent bailout fund for heavily indebted members of the eurozone. President Ilves approved it the following month, affirming Estonia's commitment to the currency. Following ratification, Estonia was required to pay 149 million euros ($193 million) into the ESM, and could contribute some 1.15 billion euros ($1.5 billion) more to the fund over coming years.

Intermittent tensions with Russia continued in 2012. In February, Aleksei Dressen, a senior official within Estonia's state security agency, was arrested on suspicion of spying for Russia's Federal Security Service. He was convicted of treason in July and sentenced to 16 years in prison.

Political Rights and Civil Liberties: Estonia is an electoral democracy. The 1992 constitution established a 101-seat, unicameral parliament, or Riigikogu, whose members are elected for four-year terms. A prime minister serves as head of government, and is chosen by the president and confirmed by the parliament. The president is elected by parliamentary ballot to a five-year term, filling the largely ceremonial role of head of state. Only citizens may participate in national elections; as a result, ethnic Russian residents of Estonia whose citizenship remains undetermined cannot vote in national polls. Resident noncitizens are permitted to vote in local elections, but may not run as candidates. Political parties organize freely, though only citizens may be members.

There are occasional problems with government corruption in Estonia. In February 2012, the parliament passed a new anticorruption law designed to increase public sector transparency and make requirements more stringent for politicians to declare their assets. In March, a former adviser to the Tallinn city government and an official in the Center Party were both sentenced to several years in jail after being convicted on bribery charges. In May, Silver Meikar, a former member of parliament with Prime Minister Andrus Ansip's Reform Party, claimed that he had personally funnelled thousands of dollars in illegitimate, anonymous donations to the Reform Party in 2009 and 2010 at the behest of Justice Minister Kristen Michal, who was the party's secretary general at the time. Meikar said dozens of party members, including members of the parliament, had participated in similar schemes. Although Ansip rejected the claims, prosecutors began an investigation, and President Toomas Hendrik Ilves called for Michal's resignation. Michal finally stepped down in December. In May, prosecutors reopened a case against two IRL members who in 2011 had been accused of improperly selling Estonian residency permits—and thus EU residency—to wealthy Russian citizens. Estonia was ranked 32 out of 176 countries surveyed in Transparency International's 2012 Corruption Perceptions Index.

The government respects freedom of the press. Both public and private television and radio stations operate in Estonia, and there are several independent newspapers, including at least one in Russian. In November 2010, lawmakers passed a measure authorizing fines for outlets that disseminated news deemed libellous, as well as for journalists who refused to reveal sources under certain circumstances, though no person or organization has been prosecuted under it. Legal guarantees for public access to government information are respected in practice. The government does not restrict access to the internet.

Religious and academic freedoms are respected in law and in practice.

The constitution guarantees freedoms of assembly and association, and the government upholds those rights in practice. Civil society is vibrant, and the government involves nongovernmental organizations in the drafting of legislation. Workers may organize freely, strike, and bargain collectively, although public servants at the municipal and state levels may not strike. The Confederation of Estonian Trade Unions has reported private sector violations of union rights, including workers being threatened with dismissal or pay cuts if they formed unions. There were a number of major strikes in Estonia in 2012, including a three-day strike by as many as 16,000 teachers in March over low pay; a 2013 draft budget submitted to the parliament in September contained a provision to raise teachers' salaries by an average of 11 percent, compared to an average wage increase of 4.4 percent for other public workers. In October, medical workers went on strike to protest low wages, as well as increasing workloads resulting from the departure of doctors and nurses for Finland, where salaries were significantly higher. Several major hospitals shut down outpatient services amid the strike, except for oncological patients, and those pregnant or under the age of 18. The strike was settled later in October after the hospitals agreed to increase pay for some medical workers and take measures to decrease workloads.

The judiciary is independent and generally free from government interference. Laws prohibiting arbitrary arrest and detention and ensuring the right to a fair trial are largely observed. However, the average length of pretrial detention is seven months, due to judicial extensions of the six-month legal limit. The country's prison system continues to suffer from overcrowding, and prisoners have poor access to health care, though new prisons were being constructed in 2012.

In 2012, about 6.8 percent of the Estonian population was of undetermined citizenship, down from about a third in 1992. Ethnic Russians, many of whom had arrived in Estonia during the Soviet era and speak Russian as their first language, make up about a quarter of Estonia's population. These Russians were regarded as immigrants after Estonia's independence and were required to apply for citizenship, a process that included demonstrating knowledge of the Estonian language. A 2011 law mandated that public, Russian-language high schools must teach 60 percent of their curriculum in the Estonian language, with the intention of readying Russian-speaking students for Estonian jobs, many of which require command of the Estonian language. The Tallinn government, which was controlled by the Center Party, planned in February 2012 to establish a public school where primary and secondary students could attend classes in Russian at no cost.

Estonia's constitution allows citizens and noncitizens holding government-issued identity documents to travel inside Estonia and abroad. In August 2012, the Justice Ministry released a draft of a new law that would allow same-sex couples to register their cohabitation. The proposed law would allow same-sex couples some protections that married opposite-sex couples receive, but would not allow such couples to adopt children.

Though women enjoy the same legal rights as men, the World Economic Forum's 2012 Global Gender Gap Report found that Estonian women earn roughly 62 percent of an average man's salary for the same job. There are currently 20 women serving in the parliament. Violence against women, including domestic violence, remains a problem. Estonia is a source, transit point, and destination for women trafficked for the purpose of prostitution. Estonia criminalized human trafficking in March 2012, becoming the last EU country to do so; the first prosecution under the new law took place in April.

Ethiopia

Political Rights: 6
Civil Liberties: 6
Status: Not Free

Population: 89,960,000
Capital: Addis Ababa

Ten-Year Ratings Timeline For Year Under Review (Political Rights, Civil Liberties, Status)

2003	2004	2005	2006	2007	2008	2009	2010	2011	2012
5,5PF	5,5P	5,5PF	5,5PF	5,5PF	5,5PF	5,5PF	6,6NF	6,6NF	6,6NF

Overview: The death of Prime Minister Meles Zenawi was announced in August 2012, following months of speculation about his declining health, and he was replaced by his former deputy, **Hailemariam Desalegn. Despite the change in personnel, the regime continued its pattern of harassing and imprisoning political opponents, journalists, and, increasingly, the country's Muslim population. Meanwhile, Ethiopian troops carried out a series of military incursions into Eritrea in March, the first since the end of the war in 2000.**

Ethiopia, one of the few African countries to avoid decades of European colonization, ended a long tradition of monarchy in 1974, when Emperor Haile Selassie was overthrown in a Marxist military coup. Colonel Mengistu Haile Mariam ruled the country until he was toppled by guerrilla groups in 1991. The main rebel group, the Ethiopian People's Revolutionary Democratic Front (EPRDF), formed a provisional government with Meles Zenawi as head of state.

In 1995, the EPRDF introduced democratic institutions and a new constitution, and Meles was elected prime minister in polls boycotted by most of the opposition, which claimed harassment of its supporters. The EPRDF easily won the 2000 legislative elections, and Meles began his second five-year term. Opposition parties and some observers criticized the government's conduct of the vote.

A border dispute with Eritrea, which had gained formal independence from Ethiopia in 1993 after a long guerrilla conflict, triggered a 1998–2000 war between the countries. Ethiopia later rejected the findings of an international commission that awarded the contested area to Eritrea, and the two neighbors have remained at odds ever since.

The EPRDF and its allies led the 2005 parliamentary elections, though the main opposition parties won a third of the seats. Claiming that voter fraud had deprived them of outright victory, opposition supporters took to the streets. The authorities responded harshly, killing at least 193 people and arresting more than 4,000. Several opposition figures received long sentences, and though all were pardoned and released in 2007, some were later rearrested.

The 2010 parliamentary and regional elections were tightly controlled by the EPRDF. Voters were threatened with losing their jobs, homes, or government services if they did not turn out for the ruling party. Opposition meetings were broken up, and candidates were threatened and detained. Opposition-aligned parties saw their 160-seat presence in Parliament virtually disappear, with the EPRDF and its allies taking all but 2 of the 547 seats in the lower house. Meles was sworn in for a third term as prime minister.

Shorn of their representation in Parliament and under pressure by the authorities, opponents of the EPRDF found it increasingly difficult to operate. In 2011, Parliament's lower house declared five groups to be terrorist entities, including the U.S.-based opposition movement Ginbot 7. Any journalist who interviewed movement members faced arrest on terrorism charges. Domestic nongovernmental organizations (NGOs) estimated that there were up to 400 political prisoners by the end of 2012. In June 2012, 24 journalists and opposition activists were found guilty of offences under the law, including the award-winning journalist Eskinder Nega, who was sentenced in July to 18 years in prison.

Ethiopia entered a new and potentially turbulent chapter when the death of Prime Minister Meles was announced in August, following months of speculation about his failing health. On the surface, there was a smooth political transition. Meles's former deputy, Hailemariam Desalegn, was quickly sworn in as prime minister and installed as chairman of the EPRDF in September.

Tensions between Ethiopia and Eritrea remained high after a 2011 UN report accused Eritrean officials of a failed plot to bomb an African Union summit in Addis Ababa. In March 2012, Ethiopian troops carried out a series of military incursions into Eritrea, the first since the end of the war. The authorities said the attacks were aimed at rebels responsible for kidnapping a group of foreign tourists in the Afar region of Ethiopia.

Also in 2012, there was halting progress in ending the conflict between the government and separatist rebels in the Ogaden region, who have fought for independence since 1991. Talks between the government and the Ogaden National Liberation Front (ONLF) were convened in Kenya but broke down in October without agreement.

Political Rights and Civil Liberties: Ethiopia is not an electoral democracy. Parliament is made up of a 108-seat upper house, the House of Federation, and a 547-seat lower house, the House of People's Representatives. The lower house is filled through popular elections, while the upper chamber is selected by the state legislatures, with both serving five-year terms. The lower house selects the prime minister, who holds most executive power, and the president, a largely ceremonial figure who serves up to two six-year terms. All of these institutions are dominated by the EPRDF, which tightly controlled the 2010 elections and the succession process following the death of Prime Minister Meles Zenawi in 2012. While the 1995 constitution grants the right of secession to ethnically based states, the government acquired powers in 2003 to intervene in states' affairs on issues of public security.

Corruption is a significant problem in Ethiopia. EPRDF officials reportedly receive preferential access to credit, land leases, and jobs. Petty corruption extends to lower level officials, who allegedly solicit bribes in return for processing documents. In a survey of 1,000 people conducted by Transparency International (TI) in 2011, 64 percent of respondents reported having had to pay a bribe to customs officials, and 55 percent to a member of the judiciary. Ethiopia was ranked 113 out of 176 countries surveyed in TI's 2012 Corruption Perceptions Index.

The media are dominated by state-owned broadcasters and government-oriented newspapers. One of the few independent papers in the capital, *Addis Neger*, closed in 2009, claiming harassment by the authorities. Privately owned papers tend to steer clear of political issues and have low circulations. A 2008 media law criminalizes defamation and allows prosecutors to seize material before publication in the name of national security.

Journalists reporting on opposition activities face serious harassment and the threat of prosecution under the country's sweeping 2009 Antiterrorism Proclamation. In July 2012, six journalists were convicted of terrorism. While five were convicted in absentia, the sixth, Eskinder Nega, received 18 years in prison. The judge said that he had consorted with the political group, Ginbot 7, a designated terrorist entity in Ethiopia. The United States, European Union, and the UN High Commissioner for Human Rights expressed dismay at the verdicts. In other cases, the courts reduced sentences handed out to journalists convicted of terrorism. In August, a columnist with the *Feteh* weekly newspaper had her 14-year sentence reduced to 5 years, while in September, two Swedish journalists who had received 11-year sentences in 2011 for assisting the ONLF were pardoned.

Due to the risks of operating inside Ethiopia, many of the country's journalists work in exile. The Committee to Protect Journalists says that Ethiopia has driven 79 journalists into exile in the past decade, more than any other nation. The authorities use high-tech jamming equipment to filter and block news websites seen as pro-opposition. Legislation adopted in May criminalizes the use of telecommunications devices to transmit any "terrorizing message." Critics said the vaguely worded law also effectively banned the use of Skype and other voice-over-internet protocol services that cannot be closely monitored by the government.

The constitution guarantees religious freedom, but the government has increasingly harassed the Muslim community, which has grown to rival the Ethiopian Orthodox Church as the country's largest religious group. Muslim groups accuse the government of trying to impose the beliefs of an obscure Islamic sect, al-Ahbash, at the expense of the dominant Sufi-influenced strain of Islam. Before his death, Meles said the Muslim community was a source of extremism, claiming it had links to al-Qaeda.

Academic freedom is restricted. The government has accused universities of being pro-opposition and prohibits political activities on campuses. There have been reports of students being pressured into joining the EPRDF in order to secure places at universities.

The presence of the EPRDF at all levels of society inhibits free private discussion. Many people are wary of speaking against the government for fear of being overheard by party officials. The EPRDF maintains a network of paid informants, and opposition politicians have accused the government of tapping their telephones.

Freedoms of assembly and association are guaranteed by the constitution but limited in practice. Organizers of large public meetings must request permission from the authorities 48 hours in advance. Applications by opposition groups are routinely denied. Peaceful demonstrations were held outside mosques in July 2012, but the security forces responded violently, detaining protestors, including several prominent Muslim leaders. A total of 29 Muslims were eventually charged with offences under the antiterrorism law. They were awaiting trial at year's end.

The 2009 Charities and Societies Proclamation restricts the activities of foreign NGOs by prohibiting work on political and human rights issues. Foreign NGOs are defined as groups receiving more than 10 percent of their funding from abroad, a classification that captures most domestic organizations as well. NGOs have struggled to maintain operations as a result of the law, which also requires them to re-register with the authorities. According to Justice Ministry figures, there were 3,522 registered NGOs before the law was passed and 1,655 afterward. In 2010, the Human Rights Council (HRCO) and the Ethiopian Women Lawyers' Association had their bank accounts frozen for violating the rules on receiving foreign funds. An appeal against the ruling by the HRCO was rejected by the Supreme Court in October 2012.

Trade union rights are tightly restricted. All unions must be registered, and the government retains the authority to cancel registration. Two-thirds of union members belong to organizations affiliated with the Confederation of Ethiopian Trade Unions, which is under government influence. Independent unions face harassment. There has not been a legal strike since 1993.

The judiciary is officially independent, but its judgments rarely deviate from government policy. The Antiterrorism Proclamation gives great discretion to the security forces, allowing the detention of suspects for up to four months without charge. It was used in 2011 to detain more than 100 members of opposition parties; terrorist suspects were denied legal assistance while they awaited trial. A total of 31 people have been convicted under the law, 12 of them journalists. Conditions in Ethiopia's prisons are harsh, and detainees frequently report abuse.

The government tends to favor Tigrayan ethnic interests in economic and political matters, and the EPRDF is dominated by the Tigrayan People's Liberation Front. Repression of the Oromo and ethnic Somalis, and government attempts to co-opt their parties into subsidiaries of the EPRDF, have fueled nationalism in both the Oromia and Ogaden regions. Persistent claims that war crimes have been committed by government troops in the Ogaden are difficult to verify, as independent media are barred from the region. However, Human Rights Watch accused government paramilitaries of executing 10 men during an operation in the Gashaamo district in March 2012.

Private business opportunities are limited by rigid state control of economic life and the prevalence of state-owned enterprises. All land must be leased from the state. The government has evicted indigenous groups from various areas to make way for projects such as hydroelectric dams. It has also leased large tracts of land to foreign governments and investors for agricultural development in opaque deals. Up to 70,000 people have been forced to move from the western Gambella region, although the government denies the resettlement plans are connected to land investments. Journalists and international organizations have persistently alleged that the government has withheld development assistance from villages perceived as being unfriendly to the ruling party.

Women are relatively well represented in Parliament, having won 152 seats in the lower house in the 2010 elections. Legislation protects women's rights, but they are routinely violated in practice. Enforcement of the law against rape and domestic abuse is patchy, with cases routinely stalling in the courts. Forced child labor is a significant problem, particularly in the agricultural sector. Same-sex sexual activity is prohibited by law and punishable with imprisonment.

Fiji

Political Rights: 6
Civil Liberties: 4
Status: Partly Free

Population: 844,000
Capital: Suva

Ten-Year Ratings Timeline For Year Under Review (Political Rights, Civil Liberties, Status)

2003	2004	2005	2006	2007	2008	2009	2010	2011	2012
4,3PF	4,3PF	4,3PF	6,4PF	6,4PF	6,4PF	6,4PF	6,4PF	6,4PF	6,4PF

Overview: The lifting of the Public Emergency Regulations in January 2012, which had been in place since 2009, eased restrictions on freedom of assembly. In December, an independent commission submitted a draft constitution to the interim government after having collected comments from the general public from July through September. Meanwhile, severe storms in April and December displaced thousands of Fijians and caused severe property damage and outbreaks of typhoid and other illnesses.

Fiji, colonized by Great Britain in 1874, became an independent member of the Commonwealth in 1970. Rivalry between indigenous Fijians and Indo-Fijians is the main source of political and social tensions in the country. Indians, who were first brought to Fiji in the 19th century to work on sugar plantations, came to control a large share of the economy. Armed coups by indigenous factions in 1987 and 2000 overthrew governments led by Indo-Fijian parties.

Following the 2000 coup, the military installed Laisenia Qarase, an indigenous Fijian of the United Fiji Party (UFP), to lead an interim government. Qarase was elected prime minister in 2001 and won a second term in 2006. In December 2006, differences between Qarase and military chief Frank Bainimarama—another indigenous Fijian—over the fate of the 2000 coup participants resulted in another military coup in which Bainimarama ousted Qarase and dissolved Parliament. As head of the interim government, he began silencing his critics, filing legal suits against opposition and labor union leaders, and harassing and detaining journalists.

In 2008, a 45-member council—handpicked by Bainimarama—drafted the People's Charter for Change, Peace, and Progress. The charter recommended replacing communal electoral rolls with a one-person-one-vote system, and designating all citizens as Fijians, a term previously reserved only for the indigenous. The charter also officially confirmed the military's role in governing Fiji, and the interim government subsequently replaced civilians with military personnel in many high-level positions.

In 2009, the court of appeals ruled that the 2006 dismissal of Qarase and his cabinet, the dissolution of Parliament, and the 2007 appointment of Bainimarama as interim prime minister were illegal. The interim president, Josefa Iloilo, was ordered to appoint a caretaker prime minister to dissolve Parliament and call elections. The next day, Iloilo suspended the 1997 constitution, nullified all judicial appointments, reconfirmed himself as president, reappointed Bainimarama as interim prime minister, and imposed Public Emergency Regulations (PER) to ban public protests and tighten government control of the media. In July 2009, Iloilo stepped down and was replaced by Vice President Epeli Nailatikau. In 2010, the interim government granted immunity from prosecution to all those not already convicted for involvement in the 2000 and 2006 coups; beneficiaries included Iloilo, Bainimarama, and members of the military, police, and prison service.

Despite international diplomatic pressure and the loss of millions of dollars in development assistance, Bainimarama announced that new parliamentary elections would not be held until September 2014, and only after the adoption of a new constitution. The interim government ended the PER on January 7, 2012, and a nationwide consultation to gather comments from the public on a new constitution was conducted from July through September. On December 22, a five-member independent constitutional commission presented a draft to the interim government. Representatives from civil society groups will be selected to recommend revisions to the draft constitution in early 2013 before it is submitted to the interim president for final approval.

To prepare for the 2014 parliamentary elections, the interim government hired a Canadian firm in 2012 to undertake electronic voter registration. In July, more than a thousand voter registration centers began operating, and in September, voter registration was expanded to Fijian citizens overseas through Fiji's embassies.

Convinced that Fiji has taken steps toward holding free and fair elections, Australia and New Zealand restored full diplomatic ties with the country in July.

Flooding and landslides caused by severe storms in April and December devastated parts of Fiji, causing significant property damage, displacing thousands of people, and resulting in a number of casualties, while a lack of clean water after the storms led to outbreaks of typhoid and leptospirosis.

Political Rights and Civil Liberties: Fiji is not an electoral democracy. Under the 1997 constitution, which was suspended in 2009, Parliament consisted of a 32-seat Senate and a 71-seat House of Representatives. The prime minister was appointed by the president and was generally the leader of the majority party or coalition in Parliament. Since the suspension of the constitution, the interim government has essentially ruled by decree.

The two main political parties are the UFP, largely supported by indigenous Fijians, and the Fiji Labour Party, which has a largely Indo-Fijian constituency.

Official corruption remains widespread, and reform agendas by multiple governments have not produced significant results. Eradicating pervasive corruption and improving bureaucratic efficiency have been central themes of the interim government.

While the 1997 constitution provided for freedoms of speech and of the press, extensive government censorship was in place under the PER. Following the end of the PER, efforts by the interim government to limit freedom of the press continued. In June 2012, the interim government threatened not to renew Fiji TV's license after it aired interviews with former prime ministers Qarase and Mahendra Chaudhry. In October, the publisher and editor of the *Fiji Times* were convicted of contempt for publishing an editorial about an ongoing court case involving the Oceania Football Federation. Access to the internet is spreading with increased competition, but remains limited outside the capital due to cost and infrastructure constraints. In November, the interim government opened the first of eight free internet centers to expand access to poor and rural populations.

Freedom of religion is generally respected, but the interim government appears to target those, including religious leaders, who speak out against the regime. Most indigenous Fijians are Christians, and Indo-Fijians are generally Hindus. Places of worship, especially Hindu temples, have been attacked, though there were no reports of major attacks in 2012. The interim government refused permits for the Methodist Church's annual conferences between 2009 and 2011 on the grounds that speakers included senior church officials critical of the government. Methodist officials were also banned from traveling overseas to attend church meetings and conferences. In August 2012, the interim government approved a permit for the Methodist Church's annual conference, which was held later that month. Throughout the year, police granted permits to several Methodist churches across the country to hold public meetings and processions.

While academic freedom is generally respected, the education system suffers from a lack of resources, and indigenous Fijians are granted special privileges in education.

Freedoms of assembly and association, which were severely restricted under the PER, improved slightly after it was lifted. The attorney general declared that, as of July 2012, public permits were no longer required for meetings as long as they were not on a public road, in public parks, playgrounds, or arenas.

The interim government has a tense relationship with labor unions. The Essential

National Industries Decree of 2011 limited trade union and collective bargaining rights for those employed in industries that are considered essential to Fiji's economy, including the sugar industry, the airline industry, utility companies, banks, and telecommunication firms. The decree also banned strikes in these industries under a penalty of $50,000 or five years in jail, and required that all union officials be employees of the company whose workers they represented. In May 2012, a court dismissed charges against Daniel Urai, president of the Fiji Trades Union Congress, who had been arrested in November 2011. He had been accused of defacing public buildings in the capital with antigovernment graffiti and charged with sedition for "urging political violence."

The suspension of the constitution in 2009 and the related dismissal of judges and their replacement by appointees of the interim government have raised serious questions about judicial independence. The 2009 dismissals exacerbated an already serious backlog of cases, which remains a problem. In April 2012, the police chief reported that there had been a 49 percent increase in complaints against police in the first quarter of the year, which he attributed to police misconduct. Prisons are seriously overcrowded, with poor sanitary and living conditions.

Race-based discrimination is pervasive. Indigenous Fijians receive preferential treatment in education, housing, land acquisition, and other areas. In March 2012, the government abolished the Great Council of Chiefs, a 135-year old body of indigenous Fijian leaders, claiming that it was in the interest of promoting Fijian citizenry for all ethnic groups. Discrimination, economic hardship, and political turmoil have prompted many Indo-Fijians to leave Fiji. A 2011 study reported that an estimated 250,000 Fijians—many of them educated and skilled Indo-Fijians—had left the country in the last 25 years.

Discrimination and violence against women are widespread. Women are also underrepresented in government and leadership positions and do not receive equal wages. Homosexuality was decriminalized in 2010. Fiji is a source country for the trafficking of children for sexual exploitation and a destination country for the trafficking of men and women for forced labor and prostitution.

Finland

Political Rights: 1
Civil Liberties: 1
Status: Free

Population: 5,414,300
Capital: Helsinki

Ten-Year Ratings Timeline For Year Under Review (Political Rights, Civil Liberties, Status)

2003	2004	2005	2006	2007	2008	2009	2010	2011	2012
1,1F	1,1F	1,1F	1,1F	1,1F	1,1F	1,1F	1,1F	1,1F	1,1F

Overview:

The February 2012 presidential election saw a clear victory for the center-right National Coalition Party's Sauli Niinistö. The True Finns, a nationalist and populist party that had enjoyed major gains in the 2011 parliamentary elections, continued to oppose the

European Union's economic bailouts for heavily indebted eurozone members. However, Parliament approved a Spanish bailout package in July.

After centuries of Swedish and then Russian rule, Finland gained independence in 1917. The country has traditionally been neutral, but its army has enjoyed broad popular support since it fended off a Soviet invasion during World War II. Finland joined the European Union (EU) in 1995 and is the only Nordic country to have adopted the euro as its currency.

Tarja Halonen of the Social Democratic Party (SDP) won the 2000 and 2006 presidential election, becoming the country's first female president. In the 2007 parliamentary elections, the ruling Center Party held on to its plurality by 1 seat, while the National Coalition Party (KOK), a moderate conservative party, gained 10 seats; the left-leaning parties performed poorly, with the SDP losing 8 seats. Acknowledging the shift to the right, Prime Minister Matti Vanhanen formed a four-party coalition consisting of his Center Party, the KOK, the Green League, and the Swedish People's Party, leaving the SDP in opposition for the first time since 1995.

In February 2010, the National Bureau of Investigation began probing accusations of malfeasance against Vanhanen over his alleged involvement in the distribution of government funds to a nongovernmental organization that had supported his campaign. The prime minister announced his resignation in June, but cited medical and family issues for his departure. Parliament then appointed Center Party leader Mari Kiviniemi as Vanhanen's replacement until the April 2011 elections. In February 2011, Parliament voted to drop the charges against Vanhanen.

The April 2011 parliamentary elections resulted in a dramatic shift in Finnish politics. The KOK and SDP took 44 seats and 42 seats, respectively, while the ruling Center Party captured 35 seats, down 16 from the previous election, and was ousted from power. The populist, nationalist party the True Finns, led by Timo Soini, gained an unprecedented 19 percent of the popular vote, increasing its seats from 5 to 39 and becoming the third-largest party in the legislature. The elections attracted an unusual amount of international attention due to the vocal opposition to eurozone bailouts from the vehemently euroskeptic True Finns.

A coalition government was formed in June 2011, led by Prime Minister Jyrki Katainen and comprised of the KOK, the SDP, the Left Alliance, the Green League, the Swedish People's Party, and the Christian Democrats. The True Finns withdrew from coalition talks in May, when Parliament approved an EU bailout package for Portugal.

Pro-EU and pro-euro former finance minister Sauli Niinistö of the KOK handily won the presidency in February 2012, defeating the Green League candidate, Pekka Haavisto, 63 percent to 37 percent of the vote. The debate about the European bailout funds—both public and within the government—continued throughout 2012. The solvent Finns, seeing themselves as fiscally prudent, expressed frustration at sending funds to southern European countries perceived as less financially responsible.

Finland is the only country in the EU that has reserved the right to put any bailout to a parliamentary vote. The bill approving the Spanish bailout package passed Parliament in July 2012, with a comfortable majority. Parliament's approval of the Spanish rescue loan was widely considered a confidence vote on Katainen's government.

Political Rights and Civil Liberties: Finland is an electoral democracy. The president, whose role is mainly ceremonial, is directly elected for a six-year term. The president appoints the prime minister and deputy prime minister from the majority party or coalition after elections; the selection must be approved by Parliament. Representatives in the 200-seat unicameral Parliament, or Eduskunta, are elected to four-year terms. The Åland Islands—an autonomous region located off the southwestern coast whose inhabitants speak Swedish—have their own 30-seat Parliament, as well as a seat in the national legislature. The indigenous Sami of northern Finland also have their own legislature, but are not represented in the Eduskunta.

Corruption is not a significant problem in Finland, which was ranked 1 out of 176 countries surveyed in Transparency International's 2012 Corruption Perceptions Index. However, a court in April 2012 found Parliament member and former foreign minister Ikka Kanerva guilty of accepting bribes and neglecting his official duties as chairman of the Regional Council of Southwest Finland's managing board, and handed down a 15-month suspended jail sentence. Three codefendants received harsher sentences: Arto Merisalo received a six-year sentence after being convicted of paying bribes and engaging in false accounting; Tapani Yli-Saunamäki was convicted on the same charges and received a three-and-a-half-year jail term; and Toivo Sukari was convicted of aggravated bribery and received an eight-month suspended sentence. A 2010 law requires candidates and parties to report campaign donations of more than 800 euros ($1,030) in local elections or 1,500 euros ($1,930) in parliamentary elections.

Finnish law provides for freedom of speech, which is respected in practice. Finland has a large variety of newspapers and magazines and protects the right to reply to public criticism. Newspapers are privately owned but publicly subsidized, and many are controlled by or support a particular political party. In March 2010, the Finnish police launched an internet tip-off system in an effort to simplify the process of reporting threats of violence and racist slander.

Finns enjoy freedom of religion. The Evangelical Lutheran Church and the Orthodox Church are both state churches and receive public money from the income taxes of members; citizens may exempt themselves from contributing to those funds, but must renounce their membership. Religious communities other than the state churches may also receive state funds. Religious education is part of the curriculum in all secondary public schools, but students may opt out in favor of more general instruction in ethics. Academic freedom is respected.

Freedoms of association and assembly are upheld in law and in practice. Workers have the right to organize and bargain collectively, though public sector workers who provide services deemed essential may not strike. Approximately 70 percent of workers belong to trade unions. In 2012, the Confederation of Finnish Industries aggressively pushed for an ahead-of-schedule renegotiation of the comprehensive labor market reform reached in 2011, on sick leave compensation, and hiring and firing, arguing the need to control labor costs due to shrinking domestic demand. The government was divided on this issue, with the Social Democrats traditionally having close ties to the Central Organization of Finnish Trade Unions, while the KOK, Swedish People's Party, and Christian Democrats favor a renegotiation.

The constitution provides for an independent judiciary. The president appoints Supreme Court judges, who in turn appoint lower-court judges. Finland has been criticized by the European Court of Human Rights for slow trial procedures. The Ministry of the Interior controls police and Frontier Guard forces. Ethnic minorities and asylum seekers report occasional police discrimination.

The criminal code covers ethnic agitation and penalizes anyone who threatens a racial, national, ethnic, or religious group. The constitution guarantees the Sami cultural autonomy and the right to pursue their traditional livelihoods, which include fishing and reindeer herding. Their language and culture are also protected through public financial support. However, representatives of the community have complained that they cannot exercise their rights in practice and that they do not have the right to self-determination with respect to land use. While Roma also make up a very small percentage of the population, they are more significantly disadvantaged and marginalized.

Immigration issues remained divisive in 2012, in part fueled by the rapid political ascent of the True Finns in 2011. The political identity of the True Finns on the subject of immigration remains a controversial subject, both within and outside the party. While leader Timo Soini has sought to maintain a more moderate stance on immigration, several high-profile party members who served in Parliament also belonged to the nationalist group Suomen Sisu, and have expressed fierce disagreement with party leadership on this issue. However, the True Finns' political emphasis in 2012 was on opposition to EU bailouts rather than immigration. Soini ran in the 2012 presidential election, but failed to advance to the second round runoff.

Women enjoy equal rights in Finland. Women hold approximately 43 percent of the seats in Parliament, and 9 of 19 cabinet ministers are women. Despite a law stipulating equal pay for equal work, women earn only about 85 percent as much as men with the same qualifications. Domestic violence is an ongoing concern. Finland remains a destination and a transit country for trafficked men, women, and children. Amendments to the Alien Act in 2006 allow trafficked victims to stay in the country and qualify for employment rights.

France

Political Rights: 1
Civil Liberties: 1
Status: Free

Population: 63,605,300
Capital: Paris

Ten-Year Ratings Timeline For Year Under Review (Political Rights, Civil Liberties, Status)

2003	2004	2005	2006	2007	2008	2009	2010	2011	2012
1,1F	1,1F	1,1F	1,1F	1,1F	1,1F	1,1F	1,1F	1,1F	1,1F

Overview: In May 2012, François Hollande defeated incumbent Nicolas Sarkozy in the second round of the presidential election, becoming France's first Socialist president since François Mitterrand left office in 1995. The Socialists also won control of the National Assembly in June legislative elections. After a self-proclaimed jihadist killed seven people in and around Toulouse in March, the government intensified its antiterrorist measures.

After the French Revolution of 1789, France experienced both republic and monarchist regimes until the creation of the Third Republic in 1871. The Fourth Republic was established after World War II, but eventually fell victim to domestic political turbulence and a series of colonial setbacks. In 1958, Charles de Gaulle, France's wartime leader, created the strong presidential system of the Fifth Republic, which stands today. De Gaulle served as president until 1969, but the right remained in power until 1981, when socialist François Mitterrand became president.

Jacques Chirac, a right-leaning Gaullist, was first elected president in 1995. In the first round of the 2002 presidential election, Jean-Marie Le Pen—head of the far-right, xenophobic National Front—unexpectedly received more votes than Lionel Jospin, the prime minister and head of the center-left Socialist Party (PS). However, with Socialist support, Chirac defeated Le Pen overwhelmingly in the second round.

In late 2005, the accidental deaths of two teenagers of North African descent who were fleeing police touched off weeks of violent riots. Most of the rioters were youths descended from immigrants from North and sub-Saharan Africa. Despite their French birth and citizenship, many reported discrimination and harassment by police. The violence provoked a major discussion about the failure to fully integrate minorities into French society.

The ruling Union for a Popular Movement (UMP) nominated party leader Nicolas Sarkozy as its candidate for the 2007 presidential elections. Sarkozy's law-and-order message and pro-American foreign policy views made him a controversial candidate. Sarkozy defeated the PS candidate Ségolène Royal in the second round, with 53 percent of the vote, and the UMP renewed its majority in subsequent parliamentary elections. The government's popularity declined in late 2007 when riots erupted after two teenagers of African descent were killed in a collision with a police car.

The government considered a number of reforms in 2010 to reduce the country's debt, the most significant of which was an increase in the retirement age from 60 to 62, which became law in November, despite weeks of protests and strikes.

In the 2011 Senate elections, parties on the left won control of the upper house for the first time in the history of France's Fifth Republic.

Sarkozy ran for reelection in 2012 amid public dissatisfaction with the weak economy. He promised a tougher immigration policy, in an attempt to appeal to right-wing voters. His main opponent was PS candidate François Hollande, who pledged more growth-oriented economic policies and less austerity. On April 22, Hollande won the first round with 28.6 percent of the vote, ahead of Sarkozy, who took 27.2 percent. Marine Le Pen, the daughter of Jean-Marie Le Pen and his successor as head of the National Front, placed third, with 17.9 percent. Hollande won the election in a runoff against Sarkozy on May 6, with 51.6 percent of the vote, to Sarkozy's 48.4 percent. Hollande named Jean-Marc Ayrault of the PS as prime minister.

On June 10 and 17, the PS and its allies won an absolute majority of 314 seats in the National Assembly, while the UMP and its allies took 229 seats.

Shortly after taking office, Hollande on June 6 announced that he would fulfill a campaign promise and reverse the increase in the retirement age for those who had started working at 18 or 19, lowering it back to 60. In September, Hollande presented a budget that would raise the tax rate for those earning more than 1 million euros ($1.3 million) a year from 41 percent to 75 percent. Lawmakers approved the budget on December 20. However, on December 29, the Constitutional Council struck down the 75 percent tax rate, ruling that it would have been applied unevenly to different household earing the same combined annual income.

Political Rights and Civil Liberties: France is an electoral democracy. The president and members of the lower house of Parliament, the 577-seat National Assembly, are elected to five-year terms. The upper house, the 348-seat Senate, is an indirectly elected body whose members serve six-year terms. The prime minister is appointed by the president. Since 1986, there have been periods lasting several years in which the president and prime minister were from rival parties. In such circumstances, the prime minister has the dominant role in domestic affairs, while the president largely guides foreign policy.

Parties organize and compete on a free and fair basis. The center-left PS and the center-right UMP are the largest parties, though the far-right National Front party receives significant support.

In 2010, Labor Minister Éric Woerth was accused of corruption for allegedly accepting illegal donations from L'Oréal heiress Liliane Bettencourt on behalf of Nicolas Sarkozy's campaign in 2007. After Sarkozy lost the presidency and his immunity from prosecution in 2012, police on July 3 searched his home and office in connection with the Bettencourt affair. He was questioned in the case in November as a witness under caution, a status that left him open to prosecution. Corruption charges had been brought against former President Jacques Chirac in 2009 for events that dated back to when he was mayor of Paris from 1977 to 1995. In December 2011, he was found guilty of diverting public funds and abusing public trust, and received a two-year suspended sentence. France was ranked 22 out of 176 countries surveyed in Transparency International's 2012 Corruption Perceptions Index.

The media operate freely and represent a wide range of political opinions. Though an 1881 law forbids "offending" various personages, including the president and foreign heads of state, the press remains lively and critical. However, journalists covering events involving the National Front or the Corsican separatist movement have been harassed, and they have also faced difficulty covering unrest in the volatile suburbs with large immigrant populations. Reporters covering criminal cases or publishing material from confidential court documents have occasionally come under pressure by the courts to reveal sources. In November 2011, the offices of the magazine *Charlie Hebdo* were burned and its website hacked the day the magazine's cover featured a cartoon depiction of the prophet Muhammad. In September 2012, *Charlie Hebdo* published more Muhammad cartoons, prompting the government to temporarily close its embassies, consulates, and other facilities in about 20 countries to avoid anti-French violence.

While internet access is generally unrestricted, a new domestic security law, which came into effect in March 2011, allows the filtering of online content. While ostensible purposed was to prevent child pornography, free media advocates called it unnecessary censorship. A separate March 2011 decree requires internet companies to provide user data, including passwords, to authorities if requested; several major companies, including Google and Microsoft, have protested.

Freedom of religion is protected by the constitution, and strong antidefamation laws prohibit religiously motivated attacks. Denial of the Nazi Holocaust is illegal. France maintains the policy of laïcité, whereby religion and government affairs are strictly separated. A 2004 law bans "ostentatious" religious symbols in schools. In

October 2010, the Senate nearly unanimously passed a bill banning clothing that covers the face, including the burqa and niqab, in public spaces. The ban went into effect in April 2011. Violators of the ban can be fined up to 150 eruos (US$215) or ordered to take citizenship lessons, and a man who forces a woman to wear a niqab can be fined 30,000 euros (US$43,000). The first fine, for 150 euros, was issued in April to a woman in the northwest of Paris. As of September 2012, according to the Interior Ministry, 425 women had been fined and 66 had been warned for violating the headscarf ban, though it reportedly was rarely enforced by police. However, a riot broke out in Marseille in July 2012 when a woman refused to remove her veil. A controversial September 2011 directive bans street prayer, affecting thousands of Muslims in Paris who had previously prayed in the street due to a lack of space in local mosques. Academic freedom is respected by French authorities.

Freedoms of assembly and association are respected. In August 2012, youth riots erupted in the northern city of Amiens, where unemployment is high; some residents said that the unrest was in response to heavy-handed policing methods. Nongovernmental organizations can operate freely. Trade union organizations are weak, and membership has been declining since 1980. Nevertheless, civil service unions remain relatively strong, and strikes generally gain wide public support.

France has an independent judiciary, and the rule of law is firmly established. In response to repeated challenges from the European Court of Human Rights, the National Assembly adopted new rules in January 2011 that extend the right to suspects to remain silent and to have an attorney present during questioning. Prisons are overcrowded, and suicides are common. The country's antiterrorism campaign has included surveillance of mosques, and terrorism suspects can be detained for up to four days without charge. In March 2012, police killed self-proclaimed jihadist Mohamed Merah in Toulouse after he killed seven people, including three children and a rabbi at a Jewish school and three soldiers. In December, the government implemented new antiterrorism legislation that made it a crime to receive terrorist training or recruit terrorists abroad, or to promote terrorism online.

French law forbids the categorization of people according to ethnic origin, and no official statistics are collected on ethnicity. However, the riots and violence in 2005 and 2007 fueled concerns about Arab and African immigration and the failure of integration policies in France, where minorities are underrepresented in leadership positions in both the private and public sectors. Discrimination against immigrants and religious and ethnic minorities remains a problem.

During 2010, France deported at least 8,000 Roma to Bulgaria and Romania and dismantled more than 400 camps on the outskirts of French cities. Although the government claimed that the deportations were part of a larger crackdown on illegal immigration, a leaked memo from the interior ministry revealed that officials had been instructed to prioritize the dismantling of Roma camps, thus constituting illegal discrimination. Deportations of thousands continued in 2011. Police in August 2012 demolished Roma camps in Paris and other cities and the government deported hundreds of people to Romania, despite François Hollande's previous criticism of Sarkozy's policy. However, the government that month said that it would ease restrictions on hiring and residency for Roma.

Corsica continues to host a sometimes violent separatist movement. Low-level attacks against property and government targets continue to occur, though people are rarely harmed. In 2001, the government devolved some legislative powers to the island and allowed teaching in the Corsican language in public schools.

Gender equality is protected in France, and constitutional reforms in 2008 institutionalized economic and social equality. However, in the 2012 Global Gender Gap report, France ranked the lowest of 131 countries that responded to a question on wage equality. Some electoral lists require the alternation of candidates by gender. After the 2012 elections, women held a record 27 percent of seats in the National Assembly. Women hold 22 percent of Senate seats, and have served in key cabinet posts, as well as serving as prime minister. Discrimination based on sexual orientation is prohibited by law. While a type of civil union for same-sex partners is recognized, the Constitutional Council upheld a ban on same-sex marriage in January 2011. Prime Minister Jean-Marc Ayrault in June 2012 said that the new government would legalize same-sex marriage and adoption by gay and lesbian couples by the first half of 2013. The cabinet approved a draft bill in November, sending it to Parliament.

Gabon

Political Rights: 6
Civil Liberties: 5
Status: Not Free

Population: 1,564,000
Capital: Libreville

Ten-Year Ratings Timeline For Year Under Review (Political Rights, Civil Liberties, Status)

2003	2004	2005	2006	2007	2008	2009	2010	2011	2012
5,4PF	5,4PF	6,4PF	6,4PF	6,4PF	6,4PF	6,5NF	6,5NF	6,5NF	6,5NF

Overview:
In 2012, several private news outlets were suspended after criticizing President Ali Bongo Ondimba or reporting on a national address by the country's main opposition leader, and an opposition-owned television station was attacked. In September, 20 opposition groups called for a national conference on governance, including discussions on overhauling the constitution, though the government continued to resist such calls at year's end.

Gabon gained independence from France in 1960. Omar Bongo Ondimba became president in 1967 and solidified the Gabonese Democratic Party's (PDG) grip on power. In 1990, protests prompted by economic hardship led to multiparty legislative elections. Bongo and the ruling PDG retained power over subsequent years through a series of flawed elections.

Bongo died in June 2009, after more than 40 years in power, and Senate president Rose Francine Rogombe became interim head of state. Defense Minister Ali Bongo Ondimba, son of the late president, was nominated as the PDG candidate for a snap presidential election. Several senior PDG figures, including former interior minister André Mba Obame, decided to run as independents. Bongo won the August 2009 election with almost 42 percent of the vote, while Mba Obame and Pierre Mamboundou each received 25 percent. Although the opposition challenged the official results amid violent protests, the Constitutional Court upheld Bongo's victory following a recount in September.

On January 25, 2011, Mba Obame declared himself the legitimate president of Gabon, occupied the UN Development Programme's headquarters in Libreville for a month, and established a parallel government. Mba Obame and his supporters tried to ignite a popular uprising, though aside from a series of demonstrations held on January 29, there were no large-scale protests. The Gabonese government subsequently outlawed Mba Obame's opposition party, the National Union (UN). In the December National Assembly elections, which were boycotted by some of the opposition over the government's failure to implement biometric technology for voter registration, the PDG captured 115 out of 120 seats.

Gabon co-hosted the Africa Cup of Nations with Equatorial Guinea in January 2012. The government was criticized for spending hundreds of millions of dollars on a soccer tournament, while about 20 percent of the population lives on less than $2 per day.

In September, 20 normally fragmented opposition groups united to call for a national conference to discuss overhauling the constitution, dissolving the government, and holding elections. This call followed the return of Mba Obame to Gabon after spending 14 months in France for medical treatment. Bongo continued at year's end to resist calls for a national conference.

Political Rights and Civil Liberties: Gabon is not an electoral democracy. The president is elected for seven-year terms, and a 2003 constitutional amendment removed the two-term limit imposed in 1991. The president has extensive powers, including the authority to appoint judges and dissolve the parliament. The bicameral legislature consists of a 102-seat Senate and a 120-seat National Assembly. Regional and municipal officials elect senators for six-year terms, while National Assembly members are elected by popular vote for five-year terms. In December 2010, the legislature approved several constitutional amendments, including one that permits the president to prolong his term during a declared national emergency.

Freedom to form and join political parties is generally respected, but civil servants face harassment and discrimination if they are affiliated with opposition groups. The PDG has held power continuously since 1968, and of the approximately 50 other registered parties, 40 are part of the PDG's ruling coalition, the Union for the Gabonese Presidential Majority. In late 2009, eight opposition parties formed a new alliance, the Coalition of Groups and Political Parties for Change (CGPPA), with presidential runner-up André Mba Obame as a leading member. In 2010, the CGPPA coalesced into the opposition UN party, which received accreditation in April. However, the UN was dissolved by the Gabonese government in response to Mba Obame appointing himself president in January 2011.

Corruption is widespread, and rampant graft prevents the country's significant natural resource revenues from benefiting most citizens. Combating corruption is touted as a priority by the government, which has, among other things, audited government agencies to expunge ghost workers from payrolls. In March, a provincial director of the Ministry of Water and Forests was arrested for taking part in illegal logging activities; he was sentenced to five years in prison. Gabon was ranked 102 out of 176 countries surveyed in Transparency International's 2012 Corruption Perceptions Index.

Press freedom is guaranteed by law but restricted at times in practice. Conviction for libel can result in fines, publishing suspension, or a prison sentence. State-controlled outlets dominate the media, but there are some private broadcasters, and foreign news sources and independent newspapers are available. In August 2012, unidentified gunmen burned down the transmitters of TV+, a private television station owned by Mba Obame, and in September, assailants stabbed a security guard and tried unsuccessfully to enter the station's studio; the government denied responsibility. The government, through the National Communication Council, frequently suspends news outlets following critical reporting. In January, TV+ and the independent weekly *Echos Du Nord* were suspended for three months and two months, respectively, for featuring coverage of a national address by Mba Obame. In August, two private newspapers, *Embozolo* and *La Une*, were suspended for six months over articles critical of President Ali Bongo Ondimba. Access to the internet is not restricted by the government.

Religious freedom is enshrined in the constitution and upheld by the authorities. The government does not restrict academic freedom.

The rights of assembly and association are legally guaranteed. Police used tear gas to disperse a student protest over financial aid policies in June 2012, after students started throwing rocks at police. In August, one demonstrator was accidentally killed and about a dozen were injured during clashes between police and supporters of Mba Obame. Due to the lack of strong opposition parties, nongovernmental organizations (NGOs) are important vehicles for scrutiny of the government. However, human rights and environmental activist Marc Ona Essangui was charged with defaming the president and his cabinet chief over statements that both men held personal stakes in Group Olam, a Singaporean agribusiness company with substantial investments in Gabon. Ona and other civil society leaders have accused Group Olam of causing environmental damage and benefiting from land-grabbing practices in Gabon. Ona's trial, which was scheduled to begin in late December 2012, was postponed until after year's end. Virtually the entire private sector workforce is unionized, and collective bargaining is allowed by industry not by firm.

The judiciary is not independent. Judges may deliver summary verdicts in some cases, and prosecutions of former government officials appear to target opposition members. However, the right to legal counsel is generally respected. The authorities do not always observe prohibitions against arbitrary arrest and detention, and torture is sometimes used to extract confessions. Lengthy pretrial detention is common, and prisons suffer from overcrowding and poor food, ventilation, and sanitation.

Discrimination against African immigrants is widespread, and security forces harass and solicit bribes from African expatriates working in the country. Though equal under the law, most of Gabon's several thousand indigenous Baka live in extreme poverty in isolated forest communities and are often exploited as cheap labor.

The law provides for gender equality in education and employment, but women continue to face discrimination, particularly in rural areas. Several women hold high-level positions in the government, including the minister of justice. Domestic violence legislation is rarely enforced, and the crime continues to be widespread. Rape is seldom prosecuted. In 2012 the government made serious efforts to reduce human trafficking, initiating prosecuting eight suspected traffickers and assisting in repatriating victims.

The Gambia

Political Rights: 6
Civil Liberties: 6*
Status: Not Free

Population: 1,825,000
Capital: Banjul

Ratings Change: The Gambia's civil liberties rating declined from 5 to 6 due to the absence of due process for defendants, as exhibited by the execution of nine prisoners—two of whom were Senegalese nationals—without access to a lawyer or a fair trial and without notification of their families.

Ten-Year Ratings Timeline For Year Under Review (Political Rights, Civil Liberties, Status)

2003	2004	2005	2006	2007	2008	2009	2010	2011	2012
4,4PF	4,4PF	5,4PF	5,4PF	5,4PF	5,4PF	5,5PF	5,5PF	5,6NF	6,6NF

Overview:
President Yaya Jammeh's ruling party secured a landslide victory in the March 2012 legislative elections after the majority of opposition parties boycotted the vote. In August, Jammeh ordered the execution of 9 of the 47 inmates on death row, without giving them access to a fair trial, attorney, or their families. The government continued to intimidate and persecute journalists, the political opposition, sexual minorities, and members of civil society throughout the year.

After gaining independence from Britain in 1965, The Gambia enjoyed nearly 30 years of civilian rule before a 1981 coup by leftist soldiers, which was reversed by intervention from Senegal. The two countries formed the Confederation of Senegambia a year later, but it was dissolved in 1989. Lieutenant Yahya Jammeh led a 1994 military coup. A new constitution adopted in a closely controlled 1996 referendum allowed Jammeh to transform his military dictatorship into a nominally civilian administration.

Jammeh defeated human rights lawyer Ousainou Darboe in the 2001 presidential election, and the ruling Alliance for Patriotic Reorientation and Construction (APRC) dominated the 2002 legislative elections. Jammeh secured a new five-year term in the 2006 presidential election, and the APRC captured all but six elected seats in the 2007 legislative poll; both elections were marred by government repression of the media and the opposition.

In March 2006, the government announced that it had foiled an attempted coup, leading to the arrest of dozens of people, including several prominent journalists and senior intelligence and defense personnel. Ten military officers were sentenced to lengthy prison terms in 2007. Eight individuals, most of whom belonged to the military, were arrested in late 2009 on suspicion of planning another coup to overthrow Jammeh and were subsequently found guilty of treason and conspiracy and received death sentences.

In the run-up to the November 2011 presidential poll, the government-controlled Independent Electoral Commission (IEC) installed a new biometric voter registration system, though it stated that 1,897 voters had nonetheless registered at least twice. The IEC failed to share the electoral register with opposition parties, significantly shortened the campaign period, and hampered the ability of opposition parties to campaign. Clashes between opposition supporters and the APRC during the campaign resulted in three deaths. Jammeh secured his fourth term as president with 72 percent of the vote; opposition parties rejected the results as fraudulent. In response, Jammeh told his critics to "go to hell." The Economic Community of West African States (ECOWAS) refused to send election observers, citing the repressive electoral environment.

After the denial of an opposition request to postpone the March 29, 2012, legislative elections to ensure a level playing field, six of the seven opposition parties boycotted the vote. Facing no opposition for over half of the available seats, the ARPC won 43 seats, the National Reconciliation Party captured 1 seat, and independent candidates took the remaining 4 seats. Observers from the African Union (AU) noted irregularities including a "gross imbalance" between the resources of the ARPC and other parties and the presence of security personnel and traditional chiefs in polling stations; ECOWAS again refused to send observers.

In August, Jammeh announced his intention to execute—for the first time in 27 years—all 47 inmates on death row by mid-September. Many of the inmates are political prisoners, including former government officials and military officers jailed by Jammeh. Nine inmates, including two Senegalese nationals, were executed by firing squad in late August without benefit of a fair trial or access to an attorney. Following international condemnation from the AU, the European Union, and the office of the United Nations High Commissioner for Human Rights, Jammeh on September 15 announced an indefinite suspension of all executions, which would be lifted if the country's murder rate increased.

Jammeh has drawn criticism for his erratic statements, including insisting that he could personally cure HIV/AIDS and infertility in women and threatening decapitation of homosexuals. He threatened to withhold government services to voters who failed to support him in the 2011 presidential election, while declaring that he could not be removed from power because he had been installed by God. In May 2012, Jammeh ordered "Operation Bulldozer," an anticrime operation targeting murderers and drug traffickers, as well as homosexuals.

As the country continued to suffer from years of severe droughts and crop failures, an increase in the number of Gambians requiring immediate food aid led to the declaration of a state of emergency in 2010 and an influx of food assistance from international donors in 2012.

Political Rights and Civil Liberties: The Gambia is not an electoral democracy. The president is elected by popular vote for unlimited five-year terms. Of the 53 members of the unicameral National Assembly, 48 are elected by popular vote, with the remainder appointed by the president; members serve five-year terms.

Official corruption remains a serious problem. However, President Yahya Jammeh's recent focus on economic development has led to increased anticorruption efforts, including the establishment of an Anti-Corruption Commission and the sentencing of several high-ranking security officials on drug and corruption charges in 2012. Gambia was ranked 105 out of 176 countries surveyed in Transparency International's 2012 Corruption Perceptions Index.

The government does not respect freedom of the press. Laws on sedition give the authorities great discretion in silencing dissent, and independent media outlets and journalists are subject to harassment, arrest, and violence. In July 2012, Abdulhamid Adiamoh, the managing editor of the newspaper *Today*, was convicted of contempt of court in connection with an opinion piece in which he criticized a defense lawyer in the trial of a former university lecturer; he was released after paying a fine of $3,100. In August, authorities shut down independent radio station Teranga FM after the station had been told to stop airing newspaper reports translated into local languages; it remained closed at year's end. In September, two independent papers, the *Daily News* and *The Standard*, were ordered by security officials to cease publication, though no official explanation was provided; both papers have reported on sensitive political issues, including the 2012 execution of nine death row prisoners. In September, Jammeh announced that he would allow the United Nations to investigate the 2004 killing of Deyda Hydara and the disappearance of Ebrima Manneh, both prominent journalists, though the process was stalled at year's end. The government runs Radio Gambia, as well as the sole television channel and the *Gambia Daily* newspaper. There are several private radio stations and newspapers, and foreign broadcasts are available. While the state generally does not restrict internet usage, some websites, including that of the U.S.-based newspaper *Gambia Echo*, have been blocked.

Freedom of religion is legally guaranteed and generally upheld by the government. However, in 2009, state forces led mass hunts for those accused of witchcraft. Nearly 1,000 people were kidnapped, with many brought to secret government detention centers, beaten, and forced to drink hallucinogenic substances, resulting in two deaths. Open and free private discussion is limited by fears of government surveillance and retaliation.

Freedoms of assembly and association are legally protected but constrained by state intimidation in practice. In September 2012, Babucarr Ceesay, first vice president of the Gambia Press Union, and Abubacarr Saidykhan, a freelance journalist who frequently reports on cases of human rights violations, were charged with conspiracy to commit a felony after asking for government permission to organize a peaceful protest against the September executions; the charges against them were subsequently dropped, though they received death threats in October. Workers, except for civil servants and members of the security forces, have the right to form unions, strike, and bargain for wages, though a climate of fear generated by the state dissuades workers from taking action.

Although the constitution provides for an independent judiciary, Jammeh has the authority to select and dismiss judges. The judicial system recognizes customary law and Sharia (Islamic law), primarily with regard to personal status and family matters. Impunity for the country's security forces, particularly the NIA, is a problem. A 1995 decree allows the NIA to search, arrest, or seize any person or property without a warrant in the name of state security. Prisons are overcrowded and unsanitary, and inmates suffer from inadequate nutrition and lack of medical attention. Torture of prisoners has been reported as routine.

Former minister of information and communication Amadou Scattred Janneh was convicted of treason and sentenced to life in prison in 2011 for printing and distributing T-shirts with antigovernment slogans. Another former government official, Tamsir Jasseh, was convicted of treason in 2007 for his alleged role in the 2006 abortive coup attempt and sentenced to 20 years in prison. Jasseh maintained that he had been tortured while in custody and had confessed under duress. In September 2012, Janneh and Jasseh—both of whom are Gambian-Americans—were pardoned and released into the custody of Revered Jesse Jackson following a personal appeal to President Jammeh.

In 2012, a number of high-profile individuals were arrested arbitrarily or held without charge for longer than the 72 hours permitted; at least nine such documented cases occurred in December alone. Former foreign affairs minister Mamury Njie—who had reportedly advised against the executions of prisoners on death row—was arrested on October 31 and held in detention without charge until November 5. On December 14, he was charged with financial crimes and abuse of office and remained in detention at year's end. Imam Baba Leigh, who had publicly condemned the August executions, was arrested on December 3; he was reportedly being held at NIA headquarters at year's end.

The Gambia's various ethnic groups coexist in relative harmony, though critics have accused Jammeh of giving preferential treatment to members of his Jola ethnic group in the military and government.

Women enjoy fewer opportunities for higher education and employment than men. While the vice president and several cabinet ministers are women, there are only 4 women in the 53-seat National Assembly. Sharia provisions regarding family law and inheritance restrict women's rights. Rape and domestic violence are common. Female genital mutilation (FGM) remains legal and widely practiced. Local groups working to combat FGM reported being harassed in 2012 by judicial authorities. The Gambia is a source, destination, and transit country for the trafficking of women and children for prostitution and forced labor. In April 2012, 18 men and women were arrested for alleged same-sex sexual conduct at a dance ceremony for tourists; the dance reportedly involved men dressing as women. After having been detained for two weeks, they were released on approximately $3,000 bail, and eventually the charges against them were dropped for lack of evidence.

Georgia

Political Rights: 3*
Civil Liberties: 3
Status: Partly Free

Population: 4,518,900
Capital: Tbilisi

Ratings Change: Georgia's political rights rating improved from 4 to 3 due to the country's first peaceful handover of power to an opposition party after parliamentary elections that were judged free and fair by international observers and featured more pluralistic media coverage.

Note: The numerical ratings and status listed above do not reflect conditions in South Ossetia or Abkhazia, which are examined in separate reports.

Ten-Year Ratings Timeline For Year Under Review (Political Rights, Civil Liberties, Status)

2003	2004	2005	2006	2007	2008	2009	2010	2011	2012
4,4PF	3,4PF	3,3PF	3,3PF	4,4PF	4,4PF	4,4PF	4,3PF	4,3PF	3,3PF

Overview: Billionaire businessman Bidzina Ivanishvili's Georgian Dream Movement defeated President Mikheil Saakash-vili's ruling United National Movement in parliamentary elections in October, leading to the country's first peaceful transfer of power through elections since independence in 1991. A prison abuse scandal that had emerged late in the campaign sparked public anger at the government over long-neglected judicial reforms. After Ivanishvili took office as prime minister, more than 20 members of the previous government were arrested and questioned regarding a variety of alleged offenses, raising concerns about political retribution by the new authorities.

Georgia gained its independence from Russia in 1918, only to become part of the Soviet Union in 1922. In 1990, shortly before the Soviet Union's collapse, an attempt by the region of South Ossetia to declare independence from Georgia and join Russia's North Ossetia republic sparked a war between the separatists and Georgian forces. Although a ceasefire was signed in 1992, South Ossetia's final political status remained unresolved.

Following a national referendum in April 1991, Georgia declared its independence from the Soviet Union. Nationalist leader and former dissident Zviad Gamsakhurdia was elected president in May. The next year, he was overthrown by opposition militias and replaced with former Georgian Communist Party head and Soviet foreign minister Eduard Shevardnadze. Parliamentary elections held in 1992 resulted in more than 30 parties and blocs winning seats, with none securing a majority.

In 1993, Georgia was shaken by the violent secession of the Abkhazia region and an insurrection by Gamsakhurdia loyalists. Shevardnadze legalized the presence of some 19,000 Russian troops in Georgia in return for Russian support against Gamsakhurdia, who reportedly committed suicide after his defeat. In early 1994,

Georgia and Abkhazia agreed to a ceasefire under which Russian-led troops were stationed along the de facto border.

In 1995, Shevardnadze and his Citizens' Union of Georgia (CUG) party won presidential and parliamentary polls. The CUG won again in the 1999 parliamentary elections, and observers from the Organization for Security and Cooperation in Europe (OSCE) concluded that, despite some irregularities, the vote was generally fair. In the 2000 presidential poll, however, Shevardnadze's wide margin of victory led to accusations of fraud that were supported by election monitors.

Shevardnadze faced growing opposition from prominent members of the CUG, including Justice Minister Mikheil Saakashvili, who criticized the president's failure to contain widespread corruption. While Shevardnadze resigned as CUG chairman in 2001, Saakashvili left to form his own party, the United National Movement (UNM).

Flawed parliamentary elections in November 2003 sparked a campaign of street protests known as the Rose Revolution. OSCE observers reported a variety of electoral violations, Shevardnadze was forced to resign, and the Supreme Court canceled the election results. Saakashvili won a snap presidential election in January 2004, running virtually unopposed and capturing 96 percent of the vote. Fresh parliamentary elections in March gave two-thirds of the seats to the UNM and allied parties.

Georgia's relations with Russia soured as Saakashvili quickly reestablished Tbilisi's control over the semiautonomous southwestern region of Ajaria and pledged to reintegrate the separatist enclaves of Abkhazia and South Ossetia, which were tacitly supported by the Kremlin.

Mounting frustration with Saakashvili's dominance of the political scene culminated in large street protests in late 2007. Demonstrations in November drew between 50,000 and 100,000 people, prompting a violent police crackdown and the imposition of a state of emergency. Responding to opposition demands for elections, Saakashvili scheduled an early presidential vote for January 2008, giving his opponents little time to prepare. Saakashvili won with roughly 53 percent of the vote, but his main challenger alleged fraud, and OSCE observers noted an array of irregularities.

An armed conflict between the government and South Ossetian separatist forces erupted in early August, and an ensuing Russian invasion pressed deep into Georgian territory before a French-brokered ceasefire took hold several days later. Russia recognized the independence of South Ossetia and Abkhazia in the wake of the conflict, but few other countries followed suit. Russia also established a substantial, long-term troop presence in both territories.

Opposition leaders renewed their demands for the president's resignation in April 2009, and his refusal led to a series of street protests, beatings, and arrests that lasted into the summer. Some opposition members were accused of plans to foment violence during the year. Political and security conditions eased considerably in 2010, and the frequent protests that characterized the preceding three-year period were largely absent.

In October 2011, billionaire businessman Bidzina Ivanishvili announced plans to establish his own opposition political party. The government initially sought to block his participation in politics on the grounds that he had improperly obtained multiple citizenships while living abroad, but under international and domestic pressure, Saakashvili signed constitutional amendments in May 2012 that cleared the way for Ivanishvili to run in the October parliamentary elections. Meanwhile, in April, Ivanishvili founded the Georgian Dream Movement, a coalition of six opposition parties that would challenge the UNM in the October balloting.

The campaign was highly competitive, but also extremely polarized, with each side criticizing the other rather than presenting distinct policy platforms. A prison abuse scandal that emerged in September helped galvanize voter opposition to Saakashvili's government, and Georgian Dream captured 85 seats, leaving the UNM in the minority with 65. In Georgia's first peaceful transfer of power through elections, Saakashvili conceded defeat and pledged to fully cooperate with the new government, including reinstating Ivanishvili's Georgian citizenship and approving him as the new prime minister.

A key Georgian Dream campaign promise was to restore the country's frayed economic ties with Russia, but there was little progress by year's end. Saakashvili had unilaterally lifted visa restrictions on Russians traveling to Georgia in March, and Moscow pledged to reciprocate if Tbilisi revised a law that bars entry to South Ossetia and Abkhazia from areas not controlled by Georgia, potentially subjecting those entering from Russia to criminal prosecution. At year's end, no changes had been made to the law, and Russian troops continued to occupy both territories.

Political Rights and Civil Liberties: Georgia is an electoral democracy. International observers generally hailed the October 2012 parliamentary elections as free and fair, noting increased competitiveness and a range of largely peaceful political activities, including mass demonstrations by the opposition. The government's acceptance of the results and the subsequent transfer of power were also welcomed as signs of progress. However, a number of electoral problems persisted, including the abuse of administrative resources, intimidation of opposition supporters, tabulation irregularities, and an apparent progovernment bias in the activities of the State Audit Office.

The unicameral Parliament has 150 seats, with 77 chosen by party list and 73 in single-member districts. According to the constitution, the president appoints the cabinet and serves up to two five-year terms, though current president Mikheil Saakashvili—first elected in 2004—was reelected in 2008 after calling an early vote. The next presidential election is expected in October 2013. Under a package of constitutional amendments adopted in October 2010, the bulk of executive authority will shift from the president to the prime minister in 2013, and new rules surrounding votes of no confidence will make it difficult for Parliament to remove the prime minister.

Saakashvili's UNM dominated Georgian politics from 2004 until 2012, when growing dissatisfaction with the ruling party's perceived consolidation of power helped fuel support for the Georgian Dream Movement. The new party merged older opposition factions and benefited from founder Bidzina Ivanishvili's extensive personal wealth.

While notable progress has been made with respect to lower- and mid-level corruption, particularly in comparison with the country's neighbors, Georgia continues to suffer from corruption at elite levels, and the UNM administration's insularity fostered opportunities for cronyism and insider deals. After Georgian Dream took power in late 2012, the authorities arrested and interrogated more than 20 former officials from the previous government on charges ranging from abuse of power to bribery. Several of the allegations related to illegal surveillance of Georgian Dream, prompting the UNM to accuse the new government of pursuing a political vendetta. The international community urged the new leadership to maintain respect for due process, warning that using prosecutions to seek political retribution could jeopardize Georgia's bid for NATO membership. Georgian Dream officials denied that the cases were politically motivated and invited NATO to monitor the investigations. The probes were ongoing at year's end, and accusations of legal violations were inconclusive.

The constitution provides guarantees for press freedom, and the print media offer a range of political views. The state television and radio outlets were converted into public-service broadcasters in 2005, but critics maintain that the stations showed a pro-UNM bias that continued even after the 2012 elections. The major private television stations received heavy subsidies from the UNM government and displayed a progovernment slant. In the weeks following the elections, ownership changes reduced the dominance of pro-UNM stations, but the media remained polarized between the two main political camps. Legal amendments that banned offshore ownership of broadcasters and required stations to reveal their ownership structures came into effect in 2012. However, some outlets' ownership remained unclear, with listed owners allegedly serving as stand-ins for others. The authorities do not restrict access to the internet, but high-speed connections are prohibitively expensive for many citizens.

Freedom of religion is respected for the country's large Georgian Orthodox Christian majority and some traditional minority groups, including Muslims and Jews. However, members of newer groups, including Baptists, Pentecostals, and Jehovah's Witnesses, have faced harassment and intimidation by law enforcement officials and Georgian Orthodox extremists. The government does not restrict academic freedom.

Freedoms of association and assembly were generally upheld in 2012, though election observers noted some instances of local officials attempting to interfere in Georgian Dream campaign rallies, particularly in Gori. Georgian Dream held unusually large demonstrations without incident in Tbilisi, drawing an estimated 80,000 participants to one event in May.

Nongovernmental organizations (NGOs) are able to register and operate without arbitrary restrictions. NGOs were active in monitoring the preelection environment. Pushback from civil society groups forced Parliament to revise changes it made in January to the Law on Political Unions, which had allowed the State Audit Office to monitor the finances of all groups—including NGOs—that were "directly or indirectly" linked to political parties. The revision limited monitoring to groups with declared electoral goals. Civil society was also instrumental in the passage of a "must carry, must offer" rule at the end of June that obliged cable providers to broadcast all television channels for the 60-day period prior to the elections, giving the public access to more diverse information. Obtaining funding for NGOs is a challenge; local business support for charities tends not to be directed toward organizations that work on government policy and reform issues. A 2011 law allows the government to provide financial support for projects administered by NGOs and universities.

The constitution and the Law on Trade Unions allow workers to organize and prohibit antiunion discrimination. The Amalgamated Trade Unions of Georgia, the successor to the Soviet-era union federation, is the principal trade union bloc. It is not affiliated with, and receives no funding from, the government. Union influence remains marginal in practice, and in 2012 civil society groups raised concerns that the current labor code does not protect employees from being fired on political grounds. The termination of employment contracts was identified as a voter intimidation tactic in the run-up to the parliamentary elections.

The judiciary has suffered from significant corruption and pressure from the executive branch. The UNM government took some steps to improve the independence and capacity of the courts, such as pay increases for judges and the implementation of jury trials in 2011, but these have had little impact. The need for comprehensive reform of the justice system came to the fore in September 2012, when leaked videos showing the apparent abuse and rape of inmates at a prison outside of Tbilisi were broadcast on television. The images sparked public outrage, leading Saakashvili to appoint the country's ombudsman as the new minister for prisons and call for an overhaul of correctional institutions. In October, the government announced that it would grant a working group of journalists, NGO representatives, and lawyers a temporary mandate to monitor prison conditions until January 2013. Since 2007, only the ombudsman has had oversight of Georgia's penitentiaries.

The government generally respects the rights of ethnic minorities in areas of the country that are not contested by separatists. Antidiscrimination regulations cover bias based on sexual orientation, but societal discrimination against LGBT (lesbian, gay, bisexual, and transgender) people remains strong. Freedom of residence and freedom to travel to and from the country are observed.

Georgia has gradually built up legislation to address the problem of domestic violence, including a law passed in June 2012 that upgraded it from an administrative to a criminal offense. However, the ombudsman and NGOs have reported that police fail to pursue rape and domestic violence cases adequately, and the crimes are believed to be underreported. Georgia is a source, transit, and destination country for trafficking in persons, but the government's efforts to comply with international standards for combating the problem have earned it a Tier 1 ranking in the U.S. State Department's annual Trafficking in Persons Report.

Germany

Political Rights: 1
Civil Liberties: 1
Status: Free

Population: 81,825,000
Capital: Berlin

Ten-Year Ratings Timeline For Year Under Review (Political Rights, Civil Liberties, Status)

2003	2004	2005	2006	2007	2008	2009	2010	2011	2012
1,1F	1,1F	1,1F	1,1F	1,1F	1,1F	1,1F	1,1F	1,1F	1,1F

Overview:

Chancellor Angela Merkel's Christian Democratic Union suffered defeats in state parliamentary elections in 2012. President Christian Wulff resigned in a corruption scandal in February and was replaced by former East German human rights activist Joachim Gauck. In June, a regional court ruled that circumcision of boys could be considered a criminal offense, raising an outcry from Jewish and Muslim groups, and prompting the federal government to adopt legislation in December guaranteeing their right to the practice.

Modern Germany emerged in 1871, when the patchwork of German states united under Prussian leadership following the Franco-Prussian war. After Germany's defeat in World War I, the German Empire was replaced in 1919 by the Weimar Republic, which gave way in 1933 to the Nazi-led Third Reich and led to World War II. Following its defeat in World War II, Germany was divided into two states—the capitalist and democratic Federal Republic in the west and the communist German Democratic Republic in the east—during the ensuing Cold War. The Berlin Wall, which had kept East Berliners from fleeing west, was opened in 1989, and East Germany was absorbed into the Federal Republic the following year.

Chancellor Helmut Kohl and a coalition of his center-right Christian Democratic Union and Christian Social Union (CDU/CSU) and the socially liberal, market-oriented Free Democratic Party (FDP) ruled Germany for 16 years. In 1998, Germans elected the so-called "red-green coalition," consisting of the Social Democratic Party (SPD) and the Green Party, with the SPD's Gerhard Schröder as chancellor. The red-green coalition won a narrow victory in the 2002 elections.

In 2005, Schröder engineered a no-confidence vote against himself to trigger national elections. Neither the red-green coalition nor the CDU/CSU-FDP opposition was able to garner an outright majority. After unusually protracted coalition negotiations, the CDU/CSU and the SPD were obliged to form a "grand coalition," and the CDU's Angela Merkel became Germany's first female chancellor. Tensions between the two parties of the grand coalition grew during the second half of its term.

In the 2009 federal parliamentary elections, the CDU/CSU won 239 seats, while the FDP took 93 seats. The SPD had its worst result in a federal election since World War II, capturing only 146 seats. Meanwhile, the left and the Greens both made large gains, receiving the highest share of votes in their histories; however, they could not offset the SPD's losses. As a result, the alliance of the CDU/CSU and FDP received an outright majority of seats and formed a new center-right government, ensuring Angela Merkel a second term as chancellor.

In November 2009, the controversial trial of John Demjanjuk—a Ukrainian-born former U.S. citizen and accused World War II Nazi concentration camp guard—began in Munich. Demjanjuk, the lowest-ranking official to go on trial for Holocaust-related crimes, was charged with facilitating the murder of thousands of Jews at the Sobibor concentration camp in Nazi-occupied Poland. In May 2011, Demjanjuk, then 91, was convicted of accessory to murder in 28,060 counts at the Sobibor camp, and was sentenced to five years in jail. However, he was released pending appeal and was living in a German nursing home when he died in March 2012.

President Horst Köhler of the CDU resigned in May 2010, after criticism over comments he made suggesting that military intervention abroad could be justified by economic interests. One month later, CDU candidate Christian Wulff was elected to replace Köhler, but only after three election rounds, which demonstrated divisions in Merkel's majority coalition.

Marked by ongoing antinuclear sentiment reignited by the nuclear incident in Fukushima, Japan, the 2011 state parliamentary elections, which were held in seven states throughout the year, saw a series of electoral defeats for Merkel's CDU (Merkel had supported nuclear energy until reversing her position in May 2011 and setting a plan to phase out the country's nuclear plants by 2022). In Baden-Württemberg, a region ruled by the CDU since 1953, a new coalition came to power led by the Green party—the first time in German political history that a member of the Green Party would preside over a state parliament. Other notable results included the election of the Pirate Party, which campaigned for issues including information privacy and internet freedom, and won 15 seats in the Berlin state parliament.

Wulff resigned in February 2012, after becoming embroiled in a corruption scandal over financial favors he had allegedly accepted while he was governor of Lower Saxony state. The Bundestag in March elected former Lutheran pastor and former East German human rights activist Joachim Gauck as president. He was backed by all major parties after Merkel, who had opposed his previous presidential candidacy in 2010, threw her support behind him.

On May 6, 2012, in Schleswig-Holstein state elections, the incumbent CDU/FDP coalition was ousted by the SPD and the Greens; the CDU had its worst result in the state since 1950, and the FDP's share of the vote dropped by nearly half from the previous election in 2009. The Pirate Party won 8.2 percent, to enter its third state parliament. On May 13, the SPD and the Greens won a majority in North Rhine-Westphalia, Germany's most populous state. The two parties had governed in a minority coalition since 2010 but were forced to call early elections after failing to pass a budget. The SPD won nearly 40 percent of the vote, the CDU took 26.3 percent, and the Greens took 11.3 percent. The Pirate Party won 7.8 percent and qualified for seats in the state parliament.

The SPD in December 2012 nominated former finance minister Peer Steinbrück as its candidate for chancellor in the 2013 election.

Political Rights and Civil Liberties: Germany is an electoral democracy. The constitution provides for a lower house of parliament, the 622-seat Bundestag (Federal Assembly), elected at least every four years through a 50-50 mixture of proportional representation and single-member districts; as well as an upper house, the Bundesrat (Federal Council), which represents the country's 16 states. The country's head of state is a largely ceremonial president, chosen jointly by the Bundestag and a group of state representatives to serve up to two five-year terms. In Germany's federal system, state governments have considerable authority over matters such as education, policing, taxation, and spending. The chancellor, the head of government, is elected by the Bundestag and usually serves for the duration of a four-year legislative session, which can be cut short only if the Bundestag chooses a replacement in a so-called constructive vote of no confidence.

For historical reasons, political pluralism is somewhat constrained. Under electoral laws intended to restrict the far left and far right, a party must receive either 5 percent of the national vote or win at least three directly elected seats to be represented in parliament. The Constitutional Court outlawed the Socialist Reich Party (a successor to the Nazi Party) in 1952 and the Communist Party of Germany in 1956 on the grounds that their goals disregarded the principles of the constitution. However, the former ruling party of communist East Germany—the Socialist Unity Party, renamed the Party of Democratic Socialism—participated in state governments after reunification. It then merged with Labor and Social Justice The Electorate Alternative, a party of former left-wing SPD members, to form the new Left Party ahead of the 2005 elections. The main extreme right party, the National Democratic Party of Germany (NPD), is hostile to immigration and the European Union (EU), and has been accused of glorifying Adolf Hitler and the Third Reich. In December 2012, the opposition-controlled Bundesrat voted to petition the Constitutional Court to ban the NPD, but the government did not back the move.

Germany is free of pervasive corruption. The government is held accountable for its performance through open parliamentary debates, which are covered widely in the media. Germany was ranked 13 out of 176 countries surveyed in Transparency International's 2012 Corruption Perceptions Index.

Freedom of expression is enshrined in the constitution, and the media are largely free and independent. However, hate speech is punishable if publicly pronounced against specific segments of the population and in a manner that incites hatred, such as racist agitation and anti-Semitism. It is also illegal to advocate Nazism, deny the Holocaust, or glorify the ideology of Hitler. Internet access is generally unrestricted. However, in October 2012, at the request of local authorities in Lower Saxony state, Twitter blocked German users from gaining access to a neo-Nazi group's account, in what was reportedly the company's first action in any nation to block "country-withheld content" at a government's request.

Freedom of belief is legally protected. However, Germany has taken a strong stance against the Church of Scientology, which it deems an organization pursuing commercial interests rather than a religion. A number of federal states have also denied the Jehovah's Witnesses the official "public law corporation" status, which has been granted to 180 other religious groups in the country. Eight states have passed laws prohibiting female Muslim schoolteachers from wearing the headscarf, while Berlin and the state of Hesse have adopted legislation banning headscarves for all civil servants. Economic uncertainties in the aftermath of the global recession have worsened xenophobic tendencies toward immigrants in general, and

Muslims in particular, as evidenced by the 2011 reelection of the extreme right NPD party in Mecklenburg-Vorpommern. In June 2012, a regional court in Cologne ruled that doctors could be prosecuted for carrying out circumcisions, calling it a form of physical abuse when carried out on boys below the age of consent, in a case concerning a four-year-old Muslim boy who suffered complications from the procedure. Both Muslim and Jewish groups protested the ruling as an infringement of their religious freedom. In July 2012, the Bundestag passed a nonbinding motion calling on the government to ensure that circumcision, "carried out with medical expertise and without unnecessary pain, is permitted." On December 12, the Bundestag approved legislation to that effect, which had been proposed by the Justice Ministry in September. Academic freedom is generally respected.

The right of peaceful assembly is not infringed upon, except in the case of outlawed groups, such as those advocating Nazism or opposing the democratic order. Civic groups and nongovernmental organizations operate without hindrance. Trade unions, farmers' groups, and business confederations are free to organize.

The judiciary is independent, and the rule of law prevails. Prison conditions are adequate, though the Council of Europe has criticized elements in the practice of preventive detention. In February 2012, Merkel led an official tribute to the victims of a neo-Nazi terrorist cell that killed 10 people—9 small business owners mostly of Turkish origin and 1 policewoman—between 2000 and 2007. The three-member cell was tracked down in November 2011, when two men committed suicide and a woman was arrested. The woman, Beate Zschape, 37, was charged with murder in November 2012; four men were charged with assisting the group. The head of the domestic intelligence agency, Heinz Fromm, resigned in July 2012, after it emerged that the agency had destroyed files on the case and made other mistakes that allowed the cell to evade capture for years.

Germany was accused by international human rights organizations in 2011 of repatriating asylum seekers to countries where their safety could be threatened, such as Afghanistan, Iraq, and Kosovo.

Women's rights are well protected under antidiscrimination laws. However, gender wage gaps persisted in 2011, with women's wages and salaries approximately 23 percent less than men's wages for the same work. Women held 6 of the 16 federal cabinet positions and 33 percent of the seats in parliament. Limited same-sex partnership rights are respected.

Ghana

Political Rights: 1
Civil Liberties: 2
Status: Free

Population: 25,546,000
Capital: Accra

Ten-Year Ratings Timeline For Year Under Review (Political Rights, Civil Liberties, Status)

2003	2004	2005	2006	2007	2008	2009	2010	2011	2012
2,3F	2,2F	1,2F	1,2F	1,2F	1,2F	1,2F	1,2F	1,2F	1,2F

Overview:　　　　In July 2012, President John Atta Mills unexpectedly died after three and a half years in office, and Vice President John Mahama was quickly sworn in for the remainder of the term. In December, Mahama was chosen as Ghana's president in a close and polarized election, with the president's party winning a majority of seats in concurrent legislative elections. Meanwhile, several high-level government officials resigned early in the year in the wake of a corruption scandal.

Ghana achieved independence from British rule in 1957. After the 1966 ouster of its independence leader, Kwame Nkrumah, the country was rocked by a series of military coups and experienced successive military and civilian governments.

In 1979, air force officer Jerry Rawlings led a coup against the ruling military junta, handing power to an elected president, Hilla Limann. However, Limann was overthrown in another coup led by Rawlings in 1981. Rawlings proved to be brutally repressive, banning political parties and quelling all dissent. While he ultimately agreed to hold multiparty elections in the late 1980s, the elections were considered neither free nor fair, and Rawlings and his National Democratic Congress (NDC) party remained in power.

The 2000 presidential and parliamentary polls led to a peaceful transfer of power from Rawlings—who was forced to step down due to term limits—and the NDC to opposition leader John Kufuor and his New Patriotic Party (NPP), after he soundly defeated NDC candidate John Atta Mills. Kufuor was reelected in 2004, once again defeating Atta Mills. The NDC alleged irregularities, though international observers judged the elections to be generally free and fair.

In the December 2008 presidential election, Atta Mills defeated former foreign minister Nana Akufo-Addo of the NPP by less than 1 percent in a runoff vote. Despite some problems with voter registration and sporadic violence at the polls, the election was ultimately viewed as a success. The NDC also won concurrent parliamentary elections.

In July 2011, Rawlings's wife, Nana Konadu Agyemang Rawlings, unsuccessfully challenged Atta Mills for the right to represent the NDC in the 2012 presidential election. In October, Rawlings was chosen as the candidate for a new party, the National Democratic Party (NDP), but was subsequently barred from running due to the late submission of her nomination forms. The NPP again nominated Akufo-Addo as its candidate.

On July 24, 2012, Atta Mills died suddenly at the age of 68 from a massive stroke. He was quickly succeeded by Vice President John Dramani Mahama, and observers praised the quick and smooth transfer of power. In August, the NDC named Mahama as its candidate in the December 2012 presidential election. Kwesi Bekoe Amissah-Arther, the head of the bank of Ghana, was chosen as Mahama's vice president and running mate.

Divisions within the NDC—heightened by personal criticism of the late Atta Mills by Rawlings and his wife—led many observers to predict that the 2012 presidential and legislative polls would be extremely contentious. In anticipation of potential violence, all major political parties agreed in 2011 to curtail vitriolic campaign language and to denounce the use of intimidation tactics. Similarly, in 2012, the Institute of Economic Affairs, a public policy think tank, created an enforcement body including civil society members and representatives from the Electoral Commission to monitor adherence to its 2012 Political Parties' Code of Conduct. The Ghana Independent Broadcasters Association also agreed to its own code of conduct.

On December 7, Mahama was elected with just 50.7 percent of the vote, while Afuko-Addo took 47.7 percent. In concurrent parliamentary elections, the NDC captured 148 seats and the NPP took 123. Limited technical problems, including the breakdown of some new biometric voter machines used to register and identify voters, led to the extension of voting by a day at many polling places. While international and domestic observers praised the elections and reported only limited violence, the opposition disputed the results and questioned the neutrality of the Electoral Commission. On December 28, the NPP filed a legal suit before the Supreme Court contesting the presidential election results.

Ghana's economy has experienced steady growth in recent years. China has become a rising source of external funding; during Atta Mills's visit to Beijing in 2010, Ghana and China signed agreements totaling $15 billion in support of infrastructure projects. The government has faced challenges managing the rapidly growing revenues—and the resulting high public expectations—from the Jubilee offshore oilfield, discovered in 2007. Ghana began producing oil for the first time in December 2010 and received a $3 billion loan in June 2012 from the China Development Bank for gas and oil development. In 2012, Mahama proceeded with setting up foreign oil contracts without authorizing legislation in place, demonstrating the level of executive authority the president has in managing this new resource.

Political Rights and Civil Liberties: Ghana is an electoral democracy. The president and vice president are directly elected on the same ticket for up to two four-year terms. Members of the unicameral, 275-seat Parliament are also elected for four-year terms. The political system is dominated by two rival parties: the NPP and the NDC. In May 2012, the Electoral Commission completed a nationwide update of the voter roster using biometric registration. The NPP accused the NDC of rigging the process, though the local Coalition of Domestic Election Observers deemed it to have been largely successful.

Government corruption continues to be a significant problem, and anticorruption laws are rarely implemented effectively. The NDC administration has used the Bureau of National Investigation to examine corruption allegations against a number of former NPP officials, leading the NPP to claim that these efforts are politicized. In February 2012, Ghana's Economic and Organized Crimes Offices released a report on the "Woyome scandal," which involved a judgment payment of around $36 million to Alfred Woyome, an NDC financier, after an alleged breach of contract for a government construction project; the report concluded that the unusually high payment was the result of corruption and incompetence. In early 2012, the government arrested Woyome, the former chief state attorney, and the legal director in the Ministry of Finance, all of whom pled not guilty and were released on bail. During the October-November United Nations Universal Periodic Review of Ghana, the government accepted several recommendations to combat corruption in the public sector, including measurers to protect freedom of expression in the judiciary. Ghana was ranked 64 out of 176 countries surveyed in Transparency International's 2012 Corruption Perceptions Index.

Freedom of expression is constitutionally guaranteed and generally respected in practice. Numerous private radio stations operate, and many independent newspapers and magazines are published in Accra. However, the government occasionally restricts press freedom through harassment and arrests of journalists reporting on politically sensitive issues. A law prohibiting "publishing false news with intent to cause fear or harm to the public or to disturb the public peace" has at times been loosely applied. In January 2012, several agents of the Bureau of National Investigations attacked a reporter for the private *Daily Guide*, when she attempted to photograph the deputy superintendent of police, who was being investigated for cocaine smuggling. In June, four police officers assaulted a reporter for the state-owned *Daily Graphic*, who was covering a drug raid conducted by the police. The government indicated that it was investigating both cases, but no charges had been brought against either by year's end.

Religious freedom is protected by law and largely respected in practice. While relations between Ghana's Christian majority and Muslim minority are generally peaceful, Muslims often report feeling politically and socially excluded, and there are few Muslims at the top levels of government. Human rights groups have reported a high incidence of exorcism-related physical abuse at Pentecostal prayer camps. Academic freedom is legally guaranteed and upheld in practice.

The rights to peaceful assembly and association are constitutionally guaranteed and generally respected. Permits are not required for meetings or demonstrations. Civil society organizations have noted that political party "foot soldiers"—activists who assist campaigns by distributing literature and generating crowds, among other activities—have been known to use violence and aggression; however, this trend seemed to subside to some extent during the 2012 election. Nongovernmental organizations are generally able to operate freely. Under the constitution and 2003 labor laws, workers have the right to form and join trade unions. However, the government forbids action in a number of essential industries, including fuel distribution, public transportation, and the prison system. In February 2012, Ghana's Trades Union Congress called off planned strikes after reaching an agreement with the government over ending subsidies for oil products.

Ghanaian courts have acted with increased autonomy, but corruption remains a problem. Scarce resources compromise the judicial process, and poorly paid judges are tempted by bribes. The Accra Fast Track High Court is specifically tasked with hearing corruption cases involving former government officials, though some observers have raised doubts about its impartiality and respect for due process. Prisons suffer from overcrowding and often life-threatening conditions, and many prisoners experience lengthy pretrial detention. In an attempt to reduce overcrowding, a new prison for 2,000 inmates received its first prisoners in 2012.

Communal and ethnic violence occasionally flares in Ghana. In June 2012, violence erupted in the Hohoe area of Ghana's Volta region between residents of Hohoe and youth from the Muslim Zongo community in response to the exhumation of the body of a local Muslim imam. At least four people were killed and several thousand residents were displaced.

Despite equal rights under the law, women suffer societal discrimination, especially in rural areas where opportunities for education and wage employment are limited. However, women's enrollment in universities is increasing, and there are a number of high-ranking women in the current government. Women won 30 of the 275 seats in the December 2012 parliamentary elections. Despite legal protections, few victims report cases of rape or domestic violence due to the associated stigma. Same-sex sexual activity among men is illegal, and individuals suspected of homosexual relations face discrimination and abuse. People with mental disabilities also face discrimination and are frequently subjected to abuse in psychiatric institutions and "prayer camps." In June 2012, Ghana's Mental Health Act, which allows those with disabilities to challenge their detention in hospitals, went into effect, though it does not apply to those living in camps.

Ghana serves as a source, transit point, and destination for the trafficking of women and children for labor and sexual exploitation. The police's Anti-Human Trafficking Unit maintains nine regional units, but they are underfunded and have limited capacity. In March 2012, the government launched a monitoring system to track children in the Volta region to prevent child labor and trafficking.

⬇ Greece

Political Rights: 2
Civil Liberties: 2
Status: Free

Population: 11,291,000
Capital: Athens

Trend Arrow: Greece received a downward trend arrow due to a significant upsurge in right-wing violence, led by the Golden Dawn party, against immigrant groups, their supporters, and the political left, as well as a lack of effective police protection from this violence.

Ten-Year Ratings Timeline For Year Under Review (Political Rights, Civil Liberties, Status)

2003	2004	2005	2006	2007	2008	2009	2010	2011	2012
1,2	1,2F	1,2F	1,2F	1,2F	1,2F	1,2F	1,2F	2,2F	2,2F

Overview:
Greece's debt crisis continued to worsen in 2012 despite the adoption of austerity measures in order to secure bailout funds from the European Union and Interna-

tional Monetary Fund. The fiscal cuts were followed by significant social unrest throughout the year. A second round of parliamentary elections held in June led to victory for New Democracy, which formed a coalition government with two other parties. Meanwhile, the right-wing extremist party Golden Dawn, which captured seats in Parliament for the first time in 2012, embarked on a campaign of terror aimed at immigrants, the political left, and gay men and lesbians.

Modern Greece gained independence from the Ottoman Empire in 1830. The ensuing century brought territorial gains, as well as domestic political struggles between royalists and republicans. Communist and royalist partisans mounted a strong resistance to Axis occupation during World War II, but national solidarity broke down in the postwar period, leading to a civil war that the royalists won. In 1967 a group of army officers staged a military coup. They were ousted in 1974, and conservative politician Konstantinos Karamanlis returned Greece to democracy. Karmanlis's New Democracy party won the ensuing elections and ruled until 1981.

The Panhellenic Socialist Movement (PASOK) governed the country for most of 1981 to 2004. New Democracy returned to power in 2004 and won another term in 2007. Prime Minister Kostas Karamanlis, nephew of Konstantinos, called national elections halfway through his four-year mandate in October 2009, partly due to corruption scandals. PASOK captured 160 seats, and New Democracy took 91; PASOK's George Papandreou became prime minister.

A growing economic and debt crisis emerged in late 2009. In May 2010, a 110 billion euro (US$135 billion) rescue plan, including financing from the International Monetary Fund (IMF) and the European Union (EU), was issued to help prevent a Greek debt default. In return for this funding, the government was required to implement a number of austerity and modernization measures to make Greece's economy more competitive. These steps were met with a series of national strikes and protests, and Greece's debt levels continued to grow as the economy contracted and tax revenues shrank.

Additional austerity packages were passed in July 2011 as a condition for the release of bailout funds, resulting in further protests and strikes across the country. After a failed attempt to hold a referendum on the bailout package, and facing pressure from the EU, the European Central Bank, and the IMF—all overseeing the bailout—Papandreou stepped down on November 11. Lucas Papademos, the former head of the Bank of Greece, was appointed to lead a new coalition government. In February 2012, his government passed additional austerity measures, thereby securing a second, 130 billion euros (US$170 billion) bailout that included a voluntary 53.5 percent write-off on privately held Greek debt that reduced the deficit by 107 billion euros (US$140 billion).

Papademos resigned in April, having shepherded through a series of politically unpalatable austerity measures, and May elections resulted in a hung Parliament. Following a second round of elections in June, New Democracy, which received 29.7 percent of the vote and 129 seats, was able to form a coalition government with PASOK, which captured 12.3 percent and 33 seats, and the Democratic Left, which took 6.3 percent and 17 seats. Antonis Samaras of New Democracy was named the new prime minister. This coalition passed yet another round of austerity measures in

October in order to assure the release of funds from the EU and IMF. The continued push for austerity has led to growing poverty and homelessness, with unemployment reaching 25 percent and youth unemployment exceeding 58 percent. The political environment was explosive, with large-scale protests occurring in February, following additional austerity measures; in April, following the public suicide of a retiree; and in October, during the visit of German Chancellor, Angela Merkel.

The right-wing extremist party Golden Dawn entered Parliament for the first time, capturing 6.9 percent of the vote and 19 seats in June. Emboldened by increasing levels of public support, the party embarked on a campaign of violence aimed at immigrants, the political left, and members of the LGBT (lesbian, gay, bisexual, and transgender) community. Those targeted by Golden Dawn supporters have reportedly experienced inadequate police protection, and there is even some evidence of police complicity in the violence.

Political Rights and Civil Liberties: Greece is an electoral democracy. All 300 members of the unicameral Parliament are elected by proportional representation for four-year terms. The largely ceremonial president is elected by a supermajority of Parliament for a five-year term. The prime minister is chosen by the president and is usually the leader of the majority party in Parliament. The installation of an unelected technocrat, Lucas Papademos, as prime minister in 2011 was condemned by many in the media as undemocratic.

The country has generally fair electoral laws, equal campaigning opportunities, and a system of compulsory voting that is weakly enforced. Since 2010, documented immigrants are allowed to vote in municipal elections.

Corruption remains a problem in Greece. In April 2012, former PASOK minister of defense Akis Tsochatzopoulos was imprisoned pending trial on charges of laundering millions of euros in bribes from European armaments manufacturers. Greek officials have avoided clamping down on tax evasion, as demonstrated by the controversy surrounding the October 2012 publication, by journalist Kostas Vaxevanis, of a list of Greek citizens who transferred funds to the Swiss bank HSBC. The list—supposedly lost after being given to Finance Minister Giorgos Papakonstantinou in 2010—was critical of Greece's political class for not pursuing tax evaders. Greece was ranked 94 out of 176 countries surveyed in Transparency International's 2012 Corruption Perceptions Index, the worst ranking of any country in Western Europe.

The constitution includes provisions for freedoms of speech and the press. Citizens enjoy access to a broad array of privately owned print and broadcast outlets, and internet access is unrestricted. There are, however, some limits on speech that incites fear, violence, and public disharmony, as well as on publications that offend religious beliefs, are obscene, or advocate the violent overthrow of the political system. Also, political interests occasionally attempt to squelch free speech. A number of journalists have been physically assaulted by police while covering anti-austerity protests over the past two years. Additionally, Vaxevanis, in retaliation for publishing the list of tax evaders, was charged with violating Greece's data privacy laws, although he was acquitted in early November 2012.

Freedom of religion is guaranteed by the constitution, though the Orthodox Church receives government subsidies and is considered the "prevailing" faith of the country. Members of some minority religions face discrimination and legal barriers, such as permit requirements to open houses of worship and restrictions on inheriting property. The constitution prohibits proselytizing, but this law is almost never enforced. Opposition to the construction of an official mosque in Athens remains substantial; Muslim inhabitants are forced to worship in improvised mosques.

Freedoms of assembly and association are guaranteed by the constitution, and the government generally protects these rights in practice, though there are some limits on groups representing ethnic minorities. Nongovernmental organizations generally operate without interference from the authorities. Workers have the right to join and form unions. Anti-austerity protests have recurred during the past three years, including large-scale demonstrations throughout 2012. The vast majority of participants are peaceful, but the protests often turn violent as anarchist elements and the police confront each other.

The judiciary is independent, and the constitution provides for public trials. Prisons suffer from overcrowding, as do immigrant detention centers. Immigrants are disproportionately affected by institutional problems in the judicial system. Bureaucratic delays force many into a semi-legal status whereby they cannot renew their documents, putting them in jeopardy of deportation. A 2010 Amnesty International report noted that asylum seekers are often treated as criminals and face inhumane conditions in detention centers.

Acts of political violence constitute a resurgent problem, in particular those by the right-wing extremist group Golden Dawn. During the first nine months of 2012, 87 acts of anti-immigrant violence were recorded in Athens and Patra, two of the epicenters of Golden Dawn activity. There is significant evidence of police complicity, with multiple reports of officers refusing to intervene. Golden Dawn also targets leftists and members of the LGBT community. The country's Romany community continues to face considerable governmental and societal discrimination.

A 2006 law designed to address domestic violence has been criticized for not giving the state the power to protect the rights of women. Women continue to face discrimination in the workplace and hold only 21 percent of the seats in Parliament, a 4 percent increase over the 2009 election, but lower than Greece's eurozone counterparts. The country serves as a transit and destination country for the trafficking of men, women, and children for the purposes of sexual exploitation and forced labor.

Grenada

Political Rights: 1
Civil Liberties: 2
Status: Free

Population: 115,000
Capital: St. George's

Ten-Year Ratings Timeline For Year Under Review (Political Rights, Civil Liberties, Status)

2003	2004	2005	2006	2007	2008	2009	2010	2011	2012
1,2F	1,2F	1,2F	1,2F	1,2F	1,2F	1,2F	1,2F	1,2F	1,2F

Overview: Dissent continued to grow within Prime Minister Tillman Thomas's government in 2012 as more of his cabinet members resigned. While Parliament defeated a no-confidence motion in May, Thomas requested that Parliament's session in September be dissolved in order to avoid a second no-confidence motion, brought against him by a member of his own party. In July, Grenada became the first Caribbean country to decriminalize defamation.

Grenada gained independence from Britain in 1974. Maurice Bishop's Marxist New Jewel Movement seized power in 1979, creating the People's Revolutionary Government (PRG). In 1983, Bishop was murdered by New Jewel hard-liners Bernard Coard and Hudson Austin, who took control of the country. However, a joint U.S.-Caribbean military intervention quickly removed the PRG and set the country on a path toward new elections.

Prime Minister Keith Mitchell of the New National Party (NNP) ruled Grenada from 1995 to 2008, when his party lost parliamentary elections to the opposition National Democratic Congress (NDC). The NDC captured 11 seats in the 15-member House of Representatives, while the NNP won the remaining 4 seats. Tillman Thomas, the NDC leader, was sworn in as prime minister in July 2008.

Infighting and dissent grew within Thomas's government and his NDC party in 2012. On May 15, Parliament debated and defeated a motion of no confidence that had been brought against the Thomas administration by former prime minister Mitchell and the NNP, who criticized Thomas for the state of the economy and the country's political instability. Several cabinet ministers have resigned or been fired from the NDC administration since 2008, including Foreign Affairs Minister Karl Hood, who resigned in May 2012 and filed a second motion of no confidence against Thomas in August. Thomas avoided a vote on the no-confidence motion by requesting that the governor-general dissolve the fourth session of Parliament in September; only 6 of the original 11 NDC seats in the House of Representatives are still held by party members. Parliament had yet to reconvene by year's end.

Political Rights and Civil Liberties: Grenada is an electoral democracy. The 2008 parliamentary elections were considered generally free and fair, though there were allegations of voter list manipulation. The bicameral Parliament consists of the directly elected, 15-seat House of Representatives, whose members serve five-year terms, and the 13-seat Senate, to which the prime minister appoints 10 members and the opposition leader appoints 3 members. The prime minister is typically the leader of the majority party in the House of Representatives and is appointed by the governor-general, who represents the British monarch as head of state.

Grenada's main political parties are the NDC, the NNP, the Grenada United Labor Party, and the People's Labor Movement.

Corruption remains a contentious political issue in Grenada. A new Financial Intelligence Unit law adopted in February 2012 shifts responsibility for investigating financial crimes from the police force to the government, and it also allows the governor-general to appoint the Unit's director, who will be protected from lawsuits. Opposition politicians have expressed serious concerns over the new Unit's ability to remain independent and worry that it will be used for politically motivated investigations. In May, Opposition Leader Keith Mitchell accused Prime Minister Tillman Thomas of failing to report a US$150,000 contribution to the NDC from a Saudi donor. Thomas denied the allegation and admitted only to having received US$50,000 from a donor in the British Virgin Islands.

The right to free expression is guaranteed in the constitution and is generally respected in practice. In July 2012, Grenada earned international praise for becoming the first Caribbean country to decriminalize defamation. However, there were reports during the year that the government attempted to pressure the media in order to influence coverage. Reporter Rawle Titus of the independent *Grenada Advocate* weekly newspaper was fired in March, after the prime minister's press secretary contacted the paper on two separate occasions to complain about an article in which Titus criticized the prime minister's selection process of the NDC candidates for the next election. Two radio stations also reportedly received similar warnings regarding their political reporting. While there are no dailies, there are several privately owned weekly newspapers. The government owns a minority stake in a private corporation that operates the principal radio and television stations, and there are several other independent radio and television stations. Access to the internet is unrestricted.

Citizens of Grenada generally enjoy the free exercise of religious beliefs, and there are no official restrictions on academic freedom.

Constitutional guarantees regarding freedoms of assembly and association are respected. Workers have the right to strike and to organize and bargain collectively, though employers are not legally bound to recognize a union if the majority of the workers do not join. Union activity has increased due to continued company layoffs and acts of retrenchment. Failure to resolve a labor dispute between Grenada Breweries Limited and its employees represented by the Technical and Allied Workers Union in December 2011 led to threats of a national strike by the trade union movement in January 2012; the dispute was resolved in February.

The constitution provides for an independent judiciary, which is generally respected by the government. Grenada is a member of the Organization of Eastern Caribbean States court system and is a charter member of the Caribbean Court of Justice, but the country still relies on the Judicial Committee of the Privy Council in London as its final court of appeal. Detainees and defendants are guaranteed a range of legal rights, which are mostly respected in practice. Protests against police brutality erupted after five police officers allegedly beat to death Oscar

Bartholomew, a Grenadian-Canadian man on holiday with his wife, on December 26, 2011. The police officers were charged with manslaughter, and a preliminary inquest was launched in January 2012; the trial continued to be delayed at year's end. Grenada's prisons are significantly overcrowded.

The constitution and law prohibit gender discrimination. However, women are underrepresented in the government, holding just 13 percent of the seats in the lower house and 23 percent in the Senate. New domestic violence legislation came into effect in May 2011; however, most instances of abuse go unreported or are settled out of court. Same-sex sexual conduct is criminalized with prison sentences of up to 10 years.

Guatemala

Political Rights: 3
Civil Liberties: 4
Status: Partly Free

Population: 15,044,000
Capital: Guatemala City

Ten-Year Ratings Timeline For Year Under Review (Political Rights, Civil Liberties, Status)

2003	2004	2005	2006	2007	2008	2009	2010	2011	2012
4,4PF	4,4PF	4,4PF	3,4PF	3,4PF	3,4PF	4,4PF	4,4PF	3,4PF	3,4PF

Overview: Clashes between government forces and indigenous people led to the deaths of seven demonstrators at Cuatro Caminos in May 2012. Student protests in Guatemala City also met with harsh responses from the police. The UN-backed International Commission Against Impunity in Guatemala continued to show progress in reforming the country's justice system and had its mandate extended to 2015. Meanwhile, prosecutions of perpetrators of past human rights atrocities continued throughout the year.

The Republic of Guatemala, which was established in 1839, has endured a history of dictatorship, foreign intervention, military coups, and guerrilla insurgencies. Civilian rule followed the 1985 elections, and a 36-year civil war—which claimed the lives of more than 200,000 people—ended with a 1996 peace agreement. The Guatemalan National Revolutionary Unit guerrilla movement became a political party, and two truth commissions began receiving complaints of human rights violations committed during the conflict. Óscar Berger of the Grand National Alliance (GANA) was elected president in 2003. In concurrent legislative elections, the Frente Republicano Guatemalteco (FRG) lost its legislative majority, while GANA captured the largest number of seats.

In the 2007 parliamentary elections, the National Unity for Hope (UNE) party captured 51 seats, followed by GANA with 37 seats. The UNE's Álvaro Colom defeated former general Otto Peréz Molina of the Patriotic Party (PP) in the November presidential runoff vote.

In 2011, Guatemalans returned to the polls to elect a president, all 158 members of the parliament, mayors for each of the 333 municipalities, and 20 members of the Central American Parliament. The PP and UNE captured two-thirds of the seats in parliamentary elections; nine other parties took the remaining 54 seats. After no candidate won a majority of votes in the first round of the presidential election, Peréz and Manuel Baldizón of the Renewed Democratic Liberty (LIDER) party advanced to a November runoff, which Peréz won with 54 percent of the vote.

The elections were generally considered free and fair despite accompanying violence, and electoral observers reported irregularities including intimidation, vote-buying, and the burning of ballots and electoral boxes. At least 36 candidates, party activists, and their relatives were killed in campaign-related violence. One high-profile case involved a mayoral candidate from the municipality of San José Pinula who murdered his two competitors. Both the LIDER and the PP violated campaign spending laws, and five municipal elections had to be repeated due to irregularities. The electoral authority, the Supreme Electoral Tribunal, was criticized for its slow transmission of election results.

The mandate of the UN-backed International Commission against Impunity in Guatemala (CICIG)—a team of police and prosecutors tasked with investigating corruption, violence, and organized crime within Guatemalan public institutions, political parties, and civil society—was extended through September 2015. The CICIG has been highly effective in prosecuting crime in Guatemala, which has one of the highest murder rates in the world. Nearly 2,000 police and government officials have been dismissed or sent to prison since the creation of the CICIG in 2006.

In May 2012, the government declared a state of seige in the town of Santa Cruz Barillas, Huehuetenango, granting security forces the right to conduct searches and detain suspects without warrants, prohibiting gun possession, and limiting freedoms of association and the press in the name of security. Indigenous residents in the town had attacked army barracks in retaliation for the killing of Andrés Francisco Miguel, a local indigenous leader who had been protesting the building of a hydroelectric plant in the area. The government sent some 200 troops to the area; more than a dozen residents were arrested, but were eventually released months later. Two employees of the hydroelectric company were arrested for the killing of Miguel. The state of siege was lifted later that month. Two states of siege had been in effect in 2011, in Alta Verapaz to fight increased drug trafficking, and in the northern province of Petén, after 27 farmworkers were murdered by the Mexican-based Zetas drug gang.

In October 2012, seven indigenous people were killed and several dozen injured at Cuatro Caminos—an intersection of roads linking Totonicapán with Quetzaltenango, Huehuetenango, and Guatemala City—when government troops opened fire on demonstrators protesting rising electricity costs and proposed educational and constitutional changes. Despite initial government claims that the soldiers had been unarmed, a colonel and eight soldiers were arrested and charged with extrajudicial killings.

Political Rights and Civil Liberties: Guatemala is an electoral democracy. The constitution stipulates a four-year presidential term and prohibits reelection. The unicameral Congress of the Republic, consisting of 158 members, is elected for four years. Elections take place within a highly fragmented and fluid multiparty system. The main political parties are the UNE, the Patriotic Party, GANA, the Nationalist Change Union, LIDER, and the Commitment, Renewal, and Order party.

Despite efforts to combat corruption, serious problems remain. The Constitutional Court ruled in August 2011 that former president Alfonso Portillo could be extradited to the United States, where he was indicted in 2010 for allegedly embezzling state funds while in office (2000-2004) and laundering the money through Guatemalan, European, and U.S. banks; his extradition was pending at the end of 2012. In October 2012, former president of Congress Eduardo Meyer was sentenced to three years in prison for involuntary embezzlement of congressional funds, dereliction of duty, and failure to report a crime. Also in October, the mayor of Antigua and nine others were arrested on various charges, including fraud, money laundering, and abuse of authority. The Law Against Illicit Enrichment was approved at the end of October. It establishes a maximum punishment for embezzlement of 10 years in prison and up to $65,000 in fines; however, other important reforms had been removed. Guatemala was ranked 113 out of 176 countries surveyed in Transparency International's 2012 Corruption Perceptions Index.

While freedom of speech is protected by the constitution, journalists often face threats and practice self-censorship when covering drug trafficking, corruption, organized crime, and human rights violations. Threats frequently come from public officials, drug traffickers, energy companies, and local security forces in communities where police are absent. A number of journalists have received death threats, been physically assaulted, and been murdered in recent years. Carolina Vásquez Araya, a journalist from *Prensa Libre*, received death threats after writing an October 2012 column addressing the rape of workers' daughters on a farm in Esquintla and blaming government agencies and institutions for contributing to the violence. The coordinator of Centro Civitas Guatemala, who helped Araya file a legal complaint over the threats, alleged that a public official at the Ministry of Justice told Araya that it was not worth reporting on cases of child rape since they are rarely investigated. Jorge Jacobs, also of *Prensa Libre*, received death threats in October, after writing about a rumored business transaction between two local companies. The daily *La Hora* was allegedly deprived of state advertising, after publishing articles about government corruption. In July, a reporter for *El Periódico*, Enrique García, released a recording of Congressman Estuardo Galdámez offering him money in exchange for favorable reporting. Congress established a commission to investigate the allegations. Galdámez was found guilty in October and received a verbal warning. The press and most broadcast outlets are privately owned. Mexican businessman Remigio Ángel González owns a monopoly of broadcast television networks and has significant holdings in radio. Newspaper ownership is concentrated in the hands of business elites, and most papers have centrist or conservative editorial views.

The constitution guarantees religious freedom. However, indigenous communities have faced discrimination for openly practicing the Mayan religion. The government does not interfere with academic freedom, but scholars have received death threats for questioning past human rights abuses or continuing injustices.

The constitution guarantees freedom of assembly, though police have at times used force against protestors. In July 2012, dozens were injured in Guatemala City during clashes between police and students, who were protesting a new rule that would increase the number of years of schooling required to become a teacher. The government claims that the majority of forceful evictions of protesters in 2012 occurred without incident, despite the deaths of seven protestors in Totonicapán in October. President Otto Peréz Molina subsequently pledged not to use the army to disrupt protests, blockades, and land seizures in the future.

The constitution guarantees freedom of association, and a variety of nongovernmental organizations operate without significant obstacles. However, the Unit for the Protection of Human Rights Defenders in Guatemala identified 305 attacks against human rights defenders in 2012, including journalists and advocates of union and environmental rights; 13 were killed.

Guatemala is home to a vigorous labor movement, but workers are frequently denied the right to organize and face mass firings and blacklisting, especially in export-processing zones. Trade union members are also subject to intimidation, violence, and murder, particularly in rural areas during land disputes. According to the International Trade Union Confederation, which reported that 10 union members were killed in 2011 and another 6 in 2012, Guatemala is the second most dangerous country in the world for trade unionists.

In 2010, the United States filed a formal complaint against Guatemala under the Dominican Republic-Central America Free Trade Agreement, alleging government failure to protect workers' rights. In August 2011, the United States further requested a dispute settlement panel to address its complaint. Representatives from Guatemala and the United States continued to discuss the issue in 2012. Two former police officers were sentenced in October 2011 to 40 years in prison for the 1984 disappearance of union leader Fernando García. Former chief of police Hector Bol de la Cruz was arrested in June 2011 for complicity in García's disappearance; he was awaiting trial at the end of 2012.

The judiciary is troubled by corruption, inefficiency, capacity shortages, and intimidation of judges, prosecutors, and witnesses. Witnesses and judicial-sector workers continue to be threatened and, in some cases, murdered. In December 2012, a federal prosecutor and six others were murdered in Huehuetenango. A November CICIG report accused 18 judges of "creating spaces of impunity" for organized crime and corrupt officials, including shielding suspected criminals from prosecution and making questionable rulings in their favor.

Prosecutions of perpetrators of past human rights atrocities continued in 2012. In August, former police chief Pedro García Arredondo was found guilty of crimes against humanity and the forced disappearance of university student Edgar Saenz Calito in 1981; he was sentenced to seventy years in jail. The landmark ruling made Garcia the highest ranking police official to be sentenced for war crimes in Guatemala. In March, Pedro Pimentel Rios became the fifth former special forces soldier sentenced for participating in the 1982 massacre of more than 250 people in Dos Erres, El Petén, joining four others who received sentences of 6,060 years in 2011 for their roles in the killings. Former head of state Efraín Ríos Montt was indicted on charges of genocide and crimes against humanity in 2012, and was awaiting trial at year's end. Five former members of right-wing Guatemalan paramilitaries were sentenced in March 2012 to a total of 7,710 years in jail for their role in a 1982 massacre in Plan de Sanchez, a rural community in northern Guatemala. In September, 15 Q'eqchi Maya Indian women who were subjected to sexual and labor slavery between 1982 and 1986 testified at a preliminary hearing against 37 members of the military.

Police continue to be accused of torture, extortion, kidnapping, extrajudicial killings, and drug-related crimes. Three prosecutors and 4 police officers were arrested in May 2012 on suspicion of ties to drug trafficking, and 11 police officers were arrested in June for attempted kidnapping of two civilians. The government uses the military to maintain internal security, despite restrictions on this practice imposed by the 1996 peace accord. Prison conditions are harsh, and facilities are overcrowded and rife with gang- and drug-related violence and corruption.

Even after three years of declining homicide rates, Guatemala remains one of the most violent countries in Latin America. Over 5,400 people were murdered in 2012. Violence related to the shipment of drugs from South America to the United States has spilled over the border from Mexico, with rival Mexican and Guatemalan drug trafficking organizations battling for territory. These groups have operated with impunity in the northern jungles, which serve as a storage and transit hub for cocaine en route to the United States. The local drug problem has also worsened, as traffickers have paid Guatemalan associates in cocaine rather than cash. The Molina administration reacted to this situation by expanding the military's role in fighting crime, including creating special task forces to investigate kidnappings, robberies, extortion, and homicides, and building five military bases along well-known drug trafficking routes. Human rights activists are concerned that the bases will be built in areas that have experienced serious conflicts over land, natural resources, and indigenous rights, and in areas that bore the brunt of military repression during the armed conflict.

Indigenous communities suffer from especially high rates of poverty, illiteracy, and infant mortality. Indigenous women are particularly marginalized. Discrimination against the Mayan community continues to be a major concern. The government in recent years has approved the eviction of indigenous groups to make way for mining, hydroelectric, and other development projects. Several large indigenous communities have reportedly been forcibly evicted in the Polochic Valley with killings, beatings, and the burning of houses and crops.

The constitution prohibits discrimination based on gender, though gender inequalities persist in practice. Sexual harassment in the workplace is not penalized. Young women who migrate to the capital for work are especially vulnerable to harassment and inhumane labor conditions. Physical and sexual violence against women and children, including domestic violence, remain widespread, with perpetrators rarely prosecuted. While Guatemala now has its first female attorney general, police reform commissioner, and vice president, women remain underrepresented in politics and hold just 13 percent of the seats in Congress. Members of the LGBT (lesbian, gay, bisexual, and transgender) community continue to be targets of violent attacks.

Guatemala has one of the highest rates of child labor in the Americas. According to the U.S. State Department, the government does not fully comply with the minimum standards for eliminating trafficking but is making efforts to do so, including launching a program to provide specialized services for trafficking victims.

⬆ Guinea

Political Rights: 5
Civil Liberties: 5
Status: Partly Free

Population: 11,498,000
Capital: Conakry

Trend Arrow: Guinea received an upward trend arrow due to steady improvements in religious freedom, open and free private discussion, the activities of local and international nongovernmental organizations, and the climate for small businesses and private enterprise.

Ten-Year Ratings Timeline For Year Under Review (Political Rights, Civil Liberties, Status)

2003	2004	2005	2006	2007	2008	2009	2010	2011	2012
6,5NF	6,5NF	6,5NF	6,5NF	6,5NF	7,5NF	7,6NF	5,5PF	5,5PF	5,5PF

Overview:
The scheduling of Guinea's next legislative elections continued to be delayed throughout 2012, and no official date had been set by year's end. In September, the National Transitional Council, the country's interim parliament, approved new legislation governing the composition of the National Electoral Commission. While security forces continued to violently suppress demonstrations during the year, small improvements were seen in the environment for nongovernmental organizations, religious groups, and private enterprise.

Guinea gained independence from France in 1958 and grew increasingly impoverished under the repressive, one-party rule of President Ahmed Sékou Touré. After Touré's death in 1984, a military junta led by Lieutenant Colonel Lansana Conté abolished all political parties and the constitution and began a program of economic liberalization.

Conté won the country's first multiparty presidential election in 1993 that international observers said was deeply flawed. Presidential and legislative elections over the next 12 years were similarly marred by serious irregularities and resulted in victories for Conté and the ruling party.

Security forces killed more than 130 people during nationwide antigovernment demonstrations in 2007, and martial law was declared. Conté died in December 2008, and Captain Moussa Dadis Camara quickly led a successful military coup, promising to hold elections in two years. Following signs that Camara might renege on a promise not to run in the 2010 presidential election, opposition forces organized a massive rally in September 2009. Security forces viciously suppressed the demonstration, killing more than 150 people and raping and beating hundreds of others. The international community condemned the crackdown and imposed sanctions on the regime. In December, the commander of the presidential guard shot and seriously injured Camara.

While Camara recuperated, his deputy, General Sékouba Konaté, became interim president and negotiated an accord with Camara that established conditions for the upcoming presidential election. Prodemocracy leader Jean-Marie Doré, who was named interim prime minister in January 2010, was charged with leading a power-sharing government and facilitating a return to civilian rule. The accord also created a broad-based, 155-member interim parliament, the National Transitional Council (CNT). In February 2010, the International Criminal Court (ICC) found that the September 2009 massacre was a crime against humanity, and called on Guinea to try the perpetrators or allow the ICC to do so.

After no candidate garnered more than 50 percent of the vote in the June 2013 presidential election, longtime opposition leader Alpha Condé of the Rally of the Guinean People (RPG) defeated former Prime Minister Cellou Dalein Diallo of the Union of Democratic Forces of Guinea (UFDG), 52.5 percent to 47.5 percent, in the November runoff. Most domestic and international observers validated the election, and Diallo eventually accepted the results. Meanwhile, violence and voter intimidation in Guinea's eastern region resulted in the displacement of thousands of ethnic Peul supporters of Diallo.

Condé had a fraught relationship with the military, parts of which had difficulty accepting their diminished status under a civilian government. In July 2011, former army officers led an unsuccessful assassination attempt; some 50 soldiers and civilians were arrested for the attack, including former members of Konaté's presidential guard.

Parliamentary elections scheduled for December 2011 were repeatedly postponed in 2011 and 2012 due to disagreements among political leaders over issues including the composition of the National Electoral Commission (CENI). In September 2012, the president of CENI resigned, and the CNT adopted a new law imposing seven-year term limits for CENI members and mandating that a specific number of members be from civil society—including the chairman—and the political opposition. Condé reshuffled his cabinet in October, dismissing the remaining members of the military serving in the government and creating the country's first cabinet post devoted to human rights issues. In December, CENI announced a timetable for holding the legislative elections in May 2013, though no official date had been set by year's end.

One person was killed during riots between the Peul and Malinké ethnic groups in Conakry in September. Tensions between the two groups have been high since the 2010 election, in which voting took place largely along ethnic lines, and Condé continued in 2012 to face accusations of awarding government posts to members of his ethnic Malinké group.

Political Rights and Civil Liberties:

Guinea is not an electoral democracy. The president is elected by popular vote for up to two five-year terms. The legislature was dissolved in 2008, and replaced in 2010 by an appointed 155-member National Transitional Council. Legislative elections originally scheduled for December 29, 2011, have been postponed repeatedly; as of the end of 2012, no official date had been set. The 2010 constitution reinforces democratic rights, including explicitly outlining the legal status of the prime minister and establishing a number of bodies such as CENI, a national human rights body, and a constitutional court.

The main political parties are the RPG and the UFDG. There are more than 130 registered parties, most of which have clear ethnic or regional bases. In October 2012, 44 political parties merged with the RPG to form the RPG-Arc-en-Ciel coalition.

Corruption is a serious problem, and many government activities are shrouded in secrecy. Despite its rich natural resources—Guinea is the world's largest exporter of bauxite, an aluminum ore—the majority of the population lives in poverty. In May 2012, nine government employees were arrested while attempting to embezzle approximately $1.94 million from the Central Bank; they remained in detention at year's end. In November, treasury director Aissatou Boiro, who was investigating the Central Bank plot, was shot to death by unidentified men in uniform; two suspects were arrested in December. Guinea was ranked 154 out of 176 countries surveyed in Transparency International's 2012 Corruption Perceptions Index.

The 2010 constitution guarantees media freedom. In June 2010, the CNT passed two new media laws, one of which decriminalized press offenses and more clearly defined defamation provisions, while the other provided for the creation of a new media regulatory body. These laws had not been implemented by the end of 2012. There are more than 200 newspapers in the country, though most have small circulations. While the state controls the national radio station and the only television broadcaster, there are more than 30 radio stations, including 16 community radio stations. In August, the government shut down private radio station Liberté FM, reportedly to prevent it from reporting on opposition-led protests in Conakry; it was allowed to resume broadcasting the following day after pressure from press freedom groups and opposition leaders. In December, a program on radio Planète FM was temporarily suspended by the National Communication Council, and a warning was issued to another station, Espace FM, due to what critics charged was the outspoken nature of political discussions on the two stations. Journalists were harassed and assaulted in 2012, including while covering public demonstrations. Due to the high illiteracy rate, most of the population accesses information via radio, while internet access remains limited to urban areas.

Religious rights are respected in practice, although there have been rare cases of discrimination against non-Muslims in government employment, as well as restrictions on Muslims' freedom to convert to other religions. Academic freedom has been hampered to some degree by government influence over hiring and curriculum content. Free private discussion, limited under previous authoritarian governments, continued to improve in 2012.

Respect for freedom of assembly is enshrined in the constitution but repressed in practice. In May and September 2012, security forces violently dispersed opposition supporters protesting ongoing delays in holding parliamentary elections, resulting in dozens of injuries and arrests. Security forces dispersed further protests in April and August with tear gas. In September, police fired tear gas at protestors calling for the departure of a South African company hired to redo the country's voter registry and which was regarded as potentially biased in favor of the Condé administration. Freedom of association is generally respected, and there were no reports of government harassment of human rights activists in 2012. Although workers are allowed to form trade unions, strike, and bargain collectively, they must provide a 10-day notice before striking, and strikes are banned in broadly defined essential services.

The judicial system demonstrated a modest degree of independence beginning in 2010. The government made modest efforts in 2012 to bring to justice perpetrators of human rights violations over the last several years. A panel of magistrates was empowered to investigate the September 2009 massacre, and Liutenant-Colonel Moussa Tiégboro Camara and Colonel Abdoulaye Chérif Diaby were indicted in February and September, respectively, for their involvement. At year's end, Tiégboro continued as the head of an office to combat drug trafficking and organized crime, while Diaby remained in the country as a civilian. However, courts are severely understaffed and underfunded, and security forces continued to engage in arbitrary arrests, torture of detainees, and extrajudicial execution with impunity. Prison conditions remain harsh and sometimes life threatening.

A new centralized Agency for the Promotion of Private Investments was established in December 2011 to improve the country's business environment by making the registration process faster and less expensive. The agency continued to promote business reforms in 2012.

While the law prohibits discrimination based on race or ethnicity, discrimination by the country's three major ethnic groups—the Peuhl, Malinké, and Soussou—in employment and place of residence is common. Ethnic clashes between the Peul and the Malinké continued in 2012, including during the September riots.

Societal discrimination against women is common. While women have legal access to land, credit, and business, inheritance laws and the traditional justice system favor men. Rape and sexual harassment are prevalent but underreported due to fears of stigmatization. Security personnel openly raped over 100 women during the 2007 and 2009 crackdowns. Advocacy groups are working to eradicate the illegal but nearly ubiquitous practice of female genital mutilation. Although the government made efforts to combat human trafficking in 2012, fewer than a quarter of those cases investigated were ultimately submitted to the courts.

Guinea-Bissau

Political Rights: 6*
Civil Liberties: 5*
Status: Not Free

Population: 1,637,000
Capital: Bissau

Status Change: Guinea-Bissau's political rights rating declined from 4 to 6, its civil liberties rating declined from 4 to 5, and its status declined from Partly Free to Not Free due to an April military coup that led to the removal of the interim president, the suspension of the national legislature, the halting of the electoral process, and increased repression of civil liberties, including harassment and arrests of regime opponents.

Ten-Year Ratings Timeline For Year Under Review (Political Rights, Civil Liberties, Status)

2003	2004	2005	2006	2007	2008	2009	2010	2011	2012
6,4PF	4,4PF	3,4PF	4,4PF	4,4PF	4,4PF	4,4PF	4,4PF	4,4PF	6,5NF

Overview:
Less than one month after the first round of the March 2012 presidential election, which was deemed free and

fair by international observers, a military coup deposed the interim president and suspended the parliament. Freedoms of speech and movement were curtailed, and several political leaders were imprisoned. The Economic Community of West African States brokered a transition pact, and a transitional civilian government was formally established in May. Nevertheless, instability continued in Guinea-Bissau throughout the year, including an alleged coup attempt in October against the interim government.

Guinea-Bissau declared independence from Portugal in 1973, following a 13-year guerrilla war by the leftist African Party for the Independence of Guinea-Bissau and Cape Verde (PAIGC). Luís Cabral became president in 1974, but disaffection with his repressive rule led to divisions within the PAIGC, and he was toppled in 1980 by prime minister and former military commander João Bernardo "Nino" Vieira. Pressure from international donors led to the country's first presidential and multiparty legislative elections in 1994, which were won by Vieira and his PAIGC.

In 1998, Vieira called on troops from neighboring Senegal and Guinea to quell an army mutiny. The ensuing war displaced hundreds of thousands of people and destroyed the country's infrastructure and economy. Vieira was ousted in 1999 and went into exile in Portugal. The 1999 legislative and presidential elections resulted in victory for the Party of Social Renewal (PRS) and the election of its leader, Kumba Yalá, as president. In 2002, Yalá dissolved the parliament and ruled by decree until he was overthrown in a 2003 coup.

The PAIGC returned to power after winning a plurality of seats in the 2004 legislative elections. Vieira returned from exile to stand in the 2005 presidential election as an independent candidate, and ultimately defeated both Yalá and Malam Bacai Sanhá of the PAIGC. In the 2008 legislative elections, the PAIGC took 67 seats in the 100-seat legislature, the PRS won 28 seats, and the Vieira-backed Republican Party for Independence and Development captured 3 seats.

In March 2009, Vieira and the chief of the armed forces, Batista Tagme Na Wai, were assassinated in separate attacks. A new presidential election was held in June despite serious political violence during the campaign. Sanhá defeated Yalá in the July runoff, 63.3 percent to 36.7 percent. International observers reported that the voting itself was peaceful, free, and transparent.

In April 2010, mutinous soldiers led by the deputy chief of the armed forces, Antonio Indjai, detained Prime Minister Carlos Gomes Júnior, as well as the armed forces chief, General José Zamora Induta, and 40 of his subordinates. Gomes was released the following day and remained in office, but Induta and the military intelligence chief, Colonel Samba Diallo, were detained without charges until late December. In June, Sanhá officially appointed Indjai as chief of the armed forces, a decision that drew condemnation from the international community. In October, Sanhá reappointed Rear Admiral José Américo Na Tchuto as chief of the navy, just months after he had been named a drug kingpin by the U.S. Treasury Department.

Following the January 2012 death of Sanhá from complications related to diabetes, Raimundo Pereira, leader of the National Assembly and a member of the PAIGC, became interim president, and an election was scheduled for March 18. Of the nine candidates, Gomes and Yalá garnered the most votes—49 percent and 23 percent, respectively—and a second round runoff was set for late April. Although the election had been deemed free and fair by international observers, five candidates, including Yalá, alleged that the election had been fraudulent and called for a boycott of the second round. Just hours after the first round vote, Colonel Diallo was shot to death near his residence, highlighting fears of further instability in the country.

On April 12, Major General Mamadu Ture Kuruma led a military coup, and Gomes and Pereira were arrested. The self-proclaimed military command announced that the coup was in response to a plot by Gomes to use Angolan troops stationed in Guinea-Bissau to suppress the country's armed forces. However, critics charged that the true purpose was merely to eliminate Gomes, who had publicly backed plans to reform the military, before his probable second-round victory. The National Assembly was suspended, and the military command took over television and radio stations and the headquarters of the PAIGC. On April 27, Gomes and Pereira were released, but forced to leave the country for nearby Côte d'Ivoire. The European Union, the African Union, and the United Nations imposed sanctions against the regime, and the UN Security Council imposed a travel ban against a number of military officers allegedly involved in the coup.

The Economic Community of West African States (ECOWAS) brokered a transition pact signed by the military command and most political parties, except the PAIGC, on May 18. The third-place candidate in the election, Manuel Serifo Nhamadjo, was named acting president. Even though the military command formally handed over power to a transitional civilian government on May 25, the country continued to be fraught with instability throughout the year. On October 21, soldiers attacked an army barracks in what was described as a coup attempt against the interim government. Just days later, Indjai and another prominent politician, Sylvestre Alves, were abducted and beaten by unknown assailants. In December, the former attorney general, Edmundo Mendes, and the former governor of Gabu, José Carlos Macedo Monteiro, were violently attacked by members of the military.

Political Rights and Civil Liberties: Guinea-Bissau is not an electoral democracy. The 100-member unicameral National Assembly was suspended following the 2012 coup; prior to the coup, its members were elected by popular vote to serve four-year terms. Before the coup, the president was elected for a five-year term, with no term limits; the president appointed the prime minister. The military currently dominates politics, and the country's leadership is increasingly under the influence of the international narcotics trade.

Political parties in Guinea-Bissau are competitive but institutionally weak. They routinely suffer from military interference and shifting personal cliques. Party leaders are often unable or unwilling to fully carry out their constitutional functions and policy agendas, as military factions have repeatedly shown a readiness to maintain or expand their own interests through coups, assassinations, and threats. Guinea-Bissau was ranked 45 out of 52 countries surveyed in the 2012 Ibrahim Index of African Governance.

Corruption is pervasive, driven in large part by the illicit drug trade. With weak institutions and porous borders, Guinea-Bissau has become a major transit point for Latin American drug traffickers moving cocaine to Europe. Powerful segments of the military, police, and government are reportedly complicit in the trade, and the judiciary—either through lack of resources or collusion in the crimes—does not investigate or prosecute corruption cases. In July 2012, the UN secretary general for West Africa stated that drug trafficking was on the rise following the April coup. Guinea-Bissau was ranked 150 out of 176 countries surveyed in Transparency International's 2012 Corruption Perceptions Index.

Although the constitution provides for freedoms of speech and the press, these freedoms are currently not respected. Television and radio stations and newspapers were shut down during the coup; they were allowed to reopen days later but were warned not to criticize the coup or report on protests. Journalists regularly face harassment and intimidation, especially regarding the military's alleged involvement in drug trafficking and its role in the coup. Antonio Aly dos Santos, Guinea-Bissau's most popular blogger, was arrested and violently beaten in April 2012 and forced to leave the country under threat in November. In October 2012, Fernando Teixeira Gomes, a Rádio Televisão Portuguesa reporter, was told to leave the country because of his critical reporting of the government. A few days later, the government revised its position, and he was allowed to stay.

Religious freedom is legally protected and usually respected in practice. Academic freedom is similarly guaranteed and upheld.

Freedom of assembly was sharply curtailed following the 2012 coup. Demonstrations, including by the National Front Against the Coup, have been banned, and protesters threatened, arrested, and violently assaulted. Nongovernmental organizations are subject to harassment, and many are reluctant to criticize the military command. Workers are allowed to form and join independent trade unions, but few work in the wage-earning formal sector. The right to strike is protected, and government workers frequently exercise this right.

Scant resources and endemic corruption severely challenge judicial independence. Judges and magistrates are poorly trained, irregularly paid, and highly susceptible to corruption and political pressure. There are essentially no resources to conduct criminal investigations, and few formal detention facilities. With support from United Nations, the government rehabilitated the Mansôa and Bafatá prisons. These facilities, currently the only secure prisons in Guinea-Bissau, started receiving their first prisoners in June 2011. A culture of impunity prevails, especially in the military. A commission formed in 2009 to probe that year's assassinations of Vieira and the chief of the armed forces, Batista Tagme Na Waie, did not make any progress in 2012.

Following the coup, freedom of movement was curtailed by roadblocks established by the military throughout the capital. Many members of government, civil society, political parties, and state institutions such as the Supreme Court have been banned from leaving the country.

Ethnic identity is an important factor in politics, and the country's largest ethnic group, the Balanta, dominates the military and thus the transitional government.

Women face significant traditional and societal discrimination, despite some legal protections. They generally do not receive equal pay for equal work and have fewer opportunities in education and employment. Women of certain ethnic groups cannot own or manage land or inherit property. Domestic violence, female genital mutilation (FGM), and early marriage are widespread. A June 2011 law bans FGM and establishes penalties of up to five years in prison for violators. Trafficking in persons, especially children, is a serious problem, despite efforts by NGOs to raise awareness, improve law enforcement, and repatriate victims.

Guyana

Political Rights: 2
Civil Liberties: 3
Status: Free

Population: 796,000
Capital: Georgetown

Ten-Year Ratings Timeline For Year Under Review (Political Rights, Civil Liberties, Status)

2003	2004	2005	2006	2007	2008	2009	2010	2011	2012
2,2F	2,2F	3,3PF	2,3F	2,3F	2,3F	2,3F	2,3F	2,3F	2,3F

Overview: The new government in Guyana was bogged down for much of 2012 with partisan disputes, allowing little legislative progress. In June, police killed three protesters in the town of Linden during a protest against high electricity prices.

Guyana gained independence from Britain in 1966 and was ruled by the autocratic, predominantly Afro-Guyanese People's National Congress (PNC) for the next 26 years. In 1992, Cheddi Jagan of the largely Indo-Guyanese People's Progressive Party (PPP) won the presidency in Guyana's first free and fair elections. He died in 1997, and the office passed to his wife, Janet, who resigned in 1999 for health reasons. She was succeeded by Finance Minister Bharrat Jagdeo of the PPP-C, an alliance of the PPP and the Civic Party. Jagdeo was elected in his own right in 2001.

Guyanese politics are dominated by a tense split between descendants of indentured workers from India, known as Indo-Guyanese, who generally back the PPP-C, and Afro-Guyanese, who largely support the PNC-Reform (PNC-R) party. In 2004, the political climate showed brief signs of improving when the PPP-C and PNC-R announced that they had reached agreement on a wide variety of issues. However, the emerging harmony was disrupted when a police informant revealed the existence of death squads that enjoyed official sanction and had killed some 64 people. An investigation exposed apparent links to the home affairs minister, Ronald Gajraj, but he was largely exonerated by an official inquiry in 2005.

In the run-up to the 2006 legislative elections, Agriculture Minister Satyadeo Sawh was brutally slain by masked gunmen, and four newspaper employees were shot dead on the outskirts of the capital. The elections were delayed by several weeks, as deep conflicts within the seven-member Guyana Elections Commission undermined the credibility of the process. Nevertheless, the elections took place without incident in August, due in part to the presence of international observers. The PPP-C emerged victorious, with Jagdeo securing another five-year term.

In the November 2011 elections, the PPP-C's reelection bid was led by 61-year-old Donald Ramotar, an economist. Denis Marshall, the chairperson of a Commonwealth Observer Group for the 2011 national and regional elections in Guyana, noted that, despite some minor issues, the elections represented progress in strengthening Guyana's democratic processes. The PPP-C captured 32 seats, while the newly established Partnership For National Unity took 26 seats, and the Alliance For Change (AFC) won 7 seats. Ramotar became president in December. Some observers contend that the parliamentary opposition's one-vote majority has resulted in a stalemate in the National Assembly, with little legislative progress being made, and that President Ramotar's role has as a result been limited to a largely ceremonial one.

Political Rights and Civil Liberties: Guyana is an electoral democracy. The 1980 constitution provides for a strong president and a 65-seat National Assembly, with members elected every five years. Two additional, nonvoting members are appointed by the president. The leader of the party with a plurality of parliamentary seats becomes president for a five-year term and appoints the prime minister and cabinet.

The 2006 elections strengthened the hand of the ruling PPP-C, but also demonstrated that some Guyanese are beginning to vote across racial lines, as symbolized by the establishment of the multiracial AFC. The main opposition party remains the PNC-R. Other significant political parties or groupings include the Alliance for Guyana, the Guyana Labor Party, the United Force, the Justice for All Party, the Working People's Alliance, and the Guyana Action Party, which enjoys strong support from indigenous communities in the south.

The country is a transshipment point for South American cocaine destined for North America and Europe, and counternarcotics efforts are undermined by corruption that reaches to high levels of the government. The informal economy is driven primarily by drug proceeds and may be equal to between 40 and 60 percent of formal economic activity. Guyana was ranked 133 out of 176 countries surveyed in Transparency International's 2012 Corruption Perceptions Index.

Although freedom of the press is generally respected, an uneasy tension between the state and the media persists. Several independent newspapers operate freely, including the daily *Stabroek News* and *Kaieteur News*. However, opposition party leaders complain that they lack access to state media. The state owns and operates the country's sole radio station, which broadcasts on three frequencies. In 2009, the Guyana Press Association denounced a government initiative to license media professionals as an attempt to impose control over the profession. Government officials occasionally use libel lawsuits to suppress criticism. The government also closed an internationally funded Media-Monitoring Unit, established in 2006 to monitor media ahead of national elections.

Guyanese generally enjoy freedom of religion, and the government does not restrict academic freedom.

The government largely respects freedoms of assembly and association. However, on June 16, 2012, police reportedly shot and killed three men who were part of a political protest against rising electricity prices in the town of Linden. An additional 20 people were injured as a result of the police firing live ammunition and teargas into the crowd of protesters. The subsequent Linden Commission of Inquiry appointed to clarify responsibility for lives lost appeared initially to be bogged down by partisan disputes. Its final report blamed the police for the fatalities, but exonerated the Minister of Home Affairs of responsibility.

The right to form labor unions is also generally upheld, and unions are well organized. However, employers are not required to recognize unions in former state enterprises.

The judicial system is independent, but due process is undermined by shortages of staff and funds. In 2005, Guyana cut all ties to the Privy Council in London, the court of last resort for other former British colonies in the region, and adopted the Trinidad-based Caribbean Court of Justice as its highest appellate court. Prisons are overcrowded, and conditions are poor.

The Guyana Defence Force and the national Guyana Police Force are under civilian control. Racial polarization has seriously eroded law enforcement, with many Indo-Guyanese complaining that they are victimized by Afro-Guyanese criminals and ignored by the predominantly Afro-Guyanese police. Meanwhile, many Afro-Guyanese claim that the police are manipulated by the government for its own purposes. Official inquiries have repeatedly called for improved investigative techniques, more funding, community-oriented policing, better disciplinary procedures, greater accountability, and a better ethnic balance in the police force, but the government has taken few concrete steps to implement the proposed reforms. Guyana is home to nine indigenous groups with a total population of about 80,000. Human rights violations against them, particularly with respect to land and resource use, are widespread and pervasive. Indigenous peoples' attempts to seek redress through the courts have been met with unwarranted delays by the judiciary. While racial clashes have diminished in the last decade, long-standing animosity between Afro- and Indo-Guyanese remains a serious concern. A 2002 Racial Hostility Bill increased penalties for race-based crimes.

Violence against women, including domestic abuse, is widespread. Rape often goes unreported and is rarely prosecuted. The Guyana Human Rights Association has charged that the legal system's treatment of victims of sexual violence is intentionally humiliating. The 2010 Sexual Offenses Act makes rape gender neutral and expands its definition to include spousal rape and coercion and child abuse; the new law also provides for offenses committed against the mentally disabled. Sodomy is punishable with a maximum sentence of life in prison, and cross-dressing is criminalized for both men and women. Along with Cuba and Uruguay, Guyana is one of only three nations in Latin America that permits elective abortion.

Haiti

Political Rights: 4
Civil Liberties: 5
Status: Partly Free

Population: 10,256,000
Capital: Port-au-Prince

Ten-Year Ratings Timeline For Year Under Review (Political Rights, Civil Liberties, Status)

2003	2004	2005	2006	2007	2008	2009	2010	2011	2012
6,6NF	7,6NF	7,6NF	4,5PF	4,5PF	4,5PF	4,5PF	4,5PF	4,5PF	4,5PF

Overview:

Controversy over constitutional amendments and the appointment of members to the Permanent Electoral Council contributed to the further postponement beyond 2012 of elections originally scheduled for 2011. The establishment of a Superior Judicial Council in July marked a positive step toward judicial independence, though President Michel Martelly was criticized for naming justices to the Court of Cassation in violation of legal requirements. Threats against and illegal arrests of civil society leaders increased during the year. Meanwhile, rising food prices and frustration with corruption and a lack of economic progress spurred large demonstrations across the country late in 2012.

Since gaining independence from France in 1804 following a slave revolt, the Republic of Haiti has endured a history of poverty, violence, instability, and dictatorship. A 1986 military coup ended 29 years of authoritarian rule by the Duvalier family, and permitted the implementation of a French-style constitution under international pressure in 1987.

Jean-Bertrand Aristide, a popular former priest, was elected president in 1990. After only eight months in office, he was deposed and exiled by a military triumvirate. While paramilitary thugs terrorized the populace, the ruling junta engaged in blatant narcotics trafficking. The United Nations ultimately authorized a multinational force to restore the civilian government, and in September 1994, facing an imminent invasion, the military rulers stepped down. U.S. troops took control of the country, and Aristide was reinstated. He dismantled the military before the June 1995 parliamentary elections, but his support began to fracture when international observers questioned the legitimacy of the balloting. Aristide retained the backing of the more radical Fanmi Lavalas (FL) party, which won an overwhelming parliamentary majority.

FL nominee René Préval, who had been Aristide's prime minister in 1991, won the 1995 presidential election; the constitution had barred Aristide from seeking a second consecutive term. U.S. forces withdrew from the country in April 1996, while the UN force extended its stay at Préval's urging.

Aristide was reelected to the presidency in 2000, and his supporters gained a majority of seats in both the upper and lower houses in that year's parliamentary elections. Aristide's second term was undermined by cuts in foreign aid, increasing levels of poverty, and conflict with business elites and opposition groups. Faced with an armed revolt by political gangs and former army officers in February 2004,

Aristide was flown out of the country in a plane chartered by the United States; he eventually accepted exile in South Africa. A UN peacekeeping force, the United Nations Stabilization Mission in Haiti (MINUSTAH), was deployed in 2004, and has remained there since. In 2006, Préval returned to power in relatively well-conducted elections, though his newly organized Front for Hope (Lespwa) party failed to win a majority in either house of parliament.

On January 12, 2010, a powerful earthquake struck near Port-au-Prince, killing more than 200,000 people and causing 1.5 million to lose their homes. Massive displacement has continued to be a problem; by the end of 2012, 350,000 people were still living in displacement camps, and many who had moved out of the formal camps remained in precarious conditions without access to adequate housing. Law enforcement and judicial infrastructures were severely damaged, compromising security and leading to lost case work and trial delays for an already overburdened court system. In October 2010, the country suffered an outbreak of cholera introduced to Haiti by UN peacekeepers stationed on a poorly maintained base. The epidemic continued through 2012 and had killed over 7,900 people by year's end. Popular discontent toward MINUSTAH rose in 2012, spurred by a lack of accountability for the organization's role in the outbreak and by regular reports of sexual abuse by soldiers.

Presidential and parliamentary elections held in November 2010 were marred by widespread reports of fraud, voter intimidation, violations of electoral laws, illegal exclusion of political parties and candidates, and problems with the composition of the Provisional Electoral Council. Supporters of popular musician Michel Martelly—who finished third in the first round of voting, according to initial results—took to the streets, claiming that fraud had prevented him from advancing to the runoff. Under pressure from the international community, Jude Célestin, Préval's chosen successor, was ultimately forced to relinquish his place in the runoff. Martelly went on to defeat first-round leader Mirlande Manigat of the opposition Rally of Progressive National Democrats (RDNP), 68 percent to 32 percent, in the March 2011 second round. Meanwhile, after parliamentary runoff elections, the Inité coalition—founded by Préval in 2010 to replace Lespwa—held 46 seats in the lower house and 6 of the 11 Senate seats at stake. Smaller parties divided the remainder.

Martelly was sworn in as president in May 2011, but the parliament rejected his first two choices for prime minister. Lawmakers finally approved Gary Conille, but he resigned in February 2012, after only four months in office, amid growing tensions with the president over his pursuit of an audit of reconstruction contracts issued by the previous administration. Foreign Minister Laurent Lamothe was nominated to take his place and was sworn in in May 2012.

Hurricane Sandy struck Haiti in October, causing heavy rains that killed over 50 people and led to a surge in cholera cases. An estimated 200,000 people were rendered homeless by flooding, and widespread destruction of crops contributed to rising food prices.

Political Rights and Civil Liberties: Haiti is not an electoral democracy, though the country has established a relatively robust electoral framework. Constitutional amendments ratified in 2011 reformed the appointment process for the Permanent Electoral Council (CEP) tasked with organizing elections by centralizing appointment powers in the three branches of government. President Michel Martelly initially annulled the amendments after lawmakers discovered that the amendments as published contained material differences from the version that was ratified. An investigative commission concluded that adoption of the faulty version would violate the rule of law, but Martelly eventually agreed under pressure from the international community to enact the published amendments in June 2012. The controversy, along with irregularities in appointments to the newly formed CEP, contributed to the postponement of midterm parliamentary and municipal elections originally planned for November 2011. In December 2012, the executive and legislative branches agreed to establish a temporary Transitional College to plan the overdue elections.

The constitution provides for a president elected for a five-year term, a bicameral parliament composed of the 30-member Senate and the 99-member Chamber of Deputies, and a prime minister appointed by the president. Senators are elected for six-year terms, with one-third coming up for election every two years, and deputies for four-year terms. There are no term limits, but a president cannot serve consecutive terms. The parliament plays a largely reactive role, opposing or accepting initiatives from the executive branch. Most factions in the country's fragmented party system are based on personal leadership or support from a particular region.

Endemic corruption continues to limit Haiti's political and economic development. Although the Martelly administration has made reducing corruption a priority, Martelly himself was embroiled in corruption allegations; in early 2012, he was accused of accepting bribes from a Dominican construction company seeking to secure reconstruction contracts and alleged mismanagement of the National Education Fund. Very few members of his cabinet have complied with the anticorruption agency's demand to provide full disclosure of their financial records. Martelly has appointed a number of individuals to political office who have been credibly accused of human rights abuses, including Jean Morose Villiena, who was appointed mayor of Les Irois despite his facing arson, murder, and attempted murder charges. Haiti was ranked 165 out of 176 countries surveyed in Transparency International's 2012 Corruption Perceptions Index.

Freedom of the press has been constrained by the absence of a viable judicial system and widespread insecurity. Violence against journalists remains a problem, and media outlets tend to practice self-censorship. After Martelly's inauguration in 2011, various media outlets protested against the president's intimidation and threats against their reporters. The country hosts two major daily newspapers and a number of less frequent publications, though the vast majority are in French, making it difficult for Creole-speaking Haitians to understand them, and their circulations are fairly small. Radio is the main form of media in Haiti. There are some 375 radio stations across Haiti, though most lack national reach. Television stations are far less common, and the total television audience in Haiti remains below 10 percent due to lack of electricity and resources. Internet access is hampered by similar problems.

The government generally respects religious and academic freedoms. However, the absence of an effective police force has led to poor protection for those who are persecuted for their views.

The 1987 constitution guarantees freedoms of assembly and association, but these rights are often not respected in practice. Popular demonstrations against the government and its inadequate response to the country's severe economic problems grew larger and more frequent toward the end of 2012 and were sometimes met by violent police responses. In November, thousands of Haitians took to the streets to protest perceived corruption in the government.

While Haiti has rich civil society traditions at the local level, many of its formally organized civil society groups have been co-opted by political and economic elites. Crackdowns on civil society activists and human rights defenders, including harassment, threats, and illegal arrests, increased in 2012. For example, prominent human rights defender Mario Joseph reported being subjected to harassment, threats, and unwarranted searches, while Newton Saint Juste and André Michel—two attorneys pursuing corruption claims against Martelly and his family—also reported similar harassment and death threats. In September, Jean Renel Senatus, the chief prosecutor of Port-au-Prince, was fired; Senatus claimed his dismissal was the result of his refusal to execute illegal arrest warrants for 36 individuals classified as government opponents, including Joseph, Saint Juste and Michel. The events drew criticism from several international human rights groups, and spurred the Inter-American Commission on Human Rights to direct the government to safeguard the life and safety of Joseph and others.

Unions are too weak to engage in collective bargaining, and their organizing efforts are undermined by the country's high unemployment rate. New labor regulations introduced in 2009 included a stratified minimum wage system for the commercial and industrial sectors that took effect on October 1, 2012, and minimum health and safety standards. However, the minimum wage increases apply only to a small segment of the population, and enforcement remains weak.

The judicial system is underfunded, inefficient, and corrupt, and is burdened by a large backlog of cases, outdated legal codes, and poor facilities. Official business is conducted in French rather than Creole, rendering large portions of court proceedings only marginally comprehensible to those involved. The ponderous legal system guarantees lengthy pretrial detentions in inhumane prison conditions. In a move widely hailed as a critical step towards improving rule of law, Martelly in July 2012 appointed members to the CSPJ, an administrative and disciplinary organ of the judiciary that had been nonoperational. Martelly also filled several vacancies on the nation's highest court, the Court of Cassation, but his appointee to chief justice exceeded the legal age of service, and two other judges were appointed without the constitutionally required Senate approval; in October, the Senate voted for the removal of the illegally appointed judges, but they remained in their positions at year's end.

Police are regularly accused of abusing suspects and detainees, and impunity continues to be a problem. The Office of Citizen Protection, which expanded to rural areas to more effectively respond to allegations of government abuse, remains underfunded. In February 2012, a judge dismissed charges against former dictator Jean-Claude Duvalier, who in 2011 had returned to the country after 25 years in exile, for human rights violations perpetrated under his reign. Appeals of the dismissal were pending at year's end.

Widespread violence against women and children worsened considerably in the aftermath of the 2010 earthquake. Rapes were reportedly pervasive in the displacement camps, where insufficient police protection and inadequate housing exacerbated the vulnerability of women and children. Efforts of the Ministry of Women, grassroots women's groups, and legal organizations have helped improve the response to sexual violence, including more effective prosecutions of perpetrators and the consideration of new laws that would better address sexual violence and discrimination. Trafficking of children out of the country, especially to the Dominican Republic, also reportedly increased sharply after the earthquake. At the end of 2012, the parliament was considering an overhaul of its adoption laws that included provisions to increase the protection of children and to make trafficking a criminal offense. Children's rights organizations reported an increase in the prevalence of restavek, or child domestic servants, during 2012.

Honduras

Political Rights: 4
Civil Liberties: 4
Status: Partly Free

Population: 8,385,000
Capital: Tegucigalpa

Ten-Year Ratings Timeline For Year Under Review (Political Rights, Civil Liberties, Status)

2003	2004	2005	2006	2007	2008	2009	2010	2011	2012
3,3PF	3,3PF	3,3PF	3,3PF	3,3PF	3,3PF	4,4PF	4,4PF	4,4PF	4,4PF

Overview: Honduras continued in 2012 to struggle with the legacy of the 2009 coup that overthrew President José Manuel Zelaya. Human rights violations and crime rates increased during the year, making Honduras the most violent country in the world. The September murder of prominent human rights attorney Antonio Trejo Cabrera has been linked to wealthy landowner and coup supporter Miguel Facussé. A constitutional crisis erupted at the end of the year when Congress voted to remove four Supreme Court justices over disputes on rulings related to two pieces of legislation, including one on purging the national police.

The Republic of Honduras was established in 1839. The country endured decades of military rule and intermittent elected governments, with the last military regime giving way to civilian authorities in 1982. However, the military remained powerful in subsequent decades; the first president to exercise his constitutional authority to veto the military and choose its leaders did so in 1999.

Under civilian rule, power alternated between the Liberal Party (PL) and the National Party (PN). In the 2005 presidential election, José Manuel Zelaya of the PL defeated the PN's Porfirio Lobo. The run-up to the balloting was marred by political violence that left several PL supporters injured and at least two dead. Political polarization increased under Zelaya's administration amid poor policy performance and faltering public institutions. The president deepened the country's political divisions, including within his own party, and pitted factions of the political and business elite against one another through increasingly populist posturing. Zelaya was removed from power and forcibly deported in a coup on June 28, 2009, after he attempted to hold a nonbinding referendum to gauge support for an overhaul of the constitution. His opponents interpreted the proposal as a power grab, as it included the elimination of presidential term limits, though the constitutional reform process would have begun after the end of his nonrenewable four-year term in 2010. Both the Supreme Court and the military participated in the coup. Roberto Micheletti of the PL, the president of Congress, was named acting president after the legislature accepted a forged resignation letter from Zelaya. The international community condemned the coup and continued to recognize Zelaya as the legitimate president.

In September 2009, Micheletti issued an executive decree that effectively curtailed civil and political liberties, banning all public meetings and granting police new powers of detention, which effectively permitted security forces to act without regard for human rights or the rule of law. Public demonstrations supporting Zelaya's reinstatement were violently suppressed, resulting in the deaths of several protesters. Media outlets and journalists faced harassment, threats, power outages, and blocked transmissions; authorities also temporarily closed radio and television stations. Civil society organizations and human rights defenders encountered harassment, including increased surveillance, threats, and physical assaults. Micheletti reversed his decree under international pressure, though many of the abuses continued.

The international community pressed for negotiations aimed at reinstating Zelaya and allowing him to serve out his legal term; many countries warned that they would not recognize the national elections scheduled for November 2009 if the coup leaders refused to comply. Nevertheless, the de facto authorities pressed ahead with the elections. Lobo won the presidency with 56 percent of the vote, defeating Zelaya's vice president, Elvin Santos Lozano of the PL. The PN captured 71 seats in Congress, followed by the PL with 45, and three smaller parties took the remainder.

Lobo was inaugurated in January 2010, though the new government made little progress toward restoring the rule of law as violent crime and human rights violations continued. Four lower-court judges who challenged the legality of the coup in 2009 were dismissed from their posts in May 2010. Also that month, a Truth and Reconciliation Commission charged with leading an impartial investigation into the events surrounding the coup began operating, though it received little institutional support.

In April 2011, the presidents of Colombia and Venezuela sponsored talks to resolve the political crisis. In May, corruption charges against Zelaya were dropped, and both he and Lobo signed the Cartagena Accords, which guaranteed Zelaya's safety and freedom upon his return to Honduras. The agreement also paved the way for Zelaya's organization, the National Front for Popular Resistance, to register as a political party, and reaffirmed the right of citizens to modify the constitution through referendums. In June, the Organization of American States (OAS) voted to readmit Honduras as a member.

The Truth and Reconciliation Commission issued its report in July 2011, finding that Zelaya's removal from office constituted an illegal coup, that Congress had no means by which to remove a sitting president, that the interim government was illegal, and that the military used disproportionate force that resulted in at least a dozen deaths following the coup. The commission also stated that Zelaya shared blame for instigating the crisis with his push for a referendum, and that the international community, and the OAS in particular, failed to stop or reverse the coup. The report contained dozens of recommendations for strengthening the rule of law, including the creation of a constitutional court and the development of clear legal procedures for political trials.

In October 2011, the Supreme Court overwhelmingly ruled against the prosecution of six army generals who had been charged with overthrowing Zelaya and transferring him to Costa Rica. The decision made it unlikely that any coup participants would be charged.

The conflict over fertile land in the Bajo Aguán region in northern Honduras intensified in 2012 as peasants, private security forces of landowners, and state forces clashed over land. More than 50 people, most of them landless peasants, have died in the conflict since 2009. In September 2012, prominent human rights attorney Antonio Trejo Cabrera was murdered shortly before he was to testify before the Inter-American Commission on Human Rights in Washington, D.C. regarding abuses committed by the landowners in the conflict. Wealthy landowner Miguel Facussé, who is the uncle of former president Carlos Facussé and a major supporter of the 2009 coup, has reportedly been linked to Trejo's murder.

A constitutional crisis erupted in December 2012, when Congress illegally voted to remove four of the five Supreme Court justices. Their dismissals followed two decisions on the constitutionality of legislation approved by the National Congress, one regarding private cities and the other related to procedures for purging the national police. The crisis continued at year's end.

Political Rights and Civil Liberties: Honduras is not an electoral democracy. General elections were held in November 2009, and the voting itself was largely considered to have met international standards. However, the elections were overseen by an interim government established after President José Manuel Zelaya was forcibly removed by the military in a June 2009 coup, and they took place in a climate of severely compromised civil liberties. The president is elected by popular vote for a single four-year term. Members of the 128-seat, unicameral National Congress are also elected for four-year terms. The proportion of the votes received by a party's presidential candidate determines its representation in the National Congress. The military has long exerted considerable influence over civilian governments.

Corruption continues to dominate the political scene. Army officers have been found guilty of involvement in drug trafficking and other crimes. A 2006 transparency law was marred by claims that it contained amendments designed to protect corrupt politicians. However, the Institute for Access to Public Information has made efforts to enforce transparency rules and punish entities that fail to respond properly to information requests. Honduras was ranked 133 out of 176 countries surveyed in Transparency International's 2012 Corruption Perceptions Index.

Since the 2009 coup, authorities have systematically violated the constitution's press freedom guarantees. Numerous radio and television stations reported continued harassment in 2012, including police surveillance, as well as assaults, threats, blocked transmissions, and power outages. In 2012, Reporters Without Borders named Miguel Facussé as the most serious threat to press freedom in Honduras; Facussé reportedly uses his private security forces to bully journalists whose work threatens his or the government's interests. Honduras is considered the second most dangerous country in the world for journalists, with 26 killed since the 2009 coup, including several known Zelaya supporters. The government has reacted with silence or dismissal of the cases as routine street crime. Media ownership is concentrated in the hands of a few powerful business interests, and many journalists practice self-censorship, particularly since the coup. Internet use is generally unrestricted, but access was impaired following the coup by multiple politically motivated power outages and cuts in telephone service.

Freedom of religion is generally respected. Academic freedom is also usually honored, but scholars have faced pressure to support the privatization of the national university.

Constitutional guarantees of freedoms of assembly and association have not been consistently upheld. In addition to the violent suppression of peaceful demonstrations in 2009, police were accused of using excessive force during confrontations with striking and demonstrating teachers in August 2010 and March 2011. The 2006 Citizen Participation Law protects the role of civil society groups and individuals in the democratic process. However, human rights defenders and political activists continued to face significant threats following the coup, including harassment, surveillance, and detentions, as well as the murder of a number of coup opponents. Labor unions are well organized and can strike, but labor actions often result in clashes with security forces. In March 2012, the American Federation of Labor Congress of Industrial Organizations filed a complaint with the U.S. Department of Labor, charging that the Honduran government had violated Central American Free Trade Agreement labor provisions, competing unfairly and violating workers' rights.

The judicial system is weak and inefficient, and there are significant tensions between the national police, the prosecutor's office, and the Ministry of Justice and Human Rights. Business elites exert excessive influence over the Supreme Court and its decisions. Approximately 80 percent of crimes committed in Honduras are never reported, according to the government, and only 3.8 percent of reported crimes are investigated by police. The vast majority of inmates are awaiting trial, prison conditions are harsh, and the facilities are notoriously overcrowded. In February 2012, a prison fire in Comayagua killed an estimated 360 inmates, nearly 60 percent of whom had not been charged or convicted of any crime. There is an official human rights ombudsman, but critics claim that the office's work is politicized. The ombudsman not only supported and justified the 2009 coup, but has also publicly declared his opposition to the Truth and Reconciliation Commission. As many as 74 lawyers have been murdered since the coup. In September 2012, Manuel Eduardo Diaz Mazariegos, human rights prosecutor in Choluteca, was murdered near his office.

Honduras had the highest murder rate in the world in 2012. In October, the UN Office on Drugs and Crime reported a homicide rate of 86 per 100,000 inhabitants. Most murders are attributed to organized crime, including transnational youth gangs and Mexican drug-trafficking syndicates. The government has made membership in a gang punishable by up to 12 years in prison and uses the military to help maintain order. However, police officers and other vigilantes have committed extrajudicial killings, arbitrary arrests, and illegal searches. Hundreds of juveniles have reportedly been killed in "social cleansing" campaigns. Police corruption has been a major impediment to fighting crime and maintaining citizen security. In May 2012, President Porfirio Lobo appointed Juan Carlos Bonilla as police chief. Bonilla, who himself was alleged to have participated in police death squad activities, initiated a widespread purge of corrupt officers.

The country's growing crime rate has increased concerns about further limitations on civil liberties. In 2011, the detention of criminal suspects was extended from 24 to 48 hours, and a new wiretapping bill was passed, both despite protests from Minister of Justice and Human Rights Ana Pineda. President Lobo and key military officials have suggested reforms that would abolish the Ministry of Security and place the police under the Defense Ministry, potentially exacerbating the existing overlap between police and military functions.

Indigenous and Afro-Honduran residents have faced various abuses by property developers and their allies in recent years, including corrupt titling processes and acts of violence. In February 2011, a special unit was established in the Attorney General's office to investigate crimes against the LGBT (lesbian, gay, bisexual, and transgender) community, and a new Sexual Diversity Unit was established in the police force to investigate crimes committed against them. More than 70 LGBT activists have been murdered since the 2009 coup.

Violence against women is a serious problem, and the female murder rate has risen dramatically in recent years. These murders, like most homicides in Honduras, go unpunished. Women remain vulnerable to exploitation by employers, particularly in the low-wage maquiladora (assembly plant) export sector. Child labor is a problem in rural areas and in the informal economy, and school dropout rates are high. A May 2012 anti-trafficking law established new penalties for forced labor and prostitution of adults.

Hungary

Political Rights: 1
Civil Liberties: 2
Status: Free

Population: 9,947,300
Capital: Budapest

Ten-Year Ratings Timeline For Year Under Review (Political Rights, Civil Liberties, Status)

2003	2004	2005	2006	2007	2008	2009	2010	2011	2012
1,2F	1,1F	1,1F	1,1F	1,1F	1,1F	1,1F	1,1F	1,2F	1,2F

Overview: Hungary's government made modest amendments to its controversial judicial and media laws in 2012, though the European Commission continued to push for additional changes. New electoral legislation introduced mandatory voter registration at least 15 days before any election and set a number of rules and restrictions on campaign-

ing in the media. The measure was passed by the parliament in November, but the Constitutional Court cast it and several other laws into doubt in late December, when it invalidated them on procedural grounds.

Hungary achieved full independence from the Austro-Hungarian Empire following World War I. Soviet occupation after World War II led to communist rule, and Soviet troops crushed a 1956 uprising by Hungarians seeking to liberalize the political and economic system. By the late 1980s, the ruling Hungarian Socialist Workers' Party had come under intense pressure to accept reforms. The Hungarian Socialist Party (MSzP) was established in late 1989 by the reform-minded elite of the old ruling party, as its legal successor. Free parliamentary elections were held in 1990, and over the next decade, power alternated between conservative and socialist blocs, both of which pursued European integration. Hungary formally entered the European Union (EU) in 2004.

A ruling coalition consisting of MSzP and the Alliance of Free Democrats (SzD-Sz) won reelection in April 2006. In September, Prime Minister Ferenc Gyurcsány's recorded admission that his government had repeatedly lied to the electorate about its budgetary and economic performance was leaked to the press, sparking major riots and severely damaging public confidence in the government as it struggled to rein in a large budget deficit. The SzDSz withdrew from the coalition in 2008, but after Gyurcsány announced his resignation in March 2009, it joined the larger MSzP in endorsing Economy Minister Gordon Bajnai, an independent, as the new prime minister in April.

In April 2010 parliamentary elections, a conservative opposition bloc consisting of the Alliance of Young Democrats–Hungarian Civic Union (Fidesz) and the much smaller Christian Democratic People's Party (KDNP) captured 263 of 386 National Assembly seats, giving it a two-thirds majority and the ability to amend the constitution. The MSzP won just 59 seats. The far-right Movement for a Better Hungary (Jobbik) entered the parliament for the first time with 47 seats, and the liberal Politics Can Be Different (LMP) party, also new to the legislature, captured 16 seats. An independent took the remaining seat. Fidesz leader Viktor Orbán, who had served as prime minister from 1998 to 2002, reclaimed the post in May. Using its dominance of the legislature, the government installed a Fidesz loyalist as president in August and increased control over a number of institutions during 2010, including the media.

The Fidesz government enacted a new constitution in April 2011, with very little input from the opposition or civil society. It placed policies on culture, religion, morality, and the economy, including issues such as public debt and pensions, under the category of "cardinal law," meaning any legislation on those topics would require a two-thirds majority.

Hungary continued to face economic challenges in 2012. The government resisted major cuts to public spending and failed to keep its budget deficit below the EU-mandated ceiling of 3 percent of gross domestic product (GDP). In October, the official economic estimate for the year was revised downward from GDP growth of 0.1 percent to a 1.2 percent contraction.

Political Rights and Civil Liberties: Hungary is an electoral democracy. Voters elect representatives every four years to the 386-seat, unicameral National Assembly under a mixed system of proportional and direct representation. The National Assembly elects both the president and the prime minister. The president's duties are mainly ceremonial, but he can influence appointments and return legislation for further consideration before signing it into law. A December 2011 electoral law redrew parliamentary electoral districts and changed the seat allocation formula. The redistricting was ostensibly designed to reduce the overall number of lawmakers and mitigate wide variation in the size of constituencies, but some analysts said the new district lines gave a clear advantage to the ruling Fidesz party. The reforms also gave ethnic Hungarians living abroad easier access to citizenship and the right to vote.

Another package of electoral legislation was passed by the parliament in November 2012, though its legal validity was undermined in late December, when the Constitutional Court found that it and several other laws had been improperly adopted as "temporary" additions to the constitution. The electoral legislation introduced mandatory voter registration at least 15 days before an election, a change that was expected to reduce turnout among uncommitted voters. The package would also limit campaign advertising to national public radio and television, nationwide print media, and billboards in public spaces—a large percentage of which are owned by businessmen close to Fidesz—and set strict limits on the amount of such material that any station may air. Hungarian websites and commercial television stations would be prohibited from carrying campaign content during the 50 days before an election (reduced from 60 days), though there were no restrictions on social-media sites like Facebook, YouTube, and Twitter.

Relations between Hungary's main political parties, the center-left MSzP and the conservative Fidesz, have deteriorated in the last several years amid growing polarization. In October 2012, former prime minister Gordon Bajnai launched the centrist umbrella organization Together 2014 in a bid to unseat Prime Minister Viktor Orbán in the 2014 elections.

The constitution guarantees the right of ethnic minorities to form self-governing bodies, and all 13 recognized minorities have done so. Despite their large population, Roma hold just four seats in the current National Assembly. The 2011 constitution restricts voting rights for people considered to have "limited mental ability," raising concerns that the mentally disabled will be legally prohibited from participating in politics.

The government released a draft anticorruption program early in 2012, but it had yet to be implemented at year's end. A study published by Transparency International in March reported rampant collusion between the public sector and privileged private businesses as well as nontransparent campaign spending by both major parties in 2010 that averaged three times the legal limit. In June 2012, several senior police officials were arrested on suspicion of accepting regular bribes to advance the business interests of restaurant and nightclub tycoon László Vizoviczki. In July, after a lengthy investigation, the government dropped its case against former prime minister Ferenc Gyurcsány, who had been accused of abusing his position in relation to a land development deal and contributing to Hungary's debt crisis while in office. The independent Fiscal Council, which is responsible for overseeing budgetary policy, was dissolved at the end of 2010 after criticizing tax measures enacted by Orbán's government. The new council, installed in January 2011, consists of Orbán allies and has the power to dismiss the parliament.

In April 2012, the European Commission referred Hungary to the European Court of Justice over the questionable independence of its new data protection authority, in operation since January. The commissioner of the previous data protection body was removed before the end of his term; the leader of the new authority was proposed by Orbán in November 2011 and appointed by then president Pál Schmitt in December. Schmitt resigned from his post in April 2012 following accusations that he had plagiarized his doctoral thesis. He was replaced by János Áder, a founding member of Fidesz. Hungary was ranked 46 out of 176 countries surveyed in Transparency International's 2012 Corruption Perceptions Index.

Under media legislation that took effect in 2011, outlets must register with the new National Media and Infocommunications Authority (NMHH), which can revoke licenses for infractions. A new Media Council under the NMHH can close outlets or impose fines of up to $950,000 for violating vaguely defined content rules. Fidesz, with its parliamentary supermajority, controlled appointments to the Media Council, whose members serve nine-year terms. The council's president, who is directly appointed by the prime minister, nominates the heads of all public media outlets for approval by a Fidesz-dominated board of trustees. Despite minor amendments to the legislation made in March 2011 and again, following a December 2011 Constitutional Court ruling, in May 2012, international press freedom organizations insist that the laws do not adequately protect media independence. European Commission vice president Neelie Kroes stated in June that the May amendments had addressed only 11 of 66 recommendations made by the Council of Europe.

While foreign ownership of Hungarian media is extensive, domestic ownership is highly concentrated in the hands of Fidesz allies. The government is the country's largest advertiser and has withdrawn most advertising from independent media since the 2010 elections. There is anecdotal evidence that private companies withhold advertising from independent media to avoid losing government contracts. In 2011, Jobbik cofounder Dániel Papp was named as editor in chief of the news office at the MTVA media fund, which is responsible for the management of all public media. Extensive layoffs followed. Klubradio, a radio station that is critical of the Fidesz government, continued in 2012 to wage a legal battle against the Media Council, which prevented it from renewing its broadcasting license for five frequencies after the license expired in early 2011. Several courts ruled in favor of the station in 2012, but it had yet to regain control of its main frequency at year's end.

The constitution guarantees religious freedom and provides for the separation of church and state. Adherents of all religions are generally free to worship. However, hundreds of religious organizations lost their registered status and budgetary allocations for social and charitable services in January 2012 in connection with a law adopted the previous year, which shifted the power to recognize religious denominations from the courts to the parliament. Many religious groups' attempts to reregister were refused without explanation in 2012. Deregistered groups were stripped of legal standing and told to apply for recognition as associations. However, the vast majority of Hungarian believers belong to one of the 32 religious organizations automatically recognized under the law.

Anti-Semitism remains a problem, particularly among far-right groups. The government has honored fascist historical figures, though it condemned verbal and physical attacks on two local Jewish leaders in June and October 2012. In July, a member of the European Parliament for Jobbik, Csanád Szegedi, was asked by the party to resign following the disclosure of his Jewish ancestry. Jobbik claimed he was being penalized not for being Jewish, but for attempting to suppress the disclosure through bribery.

The state generally does not restrict academic freedom.

The constitution provides for freedoms of assembly and association, and the government generally respects these rights in practice. Nongovernmental organizations operate without restrictions. The government recognizes workers' rights to form associations, strike, and petition public authorities. Trade unions represent less than 30 percent of the workforce.

The independence of the judiciary came under scrutiny in 2011 and 2012 following the adoption of a reform package granting extensive administrative powers to the National Judicial Office (OBH), a new body whose leader is elected by a two-thirds parliamentary majority for a nine-year term. The OBH head's discretionary powers include the appointment of the presidents of local and higher-level courts. In July 2012, the parliament amended some controversial elements of these laws, transferring the authority to use extraordinary fast-track procedures in cases of "public interest" from the OBH to the National Council of Judges (OBT), which is elected by a committee of judges. The OBH may no longer switch cases between courts or propose amendments to the law governing the judicial system without OBT approval. The head of the OBH will now serve a single term rather than being automatically extended in office until the election of a successor. A legal provision reducing the mandatory retirement age of judges, prosecutors, and notaries from 70 to 62—seen by critics as a way for the government to purge the judiciary and stack it with supporters—was also annulled in July after being struck down by the Constitutional Court. However, the over 200 judges who had already been forced into retirement were not automatically reinstated. Many filed lawsuits over their "unlawful" removal, most of which were still pending at year's end. The Constitutional Court's December 28, 2012, decision on "temporary provisions" invalidated not only electoral legislation, but the inclusion in the constitution's preamble of language on crimes of the Communist period, the right to fast-track cases, the law on churches, and the possibility of levying a tax in case of decisions by the EU, Constitutional Court, or other governing bodies that might pose a significant burden on the budget.

Prisons are generally approaching Western European standards, though overcrowding, inadequate medical care, and poor sanitation remain problems. Inmates do not have access to independent medical staff to assess abuse allegations. The 2011 constitution introduced the possibility of life sentences without parole, prompting human rights groups to argue that such sentences would conflict with the International Covenant on Civil and Political Rights.

Hungary has taken a number of steps to improve monitoring of Romany legal rights and treatment, but Roma, who form Hungary's largest ethnic minority, still face widespread discrimination. Romany students continue to be segregated and improperly placed in schools for children with mental disabilities. In August 2012, violence broke out at two anti-Roma marches organized by far-right groups. Although Fidesz generally distances itself from anti-Semitic statements, it is less vocal in its condemnation of anti-Roma behavior. In November 2012, the Constitutional Court struck down a 2011 law that prescribed fines for homeless people living in public areas.

Women possess the same legal rights as men, but they face hiring discrimination and tend to be underrepresented in high-level business and government positions. Women hold only 35 of 386 seats in the National Assembly. The right to life from conception is protected under the 2011 constitution, but access to abortions remained largely unrestricted in 2012.

Hungary is a transit point, source, and destination for trafficked persons, including women trafficked for prostitution. Same-sex couples can legally register their domestic partnerships. However, the 2011 constitution enshrines the concept of marriage as a union between man and woman and fails to directly prohibit discrimination based on sexual orientation. In April 2012, Jobbik proposed legislation that would make "promotion of sexual deviations" punishable by up to eight years in prison, but the bill did not advance past the committee phase in May. On December 17, the Constitutional Court annulled provisions of the 2011 family protection law that defined family as the marriage and offspring, biological or adopted, of one man and one woman. The same day, Hungary's parliament amended the country's Civil Code, removing references to domestic partnerships (whether same-sex or opposite-sex) except in the context of division of property and the right to demand spousal support after the dissolution of the partnership. A separate law on same-sex partnerships remained in effect at year's end.

Iceland

Political Rights: 1
Civil Liberties: 1
Status: Free

Population: 320,100
Capital: Reykjavik

Ten-Year Ratings Timeline For Year Under Review (Political Rights, Civil Liberties, Status)

2003	2004	2005	2006	2007	2008	2009	2010	2011	2012
1,1F	1,1F	1,1F	1,1F	1,1F	1,1F	1,1F	1,1F	1,1F	1,1F

Overview: Ólafur Ragnar Grímsson won an unprecedented fifth term in the June 2012 presidential election. The Social Democratic Alliance government lost its majority in June, when one of its members joined the newly formed Bright Future party. Meanwhile, voters in October approved a nonbinding referendum on a new constitution.

After gaining independence from Denmark in 1944, Iceland became a founding member of NATO in 1949, despite having no standing army. The country declared itself a nuclear-free zone in 1985. The center-right Independence Party (IP) has traditionally been a dominant force in Icelandic politics.

In the May 2007 parliamentary elections, the IP took 25 seats and formed a coalition with the center-left Social Democratic Alliance (SDA), which captured 18 seats. The IP's Geir Haarde returned as prime minister. A major credit crisis forced the government to nationalize three large banks in 2008, resulting in widespread protests and Haarde's resignation on January 26, 2009.

In February 2009, Jóhanna Sigurðardóttir of the SDA was named interim prime minister. Her center-left coalition, consisting of the SDA and the Left-Green Movement, captured 34 of 63 seats in early parliamentary elections in April 2009, marking the first time leftist parties held a majority in Iceland. The elections also resulted in the highest number of first-time members and the largest percentage of women in parliament in Iceland's history.

While the majority of Icelanders remain opposed to European Union (EU) membership, the country opened EU accession negotiations in July 2009. Negotiations were ongoing at the end of 2012.

The anti-establishment Best Party, led by comedian Jón Gnarr, rode a wave of protest votes to capture 6 of the 15 seats in the May 2010 Reykjavik City Council election, making Gnarr mayor of the Icelandic capital.

In April 2011, voters defeated a referendum on a repayment plan for British and Dutch depositors at Icesave, an online savings account brand owned and operated by the private Landsbanki, which collapsed in 2008. Landsbanki announced that a sale of its assets should fully cover repayment to all British and Dutch depositors; the sale of assets was ongoing at the end of 2012. In 2011, a case was brought before the court of the European Free Trade Association (EFTA) by EFTA's Surveillance Authority, arguing that Iceland failed to live up to its legal obligation to provide adequate compensation to the British and Dutch depositors. The case was pending at the end of 2012.

Ólafur Ragnar Grímsson won the presidential election and his fifth term in July 2012, defeating independent journalist Thóra Arnórsdóttir.

The government lost its majority in October 2012, when Robert Marshall left the SDA to join the newly formed Bright Future party. Marshall vowed to continue to support the government until the next general election in April 2013. Also in October, a referendum on a new draft constitution was put to a nonbinding referendum. Voters approved all six proposals, including one that natural resources not currently privately owned be designated national property, another allowing a certain percentage of the electorate to put issues to a referendum, and a suggestion to establish a national church. The draft must go through further steps, including approval through another referendum, before its adoption by the parliament after the April 2013 legislative elections.

Political Rights and Civil Liberties: Iceland is an electoral democracy. The constitution, adopted in 1944, vests power in a president, a prime minister, the 63-seat unicameral legislature (the Althingi), and a judiciary. The Althingi is arguably the world's oldest parliament, established in approximately AD 930. The largely ceremonial president is directly elected for a four-year term. The legislature is also elected for four years, but can be dissolved for early elections in certain circumstances. The prime minister is appointed by the president.

The center-right IP dominated politics until 2009, when Jóhanna Sigurðardóttir's center-left coalition took power. Six major political parties and several smaller parties are represented in the Althingi.

While corruption is not a serious problem in Iceland, the country has experienced politically tinged business-fraud scandals in recent years. In 2010, Steinunn Valdís Óskarsdóttir of the SDA stepped down after it was revealed that she had accepted large corporate donations for her 2006 campaign. A number of bankers—including former director of Kaupthing Iceland, Ingólfur Helgason—were arrested in 2010 in connection with the 2008 Icesave banking crash. Several members of parliament were also implicated in the crash, including former prime minister Geir Haarde, who faced charges of negligence in the wake of the financial crisis. He was found guilty on one count in April 2012 but was not sentenced to any punishment. Iceland was ranked 11 out of 176 countries surveyed in Transparency International's 2012 Corruption Perceptions Index.

The constitution guarantees freedoms of speech and the press. In June 2010, parliament unanimously passed the Icelandic Modern Media Initiative, which mandates the establishment of stringent free speech and press freedom laws and focuses on the protection of investigative journalists and media outlets. Iceland's wide range of print publications includes both independent and party-affiliated newspapers. The autonomous Icelandic National Broadcasting Service competes with private radio and television stations. Private media ownership is concentrated, with the Norðurljós (Northern Lights) Corporation controlling most of the private television and radio outlets and two of the three national newspapers. Internet access is unrestricted.

The constitution provides for freedom of religion. Almost 90 percent of Icelanders belong to the Evangelical Lutheran Church. The state supports the church through a special tax, which citizens can choose to direct to the University of Iceland instead. A 2008 law requires the teaching of theology in grades 1 through 10. Academic freedom is respected, and the education system is free of excessive political involvement.

Freedoms of association and peaceful assembly are generally upheld. Peaceful protests occurred in September and October 2011 against IMF austerity measures and the government's failure to protect Icelanders from housing foreclosures. Many nongovernmental organizations operate freely and enjoy extensive government cooperation. The labor movement is robust, with more than 80 percent of all eligible workers belonging to unions. All unions have the right to strike.

The judiciary is independent. The law does not provide for trial by jury, but many trials and appeals use panels of several judges. The constitution states that all people shall be treated equally before the law, regardless of sex, religion, ethnic origin, race, or other status. Prison conditions generally meet international standards. The Act on Foreigners was amended in 2004 to allow home searches without warrants in cases of suspected immigration fraud, among other changes. Foreigners can vote in municipal elections if they have been residents for at least five years, or three years for citizens of Scandinavian countries. In September 2010, a father and son of Cuban origin who had held Icelandic citizenship for more than a decade fled the country after intense racially motivated intimidation. Approximately 1,000 people gathered for an anti-racism rally in the same month in response to threats received by the family.

Women enjoy equal rights, and more than 80 percent of women participate in the workforce. However, a pay gap exists between men and women despite laws designed to prevent disparities. In 2009, Sigurðardóttir became Iceland's first female prime minister and the world's first openly lesbian head of government. Iceland topped the World Economic Forum's 2012 ratings on gender equality. A committee was appointed in 2008 to develop new strategies to combat human trafficking in Iceland, and parliament passed a law criminalizing human trafficking in 2009.

India

Political Rights: 2
Civil Liberties: 3
Status: Free

Population: 1,259,721,000
Capital: New Delhi

Note: The numerical ratings and status listed above do not reflect conditions in Indian-controlled Kashmir, which is examined in a separate report.

Ten-Year Ratings Timeline For Year Under Review (Political Rights, Civil Liberties, Status)

2003	2004	2005	2006	2007	2008	2009	2010	2011	2012
2,3F	2,3F	2,3F	2,3F	2,3F	2,3F	2,3F	2,3F	2,3F	2,3F

Overview: The government faced significant political and societal opposition in 2012 as it sought to implement economic and fiscal reforms. While reported fatalities associated with the country's Maoist insurgency continued to decline, an outbreak of ethnic violence in the northeastern state of Assam caused dozens of deaths and mass displacement of civilians. Separately, high-profile cases of violence against women, including the fatal gang rape of a woman on a Delhi bus in December, triggered protests and public debate about legal protections for women and the effectiveness of Indian policing in general.

India achieved independence from Britain in 1947. The secular Congress Party ruled at the federal level for nearly all of the first 50 years of independence, but the Hindu nationalist Bharatiya Janata Party (BJP) became a major factor in Parliament in the 1990s and led a governing coalition from 1998 to 2004. The 1990s also featured significant economic reforms, with a Congress government initiating a move toward market-oriented policies following a balance-of-payments crisis in 1991. Meanwhile, a pattern of single-party governments gave way to ruling coalitions involving large numbers of parties. The change stemmed in part from the rise of new parties that held power and legislative seats in a single state or region.

After recapturing power from the BJP in the 2004 national elections, the Congress Party formed a ruling coalition with regional parties, and Congress leader Sonia Gandhi handed the premiership to former finance minister Manmohan Singh. The new Congress-led United Progressive Alliance (UPA) government reversed several of its predecessor's policies, including controversial antiterrorism legislation and the introduction of Hindu nationalism into school curriculums. However, the UPA suffered internal pressures from leftist allies over economic issues, such as privatization. The government survived a contentious July 2008 confidence vote in Parliament triggered by leftist objections to a nuclear pact with the United States, though the vote was marred by bribery allegations.

The UPA gained strength in the April–May 2009 parliamentary elections, decisively defeating the BJP-led National Democratic Alliance, its closest rival. Congress itself won 206 of 543 lower-house seats, and the UPA won 260 seats overall. The UPA also made alliances with independent parties that gave it a significant majority, leading to a more stable government.

However, a recent wave of high-profile scandals implicated several politicians and bureaucrats in corruption related to government contracts. Malfeasance in the awarding of telecommunications licenses and coal mine contracts was alleged to have caused public losses of up to $33 billion and $35 billion, respectively, and prompted the February 2011 arrest of former telecommunications minister Andimuthu Raja. An anticorruption movement spearheaded that year by political and social activist Anna Hazare, backed by large street demonstrations in all major cities, was aimed at compelling Parliament to accept changes to pending legislation that would empower a Jan Lokpal, or Citizens' Ombudsman, to investigate and prosecute government corruption. A version of the bill was passed by the lower house of Parliament in December 2011, but had yet to be passed by the upper house at the end of 2012.

In 2012, in an effort to decrease fiscal deficits and stave off a potential downgrade from credit rating agencies, the UPA government undertook a set of controversial economic reforms, including reducing subsidies for diesel and cooking gas. This led to mass protests across India and the withdrawal of one partner from the governing coalition. Protests and political controversy also followed efforts by the government to permit multinational chains such as Walmart to enter the Indian retail market.

In July, violence erupted between the tribal Bodo population and the Bengali-speaking Muslim population in the northeastern state of Assam, leading to the displacement of up to half a million people. Fears of violence between Muslims and migrants from northeastern India spread to cities elsewhere in India, causing many migrants to flee. Online media and text messages played a prominent role is stoking these fears and disseminating threats.

Political Rights and Civil Liberties: India is an electoral democracy. Members of the lower house of Parliament, the 545-seat Lok Sabha (House of the People), are directly elected for five-year terms (except for two appointed members representing Indians of European descent). The Lok Sabha determines the leadership and composition of the government. Most members of the less powerful 250-seat upper house, the Rajya Sabha (Council of States), are elected by the state legislatures using a proportional representation system to serve staggered six-year terms; up to 12 members are appointed. Executive power is vested in a prime minister and cabinet. The president, who plays a largely symbolic role but possesses some important powers, is chosen for a five-year term by state and national lawmakers. In July 2012, former finance minister and senior Congress Party leader Pranab Mukherjee was selected as the 13th president of India.

Under the supervision of the Election Commission of India (ECI), elections have generally been free and fair. The 2009 national polls were mostly peaceful, though Maoist militant attacks in parts of the country led to 17 deaths during the first phase of voting. Electronic voting machines, also used in 2004, helped reduce election day irregularities. Violence declined during state-level elections in 2009 and 2010. Goa, Gujarat, Himachal Pradesh, Manipur, Punjab, Uttar Pradesh, and Uttarakhand each held assembly elections in 2012. In Uttar Pradesh, the largest state in India with approximately 200 million people, the incumbent Bahujan Samaj Party (BSP), which is dedicated to the advancement of India's Dalit communities, was defeated by the Samajwadi Party, which draws strength from Muslims and other disadvantaged groups. The declared assets of BSP leader Mayawati increased from approximately $180,000 to over $20 million from 2003 to 2012, raising suspicions of corruption. However, a case filed against Mayawati by the Central Bureau of Investigation (CBI) was quashed by the Supreme Court during the year.

Recent attempts to address political corruption, through legislation and activism, have been driven by domestic and international pressure to counter the negative effects of graft on government efficiency and economic performance. India was ranked 94 out of 176 countries surveyed in Transparency International's 2012 Corruption Perceptions Index. Though politicians and civil servants are regularly caught accepting bribes or engaging in other corrupt behavior, a great deal of corruption goes unnoticed and unpunished. The federal government has introduced a number of initiatives to tackle the problem, such as the 2005 Right to Information Act, which is widely used to improve transparency and expose corrupt activities. While this legislation has had clear positive effects, over a dozen right to information activists have reportedly been killed since late 2009.

The private media are vigorous and diverse. Investigations and scrutiny of politicians make the news media one of the most important components of India's democracy. Nevertheless, revelations of close relationships between politicians, business executives, lobbyists, and some leading media personalities have dented public confidence in the press in recent years. While radio remains dominated by the state and private radio stations are not allowed to air news content, the television and print sectors have expanded considerably over the past decade, with many of the new outlets targeting specific regional or linguistic audiences.

Despite this vibrant media landscape, journalists continue to face a number of constraints. The government has used security laws, criminal defamation legislation, hate-speech laws, and contempt of court charges to curb critical voices. In September 2012, cartoonist Aseem Trivedi was arrested in Mumbai on charges of sedition for a set of cartoons that lampooned government corruption, though the charges were dropped in October. In November, two women were arrested for expressing dissent on the social-networking site Facebook regarding public mourning after the death of a prominent politician in Maharashtra

Internet access is largely unrestricted, although some states have passed legislation that requires internet cafés to register with the state government and maintain user registries. Under Indian internet crime law, the burden is on website operators to demonstrate their innocence. Potentially inflammatory books, films, and internet sites are occasionally banned or censored.

Freedom of religion is constitutionally guaranteed in India and is generally respected. However, legislation in several states criminalizes religious conversions that take place as a result of "force" or "allurement." Hindus make up over 80 percent of the population, but the state is secular. An array of Hindu nationalist organizations and some local media outlets promote antiminority views.

Academic freedom is generally robust, though intimidation of professors and institutions over political and religious issues sometimes occurs. Scholars and activists accused of sympathizing with Maoist insurgents have faced increased pressure from authorities and alleged torture by police.

There are some restrictions on freedoms of assembly and association. Section 144 of the criminal procedure code empowers the authorities to restrict free assembly and impose curfews whenever "immediate prevention or speedy remedy" is required. State laws based on this standard are often abused to limit the holding of meetings and assemblies. Nevertheless, protest events take place regularly in practice. The peaceful demonstrations associated with anticorruption activist Anna Hazare drew tens of thousands of people into the streets during 2011, and the movement continued in 2012.

Human rights organizations operate freely, but continue to face threats, legal harassment, excessive police force, and occasionally lethal violence. While India is home to a strong civil society sector and academic community, foreign monitors are occasionally denied visas to conduct research trips in the country on human rights and other topics. Under certain circumstances, the Foreign Contributions (Regulation) Act permits the federal government to deny nongovernmental organizations access to foreign funding. The government has been accused of abusing this power to target political opponents.

While workers in the formal economy regularly exercise their rights to bargain collectively and strike, the Essential Services Maintenance Act has enabled the government to ban certain strikes. Article 23 of the constitution bans human trafficking, and bonded labor is illegal, but the practice is fairly common across the country. Estimates of the number of affected workers range from 20 to 50 million. Children are also banned from working in potentially hazardous industries, though in practice the law is routinely flouted.

The judiciary is independent of the executive branch. Judges have displayed considerable activism in response to public-interest litigation matters. However, in recent years some judges have initiated contempt of court cases against activists and journalists who expose judicial corruption or question verdicts. Contempt of court laws were reformed in 2006 to make truth a defense with respect to allegations against judges, provided the information is in the public and national interest. The lower levels of the judiciary in particular have been rife with corruption, and most citizens have great difficulty securing justice through the courts. The system is severely backlogged and understaffed, with an estimated 32 million cases pending in lower courts and 56,000 at the Supreme Court. This leads to lengthy pretrial detention for a large number of suspects, many of whom remain in jail beyond the duration of any sentence they might receive if convicted. According the National Crime Records Bureau, nearly 65 percent of prisoners were awaiting trial or on trial at the end of 2011, with more than 9,000 awaiting trial for more than three years. The creation of various fast-track courts to clear the backlog has prompted charges that due process is being denied in some instances.

The criminal justice system fails to provide equal protection to marginalized groups. Muslims, who make up some 13 percent of the population, are underrepresented in the security forces as well as in the foreign and intelligence services. Particularly in rural India, informal councils often issue edicts concerning social customs. While these bodies play a role in relieving the overburdened official courts, their decisions sometimes result in violence or persecution aimed at those perceived to have transgressed social norms, especially women and members of the lower castes.

Police torture, abuse, and corruption are entrenched in the law enforcement system. The police also suffer from understaffing in relation to the size of the population. Citizens frequently face substantial obstacles, including demands for bribes, in getting the police to file a First Information Report, which is necessary to trigger an investigation of an alleged crime. Custodial rape of female detainees continues to be a problem, as does routine abuse of ordinary prisoners, particularly minorities and members of the lower castes. According to the Working Group on Human Rights in India and the United Nations, 14,231 people died in police custody between 2001 and 2010, and approximately 1.8 million people are victims of police torture every year. This is likely an underestimate, since it only includes cases registered with the National Human Rights Commission (NHRC).

The NHRC is headed by a retired Supreme Court judge and handles roughly 8,000 complaints each year. While it monitors abuses, initiates investigations, makes independent assessments, and conducts training sessions for the police and others, its recommendations are often not implemented, and it has few enforcement powers. The commission also lacks jurisdiction over the armed forces, one of the principal agents of abuse in several parts of the country, further hampering its effectiveness. The NHRC nevertheless makes a substantial contribution to accountability by submitting reports to international bodies such as the UN Human Rights Council, often contradicting the government's account of its performance.

Security forces operating in the context of regional insurgencies continue to be implicated in extrajudicial killings, rape, torture, arbitrary detention, kidnappings, and destruction of homes. The criminal procedure code requires the government to approve the prosecution of security force members, but approval is rarely granted, leading to impunity. The Armed Forces Special Powers Act (AFSPA) grants security forces broad authority to arrest, detain, and use force against suspects in restive areas; civil society organizations and multiple UN human rights bodies have called for the act to be repealed. An activist in the "disturbed area" of Manipur, Irom Sharmila Chanu, has been on a hunger strike for 11 years to demand the revocation of the AFSPA but has faced continual arrests and force-feeding by the authorities. A number of other security laws allow detention without charge or based on vaguely worded offenses.

The Maoist insurgency in several parts of India has been of serious concern to the government. There were 367 Maoist-related deaths across nine states in 2012, according to the South Asia Terrorism Portal (SATP), though that represented a sharp decline from the previous year's 602 deaths and the 1,180 that occurred in 2010. Among other abuses, the rebels have allegedly imposed illegal taxes, seized food and shelter, and engaged in abduction and forced recruitment of children and adults. Local civilians who are perceived to be progovernment have been targeted by the Maoists. Tens of thousands of civilians have been displaced by the violence and live in government-run camps.

Separately, in India's seven northeastern states, more than 40 insurgent factions—seeking either greater autonomy or complete independence for their ethnic or tribal groups—attack security forces and engage in intertribal violence. Such fighters have been implicated in numerous bombings, killings, abductions, and rapes of civilians, and they operate extensive extortion networks. More than 40 people were killed in the July 2012 ethnic violence in Assam, where members of the indigenous Bodo community targeted Muslims who were seen as illegal migrants from Bangladesh. The number of killings of civilians, security personnel, and militants in the northeastern insurgencies increased to 317 in 2012 from 246 in 2011, according to the SATP. These levels represent a substantial reduction compared with the more than 1,000 people killed in 2007 and 2008, and the 852 killed in 2009.

The constitution bars discrimination based on caste, and laws set aside quotas in education and government jobs for the so-called scheduled tribes, scheduled castes (Dalits), and other backward classes. Women and religious and ethnic minorities are represented in government; as of 2012, the vice president was a Muslim, the prime minister was a Sikh, and the Speaker of the Lok Sabha was a Dalit woman. A number of states were headed by female chief ministers. However, members of the lower castes and minorities continue to face routine discrimination and violence. Dalits are often denied access to land and other public amenities, abused by landlords and police, and forced to work in miserable conditions. Indian Muslims are disproportionately more likely to be poor and illiterate, with less access to government employment, medical care, or loans.

Property rights are somewhat tenuous for tribal groups and other marginalized communities, and members of these groups are often denied adequate resettlement opportunities and compensation when their lands are seized for development projects. While many states have laws to prevent land transfers to nontribal groups, the practice is reportedly widespread. In 2011, the federal government introduced the Land Acquisition, Rehabilitation, and Resettlement Bill, which was still pending in Parliament at the end of 2012. If enacted, it would provide increased rights to people threatened with displacement for industrial and infrastructure projects.

Rape, harassment, and other transgressions against women are serious problems, and lower-caste and tribal women are particularly vulnerable. In July 2012, a mob of at least 18 men stripped and molested a woman leaving a bar in Assam. The incident was caught on camera and caused a national uproar. The fatal gang rape of a woman on a Delhi bus in December led to another public outcry, mass demonstrations, and major international attention. The government responded by proposing significant legal reforms. Despite the criminalization of dowry demands and hundreds of convictions each year, the practice continues. According to a recent National Health Survey, on average, one in three married women between ages 15 and 49 has experienced physical violence. A 2006 law banned dowry-related harassment, widened the definition of domestic violence to include emotional or verbal abuse, and criminalized spousal rape. However, reports indicate that enforcement is poor. The National Crime Records Bureau reports that about 6,000 females are killed every year for dowry-related issues alone.

Muslim personal laws and traditional Hindu practices discriminate against women in terms of inheritance, adoption, and property rights. The malign neglect of female children after birth remains a concern, as does the banned but growing use of prenatal sex-determination tests to selectively abort female fetuses.

A landmark court decision in 2009 struck down Section 377 of the Indian penal code, which criminalized homosexual behavior. However, an appeal of the ruling was pending at the Supreme Court at the end of 2012, and widespread discrimination continues. At a May 2011 conference on HIV/AIDS, the health minister referred to homosexuality as "unnatural" and a "disease," adding to the difficulties faced by activists combating harmful social stigmas regarding both issues.

Indonesia

Political Rights: 2
Civil Liberties: 3
Status: Free

Population: 240,989,500
Capital: Jakarta

Ten-Year Ratings Timeline For Year Under Review (Political Rights, Civil Liberties, Status)

2003	2004	2005	2006	2007	2008	2009	2010	2011	2012
3,4PF	3,4PF	2,3F	2,3F	2,3PF	2,3F	2,3F	2,3F	2,3F	2,3F

Overview: Although Indonesian authorities made progress in combating terrorism in 2012, they were increasingly criticized for inaction in the face of continued religious intolerance and violence, including an August mob attack on a Shiite community in Sampang. In another incident, a mob in Yogyakarta attacked the book launch of a Canadian author known for her support of gay rights. Also during the year, two individuals were found guilty of blasphemy in separate trials and sentenced to prison. A new election law passed in April raised the vote threshold for party representation in the parliament, to take effect in the 2014 national elections.

Indonesia declared independence from its Dutch colonial rulers in 1945, though the Netherlands did not recognize its sovereignty until 1949. The republic's first president, Sukarno, assumed authoritarian powers in 1957. The army, led by General Suharto, crushed an apparent Communist Party of Indonesia (PKI) coup attempt in 1965. Mass acts of violence followed, ostensibly against suspected PKI members, resulting in an estimated 500,000 deaths. With military backing, Suharto formally became president in 1968.

Suharto's regime created Golkar, a progovernment party based on bureaucratic and military interests, and embarked on a development program that helped the economy grow by an annual average of 7 percent for three decades. By the 1990s, Suharto's children and cronies were the major beneficiaries of state privatization schemes and in many cases ran business monopolies with little oversight. Soaring inflation and unemployment following the Asian financial crisis of 1997 prompted urban riots in 1998, and Suharto was forced to resign. He was succeeded by then vice president B. J. Habibie, who removed legal constraints on the press, labor unions, and political parties. The province of East Timor voted to separate from Indonesia in a 1999 referendum and gained independence in 2002.

Also in 1999, Indonesia held its first free legislative elections since 1955. The Indonesian Democratic Party–Struggle (PDI-P), led by Sukarno's daughter, Megawati Sukarnoputri, won the largest number of seats, followed by Golkar. The People's Consultative Assembly, made up of elected lawmakers and appointed officials, chose Muslim leader Abdurrahman Wahid as president and Megawati as vice president that year, but Megawati rose to the presidency in 2001, after Wahid was impeached over corruption allegations. Support for the PDI-P dropped in the 2004 legislative elections, and Golkar once again became the largest party. Later that year, Susilo Bambang Yudhoyono (SBY) of the new Democratic Party and his running mate, Jusuf Kalla of Golkar, won the presidency and vice presidency in the country's first direct presidential election.

The Democratic Party won the April 2009 parliamentary elections, raising its share of seats to 148, from 55 in 2004. Golkar garnered 106 seats, and the PDI-P took 94. Religious parties generally fared poorly, though the Prosperous Justice Party (PKS), with its strong anticorruption platform, captured 57 seats. SBY easily secured a second five-year term in the July presidential election, defeating Megawati and Kalla with 61 percent of the vote in the first round. SBY's new running mate, former central bank governor Boediono, became vice president.

Public awareness of the extent of corruption in the legal system and attempts to weaken anticorruption efforts grew in 2010, and corruption allegations against members of the Democratic Party continued to undermine SBY's reformist credentials during 2011 and 2012. In a key verdict in April 2012, party treasurer Muhammad Nazaruddin was convicted of bribery and sentenced to 4 years and 10 months in prison in a case related to preparations for the 2012 Southeast Asian Games in South Sumatra. Nazaruddin claimed to have provided illicit funds to support the election of Anas Urbaningrum as Democratic Party chairman at the 2010 party congress, but the court dismissed those allegations. In December, cabinet member Andi Mallarangang resigned after being named a suspect in a corruption case involving a sports complex in Bogor, West Java. Additional cases against Democratic Party officials were pending at year's end.

A multiyear pattern of violence against religious minorities continued in 2012. In July, a mob attacked a community of the Ahmadiyya sect in Bogor, West Java, and in October, vandals damaged an Ahmadi mosque. A Shiite Muslim community in Sampang was attacked by a mob in August, resulting in two deaths. As in past instances of communal violence or intolerance, senior officials, such as the national police chief and the minister for religious affairs, called for the relocation of the minority residents.

Also in keeping with previous years, the authorities uncovered and foiled several terrorist attacks in 2012. In October, officials thwarted a coordinated attack on the U.S. and Australian embassies in Jakarta, the U.S. consulate in Surabaya, and the offices of the mining company Freeport by a new group called the Sunni Movement for Indonesian Society (HASMI). Nearly a dozen suspects were arrested. Several attacks and foiled bombing attempts in Poso between August and November resulted in the deaths of two police officers and two suspected militants, at least six arrests, and the seizure of firearms and explosives. The suspected mastermind had reported links to the Indonesian terrorist group Jemaah Islamiyah (JI). Meanwhile, several people were convicted and jailed for past attacks, including Umar Patek, the last defendant in the case of a bombing that killed 202 people in Bali in 2002. He was sentenced to 20 years in prison for his role in the construction of the car bomb.

In the eastern province of Papua, where the central government's exploitation of natural resources has stirred resentment and separatist sentiment, members of the security forces continued to enjoy relative impunity for abuses against civilians. An August 2012 report by the International Crisis Group warned of escalating violence linked to resource wealth and associated rent-seeking, as well as deep distrust between security forces and local communities. In addition, delays to provincial elections and the weakness of an appointed caretaker government resulted in a lack of communication among Papuans, their representative institutions, and the central government. Corruption has undermined the central government's efforts to improve economic conditions in Papua. Special autonomy status had been introduced in 2001 to undercut separatist agitation and a low-grade insurgency dating to the early 1950s. It provided for increased economic but not political autonomy. In March, five men charged with treason were convicted for "subversion" by the Jayapura District Court for their role in the 2011 Papuan People's Congress.

In Aceh, where a devastating tsunami in 2004 paved the way for a 2005 peace agreement between the central government and the Free Aceh Movement (GAM) after almost 30 years of violent conflict, former GAM foreign minister Zaini Abdullah was elected governor in April 2012 in the region's second elections since the peace accord. Although election day was relatively calm, the preelection period was marred by intimidation and violence—apparently between rival factions of the former rebel movement—that killed at least seven people.

Separately, in a historic move in July, the National Commission on Human Rights released reports concluding that government agencies were guilty of gross human rights violations related to execution-style killings between 1982 and 1985 as well as the army-led campaign against alleged communists in the 1960s.

Political Rights and Civil Liberties: Indonesia is an electoral democracy. In 2004, for the first time, Indonesians directly elected their president and all members of the House of Representatives (DPR), as well as members of a new legislative body, the largely advisory House of Regional Representatives (DPD). Previously, presidents had been elected by the People's Consultative Assembly (MPR), then made up of elected lawmakers and appointed officials. The MPR now performs tasks involving the swearing in and dismissal of presidents and the amendment of the constitution, and consists of elected DPR and DPD members. The DPR, with 560 seats, is the main parliamentary chamber. The 132-member DPD is responsible for proposing and monitoring laws related to regional autonomy. Presidents and vice presidents can serve up to two five-year terms, and all legislators also serve five-year terms.

Parties or coalitions must attain 25 percent of the popular vote or 20 percent of the seats in the DPR to nominate candidates for president. Voters for the DPR can select either a party list or an individual candidate, but candidates are seated based on the number of direct votes they receive. The changes, introduced in 2008, were designed to increase lawmakers' accountability to voters and reduce the power of party bosses. The 2009 elections yielded a significant turnover in the DPR's membership, with approximately 75 percent of the chamber consisting of new lawmakers. In April 2012, the DPR passed an amended election law that increased the vote threshold for parties to enter the parliament from 2.5 percent to 3.5 percent, making it more difficult for small parties to win seats in the upcoming 2014 elections.

Direct elections for provincial leaders began in 2005. Combined with the decentralization of political and fiscal power to the district and subdistrict levels in 1999, these direct elections have often led to tensions between the central government and local authorities, with the latter at times ignoring court or central government rulings. Under a law passed in August 2012, the hereditary sultan of Yogyakarta will be that region's unelected governor; the position will become nonpartisan and the sultan will be subject to a verification process with minimum requirements—such as education—every five years beginning in 2016. The prince of Paku Alaman will similarly be deputy governor of the region. The central government had pressed unsuccessfully for the posts to become directly elected, as in ordinary provinces; the hereditary sultan of Yogyakarta and prince of Paku Alam have been occupying the positions of governor and vice governor since 1945, and the region avoided direct elections that were introduced in all other provinces.

Corruption remains endemic, including in the parliament and other key institutions. Indonesia was ranked 118 out of 176 countries surveyed in Transparency International's 2012 Corruption Perceptions Index. The KPK's success in a series of high-profile cases has raised public expectations that acts of corruption, even by senior officials, will be punished. In March 2012, former tax officer Gayus Tambunan received another six-year sentence in his fourth conviction, bringing his total sentence to 28 years for offenses ranging from bribery to money laundering. In May, Nunun Nurbaeti, the wife of a parliament member, was sentenced to two and a half years in prison for her role in bribery surrounding the 2004 election of Miranda Goeltom as deputy governor of the central bank. In September, Miranda herself was convicted and sentenced to three years in prison.

However, a 2009 anticorruption law diluted the authority and independence of both the KPK and the Anticorruption Court (Tipikor), allowing the creation of regional corruption courts. In August 2012, two Tipikor judges were arrested for bribery, and a September report by Indonesia Corruption Watch (ICW) found irregularities with at least 84 judges in the 14 regional courts. Moreover, ICW noted that over 70 graft suspects tried in the regional courts were found not guilty for lack of evidence. Before the regional corruption courts were opened, the KPK had a 100 percent conviction rate. Tipikor had been established partly to counteract the acquittals commonly issued in regular courts. Even those who are convicted often receive light sentences or benefit from mass pardons.

A long-running conflict between the KPK and the national police erupted again in 2012, sparked by a KPK investigation into a contract for driving simulators that implicated Inspector General Djoko Susilo. An October KPK raid on the police's traffic division resulted in a standoff that ended only after the KPK agreed to allow the police to run a parallel internal investigation, though President Susilo Bambang Yudhoyono (SBY) recommended that the KPK be given exclusive responsibility over the case. Djoko was officially named a KPK suspect after the raid, and soon thereafter, the police withdrew 20 investigators who had been assigned to the KPK, some for several years, to assist in investigations. Five refused to report to the police headquarters, and one, Novel Baswedan, was arrested on murder charges stemming from a case that was closed in 2004. The national police filed a lawsuit against the KPK for seizing documents unrelated to the simulator matter during the October raid. All three cases were pending at year's end.

Indonesia hosts a vibrant and diverse media environment, though press freedom is hampered by a number of legal and regulatory restrictions. Strict but unevenly enforced licensing rules mean that thousands of television and radio stations operate illegally. Foreign journalists are not authorized to travel to the restive provinces of Papua and West Papua without special permission. Reporters often practice self-censorship to avoid running afoul of civil and criminal libel laws.

In addition to legal obstacles, reporters sometimes face violence and intimidation, which in many cases goes unpunished. The Alliance of Independent Journalists recorded 56 cases of violence against journalists in 2012, in addition to 12 separate incidents against journalists in Papua. In January 2012, the Supreme Court reversed the 2011 acquittal of three men in the killing of journalist Ridwan Salamun in 2010. However, the convicted men escaped due to prosecutors' failure to act promptly on the new ruling. In October, five journalists were allegedly attacked by soldiers while covering a plane crash; a video recording of the incident was posted on the video-sharing website YouTube.

Freedom of expression is generally upheld, though censorship and self-censorship of books and films for allegedly obscene or blasphemous content is fairly common. Since 2011, authorities in Aceh have cracked down on "punks" for supposedly insulting Islam. Those rounded up by police are subjected to "reeducation," which includes the forcible shaving of their punk-rock hairstyles and a traditional cleansing ceremony.

The 2008 Law on Electronic Information and Transactions (ITE) extended libel and other restrictions to the internet and online media, criminalizing the distribution or accessibility of information or documents that are "contrary to the moral norms of Indonesia" or related to gambling, blackmail, or defamation. In June 2012, reversing its own 2011 ruling based on new evidence, the Supreme Court finally exonerated Prita Mulyasari, who had been criminally prosecuted under the ITE law beginning in 2009 for complaining to friends via e-mail about a hospital where she had been a patient. In 2010 the court had overturned a parallel civil defamation ruling against her.

Indonesia officially recognizes Islam, Protestantism, Roman Catholicism, Hinduism, Buddhism, and Confucianism. Members of unrecognized religions have difficulty obtaining national identity cards. Atheism is not accepted, and the criminal code contains provisions against blasphemy, penalizing those who "distort" or "misrepresent" official faiths. The central government has often failed to respond to religious intolerance in recent years, and societal discrimination has increased. A 2006 joint ministerial decree requires religious groups seeking to build houses of worship to obtain the written approval of 60 immediate neighbors. In 2010 the Supreme Court overturned the 2006 revocation of a building permit for GKI Yasmin Church in West Java, but the local administration continued to prevent the congregation from using the premises. In May 2012, the Muslim and Christian communities reached an agreement allowing the church to open provided a mosque is built next door. However, the issue was still outstanding at year's end, and local residents blocked the congregation's access to the premises for a Christmas service. In Aceh in April, local authorities closed more than 20 places of worship, primarily for allegedly lacking proper building permits. In West Sumatra in June, Alexander Aan was sentenced to two and a half years in prison for declaring himself an atheist on his Facebook page and posting comic strips featuring the prophet Muhammad, which the judge said spread information that caused hatred and enmity.

Violence and intimidation against Ahmadiyya, a heterodox Islamic sect with approximately 400,000 Indonesian followers, continued in 2012 with attacks on Ahmadi mosques and property. Hostile acts against the group have increased since 2008, when the Religious Affairs Ministry recommended that it be banned nationwide, and the government, seeking a compromise, instead barred Ahmadis from proselytizing. The Shiite Muslim minority has also suffered violence and intimidation in recent years. In late 2011, a Shiite neighborhood in Sampang, East Java, was attacked, resulting in the destruction of homes and property. In July 2012, a Shiite cleric from Sampang, Tajul Muluk, was sentenced to two years in prison for blasphemy and teachings that deviated from mainstream Islam. The East Java High Court increased the sentence to four years in September, and the case was pending before the Supreme Court at year's end. Meanwhile, in August, Shiite students from Sampang were attacked, two accompanying adults were killed, and 35 Shiite-owned houses were torched. Separately, in October, 14 people died and almost 200 were evacuated by police during a three-day clash between Muslim and Hindu-Balinese residents in Lampung. A December report by the Setara Institute noted a 25 percent increase in acts of religious intolerance and violence compared with the previous year, with 264 acts of intolerance and 371 acts of violence, primarily in the provinces of West Java, East Java, Aceh, Central Java, and South Sulawesi. State actors—most notably, the police—carried out 39 percent of the acts of violence.

Academic freedom in Indonesia is generally respected.

Freedom of assembly is usually upheld, and peaceful protests are commonplace in the capital. However, authorities have restricted the right to assembly in conflict areas. Flag-raising ceremonies and independence rallies in Papua are routinely disbanded, often violently—as was the case with a Papuan People's Congress gathering in 2011—and participants have been prosecuted. An October 2012 rally in commemoration of the 2011 Congress ended when police opened fire on a group of 300 people; several people suffered gunshot wounds. In May, one man was killed by security forces and 13 arrested during rallies by the West Papua National Committee protesting the handover of West Papua by the United Nations Temporary Executive Authority to Indonesia.

Indonesia hosts a strong and active array of civil society organizations, though some human rights groups are subject to monitoring and interference by the government. Moreover, independence activists in Papua and the Maluku Islands, and labor and political activists in Java and Sulawesi, remain targets for human rights abuses. No high-level official has been convicted for any serious human rights violation since the fall of Suharto.

Workers can join independent unions, bargain collectively, and with the exception of civil servants, stage strikes. The labor movement is generally fragmented, and enforcement of minimum-wage and other labor standards is weak. However, the labor laws include generous severance pay and strike provisions. In January 2012, the National Workers Union reached a landmark settlement with the Nike subsidiary Nikomas whereby the company would pay for almost 600,000 hours of forced overtime worked by 4,500 employees over the past two years. Some unions have resorted to violence in their negotiations with employers. In September, members of the Indonesian Metal Workers Federation took hundreds of employees hostage at a Japanese-owned factory in West Java after the company refused to upgrade contract workers to permanent employees. The hostages were released two days later when the company agreed to the union's demands. Approximately 10 percent of workers in the formal economy—which accounts for one-sixth of the total economy—belong to unions. Household workers are currently excluded from labor law protections.

The judiciary, particularly the Constitutional Court, has demonstrated its independence in some cases, but the court system remains plagued by corruption and other weaknesses. Low salaries for judicial officials and impunity for illegal activity perpetuate the problems of bribery, forced confessions, and interference in court proceedings by military personnel and government officials at all levels.

Effective police work has proven critical to Indonesia's recent successes in fighting terrorism, but the security forces in general remain rife with corruption and other abuses, and personnel regularly go unpunished or receive light sentences for human rights violations. These include ongoing abuses in conflict zones like Papua, but they are often related to land disputes and military involvement in illegal activities such as logging and mining. In 2010 the national police issued a regulation allowing officers to use live ammunition to quell anarchic violence. In February 2012, the International Crisis Group released a report highlighting the increasing rate of attacks on police by angry crowds, noting 40 specific incidents since August 2010. The report attributes the hostility to the cumulative effects of police brutality, bribery, and lack of accountability. In January, five officers were punished with three days' detention for a December 2011 incident in which police opened fire on a crowd of protesters in Bima, West Nusa Tenggara Province, resulting in three deaths.

A 2011 law gave the State Intelligence Agency (BIN) greater authority to gather information on those suspected of terrorism, espionage, or threatening national security. The law also criminalized the leaking of state secrets to the public, which critics warned could lead to abuse of power given the broad definitions of secret information.

Currently, information garnered through torture is permissible in Indonesian courts, and torture carried out by law enforcement officers is not a criminal offense. The Indonesian Legal Aid Institute found in 2010 that up to 80 percent of detainees suffered from acts of violence in police custody. Detention laws are generally respected, but there are many reports of abuse aimed at female and minority detainees. Student activists are the most prone to arbitrary arrest, followed by farmers and journalists. Poor prison governance is compounded by overcrowding.

In July 2012, the DPR passed a Juvenile Court Law that raised the minimum age of incarceration to 14 years, ordered the creation of juvenile detention centers within five years, and prohibited the publication of court details about minors. Minors are often incarcerated with adults; prior to this law, minors aged eight and above were held criminally responsible for their acts and subject to incarceration.

Since 2006, a number of districts have issued local ordinances based on Sharia (Islamic law). Many are unconstitutional, contradict Indonesia's international human rights commitments, or are unclear, leading to enforcement problems. The central government and various parties have failed to take decisive action, apparently for political reasons. Many of the ordinances seek to impose an Islamic dress code, Koranic literacy requirements, and bans on prostitution. Other measures are more extreme. In 2009, the Aceh regional parliament passed legislation that, among other provisions, allows stoning for adultery and public lashing for homosexual acts. Nineteen people were caned in Aceh in March, April, and October 2012 for gambling and other "immoral behavior." Another 10 were caned in December for gambling and adultery. Local regulations unrelated to Sharia have also been criticized for violating constitutional protections. In August, the Home Affairs Ministry announced that 824 of the country's local bylaws should be amended or repealed, with another 1,500 under evaluation.

Ethnic minority groups face considerable discrimination. The problems of mining and logging on communal land and state appropriation of land claimed by indigenous groups are most acute in Kalimantan. Ethnic Chinese, who make up less than 3 percent of the population but are resented by some for reputedly holding much of the country's wealth, continue to face harassment and occasional violence. LGBT (lesbian, gay, bisexual, and transgender) people also suffer discrimination, and gay-themed events have encountered resistance from local officials and open hostility from groups like the Islamic Defenders Front (FPI). Many local bylaws criminalize homosexuality, and a 2008 antipornography law labels homosexual acts "deviant." In May 2012, an event in Yogyakarta featuring a prominent Canadian author known for her work supporting LGBT rights was shut down after a small radical group, the Indonesian Mujahidin Council (MMI), attacked and injured participants; a related event in Jakarta was canceled after police intervened, reportedly due to pressure from other hard-line groups.

Discrimination against women persists, particularly in the workplace. A 2008 law states that 30 percent of a political party's candidates and board members must be women. While only 101 women were elected to the 560-seat DPR in 2009, this was an increase over 63 in the previous term. Trafficking of women and children for prostitution and forced labor continues, despite the passage of new laws and stricter penalties. Abortion is illegal, except to save a woman's life. Sharia-based ordinances in a number of districts infringe on women's constitutional rights. A draft Gender Equality Bill stalled in parliament in 2012 due to objections that it contradicted Sharia on issues such as inheritance and allowed interreligious marriage and same-sex marriage.

The 2008 antipornography law applies not just to published images but to speech and gestures that "incite sexual desire," drawing concerns that it could be used to persecute women. Significantly, the law invites the "public" to participate in the discouragement of pornographic acts, leading to extrajudicial enforcement. A Constitutional Court ruling in 2010 upheld the law.

Iran

Political Rights: 6
Civil Liberties: 6
Status: Not Free

Population: 78,868,700
Capital: Tehran

Ten-Year Ratings Timeline For Year Under Review (Political Rights, Civil Liberties, Status)

2003	2004	2005	2006	2007	2008	2009	2010	2011	2012
6,6NF	6,6NF	6,6NF	6,6NF	6,6NF	6,6NF	6,6NF	6,6NF	6,6NF	6,6NF

Overview: The Iranian government continued to curtail political freedoms and violate civil liberties in 2012, imposing particularly harsh conditions on journalists, civic activists, human rights defenders, women, and minorities. The authorities stepped up restrictions on the internet and suppressed demonstrations related to the worsening economic situation. The UN special rapporteur on Iran was again denied access to the country during the year, and leading opposition figures remained in detention. The tightly controlled March parliamentary elections amounted to a contest between rival factions within the conservative leadership.

A popular revolution ousted Iran's monarchy in 1979, bringing together an unwieldy coalition of diverse political interests that opposed the regime's widespread corruption, misguided modernization efforts, and pro-Western foreign policy. Subsequently, the revolution's democratic and secular elements were largely subsumed under the leadership of the formerly exiled Ayatollah Ruhollah Khomeini. Although a newly drafted constitution incorporated some democratic institutions and values, Khomeini was named supreme leader based on the religious concept of *velayat-e faqih* (guardianship of the Islamic jurist). He was vested with control over the security and intelligence services, the armed forces, the judiciary, and the state media. With Iran in political turmoil, Iraqi dictator Saddam Hussein seized the opportunity to stop the spread of the Islamic revolution and settle a long-running border dispute. The ensuing Iran-Iraq War, which lasted from 1980 to 1988, cost over a million lives.

After Khomeini's death in 1989, the title of supreme leader passed to Ayatollah Ali Khamenei, a compromise candidate who lacked the religious credentials and charisma of his predecessor. The constitution was amended, the office of prime minister was abolished, and Khamenei's power was consolidated, giving him final authority over all matters of foreign and domestic policy.

Beneath its veneer of religious probity, the Islamic Republic gave rise to a new elite that accumulated wealth through opaque and unaccountable means. Basic freedoms were revoked, and women in particular experienced a severe regression in their status and rights. By the mid-1990s, dismal economic conditions and a demographic trend toward a younger population had contributed to significant public dissatisfaction with the regime. A coalition of reformists began to emerge within the leadership, advocating a gradual process of political change, economic liberalization, and normalization of relations with the outside world that was designed to reform, but not radically alter, the existing political system.

Representing this coalition, former culture minister Mohammad Khatami was elected president in 1997 with nearly 70 percent of the vote. Under his administration, independent newspapers proliferated, and the authorities relaxed the enforcement of restrictions on social interaction between the sexes. Reformists won 80 percent of the seats in the country's first nationwide city council elections in 1999 and took the vast majority of seats in parliamentary elections the following year, with student activists playing a major role in their success.

The 2000 parliamentary elections prompted a backlash by hard-line clerics. Over the next four years, the conservative judiciary closed more than 100 reformist newspapers and jailed hundreds of liberal journalists and activists, while security forces cracked down on student protests. Khatami was reelected with 78 percent of the vote in 2001, but popular disaffection stemming from the reformists' limited accomplishments, coupled with the disqualification and exclusion of most reformist candidates by the conservative Guardian Council, allowed hard-liners to triumph in the 2003 city council and 2004 parliamentary elections. These electoral victories paved the way for the triumph of hard-line Tehran mayor Mahmoud Ahmadinejad in the 2005 presidential contest. Although Ahmadinejad had campaigned on promises to fight elite corruption and redistribute Iran's oil wealth to the poor and middle class, his ultraconservative administration oversaw a crackdown on civil liberties and harsher enforcement of the regime's strict morality laws.

The new government also adopted a more confrontational tone on foreign policy matters, feeding suspicions that its expanding uranium-enrichment activity, ostensibly devoted to generating electricity, was in fact aimed at weapons production. Beginning in 2006, in an effort to compel Iran to halt the uranium enrichment, the UN Security Council imposed multiple rounds of sanctions on the country. However, diplomatic negotiations failed to break the stalemate.

In the 2006 local council and Assembly of Experts elections, voters signaled their disapproval of the government's performance by supporting more moderate officials. Carefully vetted conservative candidates won nearly 70 percent of the seats in the 2008 parliamentary elections, but many were considered critics of Ahmadinejad, and particularly of his economic policies.

Despite crackdowns on human and women's rights activists and restrictions on internet freedom in the months prior to the June 2009 presidential election, supporters of all candidates seemed to enjoy a relatively relaxed and politically vibrant atmosphere. The Guardian Council approved only three candidates—all well-known political personalities with established revolutionary credentials—to compete against Ahmadinejad: Mir Hussein Mousavi, a former prime minister; Mohsen Rezai, a conservative former head of the Islamic Revolutionary Guard Corps (IRGC); and Mehdi Karroubi, a reformist former Speaker of parliament and cleric. Mousavi emerged as the main challenger, confronting Ahmadinejad in televised debates.

Polls indicated a close race, but Ahmadinejad was declared the winner soon after the election, credited with over 63 percent of the vote. All three challengers lodged claims of fraud, and protests broke out on a massive scale across the country as voters rejected the official results. The security forces violently cracked down on all public expressions of dissent and tightened government control of both online and traditional media. Protesters continued to mount periodic demonstrations, using mobile-telephone cameras and the internet to document abuses and communicate with the outside world. Over the course of 2010, however, the government effectively crippled the opposition's ability to mount large-scale demonstrations.

In the wake of the postelection confrontations, basic freedoms deteriorated and political affairs were further securitized. With the reformist opposition pushed to the sidelines, a power struggle between Ahmadinejad and Khamenei spilled into public view in April 2011, when the latter reinstated an intelligence minister who had been fired by the president. A dozen associates of Ahmadinejad and his controversial chief of staff, Esfandiar Rahim-Mashaei, were subsequently accused of constituting a "deviant current" within the country's leadership.

The March 2012 parliamentary elections, from which the reformist opposition was excluded, highlighted the deep divisions among conservative forces. Though there were no claims of systematic election fraud, several sitting lawmakers accused the IRGC of vote rigging. The official results were seen as favoring Khamenei's supporters rather than Ahmadinejad's. Later in March, for the first time in the history of the Islamic Republic, the parliament summoned the president to answer questions on his mismanagement of the economy, cabinet appointments, squandering of state resources, and disobedience of the supreme leader.

In October, Ahmed Shaheed, the UN special rapporteur on human rights in Iran, published a report expressing concern that the government's failure to investigate a wide range of human rights violations was indicative of a "culture of impunity." The regime has not permitted Shaheed to visit the country since his position was created in 2011.

Political Rights and Civil Liberties: Iran is not an electoral democracy. The most powerful figure in the government is the supreme leader, currently Ayatollah Ali Khamenei. He is chosen by the Assembly of Experts, a body of 86 clerics who are elected to eight-year terms by popular vote, from a list of candidates vetted by the Guardian Council. The supreme leader, who has no fixed term, is the commander in chief of the armed forces and appoints the leaders of the judiciary, the heads of state broadcast media, the Expediency Council, and half of the Guardian Council members. Although the president and the parliament, both with four-year terms, are responsible for designating cabinet ministers, the supreme leader exercises de facto control over appointments to the Ministries of Defense, Interior, Foreign Affairs, and Intelligence.

All candidates for the presidency and the 290-seat, unicameral parliament are vetted by the Guardian Council, which consists of six Islamic theologians appointed by the supreme leader and six jurists nominated by the head of the judiciary and confirmed by the parliament, all for six-year terms. The council generally disqualifies about a third of parliamentary candidates, though some are able to reverse these rulings on appeal. It also has the power to reject legislation approved by the parliament. Disputes between the two bodies are arbitrated by the Expediency Council, another unelected, conservative-dominated entity, currently headed by former president Ali Akbar Hashemi Rafsanjani.

Opposition politicians and party groupings have suffered especially harsh repression since the 2009 presidential election, with many leaders—including former lawmakers and cabinet ministers—facing arrest, prison sentences, and lengthy bans on political activity. Since February 2011, the former presidential candidates and prominent opposition leaders Mir Hussein Mousavi and Mehdi Karroubi, and Mousavi's wife, Zahra Rahnavard, have been kept under strict house arrest without trial, incommunicado, and with only limited access to family members.

Corruption is pervasive. The hard-line clerical establishment and the IRGC, to which it has many ties, have grown immensely wealthy through their control of tax-exempt foundations that dominate many sectors of the economy. The administration of President Mahmoud Ahmadinejad has gravely damaged fiscal transparency and accountability through the abolition of independent financial watchdogs and the murky transfer of profitable state companies to the IRGC and other semigovernmental conglomerates. Iran was ranked 133 out of 176 countries surveyed in Transparency International's 2012 Corruption Perceptions Index.

Freedom of expression is severely limited. The Ministry of Culture, which must approve publication of all books, has ratcheted up pressure on publishers and writers since 2009. In 2010, authorities banned the sale of any books that had received a publishing license prior to 2007. Some 250 "subversive" titles on a range of topics were banned ahead of the 2012 Tehran International Book Fair, and Cheshmeh Publications, one of the largest publishing houses in Iran, had its operating license revoked in June 2012.

The government directly controls all television and radio broadcasting. Satellite dishes are popular, despite being illegal, and there have been increasing reports of dish confiscation and steep fines. The authorities frequently issue ad hoc orders banning media coverage of specific topics and events, including the economic impact of international sanctions, the fate of opposition leaders, and criticism of the country's nuclear policy. Cooperation with Persian-language satellite news channels based abroad is banned. Fariborz Raisdana, a prominent economic analyst, began serving a one-year prison term in May 2012, having originally been arrested in December 2010, after criticizing government economic policies on the Persian service of the British Broadcasting Corporation (BBC). In an unprecedented move, the government has also placed pressure on the family members of journalists living abroad, including BBC Persian employees, who have been harassed, questioned, and detained by the security and intelligence apparatus.

The Press Court has extensive power to prosecute journalists for such vaguely worded offenses as "mutiny against Islam," "insulting legal or real persons who are lawfully respected," and "propaganda against the regime." The use of "suspicious sources" or sources that criticize the government is also forbidden. Numerous periodicals were closed for morality or security offenses in 2012, including the independent newspaper *Maghreb*, which was found in violation of press laws following its publication of a cartoon of Ahmadinejad. Among other editors arrested during the year, Ali Akbar Javanfekr, an Ahmadinejad adviser and head of the state news agency, was jailed for six months in September for publishing content "contrary to Islamic standards." Also that month, a special media court found Reuters bureau chief Parisa Hafezi guilty of "disseminating lies" for a story on women practicing martial arts in Iran and suspended the agencies accreditation. Iran ranks second in the world for the number of jailed journalists, with 45 behind bars as of December 2012, according to the New York–based Committee to Protect Journalists.

Internet penetration has skyrocketed in recent years, and many Iranians used mobile-telephone cameras and social-networking sites to provide some of the only independent coverage of the 2009 postelection crackdown. The authorities have consequently established draconian laws and practices to restrict access to communication tools, persecute dissidents for their online activity, and strengthen the government's vast censorship apparatus. Key international social-media sites like Facebook, Twitter, and YouTube were blocked after the 2009 election, and the number of disabled political sites continued to increase in 2012, hampering the opposition's ability to communicate and organize. The 2010 Computer Crimes Law is freighted with vaguely defined offenses that effectively criminalize legitimate online expression; the law also legalizes government surveillance of the internet. In January 2012, the authorities unveiled new regulations that oblige cybercafé owners to record the personal information and browsing histories of customers. The first phase of a national intranet, aimed at disconnecting the population from the global internet, was launched in September.

Iranian filmmakers are subject to tight restrictions, and many have been arrested or harassed since the 2009 election. In January 2012, the government ordered the closure of the House of Cinema, an independent professional association that supported some 5,000 Iranian filmmakers and artists.

Religious freedom is limited in Iran, whose population is largely Shiite Muslim but includes Sunni Muslim, Baha'i, Christian, Jewish, and Zoroastrian minorities. The Special Court for the Clergy investigates religious figures for alleged crimes and has generally been used to persecute clerics who stray from the official interpretation of Islam or criticize the supreme leader. Ayatollah Seyed Hussain Kazemeini Boroujerdi, a cleric who advocates the separation of religion and politics, is currently serving 11 years in prison for his beliefs. Sunnis enjoy equal rights under the law but face discrimination in practice; there is no Sunni mosque in Tehran, and few Sunnis hold senior government posts. Sufi Muslims have also faced persecution by the authorities. Since the leader of the Sufi order Nematollahi Gonabadi was arrested in 2009 and sentenced to four years in prison, security forces have repeatedly clashed with members of the order in Gonabad and Kavar.

Iranian Baha'is, thought to number between 300,000 and 350,000, are not recognized as a religious minority in the constitution, enjoy virtually no rights under the law, and are banned from practicing their faith. Under Ahmadinejad, concerted efforts to intimidate, imprison, and physically attack Baha'is have been carried out by security forces, paramilitary groups, and ordinary citizens with impunity. Baha'i students are barred from attending university and prevented from obtaining their educational records. In May 2011, 39 Baha'i students and volunteer instructors were arrested in connection with an online university initiative. In January 2012, an appeals court sentenced six of the volunteer educators to between four and five years in prison. At year's end, at least 105 Baha'is were in prison, including 7 community leaders who were sentenced in 2010 to 20 years on charges of espionage and "engaging in propaganda against Islam."

The constitution recognizes Zoroastrians, Jews, and Christians as religious minorities, and they are generally allowed to worship without interference, so long as they do not proselytize. Conversion by Muslims to a non-Muslim religion is punishable by death. In 2012, authorities shut down several churches in Tehran, Ahvaz, and Esfahan that provided services in the Persian language, which made them potentially accessible to converts.

The non-Muslim minorities are barred from election to representative bodies (though five parliament seats are allocated to the Armenian Christian, Chaldean Christian, Zoroastrian, and Jewish minorities); cannot hold senior government or military positions; and face restrictions in employment, education, and property ownership.

Academic freedom is limited. Scholars are frequently detained, threatened, and forced to retire for expressing political views. Since 2009, between 50 and 150 university faculty members have been forced to retire or dismissed based on their personal and political opinions. A 2010 government directive barred Iranian scholars and citizens from contact with over 60 European and U.S.-based foundations, think tanks, and educational institutions. Academics are prevented from freely participating in exchanges abroad. In August 2012, the government intimidated dozens of Iran-based scholars into canceling plans to attend a conference of the International Society for Iranian Studies (ISIS) in Istanbul. Students involved in organizing protests face suspension or expulsion in addition to criminal punishments. Since the 2009 presidential election, the IRGC-led Basij militia has increased its presence on campuses, and vocal critics of the regime face increased persecution and prosecution. According to Iran's largest student organization, between 2009 and 2012, 396 students were banned from pursuing their studies because of their political activities. During the same period, 634 were arrested, with 30 of them currently serving long prison terms, for exercising their rights to assembly, association, and free expression.

In 2011, as part of a government effort to bring curriculums into line with "religious and indigenous ideology and principles," the country's top humanities university, Allameh Tabatabai, eliminated 13 branches of social sciences, including political science, history, sociology, philosophy, pedagogy, and journalism. In 2012, new educational barriers for women were introduced, with 36 universities reportedly excluding women from registering in 77 fields of study.

The constitution prohibits public demonstrations that "are detrimental to the fundamental principles of Islam," a vague provision that was frequently invoked to deny permit requests after the 2009 presidential election. Vigilante and paramilitary organizations that are officially or tacitly sanctioned by the government—most notably the Basij and Ansar-i Hezbollah—regularly play major roles in breaking up demonstrations. Peaceful, nonpolitical demonstrations are increasingly met with brutal violence.

The constitution permits the establishment of political parties, professional syndicates, and other civic organizations, provided that they do not violate the principles of "freedom, sovereignty, and national unity" or question the Islamic basis of the republic. Human rights discourse and grassroots activism are integral parts of Iranian society. However, the security services routinely arrest and harass secular activists as part of a wider effort to control nongovernmental organizations (NGOs). In August 2012, security and intelligence forces raided a camp set up to deliver aid to victims of a devastating earthquake in East Azerbaijan Province. Authorities detained 35 volunteer relief workers on charges of "assembly and collusion against national security goals." Although NGO permits are not required by law, the Interior Ministry has been issuing them and shutting down organizations that do not seek or qualify for them. In 2011, the government began reviewing a new bill on the establishment and supervision of NGOs that could unduly restrict and severely impede their activities; the process continued at the end of 2012.

Iranian law does not allow independent labor unions, though workers' councils are represented in the Workers' House, the only legal labor federation. Workers' public protests and May Day gatherings are regularly suppressed by security forces. In 2012, the authorities denied workers the right to hold a May Day rally for a fifth consecutive year.

The judicial system is not independent, as the supreme leader directly appoints the head of the judiciary, who in turn appoints senior judges. Suspects are frequently tried in closed sessions without access to legal counsel. Political and other sensitive cases are tried before revolutionary courts, where due process protections are routinely disregarded and trials are often summary. Judges deny access to lawyers, commonly accept coerced confessions, and disregard torture or abuse during detention.

The government practice of pressuring lawyers to abandon the cases of political and social detainees is widespread in Iran. Lawyers who resist such pressure can face harassment, interrogation, and incarceration. Since 2009, at least 42 attorneys have been prosecuted, including prominent human rights lawyers Nasrin Sotoudeh, Mohammad Seyfzadeh, Abdolfattah Soltani, and Mohammad Ali Dadkhah, who have received long prison sentences and been barred from practicing law. In recent years, the government has progressively intervened in the affairs of the Iranian Bar Association, an independent body responsible for issuing licenses to lawyers, overseeing their performance, and legally protecting them. In early 2012, the judiciary submitted a draft bill to the parliament that would replace the association with a state-controlled body composed of lawyers appointed by the judiciary itself; the process continued at the end of 2012.

The country's penal code is based on Sharia (Islamic law) and provides for flogging, amputation, and execution by stoning or hanging for a range of social and political offenses; these punishments are carried out in practice. Iran routinely ranks second only to China in number of executions, with hundreds carried out each year. While many inmates are executed for drug-related offenses, a number of political prisoners convicted of moharebeh (enmity against God) also receive death sentences. Iran's overall execution rate has increased significantly under Ahmadinejad. In 2012 the authorities announced 292 executions, but human rights organizations estimate that as many as 230 additional individuals were executed without official acknowledgment. Amendments to Iran's penal code that were approved by the parliament and Guardian Council in 2012 but had not been signed into law by year's end would maintain many of the deeply flawed provisions of the previous code. Although it eliminates stoning, the revised code continues to mandate the death penalty for "crimes" such as drinking alcohol, consensual sexual relations outside of marriage, and vaguely defined violations of national security laws. One provision equates the age of criminal responsibility with the age of puberty under Sharia—15 years for boys and 9 for girls. Contrary to Iran's obligations under the Convention on the Rights of the Child, the judiciary continues to execute juvenile offenders. More than 100 juveniles reportedly remain on death row.

Although the constitution prohibits arbitrary arrest and detention, such abuses are increasingly employed, and family members of detainees are often not notified for days or weeks. Suspected dissidents are frequently held in unofficial, illegal detention centers. Prison conditions in general are notoriously poor, and there are regular allegations of abuse, rape, torture, and death in custody. In October 2012, at least nine female political prisoners went on hunger strike to protest unannounced inspections, impromptu body searches, and verbal abuse and beatings by female guards. In November 2012, Sattar Beheshti, a 35-year-old blogger, died while in police custody. The head of Tehran's cybercrimes unit was subsequently fired after allegations surfaced that Beheshti died while under interrogation.

The constitution and laws call for equal rights for all ethnic groups, but in practice, these rights are restricted by the regime. Minority languages are prohibited in schools and government offices. Minority rights activists are consistently threatened and arrested. Ethnic Kurds, Arabs, Baluchis, and Azeris complain of discrimination. Kurdish opposition groups suspected of separatist aspirations, such as the Democratic Party of Iranian Kurdistan (KDPI), are brutally suppressed. At least 28 Kurdish prisoners convicted of national security charges remained on death row at the end of 2012.

Sexual orientation is also a subject of government scrutiny. The penal code criminalizes all sexual relations outside of traditional marriage, and Iran is among the few countries where individuals can be put to death for consensual same-sex conduct.

Women are widely educated; a majority of university students are female. However, women currently hold just 3 percent of the seats in the parliament, and they are routinely excluded from running for higher office. Female judges may not issue final verdicts, and a woman cannot obtain a passport without the permission of her husband or a male relative. Women do not enjoy equal rights under Sharia-based statutes governing divorce, inheritance, and child custody, though some of these inequalities are accompanied by greater familial and financial obligations for men. A woman's testimony in court is given only half the weight of a man's, and the monetary compensation awarded to a female victim's family upon her death is half that owed to the family of a male victim. Women must conform to strict dress codes and are segregated from men in some public places. There has been a crackdown in recent years on women deemed to be dressed immodestly. Women's rights activists, especially members of the One Million Signatures Campaign, continue to face repression.

Iraq

Political Rights: 6*
Civil Liberties: 6
Status: Not Free

Population: 33,703,000
Capital: Baghdad

Ratings Change: Iraq's political rights rating declined from 5 to 6 due to the concentration of power by Prime Minister Nouri al-Maliki and increasing pressure on the political opposition, as exemplified by the arrest and death sentence in absentia of Vice President Tariq al-Hashimi, the country's most senior Sunni Arab politician.

Ten-Year Ratings Timeline For Year Under Review (Political Rights, Civil Liberties, Status)

2003	2004	2005	2006	2007	2008	2009	2010	2011	2012
7,5NF	7,5NF	6,5NF	6,6NF	6,6NF	6,6NF	5,6NF	5,6NF	5,6NF	6,6NF

Overview:

Immediately after the U.S. military completed its scheduled withdrawal from Iraq at the end of 2011, tensions arose again between Sunni and Shiite political parties. The Sunni Iraqiya Party boycotted the parliament in response to a perceived power grab by Prime Minister Nouri al-Maliki and the issuing of an arrest warrant for Vice President Tariq al-Hashimi, a Sunni politician. Al-Hashimi was tried and sentenced to death in absentia in September 2012 as part of a series of events that heightened political discord and coincided with one of the largest spikes in violence seen in the country in two years. In December, President Jalal Talabani left Iraq to receive treatment in Germany for a stroke.

The modern state of Iraq was established after World War I as a League of Nations mandate administered by Britain. The British installed a constitutional monarchy that privileged the Sunni Arab minority at the expense of Kurds and Shiite Arabs. Sunni Arab political dominance continued after independence in 1932 and a military coup that toppled the monarchy in 1958. The Arab nationalist Baath Party seized power in 1968, and the new regime's de facto strongman, Saddam Hussein, assumed the presidency in 1979. Over the next two decades, Iraq endured brutal political repression, a destructive war with Iran from 1980 to 1988, military defeat by a U.S.-led coalition following Hussein's 1990 invasion of Kuwait, and years of onerous postwar trade sanctions.

After the establishment of a U.S.-enforced no-fly zone north of the 36th parallel in 1991, most of the three northern provinces of Erbil, Duhok, and Sulimaniyah came under the control of the Kurdistan Democratic Party (KDP) and the Patriotic Union of Kurdistan (PUK). The two factions fought openly in the mid-1990s, but they eventually reconciled and formed an autonomous Kurdistan Regional Government (KRG).

A U.S.-led coalition invaded Iraq in March 2003 and established a Coalition Provisional Authority (CPA) to administer the country. It disbanded the Iraqi military and prevented members of the Baath Party from serving in government or the new security forces. The resulting security vacuum led to widespread looting, damage to infrastructure, and acute electricity and water shortages.

Exploiting Sunni Arab frustrations with the de-Baathification policy and the impending shift of political power toward the Shiite majority, loose networks of former Baathist officials, Sunni Arab tribe members, and Islamist militants associated with al-Qaeda began organizing and funding an insurgency that rapidly gained strength in late 2003 and 2004.

Intimidation by insurgents ensured that Sunni Arabs boycotted the 2005 elections for a Transitional National Assembly and provincial governments, resulting in a landslide victory for Shiite and Kurdish parties. A new constitution was approved by referendum in October 2005, though more than two-thirds of voters in two largely Sunni Arab provinces rejected it.

Meanwhile, Shiite party militias were able to infiltrate the Interior Ministry's police and counterinsurgency forces, and extrajudicial detentions and killings by both the militias and militia-dominated police units became common during 2005 and 2006. Sunni militias responded in kind, and an intense cycle of sectarian conflict ensued. Ethnically cleansed or segregated neighborhoods soon became a fixture in Baghdad and other multiethnic or religiously diverse provinces.

Sunni Arabs participated in the December 2005 elections for a full-term parliament, increasing their political representation. Nouri al-Maliki of the Shiite Da'wa Party was chosen as prime minister. However, further political progress remained elusive; the main Sunni Arab bloc in parliament and a Shiite faction loyal to populist cleric and militia leader Moqtada al-Sadr both began a boycott of the legislature in 2007.

The parliament adopted several symbolic measures in 2008 to bring Sunni Arabs back into the political process. Many former Baathists were permitted to return to jobs they had lost, and the government granted amnesty to thousands of mainly Sunni Arab prisoners. The largest Sunni bloc returned to government after a boycott of almost a year, and six Sunni ministers joined al-Maliki's cabinet. Also in 2008, Iraqi security forces cracked down on al-Sadr's militia network, and local, U.S.-funded Sunni militias that had formed over the previous two years began to successfully suppress the insurgencies in the western provinces.

Under electoral legislation passed in late 2008, voters in the January 2009 provincial elections could choose candidates rather than party lists, the use of religious symbols in campaigning was restricted, a 25 percent quota was set for female council members, and just 6 seats—down from 15 in an earlier draft—were set aside for Christians and other small minorities out of a total of 440 provincial council seats. The voting was largely peaceful, and turnout in most provinces ranged from 50 percent to 75 percent. On the whole, al-Maliki's Da'wa Party emerged as the winner, though it needed to form coalitions to govern in most provinces.

The 2009 provincial elections did not include the autonomous Kurdish region or the contested province of Kirkuk. Separate elections in July 2009 for the Kurdish regional parliament and presidency featured high turnout and a fairly strong showing by a new opposition bloc called Gorran (Change), which took about a quarter of the parliamentary vote. A referendum to determine whether Kirkuk would join the Kurdish region remained delayed through 2011, despite a constitutional provision that had required it before the end of 2007.

Parliamentary elections were held in March 2010, despite having been constitutionally mandated for January 2010. They were governed by a 2009 election law that called for an open-list, proportional representation voting system, with multimember districts corresponding to the 18 provinces. A total of eight seats were reserved for Christians and other religious minorities.

Despite election day violence, the polling was seen as relatively free and fair. The electoral commission took candidates' complaints seriously and conducted a partial recount, but found no evidence of significant fraud. Voters clearly demonstrated their frustration with the government by returning only 62 of the previous parliament's 275 members, but the elections resulted in political deadlock. Despite a constitutional requirement to form a government within 30 days of the election results' announcement, neither of the rival blocs were able to organize a majority, with foreign powers including Iran, Saudi Arabia, and the United States reportedly playing a role in the lengthy negotiations. The new parliament reelected Kurdish leader Jalal Talabani as president in November 2010, and in December 2010, al-Maliki finally secured parliamentary approval for a unity government that encompassed all major factions, including Iraqiya and al-Sadr's Shiite movement.

The long postelection interregnum featured an escalation in sectarian and antigovernment violence. Insurgents began targeting national institutions, especially the security services, and sites with sectarian significance. By the summer of 2010, violence had reached heights not seen in years. In the beginning of 2011, U.S. military officials estimated a 20 percent decrease in overall security incidents from 2010. However, al-Qaeda in Mesopotamia and various guerrilla groups launched attacks against civilians, politicians, Iraqi security forces, and American troops after U.S. forces killed Osama bin Laden in Pakistan in May 2011.

In keeping with a 2008 security agreement between Iraq and the United States, about 50,000 U.S. military personnel remained in Iraq through much of 2011, though they had withdrawn from Iraqi cities in 2009 and formally ended combat operations in 2010. American and Iraqi political leaders had expected to agree on a reduced presence of up to 5,000 U.S. troops beyond 2011, but the Iraqi parliament refused to grant U.S. personnel immunity from prosecution under Iraqi law. Consequently, the last U.S. troops left the country in December 2011.

One day after the completion of the U.S. military withdrawal, tension once again arose between Sunni and Shiite political parties. In an apparent power grab by al-Malaki's ruling coalition, an arrest warrant was issued for Vice President Tariq al-Hashmi, a Sunni politician, alleging him of running a "death squad" that targeted police and government officials. Al-Hashmi fled to Turkey in early 2012, but arrests of other Sunni, Baathist, and secular Shiite political figures continued, and al-Hashmi's Sunni Iraqiya Party boycotted the parliament in protest. Al-Hashmi was tried and sentenced to death in absentia in September 2012. Trials against him and members of his party continued even after his conviction, and two more death sentences were leveled against him in November 2012.

The office and home of Finance Minister and Iraqiya political coalition member Rafie al-Issawi were raided by Iraqi security forces in December 2012, and 10 of his bodyguards were arrested on terrorism charges. The episode led thousands of opponents of al-Maliki's government to participate in protests across the country. The combination of al-Hashmi's exile and conviction, the raid on al-Issawi, and the December departure of President Talabani from the country due to a stroke and failing health deepened political distrust and division between Sunni and Shiite groups in Iraq. A resulting spike in violence was seen during the second half of 2012 with death tolls similar to the most violent months of 2010.

In addition to ongoing violence and political strife, Iraq continues to suffer from economic difficulties and insecure borders. The government has remained unable to provide basic public services. While electricity provision, for example, has increased significantly in recent years, it has not kept pace with growing demand, and most Iraqis lack a reliable source of power. Unemployment hovers above 20 percent nationally, and reaches as high as 50 percent in some rural areas.

The northern and autonomous Kurdish areas have experienced economic prosperity in recent years, especially relative to the rest of the Iraqi population. However, relations between the Kurds and their Turkish, Iranian, and southern Iraqi compatriot neighbors remain strained.

Political Rights and Civil Liberties: Iraq is not an electoral democracy. Although it has conducted meaningful elections, political participation and decision making in the country remain seriously impaired by sectarian and insurgent violence, widespread corruption, and the influence of foreign powers. Under the constitution, the president and two vice presidents are elected by the parliament and appoint the prime minister, who is nominated by the largest parliamentary bloc. Elections are held every four years. The prime minister is tasked with forming a cabinet and running the executive functions of the state. The parliament consists of a 325-seat lower house, the Council of Representatives, and a still-unformed upper house, the Federal Council, which would represent provincial interests. The Independent Electoral Commission of Iraq, whose nine-member board was selected by a UN advisory committee, has sole responsibility for administering elections.

Political parties representing a wide range of viewpoints operate without legal restrictions, but the Baath Party is officially banned. Additionally, after the U.S. troop withdrawal in December 2011, Sunni and secular political actors began to face increased scrutiny and repression in light of Prime Minister Nouri al-Maliki's attempts to consolidate power.

Home to one-fifth of the country's population, the autonomous Kurdish region constitutes a distinct polity within Iraq, with its own flag, military units, and language. The 111-seat regional legislature remains dominated by the allied PUK and KDP, despite the presence of the new Gorran opposition bloc following 2009 elections. The Kurdish region's political leaders profess their commitment to remaining part of a federal Iraqi state, but Kurdish security forces maintain a de facto border with the rest of Iraq, Iraqi Arabs are often treated as foreigners, and the regional government frequently acts in its own interest over Baghdad's objections.

Iraq is plagued by pervasive corruption at all levels of government. A national Integrity Commission is tasked with fighting corruption, but it conducts its investigations in secret and does not publish its findings until the courts have issued final decisions. The overwhelming majority of offenders enjoy impunity, largely because of an amnesty law allowing ministers to intervene and dismiss charges. As a result, cases are generally brought against low- and mid-ranking officials. While the Integrity Commission had gained some momentum, it has faced a number of setbacks in recent years. Most prominently, the commission's chairman was forced to resign amid mounting political pressure in 2011, commission members have been implicated in corrupt arms deals, and there have been numerous reports of government pressure aimed at silencing corruption whistleblowers. Iraq was ranked 169 out of 176 countries surveyed in Transparency International's 2012 Corruption Perceptions Index.

Freedom of expression is protected by the constitution, but in practice it has been seriously impeded by sectarian tensions and fear of violent reprisals. Over a dozen private television stations are in operation, and major Arab satellite stations are easily accessible. Hundreds of print publications have been established since 2003 and are allowed to function without significant government interference. Internet access is not currently restricted, but the Information Technology Crimes law currently under review by the Iraqi parliament threatens to restrict free speech online. Legislation passed in 2006 criminalized the ridicule of public officials, who often file suits when journalists report on corruption allegations. Iraq's media regulatory body, the Communication and Media Commission, threatened in 2012 to close 44 radio and television outlets accused of lacking official permits before deciding to delay those efforts. The move raised tensions between media and the government. Continuing insecurity has hindered journalists' ability to report widely and objectively, with intimidation and violence against journalists increasing since the U.S. troop withdrawal. The Committee to Protect Journalists (CPJ) estimates that over 140 journalists have been killed since 2003, while Reporters Without Borders (RSF) puts the number closer to 230.

Journalists previously operated more freely in the Kurdish region, but conditions there have deteriorated in recent years. A 2008 press law imposed fines for creating instability, spreading fear or intimidation, causing harm, or violating religious beliefs. Journalists who offend local officials and top party leaders or expose high-level corruption remain subject to physical attacks, arbitrary detention, and harassment.

Freedom of religion is guaranteed by the constitution, and religious institutions are allowed to operate with little formal oversight. However, all religious communities in Iraq have been threatened by sectarian violence. An estimated 300,000 to 900,000 Christians have sought safety abroad since 2003. Religious and ethnic minorities in northern Iraq—including Turkmens, Arabs, Christians, and Shabaks—have reported instances of discrimination and harassment by Kurdish authorities, though a number have fled to the Kurdish-controlled region due to its relative security. Formerly mixed areas across Iraq are now much more homogeneous, and terrorist attacks continue to be directed toward sectarian targets.

Academic institutions operate in a highly politicized and insecure environment. Hundreds of professors were killed during the peak of sectarian and insurgent violence, and many more stopped working or fled the country, though there have been some reports of scholars returning to their jobs following relative security improvements in the last several years.

Rights to freedom of assembly and association are recognized by the constitution, though it guarantees these rights "in a way that does not violate public order and morality." Some isolated protests were held in 2011, inspired by popular uprisings in North Africa. As a result, more than 20 protesters were killed by security forces as they tried to disperse the crowds. In December 2012, large-scale protests were held by Sunnis and opponents of al-Maliki's government, leading to the temporary closure of a major trade route into Syria and Jordan. Domestic and international nongovernmental organizations (NGOs) are able to operate without legal restrictions, though safety concerns severely limit their activities in many areas. The constitution provides for the right to form and join trade unions. Union activity has flourished in nearly all industries since 2003, and strikes have not been uncommon. However, Iraq's 1987 labor law remains in effect, prohibiting unionization in the public sector, and a 2005 decree gave authorities the power to seize all union funds and prevent their disbursal.

Judicial independence is guaranteed in the constitution. The Higher Judicial Council—headed by the chief judge of the Federal Supreme Court and composed of Iraq's 17 chief appellate judges and several judges from the Federal Court of Cassation—has administrative authority over the court system. In practice, however, judges have come under immense political and sectarian pressure and have been largely unable to pursue cases involving organized crime, corruption, and militia activity, even when presented with overwhelming evidence. Iraqi citizens often turn to local militias and religious groups to arbitrate rather than seeking redress with official law enforcement bodies that are seen as corrupt or ineffective.

The criminal procedure code and the constitution prohibit arbitrary arrest and detention, though both practices are common in security-related cases. The constitution also prohibits all forms of torture and inhumane treatment and affords victims the right to compensation, but there are few effective safeguards in place. A previously unknown detention facility where credible accusations of torture were reported was found to be under the direct control of the prime minister's office in 2010. While KRG laws also prohibit inhumane treatment, it is widely acknowledged that Kurdish security forces practice illegal detention and questionable interrogation tactics. Detainees in U.S. custody also experienced torture and mistreatment, though after the 2011 U.S. withdrawal, no prisoners of war remained directly detained in Iraq.

About five million Iraqis have been displaced from their homes since 2003. While hundreds of thousands—most of them Sunni Arabs—have fled to Jordan and Syria, nearly three million Iraqis are displaced within Iraq. In regions like Kirkuk, the Saddam Hussein regime forced some 250,000 Kurdish residents to move from their homes in the name of regional "Arabization." Ethnic disputes in the region have resulted in a longstanding political impasse between the majority Kurds and minorities of Arabs, Turkmen, and Assyrian-Chaldean Christians.

The constitution promises women equal rights under the law, though in practice they face various forms of legal and societal discrimination. Women are guaranteed 25 percent of the seats in the legislature, and their participation in public life has increased in recent years. While they still face serious social pressure and restrictions, women have also returned in larger numbers to jobs and universities. Women enjoy somewhat greater legal protections and social freedoms in the Kurdish region, but their political power is limited. Moreover, domestic abuse and so-called honor killings remain serious problems both in the Kurdish region and across the country. The laws applicable outside the Kurdish region offer leniency to the perpetrators of honor killings. In July 2010, Kurdish religious leaders formally declared that female genital mutilation (FGM) was un-Islamic, but advocacy groups claim that more than 50 percent of Kurdish teenage girls are victims of FGM. The U.S. State Department placed Iraq on the Tier 2 watch list of its 2012 Trafficking in Persons Report, noting problems including the trafficking and sexual exploitation of women and children from impoverished and displaced Iraqi families, and the abuse of foreign men and women who are recruited to work in Iraq.

Ireland

Political Rights: 1
Civil Liberties: 1
Status: Free

Population: 4,683,100
Capital: Dublin

Ten-Year Ratings Timeline For Year Under Review (Political Rights, Civil Liberties, Status)

2003	2004	2005	2006	2007	2008	2009	2010	2011	2012
1,1F	1,1F	1,1F	1,1F	1,1F	1,1F	1,1F	1,1F	1,1F	1,1F

Overview: As Ireland's economy continued to struggle in 2012, the government imposed a series of new austerity measures, including the first property tax to be imposed since 1977. After 15 years of hearings, the Mahon Tribunal released its final report in March, finding that the country is affected by widespread corruption. In an effort to address gender inequality in government, new legislation adopted in July will reduce state funding for parties if fewer than 30 percent of their candidates are women in the next general elections.

The Irish Free State emerged from the United Kingdom under the Anglo-Irish Treaty of 1921, though six counties in the province of Ulster remained part of the United Kingdom. A brief civil war followed, ending in 1923. In 1937, the Irish Free State adopted a new constitution and a new name—Ireland, or Éire.

Ireland joined the European Community (now the European Union, or EU) in 1973. Thanks in part to large subsidies from the EU, Ireland enjoyed high rates of economic growth for many years, transforming into one of Europe's richest countries.

The Fianna Fáil party has generally dominated Irish politics since the 1930s. Fianna Fáil succeeded in defeating Fine Gael in the 2007 general elections, and formed a governing coalition with the Green Party and the Progressive Democrats for the first time. After three consecutive terms as prime minister, Patrick "Bertie" Ahern stepped down in May 2008, due to a long-running corruption investigation into his previous activities as finance minister. Finance Minister Brian Cowen took over as prime minister that same month.

In the fall of 2008, Ireland's economy declined sharply due to falling property values and the global financial turmoil. Ireland's economy entered a technical depression in 2009, mostly due to government bailouts of the banking system. Support for the ruling Fianna Fáil and Green parties subsequently declined in the 2009 local elections. Following a series of resignations and defections, the number of coalition backers dropped to that of the opposition, but the coalition remained in power after agreeing in October to electoral reform.

Frustration with and distrust of the government grew following the 2010 acceptance of a US$113 billion loan package from the International Monetary Fund and the EU, which ultimately led to the implementation of harsh austerity measures. Fianna Fáil was largely blamed for failing to address the reckless lending that caused housing prices to fall, and the party's popularity sank. The Green Party subsequently quit the coalition, leaving Fianna Fáil without a majority in Parliament. Cowen called for early elections, pledging to stay on in a caretaker capacity.

After holding power for 61 of the previous 79 years, Fianna Fáil suffered its worst defeat in elections held in February 2011, capturing only 20 seats in Parliament's lower house. Fine Gael won 76 seats but lacked a majority and was forced to enter into a coalition with the Labour Party, which took 37 seats. The Greens failed to enter Parliament, while Sinn Féin won 14 seats; the remaining seats were captured by independents and two smaller parties. Enda Kenny of Fine Gael was elected prime minister. With two-thirds of the seats, Kenny's Fine Gael–Labour coalition held the largest parliamentary majority in Ireland's history.

The country's economic troubles continued in 2012, with unemployment at nearly 15 percent in December. The government imposed a series of new measures, including a 100 euro (US$130) household charge, the first property tax to be imposed since 1977. In a May referendum, Irish citizens voted overwhelmingly in favor of the EU's Referendum on the Treaty on Stability, Coordination, and Governance in the Economic and Monetary Union, which serves to tighten control over the borrowing and spending of EU member states. Ireland did, however, experience manufacturing growth in 2012, mostly due to its trade relationship with the United States, whose economy improved. In December, the Irish government passed the Personal Insolvency Bill, which will overhaul the country's consumer debt and bankruptcy laws and substantially reduce the amount borrowers owe on mortgages.

Political Rights and Civil Liberties: Ireland is an electoral democracy. The Parliament (Oireachtas) consists of a lower house (the Dáil), whose 166 members are elected by proportional representation for five-year terms, and an upper house (the Seanad, or Senate) with 60 members, 11 appointed and 49 elected by various interest groups. The Senate is mainly a consultative body, in which members serve five-year terms. The prime minister, or taoiseach, is chosen by Parliament. The president, whose functions are largely ceremonial, is directly elected for a seven-year term.

Ireland's two largest parties—Fianna Fáil and Fine Gael—do not differ widely in ideology but represent the opposing sides of the 1922-23 civil war. The smaller parties include the Labour Party, Sinn Féin, and the Green Party.

Corruption—including cronyism, political patronage, and illegal donations—is a recurring problem. After 15 years of hearings, the Mahon Tribunal released its final report in March 2012, finding that corruption had affected "every level of Irish political life," and that former prime minister Patrick "Bertie" Ahern had not been forthright about money he received while finance minister; he subsequently resigned from Fianna Fáil. Ireland was ranked 25 out of 176 countries surveyed in Transparency International's 2012 Corruption Perceptions Index.

The media are free and independent, and internet access is unrestricted. The print media present a variety of viewpoints. The state may censor material deemed indecent or obscene. Reforms to Ireland's defamation legislation made in 2010 introduced the offense of blasphemous libel, with penalties of up to 25,000 euros (US$33,500). New copyright legislation was passed in March 2012, despite significant opposition from internet freedom groups, who argued that the law could result in injunctions against companies like YouTube and Facebook if copyrighted materials are posted by other parties. The law's passage through a ministerial order, rather than Parliament, meant that voters could not voice their opposition to representatives. Hi-tech companies expressed concern that the law could negatively affect the growth of online business in Ireland.

Freedom of religion is constitutionally guaranteed. Although the country is overwhelmingly Roman Catholic, there is no state religion, and adherents of other faiths face few impediments to religious expression. While the Catholic Church operates approximately 90 percent of Ireland's schools—most of which provide religious education—parents may exempt their children from religious instruction; the constitution also requires equal funding for students wishing instruction in other faiths. Academic freedom is respected.

The right of public assembly and demonstration is respected. In July 2012, protesters in Dublin marched on Parliament to oppose International Monetary Fund calls for Ireland to cut its social welfare benefits. Freedom of association is upheld, and nongovernmental organizations can operate freely. Labor unions operate without hindrance, and collective bargaining is legal and unrestricted.

The legal system is based on common law, and the judiciary is independent. Prison conditions have been highlighted as dangerous, unsanitary, and overcrowded, among other issues. According to Rape Crisis Network Ireland's 2010 National Rape Crisis Statistics and Annual Report released in November 2011, only about 30 percent of survivors of sexual violence reported the abuse to authorities, primarily due to discouragement by police.

The Irish Travellers, a traditionally nomadic group of about 25,000 people, are not recognized as an ethnic minority, and face discrimination in housing and hiring.

While employment discrimination on the basis of gender or sexual orientation is prohibited, gender inequality in wages persists, and women continue to be underrepresented in the political sphere; women comprise only 15 percent of the members of the lower house of Parliament. In July 2012, the Electoral (Amendment) (Political Funding) Act 2012 was signed into law; among other changes, the legislation reduces state funding for parties if fewer than 30 percent of their candidates are women in the next general elections. Abortion is legal only when there is a "real and substantial risk" to the mother's life. Some 150,000 Irish women have traveled to Britain for abortions since it was legalized in 1967 due to the ban on abortion inside both the Republic of Ireland and Northern Ireland. A 31-year-old dentist, Dr. Savita Halappanavar, died in a Galway hospital in October 2012 while miscarrying; she was refused an abortion by doctors, because the fetus still had a heartbeat. The case reignited discussions in Ireland in 2012 over the country's strict and unclear abortion law. In December, the Irish government claimed it would work to change the restrictions in order to allow abortions in certain circumstances, specifically when the mother's life is at risk.

The 2010 Civil Partnership and Certain Rights and Obligations of Cohabitants Act legally recognizes same-sex couples, though it denies them some rights awarded to heterosexual married couples, such as adoption rights.

Reports released by the Commission to Inquire into Child Abuse in 2009 documented decades of widespread physical and emotional abuse against children in state institutions and by Catholic priests, as well as collusion to hide the abuse. The 2011 Cloyne report revealed similar abuse and subsequent cover-ups in the diocese of Cloyne. The government has taken steps to address the abuse, which has declined in recent decades. The government has also moved to end the Catholic Church's monopoly on Ireland's primary education system, as 3,000 schools currently remain under the Church's control. A referendum on a constitutional amendment introducing a new standalone article on children, which recognizes their natural and innate rights, passed with 57 percent of the vote in November 2012.

Israel

Political Rights: 1
Civil Liberties: 2
Status: Free

Population: 7,906,000 [Note: There are an estimated 325,500 Israeli settlers in the West Bank, about 18,700 in Golan Heights, and nearly 187,000 in East Jerusalem.]
Capital: Jerusalem

Note: The numerical ratings and status above reflect conditions within Israel itself. Separate reports examine the West Bank and the Gaza Strip.

Ten-Year Ratings Timeline For Year Under Review (Political Rights, Civil Liberties, Status)

2003	2004	2005	2006	2007	2008	2009	2010	2011	2012
1,3F	1,3F	1,2F	1,2F	1,2F	1,2F	1,2F	1,2F	1,2F	1,2F

Overview:

Several pieces of legislation drafted in 2012 appeared to threaten aspects of democracy and due process, including a bill that would allow the Knesset to override Supreme Court decisions and a law permitting the lengthy detention of migrants without trial. Also during the year, informal gender segregation on buses continued, a number of women were attacked by ultra-Orthodox Jewish men for "immodest" dress, and women were regularly arrested at the Western Wall in Jerusalem for religious reasons. In November, an eight-day conflict between Gaza-based Hamas militants and Israel killed six Israelis and over 160 Palestinians.

Israel was formed in 1948 from part of the British-ruled mandate of Palestine. A 1947 UN partition plan dividing Palestine into two states, Jewish and Arab, was rejected by the Arab Higher Committee and the Arab League, and Israel's 1948 declaration of independence led to war with a coalition of Arab countries. While Israel maintained its sovereignty and expanded its borders, Jordan (then known as Transjordan) seized East Jerusalem and the West Bank, and Egypt took control of the Gaza Strip.

After its 1967 war with Egypt, Jordan, and Syria, Israel occupied the Sinai Peninsula, the West Bank, the Gaza Strip, East Jerusalem, and the Golan Heights. While it returned Sinai to Egypt in 1982 as a result of the Camp David Accords, Israel annexed East Jerusalem in 1967 and unilaterally extended Israeli law to the Golan Heights in 1981.

In 1993, following a Palestinian uprising, or intifada, that began in late 1987, Israel secured an agreement (the Oslo Agreement) with the Palestine Liberation Organization (PLO) that provided for a phased Israeli withdrawal from the West Bank and Gaza Strip and some Palestinian autonomy in those areas, in exchange for Palestinian recognition of Israel and a renunciation of terrorism. In 1994, Israel and Jordan signed a U.S.-brokered peace agreement. However, Israeli-Palestinian negotiations on a future Palestinian state broke down in 2000, and a second intifada began.

In 2002, the Israel Defense Forces (IDF) reoccupied many of the West Bank areas that the Israeli government had ceded to the Palestinian Authority (PA) in the 1990s. Israel also began building a security barrier that roughly followed the 1949 armistice line, though it frequently extended deeper into the West Bank to incorporate Jewish settlements. Although the barrier was credited with reducing attacks inside Israel by about 90 percent, critics accused Israel of confiscating Palestinian property and impeding access to land, jobs, and services for those living in the barrier's vicinity. The barrier was declared illegal by the International Court of Justice in 2004, and was rerouted six times by order of the Israeli Supreme Court in response to a series of appeals.

In 2005, an informal ceasefire between the PA and Israel led to a general decline in violence, and Israel completed a unilateral withdrawal of all 7,500 Jewish settlers and military personnel from the Gaza Strip. Because his own right-wing Likud Party opposed that move, Prime Minister Ariel Sharon left Likud and founded the centrist Kadima party. In January 2006, Sharon suffered a stroke that put him in a coma, and Deputy Prime Minister Ehud Olmert became prime minister and Kadima chairman. After the 2006 parliamentary elections, Olmert and Kadima headed a new coalition government that included the center-left Labor Party, the religious Shas party, and other factions.

Israeli-Palestinian relations deteriorated after the Islamist group Hamas won elections to the Palestinian Legislative Council (PLC) in January 2006, outpolling PA president Mahmoud Abbas's Fatah party. Over the next two years, Israel experienced regular rocket and mortar fire from Gaza, as well as some terrorist attacks; the IDF continued to stage airstrikes against militant leaders, and invaded the Gaza Strip in the summer of 2006. Also that summer, Israel went to war against the Lebanese Islamist militia Hezbollah after the group staged a cross-border attack; a UN-brokered ceasefire ended the fighting in August.

Olmert resigned in September 2008, after being charged in a corruption case. Foreign Minister Tzipi Livni replaced him, but she was unable to form a new majority coalition in the Knesset (parliament), prompting early elections in February 2009. While Kadima led with 28 seats, Likud (27 seats) ultimately formed a mostly right-wing government with the secular nationalist Yisrael Beiteinu (15 seats), Shas (11 seats), and other parties. The Labor Party (13 seats) also joined the coalition, leaving Kadima in opposition. The new government, headed by Likud leader Benjamin Netanyahu, took office in April 2009.

Meanwhile, unilateral ceasefires in January 2009 ended an almost three-week-long conflict between Israel and Hamas, which had ruled the Gaza Strip exclusively since driving out Fatah officials in a 2007 PA schism. Well over 1,000 Palestinians were killed, including hundreds of noncombatants. Thirteen Israelis were killed, including three civilians.

In 2010 and 2011, a series of private ships carrying food and goods attempted to break Israel's economic blockade of Gaza, in place since 2007. In May 2010, Israeli forces intercepted a six-ship flotilla from Turkey and killed nine activists on board one vessel—the *Mavi Marmara*—in an ensuing confrontation. A UN report concluded that Israel was legally allowed to blockade Gaza, but that it had used excessive force and should not have operated so far from Israeli shores. Israel later eased some aspects of the blockade.

In January 2011, the Labor Party quit the coalition, but Defense Minister Ehud Barak and four other lawmakers resigned from Labor and started a new party, Independence, which remained in the ruling coalition.

Bouts of fighting between Israel and Gaza-based militants broke out regularly in 2011. In May, thousands of Palestinians marched on Israel's borders from Syria, Lebanon, the West Bank, and Gaza to mark Al-Nakba Day commemorating the displacement of Palestinians following Israel's declaration of independence in 1948. Clashes with Israeli troops ensued, and a dozen protesters were killed. In June, Israeli soldiers clashed with hundreds of Syrian and Palestinian protesters who entered the Golan Heights. According to Syria, Israeli troops killed 23 demonstrators; Israel claimed that some protesters were killed by a Syrian land mine, and that fewer people died overall.

In October 2011, Israel and Hamas negotiated a prisoner exchange whereby Hamas freed IDF soldier Gilad Shalit, who had been held captive since 2006, and Israel freed 1,027 Palestinian prisoners. Fighting between Hamas and Israel intensified again in November 2012, after Hamas stepped up its rocket fire into Israel, and Israel assassinated Ahmed Jabari, the commander of Hamas's military wing. However, the IDF stopped short of a ground invasion of Gaza, and the eight-day conflict ended with an Egyptian-brokered ceasefire. Six Israelis and more than 160 Palestinians were killed. The ceasefire agreement led to a loosening of the blockade.

In May 2012, Netanyahu struck a coalition deal with Kadima leader Shaul Mofaz, bringing the coalition members to 94, but Kadima withdrew in July due to tensions over the issue of subjecting ultra-Orthodox Jews to military conscription. The remaining governing parties were unable to agree on a budget in October, prompting the dissolution of the Knesset and the scheduling of elections for January 2013.

Political Rights and Civil Liberties: Israel is an electoral democracy. A largely ceremonial president is elected by the 120-seat Knesset for seven-year terms. The prime minister is usually the leader of the largest party or coalition in the Knesset, members of which are elected by party-list proportional representation for four-year terms. At under 3 percent, Israel's vote threshold for a party to win parliamentary representation is the world's lowest, leading to the regular formation of niche parties and unstable coalitions.

Parties or candidates denying Israel's Jewish character, opposing the democratic system, or inciting racism are prohibited. In 2009, the Knesset's Central Elections Committee voted to ban two Arab parties—Balad and the United Arab List (UAL)–Ta'al—from that year's elections, citing their alleged support for Hamas in the Gaza conflict. The ban was rapidly overturned by the Supreme Court, and the parties won three and four seats, respectively. In 2010, a Knesset plenum voted to strip Balad member Haneen Zoabi of some parliamentary privileges following her participation in the Mavi Marmara flotilla. In December 2012, a special nine-judge panel of the High Court voted unanimously to overturn the Central Elections Committee's ruling, paving the way for Zoabi to run in the 2013 elections.

Arabs enjoy equal political rights under the law but face discrimination in practice. Although Israeli identity cards have not classified residents by ethnicity since 2005, Jewish Israelis can often be identified by the inclusion of their Hebrew birth date. Arab Israelis currently hold 13 seats in the Knesset—though they constitute some 20 percent of the population—and no independent Arab party has ever been formally included in a governing coalition. Arabs generally do not serve in senior positions in government. Rising calls on the political right to impose a loyalty oath have marginalized Arab Israelis, though such measures have been rejected to date. In February 2012, some right-wing politicians denounced Salim Joubran, the sole Arab Israeli judge on the Supreme Court, for remaining silent during the singing of the national anthem—which refers explicitly to the Jewish soul—at a swearing-in ceremony. However, Deputy Prime Minister Moshe Ya'alon reportedly came to his defense.

After Israel annexed East Jerusalem in 1967, the Arab residents were issued Israeli identity cards and given the option of obtaining Israeli citizenship, though most choose not to seek citizenship for political reasons. These noncitizens can vote in municipal as well as PA elections, and remain eligible to apply for Israeli citizenship. However, Israeli law strips noncitizens of their Jerusalem residency if they stay outside the city for more than three months.

A 2003 law denies citizenship and residency status to West Bank or Gaza residents married to Israeli citizens. While the measure was criticized as blatantly discriminatory, supporters cited evidence that 14 percent of suicide bombers acquired Israeli identity cards via family reunification laws. A 2011 law allows the courts to revoke the citizenship of any Israeli convicted of spying, treason, or aiding the enemy. A number of rights groups and the Shin Bet security service criticized the legislation as unnecessary and overly broad.

Under the 1948 Law of Return, Jewish immigrants and their immediate families are granted Israeli citizenship and residence rights; other immigrants must apply for these rights.

Corruption scandals in recent years have implicated several senior officials. Ehud Olmert resigned as prime minister in 2008 amid graft allegations, and was indicted in 2009. In July 2012, he was found not guilty in two cases and convicted of breach of trust in a third case; a fourth case was ongoing at year's end. Separately, Yisrael Beiteinu leader Avigdor Lieberman was indicted for fraud and breach of trust in December 2012, prompting his resignation as foreign minister. Israel was ranked 39 out of 176 countries surveyed in Transparency International's 2012 Corruption Perceptions Index.

The Israeli media are vibrant and independent and freely criticize government policy. All Israeli newspapers are privately owned, though ownership is concentrated among a small number of companies. Internet access is widespread and unrestricted. The Israel Broadcasting Authority operates public radio and television services, and commercial broadcasts are widely available. Most Israelis subscribe to cable or satellite television. In September 2011, the financially troubled Channel 10 television station was allegedly pressured by investors into apologizing for a story on a supporter of Prime Minister Benjamin Netanyahu, American businessman Sheldon Adelson; Netanyahu and his wife agreed to drop libel suits against the station in October 2012.

Print articles on security matters are subject to a military censor, and while the scope of permissible reporting is generally broad, press freedom advocates have warned of more aggressive censorship in recent years. In 2011, journalist Anat Kam was sentenced to four and a half years in prison for giving *Haaretz* newspaper reporter Uri Blau over 2,000 classified military documents during her military service. The Supreme Court reduced Kam's sentence by one year in December 2012. The Government Press Office has occasionally refused to provide press cards to journalists, especially Palestinians, to restrict them from entering Israel, citing security considerations.

Legislation passed in March 2011 requires the state to fine or withdraw funds from local authorities and other state-funded groups that hold events marking Al-Nakba on Israeli independence day; that support armed resistance or "racism" against Israel; or that desecrate the state flag or national symbols. Both Arab rights and freedom of expression groups criticized the law as an unnecessary and provocative restriction. In July 2011, the Knesset passed the so-called Boycott Law, which exposes Israeli individuals and groups to civil lawsuits if they advocate an economic, cultural, or academic boycott of the State of Israel or West Bank settlements, even without clear proof of financial damage. In December 2012, the High Court of Justice heard a petition against the law by eight civil rights groups; a ruling was pending at year's end.

While Israel's founding documents define it as a "Jewish and democratic state," freedom of religion is respected. Christian, Muslim, and Baha'i communities have jurisdiction over their own members in matters of marriage, divorce, and burial. The Orthodox establishment generally governs these matters among Jews, drawing objections from many non-Orthodox and secular Jews. In a landmark ruling in May 2012, the first non-Orthodox rabbi, Miri Gold, won the right to receive state funding (in this case, from the Ministry of Education, Culture, and Sport). In another milestone case in 2011, an Israeli Jew won the right to an identity card that excluded his Hebrew birth date. Marriages between Jews and non-Jews are not recognized by the state unless conducted abroad, and legislation allowing nonreligious civil unions is restricted to two parties with no official religion.

Ultra-Orthodox Jews were exempt from compulsory military service under the 2002 Tal Law, which expired in July 2012 after the High Court of Justice ruled it unconstitutional in February. At the end of 2012, Israeli authorities were preparing to send draft notices to thousands of ultra-Orthodox youths.

Muslim and Christian religious authorities are occasionally discriminated against in resource allocation and upkeep of religious sites, though the state budget officially assigns funds according to need. Citing security concerns, Israel occasionally restricts Muslim worshippers' access to the Temple Mount, or Haram al-Sharif, in Jerusalem. In July 2012, Knesset member Michael Ben-Ari of the National Union party was photographed destroying a copy of the Christian New Testament; national and international condemnation of the stunt ensued.

Primary and secondary education is universal, with instruction for the Arab minority based on the common curriculum used by the Jewish majority, but conducted in Arabic. In 2010, the government mandated the teaching of Arabic in all state schools. School quality is generally worse in mostly Arab municipalities, and Arab children have reportedly had difficulty registering at mostly Jewish schools. Israel's universities are open to all students based on merit, and have long been centers for dissent. In late 2012, the Council of Higher Education attempted to shut down the Department of Politics and Government at Ben Gurion University, ostensibly for political and ideological reasons. The decision was being contested at year's end. Also in late 2012, the government granted Ariel College in the West Bank university status. In response, the Council of Presidents of Israeli Universities filed a motion at the High Court of Justice to oppose the designation. Periodic road closures and other security measures restrict access to Israeli universities for West Bank and Gaza residents.

Israel hosts an active civil society, and demonstrations are widely permitted, though groups committed to the destruction of Israel are not allowed to demonstrate. Thousands of Israelis participated in social protests in 2012, following massive 2011 demonstrations over the cost of living. A law requiring nongovernmental organizations (NGOs) to submit financial reports four times a year on the support they receive from foreign government sources went into effect in early 2012.

Workers may join unions of their choice and have the right to strike and bargain collectively. Three-quarters of the workforce either belong to Histadrut, the national labor federation, or are covered by its social programs and bargaining agreements. Both sector-specific and general strikes are common, but typically last less than 24 hours. About 100,000 legal foreign workers enjoy wage protections, medical insurance, and guarantees against employer exploitation. However, those who leave their original employers can be stripped of such rights and may face deportation. A 2011 amendment to the Israel Entry Law restricts the number of times foreign workers can change employers and may limit them to working in a specific geographical area or field. Advocacy groups claim that there are at least 100,000 illegal workers in Israel, many of whom are exploited. In 2010, Israel began construction of a barrier along its border with Egypt to prevent undocumented African migrants from entering. In January 2012, the Knesset passed legislation allowing migrants and asylum seekers who entered Israel irregularly and have been involved in criminal proceedings to be administratively detained, without trial, for up to three years, or indefinitely if they come from hostile countries.The judiciary is independent and regularly rules against the government. The Supreme Court hears direct petitions from citizens and Palestinian residents of the West Bank and Gaza Strip, and the state generally adheres to court rulings. In April 2012, the Knesset debated a bill that would allow it to override Supreme Court decisions. However, following a storm of criticism, no such measure had been enacted by year's end.

The Emergency Powers (Detention) Law of 1979 provides for indefinite administrative detention without trial. According to the human rights group B'Tselem, as of the end of November 2012 there were 4,430 Palestinians in Israeli jails: 3,048 serving sentences, 216 detainees, 990 being detained until the conclusion of legal proceedings, and 178 administrative detainees. A temporary order in effect since 2006 permits the detention of suspects accused of security offenses for 96 hours without judicial oversight, compared with 24 hours for other detainees. Israel outlawed the use of torture in 2000, but milder forms of coercion are permissible when the prisoner is believed to have vital security information, leading to some criticism by human rights groups. Interrogation methods include binding detainees to a chair in painful positions, slapping, kicking, and threatening violence against detainees and their relatives. Al-Nakba Day protests in 2012 included a mass hunger strike by Palestinians held in Israeli jails. Under an Egyptian-brokered agreement, Israel pledged to improve prison conditions in exchange for an end to the strike.

According to Defence for Children International, there were 178 Palestinian children being held in Israeli jails as of November 2012, and 21 Palestinian youths aged 12 to 15. Most are serving two-month sentences—handed down by a Special Court for Minors created in 2009—for throwing stones or other projectiles at Israeli troops in the West Bank; acquittals on such charges are very rare. East Jerusalem Palestinian minors are tried in Israeli civil juvenile courts.

Arab citizens of Israel tend to receive inferior education, housing, and social services relative to the Jewish population. According to a 2010 report by the NGO Mosawa, Arab Israelis own only 3.5 percent of the land in Israel. Arab Israelis, except for the Druze minority, are not subject to the military draft, though they may volunteer. Those who do not serve are ineligible for the associated benefits, including scholarships and housing loans.

At the end of 2012, the courts were reviewing the constitutionality of 2011 legislation that would allow Jewish communities of up to 400 residents in the Negev and Galilee to exclude prospective residents based on "social suitability." The measure was seen by critics as an attempt to legalize restrictions that could be used to bar Arab residents.

There are about 110,000 Bedouin in the Negev region, most of whom live in dozens of towns and villages that are not recognized by the state. Those in unrecognized villages cannot claim social services and have no official land rights, and the government routinely demolishes their unlicensed structures. International and domestic human rights groups accuse the government of pervasive land and housing discrimination against the historically nomadic Bedouin.

The state's Israeli Lands Administration owns 93 percent of the land in Israel; 13 percent of that is owned by the Jewish National Fund (JNF). In 2005, the Supreme Court and attorney general ruled that the JNF could no longer market property only to Jews. The Knesset made several unsuccessful attempts to override those rulings.

Security measures can lead to delays at entrances to some public places, though IDF checkpoints are restricted to the West Bank. By law, all citizens must carry national identification cards. The West Bank security barrier restricts the movement of some East Jerusalem residents. Formal and informal local rules that prevent driving on Jewish holidays can also hamper freedom of movement.

Women have achieved substantial parity at almost all levels of Israeli society. However, Arab women and religious Jewish women face some discrimination. Many ultra-Orthodox Jewish communities enforce gender separation, impinging on women's rights in nearby public places and public transportation. In January 2012, the Supreme Court ruled against gender-segregated buses, though many women still sit at the rear of buses on certain bus lines in practice. In late 2011 and early 2012, ultra-Orthodox men attacked women and girls in the town of Beit Shemesh whom they deemed to be dressed immodestly. Repeatedly during 2012, Jewish women were arrested at the Western Wall for praying in shawls traditionally used by men, in violation of rules set for the location by ultra-Orthodox religious officials. In December 2012, the government formed a commission to evaluate the status of public prayer at the site in light of these ongoing gender concerns.

Both the United Nations and the U.S. State Department have identified Israel as a top destination for trafficked women in recent years. The government has opened shelters for victims, and a 2006 law mandates prison terms of up to 20 years for perpetrators.

Since 2006, Israel has recognized same-sex marriages conducted abroad. While such marriages are still not conducted in the country, a family court in Tel Aviv recognized Israel's first same-sex divorce in December 2012. Nonbiological parents in same-sex partnerships are eligible for guardianship rights. Openly gay Israelis are permitted to serve in the armed forces.

Italy

Political Rights: 2*
Civil Liberties: 1
Status: Free

Population: 60,949,900
Capital: Rome

Ratings Change: Italy's political rights rating declined from 1 to 2 due to continued, widespread grand and petty corruption, especially in the south.

Ten-Year Ratings Timeline For Year Under Review (Political Rights, Civil Liberties, Status)

2003	2004	2005	2006	2007	2008	2009	2010	2011	2012
1,1F	1,1F	1,1F	1,1F	1,1F	1,2F	1,2F	1,2F	1,1F	1,2F

Overview: In July 2012, the government approved $32 billion in spending cuts over the next three years to tackle Italy's growing public debt, a move that led to anti-austerity protests across the country. Umberto Bossi, the founder and leader of the Northern League regional party and a fierce critic of corruption, stepped down in April after accusations that he had used party funds for personal use. Meanwhile, former prime minister Silvio Berlusconi was sentenced in October to nearly four years in prison for tax fraud, a charge that he was appealing at year's end.

Italy was unified under the constitutional monarchy of Piedmont and Sardinia in the 19th century. Its liberal period ended in 1922 with the rise Benito Mussolini and his Fascist Party, which eventually led the country to defeat in World War II. A referendum in 1946 replaced the monarchy with a republican form of government.

The "clean hands" corruption trials of the early 1990s prompted the collapse of the major political factions that had dominated postwar Italian politics—the Christian Democrats, the Communists, and the Socialists. Since that time, many new parties and coalitions have emerged.

Parliamentary elections in 2006 ushered in a new center-left coalition government led by Romano Prodi, leaving outgoing prime minister Silvio Berlusconi's center-right bloc in opposition for the first time since 2001. However, Prodi's new government proved unstable; it lost key votes in Parliament over Italy's troop presence in Afghanistan in 2007, and it finally collapsed after a no-confidence vote in January 2008.

Berlusconi's rightist coalition, People of Freedom (PDL), handily won early parliamentary elections in April 2008, capturing a total of 344 seats in the lower house and 174 in the Senate in combination with two smaller allies. A center-left coalition led by Rome mayor Walter Veltroni's new Democratic Party placed second, with 246 seats in the lower house and 132 seats in the Senate. Berlusconi ran on pledges to crack down on crime and illegal immigration, and the new Parliament passed a number of measures on those issues in 2008 and 2009.

In 2011, Italy's growing public debt, at 120 percent of gross domestic product, fueled international concerns. A crucial austerity package was passed by both houses of Parliament in November, allowing the sale of state assets and hikes in the value-added tax, the retirement age, and fuel prices. The increasingly unpopular Berlusconi resigned in November 2011 and was replaced by a technocratic government led by the respected economist Mario Monti, a former member of the European Commission. The new government ushered yet another austerity package through Parliament in December. In July 2012, the government announced spending cuts of 26 billion euros (about US$32 billion) over the next three years, which will include reducing the number of public sector workers by 10 percent.

A combination of the country's financial difficulties and fraud charges against Berlusconi led to declines for both the PDL and the Northern League during local elections in May 2012, in which left-leaning parties and grassroots movements performed well. A protest movement led by the comedian Beppe Grillo that ran in opposition to austerity measures and the traditional political system won the mayor's seat in Parma. In December, Berlusconi announced his intention to lead his party in the 2013 parliamentary elections—just two months after he had stated that he would not enter the race.

A series of earthquakes and aftershocks hit towns in central and northern Italy in May, killing more than 20 people, leaving thousands homeless, and causing billions of dollars in damages. In January, the Costa Concordia cruise ship ran aground outside the Tuscan town of Giglio, killing more than 30 passengers onboard; an investigation into the disaster was ongoing at year's end.

Political Rights and Civil Liberties: Italy is an electoral democracy. The president, whose role is largely ceremonial but sometimes politically influential, is elected for a seven-year term by Parliament and regional representatives. Giorgio Napolitano, a former Communist, was selected for the post in 2006. The president chooses the prime minister, who is often, but not always, the leader of the largest party in the elected, 630-seat lower house, the Chamber of

Deputies. The upper house is the Senate, with 315 elected seats. Members of both chambers serve five-year terms. The president may appoint up to five senators for life, and in November 2011, Napolitano used this mechanism to make Mario Monti a member of Parliament, smoothing his path to the premiership. Monti's technocratic government was supported by the elected Parliament, though Monti is not an elected officeholder.

A 1993 electoral law replaced the existing system of proportional representation with single-member districts for most of the seats in Parliament. The move was designed to reduce the number of political parties that could obtain seats and ensure a more stable majority for the parties in power; Italians had seen more than 50 governments since 1945. However, in 2005, proportional representation was restored, with a provision awarding at least 54 percent of the seats in the lower house to the winning party or coalition, no matter how small its margin of victory. For the Senate, victory in a given region assures the winning party or coalition a 55 percent majority of that region's allotment of seats. Just six parties won seats in the lower house in the 2008 elections, down from 26 in the previous elections.

The Democratic Party has been the main party of the left since it was formed through a merger of multiple smaller parties in 2007. The Northern League, which was founded in 1991 as a federation of several regional parties, is allied with the right-leaning PDL.

Corruption remains a central issue in Italian politics. In October 2012, a court sentenced former prime minister Silvio Berlusconi to nearly four years in prison for tax fraud, a charge that he was appealing at year's end. This was Berlusconi's fourth lower-court conviction and the first since stepping down as prime minister. In February, a court in Milan ended a corruption trial against him for paying a British lawyer, David Mills, to lie for him in court; the court ruled that the statute of limitations had expired. Berlusconi still faces three other trials, including a criminal trial for allegedly paying an underage prostitute for sex. In May, police ordered a series of pre-dawn raids to clamp down on a growing match-fixing scandal that has tarnished the country's national sport, football (soccer). Umberto Bossi, the charismatic founder and leader of the Northern League, resigned in April after an investigation found that he had used party funds to pay for home repairs and purchase cars. Italy was ranked 72 out of 176 countries surveyed in Transparency International's 2012 Corruption Perceptions Index.

Freedoms of speech and the press are constitutionally guaranteed. There are many newspapers and news magazines, most with regional bases. Newspapers are primarily run by political parties or owned by large media groups. When Berlusconi was prime minister, he controlled up to 90 percent of the country's broadcast media through state-owned outlets and his own private media holdings. Internet access is generally unrestricted. Courts still convict individuals for criminal defamation. In June, journalists Orfeo Donatini and Tiziano Marson of the newspaper *Alto Adige* were convicted of defaming a local politician in a 2008 article alleging that he had participated in a neo-Nazi summit; the information for the article had been obtained from a police report. Both journalists were sentenced to four months in prison and fined 15,000 euros ($18,500). In September 2012, the Supreme Court upheld a 14-month prison sentence for then editor of the right-wing paper *Libero*, Alessandro Sallusti. Sallusti was originally convicted in 2011 for allowing the publication of an anonymously written article in 2007 that called for the death of a gynecologist and others over an abortion performed on a 13-year-old.

Religious freedom is constitutionally guaranteed and respected in practice. Although Roman Catholicism is the dominant faith, and the state grants some privileges to the Catholic Church, there is no official religion. The state provides support, if requested, to other sects represented in the country. Agreements between the government and a number of religious groups have been signed, but an omnibus religious freedom law has yet to be passed. In March 2011, the European Court of Human Rights ruled that crucifixes traditionally hung in school classrooms across the country do not violate the rights of non-Catholics. Academic freedom is respected.

Italians are free to assemble and form social and political associations, and about 35 percent of the workforce is unionized. The constitution recognizes the right to strike, with the exception of those employed in essential services and a number of self-employed professions, such as lawyers, doctors, and truck drivers. Protests spread across the country in November 2012 in opposition to austerity measures imposed by the government.

The judicial system is undermined by long trial delays and the influence of organized crime. Despite legal prohibitions against torture, there have been reports of excessive use of force by police, particularly against illegal immigrants. Some prisons continue to suffer from overcrowding. The country continued to make some gains against organized crime in 2012. In March, police arrested 16 judges accused of taking bribes from a crime syndicate known as the Camorra in the southern city of Naples. However, the mayor of the southern town of Monasterace in Calabria resigned in April after her business was set on fire and her car shot for in what she believed was retaliation by the local mafia for instituting financial reforms.

Italy is a major entry point for undocumented immigrants trying to reach Europe, and the government has been criticized for holding illegal immigrants in overcrowded and unhygienic conditions and denying them access to lawyers. A government crackdown on illegal immigration that began in 2008 has led to the arrest of hundreds of people. A 2009 immigration law imposes fines on illegal immigrants and grants authorities the power to detain them for up to six months without charge. In September 2012, the government began implementing a new law imposing sanctions, including fines and prison sentences, on employers who hire undocumented workers. In February, the European Court of Human Rights ruled that Italy had violated the European Convention on Human Rights in 2009 when it turned away a boat of African migrants and asylum seekers and sent them to Libya as part of its agreement with the country's former leader, Colonel Mu'ammar al-Qadhafi.

Women benefit from generous maternity-leave provisions, equality in the workforce, and considerable educational opportunities. However, violence against women continues to be a problem, and female political representation is low for the region. Women hold 21 percent of the seats in the Chamber of Deputies. Italy is a destination country for the trafficking of women and children for sexual and labor exploitation. The government has tried to tackle the problem by prosecuting more traffickers; it also finances nongovernmental organizations that work to raise awareness of the problem and support trafficking victims.

Jamaica

Political Rights: 2
Civil Liberties: 3
Status: Free

Population: 2,716,000
Capital: Kingston

Ten-Year Ratings Timeline For Year Under Review (Political Rights, Civil Liberties, Status)

2003	2004	2005	2006	2007	2008	2009	2010	2011	2012
2,3F	2,3F	2,3F	2,3F	2,3F	2,3F	2,3F	2,3F	2,3F	2,3F

Overview: In 2012, two gay Jamaicans initiated a legal challenge with the Inter-American Commission on Human Rights to laws discriminating against members of the country's LGBT (lesbian, gay, bisexual, and transgender) community. Meanwhile, the economy continued to stagnate during the year as the country struggled with high rates of inflation and unemployment.

Jamaica achieved independence from Britain in 1962. Since then, power has alternated between the social democratic People's National Party (PNP) and the more conservative Jamaica Labour Party (JLP). In September 2007, the JLP won a majority of seats in the House of Representatives, ending 18 years in power for the PNP. JLP leader Bruce Golding became the new prime minister.

Under Golding, Jamaica struggled with high levels of crime, sluggish economic growth, and a public sector in need of major reform. In 2009, an all-time high of 1,682 homicides were reported. Over half of these were gang related, and only 21 percent were resolved in court. The situation improved slightly in 2011 following police crackdowns on gang violence. According to police statistics, the murder rate during the first three months of the year fell 44 percent over the same period in 2010. The government also established a commission to investigate incidents of civilian shootings, though local human rights organizations have expressed doubt whether it will have the resources it needs to function effectively.

Long-standing relationships between elected representatives and organized crime, in which criminal gangs guaranteed voter turnout in certain neighborhoods in exchange for political favors and protection, received special scrutiny in recent years as the U.S. government pressed for the extradition of alleged drug trafficker Christopher "Dudus" Coke. The gang Coke reputedly led, the Shower Posse, was based in Tivoli Gardens, an area of Kingston that Golding represented in Parliament. In April 2010, the *Washington Post* reported that a JLP government official had signed a $400,000 contract with the U.S. lobbying firm Manatt, Phelps & Phillips to fight Coke's extradition. The public outcry in the United States and Jamaica forced Golding in May 2010 to order Jamaican security forces into Tivoli Gardens to arrest Coke, leading to days of violence, in which 73 civilians and several police officers were killed. Coke was finally apprehended in late June, reportedly on his way to surrender at the U.S. embassy. In August 2011, after being extradited to the United States, he pled guilty to drug trafficking and assault charges under a plea bargain; he was sentenced to 23 years in prison in June 2012.

Golding suddenly announced his resignation in September 2011, a move widely interpreted as fallout from the Coke affair, which had caused Golding to lose support within his own party and among the electorate. Observers speculated that the managed transition to a successor was a preemptive political maneuver to keep the JLP as a viable political contender. In October, the JLP elected Minister of Education Andrew Holness to become Golding's successor as party leader and prime minister. The transition to Holness, who was 39 years old, was seen by some as marking a generational shift within the JLP, and possibly within Jamaican party politics in general.

Holness called for early general elections at the end of the year. On December 29, the PNP captured 41 seats in Parliament, while the JLP took only 22. Portia Simpson Miller became prime minister; she had previously held the position in 2006 and 2007.

Despite continued success in the tourism industry and a surge in the real estate sector, the Jamaican economy continued to stagnate 2012, struggling with high inflation and unemployment exacerbated by high debt levels and the implementation of government austerity plans.

Political Rights and Civil Liberties: Jamaica is an electoral democracy. The bicameral Parliament consists of the 60-member House of Representatives, elected for five years, and the 21-member Senate, with 13 senators appointed on the advice of the prime minister and 8 on the advice of the opposition leader. The leader of the party or coalition holding a majority in the House of Representatives is appointed as prime minister by the governor general. The British monarch is represented as head of state by a governor general, who is nominated by the prime minister and approved by the monarch.

Powerful criminal gangs in some urban neighborhoods maintain influence over voter turnout in return for political favors, which has called into question the legitimacy of election results in those areas.

Corruption remains a serious problem in Jamaica. Government whistle-blowers who object to official acts of waste, fraud, or abuse of power are not well protected by Jamaican law, as is required under the Inter-American Convention against Corruption. Implementation of the 2002 Corruption Prevention Act has been problematic. Opposition leaders have accused the government of having connections to scams originating in Jamaica in which victims are told they have won the lottery, only to have their personal information stolen. The government has addressed the matter by amending a handful of laws, including the Evidence Act in November 2012. Jamaica was ranked 83 out of 176 countries surveyed in Transparency International's 2012 Corruption Perceptions Index.

The constitutional right to free expression is generally respected. While newspapers are independent and free of government control, circulation is generally low. Broadcast media are largely state owned but are open to pluralistic points of view. Journalists occasionally face intimidation in the run-up to elections. The country enacted an access to information law in 2002.

Freedom of religion is constitutionally protected and generally respected in practice. While laws banning Obeah—an Afro-Caribbean shamanistic religion—remain on the books, they are not actively enforced. The government does not hinder academic freedom.

Freedoms of association and assembly are generally respected. Jamaica has a small but robust civil society and active community groups. Approximately 20 percent of the workforce is unionized. Labor unions are politically influential and have the right to strike.

The judicial system is headed by the Supreme Court and includes a court of appeals and several magistrates' courts. The Trinidad-based Caribbean Court of Justice is the highest appellate court. A growing backlog of cases and a shortage of court staff at all levels continue to undermine the justice system.

Extrajudicial killings by police remain a major problem in Jamaica, accounting for 12 percent of murders each year, according to Amnesty International. Since 2006, the government has paid an estimated J$365 million (US$3.8 million) to victims of such violence, and it reportedly owes an additional J$400 million (US$4.4 million). Jamaican police killed 21 people—including a 13-year-old girl caught in the crossfire of a shootout between police and criminals—over six days in early March 2012, prompting calls for authorities to mount an investigation into police operations. In October, the Jamaica Civil Society Coalition and the human rights lobby Jamaicans for Justice criticized the lack of a preliminary report in the public investigation into the 2010 Tivoli Garden riots that led to the killing of dozens of civilians. Ill-treatment by prison guards has also been reported, and conditions in detention centers and prisons are abysmal. Vigilante violence remains a common occurrence in Jamaica. Jamaican Police Commissioner Owen Ellington in October condemned mob killings in Kingston and other parts of the island. According to recent reports, children from abusive homes are routinely placed into police custody together with common criminals for periods of up to two weeks.

Kingston's insular "garrison" communities remain the epicenter of most violence and serve as safe havens for gangs. Jamaica is a transit point for cocaine shipped from Colombia to U.S. markets, and much of the island's violence is the result of warfare between drug gangs known as posses. Contributing factors include the deportation of Jamaican-born criminals from the United States and an illegal weapons trade.

Harassment and violence against members of the LGBT (lesbian, gay, bisexual, and transgender) community remains a major concern and is frequently ignored by the police. Sodomy is punishable by 10 years in prison with hard labor. Although Prime Minister Portia Simpson Miller stated that she would hire a gay man or lesbian to serve in her cabinet, her administration has made no attempts to repeal the country's anti-gay laws. In October 2012, two gay Jamaicans initiated a legal challenge to these laws with the Inter-American Commission on Human Rights. According to the Jamaican Forum of Lesbians, All-Sexuals and Gays in 2012, nine gay men were killed in 2012.

Legal protections for women are poorly enforced, and violence and discrimination remain widespread. A number of highly publicized rape cases of young girls have led to public protests and a renewed debate about prevention and punishment of the crime. Women are underrepresented in government, holding just seven seats in the House of Representatives.

Japan

Political Rights: 1
Civil Liberties: 2
Status: Free

Population: 127,587,800
Capital: Tokyo

Ten-Year Ratings Timeline For Year Under Review (Political Rights, Civil Liberties, Status)

2003	2004	2005	2006	2007	2008	2009	2010	2011	2012
1,2F	1,2F	1,2F	1,2F	1,2F	1,2F	1,2F	1,2F	1,2F	1,2F

Overview: The Democratic Party of Japan's approval ratings plummeted throughout 2012 after the passage of legislation doubling Japan's consumption tax and the government's handling of the country's nuclear energy policy. Territorial disputes escalated with China over the Senkaku/Diaoyu Islands and with South Korea over the Tokdo/Takeshima Islands during the year. The Liberal Democratic Party won snap legislative elections in December after the lower house was dissolved in exchange for the passage of deficit financing and electoral reform bills.

Japan has been a parliamentary democracy with a largely symbolic monarchy since its defeat in World War II. The Liberal Democratic Party (LDP) presided over Japan's economic ascent while maintaining close security ties with the United States during the Cold War. The so-called iron triangle—the close relationship between the LDP, banks, and big business—fostered Japan's economic success. The LDP government mandated that corporations, specifically construction firms in charge of major public-works projects, rely on banks for capital, and the banks in turn took large equity stakes in the companies. Over time, companies engaged in politically expedient but financially unviable projects in order to reap government rewards, and the iron triangle became a major source of government corruption.

Shinzo Abe became prime minister in 2006, though his tenure was marred by scandals and political gaffes. Abe resigned in September 2007, after the LDP lost control of the legislature's upper chamber to the Democratic Party of Japan (DPJ) in the July elections.

Abe's ineffective successor, Yasuo Fukuda, resigned in September 2008. Former foreign minister Taro Aso, the LDP secretary general, succeeded him and focused on strengthening the economy and eliminating government debt equal to almost 200 percent of the country's gross domestic product.

The LDP's nearly 55-year dominance in the legislature's lower chamber ended when the DPJ captured 308 seats in the August 2009 elections, and DPJ leader Yukio Hatoyama became prime minister. The DPJ victory also led to the development of a two-party system in Japan. However, a failure to keep several campaign promises and a financial scandal involving DPJ secretary general Ichiro Ozawa prompted Hatoyama's resignation in June 2010.

Approval ratings for Hatoyama's successor, Finance Minister Naoto Kan, plummeted after he proposed doubling the country's sales tax. The DPJ subsequently lost its majority in the legislature's upper chamber elections in July to a coalition of the LDP and two smaller parties. Kan continued to face significant domestic and international challenges, including persistent inflation, a faltering economy, and diplomatic disputes with China and Russia.

On March 11, 2011, Japan was hit by a 9.0 earthquake off the east coast of Tohoku, which triggered a tsunami. Numerous buildings and critical infrastructure were damaged or destroyed, and many people died. The reactor cooling systems at the Fukushima Daiichi Nuclear Power Plant also suffered severe damage, resulting in a nuclear meltdown. Widespread radioactive contamination led to an evacuation of the surrounding area, displacing several hundred thousand residents. Amid plunging approval ratings over the government's handling of the crises, Kan resigned in August, and Finance Minister Yoshihiko Noda was chosen as his successor.

After Fukushima, the government began shutting down nuclear reactors throughout the country, the last of which was closed on May 5, 2012, both for maintenance checks and in response to growing public hostility toward nuclear energy. Prior to Fukushima, nuclear power comprised 30 percent of Japan's energy, and there had been plans to increase that share to 50 percent by 2030. During July and August, tens of thousands of antinuclear activists protested the restarting of two reactors at the Ohi Nuclear Power Plant. The largest demonstration, on July 16 in a central Tokyo park, reportedly attracted 170,000 protestors. Weekly protests outside the prime minister's office continued until August 22, when Noda invited a dozen protestors inside for a half-hour meeting that was broadcast live. Noda affirmed that the government would consider public opinion when drafting the country's energy policy. Meanwhile, approval ratings for Noda and the DPJ plummeted after the adoption in August of legislation that will increase the consumption tax rate from 5 to 10 percent by 2015 to help fund social security needed to care for the country's rapidly aging population.

In August 2012, Japan recalled its ambassador to South Korea after South Korean President Lee Myung-bak visited the Tokdo/Takeshima Islands, reviving an ongoing territorial dispute. Japan claims the islands under international law, and it asked South Korea to submit a joint request to the International Court of Justice to examine the issue. Although Seoul refused, Tokyo returned the Japanese ambassador to his post.

Tensions between Japan and China flared in September over the Senkaku/Diaoyu Islands. Japan claims the islands for itself, while private Japanese citizens have owned several of them. On September 11, Japan's cabinet secretary announced that the government would purchase the islands from their owners for 2.05 billion yen (US$26.2 million), triggering massive nationalist protests throughout China. Violence spread to more than 100 cities, particularly against Japanese citizens and businesses, leading to military exchanges in the disputed waters around the islands. Nationalist sentiment and an emphasis on national defense policies also grew in Japan.

In November, Noda offered to dissolve the legislature's lower house early in exchange for the passage of deficit financing and electoral reform bills introduced earlier in the year. Opposition leader Shinzo Abe agreed, the bills were adopted, and on November 16, Noda dissolved the lower house and called for snap elections. The LDP won a clear majority of more than 252 seats in the December 16 elections, and Abe replaced Noda as prime minister.

Political Rights and Civil Liberties: Japan is an electoral democracy. The prime minister—who leads the majority party or coalition in the bicameral legislature's (Diet's) lower chamber, the House of Representatives—serves as head of government. Members of the House of Representatives serve four-year terms. In November 2012, the lower house passed legislation that reduced its size to 475 seats, from 480, by cutting the number of voting districts to 6, from 11, thus decreasing the number of single-member seats to 295, from 300. Districts will be redrawn and the bill will be in effect after the 2013 Lower House election. The 242-seat upper chamber, the House of Councillors, consists of 146 members elected in multiseat constituencies and 96 elected by national party list; members serve six-year terms, with half facing election every three years. Proposed legislation would maintain the same number of Councillors, but the four smallest districts would be cut, and the four largest districts would be divided (-4, +4). Emperor Akihito serves as the ceremonial head of state.

Significant efforts have been made to fight corruption by reforming the iron triangle system, mostly by loosening ties between the government and big business. In January 2011, Ichiro Ozawa and three of his aides were indicted for underreporting income and violating campaign finance laws. The Tokyo District Court acquitted Ozawa in April 2012; the Tokyo High Court upheld the ruling in November after prosecutors appealed. Ozawa's aides were found guilty of falsifying financial reports of Ozawa's political fund management organization in September 2011 and received suspended prison terms, which they appealed. Japan was ranked 17 out of 176 countries surveyed in Transparency International's 2012 Corruption Perceptions Index.

Japan's press is private and independent. However, its press clubs, or kisha kurabu, ensure homogeneity of news coverage by fostering close relationships between the major media and bureaucrats and politicians. Government officials often give club members exclusive access to political information. Internet access is not restricted.

Japanese of all faiths can worship freely. Religious groups may be unlicensed, but registering with government authorities as a "religious corporation" brings tax benefits and other advantages. There are no restrictions on academic freedom.

The constitution guarantees freedoms of assembly and association, and there are active human rights, social welfare, and environmental groups. Massive peaceful antinuclear protests against the restarting of two reactors took place in July and August 2012. Anti-U.S. military protests erupted in September 2012, as tens of thousands of people rallied against the deployment of the Osprey hybrid aircraft in Okinawa. The Osprey's crash record concerned residents, and Okinawa governor Hiokazu Nakaima asked the United States to suspend deployment until the aircraft's safety could be confirmed. A case of breaking and entering and a U.S. serviceman's alleged assault of a teenage Japanese boy led to additional protests against the U.S. military in Okinawa in November.

Japan's judiciary is independent. There are several levels of courts, and suspects generally receive fair public trials by an impartial tribunal within three months of being detained. For serious criminal cases, a judicial panel composed of saiban-in (lay-judges), selected from the general public, and professional judges rule on defendants. While arbitrary arrest and imprisonment are not practiced, the police may detain suspects for up to 23 days without charge in order to extract confessions. Prison conditions comply with international standards, though prison officials sometimes use physical and psychological intimidation to enforce discipline or elicit confessions.

The constitution prohibits discrimination based on race, creed, sex, or social status. However, entrenched societal discrimination prevents Japan's estimated three million burakumin—descendants of feudal-era outcasts—and the indigenous Ainu minority from gaining equal access to housing and employment. Foreign-born populations, particularly Koreans, suffer similar disadvantages.

Although women in Japan enjoy legal equality, discrimination in employment and sexual harassment on the job are common. Violence against women often goes unreported due to concerns about family reputation and other social mores. Japanese courts have yet to provide reparations to comfort women—World War II–era sex slaves—despite international pressure. Japan is a destination, source, and transit country for people trafficked for forced labor and sexual exploitation.

⬇ Jordan

Political Rights: 6
Civil Liberties: 5
Status: Not Free

Population: 6,318,400
Capital: Amman

Trend Arrow: Jordan received a downward trend arrow due to the repression of widespread protests against a new electoral law and the lack of meaningful political reform.

Ten-Year Ratings Timeline For Year Under Review (Political Rights, Civil Liberties, Status)

2003	2004	2005	2006	2007	2008	2009	2010	2011	2012
5,5PF	5,4PF	5,4PF	5,4PF	5,4PF	5,5PF	6,5NF	6,5NF	6,5NF	6,5NF

Overview: The harassment of opposition activists continued in 2012, with the government cracking down on demonstrators protesting a new electoral law and the political status quo, as well as fuel subsidy reductions. A new press law was also widely criticized for limiting freedom of expression on the internet. Meanwhile, the threat of instability spreading from neighboring Syria remained throughout the year.

The Hashemite Kingdom of Jordan, then known as Transjordan, was established as a League of Nations mandate under British control in 1921 and won full independence in 1946. The 46-year reign of King Hussein, which began in 1953, featured a massive influx of Palestinian refugees, the occupation of the West Bank by Israel in 1967, and numerous assassinations and coup attempts. Nevertheless, with political and civil liberties tightly restricted, Hussein proved adept at co-opting his political opponents. Jordan signed a peace treaty with Israel in 1994.

Crown Prince Abdullah II succeeded his father in 1999, implementing major economic reforms to alleviate severe economic problems. Meanwhile, additional restrictions on the media, public protests, and civil society were imposed after Islamists, leftists, and Jordanians of Palestinian descent staged demonstrations to demand the annulment of the 1994 treaty and express support for the Palestinian uprising (intifada) that began in 2000. Beginning in 2001, Abdullah ruled by decree for two years, and due process and personal freedoms were curtailed. The king allowed reasonably free and transparent—though not fair—parliamentary and municipal elections in 2003. The relationship between the government and political parties remained strained, however, as the 2007 elections were marred by irregularities and the arrest of members of the Islamic Action Front (IAF), the main opposition party. A 2008 law requiring parties to have broader membership bases led to a drop in the number of registered parties from 37 to 14.

The king unexpectedly dismissed parliament in November 2009 and ruled by decree until November 2010. International observers deemed the November 2010 polls to have been technically well conducted, but the IAF boycotted them, citing structural biases that guaranteed the success of the king's traditional supporters.

Jordan largely avoided the widespread political unrest that swept the Middle East in 2011. Calls for reform escalated late in the year, however, resulting in the October resignation of Prime Minister Marouf al-Bakhit and all but four cabinet ministers. The king replaced Bakhit with Awn Khasawneh, a former judge at the International Court of Justice considered friendly to reform.

In 2012 Jordan saw further cabinet reshuffles and the promise of elections in early 2013 in response to ongoing popular discontent. Prime Minister Khasawneh resigned in April, and was replaced by Fayez El-Tarawneh, who himself resigned in early October. The king then appointed Abdullah Ensour as interim prime minister of a caretaker government tasked with overseeing the elections. In June, parliament passed a new electoral law at King Abdullah's urging. Many regime opponents, including the IAF, criticized the law and vowed to boycott the upcoming elections. Critics said that the new law continues to encourage voting based on tribal ties, rather than political and ideological affiliation, by allocating relatively few seats based on proportional representation. In protests against the electoral law, opponents also argued that the electoral weight granted to representatives from each of Jordan's governorates disadvantaged urban-based groups less likely to be loyal to King Abdullah. The government's decision to reduce fuel subsidies also touched off protests involving thousands of people in late October and early November. Dozens were injured, at least three people killed, and several hundred protesters were arrested. King Abdullah pardoned most of the protesters arrested in these demonstrations in early December.

Meanwhile, the conflict in neighboring Syria continued to impact Jordan, as an influx of refugees, cross-border fighting, and a thwarted al-Qaeda plot raised fears of insecurity. The office of the United Nations High Commissioner for Refugees estimated that there were more than 160,000 Syrian refugees in Jordan by the end of the year, with steady increases in arrivals straining Jordan's resources and social services. The difficult conditions in Zaatari refugee camp, the main facility for Syrian refugees in northern Jordan, contributed to fears of unrest.

Political Rights and Civil Liberties: Jordan is not an electoral democracy. King Abdullah II holds broad executive powers, appoints and dismisses the prime minister and cabinet, and may dissolve the bicameral National Assembly at his discretion. The members of the lower house of the National Assembly, the Chamber of Deputies, are elected through universal adult suffrage. The Chamber of Deputies may approve, reject, or amend legislation proposed by the cabinet, but it cannot enact laws without the assent of the 55-seat upper house, the Senate, whose members are appointed by the king. Members of both houses serve four-year terms. Regional governors are appointed by the central government.

The electoral law passed in June 2012 increased the total number of seats in the Chamber of Deputies from 120 to 150 and the quota of seats for women from 12 to 15. Each voter was given the right to cast one ballot for a national party list in a proportional representation system and another for a local candidate in single nontransferable vote system. Only 27 of the 140 seats are to be determined by proportional representation. The law also permits members of the security forces to vote for the first time. Constitutional amendments approved by the king in September 2011 called for the creation of an Independent Electoral Commission, which was established in May 2012.

Parliament adopted legislation in May 2012 making it easier to create new political parties, but discouraged the creation of parties founded on religious or tribal affiliations.

The Chamber of Deputies is heavily imbalanced in favor of rural districts, whose residents are generally of Transjordanian (East Bank) origin. Christian and Circassian minorities are guaranteed nine and three seats, respectively.

Efforts to combat corruption in recent years have yielded mixed results, and investigations and arrests rarely lead to serious punishment. In February 2012, former intelligence chief Mohamed al-Dahabi was arrested on charges of embezzlement, money laundering, and abuse of power, and stood trial in June. He was convicted in November, receiving the maximum sentence of 13 years in prison. Jordan was ranked 58 out of 176 countries surveyed in Transparency International's 2012 Corruption Perceptions Index.

Freedom of expression is restricted, and those who violate unwritten rules, or red lines, regarding reporting on the royal family and certain societal taboos face arrest. While imprisonment was abolished as a penalty for press offenses in 2007, journalists can still be jailed under the penal code. Self-censorship is common. Several people were arrested in 2012 for insulting or criticizing the king, his cabinet, or Jordan's system of government. Most broadcast news outlets remain under state control, but satellite dishes and the internet give residents access to foreign media. While there are dozens of private newspapers and magazines, the government has broad powers to close them. Websites are subject to similar restrictions, and police have considerable discretion in monitoring and sanctioning online content. Newspapers faced pressure in 2012 to delete or retract material critical of the government, and satellite television station JOSAT faced suspension after it aired a program on corruption.

In September 2012, parliament amended the Press and Publications Law, which further restricts the freedom of expression of electronic publications, requires journalists to join a union, requires that websites register with the government, and holds website owners responsible for all content posted to their sites, even by visitors. Activists from Jordan and international human rights organizations argued that the law was an unprecedented assault on freedom of expression and could lead to greater persecution of regime critics.

Islam is the state religion. Christians are recognized as religious minorities and can worship freely. While Baha'is and Druze are not officially recognized, they are allowed to practice their faiths. The government monitors sermons at mosques, and preachers cannot practice without written government permission. Only state-appointed councils may issue religious edicts, and it is illegal to criticize these rulings.

Academic freedom is generally respected, and Jordanians openly discuss political developments within established red lines. However, there have been reports of a heavy intelligence presence on some university campuses.

Freedom of assembly is generally restricted, though a March 2011 amendment to the Public Gatherings Law allowed demonstrations without prior permission. In 2012, police forcefully dispersed protests against the political status quo and the detention of protesters in prior demonstrations around the country, especially in Amman, Tafilah, and Mafreq, detaining demonstrators on charges of disturbing public order, insulting the king, or incitement against the regime. In July, police used violence to disperse a protest against the press law amendments. The government also used a provision prohibiting unlawful gatherings for the purpose of committing crime as a way to penalize peaceful assembly and freedom of expression. In late October and early November, police violently dispersed protests against cuts to fuel subsidies in multiple cities, arresting over 300 people and trying them in state security courts. Freedom of association is limited. The Ministry of Social Development has the authority to reject registration and foreign funding requests for nongovernmental organizations (NGOs) and can disband organizations it finds objectionable. NGOs supporting associations with political purposes are prohibited. State security must approve all NGO board members. In June 2012, the government banned the legal assistance group Tamkeen for allegedly accepting unauthorized foreign funding, an accusation international rights groups criticized as unfounded.

Workers have collective bargaining rights but must receive government permission to strike. More than 30 percent of the workforce is organized into 17 unions. Labor rights organizations have raised concerns about poor working conditions and sexual abuse in Qualifying Industrial Zones, where mostly female and foreign factory workers process goods for export. In 2012, the Ministry of Labor issued new guidelines that further restricted migrants' mobility by conditioning their exiting the country on the permission of their employers.

The judiciary is subject to executive influence through the Justice Ministry and the Higher Judiciary Council, most of whose members are appointed by the king. While most trials in civilian courts are open and procedurally sound, the State Security Court (SSC) may close its proceedings to the public. The prime minister may refer cases to the SSC, and people convicted of misdemeanors by the SSC lack the right of appeal. In 2012, numerous people arrested during demonstrations against the government were charged under terrorism provisions, which placed them under the jurisdiction of the SSC. Groups including the IAF continue to call for the SSC to be dissolved altogether. Provincial governors can order indefinite administrative detention. Constitutional amendments approved in 2011 called for the creation of a Constitutional Court, which was established in October 2012. International human rights groups continued to express concern over the use of torture in Jordanian prisons in 2012. Prison conditions are poor, and inmates reportedly experience severe beatings and other abuse by guards.

Women enjoy equal political rights but face legal discrimination in matters involving inheritance, divorce, and child custody, which fall under the jurisdiction of Sharia (Islamic law) courts. Women are guaranteed 15 seats in the lower house of parliament under the new electoral law and 20 percent of municipal council seats. The upper house of parliament currently has seven female senators. Men who commit "honor crimes" against women often receive lenient sentences. In July 2012, a man was accused of stabbing to death and running over his divorced sister; between 15 and 20 such crimes occur in Jordan each year. Jordan is a destination and transit country for human trafficking for forced labor and, to a lesser extent, sex.

⬇ Kazakhstan

Political Rights: 6
Civil Liberties: 5
Status: Not Free

Population: 16,793,000
Capital: Astana

Trend Arrow: Kazakhstan received a downward trend arrow due to the banning of several media outlets following a violent crackdown on labor unrest.

Ten-Year Ratings Timeline For Year Under Review (Political Rights, Civil Liberties, Status)

2003	2004	2005	2006	2007	2008	2009	2010	2011	2012
6,5NF	6,5NF	6,5NF	6,5NF	6,5NF	6,5NF	6,5NF	6,5NF	6,5NF	6,5NF

Overview: In January 2012, the government extended its emergency powers following December 2011 violence between police and striking oil workers in Zhanaozen that left 16 people dead. The authorities continued to harass and detain journalists attempting to report on the aftermath, arrested opposition politicians, and rushed dozens of defendants to trial. In December, a court shuttered a major group of opposition media outlets for propagating "extremism." Separately, the government strictly enforced 2011 legislation on religion, leaving up to a third of previously legal organizations outside the law and criminalizing believers who continued to meet without registration.

Kazakh Communist Party leader Nursultan Nazarbayev won an uncontested presidential election in December 1991, two weeks before Kazakhstan gained its independence from the Soviet Union. In April 1995, Nazarbayev called a referendum on extending his five-year term, due to expire in 1996, until December 2000. A reported 95 percent of voters endorsed the move. An August 1995 referendum, which was boycotted by the opposition, approved a new constitution designed to strengthen the presidency. Nazarbayev's supporters captured most of the seats in December 1995 elections for a new bicameral Parliament.

In October 1998, Parliament amended the constitution to increase the presidential term from five to seven years and moved the presidential election forward from December 2000 to January 1999. The main challenger was disqualified on a technicality, and Nazarbayev was reelected with a reported 80 percent of the vote.

Progovernment parties captured all but one seat in 2004 elections for the lower house of Parliament. International monitors from the Organization for Security and Cooperation in Europe (OSCE) found some improvements over previous polls, but criticized the lack of political balance on election commissions, media bias in favor of propresidential candidates, and the politically motivated exclusion of other candidates.

The president again secured reelection in 2005 with 91 percent of the vote amid opposition allegations of fraud. An international monitoring report found intimidation and media bias in favor of the incumbent.

Political violence flared in 2005–06, with the suspicious suicide of opposition leader Zamanbek Nurkadilov in December 2005 and the murder of Altynbek Sarsenbayev, a leading member of the opposition coalition For a Just Kazakhstan, in February 2006. The investigation of Sarsenbayev's killing pointed to the involvement of state security officers but left many questions unanswered.

Constitutional changes in May 2007 removed term limits for Nazarbayev, reduced the terms to five years, and eliminated individual district races for the lower house of Parliament, leaving only party-slate seats filled by nationwide proportional representation. Elections under the new rules in August produced a one-party legislature, with the propresidential Nur Otan party taking 88 percent of the vote and no opposition parties clearing the 7 percent threshold for representation. No opposition candidates participated in the October 2008 indirect elections for the upper house of Parliament.

Although Nazarbayev rejected a proposal to hand him the presidency for life in 2009, a constitutional amendment in 2010 gave him immunity from prosecution and made his family's property effectively inviolable. Nazarbayev won a snap presidential election in April 2011 with 96 percent of the vote. His three little-known competitors all publicly expressed support for him. Nur Otan won all 16 Senate seats at stake in indirect upper-house elections in August.

The country was shaken in 2011 by several minor bomb attacks blamed on religious extremists. The government responded by enacting new legislation that broadly restricted religious freedoms. In December of that year, an extended strike by oil workers in the city of Zhanaozen turned violent, resulting in at least 16 deaths as police cracked down, and prompting the government to declare a state of emergency.

Over the course of 2012, the courts hastily issued criminal convictions against alleged organizers and participants in the Zhanaozen unrest, opposition politicians accused of supporting them, and some local government officials who were charged with neglect or excessive force. Despite initial promises, the government rejected international requests for an independent inquiry into the Zhanaozen events. Meanwhile, the security services engaged in numerous "antiterrorism" operations around the country, drawing criticism for killing most suspects during the raids. In

December, a court in Almaty approved prosecutors' request to ban the opposition Algha (Forward) party, the People's Front movement, and some 36 independent newspapers and websites on the grounds that they were "extremist."

Also during the year, parliamentary elections held in January resulted in a new lower house that included two minor parties but no opposition representation. Nur Otan took 83 of the 107 seats, Ak Zhol won eight, and the Communist People's Party secured seven. OSCE monitors noted that the elections did not meet democratic norms. A September government shuffle ended Karim Masimov's nearly six-year tenure as prime minister, reassigning him to head the presidential administration. First Deputy Prime Minister Serik Akhmetov was named to replace him.

Throughout the year, Astana maintained good relations with China, Russia, and the United States, which continued to ship supplies for its operations in Afghanistan through Kazakh territory.

Political Rights and Civil Liberties:

Kazakhstan is not an electoral democracy. The constitution grants the president considerable control over the legislature, the judiciary, and local governments. Under the current constitutional rules, President Nursultan Nazarbayev may serve an indefinite number of five-year terms.

The upper house of the bicameral Parliament is the 47-member Senate, with 32 members chosen by directly elected regional councils and 15 appointed by the president. The senators serve six-year terms, with half of the 32 elected members up for election every three years. The lower house (Mazhilis) has 107 deputies, with 98 elected by proportional representation on party slates and 9 appointed by the Assembly of Peoples of Kazakhstan, which represents the country's various ethnic groups. Members serve five-year terms.

The ruling party, Nur Otan, is headed by the president and dominates the legislature. Parties must clear a 7 percent vote threshold to enter the Mazhilis, and once elected, deputies must vote with their party. Parties are barred from forming electoral blocs. A 2009 electoral law amendment guarantees the second-ranked party at least two seats in the Mazhilis if only one party passes the 7 percent threshold. Aside from Nur Otan, two parties—Ak Zhol and the Communist People's Party—won representation in the 2012 Mazhilis elections, with each earning just over 7 percent of the vote. However, neither is considered an opposition party.

Political parties based on ethnic origin, religion, or gender are prohibited. A 2002 law raised the number of members that a party must have to register from 3,000 to 50,000; modest amendments in 2009 lowered the number to 40,000. In December 2012, a court invoked laws against "extremism" to ban the unregistered opposition party Algha and the People's Front, another opposition movement. Algha leader Vladimir Kozlov had been sentenced to seven and a half years in prison in October for his alleged role in the Zhanaozen violence. He was found guilty of heading an illegal group, inciting social hatred, and calling for the violent overthrow of the constitutional order.

Corruption is widespread at all levels of government. Rakhat Aliyev, Nazarbayev's former son-in-law, issued allegations of corruption among top officials that were accompanied by some documentary evidence and matched reports from numerous other sources. In October 2012, prosecutors in Atyrau announced they had uncovered

$100 million in corrupt deals involving regional officials and Amanzhan Ryskali, brother of former governor Bergay Ryskaliev. Kazakhstan was ranked 133 out of 176 countries surveyed in Transparency International's 2012 Corruption Perceptions Index.

While the constitution provides for freedom of the press, the government has repeatedly harassed or shut down independent media outlets. Most of the country's outlets, including publishing houses, are controlled or influenced by members of the president's family and other powerful groups. Libel is a criminal offense, and the criminal code prohibits insulting the president; self-censorship is common. Lukpan Akhmedyarov, a journalist based in the city of Oral, was fined some $33,000 in July 2012 for criticizing a local official. He and his employer, Uralskaya Nedelya, were fined another $7,700 in November for insulting a local finance police officer. Akhmedyarov had been attacked and seriously injured by unidentified assailants in April.

Independent media frequently suffer attacks, arrests, and pressure from authorities. As the Zhanaozen violence erupted in late 2011 and protests spread to neighboring cities, police used emergency powers to arrest or detain journalists attempting to cover the unrest. The government shut down access to online social media, internet service in the affected areas, and some independent online news outlets in an attempt to control information about the violence. Many of these measures were continued into 2012, including raids on independent media outlets and harassment and detention of journalists covering the aftermath of the events. New regulations gave the Ministry of Culture and Information expanded powers to combat "unofficial or negative information" about any crisis, and in October, the ministry issued a code of ethics for journalists. It was described as a nonbinding "instrument of self-discipline," but critics said it was meant to encourage self-censorship. The December court decision designating "extremist" media outlets affected eight newspapers, including *Respublika* and *Vzglyad*, and 23 news websites. Similar rulings that month banned additional outlets, including the Kyrgyzstan-based Stan TV and Moscow-based K-Plus television stations, along with their websites.

Apart from the outlets banned for extremism in 2012, the government has a broader record of blocking websites that are critical of the regime. The list of banned websites expanded significantly during the year, with some 950 new sites added. The authorities also intensified measures to restrict circumvention tools like Tor and virtual private networks, which enable secure and uncensored internet access and are popular with opposition journalists and activists.

The constitution guarantees freedom of worship, and many religious communities practice without state interference. However, laws passed in 2005 banned all activities by unregistered religious groups and gave the government great discretion in outlawing organizations it designated as "extremist." Local officials have harassed groups defined as "nontraditional," such as Hare Krishnas, Protestant Christians, and Jehovah's Witnesses. A 2011 law required reregistration of all religious groups, gave the government unprecedented authority to regulate religious communities, and forbade religious expression in government institutions. These new rules were enforced strictly in 2012. The process of reregistration was used to cull around one-third of the country's religious organizations, exposing unregistered believers to arrest and prosecution.

The government reportedly permits academic freedom, except with respect to criticism of the president and his family. Corruption in the education system is widespread, and students frequently bribe professors for passing grades.

Despite constitutional guarantees, the government imposes restrictions on freedom of association and assembly. Unsanctioned opposition gatherings are frequently broken up by police. Nongovernmental organizations continue to operate despite government harassment surrounding politically sensitive issues.

Workers can form and join trade unions and participate in collective bargaining, although co-opted unions and close links between the authorities and big business make for an uneven playing field. Migrant workers from neighboring countries often face poor working conditions and a lack of legal protections. Child labor in agriculture has been reported. During 2012, dozens of people were convicted for participating in the 2011 Zhanaozen protests by striking oil workers and their supporters, described by prosecutors as "mass disorder." However, several police and local officials were also convicted for excessive force or corruption in relation to the deadly crackdown, and a prison official was held accountable for the death of a suspect in custody.

The constitution makes the judiciary subservient to the executive branch. Judges are subject to political bias, and corruption is evident throughout the judicial system. Conditions in pretrial facilities and prisons are harsh. Police at times abuse detainees and threaten their families, often to obtain confessions, and arbitrary arrest and detention remain problems.

Members of the sizable Russian-speaking minority have complained of discrimination in employment and education. The Russian and Kazakh languages officially have equal status, but in 2011, newly rigorous Kazakh-language testing for candidacy in the presidential election eliminated many opposition candidates. Kazakhstan decriminalized homosexual activity in 1998, but LGBT (lesbian, gay, bisexual, and transgender) people continue to face societal discrimination.

While the rights of entrepreneurship and private property are formally protected, equality of opportunity is limited by bureaucratic hurdles and the control of large segments of the economy by clannish elites and government officials. Astana residents whose homes have been demolished to make way for large construction projects have said they were denied legally guaranteed compensation.

Traditional cultural practices and the country's economic imbalances limit professional opportunities for women. Domestic violence often goes unpunished, as police are reluctant to intervene in what are regarded as internal family matters. Despite legal prohibitions, the trafficking of women for the purpose of prostitution remains a serious problem.

Kenya

Political Rights: 4
Civil Liberties: 4*
Status: Partly Free

Population: 43,013,000
Capital: Nairobi

Ratings Change: Kenya's civil liberties rating declined from 3 to 4 due to increased ethnic and religious tensions and incidents of violence throughout the country in advance of 2013 elections, driven in part by the heavy-handed counterterrorism efforts of the police and security services.

Ten-Year Ratings Timeline For Year Under Review (Political Rights, Civil Liberties, Status)

2003	2004	2005	2006	2007	2008	2009	2010	2011	2012
3,3PF	3,3PF	3,3PF	3,3PF	4,3PF	4,3PF	4,4PF	4,3PF	4,3PF	4,3PF

Overview:
In 2012, leading politicians jockeyed for position in the run-up to general elections set for March 2013, the first polls since a disputed ballot in 2007 resulted in deadly ethnic and political violence. However, the International Criminal Court's indictment of prominent Kenyans, including a top candidate for president, overshadowed the elections, with the trial scheduled to begin in the spring of 2013. Throughout 2012, ethnic and religious tensions and violence increased, exacerbated by factors including the upcoming elections, abuses by the security forces, and Kenya's military involvement in fighting the Islamist group al-Shabaab in Somalia.

Kenya achieved independence from Britain in 1963. Nationalist leader Jomo Kenyatta served as president until his death in 1978, when Vice President Daniel arap Moi succeeded him. While the Kenyan African National Union (KANU) party remained in power, Moi diminished the influence of the previously dominant Kikuyu ethnic group, favoring his own Kalenjin group.

In 1992, after a lengthy period of single-party rule, domestic unrest and pressure from international donors forced Moi to hold multiparty elections. However, he and KANU continued to win elections by using political repression, state patronage, media control, and dubious electoral procedures.

Government corruption remained endemic, as did police abuses, political influence in the judiciary, and state efforts to undermine independent civil society activity. Political polarization increased amid government-sponsored ethnic violence, perpetrated in most cases by Kalenjin or Maasai KANU supporters against members of the Kikuyu and Luhya ethnic groups, who were believed to support opposition parties. Despite these problems, political space for opposition views continued to open, and many of the core elements necessary for a democratic political system developed.

The opposition united to contest the 2002 elections as the National Rainbow Coalition. The bloc won a majority in the National Assembly, and its presidential candidate, Mwai Kibaki, emerged victorious. The new leadership's ambitious reform program achieved some successes, but the effort was blunted by the fragility of the governing coalition, a complex bid to overhaul the constitution, significant fiscal constraints, and the threat of terrorism.

A lively press and public investigative commissions became increasingly critical of the substance and slow pace of the government's reform agenda, and in 2005, referendum voters soundly rejected a draft constitution that failed to shift power away from the presidency. In 2006, John Githongo, Kibaki's former anticorruption chief, issued an authoritative report indicating that corruption had reached the highest ranks of the government, prompting the resignation of several cabinet ministers.

Kenya's democratic development and economic performance suffered sharp reversals as a result of apparent manipulation of the December 2007 presidential election, which aggravated public discontent and fostered large-scale violence. While the concurrent parliamentary polls showed major gains for the opposition Orange Democratic Movement (ODM), Kibaki was declared the winner of the presidential vote over ODM candidate Raila Odinga amid credible allegations of fraud. Kibaki had long been accused of favoring his Kikuyu group, and the presidential results sparked weeks of violence between the Kikuyu, the Luo, and other groups. Approximately 1,150 people were killed and over 350,000 were displaced. In late February 2008, Kibaki and Odinga, a Luo, negotiated a compromise agreement under intense foreign pressure in which Odinga received the newly created post of prime minister and the ODM joined Kibaki's Party of National Unity in a coalition cabinet.

A Commission of Inquiry into Post-Election Violence issued a report in 2008 that identified governmental impunity, popular anger, and systemic failures in Kenya's security institutions as the primary instigating factors in the crisis. The report called for the creation of a special tribunal to prosecute crimes committed during the postelection violence, and stated that in the absence of such a tribunal, the names of organizers of the violence should be sent to the International Criminal Court (ICC). The Kenyan government made little progress in addressing the postelection violence, prompting the ICC to initiate an investigation into crimes against humanity in 2010. In April 2011, six high-profile Kenyans, including Deputy Prime Minister Uhuru Kenyatta and former cabinet minister William Ruto, appeared before the ICC.

In an August 2010 referendum, voters overwhelmingly approved a new constitution that delineated and checked the roles and powers of the executive, legislative, and judicial branches of government. The new arrangement limited previously expansive presidential and other executive powers, and shifted some authority from the central government to local officials. Throughout 2011 and 2012, legislative bodies, government commissions, and civil society groups worked to implement the far-reaching reforms called for in the new constitution. These included the creation of the Independent Electoral and Boundaries Commission, which is tasked with organizing the first presidential and parliamentary elections since the flawed 2007 polls; these elections are scheduled for March 2013. In 2012, Kenyatta, with Ruto as his running mate, and Odinga emerged as the front-runners in the presidential campaign. Their two rival political groupings—Kenyatta's Jubilee Coalition and Odinga's Coalition for Reform and Democracy—are generally based on ethnicity, not ideology, raising concerns that postelection violence could again erupt along ethnic lines.

In January 2012, the ICC ordered Kenyatta, Ruto, and two others to stand trial for crimes against humanity in connection with the 2007–08 postelection violence, with the trial dates set for April 2013, just after a possible presidential runoff vote. The ICC charges against Kenyatta and Ruto became political capital in some circles, as anti-Western and anti-ICC rhetoric became prevalent during the campaign and attracted some voters to the defendants' ticket.

In retaliation for Kenya's military involvement in the African Union Mission in Somalia, which was battling the radical Islamist group al-Shabaab, supporters of the group perpetrated multiple attacks inside Kenya in 2012, mainly in areas of North Eastern Province and Nairobi with large ethnic Somali populations. In the deadliest incident, 17 people were killed and around 60 were injured when gunmen opened fire and threw grenades in two churches in Garissa, near the Somali border, in July. In September, the police said that they had foiled a terrorist attack in the final stages of planning in Nairobi, and that the perpetrators had ties to al-Shabaab. In a May 2012 report, Human Rights Watch documented human rights abuses against ethnic Somalis—both Kenyan citizens and refugees—by police and security forces, including sexual assault, beatings, arbitrary detention, and destruction of property. According to the UN High Commissioner for Refugees, there are more than 540,000 refugees from Somalia in Kenya, mainly in the Dadaab camp complex near the Somali border. In December, in the wake of the al-Shabaab attacks, the head of Kenya's refugee agency ordered all Somali refugees in Kenya to move to the Dadaab.

Political Rights and Civil Liberties: Kenya is not an electoral democracy. The 2007 presidential poll was undermined by several factors, including a defective voter registry and widespread fraud. However, the conduct of the constitutional referendum in August 2010 was considered legitimate and competitive, indicating an improvement in electoral transparency. Registration and other preparations for the 2013 vote were behind schedule throughout most of 2012.

Under the new constitution, the president is elected for up to two five-year terms. Following the 2013 elections, the post of prime minister—created as part of the 2008 compromise—will be abolished, and a new position of deputy president will be established. The unicameral National Assembly, which consists of 210 members elected for five-year terms, 12 members appointed by the president based on each party's share of the popular vote, and 2 ex-officio members, is set to be replaced by a bicameral legislature. The upper house, the Senate, will have at least 60 members, while the lower house is expected to number about 290 members. Ministers may not serve in the legislature, which will have the authority to approve or reject cabinet appointments. Local authorities are to be granted heightened powers. From the 2013 election on, the country will be divided into 47 counties, each of which will have a directly elected governor and assembly.

Political parties representing a range of ideological, regional, and ethnic interests are active and vocal, and there are no significant impediments to party formation. However, parties generally do not have an enduring presence, but are often amalgamated into coalitions designed only to win elections.

Kenya's new constitution includes measures for increased accountability and transparency to combat pervasive corruption, and an open government data portal is already available. However, official probes and prosecutions of corruption have yielded meager results, and no top officials have been successfully prosecuted for corruption since 2002. National and international watchdog bodies have identified the police, the judiciary, and the Ministry of Defense as some of the most corrupt institutions in the country. Transparency International's 2012 Corruption Perceptions Index ranked Kenya 139 out of 176 countries surveyed.

The new constitution strengthened protections for freedoms of speech and of the press; however, several laws restrict these rights in practice. The government monitors in some civil society meetings, and individuals run the risk of legal retaliation for expressing certain views. In addition to an existing hate speech law, the government in September announced plans to begin monitoring text messages and internet communications for hate speech; anyone caught expressing these views could face a fine of up to five million shillings ($58,100). Security forces harassed members of the media during the year. In April, two journalists were threatened by officers after covering a police raid on a supermarket in the western town of Kitale. Government officials brought several successful defamation suits against media outlets during the year. Journalists practice a degree of self-censorship, especially regarding topics such as corruption and drug trafficking. Nevertheless, Kenya's press environment remains one of the most vibrant in Africa. The government-owned Kenya Broadcasting Corporation dominates the broadcast sector, particularly outside urban centers. The government does not restrict access to the internet.

The authorities generally uphold freedom of religion in civil matters. The Islamic (Kadhi) court system is subordinate to the superior courts of Kenya. The Kadhi courts adjudicate cases related to personal status, marriage, divorce, or inheritance for people who profess the Muslim religion and who voluntarily submit to the courts' jurisdiction. Religious groups are required to register with the government, which permits them to apply for tax-exempt status. Religious tension has risen in recent years due to terrorist attacks carried out in Kenya in 2011 and 2012 by al-Shabaab, the Kenyan government's decision to send troops to Somalia to fight al-Shabaab in late 2011, and extrajudicial attacks by the Kenyan security forces against the mainly Muslim ethnic Somali population, which consists of both Kenyan citizens and refugees.

Academic freedom is the norm in Kenya, though the education system suffers from structural, funding, and other problems.

The constitution guarantees freedom of assembly. Local police must be notified in advance of any public meetings, and may prohibit such meetings from going forward. In 2012 the police regularly prohibited human rights groups from holding public meetings, and broke up meetings that had been permitted to begin. In April, police used teargas and fired live rounds into the air in order to break up a political rally near Nairobi, citing the presence of a former leader of the Mungiki, a sect of mainly Kikuyu youth that has been linked to the postelection violence and other criminal activity. In October, police used teargas to disperse demonstrators protesting a huge bonus that outgoing Kenyan legislators had awarded themselves. Kibaki later vetoed these bonuses in the wake of the protests. However, most nonpolitical protests in Kenya are tolerated. Domestic and international nongovernmental organizations are generally allowed to operate unimpeded.

There are some 40 trade unions in the country, representing about 900,000 workers. Most of the unions are affiliated with the sole approved national federation, the Central Organization of Trade Unions. The 2007 Labour Relations Act establishes broad criteria for union registration, leaving authorities with limited grounds for suspending or refusing to register a union. However, there are restrictions on the right to strike, and the relevant government bodies have been accused of failing to adequately enforce labor laws and protections.

The new constitution includes several provisions designed to enhance the independence of the judiciary, which had been subservient to the executive for much of the period since the end of colonial rule. A Supreme Court, Court of Appeal, and Constitutional Court were established, and the new Supreme Court chief justice, Willy Mutunga, has built up the court's image as a trusted institution. The new Judicial Services Commission handles the vetting and appointment of judges, and has been cited as an early success. However, the courts remain understaffed and underfinanced, leading to long trial delays that violate defendants' right to due process. A task force appointed in February 2012 to probe cases of postelection violence in 2007 and 2008 did not lead to any successful prosecutions during the year. The Truth, Justice, and Reconciliation Commission, established in 2008 to investigate gross human rights abuses and historical injustices between independence and 2008, made only minor progress in 2012, heavily overshadowed by the ICC proceedings. Prison conditions remain life threatening.

Impunity for arbitrary arrests, beatings, killings, and corruption among the security forces remained prevalent in 2012. In April, three people were killed during the forceful dispersion of a crowd by police in a suburb of Nairobi; six officers were suspended for the incident, but criminal proceedings had not begun at year's end. However, in the first conviction of police for extrajudicial killings, six officers were sentenced to death in December for the 2010 murders of seven taxi drivers; the sentence was being appealed.

At least seven prominent Muslim leaders with alleged ties to al-Shabaab were disappeared or killed by the police in 2012. In April, clerics Samir Khan and Mohammed Kassim were taken from a bus in Mombasa by armed men; Khan's mutilated body was found two days later, while Kassim remained missing. In August, Sheik Aboud Rogo Mohammed, who had been accused of involvement in funding and recruitment for al-Shabaab, was assassinated, allegedly by police. This ignited several days of violent riots in Mombasa, resulting in several deaths and injuries. Human rights organizations alleged that this is part of a targeted campaign by the security forces against terrorism suspects in Kenya.

In June, a High Court panel overturned a ban on the Mombasa Republican Council, a group that advocated the secession of mainly Muslim Coast Province. Authorities continued to target the group and its members, including incidents of beatings, raids, and killings. The ban was reinstated in October.

Kenya's population comprises more than 40 ethnic groups, and friction between them has led to frequent allegations of discrimination and periodic episodes of violence. Between December 2011 to May 2012, clashes between the Borana and Turkana groups near Isiolo, in central Kenya, displaced at least 7,500 people and killed dozens. Meanwhile, violence between the Borana and Gabra in the northern district of Moyale displaced up to 40,000, as pastoralists fought over access to land

and political control of the region in the run-up to the 2013 elections. Unresolved land usage and sharing issues also spiked in the Tana River valley in the southeast, as violent skirmishes between agricultural and pastoralist groups broke out in August and September, and again in December, killing 160 people and displacing thousands. An assistant minister was charged with inciting violence and was fired by the president, though these charges were eventually dismissed.

An estimated 200,000 internally displaced people (IDPs) from the 2007–08 postelection violence still have not returned to their homes. Approximately 118,000 IDPs were created in 2012 as a result of ethnic and resource clashes.

Consensual same-sex sexual activity is criminalized in Kenya, with a maximum of 21 years in prison for sex between men. Rape and domestic violence are widespread and rarely prosecuted, and spousal rape is not prohibited by law. Female genital mutilation is widely practiced, especially in rural areas, despite efforts to stop the practice. Women face severe discrimination in access to employment and credit, matrimonial rights, and property rights. The new constitution introduced significant reforms that could signal an improvement in equal treatment, domestic protections, inheritance rights, and government representation for women.

Kiribati

Political Rights: 1
Civil Liberties: 1
Status: Free

Population: 105,000
Capital: Tarawa

Ten-Year Ratings Timeline For Year Under Review (Political Rights, Civil Liberties, Status)

2003	2004	2005	2006	2007	2008	2009	2010	2011	2012
1,1F	1,1F	1,1F	1,1F	1,1F	1,1F	1,1F	1,1F	1,1F	1,1F

Overview: President Anote Tong was reelected on January 17, 2012. The government demanded closure of the newspaper *Kiribati Independent* for failing to be properly registered; the publisher accused the government of attempting to shut it down for printing reports critical of the government.

Kiribati gained independence from Britain in 1979. The country consists of 33 atolls scattered across nearly 1.5 million square miles of the central Pacific Ocean, as well as Banaba Island in the western Pacific.

Chinese military ambitions in the Pacific and competing offers of development assistance from China and Taiwan have been major issues in Kiribati politics. President Teburoro Tito's refusal to release details about a 15-year land lease to China for a satellite-tracking facility led to the collapse of his government in 2003. Opposition leader Anote Tong, who was elected president in 2004, immediately terminated the Chinese lease and restored diplomatic ties with Taiwan. Tong won a second four-year term in the 2007 presidential election.

Tong has vigorously called for international attention to the growing threats Kiribati faces from rising sea levels and dwindling fresh-water supplies. He has warned that relocation of the entire population might be necessary if ongoing climate change makes inundation inevitable. New Zealand has pledged to accept environmental refugees from Kiribati, and some have already moved there. In 2011, Tong said more coastal villages needed resettlement because the sea walls were no longer sufficient to protect them, and called for assistance for those who had to relocate overseas.

The government is the main employer in Kiribati, and many residents practice subsistence agriculture. The economy depends considerably on interest from a trust fund built on royalties from phosphate mining, overseas worker remittances, and foreign assistance.

Parliamentary elections took place over two rounds in 2011. The ruling Pillars of Truth party won 15 seats, and the opposition Karikirakean Tei-Kiribati and Maurin Kiribati parties took 10 seats and 3 seats, respectively.

Tong won another term in presidential elections held on January 13, 2012. Turnout nationwide was about 68 percent, and Tong defeated his closest opponent by about 2,000 votes. A new 12-member cabinet was formed on January 18.

Political Rights and Civil Liberties: Kiribati is an electoral democracy. The president is popularly elected in a two-step process, whereby Parliament nominates candidates from its own ranks and voters then choose one to be president. Forty-four representatives are popularly elected to the unicameral House of Parliament for four-year terms. The attorney general holds a seat ex officio, and the Rabi Island Council nominates one additional member. (Although Rabi Island is part of Fiji, many of its residents were originally from Kiribati's Banaba Island; British authorities forced them to move to Rabi when phosphate mining made Banaba uninhabitable.) The president, vested with executive authority by the constitution, is limited to three four-year terms.

Political parties are loosely organized and generally lack fixed ideologies or formal platforms. Geography, tribal ties, and personal loyalties influence political affiliations.

Official corruption and abuse are serious problems, and international donors have been demanding improved governance and transparency.

Freedom of speech is generally respected. There are two weekly newspapers: the state-owned *Te Uekara* and the privately owned *Kiribati Newstar*, and churches publish newsletters and periodicals. There are two radio stations and one television channel, all owned by the state. The government ordered the closure of *Kiribati Independent* in April 2012, and again in May, on the grounds that it was not properly registered. The paper's publisher, which is based in New Zealand, claimed that it had been trying to renew its license for six months but was delayed by the government; it also accused Anote Tong's administration of attempting to silence it in retaliation for running stories critical of the government. The newspaper continued its operations until June, when police arrived at its office in Tarawa to demand cessation of all publication activity, and it remained suspended at year's end. Internet access is limited outside the capital due to costs and lack of infrastructure. In October, Kiribati signed an agreement with Micronesia to add satellite and fiber cable communication links.

There have been no reports of religious oppression or restrictions on academic freedom. Access to and the quality of education at all levels, however, is seriously restricted by a lack of resources, and secondary education is not available on all islands.

Freedoms of assembly and association are generally respected. A number of nongovernmental organizations are involved in development assistance, education, health, and advocacy for women and children. Workers have the right to organize unions, strike, and bargain collectively, though only about 10 percent of the workforce is unionized. The largest union, the Kiribati Trade Union Congress, has approximately 2,500 members.

The judicial system is modeled on English common law and provides adequate due process rights. There is a high court, a court of appeal, and magistrates' courts; final appeals go to the Privy Council in London. The president makes all judicial appointments. Traditional customs permit corporal punishment. Councils on some outer islands are used to adjudicate petty theft and other minor offenses. A 260-person police force performs law enforcement and paramilitary functions. Kiribati has no military; Australia and New Zealand provide defense assistance under bilateral agreements.

Citizens enjoy freedom of movement, though village councils have used exile as a punishment.

Discrimination against women is common in the traditional, male-dominated culture. Sexual harassment is illegal and not reported to be widespread. Spousal abuse and other forms of violence against women and children are often associated with alcohol abuse. Despite domestic and international calls for greater female participation in politics, Tong has resisted efforts to reserve a set amount of seats in Parliament for female lawmakers. The president did, however, propose creating a ministry for women and youths, though an August 2012 vote in Parliament fell short of the two-thirds majority required to advance the ministry. Kiribati is a source for sex trafficking, with girls reportedly prostituted for crew members aboard foreign fishing vessels in the country's territorial waters.

Kosovo

Political Rights: 5
Civil Liberties: 4
Status: Partly Free

Population: 2,290,000
Capital: Pristina

Ten-Year Ratings Timeline For Year Under Review (Political Rights, Civil Liberties, Status)

2003	2004	2005	2006	2007	2008	2009	2010	2011	2012
5,5PF	6,5NF	6,5NF	6,5NF	6,5NF	6,5NF	5,4PF	5,4PF	5,4PF	5,4PF

Overview:
The International Steering Group ended its supervisory mandate of Kosovo in September 2012, though an international presence, including NATO peacekeepers, will continue to monitor conditions on the ground. In October, the prime ministers of Kosovo and Serbia held the first high-level meetings between the nations since 2008,

while Brussels noted progress on Kosovo's European trajectory. Meanwhile, legislators withdrew provisions from a new criminal code that threatened media independence after opposition from journalists and human rights groups.

Ethnic Albanians and Serbs competed for control over Kosovo throughout the 20th century. Following World War II, it became an autonomous Serbian province within Yugoslavia. In the late 1980s, the Yugoslav government began revoking much of Kosovo's provincial autonomy. In response, Kosovo Albanians, under longtime leader Ibrahim Rugova, developed their own quasi-governmental institutions during the 1990s, amid the chaos that accompanied the collapse of Yugoslavia.

An ethnic Albanian guerrilla movement, the Kosovo Liberation Army (KLA), began attacking Serbs and suspected ethnic Albanian collaborators in late 1997, provoking harsh responses by government forces. In March 1999, after internationally sponsored negotiations failed to halt the violence, NATO launched a 78-day bombing campaign that compelled Serbia to relinquish control over the province. After the fighting had ended, hundreds of thousands of displaced ethnic Albanians returned. NATO and the United Nations took responsibility for Kosovo's security and civilian administration, though Serbian rule remained legally intact.

After the international takeover, tens of thousands of non-Albanians were forced to flee the province. Currently, ethnic Albanians comprise about 90 percent of the population, with Serbs comprising most of the remainder. The largest Serb enclave is north of the Ibar River, while smaller Serb areas are scattered throughout Kosovo. In March 2004, two days of rioting against non-Albanian ethnic groups left some 20 people dead.

The October 2004 parliamentary elections resulted in a governing coalition between Rugova's Democratic League of Kosovo (LDK) and the Alliance for the Future of Kosovo (AAK). The Democratic Party of Kosovo (PDK), led by former KLA political leader Hashim Thaçi, won the 2007 parliamentary elections, raising Thaçi to the premiership.

The 2004 riots accelerated talks on Kosovo's final status. While ethnic Albanian negotiators demanded full independence, Serbian officials offered only autonomy. In late 2007, Finnish mediator Martti Ahtisaari recommended that the UN Security Council grant Kosovo a form of internationally supervised independence. Russia backed Serbia, however, and the international community was unable to reach consensus.

Kosovo's Assembly formally declared independence from Serbia on February 17, 2008, and the United States and most European Union (EU) members quickly recognized the new country. In June 2008, Kosovo's Serb municipalities formed a separate assembly that rejected Pristina's independence and aligned with Belgrade. The legal situation was further complicated by the ongoing supervision of Kosovo by international entities, including the UN Interim Mission in Kosovo, an EU mission known as EULEX, and NATO peacekeepers.

Following Serbia's August 2008 request for an advisory opinion, the International Court of Justice ruled in July 2010 that Kosovo's declaration of independence did not violate international law. While Kosovo joined the International Monetary Fund and the World Bank in 2009, continued resistance from Russia and China blocked its membership to the United Nations and other international organizations. As of December 2012, 98 countries recognized Kosovo.

In November 2010, Thaçi's government collapsed, leading to early elections in December. While most Serbs north of the Ibar boycotted the vote, up to 40 percent of the roughly 55,000 Serbs in the southern enclaves reportedly participated. Significant fraud in parts of Kosovo, including vote-buying, necessitated reruns in several municipalities in January 2011. Later that month, the Central Election Commission announced that the PDK won 32 percent of the vote and 34 seats in the 120-seat Assembly, while the LDK took 25 percent and 27 seats. The Vetëvendosje (Self-Determination) opposition movement finished a strong third with 13 percent and 14 seats.

A December 2010 report by Council of Europe rapporteur Dick Marty accused high-level Kosovo officials, including Thaçi, of involvement in an organized crime network that was active during and after the 1999 conflict. Most controversially, the report alleged that the group harvested organs from prisoners held by the KLA. Despite the allegations, Kosovo's parliament in February 2011 elected Thaçi to a second term as prime minister. It also elected businessman Behgjet Pacolli of the New Alliance for Kosovo as president, though the Constitutional Court overturned Pacolli's election in March, saying the vote had not been conducted properly. Atifete Jahjaga, deputy director of the Kosovo police, succeeded Pacolli in April.

In March 2011, Kosovo and Serbia began bilateral talks on technical issues regarding trade and other areas. The ongoing negotiations were repeatedly disrupted by a border conflict in northern Kosovo, the majority-Serb contested territory where Serbia funds "parallel" public services such as health care, and Pristina has scant influence. Hostilities had erupted there in July 2011, after Thaçi sent police to the border to enforce an effective embargo of Serbian goods in retaliation for a 2008 Serb ban on Kosovo imports that had followed its independence declaration. Local Serbs responded by burning checkpoints, blocking roads, and mobilizing demonstrations. NATO forces helped restore peace, and the bilateral dialogue resumed following an August 2011 NATO-brokered interim agreement.

Northern Kosovo remained restive in 2012. In January, leaders there rejected a settlement proposal by former Serbian president Boris Tadic to grant the north further autonomy. A month later, voters in northern Kosovo rejected the authority of central Kosovo institutions in a referendum held over international objections. Border blockades continued through the year.

The International Steering Group, a body representing 25 countries, ended its oversight of Kosovo on September 10. The political "milestone," as many called it, was largely symbolic, as NATO peacekeepers, EULEX, and a scaled-back UN mission continue to monitor conditions on the ground. However, this development also reflected Kosovo's state-building progress under the Ahtisaari plan, especially the decentralization process of granting self-rule to Serb enclaves south of the Ibar. In October, the EU said that Kosovo was nearly ready to begin negotiating a Stabilization and Association Agreement, a pre-accession instrument, and that talks would begin once Kosovo strengthened the rule of law, among other steps.

In September, Serbian leaders agreed to participate in regional meetings with Kosovo officials if "Kosovo" is followed on first reference in documents by an asterisk connected to a footnote explaining that, in effect, Belgrade does not recognize Kosovo's statehood. The bilateral dialogue, which had stalled after the May general elections in Serbia, resumed on October 19 in Brussels with meetings between Thaçi and Serbian prime minister Ivica Dacic; the meetings were the first high-level encounter between the nations since 2008. Nevertheless, key issues, such as the contested north, remained unresolved in 2012.

On November 29, Ramush Haradinaj, a former prime minister of Kosovo and KLA commander, was acquitted at the International Criminal Tribunal for the Former Yugoslavia in a retrial of a 2008 verdict. The UN court said that there was no evidence of charges that Haradinaj committed crimes against humanity in 1998 and 1999.

Political Rights and Civil Liberties: Kosovo is not an electoral democracy. Members of the unicameral, 120-seat Assembly are elected to four-year terms; 10 seats are reserved for ethnic Serbs and another 10 for other ethnic minorities. The Assembly elects the president, who serves a five-year term. The prime minister is nominated by the president and requires Assembly approval. The International Civilian Office, which oversaw legislation and decisions by the government, closed in 2012.

In February 2012, the National Anticorruption Council was launched to improve intergovernmental cooperation in the fight against graft and misconduct. However, corruption remains widespread in many areas, including the judiciary and law enforcement. In April, authorities arrested the Anticorruption Task Force chief for abuse of office, including extortion. Implementation of anticorruption legislation is weak, and the government should adopt and fully support a new anticorruption strategy, according to a European Commission (EC) analysis released in October. Kosovo was ranked 105 out of 176 countries surveyed in Transparency International's 2012 Corruption Perceptions Index.

The constitution protects freedoms of expression and the press, with exceptions for speech that provokes ethnic hostility. Despite a variety of technically free media, journalists report frequent harassment and intimidation. After months of public outcry, legislators in October removed provisions in the criminal code that criminalized defamation and potentially forced journalists to reveal their sources. International officials in Kosovo have been accused of occasionally restricting media independence. The government does not restrict access to the internet.

The constitution guarantees religious freedom. The predominantly Muslim ethnic Albanians enjoy this right in practice, as does the Serb minority. Nevertheless, the Muslim community increasingly complains of discrimination. In April 2012, the UN noted an apparent year-on-year rise in vandalism at Serbian Orthodox sites. Overall, however, attacks on minority religious sites have declined since 2004.

Academic freedom is not formally restricted, but appointments at the University of Pristina are politicized. Kosovo's education system is largely segregated along ethnic lines.

Freedom of assembly has occasionally been restricted for security reasons, and the constitution includes safeguards for public order and national security. In 2012, journalists held peaceful protests over the criminal code amendments. However, police forcefully dispersed a January border demonstration organized by Vetëvendosje over the government's refusal to enforce an opposition resolution to embargo Serbia. Nongovernmental organizations generally function freely. The courts can ban groups that infringe on the constitutional order or encourage ethnic hatred. The constitution protects the right to establish and join trade unions. However, workers face intimidation, and private sector unions are nearly nonexistent.

Kosovo made progress with judicial reforms in 2012. Authorities continued to implement reforms contained in 2010 laws on the Judicial and Prosecutorial Councils, a process that will lead to the introduction of a new court system in 2013. Remuneration for judges and prosecutors continued to rise, improving judicial independence. However, case backlogs remain high, enforcement of judgments is weak, courts are not fully independent, and the judiciary and prosecutor's offices are understaffed, with a particular shortage of appellate judges, according to the EC. Northern Kosovo lacks a fully functional judiciary capable of processing civil and criminal cases.

Ethnic Albanian officials rarely prosecute cases involving Albanian attacks on non-Albanians. In 2012, Amnesty International (AI) urged EULEX to prioritize the investigation of war crimes, emphasizing that very few KLA members have been prosecuted amid "a culture of impunity." AI also called for heightened witness protection following the deaths of several witnesses in high-profile war crimes cases. Prison conditions are generally in line with international standards, though living conditions, including poor ventilation, are sometimes problematic, and prisoner abuse remains a concern.

Freedom of movement for ethnic minorities is a significant problem, and returnees to Kosovo still face hostility and bleak economic prospects. In April 2012, the UN noted an apparent rise in crimes against minority communities, including intimidation and assault, and an alarming series of "tit-for-tat" arrests between Serbian and Kosovo police in February and March. Blockades in northern Kosovo restricted freedom of movement in 2012. Kosovo's Roma, Ashkali, Gorani, and other minority populations face difficult socioeconomic conditions. Property reclamation by displaced persons remains problematic.

Kosovo is a principal transit point along the heroin-trafficking route between Central Asia and Western Europe. Organized crime is endemic, especially in northern Kosovo. Kosovo authorities are cooperating with EULEX's investigation into the allegations in Dick Marty's 2010 report. Investigators are looking into a September report by Serbian prosecutors that a former KLA fighter who is a witness in a war crimes case had claimed that he removed a Serbian prisoner's heart for sale on the black market during the conflict.

Patriarchal attitudes often limit women's ability to gain an education or secure employment. Women are underrepresented in politics despite rules that they must occupy every third spot on each party's candidate list. Women in rural areas remain effectively disenfranchised through family voting—in which the male head of a household casts ballots for the entire family—though attitudes toward women's rights are liberalizing in urban areas. Domestic violence is a serious problem, as is discrimination against sexual minorities. Kosovo is a source, transit point, and destination for human trafficking.

Kuwait

Political Rights: 5*
Civil Liberties: 5
Status: Partly Free

Population: 2,818,000
Capital: Kuwait City

Ratings Change: Kuwait's political rights rating declined from 4 to 5 due to a parliamentary crisis and the government's attempts to undermine the political opposition by revising the electoral law.

Ten-Year Ratings Timeline For Year Under Review (Political Rights, Civil Liberties, Status)

2003	2004	2005	2006	2007	2008	2009	2010	2011	2012
4,5PF	4,5PF	4,5PF	4,4PF	4,4PF	4,4PF	4,4PF	4,5PF	4,5PF	5,5PF

Overview:
Kuwait's political crisis worsened in 2012, as the emir dissolved the results of the February elections in June and decreed a new electoral law in October, resulting in protests by tens of thousands of Kuwaitis and an opposition boycott of the December elections. Hundreds of demonstrators were injured, and prominent opposition figures were arrested during the year for criticizing the government. Meanwhile, opposition media outlets were shut down and bloggers charged with insulting the emir.

For more than 200 years, the al-Sabah dynasty has played a role in ruling Kuwait. A year after the country gained its independence from Britain in 1961, a new constitution gave broad powers to the emir and created the National Assembly. Iraqi forces invaded in August 1990, but a military coalition led by the United States liberated the country in February 1991.

Emirs suspended the National Assembly from 1976 to 1981 and from 1986 to 1992. After its restoration in 1992, the parliament played an active role in monitoring the emir and the government, often forcing cabinet ministers out of office and blocking legislation proposed by the ruling family. However, the legislature also served as an impediment to progressive political change by rejecting measures on women's rights and economic reform.

After 28 years of rule, Sheikh Jaber al-Ahmad al-Sabah died in 2006. The cabinet and parliament removed his heir for health reasons and elevated Sheikh Sabah al-Ahmad al-Sabah, the half-brother of the previous emir, as the new emir. In parliamentary elections that year, a coalition of liberals, Islamists, and nationalists campaigning against corruption captured a majority of seats.

In March 2009, the government resigned amid calls by parliament to question cabinet members over the misuse of public funds, prompting the emir to dissolve the parliament two days later. Parliamentary elections were held again in May with Sunni Islamists, Shiites, liberals, and tribal representatives all winning seats. The prime minister went before the parliament in December to answer to allegations of corruption and survived a subsequent vote of confidence.

Tensions between the government and the public persisted throughout 2011, sparking regular demonstrations demanding the prime minister's resignation and the eradication of systemic corruption. Protests continued into November, leading to two dozen arrests as well as the cabinet's resignation. The emir dissolved parliament in December, setting the stage for new elections in 2012.

In the February 2012 parliamentary elections, opposition candidates gained a majority of seats. A parliamentary commission formed in March claimed that it had uncovered evidence of graft and sought to question the premier. Parliamentary efforts to question government ministers led the emir to suspend parliament for a month in June. That same month, the Constitutional Court declared that the emir's 2011 dissolution of the parliament was unconstitutional, tossed out the results of the February elections, and reseated the 2009 progovernment parliament. The Court's decision prompted large-scale protests in June, with tens of thousands of people demonstrating and calling for new elections. Their efforts were bolstered when the re-seated 2009 parliament failed twice to establish a quorum.

The government exacerbated the political crisis in August when it referred Kuwait's 2006 electoral law to the Constitutional Court for review. The move, which aimed to reduce the number of electoral districts and limit opposition support, prompted more demonstrations. In September, the court rejected the government's attempt, forcing the emir to dissolve parliament and set new elections for December.

In October, the emir issued a royal decree reducing the number of candidates elected in each district from four to one, a move designed to limit the power of the opposition. Tens of thousands of Kuwaitis responded by holding regular protests in October and November, with hundreds being injured by the harsh security response. The opposition boycotted the December 1 elections, leading progovernment candidates to capture the majority of seats. Voter turnout was around 40 percent, the lowest in Kuwait's history. Opposition protests continued through the end of the year.

Political Rights and Civil Liberties: Kuwait is not an electoral democracy. The emir appoints the prime minister and cabinet and shares legislative power with the 50-member National Assembly, which is elected to four-year terms by popular vote. The emir has the authority to dissolve the National Assembly at will but must call elections within 60 days. The parliament can overturn decrees issued by the emir while it is not in session. It can also veto the appointment of the country's prime minister, but it then must choose from among three alternates put forward by the emir. The parliament also has the power to remove government ministers with a majority vote. The electorate consists of men and women over 21 years of age who have been citizens for at least 20 years; members of most security forces are barred from voting.

Formal political parties are banned. While political groupings, such as parliamentary blocs, have been allowed to emerge, the government has impeded their activities through harassment and arrests.

Corruption remains a dominant political issue, and lawmakers continue to pressure the government to address this problem. In August 2011, allegations emerged that up to 18 members of parliament received large cash deposits into their personal bank accounts. The transactions have widely been interpreted as evidence of government bribery and fueled protests in the fall of 2011 that spilled over into 2012. Parliamentary efforts to investigate corruption have been obstructed by the government. In May 2012, a commission established by the government concluded its investigation into the August case after claiming it found no evidence of fraud. In October, the public prosecutor formally ended the state's inquiry, also citing lack of evidence. Kuwait was ranked 66 out of 176 countries surveyed in Transparency International's 2012 Corruption Perceptions Index.

Kuwaiti authorities continue to limit press freedom. While press offenses have been decriminalized, offenders still face steep fines. Kuwaiti law punishes the publication of material that insults Islam, criticizes the emir, discloses secret or private information, or calls for the regime's overthrow. In March 2012, authorities shuttered the newspaper *al-Dar* for three months on charges that it was inciting sectarianism. Abdul Hussein al-Sultan, the newspaper's editor, was fined and sentenced to six months in prison. In April, parliament passed a new law criminalizing blasphemy, making insulting the prophet a capital offense, though the law was rejected by the emir. In April, police arrested blogger Hamad al-Naqi on charges that he had blasphemed the prophet as well as the leaders of Kuwait and Saudi Arabia on the social-media site Twitter; he was sentenced to 10 years in prison in June. Other prominent figures were detained for criticizing the government, including several royal family members and the former member of parliament Musallam al-Barak, who was arrested on charges of having "undermined the status of the emir" in an October speech. He was held for 10 days, and his trial was postponed through the end of the year. In January, journalist Ayyad al-Harbi was arrested for insulting the emir in comments he posted on the social-media site, Twitter; his trial was pending at year's end.

Kuwait has more than 10 daily and weekly Arabic newspapers and two English-language dailies. The state owns four television stations and nine radio stations, but there are also a number of private outlets, including the satellite television station Al-Rai. Foreign media outlets have generally operated relatively freely in Kuwait. Kuwaitis enjoy access to the internet, though the government has instructed internet service providers to block certain sites for political or moral reasons.

Islam is the state religion, but religious minorities are generally permitted to practice their faiths in private. Shiite Muslims, who make up around a third of the population, enjoy full political rights but have experienced a rise in harassment in the aftermath of the Iraq war and the uprising in Bahrain. Kuwaiti Salafis and Sunni Islamists have criticized the country's Shiites for alleged links to Iran. Academic freedom is generally respected. Kuwait allows relatively open and free private discussion, often conducted in traditional gatherings (diwaniyat) that typically include only men.

Freedoms of assembly and association are guaranteed by law, though the government constrains these rights in practice. Kuwaitis must notify authorities of a public meeting or protest but do not need a permit. Peaceful demonstrations were held throughout 2012, mostly in response to charges of government corruption and the parliamentary crisis. In October 2012, the government declared that public assemblies of more than 20 people were illegal. Tens of thousands of demonstrastors routinely defied the new restrictions, prompting police to respond with teargas and violence to disperse crowds; hundreds were injured. Members of Kuwait's more than

100,000 stateless residents, known as bidoon, have also staged regular protests over the last two years calling for greater rights. They are considered illegal residents, do not have full citizenship rights, and often live in wretched conditions. In January 2012, the government announced that it would deport bidoon who participated in protests, and throw out their citizenship applications, and dismiss those serving in the army if they or their family members were determined to have participated in demonstrations. The government routinely restricts the registration and licensing of nongovernmental organizations (NGOs), forcing dozens of groups to operate without legal standing or state assistance. Representatives of licensed NGOs must obtain government permission to attend foreign conferences. Workers have the right to join labor unions, but Kuwait's labor law mandates that there be only one union per occupational trade. Migrant workers enjoy limited legal protections against mistreatment or abuse by employers.

Kuwait lacks an independent judiciary. The emir appoints all judges, and the executive branch approves judicial promotions. Authorities may detain suspects for four days without charge. Detainees, especially bidoon, have been subjected to torture. In 2011, police arrested a Kuwaiti citizen, Mohammed al-Mutairi, for alcohol possession, which is illegal in Kuwait. A parliamentary investigation revealed that authorities tortured al-Mutairi for six days before killing him and then engaged in a cover-up. Controversy surrounding the case forced the resignation of Minister of the Interior Sheikh Jaber al-Khaled al-Sabah in February 2011, and 16 police officers were brought up on charges. In January 2012, two of the officers were sentenced to life in prison, while four others received sentences of 15 to 16 years. Three other officers received smaller sentences ranging from two years in prison to fines, while the remaining officers were acquitted. The government permits visits by human rights activists to prisons, where overcrowding remains a problem.

The 1962 constitution provides men and women with equal rights. Kuwaiti women have the right to vote and run as candidates in parliamentary and local elections. For the first time in Kuwait's history, four women won seats in the 2009 parliamentary elections. While no women were elected in the February elections, three were victorious in the December vote. Women also comprise more than 60 percent of the student body at several leading Kuwaiti universities. Nevertheless, women face discrimination in several areas of law and society and remain underrepresented in the workforce. Women are offered some legal protections from abuse and discrimination, but they are only permitted to seek a divorce in cases where they have been deserted or subject to domestic violence. Women must have a male guardian in order to marry and are eligible for only one half of their brother's inheritance. As of 2009, married women have the right to obtain passports and to travel without their husband's permission. Domestic abuse and sexual harassment are not specifically prohibited by law, and foreign domestic servants remain particularly vulnerable to abuse and sexual assault.

Kyrgyzstan

Political Rights: 5
Civil Liberties: 5
Status: Partly Free

Population: 5,667,800
Capital: Bishkek

Ten-Year Ratings Timeline For Year Under Review (Political Rights, Civil Liberties, Status)

2003	2004	2005	2006	2007	2008	2009	2010	2011	2012
6,5NF	6,5NF	5,4PF	5,4PF	5,4PF	5,4PF	6,5NF	5,5PF	5,5PF	5,5PF

Overview: A new anticorruption body within the state security service began to address one of Kyrgyzstan's most fundamental problems in 2012, but its choice of cases raised suspicions that it was pursuing President Almazbek Atambayev's political opponents. Prime Minister Omurbek Babanov's coalition government collapsed in August, reportedly due to disagreements with the president on the division of executive power. A new government formed in September was led by the president's party, with an old ally, Jantoro Satybaldiyev, as prime minister. The country continued to suffer from serious flaws in the treatment of national minorities, due process, prevention of and accountability for torture, and judicial independence.

Shortly after Kyrgyzstan gained independence from the Soviet Union in 1991, Askar Akayev, a respected physicist, was elected president. He easily won reelection in 1995, and constitutional amendments the following year substantially increased the powers of the presidency. International observers noted serious irregularities in the 2000 parliamentary and presidential elections, which yielded another term for Akayev.

Long-standing frustrations in the economically depressed and politically marginalized south culminated in public protests in 2002. Six protesters were killed when police fired into a crowd in the village of Aksy. Although several prosecutors and police officials were eventually convicted and sentenced to prison, opposition critics continued to argue that senior officials who authorized the use of force were never brought to justice.

After flawed February 2005 parliamentary elections, thousands of demonstrators protested irregularities and ultimately called for Akayev's resignation. On March 24, protesters and opposition supporters stormed the presidential headquarters in Bishkek. Akayev fled abroad and later resigned.

In the July 2005 presidential poll, former prime minister and opposition leader Kurmanbek Bakiyev captured 89 percent of the vote. His victory was regarded as nearly inevitable after Feliks Kulov, his most serious rival, withdrew his presidential candidacy in exchange for the post of prime minister. Observers from the Organization for Security and Cooperation in Europe (OSCE) nevertheless concluded that the election represented an improvement over previous votes.

After violently dispersing opposition protests in April 2007, the government enacted constitutional revisions in an October referendum, expanding the parliament from 75 to 90 seats and introducing party-slate balloting. Parliamentary elections in

December resulted in a legislature dominated by the newly formed progovernment party Ak Zhol and devoid of opposition representation.

The president consolidated his power in 2008 and 2009, sidelining the country's remaining well-known opposition figures. In March 2009, Medet Sadyrkulov, Bakiyev's former chief of staff, was found dead in a burned-out car near Bishkek. Opposition representatives charged that he had been assassinated because he was planning to join them. Bakiyev won another five-year term in the July 2009 presidential election, taking 75 percent of the vote. OSCE observers concluded that the poll failed to meet international standards, citing evidence of fraud, intimidation of opposition supporters, and the misuse of administrative resources, among other problems.

In April 2010, Bakiyev fled the country amid antigovernment protests in Bishkek, leading to the formation of an interim government. A reported 86 people were killed in the street confrontations, with most victims apparently shot by security forces. In the first half of June, ethnic rioting swept the southern cities of Osh and Jalalabad, leaving at least 470 people dead. Ethnic Uzbeks suffered the brunt of the violence, and local security forces were accused of abetting attacks on Uzbek communities. Later the same month, a referendum that international observers deemed generally fair confirmed longtime opposition figure Roza Otunbayeva as interim president through December 2011 and approved a new constitution that shifted power from the presidency to the parliament.

Parliamentary elections held in October 2010 were deemed an improvement over Bakiyev-era balloting. The nationalist Ata-Jurt party led with 28 of 120 seats, followed by Otunbayeva's Social Democratic Party of Kyrgyzstan (SDPK) with 26, Ar-Namys with 25, Respublika with 23, and Ata-Meken with 18. Ata-Jurt, the SDPK, and Respublika formed a coalition government in December, leaving Ar-Namys and Ata-Meken in opposition. Almazbek Atambayev of the SDPK became prime minister. The coalition remained stable but failed to coordinate on a legislative agenda before the October 2011 presidential election.

The presidential poll was seen by OSCE observers as free and competitive, though marred by significant irregularities on election day. Atambayev defeated 15 other candidates and took 63 percent of the vote. In December, a new coalition composed of the SDPK, Respublika, Ata-Meken, and Ar-Namys was formed, with Omurbek Babanov of Respublika as prime minister.

The coalition lasted eight months, collapsing in August 2012, after Babanov and Atambayev publicly clashed over their respective roles under the new constitution. In September, the SDPK took the lead in a new coalition with Ata-Meken and Ar-Namys, and Jantoro Satybaldiyev, a close ally of the president, became prime minister.

Separately, the party of Melis Myrzakmatov, the Kyrgyz nationalist mayor of Osh since 2009, won city council elections in March amid widespread reports of voter intimidation. However, tensions in the city began to ease as it became clear that Myrzakmatov would not implement the most ambitious versions of his controversial reconstruction and resettlement plans, which were seen as favoring ethnic Kyrgyz.

In October, three lawmakers from the opposition Ata-Jurt party were arrested after a protest in Bishkek to demand the nationalization of a gold mine run by a Canadian company. The men, who remained in pretrial detention at year's end, were accused of calling for the government's overthrow and attempting to storm the parliament.

The SDPK won the most votes in a series of local elections in November, followed by Respublika and Ata-Meken. Feliks Kulov of the Ar-Namys party, which fared poorly in the voting, stepped down as head of the ruling coalition to protest alleged electoral fraud.

Political Rights and Civil Liberties: Kyrgyzstan is not an electoral democracy, though the parliamentary and presidential elections of 2010 and 2011 were considered improvements over the deeply flawed 2007 parliamentary and 2009 presidential votes. OSCE observers praised the 2010 parliamentary campaign's pluralism and other positive features, but were more critical of the 2011 presidential vote, citing widespread problems with voter lists and numerous faults in the tabulation process.

Constitutional changes adopted in the June 2010 referendum expanded the unicameral parliament from 90 to 120 deputies, with no party allowed to hold more than 65 seats. Parliamentary elections are to be held every five years. The president, who shares executive power with the prime minister, serves a single six-year term with no possibility of reelection and has the power to veto legislation.

The aim of the 2010 reforms was to ensure political pluralism and prevent the reemergence of an authoritarian, superpresidential system. In 2012, however, observers noted signs that President Almazbek Atambayev was beginning to reclaim powers given to the prime minister's office under the new constitution and to use the executive branch to target political enemies.

Corruption is pervasive in Kyrgyz society. The nepotistic practices of former president Kurmanbek Bakiyev, whose sons and brothers were prominent in business and government, were a significant source of popular dissatisfaction prior to his ouster. The interim government charged some members of the Bakiyev regime with corruption, but the results in the largely unreformed courts have been inconclusive. In March 2012, the former president's brother, Akhmat Bakiyev, due to stand trial for corruption, escaped from a clinic where he had supposedly been receiving treatment. Also during the year, a new anticorruption service within the State Committee of National Security (GKNB) arrested an opposition lawmaker and a cabinet minister in June and July, respectively, but some observers described the cases as selective and politicized. Kyrgyzstan was ranked 154 out of 176 countries surveyed in Transparency International's 2012 Corruption Perceptions Index.

The media landscape remained bifurcated along ethnic lines in 2012, with significantly improved conditions for Kyrgyz-language media since 2010 and vastly worse conditions for both Uzbek-language outlets and critical Russian-language media. Independent Uzbek-language media virtually ceased to exist in southern Kyrgyzstan after the June 2010 ethnic violence, as several Uzbek television and radio outlets were closed down. In February 2012, the Kyrgyz State Communications Agency instructed internet service providers to block the Russia-based news website *Fergananews.com*; the parliament had previously condemned the site for its critical coverage of the situation in Osh. In July, Russian-language journalist Vitaliy Farafonov was convicted in Bishkek of "inciting ethnic hatred" in his online articles. Though the court imposed only a fine, the state prosecutor had requested eight years' imprisonment, far beyond the maximum penalty prescribed by law. Prosecutions for inciting hatred have focused exclusively on minority writers, despite the prevalence of openly racist and anti-Semitic articles in Kyrgyz-language media. In April, the GKNB disclosed plans to systematically monitor online news outlets for hate speech, raising concerns that it could stifle dissent or punish media for reporting the speech of public figures.

The government has generally permitted a broad range of religious practices, but all religious organizations must register with the authorities, a process that is often cumbersome and arbitrary. Proselytizing, private religious education, and the wearing of headscarves in schools were banned in 2009. The government monitors and restricts Islamist groups that it regards as a threat to national security, particularly Hizb ut-Tahrir, an ostensibly nonviolent international movement calling for the creation of a caliphate.

Tight official restrictions on freedom of assembly have not been altered since the Bakiyev era, but enforcement has been eased considerably in practice. Small protests are held regularly, though they sometimes encounter police violence.

Nongovernmental organizations (NGOs) participate actively in civic and political life, and public advisory councils were established in the parliament and most ministries in 2011, permitting improved monitoring and advocacy by NGOs. However, rising nationalism continues to affect both ethnic Kyrgyz and ethnic Uzbek NGO activists. Human rights workers who support Uzbek victims of abuse continue to face threats, harassment, and physical attacks.

The law provides for the formation of trade unions, and unions are generally able to operate without obstruction. However, strikes are prohibited in many sectors. Legal enforcement of union rights is weak, and collective bargaining agreements are not always respected by employers.

The judiciary is not independent and remains dominated by the executive branch. Corruption among judges, who are underpaid, is widespread. Defendants' rights, including the presumption of innocence, are not always respected, and there are credible reports of torture during arrest and interrogation.

The ongoing trials of the Bakiyev family and their accomplices, including a case against 28 former government officials and special forces members for the alleged killing of 86 demonstrators in April 2010, have been marred by numerous procedural violations and threats against lawyers in the courtroom. Human Rights Watch also documented systematic rights violations at trials of ethnic Uzbeks in 2010 and 2011, with defendants attacked in courtrooms, tortured in detention, and convicted on flimsy or fabricated evidence. In June 2012, four Jalalabad police officers charged in the August 2011 beating death of an ethnic Uzbek Russian citizen, Usman Kholimirzayev, were released to house arrest. The legal proceedings in their case have been marked by protests against prosecutors, witness intimidation, and multiple venue changes.

The widespread and extensively documented violence against the Uzbek community in southern Kyrgyzstan in 2010 cast a harsh light on the plight of ethnic minorities. Uzbeks, who make up nearly half of the population in Osh, had long demanded more political and cultural rights, including greater representation in government, more Uzbek-language schools, and official status for the Uzbek language.

The government generally respects the right of unrestricted travel to and from Kyrgyzstan. However, barriers to internal migration include a requirement that citizens obtain permits to work and settle in particular areas of the country.

Personal connections, corruption, organized crime, and widespread poverty limit business competition and equality of opportunity. Companies that had belonged to the Bakiyev family were nationalized in 2010, pending a new process of privatization. That year's ethnic violence affected property rights in the south, as many businesses, mainly owned by ethnic Uzbeks, were destroyed or seized. In 2012, nationalist politicians called for the state to seize assets held by foreign companies, especially in the mining sector. Nationalist thugs frequently attacked foreign mining operations, often with no interference from local authorities.

Despite achieving notable leadership positions, women remain underrepresented in high levels of government. Cultural traditions and apathy among law enforcement officials discourage victims of domestic violence and rape from contacting the authorities. An international inquiry criticized the government response to rape cases from the 2010 ethnic violence as "inadequate if not obstructive." The trafficking of women and girls into forced prostitution abroad is a serious problem, and some victims report that the authorities are involved in trafficking. The practice of bride abduction persists despite being illegal, and few perpetrators are prosecuted. In December 2012, the parliament voted to increase the maximum penalty from 3 to 10 years in prison, and bride kidnapping is now a "public crime" that prosecutors are legally obligated to pursue regardless of whether the victim presses charges. Previously classified as a private crime, victims and their families often faced social pressure not to press charges, and very few cases were ever prosecuted.

Homosexual activity is not illegal, but LGBT (lesbian, gay, bisexual, and transgender) people reportedly face severe discrimination and the risk of abuse, including by police.

Laos

Political Rights: 7
Civil Liberties: 6
Status: Not Free

Population: 6,520,900
Capital: Vientiane

Ten-Year Ratings Timeline For Year Under Review (Political Rights, Civil Liberties, Status)

2003	2004	2005	2006	2007	2008	2009	2010	2011	2012
7,6NF	7,6NF	7,6NF	7,6NF	7,6NF	7,6NF	7,6NF	7,6NF	7,6NF	7,6NF

Overview: **Construction of the Xayaburi dam on the Mekong River continued in 2012, despite protests and studies showing its potentially devastating environmental impact. In December, prominent antipoverty activist Sombath Somphone disappeared; video footage appeared two days later showing him being abducted by police. Also that month, the government expelled the country head of the international development agency Helvetas, who had recently criticized the government. Laos was approved for entry to the World Trade Organization in October.**

Laos won independence in 1953, after six decades of French rule and Japanese occupation during World War II. The constitutional monarchy soon fell into a civil war with Pathet Lao guerrillas, who were backed by the Vietnamese Communist Party. As the conflict raged on, Laos was drawn into the Vietnam War in 1964. The Pathet Lao seized power in 1975, and the Lao People's Revolutionary Party (LPRP) has ruled the country ever since. By the 1980s, the economy was in tatters after years of civil war and state mismanagement. The LPRP relaxed controls on prices, encouraged foreign investment, and privatized farms and some state-owned enterprises.

The party's policy of maintaining tight political control while spurring economic development continued over the subsequent decades, and the country consistently reported high macroeconomic growth rates. However, the rapid expansion of extractive industries and the influx of thousands of Chinese businesses, particularly in northern Laos, increased economic inequality and fostered greater corruption. The seizure of land from subsistence farmers and tribal communities for leasing to foreign-owned agribusinesses also triggered occasional protests and violence and resulted in environmental destruction.

In elections held in 2011, the LPRP maintained its dominance of the rubber-stamp National Assembly, winning 128 of 132 seats.

In July 2012, Hillary Clinton visited Laos, marking the first time in decades that a U.S. secretary of state had visited the country. In October, Laos was formally approved for entry to the World Trade Organization.

Construction on the controversial Xayaburi dam on the Mekong River formally began in November 2012. The project had raised concerns over its impact on the environment and local residents and stirred popular anger in Laos, as well as criticism from Vietnam and Cambodia, which could be negatively impacted by the dam. The Lao government had supposedly suspended work on the dam, though preparatory work had taken place throughout 2012, even before the formal announcement.

Political Rights and Civil Liberties: Laos is not an electoral democracy. The 1991 constitution makes the LPRP the sole legal political party and grants it a leading role at all levels of government. The party's Central Committee and Politburo dominate decision making. The LPRP vets all candidates for election to the National Assembly, whose members elect the president. In 2011, the legislature was increased in size from 115 members to 132, supposedly to make it more inclusive. The assembly featured somewhat more open debate than in previous years, but it continued to hold little real power. Laos launched a process of greater devolution of limited powers to provinces in 2012.

Corruption by government officials is widespread. Laws aimed at curbing graft are rarely enforced, and government regulation of virtually every facet of life provides many opportunities for bribery. Senior officials in government and the military are frequently involved in commercial logging, mining, and other extractive enterprises. Both Vietnam and China have significant influence in Laos, and their militaries have allegedly participated in the widespread smuggling of Lao resources. Vietnam's army reportedly plays a central role in timber smuggling in Laos. Lao activists also claim that Chinese companies involved in the rubber business have bribed many local officials for access to land. Laos was ranked 160 out of 176 countries surveyed in Transparency International's 2012 Corruption Perceptions Index.

Freedom of the press is severely restricted. Any journalist who criticizes the government or discusses controversial political topics faces legal punishment. The state owns all media. Residents within frequency range of Radio Free Asia and other foreign broadcasts from Thailand can access these alternative media sources. While very few Lao have access to the internet, its content is not heavily censored, partly because the government lacks the capability to monitor and block most web traffic. Many educated Lao obtain news about Laos through Thai online newspapers. In 2012, authorities took off the air a popular radio show, "Talk of the News," that had focused on land grabs and other political stories; the government publicly rebuked journalists, including "Talk of the News" host Ounkeo Souksavanh, for not heeding state guidance on stories, particularly related to dams on the Mekong.

Religious freedom is constrained. The religious practice of the majority Buddhist population is somewhat restricted through the LPRP's control of clergy training and supervision of temples. Lao officials reportedly continue to jail Christians or expel them from their villages for proselytizing. In 2012, Christian activist groups reported more than twice as many cases of persecution against Lao Christians as in 2011.

Academic freedom is not respected. University professors cannot teach or write about politically sensitive topics, though Laos has invited select foreign academics to teach courses in the country, and some young people go overseas for university education. Government surveillance of the population has been scaled back in recent years, but searches without warrants still occur.

The government severely restricts freedom of assembly. Laws prohibit participation in organizations that engage in demonstrations or public protests, or that in any other way cause "turmoil or social instability." Violators can receive sentences of up to five years in prison. Groups of demonstrators have sometimes disappeared. After signing the International Covenant on Civil and Political Rights in 2009, Laos created a legal framework for nongovernmental organizations (NGOs), allowing such groups to be licensed; this has affected primarily foreign NGOs, which have proliferated in the country in recent years. There are some domestic nongovernmental welfare and professional groups, but they are prohibited from pursuing political agendas and are subject to strict state control. In December 2012, the Lao government expelled Anne-Sophie Gindroz, the country director of the Swiss-based development agency Helvetas, after Gindroz penned a letter to international donors that criticized the limited freedoms allowed by the Lao regime. In December, internationally acclaimed antipoverty activist Sombath Somphone disappeared; video footage surfaced days later that showed police stopping and abducting him, and his whereabouts remained unknown at year's end.

All unions must belong to the official Federation of Lao Trade Unions. Strikes are not expressly prohibited, but workers rarely stage walkouts, and they do not have the right to bargain collectively.

The courts are corrupt and controlled by the LPRP. Long procedural delays are common, particularly for cases dealing with public grievances. Security forces often illegally detain suspects. Prisoners are frequently tortured and must bribe officials to obtain better food, medicine, family visits, and more humane treatment.

Discrimination against members of ethnic minority tribes is common. The Hmong, who fielded a guerrilla army allied with U.S. forces during the Vietnam War, are particularly distrusted by the government and face harsh treatment. Although some Hmong who are loyal to the LPRP have been elected to the national legislature, poorer and more rural Hmong have been forced off their land to make way for extractive industries. Some Hmong refugees who returned to the country from Thailand in late 2009 and early 2010 appear to have vanished, and efforts by their families, foreign diplomats, and members of the U.S. Congress to obtain information on their whereabouts have been largely unsuccessful.

Refugees who arrive in Laos often are deported; in 2012, 20 refugees from North Korea were arrested in Laos and expected to be deported.

All land is owned by the state, though citizens have rights to use it. On some occasions, the government has awarded land to citizens with government connections, money, or links to foreign companies. Traditional land rights still exist in some areas, adding to confusion and conflict over access. With no fair or robust system to protect land rights or ensure compensation for displacement, development projects often spur public resentment. In 2012, villagers in the coffee-growing region of Paksong launched public protests against an agreement the government made with a Singaporean company to plant coffee on land that local farmers claimed was illegally taken from them. Also in 2012, the Lao government rejected a proposal for a Chinese rare earth mineral plant in Laos on the grounds that it might have had a negative environmental impact.

Although laws guarantee women many of the same rights as men, gender-based discrimination and abuse are widespread. Tradition and religious practices have contributed to women's inferior access to education, employment opportunities, and worker benefits. An estimated 15,000 to 20,000 women and girls from the Mekong region, including Laos, are trafficked each year for prostitution. However, the government has made some improvements in combating trafficking over the last five years, including closer cooperation with neighboring governments.

Latvia

Political Rights: 2
Civil Liberties: 2
Status: Free

Population: 2,049,000
Capital: Riga

Ten-Year Ratings Timeline For Year Under Review (Political Rights, Civil Liberties, Status)

2003	2004	2005	2006	2007	2008	2009	2010	2011	2012
1,2F	1,2F	1,1F	1,1F	2,1F	2,1F	2,1F	2,2F	2,2F	2,2F

Overview: In September 2012, the parliament provisionally approved amendments to the country's citizenship law, including one allowing some ethnic Latvians abroad to become dual citizens. Voters in February overwhelmingly rejected a proposal to adopt Russian as Latvia's second language. Meanwhile, the results of the 2011 census, which were made public in January 2012, showed that the country's population has decreased by about 13 percent since 2000, partly as a result of the emigration of educated young people.

After centuries of foreign domination, Latvia gained its independence in 1918, only to be annexed by the Soviet Union during World War II. The long Soviet occupation featured a massive influx of ethnic Russians and the deportation, execution, and emigration of tens of thousands of ethnic Latvians. In 1991, Latvia regained its independence as the Soviet Union disintegrated, and a multiparty system developed during the 1990s. Following independence, residents who did not speak Latvian were required to learn the language in order to gain citizenship. Many Russian speakers refused, and as a result, the country is still home to some 300,000 noncitizens, most of them ethnic Russians. Latvia joined both the European Union (EU) and NATO in 2004.

A center-right coalition government headed by Prime Minister Ivars Godmanis collapsed in 2009, following violent protests sparked by a deepening economic crisis. A new center-right coalition government was formed, with Valdis Dombrovskis of the New Era Party as prime minister. Sharp spending cuts enacted to counter a severe recession caused the gross domestic product (GDP) to contract by about a quarter over 2008 and 2009.

The center-right Unity coalition, composed of New Era, the Civic Union, and the Society for Other Politics, won parliamentary elections in 2010 and subsequently formed an unstable coalition with the Union of Greens and Farmers (ZZS), a party beset by corruption allegations and which was closely linked to Aivars Lembergs, a powerful businessman and the mayor of Ventspils. Dombrovskis returned as prime minister.

In May 2011, the parliament blocked the lifting of immunity for parliament member Ainars Šlesers, thereby impeding a corruption investigation by the Bureau for the Prevention and Combating of Corruption. Exasperated, President Valdis Zatlers called for the dissolution of the parliament. Days afterward, Zatlers lost a presidential election to ZZS candidate Andris Berzinš, a multimillionaire former banker. A July 2011 referendum on Zatlers's proposal to dissolve the parliament passed with 94 percent of the vote.

In the run-up to the September 2011 snap elections, which focused largely on corruption issues, Zatlers formed the center-right, pro-transparency Zatlers Reform Party (ZRP). Harmony Center, a party largely backed by ethnic Russians, captured the majority of votes for the first time ever, winning 31 of the 100 legislative seats. The ZRP won 22 seats, the Unity coalition secured 20, the National Alliance won 14, and the ZZS captured 13. Šlesers's Latvia's First Party/Latvian Way, afterward renamed the Šlesers Reform Party, did not win any seats. Despite its first-place finish, Harmony Center was not included in the new government. Instead, the ZRP, Unity, and the conservative National Alliance formed a 56-seat governing coalition, with Dombrovskis returning as prime minister.

Latvia in 2012 continued its economic recovery, though unemployment remained high, hovering around 13.5 percent in the fall, after topping out at 20.5 percent in 2010. In May, the parliament voted to approve a new EU fiscal stability treaty, which required signatories to balance their budgets and penalized EU nations that ran large deficits. Dombrovskis in September said Latvia would adopt the euro at the start of 2014; it would become the second Baltic state to do so, following Estonia in 2011. In September, Dombrovskis signed a measure that decreased social welfare payments for the unemployed and those otherwise without income, against the advice of the International Monetary Fund (IMF), which said the measure could result in decreased economic growth.

In a February 2012 referendum initiated by a Russophone advocacy group, Latvians overwhelmingly rejected a proposal, publicly opposed by Dombrovskis and Berzinš, to make Russian the country's second official language.

The parliament in September voted to approve amendments to the country's citizenship law, sponsored by the Unity bloc, granting noncitizen and stateless children born after August 1991 Latvian citizenship if they were already permanent residents and if their parents pledged to help them learn the Latvian language. However, the Organization for Security and Cooperation in Europe criticized those conditions. The amendments also allowed some Latvians living abroad to apply for dual citizenship, and mandated that newborns be granted Latvian citizenship if at least one parent was a Latvian citizen, even if the child was not born in Latvia. The amendment had not been approved in a final reading by the end of 2012.

The results of a 2011 census, released in January 2012, showed that Latvia lost some 13 percent of its population between 2000 and 2011, as many educated young people left to find work abroad. The economy ministry has projected that the country's population, which is among the oldest in the world, could shrink from approximately 2 million in 2012 to 1.6 million by 2030.

Political Rights and Civil Liberties: Latvia is an electoral democracy. The constitution provides for a unicameral, 100-seat parliament (Saeima), whose members are elected to four-year terms. The parliament elects the president, who serves up to two four-year terms. The prime minister is nominated by the president and approved by the parliament. Latvian political candidates cannot run as independents. Political parties may generally organize and compete freely.

Approximately 15 percent of Latvia's residents are noncitizens. Those who immigrated during the Soviet period, the majority of whom are ethnic Russians, must apply for citizenship and pass a Latvian language test. Residents who do not hold Latvian citizenship cannot vote, hold public office, or work in government offices. Noncitizen residents may join political parties, as long as the party does not count more noncitizens than citizens as members.

Corruption is a serious problem and exists at every government level. In October 2012, Environmental Protection and Regional Development Minister Edmunds Sprudžs of the ZRP signed a decree suspending powerful businessman Aivars Lembergs as mayor of Ventspils; Sprudžs said he had received "shocking" information from the prosecutor general's office about decisions Lembergs had made as Ventspils city council chairman. Lembergs argued that Sprudžs did not have the authority to fire him; the city council reaffirmed that Lembergs was the mayor and asked Sprudžs for proof of his claims. Lembergs in 2007 had been charged with bribery, money laundering, and tax evasion; legal proceedings against him were ongoing at the end of 2012. Latvia was ranked 54 out of 176 countries surveyed in Transparency International's 2012 Corruption Perceptions Index.

The government generally respects freedom of the press. Journalist Leonids Jakobsons was detained for two days in late 2011 after publishing purportedly private e-mails between the mayor of Riga and a foreign diplomat. In March 2012, at least two men attacked Jakobsons in the stairwell of his apartment building; he was hospitalized with non-life-threatening injuries. Jakobsons, who was known for writing about sensitive topics, later said he thought the attack was connected to his work. Private television and radio stations broadcast programs in both Latvian and Russian. However, by law, 65 percent of both national and regional broadcasts must either be in Latvian or subtitled or dubbed in Latvian. While newspapers publish a wide range of political viewpoints, there has been evidence of increasing business and political influence on the media, including by Lembergs and former parliament member Ainars Šlesers.

Freedom of religion and academic freedom are generally respected.

Freedoms of assembly and association are protected by law and in practice. The government does not restrict the activities of nongovernmental organizations. Workers may establish trade unions, strike, and engage in collective bargaining. Roughly 15 percent of the workforce is unionized, though union membership appears to be decreasing.

While judicial independence is generally respected, inefficiency, politicization, and corruption continue to be problems. Lengthy pretrial detention remains a concern, and law enforcement officials have allegedly abused persons in custody. Prisons continue to suffer from overcrowding, and many prisoners have poor access to health care.

The IMF in February 2012 reported that income inequality in Latvia was among the highest in the EU, with the wealthiest 20 percent of the population earning seven times more than the poorest 20 percent.

In a February 2012 report, the Council of Europe's European Commission against Racism and Intolerance said that Latvia had made some improvements in combatting hate crimes, implementing nondiscrimination training for police, providing education for the children of ethnic minorities, and increasing the participation of minorities in political life. However, it said few racially motivated crimes were investigated or prosecuted, and added that ethnic Roma faced particularly severe discrimination. In March 2012, some 1,500 people took part in an annual parade honoring Latvian Legion of the Waffen-SS, sparking a smaller counterprotest attended mainly by ethnic Russians who held banners depicting Holocaust victims. In July, a Baltic Pride march took place peacefully in Riga, with several Latvian politicians participating. The country banned same-sex marriage in 2005.

Women enjoy the same legal rights as men, but they often face employment and wage discrimination, as well as domestic violence. There are 23 women in the parliament and 4 in the 13-member cabinet. Latvia is both a source and destination country for women and girls trafficked for the purpose of forced prostitution.

 Lebanon

Political Rights: 5
Civil Liberties: 4
Status: Partly Free

Population: 4,304,000
Capital: Beirut

Trend Arrow: Lebanon received a downward trend arrow due to deterioration in the security environment and increasing attacks and restrictions on journalists, activists, and refugees.

Ten-Year Ratings Timeline For Year Under Review (Political Rights, Civil Liberties, Status)

2003	2004	2005	2006	2007	2008	2009	2010	2011	2012
6,5NF	6,5NF	5,4PF	5,4PF	5,4PF	5,4PF	5,3PF	5,3PF	5,4PF	5,4PF

Overview: The conflict in neighboring Syria continued to affect developments in Lebanon in 2012, as refugees crossed into the country and supporters of the Syrian government clashed violently with rebel supporters, especially in northern Lebanon. Security chief Wissam al-Hassan was assassinated in October, likely for his role in exposing Syrian plans to destabilize Lebanon. Attacks on journalists, activists, and refugees increased, while Prime Minister Najib Miqati faced calls to resign.

Lebanon was established as a League of Nations mandate under French control in 1920. After winning independence in 1943, it maintained a precarious electoral system based on the division of power among the country's then 18 officially recognized sectarian communities. As the population's slight Christian majority waned into a minority, Muslim leaders demanded reform of the fixed 6-to-5 ratio of Christian-to-Muslim parliamentary seats and an end to exclusive Maronite Christian control of the presidency. In 1975, war erupted between a coalition of Lebanese Muslim and leftist militias aligned with Palestinian guerrilla groups, and an array of Christian militias bent on preserving the political status quo. Syrian troops entered Lebanon in 1976 to restore order; Israel launched military campaigns against Palestinian militants in Lebanon in 1978 and 1982.

In 1989, the surviving members of Lebanon's 1972 parliament convened in Taif, Saudi Arabia, and agreed to an Arab League plan that would weaken the presidency, establish equal Christian and Muslim parliamentary representation, and mandate close security cooperation with occupying Syrian troops. A new Syrian-backed government then extended its writ to most of the country, with southern Lebanon remaining under Israeli occupation until 2000. By the end of the 1990s, Lebanon's economy was in deep recession, and growing public disaffection with the postwar establishment spurred demonstrations against Syrian domination.

In 2004, the United States joined with France and most other European governments in calling for an end to Syria's power over Lebanon. Damascus moved to defend its position by seeking a constitutional amendment to extend the tenure of President Emile Lahoud, a staunch Syrian ally. On the eve of the parliamentary vote, the UN Security Council issued a resolution calling for a presidential election, the withdrawal of all foreign forces, and the disarmament of militias. The amendment nevertheless passed, provoking an international outcry.

Encouraged by the international climate, Prime Minister Rafiq Hariri and other politicians began defecting to the opposition. In February 2005, four months after resigning as prime minister, Hariri was killed along with 22 others by a car bomb. Widespread suspicions of Syrian involvement led to international pressure for an immediate Syrian withdrawal and to extensive anti-Syrian demonstrations in Beirut. An interim government was formed to oversee legislative elections. Syrian troops pulled out of Lebanon in April 2005. Allies of the late Hariri, consisting mainly of Sunni Muslims and certain Christian and Druze factions, named themselves the March 14 coalition, and won a plurality of seats in parliamentary elections; with support from the United States, Saudi Arabia, and others, the coalition went on to form a new government led by Prime Minister Fouad Siniora.

In July 2006, the Shiite Islamist movement Hezbollah attacked Israeli forces in a cross-border raid, sparking a six-week war that severely damaged Lebanon's infrastructure and killed some 1,500 people, most of them Lebanese civilians. After a UN-brokered ceasefire, Lebanese politicians struggled to stabilize the government. The March 8 Coalition—a largely Shiite and Christian bloc that included Hezbollah and was aligned with Syria and Iran—left the national unity government in November, demanding a reorganized cabinet in which it would hold veto power. In 2007, the army waged a four-month campaign against Fatah al-Islam, a Sunni Islamist militant group based in Nahr el-Bared, a Palestinian refugee camp, which killed some 400 people and displaced more than 30,000 others.

In May 2008, responding to a pair of government decisions they viewed as a threat, Hezbollah and its allies seized West Beirut by force, leading to battles across Lebanon that left nearly 100 people dead. A power-sharing agreement brokered by Qatar cleared the way for the delayed election of politically neutral army commander Michel Suleiman as president, the formation of a new national unity government, and the passage of a revised election law in September.

In June 2009 parliamentary elections, the March 14 and March 8 coalitions won 71 and 57 seats, respectively, and Saad Hariri—the son of Rafiq Hariri—was named prime minister. Although the elections were conducted peacefully and judged to be free and fair in some respects, vote-buying was reported to be rampant, and the electoral framework retained a number of fundamental structural flaws linked to the country's sectarian political system.

A 2010 investigation by the UN Special Tribunal for Lebanon (STL) of Hezbollah members' involvement in the Hariri assassination threatened to upset the new balance of power. To avoid political and sectarian fighting, political leaders chose which candidates would run in the 2010 municipal elections, effectively deciding the outcome well in advance of the balloting.

In 2011, eleven ministers allied with Hezbollah resigned to protest the STL's indictment of Hezbollah members and Saad Hariri's refusal to end the government's cooperation with the tribunal. The Hezbollah-backed Najib Miqati became prime minister as a result, spurring protests throughout the country.

The internal conflict in Syria spilled over into Lebanon in late 2011, as Syrian forces crossed the border to capture or kill fleeing military defectors and refugees. The office of the United Nations High Commissioner for Refugees (UNHCR) estimated that by the end of December 2012, more than 175,000 Syrian refugees were in Lebanon, including those registered and those awaiting registration. The Syrian conflict also sparked sectarian fighting in Lebanon, as a series of cross-border kidnappings and shootings between supporters and opponents of the Syrian government led to dozens of deaths, including December clashes that killed 17 in Tripoli. Journalists and activists were attacked on several occasions by both supporters of Syrian president Bashar al-Assad and Syrian rebels.

In February 2012, the STL announced that suspects in the 2005 attack on Rafiq Hariri would be tried in absentia in March 2013, and the United Nations renewed the STL's mandate for three years. National Dialogue sessions on security produced the June 2012 Baabda Declaration, which committed Lebanese political groups to keeping Lebanon neutral in the face of regional conflict. Hezbollah rejected calls from the United Nations to disarm, and in October claimed to have sent an Iranian-designed unmanned surveillance vehicle over Israeli airspace. Hezbollah's opponents argued that this action violated the Baabda Declaration.

In August, Michel Samaha, a former Lebanese government minister, was arrested on charges that he had coordinated with Syrian leaders to bomb rebel targets in northern Lebanon. In October, security chief Wissam al-Hassan was killed in a car bomb explosion in Beirut that also killed several bystanders. The assassination was likely due to al-Hassan's role in uncovering the Samaha plot, and prompted calls from the March 14 Coalition for Prime Minister Miqati's resignation. President Suleiman, however, insisted that the resignation would result in a power vacuum and urged Miqati to stay on. The assassination also halted the National Dialogue talks. Just before the end of the year, the March 14 Coalition demanded that integration of Hezbollah's arms into state arsenals also be a precondition for resuming the Dialogue.

Political Rights and Civil Liberties: Lebanon is not an electoral democracy. The president is selected every six years by the 128-member National Assembly, which in turn is elected for four-year terms. The president and parliament nominate the prime minister, who, along with the president, chooses the cabinet, subject to parliamentary approval. The unwritten National Pact of 1943 stipulates that the president must be a Maronite Christian, the prime minister a Sunni Muslim, and the speaker of the National Assembly a Shiite Muslim. Parliamentary seats are divided among major sects under a constitutional formula that does not reflect their current demographic weight. Shiites comprise at least a third of the population, but they are allotted only 21 percent of parliamentary seats. The sectarian political balance has been periodically reaffirmed and occasionally modified by foreign-brokered agreements like the 1989 Taif Accords and the 2008 Doha Agreement.

The 2009 parliamentary elections were conducted under an election law stemming from the Doha Agreement, which condensed nationwide voting into a single day, introduced some curbs on campaign finance and advertising, and created smaller, more religiously homogeneous districts. Parliament approved a law in April to allow Lebanese expatriates to vote in the 2013 elections. Throughout the year, parliament debated various proposals for a new electoral law in advance of the 2013 elections, but ongoing security concerns and lack of consensus prevented parliament from passing any proposal before the end of the year.

The sectarian political system and the powerful role of foreign patrons effectively limit the accountability of elected officials to the public at large. Political and bureaucratic corruption is widespread, businesses routinely pay bribes and cultivate ties with politicians to win contracts, and anticorruption laws are loosely enforced. Lebanon was ranked 128 out of 176 countries surveyed in Transparency International's 2012 Corruption Perceptions Index.

Lebanon has a long tradition of press freedom, though nearly all media outlets have ties to political groups. There are seven privately owned television stations and dozens of privately owned radio and print outlets that reflect a range of views. Internet access is not restricted. Vaguely worded laws have been applied in isolated cases to ban critical reporting on Syria, foreign leaders, the military, the judiciary, and the presidency. In 2012, the government censored and prosecuted artists and activists for presenting material deemed "indecent" or sensitive to state security, including work expressing anti-Syrian sentiment. Violent attacks on journalists covering the Syrian conflict and its impact on Lebanon increased, and security forces shot and killed a cameraman operating near the Syrian border in April. In August 2012, journalist Rami Aysha was detained for nearly a month and was tortured in detention.

In December 2012, Lebanon's internal security forces requested that the Ministry of Telecommunications share with it all text messages sent in Lebanon over a two-month period surrounding Wissam al-Hassan's assassination, along with the log-in and password information for several online services, in a move widely criticized as an invasion of Lebanese citizens' privacy.

Freedom of religion is guaranteed in the constitution and protected in practice. However, informal religious discrimination is common. The country's political system is based on sectarian quotas, and citizens who delete their religion from their national registration seriously limit their ability to hold government positions or run for political office. Academic freedom is firmly established.

Freedom of assembly has been generally unrestricted in the past, as hundreds of thousands of Lebanese have rallied in favor of or in opposition to the government. However, there have been reports of detentions of protest organizers who call for democratic change in Syria. In the past, Lebanon's civil society was vibrant, and nongovernmental organizations (NGOs), including human rights groups, operated openly. While this remains the case for many groups, constraints have increased in recent years. By law, the government only requires notification of an NGO's formation, but the Interior Ministry has at times transformed this into an approval process and has been known to conduct inquiries into an organization's founding members. NGOs must invite ministry representatives to votes on bylaws or boards of directors. All workers except those in government may establish unions, which have the right to strike and bargain collectively. In recent years, unions have been closely affiliated with political groupings, and labor concerns have taken a back seat to union-based political activity.

The judiciary, while ostensibly independent, is subject to heavy political influence in practice. The Judicial Council nominates judges, who are then approved by the Justice Ministry. Both government and opposition parties vet judicial appointments. International standards of criminal procedure are generally observed in the regular judiciary, but not in the military courts, which consist largely of military officers with no legal training. Though civilian oversight is guaranteed in theory, it is difficult for civilians to observe the trials in practice, and in some cases defendants have no right to appeal. The military courts are tasked with trying those accused of spying for Israel, as well as Fatah al-Islam militants, human rights workers, and individuals perceived to be inciting sectarian conflict.

The security forces' practice of arbitrary detention had declined until the last few years. While the government has made some progress toward ending torture, regulations on the issue are often not enforced, and the use of torture remains widespread in security-related cases. Prison conditions are poor.

About 400,000 Palestinian refugees living in Lebanon are denied citizenship rights and face employment and property restrictions. A 2010 law allowed them access to social security benefits, end-of-service compensation, and the right to bring complaints before labor courts, but closed off access to skilled professions and did not remove restrictions on property ownership. In June 2012, Lebanese security forces killed several Palestinians during protests in refugee camps in Ain al-Hilweh and Nahr al-Bared refugee camps, including several teenage boys.

The estimated 50,000 Iraqi refugees in Lebanon and the substantial Sudanese refugee population do not enjoy official refugee status and thus face arbitrary detention, deportation, harassment, and abuse. In 2012 security forces detained a number of Syrian refugees and threatened to return them to Syria, and a number of kidnappings stemming from the Syrian conflict went uninvestigated. In October 2012, army and intelligence forces raided houses in Beirut hosting migrant workers from Egypt, Sudan, and Syria, beating male workers in alleged retaliation for the harassment of local women. Human rights organizations have characterized the attacks as xenophobic. The Ministry of Tourism in 2012 issued a memorandum prohibiting discrimination on the basis of race at Lebanon's private pools and beaches.

Women enjoy many of the same rights as men, but they experience some social and legal discrimination. Since personal-status matters are adjudicated by each sect's religious authorities, women are subject to discriminatory rules governing marriage, divorce, inheritance, and child custody. Women hold only four parliamentary seats. In 2012, activists criticized a proposed law addressing violence against women, claiming it was insufficient. The public abuse and subsequent suicide of an Ethiopian domestic worker in Beirut in March drew attention to the exploitation and abuse perpetrated against female domestic workers. International rights groups have criticized the internal security forces' use of anal examinations of suspected gay men as a form of torture. According to the U.S. State Department's 2012 Trafficking in Persons Report, foreign workers from Africa and East Asia are often victims of forced labor, withheld wages, restricted movement, sexual exploitation, and verbal and physical abuse.

Lesotho

Political Rights: 2*
Civil Liberties: 3
Status: Free

Population: 2,217,000
Capital: Maseru

Status Change: Lesotho's political rights rating improved from 3 to 2 and its status improved from Partly Free to Free, due to free and fair parliamentary elections that resulted in the successful transition of power to the opposition party.

Ten-Year Ratings Timeline For Year Under Review (Political Rights, Civil Liberties, Status)

2003	2004	2005	2006	2007	2008	2009	2010	2011	2012
2,3PF	2,3F	2,3F	2,3F	2,3F	2,3F	3,3PF	3,3PF	3,3PF	2,3F

Overview: Despite another bout of preelectoral violence and a deeply divided result, the October 2012 parliamentary elections were free and fair and resulted in a peaceful transfer of power. Prime Minister Pakalitha Mosisili—whose Democratic Congress won the most votes but was unable to form a government—resigned, and All Basotho Congress leader Tom Thabane became prime minister in June.

Lesotho gained independence from Britain in 1966, and the following 30 years featured a number of military coups, annulled elections, and suspensions of constitutional rule. Parliamentary elections in 1998, although judged free and fair by international observers, set off violent protests after the results gave the ruling Lesotho Congress for Democracy (LCD) party 79 out of 80 seats with just 60.5 percent of the vote. Troops from South Africa and Botswana—under the mandate of the 14-country Southern African Development Community (SADC)—were summoned to restore order. Following an evaluation of the country's electoral process, it was decided that an independent commission would supervise future elections, and 40 proportionally determined seats would be added to the National Assembly. The LCD captured the most seats in the 2002 legislative elections.

In 2006, Prime Minister Pakalitha Mosisili called snap elections after 18 members of the LCD joined a new opposition party, the All Basotho Congress (ABC). In the 2007 polls, the LCD won 61 seats, while the ABC captured 17. Lesotho's Independent Electoral Commission allocated 21 of the 40 proportional-representation seats to the LCD-allied National Independent Party and 10 to the ABC's ally, the Lesotho Workers' Party. Six other parties were also awarded seats.

Opposition parties disputed the allocations, accusing the government of poll-rigging and gerrymandering, and called a general strike. The strike was halted after the SADC agreed to mediate, but the talks failed to formally resolve the dispute. In 2009, gunmen opened fire on Prime Minister Mosisili's house, but he escaped unharmed. Government officials and some journalists linked the assassination attempt to the ongoing election dispute, calling it a failed coup. The same year, the head SADC mediator, former Botswana president Sir Ketumile Masire, ended his mission in Lesotho, accusing the government of avoiding direct talks with the opposition.

The run-up to the May 2012 parliamentary elections was marked by political volatility and violence. In February, Mosisili left the LCD to form a new party, the Democratic Congress (DC), along with 45 of the LCD's members of Parliament. Mosisili's move was driven by a power struggle with LCD secretary general Mothetjoa Metsing. Mosisili remained prime minister, and the DC became the new ruling party. In April, alleged LCD supporters attacked attendees of a DC rally, injuring at least 10, while less high-profile instances of violence and intimidation across the party spectrum were reported throughout the campaign.

The actual polling in May was declared free and fair by a range of international and domestic observers. While the DC won 48 seats in the 120-seat National Assembly, Mosisili was unable to form a government. A few days later, ABC leader Tom Thabane—whose party won 30 seats—announced a 65-seat coalition with the LCD, which had captured 26 seats, and two smaller parties, the Popular Front for Democracy and the Marematlou Freedom Party. Despite fears that the results would be contested and that Mosisili and his supporters would refuse to hand over power, Thabane peacefully took over as prime minister later that month.

Drought has plagued the country for over a decade, leading to food shortages and the dependence of some 450,000 people on food aid. Meanwhile, a season of heavy rains in 2011 severely curtailed maize production in 2011 and exacerbated shortages in 2012. Lesotho suffers an adult HIV/AIDS prevalence rate of approximately 23 percent, one of the world's highest. The government announced in 2005 that it would offer free HIV testing to all citizens, the first such program in the world. Roughly 25 percent of the country's infected citizens receive antiretroviral treatment.

Political Rights and Civil Liberties: Lesotho is an electoral democracy. King Letsie III serves as ceremonial head of state. The lower house of Parliament, the National Assembly, is comprised of 120 seats; 80 seats are filled through first past-the-post constituency votes and 40 through proportional representation. Members serve five-year terms, and the leader of the majority party becomes the prime minister. The Senate, the upper house of Parliament, consists of Lesotho's 22 traditional principal chiefs, who wield considerable authority in rural areas, and 11 other members appointed on the advice of the prime minister. Fifteen parties and several independent candidates contested the 2012 elections.

While the government has aggressively prosecuted cases of graft, political corruption remains a problem. According to the African Peer Review Mechanism, corruption is rife in all sectors of government and public services, and cronyism is prevalent in state bidding procedures. In June 2012, the Directorate on Corruption and Economic Offences—the government's anticorruption watchdog—was made an autonomous body with full control over its budget. Also in June, Thabane announced that all government officials must declare their financial interests as a condition of office, though implementation had not begun by year's end. Lesotho was ranked 64 out of 176 countries surveyed in Transparency International's 2012 Corruption Perceptions Index.

Freedoms of speech and the press are generally respected. Independent newspapers and radio stations routinely criticize the government. However, state-owned print and broadcast media tend to reflect the views of the ruling party, and the state controls the country's largest radio station and its only television station. Critical media outlets and journalists face severe libel and defamation penalties, and reporters are occasionally harassed, threatened, and attacked. Media coverage of the May 2012 election was more professional and expansive than during previous elections. Nevertheless, the state-run Lesotho Broadcasting Service allocated more radio and television airtime to the DC party, while private broadcast coverage favored opposition parties.

The government does not restrict internet access, though access is restricted by socioeconomic constraints.

Freedom of religion in this predominantly Christian country is widely observed. The government does not restrict academic freedom.

Freedoms of assembly and association are generally respected, though demonstrations are sometimes broken up violently. In 2010, an LCD-proposed bill requiring prior authorization from government officials to hold public meetings passed through the law and public safety committee in Parliament. Following protests from the opposition and civic groups, 21 amendments were made to the bill before it became law, including less onerous requirements for gatherings in rural areas and more discretion for judges in fining violators. While labor rights are constitutionally guaranteed, the union movement is weak and fragmented, and many employers in the textile sector do not allow union activity.

Courts are nominally independent, but higher courts are subject to outside influence. The large backlog of cases often leads to trial delays and lengthy pretrial detention. Mistreatment of civilians by security forces reportedly continues. Prisons are dilapidated, severely overcrowded, and lack essential health services; instances of torture and use of excessive force have been reported. An independent ombudsman's office is tasked with protecting citizens' rights, but its enforcement powers are weak.

Tensions between the Basotho and the small Chinese business community have led to growing incidents of violence in recent years.

The constitution bars gender-based discrimination, but customary practice and law still restrict women's rights in the areas of property and inheritance. While their husbands are alive, women married under customary law have the status of minors in civil courts and may not enter into binding contracts. Women are prevalent in senior political and economic positions in Lesotho: women comprise about 26 percent of national legislators and over 50 percent of senior managers. Domestic violence is reportedly widespread.

Liberia

Political Rights: 3
Civil Liberties: 4
Status: Partly Free

Population: 4,245,000
Capital: Monrovia

Ten-Year Ratings Timeline For Year Under Review (Political Rights, Civil Liberties, Status)

2003	2004	2005	2006	2007	2008	2009	2010	2011	2012
6,6NF	5,4PF	4,4PF	3,4PF	3,4PF	3,4PF	3,4PF	3,4PF	3,4PF	3,4PF

Overview:　　President Ellen Johnson-Sirleaf began her second term facing continuing insecurity in neighboring Côte d'Ivoire, fears of an influx of repatriated Liberian refugees, and ongoing land disputes. Initially accused of dragging its feet in prosecuting mercenaries, the administration apprehended 10 suspects implicated in high-profile cross-border attacks in June 2012. In August, 46 government officials, including the president's son, were suspended following corruption charges. Former Warlord-turned-president Charles Taylor was convicted in April on 11 counts of war crimes and crimes against humanity committed in neighboring Sierra Leone.

Liberia was settled in 1822 by freed slaves from the United States and became an independent republic in 1847. During the 1970s, a number of groups agitated for multiparty democracy and an end to the marginalization of indigenous Liberians by Americo-Indians, the descendants of freed slaves. In 1980, fighters loyal to Army Master Sergeant Samuel Doe murdered President William Tolbert in a coup. Doe subsequently assumed leadership of the country; his regime concentrated power among members of his Krahn ethnic group.

In 1989, Charles Taylor, a former minister in Doe's government, recruited fighters from among the Gio and Mano ethnic groups and launched a guerrilla insurgency against Doe from neighboring Côte d'Ivoire. A year later, an armed intervention led by Nigeria—under the aegis of the Economic Community of West African States (ECOWAS)—prevented Taylor from seizing Monrovia, the capital. Doe was murdered by a splinter rebel group led by Prince Johnson.

After years of violence and numerous failed transitional arrangements, a peace accord was signed in 1995. Taylor won national elections in 1997, but subsequently made little effort to seek genuine reconciliation or implement security and economic reforms. Violence erupted again in 1999 as the rebel group Liberians United for Reconciliation and Democracy (LURD) sought to overthrow Taylor, with backing from Sierra Leone and Guinea. Meanwhile, the United Nations in 2001 imposed an arms embargo and diamond sanctions on Liberia in response to its involvement in the conflict in Sierra Leone.

By 2003, LURD controlled most of northern Liberia, while another rebel group, the Movement for Democracy in Liberia (MODEL), squeezed Taylor's government from the southeast. In June 2003, a UN-backed war crimes tribunal charged Taylor with supporting militants in Sierra Leone. With the capital threatened and calls for his resignation, Taylor stepped down in August and accepted Nigeria's offer of asylum.

Taylor's departure ended 14 years of intermittent civil war that killed some 200,000 Liberians. ECOWAS helped negotiate an end to the fighting, and West African peacekeepers became part of a 15,000-strong UN peacekeeping force. In accordance with the 2003 Comprehensive Peace Agreement, members of Taylor's government, LURD, MODEL, and civil society representatives formed the National Transitional Government of Liberia (NTGL). The NTGL governed until the 2005 elections, in which the Congress for Democratic Change (CDC) secured the largest number of seats, and Unity Party (UP) candidate Ellen Johnson-Sirleaf won the concurrent presidential poll. Taylor was apprehended in 2006, and his trial before a UN-backed special court opened in 2008 and concluded in 2011. In April 2012, he was convicted on 11 counts of war crimes and crimes against humanity committed in neighboring Sierra Leone and sentenced to 50 years in prison.

In the October 2011 parliamentary elections, the UP secured the most seats, winning 33 percent in each legislative house. In the concurrent presidential race, Johnson-Sirleaf captured 43.9 percent of the vote, while the CDC's Winston Tubman took 32.7 percent, and Prince Johnson of the National Union for Democratic Progress (NUDP) secured 11.6 percent. Johnson-Sirleaf was reelected after winning 90.7 percent of the vote in a second-round runoff, in which Tubman took only 9.3 percent. Although opposition members alleged fraud and corruption, international and local observers found that the elections had been generally free, fair and peaceful, with isolated incidents of violence before and afterwards. One day prior to the November 8 runoff vote, police clashed with demonstrators during a CDC protest, resulting in at least two deaths and numerous injuries. Radio and television stations with perceived pro-CDC biases were shut down by the government.

The first half of 2011 saw an influx of some 180,000 combatants and refugees from political crises in Côte d'Ivoire and Guinea. These crises continued to afflict Liberia in 2012, and persistent insecurity in Cote d'Ivoire hampered efforts at refugee repatriation on both sides of the border. Although the Johnson-Sirleaf administration made clear its determination to prosecute any Liberian mercenaries, many of those arrested were later released due to a lack of evidence. Despite these problems, in June, the government arrested 10 Ivoirians and Liberians suspected of involvement in cross-border attacks, and extradited dozens more. Meanwhile, Liberian refugees living throughout West Africa lost their refugee status in July as a result of the peaceful conditions in their home country; while some returned to Liberia, many others had not by year's end. Some refugees have been living abroad for as long as two decades, and prospects for successful repatriation are dim. The UN mission continued its drawdown in 2012, and finalized plans to reduce its strength by more than half by 2015.

Political Rights and Civil Liberties: Liberia is an electoral democracy. The bicameral legislature consists of a 30-member Senate and a 73-member House of Representatives; senators are elected to nine-year terms, and representatives to six-year terms. However, in 2005, as part of the peace agreement, half of the senators were elected to six-year terms only, allowing for staggered senatorial elections to be introduced in 2011. The president can serve up to two six-year terms. The National Elections Commission (NEC) successfully conducted an 2011 national referendum, and when the results were challenged in court, the NEC upheld and implemented the court's decisions.

The organizational and policy capacity of most parties remains weak, and politics continues to be largely personality-driven, with strong underlying ethnic and regional loyalties. In the lead-up to the 2011 elections, the Liberia Action Party and Liberia Unification Party merged with the UP; the CDC, Liberty Party, and Prince Johnson's NUDP are the most prominent opposition parties. The CDC has struggled to maintain internal coherence since its defeat in the 2011 polls, and suffered several high-profile defections in 2012.

Some progress was made on curbing corruption in 2012, though the problem remains endemic. In August, Ellen Johnson-Sirleaf suspended her son Charles from his post at the Central Bank over charges of corruption, though she later refused to dismiss him; 45 others were temporarily suspended. The government faced accusations in 2012 of corruption and a lack of transparency in striking deals with Chevron, Sime Darby Plantations, and other corporations; in the case of the Malaysian firm Sime Darby, the government in January admitted fraud in at least two counties. The government subsequently commissioned an external audit to review all past concession deals for malfeasance. In October, Liberian women's rights activist Leymah Gbowee, who shared the 2011 Nobel Peace Prize with Johnson-Sirleaf and a Yemeni activist, publicly disavowed Johnson-Sirleaf for failing to curb graft and nepotism. Liberia was ranked 75 out of 176 countries surveyed in Transparency International's 2012 Corruption Perceptions Index.

Liberian media have enjoyed unprecedented freedom following the departure of Charles Taylor. The 2010 Freedom of Information Act promotes unhindered access to public information and is considered a model for the region. The country hosts a variety of newspapers, which publish mainly in the capital; numerous radio stations also operate across the country. The government does not restrict internet access, but poor infrastructure and high costs limit usage to a small fraction of the population. Steps toward greater media freedom were made in 2012, including the decriminalization of libel in May and the signing in July of the Table Mountain Declaration, which aims to abolish insult and criminal libel laws in Africa.

Religious freedom is affirmed in the constitution, and there is no official religion. However, Liberia is a de facto Christian state, and the Muslim minority reports discrimination. The government does not restrict academic freedom, though educational infrastructure remains insufficient.

Freedoms of assembly and association are guaranteed and respected. Numerous civil society groups, including human rights organizations, operate in the country. The right of workers to strike, organize, and bargain collectively is recognized, but labor laws remain in need of reform. Labor disputes often turn violent, particularly at the various rubber plantations throughout the country. In June, the Liberia National Police came under fire at a Liberia Agriculture Company plantation in Grand Bassa County when alleged illegal tappers refused to vacate the plantation. Further disruptions occurred at the Salala Rubber Corporation in September and the Sime Darby Plantation in November.

Despite constitutional provisions for an independent judiciary, judges are subject to executive influence and corruption. Case backlogs, prolonged pretrial detention, and poor security at correctional facilities continue to impede judicial effectiveness. Harmonization of formal and customary justice systems remains an ongoing challenge, and ritual killings, mob violence, and vigilantism persist. Many

Liberians express a preference for these informal mechanisms of justice over the corrupt and understaffed courts.

Poor discipline, high levels of absenteeism, and corruption continue to plague the police and armed forces, and relations between the military and the police remain strained. The police were widely accused of inadequately investigating individuals tied to the postelectoral crisis in Côte d'Ivoire. Nevertheless, authorities acted swiftly in arresting 10 suspects connected to incidents of violence along the Ivoirian border, including a June 2012 attack that claimed the lives of seven UN peacekeepers. Prisons suffer from inadequate medical care, food, and sanitation, and conditions are often life threatening.

Communal tensions over land access and ownership remain a potential threat to peace. Many of these conflicts trace their origins to the civil war and subsequent patterns of internal migration, displacement, and resettlement. Others are the result of opaque concession agreements granting foreign corporations access to lands for production of palm oil and other products. While these conflicts are especially ubiquitous in rural areas, Liberia's cities have witnessed tensions over property rights as well, especially as the government has moved to demolish illegal urban slums. In May 2012, the authorities demolished a school and 60 surrounding homes in a Monrovia squatter settlement known as Coconut Plantation.

Since being established in October 2010, the Independent National Human Rights Commission has made little progress in pursuing national reconciliation and implementing recommendations of the Truth and Reconciliation Commission (TRC), which was formed in 2005. Funding shortfalls, operational deficiencies, and a lack of political determination to break with cycles of impunity have hampered progress. Although recommended by the TRC, no war crimes tribunal has been established and no prosecutions pursued. Johnson-Sirleaf has focused instead on implementing the Palava Hut program, which would use customary reconciliation processes to promote forgiveness; the program remained in the planning stages at year's end.

While female representation in the legislature remains limited, numerous cabinet ministers and senior officials are women. Violence against women and children, particularly rape, remains a problem. A specialized prosecution unit and a court with exclusive jurisdiction over sexual and gender-based violence are unable to effectively process the large number of cases brought before them.

Libya

Political Rights: 4*
Civil Liberties: 5*
Status: Not Free

Population: 6,469,000
Capital: Tripoli

Status Change: Libya's political rights rating improved from 7 to 4, its civil liberties rating improved from 6 to 5, and its status improved from Not Free to Partly Free due to successful elections for the General National Congress that included candidates from a range of political and regional backgrounds, increased transparency in drafting a constitution, and the proliferation and sustained activism of media outlets and civil society organizations.

Ten-Year Ratings Timeline For Year Under Review (Political Rights, Civil Liberties, Status)

2003	2004	2005	2006	2007	2008	2009	2010	2011	2012
7,7NF	7,7NF	7,7NF	7,7NF	7,7NF	7,7NF	7,7NF	7,7NF	7,6NF	4,5PF

Overview: Elections to a General National Congress (GNC) were held in July, and the unelected National Transitional Council handed power to the new body in August. The GNC was tasked with forming a constituent assembly to draft a permanent constitution, which would then be put to a referendum. A prime minister was chosen in October, and after some dispute, a cabinet was approved by the GNC. Despite the end of the previous year's civil war, security remained a problem in 2012. Among other incidents, a high-profile September attack on the U.S. consulate in Benghazi resulted in the death of the U.S. ambassador and three other Americans.

Libya comprised three provinces of the Ottoman Empire until the Italian conquest and occupation of the area in 1911. It became an independent country in 1951, after a brief period of UN trusteeship in the wake of World War II. Libya was then ruled by King Idris, a relatively pro-Western monarch, until 1969, when a group of young army officers led by 27-year-old captain Mu'ammar al-Qadhafi overthrew the king's government. Al-Qadhafi was Libya's undisputed leader until 2011, but he held no official title and was referred to as Brother Leader or Guide of the Revolution.

Al-Qadhafi expounded a political philosophy that fused Arab nationalism, socialism, and Islam, and adopted anti-Western policies. Immediately after taking power, he moved to nationalize oil assets, claiming that the revenues would be shared among the population. In the 1970s, his regime was implicated in several international terrorist attacks. The United States imposed sanctions on Libya in 1981 and bombed targets in the country in 1986. In 1988, a U.S. airliner exploded over Lockerbie, Scotland, killing all 259 people aboard as well as 11 residents of the town. After an exhaustive investigation, Scottish police issued arrest warrants for two Libyans, including an intelligence agent. The UN Security Council imposed trade sanctions on the country, and over the next several years, Libya became more economically and diplomatically isolated.

In 1999, al-Qadhafi moved to mend his international image. He surrendered the two Lockerbie bombing suspects for trial, accepted responsibility for past acts of terrorism, and offered compensation packages to the families of victims. The United Nations suspended its sanctions, and the European Union (EU) reestablished diplomatic and trade relations with Tripoli. In 2004, a year after al-Qadhafi's government announced that it had scrapped its nonconventional weapons programs, the United States established a liaison office in Tripoli. The U.S. government eventually removed Libya from its list of state sponsors of terrorism, reestablishing a full embassy in 2006. Despite frequent promises of reform, however, observance of political rights and civil liberties in Libya remained abysmal, and the Qadhafi regime was consistently hostile to foreign and domestic criticism.

In February 2011, Libyans in several cities took to the streets to protest al-Qadhafi's 42-year rule. Though influenced by the concurrent uprisings in neighboring Tunisia and Egypt, the protests' proximate cause was the arrest of a human rights activist in Benghazi. Security forces violently attacked the demonstrators, setting off clashes between Qadhafi loyalists and a combination of civilians and defectors from the police and military. The rebels in some areas—particularly in eastern Libya—were able to clear loyalist forces from their territory, leading to a civil war with multiple, shifting battlefronts. In March, NATO launched an air campaign to enforce a no-fly zone over the country, protect civilian protesters, and aid rebel militias in their battles against al-Qadhafi's military.

The rebel militias captured Tripoli in August 2011, and al-Qadhafi, his family, and senior regime members were forced to flee the city. Efforts to take control of the remaining loyalist strongholds continued into the fall, and militia members seized and killed al-Qadhafi near his hometown of Sirte in October. Saif al-Islam al-Qadhafi, the ousted leader's son and onetime heir apparent, was also detained, and remained in the custody of a regional militia pending trial.

An unelected National Transitional Council (NTC) that formed in Benghazi in early 2011 to represent the rebel movement eventually relocated to Tripoli and began operating as a de facto national government, but its popular legitimacy and control over territory and armed groups were tenuous. Under mounting pressure, the executive board of the NTC resigned in November 2011, and a new interim cabinet incorporated members of competing regional and tribal militias, as well as business community representatives.

After a series of delays prompted by continuing insecurity, the need to allow citizens more time to register, and the inability of the transitional government to investigate candidates and finalize preparations, Libyans voted in their first parliamentary elections since 1965 on July 7, 2012. More than 100 parties registered ahead of the balloting, which resulted in the creation of an interim, 200-member General National Congress (GNC) to replace the NTC. The National Forces Alliance, a coalition headed by the relatively liberal politician Mahmoud Jibril, led the party-list portion of the voting with 39 of 80 seats, followed by the Muslim Brotherhood's Justice and Construction Party with 17. An array of small parties divided the remaining 24 party-list seats, and only independents ran for the 120 majoritarian seats. Election-related violence caused at least two deaths, but fears of extensive fighting and corruption proved unfounded, and the voting was regarded as generally free and fair. While the GNC's initial choice for prime minister, Mustafa Abushagur, was unable to form a government, its second choice, Ali Zidan, was named in October, and his cabinet was approved by the Congress. The GNC was tasked with electing a committee that would draft a new constitution, but the composition of the panel and the timeline for the drafting process remained uncertain at the end of 2012.

Insecurity remained a major concern during 2012, with regional militias, armed Islamist groups, international actors, criminal gangs, and smugglers all contributing to the problem. In the most widely publicized incident, an armed assault on the U.S. consulate in Benghazi in September resulted in the death of the U.S. ambassador and three other Americans. Other large-scale violence included deadly bombings during the GNC elections, a series of attacks targeting government security forces in the second half of the year, and a deadly October assault by government and militia forces on the reputed Qadhafi loyalist town of Bani Walid. The southern border areas, a common locus for arms smuggling, drug trading, and human trafficking, had become so insecure by December that the national government instated martial law in the border provinces and gave military authorities jurisdiction over provincial governments.

Political Rights and Civil Liberties: Libya is an electoral democracy. The prime minister and cabinet are responsible to the 200-member General National Congress, whose election in July 2012 was considered largely free and fair. However, the nationwide authority of these officeholders is limited in practice by autonomous regional militias and underdeveloped state institutions.

The 2011 uprising created more space for free political association and participation in Libya. Under the regime of Mu'ammar al-Qadhafi, political parties were illegal, and all political activity was strictly monitored. While only a few parties initially organized after al-Qadhafi's fall, the 2012 elections prompted a proliferation of over 100 parties that spanned the political spectrum, from socialists to Islamists.

Corruption has long been pervasive in both the private sector and the government in Libya, which was ranked 160 out of 176 countries surveyed in Transparency International's 2012 Corruption Perceptions Index. The fall of the Qadhafi regime raised some hopes that the level of graft would decline, but oil interests, foreign governments, smuggling groups, and armed militias often still wield undue influence, especially in the south, and opportunities for corruption abound in the absence of effective fiscal, judicial, and commercial institutions.

The end of the Qadhafi regime, and of the civil war, brought some respite to Libya's long-repressed media sector. Citizen journalism has been on the rise, and more than 100 new print outlets have been established, representing a wide range of viewpoints. In June 2012, Libya's Supreme Court struck down a law that would have restricted any speech deemed insulting to the country's people and institutions. However, media freedom advocacy groups reported an uptick in visa restrictions, filming bans, arbitrary detentions, and deportations of journalists in the months after the election of the GNC in July 2012, especially in the name of security after the September attack on the U.S. consulate in Benghazi.

Nearly all Libyans are Muslims. The Qadhafi regime closely monitored mosques for signs of religious extremism and Islamist political activity, and Muslims of various religious and political strains have been much freer to organize and debate their points of view since his fall. In some cases, however, this has led to verbal and armed clashes. Some Salafi Muslim groups, whose extremely conservative beliefs preclude the veneration of saints, have persistently destroyed or vandalized Sufi Muslim shrines, and the government has lacked the will and capacity to halt such abuses. Two men were killed in a rare attack on buildings belonging to the Coptic Church near Misrata in late December. Despite these incidents, the few non-Muslims in Libya have generally been permitted to practice their faiths with relative freedom, and human rights organizations have called for their rights to be guaranteed in the forthcoming constitution.

Close state supervision of education has been lifted since al-Qadhafi's ouster, and his Green Book has been removed from school curriculums. However, laws have not been passed to guarantee academic freedom, and the education system has yet to resume normal operations in all parts of the country in the wake of the civil war.

Freedom of assembly has increased dramatically since 2011. Although the ongoing presence of militia groups and the proliferation of firearms in the country deter peaceful assemblies and the public expression of dissenting views in certain areas, demonstrations by various groups were common during 2012 in the context of the GNC elections and the constitutional drafting process.

Domestic nongovernmental organizations have been allowed significantly more freedom to operate since the collapse of the Qadhafi regime, and they continued to expand in number and range of activities in 2012, particularly surrounding the elections. Trade unions, previously outlawed, have made small strides since 2011, but they are in their organizational infancy and have received little official recognition.

The roles of the judiciary and Supreme Court remain unclear without an official constitution. The court system has begun to recuperate, with some functioning courts in city centers trying ordinary cases. However, investigations into a large number of cases involving torture and extrajudicial executions before and during the civil conflict, including that of Mu'ammar al-Qadhafi, have made little progress, and an estimated 9,000 individuals remain in government or militia custody without any formal trial or sentencing. Among these detainees are high-profile suspects like Saif al-Islam al-Qadhafi and former Qadhafi intelligence chief Abdullah al-Senoussi, who was extradited from Mauritania in September 2012.

Migrant workers from sub-Saharan Africa, who were subject to human rights abuses even before the civil conflict, were reportedly mistreated by militia groups during 2011. While many fled the country under perilous conditions, some remain internally displaced within Libya. Libyans from certain tribes and communities—often those perceived as pro-Qadhafi—have also faced violence and displacement since the civil war.

Women enjoyed many of the same legal protections as men under the Qadhafi regime, but certain laws and social norms perpetuated discrimination, particularly in areas such as marriage, divorce, and inheritance. The GNC has made some limited efforts to address these issues, but formal legal changes have yet to be made. Women's rights groups have organized conferences in Tripoli to discuss the role that women will play in the new political environment; women hold 33 seats in the GNC and two seats in the transitional cabinet.

Liechtenstein

Political Rights: 1
Civil Liberties: 1
Status: Free

Population: 36,600
Capital: Vaduz

Ten-Year Ratings Timeline For Year Under Review (Political Rights, Civil Liberties, Status)

2003	2004	2005	2006	2007	2008	2009	2010	2011	2012
1,1F	1,1F	1,1F	1,1F	1,1F	1,1F	1,1F	1,1F	1,1F	1,1F

Overview: In a July 2012 referendum, voters in Liechtenstein rejected a proposal to reduce the powers of the hereditary monarchy. Crown Prince Alois had threatened to abdicate if the measure were approved.

Liechtenstein was established as a principality in 1719 and gained its sovereignty in 1806. Since 1995, the country has been a member of the European Economic Area, a free-trade area that links the non-European Union (EU) members of Norway, Iceland, and Liechtenstein with the EU. From 1938 to 1997, it was governed by a coalition of the Progressive Citizens' Party (FBP) and the Fatherland Union, now the Patriotic Union (VU). The latter party then ruled alone until the FBP won the 2001 elections.

In a 2003 referendum, voters approved a constitutional amendment that granted significantly more power to the hereditary monarch, Prince Hans-Adam II. In 2004, Hans-Adam handed his constitutional powers to his son, Prince Alois, though the elder prince retained his title as head of state. Following the 2005 parliamentary elections, the conservative FBP and the liberal VU formed a grand coalition.

In the February 2009 parliamentary elections, the VU won 13 seats, and the FBP captured 11. The VU's Klaus Tschütscher, who replaced the FBP's Otmar Hasler as prime minister, maintained the coalition government with the FBP.

Liechtenstein, a leading offshore tax haven, has traditionally maintained tight bank secrecy laws. However, in 2009, the principality agreed to comply with transparency and tax information-sharing standards as outlined by the Organization for Economic Cooperation and Development (OECD). Following a 2009 agreement with the United Kingdom, Liechtenstein passed laws in July 2010, granting amnesty to those holding offshore accounts in the country if they declared their assets and paid 10 percent of taxes evaded since 1999. British officials in June 2012 said they had already collected 363 million euros (US$564 million) from 2,400 people through the disclosure agreement and expected to raise a total of 3 billion euros (US$4.6 billion) by 2016.

In a July 2012 referendum, 76 percent of voters rejected a proposal by prodemocracy advocates to prohibit the monarch from vetoing decisions made by the public in national referendums. Alois had threatened to abdicate if the proposal were approved.

Political Rights and Civil Liberties: Liechtenstein is an electoral democracy. However, the unelected monarch is the most politically powerful in Europe. The prince, as the hereditary head of state, appoints the prime minister on the recommendation of Parliament and possesses the power to veto legislation and dismiss the government. The unicameral Parliament (Landtag) consists of 25 deputies chosen by proportional representation every four years. Voting is compulsory.

Political parties can organize freely. The VU and the FBP have dominated politics over the last half-century.

Liechtenstein's politics and society are largely free of corruption, and the country continues to work to prevent money laundering in its banking system. The OECD removed Liechtenstein from its list of uncooperative tax havens in 2009. The Group of States against Corruption in October 2012 released its first report on Liechtenstein, saying it was "in the early stages of implementing effective anti-corruption measures."

The constitution guarantees freedoms of expression and the press, though the law prohibits public insults directed against a race or ethnic group. Liechtenstein has one private television station, one privately held radio station, and two main newspapers, which are roughly aligned with the major political parties. Internet access is not restricted.

The constitution protects religious freedom, and the criminal code prohibits any form of discrimination against any religion or its adherents. However, the constitution establishes Roman Catholicism as the state national religion. Catholic or Protestant religious education is mandatory in all primary schools, but exemptions are routinely granted. Islamic religious classes have been introduced in some primary schools since 2008. All religious groups are tax-exempt. The government respects academic freedom.

Freedoms of assembly and association are protected, and the principality has one small trade union. A 2008 law provides civil servants with the right to strike.

The judiciary is independent and impartial despite the appointment of judges by the hereditary monarch. Due process is respected, and prison conditions meet international standards. Switzerland is responsible for Liechtenstein's customs and defense.

A third of the population is foreign born. Some native citizens have expressed concern over the growing number of immigrants from non-German-speaking countries, such as Turkey and Bosnia-Herzegovina. The government has responded by seeking to teach recent immigrants the language and culture of Liechtenstein in formal integration programs. Foreigners have occasionally been the target of violence by right-wing groups. The laws in Liechtenstein provide for the granting of asylum or refugee status. Prince Alois in August 2012 called for "prudent" immigration reform to attract more skilled workers, including naturalization for long-term residents.

Gender discrimination has continued to limit opportunities for women in fields traditionally dominated by men, and a gender salary gap persists, with women earning on average only 80 percent of men's pay for equal work. Following a 2005 reform, abortion has been legal in the first 12 weeks of pregnancy, but only in cases where the mother's life is in danger or she was under 14 when she became pregnant. A referendum on allowing the full legalization of abortion in the country was held in September 2011 but was rejected by more than 52 percent of voters. Prince Alois had already signaled his intention to veto the referendum had it passed. In March

2011, Parliament passed a law allowing same-sex registered partnerships; it was upheld in a June referendum by nearly 69 percent of voters and went into effect on September 1, 2011.

Lithuania

Political Rights: 1
Civil Liberties: 1
Status: Free

Population: 3,178,900
Capital: Vilnius

Ten-Year Ratings Timeline For Year Under Review (Political Rights, Civil Liberties, Status)

2003	2004	2005	2006	2007	2008	2009	2010	2010	2012
1,2F	2,2F	1,1F	1,1F	1,1F	1,1F	1,1F	1,1F	1,1F	1,1F

Overview: A center-right coalition headed by Prime Minister Andrius Kubilius's Homeland Union–Lithuanian Christian Democrats was ousted from power in parliamentary elections held in October 2012. Lithuanian Social Democratic Party head Algirdas Butkevicius subsequently became prime minister, heading a four-party coalition government. Meanwhile, as the economy continued to slowly recover, Kubilius's government approved the European Union fiscal treaty and raised the minimum wage for all workers.

Lithuania became independent at the end of World War I, but was annexed by the Soviet Union during World War II. The country declared its independence from the Soviet Union in March 1990, and the move was eventually recognized by Soviet authorities in 1991. Lithuania joined NATO and the European Union (EU) in 2004.

Lithuanian politics have been characterized by shifting coalitions among several different parties. A center-left coalition led by the Social Democratic Party of Lithuania (LSDP) was ousted in 2008 parliamentary elections, and a center-right coalition government led by the newly formed Homeland Union–Lithuanian Christian Democrats (TS-LKD) took power. Andrius Kubilius of the TS-LKD, who had previously served as prime minister in 1999–2000, headed the new government, which enacted sharp austerity measures in response to a growing economic crisis that saw gross domestic product (GDP) contract by 15 percent in 2009, and unemployment peak at 18.3 percent in the second quarter of 2010. Meanwhile, citizens searched for work abroad as jobs disappeared and wages fell. Independent candidate Dalia Grybauskaite was elected president in 2009, with nearly 70 percent of the vote, becoming the first woman to hold the post.

Defections in Kubilius's government in 2010 reduced the ruling bloc to just 69 seats, forcing the TS-LKD to secure an informal alliance with the Lithuanian Peasant Popular Union (LVLS), which held 3 seats in the legislature.

In February 2012, Interior Minister Raimundas Palaitis fired Vitalijus Gailius, the director of Lithuania's financial-crime investigation service, saying he had acted on recommendations from Lithuania's state security department. Kubilius expressed disapproval of the move and asked Palaitis to resign, but Grybauskait backed the interior minister, and a subsequent rift between coalition partners TS-LKD and the Liberal and Center Union (LCS) nearly caused the collapse of the government. Palaitis resigned in March, saying he had done so to keep the government from falling apart.

The parliament in June voted overwhelmingly to approve a new EU fiscal treaty that required EU member nations to balance their budgets, and allowed for penalties if they failed to do so. The same month, Kubilius's government approved a 6.3 percent increase to the minimum wage, starting in August 2012.

Lithuanian voters, weary of the TS-LKD's austerity programs, dealt the governing coalition a major defeat in two rounds of parliamentary elections held in October 2012. After both rounds, the opposition LSDP finished first with 38 seats in the 141-seat legislature. The TS-LKD captured 33 seats, the Labor Party took 29 seats, the right-wing Order and Justice Party won 11 seats, and the Liberal Movement (LRLS) captured 10 seats.

Grybauskaite upset the LSDP's coalition talks by opposing any participation by the Labor Party in the new government, citing allegations that it had rigged the elections. She further claimed that it would be improper to include Labor Party leader Viktor Uspaskich in the new government because he was facing tax fraud charges, having been accused of participating in illegal financing activities for the Labor Party between 2004 and 2006. However, in November, Grybauskaite relented, tapping LSDP leader Algirdas Butkevicius to serve as prime minister. The parliament confirmed the nomination, and Butkevicius proposed an LSDP-led coalition with the Labor Party, the Order and Justice Party, and the Lithuanian Poles' Electoral Action, which had won eight seats in the legislature. In December, Grybauskait approved Butkevicius's cabinet, which included four Labor Party members, though not Uspaskich. The parliament confirmed the cabinet later that month.

The economy continued to recover from the country's economic crisis. Unemployment decreased to about 13 percent in October 2012, down from 13.9 percent in the fourth quarter of 2011, and the GDP expanded by 3.6 percent in 2012. However, Lithuania had the EU's highest emigration rate, with the exodus of educated young people remaining a major concern. Following the LSDP's election victory, a central bank official in November said announced that Lithuania would not adopt the euro currency until 2015 or later; the outgoing TS-LKD-led government had planned to adopt the currency in 2014. The remark came amid mounting speculation that Lithuania, under a new LSDP-led government, would miss a 2014 inflation target set by the TS-LKD.

Energy issues remain a source of tension between Lithuania and Russia. In September, the European Commission opened an investigation into whether Russia's state-owned natural gas company OAO Gazprom was illegally blocking competition in natural-gas markets in a number of Eastern European countries, including Lithuania. In October, Lithuanian officials said Lithuania would sue Gazprom for $1.9 billion at the Stockholm Arbitration Tribunal, alleging that the firm had overcharged it for gas shipments.

Political Rights and Civil Liberties: Lithuania is an electoral democracy. The 1992 constitution established a unicameral, 141-seat parliament (Seimas), with 71 members elected in single-mandate constituencies and 70 chosen by proportional representation, all for four-year terms. The prime minister is named by the president, but is subject to confirmation by the parliament. The president is directly elected, and may serve up to two five-year terms. Recent elections were deemed largely free and fair, though there were some reports of irregularities, including alleged bribery and forged ballots. In the 2012 election, candidates with criminal records and those who had worked with the "special services of other states" had a note printed beneath their names on informational materials posted in polling places, resulting in some candidates being stigmatized. Lithuania's many political parties operate freely, but the Communist Party is banned.

Corruption remains a problem, though the country has attempted to prosecute many officials suspected of abusing their power. In 2011, Lithuania's central bank took over the country's third-largest bank, Bankas Snoras AB, after some 20 percent of its claimed assets went missing. In November of that year, two of the bank's former directors—Vladimir Antonov and Raimondas Baranauskas—were arrested in London on charges of stealing some $610 million from Snoras, after Lithuanian prosecutors had issued a European arrest warrant for them. They were rearrested in London in July on expanded charges. Both men denied the allegations and were fighting extradition to Lithuania at year's end. In October 2012, the country's anticorruption office charged Vilnius deputy mayor Romas Adomavicius with taking a $15,000 bribe in exchange for promising that a certain company would win a large contract; he denied the charges, but was temporarily suspended from his job by a Vilnius court later that month. Also in October, officials in Vilnius arrested Eligijus Vilkickas, the director of the city's legal affairs department, on charges of requesting and accepting a bribe of $7,400. The fraud case against former economy minister and Labor Party leader Viktor Uspaskich was ongoing at year's end, as was a corruption case against Alytus mayor Ceslovas Daugela. Lithuania was ranked 48 out of 176 countries surveyed in Transparency International's 2012 Corruption Perceptions Index.

The government generally respects freedoms of speech and the press. Privately owned newspapers and independent broadcasters express a wide variety of views and criticize the government freely. However, private television station TV-3 terminated the contract of journalist Ruta Janutiene in November, after canceling plans to air a documentary that she had produced about President Dalia Grybauskaite, saying that the program did not meet the station's ethical standards. In June, a Vilnius court found journalist and Socialist People's Front leader Algirdas Paleckis guilty of denying Soviet aggression against Lithuania, overturning an earlier acquittal. Paleckis's supporters paid the approximately $4,000 fine, but Paleckis appealed the fine and conviction to Lithuania's Supreme Court; the case was pending at year's end. The press suffers from inadequate standards for transparency of ownership. Additionally, international rights groups continued to complain about a 2010 law banning the publication of material deemed harmful to minors, though no one has ever been prosecuted under it. The government does not restrict access to the internet.

Freedom of religion is guaranteed by law and largely upheld in practice. However, so-called traditional religious communities enjoy certain government benefits, including annual subsidies, which are not granted to other groups. Academic freedom is respected.

Freedoms of assembly and association are generally observed. Nongovernmental organizations may register without facing serious obstacles, and human rights groups operate without restrictions. Workers may form and join trade unions, strike, and engage in collective bargaining, though there have been reports of employees being punished for attempting to organize. Slightly less than 10 percent of the country's workforce is unionized.

The constitution guarantees judicial independence, which is respected in practice. Defendants generally enjoy due process rights, including the presumption of innocence and freedom from arbitrary arrest and detention, but detained suspects are not always granted timely access to an attorney. Police abuse of detainees and lengthy pretrial detentions remain problems. Prisons suffer from overcrowding, and inmates have poor access to health care.

Discrimination against ethnic minorities, who comprise about 16 percent of the population, remains a problem, especially among the small Romany population. Unlike Latvia and Estonia, which continue to have large noncitizen populations, Lithuania made it relatively easy for all residents to gain citizenship after independence. However, graduates from minority-language schools have to take the same Lithuanian-language exam as students from Lithuanian-language schools beginning in 2013.

Marriage is defined in Lithuania's constitution as the union between a man and a woman. Members of the LGBT (lesbian, gay, bisexual, and transgender) community face discrimination.

Although men and women enjoy the same legal rights, women earn 17 percent less on average than men in comparable jobs. Women occupy 24 percent of seats in the parliament, and the first female president and speaker of parliament were elected in 2009. Domestic violence, including both spousal and child abuse, remains a serious problem. Lithuania continues to be a source, transit point, and destination for the trafficking of women and girls for the purpose of prostitution.

Luxembourg

Political Rights: 1
Civil Liberties: 1
Status: Free

Population: 527,000
Capital: Luxembourg

Ten-Year Ratings Timeline For Year Under Review (Political Rights, Civil Liberties, Status)

2003	2004	2005	2006	2007	2008	2009	2010	2011	2012
1,1F	1,1F	1,1F	1,1F	1,1F	1,1F	1,1F	1,1F	1,1F	1,1F

Overview: Luxembourg continued deficit-cutting austerity measures in 2012, despite labor protests against pension reform. Meanwhile, the Council of Europe called on the government to do more to protect the rights of asylum seekers.

The Grand Duchy of Luxembourg was established in 1815, after the Napoleonic wars. Following a brief merger with Belgium, it acquired its current borders in

1839. The country was occupied by Germany during both world wars, and it abandoned neutrality to join NATO in 1949. Luxembourg became a founding member of the European Coal and Steel Community in 1952, a precursor to the European Union (EU); it adopted the euro currency in 1999.

The center-right Democratic Party (DP) performed poorly in June 2004 general elections, allowing the opposition Socialist Workers' Party of Luxembourg (LSAP) to replace the DP as the junior coalition partner of Prime Minister Jean-Claude Juncker's Christian Social Party (CSV).

In the June 2009 parliamentary elections, the CSV captured 26 seats, while the LSAP took 13 seats, and the DP won 9 seats; three other parties won the remaining 12 seats. Juncker remained prime minister for the 15th consecutive year—the longest tenure of any EU head of government—and formed a coalition government with the LSAP in July.

Luxembourg has been criticized for its bank secrecy rules and was placed on the Organization for Economic Cooperation and Development's (OECD) tax haven gray list in 2009. Luxembourg signed several agreements regarding the sharing of tax information and was removed from the list by the end of the year.

In December 2011, after failed negotiations with unions, the government unilaterally reduced the frequency of automatic inflation-based wage increases. In October 2012, Juncker defended a 2013 budget containing further austerity measures, while ruling out value-added tax increases that would be a burden for the poor.

In October 2012, Crown Prince Guillaume, the 30-year-old heir to the throne, married Belgian countess Stéphanie de Lannoy.

Political Rights and Civil Liberties: Luxembourg is an electoral democracy. The head of state is the unelected Grand Duke Henri, whose powers are largely ceremonial. The unicameral legislature, the Chamber of Deputies, consists of 60 members elected by proportional representation to five-year terms. The legislature chooses the prime minister. Voting is compulsory for Luxembourg's citizens. Foreigners constitute more than a third of the population.

The political system is open to the establishment of new parties. There are three traditionally strong parties: the CSV, historically aligned with the Catholic Church; the LSAP, a formerly radical but now center-left party representing the working class; and the DP, which favors free-market economic policies.

The government is largely free from corruption. In February 2011, Luxembourg adopted regulations implementing the OECD Anti-Corruption Convention. Luxembourg was ranked 12 out of 176 countries surveyed in Transparency International's 2012 Corruption Perceptions Index.

Freedom of expression is guaranteed by the constitution. A single conglomerate, Radio Télévision Luxembourg, dominates broadcast radio and television. Newspapers generally represent a broad range of opinion. Internet access is not restricted.

Although Roman Catholicism is the dominant religion, there is no state religion, and the state pays the salaries of clergy from a variety of Christian sects; Islamic clergy are not supported. In October 2012, a government-commissioned report said that 95.6 percent of state funding for religious institutions went to the Catholic Church, and recommended a more equitable distribution for other faiths.

Schoolchildren may choose to study either the Roman Catholic religion or ethics; most choose the former. Academic freedom is respected.

Freedoms of assembly and association are protected, and nongovernmental organizations operate freely. Luxembourgers may organize in trade unions, and approximately 40 percent of the workforce is unionized. The right to strike is constitutionally guaranteed. The LCGB trade union held a strike in October 2012 against the government's pension reform plans.

The judiciary is independent, though judges are still appointed by the grand duke. Detainees are treated humanely in police stations and prisons. However, in January 2011, prosecutors filed a complaint against prison staff at Schrassig prison, alleging that searches of prisoners and visitors were degrading and invasive. Overcrowding has been reported at Schrassig prison, and an April 2011 inspection was critical of prison conditions and the treatment of prisoners. Two minors were held at Schrassig prison for two weeks in November 2011, prompting debate on the treatment of child offenders.

Luxembourg's Muslim minority, mainly of Bosnian origin, faces no official hostility. The government passed a law in January 2011 that increased penalties for hate speech. Asylum claims in Luxembourg have more than doubled since 2010. In September 2011, 30 Iraqi asylum seekers went on a hunger strike protesting processing times for asylum applications. In March 2012, the Council of Europe's commissioner for human rights recommended that Luxembourg take steps to protect the rights of asylum seekers, citing unjustified detentions and a planned reduction in monthly financial aid.

While women comprise more than half of the labor force, they are underrepresented at the highest levels of government; 15 women currently serve in the 60-member parliament, and only 4 hold seats in the 15-member cabinet. While the law does not technically allow for abortion on demand, women can legally have abortions if in "distress." In June 2011, the coalition parties broadly agreed on legislation that would allow abortions in a greater number of cases while maintaining current penalties for unapproved abortions. The Chamber of Deputies approved the law in November 2012. According to the 2012 U.S. State Department report on human trafficking, Luxembourg has not yet implemented comprehensive protections for victims of trafficking.

Macedonia

Political Rights: 3
Civil Liberties: 3
Status: Partly Free

Population: 2,064,100
Capital: Skopje

Ten-Year Ratings Timeline For Year Under Review (Political Rights, Civil Liberties, Status)

2003	2004	2005	2006	2007	2008	2009	2010	2011	2012
3,3PF	3,3PF	3,3PF	3,3PF	3,3PF	3,3PF	3,3PF	3,3PF	3,3PF	3,3PF

Overview: Interethnic tensions flared in Macedonia in 2012, with incidents of violence between Macedonians and ethnic Albanians. In March, the former owner of a defunct opposition television station was convicted of tax evasion and other crimes amid ongoing concerns of political pressure on independent media. Meanwhile, the government survived a no-confidence vote in October, though political tensions remained high through the end of the year.

Macedonia, a republic in the communist-era Yugoslav federation, peacefully gained independence in 1991 as the federation dissolved. The country's legitimacy has since been threatened on several levels: Greece objects to the name "Macedonia," saying it implies a territorial and cultural claim to the Greek region of the same name; Bulgaria contends that the Macedonian language is a dialect of Bulgarian; and the Serbian Orthodox Church does not recognize the separation of the self-proclaimed Macedonian Orthodox Church. Internally, poor relations between the Macedonian Slav majority and the ethnic Albanian minority have raised doubts about the country's long-term viability.

Since independence, power has alternated between center-left and center-right governments, though an ethnic Albanian party has sat in each ruling coalition. In 2000 and 2001, Albanians mounted an armed insurgency, demanding better political representation. Unofficially, the insurgents also wanted control of smuggling routes in northwestern Macedonia. The August 2001 negotiations known as the Ohrid Accords prevented civil war, but violent incidents continue to erupt periodically.

The center-right Internal Macedonian Revolutionary Organization–Democratic Party for Macedonian National Unity (VMRO-DPMNE) won parliamentary elections in 2006 and 2008; both polls were marred by significant voting irregularities, including ballot-box stuffing, and preelection violence. University professor Gjorge Ivanov, running for the VMRO-DPMNE, won a 2009 presidential runoff against the SDSM's Ljubomir Frckoski; international observers noted an improvement over the 2008 polls.

The opposition Social Democratic Party of Macedonia (SDSM) boycotted the parliament in January 2011, and the legislature was dissolved in April. Early elections that June led to a third consecutive victory for the VMRO-DPMNE-led coalition, which took 56 seats. The SDSM-led coalition followed with 42 seats; the ethnic Albanian Democratic Union for Integration (DUI) took 15 seats, the Democratic Party of Albanians captured 8, and the National Democratic Revival won 2.

Nikola Gruevski secured a third term as prime minister. International observers called the polls competitive and transparent.

August 2011 marked the 10th anniversary of the Ohrid Accords. A month later, Macedonia celebrated the 20th anniversary of its declaration of independence, which the government marked by inaugurating a massive statue of Alexander the Great in downtown Skopje as part of the Skopje 2014 urban development plan. The statue exacerbated tensions with Greece, where Alexander is seen as a national hero. The dispute between the two countries over Macedonia's name remained unresolved in 2012, obstructing Macedonia's efforts to join NATO and the EU.

Interethnic tensions spiked in 2012. In January, arsonists attacked an Orthodox church near Struga, a majority Albanian Muslim village, after ethnic Macedonians wore costumes at a nearby carnival that were perceived as insulting to Islam. In early March, no fewer than 14 people were injured in interethnic clashes in Skopje and Tetovo, a majority Albanian town. A month later, five Macedonians were murdered at a lake outside Skopje. Authorities in coordinated raids in early May arrested 20 ethnic Albanians in connection with the murders, some of whom authorities described as radical Islamists. The Albanian community protested the arrests at a demonstration in the capital later in May. In December, a murder trial opened against six suspects, including four who were arrested in the May raids; the remaining two were being tried in absentia.

The government exacerbated ethnic tensions in August, when the VMRO-DPMNE proposed a bill to extend free health care and other services to members of the security forces who served in the 2001 conflict, most of whom were ethnic Macedonian, but not to the majority-Albanian paramilitary veterans. After the DUI threatened to leave the coalition over the bill, the opposition held a no-confidence vote in October, which Gruevski's government survived. In December, political tensions escalated when the government passed the 2013 budget after ejecting opposition leaders from the parliament, prompting public protests and opposition threats to boycott the March 2013 local elections.

Political Rights and Civil Liberties: Macedonia is an electoral democracy. Most postindependence elections have been deemed satisfactory by international standards. Members of the unicameral, 123-seat Sobranie (Assembly) are elected to four-year terms by proportional representation. The Assembly added three seats in 2011 for representatives of Macedonians living abroad. The president is elected to a five-year term through a direct popular vote, but the prime minister holds most executive power. Certain types of legislation must pass by a majority of legislators from both main ethnic groups.

Corruption is a serious problem. While relevant anticorruption legislation is in place, and existing measures to clarify party funding sources and prevent conflicts of interest were strengthened in 2012, implementation is weak. Graft and misconduct are particularly widespread in public procurement. The judiciary lacks a track record of handling high-level corruption cases, and greater cooperation is needed between supervisory bodies and law enforcement, according to the European Commission's (EC) 2012 progress peport. Macedonia was ranked 69 out of 176 countries surveyed in Transparency International's 2012 Corruption Perceptions Index.

The constitution provides for freedom of the press. However, the country's media face political pressure and harassment, resulting in self-censorship, and media outlets are divided along ethnic lines. In December 2010, Velija Ramkovski, the owner of the pro-opposition A1 Television channel, and more than a dozen associates were charged with crimes including money laundering and tax evasion in a case widely regarded as politically motivated. During the investigation, A1 Television and three of Ramkovski's newspapers closed due to unpaid taxes. In March 2012, Ramkovski was convicted and sentenced to 13 years in prison. In June, the Broadcasting Council shut down A2 Television, Ramkovski's last remaining media outlet, after it began broadcasting political content and hired journalists who had worked at A1 before its closure. In November, the government decriminalized libel according to European standards, though steep new fines for libel were introduced, which journalists said would have a chilling effect. While the Broadcasting Council is not fully independent, in 2012 it began to enforce a law prohibiting politicians from owning broadcast media. Internet access is unrestricted.

The constitution guarantees freedom of religion. A long-standing dispute between the breakaway Macedonian Orthodox Church and the canonically recognized Serbian Orthodox Church remained unresolved in 2012. The January Orthodox church attack agitated ethnic and religious tensions. Hard-line Islamists reportedly control several mosques, with financing from Middle Eastern countries.

Academic freedom is generally not restricted, but the education system is weak by European standards. Textbooks barely cover the postindependence period, primarily because Macedonians and Albanians interpret the 2001 conflict differently. In August 2012, the European Association of History Educators urged history education reform. Increasingly, schools are becoming ethnically segregated.

Constitutional guarantees of freedoms of assembly and association are generally respected. On May 11, 2012, some 10,000 peaceful protestors marched in Skopje over the arrest of ethnic Albanians for the murder of five Macedonians in April. Workers may organize and bargain collectively, though trade unions lack stable financing and skilled managers, and there have been reports of journalists being dismissed from their jobs due to their union activities.

The government has not implemented a judicial reform strategy to replace one that lapsed in 2009. While the EC praised Macedonia for reducing case backlogs in 2012, it noted little progress on independence, impartiality, and competence. Stricter criteria took effect for admission to the Academy for Judges and Prosecutors (AJP), but the requirement that all new first-instance judges be AJP graduates is not being implemented. Prison conditions are generally unsatisfactory, with overcrowding and poor health care.

In June 2012, the parliament passed a lustration law aimed at removing former Yugoslav secret police collaborators from public office. The law allows the names of informants to be published online, which critics say raises concerns about privacy.

Roma, ethnic Albanians, and other vulnerable groups face discrimination. Minority groups say that the Skopje 2014 project ignores their heritage. A 2010 antidiscrimination law does not prohibit discrimination on the basis of sexual orientation. While women in Macedonia enjoy the same legal rights as men, societal attitudes limit their participation in nontraditional roles, and women rarely participate in local politics. In Albanian Muslim areas, many women are subjected to proxy voting by male relatives. Thirty-four women were elected to the 123-seat legislature in

2011. Despite the ongoing implementation of a strategy against domestic violence, it remains a serious problem, as does the trafficking of women for forced labor and prostitution.

↑ Madagascar

Political Rights: 6
Civil Liberties: 4
Status: Partly Free

Population: 21,929,000
Capital: Antananarivo

Trend Arrow: Madagascar received a downward trend arrow due to increasing repression and physical and economic insecurity—including intimidation of journalists, violence in the south, and a rise in human trafficking—caused by ongoing political instability that began with a 2009 coup.

Ten-Year Ratings Timeline For Year Under Review (Political Rights, Civil Liberties, Status)

2003	2004	2005	2006	2007	2008	2009	2010	2011	2012
3,3PF	3,3PF	3,3PF	4,3PF	4,3PF	4,3PF	6,4PF	6,4PF	6,4PF	6,4PF

Overview:

Madagascar made uneven progress in implementing an internationally brokered road map intended to resolve a protracted political crisis, as presidential and legislative elections scheduled for 2012 were pushed back to 2013. De facto president Andry Rajoelina—who took power after a 2009 military coup—continued to lead a transitional government, and former president Marc Ravalomanana, who was ousted by Rajoelina, remained in exile. Meanwhile, the transitional government continued to harass and intimidate opponents and restrict press freedom, and economic and security conditions deteriorated, especially in the south.

Madagascar gained independence in 1960 after 70 years of French colonial rule. A leftist military junta seized power in 1972. Admiral Didier Ratsiraka emerged as leader in 1975 and retained power until his increasingly authoritarian regime bowed to social unrest and nonviolent mass demonstrations in 1991.

Under a new constitution, opposition leader Albert Zafy won the 1992 presidential election. Following Zafy's impeachment in 1996, Ratsiraka won that year's presidential runoff vote. Opposition candidate and Antananarivo mayor Marc Ravalomanana was eventually declared the winner of the 2001 presidential election after protracted political infighting, but Ratsiraka refused to acknowledge the result amid considerable violence between supporters of the two candidates. Sporadic clashes continued until July 2002, when Ratsiraka left the country.

Ravalomanana's party, I Love Madagascar (TIM), won a large majority in the 2002 parliamentary elections, and Ravalomanana secured a second term the 2006 presidential poll. A 2007 constitutional referendum increased presidential powers, and Ravalomanana's authority was bolstered again in parliamentary elections held later that year, in which TIM captured 106 of the 127 seats. Andry Rajoelina, a young and charismatic opposition candidate, was elected mayor of Antananarivo in December.

In December 2008, the government closed a television station run by Rajoelina, triggering months of violent protests in Antananarivo. Rajoelina called on Ravalomanana to resign, and declared himself president. The crisis deepened in early 2009, with some army officers announcing their support for the opposition. In March, Ravalomanana handed power to the military, which quickly transferred it to Rajoelina.

Rajoelina suspended the parliament, suppressed opposition protests, and limited press freedom. In August 2009, the various political factions backing Rajoelina reached a tentative power-sharing deal, brokered by the Southern African Development Community (SADC), with former presidents Ravalomanana, Zafy, and Ratsiraka. Rajoelina later reneged on the pact, and subsequent internationally mediated deals also collapsed.

The political climate became further polarized after Ravalomanana, who was living in exile in South Africa, was sentenced in absentia in August 2010 to life with hard labor for ordering the killing of at least 30 opposition protesters in February 2009. In a November 2010 referendum boycotted by the opposition, voters approved constitutional changes sought by Rajoelina, including lowering the minimum age for the president from 40 to 35. (Rajoelina turned 38 in May 2012.)

Internationally mediated talks continued, and in March 2011, SADC agreed to support a plan recognizing Rajoelina as interim president until elections, as long as the opposition was fairly represented in the transitional administration. After sustained pressure by SADC and the European Union, an amended road map was initialed in September by all the main parties except Ratsiraka. The deal legitimized Rajoelina as Madagascar's interim president, provided for the unconditional return of Ravalomanana, and called for elections to be held within one year, a transitional administration that included all parties to lead the country to the elections, and the passage of an amnesty law for those accused of political crimes. Rajoelina named a consensus prime minister in October, and in December he appointed a transitional parliament that included supporters of all signatories of the road map.

In 2012, Madagascar made halting progress in implementing the road map, including appointing a National Independent Electoral Commission of the Transition in March that was tasked with overhauling the inaccurate voter rolls and registering voters in preparation for presidential and parliamentary elections. However, the elections, originally mandated by the road map to be held by November 2012, were delayed until May 2013 for president and July 2013 for parliament.

Ravalomanana's status continued to be a main sticking point toward genuine resolution of the political crisis. In January 2012, a plane carrying the former president was forced to turn around in midair after being prevented from landing in Antananarivo, sparking protests by Ravalomanana's supporters. Despite pressure from SADC to pass an amnesty law that would allow for the unconditional return of all political exiles—as called for in the road map—the transitional parliament in April approved a law that excluded those who had committed "serious violations of human rights and fundamental freedoms," such as murder. This made Ravalomanana ineligible for the amnesty due to his August 2010 conviction. Rajoelina and

Ravalomanana held face-to-face talks led by SADC mediators in July and August but were unable to agree to conditions for the former president's return.

In a sign of increasing discontent in the army ranks, soldiers in July—just prior to Rajoelina's talks with Ravalomanana—mutinied. The mutiny, the third since Rajoelina took power, was quickly put down, and its leader and at least two others were killed.

In November, a South African court ordered Ravalomanana to surrender his passport after alleged victims of the 2009 massacre requested that he be investigated for crimes against humanity, under a law that allows South African courts to hear cases that fall under the jurisdiction of the Rome Statute of the International Criminal Court.

In December, SADC leaders endorsed a plan under which neither Rajoelina nor Ravalomanana would contest the presidential election, arguing that it was the only way for the transition to move forward successfully. Ravalomanana later that month pledged that he would not run, and Rajoelina indicated that he might follow suit.

The 2009 coup and ensuing political crisis seriously damaged Madagascar's economy. Following Rajoelina's takeover, the international community levied severe sanctions on the country—but continued to provide humanitarian aid—and tourists and foreign business stayed away. The road map, if implemented in full, could allow for the lifting of sanctions and the renewal of development assistance and budget support.

Political Rights and Civil Liberties: Madagascar is not an electoral democracy. Andry Rajoelina assumed the presidency in March 2009 in an unconstitutional manner. The elected bicameral parliament was suspended in March 2009, and the transitional parliament appointed by Rajoelina in December 2011 will remain in place until elections are held.

Prior to the 2009 coup, there were approximately 150 parties registered, although only a few had a national presence and they tended to suffer from internal divisions, shifting alliances, and a lack of resources and clear ideology. Since Rajoelina took power, opposition political activity has been circumscribed through arbitrary bans on meetings and protests, as well as harassment, arrests, and killings of opposition supporters.

Corruption remains a major problem and worsened in the wake of the coup, due in part to the transitional government's failure to enforce antigraft laws. In spite of a 2010 decree that prohibited the logging, transport, trading, and export of precious woods, the illegal trade continues. In 2011, the Extractive Industries Transparency Initiative (EITI) suspended Madagascar on the grounds that the program could not be effectively implemented under the transitional government. Nevertheless, in September 2012, Madagascar published its EITI report for 2010, showing that the government had doubled its income from natural resources, to around $145 million, including a $100 million payment from China's Wuhan Iron & Steel Co. for exploratory drilling for iron ore. Madagascar was ranked 118 out of 176 countries surveyed in Transparency International's 2012 Corruption Perceptions Index.

The constitution provides for freedoms of speech and of the press. However,

Rajoelina has largely ignored these protections, and the independent outlets that have remained in operation are subject to government censorship, harassment, and intimidation, and practice varying levels of self-censorship. In May 2012, the transitional government jailed Lalatiana Rakotondrazafy and Fidel Razara Pierre, the editors of Free FM, the last opposition radio station, in connection with a probe into libel charges brought by businessman and regime supporter Mamy Ravatomanga. In July, Free FM shut down due to intimidation from the transitional government after having broadcast statements by the leaders of the army mutiny earlier that month, and it remained closed at year's end. Rakotondrazafy and Pierre took refuge at the South African embassy in September, but left a month later after negotiations with the transitional government. In November, the two journalists were convicted of defaming Ravatomanga and sentenced to fines and three months in prison; they remained free at year's end.

The Malagasy people have traditionally enjoyed religious freedom, though religious organizations are required to register with the Ministry of the Interior. There are no limitations on academic freedom.

Freedom of assembly has been severely curtailed since the unrest in early 2009, and officials of the transitional government and the security forces routinely deny permission for demonstrations or forcibly repress gatherings. In May, the police shot two people during a rally in support of Free FM and press freedom. Freedom of association is generally respected, and hundreds of nongovernmental organizations, including human rights groups, are active. Workers have the right to join unions, engage in collective bargaining, and strike. There were strikes by several public sector unions in 2012, and the transitional government allowed most to go forward. More than 80 percent of workers are engaged in agriculture, fishing, and forestry at a subsistence level.

The judiciary remains susceptible to corruption and executive influence. Its acquiescence in the face of Rajoelina's unconstitutional rise to power highlighted its weakness as an institution, and subsequent judicial decisions were tainted by frequent intimidation. A lack of training, resources, and personnel hampers judicial effectiveness, and case backlogs are prodigious. More than half of the people held in the country's prisons are pretrial detainees, and prisoners suffer from harsh and sometimes life-threatening conditions. Customary-law courts in rural areas continue to lack due process guarantees and regularly issue summary and severe punishments.

The army and security forces have largely been beyond civilian control since the 2009 coup, and crime, violence, and insecurity have risen. Clashes in the south among villagers, security forces, and cattle thieves known as dahalos—who had come to be affiliated with criminal gangs—killed as many as 250 people in the first nine months of 2012. In September, the security forces launched a special operation to rein in the bandits, but also engaged in mass killings of civilians and indiscriminately burned villages.

Since the coup, the de facto government has proven unable or unwilling to stop the illegal trade in rare timber, minerals, and endangered wildlife. This in turn has weakened protections of the country's delicate ecosystem and undermined the ability of parts of the population to earn a living.

A political cleavage has traditionally existed between the coastal côtier and the highland Merina peoples, of continental African and Southeast Asian origins, respectively. Due to past military conquest and long-standing political dominance, the status of the Merina tends to be higher than that of the côtier. Ethnicity, caste, and regional solidarity are often factors that lead to discrimination.

Malagasy women hold significantly more government and managerial positions than women in many continental African countries. However, they still face societal discrimination and enjoy fewer opportunities than men for higher education and employment. There have been reports that domestic violence has risen in the wake of the coup, as personal conflicts arise over dwindling family resources. According to the U.S. State Department's 2012 Trafficking in Persons Report, weakened rule of law and a decline in economic development since the coup have led to an increase in the number of Malagasy women and children trafficked to the Middle East for forced labor and sex work. The transitional government has made little effort to combat trafficking or prosecute offenders.

⬇ Malawi

Political Rights: 3
Civil Liberties: 4
Status: Partly Free

Population: 15,883,000
Capital: Lilongwe

Trend Arrow: Malawi received an upward trend arrow due to the peaceful and constitutional transfer of power to new president Joyce Banda and improvements in civil liberties including academic freedom and freedom of assembly.

Ten-Year Ratings Timeline For Year Under Review (Political Rights, Civil Liberties, Status)

2003	2004	2005	2006	2007	2008	2009	2010	2011	2012
3,4PF	4,4PF	4,4PF	4,3PF	4,4PF	4,4PF	3,4PF	3,4PF	3,4PF	3,4PF

Overview: President Bingu wa Mutharika died suddenly in April 2012, and, after a brief power struggle, Vice President Joyce Banda took over as Malawi's leader. Under Banda, many of the oppressive policies implemented in the latter stages of Mutharika's rule were quickly lifted, and the government appeared to be on a path of greater transparency and respect for human rights. Banda's reforms resulted in improved relations with the international donor community, which had suffered greatly at the end of Mutharika's tenure.

Following Malawi's independence from Britain in 1963, President Hastings Kamuzu Banda ruled the country for nearly three decades, exercising dictatorial power through the Malawi Congress Party (MCP) and its paramilitary youth wing. Facing an economic crisis and strong domestic and international pressure, Banda accepted a 1993 referendum that approved multiparty rule. Bakili Muluzi of the United Democratic Front (UDF) won the 1994 presidential election, which was generally perceived as free and fair. He was reelected in 1999.

Muluzi handpicked Bingu wa Mutharika, a relative political outsider, as his successor ahead of the 2004 presidential election. Mutharika defeated his MCP opponent, but the MCP took a plurality of seats in concurrent parliamentary elections. In early 2005, a rift between Mutharika and Muluzi, who remained the UDF chairman, worsened after several powerful UDF figures were arrested as part of Mutharika's new anticorruption campaign. Mutharika resigned from the UDF and formed the Democratic Progressive Party (DPP), which many lawmakers subsequently joined.

In the run-up to the May 2009 presidential contest, Muluzi and the UDF formed an alliance with the head of the MCP, John Tembo, and backed his candidacy. Mutharika ran a highly effective campaign and defeated Tembo with approximately 66 percent of the vote. Mutharika's running mate, Joyce Banda, a grassroots women's rights activist, became Malawi's first female vice president. In concurrent parliamentary elections, Mutharika's DPP won 112 seats in the 193-seat legislature; the MCP took 26, and the UDF captured 17. According to international and domestic election observers, the polls were more free and competitive than in previous years. However, incumbents enjoyed a clear advantage due to the use of state resources during the campaign period and clear bias in the government-controlled media.

In late 2010, Mutharika attempted to dismiss Banda as vice president. This sparked a crisis, as the vice president is an elected position that cannot be removed by the president. Although Mutharika claimed he had attempted to fire Banda for missing cabinet meetings, opponents asserted that the president was trying to clear the way for his brother and heir apparent, Peter Mutharika, to assume the vice presidency. Banda refused to resign, and was supported by the courts. Also in December 2010, the DPP fired Banda as its vice president and expelled her for allegedly acting against the party's interests, and she was subsequently sidelined from cabinet meetings and other official government activities. In response, Banda created her own party, the People's Party (PP).

With Mutharika and his party enjoying dominance in the legislature, the president grew increasingly autocratic and repressive. In July, discontent over economic turmoil and increasingly authoritarian governance led to public protests. Police shot unarmed demonstrators, killing 18 people in Lilongwe; the government forces insisted that the protesters had been looting. In August 2011, the president dismissed his cabinet, and in September, he appointed a new cabinet that included his wife and brother. International donors, after years of applauding Mutharika's economic management, responded swiftly to the crackdown. In July, the U.S. Millennium Challenge Corporation (MCC) suspended its sole project in Malawi, a $351 million investment in the energy sector. The British government, Malawi's largest donor, suspended all aid, as did the World Bank, European Union, Norway, Germany, and the African Development Bank.

Mutharika's crackdown continued in March 2012, with a public threat to fine or arrest journalists and civil society actors who "insult" the president, as well as the arrest of John Kapito, chairperson of the Malawi Human Rights Commission, on the charge of "printing and distributing seditious materials."

On April 5, 2012, Mutharika died suddenly of a heart attack. According to the constitution, Banda was his lawful successor. However, his death was not officially announced for two days, as DPP leaders held meetings in an apparent attempt to find a way to install Peter Mutharika as president instead. Nevertheless, prominent figures in Malawian society, including the chief justice and army and civil society leaders, as well as the international community quickly made clear that they stood firmly behind Banda. On April 7, Banda was formally sworn in as Malawi's president and Africa's second female head of state. Her new administration has gained widespread international support for its efforts to reduce government waste and fight corruption, and for its respect for human rights and media and academic freedom. In June, the MCC lifted the suspension of its compact with Malawi, and other donors followed suit.

Political Rights and Civil Liberties: Malawi is an electoral democracy. The president is directly elected for five-year terms and exercises considerable executive authority. The unicameral National Assembly is composed of 193 members elected by popular vote to serve five-year terms. The 2009 presidential and parliamentary elections, though characterized by an uneven playing field in favor of incumbents, were the most fair and competitive since the first multiparty elections in 1994. The successful handover of power to Vice President Joyce Banda in the aftermath of President Bingu wa Mutharika's death in April 2012 was seen as a positive step in the wake of apparent moves by Mutharika's allies to subvert the constitution.

While opposition groups had questioned the impartiality and legitimacy of the Malawi Electoral Commission (MEC) in previous years, key observers concluded that it operated with sufficient transparency during the 2009 elections. In apparent contravention of a court order, Mutharika had suspended and closed the MEC in December 2010, after an audit report revealed that large sums of money allocated to run the 2009 elections were unaccounted for. This once again delayed local elections, which had already been postponed to April 2011 and are now scheduled to run concurrently with presidential and legislative elections in 2014. In May 2012, Banda, in consultation with several political parties, appointed 10 new MEC commissioners, and she named a new chairperson in October.

The main political parties are the DPP, the MCP, and the UDF. Despite being the country's newest major party, many observers believe that Banda's PP has a strong chance to make substantial gains in the 2014 elections.

While Mutharika had pledged to fight corruption, opposition and civil society groups charged that his campaign tended to be directed primarily at his political opponents. The new National Anti-Corruption Strategy launched in 2009 included a plan to establish "integrity committees" in public institutions. However, a February 2010 report by Global Integrity indicated that the Anti-Corruption Bureau (ACB) has largely focused on low-level civil servants while avoiding high-ranking officials under political pressure. On claiming the presidency, Banda made tackling corruption and waste a top priority. In a symbolic move, Banda in June 2012 promised to sell the presidential jet in an effort to pay down the national debt. Moreover, she announced in October that both she and Vice President Khumbo Kachali would take voluntary 30 percent pay cuts as part of a national austerity plan. Some nongovernmental organizations expressed concern, however, that Banda could be using the anticorruption laws to target political opponents, such as former ACB chief Alex Nampota, who was fired in May and arrested for abuse of office in June.

In November, High Court Justice Rezine Mzikamanda was named the new ACB director.

Freedom of the press is legally guaranteed, and although Mutharika cracked down on the media in 2011 and early 2012, the situation improved markedly under the Banda administration. In January 2011, Mutharika had promulgated a harsh new law granting the information minister power to ban publications deemed contrary to the public interest. After Banda took power, the National Assembly repealed the law in May 2012. Harassment and arrests of journalists—which had spiked in 2011, as journalists were beaten and detained during the July protests, and radio stations were closed—declined significantly after Banda took office. Malawi's eight independent newspapers present a diversity of opinion, and there are approximately 20 radio stations and 4 television stations in the country. However, the government-controlled Malawi Broadcasting Corporation and TV Malawi—historically the dominant outlets—display a significant bias in favor of the government.

Religious freedom is generally respected. Academic freedom was considered to be under attack during the Mutharika administration. In February 2011, a lecturer at Chancellor College was questioned by police after comparing Malawi with Tunisia and Egypt, which were undergoing profound political upheaval at the time; this prompted protests by other lecturers. Mutharika intervened and closed the university via his role as its chancellor. Banda has made assuring academic freedom a priority, particularly through her appointment of Loti Dzonzi as the new police inspector general, who visited Chancellor College and pledged to respect academic freedom.

Freedoms of assembly and association came under pressure under Mutharika, especially in light of the crackdown on the 2011 protests. Civil society activists faced harassment, intimidation, death threats, and violent treatment from government forces and the DPP's militia, known as the Cadets. However, following Banda's installation, the climate for civil society and opposition groups has improved notably. The right to organize labor unions and to strike is legally protected, with notice and mediation requirements for workers in essential services. Unions are active and collective bargaining is practiced, but workers face harassment and occasional violence during strikes. Since only a small percentage of the workforce is formally employed, union membership is low.

During Mutharika's first term, the generally independent judiciary became involved in political disputes and faced government hostility; the courts have rendered several significant decisions against the government in recent years. However, due process is not always respected by the overburdened court system, which lacks resources, personnel, and training. Banda appointed several new High Court judges in October 2012, though the impact of these appointments remains to be seen. Police brutality is reportedly common, as are arbitrary arrests and detentions. One of Banda's first actions was the replacement of the police inspector general, Peter Mukhito, with Dzonzi, a noted advocate of human rights who pledged to tackle corruption in the force. Prison conditions are appalling, with many inmates dying from AIDS and other diseases.

Consensual sexual activity between same-sex couples is illegal and is punishable with up to 14 years in prison. However, Banda upon taking office announced her intention to repeal these colonial-era laws, and in November, Justice Minister

Ralph Kasambara said the laws would be suspended while their constitutionality was examined. Malawi had faced international condemnation in 2009 when a gay couple who became engaged through a traditional ceremony was charged with gross public indecency. In May 2010, the couple was found guilty of engaging in unnatural acts, among other violations, and was sentenced to 14 years in prison. For her part, Banda has been an outspoken proponent of lesbian, gay, bisexual, and transgender rights, particularly in regards to HIV prevention.

Despite constitutional guarantees of equal protection, customary practices perpetuate discrimination against women in education, employment, business, and inheritance and property rights. Violence against women and children remains a serious concern, though in recent years there has been greater media attention on and criminal penalties for abuse and rape. Forced marriages and the secret initiation of girls into their future adult roles through forced sex with older men remain widespread. The practice of kupimbira, in which young girls are sold by families to pay off debts, still exists in some areas. However, women recorded significant gains in the 2009 elections, winning 22 percent of the seats. Banda's rise as the country's first female president also raised hopes for improved gender equality.

Trafficking in women and children, both locally and to locations abroad, is a problem. Penalties for the few successfully prosecuted traffickers have been criticized as too lenient. A 2010 Child Care, Protection, and Justice Bill details the responsibilities of parents for raising and protecting their children and outlines the duties of local authorities to protect children from harmful, exploitative, or undesirable practices.

Malaysia

Political Rights: 4
Civil Liberties: 4
Status: Partly Free

Population: 28,974,500
Capital: Kuala Lumpur

Ten-Year Ratings Timeline For Year Under Review (Political Rights, Civil Liberties, Status)

2003	2004	2005	2006	2007	2008	2009	2010	2011	2012
5,4PF	4,4PF	4,4PF	4,4PF	4,4PF	4,4PF	4,4PF	4,4PF	4,4PF	4,4PF

Overview: In 2012, the ruling Barisan Nasional coalition used a combination of economic rewards, reformist rhetoric, and continued repression of opposition voices in a bid to ensure victory in the next elections, expected to take place by spring 2013. The restrictive new Peaceful Assembly Act was used for the first time in April to impose limits on a large demonstration calling for clean elections. The protest ended in violent clashes with police, who were accused of using excessive force. Meanwhile, despite the repeal of the Internal Security Act and amendments to the Printing Presses and Publications Act, the Evidence Act, and the Sedition Act, the government retained considerable powers to curb civil liberties and control the media.

Malaya gained independence from Britain in 1957 and merged with the British colonies of Sarawak and Sabah to become the Federation of Malaysia in 1963. The ruling Barisan Nasional (National Front, or BN, known as the Alliance before 1969) won at least a two-thirds majority in 10 of the first 11 general elections after independence, the exception being the 1969 elections, which were nullified following largely anti-Chinese race riots. The BN consists of mainly ethnic parties, dominated by the conservative, Malay-based United Malays National Organization (UMNO).

Mahathir Mohamed served as prime minister from 1981 to 2003. His development policies transformed Malaysia into a hub for multinational corporations and high-technology exports. At the same time, he stunted democratic institutions, weakened the rule of law by curtailing the press and political opponents, and drew allegations of cronyism with his state-led industrial development.

In 2003, Mahathir stepped down and handed power to his deputy, Abdullah Ahmad Badawi. The BN won 198 of the 219 seats in the lower house of Parliament in the 2004 elections, though opposition allegations of vote buying and problems with the electoral roll were substantiated. A series of court rulings during 2006 denied certain religious and legal rights to non-Muslims, sparking debate on constitutional guarantees and the role of Islam in Malaysia. The government took action to suppress press coverage, public discussion, and related activism on ethnic issues by non-Malay groups, citing the need to prevent national unrest.

During 2007, public frustration skyrocketed in response to government suppression of peaceful protests, high-level political corruption cases, a related crackdown on online media, and a crisis involving alleged politicization of the judiciary. Demands for electoral reform in advance of the 2008 general elections—coupled with perceptions of rising crime, corruption, and inflation—triggered the largest antigovernment demonstrations in nearly a decade.

In the March 2008 elections, the BN secured just 140 of the 222 lower-house seats, losing its two-thirds majority—and its ability to amend the constitution unilaterally—for the first time since 1969. The opposition People's Justice Party (PKR) captured 31 seats, followed by the Democratic Action Party (DAP) with 28 and the Islamic Party of Malaysia (PAS) with 23. These opposition parties also won control of 5 of Malaysia's 13 states and formed a coalition called the People's Alliance (PR). However, the PR later suffered from infighting and lost control of the state of Perak in 2009 after a handful of crucial defections in the state assembly. Meanwhile, Abdullah stepped down as UMNO leader and prime minister and was succeeded in April 2009 by his deputy, Najib Razak.

In December 2010, PKR leader Anwar Ibrahim was suspended from Parliament for six months after he compared Najib's 1Malaysia program—designed to promote racial and religious unity—to a similar program in Israel. Three of his PKR colleagues received similar punishment for vocally objecting to the suspension. Anwar was also dogged by claims that he sodomized a young male aide in June 2008, a charge he said was a politically motivated fabrication. He was finally acquitted in January 2012.

A mass demonstration calling for electoral reform was forcibly dispersed by police in July 2011, prompting domestic and international criticism. In September, the government announced plans to repeal the draconian Internal Security Act

(ISA), amend the Police Act to expand protections for freedom of assembly, and ease media restrictions in the 1984 Printing Presses and Publications Act (PPPA). However, the Peaceful Assembly Act passed by Parliament in December further tightened the conditions for legal protests, and although the ISA was replaced in June 2012 with a new security law, critics questioned whether the change was a substantial improvement. The PPPA was amended in April 2012 to limit ministerial discretion in licensing decisions, but many media controls remained in place.

Also during 2012, the ruling coalition took a number of steps to win over key voting blocs ahead of national elections that were due by spring 2013. The government authorized raises for civil servants, one-time payments of 500 ringgit ($165) to poor families, and book vouchers for high school and college students. Another large demonstration to demand electoral reform in April 2012 was marred by police violence, and organizers faced criminal charges despite the new assembly law; the cases remained unresolved at year's end.

Political Rights and Civil Liberties: Malaysia is not an electoral democracy. The leader of the coalition that wins a plurality of seats in legislative elections becomes prime minister. Executive power is vested in the prime minister and cabinet. The paramount ruler, the titular head of state, is elected for five-year terms by fellow hereditary rulers in 9 of Malaysia's 13 states. Tuanku Abdul Halim Mu'adzam Shah was elected to the post in December 2011. The upper house of the bicameral Parliament consists of 44 appointed members and 26 members elected by the state legislatures, serving three-year terms. The lower house, with 222 seats, is popularly elected at least every five years.

The ruling BN is a coalition of 13 parties, most with an ethnic or regional base, including the dominant UMNO as well as the Malaysian Chinese Association (MCA) and the Malaysian Indian Congress (MIC). The 2008 electoral gains of the three main opposition parties—the DAP, PAS, and PKR—came despite serious obstacles, such as unequal access to the media and restrictions on campaigning and freedom of assembly, which left them unable to compete on equal terms with the BN. The first-past-the-post voting system also increases the power of the largest grouping, and national electoral outcomes have been affected by the malapportionment of constituencies in favor of East Malaysia. In 2008, the BN won just 51 percent of the vote but secured 140 of 222 lower-house seats.

The Election Commission (EC) is frequently accused of manipulating electoral rolls and gerrymandering districts to aid the ruling coalition, and the Registrar of Societies arbitrarily decides which parties can participate in politics. On April 3, 2012, a government committee issued recommendations for electoral reforms, many of which had been called for by the Coalition for Free and Fair Elections (Bersih)—an alliance of civil society organizations working for electoral reforms, transparency in government, and an end to corruption. However, there was widespread skepticism that the existing EC could be trusted to implement the recommended changes.

Government and law enforcement bodies have suffered a series of corruption scandals. The Malaysian Anti-Corruption Commission (MACC) has itself come under scrutiny for its interrogation practices, as two suspects have died after falling from MACC office buildings since 2009. Inquests ruled one death a suicide and the other an accident. In 2011, Shahrizat Abdul Jalil, the minister for women, family, and community development, became embroiled in a corruption scandal along with her husband, Mohamad Salleh Ismail, the executive chairman of National Feedlot Corporation (NFC). They were accused of using an $82 million loan to the company to buy personal real estate. In March 2012, Mohamad Salleh was formally charged with misappropriating NFC funds, and the next day Shahrizat announced her resignation as minister, though she kept her party position as head of UMNO's women's wing. The MACC declared that there was no case against her. In October, the chief minister of the state of Sabah, Musa Aman, was cleared of charges that he had accepted 40 million ringgit ($13 million) as part of a money-laundering scheme involving timber trader Michael Chia. Malaysia was ranked 54 out of 176 countries surveyed in Transparency International's 2012 Corruption Perceptions Index. A Whistleblower Protection Act took effect in December 2010, but it did not significantly improve transparency.

Freedom of expression is constitutionally guaranteed but restricted in practice. Parliament amended the PPPA in April 2012, retaining the home minister's authority to suspend or revoke publishing licenses but allowing judicial review of such decisions. The amendments also eliminated the requirement that publications and printers obtain annual operating permits. Section 114A, a 2012 amendment to the 1950 Evidence Act, holds owners and editors of websites, providers of web-hosting services, and owners of computers or mobile devices used to publish content online accountable for information published on their sites or through their services. Malaysian press freedom advocates, bloggers, and opposition politicians staged a 24-hour internet blackout to protest the legislation. Critics of the legislation also charged that it would effectively shift the burden of proof on the accused. Most private print outlets are controlled by parties or business groups allied with the BN. Privately owned television stations also have close ties to the BN and generally censor programming according to government guidelines. State outlets reflect government views. Books and films are directly censored or banned for profanity, violence, and political and religious material. In August 2012, a Malay Muslim manager at a Borders bookstore was charged with distributing a book offensive to Islam, even though she was not responsible for selecting the store's inventory. She is facing a possible 3,000 ringgit ($990) fine and two years in jail; the case was pending at year's end.

The internet has emerged as a primary outlet for free discussion and for exposing cases of political corruption. The government has responded in recent years by engaging in legal harassment of critical bloggers, charging them under defamation laws, the ISA, the Official Secrets Act, and the Sedition Act, all of which can draw several years in prison. In July 2012, Prime Minister Najib Razak announced plans to repeal the Sedition Act, but it would be replaced with a National Harmony Act that serves the same purpose of limiting free speech; the Sedition Act had not been repealed by year's end. The Malaysian Communication and Multimedia Commission (MCMC), an agency responsible in part for regulating the internet, has been known to monitor online content and order outlets or bloggers to remove material it views as provocative or subversive.

While the BN government continues to articulate the need for a tolerant and inclusive form of Islam, religious freedom is restricted in Malaysia. Ethnic Malays are defined by the constitution as Muslims, and practicing a version of Islam other than Sunni Islam is prohibited. Muslim children and civil servants are required to receive religious education using government-approved curriculums and instructors. Proselytizing among Muslims by other religious groups is prohibited, and a 2007 ruling by the country's highest court effectively made it impossible for Muslims to have their conversions to other faiths recognized by the state; in very rare exceptions, non-Malays have been allowed to revert to their previous faiths after converting to Islam for marriage. Non-Muslims are not able to build houses of worship as easily as Muslims, and the state retains the right to demolish unregistered religious statues and houses of worship. In 2012, mainstream media outlets attacked the Shiite minority, with the newspaper Utusan Malaysia labeling Shiite beliefs as "deviant teachings" and "serious threats".

A court ruling in late 2009 overturned a government ban prohibiting non-Muslims from using the word "Allah" to refer to God, touching off a wave of January 2010 arson attacks and vandalism that struck Christian churches as well as some Muslim and Sikh places of worship. Appeals in the case seemed to be in stasis by 2011, and the 2009 ruling had yet to be enforced. Public debate over the issue was rekindled in late 2012 amid disagreement between the DAP and PAS.

The government restricts academic freedom; teachers or students espousing antigovernment views or engaging in political activity have long been subject to disciplinary action under the Universities and University Colleges Act (UUCA) of 1971. However, following a 2011 court finding that the constitution protected students' involvement in political campaigns, Parliament in April 2012 amended the UUCA to allow students to take part in political activities off campus.

Freedoms of assembly and association are limited on the grounds of maintaining security and public order. The Peaceful Assembly Act, passed in late 2011, lifted a rule requiring police permits for nearly all public gatherings. However, other provisions were seen as a bid to restrict rather than safeguard freedom of assembly, including a prohibition on street protests and the levying of excessive fines for noncompliance with this rule. At the end of April 2012, Bersih held a rally of some 100,000 people to call for clean elections, the resignation of the incumbent election commission, and international monitoring of the next elections. While the rally was mostly peaceful, violence erupted after a small number of demonstrators crossed police barricades. Dozens of people were injured, and a Malaysian Bar Council report issued two weeks later found that the police's use of force was "indiscriminate, disproportionate, and excessive." Leaders of the demonstration faced criminal charges and a government civil suit seeking 122,000 ringgit ($40,000) in damages. Bersih officials in turn filed a challenge of the Peaceful Assembly Act's constitutionality; no ruling had been made as of year's end. Separately during the year, right-wing groups and individuals harassed and denigrated Bersih cochair Ambiga Sreenevasan, who was also harassed while traveling abroad.

The Societies Act of 1996 defines a society as any association of seven or more people, excluding schools, businesses, and trade unions. Societies must be approved and registered by the government, which has refused or revoked registrations for political reasons. Numerous nongovernmental organizations operate in Malaysia, but some international human rights organizations are forbidden from forming Malaysian branches. Suaram, one of the leading human rights groups in the country, faced government harassment in 2012, including allegations of financial irregularities.

Most Malaysian workers—excluding migrant workers—can join trade unions, but the law contravenes international guidelines by restricting unions to representing workers in a single or similar trade. The director general of trade unions can refuse or withdraw registration arbitrarily, and the union recognition process can take from 18 to 36 months. Collective bargaining is limited. Unions in essential services must give advance notice of strikes; various other legal conditions effectively render strikes impossible. Amendments in November 2011 to the Employment Act further weakened workers' rights by removing responsibility from employers and allowing greater use of subcontracting arrangements.

Judicial independence has been compromised by extensive executive influence. Arbitrary or politically motivated verdicts are not uncommon, with the most prominent example being the convictions of opposition leader Anwar Ibrahim in 1999 and 2000 for corruption and sodomy. The 1999 sodomy conviction was overturned in 2004, and Anwar was released from prison, but the corruption charge was upheld, delaying his return to elected office until 2008. A second sodomy case against him began that year, ending with an acquittal in January 2012.

Malaysia's secular legal system is based on English common law. However, Muslims are subject to Sharia (Islamic law), the interpretation of which varies regionally, and the constitution's Article 121 stipulates that all matters related to Islam should be dealt with in Sharia courts. This results in vastly different treatment of Muslims and non-Muslims regarding "moral" and family law issues.

Individuals may be arrested without a warrant for some offenses and held for 24 hours without being charged. The ISA, in force since 1960, gave the police sweeping powers to hold any person acting "in a manner prejudicial to the security of Malaysia" for up to 60 days, extendable to two years without trial. The law was used to jail mainstream politicians, alleged Islamist militants, trade unionists, suspected communist activists, ordinary criminal suspects, and members of "deviant" Muslim sects, among others. Detainees have reported cases of torture while in custody, but official documentation of these claims is rare. The ISA was replaced in June 2012 with the Security Offences (Special Measures) Act, which abolished preventive detention but left the definition of "security offences" so broad as to raise serious concerns about the genuine intent of the measure. The new law allows police to detain anyone without judicial review, and suspects may be held for 48 hours before being granted access to a lawyer.

Although the constitution provides for equal treatment of all citizens, the government maintains an affirmative-action program intended to boost the economic status of ethnic Malays and other indigenous people, known collectively as bumiputera. Bumiputera receive preferential treatment in areas including property ownership, higher education, civil service jobs, and business affairs, and bumiputera-owned companies receive the lion's share of large government contracts.

Foreign household workers are often subject to exploitation and abuse by employers. An estimated two million foreigners work in Malaysia illegally. If arrested and found guilty, they can be caned and detained indefinitely pending deportation.

Women are still underrepresented in politics, the professions, and the civil service. Violence against women remains a serious problem. Muslim women are legally disadvantaged, because their family grievances are heard in Sharia courts, where men are favored in matters such as inheritance and divorce, and women's testimony is not given equal weight. Despite some progress in investigating and punishing sex-trafficking offenses, government efforts to combat trafficking are criticized as inadequate.

Members of the LGBT (lesbian, gay, bisexual, and transgender) community face discrimination and harassment. In 2012, Prime Minister Najib called the LGBT community an example of a "deviant culture" that threatens Malaysia. His remarks were consistent with those found in the country's mainstream media. Homosexual conduct is punishable by up to 20 years in prison under the penal code, and some states apply their own penalties to Muslims under Sharia statutes.

Maldives

Political Rights: 5*
Civil Liberties: 4
Status: Partly Free

Population: 330,700
Capital: Malé

Ratings Change: The Maldives' political rights rating declined from 3 to 5 due to the forcible removal of democratically elected president Mohamed Nasheed, violence perpetrated against him and his party, the suspension of the parliament's summer session, and the role of the military in facilitating these events.

Ten-Year Ratings Timeline For Year Under Review (Political Rights, Civil Liberties, Status)

2003	2004	2005	2006	2007	2008	2009	2010	2011	2012
6,5NF	6,5NF	6,5NF	6,5NF	6,5NF	4,4PF	3,4PF	3,4PF	3,4PF	5,4PF

Overview: Rising political polarization and tension during 2011 came to a head in early 2012, culminating in the removal of the sitting president, Mohamed Nasheed, in February. While the new government insisted that its installation was legitimate and internationally recognized, Nasheed alleged that he had been deposed by force. Hundreds of protestors were attacked and detained by police and security forces throughout 2012 during pro-Nasheed demonstrations. Physical harassment of the media and freedom of expression activists also increased in 2012.

The Maldives achieved independence in 1965, after 78 years as a British protectorate, and a 1968 referendum replaced the centuries-old sultanate with a republican system. The first president, Amir Ibrahim Nasir, held office for 10 years. He was succeeded by Maumoon Abdul Gayoom, who served six five-year terms. Gayoom repeatedly renewed his mandate through a tightly controlled system of presidential referendums rather than competitive elections.

Gayoom initiated political reforms after the beating death of a prison inmate sparked riots in 2003. A People's Special Majlis (PSM), composed of lawmakers and other elected and appointed delegates, was tasked with amending the constitution in 2004. The next several years brought incremental improvements to the legislative, judicial, and media frameworks, interspersed with bouts of unrest, crackdowns on the opposition Maldivian Democratic Party (MDP), and restrictions on freedom of expression.

In June 2008, the PSM approved a new constitution. Under pressure from opposition demonstrators, the president in August ratified the new charter, which included protection for a range of civil liberties while maintaining restrictions on religious freedom. The country's first multiparty presidential election was held in October. Gayoom outpolled five challengers in the first round, but MDP leader and former political prisoner Mohamed Nasheed won the runoff. The poll was deemed relatively free and fair, though observers reported flaws, including some preelection violence and voter registration problems. Nasheed's immediate priorities included anticorruption measures, government decentralization, and measures to increase freedoms of expression and the press, though these reform plans were hindered by the opposition over the next few years.

Parliamentary elections held in May 2009 were largely transparent and competitive. Gayoom's Maldivian People's Party (DRP) won 28 of 77 seats, while the MDP captured 26, leading to protracted deadlock, as the DRP-controlled legislature repeatedly blocked the president's reforms.

In December 2011, an opposition alliance was formed against Nasheed, culminating in a December 23 mass rally attended by tens of thousands of demonstrators who alleged that Nasheed's government had failed to protect Islamic values.

In January 2012, Nasheed's government arrested Abdullah Mohamed, chief judge of the Maldivian criminal court, on charges of misconduct. Waves of antigovernment protests erupted. Following a police mutiny, Nasheed resigned on February 7, with power transferred to Vice President Mohammed Waheed Hassan, head of the Gaumee Ittihad Party, a small party that had no parliamentary representation when he took office. Nasheed alleged that he had been forced to resign at gunpoint in what amounted to a military-backed coup. Sitting ministers were immediately replaced, and a number of Gayoom allies were appointed to prominent positions in the new administration, raising suspicion that different factions and individuals had colluded to oust Nasheed. Thousands of MDP supporters took to the streets in support of Nasheed, and human rights groups claimed that security forces used excessive force during the clashes that followed. Meanwhile, government officials blamed the MDP for the violence and threatened demonstrators with charges of terrorism. Pro-Nasheed demonstrations continued in February, but without reports of violence.

In late February, President Waheed formed a Commission of National Inquiry (CNI) to investigate the events that led to the change in government. After complaints that the initial makeup of the commission was biased, a new CNI with the addition of a Singaporean ex-judge and an MDP representative was formed. In August, the CNI released a report stating that the transfer of power was legal and that Nasheed's resignation was voluntary. The MDP contested the report's findings, claiming that it had ignored testimony from a number of witnesses, and that the MDP representative on the commission resigned shortly before its findings were made public. The international community, including the United States and the Commonwealth states, generally accepted the transfer of power.

In July, the parliament's session was suspended indefinitely by the Speaker. Following a series of talks among the political factions, the final session of the year proceeded on schedule in October. Nasheed was arrested that month on charges of abuse of power, and although he was released shortly after his first hearing, a travel ban remained in place though year's end in which he was forbidden to leave Male.

Several violent attacks and the killing of Afrsheem Ali, a member of the ruling coalition, targeted moderate politicians and activists during the year, raising concerns regarding the growing power of conservative Islamist extremists in the country.

Political Rights and Civil Liberties: The Maldives is not an electoral democracy. The country's democratically elected president, Mohamed Nasheed, was removed from office in 2012, allegedly at gunpoint. Charges of abuse of power leveled against former president Nasheed after the change in government were seen as politically motivated, as he would be ineligible to stand for office if convicted. Under the 2008 constitution, the president is directly elected for up to two five-year terms. The unicameral People's Majlis is composed of 77 seats, with members elected from individual districts to serve five-year terms. Political violence and harassment increased in 2012 amid the February change in government. MDP members and supporters allege that they were explicitly targeted by police during a number of demonstrations that occurred during the year. Parliament functioned sporadically during the year, with the summer session of the body suspended by the Speaker, limiting the ability of key legislation to be passed.

In recent years, a new, independent auditor general and the revised constitution have provided greater transparency, shedding light on pervasive corruption. An Anti-Corruption Commission (ACC) was established in 2008 and opened dozens of cases, though the vast majority do not result in convictions.

The constitution guarantees freedoms of expression and the press. However, journalists and media outlets faced attacks and harassment throughout 2012 as they attempted to cover the political turmoil. The state-run Maldives National Broadcasting Commission, as well as several private stations, were attacked during the February change in government, while attacks on journalists, as well as on Raajje TV, occurred in July and August. The blocking of Christian websites by the Ministry of Islamic Affairs (MIA) remains an issue. Freelance journalist, blogger, and gay rights activist Ismail "Hilath" Rasheed—whose blog was blocked in November 2011 on the grounds that it contained "anti-Islamic" material and who was detained for several months after he took part in a protest advocating for greater religious tolerance—was stabbed in the throat in June and fled the country in July.

Freedom of religion remains severely restricted. Islam is the state religion, and all citizens are required to be Sunni Muslims. Imams must use government-approved sermons. Non-Muslim foreigners are allowed to observe their religions only in private. In September 2012, two men were arrested for possession of Christian books. In recent years, the rise of conservative strands of Islam has led to more rigid interpretations of behavior and dress, particularly for women. Extremists also opposed several initiatives of the Nasheed government, and during the February unrest, suspected Islamist extremists broke into the national museum and destroyed Buddhist statues, claiming they were idolatrous. There are no reported limitations on academic freedom, but many scholars self-censor.

The constitution guarantees freedom of assembly. However, during the ongoing demonstrations following Nasheed's ouster in February, police used excessive force, including teargas and pepper spray, against peaceful protestors, and also beat unarmed civilians. Nongovernmental organizations struggle with funding and issues of long-term viability in a weak civil society environment. The constitution and the 2008 Employment Act allow workers to form trade unions and to strike. The country's first labor tribunal was established in December 2008 to enforce the Employment Act. Exploitation of migrant workers is widespread.

The constitution provides for an independent judiciary, and a Judicial Services Commission (JSC) was established in 2009 to separate the judicial branch from the executive. Politicization of the judiciary increased in March 2012 following a number of appointments made to the JSC by new president Mohammed Waheed Hassan. Civil law is used in most cases, but it is subordinate to Sharia (Islamic law), which is applied in matters not covered by civil law and in cases involving divorce or adultery. As a result, the testimony of two women is equal to that of one man, and punishments such as internal exile continue to be carried out.

The constitution bans arbitrary arrest, torture, and prolonged detention without adequate judicial review. The Nasheed administration had initiated police reform and established a parole board to recommend sentence reductions for unjustly detained inmates. Amid the political turmoil of 2012, protestors and political activists were arrested, detained, and tortured in custody. MDP supporters in particular were targeted for harsh treatment.

The past several years have seen an increase in gang activity and violence, often linked to drugs and organized crime. More recently, political parties have used gangs to engage in political violence and attacks against opponents.

Women are increasingly entering the civil service and receiving pay equal to that of men, though opportunities are sometimes limited by traditional norms, and women hold few senior government positions. Domestic violence against women is widespread. International human rights groups have urged reform of severe legal punishments that primarily affect women, including the sentence of flogging for extramarital sex; a number of such sentences were handed down in 2012. In April, however, a new domestic violence law was passed that criminalized several types of violence and provided protection for victims. Efforts to address trafficking have been largely ineffective. Homosexual activity is against the law.

Mali

Political Rights: 7*
Civil Liberties: 5*
Status: Not Free

Population: 16,014,000
Capital: Bamako

Status Change: Mali's political rights rating declined from 2 to 7, its civil liberties rating declined from 3 to 5, and its status declined from Free to Not Free due to a military coup that deposed the democratically elected president; the ensuing repression of the media, political actors, and freedom of movement in the south; and the occupation of the north by militants who harshly suppressed fundamental rights in areas under their control.

Ten-Year Ratings Timeline For Year Under Review (Political Rights, Civil Liberties, Status)

2003	2004	2005	2006	2007	2008	2009	2010	2011	2012
2,2F	2,2F	2,2F	2,2F	2,3F	2,3F	2,3F	2,3F	2,3F	7,5NF

Overview:

On January 17, 2012, an ethnic Tuareg separatist group launched a rebellion in the north. Government forces fared poorly against the rebels, and on March 22, less than a month before scheduled elections, an army captain led a coup that ousted President Amadou Toumani Touré, suspended the constitution, and created a junta to rule the country. Under international pressure, the junta handed nominal power to interim president Dioncounda Traoré, but maintained a supervisory role. Meanwhile, Islamist militants sidelined the Tuareg rebels in the north, consolidated control over major towns, and committed serious human rights violations. As a result of the fighting and abuses, some 340,000 Malians were either internally displaced or became refugees. The Economic Community of West African States agreed to organize a military intervention in Mali, but it had yet to take action at the end of the year.

From independence from France in 1960 until 1991, Mali was ruled by military and one-party regimes. After soldiers killed more than 100 demonstrators demanding a multiparty system in 1991, President Moussa Traoré was overthrown by the military. Alpha Oumar Konaré of the Alliance for Democracy in Mali (ADEMA) won the presidency in the 1992 elections, which were deemed credible by most observers. He secured a second and final term in 1997 amid an opposition boycott. Several opposition parties also boycotted that year's National Assembly elections, in which ADEMA captured a majority of seats.

In the 2002 presidential election, independent candidate Amadou Toumani Touré, a popular former military officer who had led Mali during the post-Traoré transition period, defeated his ADEMA opponent. During legislative elections that year, the opposition Hope 2002 coalition emerged victorious over an ADEMA-led coalition.

In the April 2007 presidential poll, Touré was reelected with 71 percent in the first round of voting; he ran as an independent candidate, but with support from the Alliance of Democracy and Progress (ADP) coalition, led by ADEMA. In July 2007 elections to the National Assembly, the ADP secured a total of 113 seats, with 51 going to ADEMA. The main opposition coalition, the Front for Democracy and the Republic, captured 15 seats, while a smaller party and a number of independents secured the remaining 19 seats. ADEMA captured more votes than any other party in the 2009 municipal elections.

Violence in the north between government forces and the marginalized ethnic Tuareg minority, which had flared in 2007, died down following a 2009 government offensive and a subsequent peace agreement. However, Islamist militants kidnapped a number of international aid workers and European tourists beginning in 2008, and several were killed. The terrorist organization al-Qaeda in the Islamic Maghreb (AQIM) continued to threaten security in the north throughout 2010 and 2011.

In October 2011, Tuareg fighters formed the National Movement for the Liberation of the Azawad (MNLA), which demanded independence for northern Mali. Following the Libyan revolution that year, soldiers who had fought for ousted Libyan dictator Mu'ammar al-Qadhafi joined the MNLA, bringing new weapons and equipment. The movement launched a rebellion on January 17, 2012, and on January 26, its fighters killed 50 soldiers. This led to protests throughout Mali, as the public reacted to army's lack of supplies and its inability to suppress the rebellion. Nevertheless, as of late February, Touré promised that the presidential election scheduled for April 29, from which he was barred by term limits, would take place as planned.

On March 21, mutinous soldiers led by Captain Amadou Sanogo mounted a coup, removing the president, suspending the constitution, detaining government ministers, and establishing the National Committee for the Return of Democracy and the Restoration of the State to rule the country. The junta leaders argued that the coup was necessary to end what they considered incompetent management of the situation in the north. While some Malians welcomed the revolt, the international community condemned it. The African Union (AU) and the Economic Community of West African States (ECOWAS) suspended Mali's membership, and foreign aid was suspended as well. On March 28, the junta declared a new constitution, but after criticism, it restored the old charter on April 1. On April 8, Touré resigned as president, and Sanogo agreed to hand power to interim president Dioncounda Traoré, the Speaker of the National Assembly, on April 12. Nevertheless, the military maintained de facto authority over the civilian leadership. Soldiers from Touré's presidential guard attempted a countercoup, but they were quickly defeated by forces loyal to the junta. On May 21, supporters of the junta attacked Traoré in the presidential palace. He left the country for medical treatment and did not return until late July.

Taking advantage of the turmoil in the capital, the MNLA occupied the three main cities of the north—Timbuktu, Kidal, and Gao. On April 6, the rebels took the city of Douentza in central Mali and declared independence for Azawad. However, over the course of the summer, Islamist militant groups that had cooperated with the MNLA—Ansar Dine and the AQIM-linked Movement for Unity and Jihad in West Africa (MUJAO)—fought with and seized territory from the Tuareg separatist group. By July, the MNLA had shifted its demands toward a possible compromise with the government, seeking a level of autonomy short of full secession.

Meanwhile, the Islamist groups committed human rights abuses and destroyed religious monuments they deemed un-Islamic in the areas under their control.

In November, army chiefs from ECOWAS adopted a plan to expel the rebels from northern Mali and agreed to send 3,300 troops. The plan was approved by the AU, and by the UN Security Council in December. However, the Security Council required that political efforts be exhausted before the start of military operations, and the UN peacekeeping chief predicted that military action would not begin until late 2013. UN secretary general Ban Ki-moon called for the government in Bamako to hold elections before any intervention. Prime Minister Cheick Modibo Diarra resigned after being arrested by the junta on December 11, raising doubts about the government's ability to hold elections or cultivate the international legitimacy necessary to secure foreign military aid. Separately, the MNLA and Ansar Dine rebels signed a ceasefire to end their infighting on December 22.

Over 200,000 people from the north were internally displaced at year's end, while roughly 140,000 were refugees in neighboring countries.

Political Rights and Civil Liberties: Mali is not an electoral democracy. In 2012 the country was split between an interim government overseen by a military junta in the south and Islamist militant groups in the north. However, previous elections were peaceful and generally considered fair. According to the constitution, the president, who appoints the prime minister, is elected by popular vote and can serve up to two five-year terms. Members of the 160-seat unicameral National Assembly serve five-year terms, with 13 seats reserved to represent Malians living abroad.

In 2011, a wide variety of political parties formed fluid and frequently shifting coalitions in preparation for the elections scheduled for April 2012, which were canceled after the March coup. Party leaders were repeatedly harassed and arrested by the military during 2012.

A number of anticorruption initiatives had been launched under President Amadou Toumani Touré's administration, including the creation of a general auditor's office. However, corruption remained a problem in government, public procurement, and both public and private contracting. Mali was ranked 105 out of 176 countries surveyed in Transparency International's 2012 Corruption Perceptions Index.

Mali's media were considered among the freest in Africa before the 2012 rebellion and coup. Criminal libel laws had not been invoked by authorities since 2007, and there were no reports of harassment or intimidation of journalists in 2011. During 2012, however, an unprecedented number of journalists were illegally detained and tortured by the military and Islamist militants. Interviews with former president Touré and rebels were forbidden by the junta, and the national broadcaster was stormed by the military in April. The attacks on journalists decreased significantly in the second half of the year.

Mali's population is predominantly Muslim, and the High Islamic Council has a significant influence over politics. However, the state is secular, and minority religious rights are protected by law. In the north during 2012, Islamist militants imposed a crude form of Sharia (Islamic law) and destroyed Sufi Muslim shrines and other sacred sites that they deemed un-Islamic. Academic freedom was also suppressed in the rebel-held north.

Freedoms of assembly and association were respected prior to the coup, and nongovernmental organizations operated actively without interference. The constitution guarantees workers the right to form unions and to strike, with some limitations regarding essential services and compulsory arbitration. Since the rebellion and coup, people's ability to protest, engage in civic advocacy, or assert labor rights has been sharply curtailed across the country, particularly in the north.

The judiciary, whose members were appointed by the executive under the constitution, was not independent. Traditional authorities decided the majority of disputes in rural areas. A 2010 law called for the establishment of Centers for Access to Rights and Justice, which would provide citizens with information about their legal rights and judicial procedures, but the facilities were not operational by the time of the coup. Under the elected government, detainees were not always charged within the 48-hour period set by law, and police brutality had been reported, though the courts convicted some perpetrators. During 2012, however, people accused of crimes or perceived moral offenses were summarily punished and even executed in the north, while the junta regularly engaged in arbitrary arrests and detentions in the south.

No ethnic group predominates in the government or security forces. Longstanding tensions between the more populous nonpastoralist ethnic groups and the Moor and Tuareg pastoralist groups have often fueled intermittent instability, leading up to the rebellion of 2012.

Women have been underrepresented in high political posts. Mali's first woman prime minister took office in 2011. Domestic violence against women is widespread, and cultural traditions have hindered reform. Despite the creation of the National Coordinating Committee for the Fight Against Trafficking and Related Activities in 2011, adult trafficking has not been criminalized, and Mali remains a source, destination, and transit country for women and children trafficked for the purposes of sexual exploitation and forced labor. Prosecution of suspected traffickers is infrequent, with only two convictions in 2011. Traditional forms of slavery and debt bondage persist, particularly in the north, with thousands of people estimated to be living in conditions of servitude. Women faced heightened harassment, threats, and violence in the north in 2012 due to militants' enforcement of harsh restrictions on dress and behavior.

Malta

Political Rights: 1
Civil Liberties: 1
Status: Free

Population: 398,600
Capital: Valletta

Ten-Year Ratings Timeline For Year Under Review (Political Rights, Civil Liberties, Status)

2003	2004	2005	2006	2007	2008	2009	2010	2011	2012
1,1F	1,1F	1,1F	1,1F	1,1F	1,1F	1,1F	1,1F	1,1F	1,1F

Overview: Malta continued to face challenges related to immigration in 2012, including international criticism for its detention policies and poor conditions in its holding centers for refugees and asylum seekers. The deaths of at least two African immigrants during the year appeared to be linked to racist attitudes.

After gaining independence from Britain in 1964, Malta joined the Commonwealth and became a republic in 1974. Power has alternated between the pro-Western, center-right Nationalist Party (PN) and the nonaligned, leftist Malta Labour Party (MLP). The PN pursued European Union (EU) membership, which Malta finally achieved in 2004.

In the March 2008 elections, Lawrence Gonzi led the PN to a narrow victory over the Labour Party (PL), the renamed MLP. Voter turnout was 93 percent, the lowest the country had seen since 1971. Former PL leader George Abela was sworn in as president in April 2009. Abela, who was very popular with voters from both parties, was the first president to be nominated by a political party not in power and the first since 1974 to be backed by both sides of the House of Representatives.

Over the last decade, Malta, which is centrally located in the Mediterranean, has received an increasing number of immigrants, refugees, and asylum seekers, who subsequently settle in the country or proceed to other EU countries. In October 2012, Malta hosted the 5+5 meeting (Western Mediterranean Forum)—a gathering of the heads of state of 10 European and North African countries that border the Western Mediterranean—at which the creation of a joint task force to tackle migration problems in these nations was suggested.

Poor conditions at holding centers for refugees and asylum seekers have led to rioting and even death. In May 2012, the International Commission of Jurists released a report condemning Malta's mandatory detention policies—under Maltese law, refugees and asylum seekers are detained for up to 18 months—and inhumane conditions that violate the European Convention on Human Rights. In September 2012, the United Nations High Commissioner for Refugees published guidelines aimed at Malta and other countries that detain asylum seekers in order to reduce the number of detainees and increase their human rights standards. Also in September, the European Parliament proposed changing the way Malta detains child migrants who are currently held under the same regulations as adults.

A 2011 report found that a majority of immigrants faced xenophobia and discrimination in housing, employment, and services. Malta's media and political discourse were also criticized for contributing to an atmosphere of hostility and intolerance toward immigrants. In 2012, racist attitudes allegedly led to the deaths of at least two immigrants: Malian Mamadou Kamara was beaten to death by guards at the Safi detention center, and Sudanese Osama Al Shzliaoy was beaten to death by two Romanian men in Paceville one week after a man was acquitted of killing an immigrant from Darfur in the same neighborhood in 2009.

Political Rights and Civil Liberties: Malta is an electoral democracy. Members of the 69-seat unicameral legislature, the House of Representatives, are elected for five-year terms. Lawmakers elect the president, who also serves for five years. The president names the prime minister, usually the leader of the majority party or coalition.

The ruling PN and opposition PL dominate national politics. The smaller Democratic Alternative party also competes but is not currently represented in the parliament. In November, 2012, talks began to change the voting law to include the right to vote for Maltese living overseas.

A 2012 Eurobarometer revealed that 88 percent of Maltese saw corruption as a major problem plaguing the country, in both politics and business. In October 2012, John Dalli, a Maltese politician who served as the European Commissioner for Health and Consumer Policy, was forced to resign following reports by the European Anti-Fraud Office that Dalli had been aware of a bribery attempt involving the tobacco industry and tobacco legislation.

The constitution guarantees freedoms of speech and the press, though incitement to racial hatred is punishable by a jail term of six to eight months. In October 2012, Norman Lowell was cleared of inciting racial hatred in an article published in 2008. Blasphemy is also illegal, and censorship remains an ongoing issue. There are several daily newspapers and weekly publications in Maltese and English, as well as radio and television stations. Residents also have access to Italian television broadcasts. In September 2012, Malta's first Freedom of Information Act went into effect. Also in September, Claudette Pace, the presenter of a popular daytime show *Sellili*, filed a judicial review against the Public Broadcasting Services for replacing her after she announced her intention to run on the Nationalist Party ticket in the next general election. By the end of the year, she had left her TV program in order to pursue a career in politics. In October 2012, the Broadcasting Authority ruled that political parties had the right to choose which party representatives appeared on television, rather than allowing the station to choose which participants to invite to its programs. The ruling came after the PL sent one parliamentarian instead of another to appear on the show *Bondi+*. The government does not restrict internet access.

The constitution establishes Roman Catholicism as the state religion, and the state grants subsidies only to Catholic schools. While the population is overwhelmingly Roman Catholic, small communities of Muslims, Jews, and Protestants are tolerated and respected. There is one Muslim private school. Academic freedom is respected.

The constitution provides for freedoms of assembly and association, and the government generally respects these rights in practice. Nongovernmental organizations investigating human rights issues operate without state interference. The law recognizes the right to form and join trade unions, and limits on the right to strike were eased in 2002. A compulsory yet seldom-used arbitration clause in the country's labor law allows the government to force a settlement on striking workers.

The judiciary is independent, and the rule of law prevails in civil and criminal matters. Prison conditions generally meet international standards, though the Council of Europe's Commission for Human Rights has criticized poor detention conditions for irregular migrants and asylum seekers. Migrant workers are reportedly often exploited and subjected to substandard working conditions.

The constitution prohibits discrimination based on gender. However, women are underrepresented in government, occupying only about 9 percent of seats in the parliament. A law legalizing divorce came into effect in October 2011. Violence against women remains a problem. Abortion is strictly prohibited, even in cases of rape or incest. Malta is a source and destination country for human trafficking for the purposes of forced labor and sexual exploitation.

Marshall Islands

Political Rights: 1
Civil Liberties: 1
Status: Free

Population: 55,000
Capital: Majuro

Ten-Year Ratings Timeline For Year Under Review (Political Rights, Civil Liberties, Status)

2003	2004	2005	2006	2007	2008	2009	2010	2011	2012
1,1F	1,1F	1,1F	1,1F	1,1F	1,1F	1,1F	1,1F	1,1F	1,1F

Overview: Christopher Loeak was elected president of the Marshall Islands by parliament on January 3, 2012. Also during the year, the United States announced that it would hire fewer workers at its military facilities in the country, and would phase out funding for college scholarships, while focusing on supporting primary-school education.

The atolls and islands that make up the Republic of the Marshall Islands were claimed by Germany in 1885 and occupied by Japan during World War I. The islands came under U.S. control during World War II, and the United States administered them under United Nations trusteeship in 1947. The Marshall Islands became an independent state in 1986.

The Marshall Islands maintains close relations with the United States under a Compact of Free Association. The first compact, which came into force in 1986, allows the United States to maintain military facilities in the Marshall Islands in exchange for defense guarantees, development assistance, and visa-free access for Marshallese to live, work, study, and obtain health care and social services in the United States. The Marshall Islands relies on compact funds for almost 70 percent of its annual budget.

An amended compact with new funding and accountability requirements took effect in 2004 and will run through 2023. The deal provides the Marshall Islands with annual transfers of $57 million from the United States until 2013 and $62 million from 2014 to 2023. In exchange, the United States will continue its use of the Kwajalein missile-testing site—the primary U.S. testing ground for long-range nuclear missiles—through 2066.

In 2011, the United States agreed to pay a group of Kwajalein landowners $32 million through 2066 for the use of their land. Local populations have expressed concern about health and environmental hazards posed by the testing facility, asserting that the 67 nuclear bomb tests conducted in the Bikini and Enewetak Atolls have left the former uninhabitable and the latter partly contaminated. To compensate past, present, and future victims of the tests, the United States created a $150 million Nuclear Claims Fund, though critics say the fund is inadequate to fulfill the $2 billion in awards made to Marshall Island residents by the Nuclear Claims Tribunal, which was established in 1988 as part of the first compact.

The United States has rejected these calls on the grounds that it has paid $1.5 billion for personal injury and property damage in addition to its contributions to the Nuclear Claims Fund.

Although no party initially emerged as a clear winner in the November 2011 parliamentary elections, the Aelon Kein Ad (AKA) party secured a majority of 20 seats after victorious independent candidates joined the party.

As for many other small Pacific island states, rising sea levels and a shortage of safe drinking water are serious problems for the Marshall Islands. With limited education and employment opportunities, about one-third of the country's citizens are overseas, mostly in the United States. The government adopted austerity measures in 2011 in response to the global economic downtown, which prompted a drop in tourism. In May 2012, the United States announced that it would reduce the number of local employees at its military facilities, which is expected to increase the unemployment rate; the number of local workers had already dropped from 1,200 to fewer than 900 over the past four years.

On January 3, 2012, the 33-member parliament voted 21 to 11 to elect Christopher Loeak, a traditional chief and previous cabinet member, as the sixth president of the Marshall Islands, defeating incumbent, Jurelang Zedkaia. Loeak was inaugurated on January 17. He appointed Hilda Heine, the only doctoral degree holder in the Marshall Islands and the country's only female legislator, as the minister of education.

Political Rights and Civil Liberties: The Marshall Islands is an electoral democracy. The president is chosen for a four-year term by the unicameral parliament (Nitijela), from among its 33 members, who are directly elected to four-year terms. An advisory body, the Council of Chiefs (Iroij), consists of 12 traditional leaders who are consulted on customary law. The two main political parties are the AKA party and the United Democratic Party.

Corruption is a serious problem, and international donors have called on the Marshall Islands to improve accountability and transparency. A 2011 investigation into a scheme to defraud the government led to charges against 12 people, including transportation and communication minister Kenneth Tedi, marking the first time a cabinet minister faced criminal charges. Tedi received a 30-day suspended jail sentence and a fine of $1,000, which critics argued was too light a penalty.

The government generally respects freedoms of speech and the press. A privately owned newspaper, the *Marshall Islands Journal*, publishes articles in English and Marshallese. The government's *Marshall Islands Gazette* provides official news but avoids political coverage. Broadcast outlets include both government- and church-owned radio stations, and cable television offers a variety of international news and entertainment programs. Residents in some parts of the country can also access U.S. armed forces radio and television. The government does not restrict internet access, but penetration rates are low due to cost and technical difficulties.

Religious and academic freedoms are respected in practice. The quality of secondary education remains low, and four-year college education is rare. In June 2012, the U.S. government announced that it would phase out college scholarships to Marshall Island youths in three years, instead using the money to bolster basic education with an emphasis on student performance.

Citizen groups, many of which are sponsored by or affiliated with church organizations and provide social services, operate freely. The government broadly interprets constitutional guarantees of freedoms of assembly and association to cover trade unions.

The constitution provides for an independent judiciary. In 2012, the Pacific Judicial Development Program gave the Marshall Islands the highest marks among 14 Pacific island states for judiciary transparency. Nearly all judges and attorneys are recruited from overseas. To ease the backlog of land dispute cases, the government revived use of Traditional Rights Courts in 2010 to make advisory rulings to the High Court. Police brutality is generally not a problem, and detention centers and prisons meet minimum international standards.

Tensions persist between the local population and Chinese migrants, who control much of the country's retail sector.

The Marshall Islands has a tradition of matrilineal inheritance in tribal rank and personal property, but social and economic discrimination against women is widespread. The country is a destination for foreign women trafficked into prostitution in local bars.

Mauritania

Political Rights: 6
Civil Liberties: 5
Status: Not Free

Population: 3,623,000
Capital: Nouakchott

Ten-Year Ratings Timeline For Year Under Review (Political Rights, Civil Liberties, Status)

2003	2004	2005	2006	2007	2008	2009	2010	2011	2012
6,5NF	6,5NF	6,4PF	5,4PF	4,4PF	6,5NF	6,5NF	6,5NF	6,5NF	6,5NF

Overview: Legislative elections planned for March 2012 were postponed several times during the year, with the political opposition requesting that they be held only after the implementation of reforms ensuring fair elections. In October, President Mohamed Ould Abdel Aziz was shot—allegedly accidentally—by members of a military patrol, and sustained minor injuries. The authorities violently dispersed a number of protests throughout the year, including ones led by students and antislavery activists.

Following independence from France in 1960, Mauritania was ruled by a series of civilian and military authoritarian regimes. In 1984, Colonel Ahmed Taya ousted President Mohamed Khouna Ould Haidallah. Although Taya introduced a multiparty system in 1991, he secured poll victories for himself and his Democratic and Social Republican Party (PRDS) through the misuse of state resources, suppression of the opposition, and manipulation of the media and electoral institutions.

In August 2005, soldiers led by Colonel Ely Ould Mohamed Vall overthrew Taya's government in a move that received strong public support. Soon after taking power, the Military Council for Justice and Democracy (CMJD) pardoned and released hundreds of political prisoners, and dozens of political activists returned from exile. The CMJD established an independent electoral commission to administer elections. Independent candidates, mostly former PRDS members, secured a majority of seats in the 2006 legislative and municipal elections. Independents also won a majority of seats in the February 2007 Senate elections, while Sidi Ould Cheikh Abdellahi, an independent, won the presidency in March. This series of elections were the first in Mauritania's history to be broadly viewed as generally free and fair.

Abdellahi drew criticism from military leaders and members of the National Party for Democracy and Development (PNDD) for inviting hard-line Islamists and former members of Taya's regime into the cabinet. The government resigned in July 2008 under the threat of a parliamentary no-confidence vote, and Abdellahi formed a new cabinet that included only PNDD members. However, this failed to restore lawmakers' confidence, and a top military officer, General Mohamed Ould Abdel Aziz, mounted a successful coup on August 6.

Aziz and his allies announced that an 11-member junta, the High State Council (HSC), would run the country until new elections were held. While the international community strongly condemned the coup, and key donors suspended nonhumanitarian aid, the domestic reaction was mixed. A majority of lawmakers and mayors expressed support, but a coalition of four pro-Abdellahi parties formed the National Front for the Defense of Democracy and refused to participate in the junta-led government.

In April 2009, Aziz announced that he would resign from the military in order to run for president. Despite initial resistance, opposition parties agreed to participate in the presidential vote after six days of negotiations. Under international pressure, the HSC handed power in June to a transitional government to supervise an election set for July 2009.

Aziz won the election in the first round with 52.6 percent of the vote. Four opposition parties claimed that the results were predetermined, electoral lists had been tampered with, and fraudulent voters had used fake ballot papers and identity cards. The parties lodged a formal appeal with the Constitutional Council that was ultimately rejected, and the head of the electoral commission resigned over doubts about the election's conduct. While some opposition parties continued to protest the outcome, the Rally for Democratic Forces recognized Aziz's presidency in September 2010, citing the need for unity in the face of increased terrorist attacks by Islamist militants.

In May 2011, Aziz initiated a new census, the finalization of voter lists, and the automation of national identity cards. Nevertheless, municipal and legislative elections planned for October were postponed indefinitely in August. The Mauritanian Coordination of Democratic Opposition (COD) had requested the delay, claiming that a promised dialogue with Aziz on wide-ranging political and electoral reforms had yet to occur. In January 2012, legislative elections were set for March 31, but were repeatedly postponed throughout the year. The COD asked that they be postponed indefinitely pending reforms to ensure fair elections, including the establishment of a national registration process and the formation of an independent electoral commission.

On October 13, Aziz was shot and wounded while returning to Nouakchott from a weekend outside the capital city; he sustained minor injuries and was flown to France for treatment. According to official government reports, a military patrol mistakenly opened fired on his unescorted vehicle near an army checkpoint, possibly because the soldiers had been startled as he drove by and did not recognize him. However, some analysts claimed that the shooting was an assassination attempt; the investigation was ongoing at year's end.

In 2012, the Islamist rebellion in neighboring Mali continued to impact Mauritania, which had launched a joint military operation with Mali the previous year against rebel troops from al-Qaeda in the Islamic Maghreb (AQIM). In May, the Mauritanian army increased its presence along the border with Mali, though the government ruled out direct intervention. By the end of 2012, Mauritania was host to more than 100,000 Malian refugees who had fled the fighting.

Political Rights and Civil Liberties: Mauritania is not an electoral democracy. The constitutional government created after the 2006 and 2007 elections was ousted by the 2008 military coup. The legitimacy of the 2009 presidential election, which installed coup leader Mohamed Ould Abdel Aziz as the civilian president, was challenged by the opposition but declared generally free and fair by international observers. Legislative elections scheduled for October 2011 have been postponed indefinitely.

Under the 1991 constitution, the president is responsible for appointing and dismissing the prime minister and cabinet, and a 2006 amendment imposed a limit of two five-year presidential terms. The bicameral legislature consists of the 95-seat National Assembly, elected by popular vote, and the 56-seat Senate, with 53 members elected by mayors and municipal councils and 3 members chosen by the chamber to represent Mauritanians living abroad. Mauritania's party system is poorly developed, and clan and ethnic loyalties strongly influence the country's politics.

Corruption is a serious problem, and political instability has prevented fiscal transparency. While several senior officials were, for the first time, charged with corruption—including a senior military official and the former minister of finance—these cases have either been dismissed or officials have been ordered to reimburse the government for the amount they supposedly embezzled, with no further legal ramifications. Mauritania was ranked 123 out of 176 countries surveyed in Transparency International's 2012 Corruption Perceptions Index.

Despite constitutional guarantees for press freedom, some journalists practice self-censorship, and private newspapers face closure for publishing material considered offensive to Islam or threatening to the state. In 2011, the government ended a 51-year monopoly on broadcast media with a call for applications for licenses from private outlets. By the end of 2012, two private television channels and five radio stations received licenses, and applications for three other television channels were being reviewed at year's end. Defamation was decriminalized in 2011, though fines can still be levied. There were no reports of government restrictions on the internet.

Mauritania was declared an Islamic republic under the 1991 constitution, and proselytizing by non-Muslims is banned. Non-Muslims cannot be citizens, and those who convert from Islam lose their citizenship. In practice, however, non-Muslim communities have not been targeted for persecution. Academic freedom is respected.

The 1991 constitution guarantees freedom of assembly, though organizers are required to obtain consent from the authorities for large gatherings. In 2012, a series of demonstrations were organized by the opposition, led by the COD; the February 25 movement, a youth group inspired by popular uprisings in the Arab world; university students; and antislavery activists. The opposition and February 25 movement called for the resignation of the president, while students demanded educational reform and later the "demilitarization" of universities after police arrested and attacked student protestors. The largest protests occurred on March 12 and April 22, which were led predominantly by the February 25th movement, as well as on May 2, May 7, and May 10, which were organized largely by the COD. These protests, calling for the resignation of the president, were violently dispersed by security forces, often using teargas, and arrests were made. In June, one student was injured by antiriot police and had to be evacuated to Senegal for medical treatment.

The environment for civil society groups and nongovernmental organizations (NGOs) in Mauritania has improved during the last few years, with fewer restrictions on their activities. However, antislavery activists continue to face harassment and arrest.

Workers have the legal right to unionize, but unions must be approved by the public prosecutor and encounter hostility from employers. Although only about a quarter of Mauritanians are formally employed, the vast majority of workers in the industrial and commercial sectors are unionized. The right to strike is limited by notice requirements and bans on certain forms of strike action.

The judicial system is heavily influenced by the government. The Mauritanian Lawyers Association (ONA) condemned the 2011 arrests of several judges on drug-trafficking charges as politically motivated. Many judicial decisions are shaped by Sharia (Islamic law), especially in family and civil matters. Suspects are routinely held for long periods of pretrial detention, and security forces suspected of human rights abuses operate with impunity. Prison conditions are harsh, and there are reports that prisoners, particularly terrorism suspects, are subject to torture by authorities.

Members of AQIM have carried out a number of attacks in Mauritania in recent years. In 2010 an antiterrorism law removed previous restrictions on wiretaps and searches, allowed for individuals under 18 to be charged (which was illegal under Sharia), and granted immunity to terrorists that inform the authorities of a terrorism plot.

Racial and ethnic discrimination persists in all spheres of political and economic life. The country's three main ethnic groups are the politically and economically dominant White Moors of Arab and Berber descent; the black descendants of slaves, also known as Haratins or Black Moors; and black Africans who are closer in ethnic heritage to the peoples of neighboring Senegal and Mali.

Despite a 1981 law banning slavery in Mauritania, an estimated half a million black Mauritanians are believed to live in conditions of servitude. A 2007 law set penalties of 5 to 10 years in prison for all forms of slavery, but the law is hampered by a requirement that slaves themselves file a legal complaint before any prosecution can occur. In November 2011, six individuals were successfully prosecuted for enslavement and sentenced to jail, to pay a fine, and to make financial restitution to the victims. In April 2012, Biram Dah Abeid, the head of the Initiative for the Resurgence of the Abolitionist Movement (IRA) antislavery group, and seven other IRA activists were arrested for burning Islamic texts supporting slavery. In August 2012, four IRA activists were arrested for taking part in an antislavery protest and given six-month suspended sentences; police used tear gas and batons to disperse the protestors.

Under a 2005 law, party lists for the National Assembly elections must include district-based quotas for female candidates, and 20 percent of all municipal council seats are reserved for women. Nevertheless, discrimination against women persists. Under Sharia, a woman's testimony is given only half the weight of a man's. Legal protections regarding property and pay equity are rarely respected in practice. Female genital mutilation (FGM) is illegal but widely practiced. Abortion is legal only when the life of the mother is in danger. The country is a source and destination for women, men, and children trafficked for the purposes of forced labor and sexual exploitation.

Mauritius

Political Rights: 1
Civil Liberties: 2
Status: Free

Population: 1,291,000
Capital: Port Louis

Ten-Year Ratings Timeline For Year Under Review (Political Rights, Civil Liberties, Status)

2003	2004	2005	2006	2007	2008	2009	2010	2011	2012
1,2F	1,1F	1,1F	1,2F	1,2F	1,2F	1,2F	1,2F	1,2F	1,2F

Overview: President Anerood Jugnauth unexpectedly resigned in March 2012 and announced his plan to challenge Prime Minister Navinchandra Ramgoolam and his governing coalition in the 2015 parliamentary elections. A corruption case against the former health minister, finance minister, and other members of the Mauritian Socialist Movement was ongoing at year's end.

Mauritius's ethnically mixed population is primarily descended from laborers brought from the Indian subcontinent during the island's 360 years of Dutch, French, and British colonial rule. Since gaining independence from Britain in 1968, Mauritius has maintained one of the developing world's most successful democracies.

In the 2000 parliamentary elections, a coalition of the Mauritian Militant Movement (MMM) and the Militant Socialist Movement (MSM) defeated the ruling Mauritian Labour Party (MLP), and the MSM's Anerood Jugnauth became prime minister. In a planned power shift, the leader of the MMM, Paul Bérenger, took over as prime minister in 2003, becoming the first person outside the island's Indian-origin majority to hold the post. Jugnauth assumed the largely ceremonial role of president.

Frustration with rising unemployment and inflation resulted in a victory for the opposition Social Alliance in the 2005 parliamentary election, and the MLP's Navinchandra Ramgoolam was named prime minister. However, rising prices and increasing levels of crime quickly diminished the new government's popularity.

In the May 2010 legislative elections, Ramgoolam's Alliance of the Future—which included the MLP, the Mauritian Social Democratic Party, and the MSM—captured 45 seats. Bérenger's Alliance of the Heart—a coalition of the MMM, the National Union, and the Mauritanian Socialist Democratic Movement—took 20. Ramgoolam retained the premiership.

In July 2011, the Independent Commission Against Corruption (ICAC) arrested Health Minister Santi Bai Hanoomanjee of the MSM for allegedly inflating the government's bid on a private hospital. In response, all six MSM cabinet ministers—including party leader Pravind Jugnauth, the finance minister and son of Anerood Jugnauth—resigned. In August, the MSM pulled out of the governing coalition, leaving Ramgoolam with a slim parliamentary majority. Further turmoil came in September, when the ICAC arrested Pravind Jugnauth on conflict of interest charges related to the hospital bid. In December, the Director of Public Prosecution (DPP) maintained the ICAC's provisional charges against Jugnauth; an appeal was expected to be heard in early 2013. In July 2012, the ICAC completed its inquiry of the former health minister and other cabinet members and referred the case to the DPP, along with the ICAC's recommendations; the case was pending at year's end.

The MSM's troubles deepened political tensions and ultimately led to President Anerood Jugnauth's resignation in March 2012. However, he announced his return to party politics and immediately realigned his MSM party with Bérenger's MMM to create an alliance capable of defeating the MLP in 2015 parliamentary elections.

Political Rights and Civil Liberties: Mauritius is an electoral democracy. The president, whose role is largely ceremonial, is elected by the unicameral National Assembly for a five-year term. Executive power resides with the prime minister, who is appointed by the president from the party or coalition with the most seats in the legislature. Of the National Assembly's 69 members, 62 are directly elected, and 7 are appointed from among unsuccessful candidates who gained the largest number of votes; all members serve five-year terms. Decentralized structures govern the country's small island dependencies. The largest dependency, Rodrigues Island, has its own government and local councils, and two seats in the National Assembly.

The country's generally positive reputation for transparency and accountability was damaged by the 2011 arrests of two prominent MSM ministers and the ongoing scandal, as well as allegations by the MSM that the ruling party is using the ICAC as a political tool. A 2008 diplomatic cable from the U.S. Embassy in Port Louis, leaked in September 2011 by the activist organization WikiLeaks, described corruption in Mauritius as "often overlooked" and called the graft problem "pervasive and ingrained." Mauritius was ranked 43 out of 176 countries surveyed in Transparency International's 2012 Corruption Perceptions Index, and the country has been ranked first in the Ibrahim Index of African Governance since its inception in 2007.

The constitution guarantees freedom of expression. Several private daily and weekly publications criticize both the ruling and opposition parties, but the state-owned Mauritius Broadcasting Corporation's radio and television services generally reflect government viewpoints. A small number of private radio stations compete with the state-run media. In July 2012, the editor of the *Sunday Times*, Imran Hosany, was arrested and charged with outraging public and religious morality after publishing photographs of a tourist lying dead after she was murdered on her honeymoon in Mauritius; the case was pending at year's end.

Religious and academic freedoms are respected.

Freedoms of assembly and association are honored, though police have occasionally used excessive force in response to riots. There are more than 300 unions in Mauritius. Tens of thousands of foreign workers employed in export-processing zones suffer from poor living and working conditions, and their employers are reportedly hostile to unions.

The generally independent judiciary, headed by the Supreme Court, administers a legal system that combines French and British traditions. Civil rights are largely respected, though individual cases of police brutality have been reported.

Various ethnic cultures and traditions coexist peacefully, and constitutional prohibitions against discrimination are generally upheld. However, Mauritian Creoles—descendants of African slaves, who comprise about a third of the population—are culturally and economically marginalized. Tensions between the Hindu majority and Muslim minority persist. In a November 2011 report, the Truth and Justice Commission (TJC)—established to examine the country's history of slavery and indentured labor—recommended various measures to encourage national reconciliation, including building a slavery memorial and promoting increased economic and political participation by non-Hindu Mauritians. In March 2012, the chair of the Ministerial Committee of the TJC expressed his disappointment that only 3 of the 19 measures the committee chose for immediate implementation had been adopted by various government and sociocultural organizations.

Women comprise about 36 percent of the labor force, but they receive less compensation than men for similar work and hold only 13 seats in the National Assembly and two cabinet posts. A January 2012 gender quota law mandates that at least one-third of the candidates in local elections be women. Following the country's first local government elections in December, women's representation at the local government level increased from 6.4 percent to 26.2 percent. However, at year's end, Prime Minister Navinchandra Ramgoolam's plan to extend the quota to the national parliament for the 2015 elections had yet to be approved. Rape and domestic violence against women remain major concerns.

Mexico

Political Rights: 3
Civil Liberties: 3
Status: Partly Free

Population: 116,147,000
Capital: Mexico City

Ten-Year Ratings Timeline For Year Under Review (Political Rights, Civil Liberties, Status)

2003	2004	2005	2006	2007	2008	2009	2010	2011	2012
2,2F	2,2F	2,2F	2,3F	2,3F	2,3F	2,3F	3,3PF	3,3PF	3,3PF

Overview:

Enrique Peña Nieto of the Institutional Revolutionary Party (PRI) was elected president in July 2012. His victory signified the return to power of the PRI, which had used authoritarian methods to dominate Mexican politics from 1929 until 2000. Although violence between security forces and organized criminal groups, and among the criminal groups themselves, remained high, homicides decreased relative to 2011 amid signs that many of the larger crime syndicates had splintered into smaller, more localized groups.

Mexico achieved independence from Spain in 1810 and became a republic in 1822. Seven years after the Revolution of 1910, a new constitution established the United Mexican States as a federal republic. From its founding in 1929 until 2000, the Institutional Revolutionary Party (PRI) dominated the country through patronage, corruption, and repression. The formal business of government often took place in secret, and the rule of law was frequently compromised by arbitrary power.

In the landmark 2000 presidential election, Vicente Fox Quesada of the National Action Party (PAN) defeated the candidates of the PRI and the leftist Party of the Democratic Revolution (PRD), capturing 42.5 percent of the vote. Fox presided over the provision of more open and accountable government and the arrests of some leaders of the country's vicious drug-trafficking groups. However, solutions to the problems of poverty, corruption, crime, and unemployment proved elusive. Elections held in July 2003 confirmed the PRI as the most powerful party in Congress and in many state governments.

In the 2006 presidential election, PAN candidate Felipe Calderón defeated Mexico City mayor Andrés Manuel López Obrador of the PRD by a mere 244,000 votes in the initial count. López Obrador rejected the result and for several months led protests that paralyzed parts of Mexico City, but many Mexicans—and most international observers—were not convinced by the PRD's evidence of fraud. In September, after a partial recount, the Federal Electoral Tribunal formally declared Calderón the winner. Though the PAN won the most seats in the concurrent congressional elections, the PRD's share of deputies exceeded the PRI's for the first time.

In 2007, Calderón managed to forge coalitions with opposition lawmakers to pass modest pension, tax, electoral, and judicial reforms, but the PRI emerged from the July 2009 congressional elections with control of the Chamber of Deputies, forming a majority with the allied Green Party as the vote shares of the PAN and especially the PRD declined.

The PRI continued its comeback by outperforming its rivals in state and local elections, winning the governorship in 15 of 21 races held between 2009 and 2011, although alliances between the PAN and the PRD resulted in victories in several PRI bastions in 2010. In 2012 the PRI won three of six gubernatorial races, while the PRD won two as well as the mayoralty of Mexico City.

After years of deliberation and revision, a package of political reform legislation took effect in August 2012. Calderón had first proposed reforms in December 2009, aiming to alter key elements of the political system, particularly Mexico's nearly unique ban on reelection at all governmental levels. The final version was far less ambitious and did not lift the reelection ban, though it did authorize independent candidacies and create some mechanisms for citizen-initiated referendums.

Mexican politics in 2012 revolved around national elections held in July. The three main presidential candidates were the PRD's López Obrador, PAN legislator Josefina Vázquez Mota, and Enrique Peña Nieto, the former PRI governor of Mexico State. Peña Nieto entered the official campaign, which began in April, with a substantial lead in most polls. As the race proceeded, the Vázquez campaign foundered, allowing López Obrador to rise from third to second and consolidate support among the millions of Mexicans who were wary of a return to power by the PRI. Despite the Peña Nieto campaign's assurances that the party had fully embraced democratic procedures and principles, accusations that the PRI engaged in campaign improprieties—particularly collusion with the dominant broadcaster, Televisa—helped spark a significant anti-PRI student movement.

A preponderance of polls gave Peña Nieto a double-digit lead, but he won the July 1 balloting with 38 percent of the vote, followed by López Obrador with 32 percent. Vázquez trailed with 25 percent, as voters punished the PAN for its mediocre performance in improving socioeconomic conditions during 12 years in power. López Obrador initially refused to accept the results, citing alleged infractions including widespread vote-buying, manipulation of polls, overspending, and media bias. While many observers attested to the credibility of the PRD's claims, particularly regarding vote-buying and media violations, the Federal Electoral Tribunal found insufficient evidence to invalidate the election, and Peña Nieto was formally declared the winner in August.

In concurrent congressional elections, the PRI emerged as the strongest force in both the 500-member Chamber of Deputies and the 128-member Senate. Including allied parties, the PRI garnered a narrow majority of 251 seats in the lower chamber. The PRD and its allies won 135, followed by the PAN with 114. No coalition gained a majority in the Senate, where the PRI–Green Party alliance held 61 seats, the PAN took 38, and the PRD won 22.

In November, during Calderón's lame-duck period, Mexico passed a significant labor reform and a law requiring greater transparency in state budgets. As Peña Nieto took office in December, the main parties agreed to a Pact for Mexico, intended to facilitate structural reforms in areas including security, justice, education, the economy, and anticorruption. An education reform passed in December, and a reorganization of the security sector began the same month.

In 2012 Mexico registered over 20,500 murders, a majority of which were linked to violence associated with organized crime syndicates, and the issue remained the dominant concern in Mexican society. Nonetheless, the number of murders fell over 8 percent from 2011, the first decrease since violence exploded in 2008. Progress was particularly visible in Ciudad Juárez, the previous epicenter of the violence, where murders fell by over 75 percent from a peak in 2010. Despite this shift, the homicide rate remained more than twice as high as when Calderón took office; overall, the violence claimed approximately 63,000 lives during his presidency. In addition, allegations of severe human rights violations continued to surround the security operations conducted by more than 45,000 soldiers in various parts of Mexico. While a majority of Mexicans still supported the government's military-led offensive against organized crime, opinion polls also registered skepticism about official claims that the campaign was making progress. The leader of an especially feared criminal group, the Zetas, was killed by federal forces in October, marking one of the most visible successes for the Calderón administration's focus on eliminating kingpins. Many analysts noted, however, that the apparent fragmentation of larger syndicates into smaller gangs would require a strategic shift by the Peña Nieto administration.

Political Rights and Civil Liberties:

Mexico is an electoral democracy. The president is elected to a six-year term and cannot be reelected. The bicameral Congress consists of the 128-member Senate, elected for six years through a mix of direct voting and proportional representation, with at least two parties represented in each state's delegation, and the 500-member Chamber of Deputies, with 300 elected directly and 200 through proportional representation, all for three-year terms. Members of Congress are also barred from reelection. Each state has an elected governor and legislature.

The Federal Electoral Institute (IFE), which supervises elections and enforces political party laws, has come to be viewed as a model for other countries. Following complaints about the fairness of the 2006 elections, an electoral reform was passed in 2007 to strictly regulate campaign financing and the content of political advertising. Opinion has been mixed regarding the efficacy and fairness of the reform. The 2012 elections were considered generally free and fair, but complaints persisted, especially by the opposition PRD, concerning media coverage and alleged vote-buying. At the state level, allegations of abuse of public resources to favor specific gubernatorial candidates have increased in recent years.

Signs of the vulnerability of politicians and municipal governments to pressure from organized crime have mounted over the past five years. Over a dozen small-town mayors and candidates for office were killed between 2010 and 2012. In the most violence-plagued regions, provision of public services has become more difficult, and public sector employees such as teachers are subject to extortion.

Official corruption remains a serious problem. Billions of dollars in illegal drug money is believed to enter the country each year from the United States, and there is a perception that such funds affect politics, particularly on the state and local levels. Attempts to prosecute officials for alleged involvement in corrupt or criminal activity have often failed due to the weakness of the state's cases. Most punishment has focused on low- and mid-level officials, hundreds of whom have been dismissed or charged with links to drug traffickers. A former governor of Tamaulipas, Tomás Yarrington, was charged in 2012 with accepting bribes from drug traffickers and also faced civil cases in the United States; he remained a fugitive at year's end.

Several army generals were formally charged with similar offenses in July. Mexico was ranked 105 out of 176 countries surveyed in Transparency International's 2012 Corruption Perceptions Index. A 2002 freedom of information law, despite some limitations, has been considered successful at strengthening transparency at the federal level, though momentum has slowed and many states lag far behind.

Legal and constitutional guarantees of free speech have been gradually improving, but the security environment for journalists has deteriorated markedly. Some major media outlets are no longer dependent on the government for advertising and subsidies, and the competitive press has taken the lead in denouncing official corruption, though serious investigative reporting is scarce, particularly at the local level. Broadcast media are dominated by two corporations that control over 90 percent of the market. The biggest, Televisa, faced accusations in 2012 that it actively supported the PRI's Enrique Peña Nieto during both his term as governor and his presidential campaign.

Since a sharp increase in violence in 2006, reporters probing police issues, drug trafficking, and official corruption have faced a high risk of physical harm. The National Human Rights Commission (CNDH) reported 82 journalists killed between 2005 and 2012, making Mexico one of the world's most dangerous countries for media workers. Self-censorship has increased, and many newspapers in high-violence zones no longer publish stories involving in-depth reporting on organized crime. Press watchdog groups celebrated the June 2012 ratification of a constitutional amendment federalizing crimes against journalists.

The government does not restrict internet access, but criminals have extended their reach to citizens attempting to report on crime via online outlets. Three individuals killed in Nuevo Laredo in 2011 were found with notes from the Zetas gang that tied their deaths to their online crime-reporting activities. A 2011 law passed in Veracruz to criminalize the "perturbation of public order" was viewed as an attempt to intimidate users of the microblogging service Twitter; efforts by the state to revise the law in order to pass constitutional muster continued in 2012.

Religious freedom is constitutionally protected and generally respected in practice. A constitutional amendment allowing increased public worship passed Congress in March 2012 but had not yet taken effect by year's end. Political battles over issues such as abortion and equal rights for LGBT (lesbian, gay, bisexual, and transgender) people have led to an increase in religious discourse in the public sphere in recent years. The government does not restrict academic freedom.

Constitutional guarantees regarding free assembly and association are largely upheld, but political and civic expression is restricted in some regions. Civic observers criticized both protester vandalism and excessive force used by Mexico City police during demonstrations coinciding with Peña Nieto's presidential inauguration in December 2012. Nongovernmental organizations, though highly active, sometimes face violent resistance, including threats and murders. Although arrests were made in several prominent cases of activists killed in 2011, groups continued to demand greater protection by the authorities.

Trade unions' role as a pillar of the PRI has diminished significantly, but independent unions have long faced government and management interference. Informal, nontransparent negotiations between employers and politically connected union leaders often result in "protection contracts" that govern employee rights but are never seen by workers. Several large unions, particularly the teachers' union, are considered opaque and overly antagonistic to necessary policy reforms. The education reform passed by Congress in December 2012 offered a potential challenge to the power of the teachers' union, but the labor reform passed in November was viewed as a missed opportunity to increase union transparency.

The justice system remains plagued by delays and unpredictability. A 2008 constitutional reform replaced the civil-inquisitorial trial system with an oral-adversarial one. The overhaul was widely expected to strengthen due process and increase efficiency and fairness, but human rights groups raised concerns about the vague definition of organized crime and weaker protections afforded to organized crime suspects. Implementation of the new system was expected to take eight years, and in 2012 civil society groups noted progress in some states but significant delays in others.

In many areas, coordination between different branches of the federal government, as well as between federal authorities and the state and local police, is problematic. In crime-plagued zones, local police have been purged and temporarily replaced by federal troops. A 2009 law requires all members of the police to be vetted, but the process faced delays in 2012 as several states lagged behind in vetting officers or dismissing those with violations. A bill sent to Congress in 2010 that mandates the merger of state and municipal police forces again failed to pass in 2012.

Lower courts and law enforcement in general are undermined by widespread bribery and incapacity. A 2012 survey found that 92 percent of crimes go unreported, because the underpaid police are viewed as either inept or in league with criminals. Only a small minority of crimes end in convictions, even when investigations are opened. Prisons are violent and overcrowded, and several prison riots in 2012 resulted in the deaths of scores of prisoners, including 44 in a Nuevo León prison in February. Several hundred others escaped during the year, including 131 in one incident in Coahuila in September.

Presidential authority over the armed forces is extensive, but the military has historically operated beyond public scrutiny, and human rights advocates have warned that its strengthened counternarcotics role has not been accompanied by increased oversight of its conduct. Complaints of abuse, including torture, forced disappearances, and extrajudicial executions, have risen dramatically in recent years. Military personnel are generally tried in military courts, but in a series of cases starting in August 2012, the Supreme Court ruled that human rights violations against civilians must be tried in civilian courts.

The number of deaths attributed to organized crime declined in 2012 after rising sharply each year between 2007 and 2011. Although homicides plummeted in the previous epicenter of violence, Ciudad Juárez, violence remained acute in much of the north and spiked in several other cities, including Acapulco and Torreón. The murders often featured extreme brutality designed to maximize the psychological impact on civilians, authorities, and rival groups. The number, severity, and geographic range of massacres also declined in 2012, although several horrific episodes did occur, including the discovery in May of 49 bodies in Nuevo León and 18 near Guadalajara the same month.

In addition to homicides, organized criminals have engaged in kidnappings, extortion, oil theft, and other offenses. The government has taken a number of steps in recent years to curb the violence and ease popular frustration, including consultations with civic leaders, the signing of a $1.5 billion counternarcotics aid agreement with the United States, the continued deployment of troops, the reformation of the federal police, and the decriminalization of possession of small quantities of drugs. The administration of outgoing president Felipe Calderón touted the killing or arrest of 25 of the 37 most wanted criminal kingpins and the decline of violence in hot spots such as Tijuana and Ciudad Juárez as evidence of progress, but polls have revealed consistent pessimism about the effectiveness of Calderón's strategy.

Mexican law bans discrimination based on categories including ethnic origin, gender, age, and religion. Discrimination based on sexual orientation is banned in some states. Nevertheless, social and economic discrimination has marginalized indigenous peoples, with many relegated to extreme poverty in rural villages that lack essential services. The government has attempted to improve indigenous-language services in the justice system, an area of major concern. Indigenous groups have been harmed by the criminal violence in recent years. In addition, disputes over land issues within indigenous groups at times become violent.

Rights groups frequently detail the persecution and criminal predation faced by migrants from Central America, many of whom are bound for the United States. Mass graves containing hundreds of bodies found in Tamaulipas in 2011 included many migrants. In several states in recent years, criminals have impeded free movement by blocking major roads.

Domestic violence and sexual abuse are common. According to a 2012 study, 46 percent of women have suffered some form of violence, and perpetrators are rarely punished. Implementation of a 2007 law designed to protect women from such crimes remains halting, particularly at the state level, and impunity is the norm for the hundreds of women killed each year. More positively, female legislators make up over one-third of the Congress elected in 2012. Mexico is both a major source and a transit country for trafficked persons. Abortion has been a contentious issue in recent years, with many states reacting to Mexico City's 2007 liberalization of abortion laws by strengthening their own criminal bans on the procedure.

Same-sex marriage is legal in Mexico City and the state of Quintana Roo, and same-sex civil unions are permitted in the state of Coahuila.

Micronesia

Political Rights: 1
Civil Liberties: 1
Status: Free

Population: 107,000
Capital: Palikir

Ten-Year Ratings Timeline For Year Under Review (Political Rights, Civil Liberties, Status)

2003	2004	2005	2006	2007	2008	2009	2010	2011	2012
1,1F	1,1F	1,1F	1,1F	1,1F	1,1F	1,1F	1,1F	1,1F	1,1F

Overview: Congress passed legislation in 2012 to improve the collection of tax revenues, and also adopted resolutions to promote renewable energy projects. In March, Micronesia passed a National Trafficking Act, and approved the country's accession to the UN Convention Against Corruption and to two UN protocols to protect children.

The United States administered Micronesia, which included the Marshall Islands and other Pacific island groups, between 1947 and 1979 as a United Nations Trust Territory. In 1970, the Northern Marianas, Marshall Islands, and Palau demanded separate status from Kosrae, Pohnpei, Chuuk, and Yap; the latter four territories, representing 607 islands, became the Federated States of Micronesia (FSM). The FSM adopted a constitution and became an independent country in 1979.

In 1986, the FSM signed its first Compact of Free Association with the United States, which provides the FSM with economic and defense assistance in exchange for allowing U.S. military bases on the islands. FSM citizens also receive visa-free entry to the United States for health services, education, and employment.

Compact funds represent about one-third of the FSM's national income. An amended compact came into effect in 2003 to extend this core commitment for another 20 years. The federal Congress agreed in 2005 to distribute larger shares of compact funds to each of the FSM's four states. A new system to track funded projects was adopted in 2009 to improve transparency and accountability in the use of compact funds.

Legislative elections held in March 2011, in which all candidates were independents, were deemed free and fair. President Emanuel Mori and Vice President Alik L. Alik were reelected in May.

The FSM has been expanding its ties with China, which is one of four countries in which the FSM has a permanent embassy. In 2010, China was named the preferred candidate for exclusive fishing rights in FSM waters. Chinese aid to the FSM includes financing an expansion of the Chuuk airport terminal and providing scholarships for FSM students to study in China.

In 2012, Congress passed legislation to improve the efficiency of the country's tax collection system, and also adopted resolutions pledging to reduce the FSM's reliance on fossil fuels and promote renewable energy sources.

Political Rights and Civil Liberties: The FSM is an electoral democracy. The unicameral, 14-member Congress has one directly elected representative from each of the four constituent states, who serve four-year terms. The other 10 representatives are directly elected for two-year terms from single-member districts. Chuuk state, home to nearly half of the FSM's population, holds the largest number of congressional seats, which has been a source of resentment among the three smaller states. The president and vice president are chosen by Congress from among the four state representatives to serve four-year terms. By informal agreement, the two posts are rotated among the representatives of the four states. Each state has its own constitution, elected legislature, and governor; the state governments have considerable power, particularly in budgetary matters. Traditional leaders and institutions exercise significant influence in society, especially at the village level.

There are no formal political parties, but there are no restrictions on their formation. Political loyalties are based mainly on geography, clan relations, and personality.

Official corruption is a problem and a major source of public discontent. In September 2012, the public auditor reported many fundamental weaknesses in the government payroll system, with paychecks going to employees had been fired and overpayments for unauthorized work hours, among other problems. In March, lawmakers approved the FSM's accession to the United Nations Convention Against Corruption.

The news media operate freely. Print outlets include government-published newsletters and several small, privately owned weekly and monthly newspapers. Each state government runs its own radio station, and the Baptist church runs a fifth station. Television stations operate in three of the four states. Cable television is available in Pohnpei and Chuuk, and satellite television is increasingly common. Use of the internet is growing, but low income and small populations make it difficult for service providers to expand coverage.

Religious freedom is respected in this mainly Christian country. There are no reports of restrictions on academic freedom, but lack of funds negatively affects the quality of and access to education.

Freedom of assembly is respected, and citizens are free to organize civic groups. A small number of student and women's organizations are active. No labor unions exist, though there are no laws against their formation. No specific laws regulate work hours or set workplace health and safety standards. The right to strike and bargain collectively is not legally recognized. The economy is dependent on fishing, tourism, subsistence agriculture, and U.S. assistance.

The judiciary is independent, but it lacks funds to improve the functioning of the courts. The small national police force is responsible for local law enforcement matters, while the United States provides for national defense. There are no reports of abuses or inhumane treatment by police or prison officials, though there is a cultural resistance among the populace to rely on police and the judiciary.

Women enjoy equal rights under the law, including those regarding property ownership and employment. Although well represented in the lower and middle ranks of the state and federal governments, there are no women in Congress, and social and economic discrimination against women persists in this male-dominated culture. Domestic violence is a problem, and cases often go unreported because of family pressure or an expectation of inaction by the authorities. Offenders rarely face trial, and those found guilty usually receive light sentences.

Micronesia is a source country for women trafficked into prostitution. In March

2012, lawmakers adopted the Human Trafficking Act to allow prosecution of activities related to human trafficking conducted in the FSM or by FSM nationals. Lawmakers also approved FSM's accession to the Optional Protocol on the Sale of Children, Child Prostitution and Child Pornography under the United Nations Convention on the Rights of the Child and the Optional Protocol on the Involvement of Children in Armed Conflict.

Moldova

Political Rights: 3
Civil Liberties: 3
Status: Partly Free

Population: 4,114,000
Capital: Chisinau

Note: The numerical ratings and status listed above do not reflect conditions in Transnistria, which is examined in a separate report.

Ten-Year Ratings Timeline For Year Under Review (Political Rights, Civil Liberties, Status)

2003	2004	2005	2006	2007	2008	2009	2010	2011	2012
3,4PF	3,4PF	3,4PF	3,4PF	3,4PF	4,4PF	3,4PF	3,3PF	3,3PF	3,3PF

Overview: Parliament finally elected a president in March 2012, ending a political deadlock that had left the post vacant since 2009. The achievement was made possible by the weakening of the opposition Communist Party, which suffered additional defections during the year. The party was also buffeted by the closure of an allied television outlet in April, a failed attempt to block an antidiscrimination law in May, and a ban on Soviet symbols in July. The antidiscrimination law was one of several measures undertaken by the ruling Alliance for European Integration as it sought to upgrade Moldova's ties with the European Union.

Moldova gained independence from the Soviet Union in 1991, and free and fair elections followed in 1994. Centrist parties governed until 2001, when the Party of Communists of the Republic of Moldova (PCRM) won a landslide victory, promising a return to Soviet-era living standards. Communist leader Vladimir Voronin was elected president by Parliament.

The PCRM took 56 of 101 seats in the 2005 parliamentary elections and built a coalition to obtain the 61 votes needed to reelect Voronin. After charting a foreign policy course away from Russia and toward the European Union (EU) in the period surrounding the elections, Voronin steered the country back toward Russia in 2007 and 2008. The Kremlin's cooperation is seen as essential in resolving the status of Transnistria, a separatist region that has maintained de facto independence from Moldova since 1992.

The PCRM won 60 seats in April 2009 parliamentary elections, though international monitors documented problems including flaws in the voter lists, intimidation and harassment of opposition parties, and media bias. Three opposition parties won the remainder. The results triggered youth-led protests in Chisinau, and the demonstrations turned violent on the second day, with some protesters ransacking government buildings. Police responded with beatings, hundreds of arrests, and serious abuse of detainees in custody.

The PCRM failed twice to elect its choice to replace the term-limited Voronin as president, triggering fresh parliamentary elections in July 2009. Although similar electoral flaws were reported by observers, the defection of former PCRM Parliament speaker Marian Lupu to the opposition Democratic Party (PD) helped it and three other opposition parties to secure a simple majority. The new coalition, called the Alliance for European Integration (AIE), elected Liberal Democratic Party (PLD) leader Vlad Filat as prime minister, and Liberal Party (PL) leader Mihai Ghimpu as Parliament Speaker and acting president. With just 53 seats, the coalition failed twice—in November and December—to secure Lupu's election as president.

A third round of parliamentary elections was held in November 2010, after a PCRM boycott helped to thwart a September constitutional referendum that would have introduced direct presidential elections. The new balloting, which was praised by observers, strengthened the AIE parties' position overall, though they still lacked the supermajority needed to elect a president. The PCRM took 42 seats, followed by the PLD with 32, the PD with 15, and the PL with 12. Lupu was elected Parliament Speaker and acting president in late December, and Filat resumed his role as prime minister in January 2011.

Internal AIE feuding intensified during 2011, but further factional rifts in the PCRM also emerged. Three Parliament members defected from the PCRM caucus in early November, and after two abortive presidential election attempts in November and December, the AIE and the PCRM defectors finally agreed on a compromise candidate in early 2012. Nicolae Timofti, head of an entity that oversees the judiciary, was duly elected with 62 votes on March 16 and sworn in a week later. The PCRM refused to recognize the constitutional legitimacy of the process, mounting a series of large protests, but it ultimately ended a four-month boycott of Parliament in June.

The PCRM continued to suffer setbacks throughout the year. In July, the AIE majority passed a ban on Soviet symbols, such as the hammer and sickle, that were still used by the Communists; the ban took effect October 1. Voronin vowed to appeal to the European Court of Human Rights (ECHR). A group of three PCRM lawmakers left the caucus in June, and another switched to the Socialist Party in September. In October, the seven lawmakers who had quit the PCRM caucus since late 2011 announced the formation of their own bloc. Another Parliament member left the party in December, leaving the Communists with 34 seats.

Political Rights and Civil Liberties: Moldova is an electoral democracy. Voters elect the 101-seat unicameral Parliament by proportional representation for four-year terms. Parliament elects the president, who serves up to two four-year terms. The prime minister, who holds most executive power, must be approved by Parliament.

Domestic and international observers hailed the November 2010 parliamentary elections as a substantial improvement over the 2009 balloting, citing a more open and diverse media environment, impartial and transparent administration by the Central Election Commission, and a lack of restrictions on campaign activities. Some problems were reported, including flaws in the voter list, unbalanced distribution of overseas polling sites, and isolated cases of intimidation.

Corruption remains a major problem in Moldova, and the country's leading politicians regularly trade accusations of graft and illegal business activities. Under an EU-backed reform strategy adopted in May 2012, the scope of the renamed National Anticorruption Center was narrowed to exclude general economic crimes, allowing the agency—now an autonomous body under parliamentary rather than government supervision—to focus on corruption and money laundering. The new center was still recruiting staff at year's end. Moldova was ranked 94 out of 176 countries surveyed in Transparency International's 2012 Corruption Perceptions Index.

The media environment improved following the 2009 change in government. The public broadcaster, Teleradio Moldova (TRM), grew more impartial under new management, and two new private satellite television channels added to the diversity of national news coverage. However, several media outlets are perceived as party affiliates, including a number linked to AIE leaders. NIT, the only opposition-aligned television station with national reach, was known for an especially strong bias and is believed to be owned by the son of PCRM leader Vladimir Voronin. The Audiovisual Coordinating Council (CCA) had penalized it several times for politicized reporting, but the regulator's April 2012 revocation of its license—followed just a day later by the cutoff of its transmissions, before the decision had been upheld in the courts—raised concerns in some segments of civil society and the international community. NIT's appeal of the closure was still pending at year's end, following repeated court delays. Separately, unidentified attackers destroyed or stole equipment at the headquarters of regional broadcaster Elita TV in April. Reporters sometimes face physical abuse or selective exclusion from events of public interest. A cameraman for the opposition-oriented Omega news agency was hospitalized in May after four men emerged from a car and severely beat him without taking any valuables.

Although the constitution guarantees religious freedom, Moldovan law recognizes the "special significance and primary role" of the Orthodox Church. The Russian-backed Moldovan Orthodox Church accounts for more than 80 percent of the population, while the Romanian-backed Bessarabian Orthodox Church represents another 11 percent. Despite some positive steps by the AIE government in recent years, minority groups continue to encounter discrimination or hostility from local authorities, Orthodox clergy, and residents in some areas. Moldovan officials do not restrict academic freedom, though opposition parties have accused the AIE of placing political pressure on university students and seeking to inject pro-Romanian ideology into school curriculums.

The current government has generally upheld freedom of assembly. Opposition parties repeatedly mounted large antigovernment protests in 2012. Also during the year, activists who support Moldova's unification with Romania organized a series of marches, some of which had to be aborted after antiunion demonstrators pelted participants with eggs or rocks. The leader of the antiunion Social Democratic Party was facing a criminal investigation at year's end for his role in the disruptions. State relations with civil society groups have improved under the AIE, though some leading politicians have displayed wariness or hostility toward nongovernmental organizations (NGOs). Domestic NGOs have actively monitored recent election campaigns. Enforcement of union rights and labor standards is weak, with employers rarely punished for violations. Workers participating in illegal strikes face possible fines or prison time.

Although the constitution provides for an independent judiciary, reform efforts suffer from lack of funds, and judicial and law enforcement officials have a reputation for political influence and corruption. Numerous cases of malfeasance and petty bribery were reported during 2012. The election of Nicolae Timofti, a proponent of judicial reform, as president in March raised hopes for future improvements. In November, the prosecutor general's office began posting online all queries from lawmakers in an effort to deter improper requests. Prison conditions are generally harsh.

Roma suffer serious discrimination in housing, education, and employment, and have been targets of police violence. Gay men are also reportedly subject to harassment. In May 2012, the AIE overcame fierce opposition to pass the EU-backed Law on Ensuring Equality. Although the law's main article does not list sexual orientation among the banned grounds for discrimination, it was understood to be covered under a reference to "any other similar grounds." Moreover, sexual orientation is listed in a section on workplace discrimination. Opponents of the law—an alliance of opposition parties and Orthodox clergy—portrayed it as part of a general assault on traditional morality, claiming that it encouraged pederasty and Islamization. Meanwhile, municipalities including the city of Balti passed bans on "homosexual propaganda."

Women are underrepresented in public life; just 19 were elected to Parliament in 2010. Orders of protection for victims of domestic violence are inadequately enforced. Moldova is a significant source for women and girls trafficked abroad for forced prostitution. In May 2012, Parliament overrode a presidential veto on a law that imposed chemical castration on convicted pedophiles. The measure was designed to combat the problem of sex tourism by foreign pedophiles. It would also allow courts to apply the punishment to convicted rapists on a case-by-case basis.

Monaco

Political Rights: 2
Civil Liberties: 1
Status: Free

Population: 36,400
Capital: Monaco

Ten-Year Ratings Timeline For Year Under Review (Political Rights, Civil Liberties, Status)

2003	2004	2005	2006	2007	2008	2009	2010	2011	2012
2,1F	2,1F	2,1F	2,1F	2,1F	2,1F	2,1F	2,1F	2,1F	2,1F

Overview: In April 2012, the Conseil National reelected Jean-Francouis Robillon as its president. Workers went on strike over a change to Monaco's pension plans, which the government passed in September. In May, journalists were forced to evacuate the Grand Prix race temporarily after a bomb was found.

The Grimaldi family has ruled the Principality of Monaco for more than 700 years, except for a period of French occupation between 1793 and 1814. Under a treaty ratified in 1919, France pledged to protect Monaco's territorial integrity, sovereignty, and independence in return for a guarantee that Monégasque policy would conform to French political, military, and economic interests.

Prince Rainier III, who ruled from 1949 until his death in 2005, is often credited with engineering Monaco's impressive economic growth. During his reign, the country ended its dependence on gambling and nurtured other sources of revenue—principally tourism and financial services. Monaco adopted the euro currency in 2002, but remains outside of the European Union. In April 2005, Rainier was succeeded by Prince Albert II, who has made global environmental awareness a priority of his reign.

In the 2008 legislative elections, the Union of Monaco (UPM) won 21 of the 24 seats in the Conseil National, or parliament. The conservative opposition party, Rally and Issues for Monaco (REM), captured the remaining three seats. In April 2012, the Conseil National reelected Jean-Francois Robillon as president and Fabrice Notari as vice president.

On July 1, 2011, Albert wed Charlene Wittstock of South Africa. In July 2012, the son of Princess Caroline, Andrea Casiraghi, announced his engagement to Tatiana Santo Domingo.

In June and September 2012, hundreds of members of the Worker's Trade Union of Monaco went on strike against the government's proposed changes to pension laws, including an increase in contributions by both employers and employees. The law passed easily in September.

In May 2012, a bomb was found outside the media center at Monaco's famous Grand Prix race. Journalists were forced to evacuate, and the bomb was successfully detonated. No suspects or motives were found by year's end.

Political Rights and Civil Liberties: Monaco is an electoral democracy. However, only the prince, who serves as head of state, may initiate legislation and change the government. The 24 members of the unicameral Conseil National are elected for five-year terms; 16 are chosen through a majority electoral system and 8 by proportional representation.

The head of government, known as the minister of state, is traditionally appointed by the monarch from a candidate list of three French nationals submitted by the French government. The current minister of state, Michel Roger, has held the post since March 2010. The monarch also appoints five other ministers who comprise the cabinet. All legislation and the budget require the approval of the Conseil National, which is currently dominated by the UPM. The only other party represented is the REM.

Inadequate financial record keeping has traditionally made the country's level of corruption difficult to measure. However, the principality in 2009 started providing foreign tax authorities with information on accounts held by noncitizens, and by October of that year, the Organization for Economic Cooperation and Development (OECD) had removed Monaco from its list of uncooperative tax havens. Monaco took further steps toward improving financial transparency by signing tax information exchange agreements with 24 countries between 2009 and 2010, including with a number of OECD countries. The agreements ensure that Monaco will surrender relevant tax documents requested by the signatories. In March 2012, a manager at Société Monégasque d'Environnement Technologique was sentenced to eight months in prison for fraud.

The constitution provides for freedoms of speech and the press, although criticism of the ruling family is prohibited. In 2011, Robert Eringer, a California-based blogger and former employee of Prince Albert, was ordered to pay 20,000 euros (US$26,000) in damages plus 7,000 euros (US$9,100) in legal fees to Albert after a Paris court found him guilty of publishing false information about the monarchy and other prominent figures in Monaco. The court also ordered Eringer to remove his defamatory blog posts about Prince Albert.

The constitution guarantees freedom of worship, though Roman Catholicism is the state religion. There are no laws against proselytizing by formally registered religious organizations, but authorities strongly discourage proselytizing in public. Academic freedom is not restricted. The country's only institution of higher education, the private International University of Monaco, offers graduate and undergraduate programs in business administration, finance, and related fields. Monégasque students may attend French colleges and universities under various agreements between the two countries.

The constitution provides for freedom of assembly, which is generally respected in practice. No restrictions are imposed on the formation of civic and human rights groups. Workers have the legal right to organize and bargain collectively, although they rarely do so. All workers except state employees have the right to strike, as did members of the Worker's Trade Union of Monaco in 2012.

The legal rights to a fair public trial and an independent judiciary are generally respected. The justice system is based on the French legal code, and under the constitution, the prince delegates his judicial powers to the courts. The prince names five full members and two judicial assistants to the Supreme Court after the Conseil National, and other government bodies submit judicial nominations. Jail facilities generally meet international standards. Once criminal defendants receive definitive sentences, they are transferred to a French prison.

The constitution differentiates between the rights of Monégasque nationals and those of noncitizens. Of the principality's estimated 36,000 residents, only about 5,000 are citizens, and they alone may elect the Conseil National. Citizens also benefit from free education, unemployment assistance, and the ability to hold elective office. Noncitizens holding a residence permit may purchase real estate and open businesses.

Women generally receive equal pay for equal work. Women who become naturalized citizens by marriage cannot vote or run as candidates in elections until five years after the marriage. There are six women in the Conseil National. Abortion is legal only under special circumstances, including rape.

Mongolia

Political Rights: 1*
Civil Liberties: 2
Status: Free

Population: 2,873,000
Capital: Ulaanbaatar

Ratings Change: Mongolia's political rights rating improved from 2 to 1 due to significant progress in the conduct of parliamentary elections, which were regarded as free and fair.

Ten-Year Ratings Timeline For Year Under Review (Political Rights, Civil Liberties, Status)

2003	2004	2005	2006	2007	2008	2009	2010	2011	2012
2,2F	2,2F	2,2F	2,2F	2,2F	2,2F	2,2F	2,2F	2,2F	1,2F

Overview: Parliamentary elections held in June 2012 were deemed to have been free and fair, further confirming Mongolia's status as Asia's only post-socialist democracy. The election was won by a coalition of the Democratic Party, Justice Coalition, and Civil Will Green Party, led by Prime Minister Norovyn Altankhuyag. In August, former president Nambaryn Enkhbayar was convicted on corruption charges and sentenced to 2 1/2 years in jail. Pervasive corruption remained a problem in 2012, particularly in the country's mining sector.

Once the center of Genghis Khan's sprawling empire, Mongolia was ruled by China's Manchu Qing Empire for nearly 270 years. Mongolia declared its independence in 1911. After Chinese troops entered the country in 1919, Mongolia invited Russian Soviet forces to help secure control. Mongolia founded a people's republic in 1924, with the Mongolian People's Revolutionary Party (MPRP) governing the country as a one-party communist state. In response to persistent antigovernment protests, the MPRP legalized opposition parties in 1990, but easily won the first multiparty parliamentary elections that year and again in 1992.

The MPRP lost the 1996 parliamentary elections, and power was transferred peacefully to the opposition Democratic Union Coalition. After an economic downturn the following year, the MPRP won both the 1997 presidential election and the 2000 parliamentary vote. The 2004 parliamentary elections were marred by irregularities and gave neither side a majority. The MPRP consequently agreed to a power-sharing government with the opposition Motherland Democracy Coalition (MDC).

The MPRP's Nambaryn Enkhbayar, the parliament speaker and a former prime minister, won the 2005 presidential election. In January 2006, the MDC-MPRP coalition government collapsed, and the MPRP formed a new government with several small parties and MDC defectors led by MPRP prime minister Miyeegombo Enkhbold, who was replaced in November 2007 by Sanjaa Bayar after being accused of excessive political favoritism and corruption.

The initial results of the June 2008 parliamentary elections handed the MPRP a solid majority, but the opposition Democratic Party (DP) and others challenged the outcome. Small-scale protests escalated into large, violent demonstrations in the capital. Five people were killed, scores were injured, and over 700 others were arrested. The government declared a four-day state of emergency.

Former prime minister Tsakhiagiin Elbegdorj of the DP was elected president in May 2009. In October of that year, Bayar resigned as prime minister for health reasons and was replaced by Foreign Minister Sukhbaatar Batbold, who governed in a "grand coalition" with the DP until January 2012, when the DP left the coalition in preparation for parliamentary elections in June. In 2010, the MPRP renamed itself the Mongolian People's Party. In 2011, MPP members under the leadership of former president Enkhbayar broke off from the party and re-formed the MPRP.

In the parliamentary elections held on June 28, 2012, the DP won 33 seats in the elections, the MPP 25, and the Justice Coalition—which included the reformed MPRP—took 11, with the rest of the seats going to other parties. There were significantly fewer foreign election observers present for the elections, although the General Election Commission accredited domestic civil society observers for the first time. Observers, who were concentrated in Ulaanbaatar, generally deemed the election to have been free and fair. While there were some allegations of election fraud, they were relatively muted, though the victories of two MPP candidates in Övorkhangai province were invalidated by the courts.

Ulaanbaatar city elections were held in conjunction with the parliamentary elections for the first time. The MPP leadership in the capital was replaced with a DP majority under the leadership of charismatic democracy activist Erdene Bat-Uul.

Mongolia's economy continues to be shaped by the large gold and copper project in Oyu Tolgoi. In the summer of 2012, the government issued shares in the large Tavan Tolgoi coal project. After leases offered to international bidders were retracted, the government itself apparently plans to operate the mine.

Political Rights and Civil Liberties: Mongolia is an electoral democracy. The prime minister, who holds most executive power, is nominated by the party or coalition with the most seats in the 76-member parliament (the State Great Hural) and approved by the parliament with the agreement of the president. The president is head of state and of the armed forces, and can veto legislation, subject to a two-thirds parliamentary override. Candidates running for president are nominated by parties but may not be party members. Both the president and the parliament are directly elected for four-year terms.

Parliamentary balloting has varied over the years between multimember and single-member districts. The 2012 elections contained further changes; under the new rules, 48 of the parliament's 76 seats were directly awarded in direct elections, while the remaining 28 were allocated through a proportional system according to parties' share of the national vote. Among the 26 electoral districts, 18 were represented by 2 parliamentarians, 6 elected a single representative, and 2 of the districts elected 3. The elections also included several procedural changes in the registration and voting process, including the introduction of biometric voter identification papers, vote counting machines, a quota for female candidates, and a more stringent procedure by which the General Election Commission would check and approve party platforms based on their financial feasibility.

Corruption remains a serious problem in Mongolia and is viewed as pervasive. The Independent Authority Against Corruption (IAAC) has been actively investigating corruption allegations since 2007. In April 2012, the IAAC arrested former president and MPRP party leader Nambaryn Enkhbayar on corruption charges, banning him from taking part in the June elections. Although Enkhbayar claimed that the arrest was politically motivated, the ban on his participating in the elections was upheld by Mongolian courts, and many observers accepted the arrest as a consequence of the pervasive corruption that took place during his presidency. In August, Enkhbayar was convicted of relatively minor corruption and money-laundering charges, and in November, he was sentenced to 2 1/2 years in prison.

Although the government operates with limited transparency, the first Citizens' Hall was established in Ulaanbaatar in 2009 to encourage civic participation in the legislative processes. Citizens have the opportunity to provide feedback on draft laws and government services by attending such hearings or submitting their views via letter, fax, e-mail, or telephone. Mongolia was ranked 94 of 176 countries surveyed in Transparency International's 2012 Corruption Perceptions Index.

While the government generally respects press freedom, many journalists and independent publications practice a degree of self-censorship to avoid legal action under the State Secrets Law or libel laws that place the burden of proof on the defendant. Journalists have been charged in defamation suits by ministers of parliament and businesspeople; in many cases, the charges were dropped. Journalist Gantumur Uyanga, who was accused of libel by a former minister in November 2011, was elected to parliament herself in 2012. There are hundreds of privately owned print and broadcast outlets, but the main source of news in the vast countryside is the state-owned Mongolian National Broadcaster. Foreign content from satellite television and radio services like the British Broadcasting Corporation and Voice of America is also increasingly available. Some international media operations—including Bloomberg in the fall of 2012—have moved into the Mongolian market. The government does not interfere with internet access.

Freedom of religion is guaranteed by the constitution. The fall of communism led to an influx of Christian missionaries to Mongolia and a revival of Mongolia's traditional Buddhism and shamanism. Religious groups are required to register with the government and renew their status annually. The Kazakh Muslim minority generally enjoys freedom of religion. Academic freedom is respected.

Freedoms of assembly and association are observed in law and in practice. A number of environmental, human rights, and social welfare groups—while largely reliant on foreign donors—operate without government restriction. However, some journalists and nonprofit personnel have alleged government monitoring of e-mail accounts and wiretapping. Trade unions are independent and active, and the government has generally protected their rights in recent years, though the downsizing or sale of many state factories has contributed to a sharp drop in union membership. Collective bargaining is legal.

The judiciary is independent, but corruption among judges persists. The police force has been accused of making arbitrary arrests and traffic stops, holding detainees for long periods, and beating prisoners. Four senior police officers were tried for their roles in the death of rioters following the 2008 parliamentary election. Prison deaths continue to be reported, as insufficient nutrition, heat, and medical care remain problems. President Tsakhiagiin Elbegdorj issued a moratorium on the death penalty in January 2010.

While women comprise 60 percent of all university students as well as 60 percent of all judges, they hold only 9 parliamentary seats. Spousal abuse is prohibited by law, but social and cultural norms continue to discourage victims from reporting such crimes. Mongolia is a source, transit, and destination country for men, women, and children who are subjected to sex trafficking and forced labor. The government has continued efforts to eliminate trafficking though funding for such efforts has been inadequate.

Montenegro

Political Rights: 3
Civil Liberties: 2
Status: Free

Population: 621,700
Capital: Podgorica

Note: The ratings through 2002 are for the Federal Republic of Yugoslavia, of which Montenegro was a part, and those from 2003 through 2005 are for the State Union of Serbia and Montenegro.

Ten-Year Ratings Timeline For Year Under Review (Political Rights, Civil Liberties, Status)

2003	2004	2005	2006	2007	2008	2009	2010	2011	2012
3,2PF	3,2F	3,2F	3,3PF	3,3PF	3,3PF	3,2F	3,2F	3,2F	3,2F

Overview: The European Union opened accession negotiations with Montenegro in June 2012, noting improvements in the rule of law, among other areas, while urging further progress on anticorruption efforts and judicial reform. Lawmakers in July called early elections, and the ruling center-left coalition held on to power in polls that followed in October. Milo Đukanovic, who had served as prime minister or president for most of the previous two decades, was elected prime minister in December.

Montenegro was first recognized as an independent state in 1878. In 1918, it joined the newly formed Kingdom of Serbs, Croats, and Slovenes, which after World War II became the Socialist Federal Republic of Yugoslavia. As that state collapsed in the early 1990s, Montenegro maintained its ties to Serbia in the truncated Federal Republic of Yugoslavia (FRY), dominated by Serbian leader Slobodan Miloševic. In 1997, however, a group of former Miloševic cohorts in Montenegro, led by Prime Minister Milo Đukanovic, decided to break with Miloševic and pursue Montenegrin independence.

Miloševic's fall from power in 2000 did not improve relations between Montenegro and its larger federal partner. The republics signed an agreement in 2002 that loosened their bond, and the FRY became the State Union of Serbia and Montenegro in 2003. The deal allowed either republic to hold an independence referendum after three years, and Đukanovic exercised that option in May 2006. Voters supported independence, which the parliament officially declared in July.

The September 2006 parliamentary elections confirmed voter support for Montenegro's ruling proindependence coalition, comprising Đukanovic's Democratic Party of Socialists (DPS) and the Social Democratic Party (SDP). Đukanovic retired in October but returned as prime minister in February 2008. In April, President Filip Vujanovic of the DPS was elected to a second five-year term.

In January 2009, Vujanovic called snap parliamentary elections, reportedly because of fears that the global economic crisis could erode voter support for the DPS-led coalition before the legislature's full term ended. The March polls saw the coalition win a comfortable majority of 48 seats in the 81-seat parliament.

Since gaining independence, Montenegro has sought to join NATO and the European Union (EU). In December 2010, the EU granted the country candidate status. A few days later, Đukanovic resigned again, asserting that he had successfully guided the country toward European integration. However, there were indications that his continued tenure could have obstructed Montenegro's EU candidacy due to allegations that he had been involved in cigarette smuggling in the 1990s. Đukanovic remained chairman of the DPS, and Finance Minister Igor Lukšic, also a DPS member, succeeded him as prime minister.

In September 2011, the parliament broke a four-year impasse to approve a landmark new election law that ensures the representation of minorities and improves technical voting issues. The law's passage had been delayed due to a controversy over the languages officially recognized in the country. In 2010, Montenegrin had become the official language of the state broadcaster, and a Montenegrin grammar text was introduced in schools. Critics countered that the government was promoting an artificial language derived from standard Serbian, and the opposition had vowed that it would not support the election law until the Serbian language was given equal status to Montenegrin in the education system. The law was passed after legislators agreed on a class to be taught in schools called "Montenegrin-Serbian, Bosnian, Croatian language and literature."

In October 2011, the European Commission (EC), noting continued reform efforts and the election law's passage, cleared Montenegro to begin EU accession negotiations. On June 26, 2012, the EU officially invited Montenegro to begin membership talks, praising strides on rule of law and fundamental rights, while calling for the country to continue implementing needed reforms regarding judicial independence and the ongoing fight against corruption.

In July, legislators voted to dissolve the parliament and call early elections so the government could begin the EU talks with a fresh mandate. President Vujanovic scheduled the polls for October 14. The DPS-led coalition won with a simple majority of 46 percent, or 39 seats. The opposition Democratic Front took 20 seats, followed by the Socialist People's Party with 9, Positive Montenegro with 7, and the Bosniak Party with 3. The Croat Citizens' Initiative and two Albanian parties won 1 seat each. The DPS-led coalition took power with support from Albanian and Croatian minority parties, and Đukanovic was elected to his seventh term as prime minister on December 4.

Political Rights and Civil Liberties: Montenegro is an electoral democracy. International observers have deemed recent elections free and fair, despite some irregularities. Members of the unicameral, 81-seat Skupština (Assembly) are elected for four-year terms. Under a 2011 election law, parliamentary seats are awarded strictly on the basis of candidates' positions on electoral lists. The president, directly elected for up to two five-year terms, nominates the prime minister, who requires legislative approval.

Numerous political parties compete for power, though the opposition is weak, with the biggest player the Democratic Front, comprising the reform-minded Movement for Changes and New Serb Democracy. The current coalition government comprises the DPS, the SDP, and a handful of lawmakers from parties that represent Montenegro's ethnic minorities. Serbs, who comprise nearly 30 percent of the population, generally opposed independence prior to 2006 but have adjusted to the new reality.

Corruption remains a serious problem and is partly a legacy of the struggle against the Miloševic regime in the 1990s, when the small republic turned to various forms of smuggling to finance government operations. Key legislative frameworks to improve transparency in party financing and public procurement, among other anticorruption efforts, are being implemented. After an amended law on conflicts of interest took force in March, every parliamentarian who held board or executive positions in state-owned companies resigned. However, enforcement of anticorruption measures is uneven, convictions in high-profile corruption cases are low, and interagency cooperation needs improvement, especially between prosecutors and police, according to the EC's 2012 progress report. From October 2011 to September 2012, 23 officials were charged with abuse of office and bribery, including the president. Montenegro was ranked 75 out of 176 countries surveyed in Transparency International's 2012 Corruption Perceptions Index.

Freedom of the press is generally respected, and a variety of independent media operate. In 2011, Montenegro decriminalized libel under European standards. However, journalists continue to face pressure and harassment. In April 2012, a broadcast journalist who had been convicted of libel before the legislative change was sentenced to four months in prison. Also in 2012, investigative journalist Olivera Laki was attacked after reporting a series on corruption; her attacker was sentenced to nine months in prison. The public broadcaster is not fully independent. Internet access is unrestricted.

The constitution guarantees freedom of religious belief. However, the canonically recognized Serbian Orthodox Church and a self-proclaimed Montenegrin Orthodox Church continue to clash over ownership of church properties and other issues.

Academic freedom is guaranteed by law, but political debates about the nature of Montenegrin identity and history have spilled over into the educational realm, as was the case when controversy over the Montenegrin language almost blocked the adoption of the 2011 election law.

Citizens enjoy freedoms of association and assembly. Nongovernmental organizations generally operate without state interference, and the EC noted improving cooperation between civil society and government institutions in 2012. Most formally employed workers belong to unions, and the right to strike is generally protected. However, trade union members sometimes face discrimination, and dismissals of striking workers have been reported.

The EC cited progress on judicial reform in 2012. The new Judicial and Prosecutorial Councils were constituted in June and July, respectively, and independence and accountability continued to improve with the implementation of relevant legislative frameworks. In October, the EC noted that the case backlog was down 4 percent since 2010. However, the government has yet to institute a nationwide recruitment system for judges and prosecutors based on transparent criteria, and courts remain subject to political influence. Prison conditions do not meet international standards for education or health care.

Ethnic Albanians, who comprise 5 percent of the population, maintain that they are underrepresented in the civil service, particularly in the police and judiciary. Roma, Ashkali, Egyptians, members of the LGBT (lesbian, gay, bisexual, and transgender) communities, and other minority groups often face discrimination. The government adopted a strategy on inclusion of ethnic minorities in April 2012, but implementation is slow. As part of the Sarajevo Declaration Process, Montenegro continues to cooperate with Bosnia and Herzegovina, Croatia, and Serbia to reintegrate refugees from the conflicts in the former Yugoslavia.

Women in Montenegro are legally entitled to equal pay for equal work, but traditional patriarchal attitudes often limit their salary levels and educational opportunities. Women are underrepresented in government and business. New provisions requiring women to comprise 30 percent of candidate lists were implemented in the 2012 elections. Domestic violence remains problematic despite a 2011 government strategy against violence in the home. Trafficking in persons for the purposes of prostitution and forced labor remains a problem, although the government is preparing an antitrafficking strategy through 2018.

Morocco

Political Rights: 5
Civil Liberties: 4
Status: Partly Free

Population: 32,597,000
Capital: Rabat

Note: The numerical ratings and status listed above do not reflect conditions in Western Sahara, which is examined in a separate report.

Ten-Year Ratings Timeline For Year Under Review (Political Rights, Civil Liberties, Status)

2003	2004	2005	2006	2007	2008	2009	2010	2011	2012
5,5PF	5,4PF	5,4PF	5,4PF	5,4PF	5,4PF	5,4PF	5,4PF	5,4PF	5,4PF

Overview: **Prime Minister Abdelilah Benkirane of the Justice and Development Party took office in January 2012. Economic instability and unrest deepened during the year, due in part to high fuel and food costs and an economic system dominated by the king and other elites. The February 20 Movement staged nationwide protests throughout the year, including in July and September.**

Morocco gained independence in 1956, after more than four decades of French rule. The first ruler after independence, King Mohamed V, reigned until his death in 1961. His son, Hassan II, then ruled the country until his death in 1999. Thousands of his political opponents were arrested, tortured, and killed, while many simply disappeared.

In 1975, Morocco and Mauritania occupied Western Sahara. After three years of fighting the Algerian-backed Polisario Front, a Sahrawi nationalist guerrilla movement, Mauritania withdrew from the portion it claimed. Morocco then annexed the territory in full. A planned referendum on Western Sahara's future—attached to a UN-monitored ceasefire agreement in 1991—never took place.

In the last few years of Hassan's life, several political prisoners were released, independent newspapers began publishing, and a new bicameral parliament was established. King Mohamed VI, who inherited the throne in 1999, declined to expand political freedom significantly early in his reign, apparently aiming to check the increased influence of Islamist political parties. However, he removed longtime interior minister Driss Basri, who had led much of the repression under King Hassan, and allowed exiled dissidents to return to the country. Parliamentary elections held in 2002 were recognized as generally open, and more than a dozen political parties participated, though independent journalists and other critics of the king were harassed and detained.

In May 2003, local Islamist militants with purported links to al-Qaeda mounted a series of deadly suicide bombings, targeting symbols of Morocco's Jewish community in Casablanca. The government responded by enacting a harsh antiterrorism law, which was subsequently used to prosecute nonviolent opponents of the king.

In 2004, King Mohamed inaugurated the Equity and Reconciliation Commission (IER), tasked with addressing the human rights abuses perpetrated by the authorities from 1956 to 1999 and recommending forms of reparation for the victims. The commission, which featured public testimony from victims, submitted its final report in 2006, including a series of recommendations for legal and institutional reforms designed to prevent future abuses. Critics of the IER complained that it did not hold perpetrators accountable, and that its recommendations did not lead to major structural changes. Moreover, the authorities were intolerant of further discussion of past abuses. In June 2008, a court in Rabat ordered the private daily *Al-Jarida al-Oula* to stop publishing IER testimony.

In the 2007 elections for the Chamber of Representatives, the lower house of Parliament, the conservative Independence Party (Istiqlal) won a plurality, the Islamist Justice and Development Party (PJD) placed second, and the Socialist Union of People's Forces (USFP), previously the lead party in the governing coalition, came in third.

In 2011, the political environment was shaken by protests inspired by popular uprisings elsewhere in the Middle East and North Africa. Demonstrations demanding democratic political reforms were held across the country on February 20, and the resulting protest movement, named for this date and comprised of students and activists, have continued to press for change.

After naming a commission to draft a new constitution in response to the protests, the king presented the proposed document in June 2011. It preserved most of the monarch's existing powers, but would require him to choose the prime minister from the party that won the most seats in parliamentary elections, and consult the prime minister before dissolving Parliament. Other provisions included giving official status to the Berber language, calling for gender equality, and emphasizing respect for human rights. Although the February 20 movement rejected the changes as insufficient, the main political parties encouraged voters to approve the document in a July referendum, and it reportedly passed with over 98 percent of the vote.

Parliamentary elections were held in November 2011, resulting in a victory for the opposition PJD, which took 107 of the 395 seats in the lower house. Istiqlal placed second with 60 seats, followed by the National Rally of Independents with 52, the Modernity and Authenticity Party (PAM) with 47, the USFP with 39, the Popular Movement with 32, the Constitutional Union with 23, the Party of Progress and Socialism with 18, and ten small parties dividing the remainder. After the PAM's poor showing, PAM leader Fouad Ali el-Himma resigned and joined the palace as an adviser to the king.

Abdelilah Benkirane of the PJD was named prime minister, and he formed a coalition government with Istiqlal, the Popular Movement, and the Party of Progress and Socialism in January 2012. Although Morocco continued to be one of the more stable nations in the region in 2012, economic instability and unrest deepened as the year progressed due to the economic problems in Europe, high fuel and food costs, and an economic system dominated by the king and his economic and political elite.

Political Rights and Civil Liberties: Morocco is not an electoral democracy. Most power is held by the king and his close advisers. Even under the 2011 constitution, the monarch can dissolve Parliament, rule by decree, and dismiss or appoint cabinet members. He sets national and foreign policy, commands the armed forces and intelligence services, and presides over the judicial system. One of the king's constitutional titles is "commander of the faithful," giving his authority a claim to religious legitimacy. The king is also the majority stakeholder in a vast array of private and public sector firms; according to *Forbes*, Mohammed VI is worth $2.5 billion, making him one of the world's wealthiest people.

The lower house of Parliament, the Chamber of Representatives, has 395 directly elected members who serve for five-year terms. Sixty of these seats are reserved for women and 30 for men under age 40. Members of the 270-seat upper house, the Chamber of Counselors, are chosen by an electoral college to serve nine-year terms. Under a rule that took effect in 2009, women are guaranteed 12 percent of the seats in local elections.

Given the concentration of power in the monarchy, the country's fragmented political parties are generally unable to assert themselves. The PJD, which won the 2011 parliamentary vote, has long been a vocal opposition party, even as it remained respectful of the monarchy. The Islamist Justice and Charity Movement is illegal, though it is generally tolerated by the authorities. Other Islamist groups are harassed by authorities and not permitted to participate in the political process.

Despite the government's rhetoric on combating widespread corruption, it remains a problem, both in public life and in the business world. In 2012 a new book by journalists Catherine Graciet and Éric Laurent, *Le Roi Prédateur*, leveled sharp charges of corruption at the palace. Morocco was ranked 88 out of 176 countries surveyed in Transparency International's 2012 Corruption Perceptions Index.

Although the independent press enjoys a significant degree of freedom when reporting on economic and social policies, the authorities use restrictive press laws and an array of financial and other, more subtle mechanisms to punish critical journalists, particularly those who focus on the king, his family, the status of the Western Sahara, or Islam. Rachid Nini, editor of the popular daily *Al-Massae*, was sentenced in June 2011 to a year in jail on charges of spreading misinformation after publishing articles on alleged corruption involving the royal palace and PAM leader Fouad Ali el-Himma. The paper had also called for the repeal of the 2003 antiterrorism law. Nini was released in April 2012 and resigned from the paper, migrating to the internet. Other journalists have also been harassed, including Hamid Naïmi, who has investigated corruption and the marginalization of the Berber population in the northern Rif region, and Mohamed Sokrate, a blogger who has written sympathetically about the February 20 Movement and advocates secularism. The state dominates the broadcast media, but residents have access to foreign satellite television channels. The authorities occasionally disrupt websites and internet platforms, while bloggers and other internet users are sometimes arrested for posting content that offends the monarchy.

Nearly all Moroccans are Muslims. While the small Jewish community is permitted to practice its faith without government interference, Moroccan authorities are growing increasingly intolerant of social and religious diversity, as reflected in arrest campaigns against Shiites, Muslim converts to Christianity, and those opposed to a law enforcing the Ramadan fast.

While university campuses generally provide a space for open discussion, professors practice self-censorship when dealing with sensitive topics like Western Sahara, the monarchy, and Islam.

Freedom of assembly is not always respected, though frequent demonstrations by unemployed graduates and unions are generally tolerated. The February 20 Movement also holds rallies on a periodic basis; notable protests in 2012 included a demonstration in Casablanca on July 22 and in Rabat on September 23. The protests were largely peaceful, and included demands that activists be released from prison. Reduced in numbers from its height in 2011, the movement was deemed illegal by a Casablanca judge in July 2012. Although such protests often occur without incident, activists say they are harassed outside of public events.

Civil society and independent nongovernmental organizations are quite active, but the authorities monitor Islamist groups, arrest suspected extremists, and harass other groups that offend the government. Moroccan workers are permitted to form and join independent trade unions, and the 2004 labor law prevents employers from punishing workers who do so. However, the authorities have forcibly broken up labor actions that entail criticism of the government, and child laborers, especially girls working as domestic helpers, are denied basic rights.

The judiciary is not independent, and the courts are regularly used to punish opponents of the government. Arbitrary arrest and torture still occur, though they are less common than under King Hassan. The security forces are given greater leeway with detainees advocating independence for Western Sahara, leading to frequent reports of abuse and lack of due process.

Many Moroccans have a mixed Tamazight (Berber) ancestry, and the government has officially recognized Tamazight language and culture.

Women continue to face significant discrimination at the societal level. However, Moroccan authorities have a relatively progressive view on gender equality, which is recognized in the 2011 constitution. The 2004 family code has been lauded for granting women increased rights in the areas of marriage, divorce, and child custody, and various other laws aim to protect women's interests.

Mozambique

Political Rights: 4
Civil Liberties: 3
Status: Partly Free

Population: 23,702,000
Capital: Maputo

Ten-Year Ratings Timeline For Year Under Review (Political Rights, Civil Liberties, Status)

2003	2004	2005	2006	2007	2008	2009	2010	2011	2012
3,4PF	3,4PF	3,4PF	3,4PF	3,3PF	3,3PF	4,3PF	4,3PF	4,3PF	4,3PF

Overview: In October 2012, President Armando Guebuza replaced several key government figures, including the prime minister. The economy continued to grow during the year, as the country tapped into its large coal and natural gas reserves, though much of Mozambique's population remained impoverished.

Mozambique achieved independence from Portugal in 1975. The Front for the Liberation of Mozambique (FRELIMO), a guerrilla group that had long fought to oust the Portuguese, installed itself as the sole legal political party in a Marxist-style state. A 16-year civil war followed, pitting the Soviet-allied FRELIMO against the Mozambique National Resistance (RENAMO), a force sponsored by the white-minority governments of Rhodesia (Zimbabwe) and South Africa. The war resulted in nearly a million deaths and the displacement of several million others. President Samora Machel, the FRELIMO leader, was killed in a suspicious plane crash in 1986; he was succeeded by Joaquim Chissano, a reform-minded FRELIMO moderate. A new constitution was enacted, calling for a multiparty political system, a market-based economy, and free elections. A peace accord signed in 1992 brought an end to the war, and a 7,500-strong UN peacekeeping force oversaw a disarmament and demobilization program and a transition to democratic government.

Mozambique held its first democratic elections in 1994. Chissano retained the presidency, and FRELIMO secured a majority of seats in the National Assembly. RENAMO accepted the outcome, transforming itself into a peaceful opposition political movement. Chissano and FRELIMO were again victorious in the 1999 elections, which were deemed credible by the international community, despite technical difficulties and irregularities in the tabulation process. However, RENAMO accused the government of fraud and at one point threatened to form its own government in the six northern and central provinces it controlled.

Chissano announced that he would step down as president upon completion of his second elected term. In 2002, FRELIMO leaders chose Armando Guebuza, a hardliner, to lead the party. Pledging to address corruption, crime, and poverty, Guebuza and FRELIMO won presidential and legislative elections in 2004 with a wide margin of victory, though RENAMO cited evidence of fraud. The National Electoral Commission (CNE) later admitted that 1,400 vote-summary sheets favoring RENAMO had been stolen—accounting for 5 percent of the total vote—and transferred one parliamentary seat from FRELIMO to RENAMO as compensation. International election observers expressed concerns about the CNE's conduct during the tabulation process, but ultimately determined that the abuses had not altered the overall outcome.

Mozambique held presidential, legislative, and—for the first time—provincial elections in October 2009. Guebuza was reelected with 75 percent of the vote. His opponents, Afonso Dhlakama of RENAMO and Daviz Simango of the newly formed Democratic Movement of Mozambique (MDM), received 16.4 percent and 8.6 percent, respectively. In the parliamentary contest, FRELIMO captured 191 of 250 seats, while RENAMO won 51, and the MDM took 8. FRELIMO also won absolute majorities in all 10 of the country's provincial assemblies. RENAMO and the MDM both alleged fraud, and international observer groups were highly critical of many preelection processes. Observers also documented irregularities that indicated ballot stuffing and tabulation fraud at some polling stations, though they concluded that the distortions were not significant enough to have impacted the overall result of the elections.

Guebuza's government has largely continued the liberal economic reforms and poverty reduction policies of its predecessor. However, Guebuza has been criticized for his confrontational stance toward opposition parties and heavy-handed management of FRELIMO. In October 2012, he dismissed Prime Minister Aires Ali, replacing him with Alberto Vaquina. Several other cabinet members were reappointed to other positions in the executive, with the exceptions of Ali and the former ministers of Youth and Sport, Education, and Science and Technology. Governor Carvalho Muaria was promoted to Minister of Tourism.

Mozambique's macroeconomic performance remained among the strongest in sub-Saharan Africa in 2012, although gross domestic product (GDP) growth, at almost 7 percent, was almost 1 percent lower than its 2011 rate, largely because of the ongoing global economic turmoil. Inflation continued to decline, reaching an all-time low of 3 percent in mid-2012.

Nevertheless, most of the population lives in severe poverty. Mozambique was rated 184 out of 187 countries on the UN Development Program's 2012 Human Development Index. The government has begun to implement its 2011 Poverty Reduction Strategy—intended to cut poverty from its 2009 level of 55 percent to 42 percent in 2014—by starting to overhaul social protection programs. The antipoverty program nevertheless faces enormous challenges, and administrative capacity and coordination need to be improved.

Following the discovery of large quantities of natural gas by U.S.-based Anadarko and Italy's ENI, Mozambique in November 2011 held a tender for the acquisition of seismic, gravity, and magnetic data of Mozambique's onshore and offshore basins. A new licensing round for offshore blocks in the Rovuma basin was planned for late 2012 but postponed until 2013. A revised oil law was introduced in the summer of 2012 but has yet to be approved. The law has been met with resistance by civil society groups, which regard it as too favorable to the interests of oil companies.

Mozambique has long enjoyed close relations with donors, whose support has accounted for roughly half of the country's budget in recent years. However, in an effort to communicate disapproval of FRELIMO's problematic handling of the 2009 elections and its increasing dominance over the state and economy, Western donors withheld aid in 2010 until late March of that year, when the government agreed to reform the electoral system and introduce new legislation to address rampant corruption. Net aid flows declined significantly from 14.5 percent of GDP in 2009 to 10 percent of GDP in 2012.

Political Rights and Civil Liberties: Mozambique is not an electoral democracy. While international observers have deemed that the overall outcomes of Mozambique's national elections reflected the will of the people, electoral processes have repeatedly been riddled with problems. The 2009 elections were particularly criticized for the widespread rejection of party lists and for irregularities in the tabulation of results.

The president, who appoints the prime minister, is elected by popular vote for up to two five-year terms. Members of the 250-seat, unicameral Assembly of the Republic are also elected for five-year terms. The national government appoints the governors of the 10 provinces and the capital city, Maputo. Despite the introduction of elected provincial assemblies and municipal governments, power remains highly centralized, particularly in the hands of the president.

Political parties are governed by a law that expressly prohibits them from identifying exclusively with any religious or ethnic group. Although RENAMO and the MDM have won representation as opposition parties in the parliament, FRELIMO is the only party to have held power nationally, and its unbroken incumbency has allowed it to acquire significant control over state institutions. In the lead-up to the 2009 elections, the government was heavily criticized for the CNE's disqualification of MDM candidates in 7 of the country's 11 parliamentary constituencies. Elements within FRELIMO are also believed to have instigated several violent attacks against opposition candidates and their supporters during the campaign. In October 2012, RENAMO leaders called for national peaceful demonstrations to protest FRELIMO's unwillingness to negotiate with opposition groups and force it to accept a "new political order."

Corruption in government and business remains pervasive. In March 2012, former interior minister Almerino Manhenje was convicted of illegal budgetary decisions and mismanagement of expenses in 2004; the former director and deputy director of the financial department were also found guilty in the same case. In August, the government dismissed the president of the National Social Security Institute after the institution lost $100,000 in a failed attempt to acquire a building without a public tender, as required by law. In response to international pressure from countries and institutions that financially support Mozambique's government, the National Assembly passed a new anticorruption law in August 2012 and granted new powers to the Central Office for Combating Corruption. Mozambique was ranked 123 out of 176 countries surveyed in Transparency International's 2012 Corruption Perceptions Index.

While press freedom is legally protected, journalists are sometimes harassed or threatened and often practice self-censorship. Mozambique has a government-run daily, *Noticias*, and the privately owned *Diario de Moçambique*. There is also a state news agency and a state radio and television broadcaster. Independent media include several weeklies and the daily *O País*, a number of radio stations, and, more recently, news websites. These sources, however, face sustainability issues as a result of the state's dominance over advertising. Although there are no official government restrictions on internet use, opposition leaders have claimed that government intelligence services monitor e-mail.

Religious freedoms are well respected, and academic freedoms are generally upheld. In 2012 the Islamic community of Nampula declared its intention to cut all ties with the central government, demanding that it apologize for prohibiting the use of veils in schools in 2011. They also seek permission for the wearing of veils in pictures used for ID cards. The Ministry of Justice, which is responsible for religious policy, has since begun negotiations on the issue with the Islamic community.

Associational and organizational rights are broadly guaranteed, but with substantial regulations. By law, the right to assemble is subject to notification and timing restrictions, and in practice, it is also subject to governmental discretion. In several instances, campaign rallies in the lead-up to the 2009 elections were violently disrupted by rival party activists, though most events proceeded peacefully. Security forces have at times broken up protests using disproportionate force. In September 2010, security forces opened fire on rioters in Maputo, killing 12 people, including 2 children, and injuring more than 400. Nongovernmental organizations (NGOs) operate openly but face bureaucratic hurdles in registering with the government, as required by law. Workers have the right to form and join unions and to strike.

Corruption, scarce resources, and poor training undermine judicial independence. The judicial system is further challenged by a dearth of qualified judges and a backlog of cases. In September 2012, 25 judges were selected for the newly established Superior Appeals Courts, designed to relieve the Supreme Court that was previously the only court of appeal. The new courts were still not functioning as of the end of 2012.

Despite the government's public committment in 2011 to investigating all cases of arbitrary detention, ill-treatment and torture of prisoners, and excessive force by the police, abuses continue to occur. Amnesty International in 2012 cited several cases of excessive use of force, torture, and unlawful killings, including the death of two prisoners at the Quinta do Girassol detention center after being beaten by a prison guard.

Women are fairly well represented politically, holding the premiership from 2004 to 2010 and comprising some 39 percent of the parliament. However, they continue to face societal discrimination and violence. Legal protections for women and children are rarely enforced. Human trafficking has been on the rise, with Mozambicans and Asian immigrants taken to South Africa and sexually exploited. Witch hunts continue to be a major problem in Mozambique, particularly in the south, where the elderly are killed in high numbers after being accused of witchcraft.

Namibia

Political Rights: 2
Civil Liberties: 2
Status: Free

Population: 2,364,000
Capital: Windhoek

Ten-Year Ratings Timeline For Year Under Review (Political Rights, Civil Liberties, Status)

2003	2004	2005	2006	2007	2008	2009	2010	2011	2012
2,3F	2,3F	2,2F	2,2F	2,2F	2,2F	2,2F	2,2F	2,2F	2,2F

Overview: In December 2012, Hage Geingob was reelected vice president of the long-ruling SWAPO party, making him the party's likely presidential candidate for 2014. In July, in what was hailed as a landmark ruling for women's and patients' rights, the High Court found in favor of three HIV-positive women who claimed that they had been sterilized at state hospitals without giving informed consent.

Namibia, formerly known as South West Africa, was claimed by German imperial forces in the late 19th century and became a South African protectorate after World War I. In 1966, South Africa's mandate was revoked by the United Nations, and the South West Africa People's Organization (SWAPO) began a guerrilla campaign for independence. After years of war, a UN-supervised transition led to independence in 1990, and SWAPO leader Sam Nujoma was chosen as president.

Secessionist fighting in Namibia's Caprivi region between 1998 and 1999 led some 2,400 refugees to flee to neighboring Botswana. Treason trials for the alleged secessionists resulted in guilty verdicts in 2007, though the Supreme Court had yet to reach a decision on appeals of the verdicts for more than 100 defendants as of the end of 2012.

Nujoma and SWAPO retained control of the presidency and legislature in the 1994 and 1999 elections. In 2004, Nujoma's longtime ally, Hifikepunye Pohamba, was chosen as the party's presidential candidate and went on to win the elections. He was reelected in November 2009 with 75 percent of the vote, while the candidate of the Rally for Democracy and Progress (RDP), an opposition party formed in 2007 mainly by SWAPO defectors, captured just 11 percent.

In concurrent parliamentary elections, SWAPO won 54 seats in the 72-member legislature, while the RDP took 8 seats. The elections were praised as free and fair by domestic and international observers, although the latter raised some concerns about pro-SWAPO bias in the government-run Namibian Broadcast Corporation (NBC), delays in the counting process, and organizational mishaps during the polling process. Nine opposition parties filed a legal challenge calling for the nullification of the parliamentary elections due to "gross irregularities." After the High Court rejected the challenge in February 2011, the parties appealed the ruling to the Supreme Court, which heard the case in October. In July 2012, the RPD held a sit-in outside the Supreme Court building in Windhoek to protest the court's delay in issuing a decision, and in October filed a petition with the chief justice, seeking to force the judges who had heard the case to release a verdict. The Supreme Court released the verdict later that month, dismissing the case outright and ordering the RDP to pay SWAPO's legal costs.

In late November and early December, SWAPO held its much-anticipated party congress, in which it elected its leaders, including party vice president. The congress—held every five years—had been preceded by a bitter succession fight, as the SWAPO vice president would be the party's 2014 presidential candidate and, given SWAPO's previous electoral dominance, was expected to become Namibia's next president. Trade and Industry Minister Hage Geingob, the incumbent, won the race, defeating Local and Regional Government Minister Jerry Ekandjo and Justice Minister Pendukeni Iivula-Ithana, who was also the party's secretary general. Days later, Geingob was appointed prime minister, replacing Nahas Angula. Geingob, who was from the minority Damara community, would likely become the first Namibian president not to hail from the Oshiwambo-speaking majority.

The small white minority owns just under half of Namibia's arable land, and redistribution of property has been slow despite efforts to accelerate the process. In October 2012, Pohamba warned that unequal land distribution could become a threat to political stability.

Political Rights and Civil Liberties: Namibia is an electoral democracy. The bicameral legislature consists of the 26-seat National Council, whose members are appointed by regional councils for six-year terms, and the 72-seat National Assembly, whose members are popularly elected for five-year terms using party-list proportional representation. The president, who is directly elected for five-year terms, appoints the prime minister and cabinet.

SWAPO has dominated since independence. Significant opposition parties include the RDP, the Congress of Democrats, the Democratic Turnhalle Alliance, and the United Democratic Front. Since the RDP's formation, its supporters have been subject to harassment and intimidation by SWAPO members, who occasionally disrupt RDP rallies despite calls by police to disperse. While these problems have subsided somewhat in recent years, the RDP experienced some difficulty in holding rallies before the 2009 elections.

Although President Hifikepunye Pohamba has made anticorruption efforts a major theme of his presidency, official corruption remains a problem, and investigations of major cases proceed slowly. The Anti-Corruption Commission has considerable autonomy, as it reports only to the National Assembly, though it lacks prosecutorial authority. A major scandal surfaced in July 2010 over a scam that cost the Government Institutions Pension Fund N$660 million (approximately US$90 million) between 1994 and 2002. Following a forensic audit by the Office of the Auditor General, the Namibian police did not start an official investigation until January 2012, and said in October that the investigation, which cost N$6 million (US$680,000), was not expected to conclude until 2013. Namibia was ranked 58 out of 176 countries surveyed in Transparency International's 2012 Corruption Perceptions Index, and sixth overall in the 2012 Ibrahim Index of African Governance.

The constitution guarantees free speech, and Namibia's media have generally enjoyed a relatively open environment. However, government and party leaders at times issue harsh criticism and even threats against the independent press, usually in the wake of unflattering stories. While many insist that the state-owned NBC has been free to criticize the government, concerns have increased about excessive government influence over programming and personnel. In August 2011, a 10-year ban on government advertising in the daily *Namibian* was lifted; the ban had been imposed by former president Sam Nujoma, who alleged that the paper was biased against the government. In November 2012, a Windhoek High Court judge dismissed a N$300,000 (US$37,000) defamation claim filed by a former Walvis Bay municipal official against the *Namibian*. Many publications and organizations have websites that are critical of the government. The 2009 Communications Act raised concerns about privacy rights on the internet, as it allows the government to monitor telephone calls, e-mail, and internet usage without a warrant.

Freedom of religion is guaranteed and respected in practice. The government has in the past been accused of pressuring academics to withhold criticism of SWAPO, though there were no such reports in 2012.

Freedoms of assembly and association are guaranteed by law and permitted in practice, except in situations of national emergency. The government generally tolerated the RDP's peaceful protests near the Supreme Court building in 2012, though the protesters were ordered to move 500 meters away from the court. Human rights groups generally operate without interference, but government ministers have threatened and harassed nongovernmental organizations and their leadership in the past. Constitutionally guaranteed union rights are respected. However, essential public sector workers do not have the right to strike. Collective bargaining is not widely practiced outside the mining, construction, agriculture, and public service industries. The main umbrella union, the National Union of Namibian Workers, is affiliated with SWAPO and played a role in selecting the new party leaders.

The constitution provides for an independent judiciary, and the separation of powers is observed in practice. Access to justice, however, is obstructed by economic and geographic barriers, a shortage of public defenders, and delays caused by a lack of capacity in the court system, especially at lower levels. Traditional courts in rural areas have often ignored constitutional procedures. However, legislation to create greater uniformity in traditional court operations and better connect them to the formal judicial system was implemented in 2009. Allegations of police brutality persist. Conditions in prisons are improving, though overcrowding remains a problem.

Minority ethnic groups have claimed that the government favors the majority Ovambo—which also dominates SWAPO—in allocating funding and services. A colonial-era law prohibits homosexual relations between men, but the law is generally not enforced. However, members of the LGBT (lesbian, gay, bisexual, and transgender) community report that they continue to suffer discrimination and persecution, including negative rhetoric by some public officials and discrimination in employment.

Women continue to face discrimination in customary law and other traditional societal practices. Widows and orphans have been stripped of their land, livestock, and other assets in rural areas. Lack of awareness of legal rights as well as informal practices have undermined the success of legal changes. Violence against women is reportedly widespread, and rights groups have criticized the government's failure to enforce the country's progressive domestic violence laws. According to the U.S. State Department's 2012 Trafficking in Persons Report, Namibia serves as a source, transit, and destination country for human trafficking for forced labor and prostitution, and it was placed on the Tier 2 Watch List due to its failure to take legal action against offenders.

Namibia's HIV infection rate, though extremely high—13.1 percent in 2009— is much lower than its southern African neighbors. In July 2012, Namibia's High Court ruled in favor of three HIV-positive women who alleged that they had been coerced by workers at government-run hospitals into agreeing to undergo sterilization while they were delivering their babies via caesarian sections, though the court found that there was not enough evidence to prove that they had been coerced due to their HIV status.

Nauru

Political Rights: 1
Civil Liberties: 1
Status: Free

Population: 10,200
Capital: Yaren

Ten-Year Ratings Timeline For Year Under Review (Political Rights, Civil Liberties, Status)

2003	2004	2005	2006	2007	2008	2009	2010	2011	2012
1,1PF	1,1F	1,1F	1,1F	1,1F	1,1F	1,1F	1,1F	1,1F	1,1F

Overview: In September 2012, Nauru reopened a refugee detention and processing center for Australia, where harsh living conditions and delays in the processing of refugee claims led to protests and hunger strikes by asylum seekers. Also during the year, President Sprent Dabwido failed to secure passage of constitutional reforms to break political gridlock and increase stability.

Nauru, an eight-square-mile island in the South Pacific, is the world's smallest republic. It was a German protectorate from 1888 until Australian troops seized it during World War I. The League of Nations granted a joint mandate to Australia, Britain, and New Zealand to govern the island in 1919. Japan occupied Nauru during World War II, and in 1947, the United Nations designated it as a trust territory under Australia. Nauru gained independence in 1968 and joined the United Nations in 1999.

Nauru's once-plentiful supply of phosphate, mined by Australia for use as fertilizer, is almost exhausted. Mining has made more than 80 percent of the island uninhabitable, and the government has squandered much of its accumulated wealth through financial mismanagement. The country currently carries a large foreign debt, and climate change and rising sea levels threaten its survival.

With few viable methods of generating income, Nauru relies heavily on foreign development assistance. In 2011, Nauru engaged in talks with aid donors, including the Asian Development Bank, Australia, and New Zealand, about the creation of a new trust fund, with stricter rules on how funds may be accessed, to better secure the long-term needs of its citizens. Nauru has secured considerable aid from China and Taiwan by switching diplomatic recognition between the two rivals.

Between 2001 and 2008, in exchange for rent and aid, Nauru hosted a refugee detention and processing center for Australia. The center was criticized for holding refugees for years while they awaited processing; it closed in 2009, which cost Nauru approximately one-fifth of its gross domestic product. In May 2011, Nauru offered Australia renewed access to the center. Australia initially declined, citing Nauru's failure to sign the United Nations Refugee Convention. However, Nauru signed the convention in June, and the center officially reopened in September 2012. Australia promised Nauru millions of dollars to renovate the center, in addition to rent payments and other assistance. By October, nearly 400 asylum seekers were transferred from an Australian holding center on Christmas Island to the facility in Nauru, where poor living conditions sparked protests and even suicide attempts by asylum seekers. Some 300 detainees went on hunger strike in November over long delays in the processing of their refugee claims. In December, one hunger striker was evacuated to Australia for medical treatment and was subsequently returned to Nauru.

Intense political rivalries and the use of no-confidence votes have been a source of political instability. Several changes of government occurred between 2007 and 2011, with none lasting longer than a year, and the shortest lasting only days. President Sprent Dabwido, elected in November 2011, made constitutional reforms to increase political stability a priority. In January 2012, he pushed for reforms that included increasing the number of seats in Parliament to 19 to prevent legislative stalemates, selecting the speaker from outside of Parliament, adopting a code of conduct for lawmakers, establishing an Ombudsman Commission, and strengthening the Audit Department. After Parliament rejected the bill three times, Dabwido replaced his entire cabinet in June with the hope of building support for his reforms.

Political Rights and Civil Liberties: Nauru is an electoral democracy. The 18-member unicameral Parliament is popularly elected from 14 constituencies for three-year terms. Parliament chooses the president and vice president from among its members. Political parties include the Nauru First Party, the Democratic Party, and the Center Party, but many politicians are independents.

Corruption is a serious problem in Nauru. In 2011, President Marcus Stephen resigned amid allegations that he had accepted bribes from an Australian phosphate company.

The government does not restrict or censor the news media. There are several local weekly and monthly publications; foreign dailies, mostly in English, are widely available. The government publishes occasional bulletins, and the opposition publishes its own newsletters. Radio Nauru and Nauru TV, which are owned and operated by the government, broadcast content from Australia, New Zealand, and other international sources. There are no formal restrictions on internet usage.

The constitution provides for freedom of religion, which the government generally respects in practice. There have been no reports of government suppression of academic freedom.

The government respects freedoms of assembly and association. There are several advocacy groups for women, as well as development-focused and religious organizations. There are no trade unions or labor protection laws, partly because there is little large-scale, private employment.

The judiciary is independent, and defendants generally receive fair trials and representation. The Supreme Court is the highest authority on constitutional issues. Appeals in civil and criminal cases can be lodged with the high court of Australia. Traditional reconciliation mechanisms, rather than the formal legal process, are frequently used, typically by choice but sometimes under communal pressure. A civilian official controls the 100-person police force, and there have been few reported cases of abuse. Nauru has no armed forces; Australia provides defense assistance under an informal agreement.

Societal pressures limit women's ability to exercise their legal rights. No women currently serve in Parliament. Sexual harassment is a crime, but spousal rape is not. Domestic violence is frequently associated with alcohol abuse. In late 2011, Nauru pledged to decriminalize homosexuality—male homosexuality is punishable with 14 years of prison at hard labor—after a UN human rights audit, although there had been no legislative action on the issue by the end of 2012.

Nepal

Political Rights: 4
Civil Liberties: 4
Status: Partly Free

Population: 30,918,000
Capital: Kathmandu

Ten-Year Ratings Timeline For Year Under Review (Political Rights, Civil Liberties, Status)

2003	2004	2005	2006	2007	2008	2009	2010	2011	2012
5,4PF	5,5PF	6,5NF	5,4PF	5,4PF	4,4PF	4,4PF	4,4PF	4,4PF	4,4PF

Overview:
Nepal's Constituent Assembly missed yet another deadline to write a constitution in 2012, and it was forced to dissolve when its mandate expired in May. However, fresh elections had still not been held at year's end, as the main political parties disagreed over who should govern in a caretaker capacity during the balloting. Meanwhile, human rights groups protested an ordinance proposed by the government in August that would allow amnesty for many of the most serious abuses during the country's long civil war.

King Prithvi Narayan Shah unified the Himalayan state of Nepal in 1769. Following two centuries of palace rule, the left-leaning Nepali Congress (NC) party won the country's first elections in 1959. King Mahendra abruptly dissolved Parliament and banned political parties in 1960, and in 1962 he began ruling through a repressive panchayat (village council) system. Many parties went underground until early 1990, when the Jan Andolan (Peoples' Movement) organized prodemocracy rallies that led King Birendra to establish parliamentary democracy.

In Nepal's first multiparty elections in 32 years, Girija Prasad Koirala, a veteran dissident, led the NC to victory and formed a government in 1991. Torn by intraparty conflicts, the NC was forced in 1994 to call early elections. The Communist Party of Nepal/United Marxist-Leninist, or CPN-UML, won a plurality in Parliament, but it failed to build a stable governing majority. Separately, the more militant Communist Party of Nepal (Maoist) launched a guerrilla insurgency in 1996, leading to a decade-long civil conflict that ultimately claimed some 12,800 lives. Hopes for a more stable government rose after the NC won a majority in 1999 elections.

In June 2001, King Birendra's brother Gyanendra took the throne after a palace incident in which the crown prince apparently shot and killed Birendra and nine other members of the royal family before killing himself. Gyanendra declared a state of emergency in November, and for the next several years, he ruled without Parliament. Moreover, he presided over a sharp escalation in the civil conflict.

By 2005, Gyanendra's government was cracking down on political dissent and shuttering numerous media outlets and other means of communication. A seven-party alliance (SPA) of mainstream political factions entered into talks with the Maoists, yielding an agreement that called for the restoration of democracy. Facing prodemocracy protests by hundreds of thousands of people, Gyanendra in April 2006 agreed to the provisions of the SPA-Maoist pact. The restored Parliament quickly removed most of the king's powers, and the SPA announced plans to elect a Constituent Assembly (CA) that would write a new constitution.

The SPA and Maoists concluded a Comprehensive Peace Agreement (CPA) in November 2006, stipulating that the Maoists would place their weapons under UN monitoring, confine their fighters to camps, disband their parallel government, and join a new interim government alongside members of the existing Parliament. In January 2007, an interim constitution was promulgated.

After a series of delays, CA elections were finally held in April 2008, and international observers deemed them generally free and fair, with few incidents of violence on election day. However, the campaign period was marred by regular attacks on candidates and campaign workers. The Maoists won 220 of the 601 seats. Their nearest rival was the NC (110 seats), followed by the CPN-UML (103 seats); the Madhesi People's Rights Forum (52 seats), a party aiming to represent residents of the country's southern plains region; and a range of smaller parties and independents. The CA quickly voted to replace the monarchy with a republican system, and in July it chose the NC's Ram Baran Yadav as president. Maoist leader Prachanda was elected prime minister in August, and the Maoists formed a coalition government.

Frustrated by the military's resistance to integration with former Maoist fighters, Prachanda in May 2009 ordered the firing of army chief Rookmangud Katawal. However, the move drew objections from other parties, and the president, who technically controlled such decisions, ultimately rejected the dismissal. Prachanda resigned, and a new government led by the CPN-UML was formed. The Maoists subsequently mounted frequent protests and physically blockaded the CA for a time.

Continued partisan disagreement contributed to Prime Minister Madhav Kumar Nepal's decision to resign in June 2010. After months of negotiations, the CA finally chose Jhalanath Khanal of the CPN-UML as the new prime minister in February 2011. He, too, was forced from office in August, as the major parties failed to make any progress in drafting a permanent constitution. Maoist candidate Baburam Bhattarai was chosen to lead a new coalition government.

Efforts to draft a constitution in early 2012 foundered on disputes over whether the country should assume a more federal structure, with different ethnic groups having provinces of their own. Bhattarai sought to extend the CA's mandate—originally two years—yet again, but the Supreme Court rejected the move in May, ruling that any further extensions would be illegal. The CA was consequently dissolved, and Bhattarai called new elections for November. Rival parties objected to the idea that Bhattarai's caretaker government would oversee the balloting, however, and no agreement on a framework for elections had been reached by year's end.

Political Rights and Civil Liberties: Nepal is not an electoral democracy. The CA elections held in April 2008 were found by a European Union observation team to be "generally organized in a professional and transparent manner." However, the observers noted that the preelection period did not fully meet international standards due to restrictions on freedoms of assembly, movement, and expression.

The government is operating under a 2007 interim constitution. In addition to its task of writing a permanent constitution, the 601-seat CA serves as the interim legislature. Members were selected through a mixed system of first-past-the-post constituency races (240 seats), proportional representation (335 seats), and appointments by the cabinet (26 seats). Both the president and the prime minister are elected by a majority of the CA.

Unlike the 1990 constitution, the interim constitution has no limitation on parties formed along ethnic lines. A third of the seats in the CA are reserved for women, and substantial allocations are also made for Madhesis, Dalits, and other minority groups.

The CA repeatedly extended its initial two-year mandate after May 2010, but by the end of 2012, it had still not passed a permanent constitution. It was forced to dissolve that month, leaving government in the hands of a caretaker administration until elections could be held. The outgoing CA made little progress on finalizing the peace process and reintegrating former fighters into society. These and other unresolved problems, including proposals for an amnesty covering even the most severe human rights abuses committed during the civil war, have led to considerable political instability. Since 2008, Nepal has had five different prime ministers.

Corruption is endemic in Nepali politics and government. While the Commission for the Investigation of Abuse of Authority is active, high-level officials are rarely prosecuted. Many members of the legislature have been accused or convicted of corruption in the past. Graft is particularly prevalent in the judiciary, with frequent payoffs to judges for favorable rulings, and in the police force, which has been accused of extensive involvement in organized crime. Nepal was ranked 139 out of 176 countries surveyed in Transparency International's 2012 Corruption Perceptions Index.

The interim constitution provides for press freedom and specifically prohibits censorship, although these rules can be suspended during an emergency. Many restrictions on the press were lifted after Parliament was restored in 2006. However, media workers frequently face physical attacks, death threats, and harassment by armed groups, security personnel, and political cadres, and the perpetrators typically go unpunished. Throughout 2012, supporters of political parties attacked journalists who wrote critical pieces about their organizations and leaders. The government maintains control of both the influential Radio Nepal, whose coverage is supportive of official policies, and the country's main television station. However, there is a variety of independent radio and print outlets. Some have come to show a strong bias toward the Maoists, partly due to intimidation, but other outlets are critical of the party.

The interim constitution identifies Nepal as a secular state, signaling a break with the Hindu monarchy. Religious tolerance is broadly practiced, but proselytizing is prohibited, and members of some religious minorities occasionally report official harassment. Christian groups have considerable difficulty registering as religious organizations, leaving them unable to own land.

The government does not restrict academic freedom. However, Maoist strikes have repeatedly threatened the school system, and a 2011 report by Human Rights Watch charged that Nepal had largely ignored the right to education of poor and disabled children. Minorities, including Hindi- and Urdu-speaking Madhesi groups, have complained at having Nepali enforced as the language of education in government schools.

Freedom of assembly is guaranteed under the interim constitution. While security forces have allowed large protests by Maoists and other political parties, Tibetan protests have been violently suppressed in recent years. In certain cases, authorities have detained Tibetan and Nepali monks and pressured them to sign pledges not to participate in future protests.

Nongovernmental organizations (NGOs) played an active role in the movement to restore democracy in 2006, and restrictions on NGO activity imposed by the king in 2005 were lifted under the interim regime. However, Maoist cadres and the affiliated Young Communist League (YCL) have at times threatened or disrupted the activities of NGOs. Groups working on Tibetan issues in Nepal report increasing intimidation by security forces due to pressure from China, a major donor of both military and nonmilitary aid to Nepal.

Labor laws provide for the freedom to bargain collectively, and unions generally operate without state interference. A draconian labor ordinance put in place by the king's government was repealed in 2006, and restrictions on civil service members forming unions were lifted. Workers in a broad range of "essential" industries cannot stage strikes, and 60 percent of a union's membership must vote in favor of a strike for it to be legal. Bonded labor is illegal but remains a problem. Similarly, the legal minimum age for employment is 14 years, but over two million children are believed to be engaged in various forms of labor, often under hazardous conditions.

The constitution provides for an independent judiciary, but most courts suffer from endemic corruption, and many Nepalese have only limited access to justice. Rights groups in 2012 raised concerns that the government was trying to pass legislation that would make more judges political appointees, further reducing judicial independence. Because of heavy case backlogs and a slow appeals process, suspects are frequently kept in pretrial detention for periods longer than any sentences they would face if tried and convicted.

Prison conditions are poor, with overcrowding and inadequate sanitation and medical care. The government generally has refused to conduct thorough investigations or take serious disciplinary measures against police officers accused of brutality or torture. A leading Nepali group monitoring torture, the Centre for Victims of Torture, found that 74 percent of respondents in a survey conducted by the organization said that they had been tortured while in custody. The group reported that the use of torture by police declined slightly in 2012 compared with 2011. Separately, in September 2012, rights organizations were unsuccessful in their calls on the government to halt the promotion of Kuber Singh Rana to inspector general of police due to his alleged involvement in human rights abuses during the civil war period.

Human rights groups have argued that no one has been punished for abuses during the decade-long civil war, in part because of the weakness of the judiciary and a prevailing climate of impunity. Several political parties, including the Maoists, concluded an agreement in mid-2011 stating that anyone who committed abuses during the civil war would receive an amnesty; the government in August 2012 proposed the establishment of a politically appointed commission to serve as the mechanism for issuing such amnesties. However, no such measure had been enacted by the end of 2012.

A 2007 civil service law reserves 45 percent of posts for women, minorities, and Dalits, but their representation in state institutions remains inadequate, particularly at the highest levels of government. Members of the Hindu upper castes continue to dominate government and business, and low-caste Hindus, ethnic minorities, and Christians face discrimination in the civil service and courts. Despite constitutional protections and the May 2012 passage of the Caste-based Discrimination and Untouchability (Offense and Punishment) Act, which prohibits discrimination against Dalits and increases punishments for public officials found responsible of discrimination, Dalits continue to be subjected to exploitation, violence, and social exclusion. Separately, due to pressure from China, Tibetans fleeing to Nepal on their way to India in recent years have been detained and in some cases pushed back across the border by Nepali police, though such actions do not reflect official Nepali policy.

Madhesis, plains-dwelling people with close connections to groups across the border in India, comprise 35 to 50 percent of Nepal's population, but they are underrepresented in politics, receive comparatively little economic support from the government, and—until an amendment to the citizenship law in 2006—had difficulty acquiring formal citizenship due to Nepali language requirements. In recent years, the Madhesi People's Rights Forum has organized armed cadres and mounted general strikes and protests to bolster their demands for regional autonomy and other goals, especially in the context of the drafting of the permanent constitution. Combined with attacks by more radical Madhesi groups, such activities have triggered curfews and increased violence from the state.

In 2007, the Supreme Court ordered the government to abolish all laws that discriminate against LGBT (lesbian, gay, bisexual, and transgender) people, and in 2008 it gave its consent to same-sex marriage. The government has yet to implement these rulings, though citizens can now obtain third-gender identity documents. LGBT people reportedly face harassment by the authorities and other citizens, particularly in rural areas.

Forcible evictions to make way for development projects has become a problem. In May 2012, human rights organizations warned that the Kathmandu police had begun forcibly removing residents of settlements along the Bagmati River to make way for a planned urban development project.

Women rarely receive the same educational and employment opportunities as men, and domestic violence against women continues to be a major problem. The 2009 Domestic Violence Act provides for monetary compensation and psychological treatment for victims, but authorities generally do not prosecute domestic violence cases. The commission charged with providing reparations to women subjected to gender-based violence has also been severely criticized for nonimplementation of its mandate and for politicized distribution of resources. Trafficking of young women from Nepal for prostitution in India is common. According to Human Rights Watch, kidnapping gangs have become rampant in recent years, abducting children to obtain small ransoms. Police rarely intervene in the kidnappings. Underage marriage of girls is widespread, particularly among lower-status groups.

Netherlands

Political Rights: 1
Civil Liberties: 1
Status: Free

Population: 16,749,000
Capital: Amsterdam

Ten-Year Ratings Timeline For Year Under Review (Political Rights, Civil Liberties, Status)

2003	2004	2005	2006	2007	2008	2009	2010	2011	2012
1,1F	1,1F	1,1F	1,1F	1,1F	1,1F	1,1F	1,1F	1,1F	1,1F

Overview: The coalition government collapsed in April 2012, when right-wing politician Geert Wilders withdrew his party's support for an austerity budget. Prime Minister Mark Rutte led his center-right VVD party to a first-place finish in the September general election. Rutte struck a coalition deal with the Labor Party in October, reaching agreement on further budget cuts to reduce the deficit.

After the Dutch won their independence from Spain in the 16th century, the princely House of Orange assumed the leadership of the Dutch Republic, which later became the Republic of the United Netherlands. Following a brief period of rule by Napoleonic France, the Kingdom of the Netherlands emerged in the 19th century as a constitutional monarchy with a representative government. The Netherlands remained neutral in both world wars, though the 1940 invasion by Nazi Germany influenced the country to join NATO in 1949. In 1952, it became a founding member of the European Coal and Steel Community, a precursor to the European Union (EU).

In May 2002, right-wing politician Pim Fortuyn was murdered a few days before general elections. His newly formed party, the Pim Fortuyn List (LPF), had been running on an anti-immigrant platform, returning issues of immigrant integration to the forefront of Dutch politics. Following the elections, a new coalition—consisting of the center-right Christian Democratic Appeal party (CDA), the far-right populist LPF, and the center-right People's Party for Freedom and Democracy (VVD)—took office in July, only to collapse that October due to party infighting. The CDA narrowly won ensuing elections in January 2003, and subsequently formed a center-right coalition government with the VVD and the smaller Democrats-66 (D66) party.

In May 2006, immigration and integration minister Rita Verdonk moved to annul the citizenship of a fellow VVD member of parliament, the Somali-born Ayaan Hirsi Ali, after it was discovered that Hirsi Ali had lied in her 1992 asylum application. Hirsi Ali had received death threats for being an outspoken critic of Islam and for a film made in collaboration with controversial filmmaker Theo Van Gogh, who was killed by a radical Islamist in 2004. D66 quit the government over the handling of the incident, causing the coalition to collapse in June 2006.

The CDA won the November 2006 elections and formed a centrist coalition government with the Labor Party (PvdA) and the conservative Christian Union party in February 2007. The CDA's Jan-Peter Balkenende continued as prime minister. The coalition government included the country's first Muslim cabinet ministers and marked the Christian Union's debut in government. The LPF later disbanded.

Elections were held again in June 2010 following the collapse of the CDA-led government in February. The VVD finished first with 31 seats, while Geert Wilder's right-wing Party for Freedom (PVV) won 24 seats, nearly tripling the number of votes it received in 2006. The VVD and the CDA formed a coalition, but lacked a parliamentary majority. The PVV was not included in the government but pledged to give it voting support. In exchange, the new government backed several anti-immigration initiatives endorsed by the PVV. Mark Rutte of the VVD became prime minister, with his party leading the government for the first time.

The government collapsed in April 2012, after Wilders rejected proposed budget austerity measures as too severe. In the September general election, Rutte led the VVD to first place, winning 41 seats, while the PvdA took 38 seats. The PVV, which campaigned for leaving the EU and the euro, dropped to 15 seats. The Socialist Party also captured 15 seats, and the CDA fell to fifth place, with 13 seats. Six other parties took the remaining 28 seats.

In October, Rutte and Labor Party leader Diederik Samsom announced a coalition agreement following 47 days of talks. The deal called for budget cuts of 16 billion euros (US$25 billion) over the next four years. Among the austerity measures was a ban on income assistance for immigrants who could not speak Dutch. Rutte and his new government were sworn in by the queen in November.

Political Rights and Civil Liberties: The Netherlands is an electoral democracy. The 150-member lower house of parliament, or Second Chamber, is elected every four years by proportional representation. The 75-member upper house, or First Chamber, is elected for four-year terms by the country's provincial councils. Foreigners residing in the country for five years or more are eligible to vote in local elections. The Netherlands extended voting rights to Aruba and the Netherlands Antilles for the first time in the June 2009 European Parliament elections.

The leader of the majority party or coalition is usually appointed prime minister by the monarch, currently Queen Beatrix. Mayors are appointed from a list of candidates submitted by the municipal councils. The monarch appoints the Council of Ministers (cabinet) and the governor of each province on the recommendation of the majority in parliament.

The country has few problems with political corruption. The Netherlands was ranked 9 out of 176 countries surveyed in Transparency International's 2012 Corruption Perceptions Index.

The news media are free and independent. The 1881 lèse majesté laws restricting defamation of the monarch are rarely enforced. In June 2011, PVV leader Geert Wilders was acquitted on charges of discrimination and inciting hatred of Muslims through his editorials and his film *Fitna*; the court ruled that Wilders's comments were part of public debate and were not a direct call for violence.

The constitution guarantees freedom of religion. Religious organizations that provide educational facilities can receive subsidies from the government. Members of the country's Muslim community have encountered increased hostility in recent years, including harassment and verbal abuse, as well as vandalism and arson attacks on mosques. The government requires all imams and other spiritual leaders recruited from Muslim countries to take a one-year integration course before practicing in the Netherlands. In September 2011, the cabinet introduced a ban on clothing that covers the face, imposing a maximum fine of 380 euros (US$460) for the first violation. However, the measure did not come to a vote in parliament and was shelved after the Wilders-backed government fell in 2012. The VVD-PvdA October 2012 coalition agreement called for a ban on face-covering clothing in public settings, including schools, hospitals, public transportation, and government buildings, and for withholding social security benefits from people who wore such garments. The government does not restrict academic freedom.

Freedoms of assembly and association are respected in law and in practice. National and international human rights organizations operate freely without government intervention. Workers have the right to organize, bargain collectively, and strike. Teachers at 2,000 schools went on strike in March 2012 to protest budget cuts.

The judiciary is independent, and the rule of law prevails in civil and criminal matters. The police are under civilian control, and prison conditions meet international standards. The population is generally treated equally under the law, although human rights groups have criticized the country's asylum policies for being unduly harsh and violating international standards. The CDA proposed a bill in 2011 that would allow underage asylum seekers to receive residence permits if they have been in the country for eight years or more due to delays in their applications. In December 2012, the government announced that it would propose legislation to criminalize living in the country without permission, with illegal residency punishable by fines and an entry ban of up to five years. Requirements for passing the integration exam became more stringent in 2011, while failure to pass would result in revocation of one's residence permit. The October 2012 coalition agreement called for granting residency to children who had been in the country for more than five years, as well as their relatives.

In 2001, the Netherlands became the first country in the world to legalize same-sex marriage. In November 2011, a Dutch court ruled in favor of a gay teacher who had been fired by a Christian school because he was living with another man, clarifying a law that schools may not dismiss teachers on the basis of their sexual orientation.

In April 2010, the Dutch high court ruled that the Calvinist political party, which holds three seats in parliament, must allow women to run on the party's ballot; the party believes women should not have the right to vote, and has fielded only male candidates. In 2012, the European Court of Human Rights dismissed the party's appeal against the ruling. The Netherlands is a destination and transit point for human trafficking, particularly in women and girls for sexual exploitation. A 2005 law expanded the legal definition of trafficking to include forced labor and increased the maximum penalty for convicted offenders. Prostitution is legal and regulated in the Netherlands, though links between prostitution and organized crime have been reported.

New Zealand

Political Rights: 1
Civil Liberties: 1
Status: Free

Population: 4,437,000
Capital: Wellington

Ten-Year Ratings Timeline For Year Under Review (Political Rights, Civil Liberties, Status)

2003	2004	2005	2006	2007	2008	2009	2010	2011	2012
1,1F	1,1F	1,1F	1,1F	1,1F	1,1F	1,1F	1,1F	1,1F	1,1F

Overview: The government introduced controversial changes to New Zealand's immigration laws in 2012, giving preference to higher-income applicants, allowing the detention of mass arrivals of refugees for up to six months during processing, and restricting the rights of detainees to judicial review. Although the reforms were criticized as being discriminatory, the government insisted they were necessary to attract more skilled immigrants, reduce taxpayer expenditures, and deter human traffickers.

British sovereignty in New Zealand was established in 1840 under the Treaty of Waitangi, a pact between the British government and Maori chiefs that also guaranteed Maori land rights. New Zealand gained full independence from Britain in 1947, though the British monarch remained head of state.

Prime Minister Helen Clark dissolved Parliament in October 2008 and called snap elections in November. John Key's center-right National Party, which took 58 seats, also garnered support from the Maori Party (5 seats), the ACT New Zealand Party (5 seats), and the United Future Party (1 seat). The Labour Party—which had been in office since 1999—captured 43 seats. Key became prime minister.

The rights and welfare of the Maori population are major issues in New Zealand politics. In the first official designation of intellectual property protection for the Maori, the government in 2009 officially acknowledged that the war dance (haka) performed by the national rugby team belonged to the Ngati Toa tribe. Although the tribe will not be awarded royalty claims, it can address grievances over inappropriate use of the haka. In addition, the government agreed to pay $111 million in compensation—including both rent payments from state-owned forests and greenhouse gas emission credits—to eight tribes as a comprehensive settlement for grievances over land seizures and other breaches of the Treaty of Waitangi. In 2010, the government signed a new agreement with the Maori over contentious foreshore and seabed rights, replacing a 2006 deal that had ended Maori rights to claim customary title in courts of law. Tribes can now claim customary title to areas proven to have been under continuous indigenous occupation since 1840.

In 2010, New Zealand restored full bilateral defense ties with the United States, which marked a significant change in the country's defense and security policies. The United States had ended its previous treaty obligations with New Zealand in 1986, after New Zealand banned nuclear weapons from its ports, a restriction that still stands.

Two disasters struck New Zealand in 2011. In February, a major earthquake hit Christchurch, killing more than 180 people and leaving thousands injured and homeless. Rescue and recovery costs prompted the government to impose major spending cuts to limit an expected budget deficit. In October, a cargo ship ran aground on a coral reef near the North Island port of Tauranga, spilling at least 70 containers of oil and hazardous materials into the water.

In the November 2011 legislative elections, the National Party took 59 seats, and the Labour Party captured 34 seats. Key secured a second term as prime minister by forming a coalition government with the ACT New Zealand Party and the United Future Party.

In 2012, the government introduced controversial revisions to its immigration laws. The changes would allow the government to detain mass arrivals under a group warrant for a period of up to six months for processing. Detainees would have limited rights to judicial review, and family reunifications would be limited for those granted refugee status. While the government maintains that the changes are necessary to deter mass arrivals of asylum seekers and make New Zealand a less attractive destination for human smugglers and traffickers, critics charge that the proposals are xenophobic and unnecessary and run counter to the country's obligations under the United Nations Refugee Convention; New Zealand annually accepts 750 refugees for resettlement through the United Nations High Commissioner for Refugees, and also considers claims from asylum seekers when they arrive in New Zealand. In addition, processing under the new rules would favor those with higher incomes, which the government insists will save taxpayers money and attract more skilled talent to settle in New Zealand. The proposed changes had not been enacted by year's end.

Political Rights and Civil Liberties: New Zealand is an electoral democracy. A mixed-member electoral system combines voting in geographic districts with proportional representation balloting. As a member of the Commonwealth, a governor-general represents Britain's Queen Elizabeth II as the ceremonial head of state. The prime minister, the head of government, is the leader of the majority party or coalition and is appointed by the governor-general. In 2011, Jerry Mateparae, a former military chief and head of the intelligence agency, was named governor-general, becoming the second Maori to hold this ceremonial post. The unicameral Parliament, or House of Representatives, has 121 members who are elected to three-year terms.

The two main political parties are the center-left Labour Party and the center-right National Party. Smaller parties include the Maori Party, the ACT New Zealand Party, and the United Future Party. Seven of Parliament's constituency seats are reserved for the native Maori population. The Maori Party, the country's first ethnic party, was formed in 2004 to advance Maori rights and interests.

New Zealand is one of the least corrupt countries in the world. It was tied with Finland and Denmark for first place out of 176 countries surveyed in Transparency International's 2012 Corruption Perceptions Index.

The media are free and competitive. Newspapers are published nationally and locally in English and in other languages for the growing immigrant population. Television outlets include the state-run Television New Zealand, three private channels, and a Maori-language public network. There is also a Maori-language radio station. The New Zealand Press Association (NZPA), which once dominated the distribution of domestic and world news to New Zealand media outlets, closed in 2011 as a result of competition from internet-based news sources and the dominance of Australian newspaper chains, which did not use the NZPA's services. The government does not control or censor internet access, and competitive pricing promotes large-scale diffusion.

Freedom of religion is provided by law and respected in practice. Only religious organizations that collect donations need to register with the government. Although New Zealand is a secular state, the government has fined businesses for operating on the official holidays of Christmas Day, Good Friday, and Easter Sunday. A 2001 law grants exemptions to several categories of stores in response to demands from non-Christian populations. Academic freedom is enjoyed at all levels of instruction.

The government respects freedoms of assembly and association. Nongovernmental organizations are active throughout the country, and many receive considerable financial support from the government. In 2011, protesters disrupted oil and gas exploration conducted by Brazil's state-owned energy company Petrobas off the North Island, claiming that development would threaten marine wildlife and coastal environments. The New Zealand Council of Trade Unions is the main labor federation. Fewer than 20 percent of the country's wage earners are union members. Under the 2001 Employment Relations Act, workers can organize, strike, and bargain collectively, with the exception of uniformed personnel.

The judiciary is independent, and defendants can appeal to the Privy Council in London. Prison conditions generally meet international standards, though there have been allegations of discrimination against the Maori, who make up more than half of the prison population. Over the past decade, the police have introduced training to better deal with an increasingly racially and culturally diverse population.

Approximately 15 percent of the country's 4.4 million people identify themselves as Maori. Although no laws explicitly discriminate against the Maori and their living standards have generally improved, most Maori and Pacific Islanders continue to lag behind the European-descended majority in social and economic status. The Maori population has become more assertive in its claims for land, resources, and compensation from the government. A special permanent commission hears Maori tribal claims tied to the Treaty of Waitangi.

Violence against women and children remains a significant problem, particularly among the Maori and Pacific Islander populations. Many governmental and nongovernmental programs work to prevent domestic violence and support victims, with special programs for the Maori community. A 2007 law banning the spanking of children remains controversial because it gives police the authority to determine whether a parent should be charged with abuse. A majority of voters rejected the law in a nonbinding referendum in 2009, but the government has kept it in place. The 2005 Civil Union Bill grants same-sex partnerships recognition and legal rights similar to those of married couples.

Nicaragua

Political Rights: 5
Civil Liberties: 4
Status: Partly Free

Population: 5,955,000
Capital: Managua

Ten-Year Ratings Timeline For Year Under Review (Political Rights, Civil Liberties, Status)

2003	2004	2005	2006	2007	2008	2009	2010	2011	2012
3,3PF	3,3PF	3,3PF	3,3PF	3,3PF	4,3PF	4,4PF	4,4PF	5,4PF	5,4PF

Overview: President Daniel Ortega and his party, the Sandanista National Liberation Front (FSLN), continued to consolidate power in 2012, with an overwhelming victory in the November municipal elections giving the FSLN near complete dominance over most of the country's institutions. Serious concerns remained about the politicization of institutions, particularly the Supreme Electoral Council. Meanwhile, the Comprehensive Law Against Violence Toward Women went into effect in June.

The independent Republic of Nicaragua was established in 1838, 17 years after the end of Spanish rule. Its subsequent history has been marked by internal strife and dictatorship. The Sandinista National Liberation Front (FSLN), a leftist rebel group, overthrew the authoritarian regime of the Somoza family in 1979. The FSLN then moved to establish a left-wing government, leading to a civil war. The United States intervened, in part by supporting irregular rebel forces known as the contras.

In 1990, National Opposition Union presidential candidate Violeta Chamorro defeated the FSLN's Daniel Ortega in free and open elections, leading to a peaceful transfer of power. Before leaving office, however, the Sandinistas revised laws and sold off state property to party leaders, ensuring that they would retain political and economic clout.

Former Managua mayor Arnoldo Alemán of the Liberal Constitutionalist Party (PLC) defeated Ortega in the 1996 presidential election, but he was accused of corruption throughout his ensuing presidency. In 1999, the PLC and FSLN agreed to a governing pact that guaranteed Alemán a seat in both the Nicaraguan and the Central American parliaments, ensuring him immunity from prosecution. It also included reforms that lowered the vote threshold for winning an election without a runoff from 45 to 40 percent (or 35 percent if the winner had a lead of five percentage points). Using their combined bloc in the legislature, the two parties solidified their control over the Supreme Court and the electoral tribunal, among other institutions.

In the 2001 election, PLC presidential candidate Enrique Bolaños, a respected conservative businessman and former vice president to Alemán, defeated Ortega. He vowed to prosecute Alemán and his aides for corruption, causing a break with the PLC; Bolaños later formed the Alliance for the Republic (APRE) party. The protracted effort to convict Alemán eventually led to a 20-year prison sentence for money laundering in 2003. However, the former leader used his alliance with Ortega to secure his release from parole conditions in March 2007, as long as he did not leave the country.

Ortega won the 2006 presidential election with 38 percent of the vote in the first round. Eduardo Montealegre of the Nicaraguan Liberal Alliance (ALN), who had served as finance minister under Bolaños, took 29 percent.

In 2007, Ortega consolidated his power over the central bank, the police, and the military through a series of legislative changes. His administration also established a system of Citizens' Power Councils (CPCs), from the neighborhood to the federal level, to promote direct democracy and participation in the government's Zero Hunger food production project. Critics argued that the bodies would blur the lines between state and party institutions.

Prior to the November 2008 municipal elections, the Supreme Electoral Council (CSE) took a number of steps that appeared designed to ensure FSLN victories, including postponing elections in several municipalities in the Northern Atlantic Autonomous Region (RAAN), where anti-FSLN sentiment was high, and preventing two opposition parties from contesting the elections. The CSE also refused accreditations to local and international electoral observers for the first time since 1990. After the balloting, the CSE announced that the FSLN had won 105 of 146 municipalities, including Managua. However, independent observers documented fraud in at least 40 municipalities, and the international community condemned the election results, leading to the suspension of more than $150 million in U.S. and European Union (EU) aid in 2009.

In July 2009, Ortega publicly stated that the constitutional ban on consecutive presidential terms should be eliminated. The National Assembly opposed his initiative, and Ortega lacked the support to pass a constitutional amendment on the issue. Ortega and more than 100 FLSN mayors subsequently filed a petition with the Constitutional Chamber of the Supreme Court claiming that the ban on consecutive terms violated their rights to participate in the political process. In October 2009, the Supreme Court found in favor of Ortega and the mayors, lifting the ban on consecutive terms; the ruling, however, did not amend the constitution.

In January 2010, Ortega decreed that appointed officials could remain in their posts until the National Assembly selected replacements, even if that occurred after the end of their terms. The decree affected 25 high-level posts, including the presidency and magistrates of the CSE, who had supported allowing Ortega to run for a second consecutive presidential term in 2011. The struggle over these appointments sent Nicaragua into a political crisis in 2010, as members of the National Assembly were unable to achieve the majority necessary to select replacements. In keeping with Ortega's decree, many officials remained in their posts after their terms expired in June, including the CSE president and members of the Supreme Court, which moved ahead with preparations for the 2011 elections.

Ortega's candidacy for another term was officially approved by the CSE in April 2011, effectively ending legal challenges to his candidacy. Fabio Gadea Mantilla's Nicaraguan Unity for Hope (UNE) attempted to unite the opposition against Ortega, but former president Alemán refused to abandon his candidacy. Instead, Gadea became the candidate for the Liberal Independent Party (PLI) coalition, which united parties from Montealegre's ALN and the Sandinista Renovation Movement. Alemán was selected as the presidential candidate for the PLC-Conservative Party alliance.

The CSE delayed issuing invitations to international observer teams until August 2011, significantly reducing the time available for observers to conduct their work. As with the 2008 municipal elections, several domestic observer groups with significant experience in electoral observation did not receive accreditation, though several international observer missions that were excluded in 2008—including the EU, the Organization of American States, and the Carter Center—were invited to observe. There was some controversy over the rules for accompaniment issued by the CSE, which some observer teams feared would limit their capacity to effectively observe the electoral process.

Ortega won the election in November 2011 with almost 63 percent of the vote, followed by Gadea with 31 percent and Alemán with almost 6 percent. The FSLN won 63 seats in the National Assembly, followed by the PLI with 27 and the PLC with 2. Though international observation teams noted irregularities and lamented a lack of transparency, there was no conclusive evidence of fraud. Observers did, however, report issues with the distribution of voting cards, the voter registry, difficulty accessing polling places, and concerns about the composition of electoral boards. Both Gadea and Alemán denounced the outcome and refused to recognize the results. Several protestors were killed and dozens of police officers were injured in postelection violence between supporters of the government and the opposition. In June 2012, the United States canceled its fiscal-transparency waiver—a policy in which U.S. aid to Nicaragua is contingent on financial and electoral transparency—over concerns about the 2011 elections, cutting approximately $3 million in aid.

In May 2012, the National Assembly approved numerous changes to the municipal electoral law, including adding the provision that mayors could run for reelection and instating a requirement that half of each party's candidates for mayor and council seats be women. The Assembly also approved an increase of municipal councilors from 2,178 to 6,534.

Municipal elections were held in November 2012. The FSLN won 134 of 153 municipalities, the PLI took 13, the PLC captured 2, Yatama won 3, and the Liberal Alliance took 1. The PLI and PLC challenged results in five municipalities, but the challenges were rejected by the CSE on procedural grounds. Opposition parties and observer groups noted irregularities in the electoral process, including outdated voter rosters, the presence of "phantom" parties and candidates, voters being turned away at the polls, and repeat voters. The abstention rate was also a matter of concern, though that number has been disputed by the CSE.

Political Rights and Civil Liberties: Nicaragua is an electoral democracy. The constitution provides for a directly elected president and a 92-member unicameral National Assembly. Two seats in the legislature are reserved for the previous president and the runner-up in the most recent presidential election. Both presidential and legislative elections are held every five years. While the president is limited to two nonconsecutive terms under the constitution, the Supreme Court lifted the restriction in October 2009 following a petition by Ortega.

Corruption cases against opposition figures are often criticized for being politically motivated. The 2007 Law on Access to Public Information requires public entities and private companies doing business with the state to disclose certain information. However, it preserved the government's right to protect information related to state security. Concerns about the transparency of funds from the Bolivarian Alliance for the Peoples of our America organization, of which Nicaragua is a member, persisted in 2012, as did those over the appointments of officials whose terms have expired and the electoral process. Nicaragua was ranked 130 out of 176 countries surveyed in Transparency International's 2012 Corruption Perceptions Index.

In May 2012, CSE alternate magistrate Julio César Osuna of the PLC was arrested on charges of money laundering, using his office to smuggle drugs, and selling false identification to drug traffickers. He was later stripped of his immunity by the National Assembly so that he could stand trial. Osuna, who has been linked to the traffickers who ordered the 2011 murder of Argentine folk singer/songwriter Facundo Cabral in Guatemala City, pled guilty to racketeering and falsifying documents in exchange for a reduced sentence of 23 years. CSE President Roberto Rivas insisted that Osuna had been working alone and that there was no wider scandal involving the CSE, though critics have suggested that is unlikely.

The constitution calls for a free press but allows some censorship. Radio remains the main source of information. Before leaving office in 1990, the Sandinistas privatized some radio stations and handed them to party loyalists. There are six television networks based in the capital, including a state-owned network, and many favor particular political factions. Three national newspapers cover the news from a variety of political viewpoints. The Communications and Citizenry Council, which oversees the government's press relations and is directed by First Lady Rosario Murillo, has been accused of limiting access to information and censoring the opposition. Access to the internet is unrestricted.

The press has faced increased political and judicial harassment since 2007, and the Ortega administration engages in systematic efforts to obstruct and discredit media critics. Journalists have received death threats, and some have been killed in recent years, with a number of attacks attributed to FSLN sympathizers. Luis Galeano, a reporter for *El Nuevo Diario*, received death threats in February 2011, following a series of articles on government corruption that included allegations against CSE president Roberto Rivas Reyes. Another *El Nuevo Diario* reporter, Silvia González, reported receiving death threats following a series of articles on corruption and the mysterious death of a former Contra leader; she fled the country in September 2011. Though the Ortega administration condemned the attacks, González ultimately fled the country. In addition, members of the ruling elite have acquired stakes in media outlets and used their ownership influence to sideline independent journalists.

Religious and academic freedoms are generally respected.

Freedoms of assembly and association are recognized by law, but their observance in practice has come under mounting pressure. While public demonstrations are generally allowed, opposition members have accused the police of partisan behavior and failing to protect demonstrators. Although nongovernmental organizations are active and operate freely, they have faced harassment in recent years, and the emergence of the CPCs has weakened their influence. The FSLN controls many of the country's labor unions, and the legal rights of non-FSLN unions are not fully guaranteed. Although the law recognizes the right to strike, unions must clear a number of hurdles, and approval from the Ministry of Labor is almost never granted.

Employers sometimes form their own unions to avoid recognizing legitimate organizations. Employees have reportedly been dismissed for union activities, and citizens have no effective recourse when labor laws are violated by those in power. Child labor and other abuses in export-processing zones remain problems, though child labor occurs most often in the agricultural sector.

The judiciary remains dominated by FSLN and PLC appointees, and the Supreme Court is a largely politicized body controlled by Sandinista judges. The court system also suffers from corruption, long delays, a large backlog of cases, and a severe shortage of public defenders. Access to justice is especially deficient in rural areas and on the Caribbean coast.

Despite long-term improvements, the security forces remain understaffed and poorly funded, and human rights abuses still occur. Forced confessions are also a problem, as are arbitrary arrests. Though Nicaragua has generally been spared the high rates of crime and gang violence that plague its neighbors to its north, the country—specifically the Atlantic coast—is an important transshipment point for South American drugs. The police have been active in combating trafficking and organized crime. Prison conditions are poor.

The constitution and laws nominally recognize the rights of indigenous communities, but those rights have not been respected in practice. Approximately 5 percent of the population is indigenous and lives mostly in the RAAN and the Southern Atlantic Autonomous Region (RAAS). In 2009, the Miskito Council of Elders in the RAAS announced the creation of a separatist movement demanding independence, citing government neglect and grievances related to the exploitation of natural resources. In 2012 the constitution was translated into Miskito and Mayangna for the first time.

Violence against women and children, including sexual and domestic abuse, remains widespread and underreported; few cases are ever prosecuted. Additionally, the murder rate among females increased significantly in recent years. In January 2012, the Comprehensive Law Against Violence Toward Women was passed by the National Assembly. The law, which went into effect in June 2012, addresses both physical and structural forms of violence, and recognizes violence against women as a matter of public health and safety. The law also sets forth sentencing guidelines for physical and psychological abuses against women, as well as the newly established crime of femicide. Abortion is illegal and punishable by imprisonment, even when performed to save the mother's life or in cases of rape or incest. Scores of deaths stemming from the ban have been reported in recent years.

Nicaragua is a source country for women and children trafficked for prostitution. In September 2010, the government passed a law that classifies human trafficking as a form of organized crime. In 2012 Nicaragua moved from Tier 2 to Tier 1 in the U.S. State Department's Trafficking in Persons Report, which stated that Nicaragua fully complied with minimal standards. The report noted that the number of investigations and prosecutions of trafficking rose and penalties for trafficking-related offenses were increased.

Niger

Political Rights: 3
Civil Liberties: 4
Status: Partly Free

Population: 16,276,000
Capital: Niamey

Ten-Year Ratings Timeline For Year Under Review (Political Rights, Civil Liberties, Status)

2003	2004	2005	2006	2007	2008	2009	2010	2011	2012
4,4PF	3,3PF	3,3PF	3,3PF	3,4PF	3,4PF	5,4PF	5,4PF	3,4PF	3,4PF

Overview:
Niger experienced economic growth in 2012, largely due to revenues from the country's extractive industries and higher agricultural production, along with ongoing stability. Nevertheless, the crisis in neighboring Mali led some 60,000 refugees to flee to northern Niger, and insecurity continued in the area, where six aid workers were kidnapped. Meanwhile, floods and cholera claimed 162 lives and left 125,000 homeless.

Since gaining independence from France in 1960, Niger was governed by a series of one-party and military regimes. Under international and domestic pressure, General Ali Seibou allowed for the adoption of a new constitution by popular referendum in 1992. Mahamane Ousmane of the Alliance of Forces for Change was elected president in 1993, but overthrown in January 1996 by Colonel Ibrahim Baré Maïnassara, who became president in a sham election six months later.

After members of the presidential guard assassinated Maïnassara in April 1999, the guard commander led a transitional government that organized a constitutional referendum in July and competitive elections in November. Retired lieutenant colonel Mamadou Tandja—supported by the National Movement for a Developing Society (MNSD) and the Democratic and Social Convention (CDS) parties—won the presidency in generally free and fair balloting, and the MNSD and CDS took a majority of seats in the National Assembly. Tandja was reelected in 2004, and in concurrent legislative elections, four parties joined the MNSD and CDS to again secure a majority.

Prime Minister Hama Amadou's government lost a vote of confidence in 2007, and Amadou was arrested in 2008 on embezzlement charges. In May 2009, Tandja dissolved the National Assembly after lawmakers refused to approve a constitutional referendum that would delay the next presidential election until 2012, expand executive powers, and eliminate executive term limits. Tandja then dissolved the Constitutional Court—after it ruled against the referendum—and announced that he would rule by decree under emergency powers. The controversial constitutional changes were adopted by referendum in August, but observers rejected the results as fraudulent. Later that month, Tandja lifted emergency rule and announced that legislative elections would be held in October. Key opposition parties boycotted the vote, allowing Tandja's MNSD to capture a majority of seats. The international community denounced the elections.

In February 2010, the Supreme Council for the Restoration of Democracy (CSRD), a military junta led by Major Salou Djibo, placed Tandja under house arrest, suspended the constitution, and dissolved all government institutions. The junta appointed a transitional government, which created the National Consultative Council, a 131-member body tasked with drafting a new constitution and electoral code, and a Transition Constitutional Council to replace the Constitutional Court. Djibo remained the de facto head of state. In a referendum held in October 2010, 90 percent of participating voters approved the new constitution.

Presidential, legislative, and municipal elections were held on January 31, 2011. The junta had forbidden its members and representatives of the transitional government from running for office. The Nigerien Party for Democracy and Socialism (PNDS), led by opposition leader Mahamadou Issoufou, took the most seats, with 37. The MNSD—led by former prime minister Seini Oumarou—placed second with 26 seats, while Amadou's Nigerien Democratic Movement for an African Federation took 25. In the first round of the presidential election, Issoufou and Oumarou emerged as the top two candidates; Issoufou claimed victory with 58 percent of the vote in a March runoff election. Both the presidential and legislative elections were declared free and fair by international observers. The PNDS and MNSD won the majority of positions across the country in local elections. In May, the Niamey Court of Appeals ordered that Tandja be released from prison.

Already one of the world's poorest countries, Niger has been ravaged by extreme food shortages since a 2009 drought. In January 2012, the number of people at risk of food insecurity was estimated at 3 million, with 400,000 children requiring treatment for malnutrition. In September, however, the government announced that agricultural production was higher than had been expected and that the crisis should be alleviated in 2013. Floods and cholera claimed 162 lives in 2012 and left 125,000 people homeless. Economic growth is projected at about 12 percent for 2012, mainly due to the uranium mining and oil industries, although that estimate might be revised downward due to lower than expected oil output.

The crisis in neighboring Mali led to an influx of some 60,000 Malian refugees in 2012, as well as 3,000 returned Nigeriens, raising pressures on food provisions. The government increased the number of troops in the north to avoid a spillover of the conflict and proposed a $2.5 billion development project in the area, although it is unclear whether the government has the necessary funds for the operation. In October, the government signed a Joint Commission for Cooperation with Nigeria against the Islamist militant groups Boko Haram and al-Qaeda in the Islamic Maghreb (AQIM).

Political Rights and Civil Liberties: Niger is an electoral democracy. In 2011, the transitional government restored democratic civilian rule by holding successful legislative and presidential elections. After the 2010 military coup, former prime minister and presidential hopeful Hama Amadou returned from exile, three former legislators were released from jail, and there was a decrease in harassment of opposition politicians. The 2010 constitution, written in broad consultation with civil society, reinstated executive term limits, curbed executive power, and provided amnesty for members of the CSRD. Under the constitution, the president is elected by popular vote for up to two five-year terms, and members of the 113-seat, unicameral National Assembly serve five-year terms. Since assuming power, President Mahamadou Issoufou has appointed former opponents and members of civil society to high positions in government to foster inclusivity.

Corruption is a serious problem in Niger, and observers have raised concerns regarding uranium-mining contracts. However, the 2010 constitution contains provisions for greater transparency in government reporting of revenues from the extractive industries, as well as the declaration of personal assets by government officials, including the president. In July 2011, the government created the High Authority to Combat Corruption, and it opened an anticorruption hotline in August. Key officials from the previous administration were indicted for fraud and corruption during 2011, and in July, Issoufou was the target of a foiled assassination attempt thought to be motivated by his crackdowns on corruption in the military. Niger was ranked 113 out of 176 countries surveyed in Transparency International's 2012 Corruption Perceptions Index.

In 2010, the transitional government made significant efforts to restore freedoms of speech and of the press. In June of that year, the National Assembly adopted a new press law that eliminated prison terms for journalists, and removed the threat of libel cases that journalists had faced under Tandja. In November, Issoufou became the first head of state to sign the Table Mountain Declaration, which calls on African governments to promote press freedom. In 2012, the media were largely allowed to freely publish political facts and critiques. The government does not restrict internet use, though less than 1 percent of the population has access.

Freedom of religion is generally respected in this overwhelmingly Muslim country. In the aftermath of the coup, both Muslim and Christian leaders worked with the CSRD to restore peace and democracy. Academic freedom is guaranteed but not always observed in practice.

Constitutional guarantees of freedoms of assembly and association are largely upheld. The government does not restrict the operations of nongovernmental organizations (NGOs), although a lack of security in the north prevents NGOs from adequately assessing human rights conditions there. The constitution and other laws guarantee workers the right to join unions and bargain for wages, although over 95 percent of the workforce is employed in subsistence agriculture and small trading. In April 2012, workers in the mining and oil industries organized a weeklong strike that was peacefully resolved.

The constitution provides for an independent judiciary, and courts have shown some autonomy in the past, though the judicial system has at times been subject to executive interference. The Ministry of Justice supervises public prosecutors, and the president has the power to appoint judges. Judicial corruption is fueled partly by low salaries and inadequate training. Prolonged pretrial detention is common, and police forces are underfunded and poorly trained. Prisons are characterized by overcrowding and poor health conditions.

Insecurity continues to plague the northwest of the country along the Malian border, and several people have been kidnapped in the area by groups such as AQIM. In October 2012, six aid workers were kidnapped by unidentified gunmen; five of the workers were released the following month, though the sixth died from wounds inflicted during the abduction.

Constitutional protections provide for a quota of eight seats in the National Assembly for minorities and the nomadic population, who continue to have poor access to government services.

Under a 2002 quota system, political parties must allocate 10 percent of their elected positions to women. Although the 2010 constitution prohibits gender discrimination, women suffer discrimination in practice. Family law gives women inferior status in property disputes, inheritance rights, and divorce. Sexual and domestic violence are reportedly widespread. Female genital mutilation was criminalized in 2003 but continues.

While slavery was criminalized in 2003 and banned in the 2010 constitution, an estimated 115,000 adults and children still live in conditions of forced labor. Niger remains a source, transit point, and destination for human trafficking. Despite a 2010 antitrafficking law and a five-year antitrafficking plan, investigation and prosecution efforts remained weak in 2012.

⬇ Nigeria

Political Rights: 4
Civil Liberties: 4
Status: Partly Free

Population: 170,124,000
Capital: Abuja

Trend Arrow: Nigeria received a downward trend arrow due to continued rampant corruption, the suppression of civil society during fuel-subsidy protests as well as restrictions on its activity in the north, and limitations on freedom of movement as a result of violence associated with the militant group Boko Haram.

Ten-Year Ratings Timeline For Year Under Review (Political Rights, Civil Liberties, Status)

2003	2004	2005	2006	2007	2008	2009	2010	2011	2012
4,4PF	4,4PF	4,4PF	4,4PF	4,4PF	4,4PF	5,4PF	4,4PF	4,4PF	4,4PF

Overview:
Human rights conditions worsened in the north of the country in 2012, as the radical Islamist group Boko Haram stepped up its attacks on civilians and the security forces were accused of committing abuses in the course of their counterterrorism efforts. Separately, in January, police reportedly used excessive force in response to strikes and mass protests against a proposed fuel-price increase. Unchecked government corruption has resulted in billions of dollars of lost public revenue over the last decade.

The armed forces ruled Nigeria for much of the period after independence from Great Britain in 1960. Beginning with the first coup in January 1966, military officers consistently claimed that only they could manage simmering tensions among the country's 250 ethnic groups and its different religious communities. Muslims, who constitute a majority in the north, make up about 50 percent of the overall population, while Christians, who dominate in the south, account for most of the remaining 50 percent. Ethnic and regional friction led to the attempted secession of Nigeria's oil-rich southeast as the Republic of Biafra in 1967, which touched off a three-year civil war and a devastating famine that together caused more than one million deaths.

A military-supervised political transition led to the inauguration of a civilian government in 1979, but the new democratic regime was burdened by factionalism, corruption, and communal polarization. Economic mismanagement and deeply flawed elections triggered another military intervention in 1983, followed by 16 more years of military rule.

After several years under the leadership of General Ibrahim Babangida, the country held a presidential election in June 1993. Moshood Abiola, a Muslim Yoruba from the south, was widely considered the winner, but Babangida annulled the election. A civilian caretaker administration governed briefly until General Sani Abacha, a principal architect of previous coups, took power in November 1993. Abacha's dictatorial regime dissolved all democratic structures and banned political parties, governing through a predominantly military Provisional Ruling Council. Abiola was jailed in 1994 and ultimately died in detention, just weeks after Abacha's unexpected demise in 1998.

General Abdulsalami Abubakar emerged as the new military leader and presided over a transition to civilian rule. In 1999, Olusegun Obasanjo—a former general who had led a military regime from 1976 to 1979 and spent a number of years in prison under Abacha—won the presidential election on the ticket of the People's Democratic Party (PDP), which also captured the most seats in the National Assembly. While hailed internationally for bringing an end to almost two decades of military dictatorship, the 1999 elections featured numerous instances of voter intimidation and fraud.

Obasanjo was reelected in 2003, but the voting was again marred by fraud and violence. The runner-up, former general Muhammadu Buhari, a northern Muslim and member of the All Nigeria People's Party (ANPP), filed a petition to nullify the results. However, the Supreme Court in 2005 unanimously rejected the challenge.

The April 2007 elections were also marred by bloodshed and reports of massive vote-rigging and fraud. Umaru Yar'Adua, the PDP candidate and Obasanjo's handpicked successor, was credited with 70 percent of the presidential ballots. In the parliamentary vote, the PDP won 85 of 109 Senate seats and 262 of 360 seats in the House of Representatives. The PDP also captured 29 out of 36 governorships. International and local election monitors were highly critical of the vote, and the official results drew public complaints and legal challenges from the opposition. The Supreme Court upheld Yar'Adua's victory in December 2008.

In November 2009, an ailing Yar'Adua left the country to seek medical treatment in Saudi Arabia. The National Assembly provisionally handed power to Vice President Goodluck Jonathan in February 2010. Yar'Adua died in May, allowing Jonathan to formally assume the presidency. In September, Jonathan replaced leaders in the security forces and appointed the widely respected Attahiru Jega to head the Independent National Electoral Commission (INEC).

Presidential, legislative, and gubernatorial elections were held in April 2011. Jonathan won the April 16 presidential contest, defeating Buhari, the Congress for Progressive Change (CPC) candidate, 58.9 percent to 32 percent. The vote divided the country along ethnic and sectarian lines, with Buhari winning the northern states and Jonathan taking the south. Meanwhile, PDP candidates won a reduced majority in legislative elections on April 9 and 26. In the House of Representatives, the PDP claimed 202 of 360 seats, while the Action Congress of Nigeria (ACN) won 66, the CPC took 35, and the ANPP garnered 25. In the Senate, the PDP lost its two-thirds majority, winning 71 of 109 seats; the ACN took 18 seats, and the CPC and ANPP won 7 each. The PDP captured 18 of the 26 contested governorships.

The elections were followed by pro-Buhari protests in parts of 12 northern and so-called Middle Belt states. These degenerated into sectarian riots and retaliatory killings, leaving over 800 people dead and 65,000 internally displaced.

Despite the election-related violence and a high number of dubious official results, most observers deemed the 2011 elections an improvement over those in 2007, citing more orderly polling stations and competent INEC personnel.

Also in 2011, the radical Islamist movement Boko Haram became a serious threat to internal security in Nigeria. Whereas it had previously been restricted largely to northeastern Borno State and focused its attacks on government officials, security forces, and traditional leaders it perceived as complicit with the government, the group increasingly targeted ordinary civilians and moved into new areas. Both the scale and the geographic reach of Boko Haram attacks continued to expand in 2012. In January, coordinated bombings and gunfire in the city of Kano killed some 180 people, and approximately 100 people were killed in Kaduna in June when Boko Haram bombed three churches. There were more frequent, smaller attacks in the states of Borno, Yobe, Gombe, Adamawa, and Bauchi, though these mainly targeted security forces and other government personnel. The escalation of Boko Haram activity was matched by a harsh and somewhat indiscriminate response from the military and police, reportedly including extrajudicial killings and arbitrary arrests.

Nigeria's economy is dominated by hydrocarbons, which account for 95 percent of export revenues and 80 percent of government revenue. It is estimated that nearly $400 billion in oil revenue has been stolen or squandered since independence. Wealth and political power are concentrated in the hands of a narrow elite, and much of the regular violence in the oil-rich yet impoverished Niger Delta region stems from unequal distribution of oil revenue.

Political Rights and Civil Liberties:

Nigeria is not an electoral democracy. According to the constitution, the president is elected by popular vote for no more than two four-year terms. Members of the bicameral National Assembly, consisting of the 109-seat Senate and the 360-seat House of Representatives, are elected for four-year terms. However, since the return of civilian rule in 1999, elections have by and large been chaotic affairs marked by vote rigging and violence. This has been particularly the case in the Niger Delta, where many prominent politicians reportedly sponsor criminal gangs to target opponents, but violence and intimidation are also strategically used by political elites or "godfathers" in other parts of the country.

The ruling PDP, the ACN, and the CPC are currently the largest political parties. The ACN and CPC derive much of their support from regional strongholds (the Yoruba-speaking southwest and Muslim north, respectively), while the PDP enjoys the backing of patronage networks consisting of elites from every section of Nigeria. Other prominent parties include the ANPP and the All-Progressive Grand Alliance. Although the PDP has dominated the political landscape since 1999, its grip on power was weakened following the April 2011 elections. INEC chief Attahiru Jega has won praise for addressing opposition complaints that the commission functioned as an appendage of the PDP.

Corruption remains pervasive, and government efforts to improve transparency and reduce graft have been inadequate. A 2011 report by Human Rights Watch found that the Economic and Financial Crimes Commission, Nigeria's main anti-corruption agency, arraigned 30 prominent politicians on corruption charges since it began work in 2002. However, it won only four convictions, resulting in little or no jail time. The body is hampered by political interference, an inefficient judiciary, and its own institutional weaknesses, and is subject to accusations that it targets those who have lost favor with the government. In a sign of ongoing, large-scale graft, an internal Petroleum Resources Ministry report leaked in October 2012 found that $29 billion in public revenue was lost over the past decade to a natural gas price-fixing scheme. Nigeria was ranked 139 out of 176 countries surveyed in Transparency International's 2012 Corruption Perceptions Index.

Freedom of speech and expression is constitutionally guaranteed, and Nigeria has a lively independent media sector. However, state security agents occasionally arrest journalists, confiscate newspapers, and harass vendors, notably when journalists are covering corruption or separatist and communal violence. Local authorities frequently condemn those who criticize them, and cases of violence against journalists often go unsolved. Sharia (Islamic law) statutes in 12 northern states impose severe penalties for alleged press offenses. Media outlets have also been the victims of terrorist attacks. In June 2012, Boko Haram bombed the offices of a major newspaper, *This Day*. The effects of the 2011 Freedom of Information Act remained uncertain in 2012; observers have argued that the measure has yet to be implemented, noting that as of September 2012, no requests for information had been granted by any significant government agency. The government does not restrict internet access.

Religious freedom is guaranteed by the constitution, though many Nigerians, including government officials, discriminate against adherents of other religions. Religious violence is frequently intertwined with regional and ethnic differences and accompanying competition for land and resources. In recent years, sectarian clashes have erupted in and around the city of Jos, leaving hundreds dead and displacing thousands more. In terms of terrorism, Christians and their houses of worship have been explicitly targeted by Boko Haram, though Muslims still account for the majority of the group's victims.

Academic freedom is generally honored, although government officials frequently pressure university administrators and faculty to ensure special treatment for their relatives and associates. At the state level, student admission and faculty hiring policies are subject to ethnic politics. The public education system remains dismal; more than a third of the population is illiterate.

Freedoms of assembly and association are generally respected in practice. However, protests are often suppressed by state and private security forces, especially demonstrations organized by youth groups or in the Niger Delta. Human rights groups report that dozens of activists have been killed in recent years and hundreds have been detained. Workers, except those in the military or "essential services," may join trade unions and have the right to bargain collectively. Public health workers strike frequently. In January 2012, labor and other activists led large-scale strikes and protests against official corruption and a government plan to reduce fuel subsidies. The demonstrations were at times met with live fire and excessive force by police and the military, leading to several deaths. In November, at least 100 people were charged with treason for taking part in a Biafran independence march.

The higher courts are relatively competent and independent, but they remain subject to political influence, corruption, and lack of funding, equipment, and training. Certain departments, particularly the Court of Appeals, have often overturned decisions on election challenges or allegations of corruption against powerful elites, raising doubts about their independence.

Ordinary defendants frequently lack legal representation and are often ill-informed about court procedures and their rights. Human rights groups have alleged that Islamic courts in the 12 northern states with Sharia statutes fail to respect due process and discriminate against non-Muslims. Pretrial detainees, many of whom are held for several years, account for about 70 percent of the country's inmates, and few have access to a lawyer. Children and the mentally disabled are often held with the general prison population. Prison facilities are rife with disease, as they commonly lack water, adequate sewage facilities, and medical services.

Security forces commit abuses with near impunity, and corruption pervades their ranks. Amnesty International has accused military forces currently deployed to quell the terrorist activities of Boko Haram of worsening human rights conditions through extreme, extralegal tactics. In an October 2012 report, Human Rights Watch estimated that Boko Haram attacks accounted for over 1,500 of the roughly 2,800 deaths in the conflict since 2009, suggesting that government forces were responsible for the remainder. In one case during 2012, Amnesty International called for an independent inquiry into the alleged extrajudicial killing of at least 30 young men by security forces in the city of Maiduguri in late October. Many of the tactics used by the military, such as cordon-and-sweep searches, result in other forms of rights abuses in areas where Boko Haram operates, and security forces have engaged in arbitrary mass arrests of young Muslim men in these areas.

In addition to extrajudicial killings of criminal suspects and prisoners, torture and general ill-treatment of detainees are widespread in Nigeria, and such abuses are reportedly used to force confessions and extort bribes. Corrupt officers are often supported by a chain of command that encourages and institutionalizes graft. Violent crime in certain cities and areas remains a serious problem, and the trafficking of drugs and small arms is reportedly on the rise.

The constitution prohibits ethnic discrimination by the government and requires government offices to reflect the country's ethnic diversity, but societal discrimination is widely practiced, and ethnic clashes frequently erupt. Ethnocultural groups in the southern Niger Delta area feel particular discrimination, primarily with regard to distribution of the country's oil wealth, and their grievances have fueled militant violence in the region.

No laws prohibit discrimination against the physically and mentally disabled, and people with disabilities face social stigma, exploitation, and discrimination. Homosexual activity is illegal and punishable by up to 14 years in prison. The northern states' Sharia statutes allow the death penalty for sexual activity between men, but no such sentences have been applied in practice.

Nigerian women's educational opportunities have improved, and women hold several key governmental positions. However, women throughout the country experience discrimination in employment and are often relegated to inferior positions. In the northern states governed under Sharia statutes, women's rights have suffered particularly serious setbacks. Rape and spousal rape are considered separate offenses, though both have low rates of reporting and prosecution. Domestic violence is common and accepted in most parts of society. Women in some ethnic groups are denied equal rights to inherit property, and various forms of gender-based violence are not considered crimes. Although the federal government publicly opposes female genital mutilation, it has taken no action to ban the practice.

While illegal, human trafficking to, from, and within the country for the purposes of labor and prostitution is reported to be on the rise. Forced labor is illegal but common, especially bonded labor and domestic servitude, and the government makes very little effort to combat the practice. Several organizations have reported on an illegal trade in which pregnant teenagers are promised abortions, only to be held until their babies are delivered and sold.

North Korea

Political Rights: 7
Civil Liberties: 7
Status: Not Free

Population: 24,589,100
Capital: Pyongyang

Ten-Year Ratings Timeline For Year Under Review (Political Rights, Civil Liberties, Status)

2003	2004	2005	2006	2007	2008	2009	2010	2011	2012
7,7NF	7,7NF	7,7NF	7,7NF	7,7NF	7,7NF	7,7NF	7,7NF	7,7NF	7,7NF

Overview: Efforts were made to quickly solidify and legitimize Kim Jong-un's rule in 2012, after his father's death the previous year. In April, North Korea conducted a controversial, though ultimately unsuccessful, rocket launch, attracting international condemnation and nullifying a recent agreement with the United States. A number of new economic and agricultural policies were announced during the year to address key deficiencies in the country's economy. Meanwhile, tensions with South Korea flared late in the year prior to the South Korean presidential election.

The Democratic People's Republic of Korea (DPRK, or North Korea) was established in 1948, after three years of post–World War II Soviet occupation. The Soviet Union installed Kim Il-sung, an anti-Japanese resistance fighter, as the country's leader. In 1950, North Korea invaded South Korea in an attempt to reunify the peninsula under communist rule. Drawing in the United States and then China, the three-year conflict resulted in the deaths of at least 2.5 million people and ended with a ceasefire rather than a full peace treaty. Since then, the two Koreas have been on a continuous war footing, and the border remains one of the most heavily militarized places in the world.

Kim Il-sung solidified his control after the war, purging rivals, consigning thousands of political prisoners to labor camps, and fostering an extreme personality cult that promoted him as North Korea's "Great Leader." Marxism was replaced by the "Juche" (translated as "self-reliance") ideology, which combines extreme nationalism, xenophobia, and the use of state terror. After Kim Il-sung died in 1994, he was proclaimed "Eternal President," but power passed to his son, Kim Jong-il.

The end of the Cold War and associated subsidies from the Soviet Union and China led to the collapse of North Korea's command economy. Decades of severe economic mismanagement were exacerbated by harsh floods in 1995 and 1996, resulting in a famine that killed at least a million people. As many as 300,000 North Koreans fled to China in search of food, despite a legal ban on leaving the country. The emergence of black markets helped to deal with extreme shortages of food and other goods, and illicit traders smuggled in various items from China. In 1995, North Korea allowed the United Nations and private humanitarian aid organizations to undertake one of the world's largest famine-relief operations. The DPRK continues to force the international community to bear the burden of feeding its citizens while it devotes resources to its military.

The regime instituted halting economic reforms in 2002, easing price controls, raising wages, devaluing the currency, and giving factory managers more autonomy. China and South Korea also continued to provide aid, fearing that state collapse could lead to massive refugee outflows, military disorder, the emergence of criminal gangs and regional warlords, and a loss of state control over nuclear weapons.

The DPRK withdrew from the Nuclear Non-Proliferation Treaty in 2003 and proceeded to test ballistic missiles and a nuclear device in 2006. In early 2007, the regime agreed to denuclearize in exchange for fuel aid and other concessions from its four neighbors—China, South Korea, Japan, and Russia—and the United States, but further negotiations and implementation of the deal proceeded haltingly. In 2008, Pyongyang handed over its declaration of nuclear assets and disabled its Yongbyon nuclear plant, and the United States removed North Korea from its list of state sponsors of terrorism.

In April 2009, the DPRK tested a long-range missile and announced its withdrawal from the Six-Party Talks. In response, the UN Security Council unanimously passed Resolution 1874, which tightened weapons-related financial sanctions and called on all governments to search North Korean shipments for illicit weapons.

In November, the government announced a currency revaluation and other measures designed to curb private trading and reassert state control over the economy. With the crippled black market unable to meet demand, prices rose sharply. The economy was disrupted further in early 2010 when the government banned the use of foreign currency. In February 2010, the government backtracked on the currency revaluation, issuing a rare formal apology and allowing markets to reopen.

North Korea responded to joint U.S.-South Korean military exercises in the West Sea with a surprise attack on South Korea's Yeonpyeong Island in November. South Korea launched a brief counterattack, which resulted in several South Korean casualties, including the first civilian deaths since the Korean War. North Korean authorities also revealed to the international community that they had built a uranium enrichment facility.

With inter-Korean tensions high, South Korea denounced North Korean requests for food aid in early 2011, and the United States followed suit. All inter-Korean cooperative activities were stalled except for the operation of the Gaeseong Industrial Complex, a joint North-South Korean economic venture. In February, a series of food assessments found chronic malnutrition in North Korea. In May, the U.S. Special Envoy for North Korean Human Rights led another food assessment team into North Korea, marking the first time a designated human rights envoy had been allowed in the country, though he was not there for formal negotiations. In June, the European Union pledged $14.5 million in food aid to North Korea, and South Korea approved humanitarian efforts and food aid through third party organizations.

In October, U.S. and North Korean officials met in Geneva to move the two countries toward renewing dialogue on nuclear disarmament and improving relations. Prospects for resuming multilateral nuclear negotiations seemed high until December 17, when Kim Jong-il died of a heart attack at the age of 69. Kim Jong-un, Kim Jong-il's third son, succeeded his father as the country's leader without a major power struggle.

Efforts to solidify and legitimize Kim Jong-un's power were swift. On December 30, a special meeting of the Politburo officially appointed him Supreme Commander of the Korean People's Army. On April 11, 2012, the Korean Workers' Party convened the Fourth Party Conference and anointed Kim Jong-un as First Secretary—the official head of the party—along with other titles formerly held by his father, including "eternal general secretary." On April 13, the Supreme People's Assembly met and appointed Kim Jong-un to the helm of the National Defense Commission, while elevating his father to the post of eternal chairman.

Meetings between the United States and the DPRK continued in early 2012, culminating on February 29 with an accord known as the "Leap Day Agreement." While the specifics of the agreement were ambiguous, the general terms were for North Korea to put a moratorium on uranium enrichment and missile testing in exchange for food aid from the United States, with more substantive negotiations to follow. The agreement was nullified within days, however, when the DPRK announced its intent to launch a satellite into space.

The April 13 rocket launch, which was ultimately unsuccessful, was part of a number of activities arranged for the centenary birthday celebrations of Kim Il-sung. On April 15, Kim Jong-un addressed the public, vowing that the North Korean people would "not have to tighten their belts again." Many experts believed the statement, as well as several key cabinet appointments, indicated a shift in policy focus from the military to the economy.

In July, the replacement of the chief of the Korean People's Army (KPA) sparked a number of military defections. In October, additional North Korean leaders were purged, and the vice minister of the KPA was reportedly executed. Meanwhile, a soldier from the Minkyung Unit—which generally consists of soldiers chosen specifically for their perceived loyalty to the regime—shot and killed two of his superiors before escaping across the Military Demarcation Line.

Inter-Korean tensions rose toward the end of the year, when North Korea attempted to influence the South's December elections through a series of small provocations and threats. Also in December, North Korea conducted another rocket launch, successfully putting a satellite into orbit. Although this was a weather satellite, the international community feared the implications for North Korea's ability to develop nuclear warhead technology.

Political Rights and Civil Liberties: North Korea is not an electoral democracy. Kim Jong-il led the DPRK following the 1994 death of his father, Kim Il-sung, to whom the office of president was permanently dedicated in a 1998 constitutional revision. Kim Jong-un became the country's new leader after his father's death in December 2011. North Korea's parliament, the Supreme People's Assembly (SPA), is a rubber-stamp institution elected to five-year terms. All candidates for office, who run unopposed, are preselected by the ruling Korean Workers' Party and two subordinate minor parties.

Corruption is believed to be endemic at every level of the state and economy. North Korea was ranked 174 out of 176 countries surveyed in Transparency International's 2012 Corruption Perceptions Index.

All media outlets are run by the state. Televisions and radios are permanently fixed to state channels, and all publications are subject to strict supervision and censorship. In January 2012, the Associated Press opened a bureau office in Pyongyang. Internet access is restricted to a few thousand people, and foreign websites are blocked. The black market provides alternative information sources, including cellular telephones, pirated recordings of South Korean dramas, and radios capable of receiving foreign programs. Cell phones were introduced to North Korea in 2010, and the one millionth subscriber was signed in 2012. The cell phone network is limited to domestic use only, with foreign residents on separate networks.

Although freedom of religion is guaranteed by the constitution, it does not exist in practice. State-sanctioned churches maintain a token presence in Pyongyang, and some North Koreans who live near the Chinese border are known to practice their faiths furtively. However, intense state indoctrination and repression preclude free exercise of religion as well as academic freedom. Nearly all forms of private communication are monitored by a huge network of informers.

Freedom of assembly is not recognized, and there are no known associations or organizations other than those created by the state. Strikes, collective bargaining, and other organized-labor activities are illegal.

North Korea does not have an independent judiciary. The UN General Assembly has recognized and condemned severe DPRK human rights violations, including torture, public executions, extrajudicial and arbitrary detention, and forced labor; the absence of due process and the rule of law; and death sentences for political offenses. South Korean reports suggest that up to 154,000 political prisoners are held in six detention camps. Inmates face brutal conditions, and collective or familial punishment for suspected dissent by an individual is a common practice.

The government operates a semihereditary system of social discrimination, whereby all citizens are classified into 53 subgroups under overall security ratings—"core," "wavering," and "hostile"—based on their family's perceived loyalty to the regime. This rating determines virtually every facet of a person's life, including employment and educational opportunities, place of residence, access to medical facilities, and even access to stores.

There is no freedom of movement, and forced internal resettlement is routine. Access to Pyongyang is tightly restricted; the availability of food, housing, and health care is somewhat better in the capital than in the rest of the country. This disparity has increased, with the capital featuring more luxuries for a growing middle class. Emigration is illegal, but many North Koreans have escaped to China or engaged in cross-border trade. Ignoring international objections, the Chinese government continues to return refugees and defectors to North Korea, where they are subject to torture, harsh imprisonment, or execution.

The economy remains both centrally planned and grossly mismanaged. Development is also hobbled by a lack of infrastructure, a scarcity of energy and raw materials, an inability to borrow on world markets or from multilateral banks because of sanctions, lingering foreign debt, and ideological isolationism. However, the growth of the black market has provided many North Koreans with a field of activity that is largely free from government control. In 2012 a number of new laws were announced to improve the business environment for foreign investment. New agricultural policies, meanwhile, would introduce smaller work teams on the collective farms and permit farmers to keep 30 percent of their output. The new policies were proposed for three counties as a trial phase, and there is skepticism as to how the changes, if successful, would be implemented on a national scale.

There have been widespread reports of trafficked women and girls among the tens of thousands of North Koreans who have recently crossed into China. UN bodies have noted the use of forced abortions and infanticide against pregnant women who are forcibly repatriated from China.

Norway

Political Rights: 1
Civil Liberties: 1
Status: Free

Population: 5,019,000
Capital: Oslo

Ten-Year Ratings Timeline For Year Under Review (Political Rights, Civil Liberties, Status)

2003	2004	2005	2006	2007	2008	2009	2010	2011	2012
1,1F	1,1F	1,1F	1,1F	1,1F	1,1F	1,1F	1,1F	1,1F	1,1F

Overview: Far-right, anti-immigrant militant Anders Breivik was found guilty in July 2012 and sentenced to 21 years in prison for deadly attacks in 2011 that killed more than 70 people, many of them children. Immigration continued to be a sensitive topic throughout the year, as authorities conducted raids on asylum centers and forcibly repatriated rejected asylum applicants. Meanwhile, the country experienced some of the largest public sector strikes in nearly three decades.

Norway's constitution, the Eidsvoll Convention, was first adopted in 1814, during a brief period of independence after nearly four centuries of Danish rule. Subsequently, Norway became part of a Swedish-headed monarchy. Since gaining independence in 1905, it has functioned as a constitutional monarchy with a multiparty parliamentary structure. Norway became a founding member of NATO in 1949.

Norwegian citizens narrowly rejected membership in the European Union (EU) in 1972 and 1994, despite government support for joining. Norwegians wanted to preserve their sovereignty and feared that membership would threaten the country's energy, agriculture, and fishing industries. As part of the European Economic Area (EEA), Norway has nearly full access to EU markets and exports approximately 75 percent of its goods to EU countries. While Norway has adopted almost all EU directives, it has little power to influence EU decisions.

In the September 2005 legislative elections, the center-left Red-Green coalition—led by the Labor Party and including the Socialist Left Party and the Center Party (Agrarians)—won 48 percent of the vote and 87 of 169 seats. Prime Minister Jens Stoltenberg reshuffled members of his coalition government in October 2007, resulting in a historic female-majority cabinet, with 10 female and 9 male ministers.

Stoltenberg's coalition was reelected in the September 2009 parliamentary elections, making it the first government to win reelection in 16 years. In concurrent elections for the Sami Assembly, the Norwegian Labor Party captured 14 seats, the Norwegian Sami Association received 11, and various other Sami parties won a total of 14. Municipal and county elections in September 2011 saw a loss of votes for the anti-immigration Progress Party, but gains for the Conservatives, Liberals, and Labour parties.

On July 22, 2011, Norwegian national and right-wing fundamentalist Anders Breivik detonated a powerful bomb in the center of Oslo near several government buildings, killing eight people and inflicting widespread material damage. Breivik then proceeded to shoot and kill 69 people attending a Labor Party summer youth camp on the island of Uttoya. The attacks—the deadliest in Scandinavia since World War II—prompted a national and regional discussion of Breivik's extreme-right, anti-immigrant, anti-Muslim ideology, which included a radical resistance and hostility to Norway's multicultural agenda and its native Norwegian supporters. Minister of Justice Knut Storberget resigned in November 2011, citing personal reasons, but tacitly acknowledged the intense criticism he received over the poor police response to the Breivik massacre as significant to his decision.

Breivik's trial began in April 2012. He was initially declared legally insane and thus likely to be detained in a psychiatric institution, provoking a public outcry. The court, however, found Breivik legally competent, and he was sentenced to 21 years in prison with the possibility of "preventative detention," extending his sentence if he is deemed to be a continued threat to society. The independent 22 July Commission, which was appointed by the government, published its report in August 2012. The report found serious shortcomings in Norway's police force, including inadequate response times regarding its arrival at Uttoya and arrest of Breivik. The government subsequently announced that it would strengthen emergency preparedness measures.

Immigration to Norway has increased fivefold since the 1970s, including recent asylum seekers predominantly from Afghanistan, Iraq, Somalia, and Eritrea. More than 10 percent of Norway's population was foreign born in 2012, and more than 7,000 asylum seekers from some 100 countries arrived in Norway in 2012. In 2012, Norwegian police executed a series of raids on asylum centers and arranged forced repatriation of the more than 10,000 rejected asylum seekers still living illegally in Norway. The national debate on immigration was affected by the attacks by

Breivik, resulting in numerous public demonstrations and calls for strengthening Norway's tolerance and multiculturalism.

Political Rights and Civil Liberties: Norway is an electoral democracy. The unicameral Parliament, called the Storting, has 169 members who are directly elected for four-year terms through a system of proportional representation. The constitutional monarch, currently King Harald V, appoints the prime minister, who is the leader of the majority party or coalition in the Storting. While the monarch is officially the head of state and commander in chief of the armed forces, his duties are largely ceremonial.

The indigenous Sami population, in addition to participating in the national political process, has its own Consultative Constituent Assembly, or Sameting, which has worked to protect the group's language and cultural rights and influence the national government's decisions about Sami land and its resources. The Sameting is comprised of 39 representatives who are elected for four-year terms. The government supports Sami-language instruction, broadcast programs, and subsidized newspapers in Sami regions. A deputy minister in the national government deals specifically with Sami issues.

Norway remains one of the least corrupt countries in the world. However, isolated incidents of bribery and misconduct have occurred, and Norway's role in the international energy and mining industries has received particular scrutiny. In 2012, opposition parties strongly criticized Trade and Industry minister Trond Giske for appointing friends and family to state bodies and state-owned firms. Parliament started an inquiry into the matter in November 2012, which was ongoing at year's end. Norway was ranked 7 out of 176 countries surveyed in Transparency International's 2012 Corruption Perceptions Index.

Freedom of the press is constitutionally guaranteed. In an effort to promote political pluralism, the state subsidizes many newspapers, the majority of which are privately owned and openly partisan. Internet access is not impeded by the government.

Freedom of religion is protected by the constitution and respected in practice. The monarch is the constitutional head of the official Evangelical Lutheran Church of Norway, and at least half of the cabinet must belong to the church. Other denominations must register with the state to receive financial support, which is determined by size of membership. Students must take a course on religion and ethics focusing on Christianity, though it is thought to violate international human rights conventions. Contrary to a decision reached in 2009 by the National Courts Administration, the Equality Tribunal in August 2010 issued a nonbinding opinion that banning female police officers from wearing the hijab (headscarf) violates Norway's freedom of religion and antidiscrimination laws. A 2012 poll showed a rise in anti-Semitic attitudes, which prompted the Organization for Security and Cooperation in Europe to criticize Norwegian officials for inadequately addressing the issue. Ubaydullah Hussain, leader of the Norwegian Muslim extremist group "Prophet's Ummah," was arrested in November and held in custody for several weeks for posting threatening messages on social media sites against "certain individuals" in the Jewish community, as well as two journalists. Investigations were continuing at year's end.

The constitution guarantees freedoms of assembly and association. Norwegians are very active in nongovernmental organizations. Labor unions play an important role in consulting with the government on social and economic issues, and approximately 53 percent of the workforce is unionized. The right to strike is legally guaranteed, except for members of the military and senior civil servants, and is practiced without restrictions. All workers have the right to bargain collectively. The summer of 2012 saw the largest public sector strikes since 1984 over wages, affecting schools and prisons, as well as strikes in the private sector, including the crucial oil industry. The government imposed forced arbitration in September, but also formed a commission to evaluate the collective bargaining process.

The judiciary is independent, and the court system, headed by the Supreme Court, operates fairly at the local and national levels. The king appoints judges on the advice of the Ministry of Justice. The police are under civilian control, and human rights abuses by law enforcement authorities are rare. Prison conditions generally meet international standards. Three suspects were arrested in 2010 and charged with conspiracy to commit terrorism for their plan to attack the headquarters of *Jyllands-Posten*, the Danish newspaper that had published cartoons featuring the prophet Muhammad in 2005; they were found guilty of terrorism in January 2012, and sentenced to between four months and seven years in prison.

The mandate of the Office of the Ombudsman was expanded in 2006 to include all forms of discrimination, and it is responsible for enforcing the country's Gender Equality Act, the Discrimination Act, and the Worker Protection and Working Environment Act. While citizens within the EEA no longer need a residence permit to work in Norway, the agreement excludes Romanians and Bulgarians.

The Gender Equality Act provides equal rights for men and women. In 2009, women won nearly 40 percent of the seats in Parliament, a slight increase over previous elections. Norway is a destination country for human trafficking for the purposes of labor and sexual exploitation. The country, however, remains a leader in antitrafficking efforts, according to the U.S. State Department's 2012 Trafficking in Persons Report.

⬇ Oman

Political Rights: 6
Civil Liberties: 5
Status: Not Free

Population: 3,090,200
Capital: Muscat

Trend Arrow: Oman received a downward trend arrow due to arrests of human rights and political reform advocates and increased restrictions on free expression in online forums.

Ten-Year Ratings Timeline For Year Under Review (Political Rights, Civil Liberties, Status)

2003	2004	2005	2006	2007	2008	2009	2010	2011	2012
6,5NF	6,5NF	6,5NF	6,5NF	6,5NF	6,5NF	6,5NF	6,5NF	6,5NF	6,5NF

Overview:　　　　After Sultan Qaboos bin Said was slow to institute promised economic and political reforms, a series of antigovernment protests in 2012 led to crackdowns on freedoms of expression and assembly, with dozens of activists arrested throughout the year. The 2011 convictions of two journalists who wrote about corruption in the Ministry of Justice were upheld following an appeal. In December, municipal elections were held for the first time in Oman's history.

Except for a brief period of Persian rule, Oman has been an independent state since a native dynasty expelled the Portuguese from Muscat in 1650. The sultan subsequently conquered neighboring territories and built a small empire that included parts of the eastern coast of Africa and the southern Arabian Peninsula. The overseas possessions were gradually lost beginning in the mid-19th century.

During the 1950s and 1960s, Oman experienced a period of civil unrest centered mostly in the interior regions of the country. In 1964, a group of separatists supported by Marxist governments, including that of the neighboring People's Democratic Republic of Yemen (South Yemen), started a revolt in Oman's Dhofar province, which lasted until the mid-1970s. Sultan Qaboos bin Said al-Said seized power in 1970 by overthrowing his father, Sultan Said bin Taimur, who had ruled for nearly four decades. The new sultan launched a program to modernize Oman's infrastructure, educational system, government, and economy.

In 1991 Qaboos replaced the appointed State Consultative Council, established in 1981, with a partially elected Consultative Council (Majlis al-Shura) designed to provide the sultan with a wider range of opinions on ruling the country. A limited number of women gained the right to vote and run as candidates in 1994. The 1996 basic law, promulgated by royal decree, created a bicameral parliament consisting of an appointed Council of State (Majlis al-Dawla) and a wholly elected Consultative Council. Only a limited number of citizens selected by tribal leaders were allowed to vote in the first elections. The basic law granted certain civil liberties; banned discrimination on the basis of sex, religion, ethnicity, and social class; and clarified the process for royal succession.

This limited political reform in the 1990s was overshadowed by a stronger effort, spearheaded by Qaboos in 1995, to liberalize and diversify Oman's oil-dependent economy. In preparation for Oman's accession to the World Trade Organization in 2000, the government lifted restrictions on foreign investment and ownership of enterprises in the country.

In 2003, the sultan decreed universal suffrage for all Omanis over the age of 21. Parliamentary elections have been held twice since, once in 2007 and again in 2011, when Omanis elected 84 members of the new Majlis al-Shura from over 1,100 candidates.

Oman held its first ever municipal elections in December 2012. Fifty percent of eligible voters participated, choosing between 1,475 candidates for seats on 192 local councils. Four women won seats in the elections.

Following demonstrations in 2011 calling for economic and political reforms, Sultan Qaboos promised new jobs, an increase in social benefits, and measures to address government corruption. After three human rights activists were arrested in May 2012 while traveling to observe a strike by oil workers, the government began arresting bloggers and writers who had been critical of the government in online forums and social media. New protests were held in June, calling for the release of the imprisoned activists, for greater freedom of expression, as well as for faster implementation of promised economic reforms. By year's end, more than 30 activists, writers, and bloggers had been arrested or detained.

Political Rights and Civil Liberties: Oman is not an electoral democracy. Citizens elect the 84-member Consultative Council for four-year terms, but the chamber has no legislative powers and can only recommend changes to new laws. The Consultative Council is part of a bicameral body known as the Council of Oman. The other chamber, the 59-member State Council, is appointed by the sultan, who has absolute power and issues laws by decree. The sultan serves as the country's prime minister; heads the ministries of defense, foreign affairs, and finance; and is the governor of Oman's central bank.

Political parties are not permitted, and no meaningful organized political opposition exists. However, mechanisms exist for citizens to petition the government through local officials, and certain citizens are afforded limited opportunities to petition the sultan in direct meetings.

Although corruption has not been perceived to be a serious problem, the issue was a factor in mobilizing protests in 2011 and 2012. The legal code does not include freedom of information provisions. Oman was ranked 61 out of 176 countries surveyed in Transparency International's 2012 Corruption Perceptions Index.

Freedom of expression is limited, and criticism of the sultan is prohibited. The 2004 Private Radio and Television Companies Law allows for the establishment of private broadcast media outlets. The government permits private print publications, but many of these accept government subsidies, practice self-censorship, or face punishment for crossing political red-lines. In September 2011, Youssef al-Haj and Ibrahim Ma'mari of the newspaper *Al-Zaman* were convicted of "insulting" the minister of justice and sentenced to five months in prison after reporting in May on allegations of corruption at the ministry. In January 2012, an appeals court upheld the convictions, but suspended their sentences.

Omanis have access to the internet through the national telecommunications company, and the government censors politically sensitive and pornographic content. The sultan issued a decree in 2008 expanding government oversight and regulation of electronic communications, including on personal blogs. Throughout 2012, authorities increased the monitoring of social media and arrested several Omanis for posting "negative" or "insulting" material, spreading rumors about national security, or inciting protests. Thirty-two activists received prison sentences ranging from 6 to 18 months for posting comments on social media that were considered slanderous to Sultan Qaboos.

Islam is the state religion. Non-Muslims have the right to worship, though they are banned from proselytizing. Non-Muslim religious organizations must register with the government. The Ministry of Awqaf (Religious Charitable Bequests) and Religious Affairs distributes standardized texts for mosque sermons and expects imams to stay within the outlines of these texts. The government restricts academic freedom by preventing the publication of material on politically sensitive topics.

The right to peaceful assembly within limits is provided for by the basic law. However, all public gatherings require official permission, and the government has the authority to prevent organized public meetings without any appeal process. In

2012, a dozen activists were fined and sentenced to one year in prison for participating in protests held in support of writers and bloggers who had been arrested for libeling the Sultan. The basic law allows the formation of nongovernmental organizations, but civic life remains limited. The government has not permitted the establishment of independent human rights organizations and generally uses the registration and licensing process to block the formation of groups that are seen as a threat to stability.

Oman's 2003 labor law allows workers to select a committee to represent their interests but prevents them from organizing unions. Additional labor reforms enacted in 2006 brought a number of improvements, including protections for union activity, collective bargaining, and strikes. However, legal provisions covering migrant workers remain inadequate, and domestic servants are particularly vulnerable to abuse. In May 2012, over a thousand oil workers from contracted companies went on strike calling for increased wages, health insurance, and risk compensation. Most of the strikers were fired form their positions but later rehired after signing oaths stating that their strike was illegal and that they would not strike again.

The judiciary is not independent and remains subordinate to the sultan and the Ministry of Justice. Sharia (Islamic law) is the source of all legislation, and Sharia Court Departments within the civil court system are responsible for family law matters, such as divorce and inheritance. In less populated areas, tribal laws and customs are frequently used to adjudicate disputes. The authorities do not regularly follow requirements to obtain court orders to hold suspects in pretrial detention. The penal code contains vague provisions for offenses against national security, and such charges are prosecuted before the State Security Court, which usually holds proceedings that are closed to the public. Prisons are not accessible to independent monitors, but former prisoners report overcrowding.

Omani law does not protect noncitizens from discrimination. Foreign workers risk deportation if they abandon their contracts without documentation releasing them from their previous employment agreement. Under these regulations, employers can effectively keep workers from switching jobs and hold them in conditions susceptible to exploitation.

Although the basic law prohibits discrimination on the basis of sex, women suffer from legal and social discrimination. Oman's personal status law, based on Sharia, favors the rights of men over those of women in marriage, divorce, inheritance, and child custody. According to official statistics, women constitute a very small percentage of the total labor force in Oman. Despite a 2008 antitrafficking law, Oman remains a destination and transit country for the trafficking of women and men.

Pakistan

Political Rights: 4
Civil Liberties: 5
Status: Partly Free

Population: 180,427,600
Capital: Islamabad

Note: The numerical ratings and status listed above do not reflect conditions in Pakistani-controlled Kashmir, which is examined in a separate report.

Ten-Year Ratings Timeline For Year Under Review (Political Rights, Civil Liberties, Status)

2003	2004	2005	2006	2007	2008	2009	2010	2011	2012
6,5NF	6,5NF	6,5NF	6,5NF	6,5NF	4,5PF	4,5PF	4,5PF	4,5PF	4,5PF

Overview:
In 2012, despite ongoing tensions between the civilian government, the military and intelligence agencies, and the judiciary, the government managed to remain in power, albeit with a change in prime minister in June. Societal discrimination and attacks against religious minorities and women, as well as weak rule of law and impunity, remained issues of concern. Journalists, human rights defenders, and humanitarian aid workers faced significant pressure and threats, particularly those whose work focused on sensitive topics such as Pakistan's blasphemy laws or abuses by security and intelligence agencies. The army's campaigns against Islamist militants in the tribal areas led to a range of human rights abuses, displacement of civilians, and retaliatory terrorist attacks across the country, while sectarian attacks, as well as violence in Balochistan and the city of Karachi, worsened during the year.

Pakistan was created as a Muslim homeland during the partition of British India in 1947, and the military has directly or indirectly ruled the country for much of its independent history. As part of his effort to consolidate power, military dictator Mohammad Zia ul-Haq amended the constitution in 1985 to allow the president to dismiss elected governments. After Zia's death in 1988, successive civilian presidents cited corruption and abuse of power in sacking elected governments headed by prime ministers Benazir Bhutto of the Pakistan People's Party (PPP) in 1990 and 1996, and Nawaz Sharif of the Pakistan Muslim League (PML) in 1993.

Sharif, who returned to power in the 1997 elections, was deposed in a military coup after he attempted to fire the army chief, General Pervez Musharraf, in 1999. Musharraf appointed himself "chief executive" (and later president), declared a state of emergency, and suspended democratic institutions. The 2002 Legal Framework Order (LFO) gave Musharraf effective control over Parliament and changed the electoral rules to the detriment of opposition parties. The regime also openly promoted progovernment parties, such as the newly formed Pakistan Muslim League Quaid-i-Azam (PML-Q), which captured the largest share of seats in the 2002 parliamentary elections and led the new government.

While he managed to contain the secular opposition over the next several years, Musharraf was less willing to rein in radical Islamist groups, with which the military traditionally had a close relationship. These groups gradually extended their influence from outlying regions like the Federally Administered Tribal Areas (FATA) to major urban centers, carrying out attacks on both military and civilian targets.

Tensions between Musharraf and the increasingly activist judiciary came to a head in 2007 when he suspended Iftikhar Chaudhry, the chief justice of the Supreme Court, sparking political unrest. When the court attempted to rule on the validity of Musharraf's victory in the October presidential election, he again took preemptive action and imposed martial law on November 3. The state of emergency was lifted in mid-December and an amended version of the constitution was restored. Following the December 27 assassination of former prime minister Bhutto, parliamentary elections were postponed until February 2008 and Bhutto's widower, Asif Ali Zardari, assumed de facto leadership of the PPP.

The PPP led the February voting, taking 97 of 272 directly elected seats in the National Assembly, followed by Sharif's PML-N with 71. The ruling PML-Q was routed, taking only 42 seats, and the Muttahida Majlis-i-Amal (MMA), an alliance of Islamic parties, was also severely weakened. At the provincial level, the PML-N triumphed in its traditional stronghold of Punjab, the PPP dominated in Sindh, and the Awami National Party (ANP), a secular and ethnic Pashtun group, won the most seats in North-West Frontier Province (NWFP).

In August 2008, Musharraf resigned as president in the face of impeachment efforts. The next month, Zardari won an indirect presidential election with 481 of the 702 votes cast; 368 national and provincial lawmakers abstained or boycotted the vote. In addition, the PPP and its allies gained a plurality in the March 2009 Senate elections. After Chaudhry was reinstated as chief justice, also in March, the Supreme Court began dismantling the actions taken by Musharraf, declaring them illegal and calling on Parliament to "regularize" them through ordinary legislation.

During 2010, tensions between the civilian PPP-led government, the judiciary, and the military persisted, as the government faced pressure from the military to replace Zardari, the judiciary repeated its calls for Zardari's old corruption cases to be reopened, and the military and intelligence agencies attempted to undercut the government's policies and decision making. Despite the government's increasingly tenuous hold on power in 2011 and 2012, it managed to remain in office through year's end amid a delicate power struggle between the politicians, military, and judiciary. In January 2012, the Supreme Court initiated contempt proceedings against Prime Minister Yousaf Raza Gilani, and he was found guilty in April of refusing to address corruption allegations against Zardari, prompting calls for his resignation. In June, the National Assembly voted to replace Gilani as prime minister with Raja Pervez Ashraf.

Armed conflict between the military and Islamist militants affiliated with the Tehrik-i-Taliban Pakistan (TTP, or Pakistani Taliban) network persisted during 2012, as did regular missile attacks by U.S. drone aircraft that killed militant leaders but also caused civilian casualties and stoked resentment among many Pakistanis. Meanwhile, a range of Islamist militant groups continued to stage bombing and other attacks against official buildings, prominent politicians and military personnel, and religious ceremonies and places of worship. While the level of killings overall in 2012 remained roughly equivalent to the previous year, the number of civilians affected by the violence increased.

Political Rights and Civil Liberties: Pakistan is not an electoral democracy. A civilian government and president were elected in 2008, ending years of military rule, but the military continues to exercise de facto control over many areas of government policy. The political environment is also troubled by corruption, partisan clashes, and Islamist militancy, among other problems.

The lower house of the bicameral Parliament is the 342-seat National Assembly, which has 272 directly elected members and additional seats reserved for women (60 seats) and non-Muslim minorities (10 seats), all with five-year terms. The upper house is the 100-seat Senate, most of whose members are elected by the four provincial assemblies for six-year terms, with half up for election every three years. The president is elected for a five-year term by an electoral college consisting of the national and provincial legislatures, and cannot be elected for more than two consecutive terms. The Constitution (18th Amendment) Act of 2010 rescinded the president's right (granted by the 2002 LFO) to unilaterally dismiss the prime minister and the national and provincial legislatures and to impose a provincial state of emergency. The president also lost the power to appoint the head of the army and the chief election commissioner. The reforms were intended to strengthen the premiership and Parliament.

The 2008 parliamentary elections were not completely free and fair. A European Union observer mission noted the abuse of state resources and media, inaccuracies in the voter rolls, and rigging of the vote tallies in some areas. Opposition party workers faced police harassment, and more than 100 people were killed in political violence during the campaign period. However, private media and civil society groups played a significant watchdog role, and despite the irregularities, the balloting led to an orderly rotation of power that reflected the will of the people. In preparation for general elections scheduled for early 2013, an amendment to the Election Law passed in April 2011 was designed to strengthen the independence of the Election Commission and improve procedures for voter registration, while limiting opportunities for rigging, and an amended code of electoral conduct and other rules designed to limit fraud and misuse of resources were announced in June 2012. However, concerns remained about revised electoral rolls and the possibility that a significant number of voters may not have been registered properly.

The institutional capacity and internal democratic structures of political parties—some of which are based more on personalities than ideologies or platforms—remain weak. Some political parties also have armed or militant wings, which led to continued concern in 2012 as turf battles among various factions worsened in Karachi, leading to the killings of a number of political activists.

A certain number of legislative seats are reserved for women and religious minorities at the national, provincial, and local levels. In some parts of the country, women have difficulty voting and running for office due to objections from social and religious conservatives, though women won an additional unreserved 16 National Assembly seats in the 2008 elections. At least 17 seats in the Senate are reserved for women, and religious minorities were allotted 4 seats in the Senate as part of the 18th Amendment. Members of the heterodox Ahmadiyya sect, who consider themselves Muslims but are deemed a non-Muslim minority by the constitution, largely boycotted the 2008 elections to protest this official designation.

The FATA are governed by the president through unelected civil servants, though elected local councils were set up in 2007. In another positive step, a system introduced in August 2012 gave local government bodies greater autonomy in financial, administrative, and legislative matters, as well as the ability to levy taxes.

Pakistan's government operates with limited transparency and accountability, though this has improved with the resumption of civilian rule. The military has a stake in continuing to influence both commercial and political decision-making processes, in addition to its traditional dominance of foreign policy and security issues. Serving and retired officers have received top jobs in ministries, state-run corporations, and universities, and they enjoy a range of other privileges. A tenth of all civilian jobs remain reserved for officers.

Corruption is pervasive at all levels of politics and the bureaucracy, and oversight mechanisms to ensure transparency remain weak. Hundreds of politicians, diplomats, and officials, including President Asif Ali Zardari, were granted immunity in ongoing corruption cases under the 2007 National Reconciliation Ordinance (NRO). Though the Supreme Court revoked the NRO in 2009 and upheld this decision in a 2011 ruling, prosecution of reopened cases remains uneven and ineffective. In March 2012, the Supreme Court ordered that a key corruption case against the president be reopened. However, also during the year, Chief Justice Iftikhar Chaudhry, who has been at the forefront of initiating corruption investigations against elected politicians, faced allegations that he had intentionally overlooked his son's corrupt relationship with the prominent and politically connected businessman Malik Riaz. Pakistan was ranked 139 out of 176 countries surveyed in Transparency International's 2012 Corruption Perceptions Index. Transparency International's local branch in Pakistan continued to face harassment and threats over its efforts to monitor the disbursement of foreign aid, as well as to highlight corrupt practices under the Zardari administration. In general, Pakistan has an extremely low level of tax collection, as many of the country's wealthiest citizens, including members of Parliament, use legal loopholes to avoid paying taxes. A December 2012 report by Pakistan's Center for Investigative Journalism found that around 70 percent of current lawmakers did not file tax returns the previous year.

Pakistan's outspoken newspapers and private television stations present a diverse range of news and opinion. However, powerful figures, including military officials and members of the higher judiciary, attempt to silence critical reporting, and the very high level of violence against journalists continued in 2012. The constitution and other laws authorize the government to curb speech on subjects including the armed forces, the judiciary, and religion. Blasphemy laws are occasionally used against the media, and since 2010, broadly defined contempt laws have increasingly been employed to restrict reporting on particular court cases or judges. The government also continued to engage in efforts to suspend and temporarily block broadcasts or otherwise restrict media content related to certain extremist groups, as well as political satire. In August, the Supreme Court ordered the broadcast regulatory body to define obscenity in order to be able to censor media content.

According to the Committee to Protect Journalists, at least seven journalists were murdered because of their work in 2012, making Pakistan the world's third-deadliest country for members of the press. Impunity in cases concerning murdered journalists remains the norm. Intimidation by the security forces—including verbal threats, physical attacks, and arbitrary, incommunicado detention—continues to occur, as do harassment and attacks by Islamic fundamentalists and hired thugs working for feudal landlords or local politicians. A number of reporters covering the conflict between the military and Islamist militants in Khyber Pakhtunkhwa (or KP, as NWFP was renamed in 2010) and the FATA were detained, threatened, expelled, or otherwise obstructed in 2012, by either government forces or militants. Conditions for journalists in Balochistan also remained grim.

While websites addressing sensitive subjects, particularly Balochi separatism, have routinely been blocked by the authorities, starting in 2010 the government moved more aggressively to block "blasphemous" material. This trend continued in 2012, affecting websites as well as mobile phone content, and including more material of a political nature. The social-networking website Twitter was blocked briefly in May, and in September, in response to protests sparked by a video concerning the prophet Muhammad, the Supreme Court ordered a block of the video-sharing website YouTube, which remained in place at year's end.

Pakistan is an Islamic republic, and there are numerous legal restrictions on religious freedom. Violations of blasphemy laws draw harsh sentences, including the death penalty, and injuring the "religious feelings" of individual citizens is prohibited. Incidents in which police take bribes to file false blasphemy charges against Ahmadis, Christians, Hindus, and occasionally Muslims continue to occur, with several dozen cases reported each year. No executions on blasphemy charges have been carried out to date, but accusations or the charges alone can lead to years of imprisonment, ill-treatment in custody, and extralegal persecution by religious extremists or mob violence. Aasia Bibi, a Christian woman sentenced to death for blasphemy in 2010, remained in jail pending an appeal. Meanwhile, the arrest of a 14-year-old mentally impaired girl, Rimsha Masih, on blasphemy charges in August 2012 led to widespread condemnation; several hundred Christian families in her neighborhood were then forced to flee their homes as a result of the case. The Islamabad High Court dismissed the case in November. Religious hard-liners have argued that even advocacy of reforming the blasphemy laws constitutes an act of blasphemy. In 2011, two reformist PPP politicians—Punjab governor Salman Taseer and Shahbaz Bhatti, the minister for minorities affairs and a Christian—were murdered after they spoke out against abuse of the blasphemy laws, and others have faced death threats and legal harassment.

The penal code severely restricts the religious practice of Ahmadis, who comprise a small percentage of the population, and they must effectively renounce their beliefs to vote or gain admission to educational institutions. Authorities occasionally confiscate or close Ahmadiyya publications and harass their staff, and dozens of Ahmadis faced criminal charges under blasphemy or other discriminatory laws during 2012.

Religious minorities also face unofficial economic and social discrimination, and they are occasionally subject to violence and harassment. In a growing trend, particularly in Sindh Province, Hindu girls are kidnapped, forcibly converted to Islam, and compelled to marry their kidnappers. Terrorist and other attacks on places of worship and religious gatherings occur frequently, leading to the deaths of dozens of people every year. There has been a notable upsurge in violence between members of the Sunni Muslim majority and the Shiite Muslim minority since 2009, with largely Shiite ethnic Hazaras in Balochistan facing particular threats during 2012. Recent waves of attacks on Christians have also been attributed to the spread of Sunni extremist ideology.

The government generally does not restrict academic freedom. However, the university cadres of political parties and Islamist groups intimidate students, teachers, and administrators; aim to impose "Islamic" moral codes by blocking certain types of classes or behavior; and try to influence university policies. Schools and female teachers, particularly in the FATA and KP, continue to face threats and attacks by Islamist militants. In October 2012, Malala Yousufzai, a teenage activist for girls' education, was shot in the head and seriously injured by the Taliban, provoking international condemnation.

The rights to freedom of assembly and association are selectively upheld. Authorities sometimes restrict public gatherings, disperse protests with excessive force, and use preventive detention to forestall planned demonstrations. However, such tactics were employed less in 2012 than in previous years.

Authorities generally tolerate the work of nongovernmental organizations (NGOs) and allow them to publish critical material. However, NGOs that focus on female education and empowerment, and female NGO staff in general, have faced threats, attacks, and a number of murders by radical Islamists, particularly in the FATA and KP. Citing security concerns, the government has at times prevented aid groups from operating in Balochistan, exacerbating the province's humanitarian situation, and access to KP and the FATA remains challenging. Working or commenting on issues concerning blasphemy or the intelligence services has become more risky for both local and international activists, and attacks on human rights defenders also appeared to be on the rise. Pakistan is home to a large number of charitable or cultural organizations, such as the Jamaat-ud-Dawa, that have links to Islamist militant groups.

An April 2010 constitutional amendment placed labor law and policy under the purview of the provinces. Provincial labor laws allow workers to form and join trade unions, but place restrictions on union membership, the right to strike, and collective bargaining, particular in industries deemed essential. Although protests and strikes occur regularly, many workers have been fired for union activity, and union leaders have faced harassment. Illegal bonded labor is widespread, though the authorities in 2012 continued efforts to combat the practice in the brick-kiln industry. Enforcement of child labor laws remains inadequate; recent surveys have indicated that there are at least 10 million child workers in Pakistan.

The judiciary consists of civil and criminal courts and a special Sharia (Islamic law) court for certain offenses. Lower courts remain plagued by corruption, intimidation, and a backlog of more than a million cases that results in lengthy pretrial detention. The 2009 National Judicial Policy aimed to tackle all three problems, and appears to have had some positive effects, with backlogs dramatically reduced in certain provinces.

Provisions of the 18th Amendment granted power over judicial appointments to a judicial commission rather than the president, and the 19th Amendment further strengthened the role of the chief justice and other senior judges in the commission and appointments process. However, tensions between the judiciary and the executive persisted in 2012. The Supreme Court continued to push for the revival of corruption cases against Zardari and engaged in activism in politically popular cases concerning blasphemy and economic policy. Observers voiced concern that the judiciary was becoming increasingly close to the army, supporting its agenda while trying to undermine the executive.

Other parts of the judicial system, such as the antiterrorism courts, operate with limited due process rights. The Sharia court enforces the 1979 Hudood Ordinances, which criminalize extramarital sex and several alcohol, gambling, and property offenses. They provide for Koranic punishments, including death by stoning for adultery, as well as jail terms and fines. In part because of strict evidentiary standards, authorities have never carried out the Koranic punishments. The justice system in the FATA is governed by the Frontier Crimes Regulation, which allows collective punishment for individual crimes and preventive detention of up to three years. It also authorizes tribal leaders to administer justice according to Sharia and tribal custom. In designated parts of the Provincially Administered Tribal Areas—districts of KP and Balochistan outside of federal and provincial legislative and judicial control—Sharia is imposed under the 2009 Nizam-e-Adl regulation, and judges are assisted by Islamic scholars.

Feudal landlords and tribal elders throughout Pakistan adjudicate some disputes and impose punishments—including the death penalty and the forced exchange of brides between tribes—in unsanctioned parallel courts called jirgas. Human rights groups have noted that such jirgas impose hundreds of death sentences each year, the majority on women. Militants in the tribal areas and parts of KP have reportedly set up their own courts, enforcing a strict interpretation of Islamic law and dispensing harsh penalties with little regard for due process.

Police and other security services routinely engage in excessive force, torture, extortion, arbitrary detention, rape of female detainees, and extrajudicial killings. Conditions in the overcrowded prisons are extremely poor, and case backlogs mean that the majority of inmates are awaiting trial. Feudal landlords, tribal groups, and some militant groups operate private jails where detainees are regularly maltreated. While a number of cases are investigated and some prosecutions do occur, impunity for human rights abuses remains the norm. In a positive step, in May 2012, Zardari authorized the creation of an independent National Human Rights Commission, which would be empowered to monitor human rights conditions, investigate cases of violations, and provide recommendations to the government. However, critics raised concern that the new body would not be able to address violations committed by the military or intelligence agencies.

The high number of cases of "disappearance," in which people are illegally detained incommunicado by state agencies, continued to be a key issue of concern, with hundreds of unresolved cases pending. Some victims were suspected of links to radical Islamist groups, but such detentions have also affected Balochi and Sindhi nationalists, journalists, researchers, and social workers. The military's powerful Directorate for Inter-Services Intelligence (ISI), which operates largely outside the control of civilian leaders and the courts, has faced intermittent pressure from the Supreme Court to end the practice of secret detentions, but the court's ability to resolve cases has been mixed. In 2012, the Supreme Court held ongoing hearings for a case regarding the role of the paramilitary Frontier Corps in disappearances in Balochistan. While official commissions of inquiry established by the government to trace individual cases have also had limited success, new cases continued to be reported. According to the Human Rights Commission of Pakistan (HRCP), an NGO, of the 87 new disappearances reported in 2012, 72 individuals were traced or eventually released.

Tens of thousands of armed militants belonging to radical Sunni Islamist groups have varying agendas and carry out terrorist attacks against foreign, government, and religious minority targets, killing hundreds of civilians each year. Sunni and Shiite groups engage in tit-for-tat sectarian violence, mostly bomb attacks against places of worship and religious gatherings. The New Delhi–based South Asia Terrorism Portal (SATP) reported that 507 people were killed and 577 were injured in sectarian violence in 2012, a substantial increase from the previous year.

The military's campaigns against Islamist fighters in the tribal areas since 2002 have been accompanied by human rights abuses, and missile strikes attributed to U.S. drone aircraft have reportedly killed or injured civilians along with their intended targets. In total, more than 340 people were killed by alleged drone attacks in 2012. The authorities are sponsoring tribal militias, or lashkars, to help control the FATA, creating yet another unaccountable armed force. Islamist militants' expanding influence over territory in KP and the FATA has led to severe practical restrictions on local inhabitants' dress, social behavior, educational opportunities, and legal rights. The militant groups also target political leaders (particularly from the ANP), tribal elders, teachers, and aid workers in their quest for control over local populations. In July 2012, women's rights advocate Farida Afridi was murdered outside her home; she had previously received threats regarding her work. Although many of the internally displaced civilians in KP have returned to their homes over the past several years, hundreds of thousands remained displaced in the FATA. The SATP reported that 6,211 people were killed nationwide in terrorist- or insurgent-related violence in 2012, including 3,007 civilians, 732 security force personnel, and 2,472 militants, a level roughly comparable to the previous year but an increase in the number of civilians affected.

A simmering insurgency continued in Balochistan, with ethnic Balochi activists demanding either enhanced political autonomy or outright independence as well as more local control over the province's natural resources. Armed militants carried out a growing number of attacks on infrastructure, security forces, and non-Balochi teachers and educational institutions during the year. The army's counterinsurgency operations have led to increasing human rights violations and the displacement of civilians. Thousands of activists, political leaders, and other locals with suspected separatist sympathies have been detained, according to the International Crisis Group, with scores killed in apparent extrajudicial executions. Sunni militants, seen to operate under the protection of the security forces, carried out a campaign against mostly ethnic Hazara Shiites in Balochistan, killing dozens of Hazaras in a series of targeted attacks in 2012. After years of inaction, in May a number of key stakeholders agreed to a change of approach by the federal government that emphasized a political rather than a military solution to the crisis, including opening talks with insurgents and placing the paramilitary forces responsible for many of the abuses under political rather than military control.

Ethnic violence in Karachi escalated further in 2012, killing nearly 2,000 people, mostly ordinary civilians. The turf battles are exacerbated by the fact that each faction has the support of a political party, including the traditionally dominant Muttahida Qaumi Movement (MQM), which represents refugees from India who settled in Karachi in 1947; the ANP, representing ethnic Pashtun migrants from other areas of Pakistan; and the PPP, which is allied with Balochi gangs. The criminal gangs that carry out much of the violence also regularly extort money from businesses in Karachi, a crucial economic hub.

Pakistan hosts approximately 1.65 million registered Afghan refugees and more than a million undocumented Afghans, with the majority living in urban areas rather than refugee settlements on the border. They face societal and official discrimination as well as economic exploitation, since even registered refugees are not allowed to work legally. Other marginalized groups, including Dalits, or lower castes, also face multiple forms of discrimination.

Traditional norms, discriminatory laws, and weak policing contribute to a high incidence of rape, domestic abuse, and other forms of violence—including acid attacks—against women. According to the HRCP, up to 80 percent of women are victims of such abuse during their lifetimes. Female victims of sexual crimes are often pressured by police not to file charges, and they are sometimes urged by their families to commit suicide. Gang rapes sanctioned by village councils to punish the targeted woman's relatives continue to be reported, even though perpetrators in some cases have received harsh sentences. The 2006 Women's Protection Act requires judges to try rape cases under criminal law rather than Sharia. However, extramarital sex is still criminalized, and spousal rape is not recognized as a crime. According to the HRCP, at least 913 women were killed by family members in so-called honor killings in 2012, a level similar to the previous year, but many such crimes may go unreported. Illegal forms of child and forced marriage remain problems, and women who attempt to choose their own spouse often face severe pressure and retribution from family members, including murder. Most interfaith marriages are considered illegal, and the children of such unions would be illegitimate.

However, in the past several years, a number of laws have attempted to improve women's legal rights and avenues for redress against abuse and discrimination. In 2011, the Prevention of Anti-Women Practices Act explicitly recognized a range of practices—including acid attacks, forced marriage, and honor killings—as criminal acts, and afforded protection to victims, while the Acid Control and Acid Crime Prevention (Amendment) Bill provided guidelines on jail terms and fines for perpetrators of acid attacks. In March 2012, Zardari signed the National Commission on the Status of Women Bill, which strengthened the commission's autonomy and ability to investigate violations.

Pakistani inheritance law discriminates against women, who also face unofficial discrimination in educational and employment opportunities. Two laws were enacted in 2010 to criminalize sexual harassment in the workplace and establish related codes of conduct and mechanisms for complaints. The trafficking of women and children remains a serious concern, with female victims used for forced labor or sexual exploitation.

Legal and societal discrimination against gay men and lesbians is pervasive, and most individuals do not identify themselves as such openly. In 2009, the Supreme Court ordered that hijras (a term covering transvestites, hermaphrodites, and eunuchs) be considered equal citizens and allowed to classify themselves as a distinct gender on national identity cards. In late 2012, transgender citizens were included as a category in the country's computerized national identity card process, which would allow this group voting rights in the forthcoming elections.

Palau

Political Rights: 1
Civil Liberties: 1
Status: Free

Population: 20,600
Capital: Melekeok

Ten-Year Ratings Timeline For Year Under Review (Political Rights, Civil Liberties, Status)

2003	2004	2005	2006	2007	2008	2009	2010	2011	2012
1,1F	1,1F	1,1F	1,1F	1,1F	1,1F	1,1F	1,1F	1,1F	1,1F

Overview: Former president Tommy Remengesau Jr. was reelected in November 2012, defeating incumbent Johnson Toribiong. In October, Palau concluded its first-ever trial by jury. Meanwhile, Typhoon Bopha caused millions of dollars of damage in the country in December.

The United States administered Palau, which consists of 8 main islands and more than 250 smaller islands, as a UN Trust Territory from 1947 until 1981, when it became self-governing. Palau gained full independence in 1994 under a Compact of Free Association with the United States; the compact granted Palau $442 million in U.S. economic aid between 1994 and 2009 and allowed Palauan citizens to reside, work, study, and access federal government programs in the United States in exchange for U.S. military access to the archipelago until 2044. A financial agreement signed in September 2010 under the compact promises more than $250 million in total assistance through 2024. However, the U.S. Congress had yet to ratify the agreement by the end of 2012.

Johnson Toribiong was elected president in November 2008. Parliamentary elections were held the same month with all candidates running as independents.

Development assistance from Taiwan and other donors, remittances from citizens overseas, and tourism are major sources of revenue. Some legislators have advocated closer ties with China in order to attract Chinese tourists and investments. The 2011 Petroleum Act seeks to expand revenue sources by allowing exploration, extraction, and development and production of oil and gas resources in Palau's 200-nautical mile exclusive economic zone.

A power plant fire in November 2011 led to a two-week state of emergency and electricity rationing, affecting hospitals, the sewage system, schools, and public services. In December, Typhoon Bopha destroyed homes and disrupted water, electricity, and telecommunications systems; recovery efforts are expected to cost as much as $20 million. To reduce Palau's dependence on fossil fuel-generated electricity, the legislature in January 2012 approved the greater use of renewable energy. However, Palau lacks funding for equipment, and its remoteness means that the shipping of construction equipment can take weeks or months.

More than 12,000 voters registered for the September 26, 2012, primary election. The top two winners among three presidential candidates and four vice-presidential candidates competed in the general elections on November 6. Tommy Remengesau, Jr., who was president from 2001 to 2009, was declared the winner with 58 percent of the vote, defeating Toribiong. Antonio Bells defeated incumbent Kerai Mariur to secure the vice presidency with 52 percent of the vote. In concurrent parliamentary elections, all candidates ran as independents.

Political Rights and Civil Liberties: Palau is an electoral democracy. The bicameral legislature, the Olbiil Era Kelulau, consists of the 9-member Senate and the 16-member House of Delegates. Legislators are elected to four-year terms by popular vote, as are the president and vice president. The president may serve only two consecutive terms. Palau is organized into 16 states, each of which is headed by a governor and has a seat in the House of Delegates. Every state is also allowed its own constitutional convention and to elect a legislature and head of state.

There are no political parties, though no laws prevent their formation. The current system of loose political alliances that can quickly form and dismantle has had a destabilizing effect on governance.

Government corruption and abuse are problems, with several high-ranking public officials having faced charges in recent years. Although anti-money laundering measures were introduced in 2007, significant deficiencies in due diligence, record keeping, and monitoring have been found, and the attorney general's office generally lacks the resources to oversee implementation of these measures.

Freedoms of speech and the press are respected. There are several print publications, five privately owned radio stations, and one privately owned television station. Cable television rebroadcasts U.S. and other foreign programs. The government does not impede internet access, but high costs and a lack of connectivity outside the main islands limit diffusion. Palau is seeking assistance from multilateral development banks to finance an underwater cable that would expand internet access.

Citizens of Palau enjoy freedom of religion. Although religious organizations are required to register with the government, applications have never been denied. There have been no reports of restrictions on academic freedom, and the government provides well-funded basic education for all. A December 2012 law requires Palauan language instruction in all primary and secondary schools chartered in Palau or receiving public funds.

Freedoms of assembly and association are respected. Many nongovernmental groups represent youth, health, and women's issues. Workers can freely organize unions and bargain collectively, though the economy is largely based on subsistence agriculture and is heavily dependent on U.S. aid, as well as rent payments and remittances from Palauans working overseas.

The judiciary is independent, and trials are generally fair. In October 2012, Palau concluded its first-ever jury trial; previously, all trials were decided by a judge. A 300-member police and first-response force maintains internal order. Palau has no military. There have been no reports of prisoner abuse, though overcrowding is a problem in the country's only prison.

Foreign workers account for about one-third of the population and 75 percent of the workforce. There have been reports of discrimination against and abuse of foreign workers, who cannot legally change employers once they arrive in Palau. In response to social tensions and a slower economy, the government in 2009 decided to limit the total number of foreign workers in the country at any time to 6,000.

Women are highly regarded in this matrilineal society; land rights and familial descent are traced through women. Women are active in the economy and politics. The number of domestic violence and child abuse cases is small. Sexual harassment and rape, including spousal rape, are illegal. The U.S. State Department's 2012 Human Trafficking Report cites Palau as a destination country for forced prostitution (women) and labor (men and women). In 2012, police investigated several cases of forced labor and offered assistance and housing to victims, but law enforcement in general lacks training and resources to fight human trafficking. In October 2011, Palau pledged to end discrimination against gay men and lesbians following a UN audit of human rights in the island state, but no concrete changes had been implemented as of the end of 2012.

Panama

Political Rights: 1
Civil Liberties: 2
Status: Free

Population: 3,610,000
Capital: Panama City

Ten-Year Ratings Timeline For Year Under Review (Political Rights, Civil Liberties, Status)

2003	2004	2005	2006	2007	2008	2009	2010	2011	2012
1,2F	1,2F	1,2F	1,2F	1,2F	1,2F	1,2F	1,2F	1,2F	1,2F

Overview: President Ricardo Martinelli confronted serious challenges from opposition parties while attempting to pass electoral reforms in October 2012. In September, security forces clashed violently with protesters opposing the proposed sale of state land to private companies.

Panama was part of Colombia until 1903, when a U.S.-supported revolt resulted in the proclamation of an independent republic. A period of weak civilian rule ended with a 1968 military coup that brought General Omar Torrijos to power. After signing the 1977 Panama Canal Treaty with the United States, under which the canal was gradually transferred to Panamanian control by 1999, Torrijos promised democratization.

After Torrijos's death in 1981, General Manuel Noriega emerged as Panamanian Defense Force (PDF) chief. He rigged the 1984 elections to bring the Democratic Revolutionary Party (PRD), then the PDF's political arm, to power. The Democratic Alliance of Civic Opposition (ADOC) won the 1989 elections, but Noriega annulled the vote and declared himself head of state. He was removed during a U.S. military invasion later that year, and ADOC's Guillermo Endara became president. Presidential and legislative elections in 2004 returned the PRD to power, with Martín Torrijos, son of the former strongman, winning the presidency. In the 2009 elections, Ricardo Martinelli of the center-right, business-oriented Democratic Change (CD) party won the presidency as part of the Alliance for Change coalition with the Panameñista Party (PP), capturing 60 percent of the vote.

The CD's alliance with the PP collapsed in August 2011, when Martinelli announced plans to hold a referendum on proposed electoral reforms, which included allowing consecutive terms in office for the president. In September 2012, the government passed an electoral law that would eliminate voting by party lists and establish primaries six months before elections, in which independent candidates would have to collect at least 2 percent of the total number of valid votes from the previous elections in order to compete. Opposition parties argued that the reforms violated the constitution and could allow Martinelli to seek reelection in 2014.

In September 2012, the legislature passed a law allowing commerce officials to fine offenders accused of copyright infringement by up to $100,000 without a trial. Opponents argued that the law could curtail free speech, though the government said that it was necessary to bring Panama into compliance with its free-trade agreement with the United States, which went into effect on October 31, 2012.

In October, the government canceled plans to sell state-owned land in the duty-free zone in Colón following massive protests from local residents, who feared the sale of the land would result in job losses. Three people were killed, at least six were injured, and over two hundred were arrested in violent clashes between protesters and security forces. After canceling the plan, the government announced that it would instead increase commercial rents and reinvest money in the impoverished and crime-ridden area.

Political Rights and Civil Liberties: Panama is an electoral democracy. The 2009 national elections were considered free and fair by international observers. The president and deputies of the 71-seat unicameral National Assembly are elected by popular vote for five-year terms. Presidents may not seek consecutive terms and must wait two terms before running again.

Corruption remains widespread, and electoral reforms have been criticized for failing to improve the transparency of campaign financing. Panama and the UN Office on Drugs and Crime signed an agreement in June 2011 to establish a regional anticorruption academy. After serving 20 years in a U.S. jail for drug trafficking, racketeering, and money laundering and a term in France on money-laundering charges, former dictator Manuel Noriega was extradited in December 2011 to Panama to serve a 20-year sentence related to human rights violations. In September 2012, Vice President Juan Carlos Varela accused officials associated with President Ricardo Martinelli of accepting bribes when signing a $250 million contract to buy helicopters and other equipment from Italy. In October, a criminal complaint was filed against the secretary general of the ruling CD, alleging that he misused government funds. A new shield law went into effect in November, making it more difficult to file charges against public officials by requiring evidence of guilt before a complaint may be filed. Panama was ranked 83 out of 176 countries surveyed in Transparency International's 2012 Corruption Perceptions Index.

The country's media outlets are privately owned, with the exceptions of the state-owned television network and a network operated by the Roman Catholic

Church. However, media ownership is generally concentrated among relatives and associates of former president Ernesto Pérez Balladares (1994–99) of the PRD. Panama maintains a harsh legal environment for journalists. The legislature considered a bill to make it illegal to criticize the country's president and other top officials, but it abandoned the proposal in January 2011 amid international and national pressure. Darío Fernández Jaén, owner of radio station Radio Mi Favorita and an outspoken critic of Martinelli, was murdered in November 2011; one of the suspects arrested allegedly confessed to being hired to commit the crime. There were several instances in 2012 of public officials striking journalists during interviews, increasing pressure on the media. President Martinelli publicly berated a journalist who was a recovering drug addict. Journalists have also been the subject of government attack ads. Internet access is unrestricted.

Freedom of religion is respected, and academic freedom is generally honored.

Freedom of assembly is recognized, and nongovernmental organizations are free to operate. In March 2011, public protests forced the government to repeal Law 8, which had imposed controversial reforms to the Mining Code; this was regarded as a victory for environmental and indigenous groups. Congress' voting on the 2012 electoral reforms was disrupted by protesters who on one occasion forced their way into the building. Although only about 10 percent of the labor force is organized, unions are cohesive and powerful.

The judicial system remains overburdened, inefficient, politicized, and prone to corruption. Panama's Accusatory Penal System became operational on September 2, 2011, and is gradually being introduced throughout the country. The new system is intended to reduce congestion in the courts by resolving complaints more efficiently while reducing the number of people held in detention without conviction. The prison system is marked by violent disturbances in decrepit, overcrowded facilities. As of September 2012, the prison system held more than 6,000 inmates than it was designed to.

The police and other security forces are poorly disciplined and corrupt. Security decrees issued by the Torrijos government in 2008 included the creation of a national aero-naval service, a border service, a council for public security and national defense, and a national intelligence service. Opponents warned of a return to Panama's military past and said the changes lacked safeguards against abuse of power. In September 2012, Jaime Abad of the now defunct Judicial Technical Police asserted that Panama's security forces must be depoliticized. Panama's growing importance as a regional transport center makes it appealing to drug traffickers and money launderers.

Refugees from Colombia have faced difficulty obtaining work permits and other forms of legal recognition. The Martinelli administration had suggested measures to normalize the status of thousands of undocumented Colombians living in Panama without official refugee status, but minimal progress had been made on these measures. New immigration rules that took effect in 2008 tightened controls on foreigners, but other legislation grants recognized refugees who have lived in Panama for more than 10 years the right to apply for permanent residency.

Discrimination against darker-skinned Panamanians is widespread. The country's Asian, Middle Eastern, and indigenous populations are similarly singled out. Indigenous communities enjoy a degree of autonomy and self-government, but some 90 percent of the indigenous population lives in extreme poverty. Since 1993, indigenous groups have protested the encroachment of illegal settlers on their lands and government delays in formal land demarcations. In January 2012, protestors opposing the building of hydroelectric dams on their land blocked the Interamericana road linking Panama to other Central American countries. In March, two people were killed—Plantares community leader Arquilio Opúa and a logger—in fights over illegal logging in Wounaan communities in the country's east. In September, indigenous Naso in the Bocas del Toro province blocked access for several days to the Bonyic Hydroelectric project, protesting the construction of a road they feared would cut through an ancient archeological site; fifteen were arrested before a dialogue was brokered to protect burial grounds at the site.

Violence against women and children is widespread and common. Panama is a source, destination, and transit country for human trafficking. The government has worked with the International Labour Organization on information campaigns addressing the issue, and it has created a special unit to investigate cases of trafficking for the purpose of prostitution. However, law enforcement is weak, the penal code does not prohibit trafficking for forced labor, and the government provides inadequate assistance to victims.

Papua New Guinea

Political Rights: 4
Civil Liberties: 3
Status: Partly Free

Population: 7,034,000
Capital: Port Moresby

Ten-Year Ratings Timeline For Year Under Review (Political Rights, Civil Liberties, Status)

2003	2004	2005	2006	2007	2008	2009	2010	2011	2012
3,3PF	3,3PF	3,3PF	3,3PF	3,3PF	4,3PF	4,3PF	4,3PF	4,3PF	4,3PF

Overview: General elections were held in June and July 2012, after months of legal battles between Peter O'Neill and Michael Somare, each of whom claimed to be the legitimate prime minister. O'Neill's People's National Congress Party was victorious, cementing O'Neill's status as prime minister. In September, Papua New Guinea and Australia signed an agreement to reopen a processing center for asylum seekers.

Papua New Guinea (PNG) gained independence from Australia in 1975. The Autonomous Bougainville Government was created in 2005 following a multi-year, low-grade secessionist war in which landowners on Bougainville Island waged guerrilla attacks on a major Australian-owned copper mine, demanding compensation and profit-sharing. Natural-resource exploitation, including mining and logging, provide the bulk of government revenue, though economic growth has not brought greater political stability.

Prime Minister Michael Somare's ruling National Alliance (NA) won 27 out of 109 seats in the 2007 parliamentary elections, and the 71-year-old Somare was chosen for a second five-year term.

In December 2010, Somare stepped down to face a leadership tribunal for filing improper financial statements. In March 2011, he was convicted on 13 charges of misconduct and sentenced to two weeks of suspension from office without pay. Days after sentencing, Somare traveled to Singapore for medical treatment. In May, his family announced his retirement due to poor health, and Parliament elected the NA's Peter O'Neill prime minister in August. However, in October, Somare, who had returned to PNG, claimed that he never formally left office and sued to reclaim the top post. In December, the Supreme Court ruled that O'Neill's election was unconstitutional and that Somare should be reinstated. The speaker of Parliament refused to implement the decision, and Parliament voted on December 21 to restrict anyone aged 72 or older from becoming or remaining prime minister, which effectively blocked Somare from returning to office.

In early 2012, the Supreme Court and Parliament each reaffirmed its position that Somare and O'Neill, respectively, was the rightful prime minister, causing considerable confusion. Each man, for example, appointed his own police commissioner and claimed control over security forces. In January, Francis Agwi, the defense force commander, declared support for O'Neill and was arrested by soldiers loyal to Somare; Agwi was released after one day, and Somare admitted to ordering the arrest. To restore calm, the Supreme Court ruled that Agwi should remain in his post until the dispute between Somare and O'Neill was resolved.

Somare filed another suit in February to reclaim the top post. After the Supreme Court agreed again to hear the case, O'Neill attempted to remove Chief Justice Salamo Injia, arresting him in March for allegedly obstructing a police investigation. The National Court put a stay on the charge and ordered Injia released. Within days, Parliament passed a law giving it the power to refer a judge to the governor-general for investigation. On May 20, the Supreme Court again ordered that Somare be restored as prime minister. Tensions heightened as O'Neill refused to comply, arguing that the decision was unconstitutional and threatening to arrest the three judges who made the ruling. After Parliament again elected O'Neill as prime minister, the government called for new general elections in June and July to resolve the impasse.

The elections were marked by violence; in Southern Highlands alone, 18 people were killed and many more injured before the polling stations even opened. Across the country, there were allegations of inadequate security, stolen or stuffed ballot boxes, underage voters, names absent from electoral rolls, and other irregularities. Postelection violence also occurred in many locations. Despite these problems, international observers from Australia, New Zealand, and other countries deemed the elections largely free and fair.

O'Neill's People's National Congress Party took the most seats—22—and O'Neill was tapped to form a new government. On August 8, O'Neill and his new cabinet were officially sworn in. With the legitimacy issue settled, the O'Neill government continued its push to undo some of the most controversial decisions of the Somare government. For example, Parliament repealed a measure that allowed a Chinese-owned mining firm to dump waste into the sea, and another that limited people's rights to challenge government decisions in court. In November, a bill that would extend from 18 to 30 months the grace period before a vote of no-confidence could be held passed its first reading in Parliament. The change could increase political stability by ensuring that a government would serve at least half of its regular term before a no-confidence vote.

In September, PNG and Australia agreed to reopen a processing center in Manus Island for people seeking asylum in Australia. Australia agreed to provide hundreds of millions of dollars in rent, assistance, and funds to build, operate, and maintain the facility. The processing center, expected to hold about 600 asylum seekers, was host to 130 by year's end.

Political Rights and Civil Liberties: PNG is an electoral democracy. Voters elect a unicameral, 109-member National Parliament to serve five-year terms. A limited preferential voting system allows voters to choose up to three preferred candidates on their ballots. The prime minister, the leader of the majority party or coalition, is formally appointed by the governor general, who represents Britain's Queen Elizabeth II as head of state.

Major parties include the People's National Congress Party, the Triumph Heritage Party, the NA, and the People's Progressive Party. Political loyalties are driven more by tribal, linguistic, geographic, and personal ties than party affiliation. Many candidates run as independents, aligning with parties after they are elected.

Official abuse and corruption are widespread. The Task Force Sweep (TFS)—an anticorruption organization created in 2011—has launched investigations into many current and former officials, including Michael Somare and his wife. In November 2012, the TFS reported that it had investigated 52 cases of corruption and recovered some $27 million, while dozens of politicians and businesspeople had been arrested. According to the TFS, almost half of the country's development budget from 2009 through 2011 had been lost to corrupt practices. PNG was ranked 150 out of 176 countries surveyed in Transparency International's 2012 Corruption Perceptions Index.

Freedom of speech is generally respected, and the media provide independent coverage of controversial issues such as alleged police abuse, official corruption, and opposition views. However, the government and politicians have occasionally used media laws and libel and defamation lawsuits to limit critical reporting. There are several private and state-owned local and national radio and television stations. Internet use is growing, but cost and lack of infrastructure limits its spread outside urban centers.

The government upholds freedom of religion. Academic freedom is generally respected, but the government does not always tolerate criticism.

The constitution provides for freedoms of assembly and association, and the government generally observes these rights in practice. Marches and demonstrations require 14 days' notice and police approval. Many civil society groups provide social services and advocate for women's rights, the environment, and other causes. The government recognizes workers' rights to strike, organize, and engage in collective bargaining. In October 2012, miners in Enga province stopped working to demand improved safety.

The judiciary is independent. The legal system is based on English common law. The Supreme Court is the final court of appeal and has jurisdiction on constitutional matters. Laypeople sit on village courts to adjudicate minor offenses under customary and statutory law. Suspects often suffer lengthy detentions and trial delays because of a shortage of trained judicial personnel.

Law enforcement officials have been accused of corruption, unlawful killings, extortion, rape, theft, the sale of firearms, and the use of excessive force in the arrest and interrogation of suspects. The correctional service is understaffed, prison conditions are poor, and prisoners have reported torture while in detention. Prison breaks are frequent, and reports of violent crimes continue to increase. Weak governance and law enforcement have allegedly made PNG a base for organized Asian criminal groups. In November 2012, the National Court ordered the government to pay nearly $1 million in compensation to individuals who claimed that police had violated their human rights.

Native tribal feuds over land, titles, religious beliefs, and perceived insults frequently lead to violence and deaths. Inadequate law enforcement and the increased availability of guns have exacerbated the problem. In 2012, ethnic clashes in the city of Lae displaced more than 700 people, and 15 were killed in tribal clash in the Eastern Highlands province. A number of people are killed and injured each year for allegedly practicing sorcery, which was criminalized in 1971. In July 2012, 29 were arrested for alleged sorcery-related killings and cannibalism in Madang province.

Discrimination and violence against women and children are widespread. Although domestic violence is punishable by law, prosecutions are rare; police commonly treat it as a private matter. Family pressure and fear of reprisal also discourage victims from pressing charges. Women are frequently barred from voting by their husbands. Women are underrepresented in government and other sectors. Three women were elected to Parliament in the 2012 elections, the highest number ever. In 2011, the government rejected a call by the United Nations to decriminalize homosexuality. The PNG is a source, transit, and destination country for forced prostitution and labor.

Paraguay

Political Rights: 3
Civil Liberties: 3
Status: Partly Free

Population: 6,683,000
Capital: Asuncion

Trend Arrow: Paraguay received a downward trend arrow due to the swift parliamentary ouster of President Fernando Lugo without due process and a worsening press environment under the new administration.

Ten-Year Ratings Timeline For Year Under Review (Political Rights, Civil Liberties, Status)

2003	2004	2005	2006	2007	2008	2009	2010	2011	2012
3,3PF	3,3PF	3,3PF	3,3PF	3,3PF	3,3PF	3,3PF	3,3PF	3,3PF	3,3PF

Overview: The Paraguayan parliament controversially ousted President Fernando Lugo on June 22, 2012, replacing him with Vice President Federico Franco. The new administration proceeded to purge and assume greater control of state-owned media, while also implementing important tax reform. Separately, the Paraguayan People's Army, a

radical socialist guerrilla group, continued attacks, targeting a radio station in October 2012.

Paraguay, which achieved independence from Spain in 1811, was racked by a series of crises following the 1989 ouster of authoritarian president Alfredo Stroessner of the right-wing Colorado Party after 35 years in power. The fragility of the country's emerging democratic institutions resulted in nearly 15 years of popular uprisings, military mutinies, antigovernment demonstrations, bitter political rivalries, and continued rule by the Colorados.

Senate leader Luis González Macchi assumed the presidency in 1999, after the incumbent fled the country amid murder charges. In 2002 González Macchi offered to leave office early to avoid pending impeachment hearings against him for embezzlement. Former education minister Nicanor Duarte Frutos of the Colorado Party emerged victorious in the 2003 national elections. After taking office, Duarte moved to assume control of the tax, port, and customs authorities to combat rampant tax evasion and smuggling.

Fernando Lugo, a former Roman Catholic priest and the leader of the Patriotic Alliance for Change (APC) coalition, was elected president in 2008, representing the first time in Paraguay's history that power was transferred peacefully to an opposing party. In concurrent legislative elections, the Authentic Liberal Radical Party (PLRA), part of Lugo's coalition that included both conservative and leftist parties, performed strongly, though it captured slightly fewer seats than the Colorado Party. Lugo's election raised expectations that the standard of living for Paraguay's poor majority would improve. However, Lugo was never able to implement the land reform necessary to address Paraguay's highly skewed land distribution. He also lost support when evidence emerged starting in 2009 that he fathered up to four children while he was still a priest.

The rise of the Paraguayan People's Army (EPP)—an armed leftist guerrilla group—forced Lugo to declare a month-long state of emergency in half of the country in April 2010. After a lull, the group reemerged in January 2011 with a series of bombings and attacks across the country that continued periodically into 2012. While several senior EPP members have been captured, the group continued its campaign of kidnapping, extortion, and bombing attacks. The EPP claimed responsibility for the October 2012 bombing of a privately owned radio station in the northern department of Concepción, and also announced its intention to kill three journalists for repeatedly criticizing the EPP.

Representing a major victory for Paraguay, Congress ratified an agreement with Brazil in 2011 that settled a decades-long dispute over payments for energy produced by the Itaipú hydroelectric dam. As a result, it was expected that Paraguay's income from the dam would triple. A law passed in September 2012 earmarked approximately $40 million annually from dam proceeds in support of information technology in schools.

In addition to the paternity scandals, Lugo's presidency was complicated by a publically unsupportive vice president, strong Colorado opposition in Congress, his struggle with lymphatic cancer, and intermittent rumors of a military coup. But the June 22, 2012, near-unanimous Congressional vote that impeached President Lugo due to "poor performance of his duties" still shocked the nation. Lugo stepped down peacefully after the swift two-day trial, and Vice President Federico Franco was sworn in as president. The reported catalyst was the violent eviction of landless protesters the week before in which 11 peasants and 6 policemen were killed. While Paraguay's neighbors condemned the impeachment for its lack of due process, the move did not provoke domestic outrage in a large-scale or sustained manner. During the second half of 2012, Franco was able to implement important reforms, including passing Paraguay's first ever personal income tax, and more quickly and efficiently awarding land titles to rural squatters. His successor will be elected in April 2013.

Political Rights and Civil Liberties: Paraguay is an electoral democracy. However, while the congressional vote impeaching Fernando Lugo was technically constitutional, his swift ouster raised questions about the absence of due process. The 1992 constitution provides for a president, a vice president, and a bicameral Congress consisting of a 45-member Senate and an 80-member Chamber of Deputies, all elected for five-year terms. The president is elected by a simple majority vote to a five-year term, and reelection is prohibited. The constitution bans active-duty military from engaging in politics.

Before President Fernando Lugo and the APC came to power in 2008, the Colorado Party had ruled Paraguay for over 60 years. The other major political groupings include the PLRA, the Beloved Fatherland Party, the National Union of Ethical Citizens, and the National Agreement Party.

Corruption cases languish for years in the courts without resolution, and corruption often goes unpunished as judges favor the powerful and wealthy. The Lugo administration pledged to increase overall transparency in government and reduce corruption, specifically in the judiciary. However, the president was unable to depoliticize Paraguay's corrupt Supreme Court. Paraguay was ranked 150 out of 176 countries surveyed in Transparency International's 2012 Corruption Perceptions Index.

The constitution provides for freedoms of expression and the press, but the de facto respect of these rights by the government sharply deteriorated with the onset of the Franco government. For example, 27 journalists and other employees—individuals the Lugo administration initially recruited —were fired from TV Publica in September 2012, and its airtime was disrupted immediately following Lugo's impeachment. In 2012 journalists investigating corruption and organized crime or who were vocally critical of the government suffered threats and violent attacks by drug cartels, government officials, and the EPP. Direct pressure by criminal groups and corrupt authorities led journalists to censor themselves in 2012, especially in remote border areas. There are a number of private television and radio stations and independent newspapers, as well as two state-owned media outlets, Radio Nacional and TV Publica. Paraguay does not have a right to information law and continues to use defamation laws against the press. The government does not restrict internet use, nor does it censor its content.

The government generally respects freedom of religion. All religious groups are required to register with the Ministry of Education and Culture, but no controls are imposed on these groups, and many informal churches exist. The government does not restrict academic freedom.

The constitution guarantees freedoms of association and assembly, and these rights are respected in practice. There are a number of trade unions, but they are weak and riddled with corruption. The labor code provides for the right to strike and prohibits retribution against strikers, though the government generally has failed to address or prevent employer retaliation. Employers often illegally and dismiss strikers and union leaders.

The judiciary is nominally independent but is highly corrupt and dominated by judges who are members of the Colorado Party. Courts are inefficient, and political interference in the judiciary is a serious problem, as politicians routinely pressure judges and block investigations. The constitution permits detention without trial until the accused has completed the minimum sentence for the alleged crime. Illegal detention by police and torture during incarceration still occur, particularly in rural areas. Overcrowding, unsanitary conditions, and mistreatment of inmates are serious problems in the country's prisons.

The lack of security in border areas, particularly in the tri-border region adjacent to Brazil and Argentina, has allowed organized crime groups to engage in money laundering and the smuggling of weapons and narcotics. The Shiite Islamist movement Hezbollah has long been involved in narcotics and human trafficking in the largely ungoverned tri-border area. In recent years, Hezbollah has developed ties with Mexican drug cartels.

The constitution provides Paraguay's estimated 108,000 indigenous people with the right to participate in the economic, social, and political life of the country. In practice, however, the indigenous population is unassimilated and neglected. Peasant organizations sometimes occupy land illegally, and landowners often respond with death threats and forced evictions by hired vigilante groups. On a positive note, the government made additional progress in 2012 in returning ancestral land to indigenous groups. After almost two decades of legal battles, Paraguayan authorities and a landowner finalized a deal in February to allow the Yakye Axa indigenous community to return to more than 12,000 hectares of ancestral land. This deal followed a September 2011 agreement outlining a government purchase eventually return land to the Sawhoyamaxa indigenous community.

Employment discrimination against women is pervasive. Sexual and domestic abuse of women continues to be a serious problem. Although the government generally prosecutes rape allegations and often obtains convictions, many rapes go unreported because victims fear their attackers or are concerned that the law will not respect their privacy. Trafficking in persons is proscribed by the constitution and criminalized in the penal code, but there have been occasional reports of trafficking for sexual purposes and domestic servitude.

Peru

Political Rights: 2
Civil Liberties: 3
Status: Free

Population: 30,136,000
Capital: Lima

Ten-Year Ratings Timeline For Year Under Review (Political Rights, Civil Liberties, Status)

2003	2004	2005	2006	2007	2008	2009	2010	2011	2012
2,3F	2,3F	2,3F	2,3F	2,3F	2,3F	2,3F	2,3F	2,3F	2,3F

Overview: Significant social conflict, mostly involving local protests against mining industry projects, continued to afflict Peru throughout 2012. The government led by President Ollanta Humala responded with a mix of force and dialogue, but took few steps toward providing clear frameworks for dispute resolution. A recall referendum against Lima mayor Susana Villarán was approved in November despite serious questions about the legitimacy of the signature-gathering process.

After achieving independence from Spain in 1821, Peru experienced alternating periods of civilian and military rule. Civilians have held office since a 12-year dictatorship ended in 1980. However, that year, a Maoist guerrilla group known as the Shining Path launched a vicious two-decade insurgency. The conflict led to the deaths of some 69,000 people, nearly three-fourths of whom were residents of poor highland villages.

Alberto Fujimori, a university rector and engineer, was elected president in 1990. In 1992, backed by the military, he suspended the constitution, took over the judiciary, and dissolved Congress. A new constitution featuring a stronger presidency and a unicameral Congress was approved in a state-controlled 1993 referendum. Congress passed a law in 1996 that allowed Fujimori to run for a third term, despite a constitutional two-term limit.

According to official results, Fujimori outpolled Alejandro Toledo—a U.S.-educated economist who had been raised in one of Peru's urban squatter settlements—in the first round of the 2000 presidential election. Toledo boycotted the runoff, pointing to widespread doubts about the process's legitimacy.

Beginning in September 2000, a series of videotapes emerged showing intelligence chief Vladimiro Montesinos bribing congressmen and other figures. As a result, in late November, opposition forces assumed control of Congress, Fujimori fled to Japan and resigned, and respected opposition leader Valentín Paniagua was chosen as interim president. Toledo's Perú Posible party led the April 2001 congressional elections, and he bested former president Alan García (1985–90) in a runoff presidential election in June of that year.

In 2004, a special anticorruption court convicted Montesinos in the first of many cases against him, sentencing him to 15 years in prison. Fujimori flew to Chile from Japan in 2005 in the hopes of mounting a 2006 presidential bid in Peru, but he was immediately detained as Peru requested his extradition. García won the 2006 presidential election, defeating Ollanta Humala of the Peruvian Nationalist Party (PNP), while the PNP and its allies led the congressional elections. Once in office, García focused on macroeconomic growth and stability for foreign investors.

Fujimori was extradited from Chile in 2007, and in April 2009 he was sentenced to 25 years in prison for overseeing death-squad killings and two kidnappings. International observers and local rights groups hailed the verdict as an unprecedented example of a democratically elected head of state convicted of human rights violations in his home country.

In June 2009, a violent confrontation in the town of Bagua between police and a group of mainly indigenous protesters left 10 protesters and 23 police officers dead and over 200 people injured. The protesters had objected to June 2008 government decrees that they said violated their land rights. The disputed decrees were rescinded, and the government acknowledged its failure to consult with locals, though it blamed outside agitators for raising tensions.

The 2011 presidential election was characterized by sharp polarization. With various candidates dividing the center, the leftist Humala and right-wing Keiko Fujimori—daughter of the former president—were the top finishers in the first round. In concurrent legislative elections, an alliance led by the PNP captured 47 of the 130 seats, followed by Fujimori's Force 2011 party with 38 seats and Perú Posible with 21 seats. García's Peruvian Aprista Party (APRA) captured just four seats.

During the run-up to the presidential second round in June, Fujimori portrayed Humala as a dangerous leftist, while Humala sought to soften his image while tying Fujimori to her father's authoritarianism. Despite Fujimori being the clear favorite among much of the country's elite class, including major print and broadcast media outlets, Humala ultimately won by a margin of three percentage points.

The new president's Peru Wins alliance forged a congressional majority with Perú Posible. The administration was successful in securing unanimous passage of the Law of Prior Consultation, which holds that native communities must be consulted on development projects in their areas. However, social conflict reemerged, as opposition to a proposed gold mine in the northern region of Cajamarca led to large-scale protests and scores of injuries. Humala suspended the project, but in early December he reversed course, declaring a state of emergency in several of the affected areas and breaking off talks. He also oversaw a cabinet shuffle that included the replacement of Prime Minister Salomón Lerner with former army officer Oscar Valdés. This move added to suspicions among some initial Humala supporters that the government was moving to the right and undergoing a process of militarization.

Tension remained high during the first half of 2012, as mining-related protests in Cajamarca, Cuzco, and other regions resulted in clashes with the police that caused several deaths. In July, Valdés and five other ministers were replaced; new cabinet chief Juan José Jiménez instituted more active conflict management, and violent clashes decreased in the second half of the year.

Meanwhile, economic growth and expanded social programs helped raise Humala's approval rating to around 48 percent—a high figure by Peruvian standards—by year's end. His relative success fueled speculation that his wife, Nadine Heredia, whose approval was even higher, would seek to succeed him in the presidency, despite both her frequent denials and a legal ban on the election of direct relatives of the current president.

In November 2012, opponents of Lima mayor Susana Villarán gathered sufficient signatures to force a recall referendum in March 2013. The process was allowed to move forward despite serious questions about the legitimacy of the process, including opaque financing, the validity of many of the signatures, and a series of contradictory rulings by the National Election Board. The mayor's opponents pointed to her low approval ratings, while supporters alleged that opponents were motivated by the mayor's efforts to investigate corrupt practices committed during the previous administration.

Political Rights and Civil Liberties: Peru is an electoral democracy. The 2011 elections were generally free and fair, according to international observers. However, shortcomings included lack of enforcement of campaign finance norms and pressure on media outlets by powerful economic interests in support of losing candidate Keiko Fujimori.

The president and the 130-member, unicameral Congress are elected for five-year terms. Congressional balloting employs an open-list, region-based system of proportional representation with a 5 percent vote hurdle for a party to enter the legislature. A lack of programmatic coherence among parties and occasional party-switching by politicians have reinforced a broader trend toward political fragmentation. However, regional presidents have become important actors, and the regional and local elections in October 2010 resulted in a moderately increased consolidation of regional political movements. In 2012, controversy continued to surround a group advocating for the release of Shining Path prisoners. The group's petition to register as a political party was rejected in 2011.

Corruption is a serious problem. Checks on campaign financing are particularly weak at the local level, where drug traffickers' influence is perceived to have grown in recent years. Peruvians rated corruption as the most negative aspect of President García's administration, but a congressional commission charged with investigating corruption among García administration officials produced few criminal accusations in 2012. Some government agencies have made progress on transparency, but a December 2012 decree labeled as secret all information related to defense and security policies, drawing an outcry from government watchdogs. Peru was ranked 83 out of 176 countries surveyed in Transparency International's 2012 Corruption Perceptions Index.

The lively press is for the most part privately owned. Officials and private actors sometimes intimidate or even attack journalists in response to negative coverage. Low pay leaves reporters susceptible to bribery, and media outlets remain dependent on advertising by large retailers. The local press watchdog Institute for Press and Society registered 95 violations of press freedom during 2012. Defamation remains criminalized, and several journalists were convicted in 2012, including prominent reporter Juan Carlos Tafur and colleague Robert More, who each received a fine and suspended sentence in June for defaming a former army general. The government does not limit access to the internet.

The constitution provides for freedom of religion, and the government generally respects this right in practice. However, the Roman Catholic Church receives preferential treatment from the state. The government does not restrict academic freedom. The constitution provides for the right to peaceful assembly, and the authorities uphold this right for the most part. However, the executive branch has issued several decrees in recent years that limit police and military responsibility in the event of injury or death during demonstrations, and the government has both frequently resorted to declarations of states of emergency and done little to prevent excessive use of force by security forces when confronting protests. According to the government, 191 Peruvians died in episodes of social conflict during the García administration, including 38 police and soldiers; several thousand others faced charges for protest-related incidents. At least 24 more protesters were killed by government forces during 2012. Analysts frequently observe that the government's approach to local grievances, which often involve environmental issues, typically eschews mediation and early intervention in favor of reaction in the form of repression by militarized police units and sometimes military forces. Over 50 community members involved in the 2009 Bagua protests are facing trial, while very few members of the police or military have faced charges for protest-related incidents in recent years.

Freedom of association is generally respected, but conservative politicians frequently allege that nongovernmental organizations (NGOs) hinder economic development. Anti-mining activists, including noted environmental leader Marco Arana, have been subjected to arbitrary arrest or faced questionable legal charges in recent years, while several NGOs have experienced various forms of intimidation.

Peruvian law recognizes the right of workers to organize and bargain collectively. Workers must notify the Ministry of Labor in advance of a strike, with the result that nearly all strikes are categorized as illegal in practice. Less than 10 percent of the formal-sector workforce is unionized. Parallel unionism and criminal infiltration of the construction sector in Lima have led to a series of disputes and murders.

The judiciary is widely distrusted and prone to corruption scandals. While the Constitutional Court is relatively independent, its autonomy has undergone a mix of setbacks and advances in recent years. A 2008 Judicial Career Law improved the entry, promotion, and evaluation system for judges, and the judiciary's internal disciplinary body has been highly active. By the end of 2012, however, the terms of six of the Constitutional Court's seven members had expired amid delays in the process of appointing new justices.

A significant majority of inmates are in pretrial detention, and the inmate population is far above the system's intended capacity. Since 2006, an adversarial justice system designed to improve the speed and fairness of judicial proceedings has slowly been implemented. Access to justice, particularly for poor Peruvians, remains problematic, and crime has risen. In an October 2012 poll, 43 percent of residents of 10 major cities reported being the victim of a crime in the previous year.

The military continues to place numerous obstacles in the path of investigators regarding past violations. The García government made almost no efforts to prioritize justice for cases of human rights abuses by state actors during the 1980s and 1990s, and the Humala administration has remained similarly passive. In 2010, the government announced a decree that would have applied a statute of limitations to grave human rights abuses committed during the internal conflict, but domestic and international outcry forced a retreat, and the Constitutional Court subsequently declared the decree unconstitutional. Other decrees announced that month—expanding the military's internal role and extending the reach of the military justice system—remained in force. In August 2012, the Supreme Court (CSJ) issued a controversial decision stating that the actions of a state-sponsored death squad in the 1990s did not constitute crimes against humanity. Rights groups immediately sought guidance from the Inter-American Court of Human Rights, which urged the CSJ to revoke the decision, which it did in September. In October, relatives of former president Alberto Fujimori formally presented a request for a medical pardon, which was under examination at year's end.

Remnants of the Shining Path, which are involved in the drug trade, continue to clash with security forces in the Apurimac-Ene River Valley and Upper Huallaga zones. The coca-eradication efforts and economic development programs in other regions have failed to reverse a trend toward increased coca production. In February 2012, the government captured the main leader of the Alto Huallaga faction, known only as Comrade Artemio, though attacks during the year killed over 20 members of the security forces. In August, the government sent Congress a bill that would criminalize the denial of terrorism; following complaints about the law's scope, the government submitted a narrower version that remained under consideration at year's end but remained subject to sharp criticism by human rights groups. Discrimination against the indigenous population remains pervasive. Regulations to implement the Law of Prior Consultation passed in September 2011 were issued in April, and government agencies began establishing consultation mechanisms, but delays in initiating the first formal process fueled worries that the government's need for mining revenue would continue to take precedence over indigenous people's environmental concerns.

In recent years, women have advanced into leadership roles in various companies and government agencies. Although legal protections have improved, domestic violence is epidemic, with over half of Peruvian women reporting instances of physical or emotional abuse. Forced labor, including child labor, persists in the gold-mining region of the Amazon.

Philippines

Political Rights: 3
Civil Liberties: 3
Status: Partly Free

Population: 96,218,400
Capital: Manila

Ten-Year Ratings Timeline For Year Under Review (Political Rights, Civil Liberties, Status)

2003	2004	2005	2006	2007	2008	2009	2010	2011	2012
2,3F	2,3F	3,3PF	3,3PF	4,3PF	4,3PF	4,3PF	3,3PF	3,3PF	3,3PF

Overview: In October 2012, the government signed an agreement with the Moro Islamic Liberation Front that established a framework for peace on the southern island of Mindanao. Separately, in September the president signed the Cybercrime Prevention Act despite critics' warnings that it would curtail freedom of expression and undermine due process. The Supreme Court quickly suspended the law's implementation pending a review of its constitutionality. Former president Gloria Macapagal-

Arroyo remained in pretrial detention on corruption charges at year's end, having initially been arrested in late 2011, released on bail in July, then rearrested under new charges in October.

After centuries of Spanish rule, the Philippines came under U.S. control in 1898 and won independence in 1946. The country has been plagued by insurgencies, economic mismanagement by powerful elites, and widespread corruption since the 1960s. In 1986, a popular protest movement ended the 14-year dictatorship of President Ferdinand Marcos and replaced him with Corazon Aquino, whom the regime had cheated out of an electoral victory weeks earlier.

Aquino's administration ultimately failed to implement substantial reforms and was unable to dislodge entrenched social and economic elites. Fidel Ramos, a key figure in the 1986 protests and former national defense secretary under Aquino, won the 1992 presidential election. The country was relatively stable and experienced significant if uneven economic growth under his administration. Ramos's vice president, Joseph Estrada, won the 1998 presidential election by promising concrete socioeconomic reform, but his administration was dogged by allegations of corruption. Massive street protests forced him from office in 2001 after a formal impeachment process failed.

Gloria Macapagal-Arroyo, Estrada's vice president, assumed the presidency, and her political coalition won the May 2001 legislative elections. In the 2004 presidential election, Arroyo initially seemed to have defeated her challenger by some 1.1 million votes. However, claims of massive fraud triggered demonstrations and were verified by some members of the administration. When an audiotape of a conversation between the president and election officials surfaced in June 2005, supporting the previous year's vote-rigging allegations, many cabinet officials resigned to join a new opposition movement. An ultimately unsuccessful impeachment bid was launched, and the first of years of frequent protests called for the president's resignation.

The administration mounted several efforts to undercut the opposition movement, including punitive prosecutions and executive orders in 2005 and a weeklong state of emergency in 2006 in response to an alleged coup attempt. The congressional opposition initiated a second unsuccessful impeachment bid that June.

Although the president's coalition increased its lower house majority in May 2007 legislative elections, the opposition bolstered its control of the Senate. Later that year, Arroyo was implicated in a major corruption scandal involving a national broadband contract with the Chinese company ZTE that had been approved in April. Separately, Arroyo pardoned Estrada in October, a month after the country's antigraft court sentenced him to life in prison. His conviction had been the first of a former president, and the pardon was widely perceived as a bid to set a favorable precedent for Arroyo's own treatment after leaving office. Leaders of an unsuccessful coup attempt in November called for Arroyo's removal on the grounds of electoral fraud and corruption, and yet another failed impeachment bid was launched in October 2008.

In November 2009, the wife of a local vice mayor was ambushed by 100 armed men as she traveled with other family members and supporters to file her husband's candidacy for the Maguindanao provincial governorship. A total of 58 people were massacred in the incident, including 29 journalists and 3 other media workers who were accompanying the unarmed group. Evidence soon emerged to implicate the Ampatuan clan, which dominated the province's politics and was closely allied with the Arroyo administration.

Arroyo responded in early December by declaring martial law for the first time in nearly 30 years, as well as a state of emergency, which remained in place in three provinces even after martial law was lifted in mid-December. At least 62 people were arrested, including Maguindanao governor Andal Ampatuan Sr., and the authorities dug up arms caches amid an effort to weaken local clans. Nevertheless, the Arroyo administration was widely criticized for its longtime policy of tolerating local warlords and supporting clan patronage as part of its counterinsurgency strategy.

In the May 2010 presidential election, the reformist Liberal Party (LP) candidate Benigno "Noynoy" Aquino—the son of former president Corazon Aquino—prevailed with 42 percent of the vote. In concurrent congressional balloting, half of the 24 Senate seats were up for election. Three went to LP candidates; two each to Arroyo's Lakas-Kampi CMD party, the Force of the Filipino Masses, and the Nationalist Party; and one each to the National People's Coalition, the People's Reform Party, and an independent. In the 280-member lower house, the LP ultimately won 119 seats, while Lakas-Kampi CMD took 46 and other parties split the remainder. In keeping with a long-standing pattern, the LP's predominance resulted from a number of lawmakers defecting to join the new president's party.

Soon after taking office, Aquino established a Truth Commission to investigate the corruption and electoral fraud allegations against Arroyo. The former president was arrested on vote-rigging charges in November 2011, then released in July 2012 after posting nearly $25,000 bail. She was arrested again in October, this time on charges that she and members of her administration had stolen money from the national lottery. She remained in custody at year's end, and further corruption charges were expected.

In October 2012, the Moro Islamic Liberation Front (MILF) signed a peace agreement with the government, aiming to end a Muslim insurgency that had plagued the southern provinces since the early 1970s. The pact would create a new, larger autonomous region to be known as Bangsamoro, replacing the existing Autonomous Region of Muslim Mindanao (ARMM). However, some rebel factions did not accept the terms of the agreement. Elements of the Moro National Liberation Front argued that the terms of the MILF deal abrogated their separate 1996 agreement with the government, but they remained peaceful. Another group, the Bangsamoro Islamic Freedom Fighters, which broke away from the MILF after disagreements on the peace process, vowed to continue its insurgency.

Political Rights and Civil Liberties: The Republic of the Philippines is an electoral democracy. The May 2010 elections marked a significant improvement over previous polls that were marred by fraud, intimidation, and political violence. The country has a presidential system of government, with the directly elected president limited to a single six-year term. The national legislature, Congress, is bicameral. The 24 members of the Senate are elected on a nationwide ballot and serve six-year terms, with half of the seats up for election every three years. The 280 members of the House of Representatives serve three-year terms, with 228 elected in single-member constituencies and the remainder elected by party list to represent ethnic minorities. Legislative coalitions are exceptionally fluid, and members of Congress often change party affiliation.

The Commission on Elections (Comelec) is appointed by the president, and with the president's permission it has the authority to unseat military, police, and government officials. Comelec was widely discredited by the 2005 audiotape scandal regarding cheating in the 2004 elections, and the 2007 legislative elections were overseen by the same tainted officials. However, during the 2010 balloting, the commission was led by the respected lawyer Jose Melo, and its push for a fully automated election system was seen as an effort to restore its reputation. In a positive step for human rights, detainees were permitted to vote for the first time in 2010. Another significant improvement was the reduction in political violence, aided by restrictions on firearms during the campaign. Such bloodshed is typically tied to local rivalries and clan competition. Persistent problems included media bias, which tended to favor wealthier candidates, and vote-buying.

As the 2013 elections approached, teachers raised concerns in 2012 about their potential disenfranchisement, as they often serve as election inspectors and miss the opportunity to vote themselves. About 120,000 teachers were reportedly deregistered in 2010 because their poll duties had prevented them from voting in the past two elections. Political violence also remained a concern in 2012, as widespread intimidation, bombing incidents, and low-level violence continued in the ARMM. Separately, Raul Matamorosa, the mayor of Lupi in the eastern Bicol region and an ally of President Benigno Aquino, was shot and killed by unidentified assailants in October.

Corruption and cronyism are rife in business and government. A few dozen leading families continue to hold an outsized share of land, corporate wealth, and political power. Local bosses often control their respective areas, limiting accountability and encouraging abuses of power. High-level corruption also abounds. In addition to the ongoing cases against former president Gloria Macapagal-Arroyo, Supreme Court chief justice Renato Corona, an Arroyo appointee, was ousted by the Senate after an impeachment trial in May 2012, having been found guilty of submitting false asset declarations.

A culture of impunity, stemming in part from a case backlog in the judicial system, hampers the fight against corruption. More high-profile cases have been filed in recent years, and several civic organizations have emerged to combat corruption, but cases take an average of six to seven years to be resolved in the Sandiganbayan anticorruption court. The country's official anticorruption agencies, the Office of the Ombudsman and the Presidential Anti-Graft Commission (PAGC), have mixed records. Many observers maintain that the former was compromised under the Arroyo administration, as convictions declined, while the PAGC lacks enforcement capabilities. The Arroyo-era ombudsman was forced from office in 2011 after Aquino's congressional allies voted to impeach her. The Philippines was ranked 105 out of 176 countries surveyed in Transparency International's 2012 Corruption Perceptions Index.

The constitution provides for freedoms of expression and the press. The private media are vibrant and outspoken, although newspaper reports often consist more of innuendo and sensationalism than substantive investigative reporting. The country's many state-owned television and radio stations cover controversial topics and are willing to criticize the government, but they too lack strict journalistic ethics. While the censorship board has broad powers to edit or ban content, government censorship is generally not a serious problem. The internet is widely available and uncensored.

Potential legal obstacles to press freedom include Executive Order 608, which established a National Security Clearance System to protect classified information, and the Human Security Act, which allows journalists to be wiretapped based on mere suspicion of involvement in terrorism. Libel is a criminal offense, and libel cases have been used frequently to quiet criticism of public officials. Despite persistent lobbying by press freedom groups, Congress has yet to pass a draft Freedom of Information Act, which remained stalled in the lower house at the end of 2012. In September the president signed the Cybercrime Prevention Act, which would extend criminal libel law to online content, potentially criminalizing simple activities like forwarding or recommending material created by others. The maximum penalty for online libel would be 12 years in prison, twice as long as for libel in traditional media. The law also allows the authorities to shut down websites and monitor traffic data without a court order. In early October, the Supreme Court suspended implementation of the law pending a review of its constitutionality.

The Philippines remains one of the most dangerous places in the world for journalists to work, and impunity for crimes against them is the norm. The Maguindanao massacre trial was ongoing in 2012, and although it was transferred to Manila to prevent local interference and has moved forward with unusual speed, a number of complications have been noted, including witness intimidation, flawed forensic investigations, and the fact that only 19 of the 196 suspects were on trial. Three journalists were killed in the Philippines during 2012, according to the Committee to Protect Journalists, but only one murder was confirmed as being related to the victim's work.

Freedom of religion is guaranteed under the constitution and generally respected in practice. While church and state are separate, the Catholic Church exerts political influence. The population is mostly Christian, with a Roman Catholic majority. The Muslim minority is concentrated on the southern island of Mindanao and, according to the most recent census, represents 5 to 9 percent of the total population. Perceptions of relative socioeconomic deprivation and political disenfranchisement, and resentment toward Christian settlement in traditionally Muslim areas, have played a central role in Muslim separatist movements.

Academic freedom is generally respected in the Philippines; professors and other teachers can lecture and publish freely. However, in August 2012, the president of a respected Catholic university threatened to investigate—and potentially dismiss—faculty who had expressed support for the proposed Reproductive Health Bill, which would provide increased access to and government funding for contraceptives. The legislation was passed in December.

Citizen activism is robust, and demonstrations are common. However, permits are required for rallies, and antigovernment protests are often dispersed. The Philippines has many active human rights, social welfare, and other nongovernmental groups, as well as lawyers' and business associations. Various labor and farmers' organizations that are dedicated to ending extrajudicial killings and helping families of the disappeared face serious threats, and their offices are occasionally raided.

Trade unions are independent and may align with international groups. However, in order to register, a union must represent at least 20 percent of a given bargaining unit. Moreover, large firms are stepping up the use of contract workers, who are prohibited from joining unions. Only about 5 percent of the labor force is unionized. Collective bargaining is common, and strikes may be called, though unions must provide notice and obtain majority approval from their members. Violence against labor leaders remains a problem and has been part of the broader trend of extrajudicial killings over the last decade.

Judicial independence has traditionally been strong, particularly with respect to the Supreme Court. However, by late 2010 all members of the Supreme Court were Arroyo appointees, and they continue to dominate the body, despite the 2012 impeachment of Chief Justice Corona. Rule of law in the country is generally weak. A backlog of more than 800,000 cases in the court system contributes to impunity, and low pay encourages rampant corruption. The judiciary receives less than 1 percent of the national budget, and judges and lawyers often depend on local power holders for basic resources and salaries, leading to compromised verdicts. At least 12 judges have been killed since 1999, but there have been no convictions for the attacks.

Arbitrary detention, disappearances, kidnappings, and abuse of suspects continue to be reported. Mounting evidence has confirmed the military's responsibility for many of the numerous killings of leftist journalists, labor leaders, and senior members of legal left-wing political parties in the context of the Arroyo administration's counterinsurgency against the New People's Army, a communist rebel group. Military officers maintain that such killings were the result of purges within the communist movement. The lack of effective witness protection has been a key obstacle to investigations. About 90 percent of extrajudicial killing and abduction cases have no cooperating witnesses. Especially problematic is the fact that the Department of Justice oversees both the witness-protection program and the entity that serves as counsel to the military. Similarly, the Philippine National Police, tasked with investigating murders of journalists, falls under the jurisdiction of the military. Convictions for extrajudicial killings are extremely rare, and no military personnel were found guilty during Arroyo's presidency. At the end of 2012, Aquino signed a new law criminalizing enforced disappearances.

Local officials are believed to keep lists of suspected criminals who are abducted or killed by death squads if they fail to heed warnings to reform or leave the area. The Commission on Human Rights launched independent investigations into death squads in March 2009, but many witnesses and advocates fear for their safety if they testify. Kidnappings for ransom remained common in the Southern region, with several high-profile abductions of Australian, American, and European tourists in 2012 by militants affiliated with Abu Sayyaf. Abu Sayyaf continued to attack civilians and battle security forces in 2012; in July the militants staged ambushes on rubber plantations, the largest of which killed 6 workers and wounded 22.

The Muslim separatist conflict has caused severe hardship for many of the 15 million inhabitants of Mindanao and nearby islands, and has resulted in more than 120,000 deaths since it erupted in 1972. Both government and rebel forces have committed summary killings and other human rights abuses. More than 11,000 people remained displaced in Mindanao at the end of 2012. An estimated 300,000 people were displaced throughout the year; two thirds were due to the separatist conflict and clan violence, while others were the result of tropical storms and flooding.

Citizens may travel freely outside conflict zones, and there are no restrictions on employment or place of residence. The poor security situation inhibits individuals' ability to operate businesses.

Women have made many social and economic gains in recent years. The UN Development Programme notes that the Philippines is one of the few countries in Asia to have significantly closed the gender gap in the areas of health and education. Although more women than men now enter high school and university, women face some discrimination in private sector employment, and those in Mindanao enjoy considerably fewer rights in practice. Divorce is illegal in the Philippines, though annulments are allowed under specified circumstances. A 2009 law known informally as the Magna Carta of Women included provisions calling for women to fill half of third-level government positions, requiring that each barangay (local administrative unit) have a "violence against women desk," and recognizing women's rights as human rights. Despite these measures, enforcement has been uneven. The trafficking of women and girls abroad and internally for forced labor and prostitution remains a major problem, despite antitrafficking efforts by the government and civil society. The country's various insurgent groups have been accused of using child soldiers.

Poland

Political Rights: 1
Civil Liberties: 1
Status: Free

Population: 38,222,000
Capital: Warsaw

Ten-Year Ratings Timeline For Year Under Review (Political Rights, Civil Liberties, Status)

2003	2004	2005	2006	2007	2008	2009	2010	2011	2012
1,2F	1,1F	1,1F	1,1F	1,1F	1,1F	1,1F	1,1F	1,1F	1,1F

Overview: **Poland's two largest political parties—Civic Platform and Law and Justice—remained polarized in 2012. In September, a website designer was convicted of defaming the president with his blog. Legislation limiting rights to public information and public assembly were signed in 2012. The unregulated Polish lender and investment company Amber Gold collapsed, drawing widespread attention to the sometimes weak enforcement of financial regulations. One long-standing case under Poland's controversial blasphemy law resulted in a fine for the defendant, while another dismissed in 2011 was under appeal at the end of 2012.**

After being dismantled by neighboring empires in a series of 18th-century partitions, Poland enjoyed independence from 1918 to 1939, only to be invaded by Germany and the Soviet Union at the opening of World War II. The country was exploited as a Soviet satellite state until the Solidarity trade union movement forced the government to accept democratic elections in 1989.

Fundamental democratic and free-market reforms were introduced starting in 1989 and continued until Poland became a member of the European Union (EU) in 2004. In the 1990s, power shifted between political parties rooted in the Solidarity movement and those with communist origins. Former Communist Party member Alexander Kwasniewski of the Democratic Left Alliance (SLD) replaced Solidarity's Lech Wałesa as president in 1995 and was reelected by a wide margin in 2000.

Promising to eliminate corruption and protect Polish values under EU pressure, the conservative Law and Justice (PiS) party, headed by twin brothers Lech and Jarosław Kaczynski, won the September 2005 parliamentary elections. Lech Kaczy ski became president in October, and Jarosław Kaczynski later became prime minister. PiS formed a fragile majority coalition with the leftist-populist, agrarian Self-Defense Party (Samoobrona) and the socially conservative, Catholic-oriented League of Polish Families (LPR). The coalition finally collapsed in 2007, prompting legislative elections that yielded a government led by Prime Minister Donald Tusk of the center-right Civic Platform (PO) party, in coalition with the Polish People's Party (PSL). The relationship between Tusk and President Lech Kaczy ski remained tense in 2008 and 2009, as Kaczynski resisted the government's generally pro-EU policy initiatives and its less antagonistic stance toward Russia. Following the deaths of President Kaczy ski and 95 other passengers in an April 2010 plane crash in Smolenk, Russia, Sejm speaker Bronisław Komorowski of PO served as interim president until June elections, in which he won 53 percent of the vote in the second round.

Komorowski's presidency has seen increasing polarization between supporters of PiS and PO. In October 2011 elections to the lower house of parliament, PO won 207 seats, followed by PiS with 157. The liberal Palikot Movement captured 40 seats, PSL took 28, and SLD won 27. A representative of the ethnic German minority held the remaining seat. In the Senate, PO took 63 seats, PiS won 31, PSL received 2 seats, and the remainder went to independents. The elections marked the first time in Poland's postcommunist history that a prime minister won a second consecutive term.

In 2012, Poland remained the fastest-growing economy in the EU, though growth slowed throughout the year. Pension reforms in March raised the retirement age to 67, despite widespread protests. Although Prime Minister Tusk promised to end partisan hiring practices in publicly funded positions, the daily *Puls Biznesu* in November published a list of 428 people associated with PO working for government-owned businesses at a total cost of 48 million euros (US$65.3 million) over the last five years.

Political Rights and Civil Liberties: Poland is an electoral democracy. Voters elect the president for up to two five-year terms and members of the bicameral National Assembly for four-year terms. The president's appointment of the prime minister must be confirmed by the 460-seat Sejm, the National Assembly's lower house, which is elected by proportional representation. While the prime minister is responsible for most government policy, the president's position also has influence, particularly over defense and foreign policy matters. The 100 Senate members can delay and amend legislation but have few other powers.

Anticorruption laws are not always effectively implemented, and official corruption remains a problem. In May 2012, former PO deputy Beata Sawicka and the mayor of Hel peninsula received three- and two-year sentences, respectively, for fixing a tender for the purchase of Hel land. In July, journalists released recordings of a January conversation between Władysław Serafin of PSL and the former head of the Agricultural Market Agency (ARR), Władysław Łukasik. The speakers implicated PSL in nepotism and irregularities in the distribution of EU farm subsidies, particularly to a grain company owned by the ARR. Minister of Agriculture and PSL head Marek Sawicki resigned in July, and an investigation was launched, but made no progress by year's end

The collapse of Amber Gold, an unregulated Polish lender and investment company, revealed corrupt dealings between PO officials, business interests, and the judiciary. The company's founder, Marcin Plichta, who had past fraud convictions, was arrested on August 27 and was awaiting trial on various corruption charges at year's end. In response to the scandal, the attorney general asked for a recall of prosecutors in Gdansk, where Amber Gold was based, for having ignored warnings of wrongdoing from the Financial Supervision Authority.

The constitution guarantees freedom of expression and forbids censorship. Libel remains a criminal offense, though a 2009 amendment to the criminal code eased possible penalties. In September 2012, the creator of the website *Antykomor.pl* that satirized President Komorowski was sentenced to 15 months of restricted liberty and 600 hours of community service for defaming the president. Poland's print media are diverse and mostly privately owned. The dominant state-owned Polish Television and Polish Radio face growing competition from private domestic and foreign outlets. When the PO-controlled National Broadcasting Council refused a digital broadcast license to TV Trwam, an ultraconservative TV station linked to PO's major political rival, PiS, PiS supporters protested, and the Constitutional Court ruled to license TV Trwam through 2022. In September 2011, the parliament enacted changes to the freedom of information law intended to bring Poland in line with EU regulations. One controversial provision, submitted after the rest of the changes had already been debated in the Sejm, would have limited access to information deemed threatening to the country's political and economic interests. In April 2012, the Polish Constitutional Tribunal nullified the provision in question on procedural grounds. A May 2012 court ruling found that the Central Anti-Corruption Bureau (CBA) had violated journalist Bogdan Wróblewski's privacy rights by monitoring his phone records in the 2005–2007 period. Wróblewski was one of ten journalists considered critical of the PiS-Samoobrona-LPR coalition government whose phone records were monitored during this time. The CBA appealed the verdict, and a new trial was pending at year's end.

The government does not restrict internet access. However, in January, thousands protested Prime Minister Tusk's signing of the Anti-Counterfeiting Trade Agreement establishing international standards for enforcing intellectual property rights, accusing it of facilitating internet censorship.

The state respects freedom of religion. Religious groups are not required to register with the authorities but receive tax benefits if they do. In August 2011, a judge ruled that death-metal singer Adam Darski was not guilty of blasphemy for tearing up a Bible during a 2007 concert. However, in 2012, the acquittal was appealed and brought before the Supreme Court, which ruled in October that a person may be found guilty of blasphemy, a crime punishable by up to two years in prison, even if it was unintentional. In 2013, Darski's case will be reexamined by a district court. In January, popstar Dorota "Doda" Rabczewska was also fined about 1,200 euros for having violated the blasphemy law during a 2009 interview. Academic freedom in Poland is generally respected.

Polish citizens are free to assemble legally, and various demonstrations took place throughout 2012 on issues ranging from internet freedom to economic austerity measures. A controversial amendment passed in October 2012 grants local authorities increased discretion to limit demonstrations in their districts, allegedly to maintain public order. Freedom of association is respected in law and in practice. Poland has a robust labor movement, though certain groups—including the self-employed and private contractors—may not join unions. Complicated legal procedures hinder workers' ability to strike, and labor leaders have complained of harassment by employers.

The judiciary is independent, but the courts are notorious for delays in adjudicating cases. Prosecutors' slow action on corruption investigations have prompted concerns that they are subject to political pressure. Pretrial detention periods can be lengthy, and prison conditions are poor by European standards.

Ethnic minorities generally enjoy generous legal rights and protections, including funding for bilingual education and publications. They also receive privileged representation in the parliament, as their political parties are not subject to the minimum vote threshold of 5 percent to achieve representation. Some groups, particularly the Roma, experience employment and housing discrimination, racially motivated insults, and, sometimes, physical attacks. Sexual minorities continue to face discrimination, though the first openly gay and transgender lawmakers entered the Sejm in November 2011.

Women hold senior positions in government and the private sector, including 24 percent of the seats in the Sejm. Poland's abortion laws are among the strictest in Europe. Women who undergo illegal abortions do not face criminal charges, but those who assist in the procedures—including medical staff—can face up to three years in prison. In November 2012, the European Court of Human Rights ordered Poland to pay a 14-year-old rape victim 61,000 euros for failing to provide her with "unhindered" access to an abortion. Domestic violence against women remains a serious concern, as does trafficking in women and girls for the purpose of prostitution.

Portugal

Political Rights: 1
Civil Liberties: 1
Status: Free

Population: 10,560,700
Capital: Lisbon

Ten-Year Ratings Timeline For Year Under Review (Political Rights, Civil Liberties, Status)

2003	2004	2005	2006	2007	2008	2009	2010	2011	2012
1,1F	1,1F	1,1F	1,1F	1,1F	1,1F	1,1F	1,1F	1,1F	1,1F

Overview:
Massive protests continued to sweep Portugal in 2012 in response to the country's ongoing financial crisis and the government's proposed budget and austerity measures. Meanwhile, a new immigration law more closely aligned with European Union migration policy went into effect in September.

Portugal was proclaimed a republic in 1910, after King Manuel II abdicated during a bloodless revolution. António de Oliveira Salazar became prime minister in 1932 and ruled the country as a fascist dictatorship until 1968, when his lieutenant, Marcello Caetano, replaced him. During the "Marcello Spring," repression and censorship were relaxed somewhat, and a liberal wing developed inside the one-party National Assembly. In 1974, a bloodless coup by the Armed Forces Movement, which opposed the ongoing colonial wars in Mozambique and Angola, overthrew Caetano.

A transition to democracy began with the election of a Constitutional Assembly that adopted a democratic constitution in 1976. A civilian government was formally established in 1982 after a revision to the constitution brought the military under civilian control, curbed the president's powers, and abolished the unelected Revolutionary Council. Portugal became a member of the European Economic Community (later the European Union, or EU) in 1986, and formally adopted the euro currency in 2002. The country handed over its last colonial territory, Macao, to the People's Republic of China in 1999.

Aníbal Cavaco Silva, a center-right candidate who had served as prime minister from 1985 to 1995, won the 2006 presidential election; he was reelected in January 2011. The Socialist Party captured the largest number of seats in the 2009 legislative elections, followed by the Social Democratic Party (PSD).

In March 2011, Jóse Sócrates of the Socialist Party stepped down as prime minister after his government's fourth austerity budget proposal was rejected by all five opposition parties. Early legislative elections were held in June and saw the victory of the PSD with 39 percent of the vote, compared to the Socialist Party's 28 percent. PSD leader Pedro Passos Coelho immediately formed a coalition government with the Popular Party.

A series of protests swept the nation in 2012 in response to the financial crisis that has gripped the country for several years. More than 100,000 people took to the streets in Lisbon on September 15, as well as tens of thousands more in more than 40 towns across Portugal, to protest a proposed austerity budget, which the government ultimately rejected. It was the largest protest since 1974, but resulted in only two arrests. Protests took place in Lisbon throughout October in response to the government's tax hikes proposed in the draft 2013 budget, which was passed on October 31. During a protest on October 15, 10 police officers and 1 protester were injured after police tried to dispurse crowds using batons. Two of Portugal's largest trade unions, the General Confederation of Portuguese Workers and the General Workers' Union, organized a massive strike on November 14 to protest the worsening economy and the recently passed 2013 budget. A challenge to the budget—and specifically, the tax increases, which were the highest in Portugal's modern history—was pending with the Constitutional Court at year's end.

Political Rights and Civil Liberties: Portugal is an electoral democracy. The 230 members of the unicameral legislature, the Assembly of the Republic, are elected every four years using a system of proportional representation. The president can serve up to two five-year terms; while the position is largely ceremonial, the president can delay legislation through a veto, dissolve the assembly to trigger early elections, and is the commander in chief of the armed forces with the power to declare war. The legislature nominates the prime minister, who is then confirmed by the president. The constitution was amended in 1997 to allow Portuguese citizens living abroad to vote in presidential and legislative elections, as well as national referendums.

The main political parties are the Socialist Party, the PSD, and the Social Centre/People's Party. The autonomous regions of Azores and Madeira—two island groups in the Atlantic—have their own political structures with legislative and executive powers.

Portugal continued to struggle with corruption issues throughout 2012. Portuguese police carried out a widespread operation in 2009 to expose companies engaged in illicitly obtaining industrial waste contracts. A number of officials linked to Socialist Prime Minister Jose Sócrates were implicated in the scandal, known as "Hidden Face." While Sócrates himself was not implicated, the scandal damaged his government's credibility. More than 30 people were charged with graft, money laundering, and influence peddling. Their trials opened in November 2011 and continued throughout 2012, though no one had been prosecuted by the end of the year. With new evidence against Sócrates in the 2002 Freeport scandal—in which Sócrates and two other plaintifs were charged with illegally accepting bribes for the construction of a shopping mall on protected lands outside Lisbon—prosecutors tried but failed to reopen the case against him in October 2012. In 2012, Transparency International released a report recommending that Portugal change its process of choosing a prosecutor general to allow for greater autonomy and less government influence. Portugal was ranked 33 out of 176 countries surveyed in Transparency International's 2012 Corruption Perceptions Index.

Freedom of the press is constitutionally guaranteed, and laws against insulting the government or armed forces are rarely enforced. In October 2012, Portugal's national news agency, Lusa, went on strike for four days, including a news blackout, after it was announced that the government planned to cut its budget by more than 30 percent. Poorly funded public broadcasting channels already face serious competition from commercial television outlets. Internet access in Portugal is not restricted.

Although the country is overwhelmingly Roman Catholic, the constitution guarantees freedom of religion and forbids religious discrimination. The Religious Freedom Act provides religions that have been established in the country for at least 30 years (or recognized internationally for at least 60 years) with a number of benefits formerly reserved only for the Catholic Church, such as tax exemptions, legal recognition of marriage and other rites, and respect for traditional holidays. Academic freedom is respected.

Freedoms of assembly and association are honored, and national and international nongovernmental organizations, including human rights groups, operate in the country without interference. Workers enjoy the right to organize, bargain collectively, and strike. However, a 2003 labor law mandated that workers assess a proposed strike's impact on citizens, and provide minimal services during such an event. Thousands of people in 2012 participated in public protests and strikes amid high unemployment and other economic struggles, including the massive November strike against the government's 2013 budget. Only 19 percent of the workforce is unionized.

The constitution provides for an independent judiciary, though staff shortages and inefficiency have contributed to a considerable backlog of pending trials. Human rights groups have expressed concern over unlawful police shootings and deaths in custody. Criticism also continues over poor prison conditions, including overcrowding, poor sanitary conditions, mistreatment of prisoners by police and prison guards, and relatively high rates of HIV/AIDS among inmates.

The constitution guarantees equal treatment under the law. The government has taken a number of steps to combat racism, including passing antidiscrimination laws and launching initiatives to promote the integration of immigrants and Roma. A 2007 immigration law facilitates family reunification and legalization for immigrants in specific circumstances. According to a 2008 study by the Observatory for Immigration, immigrants pay excessively high taxes, though little revenue is channeled to projects that benefit them directly. In September 2012, a new immigration law went into effect that more closely aligns with EU migration policy, including extending temporary visas and imposing higher penalties for employers who hire staff that are in the country illegally.

Domestic violence against women and children remains a problem, and few domestic violence cases are prosecuted. Portugal is a destination and transit point for trafficked persons, particularly women from Eastern Europe and former Portuguese colonies in South America and Africa. Portugal legalized same-sex marriage in 2010.

Qatar

Political Rights: 6
Civil Liberties: 5
Status: Not Free

Population: 1,881,600
Capital: Doha

Ten-Year Ratings Timeline For Year Under Review (Political Rights, Civil Liberties, Status)

2003	2004	2005	2006	2007	2008	2009	2010	2011	2012
6,6NF	6,5NF	6,5NF	6,5NF	6,5NF	6,5NF	6,5NF	6,5NF	6,5NF	6,5NF

Overview:

In June 2012, Qatar's Advisory Council passed a draft media law that would criminalize criticism of the Qatari government or its allies, and a poet was sentenced to life in prison in December for insulting the emir. Meanwhile, Qatar provided support during the year to opposition forces attempting to overthrow Syria's government.

Qatar gained independence from Britain in 1971. The following year, Khalifa bin Hamad al-Thani deposed his cousin, Emir Ahmad bin Ali al-Thani, and ruled for 23 years as an absolute monarch. In 1995, the emir was deposed by his son, Hamad bin Khalifa al-Thani, who began a program of gradual political, social, and economic reforms. Hamad dissolved the Ministry of Information shortly after taking power, an action designed to demonstrate his commitment to expanding press freedom.

In 1996, Hamad permitted the creation of Al-Jazeera, which has become one of the most popular Arabic-language satellite television channels in the Middle East. However, Al-Jazeera generally does not cover Qatari politics and focuses instead on regional issues.

The country held its first elections in 1999 for a 29-member Central Municipal Council, a body designed to advise the minister on municipal affairs and agriculture. The poll made Qatar the first state of the Gulf Cooperation Council to introduce widespread voting rights for men and women over 18 years of age. Hamad also accelerated a program to strengthen Qatar's educational institutions, inviting foreign universities to establish branches in the country.

In addition to Central Municipal Council elections in 2003, Qataris voted in a referendum that overwhelmingly approved the country's first constitution, which came into force in 2005. The new constitution slightly broadened the scope of political participation without eliminating the ruling family's monopoly on power, and most rights do not apply to noncitizen residents, who form a majority of the population.

The most recent Municipal Council elections were held in May 2011. Four of the 101 candidates were women; the only woman who had previously served on the Council was reelected. Voter turnout was 43 percent, with just 13,606 registered voters participating.

Qatar has hosted U.S. military forces for a number of years, and the U.S. presence grew significantly after 2001. The country has faced severe criticism in the region for its ties to the United States and its tentative links with Israel. Qatar is deeply involved in regional politics. It provided military and political support for the 2011 revolution in Libya, and it has provided material support to opposition forces attempting to overthrow Bashar al-Assad in Syria. In November 2012, the Syrian National Council—the Syrian opposition's primary political group—held four days of talks in Qatar's capital, Doha to discuss overhauling its structure.

Political Rights and Civil Liberties: Qatar is not an electoral democracy. The head of state is the emir, whose family holds a monopoly on political power. The emir appoints the prime minister and cabinet, and also appoints an heir apparent after consulting with the ruling family and other notables. The constitution stipulates the formation of an elected parliament, the Advisory Council (Majlis Al-Shura). Elections are to be held for 30 of the 45 seats for four-year terms, while the emir has the power to appoint the other 15 members. Although elections for this body were scheduled for 2010, Emir Hamad bin Khalifa al-Thani in 2011 again extended the existing 35-member Council's current session until 2013; all its members are appointed. Central Municipal Council members, who are elected to serve four-year terms, enjoy limited powers.

Only a small percentage of the country's population is permitted to vote or hold office. The government does not permit the existence of political parties.

Critics continue to complain of a lack of transparency in government procurement. However, Qatar was ranked 27 out of 176 countries surveyed in Transparency International's 2012 Corruption Perceptions Index, tied with the United Arab Emirates as the best performer in the Middle East.

Although the constitution guarantees freedom of expression, both print and broadcast media content are influenced by leading families. Journalists practice a high degree of self-censorship and face possible jail sentences for slander. In June 2012, the Advisory Council approved a draft media law which was awaiting final approval by Sheikh Hamad at year's end. The law would prevent journalists from being detained by authorities without a court order, and would allow them to protect their sources unless required to do so by a court. However, it also would impose fines of up to $275,000 for publishing or broadcasting material that criticizes the Qatari regime or its allies, insults the ruling family, or damages national interests. While state censorship is supposedly forbidden under the law, journalists would be required to obtain licenses and would be monitored by the Ministry of Arts, Heritage and Culture. In December, poet Mohamed Ibn al-Dheeb al-Ajami was sentenced to life in prison for insulting the emir after videos of him reciting his poetry were posted on the internet.

The top five daily newspapers are privately owned, but their owners and boards include members of the ruling family. Although the satellite television channel Al-Jazeera is privately held, the government has reportedly paid for the channel's operating costs since its inception. As a result, Al-Jazeera rarely criticizes the ruling family. Qataris have access to the internet, but the government censors content and blocks access to sites that are deemed pornographic or politically sensitive.

Islam is Qatar's official religion, though the constitution explicitly provides for freedom of worship. The Ministry of Islamic Affairs regulates clerical matters and the construction of mosques. Several churches have been built for Qatar's Christian community in recent years. The constitution guarantees freedom of opinion and academic research, but scholars often practice self-censorship on politically sensitive topics.

While the constitution grants freedoms of assembly and association, these rights are limited in practice. Protests are rare, with the government restricting the public's ability to organize demonstrations. In spite of early 2011 Facebook campaign efforts to mobilize protests in Qatar, the country did not experience the "Arab Spring" unrest that took place in other countries in the region during the year. In December 2012, the government permitted a 300-person demonstration calling for Arab leadership on climate change and for improved migrant worker rights. All nongovernmental organizations need state permission to operate, and the government closely monitors their activities. After hosting the 2007 Conference on Democracy and Reform in Doha, the Ministry of Foreign Affairs established the Arab Foundation for Democracy to monitor progress on reform in the region; Sheikh Hamad has contributed $10 million to the foundation. There are no independent human rights organizations, but a government-appointed National Human Rights

Committee, which includes members of civil society and government ministries, investigates alleged abuses.

A 2005 labor law expanded some protections, but restricts the right to form unions and to strike. The only trade union allowed to operate in the country is the General Union of Workers of Qatar, which prohibits the membership of noncitizens or government sector employees. Foreign nationals comprise 94 percent of the workforce. Many foreign workers face economic abuses, including the withholding of salaries or contract manipulation, while others endure poor living conditions and excessive work hours. However, fear of job loss and deportation often prevents them from exercising their limited rights. Female domestic workers are particularly vulnerable to abuse and exploitation. In order to support infrastructure projects in preparation for the 2022 World Cup, Qatar is projected to import over 1 million migrant laborers.

Despite constitutional guarantees, the judiciary is not independent in practice. The majority of Qatar's judges are foreign nationals who are appointed and removed by the emir. The judicial system consists of Sharia (Islamic law) courts, which have jurisdiction over a narrow range of issues including family law, and civil law courts, which have jurisdiction over criminal, commercial, and civil cases. Although the constitution protects individuals from arbitrary arrest and detention and bans torture, a 2002 law allows the suspension of these guarantees for the "protection of society." The law empowers the minister of the interior to detain a defendant for crimes related to national security on the recommendation of the director-general of public security.

While the constitution prohibits discrimination based on nationality, the government discriminates against noncitizens in the areas of education, housing, healthcare, and other services that are offered free of charge to citizens.

The constitution treats women as full and equal persons, and discrimination based on gender, country of origin, language, or religion is banned. In March 2010, Qatar swore in Sheikha Maha Mansour Salman Jassim al-Thani as its first woman judge. In 2006, Qatar implemented a codified family law, which regulates issues such as inheritance, child custody, marriage, and divorce. While this law offers more protections for women than they previously enjoyed, they continue to face some disadvantages, including societal discrimination, and few effective legal mechanisms are available for them to contest incidents of bias. Domestic violence is not criminalized and is prevalent. The Qatar Foundation for Child and Woman Protection has noted a significant increase in cases of violence since 2004. The proposed Qatari 2011-2016 National Development Strategy includes measures to better protect victims of abuse, including laws against domestic violence, increased legal protections for victims, and robust social support services. However, these measures had not been instituted as of 2012. Qatar is a destination for the trafficking of men and women, particularly for forced labor and prostitution.

Romania

Political Rights: 2
Civil Liberties: 2
Status: Free

Population: 21,408,000
Capital: Bucharest

Ten-Year Ratings Timeline For Year Under Review (Political Rights, Civil Liberties, Status)

2003	2004	2005	2006	2007	2008	2009	2010	2011	2012
2,2F	3,2F	2,2F	2,2F	2,2F	2,2F	2,2F	2,2F	2,2F	2,2F

Overview:
Public frustration with austerity measures brought down two center-right prime ministers in February and April 2012, leading to a new center-left government headed by Victor Ponta in May. Ponta called a referendum in July to impeach President Traian Basescu, a political rival, and pressured the Constitutional Court to ease his ouster, but the vote failed amid low turnout. Ponta's coalition easily won parliamentary elections in December.

In 1989, longtime dictator Nicolae Ceausescu was overthrown and executed by disgruntled Communists. A provisional government was formed, and regular multiparty elections soon followed, with power changing hands between right-leaning parties and the former Communist Party, renamed the Social Democratic Party (PSD), during the 1990s. The PSD returned to power in the 2000 parliamentary elections, with Adrian Nastase as prime minister.

In 2004, Traian Basescu of the Alliance for Truth and Justice (comprising the National Liberal Party, or PNL, and the Democratic Party, or PD) defeated N stase in a presidential runoff. The PNL and PD then formed a coalition government with the Humanist Party (later renamed the Conservative Party, or PC) and the Democratic Union of Hungarians in Romania (UDMR). C lin Popescu-Tariceanu of the PNL became prime minister.

The ruling coalition proved unstable, and after Romania's accession to the European Union (EU) in January 2007, Popescu-Tariceanu ousted the Basescu-allied PD from the cabinet in April. At the PSD's urging, Parliament voted to suspend Basescu and organize a referendum on his removal, but he easily won the vote that May.

The new Democratic Liberal Party (PDL), a union of the PD and a PNL splinter faction, won parliamentary elections in November 2008. PDL leader Emil Boc was confirmed by Parliament as the new prime minister. B sescu narrowly defeated his PSD challenger, Mircea Geoana, in the 2009 presidential election, and Parliament subsequently approved a new PDL-UDMR coalition government led by Boc.

The government struggled throughout 2010 and 2011 to implement a harsh fiscal austerity package as part of a 2009 emergency loan agreement with the International Monetary Fund. The budgetary measures and labor reforms drew repeated protests by workers and criticism from opposition parties. Boc finally resigned in February 2012, after weeks of sometimes violent demonstrations, and his successor, Mihai Razvan Ungureanu, was toppled by a parliamentary no-confidence vote in late April.

With the PDL unable to gather a majority, Basescu named PSD leader Victor

Ponta as prime minister, and his Social Liberal Union (USL) government—an alliance of the PSD, PNL, and PC—was approved by Parliament in early May. The new government took a rapid series of legally dubious steps to consolidate control over state institutions.

Over the course of a few days in late June and early July, Ponta and the USL shifted control of the official gazette, used to promulgate laws, from Parliament to the government; removed, without clear justification, the ombudsman, the only official with the authority to challenge government decrees before the Constitutional Court; replaced the PDL Speakers of both chambers of Parliament; and passed a motion to suspend the president, setting the stage for a referendum to permanently oust Basescu at the end of July.

As the Constitutional Court moved to curb some of these actions, for instance by initially rejecting the government's claims that B sescu had abused his authority, Ponta and the USL issued emergency decrees that attempted, ultimately without success, to limit its jurisdiction. The court's judges complained to EU officials of threats and political pressure. Nevertheless, the Constitutional Court was able to block the government's attempt to remove a 50 percent turnout threshold for the impeachment referendum to be valid. The vote consequently failed, with 87 percent backing impeachment amid 46 percent turnout.

In the weeks between the balloting and the court's final ruling on its annulment in late August, Ponta continued to push for Basescu's removal, arguing that the voter rolls were inaccurate and the actual turnout was higher. The interior minister and a subordinate responsible for organizing the referendum resigned in early August due to intense political pressure, triggering a cabinet reshuffle.

The crisis eased over the subsequent months, and the December 9 parliamentary elections proceeded without incident. The USL won handily, taking 273 of 412 seats in the lower house and 122 of 176 seats in the Senate. The PDL's Right Romania Alliance placed a distant second with 56 lower house seats and 24 Senate seats, followed by the People's Party–Dan Diaconescu with 47 and 21, the UDMR with 18 and 9, and various national minority representatives with a total of 18 seats in the lower house. Basescu duly nominated Ponta for a new term as prime minister, and Parliament approved the new USL government on December 21.

Political Rights and Civil Liberties:

Romania is an electoral democracy. Elections since 1991 have been considered generally free and fair. The president is directly elected for up to two five-year terms and appoints the prime minister with the approval of Parliament. Members of the bicameral Parliament, consisting of the 176-seat Senate and 412-seat Chamber of Deputies, are elected for four-year terms.

In January 2012, the Constitutional Court struck down a PDL-backed plan to postpone local elections and hold them jointly with the parliamentary polls. The move had been seen as an attempt to keep the PDL's local allies in power to influence the legislative elections. The local balloting was held on schedule in June, and the USL won the mayors' posts in all major cities.

The constitution grants one lower-house seat to each national minority whose representative party or organization fails to win any seats under the normal rules, and 18 such seats were allotted in 2012. The UDMR has long represented the ethnic

Hungarian minority. Political participation and representation of Roma are weak, though two Romany candidates with the USL and one representing a national minority party won seats in Parliament in 2012.

Romania has struggled to meet EU anticorruption requirements. A July 2012 EU monitoring report praised the National Anticorruption Directorate and the National Integrity Agency (ANI) for increasing impartial investigations and successful prosecutions, but cited ongoing problems with follow-up by administrative and judicial bodies, including a pattern of minimum or suspended sentences. Romania's corruption problems kept it out of the EU's passport-free travel zone in 2012, and prompted the suspension of about 500 million euros ($648 million) in EU economic development funds in October. Romania was ranked 66 out of 176 countries surveyed in Transparency International's 2012 Corruption Perceptions Index.

Some significant progress against corruption was reported in 2012. In a landmark case, former prime minister Adrian N stase was sentenced to two years in prison in January for misappropriating state funds for his 2004 presidential campaign. He also received a three-year suspended prison sentence for blackmail in March. Although he allegedly shot himself in a bid to avoid prison after losing a Supreme Court appeal in June, he was duly incarcerated after a brief hospital stay. In October, the Senate defied a Supreme Court ruling by voting that Mircea Diaconu, who had resigned as culture minister in June due to a conflict of interest, could remain a senator; he later announced that he would not seek reelection. Also in October, the health minister resigned over embezzlement allegations. Separately, two former agriculture ministers were convicted of corruption-related offenses in February. Prime Minister Victor Ponta fired a cabinet official in November after the ANI accused him of a conflict of interest, but three ministers who were similarly accused refused to resign.

The constitution protects freedom of the press, and the media have been characterized by considerable pluralism. However, a weakening advertising market has led foreign media companies to sell their Romanian assets, leaving a larger share of important outlets in the hands of wealthy Romanian businessmen, who typically use them to advance their political and economic interests. State-owned media remain vulnerable to political influence. New leadership was installed at the public broadcaster after the change in government in 2012, and planned staff cuts raised concerns that employees would be laid off based on political criteria. The Ponta government and allied media repeatedly smeared critical journalists during 2012, accusing them of being paid by the president's faction to spread misinformation. Several journalists were attacked by protesters or police during the antigovernment protests in January. The government does not restrict access to the internet, and penetration is estimated at 39 percent.

Religious freedom is generally respected, but the Romanian Orthodox Church remains dominant and politically powerful. The government formally recognizes 18 religions, each of which is eligible for proportional state support. Minorities encounter discrimination by some local officials and hostility from Orthodox priests. Anti-Semitism remains a problem. Senator Dan Sova, who was fired as PSD spokesman in March 2012 after denying Holocaust-related historical events in a televised interview, was nevertheless appointed as a cabinet minister in August.

The government does not restrict academic freedom, but the education system is weakened by rampant corruption. Ponta's first education minister, Ioan Mang, was forced to resign in May 2012 over allegations of plagiarism. In June, the British science magazine *Nature* accused Ponta of plagiarizing his 2003 doctoral thesis, for which Nastase had served as adviser. Inquiries by the Romanian Academy and the University of Bucharest confirmed the claims, but a council overseen by the Education Ministry rejected them, and Education Minister Ecaterina Andronescu said the latter finding prevailed.

The constitution guarantees freedoms of assembly and association, and the government respects these rights in practice, though the January 2012 protests featured violence between police and demonstrators. Workers have the right to form unions and a limited right to strike, but in practice many employers work against unions, and enforcement of union and labor protections is weak.

Judicial independence was threatened in 2012 by political pressure surrounding the impeachment effort, and the courts continued to suffer from chronic problems such as corruption, political influence, staffing shortages, and inefficient resource allocation. Conditions in Romanian prisons remain poor.

Roma, members of the LGBT (lesbian, gay, bisexual, and transgender) community, people with disabilities, and HIV-positive children and adults face discrimination in education, employment, and other areas. Romania is home to the EU's largest population of Roma, but has struggled to obtain and spend EU funding dedicated to improving their living conditions. The mayor of Baia Mare, who was fined for building a wall around Romany homes in 2011, drew new criticism in 2012 for relocating about 150 Roma to the polluted site of a shuttered chemical plant.

The constitution guarantees women equal rights, but gender discrimination is a problem. Less than 12 percent of the seats in Parliament are held by women. A March 2012 legal amendment provided for restraining orders in domestic violence cases, which are rarely prosecuted. Trafficking of women and girls for forced prostitution remains a major concern, as does trafficking of children for forced begging.

Russia

Political Rights: 6
Civil Liberties: 5
Status: Not Free

Population: 143,165,000
Capital: Moscow

Trend Arrow: Russia received a downward trend arrow due to the imposition of harsh penalties on protesters participating in unsanctioned rallies and new rules requiring civil society organizations with foreign funding to register as "foreign agents."

Ten-Year Ratings Timeline For Year Under Review (Political Rights, Civil Liberties, Status)

2003	2004	2005	2006	2007	2008	2009	2010	2011	2012
5,5PF	6,5NF	6,5NF	6,5NF	6,5NF	6,5NF	6,5NF	6,5NF	6,5NF	6,5NF

Overview: Prime Minister Vladimir Putin won the tightly controlled March 2012 presidential election and returned to the Kremlin after a four-year interlude, during which his chosen placeholder, Dmitry Medvedev, had continued Putin's policies and allowed him to avoid

violating constitutional term limits. Putin immediately imposed greater restrictions on public assemblies, nongovernmental organizations, and the internet, seeking to squelch the nascent protest movement that had arisen in response to fraudulent December 2011 parliamentary elections. Vaguely defined amendments to the law on treason potentially criminalized a variety of activities, including ordinary interactions with foreigners. The authorities also launched anticorruption investigations during the year, exposing high levels of fraud in state spending, but as with past anticorruption drives, actual arrests were limited to lower-level officials rather than members of the elite.

With the collapse of the Soviet Union in December 1991, the Russian Federation emerged as an independent state under the leadership of President Boris Yeltsin. In 1993, Yeltsin used force to thwart an attempted coup by parliamentary opponents of radical reform, after which voters approved a new constitution establishing a powerful presidency and a bicameral national legislature, the Federal Assembly. The 1995 parliamentary elections featured strong support for the Communist Party and ultranationalist forces. Nevertheless, in the 1996 presidential poll, which suffered from electoral manipulation by all sides, Yeltsin defeated Communist leader Gennady Zyuganov with the financial backing of powerful business magnates, who used the media empires they controlled to ensure victory. In 1999, Yeltsin appointed Vladimir Putin, then the head of the Federal Security Service (FSB), as prime minister.

Conflict with the separatist republic of Chechnya, which had secured de facto independence from Moscow after a brutal 1994–96 war, resumed in 1999. Government forces reinvaded the breakaway region after Chechen rebels led an incursion into the neighboring Russian republic of Dagestan in August and a series of deadly apartment bombings—which the Kremlin blamed on Chechen militants and some of Putin's critics blamed on him—struck Russian cities in September. The prosecution of the second Chechen war dramatically increased Putin's popularity, and after the December 1999 elections for the State Duma, the lower house of the Federal Assembly, progovernment parties were able to form a majority coalition.

An ailing and unpopular Yeltsin, who was constitutionally barred from a third presidential term, resigned several months early on December 31, 1999, transferring power to Putin—allegedly in exchange for immunity from prosecution for corruption. The new acting president subsequently secured a first-round victory over Zyuganov, 53 percent to 29 percent, in the March 2000 presidential election. After taking office, Putin moved quickly to reduce the influence of the legislature, tame the business community and the news media, and strengthen the FSB. He considerably altered the composition of the ruling elite through an influx of personnel from the security and military services. Overall, Putin garnered enormous personal popularity by overseeing a gradual increase in the standard of living for most of the population; the improvements were driven largely by an oil and gas boom and economic reforms that had followed a 1998 financial crisis.

In the December 2003 Duma elections, the Kremlin-controlled United Russia party captured 306 out of 450 seats. With the national broadcast media and most print outlets favoring the incumbent, no opponent was able to mount a significant challenge in the March 2004 presidential election. Putin, who refused to debate the other candidates, received 71.4 percent of the vote in a first-round victory, compared with 13.7 percent for his closest rival, the Communist-backed Nikolai Kharitonov.

Putin introduced legislative changes in 2004 that eliminated direct gubernatorial elections in favor of presidential appointments, citing a need to unify the country in the face of terrorist violence. The government also began a crackdown on democracy-promotion groups and other nongovernmental organizations (NGOs), especially those receiving foreign funding. The authorities removed another possible threat in 2005, when a court sentenced billionaire energy magnate Mikhail Khodorkovsky, a supporter of liberal opposition parties, to eight years in prison. The case was seen as a warning to other business leaders to stay out of politics.

A law enacted in 2006 handed bureaucrats wide discretion in monitoring and shutting down NGOs, which the authorities used to target organizations that were critical of official policy. In another sign that safe avenues for dissent were disappearing, an assassin murdered investigative journalist Anna Politkovskaya in October of that year. She had frequently criticized the Kremlin's ongoing military campaign in Chechnya and the excesses of Russian troops in the region.

The heavily manipulated December 2007 parliamentary elections gave United Russia 315 of the 450 Duma seats, while two other parties that generally supported the Kremlin, A Just Russia and the nationalist Liberal Democratic Party of Russia (LDPR), took 38 and 40 seats, respectively. The opposition Communists won 57 seats in the effectively toothless legislature.

Constitutionally barred from a third consecutive term, Putin handpicked his successor, First Deputy Prime Minister Dmitry Medvedev, who won the March 2008 presidential election with 70.3 percent of the vote. Medvedev appointed Putin as his prime minister, and the former president continued to play the dominant role in government. At the end of 2008, the leadership amended the constitution for the first time since it was adopted in 1993, extending future presidential terms from four to six years. Even as Medvedev continued to implement Putin's policies, civil society became more active during his presidency on issues including corruption and environmental protection.

In September 2011, Medvedev announced that he would step aside so that Putin could return to the presidency in elections set for March 2012. The controversial move came as Putin's popularity was declining, largely as a result of Russia's unchecked corruption and a plateau in the improvement of living standards.

Although the authorities made extensive use of their incumbency in the December 2011 elections, United Russia captured just 238 seats, a significant drop from the 2007 elections. The Communist Party placed second with 92 seats, followed by A Just Russia with 64 and the LDPR with 56. Truly independent parties were not allowed to run. In the weeks following the elections, the largest antigovernment demonstrations since Putin came to power were held in Moscow, with smaller protests taking place in other cities in Russia. The demonstrators called for the annulment of the election results, an investigation into vote fraud, and freedom for political prisoners. Hundreds of people were arrested, and several protest leaders were jailed for short periods.

Despite the growing discontent in Russia at the beginning of 2012, Putin was able to secure victory in the March presidential election, officially winning 63.6 percent of the vote against a field of weak, hand-chosen opponents. Zyuganov, the Communist leader, was his closest challenger with 17.2 percent. With his return to the Kremlin assured, Putin quickly toughened the authorities' response to the protests. The police used violence to suppress a Moscow demonstration linked to his inauguration in May, arresting many of the participants. Putin also pushed through new laws limiting the actions of NGOs, placing new restrictions on the internet, recriminalizing slander, and expanding the definition of treason to include a wide variety of activities in an effort to frighten the population into passivity.

Political Rights and Civil Liberties: Russia is not an electoral democracy. The 2012 presidential election was skewed in favor of prime minister and former president Vladimir Putin, who benefited from preferential media treatment, numerous abuses of incumbency, and procedural irregularities during the vote count, among other advantages. The deeply flawed 2011 Duma elections were marked by a "convergence of the state and the governing party, limited political competition and a lack of fairness," according to the Organization for Security and Cooperation in Europe, but many voters used them to express a protest against the status quo.

The 1993 constitution established a strong presidency with the power to dismiss and appoint, pending parliamentary confirmation, the prime minister. Putin's decision to place Dmitry Medvedev in the presidency for four years so that he could return to office for a third term, now extended from four to six years, violated the spirit of the constitution's two-term limit. The Federal Assembly consists of the 450-seat State Duma and an upper chamber, the 166-seat Federation Council. The 2008 constitutional amendment extended Duma terms from four to five years.

Since the 2007 elections, all Duma deputies have been elected on the basis of party-list proportional representation. Parties must gain at least 7 percent of the vote to enter the Duma. Furthermore, parties cannot form electoral coalitions. Medvedev signed legislation in April 2012 that liberalized party registration rules, allowing 42 parties to register by year's end. However, none posed a significant threat to the authorities, and many seemed designed to encourage division and confusion among the opposition.

Half the members of the upper chamber are appointed by governors and half by regional legislatures, usually with strong federal input. As of January 2011, only locally elected politicians are eligible to serve in the Federation Council; the change was expected to benefit United Russia, as most local officeholders are party members. A law signed by Medvedev in May 2012 restored gubernatorial elections, ending the system of presidential appointments dating to 2004. The first set of elections was held in five regions in October. However, the new rules allowed regional officials to screen the candidates for governor, eliminating strong opposition contenders and helping to ensure that pro-Kremlin incumbents won all five races. These included one in Ryazan, where the governor was extremely unpopular.

Corruption in the government and business world is pervasive, and a growing lack of accountability enables bureaucrats to act with impunity. The leadership frequently announces anticorruption campaigns, but they are typically superficial in nature. In November 2012, Putin fired Defense Minister Anatoly Serdyukov amid allegations of fraud in the Ministry of Defense. Other investigations during the year implicated the head of the presidential administration, Sergei Ivanov, and First Deputy Prime Minister Igor Shuvalov. By year's end, it was not clear how far the campaign would go, or whether it reflected destabilizing conflict among the elite. The top leaders had yet to face prosecution, though some lower-level officials were formally charged.

Although the constitution provides for freedom of speech, the government controls, directly or through state-owned companies, all of the national television networks. Only a handful of radio stations and publications with limited audiences offer a wide range of viewpoints. At least 19 journalists have been killed since Putin came to power, including 3 in 2009, and in no cases have the organizers of the murders been prosecuted. Vague laws on extremism make it possible to crack down on any speech, organization, or activity that lacks official support. Discussion on the internet is largely unrestricted, but the government devotes extensive resources to manipulating online information and analysis. In November 2012, a broadly worded new law, ostensibly targeting information that is unsuitable for children, created a blacklist of internet outlets that initially led to the shuttering of more than 180 sites.

Freedom of religion is respected unevenly. A 1997 law on religion gives the state extensive control and makes it difficult for new or independent groups to operate. Orthodox Christianity has a privileged position, and in 2009 the president authorized religious instruction in the public schools. Regional authorities continue to harass nontraditional groups, such as Jehovah's Witnesses and Mormons. While Russia has long struggled with anti-Semitism, Putin supported the creation of a $50 million Jewish museum that opened in Moscow in late 2012.

Academic freedom is generally respected, though the education system is marred by corruption and low salaries. The arrest and prosecution of scientists and researchers on charges of treason, usually for discussing sensitive technology with foreigners, has effectively restricted international contacts in recent years. Historians who seek to examine controversial aspects of Russian and Soviet history, such as the fate of ethnic minority populations that were deported to Siberia during World War II, and the Ukrainian famine of 1932–33, face severe pressure from the authorities.

The government has consistently reduced the space for freedoms of assembly and association. Overwhelming police responses, the use of force, and routine arrests have discouraged unsanctioned protests, though pro-Kremlin groups are able to demonstrate freely. At least 18 people were arrested at a rally on the eve of Putin's inauguration in May 2012, and the one person tried and convicted to date received four and a half years in prison after he admitted to attacking the police. In August, a Moscow court sentenced three members of the performance group Pussy Riot to two years in prison for filming and posting on YouTube an anti-Putin "punk prayer" in an Orthodox cathedral in February. Amid international criticism of the verdict, one of the three was freed by an appellate court in October.

A 2006 law imposed onerous new reporting requirements on NGOs, giving bureaucrats extensive discretion in deciding which groups could register and hampering activities that the state deemed objectionable. The law also places tight controls on the use of foreign funds. A law enacted in 2012 required all organizations receiving foreign funding and involved in vaguely defined "political activities" to register as "foreign agents" with the Justice Ministry. Noncompliance can be punished by steep fines and prison terms. In November, the Justice Ministry shut down the Russian Association of Indigenous Peoples of the North (RAIPON), which apparently drew the authorities' ire by opposing development projects. The state has sought to provide alternative sources of funding to local NGOs, including a handful of organizations that are critical of government policy, though such support generally limits the scope of the recipient groups' activities.

While trade union rights are legally protected, they are limited in practice. Strikes and worker protests have occurred in prominent industries, such as automobile manufacturing, but antiunion discrimination and reprisals for strikes are not uncommon, and employers often ignore collective-bargaining rights. The largest labor federation works in close cooperation with the Kremlin.

The judiciary lacks independence from the executive branch, and career advancement is effectively tied to compliance with Kremlin preferences. The justice system has been tarnished by politically fraught cases such as that of Mikhail Khodorkovsky. The criminal procedure code allows jury trials for serious cases, though they occur rarely in practice. While juries are more likely than judges to acquit defendants, such verdicts are frequently overturned by higher courts, which can order retrials until the desired outcome is achieved. Russia ended the use of jury trials in terrorism cases in 2008. Russian citizens often feel that domestic courts do not provide a fair hearing and have increasingly turned to the European Court of Human Rights.

Critics charge that Russia has failed to address ongoing criminal justice problems, such as poor prison conditions and the widespread use of illegal detention and torture to extract confessions. In October 2012, opposition activist Leonid Razvozzhayev was allegedly abducted by Russian authorities in Ukraine, where he was preparing an asylum application; forcibly repatriated; and compelled to signed a confession to charges of planning mass riots. Russian officials insisted that he had turned himself in. The circumstances surrounding the 2009 death of lawyer Sergei Magnitsky in pretrial detention, after he accused government employees of embezzling millions of dollars, suggested that the authorities had deliberately denied him medical treatment. As many as 50 to 60 people die each year in investigative isolation wards (SIZOs), according to the Moscow Helsinki Group. In some cases, there has also been a return to the Soviet-era practice of punitive psychiatric treatment.

Parts of the country, especially the North Caucasus area, suffer from high levels of violence. Chechen president Ramzan Kadyrov's relative success in suppressing major rebel activity in his republic has been accompanied by numerous reports of extrajudicial killings and collective punishment. Moreover, related rebel movements have appeared in surrounding Russian republics, including Ingushetia, Dagestan, and Kabardino-Balkaria. Hundreds of officials, insurgents, and civilians die each year in bombings, gun battles, and assassinations.

Immigrants and ethnic minorities—particularly those who appear to be from the Caucasus or Central Asia—face governmental and societal discrimination and harassment. Institutions representing Russia's large Ukrainian minority have come under selective government pressure. LGBT (lesbian, gay, bisexual, and transgender) people also encounter discrimination and abuse, and gay rights demonstrations are often attacked by counterdemonstrators or suppressed by the authorities. In 2012, St. Petersburg and some other cities passed criminal bans on LGBT "propaganda."

The government places some restrictions on freedom of movement and residence. Adults must carry internal passports while traveling and to obtain many government services. Some regional authorities impose registration rules that limit the right of citizens to choose their place of residence. In the majority of cases, the targets are ethnic minorities and migrants from the Caucasus and Central Asia.

In December 2012, Putin signed a ban on the adoption of Russian children by families in the United States. The measure was seen as retaliation for a new U.S. law, named for Sergei Magnitsky, that imposes asset freezes and travel restrictions on Russian officials found to have committed human rights abuses.

State takeovers of key industries and large tax penalties imposed on select companies have illustrated the precarious nature of property rights in the country, especially when political interests are involved.

Women have particular difficulty achieving political power. They hold 13 percent of the Duma's seats (down from 14 percent in the previous term) and less than 5 percent of the seats in the Federation Council. Only 3 of 26 cabinet members are women. Domestic violence against women continues to be a serious problem, and police are often reluctant to intervene in what they regard as internal family matters. Economic hardships contribute to widespread trafficking of women abroad for prostitution.

Rwanda

Political Rights: 6
Civil Liberties: 6*
Status: Not Free

Population: 10,815,000
Capital: Kigali

Ratings Change: Rwanda's civil liberties rating declined from 5 to 6 due to numerous documented cases of unlawful detention, torture, and ill-treatment of civilians by military intelligence agents in secret locations.

Ten-Year Ratings Timeline For Year Under Review (Political Rights, Civil Liberties, Status)

2003	2004	2005	2006	2007	2008	2009	2010	2011	2013
6,5NF	6,5NF	6,5NF	6,5NF	6,5NF	6,5NF	6,5NF	6,5NF	6,5NF	6,6NF

Overview: **The Rwandan Patriotic Front under President Paul Kagame continued to prosecute journalists and opposition politicians in 2012, with harsh sentences delivered in several cases. An October report by an international human rights group noted numerous instances of torture, ill-treatment, and enforced disappearances in secret detention centers at the hands of Rwanda's military intelligence between March 2010 and June 2012. Meanwhile, the community-based gacaca genocide courts officially completed their work in June.**

Belgian colonial rule in Rwanda, which began after World War I, exacerbated tensions between the minority Tutsi ethnic group and the majority Hutu. A Hutu rebellion beginning in 1959 overthrew the Tutsi monarchy, and independence from Belgium followed in 1962. Hundreds of thousands of Tutsi were killed in recurring violence or fled the country over the subsequent decades. In 1990, the Tutsi-dominated Rwandan Patriotic Front (RPF) launched a guerrilla war from Uganda to force the Hutu regime, led by President Juvénal Habyarimana, to accept power sharing and the return of Tutsi refugees.

Habyarimana was killed when his plane was shot down near Kigali in April 1994. Hutu extremists immediately pursued the complete elimination of the Tutsi. During the genocide, which lasted approximately three and a half months, as many as one million Tutsi and moderate Hutu were killed. By July, however, the RPF had succeeded in taking control of Kigali and establishing an interim government of national unity.

The Hutu-dominated army and militia, along with as many as two million Hutu refugees, fled into neighboring countries, especially the Democratic Republic of Congo (DRC). These forces were able to retrain and rearm in the midst of international relief efforts to assist the refugees. The RPF responded by attacking refugee camps in the DRC in 1996. A 2010 UN report provided strong evidence of war crimes committed by RPF forces in incursions in the DRC from 1996 to 1997 and from 1998 to 2003, while a November 2012 UN report documented evidence of direct RPF support for the Mouvement du 23 mars (M23), a new rebel group in the DRC seeking secession from Kinshasa.

Nearly three million refugees returned to Rwanda between 1996 and 1998 and were reintegrated into society. Security improved considerably after 1997, although isolated killings and disappearances continued. In 2000, President Pasteur Bizimungu, a moderate Hutu installed by the RPF, resigned and was replaced by Vice President Paul Kagame, a Tutsi.

Rwanda's extended postgenocide political transition officially ended in 2003 with a new constitution and national elections. The RPF's preeminent position—combined with a short campaign period, the RPF's ability to suppress opposition, and a pliant political culture traumatized by the effects of the genocide—ensured victory for Kagame in the presidential vote and for the RPF and its allies in subsequent parliamentary elections. The largest opposition party, the Hutu-based Democratic Republican Movement, was declared illegal before the elections for allegedly promoting ethnic hatred, as was a new party created by Bizimungu in 2001.

A series of four parliamentary commissions between 2003 and 2008 investigated allegations of "genocide ideology" and "divisionism" in domestic and international nongovernmental organizations (NGOs), opposition political parties, the media, and schools. These commissions equated criticism of the RPF-led government with denial of the genocide, and made accusations against numerous individuals and organizations without recourse to due process, driving a number of government critics into exile and pushing some NGOs and political parties to curtail their activities.

The RPF-led coalition handily won the 2008 parliamentary elections, taking 42 out of 53 elected seats in the lower house. Monitoring by a European Union observer team indicated that the actual RPF share of the vote was higher than reported, suggesting a manipulation of results to make the elections appear more democratic.

In advance of the August 2010 presidential poll, the government prevented new political parties from registering and arrested the leaders of several parties, effectively preventing them from fielding candidates. The most credible opposition candidate, Victoire Ingabire, the leader of the United Democratic Forces–Inkingi (FDU-Inkingi), was arrested and released in April on charges of denying the genocide and collaborating with a terrorist group. With no serious challengers on the ballot, Kagame won reelection with 93 percent of the vote.

Ingabire was arrested again in October 2010, accused of engaging in terrorist activities, while three members of FDU-Inkingi were given heavy fines in February 2011 for supporting "divisionism" by conspiring to participate in unauthorized demonstrations in June 2010. Also in February, Bernard Ntaganda of the Social Party-Imberakuri was sentenced to four years in prison for threatening state security and fomenting "divisionism" in his 2010 election campaign speeches, as well as for planning unauthorized demonstrations. The Supreme Court upheld these charges against Ntaganda in April 2012. Ingabire's trial, which began in September 2011, ended in October 2012 with an eight-year prison sentence for conspiring to harm the country through terrorist activities and minimizing the 1994 genocide.

The community-based gacaca courts officially completed their work in June 2012, after prosecuting hundreds of thousands of people accused of being involved in the genocide. Meanwhile, the national criminal court system continued to try special cases of those accused of more serious crimes related to the genocide, including those transferred from the International Criminal Tribunal for Rwanda (ICTR). By the end of 2012, the ICTR had completed cases against 72 individuals, with 1 trial ongoing and 16 on appeal; it aims to complete its work by the end of 2014. In February 2012, an international crimes chamber was created within Rwanda's High Court to prosecute extradited suspects.

Political Rights and Civil Liberties:

Rwanda is not an electoral democracy. International observers noted that the 2010 presidential and 2008 parliamentary elections, while administratively acceptable, presented Rwandans with only a limited degree of political choice. The 2003 constitution grants broad powers to the president, who can serve up to two seven-year terms and has the authority to appoint the prime minister and dissolve the bicameral Parliament. The 26-seat upper house, the Senate, consists of 12 members elected by regional councils, 8 appointed by the president, 4 chosen by a forum of political parties, and 2 representatives of universities, all serving eight-year terms. The Chamber of Deputies, or lower house, includes 53 directly elected members, 24 women chosen by local councils, 2 from the National Youth Council, and 1 from the Federation of Associations of the Disabled; all serve five-year terms. Parliament generally lacks independence, merely endorsing government initiatives. However, parliamentary committees have begun to question ministers and other executive branch officers more energetically, and some of these deliberations are reported in the local press.

The constitution officially permits political parties to exist, but only under strict controls. The charter's emphasis on "national unity" effectively limits political pluralism. The RPF dominates the political arena, and parties closely identified with the 1994 genocide are banned, as are parties based on ethnicity or religion. These restrictions have been used to ban other political parties that might pose a challenge to RPF rule. The constitutionally mandated Political Party Forum vets proposed policies and draft legislation before they are introduced in Parliament. All parties must belong to the forum, which operates on the principle of consensus, though in practice the RPF guides its deliberations.

Government countermeasures have helped limit corruption, though graft remains a problem. In recent years, a number of senior government officials have been fired and faced prosecution for alleged corruption, embezzlement, and abuse of power. Government institutions focused on combating corruption include the Office of the Ombudsman, the auditor general, and the National Tender Board. Rwanda was ranked 50 out of 176 countries surveyed in Transparency International's 2012 Corruption Perceptions Index.

The RPF has imposed various legal restrictions and informal controls on the media, and press freedom groups have accused the government of intimidating independent journalists. In February 2011, Umurabyo newspaper journalists Agnès Uwimana Nkusi and Saïdati Mukakibibi were sentenced to 17 and 7 years, respectively, for denying the genocide, inciting civil disobedience, and defaming public officials based on a 2009 article criticizing President Paul Kagame. Nkusi and Mukakibibi appealed their case in January 2012, and in April, the Supreme Court reduced their sentences to four and three years, respectively. In July, Idriss Gasana Byiringiro, a reporter for the private weekly *Chronicles*, was detained for 30 days shortly after he submitted a police request to investigate an incident of state security agents interrogating him about his reporting and confiscating his telephone and laptop. In November, the editor of the Kinyarwandan-language paper *Umusingi*, Stanley Gatera, was fined and sentenced to one year in prison for gender discrimination and inciting "divisionism" in a June opinion piece.

Rwanda's repressive media environment has led many journalists to flee the country and work in exile. In November 2011, Charles Ingabire, editor of the Uganda-based online publication *Inyenyeri News* and an outspoken critic of the Kagame regime who had fled Rwanda in 2007 due to threats, was shot dead in Uganda. His murder remained unsolved at the end of 2012. There are increasing indications that e-mail and other private communications are being monitored. In August 2012, the lower house adopted a constitutional amendment expanding the surveillance and interception capabilities of security authorities.

Religious freedom is generally respected, though relations between religious leaders and the government are sometimes tense, in part because of the involvement of clergy in the 1994 genocide. Fear among teachers and students of being labeled "divisionist" restrains academic freedom. Following the 2004 and 2008 parliamentary commission reports on "divisionism," numerous students and teachers were expelled or dismissed without due process. The crackdown ahead of the 2010 presidential election that severely stifled general free discussion—with the Department of Military Intelligence closely monitoring the population—did not ease in 2012.

Although the constitution codifies freedoms of assembly and association, these rights are limited in practice. Some NGOs cite registration and reporting procedures as excessively onerous, and activities that the government defines as "divisive" are prohibited. Several organizations have been banned in recent years, leading others to refrain from criticizing the RPF. In August 2011, leaders of the League for Human Rights in the Great Lakes Region, one of the remaining independent human rights groups in Rwanda, were detained and prevented from traveling. However, most civil society organizations that are not focused on sensitive subjects, such as democracy and human rights, function without direct government interference.

The constitution provides for the rights to form trade unions, engage in collective bargaining, and strike. However, public workers are not allowed to unionize, and employees of the many "essential services" are not allowed to strike. The International Trade Union Confederation reported that although a 2009 labor code improved workers' rights, the government continues to pressure unions in indirect ways.

Recent improvements in the judicial system include an increased presence of defense lawyers at trials, improved training for court staff, and revisions to the legal code, but the judiciary has yet to secure full independence from the executive. The gacaca courts faced criticism from legal experts over their failure to address genocide-era crimes allegedly committed by the RPF, and because they routinely tried politically motivated cases. Individual police officers sometimes use excessive force, and local officials periodically ignore due process protections. The construction of new prisons during the past decade has improved prison conditions, even as the gacaca trials increased the prison population. Nevertheless, an October 2012 report by Amnesty International documented 45 cases of unlawful imprisonment and 18 cases of torture and ill-treatment in secret military detention centers between March 2010 and June 2012.

Equal treatment for all citizens under the law is guaranteed, and legal protections against discrimination have increased in recent years. A national identity card is required when Rwandans wish to move within the country, but these are issued regularly and no longer indicate ethnicity.

The 2003 constitution requires women to occupy at least 30 percent of the seats in each chamber of Parliament; women currently fill 10 of the 26 Senate seats. Legislation has strengthened women's rights to inherit land. However, de facto discrimination against women continues. Domestic violence is illegal, but remains widespread.

Saint Kitts and Nevis

Political Rights: 1
Civil Liberties: 1
Status: Free

Population: 54,000
Capital: Basseterre

Ten-Year Ratings Timeline For Year Under Review (Political Rights, Civil Liberties, Status)

2003	2004	2005	2006	2007	2008	2009	2010	2011	2012
1,2F	1,2F	1,1F	1,1F	1,1F	1,1F	1,1F	1,1F	1,1F	1,1F

Overview: In response to a legal challenge brought by the Concerned Citizens Movement, the High Court ruled in March 2012 that there were irregularities in the 2011 Nevis Island Assembly elections. The newly elected Nevis premier dissolved the Nevis parliament in November and called for general elections. Meanwhile, the national government took steps during the year to reform and modernize the criminal justice system and to address the country's significant debt problem.

Saint Kitts and Nevis gained independence from Britain in 1983 but remains a member of the Commonwealth. Denzil Douglas of the ruling Saint Kitts and Nevis Labour Party (SKNLP) has been prime minister since 1995. In the 2000 elections, the SKNLP won all eight Saint Kitts seats in the National Assembly, shutting out the opposition People's Action Movement (PAM). In the 2004 elections, the SKNLP captured seven Saint Kitts seats, and the PAM took one seat. The proindependence Concerned Citizens Movement (CCM) retained two of Nevis's three parliamentary seats, while the third went to the Nevis Reformation Party (NRP).

The January 2010 parliamentary elections were the first to take place under a new electoral law. International monitors found the elections to be generally free and fair, but noted the need for the electoral law to address several important issues, including campaign finance, media access, and civil society participation. Douglas won a fourth term as prime minister, as the SKNLP won six seats, and the PAM gained an additional Saint Kitts seat for a total of two. The CCM and NRP retained two and one Nevis seats, respectively.

In July 2011 elections for the Nevis Island Assembly (NIA), the NRP captured three seats and the CCM took two seats. However, the CCM challenged the results of the St. Johns seat, which they lost by only 14 votes, and accused the NRP of unlawfully disenfranchising more than 200 voters by removing them from the voter list prior to the election. In March 2012, the High Court declared the July 2011 election results for the St. Johns seat to be null and void; this decision was upheld by the Organisation of Eastern Caribbean States Court of Appeal in August. The NIA was dissolved on November 8 in preparation for what the premier of Nevis determined would be new general elections, instead of a by-election.

The Douglas administration continued to focus on economic development, the reduction of public debt, and crime prevention in 2012. St. Kitts and Nevis has one of the highest debt-to-gross domestic product ratios (154 percent) in the world. In addition to tourism and offshore financial services, the government has promoted economic citizenship programs—attracting foreign direct investment in exchange for passports. The U.S. State Department has criticized this program as being ineffectively regulated, which may increase the risk of money laundering.

Political Rights and Civil Liberties: Saint Kitts and Nevis is an electoral democracy. The federal government consists of the prime minister, the cabinet, and the unicameral National Assembly. A governor-general represents Britain's Queen Elizabeth II as ceremonial head of state. Elected National Assembly members—eight from Saint Kitts and three from Nevis—serve five-year terms. The governor-general appoints three senators and the attorney general under the advice of the prime minister and the leader of the opposition.

The NIA is composed of five elected and three appointed members, and the local government pays for all of its own services, except for those involving police and foreign relations. Saint Kitts has no similar body. The constitution grants Nevis the option to secede, but a referendum on secession held in 1998 failed to gain the required approval of two-thirds of the electorate. Nevisians continue to express discontent over the central government's neglect of the island.

Saint Kitts and Nevis has generally implemented its anticorruption laws effectively, though government officials are not required to disclose financial assets, and there is no freedom of information legislation. A Financial Intelligence Unit investigates financial crimes, such as money laundering and the financing of terrorism, but there is no independent body to address allegations of governmental corruption.

Constitutional guarantees of freedom of expression are generally respected. The prime minister voiced his support for Freedom of Information legislation in 2012, but a bill had yet to pass at year's end. The government owns the sole local television station, to which the opposition faces some restrictions on access. In addition to both government and private radio stations, there is one privately owned daily newspaper, and political parties publish weekly newspapers. Internet access is not restricted.

Freedom of religion is constitutionally protected, and academic freedom is generally honored.

The right to form civic organizations is generally respected, as is freedom of assembly. Workers may legally form unions, though a union can engage in collective bargaining only if more than 50 percent of the company's employees are union members. The right to strike, while not specified by law, is recognized and generally respected in practice.

The judiciary is largely independent, and legal provisions for a fair and speedy trial are generally observed. The highest court is the Eastern Caribbean Supreme Court on Saint Lucia, but under certain circumstances, there is a right of appeal to the Trinidad-based Caribbean Court of Justice. Additionally, an appeal may be made to the Privy Council in London.

The islands' traditionally strong rule of law continues to be tested by the prevalence of drug-related crime and corruption. The government took steps to reform and modernize the criminal justice system in 2012 by introducing a number of bills to improve the jury system, initiate the use of DNA testing, revise legislation relating to sexual offenses, and codify the criminal law. The attorney general also announced plans to create a Criminal Division Court within the High Court. The national prison, however, remains severely overcrowded.

While domestic violence is criminalized, violence against women remains a serious problem. Only one woman serves in the National Assembly. Legal and social discrimination against sexual minorities persists; same-sex sexual conduct between men is criminalized with prison sentences of up to 10 years.

Saint Lucia

Political Rights: 1
Civil Liberties: 1
Status: Free

Population: 169,000
Capital: Castries

Ten-Year Ratings Timeline For Year Under Review (Political Rights, Civil Liberties, Status)

2003	2004	2005	2006	2007	2008	2009	2010	2011	2012
1,2F	1,2F	1,1F	1,1F	1,1F	1,1F	1,1F	1,1F	1,1F	1,1F

Overview: Prime Minister Kenny Anthony's government struggled to tackle the country's high rates of unemployment and crime during 2012. Critics also highlighted the government's inability to control government spending, borrowing, and public debt.

Saint Lucia, a member of the Commonwealth, achieved independence from Britain in 1979. Kenny Anthony led the Saint Lucia Labour Party (SLP) to victory in the 1997 legislative elections, defeating the United Workers' Party (UWP). As prime minister, Anthony attempted to improve the economy and address official corruption. In the 2001 general elections, the SLP retained a majority of seats in the House of Assembly, and Anthony returned to the premiership.

John Compton, Saint Lucia's first prime minister after independence, came out of retirement to lead the UWP to an unexpected victory in the December 2006 elections by winning 11 seats in the House of Assembly. Compton was sworn in again as prime minister at the age of 81. However, he soon became ill and died in September 2007. He was replaced by Stephenson King, a UWP cabinet member who had served as acting prime minister for several months before Compton's death.

During 2008, the opposition SLP repeatedly threatened to mount public demonstrations and called for King's resignation. The SLP was particularly critical of the government's intention to ratify the Rome Statute of the International Criminal Court, while opting out of a drug interdiction agreement with Britain. The Rome Statute was eventually ratified in August 2010.

In 2009, King reshuffled his cabinet for the second time since taking office in an effort to regain political momentum in the face of a deteriorating economic situation. Damage inflicted by Hurricane Tomas in 2010 adversely affected agriculture and tourism and contributed to Saint Lucia's budget deficit.

Weak economic growth, an unemployment rate of 20 percent, and a substantial rise in violent crime were major factors in the November 2011 general elections, in which the SLP unseated the UWP, giving it an 11-to-6 seat majority in the House of Assembly. Anthony was returned to the position of prime minister in late November.

As Anthony and his new government struggled to reduce the country's high rates of unemployment and crime in 2012, the opposition complained of increasing government spending, borrowing, and public debt. A value-added tax was introduced in October in an attempt to encourage investment and prompt economic growth.

Political Rights and Civil Liberties: Saint Lucia is an electoral democracy. A governor-general represents the British monarch as head of state. Under the 1979 constitution, the bicameral Parliament consists of the 17-member House of Assembly, elected for five years, and an appointed 11-member Senate. The prime minister is chosen by the majority party in the House of Assembly. Six members of the Senate are chosen by the prime minister, three by the leader of the parliamentary opposition, and two in consultation with civic and religious organizations. The island is divided into 11 quarters (districts), each with its own elected council and administrative services.

Political parties are free to organize, but two parties—the UWP and the SLP—dominate politics.

Saint Lucia has low levels of corruption and was ranked 22 out of 176 countries surveyed in Transparency International's 2012 Corruption Perceptions Index. Access to information is legally guaranteed, and government officials are required by law to present their financial assets annually to the Integrity Commission. Prime Minister Anthony announced in September 2012 that the government would continue to maintain diplomatic ties with Taiwan, despite earlier accusations that the former Taiwan Ambassador Tom Chou had been meddling in the country's politics by giving millions of dollars to local UWP politicians during the King administration and leading up to the 2011 elections.

The constitution guarantees freedom of speech, which is respected in practice. Libel offenses were removed from the criminal code in 2006. The media carry a wide spectrum of views and are largely independent. While there are no daily newspapers, there are numerous privately owned newspapers that publish three issues per week. In addition to privately held radio and television stations, the government operates Radio Saint Lucia and a television station. Internet access is not restricted.

The constitution guarantees freedom of religion, and that right is respected in practice. Academic freedom is generally honored.

Constitutional guarantees regarding freedoms of assembly and association are largely upheld. Civic groups are well organized and politically active, as are labor unions, which represent the majority of wage earners. However, the Trade Union Federation faced lengthy governmental delays in its attempts to negotiate a salary increase for public sector workers for the 2010–2013 period. Negotiations finally began in November 2012 but were immediately halted, when union representatives walked out after being offered a zero percent increase and a one-time holiday bonus of EC$1,000 (roughly US$370) per worker. Negotiations were ongoing at year's end. The long-awaited Labour Act, which was finally implemented in August, will govern the enforcement of the country's labor laws.

The judicial system is independent and includes a high court under the Saint Lucia–based Eastern Caribbean Supreme Court. In recent years, the record of Saint Lucia's police and judicial system has been blemished by a series of incidents, including the severe beatings of inmates by police and cases of police assault and unlawful killings that have gone unpunished.

Citizens have traditionally enjoyed a high degree of personal security, though rising crime levels has caused widespread concern. High rates of violence continued in 2012, largely attributed to gang-related crimes, such as drug trafficking, drive-by shootings, and armed robbery. Prison overcrowding remains a problem, with major backlogs in the judicial system leading to prolonged pretrial detentions.

Women are underrepresented in politics and other professions; there are currently three women serving in Parliament and two women in the Senate. Domestic violence is a serious concern and often goes unreported. Same-sex sexual relations are criminalized, with punishments of up to 10 years in prison.

Saint Vincent and the Grenadines

Political Rights: 1
Civil Liberties: 1
Status: Free

Population: 108,000
Capital: Kingstown

Ten-Year Ratings Timeline For Year Under Review (Political Rights, Civil Liberties, Status)

2003	2004	2005	2006	2007	2008	2009	2010	2011	2012
2,1F	2,1F	2,1F	2,1F	2,1F	2,1F	2,1F	1,1F	1,1F	1,1F

Overview: Improvements in the tourism and manufacturing sectors in 2012 contributed to a slow recovery of the economy, which has struggled to rebound from a series of natural disasters and the global financial crisis. Overcrowded prison conditions were relieved in April with the long-awaited transfer of prisoners to the Belle Isle Correctional Facility, which had opened in 2009 but had remained empty.

Saint Vincent and the Grenadines achieved independence from Britain in 1979, with jurisdiction over the northern Grenadine islands, which include Bequia, Canouan, Mayreau, Mustique, Palm Island, Petit Saint Vincent, and Union Island, in addition to a number of smaller islets.

In the 2001 elections, the social-democratic Unity Labour Party (ULP) captured 12 of the 15 contested legislative seats, and Ralph Gonsalves became prime minister. The incumbent, conservative New Democratic Party (NDP) was reduced to three seats. In the 2005 polls, Gonsalves led the ULP to reelection, again taking 12 seats, while the NDP took the remaining 3 seats.

In 2009, the country was polarized over a November national referendum to replace its 1979 constitution with one produced by a government-appointed Constitutional Review Commission. Among other changes, the proposed constitution would have made the country a republic, facilitated the process of replacing the British Privy Council as the country's highest appeals court, and limited marriage to that between a man and a woman. The opposition strongly opposed the new constitution for falling short of fully reforming the government. The measure failed to reach two-thirds majority, receiving support from only 43 percent of voters.

In the December 2010 general elections, the ULP, still reeling from the defeat of the proposed constitutional reform referendum, won a slim majority of eight seats, and Gonsalves retained the post of prime minister. Meanwhile, the NDP more than doubled its representation, taking seven seats. Despite threats of legal challenges from NDP leaders, observers from the Caribbean Community, the Organization of American States, and the National Monitoring and Consultative Mechanism deemed the elections free and fair.

The International Monetary Fund reported that improvements in the tourism and manufacturing sectors in 2012 contributed to a slow recovery of the economy, which had been hard hit by torrential rains that wiped out the country's banana industry in 2011, destruction caused by Hurricane Tomas in 2010, and the global financial crisis. Part of Gonsalves's economic plan to bolster the tourism industry has included the construction of the Argyle International Airport, which continued to be under construction at the end of 2012.

Political Rights and Civil Liberties: Saint Vincent and the Grenadines is an electoral democracy. The constitution provides for the election of 15 representatives to the unicameral House of Assembly. The governor general appoints six senators to the chamber, four selected on the advice of the prime minister and two on the advice of the opposition leader; all serve five-year terms. The prime minister is the leader of the majority party. A governor general represents the British monarch as head of state.

In recent years, there have been allegations of money laundering through Saint Vincent banks and drug-related corruption within the government and the police force. However, the government has taken some measures to prevent and prosecute such crimes, such as enacting the Proceeds of Crime and Money Laundering (Prevention) (Amendment) Act 2012 in April. However, there is no independent body to investigate government corruption. Saint Vincent was ranked 36 out of 176 countries surveyed in Transparency International's 2012 Corruption Perceptions Index.

The press is independent, and the constitution guarantees freedoms of speech and the press. While Freedom of Information legislation was enacted in 2003, it has yet to be fully implemented. Government officials use libel lawsuits against members of the media. There are several privately owned, independent weeklies and one daily newspaper. The national newspapers publish opinions critical of the government. The St. Vincent and the Grenadines Broadcasting Corporation operates a television station. Satellite dishes and cable television are available. The main news radio station is partly government owned, but radio talk shows are increasing. Equal access to radio is mandated during electoral campaigns, but there have been allegations that the ruling party has taken advantage of state control over programming. Some journalists also allege that government advertising is used as a political tool. Internet access is not restricted.

Freedom of religion is constitutionally protected and respected in practice, and academic freedom is generally honored.

Freedoms of assembly and association are constitutionally protected, and nongovernmental organizations are free from government interference. Labor unions are active and permitted to strike and engage in collective bargaining.

The government generally respects judicial independence. The highest court is the Saint Lucia–based Eastern Caribbean Supreme Court, which includes a court of appeals and a high court. The country recognizes the original jurisdiction of the Trinidad-based Caribbean Court of Justice, but the final court of appeal is still the

Judicial Committee of the Privy Council in London. There are often long judicial delays and a large backlog of cases caused by personnel shortages in the local judiciary. Crowded prison conditions improved in 2012 with the long-awaited transfer of prisoners to the Belle Isle Correctional Facility in April; the prison officially opened in 2009 but had remained empty until 2012.

Women are underrepresented in political decision-making positions. Violence against women, particularly domestic violence, is a major problem. The Domestic Violence Summary Proceedings Act, which provides for protective orders, offers some tools that benefit victims. Same-sex sexual relations remain a criminal offense and carry sentences of up to 10 years in prison. In 2011, the government rejected a call by the UN Human Rights Council to repeal laws criminalizing same-sex relations.

Samoa

Political Rights: 2
Civil Liberties: 2
Status: Free

Population: 187,000
Capital: Apia

Ten-Year Ratings Timeline For Year Under Review (Political Rights, Civil Liberties, Status)

2003	2004	2005	2006	2007	2008	2008	2010	2011	2012
2,2F	2,2F	2,2F	2,2F	2,2F	2,2F	2,2F	2,2F	2,2F	2,2F

Overview: **Samoa officially joined the World Trade Organization in May 2012. Protests over land rights turned violent in August, resulting in one police officer being injured. In November, Samoa launched the first internet-based television station in the Pacific Islands.**

Germany controlled what is now Samoa between 1899 and World War I. New Zealand administered the islands under a UN mandate after World War II. The country gained independence in 1962.

The centrist Human Rights Protection Party (HRPP) has dominated politics since independence. Tuilaepa Aiono Sailele Malielegaoi of the HRPP secured a second term as prime minister in the 2006 legislative elections, in which the HRPP captured the most seats. Former prime minister Tuiatua Tupua Tamasese Efi was elected head of state by the legislature in June 2007.

In the March 2011 parliamentary elections, the HRPP took 36 seats, while the Tautua Somoa Party (TSP) captured the remaining 13. The elections were generally regarded as fair and open, though the electoral court found four lawmakers from both the HRPP and the TSP guilty of bribing voters, and stripped them of their seats. Special by-elections were held in July 2012 to fill the 4 seats; the HRPP captured all of them, boosting its majority to 40 seats. Prime Minister Tuilaepa was elected to a third term.

In April 2012, the Supreme Court rejected claims from villagers from Satapuala over 8,000 acres of land near the airport that they claimed were unlawfully taken from them by colonial authorities and kept by subsequent governments on the grounds that the villagers had accepted new land for resettlement. About 200 villagers protested at the prime minister's office in July. Demonstrations continued into August, turning violent when police attempted to remove a roadblock set up by villagers to block traffic to and from the airport. Witnesses reported gunshots, and a police officer was injured. In November, a member of parliament from Satapuala and 17 matai from the village pleaded not guilty to charges including obstruction and unlawful assembly. The hearing was adjourned until 2013.

Samoa depends heavily on tourism and remittances from Samoans living abroad, both of which have fallen in recent year. Samoa has been forging closer ties with China, including through the sale of fishing licenses—an important local source of employment—though the rapid expansion of China's presence in the local economy has local business leaders warning of rising social tensions. Samoa formally joined the World Trade Organization in May 2012.

In December, Cyclone Evan—the worst cyclone to hit Samoa in two decades—caused widespread damage to crops and infrastructure, and resulted in more than a dozen fatalities.

Political Rights and Civil Liberties: Samoa is an electoral democracy. The head of state, who is elected by the 49-member Legislative Assembly, appoints the prime minister. Two legislative seats are reserved for at-large voters, mostly citizens of mixed or non-Samoan heritage who have no ties to the 47 village-based constituencies. All lawmakers serve five-year terms.

Matai, or chiefs of extended families, control local government and churches through the village fono, or legislature, which is open only to them. The Supreme Court ruled in 2000 that the village fono could not infringe on freedoms of religion, speech, assembly, or association. Nevertheless, entire families have been forced to leave their villages for allegedly insulting a matai, embracing a different religion, or voting for political candidates not endorsed by the matai. Approval of the matai is essential for most candidates for elected office.

Official corruption and abuses are a source of increasing public discontent. In September 2012, local media published an anonymous letter to the prime minister alleging widespread corruption in the police force, conflicts of interest, and immoral behavioral among senior officers. The police launched an internal investigation, though no progress on the investigation had been reported at year's end.

Freedoms of speech and the press are generally respected. The government operates one of three television stations, and there are several English-language and Samoan newspapers. In September 2012, the Samoan Reform Commission recommended the creation of a self-regulating media council to set standards for fairness, accuracy, and balance in the news media. It also suggested repealing legislation requiring journalists to reveal their sources in court. No actions were taken on these recommendations by year's end. In 2011, the government ended its monopoly on telephone and internet services. In November 2012, Bluesky Samoa launched Moana TV, the first internet-based station in the South Pacific.

The government respects freedom of religion in practice, and relations among religious groups are generally amicable. There were no reports of restrictions on academic freedom.

Freedoms of assembly and association are respected, and human rights groups operate freely. Workers, including civil servants, can strike and bargain collectively. Approximately 60 percent of adults work in subsistence agriculture, and about 20 percent of wage earners belong to trade unions.

The judiciary is independent and upholds the right to a fair trial. The Supreme Court is the highest court, with full jurisdiction over civil, criminal, and constitutional matters. The head of state, on the recommendation of the prime minister, appoints the chief justice. Prisons generally meet minimum international standards.

Samoa has no military, and the small police force has little impact in the villages, where the fono settles most disputes. The councils vary considerably in their decision-making styles and in the number of matai involved. Light offenses are usually punished with fines; serious offenses result in banishment from the village.

Domestic violence against women and children is widespread. Spousal rape is not illegal, and social pressure and fear of reprisal inhibit reporting of domestic abuse. In 2011, the government rejected a call by the United Nations to decriminalize homosexuality, arguing that it was contrary to Samoan culture and values.

San Marino

Political Rights: 1
Civil Liberties: 1
Status: Free

Population: 32,300
Capital: San Marino

Ten-Year Ratings Timeline For Year Under Review (Political Rights, Civil Liberties, Status)

2003	2004	2005	2006	2007	2008	2009	2010	2011	2012
1,1F	1,1F	1,1F	1,1F	1,1F	1,1F	1,1F	1,1F	1,1F	1,1F

Overview: The Sammarinese Christian Democratic Party captured the most seats in the November 2012 parliamentary elections and formed a three-party ruling coalition, the San Marino Common Good. The country took steps to be removed from the Organisation for Economic Cooperation and Development's blacklist of tax havens. Meanwhile, several arrests were made during the year of suspected organized crime figures.

Founded in the year 301, according to tradition, San Marino is considered the world's oldest republic and is one of the world's smallest states. The papacy recognized San Marino's independence in 1631, as did the Congress of Vienna in 1815. In 1862, Italy and San Marino signed a treaty of friendship and economic cooperation. Despite its dependence on Italy, from which it currently receives budget subsidies, San Marino maintains its own political institutions. Tourism and banking dominate the country's economy.

In early parliamentary elections in 2008, the center-right Pact for San Marino coalition captured 35 of the 60 seats in the legislature, with 22 of those seats going to the Sammarinese Christian Democratic Party (PDCS).

In March 2011, the government canceled a referendum on joining the European Union (EU), despite popular support for accession. In June, the government chose to push for stronger adherence to EU standards without becoming a full-fledged EU member or giving the people the opportunity to vote in a referendum.

After the resignations of two members of parliament, Augusto Casali (Nuovo Partito Socialista) and Romeo Morri (Moderati Sammarinesi) on July 16, 2012, the leading coalition no longer had a parliamentary majority. The legislature was dissolved in August, forcing the country to hold early elections on November 11. The PDCS captured 21 seats and formed a three-party coalition—the San Marino Common Good—with the Party of Social Democrats, which won 10 seats, and the Popular Alliance, which took 4 seats.

In June 2012, San Marino signed a protocol to exchange tax information with Italy, a step toward being removed from the Organisation for Economic Cooperation and Development in Europe's blacklist of tax havens. The agreement would help San Marino crackdown on Italian tax evaders.

Political Rights and Civil Liberties: San Marino is an electoral democracy. The 60 members of the Great and General Council, the unicameral legislature, are elected every five years by proportional representation. Executive power rests with the 10-member Congress of State (cabinet), which is headed by two captains regent. As the joint heads of state, the captains regent are elected every six months by the Great and General Council from among its own members. Although there is no official prime minister, the secretary of state for foreign and political affairs is regarded as the head of government; Antonella Mularoni was elected to the post in December 2008. Under changes made to the electoral law in 2008, the winning coalition must capture a majority of 50 percent plus 1 and at least 30 of the 60 parliamentary seats.

There is little government corruption in the country, though financial corruption has prompted the government to explore laws that provide greater financial transparency. In August 2010, San Marino became the 48th state to join the Council of Europe's Group of States against Corruption. In 2012, among those arrested for suspected criminal activity under a new anti-mafia commission established in 2011 were Livio Bacciocchi of the financial institution Fincapital, who was accused of money laundering. Roberto Zavoli, Bacciocchi's collaborator, was also arrested, and the bank's president, Oriano Zonzini, was placed under house arrest but released in June 2012. In January 2012, Marco Bianchini, the former head of the financial firm Karnak, was accused of extortion and corruption related to the Camorra, a Neapolitan mafia, in a scandal known as Criminal Minds; he was arrested after transferring 5 million euros (US$6.5 million) into a Maltese bank. No one had been prosecuted by year's end. The anti-mafia commission is expected to release a comprehensive report detailing the state of organized crime in San Marino in April 2013.

Freedoms of speech and the press are guaranteed. There are several daily private newspapers; a state-run broadcast system for radio and television, RTV; and a private FM station, Radio Titiano. The Sammarinese have access to all Italian print media and certain Italian broadcast stations. Access to the internet is unrestricted.

Religious discrimination is prohibited by law. Roman Catholicism is the dominant, but not the state, religion. Academic freedom is respected.

Freedom of assembly is respected, and civic organizations are active. Workers are free to strike, organize trade unions, and bargain collectively, unless they work in military occupations. Approximately half of the country's workforce is unionized.

The judiciary is independent. Lower-court judges are required to be noncitizens—generally Italians—to assure impartiality. The final court of review is the Council of Twelve, a group of judges chosen for six-year terms from among the members of the Great and General Council. Civilian authorities maintain effective control over the police and security forces, and the country's prison system generally meets international standards.

The European Commission against Racism and Intolerance has raised some concerns in the past about the status of foreigners in the country. San Marino has no formal asylum policy, and a foreigner must live in the country for 30 years to be eligible for citizenship. The European Convention on Nationality recommends that such residence requirements not exceed 10 years.

Women are given legal protections from violence and spousal abuse, and gender equality exists in the workplace and elsewhere. There are, however, slight differences in the way men and women can transmit citizenship to their children. Abortion is permitted only to save the life of the mother, though abortion laws in neighboring Italy are more liberal, and some women living in San Marino seek abortions there. Under a 2008 electoral law, no more than two-thirds of candidates from each party can be of the same gender. Ten women were elected to the Great and General Council in 2012, and two to the 10-member Congress of State in 2008.

São Tomé and Príncipe

Political Rights: 2
Civil Liberties: 2
Status: Free

Population: 183,000
Capital: São Tomé

Ten-Year Ratings Timeline For Year Under Review (Political Rights, Civil Liberties, Status)

2003	2004	2005	2006	2007	2008	2008	2010	2011	2012
2,2F	2,2F	2,2F	2,2F	2,2F	2,2F	2,2F	2,2F	2,2F	2,2F

Overview: Tensions between Prime Minister Patrice Trovoada and the opposition grew during 2012, resulting in a no-confidence vote against Trovoada and President Pinto da Costa's decision to dissolve the government on December 4. The president invited the party that had placed second in the 2010 legislative elections to form a new government, and Gabriel da Costa assumed office as the new prime minister on December 10.

São Tomé and Príncipe gained independence from Portugal in 1975. President Manuel Pinto da Costa's Movement for the Liberation of São Tomé and Principe— later the Movement for the Liberation of São Tomé and Príncipe–Social Democratic Party (MLSTP-PSD)—was the only legal political party until a 1990 referendum established multiparty democracy. Former prime minister Miguel dos Anjos Trovoada returned from exile and won the first democratic presidential election in 1991. He was reelected for a final term in 1996.

Fradique de Menezes, backed by Trovoada's Independent Democratic Action (ADI) party, won the 2001 presidential election. In 2003, a group of military officers briefly ousted Menezes, but he was returned to power one week later.

The Force for Change Democratic Movement–Liberal Party (MDFM-PL), in coalition with the Democratic Convergence Party (PCD), captured more seats than any other party in the 2006 parliamentary elections. While peaceful protesters had prevented thousands from voting in several parts of the country, a rerun for affected districts was subsequently held without incident. Negotiations on the formation of a new coalition government led to the appointment of a new prime minister, MDFM leader Tomé Soares da Vera Cruz. In the July presidential election, Menezes was chosen for a second term.

Following growing criticism over price increases and the handling of a police mutiny in 2007, the government collapsed twice in 2008. A new ruling coalition was formed in June with Joaquim Rafael Branco, leader of the MLSTP-PSD, as prime minister. The ADI refused to join, but the government gained a majority of seats in the National Assembly.

In the August 2010 parliamentary elections, the ADI captured 26 seats, followed by the MLSTP-PSD with 21 seats and the PCD with 7; the MDFM-PL captured only 1 seat. The Supreme Court validated the results, and ADI leader Patrice Trovoada was appointed prime minister.

After two unsuccessful electoral bids in 1996 and 2001, former president Pinto da Costa won the August 2011 presidential election. He defeated the ruling party's candidate, Evaristo Carvalho, in a run-off election with 52.9 percent of the vote. Foreign observers deemed the highly contested elections credible and fair.

On November 29, 2012, the parliament passed a vote of no confidence in the government of Prime Minister Trovoada while the members of the ruling ADI were not present. The ADI described the action as illegal and organized public demonstrations calling for early elections. President Pinto da Costa urged the parties to reconcile, but after several failed meetings, he formally dissolved the Trovoada-led government on December 4. Pinto da Costa gave the ADI 24 hours to appoint a leader to form the new government. The ADI rejected the timeline as too brief and insisted on Trovoada's reinstatement and the holding of early elections. The president responded by inviting the party that had received the second largest number of votes in the 2010 legislative election—the MLSTP-PSD—to head a new government. On December 10, the president announced that he had accepted the MLSTP-PSD's candidate, Gabriel Ferreiro da Costa, who appointed all of his cabinet members on December 22.

Political Rights and Civil Liberties: São Tomé and Príncipe is an electoral democracy. The 2010 parliamentary elections were free and fair, as were the presidential elections in 2011. The president is elected for up to two five-year terms. Members of the unicameral, 55-seat National Assembly are elected by popular vote to four-year terms.

Development aid and potential oil wealth have fueled corruption among the ruling elite. President Manuel Pinto da Costa named 2012 the year of anticorruption.

In September, a new anticorruption law came into force. Shortly thereafter, the Public Integrity Center was established with the support of Transparency International, the United Nations, and the U.S. Embassy. The main goal of this nongovernmental organization is to mobilize public opinion and promote good governance, transparency, and honesty. São Tomé and Principe was ranked 72 out of 176 countries surveyed in Transparency International's 2012 Corruption Perceptions Index.

Freedom of expression is guaranteed and respected. While the state controls a local press agency and the only radio and television stations, no law forbids independent broadcasting. Opposition parties receive free airtime, and newsletters and pamphlets criticizing the government circulate freely. Residents also have access to foreign broadcasters. Internet access is not restricted, though a lack of infrastructure limits penetration.

Freedom of religion is respected within this predominantly Roman Catholic country. The government does not restrict academic freedom.

Freedoms of assembly and association are respected. Citizens have the constitutional right to demonstrate with two days' advance notice to the government. Workers' rights to organize, strike, and bargain collectively are guaranteed and respected.

The constitution provides for an independent judiciary, though it is susceptible to political influence, and is understaffed and inadequately funded. The Supreme Court has ruled in the past against both the government and the president. However, in August 2012, the court cited lack of evidence for dismissing corruption charges against three businessmen involved in the controversial STP Trading case, which involved government officials. The decision was contested by the attorney general but confirmed in November by the Supreme Court. The country's one prison is overcrowded, and inmates suffer from inadequate food and medical care.

The constitution provides equal rights for men and women, but women encounter discrimination in all sectors of society. Domestic violence is common and rarely prosecuted.

Saudi Arabia

Political Rights: 7
Civil Liberties: 7
Status: Not Free

Population: 28,705,100
Capital: Riyadh

Ten-Year Ratings Timeline For Year Under Review (Political Rights, Civil Liberties, Status)

2003	2004	2005	2006	2007	2008	2009	2010	2011	2012
7,7NF	7,7NF	7,6NF	7,6NF	7,6NF	7,6NF	7,6NF	7,6NF	7,7NF	7,7NF

Overview: Saudi authorities continued to crack down on Shiite activists and protestors in the Eastern Province throughout 2012. Smaller protests occurred in other parts of the country during the year, including in Riyadh and the southwestern city of Abha. The kingdom systematically arrested, tried, and imprisoned some of the country's most visible human rights activists, including the cofounders of the Saudi Civil and

Political Rights Association. In June, Crown Prince Nayef bin Abdul Aziz died and was succeeded by his brother, Salman bin Abdul Aziz.

Since its unification in 1932 by King Abdul Aziz Ibn Saud, Saudi Arabia has been governed by the Saud family in accordance with a conservative school of Sunni Islam. In the early 1990s, Saudi Arabia embarked on a limited program of political reform, introducing an appointed Consultative Council, or Majlis al-Shura. However, this did not lead to any substantial shift in political power. In 1995, King Fahd bin Abdul Aziz al-Saud suffered a stroke, and his half-brother, Crown Prince Abdullah bin Abdul Aziz al-Saud, took control of most decision making in 1997.

The formal transfer of power from King Fahd, who died in 2005, to Crown Prince Abdullah led to increased expectations of political reform. However, now King Abdullah enacted few significant changes. The 2005 municipal council elections gave Saudi men a limited opportunity to select some of their leaders at the local level, but women were completely excluded. The eligible electorate consisted of less than 20 percent of the population: male citizens who were at least 21 years old, not serving in the military, and resident in their district for at least 12 months. Half of the council seats were open for election, and the other half were appointed by the monarchy. Candidates supported by conservative Muslim scholars triumphed in the large cities of Riyadh and Jeddah, and minority Shiite Muslim voters participated in large numbers. The government ultimately determined that the councils would serve only in an advisory capacity.

In 2006, Abdullah issued the bylaws for the Allegiance Commission, a new body to be composed of the sons (or grandsons, if sons are deceased, incapacitated, or unwilling) of the founding king. The commission, to be chaired by the oldest surviving son, would make decisions on appointing successors to the throne, using secret ballots and a quorum of two-thirds of the members. The commission was also granted the authority to deem a king or crown prince medically unfit to rule.

After being named crown prince in 2011, Nayef bin Abdul Aziz died in June 2012. He was succeeded by his brother, Salman bin Abdul Aziz. A cabinet reshuffle in 2009 resulted in the appointment of the first-ever female cabinet member, Noura al-Fayez. The king also fired two controversial religious figures, one of whom headed the religious police force. The move was interpreted as a sign that the monarchy felt less beholden to hard-line religious leaders and was seeking to promote more moderate clerics. This trend continued in 2010, with Abdullah decreeing in August that the issuing of religious edicts (fatwas) would be restricted to the Official Council of Senior Clergy. The decree was intended to outlaw the declaration of controversial fatwas and rein in radicalism.

Saudi Arabia has not experienced the kind of popular protests that have occurred elsewhere in the Middle East and North Africa in recent years. Saudi activists used social media to call for a "Day of Rage" to be held in March 2011. However, authorities dispatched security personnel across the country as preemptive measures, and large protests failed to materialize. In an effort to prevent wide-scale social unrest, Abdullah committed over $130 billion to address some of the social and economic complaints of the country's citizens; between two and four million Saudis live below the poverty line. Improvements included plans to construct affordable housing, provide unemployment benefits, and increase the salaries of government employees.

Nevertheless, smaller demonstrations were common, including in predominantly Shiite villages in the country's Eastern Province, where protestors demanded an end to discrimination and improvements in their economic conditions. Similar demands were made by others, including Sunnis, across the kingdom in 2012.

Saudi Arabia's growing youth population—which suffers from an unemployment rate estimated as high as 30 percent for those between the ages of 15 and 24—has placed additional pressure on the authorities to create new jobs. In response, the government has deployed its immense oil wealth to strengthen the nonpetroleum sector and sought to encourage private investment, though the results of these efforts remain unclear.

Political Rights and Civil Liberties: Saudi Arabia is not an electoral democracy. The 1992 Basic Law declares that the Koran and the Sunna (the guidance set by the deeds and sayings of the prophet Muhammad) are the country's constitution. The cabinet, which is appointed by the king, passes legislation that becomes law once ratified by royal decree. The king also appoints a 150-member Majlis al-Shura (Consultative Council) every four years, though it serves only in an advisory capacity. Limited elections for advisory councils at the municipal level were introduced in 2005, and the second round of elections was held in September 2011. In addition to the advisory councils, the monarchy has a tradition of consulting with select members of Saudi society, but the process is not equally open to all citizens. Political parties are forbidden, and organized political opposition exists only outside the country.

Corruption remains a significant problem. After widespread floods killed more than 120 people in November 2009, King Abdullah in May 2010 ordered the prosecution of over 40 officials in the city of Jeddah on charges of corruption and mismanagement related to improper construction and engineering practices. A second round of floods in January 2011 killed over 10 people and displaced several thousand, sparking small protests that alleged ongoing corruption. In May 2012, a government official and a local businessman were fined and sentenced to five years in prison on charges of corruption related to the 2009 floods. Several cases remained pending at the end of 2012 A 2011 royal decree established an anticorruption commission to monitor government departments, though administrative obstacles continued to hinder the commission's success in 2012. Saudi Arabia was ranked 66 out of 176 countries surveyed in Transparency International's 2012 Corruption Perceptions Index.

The government tightly controls domestic media content and dominates regional print and satellite-television coverage, with members of the royal family owning major stakes in news outlets in multiple countries. Government officials have banned journalists and editors who publish articles deemed offensive to the religious establishment or the ruling authorities. In April 2011, Abdullah issued a royal decree amending the country's press law, criminalizing any criticism of the country's grand mufti, the Council of Senior Religious Scholars, or government officials; violations could result in fines and forced closure. In March 2011, Khaled al-Johani, a teacher, was arrested after calling for greater rights and democracy during an interview recorded in Riyadh and broadcast by the television station BBC Arabic. He was imprisoned shortly afterwards and remained in jail in 2012.

In December, prominent Saudi author and intellectual Turki al-Hamad was arrested for criticizing Islamists on the social-media site, Twitter; he remained in prison at year's end.

The regime has taken steps to limit the influence of new media, blocking access to over 400,000 websites that are considered immoral or politically sensitive. A January 2011 law requires all blogs and websites, or anyone posting news or commentary online, to have a license from the Ministry of Information or face fines and/or the closure of the website. In February 2012, Saudi writer Hamza Kashgari was arrested in Malaysia and deported back to Saudi Arabia while trying to flee prosecution for apostasy, which carries a mandatory death sentence, after using Twitter to express views of Islam and the prophet Muhammad that are criminalized in the kingdom; he remained in jail at year's end.

Islam is the official religion, and all Saudis are required by law to be Muslims. The government prohibits the public practice of any religion other than Islam and restricts the religious practices of the Shiite and Sufi Muslim minority sects. Although the government recognizes the right of non-Muslims to worship in private, it does not always respect this right in practice. The building of Shiite mosques is banned. In April 2012, religious scholar Yusuf Ahmed was sentenced to five years in prison for calling for the destruction of the Mecca mosque and for other criticisms of the regime. In June, authorities arrested Raef Badawi, creator of a website for the discussion of religion called *Free Saudi Liberals*, and charged him with apostasy; he remained in prison at year's end.

Academic freedom is restricted, and informers monitor classrooms for compliance with curriculum rules, such as a ban on teaching secular philosophy and religions other than Islam. Despite changes to textbooks in recent years, intolerance in the classroom remains an important problem, as some teachers continue to espouse discriminatory and hateful views of non-Muslims and Muslim minority sects.

Freedoms of assembly and association are not upheld. The government frequently detains political activists who stage demonstrations or engage in other civic advocacy. While there have been no large-scale protests in the kingdom, smaller demonstrations have become more common. Several protests by relatives of political prisoners took place outside the Ministry of the Interior in Riyadh in 2012. The most visible demonstrations occurred in predominantly Shiite villages in the country's Eastern Province, where hundreds of Shiite protestors regularly took to the streets demanding political reform, as well as in support of the uprising in neighboring Bahrain. In March, over 50 women students at the University of Abha in southwestern Saudi Arabia protested poor facilities and material conditions on campus; several were wounded by police. In April, Muhammad al-Bajadi, cofounder of the Saudi Civil and Political Rights Association (ACPRA), was sentenced to four years in prison for "tarnishing the image of the state." In September, Muhammad al-Qahtani, and Abdullah al-Hamad, also cofounders of ACPRA, were put on trial for similar charges and forbidden from travelling outside the country Their trials were pending at the end of 2012.

A 2005 labor law extended various protections and benefits to previously unregulated categories of workers. The legislation also banned child labor, set provisions for resolving labor disputes, and established a 75 percent quota for Saudi citizens in each company's workforce. However, the more than six million foreign workers in the country have virtually no legal protections. Many are lured to the kingdom under false pretenses and forced to endure dangerous working and living conditions. Female migrants employed in Saudi homes as domestic workers report regular physical, sexual, and emotional abuse.

The judiciary, which must coordinate its decisions with the executive branch, is not independent. A Special Higher Commission of judicial experts was formed in 2008 to write laws that would serve as the foundation for verdicts in the court system, which is grounded in Sharia (Islamic law). While Saudi courts have historically relied on the Hanbali school of Islamic jurisprudence, the commission incorporates all four Sunni Muslim legal schools in drafting new laws. The penal code bans torture, but allegations of torture by police and prison officials are common, and access to prisoners by independent human rights and legal organizations is strictly limited. In July 2011, Saudi Arabia issued a draft of a sweeping new antiterrorism law, which includes significant prison sentences for criticizing the government or questioning the integrity of the king or crown prince; it had not been adopted by the end of 2012, though elements of the law, including outlawing criticism of the royal family, appeared to have been implemented.

Substantial prejudice against ethnic, religious, and national minorities prevails. Shiites, who represent 10 to 15 percent of the population, are underrepresented in major government positions and have also faced physical assaults. As a result, Shiite activists and demonstration organizers became more confrontational in 2012. Authorities responded harshly, issuing a most-wanted list targeting activists and violently cracking down on protests. Several were killed, including Akbar al-Shakuri and Mohammed al-Filfil in July and Ali al-Marar in December, and many more were arrested over the course of the year. In July, police arrested popular Shiite cleric Nimr al-Nimr on charges of sedition.

Freedom of movement is restricted in some cases. The government punishes activists and critics by limiting their ability to travel outside the country, and reform advocates are routinely stripped of their passports. In March 2012, human rights lawyer Waleed Abu al-Khair, creator of the Monitor of Human Rights in Saudi Arabia, was barred from leaving the country as he faced charges of "insulting the judiciary" and "harming the reputation of the kingdom" after providing information about one of his cases to an international human rights organization.

While a great deal of business activity is connected to members of the government, the ruling family, or other elite families, officials have given assurances that industrial and commercial zones will be free from royal family interference.

Women are not treated as equal members of society, and many laws discriminate against them. They are not permitted to vote in municipal elections, drive cars, or travel within or outside of the country without a male relative. According to interpretations of Sharia in Saudi Arabia, daughters generally receive half the inheritance awarded to their brothers, and the testimony of one man is equal to that of two women. Moreover, Saudi women seeking access to the courts must be represented by a male. The religious police enforce a strict policy of gender segregation and often harass women, using physical punishment to ensure that they meet conservative standards of dress in public. In May 2011, Saudi women launched a highly visible campaign demanding the expansion of their rights, including the right to drive. A 32-year-old Saudi woman, Manal al-Sharif, was arrested the same month, after posting a video of herself driving on YouTube; she was released after being detained for 10 days. Education and economic rights for Saudi women have improved somewhat in recent years, with more than half of the country's university students now female, though they do not enjoy equal access to classes and facilities. Women gained the right to hold commercial licenses in 2004. In 2008 the Saudi Human Rights Commission established a women's branch to investigate cases of human rights violations against women and children, though it has not consistently carried out any serious investigations or brought cases against violators. A 2009 law imposes fines of up to $266,000 for those found guilty of human trafficking.

Senegal

Political Rights: 2*
Civil Liberties: 3
Status: Free

Population: 13,108,000
Capital: Dakar

Status Change: Senegal's political rights rating improved from 3 to 2, and its status improved from Partly Free to Free, due to free and fair presidential and parliamentary elections that resulted in a peaceful rotation of power, as well as nascent efforts by the new president to increase government accountability and transparency.

Ten-Year Ratings Timeline For Year Under Review (Political Rights, Civil Liberties, Status)

2003	2004	2005	2006	2007	2008	2009	2010	2011	2012
2,3F	2,3F	2,3F	2,3F	2,3F	3,3PF	3,3PF	3,3PF	3,3PF	2,3F

Overview: Tensions rose in the run-up to the February 2012 presidential election, in which Abdoulaye Wade ran for a constitutionally questionable third term. Wade's candidacy sparked demonstrations, leading to several deadly clashes between protesters and police. After losing to opposition candidate Macky Sall, Wade quickly conceded defeat, leading to a peaceful transfer of power. Legislative elections held in June saw an overwhelming victory for Sall's United in Hope coalition. Shortly after his election, Sall launched an audit of state institutions and initiated talks with rebel groups over the long-running conflict in the Casamance region.

Since gaining independence from France in 1960, Senegal has avoided military or harsh authoritarian rule and has never suffered a successful coup d'état. President Leopold Senghor exercised de facto one-party rule through the Socialist Party (PS) for nearly two decades after independence. Most political restrictions were lifted after 1981, when Abdou Diouf of the PS succeeded Senghor. Diouf secured victories in the 1988 and 1993 elections.

Four decades of PS rule ended when Senegalese Democratic Party (PDS) leader Abdoulaye Wade defeated Diouf in the 2000 presidential runoff vote, which was deemed free and fair by international observers. A new constitution was approved in 2001, reducing presidential terms from seven to five years, setting the maximum number of terms at two, and abolishing the Senate. A coalition led by the PDS won a majority of seats in the 2001 legislative elections.

After taking office in 2000, Wade worked to increase the power of the presidency and demonstrated a willingness to persecute those threatening his authority, including former prime minister Idrissa Seck, who was stripped of his position and charged with undermining state security. In 2006, Wade led a successful drive to amend the constitution to postpone legislative elections by a year and reestablish the Senate, where most of the members would be appointed by the president. Wade secured a second term in the 2007 presidential election amid opposition accusations of vote rigging. The opposition coalition, including the PS and 11 other parties, boycotted legislative polls later that year, leading to an overwhelming victory for the PDS. In 2008, the National Assembly approved Wade's proposal to restore the seven-year presidential term beginning in 2012.

In September 2009, Wade announced his intention to run for a third term in 2012, prompting critics to allege that he was trying to circumvent the constitution's stated two-term limit. Supporters contended that Wade's current term was his first under the 2001 constitution, which introduced term limits, making his run for a possible third term legal. In October 2010, Wade appointed his son, Karim, as energy minister, in addition to his existing role as minister of international cooperation, national planning, air transport, and infrastructure. The move prompted fears that the president was positioning his son to succeed him. In January 2012, Senegal's Constitutional Council, made up of presidential appointees, ruled in favor of Wade's bid for candidacy in the 2012 election.

Throughout 2011 and early 2012, those opposed to Wade's candidacy organized demonstrations and riots in Dakar and other urban areas. In June 2011, a wave of protests broke out in response to a constitutional amendment proposed by Wade to lower the threshold for victory in the first round of a presidential election from 50 percent to 25 percent and to include the vice president on the presidential ticket. The protests resulted in numerous injuries, and prompted the PDS to withdraw the bill. In early 2012, government authorities repressed public demonstrations, and a number of protestors opposing Wade were beaten or killed by security forces.

Despite apprehension about escalating public unrest, the first round of the presidential election took place on February 26 without incident. Wade won 32 percent of the vote against 13 opponents, and a runoff against front-runner Macky Sall, of the Alliance for the Republic party, was held on March 25. Sall won 66 percent of the vote in the second round, and Wade quickly conceded defeat. The election results were internationally hailed as a victory for democracy in Senegal and West Africa more broadly. On April 3, Sall appointed Abdoul Mbaye, a former banker, as prime minister. In the July 1 parliamentary elections, which were deemed free and fair, Sall's United in Hope coalition, which includes the Alliance for the Republic, captured 119 of the 150 seats, followed by the PDS with 12 seats. Around a dozen parties captured the remaining seats.

The separatist conflict in the Casamance region remained unresolved at the end of 2012. The peace process had wavered since the 2007 death of the head of the separatist Movement of the Democratic Forces of Casamance (MFDC), Augustin Diamacoune Senghor. Throughout 2012, at least 10 individuals were killed as a result of the conflict, compared to 83 related deaths in 2011. The level of violence related to the conflict declined after Sall led a new round of peace negotiations with the rebels in Rome in October 2012. Subsequently, the MFDC released eight Senegalese military prisoners. From October through December, the armed forces did not undertake any offensive operations. Meanwhile, progress has been made in recent years in clearing the region of land mines, which have caused nearly 800 deaths and 60,000 displacements since 1988.

Political Rights and Civil Liberties: Senegal is an electoral democracy. The National Observatory of Elections has credibly overseen legislative and presidential polls since its creation in 1997. The president is elected by popular vote for up to two terms, and the length of the term was extended from five to seven years by a constitutional amendment in 2008. The president appoints the prime minister. Constitutional amendments that took effect in 2007 converted the National Assembly into a 150-seat lower house and created an upper house, the 100-member Senate. Members of the National Assembly are popularly elected every five years. In September 2012, members of parliament voted to abolish the Senate in order to increase funds for the prevention of flooding in Dakar.

There are 73 legally registered political parties in Senegal. The preelection protests led to the creation of a the June 23 Movement (M23), a coalition made up of approximately 60 opposition parties and nongovernmental organizations (NGOs), which united against former president Abdoulaye Wade in March 2012 and endorsed Macky Sall in the runoff election. The June 23 protests were sparked in part by a younger group of activists led by rap musicians known as the Y'en A Marre (Enough Is Enough) movement. Both groups have drawn comparisons to the Arab Spring movements in 2011.

Corruption has long been a serious problem in Senegal and provoked growing public outrage under Wade's second term. To address corruption and increase transparency, President Sall began a far-reaching public-works audit to investigate all members of the Wade regime, shut down 59 state bodies to save public money and attract investors, and reshuffled his cabinet. Senegal was ranked 94 out of 176 countries surveyed in Transparency International's 2012 Corruption Perceptions Index.

Freedom of expression is generally respected, and members of the independent media are often highly critical of the government despite the risk of criminal defamation charges. In recent years, several journalists have been targeted for expressing opposition to the government. In the run-up to the 2012 presidential election, at least a dozen incidents of security or other government officials harassing, threatening, or physically harming journalists were documented. After the Constitutional Council's January 2012 decision to allow Wade to run for reelection, three journalists covering the event were beaten by police, including Malick Rokhy Bâ, a correspondent from Agence France-Presse, and two female reporters from the Senegalese daily *Le Populaire*. A French freelance photographer, Romain Laurondeau, was also injured during anti-Wade demonstrations. There are a variety of public, private, and community radio stations and many independent print outlets. The government operates a television station, and there are several private television stations, which are subject to government censorship. Access to the internet is not restricted.

Religious freedom is respected, and the government provides free airline tickets to Senegalese Muslims and Christians undertaking pilgrimages overseas. Senegal is a predominantly Muslim country, with 94 percent of the population practicing Islam. The country's Sufi Muslim brotherhoods are very influential, including in the political arena. Academic freedom is legally guaranteed and respected in practice.

Freedoms of association and assembly are legally guaranteed. Street protests and demonstrations have been on the rise in recent years, and the government has taken action to repress some of them, including in the run-up to the presidential election. There were sporadic demonstrations throughout 2011 and 2012 against Wade's bid for a third term. During several of these demonstrations, including in January and February 2012, several protestors were assaulted and imprisoned by security forces. Six protestors were killed, including four who were shot, one who was hit by a gas grenade, and another who was run over by a police vehicle. On January 23, the interior minister passed an order temporarily prohibiting public demonstrations without clear rationale. On February 16, security agents used force to prevent members of the opposition movement from organizing a sit-in in Dakar.

Human rights groups and other NGOs generally operate freely in Senegal, but the political tensions in 2011 and early 2012 resulted in some efforts by the government to curb their work. On January 30, 2012, Alioune Tine, the secretary general of the human rights group Rencontre Africaine pour la Défense des Droits de l'Homme, was arrested for his involvement with the M23 movement and held in police custody for 48 hours before being released. Although workers' rights to organize, bargain collectively, and strike are legally protected for all except security employees, the labor code requires the approval of the Interior Ministry for the initial formation of a trade union.

The judiciary is independent by law, but inadequate pay and lack of tenure expose judges to external influences and prevent the courts from providing a proper check on the other branches of government. Uncharged detainees are incarcerated without legal counsel far beyond the lengthy periods already permitted by law. Prisons are overcrowded, often leading to hygiene and health issues for inmates, and Amnesty International documented several cases of torture of prisoners in 2012. Human rights groups praised Sall's decision in August to sign an agreement with the African Union to establish special chambers in the Senegalese judicial system to prosecute former Chadian president Hissène Habré, who has been living in Senegal for 21 years, for crimes committed under his regime in Chad in the 1980s. Senegal had been criticized for several years after the government had stalled his prosecution and refused four extradition requests.

Women's constitutional rights are often disregarded, especially in rural areas, and women enjoy fewer opportunities than men for education and formal employment. In May 2010, the National Assembly passed legislation requiring parity between men and women on candidate lists for public office. Women hold 64 seats in the 150-seat National Assembly. Many elements of Islamic and local customary law, particularly regarding inheritance and marital relations, discriminate against women. Rape and domestic abuse are widespread problems.

Child trafficking is a problem in Senegal. In particular, boys are often drawn in by Koranic teachers' promises to provide religious education, only to be physically abused and forced to beg in the streets. According to the U.S. State Department's 2012 Trafficking in Persons Report, approximately 50,000 child beggars lived under these circumstances.

Serbia

Political Rights: 2
Civil Liberties: 2
Status: Free

Population: 7,101,600
Capital: Belgrade

Note: The ratings through 2002 are for the Federal Republic of Yugoslavia, of which Serbia was a part, and those from 2003 through 2005 are for the State Union of Serbia and Montenegro. Kosovo is examined in a separate report.

Ten-Year Ratings Timeline For Year Under Review (Political Rights, Civil Liberties, Status)

2003	2004	2005	2006	2007	2008	2009	2010	2011	2012
3,2PF	3,2F	3,2F	3,2F	3,2F	3,2F	2,2F	2,2F	2,2F	2,2F

Overview: **In the May 2012 general elections, former ultranationalist Tomislav Nikolic upset Boris Tadic to win the presidency, and his Serbian Progressive Party subsequently formed a government with the Socialist Party of Serbia. In March, Serbia won European Union candidacy on progress in negotiations with Kosovo over customs and other technical issues. Those negotiations, which had stalled after the election, resumed in October, though the deadlock between Belgrade and Pristina over Kosovo's sovereignty remained unresolved at year's end.**

Serbia, which was recognized as an independent state in 1878 following several centuries of Ottoman rule, anchored the Kingdom of Serbs, Croats, and Slovenes proclaimed in 1918. After World War II, Serbia became a constituent republic of the Socialist Federal Republic of Yugoslavia, under the rule of Josip Broz Tito. Within the boundaries of the Serbian republic as drawn then were two autonomous provinces: the majority-Albanian Kosovo in the south, and Vojvodina, with a significant Hungarian minority, in the north.

Following the disintegration of socialist Yugoslavia in the early 1990s, the republics of Serbia and Montenegro in 1992 formed the Federal Republic of Yugoslavia (FRY). Slobodan Miloševic and his Socialist Party of Serbia (SPS, the former League of Communists of Serbia) ruled Serbia throughout the 1990s by controlling its security forces, financial institutions, and state-owned media. An avowed Serb nationalist, Miloševic oversaw extensive Serbian involvement in the 1991–95 wars that accompanied the old federation's breakup, supporting local Serb forces both in Bosnia and Herzegovina and in Croatia.

In 1998–99 an ethnic Albanian insurgency in Kosovo provoked increasingly violent reprisals by state forces against the guerrillas and Kosovo's civilian population. In March 1999, NATO launched a 78-day bombing campaign to force the withdrawal of FRY and Serbian forces from Kosovo. A NATO-led force then occupied Kosovo, and the United Nations oversaw institution-building efforts there. Miloševi was ousted in October 2000, after his attempt to steal the September Yugoslav presidential election from opposition candidate Vojislav Koštunica of the Democratic Party of Serbia (DSS) triggered massive protests. An anti-Miloševi coalition took power following Serbian parliamentary elections in December, and Zoran Đindic of the Democratic Party (DS) became Serbia's prime minister. The FRY was replaced in February 2003 with a looser State Union of Serbia and Montenegro, and each republic was granted the option of holding an independence referendum after three years.

Đindic was assassinated by organized crime groups allied with Miloševi - era security structures in March 2003. After December parliamentary elections, Koštunica became Serbia's prime minister. The new DS leader, Boris Tadi , won the presidency in June 2004.

After a successful independence referendum in May 2006, Montenegro declared independence in June, necessitating new Serbian elections. In the January 2007 vote, the main anti-Miloševi parties—including the DS, the DSS, and the liberal G17 Plus—collectively outpolled the ultranationalist Serbian Radical Party (SRS) and the SPS. In May, Koštunica formed another coalition government. President Tadic won a second term in February 2008.

Later that month, Kosovo unilaterally declared independence from Serbia. Debate over the proper response increased tensions in the Koštunica government, which ultimately resigned in March. The DS and its pro-European Union (EU) allies won elections in May and formed a coalition government with an SPS-led bloc and smaller parties representing ethnic minorities.

The new government, led by Mirko Cvetkovic, was the first since 2000 to include the SPS, which had sought to reinvent itself as a mainstream center-left party. The outcome also marked the first time since 2000 that a single party, the DS, controlled the presidency, the premiership, and a working parliamentary majority. In September 2008, hard-liners in the SRS were further isolated when the party's moderate wing broke off to form the Serbian Progressive Party (SNS).

In 2009, the parliament passed a statute that defined and expanded Vojvodina's autonomy. Also in 2009, Serbia secured visa-free travel to most EU countries for Serbian citizens. The European Commission (EC) praised Serbia for its cooperation with the International Criminal Tribunal for the former Yugoslavia (ICTY) following the July 2008 arrest in Serbia of former Bosnian Serb leader Radovan Karadži ; he had been indicted on genocide and war crimes charges and was extradited to the ICTY that month. Serbia submitted its EU membership application in December 2009. In July 2010, the International Court of Justice decided against Serbia in ruling that Kosovo's declaration of independence had not violated international law.

In May 2011, Serbian authorities arrested and extradited former Bosnian Serb military commander Ratko Mladic, a longtime fugitive wanted by the ICTY on war crimes charges. Croatian Serb wartime leader Goran Hadžic, the last of 161 suspected war criminals indicted by the ICTY still at large, was arrested and extradited from Serbia in July. The arrests marked a step forward in Serbia's EU candidacy bid.

While EU-brokered negotiations yielded some progress on trade and travel issues between Serbia and Kosovo during 2011, Belgrade maintained its opposition to Kosovo's sovereignty. In August, Germany warned that Serbia must abolish its parallel governing structures in the Serb-populated northern portion of Kosovo before it could join the EU. Though Serbia had been expected to receive EU candidacy that December, Berlin blocked the milestone until March 2012, when the country was officially invited to join the 27-member bloc on progress in the Kosovo negotiations, including a complex deal whereby Belgrade agreed to participate in regional meetings with Pristina. Previously, Serbian leaders had boycotted or walked out of such meetings attended by Kosovo officials.

On May 6, 2012, the SNS, led by former ultranationalist Tomislav Nikolic, and its allies won parliamentary elections with 73 seats. The DS-led bloc took 67 seats, followed by the SPS with a surprisingly strong 44. On May 20, Nikolic upset Tadic in a presidential runoff with 51.2 percent of the vote. His SNS formed a coalition with the SPS in July, with Ivica Dacic, SPS president and one-time Miloševic spokesman, as prime minister. The DS went into opposition, and Tadic effectively assumed blame for its electoral loss by giving up party leadership in November. The negotiations with Kosovo, stalled since the elections, resumed on October 19 with meetings in Brussels between Dacic and Kosovo prime minister Hashim Thaçi, the first high-level encounter between the nations since 2008. However, key issues, including northern Kosovo, remained unresolved in 2012.

Political Rights and Civil Liberties: Serbia is an electoral democracy. The president, elected to up to two five-year terms, plays a largely ceremonial role. The National Assembly is a unicameral, 250-seat legislature, with deputies elected to four-year terms according to party lists. The prime minister is elected by the assembly. International monitors deemed the 2008 and 2012 elections largely free and fair.

In addition to the main political parties, numerous smaller parties compete for influence, including factions representing ethnic minorities. In April 2011, the Constitutional Court clarified and extended its 2010 decision to prohibit a practice whereby politicians elected on a party ticket had to deposit a letter of resignation with the party before taking office. This had allowed party leaders to replace elected officials who proved disloyal. The court declared the system unconstitutional and invalidated any postelection reallocation of parliamentary seats.

Corruption remains a serious concern. In 2012, a new Anticorruption Agency continued to monitor conflicts of interest and political party funding, among other areas, and organized an extensive election-monitoring network. However, graft and misconduct remain widespread, especially in public procurement and privatization. The government has yet to establish a track record of investigating and prosecuting corruption, especially in high-profile cases, and political will is generally lacking. A 2012–16 anticorruption strategy is still pending, according to a 2012 progress report by the EC. Serbia was ranked 80 out of 176 countries surveyed in Transparency International's 2012 Corruption Perceptions Index.

The press is generally free, although most media outlets are thought to be aligned with specific political parties. In May 2011, public broadcaster RTS apologized for its role in supporting authoritarian governments during the 1990s, but advocacy groups noted that RTS remains subject to strong government influence. Media advertising dollars are controlled by a few economic and political actors, creating a backdrop for self-censorship. Press ownership is not fully transparent. In October, the government backtracked on plans to decriminalize defamation, saying it was not a condition for EU membership. That month, a Molotov cocktail was thrown at the home of the director of a tabloid newspaper, and a bomb was found at the house of the parents of B92 television reporter Tanja Jankovic. The EC urged the government to expedite implementation of its 2011 Media Strategy, though some journalists say the most recent draft includes continued state ownership of media outlets. Internet access is unrestricted.

The constitution guarantees freedom of religion, which is generally respected in practice. Religiously motivated incidents declined in 2012 but remain a concern. Critics say that the 2006 Law on Churches and Religious Communities privileges seven "traditional" religious communities by giving them tax-exempt status, while forcing other groups to go through cumbersome and inconsistent registration procedures. A Constitutional Court ruling on the law is still pending. Relations between factions within the Islamic community in the Sandžak region, and between one of the factions and the Serbian government, have been deteriorating in recent years. There were no reports of government restrictions on academic freedom in 2012.

Citizens enjoy freedoms of assembly and association, though a 2009 law banned meetings of fascist organizations and the use of neo-Nazi symbols. Authorities barred all public demonstrations on October 6, 2012, due to security concerns over a gay pride parade scheduled that day. The 2010 parade was attacked by several thousand counterdemonstrators, and Belgrade has banned the event two years running, despite the objection of rights groups. Radical right-wing organizations and violent "sports fans" remain a serious concern, and the Constitutional Court banned a second such group in 2012. Foreign and domestic NGOs generally operate freely. Workers may join unions, engage in collective bargaining, and strike, but the International Confederation of Trade Unions has reported that organizing efforts and strikes are substantially restricted in practice.

In July 2012, the Constitutional Court abrogated a controversial reappointment procedure in effect during 2009 and 2010 that cost hundreds of judges and prosecutors their jobs, and the officials who had appealed their "nonreappointment" were reinstated. To reintegrate these judges and prosecutors, the government announced plans in October to roughly double the court network, to 65 courts in 2013. Officials said this would also improve citizens' access to justice, following a 2010 judicial overhaul that merged the country's 138 municipal courts into 34 basic courts. In October, the EC said judicial independence and accountability needed to be improved through transparent criteria for appointments and evaluations, improved training, and effective disciplinary rules. At the end of 2011, courts had a backlog of 3.34 million cases. Prisons generally meet international standards, though overcrowding is an issue, and health-care facilities are often inadequate. Legislation passed in October granted early release to 3,600 prisoners to reduce chronic overcrowding.

Ethnic minorities are underrepresented in government. The country's main minority groups are the Bosniaks (Muslim Slavs), concentrated in the Sandžak region; an ethnic Albanian population in the Preševo Valley; and the Hungarian community in Vojvodina. Discrimination against ethnic and other minorities is widespread, and the EC has urged lawmakers to develop a strategy for inclusion of the LGBT (lesbian, gay, bisexual, and transgender) community. After nearly 1,000 Roma were removed from a settlement in New Belgrade in April 2012, Amnesty International called for a ban on forced evictions. However, it also praised a September law enabling the roughly 6,500 people in Serbia, mostly Roma, without a birth certificate to obtain documentation.

Women comprise 34 percent of the parliament. According to electoral regulations, women must account for at least 30 percent of a party's candidate list. Although women are legally entitled to equal pay for equal work, traditional attitudes often limit them economically. A 2009 law on gender equality provides a range of protections in employment, health, education, and politics. Domestic violence is a serious problem. Serbia is a source, transit, and destination country for the trafficking of men, women, and children for forced labor and prostitution.

Seychelles

Political Rights: 3
Civil Liberties: 3
Status: Partly Free

Population: 92,900
Capital: Victoria

Ten-Year Ratings Timeline For Year Under Review (Political Rights, Civil Liberties, Status)

2003	2004	2005	2006	2007	2008	2009	2010	2011	2012
3,3PF	3,3PF	3,3PF	3,3PF	3,3PF	3,3PF	3,3PF	3,3PF	3,3PF	3,3PF

Overview: **A draft law containing stronger protections for freedom of assembly was pending at the end of 2012. Following a December 2011 report by the auditor-general revealing severe financial mismanagement by the government over the past two decades, President James Michel launched an investigation into the matter in 2012**

The Seychelles gained independence from Britain in 1976, remaining a member of the Commonwealth. In 1977, Prime Minister France-Albert René seized power from President James Mancham and made his Seychelles People's Progressive Front (SPPF) the sole legal party. In 1992, however, the SPPF passed a constitutional amendment legalizing opposition parties, and many exiled leaders returned.

René stepped down in 2004 and was replaced by Vice President James Michel. Michel defeated Wavel Ramkalawan, the leader of the opposition Seychelles National Party (SNP), in the 2006 presidential poll, while the SPPF retained its majority in the 2007 legislative elections.

Michel, running for the People's Party (Parti Lepep, or PP)—the new name for the SPPF— defeated Ramkalawan with 55 percent of the vote in the May 2011 presidential election. Ramkalawan accused the PP of bribing voters, though observers called the election credible. The SNP boycotted parliamentary elections held in late September and early October 2011, citing alleged misconduct by the PP in the presidential vote and Michel's failure to implement electoral reforms. The PP captured all 25 directly elected seats and 8 of the 9 proportional seats; the Popular Democratic Movement, formed by a dissident SNP member who disagreed with the boycott, took the remaining seat. Observers from the Southern African Development Community said the voting was credible and transparent.

Discussions between the PP and SNP over political and electoral reforms led to the establishment of the Forum on Electoral Reform by the Electoral Commission (EC). In 2012, the EC submitted a proposal to President Michel outlining a new Public Order Act to modernize outdated statutes accompanying constitutional guarantees for freedoms of speech and assembly. Passage of the law, which would allow political parties to hold public meetings upon giving five days' notice to the police commissioner instead of requiring permission, was pending at year's end.

In 2011, the country modified its law to allow pirates captured anywhere beyond its territorial waters to be prosecuted in the Seychelles. In March 2012, the United States handed over 15 suspected Somali pirates to the Seychelles to stand trial. In November, all were convicted of attacking a merchant ship and abducting an Iranian fisherman and sentenced to 18 years in prison.

Political Rights and Civil Liberties: The Seychelles is an electoral democracy. The 2011 presidential and parliamentary elections were generally regarded as having met basic international norms, despite the opposition boycott of the latter. The president and the unicameral National Assembly are elected by universal adult suffrage for five-year terms. The head of government is the president, who appoints the cabinet. Of the National Assembly's 34 members, 25 are directly elected, and 9 are allocated on a proportional basis to parties gaining at least 10 percent of the vote.

The ruling PP remains the dominant party, and the opposition SNP has claimed that its sympathizers face job discrimination in the public sector and police harassment.

Concerns over government corruption have focused on a lack of transparency in the privatization and allocation of government-owned land. A December 2011 report released by the auditor-general revealed nearly two decades of dysfunction in government finances, including unprofessional bookkeeping, illegal procedures, and embezzlement. President James Michel launched an investigation that was pending at the end of 2012. Seychelles was ranked 51 out of 176 countries surveyed in Transparency International's 2012 Corruption Perceptions Index.

The government controls much of the nation's print and broadcast media, including the daily *Seychelles Nation* newspaper. Strict libel laws are sometimes used to harass journalists, leading to self-censorship. In October 2012, the chief editor of Le Nouveau *Seychelles Weekly* was convicted of contempt for discrediting a judge in a 2011 article, and was sentenced to apologize to the judge. The government can restrict the broadcast of material considered to be objectionable. The board of directors of the officially nonpartisan Seychelles Broadcasting Corporation includes several non-PP members, though coverage is biased in favor of the ruling party. There have been reports that the state monitors e-mail, chat rooms, and blogs, and opposition activists claim that the government blocks access to opposition party websites.

Religious freedom is constitutionally guaranteed and respected in practice. Churches in this predominantly Roman Catholic country have been strong voices for human rights and democratization, and they generally function without government interference. Academic freedom is generally respected, though PP loyalists are reportedly favored in high-level academic appointments.

The constitution protects freedoms of assembly and association. While public demonstrations are generally tolerated, the government has occasionally impeded opposition gatherings. In May 2012, police beat and charged a man with breaching the peace after he held a sign protesting the authorities' ineffectiveness in dealing with narcotics in his neighborhood. Human rights groups and other nongovernmental organizations operate in the country. Workers have the right to strike, though strikes are illegal until all arbitration procedures have been exhausted. Collective bargaining is rare.

Judges generally decide cases fairly, but face interference in those involving major economic or political interests. The majority of the members of the judiciary are naturalized citizens or foreign nationals from other Commonwealth countries, and the impartiality of the non-Seychellois magistrates can be compromised because they are subject to contract renewal. Security forces have at times been accused of using excessive force, including torture and arbitrary detention. Prolonged pretrial detention and overcrowding in prisons are common.

The country's political and economic life is dominated by people of European and South Asian origin. Islanders of Creole extraction face discrimination, and prejudice against foreign workers has been reported. The government does not restrict domestic travel but may deny passports for unspecified reasons of "national interest."

The Seychelles boasts one of the world's highest percentages of women in parliament, reaching 44 percent in 2011. Most women are engaged in subsistence agriculture. Despite a 2008 National Strategy on Domestic Violence, rape and domestic violence remain widespread.

Sierra Leone

Political Rights: 2*
Civil Liberties: 3
Status: Free

Population: 6,126,000
Capital: Freetown

Status Change: Sierra Leone's political rights rating improved from 3 to 2, and its status improved from Partly Free to Free, due to free and fair presidential and parliamentary elections during which reformed electoral institutions operated with transparency and demonstrated the ability to function without undue influence from the international community.

Ten-Year Ratings Timeline For Year Under Review (Political Rights, Civil Liberties, Status)

2003	2004	2005	2006	2007	2008	2008	2010	2011	2012
4,4PF	4,3PF	4,3PF	4,3PF	3,3PF	3,3PF	3,3PF	3,3PF	3,3PF	2,3F

Overview: Much of the year was consumed by preparations for November general elections. While tensions simmered in the months leading up to the elections and some irregularities were reported as ballots were cast, international observers deemed the elections free, fair, and peaceful. Incumbent president Ernest Bai Koroma won with 59 percent of the vote, and the ruling All People's Congress increased its parliamentary majority. The government made significant progress toward reforming and strengthening electoral institutions and soliciting assistance from civil society organizations in monitoring political parties, and the election was considered a milestone for the consolidation of peace in the country.

Founded by Britain in 1787 as a haven for liberated slaves, Sierra Leone achieved independence in 1961. Siaka Stevens, who became prime minister in 1967 and then president in 1971, transformed Sierra Leone into a one-party state under his All People's Congress (APC) party. In 1985, Stevens retired and handed power to his designated successor, General Joseph Momoh. The Revolutionary United Front (RUF) launched a guerrilla insurgency from Liberia in 1991, sparking a civil war that lasted for more than a decade. Military officer Valentine Strasser ousted Momoh the following year, but failed to deliver on the promise of elections. Brigadier General Julius Maada Bio deposed Strasser in 1996, and elections were held despite military and rebel intimidation. Voters chose former UN diplomat Ahmad Tejan Kabbah of the Sierra Leone People's Party (SLPP) as president.

In 1997, Major Johnny Paul Koroma toppled the Kabbah government and invited the RUF to join his ruling junta. Nigerian-led troops under the aegis of the Economic Community of West African States Monitoring Group (ECOMOG) restored Kabbah to power in 1998, and the 1999 Lomé peace agreement led to the deployment of UN peacekeepers. By 2002, the 17,000-strong UN peacekeeping force had started disarmament in rebel-held areas and the war was declared over.

Kabbah won a new term in the 2002 presidential elections, defeating the APC's Ernest Bai Koroma (no relation to Johnny Paul Koroma), and the SLPP claimed a parliamentary majority. However, the SLPP government failed to adequately address the country's entrenched poverty, dilapidated infrastructure, and endemic corruption, and in 2007, Ernest Bai Koroma won a presidential runoff election, with 55 percent of the vote, to SLPP candidate Solomon Berewa's 45 percent. The APC also gained a slight majority in Parliament.

Chieftaincy elections and parliamentary and local council by-elections held between 2009 and 2011 were marred by political violence initiated by APC and SLPP supporters. Serious clashes preceded a local by-election in the Pujehun district in March 2009, when APC operatives were accused of stabbing the wife of the district's SLPP chairman, provoking clashes between supporters of the two parties. The incident led to the publication of an APC/SLPP joint communiqué disavowing political violence, the establishment of a Commission of Inquiry, and an independent review in 2010 of the causes of the violence. In March 2012, the commission produced a report containing mostly vague, insubstantial recommendations. The government declined to act on the commission's most substantive recommendation: that those implicated in the violence be banned from public office. The by-elections confirmed a regional polarization, whereby the APC enjoys support in the north and west, while the SLPP dominates the south and east.

Political violence continued in 2011 but subsided in 2012, although election-related tensions continued to simmer. In December 2011, most of the country's political parties signed an agreement promoting cooperation with the police and increased security during political processions. However, in January 2012, violence erupted between APC and SLPP partisans during a local council by-election in Freetown, requiring police intervention and resulting in four injuries. In February, the SLPP accused the APC of arming and mobilizing ex-combatants in order to disrupt the vote, provoking counteraccusations from the APC. All parties signed an agreement in May committing to free, fair, and peaceful elections, and no major incidents of political violence were reported after the agreement was signed.

The day of the presidential and parliamentary elections—November 17—was generally peaceful, and the police capably responded to the few instances of electoral misconduct reported as ballots were cast. Voter turnout was estimated at 87 percent. Koroma of the APC won 59 percent of the presidential vote, obviating the need for a runoff; the SLPP's candidate, former military ruler Bio, secured 37 percent. In the parliamentary elections, the APC increased its majority from 59 to 69 seats, and the SLPP held on to its 43 seats. The SLPP refused to accept the results and filed a petition later in November alleging numerous irregularities, including the absence of voter registers in some parts of the APC-dominated north, and the intimidation of SLPP partisans by the police. In December, however, Koroma and Bio issued a joint statement recognizing the APC's victory, and reversing the SLPP's earlier threat of a government boycott.

Political Rights and Civil Liberties:

Sierra Leone is an electoral democracy. International observers determined that the 2012 presidential and parliamentary elections were free and fair, and they were widely considered a milestone for the consolidation of peace in the country. Of the unicameral Parliament's 124 members, 112 are chosen by popular vote, and 12 seats are reserved for indirectly elected paramount chiefs. Parliamentary and presidential elections are held every five years, and presidents may seek a second term.

The APC and SLPP are the main political parties. Other parties include the People's Movement for Democratic Change, the National Democratic Alliance, and the United Democratic Movement. Both the All Political Parties Women's Association and the All Political Parties Youth Association, which became operational in 2011, play important roles in promoting peaceful electoral campaigning, dialogue, and participation.

Much of the administration's efforts in 2012 were focused on cementing the electoral framework in preparation for November elections, which were widely considered a crucial test for Sierra Leone's democracy. The country's first biometric voting registration system was implemented between January and March. The UN Integrated Peacebuilding Office in Sierra Leone (UNIPSIL) implemented a project to incorporate nongovernmental organizations (NGOs) and other stakeholders into the planning process; its accomplishments included the convening of district-wide electoral "code of conduct" monitoring committees, which trained party representatives, civil society organizations, and other stakeholders in mediation and dispute resolution. The initiative was expanded to all of the country's 14 districts in the months leading up to the elections. The Political Parties Registration Commission, created in 2002 to monitor the conduct of political parties during elections, trained and deployed monitors throughout the country and publicized irregularities and violations of electoral laws committed by both the APC and SLPP. The National Electoral Commission hired over 70,000 temporary staff to oversee voting in more than 9,000 polling stations throughout the country.

While corruption remains a serious problem, President Ernest Bai Koroma has actively encouraged and supported the work of the Anti-Corruption Commission. The commission has established a secretariat to oversee implementation of the National Anti-Corruption Strategy, and has continued its efforts to investigate and prosecute corrupt officials—notably, the mayor of Freetown, who was indicted on 25 counts of corruption despite his membership in the ruling party. He was convicted on two of those counts in August 2012, and fined 170 million leones ($39,000). Sierra Leone was ranked 134 out of 176 countries surveyed in Transparency International's 2012 Corruption Perceptions Index.

Freedoms of speech and the press are constitutionally guaranteed, but not always respected in practice. In June 2010, the Sierra Leone Broadcasting Corporation (SLBC) was officially launched as the independent national broadcaster. The APC and SLPP relinquished control of their radio stations in 2010, allowing for incorporation into the SLBC. All political parties and the SLBC signed guidelines to ensure equitable airtime and access in the run-up to the 2012 elections. In March 2012, SLPP partisans attacked a cameraman for the SLBC during interviews with party officials at SLPP headquarters. In August, uniformed soldiers attacked two journalists who were covering a protest against the Ministry of Defense for military discharges and alleged nonpayment of salaries. Numerous independent newspapers circulate freely, and there are dozens of public and private radio and television outlets. A Freedom of Information Bill was proposed in 2010, but despite multiple rounds of legislative review and persistent pressure from international human rights organizations, passage remains stalled. The government does not restrict internet access, though the medium is not widely used.

Freedom of religion is protected by the constitution and respected in practice. Academic freedom is similarly upheld.

Freedoms of assembly and association are constitutionally guaranteed and generally observed in practice. NGOs and civic groups operate freely, though a 2008 law requires NGOs to submit annual activity reports and renew their registration every two years. While workers have the right to join independent trade unions, serious violations of core labor standards occur regularly.

The judiciary has demonstrated a degree of independence, and a number of trials have been free and fair. However, corruption, poor salaries, police unprofessionalism, prison overcrowding, and a lack of resources threaten to impede judicial effectiveness.

The Special Court for Sierra Leone, a hybrid international and domestic war crimes tribunal, has been working since 2004 to convict those responsible for large-scale human rights abuses during the civil war. The trial of former Liberian president Charles Taylor, accused of fostering the RUF insurgency, concluded in March 2011, and in April 2012, Taylor was convicted on 11 counts of war crimes and crimes against humanity. In May, Taylor was sentenced to 50 years in prison.

The Human Rights Commission of Sierra Leone—established in 2004 to investigate human rights abuses and conduct nationwide public education campaigns on human rights issues—continued its work in 2012, despite funding and logistical shortcomings. In June, the commission initiated investigations into allegations of police brutality following a protest by workers at Africa Minerals Ltd.; the body released its report in October, finding the police at fault for overreacting to the protest. The commission also played a role in monitoring the behavior of the political parties in advance of the elections; in November it chastised the APC and SLPP for using provocative and obscene language at campaign rallies.

Drug trafficking and other crimes pose a threat to the rule of law and the stability of the wider Mano River region. The Sierra Leone Transnational Organized Crime Unit, organized through the UN's West Africa Coast Initiative, continued to register successes in 2012.

Continued progress was made in 2012 in rendering Sierra Leone more attractive for business. A variety of multinational corporations have expanded their interests in the country's lucrative diamond mines, stimulating increased investments in roads and other infrastructure. The country rose eight slots in the World Bank's October 2012 Doing Business report, from 148 to 140, based largely on expanding access to credit. Still, weak rule of law, insecure property rights, and endemic corruption continued to hamper the growth of business, and the country remains overly dependent on agriculture and proceeds from natural resource extraction.

Laws passed in 2007 prohibit domestic violence, grant women the right to inherit property, and outlaw forced marriage. Despite these laws and constitutionally guaranteed equality, gender discrimination remains widespread, and female genital mutilation and child marriages are common. In 2011, the government and UNIPSIL drafted a gender equality bill recommended by the Truth and Reconciliation Commission. If passed, the law would reserve a minimum of 30 percent of parliamentary seats and one ward per local council for women. In the Parliament elected in November 2012, women won 15, or about 12 percent, of the seats. There were also 2 female cabinet ministers, out of 22 total, and three of the seven Supreme Court justices were women, including the chief justice.

Singapore

Political Rights: 4
Civil Liberties: 4
Status: Partly Free

Population: 5,293,700
Capital: Singapore

Ten-Year Ratings Timeline For Year Under Review (Political Rights, Civil Liberties, Status)

2003	2004	2005	2006	2007	2008	2009	2010	2011	2012
5,4PF	5,4PF	5,4PF	5,4PF	5,4PF	5,4PF	5,4PF	5,4PF	4,4PF	4,4PF

Overview: In 2012, journalists, academics, and others gathered at Nanyang Technological University to discuss the question of reviewing the Newspapers and Printing Presses Act, of which participants were highly critical. The government created a Media Literacy Council in August to provide advice on media policy, though critics feared that the council would be use to restrict internet freedom. The opposition Workers' Party of Singapore won a by-election in May by a large margin. In November, Singapore saw its first strike in more than two decades when over 100 public bus drivers walked off the job to protest wage discrimination.

The British colony of Singapore obtained home rule in 1959, entered the Malaysian Federation in 1963, and gained full independence in 1965. During three decades as prime minister, Lee Kuan Yew and his People's Action Party (PAP) transformed the port city into a regional financial center and exporter of high-technology goods but restricted individual freedoms and stunted political development.

Lee transferred the premiership to Goh Chok Tong in 1990 but stayed on as "senior minister," and the PAP retained its dominance. Lee's son, Lee Hsien Loong, became prime minister in 2004, and the elder Lee assumed the title of "minister mentor." The 2006 parliamentary elections, in which the PAP took 82 of 84 elected seats, resembled past elections in serving more as a referendum on the prime minister's popularity than as an actual contest for power, with both the electoral framework and the restrictive media environment favoring the ruling party.

Lee Hsien Loong continued to pursue economic growth while using the legal system and other tools to keep media criticism and the opposition in check. The government maintained that racial sensitivities and the threat of Islamist terrorism justified draconian restrictions on freedoms of speech and assembly, but such rules were repeatedly used to silence criticism of the authorities.

The May 2011 parliamentary elections featured a more vigorous and coordinated campaign effort by the opposition. Candidates ran for 82 of the 87 directly elected seats, the highest number since independence. The opposition Workers' Party took an unprecedented six directly elected seats, plus two under a system that guarantees the opposition at least nine seats in Parliament. Another party, the Singapore People's Party (SPP), was awarded the remaining seat allocated to the opposition. The PAP took 81 seats, even though it had secured only 60 percent of the overall vote. Shortly thereafter, Lee Kuan Yew resigned from his "minister mentor" position, ending over half a century in government.

The first contested presidential election since 1993 was held in August 2011, with all candidates running as independents in keeping with the constitution. Former deputy prime minister Tony Tan, the PAP-backed candidate, won with 35.2 percent of the vote, narrowly defeating three opponents. His closest challenger, former PAP lawmaker Tan Cheng Bock, took 34.9 percent, and the opposition-backed Tan Jee Say placed third with 25.1 percent. Businessman Tan Kin Lian, a former PAP district official, secured the remainder. The results confirmed the growing strength of the opposition, and the increased willingness of the electorate to vote against the ruling party. In a May 2012 by-election for the Hougang single-member constituency, Png Eng Huat of the Workers' Party defeated the PAP candidate, 62 percent to 38 percent.

Political Rights and Civil Liberties: Singapore is not an electoral democracy. Elections are free from irregularities and vote rigging, but the ruling PAP dominates the political process. The country lacks an independent election authority. Opposition campaigns have typically been hamstrung by a ban on political films and television programs, the threat of libel suits, strict regulations on political associations, and the PAP's influence on the media and the courts.

The largely ceremonial president is elected by popular vote for six-year terms, and a special committee is empowered to vet candidates. The prime minister and cabinet are appointed by the president. Singapore has had only three prime ministers since independence. Of the unicameral legislature's 87 elected members, who serve five-year terms, 12 are elected from single-member constituencies, while 75 are elected in Group Representation Constituencies (GRCs), a mechanism intended to foster minority representation. Historically, the top-polling party in each GRC won all of its four to six seats, so the system effectively bolstered the majority of the dominant party. However, the 2011 election demonstrated that this system could be challenged. Notably, the opposition Workers' Party captured a five-seat GRC in the May 2011 elections. As of 2012, up to nine members can be appointed from among leading opposition parties to ensure a minimum of opposition representation, up from three in previous years, though only three of these seats needed to be awarded in the latest elections. Up to nine additional, nonpartisan members can be appointed by the president.

Singapore has traditionally been lauded for its lack of corruption, though issues of transparency remain a concern. The country was ranked 5 out of 176 countries surveyed in Transparency International's 2012 Corruption Perceptions Index.

Singapore's media remain tightly constrained. All domestic newspapers, radio stations, and television channels are owned by companies linked to the government. Although editorials and news coverage generally support state policies, newspapers occasionally publish critical pieces. Mainstream media offered more balanced coverage of the opposition ahead of the 2011 elections. Self-censorship is common among journalists. The Sedition Act, in effect since the colonial period, outlaws seditious speech, the distribution of seditious materials, and acts with "seditious tendency." Popular videos, music, and books that reference sex, violence, or drugs are also subject to censorship. Foreign broadcasters and periodicals can be restricted for engaging in domestic politics, and all foreign publications must appoint legal representatives and provide significant financial deposits.

The internet is widely accessible, but authorities monitor online material and block some content through directives to licensed service providers. Singaporeans' increased use of social-networking websites has sparked interest in social activism and opposition parties, contributing to opposition electoral gains in 2011. The enforcement of internet restrictions was eased in the run-up to the 2011 voting, allowing broader online discussion of political issues. A panel organized at Nanyang Technological University in the summer of 2012 brought together activists, journalists, and academics to discuss the question of reviewing the Newspapers and Printing Presses Act; panelists were largely critical of requirements such as shareholders of newspaper companies being appointed by the government and the government's role in issuing permits for newspapers and magazines. In August, the government set up a 21-member Media Literacy Council, intended to provide advice on appropriate policy responses to the country's increasingly complex media landscape. Critics criticized the council as a potential additional tool for restricting internet freedom.

The constitution guarantees freedom of religion as long as its practice does not violate any other regulations, and most groups worship freely. However, religious actions perceived as threats to racial or religious harmony are not tolerated, and unconventional groups like the Jehovah's Witnesses and the Unification Church are banned. All religious groups are required to register with the government under the 1966 Societies Act. Adherents of the Falun Gong spiritual movement have been arrested and prosecuted on vandalism charges in recent years for displaying posters in a public park that detail the persecution of fellow practitioners in China.

All public universities and political research institutions have direct government links that exercise at least some influence. Academics engage in political debate, but their publications rarely deviate from the government line on matters related to Singapore.

Public assemblies must be approved by police. A 2009 law eliminated a previous threshold requiring permits for public assemblies of five or more people, meaning political events involving just one person could require official approval. Permits are not needed for indoor gatherings as long as the topic of discussion does not relate to race or religion. In the 2011 campaign period, opposition parties held rallies without significant interference.

The Societies Act restricts freedom of association by requiring most organizations of more than 10 people to register with the government, and the government enjoys full discretion to register or dissolve such groups. Only registered parties and associations may engage in organized political activity, and political speeches are tightly regulated. Singaporeans for Democracy, a civil society organization active in promoting greater political and civil rights, dissolved in August 2012, asserting that government rules and regulations had made their activities increasingly impossible; by dissolving the group, its leaders sought to call attention to the restrictive laws.

Unions are granted fairly broad rights under the Trade Unions Act, though restrictions include a ban on government employees joining unions. Union members are prohibited from voting on collective agreements negotiated by union representatives and employers. Strikes must be approved by a majority of a union's members, as opposed to the internationally accepted standard of at least 50 percent of the members who vote. In practice, many restrictions are not applied. Nearly all unions are affiliated with the National Trade Union Congress, which is openly allied with the PAP. Singapore's 180,000 household workers are excluded from the Employment Act and regularly exploited. A 2006 standard contract for foreign household workers addresses food deprivation and entitles replaced workers to seek other employment in Singapore, but it fails to provide other basic protections, such as vacation days. Workers in "essential services" are required to give 14 days' notice to an employer before striking. In November 2012, Singapore saw its first strike in more than two decades, when 171 migrant Chinese public bus drivers went on strike to protest wage discrimination. The action was regarded as illegal because public transportation is considered an essential service, and the strikers had not provided 14 days' notice. Three of the strikers were dismissed from their jobs, 29 were deported, and 1 was sentenced to six weeks in prison.

The government's overwhelming success in court cases raises questions about judicial independence, particularly because lawsuits against opposition politicians and parties often drive them into bankruptcy. It is unclear whether the government pressures judges or simply appoints those who share its conservative philosophy. Defendants in criminal cases enjoy most due process rights. Prisons generally meet international standards.

Citizens generally have the right to privacy, but the Internal Security Act (ISA) and Criminal Law Act (CLA) allow warrantless searches and arrests to preserve national security, order, and the public interest. Government agencies, including the Internal Security Department, conduct surveillance using extensive networks and sophisticated methods to monitor telephone and other private conversations. The ISA, previously aimed at communist threats, is now used against suspected Islamist terrorists. Suspects can be detained without charge or trial for an unlimited number of two-year periods. A 1989 constitutional amendment prohibits judicial review of the substantive grounds for detention under the ISA and of the constitutionality of the law itself. The CLA is mainly used to detain organized crime suspects; it allows preventive detention for an extendable one-year period. The Misuse of Drugs Act empowers authorities to commit suspected drug users, without trial, to rehabilitation centers for up to three years. The penal code mandates caning, in addition to imprisonment, for about 30 offenses, though the punishment is applied inconsistently.

There is no legal racial discrimination, though ethnic Malays reportedly face discrimination in both private- and public sector employment.

Citizens enjoy freedom of movement, though the government occasionally enforces its policy of ethnic balance in public housing, in which most Singaporeans live. Opposition politicians have been denied the right to travel.

Women enjoy the same legal rights as men on most issues, and many are well-educated professionals. There are no explicit constitutional guarantees of equal rights for women, and no laws that mandate nondiscrimination in hiring practice on the basis of gender. Few women hold top positions in government and the private sector. Twenty women won seats in the 2011 parliamentary elections. Section 377A of the Penal Code criminalizes mutually consensual sex between adult men, which is punishable by up to two years in prison. In August 2012, Singapore's Court of Appeal reversed a previous High Court decision regarding a challenge to Section 377A, saying that it "affects the lives of a not insignificant portion of our community in a very real and intimate way."

Slovakia

Political Rights: 1
Civil Liberties: 1
Status: Free

Population: 5,440,000
Capital: Bratislava

Ten-Year Ratings Timeline For Year Under Review (Political Rights, Civil Liberties, Status)

2003	2004	2005	2006	2007	2007	2009	2010	2011	2012
1,2F	1,1F	1,1F	1,1F	1,1F	1,1F	1,1F	1,1F	1,1F	1,1F

Overview: **Early elections in March 2012 saw a landslide victory for the center-left Direction–Social Democracy party, resulting in Slovakia's first ever one-party parliamentary majority. In July, the parliament voted unanimously to end the practice of parliamentary immunity. Meanwhile, a new labor code adopted in August provided additional protections for workers, including guarantees related to overtime and severance pay.**

Czechoslovakia was created in 1918 amid the collapse of the Austro-Hungarian Empire, and Soviet forces helped establish a communist government after World War II. A series of peaceful anticommunist demonstrations in 1989 brought about the collapse of the communist regime, and open elections were held the following year. In 1992, negotiations began on increased Slovak autonomy within the Czech and Slovak Federative Republic. This process led to a peaceful dissolution of the federation and the establishment of an independent Slovak Republic in 1993.

From 1993 to 1998, Prime Minister Vladimír Meciar and his Movement for a Democratic Slovakia (HZDS) flouted the rule of law and intimidated independent media. In the 1998 parliamentary elections, voters rejected Meciar's rule and empowered a broad right-left coalition that worked to enhance judicial independence, combat corruption, and undertake economic reforms.

The HZDS led the 2002 parliamentary elections, but Mikuláš Dzurinda's Slovak Democratic and Christian Union (SDKÚ) formed a center-right government with three other parties, allowing the country to complete reforms associated with European Union (EU) and NATO membership. Slovakia formally joined both organizations in 2004.

Meciar lost the 2004 presidential election to a former HZDS ally, Ivan Gašparovic. The SDKÚ-led governing coalition fractured in February 2006 amid unpopular economic reforms, prompting early parliamentary elections in June. The left-leaning, populist Direction–Social Democracy (Smer) party led the voting and formed an unusual coalition with the HZDS—now allied with the People's Party—and the far-right Slovak National Party (SNS). The government, which served until 2010 and was led by Prime Minister Robert Fico, was characterized by the concentration of political power and hostility to the media, the EU, and nongovernmental organizations (NGOs). Supported by Smer and the SNS, President Gašparovic won a second term in 2009, narrowly defeating Iveta Radicová of the SDKÚ (now allied with the Democratic Party, or DS).

The SDKÚ-DS placed a distant second to Smer in the June 2010 elections, but was able to form a center-right coalition in July with three smaller parties—the Freedom and Solidarity party (SaS), the Christian Democratic Movement (KDH), and the Most-Híd, ("Bridge") party, which campaigns to improve relations between Slovakia's ethnic majority and Hungarian minority; Radicová became prime minister. The government collapsed in October 2011 when Radicová tied a parliamentary vote on the expansion of the European Financial Stability Facility, a bailout fund for heavily indebted eurozone nations, to a vote of confidence in her own government.

Early elections held in March 2012 elections saw a landslide victory for Smer. With 83 seats, Smer was able to form Slovakia's first-ever one-party parliamentary majority, with Fico returning as prime minister. Following two major corruption scandals, parties included in the previous ruling coalition fared poorly in the elections: KDH took 16 seats, while former coalition leader SDKÚ-DS captured 11 seats. Most-Hid took 13 seats, and the SaS won 11 seats. A new party composed of former SaS members, the Ordinary People and Independent Personalities party (OlaNO), secured 16 seats by appealing to Slovaks disillusioned with the government. The SNS failed to cross the 5 percent threshold for parliamentary representation.

Fico's new administration pledged a pro-European outlook and support for planned economic reforms, including the abolition of Slovakia's 19 percent flat tax in favor of progressive taxation, with significant increases to be paid by banks, large companies, and the wealthy. The EU has demanded that Slovakia reduce its budget deficit to 3 percent of GDP by 2013, down from a projected 4.5 percent at the end of 2012.

Political Rights and Civil Liberties: Slovakia is an electoral democracy. Voters elect the president for up to two five-year terms and members of the

150-seat, unicameral National Council for four-year terms. The prime minister is appointed by the president but must have majority support in the parliament to govern. The March 2012 parliamentary elections were deemed free and fair by international monitors, though the Organization for Security and Cooperation in Europe expressed concern about a lack of oversight and transparency in campaign financing.

Corruption is widespread, most notably in public procurement and the health-care sector. Iveta Radicová's SDKÚ-led government in 2011 pushed through legislation requiring mandatory online disclosure of contracts involving public authorities and state-owned companies. However, according to Transparency International (TI), many state-owned companies still do not publish even basic information, including annual reports. In September 2012, Interior Minister Robert Kalinák introduced a revision to the public procurement law requiring deals worth 10 million eruos ($13.6 million) or more and deemed to be of societal significance to go through a special procurement process. Critics charge that the subjectivity of this process would allow for government manipulation. The law had yet to be adopted by year's end. In January, a collection of videotaped conversations and transcripts of text messages suggested that lawmakers within Radicová's coalition government had been offered large bribes in exchange for loyalty in a 2010 vote to replace prosecutor general Dobroslav Trnka. In July, Slovakia's parliament voted unanimously to lift the immunity of its deputies from criminal prosecution; only judges remain immune from prosecution. Slovakia was ranked 62 out of 176 countries surveyed in TI's 2012 Corruption Perceptions Index.

Freedoms of speech and of the press are protected by the constitution, but media outlets sometimes face political interference. In June 2012, Miloslava Zemková, the director general of Slovakia's public television and radio broadcaster, Radio and Television Slovakia, was dismissed over allegations of misconduct in a public tender. Zemková said her dismissal had been politically motivated and filed a complaint with the Constitutional Court, but the court in December refused to hear the case. The director of the European Broadcasting Union called her firing, "a sign of increasing interference and political pressure which will destabilize public service media." Journalists continue to face verbal attacks and libel suits by public officials, though these have decreased in frequency in recent years. A September 2011 amendment to the controversial Press Act reduced pressure on editors by removing a requirement that media publish responses or corrections from public officials if they are criticized for their performance in office. In a January 2012 decision contravening an EU Court of Justice ruling, a Slovak regional court ruled that newspaper articles were not copyright protected in a case brought by the country's major publishers against a media tracking company that repackaged and resold article content at a profit.

The government respects religious freedom in this largely Roman Catholic country. Registered religious organizations are eligible for tax exemptions and government subsidies. However, religious groups must have at least 20,000 members to register, effectively preventing the small Muslim community and other groups from claiming government benefits. Academic freedom is respected.

Authorities uphold freedoms of assembly and association. Thousands of Slovak citizens participated in a protest against government corruption in February 2012. NGOs generally operate without government interference. Labor unions are active, and organized workers freely exercise their right to strike. The government passed a new labor code in August that includes guarantees related to overtime and severance pay, as well as rules on hiring temporary workers; the measures were expected to take effect in 2013.

The constitution provides for an independent judiciary. Despite some reforms pushed through by Radicová's government in 2011, including removing 14 judges accused of processing cases too slowly, the court system continues to suffer from corruption, intimidation of judges, and a significant backlog of cases. Prison conditions meet most international standards, but overcrowding remains a concern. NGOs and members of the Romany community report that Romany suspects are often mistreated by police during arrest and while in custody.

The Roma, who comprise roughly 10 percent of Slovakia's population, continue to experience widespread discrimination, including forced evictions and segregation of Romany children in schools. However, in October 2012, a court in Eastern Slovakia ruled that the segregation of Roma in schools is unlawful. In September, the leader of the far-right Peoples Party–Our Slovakia invited his Facebook friends to help him "clean up" a piece of his land by demolishing the dwellings of Roma squatters; police prevented the event from taking place. Slovakia's first-ever Roma representative, Peter Pollak, was elected to the legislature in March 2012 and later became the government proxy for minorities.

Although women enjoy the same legal rights as men, they continue to be underrepresented in senior-level government and business positions. Domestic violence is punishable by imprisonment but remains widespread. Romany women have been sterilized by doctors without their consent. Slovakia is a source, transit, and destination for the trafficking of men, women, and children for forced labor and prostitution. Bratislava's third annual gay pride parade took place in June 2012, without serious incident. However, one member of parliament from OlaNO called homosexuality "sick" and expressed approval of the Russian government's ban on gay pride parades. The comment prompted Slovakia's LGBT (lesbian, gay, bisexual, transgender) community to call for a ban on hate speech.

Slovenia

Political Rights: 1
Civil Liberties: 1
Status: Free

Population: 2,052,000
Capital: Ljubljana

Ten-Year Ratings Timeline For Year Under Review (Political Rights, Civil Liberties, Status)

2003	2004	2005	2006	2007	2008	2009	2010	2011	2012
1,1F	1,1F	1,1F	1,1F	1,1F	1,1F	1,1F	1,1F	1,1F	1,1F

Overview: Following elections in December 2011, Parliament elected Janez Janša prime minister in January 2012 and approved a new center-right government. In early 2012, the government proposed austerity measures amid a dual economic and banking crisis,

leading to Slovenia's largest public sector strike in 20 years in April. The government approved the measures in May, and by November, was working on further emergency measures to stabilize the economy and avoid an international bailout. Former prime minister Borut Pahor won presidential elections in December.

The territory of modern Slovenia, long ruled by the Austro-Hungarian Empire, became part of the Kingdom of Serbs, Croats, and Slovenes (renamed the Kingdom of Yugoslavia in 1929) after World War I, and a constituent republic of the Socialist Federal Republic of Yugoslavia following World War II. After decades of relative prosperity in Josip Broz Tito's Yugoslavia, various elements in Slovene civil society began to break with the Communist system in the 1980s. In 1990, the Democratic United Opposition defeated the ruling Democratic Renewal Party (previously the Slovene branch of the League of Communists) in democratic elections, although former Communist leader Milan Kucan was elected president. The country declared independence from Yugoslavia in June 1991 and secured its status after a 10-day conflict.

After 1990, center-left governments led Slovenia for more than a decade, with Janez Drnovšek's Liberal Democracy of Slovenia (LDS) dominating the political stage. Drnovšek served as prime minister almost continuously from 1992 to 2002, when he was elected president. In the 2004 parliamentary elections, Janez Janša's center-right Slovenian Democratic Party (SDS) finally unseated the LDS-led government, and Janša became prime minister. Slovenia joined the European Union (EU) and NATO in 2004 and adopted the euro in 2007.

In the 2007 presidential election, Danilo Türk, a law professor and former diplomat, ran as an independent, backed by the Social Democrats (SD) and several other parties. He defeated SDS candidate Alojz Peterle.

In the September 2008 parliamentary elections, the SD captured 29 seats, followed by the SDS with 28. SD leader Borut Pahor became prime minister and formed a coalition government with three smaller parties.

Partly due to the effects of the global economic crisis, the Pahor government weakened in 2010, and the SDS had a strong showing in the October municipal elections. Ghanian-born doctor Peter Bossman was elected mayor of Piran, making him the first black mayor of an Eastern European city.

At the urging of several international economic watchdogs, the government proposed reforms in December 2010 to reduce public debt by increasing the retirement age to 65, implementing pension reform, and cutting social benefits. However, voters rejected the measures in a June 2011 referendum. Faulted for its handling of the economy, Pahor's government fell after a September no-confidence vote. After Parliament failed to elect a new premier, President Türk called early elections for December 4. Ljubljana mayor Zoran Jankovic's center-left Positive Slovenia won with 28 seats, upsetting the SDS, which took 26 seats, followed by the SD with 10. However, Jankovic failed to secure a parliamentary majority to form a government or become prime minister. In January 2012, Parliament elected Janša prime minister and, a month later, approved a new SDS-led coalition government; Positive Slovenia went into opposition.

With Slovenia in recession and its banking industry saddled with over $8 billion in bad loans, concern mounted that it would need an international bailout. In response, Janša's government proposed a range of austerity measures, including cuts to public wages and benefits; the proposal prompted Slovenia's largest public sector strike in 20 years on April 18. The government nonetheless approved the austerity measures in May. It also passed a law, effective from November, enabling the state to buy bad loans.

In a presidential runoff on December 2, former prime minister Pahor defeated Türk with 67.4 percent of the vote to Türk's 32.6 percent. Pahor called for broad political cooperation to tackle the country's economic crisis.

A two-decade border dispute with Croatia—which concerns the delineation of the countries' maritime border in the Bay of Piran, and parts of their common territorial border—remains a key foreign policy issue in Slovenia. In 2009, Pahor and his Croatian counterpart, Jadranka Kosor, agreed that Slovenia would lift its veto of Croatia's EU accession and allow an international arbitration panel to settle the dispute. Following parliamentary approval in both states and a successful 2010 referendum in Slovenia, the Arbitral Tribunal held its first meeting in April 2012. No decision was reached by year's end.

Political Rights and Civil Liberties: Slovenia is an electoral democracy. The country has a bicameral Parliament. Members of the 90-seat National Assembly, which chooses the prime minister, are elected to four-year terms. Members of the 40-seat National Council, a largely advisory body representing professional groups and local interests, are elected to five-year terms. The president is directly elected for up to two five-year terms. One seat each is reserved in the National Assembly for Slovenia's Hungarian and Italian minorities. Roma are automatically given seats on 20 municipal councils.

Corruption, while less extensive than in some other Central European countries, remains a problem in Slovenia, usually taking the form of conflicts of interest and contracting links between government officials and private businesses. Only 5,000 of Slovenia's 80,000 public servants are subject to financial disclosure laws. Prime Minister Janez Janša faces an ongoing bribery investigation from his first term as prime minister, and opposition leader Zoran Jankovic was briefly detained in September 2012 in connection with a corruption probe into the construction of a sports complex. Slovenia was ranked 37 out of 176 countries surveyed in Transparency International's 2012 Corruption Perceptions Index.

Freedoms of speech and the press are constitutionally guaranteed. However, laws that prohibit hate speech and criminalize defamation are in effect. The government maintains stakes in a number of media outlets. In August 2012, Reporters Without Borders condemned a move by Janša's government to dismiss four members of public broadcaster Radio Televizija Slovenija's supervisory board before the expiration of their terms; the four had been appointed by the previous government. Internet access is unrestricted.

The constitution guarantees freedom of religion and contains provisions that prohibit incitement to religious intolerance or discrimination. Approximately 58 percent of Slovenians identify themselves as Roman Catholics. In June 2010, the Constitutional Court annulled certain provisions of the 2007 Religious Freedoms Law, including requirements for legal registration of religious communities and the payment of social security contributions to priests working in prisons and hospitals. Though societal discrimination against the small Muslim community has been problematic in the past, interfaith relations were generally civil during the year. After a 40-year struggle to build a mosque in Ljubljana, a design was selected in November 2011, with construction to begin once the Muslim community finalizes funding. There were no reports of government restrictions on academic freedom during the year.

The government respects freedoms of assembly and association. Numerous nongovernmental organizations operate freely and play a role in policymaking. Workers may establish and join trade unions, strike, and bargain collectively. The Association of Free Trade Unions of Slovenia has some 300,000 members and controls the four trade union seats in the National Council. In April 2012, nearly 80,000 clerks, police officers, doctors, and teachers demonstrated over planned wage and benefit cuts in the country's largest public sector strike in 20 years.

The constitution provides for an independent judiciary, and the government respects judicial freedom. Although the judiciary has an extensive backlog of cases, the government responded with the Lukenda Project, an initiative begun in 2005 to reduce the backlog and subsequently extended until the end of 2012. Prison conditions meet international standards, though overcrowding has been reported. Incitement to racial hatred is a criminal offense. The so-called "erasure" of citizens of the former Yugoslavia remains an issue. More than 25,000 non-Slovene citizens, mostly from other constituent republics within the former federation who had remained in Slovenia after independence, were removed from official records after they failed to apply for citizenship or permanent residency during a brief window of opportunity in 1992. In 2009, Pahor's government began enforcing a 2003 Constitutional Court ruling intended to provide retroactive permanent residency status to those who had been "erased." In March 2010, Parliament adopted legislation to reinstate the legal status of those "erased" in 1992, but implementation has been problematic. In June 2012, the European Court for Human Rights ruled that the "erasures" had been grave human rights violations. Amnesty International urged Slovenian authorities to review the verdict and resolve the thousands of remaining erasure cases. Roma face widespread poverty and societal marginalization.

Women hold the same legal rights as men, but they remain underrepresented in political life and face discrimination in the workplace. There are 29 women in the National Assembly and 3 in the National Council. Domestic violence remains a concern. Prostitution has been decriminalized in Slovenia. Slovenia is a transit point and destination for women and girls trafficked for the purpose of prostitution.

Solomon Islands

Political Rights: 4
Civil Liberties: 3
Status: Partly Free

Population: 552,000
Capital: Honiara

Ten-Year Ratings Timeline For Year Under Review (Political Rights, Civil Liberties, Status)

2003	2004	2005	2006	2007	2008	2009	2010	2011	2012
3,3PF	3,3PF	3,3PF	4,3PF	4,3PF	4,3PF	4,3PF	4,3PF	4,3PF	4,3PF

Overview: In August 2012, Vika Lusibaea, the wife of convicted lawmaker Jimmy Lusibaea, won a by-election to fill his seat in Parliament, becoming the second female parliamentarian in the country's history. In January, the Australian-led Regional Assistance Mission to the Solomon Islands announced a shift in its police activities to training and technical assistance. In October, Prime Minister Gordon Darcy Lilo reshuffled his cabinet in an apparent bid to surviv a no-confidence vote.

The Solomon Islands gained independence from Britain in 1978. Tensions between the two largest ethnic groups—the Gwale and the Malaitans—over jobs and land rights turned into open warfare in 1998. Scores were injured or killed before peace was gradually restored through the 2000 Townsville Peace Agreement, brokered by Australia and New Zealand. A UN mission initially maintained order, while the Australian-led Regional Assistance Mission to the Solomon Islands (RAMSI) has kept the peace since 2003.

In 2007, Derek Sikua was elected prime minister and made political stability a priority in his government. A Truth and Reconciliation Commission, modeled after South Africa's, was launched in 2009 to investigate crimes and address impunity connected to the 1998–2003 violence. In 2010, the commission began its first hearings, during which witnesses told stories of threats, torture, and death. The commission's report was submitted to the prime minister, who by year's end had not yet released it to the public.

In the 2010 general elections, independents won 19 seats, the Solomon Islands Democratic Party captured 13 seats, the Reform Democratic Party (RDP) and the Ownership, Unity, and Responsibility Party each took 3 seats, and smaller parties captured the remainder. RDP leader Danny Philip, who was chosen as the new prime minister, resigned in November 2011 amid allegations of corruption. Parliament selected Philip's former finance minister, Gordon Darcy Lilo, to replace him. In October 2012, Lilo reshuffled his cabinet in what some said was a bid to secure support ahead of a no-confidence motion engineered by Sikua; the motion failed when Sikua did not appear for the vote.

In January 2012, RAMSI announced a scaling back of its police activity, shifting attention to police training and technical assistance. Despite being criticized by some local leaders who disapprove of its foreign influence, a recent poll indicated that 86 percent of the country's residents believe RAMSI should stay in the Solomon Islands. In February, John Michael Langsley, a British national who had worked with RAMSI, was named police commissioner; the position had been vacant since early 2011.

Also in February, foreign minister Peter Shanel Agovaka was fired for holding an unauthorized meeting with his Russian counterpart. Recent Russian offers of developmental assistance to the Solomon Islands have been met with skepticism from many critics, including prime minister Lilo, who believe that Russia has ulterior motives and that the Solomon Islands should instead strengthen ties with traditional partners like Australia, New Zealand, and the United States.

Political Rights and Civil Liberties: The Solomon Islands are not an electoral democracy. Members of the 50-seat, unicameral National Parliament are elected for four-year terms. A parliamentary majority elects the prime minister. A governor-general, appointed on the advice of Parliament for a five-year term, represents the British monarch as head of state. The governor-general appoints the cabinet on the advice of the prime minister.

New parties often form before elections and are disbanded afterward as lawmakers switch allegiance after taking office. Political activity is driven more by personalities and clan identities than party affiliation.

Corruption is rampant, and public offices are seen as opportunities for personal enrichment. Many current and former lawmakers have faced a variety of corruption charges. In 2012, lawmakers decided to give themselves a 4 percent pay raise and to spend $578,000 to buy themselves new vehicles. In October, former prime minister Danny Philip was found guilty of misconduct and fined $540 for having sold government property to a political supporter while he was premier. In January 2012, the government ratified the United Nations Convention Against Corruption.

Freedoms of expression and of the press are generally respected, but politicians and elites sometimes use legal and extralegal means to intimidate journalists. The print media include a privately owned daily, a weekly, and two monthly publications. The government operates the only radio station. There is no local television station, but foreign broadcasts can be received via satellite. Internet use is growing, but access is limited by lack of infrastructure and high costs.

Freedom of religion is generally respected, as is academic freedom.

The constitution guarantees freedom of assembly, and the government generally recognizes this right in practice. Organizers of demonstrations must obtain permits, which are typically granted. Civil society groups operate without interference. Workers are free to organize, and strikes are permitted. In 2012, lawyers, teachers, and health-care workers threatened to strike or resign over pay and work conditions.

Threats against judges and prosecutors have weakened the independence and rigor of the judicial system. Judges and prosecutors have also been implicated in scandals relating to corruption and abuse of power. A lack of resources limits the government's ability to provide legal counsel and timely trials. Victims in rural areas have even less access to the formal justice system. The ombudsman's office has far-reaching powers to investigate complaints of official abuse and unfair treatment, but generally lacks funds to do so. Poor training, abuse of power, and factional and ethnic rivalries are common in the police force.

Discrimination limits the economic and political roles of women. In August

2012, Vika Lusibaea became the second woman elected to Parliament after she won a special by-election to fill a seat left empty by her husband Jimmy Lusibaea, who was sentenced to prison for assault, attempted murder and other crimes committed in 2000. Rape and other forms of abuse against women and girls are widespread. While rape is illegal, no law prohibits domestic violence and marital rape is not a crime. The World Bank ranked the Solomon Islands the worst country in the world for violence against women in 2012, and a United Nations Special Rapporteur on violence against women concluded that existing laws do not offer sufficient protection to women. The Solomon Islands is both a source and destination country for men and women trafficked for the purposes of forced prostitution and labor.

In 2011, the government rejected a call by the United Nations to decriminalize homosexuality, saying that it is against traditional values.

Somalia

Political Rights: 7
Civil Liberties: 7
Status: Not Free

Population: 10,086,000
Capital: Mogadishu

Note: The numerical ratings and status listed above do not reflect conditions in Somaliland, which is examined in a separate report.

Ten-Year Ratings Timeline For Year Under Review (Political Rights, Civil Liberties, Status)

2003	2004	2005	2006	2007	2008	2009	2010	2011	2012
6,7NF	6,7NF	6,7NF	7,7NF	7,7NF	7,7NF	7,7NF	7,7NF	7,7NF	7,7NF

Overview: The African Union force made major strides against the Shabaab—an extremist movement—which was forced from its major strongholds and sources of revenue, and saw a series of defections in 2012. The expiration of the Transitional Federal Institutions ushered in the inauguration of a new constitution, parliament, president, and prime minister in Somalia as the country began its transition toward a permanent government.

Somalia gained independence in 1960 as an amalgam of former British and Italian colonies populated largely by ethnic Somalis. A 1969 coup by General Siad Barre led to two decades of instability, civil strife, and the manipulation of clan loyalties for political purposes. After Barre's regime was finally toppled in 1991, the country descended into warfare between clan-based militias for over two decades.

Famine and fighting killed approximately 300,000 people in 1991 and 1992, prompting a UN humanitarian mission led by U.S. forces. The intervention soon deteriorated into urban guerrilla warfare with Somali militias. Over 100 UN peacekeepers, including 18 U.S. soldiers, were killed. The international community withdrew, largely turning its back on Somalia's civil strife for the next decade.

Attempts to revitalize the political process began in 2000 with a peace conference in Djibouti, where many of Somalia's factional leaders agreed to participate in a three-year transitional government. While this initiative quickly unraveled, a fresh effort in 2004 resulted in the establishment of a 275-seat Transitional Federal Assembly (TFA), in which the leading clans took an equal number of seats, and a new Transitional Federal Government (TFG). That year, TFA members elected the Ethiopian-backed warlord Abdullahi Yusuf Ahmed to serve a five-year term as president. Divisions soon emerged within the TFG between his supporters and an alliance of Islamists and clan leaders. The Islamic Courts Union (ICU), a broad coalition of Islamists, eventually emerged as the dominant force within Mogadishu, and the group gained control of most of southern Somalia during 2006. The TFG retreated to the town of Baidoa, north of Mogadishu. Meanwhile, hard-liners within the ICU, backed by Eritrea, grew increasingly hostile toward neighboring Ethiopia. With tacit U.S. support, Ethiopia invaded Somalia to oust the ICU in December 2006, forcing the Islamists to the extreme south of the country.

The departure of the ICU prompted an insurgency against the Ethiopian-backed TFG by groups including the Shabaab, a radical ICU faction. All sides in the conflict committed severe human rights abuses, and as many as 400,000 people were displaced from Mogadishu in 2007.

Hopes for a political breakthrough were raised when a group of moderate exiled ICU leaders joined forces with non-Islamist opposition members to form the Alliance for the Reliberation of Somalia (ARS). UN-sponsored negotiations between the TFG and a faction of the ARS led to a 2008 power-sharing arrangement that doubled the size of the TFA. The Shabaab did not participate in negotiations and vowed to fight on. Ethiopian forces withdrew from Somalia in early 2009, and the expanded TFA was sworn in, electing the chairman of the ARS, Sheikh Sharif Sheikh Ahmed, as its new president.

Rampant corruption and infighting among the TFG's leaders paralyzed government business and destroyed much of the TFG's credibility. Prime Minister Omar Abdirashid Ali Sharmarke resigned in September 2010, and his replacement, Mohamed Abdullahi Mohamed, became embroiled in a dispute between President Sharif and the Speaker of parliament over whether to extend the mandates of the Transitional Federal Institutions, which were due to expire in August 2011. Under a deal negotiated by Uganda in June of 2011, Mohamed was fired, and the president, the Speaker, and his deputies had their terms extended until August 2012. A new prime minister, Abdiweli Mohamed Ali, was appointed.

Insurgents kept up their attacks, led by the Shabaab, which declared a formal alliance with al-Qaeda at the start of 2010. Mogadishu was the epicenter of the fighting; at least 2,000 civilians were killed there in 2010, including 5 government officials and 6 members of parliament, who were caught up in an attack on a hotel.

Despite ongoing assaults, the Shabaab was unable to oust the TFG from Mogadishu, which relied upon a contingent of African Union (AU) troops to shift the momentum in its favor. The African Union Mission in Somalia (AMISOM) forced the Shabaab into what it described as a "tactical withdrawal" from Mogadishu in August 2011. The Shabaab was under increasing strain, deeply unpopular with the public, militarily weak, and undermined by internal splits. It came under further pressure in October 2011, when in response to a series of kidnappings across its border, Kenyan troops invaded southern Somalia. Ethiopian forces entered Somali territory from the west, squeezing the area under direct control of the Shabaab. In February 2012, the UN Security Council, which authorizes and largely funds the AMISOM mission, unanimously approved a troop surge, bringing the total force to 17,731. The Shabaab's losses grew as the year progressed as AMISOM forces slowly gained control over its remaining strongholds and defections increased. By late September 2012, the Shabaab had retreated from the city of Kismayo, its final significant stronghold, whose port was a major source of revenue.

In August 2012, a meeting of the country's National Constituent Assembly, consisting of clan elders and local leaders, youth, and women, overwhelmingly passed a new constitution by a margin of 621-13, though the security situation did not allow for them to put the document to a national vote. Clan elders subsequently selected a 275-member parliament. In September, Hassan Sheikh Mohamud became the first president chosen on the country's soil since the beginning of the 21-year civil war. The parliament's selection of Mohamud—a relative political novice—and Ahmed's immediate acceptance of the result were seen as positive signs, though several allegations of corruption and fraud were documented during the election process. Al Jazeera reported that votes were bought and sold for payments as high as $50,000. In October, President Mohamud appointed, and parliament approved, Abdi Farah Shirdon as prime minister, and a new cabinet was sworn in in November. The new government was the target of increasing terrorist violence. A suicide bombing targeted Mohamud two days into his new role, and unknown gunmen shot and killed new member of parliament Mustafa Haji Maalim in front his home in September.

The crisis in Somalia was exacerbated in 2011 by the Horn of Africa's worst drought in six decades, which combined with the absence of security and a functioning government to create a humanitarian emergency. The Shabaab impeded efforts to assist the victims, banning 16 international organizations from operating in areas under its control in November 2011. Although conditions began to improve in 2012, more than 2 million people faced food insecurity at crisis levels through December.

The security situation continued to fluctuate in the semiautonomous region of Puntland in northeastern Somalia where the authorities struggled to contain pro-Shabaab militias in the Galgala Mountains in the Bari region. While pirates used Somalia as a launch pad for attacks, the number of attacks declined by 65 percent in 2012 to the lowest level since 2009. According to the EU Naval Force-Somalia, there were 35 attacks in 2012, down from 176 the previous year. The last successful hijacking in the region occurred in May 2012.

Political Rights and Civil Liberties: Somalia is not an electoral democracy. Prior to the expiration of the TFI and the appointment of the new president and prime minister, the state largely ceased to exist in most respects and had no governing authority with the ability to protect political rights and civil liberties. The TFG, though recognized internationally, was deeply unpopular domestically, and its actual territorial control was minimal. Though the country is now transitioning to more permanent governing institutions, the government still retains little control of the territory and has little capacity to govern beyond Mogadishu. No effective political parties yet exist, and the political process continues to be driven by clan loyalty.

Since 1991, the northwestern region of Somaliland has functioned with relative stability as a self-declared independent state, though it has not received international recognition. The region of Puntland has declared a temporary secession until Somalia is stabilized, although calls for full independence have been on the rise. Elections for Puntland's 66-member legislature were held in 2008. The new parliament elected Abdirahman Muhammad Mahmud "Farole" for a four-year term as president in January 2009. The result was seen as a fair reflection of the will of the legislature, and power was transferred peacefully from the defeated incumbent. The Puntland authority briefly broke off cooperation with the TFG in 2011 in frustration at the underrepresentation of its interests in Mogadishu; the two sides reconciled at a conference the same year, but relations remain tense.

Corruption in Somalia is rampant, especially among TFG officials and parliamentarians. A leaked report of the UN Monitoring Group on Somalia and Eritrea suggested that 70 percent of revenues to Somalia between 2009 and 2010 were unaccounted for, and that up to 25 percent of total TFG expenditures in 2011 occurred within the offices of the president, prime minister, and speaker of parliament. TFG-affiliated militias in Mogadishu diverted emergency food aid meant for victims of Somalia's famine in 2011. Corruption is also pervasive in Puntland, where the authorities have been complicit in piracy. Somalia was ranked 174 out of 176 countries surveyed in Transparency International's 2012 Corruption Perceptions Index.

The new constitution calls for freedoms of speech and the press, though Somalia is one of the most dangerous countries in the world for journalists. According to Reporters Without Borders, 17 media workers were killed in Somalia in 2012, many at the hands of the Shabaab or unknown gunmen. The last of these incidents occurred in October, when well-known Radio Kulmiye satirist Warsame Shire Awale was killed in Mogadishu after his on-air parody of the Shabaab. He was the fifth Radio Kulmiye victim in 2012. Radio is the primary news medium in Somalia. Internet and mobile telephone services are widely available in large cities, though poverty, illiteracy, and displacement limit access to these resources.

Freedom of assembly and the press were also seriously stifled in Puntland in 2012. After a round of protests in September—which sought to draw attention to perceived moves by Puntland's president Farole to postpone the January 2013 elections and extend his term by one year—Farole threatened to prosecute opposition, including "failed politicians and so called websites and media" for "supporting Puntland's enemies." In November, presidential guards fired on unarmed protestors and journalists in Gardo, resulting in at least four injuries. In early 2013, it was announced that the president's term would be extended to January 2014.

Nearly all Somalis are Sunni Muslims, but there is a very small Christian community. Both Somalia's new constitution and Puntland's charter recognize Islam as the official religion, though the constitution does include religious freedom clauses. The Shabaab has imposed crude versions of Islamic law in areas under its control, banning music, films, certain clothing, and in one area prohibiting men and women from walking together or talking in public. Anyone accused of apostasy risks execution. According to Compass Direct, a Christian nongovernmental organization (NGO) that tracks religious persecution, Zakaria Hussein Omar, a Christian, was publicly executed by the Shabaab outside Mogadishu after being accused of working for a banned Christian humanitarian organization in January 2012. The Shabaab has also denied religious freedom to moderate Muslims and caused deep offense among many Somalis by destroying the graves of Sufi saints. The education system is severely degraded due to the breakdown of the state.

Freedom of assembly is not respected amid the ongoing violence. Many NGOs and UN agencies operating in Somalia have reduced or suspended their activities. In October 2012, Shabaab banned Islamic Relief, one of the few remaining aid organizations, claiming it was "covertly extending the operations of banned organizations." According to the Aid Worker Security Database, in 2012 alone, nine aid workers were killed, one was wounded, and four were kidnapped, including two international aid workers. In January, two aid workers abducted in October 2011 by Somali pirates were rescued by a team of American Navy SEALs. In August 2012, a representative of the UN Food and Agricultural Organization was killed in Marka, in southern Somalia. The Shabaab has blocked or impeded international aid agencies from getting supplies to food insecure regions.

Existing labor laws are not adequately enforced. With the exception of a journalists' association, unions in the country are not active.

There is no judicial system functioning effectively at the national level. The new constitution offers a judicial framework that includes the creation of a Constitutional Court, federal government courts, and federal member state courts, though these institutions have yet to be established. TFG authorities administered a mix of Sharia (Islamic law) and traditional Somali forms of justice and reconciliation. The harshest codes are enforced in areas under the control of the Shabaab, where people convicted of theft or other minor crimes are flogged or have their limbs amputated, usually in public. Independent monitors have been denied access to the detention facility run by the TFG's National Security Agency in Mogadishu, where interrogations of Shabaab suspects take place.

The rights of Somali citizens are routinely abused by the various warring factions. The TFG, the AU, and insurgent groups have fired shells indiscriminately into neighborhoods in Mogadishu. Children make up a large proportion of the civilian casualties. According to Amnesty International, both the TFG and the Shabaab have unlawfully recruited child soldiers, some as young as eight. The new constitution includes a section on the rights of children, which outlaws the use of children in armed conflict. By restricting the movement of the population in the drought-hit areas it controls, the Shabaab has exposed hundreds of thousands of people to the risk of starvation.

Most Somalis share the same ethnicity, but clan divisions have long fueled violence in the country. The larger, more powerful clans continue to dominate political life and are able to use their strength to harass weaker clans.

Women in Somalia face considerable discrimination. Although outlawed under the new constitution, female genital mutilation is still practiced in some form on nearly all Somali girls. Sexual violence is rampant due to lawlessness and impunity for perpetrators, and rape victims are often stigmatized. The new constitution outlines the expectation that women be included in all branches of government and includes a nondiscrimination clause that makes specific mention of women. As of August 2012, 30 members of Somalia's new parliament were female, about half of the 30 percent country's new quota.

South Africa

Political Rights: 2
Civil Liberties: 2
Status: Free

Population: 51,147,000
Capital: Tshwane/Pretoria

Ten-Year Ratings Timeline For Year Under Review (Political Rights, Civil Liberties, Status)

2003	2004	2005	2006	2007	2008	2009	2010	2011	2012
1,2F	1,2F	1,2F	2,2F	2,2F	2,2F	2,2F	2,2F	2,2F	2,2F

Overview:
Following a heated leadership battle within the ruling African National Congress (ANC) and a related increase in political violence, President Jacob Zuma was reelected as president of the ruling party in December 2012, putting him in prime position to win a second term as state president in 2014. Also during the year, South Africa was rocked by a wave of violent strikes in the mining, agricultural, and transport sectors that resulted in over 50 deaths, including the August killing of 34 mineworkers by police near Marikana.

In 1910, the Union of South Africa was created as a self-governing dominion of the British Empire. The Afrikaner-dominated National Party (NP) came to power in 1948 on a platform of institutionalized racial separation, or "apartheid," designed to maintain white minority rule. Facing growing British and regional pressure to end apartheid, South Africa declared formal independence in 1961 and withdrew from the Commonwealth. The NP went on to govern South Africa under the apartheid system for 33 years. Mounting domestic and international pressure prompted President F. W. de Klerk to legalize the antiapartheid African National Congress (ANC) and release ANC leader Nelson Mandela from prison in 1990. Between then and the first multiracial elections in 1994, almost all apartheid-related legislation was abolished, and an interim constitution was negotiated and enacted.

The ANC won the 1994 elections in a landslide, and Mandela was elected president by the National Assembly, the lower house of Parliament. As required by the interim constitution, a national unity government was formed, including the ANC, the NP, and the Zulu-nationalist Inkatha Freedom Party (IFP). A Constitutional Assembly produced a permanent constitution, which was signed into law in 1996. The ANC claimed almost two-thirds of the vote in 1999 elections, and Thabo Mbeki, Mandela's successor as head of the ANC, won the presidency. In 2004 balloting, the ANC won nearly 70 percent of the national vote and majorities in seven of nine provincial legislatures. Mbeki easily secured a second five-year term.

In late 2007, former deputy president Jacob Zuma defeated Mbeki in a heated battle for the ANC presidency; Mbeki had sacked Zuma in 2005 after he was implicated in the corruption trial of his financial adviser, Schabir Shaik. Relations between the ANC and Mbeki's government were strained throughout 2008, and in September—after the remaining corruption charges against Zuma were set aside due to prosecutorial misconduct—the ANC's national executive committee forced Mbeki to resign as state president. The party nominated its deputy president, Kgalema Motlanthe, to serve as interim state president, and he was quickly confirmed by the National Assembly. After Mbeki's ouster, recently resigned defense minister Mosiuoa "Terror" Lekota quit the ANC and formed the opposition Congress of the People (COPE) party; he was joined by a series of ANC leaders, nearly all of them Mbeki allies.

Despite new competition from COPE, the ANC won another sweeping victory in the April 2009 elections, taking 65.9 percent of the national vote, 264 seats in the 400-seat National Assembly, and clear majorities in eight of nine provinces. The Democratic Alliance (DA) remained the largest opposition party, winning 67 National Assembly seats and outright control of Western Cape Province. COPE won 30 seats, and the IFP took 18. Zuma was easily elected state president by the National Assembly the following month, winning 277 of the 400 votes.

The ANC won 62 percent of the vote in May 2011 municipal elections, while the DA took just under 24 percent, including outright control of Cape Town and 11 of 24 municipalities in the Western Cape. The ANC won the vast majority of municipalities in every other province. The IFP secured just over 3.5 percent of the vote, and COPE took just over 2 percent.

Another leadership battle within the ANC—this time pitting Zuma against backers of Deputy President Motlanthe—dominated politics in 2012. Although Zuma defeated Motlanthe decisively at the party's December conference at Mangaung, the run-up to the gathering was marked by significant political violence and allegations of fraud and vote-buying. Court challenges by ANC members from Free State and North West Provinces disqualified some Free State delegates from voting. The prominent ANC figure and business tycoon Cyril Ramaphosa, a former labor leader, was elected deputy president of the party, replacing Motlanthe, who remained deputy president of the republic at year's end.

Also during the year, police killed 34 striking mineworkers during a violent confrontation near Marikana in August, marking the worst incident of state violence in the postapartheid era. Earlier clashes between rival unions had left 10 dead, and subsequent violence during a spate of wildcat strikes resulted in at least another 6 fatalities and scores of injuries. A government-sponsored inquiry into the violence at Marikana was pending at year's end.

Political Rights and Civil Liberties: South Africa is an electoral democracy. Elections for the 400-seat National Assembly, the lower house of the bicameral Parliament, are determined by party-list proportional representation. The 90 members of the upper chamber, the National Council of Provinces (NCOP), are selected by the provincial legislatures. The National Assembly elects the president to serve concurrently with its five-year term, and presidents can serve a maximum of two terms.

The ANC, which is part of a tripartite governing alliance with the Congress of South African Trade Unions (COSATU) and the South African Communist Party, dominates the political landscape. The DA is the leading opposition party, followed by COPE and the IFP. Factionalism within the ANC and COSATU, as well as tensions between the alliance partners, has been a hallmark of South African politics in recent years and was especially pronounced in advance of the ANC's December 2012 conference. Political violence marked ANC nomination contests in North

West, Mpumalanga, and most severely in Kwa-Zulu Natal, where at least 38 ANC members were killed in 2011 and 2012, along with at least 13 other political killings in that province. Meanwhile, allegations of "ghost voters" and vote-buying delayed ANC nominations at conferences in Limpopo, North West, and Western Cape. In December, the Constitutional Court (CC) ruled the election of the ANC's Free State executive committee null and void, disqualifying those delegates from voting at the national conference.

Several agencies are tasked with combating corruption, but enforcement is inadequate. Public servants regularly fail to declare their business interests as required by law, and the ANC has been criticized for charging fees to business leaders for access to top government officials. The tender process for public contracts is often politically driven and opaque, while the delivery of government services is undermined by maladministration. In an especially notable example from 2012, textbooks destined for schoolchildren in Limpopo were dumped as part of a wide-ranging corruption scandal. President Jacob Zuma, who was charged with corruption three times between 2005 and 2009 in connection with the so-called arms deal scandal, continued to face scrutiny in 2012 over past charges and his use of state funds to build a homestead near Nkandla. A Zuma-appointed commission to reinvestigate the arms-deal scandal ran into a number of obstacles in 2012, including accusations of bias and corruption against the panel's head, Judge Willie Seriti. South Africa was ranked 69 out of 176 countries surveyed in Transparency International's 2012 Corruption Perceptions Index.

Freedoms of expression and the press are protected in the constitution and generally respected in practice, though press freedom has deteriorated in recent years. A number of private newspapers and magazines are sharply critical of powerful figures and institutions. Most South Africans receive the news via radio outlets, a majority of which are controlled by the South African Broadcasting Corporation (SABC). The SABC also dominates the television market, but two commercial stations are expanding their reach. Internet access is unrestricted and growing rapidly, though many South Africans cannot afford the service fee.

The government is highly sensitive to media criticism and has increasingly encroached on the editorial independence of the SABC. Some government critics have been barred from SABC programs, and a number of documentaries and specials produced by the broadcaster have been canceled due to political considerations. In December 2012, editors at the SABC radio station Metro FM quashed an interview about the ANC national conference with three political journalists because no ANC representative was present. The government has also recently enacted or proposed several potentially restrictive laws. In September 2012, the CC found sections of the 2009 Film and Publications Amendment Act that require prepublication classification of material dealing with "sexual conduct" to be unconstitutional; the act obliged any publisher not recognized by the press ombudsman to submit potentially pornographic or violence-inciting materials to a government board for approval.

The National Assembly passed the controversial Protection of Information Bill in 2011, allowing state agencies to classify a wide range of information as in the "national interest" and thus subject to significant restrictions on publication. Vociferous objections from civic groups and opposition parties forced the government to amend the legislation. The NCOP passed a revised version in November 2012 that removed a clause criminalizing the disclosure of information about state security, though the bill still did not allow a "public interest" defense for violations. The amended measure awaited review by the lower house at year's end.

In recent years, government officials have used gag orders to block reporting on alleged corruption, and journalists are occasionally subject to harassment and legal action. Three *Mail & Guardian* reporters are still facing criminal charges for their November 2011 investigation into allegedly corrupt dealings by Zuma's spokesman, Mac Maharaj, which was censored by legal order. Journalists' coverage of wildcat mining strikes in August and September 2012 were occasionally inhibited by security forces.

Freedom of religion and academic freedom are constitutionally guaranteed and actively protected by the government.

Freedoms of association and peaceful assembly are secured by the constitution. South Africa hosts a vibrant civil society. Nongovernmental organizations (NGOs) can register and operate freely, and lawmakers regularly accept input from NGOs on pending legislation. Freedom of assembly is generally respected, and South Africa has a vibrant protest culture; demonstrators must notify police ahead of time but are rarely prohibited from gathering. In recent years, however, a growing number of community protests over public service delivery have turned violent and been forcibly dispersed by police. In September 2012, the government deployed security forces and banned all demonstrations in the Marikana and Rustenberg areas to contain a spate of violent marches and wildcat strikes following the previous month's fatal confrontation between strikers and police at a Marikana mine operated by the London-based firm Lonmin. In the process, some nonviolent protests were forcibly broken up by police. Police also conducted a number of raids in nearby informal settlements to confiscate weapons from strikers and their supporters.

South Africans are free to form, join, and participate in independent trade unions, and the country's labor laws offer unionized workers a litany of protections; contract workers and those in the informal sector enjoy fewer safeguards. COSATU, the nation's largest trade union federation, claims about two million members. Strike activity is very common, and unionized workers often secure above-inflation wage increases. Strikes are increasingly violent; the wildcat strikes in the mining sector during 2012 resulted in at least 50 deaths and massive damage to the economy. In September, the South African Transport and Allied Workers Union (SATWAU) and other unions staged a legal three-week strike that turned violent, leaving one worker dead and several injured. In November, wildcat strikes by vineyard workers in the Western Cape resulted in one death and the temporary deployment of police to the de Doorns area.

Judicial independence is guaranteed by the constitution, and the courts—particularly the CC and the Supreme Court—operate with substantial autonomy. Nevertheless, judicial and prosecutorial independence has come under pressure in recent years amid the Zuma corruption cases, prompting several instances of judicial and political misconduct. In a positive step for judicial independence, Parliament in September 2012 approved a 17th amendment to the constitution, making the CC the apex court and the Supreme Court of Appeal a general appellate court. An accompanying Superior Court Bill made the CC chief justice—and not the justice minister—South Africa's chief judicial authority. In October, the CC confirmed lower court rulings that Zuma's appointment of an ally, Menzi Simelane, as head of the National Prosecuting Authority (NPA) was invalid because Simelane gave dishonest testimony to a commission investigating former NPA head Vusi Pikoli.

Judicial staff and resource shortages undermine defendants' procedural rights, including the rights to a timely trial and state-funded legal counsel. Pretrial detainees, who make up 30 percent of the prison population, wait an average of three months before trial, and some wait up to two years. Lower courts have proven more susceptible to corruption than the higher panels, and there have been reports of physical intimidation of judges and magistrates.

Despite constitutional prohibitions and government countermeasures, there have been many reports of police torture and excessive force during arrest, interrogation, and detention. Prisons often feature overcrowding, inadequate health care, and abuse of inmates by staff or other prisoners; both HIV/AIDS and tuberculosis are problems. The Judicial Inspectorate for Correctional Services (JICS) investigates prisoners' complaints but has limited resources and capacity. A October 2012 JICS report found that 17 percent of prison assaults are committed by guards, and that of 71 complaints of abuse in 2011–12, only 1 resulted in disciplinary action. The government paid out R1.3 billion ($161 million) to compensate prisoners and families for assaults and rape during the report's coverage period, but prevention programs are almost nonexistent.

South Africa has one of the highest rates of violent crime in the world. As in 2011, however, rates of murder, attempted murder, armed robbery, and carjacking declined significantly in 2012. The Zuma administration has given the police more latitude to use force against criminals. Mostly due to police incapacity, vigilantism is a problem.

The constitution prohibits discrimination based on a range of categories, including race, sexual orientation, and culture. State bodies such as the South African Human Rights Commission and the Office of the Public Protector are empowered to investigate and prosecute cases of discrimination. Affirmative-action legislation has benefited previously disadvantaged groups (defined as "Africans," "Coloureds," "Asians," and as of 2008, "Chinese") in public and private employment as well as in education. Racial imbalances in the workforce persist, and a majority of the country's business assets remain white owned. The government's Black Economic Empowerment program aims to increase the black stake in the economy, mostly by establishing race-based ownership thresholds for government tenders and licenses.

Increased illegal immigration, particularly from Zimbabwe, Mozambique, and Somalia, has spurred xenophobic violence by police and vigilantes. Sporadic attacks occurred in 2012, often tied to wider service-delivery protests in which immigrants were scapegoated.

The number of foreign nationals in South Africa is contested, with estimates ranging from two to seven million, including between one and three million Zimbabweans. Although the country had a backlog of over 400,000 asylum applications by the end of 2012, the government closed three of seven refugee reception offices during the year. The 2011 Immigration Amendment Act reduced the period asylum seekers have to make a formal application at refugee reception centers after entering the country, from 14 days to 5 days; also that year, the government resumed deportations of Zimbabwean migrants, which had been halted in 2009. About 40,000

Zimbabweans were deported in 2012, including 600 unaccompanied minors. Conditions at migrant detention centers are poor, and deportees are subject to physical and sexual abuse by police and immigration officers.

Separately, the nomadic Khoikhoi and Khomani San peoples, indigenous to South Africa, suffer from social and legal discrimination.

South Africa has one of the world's most liberal legal environments for LGBT (lesbian, gay, bisexual, and transgender) people. The 2006 Civil Unions Act legalized same-sex marriage, and a 2002 Constitutional Court ruling held that gay couples should be allowed to adopt children. Nevertheless, societal bias remains strong. LGBT people are routinely subject to physical attacks, including an increase in instances of so-called corrective rape, in which lesbians are raped by men who believe this can change the victim's sexual orientation.

The state generally protects citizens from arbitrary deprivation of property. However, some 80 percent of farmland is owned by white South Africans, who make up 14 percent of the population. As a result, thousands of black and colored farmworkers suffer from insecure tenure rights; illegal squatting on white-owned farms is a serious problem, as are attacks on white owners. The government has vowed to transfer 30 percent of land to black owners by 2014; however, only about 6 percent of land had been transferred by the end of 2011, and about 90 percent of the redistributed farms had failed or were failing, according to the Ministry for Land Reform and Rural Development. In 2012, the ANC resolved to replace the government's "willing buyer, willing seller" approach to land reform with a more aggressive "just and equitable" approach, although the details of transfer and compensation under such a framework have not been articulated. The government will complete a long-awaited audit of land ownership in early 2013.

Equal rights for women are guaranteed by the constitution and promoted by the Commission on Gender Equality. While the constitution allows the option and practice of customary law, it does not allow such law to supersede women's rights as citizens. Nevertheless, women suffer de facto discrimination with regard to marriage (including forced marriage), divorce, inheritance, and property rights, particularly in rural areas. A draft Traditional Courts Bill, set for a vote in Parliament in 2013, would strengthen the legal authority of traditional leaders, sparking concerns among civic groups about women's rights. Despite a robust legal framework criminalizing domestic violence and rape, both are extremely grave problems. South Africa has one of the world's highest rates of sexual abuse, although the reported rate of "sexual offenses" declined by 3.7 percent in 2012, and rape declined by 1.9 percent. About 60,000 women reported having been raped in 2012, with many more cases likely going unreported. Women are also subject to sexual harassment and wage discrimination in the workplace, and are not well represented in top management positions. Women are better represented in government, holding some 42 percent of the seats in the National Assembly and leading five of nine provincial governments. The main opposition DA party is led by Helen Zille, the premier of Western Cape Province.

South Korea

Political Rights: 1
Civil Liberties: 2
Status: Free

Population: 48,906,300
Capital: Seoul

Ten-Year Ratings Timeline For Year Under Review (Political Rights, Civil Liberties, Status)

2003	2004	2005	2006	2007	2008	2009	2010	2011	2012
2,2F	1,2F	1,2F	1,2F	1,2F	1,2F	1,2F	1,2F	1,2F	1,2F

Overview: The Saenuri Party secured the largest number of seats in the April 2012 legislative elections, while in December, the Saenuri Party's Park Guen-hye was elected the first female president in the country's history. Several political and corruption scandals, especially within the Lee Myung-bak administration, occurred throughout the year. Meanwhile, tensions with North Korea increased, as the North launched a rocket that successfully sent a satellite into orbit, causing many to fear growing missile and warhead capabilities.

The Republic of Korea (ROK) was established on the southern portion of the Korean Peninsula in 1948, three years after the Allied victory in World War II ended Japan's 35-year occupation. U.S. and Soviet forces divided the peninsula between them as a condition of Japan's surrender. The subsequent Korean War (1950–53) pitted the U.S.- and UN-backed ROK, or South Korea, against the Soviet- and Chinese-backed Democratic People's Republic of Korea, or North Korea, and left some 3 million Koreans dead or wounded. In the decades following the 1953 armistice, South Korea's mainly military rulers crushed dissent and maintained tight control over society in response to the continuing threat from the North. During this period, South Korea's export-led industrialization drive transformed the poor, agrarian country into one of the world's leading economies.

South Korea began its democratic transition in 1987, when military strongman Chun Doo-hwan allowed direct presidential elections. In the December balloting, Chun's ally and fellow general Roh Tae-woo defeated the country's two best-known dissidents, Kim Young-sam and Kim Dae-jung.

After joining the ruling party in 1990, Kim Young-sam won the 1992 presidential election, becoming South Korea's first civilian president since 1961. He sacked hard-line military officers, curbed domestic security services, and successfully prosecuted Chun and Roh for corruption and treason. Kim Dae-jung was elected president in 1997.

Kim Dae-jung's efforts to reach out to North Korea culminated in a historic Inter-Korean summit in 2000 with North Korean leader Kim Jong-il. Roh Moo-hyun, a human rights lawyer and former cabinet minister, won the 2002 presidential election on the ruling liberal party's ticket facing an economic slowdown, an opposition-led parliament, and North Korea's revival of its nuclear weapons program. Former Seoul mayor Lee Myung-bak of the conservative Grand National Party (GNP) won the 2007 presidential election. The GNP also won the majority of seats in the 2008 parliamentary elections.

Lee focused on strengthening relations with the United States while taking a hard line against North Korea. Although the president and his party were heavily criticized for their alleged "authoritarian style" of governance, aggressive fiscal intervention and heavy spending enabled the Lee administration to stabilize the financial sector, prevent massive layoffs, and engineer an economic recovery after the 2008 global financial crisis.

Tensions with North Korea increased starting in April 2009 after Pyongyang withdrew from the Six-Party Talks on its nuclear weapons program and tested a long-range missile, followed by another nuclear test in May. Then, in March 2010, the North allegedly torpedoed the South Korean naval vessel Cheonan, killing 46 crew members. In response to joint U.S.–South Korean live-fire naval exercises in November 2010, North Korea launched a surprise attack on South Korea's Yeonpyeong Island. The South mounted an hour-long counterattack, causing a number of South Korean casualties, including the first civilian deaths since the Korean War. Renewed Inter-Korean talks in February 2011 made little progress.

On October 12, 2011, the U.S. Congress ratified the Korea–United States Free Trade Agreement (KORUS FTA). After heated debate, the Korean National Assembly ratified it on November 22, 2011, and it went into effect on March 15, 2012. Also in November, South Korea, Japan, and the United States reaffirmed their commitment to cooperate in their dealings with North Korea.

In the April 11, 2012, National Assembly elections, the Saenuri Party won 152 seats, while the Democratic United Party (DUP) took 127 seats. The United Progressive Party (UPP) captured 13 seats, the Liberty Forward Party took 5 seats, and independent candidates won 3 seats. Just days later, North Korea's attempt to launch a communications satellite to celebrate the centenary of Kim Il-sung's birth failed. South Korea and the international community viewed the launch as a test of the North's long-range ballistic missiles, prohibited under UN Security Council resolutions, and a nullification of the US-DPRK agreement concluded just weeks beforehand.

In August, President Lee made an unprecedented visit to the disputed Dokdo/Takeshima Island, reigniting nationalistic tensions with Japan, which claims the island for itself. Japan responded by temporarily recalling its ambassador to Seoul.

In the December 19 presidential election, the Saenuri Party's Park Geun-hye, the daughter of former president Park Chung-hee (1961-1979), defeated DUP candidate and former human rights lawyer Moon Jae-in, 52 percent to 48 percent. Park, who had publicly apologized for her father's legacy as a brutal dictator, became the first female president in the nation's history.

North Korean provocations increased in 2012, including skirmishes along the disputed Northern Limit Line that divides Northern from Southern waters. A successful North Korean rocket launch on December 12 alarmed South Korea and many in the international community, who expressed concern that the launch was indicative of continued missile and warhead development and posed serious security threats both in the region and to the United States.

Political Rights and Civil Liberties: South Korea is an electoral democracy. The 1988 constitution vests executive power in a directly elected president, who is limited to a single five-year term. Of the unicameral National Assembly's 300 members, 246 are elected in single-member districts and 54 are chosen through proportional representation, all for four-year terms. Political pluralism is robust, with multiple parties competing for power.

Despite the overall health of the political system, bribery, influence peddling, and extortion remain in politics, business, and everyday life. In December 2011, Kwak No-hyun, Seoul's education superintendent, was indicted for paying 200 million won ($178,842) to a fellow liberal candidate to withdraw from the 2010 election. A regional Seoul court in January 2012 fined him 30 million won ($26,850) for violating the election law, but a Seoul appellate court sentenced him to a year in prison, finding the regional court's fine too light. The Supreme Court upheld the ruling in September, stripping him of his post. In February 2012, the Speaker of South Korea's National Assembly, Park Hee-tae, resigned after allegations surfaced that he had obtained his post through bribery. A month before the April 2012 general elections, Lee Jung-hee, co-chair of the UPP, withdrew from the race for trying to rig the primary outcome against her DUP rival. In September, Choi See-joong, one of President Lee's closest advisers and former chairman of the Korea Communications Commission, was arrested for accepting bribes from a real estate developer and sentenced to two and a half years in prison and a fine of 600 million won ($537,000). South Korea was ranked 45 out of 176 countries surveyed in Transparency International's 2012 Corruption Perceptions Index.

The news media are free and competitive. Newspapers are privately owned and report aggressively on government policies and alleged official and corporate wrongdoing. Although media censorship is illegal, official censorship, particularly of online content, increased under Lee Myung-bak's administration. Reporters Without Borders has listed South Korea as a country "under surveillance" in its "Enemies of the Internet" report. Under the National Security Law, enacted in 1948 to prevent espionage and other threats from the North, listening to North Korean radio is illegal, as is posting pro-North messages online; authorities have deleted tens of thousands of web posts deemed to be pro-North. The United Nations Human Rights Commission and Amnesty International have called for the law to be scaled back or repealed, insisting that its broadly written provisions are being abused to silence political opposition. The government has also attempted to influence reporting by media outlets and has interfered with the management of major broadcast media. In July 2012, the labor union of Munhwa Broadcasting Corporation ended a 170-day strike of almost 700 employees that started in January over complaints that network president Kim Jae-chul demanded that news reports be favorable to the Lee administration. Striking workers called for Kim Jae-chul's resignation; he had not stepped down as of year's end.

The constitution provides for freedom of religion. However, Buddhist groups have accused the Lee government of religious bias.

Academic freedom is unrestricted, though the National Security Law limits statements supporting the North Korean regime or communism. A January 2012 students' rights ordinance for all Seoul-based elementary, middle, and high schools bans corporal punishment and discrimination against students on the basis of gender, religion, age, race, sexual identity, or pregnancy and allows students to stage rallies. A related teachers' rights ordinance was also announced. The Ministry of Education, Science and Technology filed a lawsuit with the Supreme Court challenging the ordinance and filed an injunction to suspend its implementation, which the Supreme Court did in November. No further decisions on the two ordinances had been reached by the end of the year.

The government generally respects citizens' right to privacy. An Anti-Wiretap Law sets the conditions under which the government may monitor telephone calls, mail, and e-mail. In March 2012, the Korean Broadcasting System reported that it had obtained 2,691 reports written by officials of the prime minister's public ethics office evidencing illegal surveillance of a number of people, mostly those critical of the Lee administration, from 2009–2012. Although the public ethics office may legally monitor the government, these reports dealt mostly with personal information and attitudes towards the Lee administration. Travel both within South Korea and abroad is unrestricted, except for travel to North Korea, which requires government approval.

South Korea respects freedom of assembly, but police must receive advance notice of all demonstrations, which may not undermine public order. Local nongovernmental organizations (NGOs) have alleged that police who mistreat demonstrators have not been penalized equally with protestors under this law. In response to protests on Jeju Island in 2011, in September 2012, participants of the World Conservation Congress passed a resolution to block construction of a naval base there. Korea's Ministry of Defense publicly criticized the resolution as being intrusive and infringing on sovereignty.

Human rights groups, social welfare organizations, and other NGOs are active and generally operate freely. The country's independent labor unions advocate workers' interests, organizing high-profile strikes and demonstrations that sometimes lead to arrests. However, labor unions in general have diminished in strength and popularity, especially amid the economic downturn.

South Korea's judiciary is generally considered to be independent. There is no trial by jury; judges render verdicts in all cases. Police occasionally verbally and physically abuse detainees. In 2012 a number of violent crimes against women and children reignited a debate over resuming the death penalty for heinous crimes. As of September, there were about 60 death row inmates, though no execution has taken place since December 1997. While South Korea's prisons lack certain amenities, such as hot water in the winter, there have been few reports of beatings or intimidation by guards.

The country's few ethnic minorities face legal and societal discrimination. Residents who are not ethnic Koreans have extreme difficulties obtaining citizenship, which is based on parentage rather than place of birth. Lack of citizenship bars them from the civil service and limits job opportunities at some major corporations.

Although South Korean women enjoy legal equality, they face social and employment discrimination in practice. However, a 2005 Supreme Court ruling granted married women equal rights with respect to inheritance. Women continued to be underrepresented in government following the December 2012 elections, comprising just 15.7 percent of National Assembly seats. In November 2012, five new bills were passed to strengthen punishment for sex crimes, including raising maximum sentences to lifetime imprisonment, increasing public access to sex offender identities, removing statutes of limitations, and increasing the age range for chemical castration.

South Sudan

Political Rights: 6
Civil Liberties: 5
Status: Not Free

Population: 9,385,000
Capital: Juba

Ten-Year Ratings Timeline For Year Under Review (Political Rights, Civil Liberties, Status)

2003	2004	2005	2006	2007	2008	2009	2010	2011	2012
--	--	--	--	--	--	--	--	6,5NF	6,5NF

Overview:
South Sudan's first full year of independence was marred by disputes with Sudan over border demarcations and management of the oil sector that brought both countries to the brink of war. A self-imposed oil shutdown following Sudan's excessive fee demands for the use of its pipeline crippled South Sudan's economy. Meanwhile, interethnic violence caused hundreds of deaths in Jonglei state.

The Republic of South Sudan achieved independence from Sudan in 2011, ending a decades-long struggle that included 39 years of civil war. The conflict was motivated by Southern alienation from the Northern government in Khartoum and attempts by successive regimes in the North to impose an Arab and Islamic identity on the South. South Sudan's more than 60 cultural and linguistic groups are predominantly African and practice Christianity or indigenous religions.

Resistance to the Northern government was led from 1983 by the Sudan Peoples' Liberation Army (SPLA) and its political arm, the Sudan Peoples' Liberation Movement (SPLM). The group's leader, John Garang, called not for secession of the South but for a new Sudan, governed under inclusive, secular principles. The Southern struggle was undermined by internal divisions over strategy and splits fomented by Khartoum, which often played out along ethnic lines. Shortly after the signing of the Comprehensive Peace Agreement (CPA) that ended the war in 2005, Garang died in a helicopter crash. His successor, Salva Kiir, pursued a more overtly separatist agenda.

The CPA formalized power sharing between the SPLM and the ruling political faction in Khartoum, the National Congress Party (NCP), in 2005. The two parties held seats in a national unity government, and the South, ruled by the SPLM-dominated Government of Southern Sudan (GOSS) in Juba, was granted a large degree of autonomy. While the aim of the CPA was to "make unity attractive," neither side was committed to the system it established. The GOSS focused on a provision allowing the South to hold a referendum on self-determination after six years.

The referendum was held in a peaceful and orderly fashion in January 2011. Almost 99 percent of those who participated cast their votes in favor of independence. Six months later, on July 9, 2011, South Sudan became the world's newest nation. A separate referendum to decide the future status of Abyei, a contested area on the border with Sudan, did not take place as scheduled.

Arguments over who was eligible to vote led to increased tensions, which resulted in Sudanese forces occupying Abyei, causing approximately 100,000 people to flee. In June, both sides agreed to withdraw their forces to make way for a UN peacekeeping force.

South Sudan endured a rocky start to life as an independent nation, struggling to provide basic services, tackle corruption, and bridge ethnic divisions among its impoverished citizens. Internal insecurity was a serious problem. The SPLA faced a series of armed rebellions and inter-ethnic clashes, which killed nearly 2,400 people in the first half of 2011. The situation further deteriorated in early 2012, when weeks of fighting in Jonglei state among the Lou Nuer, Bor Dinka, and Merle communities resulted in hundreds of deaths, abductions, the destruction of villages, and the displacement of thousands of people. Heavily outnumbered, the state security authorities were powerless to intervene. The UN Mission in South Sudan estimated that nearly 900 people were killed between December 2011 and February 2012 alone.

Relations with Sudan were hostile throughout 2012. Negotiations over the terms of South Sudan's independence foundered over issues including border demarcation, management of the oil sector, and the status of Southerners living in the North. In January, the government halted oil production, the source of 98 percent of its revenue, after Sudan demanded excessive fees for use of its pipeline. The decision catastrophically impacted South Sudan's economy, forcing the government to adopt austerity measures and freezing its development plans. Following a series of provocations on the disputed border with Sudan, the SPLA occupied Sudan's main oil field in March, drawing international condemnation that forced it to withdraw a month later. The two sides resumed negotiations, signing an agreement in September to resume oil production in South Sudan. The agreement addressed many of the outstanding disputes but did not include a deal on the future of Abyei. Implementation stalled, and oil production remained on hold at the end of the year.

Political Rights and Civil Liberties: South Sudan is not an electoral democracy. The transitional constitution, passed at independence, gives broad powers to the executive. The president cannot be impeached and has the authority to fire state governors and dissolve the parliament and state assemblies. A permanent constitution is due to be passed by 2015. A 60-member National Constitutional Review Commission established in January 2012 is charged with writing a draft text by early 2013, but its work has been hamstrung by administrative delays and lack of an operational budget. Some opposition politicians boycotted the constitutional consultation process, claiming it was insufficiently inclusive and dominated by SPLM loyalists. The government has begun preparations for the country's first national elections, which are scheduled for 2015, by passing an elections act in June 2012 and establishing a National Elections Commission in August.

South Sudan's parliament was reconfigured after independence. The SPLM holds 90 percent of the 332 seats in the lower house, the National Legislative Assembly (NLA). In addition to members of the old Southern legislature, the chamber includes 96 former members of the National Assembly in Khartoum and 66 additional members appointed by the president. The upper chamber, the Council of States, includes 20 former members of Sudan's Council of States, plus 30 members appointed by President Kiir. The SPLM was given all but five posts in a 29-member cabinet. South Sudan has a decentralized system, with significant powers devolved to the 10 state assemblies. Nine of the 10 state governors are members of the SPLM.

Five opposition parties are represented in the NLA, but they lack both the resources to operate effectively and the experience to formulate policy and set party platforms. The SPLM is intolerant of opposition. It has repeatedly accused the largest opposition party, the SPLM–Democratic Change (DC), of supporting armed groups and threatened to rescind its party registration. The SPLM-DC said the allegations were part of a campaign of harassment. Accusations persist that members of the country's largest ethnic group, the Dinka, dominate the SPLM's leadership and the security services to the detriment of other groups, such as the Nuer.

Corruption is endemic and a major source of public frustration. Government appointments are typically handed to SPLM loyalists or potential spoilers with little regard to merit, and corrupt officials take advantage of inadequate budget monitoring to divert public funds. In June 2012, President Kiir offered 75 current and former officials amnesty if they returned a total of $4 billion of public money he said they had stolen. A leading anticorruption campaigner who called for the names of the officials to be made public was kidnapped and tortured by unknown assailants. The interim constitution gives authority to the country's Anti-Corruption Commission to launch prosecutions, but it has not yet done so.

Private media in South Sudan has proliferated, with 37 FM radio stations, more than half a dozen newspapers, and several online news sites. The sole national television channel is government owned. There is one private satellite television channel, Ebony TV. Journalists currently operate in a legal vacuum. Parliament has yet to pass three draft bills to regulate the media and establish the right of journalists to operate freely. According to the Union of Journalists of Southern Sudan, media workers avoid covering sensitive subjects such as human rights abuses and official corruption, for fear of harassment. In December 2012, Diing Chan Awuol, an online journalist who had received anonymous threats over articles critical of the SPLM leadership, was shot dead on his doorstep by unknown assailants. He was the first journalist killed since South Sudan became independent. The authorities promised a thorough investigation, though noone had been arrested by year's end. In February, a presenter with Bakhita Radio who tried to attend proceedings of the National Assembly was assaulted by security guards, ejected from the building, and banned indefinitely from returning. In May, a radio disc jockey was detained for hosting a phone-in program to discuss police abuses. Two newspapers—*The Citizen* and *Al Masir*—that reported on corruption allegations against the SPLM secretary general were ordered to pay damages running to tens of thousands of dollars after a court threw out the case in March. The sale of foreign newspapers from East Africa was restricted for several months, apparently because the government disapproved of the coverage it was receiving.

Religious freedom is guaranteed by the interim constitution and generally respected in practice. There are no restrictions on academic freedom. The constitution guarantees the right to free education, although access to schools is limited outside state capitals. The university system was seriously disrupted in 2012 by austerity measures and ethnic violence, which forced the closure of the country's main institution of higher learning, Juba University, for three months.

Freedoms of assembly and association are enshrined in the interim charter, and authorities typically uphold them in practice. South Sudan is highly dependent on assistance from foreign nongovernmental organizations, which operate freely in the country. However, the government has hindered the approval of visas for some nationalities and obstructed the work of international organizations it considers unhelpful. A UN human rights official was expelled in November 2012 in response to a report accusing the SPLA of committing abuses in Jonglei state. Domestic civil society organizations, including unions, remain nascent. A Workers' Trade Union Federation, formed in 2010, has 65,000 members. Legislation to codify labor rights has stalled in the National Assembly.

The interim constitution provides for an independent judiciary. The president's Supreme Court appointments must be confirmed by a two-thirds majority in the NLA. The court system is under huge strain. In 2011, the chief justice said that the courts had the capacity to handle 100,000 cases a year, but faced four times that number. He called for greater use of traditional dispute-resolution systems and mobile courts to ease the backlog.

The South Sudan Police Service (SSPS) is ill-equipped, unprofessional, and overwhelmed by the country's security challenges. There were numerous reports in 2012 of arbitrary arrest and police brutality. Factions of the SSPS are believed to be responsible for a spate of violent crime and robberies in Juba. In 2011, UN inspectors uncovered evidence of brutality and rape at the main police training academy; at least two recruits died of their injuries, and no one has been prosecuted. The National Security Service, an unregulated agency reporting directly to the president, has been responsible for arbitrary arrests and abuses.

Prison facilities are poor, with insanitary conditions and insufficient food for inmates. Children and the mentally ill are routinely detained with adult prisoners. According to Human Rights Watch, one-third of detainees are on remand. Inefficiencies in the justice system have led to indefinite detention. Approximately 200 inmates are on death row, and at least 8 have been executed. Several human rights groups have called for a moratorium on the death penalty, arguing that weak rule of law means that irreversible miscarriages of justice are likely.

The state authorities are unable to protect vulnerable populations from violence, particularly in Jonglei state, where ethnic clashes have caused thousands of deaths and displacements. The government set up a commission of inquiry to investigate the violence, but it had not begun work by year's end. The army routinely performs policing functions, and the SPLA has committed serious abuses while carrying out such duties, including beating and torturing civilians during a disarmament campaign in Jonglei between March and August 2012. In December, the security services used excessive force to break up demonstrations in Western Bahr el-Ghazal, killing at least 13 civilians during several days of violence. Kenya has raised concerns about the impact of insecurity on its citizens working in South Sudan. At least five Kenyans were murdered in 2012, including a pharmacist who was assaulted by police officers.

Since 2005, more than two million refugees and internally displaced people have moved back to the South. The GRSS encouraged their return but has largely failed to provide them with even the most basic assistance.

Land use and ownership are frequent causes of conflict in South Sudan, and returning refugees have exacerbated the problem. Unclear or nonexistent laws have been exploited by SPLM officials and overseas investors to uproot people from their land.

The interim constitution guarantees the rights of women to equal pay and property ownership. Nonetheless, women are routinely exposed to discriminatory practices and domestic abuse. Women hold a quarter of the posts in the cabinet, fulfilling a constitutional gender quota. The SPLA continues to use child soldiers, despite a pledge to end the practice.

Spain

Political Rights: 1
Civil Liberties: 1
Status: Free

Population: 46,195,000
Capital: Madrid

Ten-Year Ratings Timeline For Year Under Review (Political Rights, Civil Liberties, Status)

2003	2004	2005	2006	2007	2008	2009	2010	2011	2012
1,1F	1,1F	1,1F	1,1F	1,1F	1,1F	1,1F	1,1F	1,1F	1,1F

Overview: **Austerity measures introduced by the government to address Spain's economic crisis led to widespread strikes and protests throughout the country in 2012. In October, unemployment hit a new high at about 25 percent of the working-age population, with youth unemployment at more than 50 percent. Meanwhile, a controversial judge who had investigated human rights abuses committed during the Francisco Franco dictatorship was found guilty of illegal wiretapping and suspended from the bench for 11 years.**

Peninsular Spain's current borders were largely established by the 16th century, and after a period of great colonial expansion and wealth, the country declined in relation to its European rivals. The Spanish Civil War of 1936–39 ended in victory for General Francisco Franco's right-wing Nationalists, who executed, jailed, and exiled the leftist Republicans. During Franco's long rule, many countries cut off diplomatic ties with Spain, and his regime was ostracized by the United Nations from 1946 to 1955. The militant Basque separatist group Euskadi Ta Askatasuna (ETA), or Basque Fatherland and Freedom, was formed in 1959 to create an independent Basque homeland, and carried out a campaign of terrorist bombings and other illegal activities. After a transitional period following Franco's death in 1975, Spain emerged as a parliamentary democracy, joining the European Economic Community, the precursor to the European Union (EU), in 1986.

In the 2004 parliamentary elections, the Spanish Socialist Workers' Party (PSOE) defeated the conservative Popular Party (PP), which had been in power for 11 years. However, lacking an outright majority, the PSOE relied on regionalist parties to support its legislation. The elections came only days after multiple terrorist bombings of Madrid commuter trains that killed almost 200 people. The PP government initially blamed ETA, but it was later discovered that the attacks had been carried out by Islamic fundamentalists in response to the government's support of the U.S.-led war in Iraq. After becoming prime minister, the PSOE's José Luis Rodríguez Zapatero pulled Spain's troops out of Iraq. In 2007, a Spanish court handed down long prison sentences to 21 of the 28 defendants charged in connection with the bombings; 7 were acquitted. In 2008, another key suspect in the bombings was sentenced to 20 years in prison.

ETA announced a ceasefire in 2006, but peace talks with the government broke down in January 2007 after the group claimed responsibility for a December 2006 bombing in a parking garage at Madrid's Barajas Airport. The Supreme Court banned hundreds of candidates with alleged links to ETA from participating in 2007 local elections in the Basque region. In March 2009, the Basque Nationalist Party lost its absolute majority in the Basque parliament elections for the first time in 30 years. The coalition of the PSOE and the PP pledged to focus on security and the economy in the Basque region, and not press for regional autonomy. In October 2011, ETA declared a "definitive cessation of armed activities," which was just shy of a full surrender and disarmament. In May 2012, the Spanish government rebuffed ETA's request for talks, calling for the former separatist group to disband.

Spain's economic woes, which began with the global recession in 2008, continued in 2011, as official unemployment topped 20 percent. The European debt crisis led to the implementation of unpopular austerity measures in Spain, such as increasing the retirement age from 65 to 67. Zapatero, who had been suffering from low approval ratings due to the country's economic crisis and the government's response, called for early general elections in November. The conservative PP trounced the PSOE, capturing 186 out of 350 seats in the lower house, while the PSOE took only 111 seats, its worst showing in 30 years. PP leader Mariano Rajoy replaced Zapatero as prime minister.

The government continued to introduce austerity measures—with more than 150 billion euros ($196 billion) of spending cuts planned for between 2012 and 2014—in order to prevent a full-scale bailout by the European Union. In response, thousands participated in general strikes in March and November 2012, with police firing on protesters during the March strike. In May, tens of thousands of people marched to mark the anniversary of the "Indignant" protest movement, which had begun the previous year as protesters, led by unemployed youth, occupied a central square in Madrid. The movement had inspired similar international movements, such as Occupy Wall Street in the United States. With the unemployment rate at about 25 percent and youth unemployment at more than 50 percent, anti-austerity protests spread to more than 50 cities throughout Spain in October.

Political Rights and Civil Liberties: Spain is an electoral democracy. The Congress of Deputies, the lower house of the bicameral parliament, has 350 members elected in multimember constituencies, except for the North African enclaves of Ceuta and Melilla, which are each assigned one single-member constituency. The Senate has 264 members, with 208 elected directly and 56 chosen by regional legislatures. Members of both the Senate and Congress serve four-year terms. Following legislative elections, the prime minister is selected by the monarch and is usually the leader of the majority party or coalition. The candidate must also be elected by the parliament. The country's 50 provinces are divided into 17 autonomous regions with varying degrees of power.

People generally have the right to organize in political parties and other competitive groups of their choice. The Bidu party in the Basque region, which was formed after the political wing of the ETA was permanently banned in 2002, won 21 seats in regional elections in October 2012. The party is expected to form a coalition with the Basque Nationalist Party and push for a referendum on independence. The government rebuffed the region of Catalonia, which produces a fifth of the country's economic output, in September 2012, when Catalonia asked for the power to raise and spend its own taxes. At the end of December, the president of Catalonia called for a referendum for the region on independence.

In recent years, incidents of political corruption have increased along with the downturn in the economy. In August 2012, the largest corruption trial in the country's history ended after 22 months. The trial involved 95 defendants—including two former mayors and 15 town counselors—who were accused of participating in a widespread system of graft, with local businesspeople bribing town officials for favorable decisions, primarily in city planning in the town of Marbella. Sentencing will take place in 2013. In March 2012, Juame Matas, the former regional head of Spain's Balearic Islands and former environment minister, was found guilty of paying a journalist with public funds to write articles praising him. Spain was ranked 30 out of 176 countries surveyed in Transparency International's 2012 Corruption Perceptions Index.

Spain has a free and lively press, with more than 100 newspapers covering a wide range of perspectives and actively investigating high-level corruption. Daily newspaper ownership, however, is concentrated within large media groups, such as Prisa and Zeta. Journalists who oppose ETA's political views have in the past been targeted by the group. In June 2012, the economic downturn led the government to lift a ban on advertising sexual services in print ads. The explicit advertisements bring in more than 40 million euros (approximately $57 million) annually for the economically struggling newspaper industry. In August 2012, the state-owned broadcaster, RTVE, removed several journalists who strongly criticized the ruling Popular Party.

Freedom of religion is guaranteed through constitutional and legal protections. Roman Catholicism is the dominant religion and enjoys privileges that other religions do not, such as financing through the tax system. Jews, Muslims, and Protestants have official status through bilateral agreements with the state, while other groups, including Jehovah's Witnesses and Mormons, have no such agreements. The government does not restrict academic freedom.

The constitution provides for freedom of assembly, and the government respects this right in practice. Large anti-austerity protests and strikes took place across the country throughout 2012. Domestic and international nongovernmental organizations operate without government restrictions. With the exception of members of the military, workers are free to strike, organize, and join unions of their choice. About 15 percent of the workforce is unionized.

The constitution provides for an independent judiciary. However, media pressure has been suspected of impacting sensitive rulings, such as immigration and Basque terrorism. Spain's universal jurisdiction law permits trying suspects for crimes committed abroad if they are not facing prosecution in their home country. In August 2011, a Spanish judge indicted nine Salvadoran soldiers under that law for the murder of six priests in El Salvador in 1989 during that country's civil war. In February 2012, the controversial judge Baltasar Garzón—who had investigated abuses committed by former dictator Francisco Franco and had ordered the arrest of Chile's former dictator Augusto Pinochet—was found guilty of illegally wire-tapping conversations between detainees accused of bribing politicians and their lawyers; he was suspended from the bench for 11 years. Critics charged that his conviction was at least partly politically motivated. Police abuse of prisoners, especially immigrants, has been reported. Those suspected of certain terrorism-related crimes can be held by police for up to five days with access only to a public lawyer. Prison conditions generally meet international standards.

Roma continue to face discrimination in the labor market and judicial system. In March 2012, the government approved the National Roma Integration Strategy, intended to help that community in health, education, employment, and housing.

Women enjoy legal protections against rape, domestic abuse, and sexual harassment in the workplace. However, violence against women, particularly within the home, remains a serious problem. Women currently hold 36 percent of the seats in the lower house and 34 percent in the upper house. Same-sex marriages are legal, and same-sex couples may adopt children. Trafficking in men, women, and children for the purposes of sexual exploitation and forced labor remains a problem.

↓ Sri Lanka

Political Rights: 5　　　　　　　　　　　　　　　　**Population:** 21,166,000
Civil Liberties: 4　　　　　　　　　　　　　　　　　　**Capital:** Colombo
Status: Partly Free

Trend arrow: Sri Lanka received a downward trend arrow due to evidence of increasing corruption and a politicized attempt to impeach the chief justice of the Supreme Court.

Ten-Year Ratings Timeline For Year Under Review (Political Rights, Civil Liberties, Status)

2003	2004	2005	2006	2007	2008	2009	2010	2011	2012
3,4PF	3,3PF	3,3PF	4,4PF	4,4PF	4,4PF	4,4PF	5,4PF	5,4PF	5,4PF

Overview:　　　　　　**President Mahinda Rajapaksa maintained a firm grip on power in 2012, and the judiciary's independence from the executive and legislative branches was seriously compromised by the start of impeachment procedures against the chief justice of the Supreme Court in November, following a ruling that was unfavorable to the government. The situation for human rights defenders and journalists remained grim, with numerous attacks and cases of intimidation occurring amid a climate of nationalist rhetoric and impunity. The government continued to reject credible allegations of war crimes committed in the final phase of its military campaign against the Tamil Tiger rebel group in 2009, even as the UN Human Rights Council passed a critical resolution calling for an investigation into these issues.**

After Sri Lanka gained independence from Britain in 1948, political power alternated between the conservative United National Party (UNP) and the leftist Sri

Lanka Freedom Party (SLFP). While the country made impressive gains in literacy, basic health care, and other social needs, its economic development was later stunted and its social fabric tested by a long-running civil war between the government and ethnic Tamil rebels. The conflict was triggered by anti-Tamil riots in 1983 that claimed hundreds of lives, but it came in the context of broader Tamil claims of discrimination by the Sinhalese majority. By 1986, the Liberation Tigers of Tamil Eelam (LTTE, or Tamil Tigers), which called for an independent Tamil homeland in the northeast, was in control of much of the northern Jaffna Peninsula. At the same time, the government was also fighting an insurgency in the south by the leftist People's Liberation Front (JVP). The JVP insurgency, and the brutal methods used by the army to quell it in 1989, killed an estimated 60,000 people.

Following a 2002 ceasefire accord (CFA), the government and LTTE agreed to explore a political settlement based on a federal system. However, the peace process was weakened by the Tigers's pullout from negotiations in 2003, as well as infighting between the main political parties about how to approach the LTTE.

After parliamentary elections held in 2004, President Chandrika Kumaratunga's United People's Freedom Alliance (UPFA) coalition, led by the SLFP and bolstered by the support of the JVP, formed a minority government. The addition of the JVP to the ruling coalition and the presence of Sinhalese nationalist forces in Parliament further hampered the peace process, as did the emergence of a breakaway faction of the Tigers, the Tamil People's Liberation Tigers (TMVP). By 2006, the splinter faction had become loosely allied with the government. Prime Minister Mahinda Rajapaksa of the SLFP narrowly won the 2005 presidential election, largely due to an LTTE boycott enforced by voter intimidation in the areas under its influence. Rajapaksa cultivated a more authoritarian style of rule, relegating Parliament to a secondary role, and appointed his brothers to key positions.

Fighting with the LTTE escalated in 2007, and the government formally annulled the CFA in January 2008. A sustained government offensive, accompanied by a deepening humanitarian crisis, culminated in a final battle in May 2009, in which the Tigers's leadership was annihilated. At least 100,000 people were killed in the 26-year conflict, including as many as 40,000 in May 2009 alone, according to the United Nations. Approximately 300,000 civilians were displaced during the final phase of the war, and many of those were interned in government-run camps, where they faced severe food shortages and outbreaks of disease. The government initially limited aid groups' access to the camps and did not allow inmates to leave, with the primary aim of screening all residents for any rebels hiding among them. At the end of 2012, more than 9,800 internally displaced persons (IDPs) remained in the camps, while tens of thousands more had left but were unable to return to their homes due to war damage and mines.

Rajapaksa called a presidential election for January 2010, almost two years early, and went on to win nearly 58 percent of the vote. His main opponent, former head of the armed forces Sarath Fonseka, received around 40 percent. Voting was divided along ethnic lines, with most Tamils and Muslims supporting Fonseka and most Sinhalese supporting the president. In February, Fonseka was arrested on charges of plotting a coup, and in September he was sentenced to a 30-month prison term for engaging in politics while still an active service member and for not adhering to procurement rules. Most analysts viewed the charges as politically motivated. He was released in May 2012, but on terms that forbade him from holding office for seven years.

In April 2010 parliamentary elections, the ruling UPFA secured 144 of 225 seats, but fell short of a two-thirds majority. The opposition UNP won 60 seats, while the Democratic National Alliance (DNA) coalition, led by the JVP, won 7, and the Tamil National Alliance (TNA) took 14. Parliament passed the government-backed 18th Amendment to the constitution in September. The package of revisions extended political control over state institutions by abolishing the constitutional council mandated by the 17th Amendment and replacing it with a government-dominated parliamentary council tasked with selecting key members of the judiciary and nominally independent commissions. The new amendment also reduced the powers of the electoral and police commissions and removed the two-term limit on presidents.

In July 2011, the ruling coalition swept local council elections in most of the country. But in a sign of continued ethnic polarization, the TNA, long allied with the Tigers, won most council contests in the north and east. Similarly, in elections held in three of the nine provinces in September 2012, the UPFA won clear majorities in the two Sinhalese-majority provinces and prevailed in the predominantly Tamil Eastern Province with the help of its coalition partner, the Sri Lanka Muslim Congress, although the TNA did win a substantial portion of the Tamil vote.

The issue of whether war crimes were committed in the final phases of the civil conflict remained a source of contention. In April 2011, an expert panel formed by the UN secretary general released a report assigning blame to both sides for a range of atrocities, and recommending the establishment of an international mechanism to investigate alleged breaches of international law and to ensure justice. Although the government maintained that a full international investigative mechanism or tribunal was unnecessary, the report was forwarded to the UN Human Rights Council (UNHRC), which in March 2012 adopted a resolution calling on the Sri Lankan government to investigate the civilian deaths that occurred near the end of the war. Sri Lankan human rights advocates and journalists attending the UN session were branded traitors and threatened with bodily harm upon returning home. Largely as a result of disagreement over the UNHRC vote, Sri Lanka's relations with the United Nations and major world democracies soured further during the year, and the government increasingly turned to nondemocratic powers such as China, Iran, and Russia for foreign investment and diplomatic support.

Meanwhile, the Lessons Learnt and Reconciliation Commission (LLRC), a government-backed investigative body whose primary mandate was to assess the reasons behind the collapse of the 2002 ceasefire, released its final report in December 2011. Among other issues, the LLRC called on the government to gradually remove security forces from civilian affairs and activity, establish a more distanced relationship between the police and institutions managing the armed forces, implement a policy of trilingualism, devolve power to local government institutions, and commence investigations into the myriad abductions, disappearances, and harassment of journalists. As part of its resolution, the UNHRC urged Sri Lanka to demonstrate how it planned to carry out the LLRC's proposals, while at the same time criticizing its report for not addressing violations of international law. In July 2012, the government released a National Action Plan with details and timeframes for implementing 120 of the report's 167 recommendations. While some progress was made on the language issue during the year, virtually none occurred in the realm of investigations into violations of human rights and international humanitarian law.

Political Rights and Civil Liberties: Sri Lanka is not an electoral democracy. The 1978 constitution vested strong executive powers in the president, who is directly elected for six-year terms and can dissolve Parliament. The prime minister heads the leading party in Parliament but has limited powers. The 225-member unicameral legislature is elected for six-year terms through a mixed proportional-representation system.

In the January 2010 presidential election, monitoring groups alleged inappropriate use of state resources—particularly transport, infrastructure, police services, and the media—to benefit the incumbent, in violation of orders issued by election officials. More than 1,000 incidents of violence, including at least four deaths, were reported in the preelection period. In the northern and eastern provinces, inadequate provisions for transport and registration of IDPs contributed to a low turnout. Election officials' orders were similarly disregarded prior to the April 2010 parliamentary elections, which also featured extensive misuse of state resources. The independent Center for Monitoring Election Violence noted that the elections were considerably less beleaguered by violence than the presidential vote, with 84 major and 202 minor incidents reported. Nevertheless, irregularities led to the nullification or suspension of results in several districts. Provincial elections held in 2012, though mostly peaceful, were marred by some reports of violence, and civil society groups accused the government and party cadres of engaging in intimidation prior to the voting, misuse of state resources, and other violations of election laws.

Some observers charge that President Mahinda Rajapaksa's centralized, authoritarian style of rule has led to a lack of transparent, inclusive policy formulation. The Centre for Policy Alternatives (CPA) and others have noted the concentration of power in the hands of the Rajapaksa family. The president himself holds multiple ministerial portfolios, and his brothers serve in other key posts: Gotabaya serves as defense secretary, Basil is minister for economic development, and Chamal was elected as speaker of Parliament in 2010. A growing number of other relatives, including the president's son Namal, also hold important political or diplomatic positions. The president and his family consequently control approximately 70 percent of the national budget. The controversial Divi Neguma Bill, which proposed combining all provincial development agencies under the minister of economic development, would transfer an additional fund of 80 billion rupees (about $630 million) to Basil Rajapaksa without oversight provisions; the bill had not passed at year's end. During 2012, the president took further steps to enhance Namal's profile in international and domestic forums, fueling speculation that he was being groomed as a potential successor.

The 18th Amendment to the constitution in 2010 effectively reversed efforts to depoliticize certain institutions under the 17th Amendment, giving a government-dominated parliamentary council powers to advise the president regarding appointments to independent commissions that oversee the police, the judiciary, human rights, and civil servants.

Official corruption worsened in 2012, notably in the education sector and within several government ministries. The current legal and administrative framework is inadequate for promoting integrity and punishing corrupt behavior, and weak enforcement of existing safeguards has been a problem. The Commission to Investigate Allegations of Bribery or Corruption was reinstated in 2011 after more than a year of inaction, with a new chairman and two commissioners appointed by the president, although it still has insufficient resources and personnel to deal with the heightened level of complaints. In 2012, the commission received 3,163 complaints, of which 440 involved the education sector and 318 the police department. For example, rampant corruption in the education sector forced parents to pay bribes of up to 60,000 rupees (about $475) for admission, materials, and unofficial projects. Graft investigations were launched in 2012 against dozens of federal, provincial, and local officials, including Public Relations Minister Mervyn Silva, who faced charges including extortion. A March parliamentary report also alleged widespread corruption in 229 public enterprises, leading to the removal of a number of chairmen. Sri Lanka was ranked 79 out of 176 countries surveyed in Transparency International's 2012 Corruption Perceptions Index.

Although freedom of expression is guaranteed in the constitution, a number of laws and regulations restrict this right, including the Official Secrets Act, the Prevention of Terrorism Act (PTA), additional antiterrorism regulations issued in 2006, and laws on defamation and contempt of court. State-run media outlets have fallen under government influence, while official rhetoric toward critical journalists and outlets grew increasingly hostile in 2012, often equating any form of criticism with treason and threatening physical violence. In particular, the government used state media to engage in a smear campaign against journalists and activists who participated in or otherwise supported the UNHRC sessions and resolution, airing their pictures alongside denunciations for "betraying the motherland."

Journalists throughout Sri Lanka, particularly those who cover human rights or military issues, encounter considerable levels of intimidation, which has led over the past several years to increased self-censorship. A number of journalists received death threats in 2012, while others were assaulted. In June, police raided the joint office of two opposition news websites, the *Sri Lanka Mirror* and *Sri Lanka X News*, for publishing antigovernment material. Eight journalists and an office assistant were arrested and their equipment confiscated. In July, the editor of the *Sunday Leader*, Federica Jansz, received death threats directly from Defense Secretary Gotabaya Rajapaksa following a story alleging he misused his authority to divert a passenger jet to pick up a puppy. Two months later, Jansz was fired after the paper was sold to an associate of the Rajapaksa family. Past attacks on journalists and media outlets, such as the murder of Lasantha Wickrematunga in 2009 and the disappearance of Prageeth Eknaligoda in 2010, have not been adequately investigated, leading to a climate of complete impunity.

The government continued efforts to censor the internet in 2012, temporarily blocking access to the independent news site *Colombo Telegraph*, as well as the websites of Tamil language news sites. In May, the Free Media Movement, a press advocacy group, brought a case to the Supreme Court on behalf of five websites that had been shut down in 2011, but the case was quickly dismissed.

Religious freedom is respected, and members of all faiths are generally allowed to worship freely. However, the constitution gives special status to Buddhism, and there is some discrimination and occasional violence against religious minorities.

Tensions between the Buddhist majority and the Christian minority—particularly evangelical Christian groups, which are accused of forced conversions—sporadically flare into attacks on churches and individuals by Buddhist extremists. Muslims have also faced harassment: in April 2012, hard-line Buddhist monks stormed a mosque in Dambulla and demanded its destruction. The government complied, ordering that the mosque would be demolished and relocated, leading to a strike in Muslim areas; the issue was pending at year's end. Work permits for foreign clergy, formerly valid for five years, were shortened to one year, leading many to opt to enter as tourists. However, in January, 161 foreign Muslim clerics were expelled for preaching on tourist visas. In recent years, the minority Ahmadiyya Muslim sect has faced increased threats and attacks from Sunni Muslims who accuse Ahmadis of being apostates.

Academic freedom is generally respected. However, some commentators report increasing politicization on university campuses, lack of tolerance for antigovernment views, and a rise in self-censorship by professors and students. In 2011, the authorities introduced mandatory "leadership training" for all university undergraduates, conducted by the army at military camps. Concerns have been raised that the curriculum promotes Sinhalese nationalist viewpoints and discourages respect for ethnic diversity and political dissent. In August 2012, the government temporarily closed down 13 of 15 state-funded universities following a strike by academics denouncing government meddling in campus life and plans to partially privatize universities; however, they were reopened the following month.

Emergency regulations that empowered the president to restrict rallies and gatherings lapsed in 2011, and permission for demonstrations is usually granted. However, police occasionally use excessive force to disperse protesters. In January 2012, authorities disrupted a protest commemorating a series of attacks on journalists by limiting demonstrators to a small area and bringing in government supporters who denounced the demonstrators as traitors. The army has placed some restrictions on assembly, particularly for planned memorial events in the north and east concerning the end of the war, according to the International Crisis Group.

Nongovernmental organizations (NGOs) experience some official harassment and curbs on their activities, and since 2010 the Defense Ministry has controlled the registration of both local and foreign NGOs. Human rights and peace-seeking groups—particularly those willing to document abuses of human rights or accountability, such as the CPA, National Peace Council, or the local branch of Transparency International—face surveillance, smear campaigns, threats to their staff, and criminal investigations into their funding and activities. In 2012, human rights advocates attending the UNHRC sessions were labeled LTTE sympathizers and their photographs broadcast on state television. Many NGOs had difficulty acquiring work permits in the northern and eastern areas of the country. However, the United Nations and other humanitarian organizations were generally given adequate access to conflict zones. No progress was made in the investigation of the disappearance and murder of human rights defender Pattani Razeek, whose body was recovered in 2011.

Most of Sri Lanka's 1,500 trade unions are independent and legally allowed to engage in collective bargaining, but this right is poorly upheld in practice. Except for civil servants, most workers can hold strikes, though the 1989 Essential Services Act allows the president to declare a strike in any industry illegal. While more than

70 percent of the mainly Tamil workers on tea plantations are unionized, employers routinely violate their rights. Harassment of labor activists and official intolerance of union activities, particularly in export processing zones, are regularly reported. The government has increased penalties for employing minors, and complaints involving child labor have risen significantly. Nevertheless, thousands of children continue to be employed as household servants, and many face abuse.

Judicial independence was significantly threatened in 2012. A growing culture of physical threats, intimidation, and political interference toward the judiciary culminated in November with Parliament commencing formal impeachment proceedings against the chief justice of the Supreme Court, Shirani Bandaranayake, immediately following a ruling unfavorable to the UPFA on the Divi Neguma Bill. State media launched a simultaneous smear campaign to vilify Bandaranayake. The International Commission of Jurists condemned the proceedings as violating due process and the fundamentals of a fair trial. The case was ongoing at year's end. Concerns about politicization of the judiciary have grown in recent years, and judicial independence had been further eroded by the 18th amendment, which granted a parliamentary council advisory powers and the president greater responsibility to make judicial appointments. Corruption remains common in the lower courts, and those willing to pay bribes have better access to the legal system.

The last years of the war featured a sharp rise in human rights abuses by security forces, including arbitrary arrest, extrajudicial execution, forced disappearance, custodial rape, and prolonged detention without trial, all of which predominantly affected Tamils. Torture occurred in the context of the insurgency but also takes place during routine interrogations. Abusive practices have been facilitated by the emergency regulations, the PTA, and the 2006 antiterrorism regulations. Under the PTA, suspects can be detained for up to 18 months without trial. These laws have been used to detain a variety of perceived enemies of the government, including political opponents, critical journalists, members of civil society, and Tamil civilians suspected of supporting the LTTE. The government allowed the emergency regulations to lapse in August 2011, but shortly thereafter authorized the expansion of law enforcement powers under the PTA. Several thousand remained in detention without charge at the end of 2012, according to Human Rights Watch. Separately, of the roughly 11,000 Tiger cadres who surrendered in the war's final stages, fewer than 1,000 remained in military-run "rehabilitation" programs during 2012.

Most past human rights abuses are not aggressively prosecuted, and victims and witnesses are inadequately protected. The National Human Rights Commission (NHRC) is empowered to investigate abuses, but has traditionally suffered from insufficient authority and resources. The independence of the NHRC and other commissions was weakened by the adoption of the 18th Amendment in 2010.

Tamils maintain that they face systematic discrimination in areas including government employment, university education, and access to justice. Legislation that replaced English with Sinhala as the official language in 1956 continues to disadvantage Tamils and other non–Sinhala speakers. Tensions between the three major ethnic groups (Sinhalese, Tamils, and Muslims) occasionally led to violence, and the government generally does not take adequate measures to prevent or contain it. In 2012, the police announced that former Tamil Tigers were welcome to join the force and began training of new Tamil-speaking recruits.

Since the end of the war, the government has ostensibly concentrated on rehabilitating former LTTE-controlled territory in the north and east (about 10–15 percent of the country) through economic development programs, but Tamil hopes for greater political autonomy remained unfulfilled. LTTE rule has been replaced by that of the army, which controls most aspects of daily life, including local government in some districts.

Human rights groups have claimed that insufficient registration policies in the postwar IDP camps contributed to widespread disappearances and removals without accountability, and the status of hundreds of Tamils who disappeared during the war's final phase remains unclear. In September 2012, the Menik Farm displacement camp, which had once housed 300,000 people displaced by the civil war, was officially closed. While more than 480,000 IDPs have returned to their home districts, in many cases they were unable to occupy their former property due to land mines, destruction of their homes, or appropriation of their land by the military or government. According to the Internal Displacement Monitoring Centre, as of December 31, 2012, over 93,000 people remained displaced, the vast majority of whom were residing with host families. Muslims forcibly ejected from the north by the LTTE in the early 1990s noted during the course of LLRC hearings in 2010 that many were unable to return to their homes, as their land was still being occupied by Tamils. In general, there are few official attempts to help this group of returnees. Other former residents of the conflict area live as refugees in India.

Observers have expressed concern that government appropriation of land in the north and east as part of economic development projects or "high security zones" has impinged on freedom of movement and the ability of local people to return to their property, and that the land will be allotted to southerners or on politically motivated grounds. The military has expanded its economic activities in the north and east, running shops and growing agricultural produce for sale in the south, while local businesspeople are pushed out of the market. Throughout the country, the military's role in a variety of economic activities—from tourism to agriculture and infrastructure projects—has expanded significantly, providing jobs and revenue for a force that has tripled in size under the current president.

Women are underrepresented in politics and the civil service. Female employees in the private sector face some sexual harassment and discrimination in salary and promotion opportunities. Rape and domestic violence remain serious problems, with hundreds of complaints reported annually; existing laws are weakly enforced. Violence against women increased along with the general fighting in the civil conflict, and has also affected female prisoners and interned IDPs. The entrenchment of the army in the north and east has increased the risk of harassment and sexual abuse for female civilians (many of whom are widows) in those areas. Although women have equal rights under civil and criminal law, matters related to the family—including marriage, divorce, child custody, and inheritance—are adjudicated under the customary law of each ethnic or religious group, and the application of these laws sometimes results in discrimination against women. The government remains committed to ensuring that children have access to free education and health care, and it has also taken steps to prosecute those suspected of sex crimes against children. However, child rape is a serious problem. Members of the LGBT (lesbian, gay, bisexual, and transgender) community face social discrimination and some instances of official harassment, and same-sex sexual activity is criminalized, though rarely prosecuted.

Sudan

Political Rights: 7
Civil Liberties: 7
Status: Not Free

Population: 33,494,000
Capital: Khartoum

Ten-Year Ratings Timeline For Year Under Review (Political Rights, Civil Liberties, Status)

2003	2004	2005	2006	2007	2008	2009	2010	2011	2012
7,7NF	7,7NF	7,7NF	7,7NF	7,7NF	7,7NF	7,7NF	7,7NF	7,7NF	7,7NF

Overview: Sudan's government struggled during 2012 to contain an economic crisis triggered by the 2011 independence of South Sudan. The two nations came close to war after South Sudan halted oil production and occupied Sudan's main oil field. An agreement to end many of their outstanding disputes was reached in September but failed to resolve the status of the Abyei region. Sudan's government responded brutally to social protests in June, conducting mass arrests and placing further restrictions on the embattled media. An armed uprising continued unabated in Southern Kordofan and Blue Nile states, worsening a dire humanitarian situation. A peace agreement in Darfur was in danger of unraveling following an upsurge of fighting.

Sudan has been embroiled in nearly continuous civil wars since gaining independence from Britain and Egypt in 1956. Between 1956 and 1972, the Anyanya movement, representing mainly black Africans in southern Sudan, battled Arab Muslim–dominated government forces. In 1969 General Jafar Numeiri took power in a coup. The South gained extensive autonomy under a 1972 accord, but Numeiri reneged on the deal in 1983 and imposed Sharia (Islamic law), igniting a civil war with the main rebel group, the Sudan People's Liberation Army (SPLA). The fighting lasted until 2004, causing the deaths of an estimated two million people. Numeiri was ousted in a popular uprising in 1985, and a civilian government elected in 1986 was overthrown three years later by General Omar al-Bashir. Over the next decade, al-Bashir governed with the support of senior Muslim clerics.

Al-Bashir oversaw flawed presidential and parliamentary elections in 2000, which the National Congress Party (NCP; formerly the National Islamic Front) won overwhelmingly. The government ended the civil war with the South in January 2005 by signing the Comprehensive Peace Agreement (CPA) with the SPLA and its political arm, the Sudan People's Liberation Movement (SPLM). The pact established a power-sharing government in Khartoum between the SPLM and the NCP, granted autonomy to a Government of Southern Sudan (GoSS) led by the SPLM, and allowed for a referendum on Southern independence to be held after a six-year transitional period.

While the CPA was being negotiated, a separate conflict erupted in Darfur. Rebels from Muslim but non-Arab ethnic groups attacked military positions in 2003, citing discrimination and marginalization by the government. In 2004, government-supported Arab militias known as janjaweed began torching villages, massacring the inhabitants, and raping women and girls. The military also bombed settlements from the air. More than two million civilians were displaced. The scale of the violence led to accusations of genocide by international human rights groups and the United States.

The government reached a peace agreement with one of Darfur's multiple rebel groups in 2006, but the others refused to sign the pact, and fighting continued despite the presence of international peacekeepers. In March 2009, the International Criminal Court (ICC) issued an arrest warrant for al-Bashir on charges of war crimes and crimes against humanity in Darfur; a charge of genocide was added in 2010.

National elections mandated by the CPA were held in 2010. The process was undermined by intimidation, vote rigging, and restrictions on freedom of expression by the NCP in the North and the SPLM in the South. The SPLM and other parties ultimately boycotted the national presidential election, citing unfair campaign conditions. As a result, al-Bashir won convincingly, capturing 68 percent of the vote. The NCP won 323 of 450 seats in the National Assembly, the lower house of parliament, 91 percent of the state assembly seats in the North, and 32 seats in the 50-seat upper chamber, the Council of States, which is indirectly elected by the state legislatures. In the South, Salva Kiir of the SPLM was elected president of the GoSS.

The Southern referendum on independence took place in January 2011. The largely peaceful process resulted in an overwhelming vote—almost 99 percent—in favor of independence. A separate referendum to decide the future of the contested border enclave of Abyei did not go ahead as planned because of disagreements over who was eligible to vote. Sudan occupied the region in May, only withdrawing following the deployment of UN peacekeepers.

The state of Southern Kordofan, close to the border with the South, became the next flashpoint. Much-delayed state elections were held in May 2011, resulting in a narrow victory for the NCP candidate, which was rejected by the SPLM. Clashes erupted the following month when Khartoum brought forward a deadline for Southern-aligned forces in the state to disarm. In the following weeks, Sudan's military launched aerial bombardments and indiscriminate shelling of civilian areas. The United Nations accused Northern troops of carrying out "targeted killings and summary executions."

The violence quickly spread eastwards to Blue Nile State. Khartoum accused the SPLM-North (SPLM-N), an offshoot of the liberation movement in the South, of leading a rebellion. Al-Bashir declared a state of emergency and banned the SPLM-N as a political party in September 2011, detaining scores of its members throughout the country. For its part, the SPLM-N pledged to work for regime change in Khartoum and announced the formation of the Sudan Revolutionary Front, an alliance with other rebel groups intent on toppling the NCP.

The fighting in Southern Kordofan and Blue Nile continued in 2012, with only a brief pause during the rainy season. It resulted in a devastating humanitarian crisis that was compounded by the refusal of the authorities in Khartoum to allow relief organizations to access areas controlled by the SPLM-N. At the end of 2012, the United Nations estimated that more than 200,000 refugees had fled to Ethiopia and South Sudan and another 700,000 people had been either internally displaced or "severely affected" by the fighting. A food security assessment conducted in

SPLM-N controlled areas in August found that more than 80 percent of households were surviving on only one meal a day.

The border conflicts soured relations with the South, which formally became the independent Republic of South Sudan on July 9, 2011. Khartoum accused the SPLM of aiding the rebels, and negotiations stalled on a host of bilateral issues, including border demarcation, management of the oil industry, and defining citizenship in the two new countries. These disputes peaked in January 2012, when the government in Juba, angered by Khartoum's refusal to set a fair price for use of its oil pipeline, shut off oil production entirely. The decision had a catastrophic effect on both countries' economies and led to border skirmishes between the two militaries which resulted in the SPLA occupying Sudan's main oil field, Heglig, in March. The United Nations demanded an end to hostilities and set a deadline of May for the two sides to resolve their outstanding disputes. The SPLA withdrew in April and talks resumed. A deal was signed in September to demilitarize the border and open the way for the resumption of oil production. No agreement was reached by year's end on the disputed border enclave of Abyei.

In Darfur, a 2011 peace agreement signed by the government with one of the minor rebel groups led to the establishment of a Darfur Regional Authority in February 2012, which included provisions to compensate victims of the war and return displaced people to their homes. However, the security situation deteriorated in the second half of 2012. There were renewed clashes between the main rebel groups and government forces. In July, the security forces used live ammunition in Nyala to end a peaceful protest against rising prices by high school students. At least a dozen people were killed and about 100 others injured. In September, the United States condemned Khartoum for launching indiscriminate bombing raids in North Darfur, reporting that at least 70 civilians were killed in the violence.

The incident in Nyala was the deadliest episode in a series of protests against the regime in Khartoum, led mainly by university students and young people. The authorities used violence and mass arrests to restore order following a series of demonstrations in Khartoum and other major towns in June. Many of the detained said they were tortured in custody. Journalists and human rights groups who tried to report on the protests were arrested and harassed. Human Rights Watch and Amnesty International estimated that at the height of the demonstrations, approximately 2,000 people were held in detention. Most were released without charge within days after promising to refrain from political activities but scores of others were convicted of public order offences, receiving fines or lashings. Unrest within the ruling party broke into the open in November when the authorities announced that a coup plot had been foiled. Several high-profile military and security officials were detained and were awaiting formal charges at year's end.

Political Rights and Civil Liberties: Sudan is not an electoral democracy. Although the first multiparty elections in 24 years were held in 2010, they were plagued by irregularities and failed to meet international standards, according to monitors from the United States, the European Union, and Sudan itself.

The country is governed according to the 2005 interim constitution. The document is being redrafted following the independence of South Sudan, though the process has stalled. Members of the opposition and civil society have so far been excluded from consultations over the constitution-writing process and claim that proposed revisions would lead to a more repressive system of governance. According to the interim constitution, the president is currently elected to serve a maximum of two five-year terms. Members of the lower house of the bicameral legislature, the 450-seat National Assembly, were elected in 2010 using a mixed majoritarian and party-list system. State legislatures chose the 50 members of the upper house, the Council of States. All lawmakers are to serve six five-year terms. As a result of South Sudan's secession, the two chambers were reduced to 340 and 30 seats, respectively.

Ahead of the 2010 elections, the NCP manipulated the census used to compile the electoral roll, overstating the population in areas of core support and under-counting opposition strongholds. Although 72 political parties nominated candidates for the elections, many of them were not allowed to campaign freely and rarely received official permission to hold public events. The leading opposition parties boycotted the presidential election in the North, and several also withdrew from the legislative polls. The voting period was plagued by irregularities, with reports of inaccurate voter rolls, ballot stuffing, and cash handouts to NCP voters.

The NCP's dominance of the political system in the North was reinforced by the independence of South Sudan, which signaled the end of the Government of National Unity and the withdrawal of the South's representatives from parliament. The Khartoum government also launched a crackdown on other political parties. The SPLM-N was banned from operating in September 2011, following the outbreak of fighting in Blue Nile State. Senior members of opposition parties, including the Popular Congress Party, Umma, and the Sudanese Communist Party, were detained for short periods without charge during student-led protests in June 2012. Two leading figures in the PCP were held for five months before being released without charge in June.

The influence of the military clique within the NCP has subverted the political system to such an extent that analysts believe a "soft coup" may have taken place in 2011, with senior generals taking over responsibility for key government decisions,

Sudan is considered one of the world's most corrupt countries. Power and resources are concentrated in and around Khartoum, while outlying states are neglected and impoverished. Members of the NCP, particularly those from favored ethnic groups, tightly control the national economy and use the wealth they have amassed in banking and business to buy political support. The International Crisis Group estimates that the party's top leadership owns more than 164 companies, which get the pick of the government's contracts. Sudan was ranked 172 out of 176 countries surveyed in Transparency International's 2012 Corruption Perceptions Index.

The 2005 interim constitution recognizes freedom of the press, but the media face significant obstacles in practice. The 2009 Press and Publication Act allows a government-appointed Press Council to prevent publication or broadcast of material it deems unsuitable, temporarily shut down newspapers, and impose heavy fines for violations of media regulations. Members of the National Intelligence and Security Services (NISS) routinely raided printing facilities in 2012 to confiscate editions of newspapers considered to be in violation of the Act. By waiting until editions had been printed, the authorities imposed crippling financial losses on newspapers, forcing at least five out of business. Other papers were shut down for extended periods, including *Alwan* and *Rai al-Shaab*, which halted production in January, and *Al-Tayar*, which was suspended in February and closed in June on the orders of the NISS. Newspaper editors were told not to publish articles by at least a dozen individual reporters.

Journalists risked prosecution for reporting on the antigovernment protests of June 2012 and a long list of other proscribed topics. According to the Committee to Protect Journalists, at least seven reporters were detained for covering the demonstrations and held until the end of August without charge. Foreign media organizations were also targeted, including Agence France Presse, whose offices were raided in June after one of its reporters photographed a protest in Omdurman, and Bloomberg, whose correspondent was deported for covering the demonstrations.

Religious freedom, though guaranteed by the 2005 interim constitution, is not upheld in practice. Approximately 97 percent of Sudan's population is Muslim, nearly all of whom are Sunni. The law prohibits apostasy, blasphemy, and conversion to any religion apart from Islam. The government uses religious laws to persecute political opponents. In 2011, 129 Darfuris were charged with apostasy, which carries a maximum sentence of death, although they were released after agreeing to follow the government's interpretation of Islam. During the fighting in Southern Kordofan state in 2012, government forces shelled churches, claiming that rebels used them as safe houses.

Respect for academic freedom is limited. The government administers public universities, monitors appointments, and sets the curriculum. Authorities do not directly control private universities, but self-censorship among instructors is common. Student associations are closely monitored for signs of antigovernment activities. Khartoum University was closed for two months following protests at the end of 2011. The authorities responded harshly to renewed demonstrations in 2012, many of which originated in universities. The security services burned dormitories at Omburman University, attacked female students protesting against increased fees at Khartoum University, and raided campuses across the country, rounding up hundreds of students.

The student-led protests of June and July 2012 led to broad restrictions on freedom of assembly. Peaceful demonstrations calling for political and economic reform were met with violence by security personnel, who attacked protesters and in one case, fired live ammunition on a crowd of young students in Nyala in Darfur.

The operating environment for nongovernmental organizations (NGOs) is difficult. In Darfur, government-backed forces and the main rebel groups place restrictions on the movements of aid workers and peacekeepers. A total of 43 members of the joint United Nations–African Union peacekeeping force in Darfur have been killed since 2007. They include four peacekeepers whose convoy was attacked by unknown assailants in September 2012 near Geneina. Independent NGOs continue to be denied access to the conflict-affected states of Southern Kordofan and Blue Nile.

Trade union rights are minimal, and there are no independent unions. The Sudan Workers' Trade Unions Federation has been co-opted by the government. All strikes must be approved by the government.

The judiciary is not independent. Lower courts provide some due process safeguards, but the higher courts are subject to political control, and special security and military courts do not apply accepted legal standards. Sudanese criminal law is based on Sharia and allows punishments such as flogging.

The National Security Act, which took effect in 2010, gives the NISS sweeping authority to seize property, conduct surveillance, search premises, and detain suspects for up to four and a half months without judicial review. The police and security forces routinely exceed these broad powers, carrying out arbitrary arrests and holding people at secret locations without access to lawyers or their relatives. Human rights groups accuse the NISS of systematically detaining and torturing opponents of the government, including Darfuri activists, journalists, and members of the youth Girifna movement. Approximately 2,000 people were arrested following antigovernment protests in June 2012. Most were held without charge before being released in August. Some activists were singled out for harsh sentences. They included Jalila Khamis Koko, an SPLM-N activist who was convicted of crimes against the state in September and sentenced to death.

It is widely accepted that the government has directed and assisted with the systematic killing of tens or even hundreds of thousands of people in Darfur since 2003, including through its support for militia groups that have terrorized civilians. Human rights groups have documented the widespread use of rape, the organized burning of villages, and the forced displacement of entire communities. The government continued to wage war against its own citizens in Southern Kordofan and Blue Nile in 2012, using indiscriminate force against civilians, including aerial bombardments. NGOs accused the government of pursuing "starvation warfare" by denying humanitarian access to populations caught up in the fighting. Ethnic groups considered unfriendly to the government were targeted for attack, notably the Nuba people, who largely sided with the SPLM during the civil war.

The approximately one million Southerners who remained in the North following South Sudan's independence face serious discrimination. Under the political agreement reached by Khartoum and Juba in September, Southerners living in Sudan will be guaranteed rights of residency and movement as well as the right to engage in economic activity and acquire property. However, the agreement does not address the question of citizenship, putting some people at risk of being reclassified as "foreigners," even if they have lived in Sudan their entire lives.

Ongoing disputes over portions of the new international boundary between Sudan and South Sudan have curtailed freedom of movement and trade across the border and caused serious hardship to pastoralist groups whose migratory routes have been severed.

Female politicians and activists play a role in public life in Sudan, and women are guaranteed a quarter of the seats in the National Assembly. In daily life, however, women face extensive discrimination. Islamic law denies women equitable rights in marriage, inheritance, and divorce. Police use provisions of Sudan's Criminal Act outlawing "indecent and immoral acts" to prohibit women from wearing clothing of which they disapprove. Female genital mutilation is widely practiced. Rape has been used as a weapon of war in Darfur and other conflict zones in Sudan.

The U.S. State Department considers Sudan to be a source, transit, and destination country for persons trafficked for forced labor and sexual exploitation. The Sudanese military and Darfur rebel groups continue to use child soldiers.

⬇ Suriname

Political Rights: 0
Civil Liberties: 2
Status: Free

Population: 542,400
Capital: Paramaribo

Trend Arrow: Suriname received a downward trend arrow due to an amended amnesty law that granted immunity to President Desiré Bouterse and 24 other suspects on trial for the 1982 murder of 15 political opponents.

Ten-Year Ratings Timeline For Year Under Review (Political Rights, Civil Liberties, Status)

2003	2004	2005	2006	2007	2008	2009	2010	2011	2012
1,2F	1,2F	2,2F	2,2F	2,2F	2,2F	2,2F	2,2F	2,2F	2,2F

Overview: A long-awaited verdict was close to being delivered in the trial against President Desiré Bouterse and 24 other suspects for the murder of 15 political opponents in December 1982, when the National Assembly passed legislation in April 2012 that granted amnesty to all defendants. Amid national and international protests, the "December murders" trial was adjourned in May for a constitutional examination of the amnesty legislation; the trial had yet to reconvene at year's end.

The Republic of Suriname achieved independence from the Netherlands in 1975, after more than three centuries of colonial rule. A 1980 military coup led by Desiré Bouterse established a regime that brutally suppressed civic and political opposition and initiated a decade of military intervention in politics. In 1987, Bouterse permitted elections, which were won by the center-right New Front for Democracy and Development (NF), a coalition of mainly East Indian, Creole, and Javanese parties. The National Democratic Party (NDP), organized by the military, captured just 3 out of 51 seats in the National Assembly.

The army ousted the elected government in 1990, and Bouterse again took power in a bloodless coup, but international pressure led to new elections in 1991. The NF again won a majority in the parliament, which chose the NF's candidate, Ronald Venetiaan, as president. Power passed to the NDP in the 1996 elections, with Bouterse ally Jules Wijdenbosch as president, but returned to the NF and Venetiaan after early elections in 2000.

A judicial investigation was launched in 2000 into the abduction and murder of 15 political opponents who were allegedly killed by Bouterse and members of his military government in December 1982. The victims of the "December murders" included labor union leaders, attorneys, military officers, professors, businessmen, and journalists. In 2001, Fred Derby, who was to be the star witness in the trial, suffered a fatal heart attack. However, the government vowed that testimony Derby gave during a preliminary hearing would be submitted at trial.

In the 2005 elections, the NF managed to remain the single largest political force, but its failure to win a two-thirds majority in the National Assembly prevented it from electing a president. In August, a United People's Assembly consisting of 891 members—including national, regional, and local lawmakers—gave Venetiaan his third term as president, with 560 votes for the incumbent versus 315 for the NDP's Rabin Parmessar.

While Bouterse continued to deny direct involvement in the 1982 "December murders," he accepted "political responsibility" and offered a public apology in March 2007. The long-awaited trial of Bouterse and 24 other suspects began in November 2007. Numerous key witnesses who had fled the country following the executions and settled in the Netherlands returned to testify in the trial.

Bouterse's Mega Combination coalition—comprising the NDP and three smaller parties—captured 23 seats in the May 2010 legislative elections, while the NF took 14 seats. In July, Bouterse was elected president with 71 percent of the parliamentary vote, defeating NF candidate Chandrikapersad Santokhi.

International travel has occasionally proven difficult for Bouterse due to a Europol warrant for his arrest that was issued after his conviction in absentia for drug trafficking in the Netherlands in 1999. However, he remains protected from arrest in Suriname due to the country's lack of an extradition treaty with the Netherlands and his current position as head of state.

There have been numerous delays in the "December murders" trial. However, on April 4, 2012, just as the trial was concluding, with a final verdict expected in May, the National Assembly passed legislation in a 28–12 vote to extend the country's 1992 amnesty law for crimes committed in defense of the state to include the period during which the December 1982 murders were committed. Immunity was therefore granted to Bouterse and the 24 other suspects. International and national protests condemned the amnesty legislation, and the Netherlands recalled its ambassador and suspended aid payments to Suriname. Questions on the constitutionality of the new amnesty law and whether a trial against the defendants who were granted immunity could proceed led to the trial's adjournment in May. The *Guyana Stabroek News* reported in June that the judges involved in the case were being threatened to permanently dismiss the case. One of the challenges to the trial's continuance is that the amnesty law's constitutionality must be reviewed in a constitutional court, which has yet to be established. The trial was expected to resume on December 12 but was once again postponed and had yet to reconvene by year's end.

Political Rights and Civil Liberties: Suriname is an electoral democracy. The 1987 constitution provides for a unicameral, 51-seat National Assembly, elected by proportional representation for five-year terms. The body elects the president to five-year terms with a two-thirds majority. If it is unable to do so, a United People's Assembly—consisting of lawmakers from the national, regional, and local levels—convenes to choose the president by a simple majority. A Council of State made up of the president and representatives of major societal groupings—including labor unions, business, the military, and the legislature—has veto power over legislation deemed to violate the constitution. Suriname's political parties largely reflect the cleavages in the country's ethnically diverse society and often form coalitions in order to gain power, including the NF, a coalition of the National Party of Suriname, and several smaller parties; the People's Alliance for Progress; the Mega Combination coalition, led by the

NDP and three smaller parties; and the A-Combination, representing the Maroons (descendants of former slaves).

Suriname has been plagued by corruption cases in recent years, and organized crime and drug networks continue to hamper governance and undermine the judicial system. The U.S. Bureau of Economic and Business Affairs reported in 2012 that the areas of government most affected by corruption are in procurement, land policy, taxation, and license issuance. Suriname was ranked 88 out of 176 countries surveyed in Transparency International's 2012 Corruptions Perception Index.

The constitution provides for freedoms of expression and the press, and the government generally respects these rights in practice. Defamation and libel remain criminal offenses, with punishments ranging from fines to imprisonment. Some media outlets engage in occasional self-censorship due to fear of reprisal from members of the former military leadership or pressure from senior government officials and others who object to critical stories about the administration. There are two privately owned daily newspapers, *De Ware Tijd* and *De West*. A number of small commercial radio stations compete with the government-owned radio and television broadcasting systems, resulting in a generally pluralistic range of viewpoints. Public access to government information is legally recognized, though it is very limited in practice. The government does not restrict internet access.

The authorities generally respect freedom of religion, which is protected by law and the constitution, and do not infringe on academic freedom.

The constitution provides for freedoms of assembly and association, and the government respects these rights in practice. Workers can join independent trade unions, though civil servants have no legal right to strike. Collective bargaining is legal and conducted fairly widely. The labor movement is active in politics.

The judiciary is susceptible to political influence and suffers from a significant shortage of judges and a large backlog of cases. Suriname is a signatory to the 2001 agreement establishing the Trinidad-based Caribbean Court of Justice (CCJ) as the final venue of appeal for member states of the Caribbean Community, but has yet to ratify the CCJ as its own final court of appeal. Police abuse detainees, particularly during arrests. Suriname is a major transit point for cocaine en route to Africa, Europe, and the United States, which has contributed to a rising tide of narcotics-related money laundering and organized crime. Prisons and detention centers are overcrowded and in poor condition.

Discrimination based on race or ethnicity is prohibited by law. However, the government does not recognize or offer any special protections for indigenous or native groups. Indigenous Amerindians and Maroons, who live primarily in the country's interior, are significantly disadvantaged in the areas of socioeconomic development and infrastructure, employment, education, and access to government services, and they have limited abilities to participate in the decision-making processes that affect their lands, traditions, and natural resources. Collective land rights are not acknowledged, and these populations continue to face problems due to illegal logging and mining on their land.

Constitutional guarantees of gender equality are not adequately enforced. Women are underrepresented in government; they hold less than 12 percent of seats in the National Assembly and just 2 of the 17 cabinet minister posts. Domestic violence remains a serious problem. While the law provides for women's equal access to education and employment, women do not receive the same wages as men for performing the same work. Suriname serves as a source, destination, and transit country for the trafficking of men, women, and children for the purposes of forced labor and prostitution.

Swaziland

Political Rights: 7
Civil Liberties: 5
Status: Not Free

Population: 1,220,300
Capital: Mbabane

Ten-Year Ratings Timeline For Year Under Review (Political Rights, Civil Liberties, Status)

2003	2004	2005	2006	2007	2008	2009	2010	2011	2012
7,5NF	7,5NF	7,5NF	7,5NF	7,5NF	7,5NF	7,5NF	7,5NF	7,5NF	7,5NF

Overview: **Antiregime protests in April and a teachers' union strike in June were violently dispersed by security forces. Press freedom in the kingdom took a further hit after senior editors at the *Swazi Observer* were suspended for political reasons in July and not reinstated by year's end.**

Swaziland regained its independence from Britain in 1968, and an elected Parliament was added to the traditional monarchy. In 1973, King Sobhuza II repealed the 1968 constitution, ended the multiparty system in favor of a tinkhundla (local council) system, and declared himself an absolute monarch. After Sobhuza's death in 1982, a protracted power struggle ended with the coronation of King Mswati III in 1986.

A new constitution implemented in 2006 removed the king's ability to rule by decree, but reaffirmed his absolute authority over the cabinet, Parliament, and judiciary. It also maintained the tinkhundla system—in which local chiefs control elections for 55 of the 65 seats in the lower house—and did not overturn the ban on political parties. The charter provided for limited freedoms of speech, assembly, and association, as well as limited rights for women, but the king could suspend these at his discretion.

The country remains mired in a deep financial crisis, which was brought on by a sharp drop in revenue from a regional customs union, maladministration of public funds, and lavish spending by the royal family. The crisis has led to massive cuts in public services, including pensions, education, and health care since 2010. In 2011, South Africa agreed to extend a $355 million loan if Swaziland met fiscal reforms approved by the International Monetary Fund (IMF) and "confidence-building measures" on democracy and human rights; the kingdom rejected these conditions. In May 2012, the IMF withdrew its advisory team from Swaziland, citing government intransigence.

The crisis has helped drive an uptick in antigovernment protests and strikes, most of which have been banned or violently dispersed by security forces. Despite court-ordered prohibitions and a strong police presence, April 2012 protests by trade unionists and prodemocracy groups in Mbabane went forward. Hundreds were reportedly detained and interrogated, and scores of cell phones and cameras were confiscated. A six-week strike beginning in June by teachers demanding salary increases saw instances of violence by both strikers and police. Thirty people were arrested, and the government fired more than 100 teachers, though King Mswati reinstated them in August.

Swaziland has the world's highest rate of HIV infection: 26 percent of Swazis between 15 and 49 are living with the disease. The financial crisis has led to shortages in antiretroviral drugs, as well as HIV testing.

Political Rights and Civil Liberties: Swaziland is not an electoral democracy. King Mswati III is an absolute monarch with ultimate authority over the cabinet, legislature, and judiciary. Of the House of Assembly's 65 members, 55 are elected by popular vote within the tinkhundla system, in which local chiefs vet all candidates; the king appoints the other 10 members. The king also appoints 20 members of the 30-seat Senate, with the remainder selected by the House of Assembly. Members of the bicameral Parliament, all of whom serve five-year terms, are not allowed to initiate legislation. Traditional chiefs govern designated localities and typically report directly to the king.

Political parties are illegal, but there are political associations, the two largest being the banned People's United Democratic Movement (PUDEMO) and the Ngwane National Liberatory Congress.

Corruption is a major problem, and government corruption was widely blamed for contributing to Swaziland's financial crisis. In March 2012, legislators voted to revoke their own 10 percent pay cuts implemented in the face of financial crisis. Swaziland was ranked 88 out of 176 countries surveyed in Transparency International's 2012 Corruption Perceptions Index.

Constitutional rights to free expression are severely restricted in practice and can be suspended by the king. Publishing criticism of the ruling family is banned. Self-censorship is widespread, as journalists are routinely threatened and attacked by the authorities. However, South African media are available, and both the *Swazi Observer* and the independent *Times of Swaziland* occasionally criticize the government. In April 2012, two South African reporters from eTV were temporarily detained outside a roadblock in Mbabane for lacking accreditation to cover the demonstrations that month. In July, two senior editors at the private, royal-owned *Swazi Observer* were suspended for one month for reporting too negatively on the king; the editors remained suspended at year's end. The government does not restrict access to the internet, but few Swazis can afford access.

Freedom of religion is not explicitly protected under the constitution, but is mostly respected in practice, although security forces have been accused of intimidating church leaders deemed sympathetic to the prodemocracy movement. Academic freedom is limited by prohibitions against criticizing the monarchy.

The government restricts freedoms of assembly and association, and permission to hold political gatherings is frequently denied. Demonstrators routinely face violence and arrests by police. The government has sweeping powers under the 2008 Suppression of Terrorism Act to declare any organization a "terrorist group," a practice that has been abused by authorities. In April 2012, the government secured an Industrial Court order prohibiting antigovernment marches planned for the middle of the month. In July, PUDEMO leader Mario Masuku was placed under house arrest to prevent him from attending a rally in support of striking teachers. Police harassment and surveillance of civil society organizations has increased in recent years, as have forced searches of homes and offices, torture in interrogations, and the use of roadblocks to prevent demonstrations.

Swaziland has active labor unions, with the largest, the Swaziland Federation of Trade Unions (SFTU), leading demands for democratization. The government is the country's largest employer, and recent retrenchments in the public sector have spurred increased activism by government employees. Workers in all areas of the economy can join unions, and 80 percent of the private workforce is unionized. However, government pressure and crackdowns on strikes have limited union operations. After approving the registration of the new Trade Union Congress of Swaziland—a merger between SFTU, the Swaziland Federation of Labour, and the Swaziland National Association of Teachers—in January 2012, the government deregistered the union before the April marches.

The dual judicial system includes courts based on Roman-Dutch law and traditional courts using customary law. The judiciary is independent in most civil cases, though the king has ultimate judicial powers, and the royal family and government often refuse to respect rulings with which they disagree. However, the Swazi High Court has made a number of notable antigovernment rulings in recent years. In 2011, Judge Thomas Masuku—head of the Judicial Services Commission—was suspended for allegedly insulting the king in a ruling, and remained so in 2012.

Incidents of police torture, beatings, and suspicious deaths in custody continued in 2012, particularly of leaders and participants in antigovernment protests. Security forces generally operate with impunity. Prisons are overcrowded, and inmates are subject to rape, beatings, and torture.

The constitution grants women equal rights and legal status as adults, but these rights remain restricted in practice. While both the legal code and customary law provide some protection against gender-based violence, it is common and often tolerated with impunity. Discrimination against members of the LGBT (lesbian, gay, bisexual, and transgender) community is widespread.

Sweden

Political Rights: 1
Civil Liberties: 1
Status: Free

Population: 9,513,500
Capital: Stockholm

Ten-Year Ratings Timeline For Year Under Review (Political Rights, Civil Liberties, Status)

2003	2004	2005	2006	2007	2008	2008	2010	2011	2012
1,1F	1,1F	1,1F	1,1F	1,1F	1,1F	1,1F	1,1F	1,1F	1,1F

Overview: The leader of the Social Democratic Party was forced to resign in January 2012, after he became the subject of a corruption investigation. In March, Sweden adopted a controversial data retention law over concerns by privacy advocates.

After centuries of wars and monarchical unions with its neighbors, Sweden emerged as a liberal constitutional monarchy in the 19th century. Norway ended its union with the country in 1905, leaving Sweden with its current borders. Its tradition of neutrality, beginning with World War I, was altered somewhat by its admission to the European Union (EU) in 1995, and was further eroded by a more pragmatic approach to security in 2002. However, Sweden has continued to avoid military alliances, including NATO.

Voters rejected adoption of the euro currency in a 2003 referendum, despite support from government and business leaders. The rejection was attributed to skepticism about the EU and fears regarding the possible deterioration of welfare benefits and damage to the economy. Just days before the referendum, Foreign Minister Anna Lindh was killed in a knife attack in Stockholm. Her killer, a Swedish national of Serbian descent who had no clear political agenda, was sentenced to life in prison. In the 2006 parliamentary elections, a four-party, center-right alliance headed by Fredrik Reinfeldt of the Moderate Party defeated the Social Democratic Party (SAP), which had been in power for 12 years.

Parliament passed the Signals Intelligence Act in 2008, giving Sweden's National Defense Radio Establishment the authority to monitor communications without a court order. Following widespread public protest, the law was changed to allow such wiretapping only in cases where external military threats were suspected. Only military and government can request surveillance, and those who have been monitored must be notified.

In the September 2010 parliamentary elections, Reinfeldt won a second term as prime minister. However, his coalition failed to win an outright majority and would instead rule as a minority government, with the Moderate Party, Center Party, and Liberal People's Party, as well as the Christian Democrats. The controversial far-right Swedish Democrats (SD) entered Parliament for the first time with 20 seats, though the other seven parties represented in Parliament vowed not to rely on the SD for significant votes, which left it politically isolated.

In October 2011, opposition and SAP leader Håkan Juholt became the subject of a fraud investigation over housing reimbursements he received beginning in 2007. He resigned in January 2012 and was replaced by Stefan Löfven.

Political Rights and Civil Liberties: Sweden is an electoral democracy. The unicameral Parliament, the Riksdag, has 349 members elected every four years by proportional representation. A party must receive at least 4 percent of the vote nationwide or 12 percent in one of the 29 electoral districts to win representation. The prime minister is appointed by the speaker of the Riksdag and confirmed by the body as a whole. King Carl XVI Gustaf, crowned in 1973, is the ceremonial head of state.

Eight political parties are currently represented in the Riksdag. The largest single party is the opposition SAP, also known as the Workers' Party, which ruled for most of the last century with the aid of the Left Party and, in later decades, the Green Party. The SD moved toward broader public acceptance in 2012, becoming the third most popular party in Sweden, according to a series of polls at year's end.

The country's principal religious, ethnic, and immigrant groups are represented in Parliament. Since 1993, the indigenous Sami community has elected its own parliament, which has significant powers over community education and culture and serves as an advisory body to the government. In April 2011, the Supreme Court issued a landmark ruling in the so-called Nordmaling case, granting Sami reindeer herders common-law rights to disputed lands; the case had been ongoing for 14 years.

Corruption rates are generally low in Sweden, which was ranked 4 out of 176 countries surveyed in Transparency International's 2012 Corruption Perceptions Index. However, the Organization for Economic Cooperation and Development published a critical report in June 2012, admonishing Sweden for insufficient enforcement of its foreign bribery laws. TeliaSonora, a telecommunications company partly owned by the Swedish government, was criticized in 2012 for giving access to its users' data to the governments of Uzbekistan, Belarus, and Azerbaijan— facilitating illegal surveillance of their citizens—in exchange for obtaining lucrative contracts. The head of TeliaSonora, Lars Nyberg, resigned in October 2012 as a consequence.

Freedom of speech is guaranteed by law, and the country has one of the most robust freedom of information statutes in the world. However, hate-speech laws prohibit threats or expressions of contempt based on race, color, national or ethnic origin, religious belief, or sexual orientation.

Sweden's media are independent. Most newspapers and periodicals are privately owned, and the government subsidizes daily newspapers regardless of their political affiliation. Public broadcasters air weekly radio and television programs in several immigrant languages. The ethnic press is entitled to the same subsidies as the Swedish-language press. Under the 2009 Intellectual Property Rights Enforcement Directive (IPRED), internet service providers must reveal information about users who are found to be engaged in illegal file sharing. However, the first case was referred to the European Court of Justice to determine whether the law was in accordance with European legislation on privacy and data protection. A ruling in April 2012 determined that IPRED followed European law. In March, Sweden adopted a data retention law after a six-year delay due to privacy concerns. The law, which puts Sweden in compliance with EU directives, requires Swedish telecommunications carriers to store data, including phone call records and internet traffic, for three years.

Religious freedom is constitutionally guaranteed. Although the population is 87 percent Lutheran, all churches, as well as synagogues and mosques, receive some state financial support. The number of reported hate crimes against the Jewish community has slowly declined in recent years, but the figures for those targeting the Muslim community have remained steady. Academic freedom is ensured for all.

Freedoms of assembly and association are respected in law and in practice. Peaceful protests were mounted against the SD and racism in the period surrounding the 2010 elections. The rights to strike and organize in labor unions are guaranteed. Trade union federations, which represent about 80 percent of the workforce, are strong and well organized. The Swedish labor code was amended in 2010, after the European Court of Justice ruled that employees at the Swedish branches of foreign companies are subject to their home country's collective agreements, and not those of Swedish unions.

The judiciary is independent. Swedish courts are allowed to try suspects for genocide committed abroad. In 2011, Sweden sought the extradition of controversial WikiLeaks founder Julian Assange from the United Kingdom so that he could be questioned regarding rape and sexual assault allegations stemming from two incidents in Stockholm in 2010. In June 2012, Assange sought refuge in the Ecuadorean embassy in London, where he was granted diplomatic asylum; he remained there at year's end.

An Equality Ombudsman position was created in 2008 to oversee efforts to prevent discrimination on the basis of gender, ethnicity, disability, and sexual orientation, and a permanent national hate-crime police unit was established in 2009. In recent years, the government has faced resistance from local communities in its efforts to establish temporary housing for asylum seekers. In 2007 Sweden changed its immigration policy, disallowing family reunification for "quota refugees"; family members must now apply separately for visas. In March 2011, the government reached an agreement on a framework for immigration reform that would increase immigrants' access to public services, though it had not been implemented by the end of 2012. In July 2012, Peter Mangs was found guilty of killing 3 people and wounding at least 10 in a series of shootings targeting primarily foreign-born individuals in the city of Malmo. In November, he was sentenced to life in prison and ordered to pay damages of over 1.1 million kronor ($165,000), after a psychiatric evaluation failed to find him legally insane.

Same-sex couples were legally allowed to adopt for the first time in 2003. The country granted lesbian couples the same rights to artificial insemination and in vitro fertilization as heterosexual couples in 2005.

Sweden is a global leader in gender equality. Approximately 45 percent of Riksdag members are women. Of the 24 government ministers, 11 are women. Although 80 percent of women work outside of the home, they still earn only 70 percent of men's wages in the public sector and 76 percent in the private sector. The country is a destination and transit point for women and children trafficked for the purpose of sexual exploitation. The 2004 Aliens Act helped to provide more assistance to trafficking victims, and a special ambassador has been appointed to aid in combating human trafficking.

Switzerland

Political Rights: 1
Civil Liberties: 1
Status: Free

Population: 7,994,200
Capital: Bern

Ten-Year Ratings Timeline For Year Under Review (Political Rights, Civil Liberties, Status)

2003	2004	2005	2006	2007	2008	2009	2010	2011	2012
1,1F	1,1F	1,1F	1,1F	1,1F	1,1F	1,1F	1,1F	1,1F	1,1F

Overview: The Swiss parliament rejected a ban on Muslim veils in 2012. However, it further tightened the country's asylum laws, and rejected a recommendation from the United Nations Human Rights Council to overturn a 2009 ban on new construction of mosque minarets.

Switzerland, which has existed as a confederation of cantons since 1291, emerged with its current borders and a tradition of neutrality at the end of the Napoleonic wars in 1815. The country's four official ethnic communities are based on language: German, French, Italian, and Romansh (the smallest community).

Switzerland remained neutral during the wars of the 20th century, and it joined the United Nations only after a referendum in 2002. Membership in international institutions has long been a controversial issue in Switzerland. The Swiss have resisted joining the European Union (EU), and even rejected membership in the European Economic Area, a free-trade area that links non-EU members with the EU. However, Switzerland has joined international financial institutions and signed a range of free-trade agreements.

During the 2003 federal elections, the far-right Swiss People's Party (SVP), hostile to both EU membership and immigration, made blatantly xenophobic appeals. It led the vote, followed closely by the center-left Social Democratic Party (SPS).

The SVP successfully championed a 2006 referendum on tightening asylum and immigration laws. The new laws require asylum seekers to produce an identity document within 48 hours of arrival or risk repatriation, and effectively limit immigration to those coming from EU countries; prospective immigrants from outside the EU would have to possess skills lacking in the Swiss economy.

In the October 2007 federal elections, the SVP captured 29 percent of the vote, more than any party since 1919. The SVP campaign received international attention for its anti-immigrant appeals, and an SVP rally and counterdemonstration in Bern resulted in violence rarely seen in Switzerland.

In December 2007, the SVP temporarily placed itself in opposition to the government after the parliament refused to reappoint SVP leader Christoph Blocher to the cabinet, choosing instead Eveline Widmer-Schlumpf, from the party's more moderate wing. The SVP subsequently expelled Widmer-Schlumpf, who then became part of the new center-right Conservative Democratic Party (BDP).

Following successful petitioning by the SVP, a referendum calling for a ban on the future construction of minarets on mosques was held in November 2009. Nearly 58 percent of the population and 22 out of 26 cantons voted in favor of the ban. However, the four mosques with existing minarets would not be affected. In November 2010, a referendum mandating the automatic deportation of foreigners convicted of certain crimes passed with 53 percent of the vote. Both referendums met with considerable domestic and international criticism.

The federal elections held in October 2011 saw a modest strengthening of the political center in Switzerland. In National Council elections, the SVP, while still the leading party, lost seats for the first time since 1975, retaining 54 seats—8 fewer than it won in 2007.

Facing renewed international criticism of its strict bank secrecy laws, in 2009 Switzerland agreed to adopt international transparency standards established by the Organization for Economic Cooperation and Development (OECD) by providing foreign governments with financial information in tax evasion cases and tax fraud investigations. In June 2012, the United States announced an agreement with Switzerland that would allow Swiss banks to report suspected tax evasion by U.S. clients to U.S. authorities. Switzerland also reached a deal with Germany in April to tax secret Swiss bank accounts held by Germans at a rate of up to 41 percent, but the upper house of the German parliament rejected the agreement in November.

Political Rights and Civil Liberties: Switzerland is an electoral democracy. The 1848 constitution, significantly revised in 1874 and 2000, provides for a Federal Assembly with two directly elected chambers: the 46-member Council of States (in which each canton has two members and each half-canton has one) and the 200-member National Council. All lawmakers serve four-year terms. The Federal Council (cabinet) is a seven-person executive council, with each member elected by the Federal Assembly. The presidency is largely ceremonial and rotates annually among the Federal Council's members.

The Swiss political system is characterized by decentralization and direct democracy. The cantons and half-cantons have significant control over economic and social policy, with the federal government's powers largely limited to foreign affairs and some economic matters. Referendums, which have been used extensively since the 1848 constitution, are mandatory for any amendments to the Federal Constitution, the joining of international organizations, or major changes to federal laws.

The government is free from pervasive corruption. However, Philipp Hildebrand, the head of the Swiss Central Bank, resigned in January 2012 over allegations that he and his wife had engaged in improper currency trading. As the world's largest offshore financial center, the country was criticized for failing to comply with recommended international norms on money laundering and terrorist financing. Switzerland has reached bilateral deals with several countries on financial information sharing and was removed from the OECD's "gry list" of tax havens in 2009. Switzerland was ranked 6 out of 176 countries surveyed in Transparency International's 2012 Corruption Perceptions Index.

Freedom of speech is guaranteed by the constitution. Switzerland has a free media environment, although the state-owned Swiss Broadcasting Corporation dominates the broadcast market. Consolidation of newspaper ownership in large media conglomerates has forced the closure of some small and local newspapers. The law penalizes public incitement to racial hatred or discrimination and denying crimes against humanity. There is no government restriction on access to the internet.

Freedom of religion is guaranteed by the constitution, and most cantons support one or several churches. The country is split roughly between Roman Catholicism and Protestantism, though some 400,000 Muslims form the largest non-Christian minority, according to the 2000 census. A 2008 law requires that immigrant clerics receive integration training, including language instruction, before practicing. The Swiss parliament in September 2012 rejected a proposal to ban face-covering veils for Muslim women in public spaces, following the implementation of similar bans in France and Belgium. Opponents of the ban argued that it was unnecessary, since relatively few women wore such veils in Switzerland, while supporters cited public safety and gender equality concerns. Most public schools provide religious education, depending on the predominant creed in each canton. Religion classes are mandatory in some schools, although waivers are regularly granted upon request. The government respects academic freedom.

Freedoms of assembly and association are provided by the constitution. The right to collective bargaining is respected, and approximately 25 percent of the workforce is unionized.

The judiciary is independent, and the rule of law prevails in civil and criminal matters. Most judicial decisions are made at the cantonal level, except for the federal Supreme Court, which reviews cantonal court decisions when they pertain to federal law. Some incidents of police discrimination and excessive use of force have been documented. Prison and detention center conditions generally meet international standards, and the Swiss government permits visits by independent human rights observers.

The rights of cultural, religious, and linguistic minorities are legally protected, though minorities—especially those of African and Central European descent, as well as Roma—face increasing societal discrimination. Increasing anxiety about the growing foreign-born population has led to the passage of stricter asylum laws. Parliament further tightened those laws in September 2012, including barring applications for asylum at Swiss embassies abroad and cutting benefits. In 2012, 28,631 people applied for asylum in Switzerland, the highest number since 1999, and up 27 percent from 2011. In response to concerns put forward by the UN Committee against Torture in 2010, the government took steps in 2011 to address the treatment of asylum seekers, including training observers present during repatriation flights and instituting a monitoring system in cases of forced repatriation. In October 2012, the UN Human Rights Council made a number of recommendations to Switzerland to improve its practices and address racism, xenophobia, and the treatment of asylum seekers. The Swiss government rejected four of the recommendations, one of which was to overturn the 2009 minaret construction ban.

Women were only granted universal suffrage at the federal level in 1971, and the half-canton of Appenzell-Innerrhoden denied women the right to vote until 1990. Fifty-eight women sit in the 200-member National Council and 9 in the Council of States. The constitution guarantees men and women equal pay for equal work, but pay differentials remain. Switzerland was ranked 10 out of 135 countries surveyed in the World Economic Forum's 2012 Gender Gap Report, which analyzes equality in the division of resources and opportunities between men and women.

Syria

Political Rights: 7
Civil Liberties: 7
Status: Not Free

Population: 22,530,700
Capital: Damascus

Trend Arrow: Syria received a downward trend arrow due to rising sectarian violence and displacement, including targeted attacks on Sunni Muslim populations that oppose the regime.

Ten-Year Ratings Timeline For Year Under Review (Political Rights, Civil Liberties, Status)

2002	2003	2004	2005	2006	2007	2008	2009	2010	2011
7,7NF	7,7NF	7,7NF	7,6NF	7,6NF	7,6NF	7,6NF	7,6NF	7,7NF	7,7NF

Overview:
The civil war that gripped Syria in 2011 continued in 2012, devastating the country and leading to widespread displacement and regional instability. More than 45,000 people were believed to have been killed—many of them civilians—in the conflict by the end of 2012, and thousands of others were injured, missing, or arrested. More than 470,000 Syrian refugees were registered with the United Nations in Turkey, Jordan, Lebanon, and Iraq, while tens of thousands more crossed borders without registering. In addition, over 2.5 million Syrians inside the country required aid, including over 1.5 million internally displaced persons. International efforts to broker a ceasefire or political agreement between the regime and opposition forces failed, and the war took on an increasingly sectarian tone.

The modern state of Syria was established as a League of Nations mandate under French control after World War I and gained formal independence in 1946. Periods of military and elected civilian rule alternated until the Arab Socialist Baath Party seized power in a 1963 coup, transforming Syria into a one-party state governed under emergency law. During the 1960s, power shifted from the party's civilian ideologues to army officers, most of whom were Alawites (adherents of a heterodox Islamic sect that makes up 12 percent of the population). This trend culminated in General Hafez al-Assad's rise to power in 1970.

The regime cultivated a base of support that spanned sectarian and ethnic divisions, but relied on Alawite domination of the security establishment and the forcible suppression of dissent. In 1982, government forces stormed the city of Hama to crush a rebellion by the opposition Muslim Brotherhood, killing as many as 20,000 insurgents and civilians.

Bashar al-Assad took power after his father's death in 2000, pledging to liberalize Syria's politics and economy. The first six months of his presidency featured the release of political prisoners, the return of exiled dissidents, and open discussion of the country's problems. But in February 2001, the regime began to reverse this so-called Damascus Spring. Leading reformists were arrested and sentenced to lengthy prison terms, while others faced constant surveillance and intimidation by the secret police.

Reinvigorated by the toppling of Iraq's Baathist regime in 2003, Syria's dissidents began cooperating and pushing for the release of political prisoners, the cancellation of the emergency law, and the legalization of opposition parties. Despite hints that sweeping political reforms would be drafted at a major Baath Party conference in 2005, no substantial measures were taken. In October 2005, representatives of all three segments of the opposition—Islamists, Kurds, and secular liberals—signed the Damascus Declaration for Democratic National Change (DDDNC), which called for the country's leaders to step down and endorsed a broad set of liberal democratic principles.

In May 2006, a number of Syrian political and human rights activists signed the Beirut-Damascus Declaration, which called for a change in Syrian-Lebanese relations and the recognition of Lebanese sovereignty. Many who signed were detained or sentenced to prison in a renewed crackdown on personal freedoms.

Al-Assad won another presidential term in 2007, with 97.6 percent of the vote. In results that were similarly predetermined, the ruling Baath-dominated coalition won the majority of seats in that year's parliamentary and municipal polls. Meanwhile, supporters of the DDDNC formed governing bodies for their alliance and renewed their activities, prompting another government crackdown. Over the subsequent three years, the state continued to suppress dissenting views and punish government opponents. Nevertheless, the United States and European countries took tentative steps in 2010 to improve relations with Damascus.

The regime's brutal response to an antigovernment uprising in 2011 dashed any hopes of further progress in its foreign relations. The initially peaceful protests were sparked by the detention and reported torture of several children for writing antigovernment graffiti in the southern city of Dara'a in March, and they soon spread to central cities like Hama and Homs, as well as towns along the Syrian-Turkish border. The authorities' extensive use of live fire and military hardware against civilian demonstrators led small groups of soldiers to desert and organize antigovernment militias. Fighting between the two sides soon escalated into a civil war.

Despite the regime's consistent claims that it was under attack from foreign-backed terrorists, not a domestic opposition with political aims, the government made some symbolic concessions in 2011, including repealing the country's long-standing emergency law and revising the constitution. The new charter, which removed language cementing the Baath Party's leadership role and added a two-term limit for presidents, was adopted with a reported 89 percent of the vote in a February 2012 referendum that the opposition dismissed as a sham. Parliamentary elections were held in May amid open warfare and an opposition boycott, producing a legislature that included only the Baath Party and allied factions with 168 seats, progovernment independents with 77 seats, and a nominal opposition group with 5 seats.

As the fighting wore on, high-ranking government and military officials continued to defect. Most notably, Riyad Farid Hijab, the prime minister since June, fled to Jordan in August. However, the opposition remained relatively disorganized. Many local militias were loosely affiliated with the Turkey-based Free Syrian Army, while others, particularly hardline Salafi-jihadi factions like Jabhat al-Nusra, cooperated with fellow rebel groups on an ad hoc basis. Various civilian opposition organizations continued to operate as well, including a national network of Local Coordination Committees and the Syrian National Council, a grouping of exiled political leaders based in Turkey.

The conflict greatly increased in tempo and violence over the course of the year, with the government using airstrikes, artillery bombardments, and even ballistic missiles to devastate rebel-held neighborhoods, and some opposition groups engaging in car bombings near government buildings. Regular massacres of civilians were reported. By year's end, the conflict was estimated to have caused over 45,000 deaths and displaced over 1.5 million people within Syria. Hundreds of thousands of Syrians also fled to neighboring countries, straining those governments' resources and testing their political stability.

UN-led efforts to forge a cease-fire agreement made little progress during the year. UN General Assembly resolutions passed in February and August condemned the Syrian government for its conduct in the war and called on al-Assad to resign as part of political transition, but Russia and China blocked any stronger action against Damascus at the UN Security Council.

At a gathering in Qatar in November 2012, a broad array of opposition military and political groups active both inside and outside Syria formed a new umbrella organization, the National Coalition of Syrian Revolutionary and Opposition Forces. The entity was designed to replace the discredited Syrian National Council as the opposition's diplomatic representative and improve coordination of funding and military supplies from Western and Arab donor countries. Key Islamist militias refused to join the group. Meanwhile, the Syrian regime reportedly continued to receive military aid from Iran and the Lebanese militant group Hezbollah.

Political Rights and Civil Liberties: Syria is not an electoral democracy. The president is nominated by the ruling Baath Party and approved by popular referendum for seven-year terms. In practice, these referendums are orchestrated by the regime, as are elections for the 250-seat, unicameral People's Council, whose members serve four-year terms and hold little independent legislative power. Almost all power rests in the executive branch.

Political parties based on religious, tribal, or regional affiliation are banned. Until a 2011 decree allowed the formation of new parties, the only legal factions were the Baath Party and its several small coalition partners in the ruling National Progressive Front (NPF). Independent candidates, who are heavily vetted and closely allied with the regime, are permitted to contest about a third of the People's Council seats. A 2012 constitutional referendum relaxed rules regarding the participation of non-Baathist parties and imposed a limit of two terms on the presidency, but parliamentary elections in May resulted in minimal changes to the composition of the government.

Corruption is widespread and rarely carries serious punishment, and bribery is often necessary to navigate the bureaucracy. Regime officials and their families benefit from a range of illicit economic activities. Syria was ranked 144 out of 176 countries surveyed in Transparency International's 2012 Corruption Perceptions Index.

Freedom of expression is heavily restricted. The penal code and a 2001 Publications Law criminalize the publication of material that harms national unity, tarnishes the state's image, or threatens the "goals of the revolution." A 2011 media law contained similar, broadly worded content restrictions, and journalists continued to be detained despite its provisions barring arrests or imprisonment for press offenses. Apart from a few stations with non-news formats, all broadcast media are state owned. However, satellite dishes are common, giving most Syrians access to foreign broadcasts. More than a dozen privately owned newspapers and magazines had opened in the years before the 2011 uprising, but their news coverage is tightly circumscribed. In areas under tenuous rebel control, opposition-oriented media outlets have begun to emerge, for the most part in print or online.

Journalists were frequently killed, tortured, jailed, or reported missing during 2012. Reporters Without Borders estimated in December that at least 18 professional journalists from domestic and international outlets had been killed by regime and opposition forces since the conflict began in 2011. This number does not include over 40 citizen journalists who have been targeted and killed because of their role in disseminating information. Foreign journalists continue to face detention and travel restrictions, and some—such as American freelance journalist Austin Tice, who was abducted by progovernment forces in August—remained missing at year's end. Meanwhile, numerous domestic reporters and citizen journalists have been detained and subjected to torture and military tribunals for their coverage.

Most Syrians access the internet through state-run servers, which block more than 200 sites associated with the opposition, Kurdish politics, Islamic organizations, human rights, and certain foreign news services, particularly those in Lebanon. Social-networking and video-sharing websites were unblocked in 2011, but they have been used to track and punish opposition supporters and activists. Online communications are reportedly monitored by intelligence agencies, and the government has fostered self-censorship through intimidation. The Syrian Electronic Army, a progovernment hacking group, has attacked opposition websites with apparent backing from the regime.

Although the constitution requires that the president be a Muslim, there is no state religion in Syria, and freedom of worship is generally respected. However, the government tightly monitors mosques and controls the appointment of Muslim religious leaders. All non-worship meetings of religious groups require permits. Mosques have frequently become sites of violence since 2011, as government forces attempt to prevent gatherings of worshipers from turning into protests. The Alawite minority dominates the internal security forces and the officer corps of the military, while Sunni Muslims make up the bulk of rebel forces. The conflict has taken on an increasingly sectarian character, with Sunni-populated areas bearing the brunt of government attacks, some Islamist factions declaring their hostility toward minorities and secularists, and civilians of all confessions seeking safety among their respective groups.

Academic freedom is heavily restricted. Several private universities have been founded in recent years, and the extent of academic freedom within them varies. University professors have been dismissed or imprisoned for expressing dissent, and some have been killed in response to their outspoken support for regime opponents. Education in general has been greatly disrupted by the civil war.

Freedom of assembly is closely circumscribed. Public demonstrations are illegal without official permission, which is typically granted only to progovernment groups. The security services intensified their ban on public and private gatherings starting in 2006, forbidding any group of five or more people from discussing political and economic topics. Surveillance and extensive informant networks have enforced this rule and, until the 2011 uprising, ensured that a culture of self-censorship and fear prevailed. Illegal protests have since been met with gunfire, arrests, and alleged torture.

Freedom of association is severely restricted. All nongovernmental organizations must register with the government, which generally denies registration to reformist or human rights groups. Leaders of unlicensed human rights groups have frequently been jailed for publicizing state abuses. Despite grave risks, opposition activist networks have continued to operate across Syria since 2011.

Professional syndicates are controlled by the Baath Party, and all labor unions must belong to the General Federation of Trade Unions, a nominally independent grouping that the government uses to control union activity. Strikes in nonagricultural sectors are legal, but they rarely occur.

While the lower courts in previous years operated with some independence and generally safeguarded ordinary defendants' rights, politically sensitive cases were usually tried by the Supreme State Security Court (SSSC), an exceptional tribunal appointed by the executive branch that denied the right to appeal, limited access to legal counsel, tried many cases behind closed doors, and routinely accepted confessions obtained through torture. The SSSC was abolished in response to the uprisings in 2011, but this did not bring any tangible gains in the rights of the accused.

The security agencies, which operate independently of the judiciary, routinely extract confessions by torturing suspects and detaining their family members. The government lifted its emergency law in April 2011, but security agencies still have virtually unlimited authority to arrest suspects and hold them incommunicado for prolonged periods without charge. Political activists are often monitored and harassed by security services even after release from prison. At the end of 2012, an estimated 100,000 people were missing or detained for political reasons. Extrajudicial killings have also increased dramatically since the civil conflict began.

The Kurdish minority faces severe restrictions on cultural and linguistic expression. The 2001 press law requires that owners and top editors of print publications be Arabs. Kurdish exile groups estimate that as many as 300,000 Syrian Kurds have traditionally been unable to obtain citizenship, passports, identity cards, or birth certificates, preventing them from owning land, obtaining government employment, and voting. Suspected Kurdish activists are routinely dismissed from schools and public sector jobs. While the government pledged in 2011 to give citizenship rights to thousands of Kurds in eastern Syria, conditions for Kurds remained harsh, and Kurdish militias have taken up arms to defend their areas amid the civil war.

The proliferation of military checkpoints, open fighting, and general insecurity have severely restricted travel and the movement of vital supplies since 2011, affecting resident civilians, the internally displaced, and those attempting to flee abroad.

While Syria was one of the first Arab countries to grant female suffrage, women remain underrepresented in Syrian politics and government. They hold 12 percent of the seats in the legislature, though the government has appointed some women to senior positions, including one of the two vice-presidential posts. The government provides women with equal access to education, but many discriminatory laws remain in force. A husband may request that the Interior Ministry block his wife from traveling abroad, and women, unlike men, are generally barred from taking their children out of the country without proof of the spouse's permission. Violence against women is common, particularly in rural areas. Perpetrators of killings classified as "honor crimes" are punished with reduced sentences ranging from five to seven years in prison. Women's rights groups estimate that there are hundreds of such killings each year. Personal status law for Muslims is governed by Sharia (Islamic law) and is discriminatory in marriage, divorce, and inheritance matters. Church law governs personal status issues for Christians, in some cases barring divorce. Homosexual acts are punishable with up to three years in prison.

Taiwan

Political Rights: 1
Civil Liberties: 2
Status: Free

Population: 23,257,700
Capital: Taipei

Ten-Year Ratings Timeline For Year Under Review (Political Rights, Civil Liberties, Status)

2003	2004	2005	2006	2007	2008	2009	2010	2011	2012
2,2F	2,1F	1,1F	2,1F	2,1F	2,1F	1,2F	1,2F	1,2F	1,2F

Overview:

Taiwan held its fifth direct presidential election in January 2012, resulting in a new term for incumbent Ma Ying-jeou of the Chinese nationalist Kuomintang (KMT). The KMT also retained control of the parliament in concurrent legislative elections. High-profile corruption cases against former officials continued to work their way through the courts, with a former cabinet secretary general facing indictment and jailed former president Chen Shui-bian receiving an additional 10 years in prison for bribery. Also during the year, private media owners initiated two deals that triggered objections from press freedom advocates, who warned that they could lead to excessive concentration and reduced diversity of content.

In 1949, Taiwan became home to defeated nationalist Kuomintang (KMT) authorities as they fled the mainland in the wake of the Chinese civil war. Still formally known as the Republic of China (ROC), the island is independent in all but name, though it lacks formal recognition by most countries and international organizations. The People's Republic of China (PRC) considers it a renegade province and has threatened to take military action if de jure independence is declared.

Taiwan's transition to democracy began in 1987, when the KMT ended 38 years of martial law. In 1988, Lee Teng-hui became the first Taiwanese-born president, breaking the political dominance previously enjoyed by mainland émigrés. Liberalization of the media and legalization of opposition political parties followed in 1989. Lee oversaw Taiwan's first full multiparty legislative elections in 1991–92 and won the first direct presidential election in 1996. Chen Shui-bian of the pro-independence Democratic Progressive Party (DPP) won the 2000 presidential election, ending 55 years of KMT rule. After a narrow reelection victory in 2004, Chen remained in office until 2008, when candidate Ma Ying-jeou recaptured the presidency for the KMT in Taiwan's second democratic transfer of power.

In January 2012, Ma won a second term, with 51.6 percent of the vote, following a vigorous race against DPP candidate Tsai Ing-wen, who took 45.6 percent. The KMT also retained control of the 113-seat parliament in concurrent legislative elections, though with a reduced majority of 64 seats. The DPP took 40, and the remainder went to independents and smaller parties.

In the first high-profile corruption scandal of the Ma administration, former cabinet secretary general and KMT lawmaker Lin Yi-shih was indicted in October 2012 for allegedly demanding and accepting bribes from a businessman. Separately, former president Chen, who was already serving corruption-related prison sentences handed down in 2010 and 2011, was sentenced to another 10 years in December for bribery. Chen's supporters and a number of independent observers called for him to be released on medical parole, citing his worsening physical and mental health, but the government said his ailments did not reach the threshold set by law and could be treated in prison or through hospital visits.

Also during the year, two proposed media sales triggered street protests in which press freedom advocates warned against ownership concentration and a decline in diversity of content. In July, media regulators gave conditional approval to a deal in which a Beijing-friendly conglomerate with already significant media holdings would acquire the country's second-largest cable television system. In November, a Hong Kong–based media group agreed to sell its Taiwan assets to a consortium of Taiwanese businessmen, some of whom have major investments in China. The sale included a popular newspaper known for its nonpartisan and investigative reporting. Both deals were still awaiting final regulatory approval at year's end.

Having signed the Economic Cooperation Framework Agreement (ECFA) trade pact with Beijing in 2010, the Ma administration continued pursuing closer ties with China in 2012. In October, a former DPP chairman visited Beijing, marking the first time that Taiwan's proindependence camp discussed cross-strait policy with the Chinese Communist Party. However, China's ongoing military buildup remained a concern. According to a September report by Taiwan's Ministry of National Defense, the Chinese military had increased the number of missiles aimed at the island to more than 1,600, from 1,400 the previous year.

Political Rights and Civil Liberties: Taiwan is an electoral democracy. The 1946 constitution created a unique government structure comprising five distinct branches (yuan). The president, who is directly elected for up to two four-year terms, wields executive power, appoints the prime minister, and can dissolve the legislature. The Executive Yuan, or cabinet, consists of ministers appointed by the president on the recommendation of the prime minister. The prime minister is responsible to the national legislature (Legislative Yuan), which consists of 113 members serving four-year terms. The three other branches of government are the judiciary (Judicial Yuan), a watchdog body (Control Yuan), and a branch responsible for civil-service examinations (Examination Yuan).

Two main parties, the proindependence DPP and the Chinese nationalist KMT, dominate the political landscape. Opposition parties are able to function freely. The combined presidential and legislative elections in January 2012 were deemed free and peaceful, despite the KMT's clear advantage in campaign funds and partisan polarization in media coverage of the candidates.

Though significantly less pervasive than in the past, corruption remains a problem. Politics and big business are closely intertwined, and instances of vote buying occur at the local level during elections. In October 2012, former Executive Yuan secretary general Lin Yi-shih was indicted for reportedly taking and demanding bribes from a businessman in exchange for a contract in 2010, while he was serving as a KMT legislator. In November, a DPP county magistrate was charged along with 19 other individuals for taking money from several companies to help them secure government contracts. Both cases were pending at year's end. Former president Chen Shui-bian, who was already serving a sentence of 18 and a half years in prison for corruption, was given another 10-year prison term in December for taking bribes from a financial group while in office. A 2011 indictment against another former president, Lee Teng-hui, for alleged embezzlement and money laundering was still pending at the end of 2012. During the year, an anticorruption agency created in 2011 continued to focus on local officials and civil servants. Separately, the opposition questioned the impartiality of the Special Investigation Division (SID) of the Supreme Prosecutor's Office, which is administered by the Ministry of Justice and tasked with investigating high-profile cases. In recent years, the SID has pursued a string of prosecutions against former DPP officials, many of whom were eventually acquitted.

Taiwan was ranked 37 out of 176 countries surveyed in Transparency International's 2012 Corruption Perceptions Index.

Taiwanese media reflect a diversity of views and report aggressively on government policies and corruption allegations. Following reforms in recent years, broadcast media are no longer subject to licensing and programming reviews by the Government Information Office (GIO), which was formally dissolved in May 2012. However, media outlets display strong party affiliations and grant preferential treatment to their respective candidates. Disputes over the leadership of the Public Television Service (PTS) continued in 2012, following a failed legislative attempt to establish a new board of directors. In June, the Taiwan High Court handed down a final ruling in favor of the former PTS president, who had sued after she was removed by the board in 2010, challenging its assertion that the dismissal was based on poor performance.

After a lengthy review, the National Communications Commission (NCC) in July 2012 conditionally approved a bid by Want Want Broadband, a subsidiary of Want Want Group, to purchase China Network Systems (CNS), the country's second-largest cable provider. Critics of the proposed merger warned that it could threaten Taiwan's media pluralism and independence, given Want Want owner Tsai Eng-meng's considerable business interests in China and his ties to the PRC authorities. Among an array of conditions imposed by the NCC, Tsai and his associates were required to avoid any involvement in the management of a news channel controlled by Want Want and to establish guidelines to ensure the editorial independence of another television network. Also in July, the Taipei district prosecutor's office issued a final ruling in favor of a reporter who was sued for criminal defamation in 2011 by a KMT lawmaker. The defendant had written an article implying that the lawmaker pressured the NCC to expedite its review of the CNS merger. Final approval for the CNS purchase was still pending at year's end.

The possible buyout of the Taiwan assets of Next Media Group raised similar concerns regarding the concentration of media ownership during 2012. The prospective seller was Hong Kong media mogul Jimmy Lai, a vocal critic of the Chinese authorities. In November, he announced an agreement to sell the group's print and television outlets in Taiwan to a consortium of Taiwanese businessmen after the company suffered significant losses, due in part to regulatory delays related to its television stations. Among the outlets for sale was *Apple Daily*, one of the island's most popular newspapers, known for its nonpartisan and investigative—though at times salacious—reporting. Most of the buyers, including the son of Tsai Eng-meng, had other significant business operations in China and Taiwan, prompting press freedom watchdogs to express concerns that self-censorship on topics related to these business interests would increase after the change in ownership. The deal was awaiting regulatory review at the end of 2012.

Taiwanese of all faiths can worship freely. Religious organizations that choose to register with the government receive tax-exempt status. In November 2012, the government barred Tibet's exiled spiritual leader, the Dalai Lama, from entering the country for a conference with little explanation, though it denied that Beijing was involved in the decision.

Educators in Taiwan can generally write and lecture without interference. In April 2012, a Taiwanese petrochemical conglomerate sued a university professor for defamation, seeking US$1.4 million in compensation for a report that said one of its factories was emitting a carcinogen. More than 400 Taiwanese scholars signed a petition urging the company to drop the lawsuit, which was pending at year's end.

Freedom of assembly is generally respected in Taiwan, and several large-scale demonstrations and campaign rallies took place in 2012. However, in December, the Ministry of Education was forced to apologize for a leaked directive in which it appeared to instruct universities to discourage student participation in a grassroots protest movement against the growing media dominance of pro-China tycoons. Taiwan's Assembly and Parade Law enables police to prosecute protesters who fail to obtain a permit or follow orders to disperse. Despite increased public support, the legislature voted in May 2012 to reject a bill that would have eased the existing law's permit process and eliminated its criminal penalties.

All civic organizations must register with the government, though registration is freely granted. Nongovernmental organizations (NGOs) typically operate without harassment.

Trade unions are independent, and most workers enjoy freedom of association. However, military personnel and government employees (with the exception of teachers) are barred from joining unions and bargaining collectively. According to official statistics, there were at least 444,600 foreign workers in Taiwan in 2012. The Employment Services Act, as amended in January 2012, enables foreign workers to extend their employment period to a maximum of 12 years. Migrant workers are not covered by the Fair Labor Standards Act or the Labor Safety and Health Act. International critics have voiced concerns that household workers in Taiwan are vulnerable to excessive working hours, low wages, and sexual harassment.

Taiwan's judiciary is independent, and trials are generally fair. The Judges Law, which took effect in July 2012, established a rating and removal system to address concerns about corrupt or incompetent judges. However, civil society groups tasked with screening cases for problematic rulings complained that the Ministry of Justice had denied them access to information on privacy grounds, which hindered them from evaluating citizen complaints. A total of three judges were warned or demoted during the year.

Police largely respect the ban on arbitrary detention, and attorneys are allowed to monitor interrogations to prevent torture. In August 2012, the Taiwan High Court acquitted three men who were sentenced to death in 1992 for the murder of a couple. The court said previous verdicts were based on flawed confessions extracted by torture, adding that the case was closed to further appeals under the amended Criminal Speedy Trial Act of 2011. Taiwan executed six inmates in 2012. Despite international criticism, polls suggested that majority of the population opposed abolition of the death penalty. Watchdog groups have expressed concerns about prison conditions, including overcrowding, limited opportunities for exercise, and lack of access to medical treatment. The issue gained greater public attention during the year due to cases involving high-profile prisoners such as former president Chen.

Police corruption remains a problem in parts of Taiwan. In August 2012, seven officers received sentences ranging from six months to six years in prison after they were convicted of frequenting and leaking information to illegal bars that were targeted for raids; the officers appealed their convictions. In December, prosecutors requested a 15-year jail term for a former Criminal Investigation Bureau chief secretary accused of investing in and protecting an illegal gambling parlor. Both cases were pending at year's end.

The constitution provides for the equality of all citizens. While social and political divisions between descendants of 1949 mainland émigrés and long-established ethnic Chinese residents have eroded, the island's non-Chinese indigenous people continue to face social and economic discrimination. Six seats in the legislature are reserved for indigenous people, giving them representation that exceeds their share of the population. A draft Indigenous Autonomy Act that would allow indigenous people to establish tribal offices and councils was still under legislative review at the end of 2012. Disputes over indigenous people's reserve lands continued. Critics note that some have already been appropriated for large-scale development projects.

Taiwanese law does not allow for asylum or refugee status, and a 2010 bill that would address the problem remains under consideration in the parliament. The measure was proposed as part of official efforts to honor two UN human rights treaties—the International Covenant on Civil and Political Rights and the International Covenant on Economic, Social, and Cultural Rights. The Taiwanese government ratified their content in 2009, despite the fact that the ROC's lack of international recognition barred its formal admission as a signatory state.

Amid warming relations and increased travel across the Taiwan Strait, the government launched a program in 2011 that allowed a quota of 500 Chinese tourists per day from select cities to travel to Taiwan without the supervision of organized tour groups. The quota was increased to 1,000 in April 2012. Taiwanese citizens are generally permitted to travel to the PRC without restrictions. However, a Taiwanese citizen was detained and interrogated for nearly two months during a trip to the country in 2012 due to his previous activities in Taiwan aimed at disseminating information in China about the Falun Gong spiritual group, which is banned on the mainland. He was released in August following a campaign on his behalf by Taiwanese politicians and activists.

After the 2012 elections, women held 30 percent of the seats in the national legislature, and a KMT lawmaker became the body's first female deputy Speaker. In January, authorities established the Department of Gender Equality to address disparities within government agencies. Taiwanese women continue to face discrimination in employment and compensation. Rape and domestic violence remain problems, though a law that took effect in January 2012 barred parole for repeat or serious sex offenders. Women from China and Southeast Asian countries, many of whom arrive in Taiwan through fraudulent marriages and deceptive employment offers, are often at risk for sex trafficking and forced labor. However, the government has stepped up efforts to combat human trafficking in recent years.

Tajikistan

Political Rights: 6
Civil Liberties: 6*
Status: Not Free

Population: 7,078,800
Capital: Dushanbe

Ratings Change: Tajikistan's civil liberties rating declined from 5 to 6 due to a ban on students attending international seminars and a military operation in Gorno-Badakhshan that resulted in scores of deaths, extrajudicial killings, and a media crackdown.

Ten-Year Ratings Timeline For Year Under Review (Political Rights, Civil Liberties, Status)

2003	2004	2005	2006	2007	2008	2009	2010	2011	2012
6,5NF	6,5NF	6,5NF	6,5NF	6,5NF	6,5NF	6,5NF	6,5NF	6,5NF	6,6NF

Overview: The government of Tajikistan in 2012 conducted a large-scale military operation in the autonomous Gorno-Badakhshan province. After a ceasefire in early August, a local strongman and former opposition commander was killed in his home. The assassination sparked riots in Khorog, the region's largest city, forcing Dushanbe to withdraw forces from the region. Authorities took new steps to cut off public access to information and communication networks during and after the fighting.

Former Communist Party leader Rakhmon Nabiyev was elected president of Tajikistan after the country declared independence from the Soviet Union in 1991. Long-simmering tensions between regional elites, combined with various anticommunist and Islamist movements, soon plunged the country into a five-year civil war. In September 1992, Communist hard-liners forced Nabiyev's resignation; he was replaced by Emomali Rakhmonov, a senior member of the Communist Party. Rakhmonov was elected president in 1994, after most opposition candidates either boycotted or were prevented from competing in the poll. Similarly, progovernment candidates won the 1995 parliamentary elections amid a boycott by the United Tajik Opposition (UTO), a coalition of secular and Islamist groups that had emerged as the main force fighting against Rakhmonov's government.

Following a December 1996 ceasefire, Rakhmonov and UTO leader Said Abdullo Nuri signed a formal peace agreement in 1997, with a reintegration process to be overseen by a politically balanced National Reconciliation Commission. A September 1999 referendum that permitted the formation of religion-based political parties paved the way for the legal operation of the Islamist opposition, including the Islamic Renaissance Party (IRP). The referendum also extended the president's term from five to seven years. In November, Rakhmonov was reelected with a reported 97 percent of the vote in a poll criticized by international observers.

Rakhmonov's People's Democratic Party (PDP) dominated the February 2000 legislative elections, which international monitors said had been flawed. After the elections, the National Reconciliation Commission was formally disbanded. However, important provisions of the 1997 peace accord remained unimplemented, with the demobilization of opposition factions incomplete and the government having failed to meet a 30 percent quota for UTO members in senior government posts.

A 2003 constitutional referendum cleared a path for Rakhmonov to seek two additional terms and remain in office until 2020. The PDP easily won 2005 parliamentary elections amid reports of large-scale irregularities.

Rakhmonov won the November 2006 presidential election with more than 70 percent of the vote, although the Organization for Security and Cooperation in Europe (OSCE) noted a lack of real competition. The president broadened his influence to the cultural sphere in 2007, de-Russifying his surname to "Rahmon" in March. He also signed legislation in May that established spending limits on birthday and wedding celebrations. The ruling PDP won 55 of 63 lower-house seats in February 2010 parliamentary elections, which failed to meet basic democratic standards, according to OSCE monitors.

Also during 2010, the security situation experienced its worst deterioration since the 1992–97 civil war, with violence including a mass prison break, an attack on a police station in the northern city of Khujand that featured the country's first suicide bombing, and a guerrilla ambush that killed 30 soldiers in the remote Rasht Valley. In 2011, the government dispatched special forces to Rasht in a bid to extend control over one of the last areas left unofficially to former opposition commanders. The operations resulted in the deaths of several of these local strongmen.

In July, the government undertook a large-scale military operation in the autonomous Gorno-Badakhshan province after a senior provincial security official was killed there earlier that month. The operation, which left some 70 people dead, targeted former opposition commanders who had since taken on government posts, but were accused of involvement in the security official's death as well as drug trafficking and other crimes. In August, one target, Tolib Ayombekov, surrendered arms and men after several days of fighting and was placed under house arrest. Another, Imomnazar Imomnazarov, was murdered in a reported grenade attack in his home that was widely believed to be an extrajudicial killing, which sparked violent public protests and the subsequent withdrawal of troops.

In October, Russia reached a deal to keep troops dating to the Soviet era in Tajikistan through 2042. Iran, meanwhile, continued to fund construction of the Sangtuda-2 hydropower plant, and pledged to build an industrial center outside Dushanbe.

Political Rights and Civil Liberties: Tajikistan is not an electoral democracy. The 1994 constitution provides for a strong, directly elected president who enjoys broad authority to appoint and dismiss officials. In the Assembly of Representatives (lower chamber), 63 members are elected by popular vote to serve five-year terms. In the 33-seat National Assembly (upper chamber), 25 members are chosen by local assemblies, and 8 are appointed by the president, all for five-year terms.

Corruption is pervasive. Patronage networks and regional affiliations are central to political life, with officials from the president's native Kulyob region dominant in government. At least two of President Emomali Rahmon's children hold senior government posts, and various family members reportedly maintain extensive business interests in the country. Major irregularities at the National Bank of Tajikistan and the country's largest industrial company, TALCO Aluminum, have been documented. Tajikistan was ranked 157 out of 176 countries surveyed in Transparency International's 2012 Corruption Perceptions Index.

Despite constitutional guarantees of freedom of speech and the press, independent journalists face harassment and intimidation, and the penal code criminalizes defamation. Crippling libel judgments are common, particularly against newspapers that are critical of the government, though in July 2012 Tajikistan decriminalized libel, reclassifying it as a civil offense. However, the act of publicly insulting the president remains punishable by a jail term of up to five years. The government controls most printing presses, newsprint supplies, and broadcasting facilities, and most television stations are state-owned or only nominally independent. The government blocks some critical websites and online news outlets. During the 2012 military operations in Gorno-Badakhshan, the government shut down access not only to domestic news, but also international social media sites and self-publishing platforms. Cell phone communication was also shut down for days in the remote region, giving the government unprecedented information control over the situation.

The government has imposed a number of restrictions on religious freedom. A 2009 law restricts religious activities to state-approved houses of prayer. Authorities limit the number of mosques allowed in the country's towns, and in recent years have undertaken a campaign to shutter those that are not properly registered. Throughout 2012, Tajikistan continued to prosecute dozens of citizens for alleged membership in extremist religious organizations, and stepped up pressure against the legal IRP, whose Gorno-Badakhshan chief was killed under mysterious circumstances in the first days of the government's military operation there in July.

The country's limited religious education institutions have failed to integrate most of the 1,500 students who were pressured to return from religious schools abroad in 2010, and some have faced prosecution. In 2011, unprecedented new legislation on "parental responsibility" that came into force banned minors from attending regular religious services in mosques, and banned private religious education. Many religious leaders criticized the law or quietly refused to obey it. Wearing of the hijab (headscarf) in schools and higher educational institutions has been banned since 2005.

In October 2012, the government banned all university students from attending events or conferences organized by international or foreign organizations.

The government limits freedoms of assembly and association. Local government approval is required to hold public demonstrations, and officials reportedly refuse to grant permission in many cases. In August 2012, some 2,000 protesters gathered in Khorog to protest the murder of a former rebel leader and to demand that the government cease military activities in the area. The protesters vandalized the police office, and two people were reportedly wounded. The standoff ended after the government said it would withdraw troops from the area. In September, hundreds of people called for the government to provide compensation after a fire at a market in Dushanbe destroyed a number of vendors' stalls and killed at least one person. Security forces reportedly prevented the demonstrators from reaching the city center, and journalists attempting to cover the event were reportedly beaten and arrested.

Nongovernmental organizations must register with the Ministry of Justice. In October 2012, courts in Khujand shut down the rights group Amparo on a technicality, drawing protests from the international community. Citizens have the legal right to form and join trade unions and to bargain collectively, but trade unions are largely subservient to the authorities.

The judiciary lacks independence. Many judges are poorly trained and inexperienced, and bribery is reportedly widespread. Police frequently make arbitrary arrests and beat detainees to extract confessions. Overcrowding and disease contribute to often life-threatening conditions in prisons. Tajikistan is a major conduit for the smuggling of narcotics from Afghanistan to Russia and Europe, which has led to an increase in drug addiction within Tajikistan.

Sexual harassment, discrimination, and violence against women, including spousal abuse, are reportedly common, but cases are rarely investigated. Reports indicate that women sometimes face societal pressure to wear headscarves, even though official policy discourages the practice. Despite some government efforts to address human trafficking, Tajikistan remains a source and transit country for persons trafficked for prostitution. Child labor, particularly on cotton farms, also remains a problem.

Tanzania

Political Rights: 3
Civil Liberties: 3
Status: Partly Free

Population: 47,656,000
Capital: Dar-es-Salaam

Ten-Year Ratings Timeline For Year Under Review (Political Rights, Civil Liberties, Status)

2003	2004	2005	2006	2007	2008	2009	2010	2011	2012
4,3PF	4,3PF	4,3PF	4,3PF	4,3PF	4,3PF	4,3PF	3,3PF	3,3PF	3,3PF

Overview: Debate over constitutional reform was ongoing in 2012, led by calls for new limits on presidential power from the opposition, which continued to stage protests throughout the year. In September, a television journalist was killed by police at an opposition rally in the southern city of Iringa. Meanwhile, in Zanzibar, a separatist Islamist group clashed with police on several occasions.

Three years after mainland Tanganyika gained independence from Britain in 1961, the Zanzibar archipelago merged with Tanganyika to become the United Republic of Tanzania. The ruling Chama Cha Mapinduzi (CCM) party, under longtime president Julius Nyerere, dominated the country's political life and promoted a collectivist economic philosophy. Nyerere's successor, Ali Hassan Mwinyi, was president from 1985 to 1995 and oversaw a political liberalization process.

CCM victories in the 1995 and 2000 presidential and parliamentary elections on the mainland and on Zanzibar were tainted by fraud and irregularities. The CCM captured a majority in the 2005 elections, and Foreign Minister Jakaya Kikwete, a CCM stalwart, was elected president, although the opposition Civic United Front (CUF) once again alleged fraud. Negotiations to legitimate the 2005 elections remained deadlocked until a July 2010 referendum led to a constitutional change creating two vice-presidential positions to be divided between the CCM and CUF.

In October 2010, Kikwete was reelected to a second five-year term with 61 percent of the vote, defeating five challengers. While the CCM retained its majority in concurrent National Assembly elections, winning 186 seats, the opposition gained its largest representation in Tanzania's history. The CUF took 24 seats, and Chama Cha Demokrasia na Maendeleo (CHADEMA) won 23. While there were some protests alleging vote rigging and poor administration, the 2010 polls represented a considerable improvement over previous elections. In the separate Zanzibar polls, the CCM presidential candidate also won a narrow victory. Unlike past elections, the opposition CUF accepted the results in Zanzibar, due in large part to a July referendum that had provided for the creation of a national unity government after the polls with two vice president posts, one for the CCM and one for the CUF.

In November 2011, the National Assembly passed the Constitution Review Act, which called for the creation of a commission to begin reforming the constitution. Throughout 2012, political debate heightened around the constitutional review process, which officially began in May with the appointment of a commission tasked with collecting citizens' views on the reforms. Potential contentious issues in the new constitution, slated for a completion in 2014, include CHADEMA-supported proposals that would limit presidential powers and restore the government of Tanganyika, and calls for increased autonomy for Zanzibar.

CHADEMA-led antigovernment protests that had begun in 2011 continued in 2012, despite an ongoing ban on CHADEMA demonstrations. After an April by-election in the Arumeru district, a local CHADEMA party chairperson was killed, and soldiers used teargas to break up crowds of CHADEMA protesters calling for the quick release of results. In August, one person was killed and many others were injured during clashes between police and CHADEMA supporters the town of Msamvu in Morogoro region.

Political Rights and Civil Liberties: Tanzania is an electoral democracy. The October 2010 national elections were judged to be the most competitive and legitimate in Tanzania's history. Executive power rests with the president, who is elected by direct popular vote for a maximum of two five-year terms. Legislative power is held by a unicameral National Assembly, the Bunge, which currently has 357 members serving five-year terms. Of these, 239 are directly elected in single-seat constituencies; 102 are women chosen by the political parties according to their representation in the Bunge; 10 are appointed by the president; 1 is awarded to the Attorney General; and 5 are members of the Zanzibar legislature, whose 50 deputies are elected to five-year terms. Along with the legislature, Zanzibar has its own president and cabinet with largely autonomous jurisdiction over the archipelago's internal affairs.

Although opposition parties were legalized in 1992, the ruling CCM continues to dominate the country's political life. The other main parties are the CUF and CHADEMA. The constitution prohibits political coalitions, which has impeded efforts by other parties to seriously contest the CCM's dominance. Opposition politics have also tended to be highly fractious. To register in Tanzania, political parties must not be formed on religious, ethnic, or regional bases, and cannot oppose the union of Zanzibar and the mainland.

Corruption remains a serious problem, and is pervasive in all aspects of political and commercial life, but especially in the energy and natural resources sectors. In response to an April 2012 report by the auditor general that millions of dollars in public funds from several ministries could not be accounted for, President Jakaya Kikwete in May fired six cabinet ministers, including the energy and minerals minister. Tanzania was ranked 102 out of 176 countries surveyed in Transparency International's 2012 Corruption Perceptions Index.

Although the constitution provides for freedom of speech, it does not specifically guarantee freedom of the press. Current laws allow authorities broad discretion to restrict media on the basis of national security or public interest, which is frequently interpreted in ways beneficial to the CCM. Print and electronic media are active, though hindered by a difficult registration process and largely limited to major urban areas. The growth of broadcast media has been slowed by a lack of capital investment; however, the number of independent television and private FM radio stations has risen in recent years. Government-owned media outlets are largely biased toward the ruling party. In July, the government imposed an indefinite ban on the weekly investigative newspaper *MwanaHalisi*, accusing it of sedition. In September, Channel Ten television journalist Daudi Mwangosi was killed during a confrontation with police at a CHADEMA rally in the southern city of Iringa. A government probe absolved the police of wrongdoing; however, separate investigations by the Commission for Human Rights and Good Governance and the Media Council of Tanzania linked the killing to police officers, and one officer was later charged with murder.

Press freedom in Zanzibar is even more constrained. The Zanzibari government owns the only daily newspaper, though many islanders receive mainland broadcasts and read the mainland press. The government largely controls radio and television content; mainland television broadcasts are delayed in Zanzibar to allow authorities to censor content. The Zanzibari government often reacts to media criticism by accusing the press of being a "threat to national unity."

Internet access, while limited to urban areas, is growing. The authorities monitor websites that are critical of the government.

Freedom of religion is generally respected, and relations between the various faiths are largely peaceful. In recent years, however, tensions between Muslims and Christians have increased, especially in Zanzibar. In 2012, there were at least three outbreaks of violence between the police and the separatist Islamist nongovernmental organization (NGO) Uamsho, which recently had grown in prominence. The worst violence came in October, when two people were killed and churches were set alight, during several days of rioting, after the group's leader temporarily disappeared. The Zanzibari government appoints a mufti, a professional jurist who interprets Islamic law, to oversee Muslim organizations. Some Muslims have criticized this practice, arguing that it represents excessive government interference.

There are no government restrictions on academic freedom.

The constitution guarantees freedoms of assembly and association. However, these rights are not always respected. Organizers of political events are required to obtain permission from the police, and critical political demonstrations are actively discouraged, as seen with the recent crackdowns on CHADEMA rallies. Many NGOs are active, and some have influenced the public policy process. However, the 2002 NGO Act has been criticized for increasing government control over NGOs and restricting their operation. Essential public service workers are barred from striking, and other workers are restricted by complex notification and mediation requirements. Strikes are infrequent on both the mainland and in Zanzibar. In July, the teachers' union attempted to strike for better pay, but the action was declared illegal by the High Court because the union had not given the required 48-hour notice.

Tanzania's judiciary remains under political influence, and suffers from underfunding and corruption. Arrest and pretrial detention rules are often ignored. Prisons suffer from harsh conditions, including overcrowding and safety and health concerns. Narcotics trafficking is a growing problem, especially given the challenge of controlling Tanzania's borders. Security forces reportedly routinely abused, threatened, and mistreated civilians with limited accountability throughout 2012.

The 2002 Prevention of Terrorism Act has been criticized by NGOs for its inconsistencies and anomalies. Acts of terrorism include attacks on a person's life, kidnapping, and serious damage to property. The law gives the police and immigration officials sweeping powers to arrest suspected illegal immigrants or anyone thought to have links with terrorists.

Tanzania has enjoyed relatively tranquil relations among its many ethnic groups. A large number of refugees from conflicts in Burundi, the Democratic Republic of Congo, and Somalia live in Tanzania. Tanzania won praise in 2010 for granting citizenship to 162,000 Burundian refugees, the largest-ever single naturalization of refugees, but those who were not granted citizenship faced mounting pressure in 2012 to return home.

Albinos continue to be subject to discrimination and violence, including killings and mutilations to obtain their body parts by practitioners of witchcraft. In both mainland Tanzania and Zanzibar, consensual same-sex sexual relations are illegal and punishable by lengthy prison terms, and members of the LBGT (lesbian, gay, bisexual, and transgender) community face societal discrimination. In July, LGBT activist Morris Mjomba was murdered in Dar-es-Salaam; no one had been arrested for the crime by year's end.

Women's rights are constitutionally guaranteed but not uniformly protected. Traditional and Islamic customs frequently discriminate against women in family law, especially in rural areas and in Zanzibar. Rape continues to be a serious problem, and domestic violence is reportedly common and rarely prosecuted. Nevertheless, women are relatively well represented in parliament, with about 36 percent of seats.

Thailand

Political Rights: 4
Civil Liberties: 4
Status: Partly Free

Population: 69,892,000
Capital: Bangkok

Ten-Year Ratings Timeline For Year Under Review (Political Rights, Civil Liberties, Status)

2003	2004	2005	2006	2007	2008	2009	2010	2011	2012
2,3F	2,3F	3,3PF	7,4NF	6,4PF	5,4PF	5,4PF	5,4PF	4,4PF	4,4PF

Overview:
The government of Prime Minister Yingluck Shinawatra, elected in 2011, consolidated its grip on power during 2012. However, Yingluck's links to her brother, deposed former prime minister Thaksin Shinawatra, remained a matter of contention, and new opposition protests called for another military coup. Separately, prosecutors and security agencies continued to employ lèse-majesté laws to curb freedom of expression and political speech, and rights abuses associated with the insurgency and counterinsurgency in southern Thailand persisted.

Thailand was the only Southeast Asian country to avoid direct colonial rule. An elite-led revolution in 1932 transformed the kingdom into a constitutional monarchy. Over the next 60 years, Thailand endured multiple military coups, constitutional overhauls, and popular uprisings. The army dominated politics during these years, with intermittent periods of unstable civilian government. Under the leadership of General Prem Tinsulanonda in the 1980s, the country experienced rapid economic growth and a gradual and heavily contested transition toward democratic rule. The military seized power again in 1991, but Thailand's monarch, King Bhumipol Adulyadej, intervened to appoint a civilian prime minister in 1992. Fresh elections held in September of that year ushered in a 14-year period of elected civilian leadership.

Thaksin Shinawatra, a former deputy prime minister who built his substantial fortune in telecommunications, unseated the ruling Democratic Party (DP) in the 2001 elections. He and his Thai Rak Thai (TRT, or Thais Love Thais) party mobilized voters in rural areas in part by criticizing the government for favoring urban, middle class Thais. As prime minister, Thaksin won praise for pursuing populist policies designed to stimulate the economy, especially in rural provinces. However, critics accused him and his government of undermining the progressive intent of the 1997 constitution. Human rights groups condemned Thaksin for seeking to suppress independent media. In 2003 a violent counternarcotics campaign resulted in at least 2,500 killings in a three-month period; in most cases the perpetrators were not brought to justice.

In 2004, separatist violence accelerated in Thailand's four southernmost provinces, home to most of the country's four million Muslims. Thaksin mounted a hardline response, and the government placed the Muslim-majority provinces of Narathiwat, Yala, and Pattani under martial law. The government was accused of human rights abuses in its effort to stamp out the insurgency.

The TRT dominated the February 2005 parliamentary elections, making Thaksin the first prime minister to serve a full four-year term and be elected to two consecutive terms. However, anti-Thaksin sentiment rose during the year, particularly in Bangkok and the south, where the DP was most popular. In January 2006, the prime minister's family was criticized for the tax-free, $1.9 billion sale of its Shin Corporation to the investment arm of the Singaporean government, which opponents said put the family's interests before the national interest. Facing a wave of protests led by the People's Alliance for Democracy (PAD)—a coalition of royalists, business elites, and military leaders with support among the urban middle class—Thaksin called snap elections in early April 2006. All three opposition parties boycotted the vote, and a fresh round of elections was ultimately scheduled for October.

A military coup in September 2006 preempted the new vote and ousted Thaksin, who was abroad at the time. The coup leaders' Council for National Security (CNS) abrogated the constitution, dissolved the parliament, and replaced the Constitutional Court with its own tribunal. In May 2007, the tribunal found the TRT guilty of bribing smaller parties in the April 2006 elections and dissolved it, specifically prohibiting Thaksin and 111 other party leaders from participating in politics for the next five years. About 57 percent of referendum voters in August 2007 approved a new constitution that contained a number of antidemocratic provisions.

Former TRT members regrouped under the banner of the People's Power Party (PPP) and won the December 2007 parliamentary elections. Throughout 2008, yellow-shirted PAD supporters marched in protests accusing the new government of serving as a corrupt proxy for Thaksin and demanding its dissolution. Meanwhile, in October the Supreme Court sentenced Thaksin in absentia to two years in prison for abuse of office.

The PPP-led government—under intense pressure from the PAD, military commanders, and the judiciary—finally fell in December 2008, when the Constitutional Court disbanded the ruling party on the grounds that it had engaged in fraud during the December 2007 elections. DP leader Abhisit Vejjajiva subsequently formed a new coalition and won a lower-house vote to become prime minister. The red-shirted United Front for Democracy against Dictatorship (UDD), which had opposed the 2006 coup, mounted large protests against the PPP's dissolution and the new government. Abhisit imposed emergency rule in Bangkok for nearly two weeks in April 2009, arresting red-shirt leaders and shutting down pro-UDD radio stations.

Reconciliation efforts later in 2009 made little progress, and UDD protests escalated again in the spring of 2010, with red shirts occupying the heart of Bangkok's commercial district in April. The government, which accused the UDD of intending to overthrow the monarchy, declared another state of emergency, and the army finally dispersed the entrenched protesters in May, at times using live fire. Between March and the end of May, a total of 92 people were killed in clashes between protesters and security forces.

Abhisit established two committees on national reform to advance reconciliation, and his government attempted to garner public support with populist economic policies. However, these efforts largely failed to win over opposition supporters, and in early 2011 Abhisit called new elections for July.

In the run-up to the elections, many elements of the Thai elite, including the military, clearly indicated to voters their preference for the DP, with the army chief appearing on national television to counsel against votes for Puea Thai, the successor to the PPP, led by Thaksin's younger sister Yingluck Shinawatra. The military also allegedly worked behind the scenes to convince smaller parties to ally themselves with the DP following the vote. Some expressed worries that Yingluck would become a proxy for Thaksin, who called her his "clone." Political tensions were heightened by concerns about the future of the monarchy.

Puea Thai ultimately won the parliamentary elections outright, taking 265 of 500 seats in the lower house. The DP placed second with 159 seats, and small parties divided the remainder. The army accepted the results, in part because Puea Thai leaders reportedly assured the military that they would not interfere in military promotions or seek trials for officers involved in the 2010 political violence. Yingluck became prime minister and installed several Thaksin loyalists in top cabinet positions. They advocated an amnesty for Thaksin, but no such action was taken. While he remained in exile, he maintained political influence through regular telephone calls, video appearances, and visits to neighboring countries.

During 2011, Yingluck suggested that she would consider reforming the country's lèse-majesté laws, which had been enforced more aggressively since 2006, and revising the constitution to bring it closer to the 1997 charter. However, in 2012 she appeared to steer a relatively conciliatory course, attempting to accommodate military, palace, and activist priorities. Her public appearances with senior royalist figures have been read as part of this rapprochement. Nevertheless, the competing interests continued to clash in the courts, media, and parliament, and street protests escalated late in the year. In October and November 2012, a new group, Pitak Siam (Protect Siam), began calling for a coup to oust the Yingluck government, though its public events did not generate a groundswell of popular support and were widely described as failures. There were also those among the UDD hardliners who became more consistent in their campaigning on behalf of those killed in April and May 2010. For instance, in December 2012, Abhisit and his former deputy were charged with murder for issuing orders that resulted in the death of a taxi driver during the 2010 crackdown on UDD protesters.

Political Rights and Civil Liberties: Thailand is an electoral democracy. The July 2011 elections were considered relatively free and fair, yielding a strong victory for the opposition party Peua Thai. The polls replaced a government that had come to power as a result of judicial action and lacked a popular mandate. Although the influential military weighed in against Puea Thai during the run-up to the vote, it was unable to decisively affect the outcome. However, the Asian Network for Free Elections, a leading monitoring organization, reported that several political parties had representatives inside polling stations trying to influence voters' choices, and that vote buying had increased compared with previous parliamentary polls.

The current constitution was drafted under the supervision of a military-backed government and approved in an August 2007 referendum. It included an amnesty for the 2006 coup leaders, and in a clear response to the premiership of Thaksin Shinawatra, whose government the coup overthrew, the charter limited prime ministers to two four-year terms and set a lower threshold for launching no-confidence motions. The constitution also reduced the role of elected lawmakers. Whereas the old Senate was fully elected, the Senate created by the new charter consists of 77 elected members and 73 appointed by a committee of judges and members of independent government bodies. Senators, who serve six-year terms, cannot belong to political parties. For the 500-seat lower chamber, the House of Representatives, the new constitution altered the system of proportional representation to curtail the voting power of the northern and northeastern provinces, where support for Thaksin remains strong.

Corruption is widespread at all levels of Thai society. Both the DP and Puea Thai include numerous lawmakers who have faced persistent corruption allegations. Thailand was ranked 88 out of 176 countries and territories surveyed in Transparency International's 2012 Corruption Perceptions Index.

The 2007 constitution restored freedom of expression guarantees that were eliminated by the 2006 coup, though the use of laws to silence critics is growing. The 2007 Computer Crimes Act assigns significant prison terms for the publication of false information deemed to endanger the public or national security. In recent years, the government has blocked very large numbers of websites for allegedly insulting the monarchy, and this blocking did not completely stop under the Peua Thai government in 2012. The authorities did ease restrictions on some red-shirt websites and community radio stations, but DP supporters have criticized the government for its unsympathetic approach to media and artists associated with their side of the political divide, including with respect to the April 2012 banning of *Shakespeare Must Die*, an adaptation of Macbeth widely considered critical of Thaksin.

The government and military control licensing and transmission for Thailand's six main television stations and all 525 radio frequencies. Community radio stations are generally unlicensed. Print publications are for the most part privately owned and are subject to fewer restrictions than the broadcast media. However, most print outlets continue to take a clearly partisan political position.

Aggressive enforcement of the country's lèse-majesté laws since the 2006 coup has created widespread anxiety and stifled freedom of expression in the media. Due to the secrecy surrounding most such cases, it is unclear exactly how many went to trial in 2012, but previous estimates suggest that the figure is in the hundreds. The laws strictly prohibit defamation of the monarchy, but the authorities have used them to target activists, scholars, students, journalists, foreign authors, and politicians who are critical of the government, exacerbating self-censorship. Defendants can face decades in prison for multiple counts, and it is often only through media and activist pressure that any leniency is shown. Some of those accused in 2012, such as Thammasat University academic Somsak Jeamteerasakul, have actively questioned the legal basis for their prosecutions. Some, including editor Somyot Prueksakakasemsuk, have recently received lengthy prison terms.

The constitution explicitly prohibits discrimination based on religious belief. However, while there is no official state religion, the constitution requires the monarch to be a Buddhist, and speech considered insulting to Buddhism is prohibited by law. The conflict in the south, which pits ethnic Malay Muslims against ethnic Thai Buddhists, continues to undermine citizens' ability to practice their religions. Buddhist monks report that they are unable to travel freely through southern communities to receive alms, and many Buddhist schoolteachers have been attacked by insurgents. Meanwhile, a significant number of Muslim religious leaders have allegedly been targeted by government security forces.

The 2007 constitution restored freedom of assembly guarantees, though the government may invoke the Internal Security Act (ISA) or declare a state of emergency to curtail major demonstrations. There was no state of emergency in most of the country in 2012, but it remained in place in the restive south. Political parties and organizations campaigned and met freely during the year, engaging in regular pro- or antigovernment demonstrations. The tempo of these protests increased toward year's end, but demonstrators' interactions with security forces were less violent than in 2008–10.

Thailand has a vibrant civil society sector, with groups representing farmers, laborers, women, students, environmentalists, and human rights interests. Attacks on civil society leaders have been reported, and even in cases where prosecutions occur, there is a perception of impunity for the ultimate sponsors of the violence.

Thai trade unions are independent, and more than 50 percent of state-enterprise workers belong to unions, but less than 2 percent of the total workforce is unionized. Antiunion discrimination in the private sector is common, and legal protections for union members are weak and poorly enforced. Exploitation and trafficking of migrant workers from Burma, Cambodia, and Laos are serious and ongoing problems, as are child and sweatshop labor. In 2012, trafficking of migrants, especially from Burma, into the fishing industry was identified as a particular issue of concern.

The 2007 constitution restored judicial independence and reestablished an independent Constitutional Court. A separate military court adjudicates criminal and civil cases involving members of the military, as well as cases brought under martial law. Sharia (Islamic law) courts hear certain types of cases pertaining to Muslims. The Thai courts have played a decisive role in determining the outcome of political disputes, for example in the ouster of the PPP government in 2008, generating complaints of judicial activism and political bias.

A combination of martial law and emergency rule remains in effect in the four southernmost provinces. Counterinsurgency operations have involved the indiscriminate detention of thousands of suspected insurgents and sympathizers, and there are long-standing and credible reports of torture and other human rights violations, including extrajudicial killings, by security forces. To date there have been no successful criminal prosecutions of security personnel for these transgressions. Separatist fighters and armed criminal groups regularly attack government workers, police, teachers, religious figures, and civilians. More than 5,000 people have been killed and almost 9,000 injured in the conflict in the past decade.

In the north of the country, so-called hill tribes are not fully integrated into Thai society and face restrictions on their freedom of movement. Many continue to struggle without formal citizenship, which renders them ineligible to vote, own land, attend state schools, or receive protection under labor laws. Thailand has not ratified UN conventions on refugees, and the authorities have forcibly repatriated Burmese and Laotian refugees. The place of Burmese refugees in Thailand is especially tenuous at this stage with the prospect of repatriation looming as a significant issue. Reports of the abuse of refugees and migrants workers from Burma also continue to emerge, and have been met by increased labor activism.

While women have the same legal rights as men, they remain subject to economic discrimination in practice, and vulnerable to domestic abuse, rape, and sex trafficking. Sex tourism has been a key part of the economy in some urban and resort areas. While Yingluck Shinawatra is the country's first female prime minister, her administration has not made women's rights a priority.

Togo

Political Rights: 5
Civil Liberties: 4
Status: Partly Free

Population: 6,011,000
Capital: Lomé

Ten-Year Ratings Timeline For Year Under Review (Political Rights, Civil Liberties, Status)

2003	2004	2005	2006	2007	2008	2009	2010	2011	2012
6,5NF	6,5NF	6,5NF	6,5NF	5,5PF	5,5PF	5,4PF	5,4PF	5,4PF	5,4PF

Overview: **Parliamentary elections planned for October 2012 were delayed beyond the end of the year following a planned boycott by opposition parties over the adoption of a new electoral code containing provisions favoring the ruling party. Security forces cracked down on subsequent opposition-led protests, including a demonstration in August in which more than 100 people were injured.**

Originally part of a German colony that fell under the control of France after World War I, Togo gained its independence in 1960. Gnassingbé Eyadéma, a demobilized sergeant, overthrew the civilian government in a bloodless coup in 1967. Using mock elections and a loyal military, he then presided over close to 40 years of repressive rule.

In 1991, under pressure from European governments, Eyadéma set up a transitional government and prepared for free elections. However, security forces attacked opposition supporters, forcing thousands to flee abroad, and the transitional government was later dissolved. A series of elections were held during the 1990s, but military harassment and legal manipulation ensured that Eyadéma and his Rally of the Togolese People (RPT) party remained in power. Eyadéma secured a new five-year term in 2003. Gilchrist Olympio, the most prominent opposition politician from the Union of Forces for Change (UFC), was prevented from running through a manufactured technicality.

Eyadéma died in February 2005. The military quickly installed his son, Faure Gnassingbé, as president, and violently repressed opposition protests. Under international pressure, Gnassingbé held an April 2005 election, in which he was elected amid significant irregularities and fraud. Subsequent clashes between opposition supporters and security forces killed almost 500 people, injured thousands, and forced 40,000 to flee the country.

In 2006, the promise of renewed economic aid from the European Union (EU)—which had cut off support in 1993—spurred the RPT and opposition parties to schedule legislative elections. In the October 2007 polls, the RPT won 50 of the 81 National Assembly seats, the UFC secured 27 seats, and the Action Committee for Renewal captured the remainder. The polls were deemed relatively fair, though the electoral system enabled the RPT to win 62 percent of the seats with just 39 percent of the vote. By the end of 2008, the EU, as well as the World Bank and International Monetary Fund, had restored economic aid.

The electoral code was reformed in 2009 in preparation for the 2010 presidential election, lifting the residency requirements that previously barred Olympio from running. Nonetheless, Olympio was disqualified again for missing a mandatory physical, leading the UFC to back Jean-Pierre Fabre instead. In March, against a divided opposition, Gnassingbé won reelection with more than 60 percent of the vote amid numerous irregularities, including vote-buying by the RPT and partisanship within the electoral commission. However, the problems were not considered serious enough to have influenced the outcome of the vote.

Following the election, the UFC splintered over how to address the contested election results. Fabre created a new party, the National Alliance for Change (ANC), which refused to accept the results and boycotted parliament, leading to large-scale demonstrations in the capital. In response, the government banned demonstrations and dispersed Fabre's supporters with tear gas and water cannons. Meanwhile, a faction led by Olympio retained the UFC title and agreed to enter into a coalition government with the RPT, and UFC members aligned with Olymipio were subsequently appointed to high-level cabinet and ministry positions. The RPT-UFC coalition agreement included a Monitoring Committee chaired by Olympio to help resolve interparty disputes and marked the first time the opposition had been included in the government since 1990.

Just five months before legislative elections scheduled for October 2012, parliament adopted a new electoral law in May that violated an Economic Community Of West African States protocol forbidding changes to a country's electoral laws less than six months prior to an election. The ANC, which accused the government of pushing through the new law without the input of the opposition beyond Olympio's UFC, organized demonstrations against the law—many of which were forcibly dispersed by the authorities. It also threatened to boycott the election over redistricting provisions heavily favoring members of the Union for the Republic (UNIR), a rebranded RPT that wanted to discard its repressive reputation. In July, Prime Minister Gilbert Fossoun Hounbgo and his cabinet stepped down, reportedly to fulfill a requirement of the new electoral law that officeholders intending to be candidates in the next parliamentary elections first resign their current positions. He was replaced by former trade minister and Gnassingbé ally Kwessi Ahoomey-Zunu.

In response to opposition and international pressure, the government agreed to delay the parliamentary elections until March 2013. In September, the government invited representatives from 11 political parties to a conference to discuss the new electoral law and pave the way for the legislative elections. The Rainbow Coalition—an alliance of six parties, including the ANC—refused to take part, accusing the conference of being no more than a façade to appease protesters. Among those who did participate, no agreement was reached on the main issue of redistricting, though they did agree on the composition of a new electoral commission (CENI). In October, the National Assembly had sworn in all CENI members, most of whom had served on previous electoral commissions. The Rainbow Coalition condemned CENI for its lack of independence and maintained its plans for an electoral boycott. By year's end, the proposed March election date remained tentative.

Political Rights and Civil Liberties: Togo is not an electoral democracy. The structure of the electoral system has largely ensured that President Faure Gnassingbé and his party remain in power, and as of October 2012, the National Assembly had overstayed its mandate. The May 2012 electoral code, which includes redistricting provisions favoring the ruling party, further limits the opposition's ability to gain power, though the code continued to be under negotiation at year's end. The president is elected to five-year terms and appoints the prime minister.

Corruption is a serious problem. In 2011, the government conducted a large-scale audit of all ministries and public services to trim government spending, but no further progress was apparent in 2012. Togo was ranked 128 out of 176 countries surveyed in Transparency International's 2012 Corruption Perceptions Index.

Freedom of the press is guaranteed by law, though often disregarded in practice. Impunity for crimes against journalists and frequent defamation suits encourage self-censorship. A 2009 law gives the state broadcasting council, the High Authority of Broadcasting and Communications (HAAC), the power to impose severe penalties—including the suspension of publications or broadcasts and the confiscation of press cards—if journalists are found to have made "serious errors" or are "endangering national security." In July 2012, the HAAC ordered the indefinite suspension of all interactive programming on the private radio station, Legende FM, accusing it of inciting racial and ethnic hatred by allowing listeners to call in and criticize the crackdowns against antigovernment protesters in June. When it refused to prevent callers from voicing critical opinions, the station itself was suspended; it had resumed some of its operations, though not its call-in programs, by year's end. In October, journalist Justin Anani was attacked by security forces while he was reporting on an antigovernment demonstration. Private print and broadcast outlets have low capacity and are often politicized. Access to the internet is generally unrestricted, but few people use the medium due to high costs.

Religious freedom is constitutionally protected and generally respected. Islam and Christianity are recognized as official religions, but other religious groups must register as associations. In September 2012, the Pew Forum on Religion and Public Life ranked Togo among the highest in the world in a study on global religious tolerance. While political discussion is prohibited on religious radio and television outlets, citizens are increasingly able to speak openly. Government security forces are believed to maintain a presence on university campuses and have cracked down on student protests in the past, though no such overt repression took place in 2012.

Freedom of assembly is sometimes restricted. A 2011 law requires that demonstrations receive prior authorization and only be held during certain times of the day. Throughout the year, the government repeatedly forcibly dispersed demonstrators protesting the adoption of the May 2012 electoral law. In August, about 100 people were injured and 125 arrested and briefly detained following clashes between protesters and police. Former prime minister and leading opposition figure, Agbeyome Kodjo, was temporarily detained in June in connection with the protests. Freedom of association is largely respected, and various human rights organizations generally operate without government interference. Togo's constitution guarantees the right to form and join labor unions. Most workers, except those working in export processing zones, have the right to strike, though they do not have the right to protection against employer retaliation.

The judicial system, including the Constitutional Court, lacks resources and is heavily influenced by the presidency. Lengthy pretrial detention is a serious problem. Prisons suffer from overcrowding and inadequate food and medical care. In June 2012, the government moved to reduce prison overcrowding by releasing on parole hundreds of prisoners who had already served two thirds of their sentence.

After widespread domestic and international demands for investigations into the political violence and human rights violations that occurred in Togo between 1958 and 2005, the Truth, Justice and Reconciliation Commission (TJRC)—which includes a diverse array of civil society representatives—was launched in 2009. However, the TJRC has no punitive power and can only recommend prosecutions, reparations, and future state actions. After examining 22,415 depositions and hearing from 523 witnesses, the TJRC released its findings in April 2012, recommending that victims receive financial and medical compensation. In a widely anticipated ruling, it concluded that injustices had indeed occurred during the 2005 political crisis. The TJRC also recommended the abolition of the death penalty, the implementation of mechanisms for the prevention of torture, constitutional reform ensuring the separation of powers, a return to a two-term limit for the presidency, and improved oversight of the police and the military. The report elicited a formal apology from the president, though no formal compensation had been administered by year's end.

Ethnic tensions have historically divided the country between the north and south along political, ethnic, and religious lines. Discrimination between the country's 40 ethnic groups occurs.

Despite constitutional guarantees of equality, women's opportunities for education and employment are limited. Customary law discriminates against women in divorce and inheritance, giving them the legal rights of minors, and children can only inherit citizenship from their father. Spousal abuse is widespread, and spousal rape is not a crime. Child trafficking for the purpose of slavery remains a serious problem, and prosecutions under a 2005 child-trafficking law are rare. Same-sex sexual activity is punishable by fines and up to three years in prison.

Tonga

Political Rights: 3
Civil Liberties: 3
Status: Partly Free

Population: 103,000
Capital: Nuku'alofa

Ten-Year Ratings Timeline For Year Under Review (Political Rights, Civil Liberties, Status)

2003	2004	2005	2006	2007	2008	2009	2010	2011	2012
5,3PF	5,3PF	5,3PF	5,3PF	5,3PF	5,3PF	5,3PF	3,3PF	3,3PF	3,3PF

Overview: King Tupou V died in Hong Kong in March 2012. His brother, Prince Tupouto'a Lavaka Ata succeeded him, taking the title King Tupou VI. In one of his final acts before his death, King Tupou V withheld royal consent for a 2011 law that would have reduced penalties for unlawful possession of firearms and ammunition. Meanwhile, several

police officers were charged with manslaughter in two separate cases during the year.

Tonga consists of 169 islands that King Siaosi I united under his rule in 1845. It became a constitutional monarchy in 1875 and a British protectorate in 1900, gaining independence in 1970 as a member of the Commonwealth. King Taufa'ahau Tupou IV ruled from 1945 to 2006. His son, Crown Prince Tupouto'a, assumed the title King Siaosi Tupou V in 2006 and was officially crowned in 2008.

The monarchy, hereditary nobles, and a few prominent commoners dominate politics and the economy. A public protest by prodemocracy activists in November 2006 escalated into rioting that destroyed the country's central business district, and the government declared a state of emergency. King Tupou V entered into talks with activists, reaching an agreement in December 2009 to create a new 26-member parliament with 17 popularly elected representatives.

Parliamentary elections were held under the new government structure in November 2010. Prodemocracy candidates of the Democratic Party of the Friendly Islands (DPFI) won 12 of the 17 commoners' seats. In December, the new parliament chose Lord Tu'ivakano as prime minister. The state of emergency that had been in effect since 2006 was lifted in February 2011.

On March 18, 2012, King Tupou V died at the age of 63, while receiving medical treatment in Hong Kong. The king had no children, and his 53-year-old brother, Prince Tupouto'a Lavaka, assumed the throne, taking the title King Tupou VI. The new king, who had previously been serving as Tonga's High Commissioner to Australia, named his 27-year-old son, Prince 'Ulukalala, as the new crown prince.

In one of his final official decisions before his death, King Tupou V in January vetoed the Arms and Ammunitions Act of 2011, which would have reduced the prison terms and fines for the unlawful possession of firearms and ammunition. The law was passed as three nobles in parliament, including house Speaker Lord Lasike, faced charges for illegally possessing firearms and other crimes. In July, Lasike was found guilty and fined $283 and stripped of his seat in parliament; he was replaced by Lord Fakafanua. Court hearings for the other two nobles, Lord Tu'ilakepa and Lord Tu'iha'ateiho, were scheduled for January and February 2013, respectively. Meanwhile, in October, the parliament failed to adopt the same bill to reduce prison terms for illegal weapons possession after Lord Fakafanua joined opposition members to block its passage.

Tonga's economy is heavily dependent on foreign aid and remittances from Tongans living abroad. The global economic downturn has reduced tourist arrivals, overseas remittances, and returns from government investments. In addition to raising fees for government licenses and services, Tonga is seeking more economic assistance from China. In 2012, China funded reconstruction of the downtown central business district with a $70 million loan.

Political Rights and Civil Liberties: Tonga is an electoral democracy. The unicameral Legislative Assembly has 26 members, including 17 popularly elected representatives and 9 nobles elected by their peers; all members serve four-year terms. The king retains the power to appoint the chief justice, judges of the court of appeal, and the attorney general on the advice of the privy council. The privy council, whose members are appointed by the king, lost its power to pass legislation following changes to the government structure in 2010. Additionally, the Legislative Assembly—rather than the king—now selects the prime minister.

Prodemocracy candidates have typically aligned with the Human Rights and Democracy Movement, which is not a formal party. Several new parties were formed to compete in the 2010 general elections, including the DPFI, the Democratic Labor Party, the Sustainable Nation-Building Party, and the People's Democratic Party.

Corruption is widespread, with royals, nobles, and their top associates allegedly having used state assets for personal benefit, and transparency and accountability are lacking. The government announced in 2012 that it would revive the Anti-Corruption Commission formed by King Tupou V in 2007, but which was never given the powers it needed to operate.

The constitution guarantees freedom of the press. Although commentaries critical of the government appear regularly in all newspapers, including those owned by the state or in which the state owns shares, the government has a history of suppressing media criticism. In 2012, the government granted a broadcast license to a new community radio station that focuses on women's issues. Funded by international donors and operated by volunteers, the station began broadcasting two days a week in February. In December, China Radio International, a 24-hour Chinese-government owned and operated FM radio station, began broadcasting in English and Chinese. Internet access is not restricted, and the number of users has increased despite high costs and lack of infrastructure.

Freedom of religion is generally respected, but the government requires all religious references on broadcast media to conform to mainstream Christian beliefs. Academics reportedly practice self-censorship to avoid conflicts with the government. In February 2012, the government mandated that Tongan be the only language taught at early education levels; the new rules add English to the curriculum in later grades, and exempt children whose mother tongue is not Tongan.

Freedoms of assembly and association are upheld. There has been a gradual decline in actions by the government and powerful elites to limit the creation or activities of nongovernmental organizations, including those that engage in work of a political nature. The 1963 Trade Union Act gives workers the right to form unions and to strike, but regulations for union formation were never promulgated.

The judiciary is generally independent, though a shortage of judges has created serious case backlogs. Traditional village elders frequently adjudicate local disputes, and nobles have increasingly faced scrutiny in society and the courts. Five police officers and one civilian were charged with manslaughter after a New Zealand police officer of Tongan origin was fatally injured in August 2012 while in police custody; an inquiry was set for February 2013. In November 2012, three police officers were charged with manslaughter in the death of a 20-year-old after a fight; they were released on bail pending a court hearing scheduled for January 2013.

Prisons are basic, and are only lightly guarded, as violent crimes are rare.

Women enjoy equal access to education and hold several senior government jobs, though no women were elected in the 2010 elections. Women cannot own land, and domestic violence is common. The government announced in 2012 that it would work to end violence against women through various measures, including the ratification of the United Nations Convention for the Elimination of Discrimination Against Women; no concrete measures had been taken by year's end.

Trinidad and Tobago

Political Rights: 2
Civil Liberties: 2
Status: Free

Population: 1,315,000
Capital: Port-of-Spain

Ten-Year Ratings Timeline For Year Under Review (Political Rights, Civil Liberties, Status)

2003	2004	2005	2006	2007	2008	2009	2010	2011	2012
3,3PF	3,3PF	3,2F	2,2F	2,2F	2,2F	2,2F	2,2F	2,2F	2,2F

Overview: After the December 2011 lifting of a state of emergency declared in response to a spike in violent crime, serious crime rates rose again in 2012. Minister of National Security Jack Warner ordered the police in October to stop publicizing crime statistics.

Trinidad and Tobago, a member of the Commonwealth, achieved independence from Britain in 1962 and became a republic in 1976.

In the November 2007 parliamentary elections, the People's National Movement (PNM) captured the largest number of seats. A Caribbean Community observer mission reported that voting was orderly and peaceful, representing a marked reduction in tension compared with previous polls. The PNM's Patrick Manning was reelected prime minister.

Faced with a no-confidence vote, Manning dissolved Parliament in April 2010 and called for elections in May. Kamla Persad-Bissessar's People's Partnership (PP) coalition—comprising the United National Congress (UNC), the Congress of the People, and the Tobago Organization of the People—won 29 of 41 seats, while the PNM took only 12. The PP's victory ended nearly 40 years of PNM rule. Persad-Bissessar pledged to bring transparency and accountability to all areas of government.

Soon after becoming prime minister, Persad-Bissessar in July allowed the first local elections since 2003; the Manning government had postponed them four times. The PP dominated in the country's 14 city, borough, and regional corporations.

In August 2011, a state of emergency was imposed to address an increase in violent crime. Related provisions included an 11 p.m. curfew and police authority to conduct searches and seizures without warrants. In September, the state of emergency was extended by three months, with the government citing continuing security concerns. By early October, almost 4,000 people had been arrested and about TT$750 million (US$117 million) in drugs had been seized. The Trinidad & Tobago Transparency Institute demanded the names and locations of detainees, and the Law Association of Trinidad and Tobago called on police to discipline officers who used excessive force during the state of emergency, which was lifted on December 5, 2011. Serious crimes rose subsequently; in 2012, there were an estimated 383 homicides, but the police department claims actual figures were probably lower.

Political Rights and Civil Liberties: Trinidad and Tobago is an electoral democracy. Tobago is a ward of Trinidad. The president is elected to a five-year term by a majority of the combined houses of Parliament, though executive authority rests with the prime minister. Parliament consists of the 41-member House of Representatives and the 31-member Senate; members of both houses are elected to five-year terms. The president appoints 16 senators on the advice of the prime minister, 6 on the advice of the opposition, and 9 at his or her own discretion.

Political parties are technically multiethnic, though the PNM is favored by Afro-Trinidadians, while the UNC is affiliated with Indo-Trinidadians. The PP coalition was multiethnic.

The country is believed to suffer from high-level corruption. Trinidad's Integrity Commission, established in 2000, has the power to investigate public officials' financial and ethical performance. Following the resignations of several commission members in 2009 due to suspicions of their ineligibility to serve, including because of allegations of malfeasance, a new Integrity Commission was appointed in 2010. Drug-related corruption extends to the business community, and a significant amount of money is believed to be laundered through front companies. The 2000 Proceeds of Crime Act imposes severe penalties for money laundering and requires that major financial transactions be strictly monitored. Trinidad and Tobago was ranked 80 out of 176 countries surveyed in Transparency International's 2012 Corruption Perceptions Index.

Freedom of speech is constitutionally guaranteed. Press outlets are privately owned and vigorously pluralistic. There are four daily newspapers and several weeklies, as well as private and public broadcast media outlets. Internet access is unrestricted.

The constitution guarantees freedom of religion, and the government honors this provision in practice. Academic freedom is generally observed.

Freedoms of association and assembly are respected. Civil society is relatively robust, with a range of interest groups engaged in the political process. Labor unions are well organized and politically active, though union membership has declined in recent years. Strikes are legal and occur frequently.

The judicial branch is independent, though subject to some political pressure and corruption. Rising crime rates have produced a severe backlog in the court system. Corruption in the police force, which is often drug related, is endemic, and inefficiencies result in the dismissal of some criminal cases. Trinidad and Tobago is the only country in the region that imposes a mandatory death sentences for murder. In 2012, the Trinidad and Tobago Coalition Against the Death Penalty called for a reconsideration of such sentences, which are prohibited under international human rights law. Prisons are severely overcrowded.

The government has struggled in recent years to address violent crime. Many Trinidadians of East Indian descent, who are disproportionately targeted for abduction, blame the increase in violence and kidnapping on government and police corruption. Most abuses by the authorities go unpunished. An October 2011 Amnesty International report criticized the use of excessive force by police and noted that such violence was seldom investigated. In October 2012, Minister of National Security Jack Warner controversially ordered the police to stop publicizing crime statistics.

The multiethnic population consists of Afro-Trinidadians, Indo-Trinidadians, and those of mixed race. The Indo-Trinidadian community continues to edge toward numerical, and thus political, advantage. Racial disparities persist, with Indo-Trinidadians comprising a disproportionate percentage of the country's upper class.

Women hold 12 seats in the House of Representatives and 7 seats in the Senate. Domestic violence remains a significant concern. A draft National Gender and Development Policy, which will provide a framework for promoting gender equality, was submitted to the Cabinet in 2012 for approval. Human rights groups have criticized the government's unwillingness to address the question of LGBT (lesbian, gay, bisexual, and transgender) rights in Trinidad and Tobago.

Tunisia

Political Rights: 3
Civil Liberties: 4
Status: Partly Free

Population: 10,800,000
Capital: Tunis

Ten-Year Ratings Timeline For Year Under Review (Political Rights, Civil Liberties, Status)

2003	2004	2005	2006	2007	2008	2009	2010	2011	2012
6,5NF	6,5NF	6,5NF	6,5NF	7,5NF	7,5NF	7,5NF	7,5NF	3,4PF	3,4PF

Overview: In 2012, the Constituent Assembly elected in 2011 attempted to balance its governing responsibilities with the need to draft and pass a new constitution, which remained incomplete at year's end. Security issues were a major concern for the coalition government during the year. Among other violent incidents, demonstrators protesting an online anti-Islam video clip in September attacked the U.S. embassy and an international school in Tunis.

Tunisia, which had been a French protectorate since 1881, gained its independence in 1956. The country was then ruled for more than 30 years by President Habib Bourguiba, a secular nationalist who favored economic and social modernization along Western lines but severely limited political liberties. Bourguiba succeeded in advancing women's rights and economic development, and his government maintained strong relations with the West and fellow Arab states.

In 1987, Prime Minister Zine el-Abidine Ben Ali ousted Bourguiba and seized the presidency in a bloodless coup. Ben Ali's rise to power had little effect on state policy. He continued to push market-based economic development and women's rights, but he also repressed political opponents. Independent journalists, secular activists, and Islamists faced imprisonment, torture, and harassment. Many Islamists, particularly supporters of the banned movement Ennahda, were jailed following sham trials in the early 1990s.

Ben Ali's hold on government institutions remained strong over subsequent years, and he won a fifth five-year term in the 2009 presidential election, taking nearly 90 percent of the vote amid tight media and candidacy restrictions.

The government's repressive measures continued through 2010 and included a harsh crackdown on journalists and bloggers. A state media campaign during the year advocated constitutional amendments that would allow Ben Ali to run for a sixth term in 2014.

The strict state controls enforced by the Ben Ali regime, combined with high unemployment and a lack of economic opportunities for young adults, led to nationwide antigovernment protests in December 2010 and January 2011. The uprising was triggered by the self-immolation of a fruit vendor protesting police harassment. As a result of the protests, which featured at least 219 deaths as demonstrators clashed with police, Ben Ali was forced to flee to Saudi Arabia on January 14.

Prime Minister Mohammed Ghannouchi assumed the role of head of state after Ben Ali's departure, but he too was forced from office by the continuing protests. Ben Ali's party, the Democratic Constitutional Rally (RCD), was dissolved by court order in March, all members of the party were forced to resign from the transitional government, and a court decision in June found Ben Ali guilty of theft and sentenced him in absentia to 35 years in prison and a $65 million fine.

Originally scheduled for June, elections for a Constituent Assembly were held in October 2011. The voting was observed by international monitoring groups, and they were widely touted as the first orderly, free, and fair elections in the country's history. There were isolated reports of irregularities and one documented violation of campaign finance rules, but the transitional authorities sought to act quickly on those problems, in some instances invalidating seats that were gained unfairly. Turnout was 52 percent, a substantially higher rate than in previous Tunisian elections.

Ennahda, the formerly outlawed Islamist party, won a plurality of the vote and 89 of the 217 seats. Two left-leaning parties, the Congress for the Republic (CPR) and Ettakatol, joined Ennahda in a governing coalition after winning 29 and 20 seats, respectively. Ennahda's Hamadi Jebali became prime minster, Ettakatol's Mustafa Ben Jaafar was chosen as Speaker of the assembly, and the CPR's Moncef Marzouki was named to hold a largely ceremonial presidency. The Constituent Assembly was tasked with drafting a new constitution and holding new elections within a year, and would serve as a legislature in the interim.

In 2012, the Constituent Assembly attempted to balance the need to draft a constitution with more basic governing responsibilities. As a result, it made little concrete progress on key issues like the role of the central and local governments, reform of the judicial system, and the respective powers of the president and prime minister. The constitutional drafting process continued during the year, but without an officially sanctioned deadline, a final document was not expected until early 2013. It remained unclear whether a referendum or a two-thirds vote in the Constituent Assembly would be necessary to adopt the constitution.

The authorities largely maintained security in the country during 2012, though there were sporadic clashes between rival political factions, crackdowns on protests related to economic issues, and threats from some Salafi Muslim groups against civilians and the state. In September, demonstrators protesting an online video that ridiculed Islam stormed the U.S. embassy and an international school in Tunis. Police reported that at least three protesters were killed and 28 people were wounded. Police and protesters also clashed violently in the town of Siliana in early December. Five days of protests over economic issues left unaddressed since the 2011 revolution were finally quashed by security forces.

Political Rights and Civil Liberties: Tunisia is an electoral democracy. The balloting of October 2011 represented a dramatic improvement in electoral freedoms and practices. Under the former regime of Zine el-Abidine Ben Ali, the president had directly appointed the cabinet, much of the legislature, and many regional officials. Elections were tightly controlled, and term limits were extended to allow Ben Ali to remain in power.

By contrast, in the 2011 elections, all 217 members of the Constituent Assembly were directly elected through party-list voting in 33 multimember constituencies, and voters were able to choose from political parties representing a wide range of ideologies and political philosophies, including Islamist and secularist groups. Many of the parties that competed were excluded from political participation under Ben Ali. It should be noted, however, that the government appoints many local officials. The appointment process for many key positions is not entirely transparent, and oversight is incomplete.

The removal of Ben Ali and his close relatives and associates, who had used their positions to create private monopolies in several sectors of the economy, represented an important first step in combating corruption and conflicts of interest. An anticorruption commission was established soon after the former president's ouster, the unelected transitional cabinet was far more subject to popular scrutiny than its predecessors, and the government elected in October 2011 also seemed inclined to operate with greater transparency. However, a strong legal framework and systematic practices aimed at curbing corruption had yet to take shape at the end of 2012. Tunisia was ranked 75 out of 176 countries surveyed in Transparency International's 2012 Corruption Perceptions Index.

The Ben Ali regime had used an array of legal, penal, and economic measures to silence dissenting voices in the media, and the transitional government almost immediately proclaimed freedom of information and expression as a foundational principle for the country. Conditions improved significantly in practice, but many problems persist, and it remains uncertain whether long-promised legal or institutional frameworks will be established to guarantee media freedoms. In May 2012, El Hiwar Ettounsi, one of five new private television stations to receive broadcast permits since the revolution, had its broadcasting equipment vandalized and stolen. Also in May, Nabil Karoui, owner of the private Nessma TV station, was ordered to pay a 2,400 dinar fine after a court found him guilty of violating moral values and disrupting public order for airing the movie *Persepolis*, which includes a cartoon depiction of Allah that religious conservatives found offensive.

Muslims form the dominant religious group in Tunisia, but the small populations of Jews and Christians have generally been free to practice their faiths. Draft constitutional language under consideration at the end of 2012 would protect religious expression, but would not give complete equality to people of all religions. Non-Muslims would be barred from the presidency, and the right to change one's faith or choose no faith was not explicitly protected. After Ben Ali's ouster, conservative and Salafi Muslims, like all religious groups, had more freedom to openly discuss the role that religion should play in the public sphere and to express their beliefs without state interference. However, this has resulted in periodic violent clashes with their political and ideological opponents, attacks on purveyors of alcohol or allegedly blasphemous art, and public threats by Salafis against state institutions. At least four Sufi Muslim shrines, which Salafi Muslims consider un-Islamic, have been destroyed, and several others have been forced to close.

Authorities limited academic discussion of sensitive topics under the Ben Ali regime, and its removal created a more open environment for students and faculties. Some small institutional improvements were made in 2012, including the reopening of the moderate 8th-century Zaitouna mosque and madrasa, which had been closed since the Bourguiba era. However, without a constitution, there is no legal framework to protect even such marginal advances.

Some human rights groups questioned the government's commitment to freedom of assembly in 2012. Although demonstrations on political, social, and economic issues took place throughout the year, many featured violent clashes with police, who were criticized for using excessive force. Temporary curfews were imposed in some cases.

Nongovernmental organizations (NGOs) were legally prohibited from pursuing political objectives and activities under the Ben Ali regime. However, many new groups began operating after the revolution. A number of conferences were held by NGOs across the country during 2012, and advocacy groups have mounted protests on issues such as women's rights, the role of religion in the state, and the needs of nomadic Berber communities. No formal registration process has been instated for these organizations, and their existence is not protected by a legal framework.

New labor organizations were established in 2011, including the Tunisian Labor Union (UTT) and the General Confederation of Tunisian Workers (CGTT). In 2012, these organizations, along with the oldest labor union in Tunisia, the General Union of Tunisian Workers (UGTT), continued to call for substantial governmental labor reform, better wages, and improved workplace conditions. However, the Constituent Assembly gave the issue little attention, leading the UGTT to both call for strikes and support protests against the authorities.

Under Ben Ali, the judicial system was carefully managed by the executive branch, which controlled the appointment and assignment of judges. Trials of suspected Islamists, human rights activists, and journalists were typically condemned as grossly unfair and politically biased by domestic and international observers. Politicized imprisonment and similar abuses declined significantly in 2011 and 2012, and the judiciary experienced some changes, reflected partly in the trial of Ben Ali in absentia. However, the court system and law enforcement agencies have not been thoroughly reformed since the fall of Ben Ali, and few within the government have shown the political will to undertake such reforms, despite significant domestic and international pressure.

Tunisia has long been praised for relatively progressive social policies, especially in the areas of family law and women's rights. The personal status code grants women equal rights in divorce, and children born to Tunisian mothers and foreign fathers are automatically granted citizenship. The country legalized medical abortion in 1973. There are currently 49 women in the Constituent Assembly, representing the largest proportion of female representatives in the Arab world, though only 7 are from a secularist party. In 2012, women's rights advocates criticized language in the draft constitution that referred to "complementarity" rather than equality between the sexes. Government officials backtracked on those provisions after the public outcry.

Turkey

Political Rights: 3
Civil Liberties: 4*
Status: Partly Free

Population: 74,885,000
Capital: Ankara

Ratings Change: Turkey's civil liberties rating declined from 3 to 4 due to the pretrial detention of thousands of individuals—including Kurdish activists, journalists, union leaders, students, and military officers—in campaigns that many believe to be politically motivated.

Ten-Year Ratings Timeline For Year Under Review (Political Rights, Civil Liberties, Status)

2003	2004	2005	2006	2007	2008	2009	2010	2011	2012
3,4PF	3,3PF	3,3PF	3,3PF	3,3PF	3,3PF	3,3PF	3,3PF	3,3PF	3,4PF

Overview: In September 2012, the courts delivered the first verdicts in a series of cases against military officers for alleged coup plots. The conduct of the trials, together with mass arrests of Kurdish activists in other cases, prompted widespread concern about the government's commitment to civil liberties and the rule of law. Meanwhile, the country struggled to cope with over 100,000 refugees fleeing the Syrian civil war, and a cross-border exchange of fire between Syrian and Turkish forces in September sparked fears of wider regional conflict.

The Republic of Turkey was formally established in 1923, following the end of World War I and the breakup of the Ottoman Empire. Its founder and first president was the military hero Mustafa Kemal, later dubbed Atatürk (Father of the Turks). He abolished both the Ottoman sultanate and the Muslim caliphate and declared Turkey a secular state. He also embraced numerous modernizing and Western-oriented reforms, including European-style education, the Latin alphabet for written Turkish, gender equality, and Western legal codes. Under Atatürk, however, Turkey was a nondemocratic one-party state.

Atatürk died in November 1938. Turkey remained neutral in World War II until February 1945, when it joined the Allies. In 1952, Turkey joined NATO to secure protection from the Soviet Union, and in 1964 it concluded an Association Agreement with the European Economic Community, the precursor to the European Union (EU). However, Turkey's domestic politics were often unstable, and the military forced out civilian governments on four occasions between 1960 and 1997. After a coup in 1980, the military government drafted a constitution that severely restricted civil liberties and political freedoms. It was ratified by referendum in November 1982.

In the 1990s and early 2000s, Turkey experienced a series of weak coalition governments, economic difficulties, corruption scandals, and continued fighting, mostly in the southeast, between the military and the separatist Kurdistan Workers' Party (PKK). In November 2002 parliamentary elections, the Justice and Development Party (AKP) won a sweeping victory. The AKP had roots in the Islamic-oriented Welfare (Refah) Party, which had been removed from power due to military pressure in 1997 and subsequently banned for antisecular activities. However, the AKP presented itself as a modern, Western-oriented party. Its leader, Recep Tayyip Erdogan, was banned from politics in 1998 for allegedly inciting religious intolerance while serving as mayor of Istanbul. Once in power, the AKP amended the constitution to allow Erdogan to become prime minister.

In its first years in government, the AKP oversaw numerous reforms linked to Turkey's bid to join the EU, including a ban on capital punishment, greater rights for free expression, greater cultural rights for the Kurdish minority, and limits on the powers of the military. Accession talks with the EU officially began in October 2005, but difficulties, including disputes with Cyprus and skepticism among some EU leaders and citizens about Turkish membership, slowed the process. Turkish popular support for EU membership also declined, and the momentum for reform began to flag.

In 2007, staunch secularist Ahmet Necdet Sezer completed his term as president, and despite objections from the military and the secularist opposition Republican People's Party (CHP), the AKP nominated its own Abdullah Gül to succeed him. The military tacitly threatened to intervene if Gül's nomination were approved by parliament, and AKP opponents mounted street demonstrations. Erdogan called early parliamentary elections for July 2007 to overcome parliamentary opposition. The AKP handily won the voting, allowing Gül to be elected president.

However, partisan disputes continued. In 2008 AKP opponents brought a case before the Constitutional Court to ban the AKP for violating principles of secularism, but the court rejected the move by one vote in July. For its part, the AKP launched an investigation into alleged coup plots by a secretive group called Ergenekon, which was accused of conspiring to stage terrorist attacks and thus provoke political intervention by the military. Numerous military and police officers, academics, publishers, and journalists were indicted in connection with the Ergenekon case. However, critics argued that the AKP was using unsubstantiated charges to suppress its political opponents. Trials began in October 2008.

In September 2010, the government called a referendum on constitutional amendments to further curtail the power of the military and judiciary and to make it more difficult to ban political parties. In addition to the attempt to ban the AKP, the largely Kurdish Democratic Society Party (DTP) in December 2009 had become the most recent of several Kurdish parties to be banned for alleged links to separatist activity. The constitutional reforms were largely supported by the EU, but critics expressed fears that they amounted to a power grab by the AKP. The proposed amendments passed with 58 percent of the vote.

The AKP's 2009–10 "Kurdish initiative," which included clandestine talks with some officials from the PKK, produced no major breakthroughs. In February 2011, the PKK ended its latest ceasefire, and armed clashes between the group and Turkish forces over the next two years killed hundreds of soldiers, police, militants, and civilians. At the same time, the government accelerated its actions against the Union of Communities of Kurdistan (KCK), which authorities described as the PKK's urban arm. Special courts, using antiterrorism laws, rendered convictions in dozens of cases against alleged KCK members.

In June 2011 parliamentary elections, the AKP won nearly 50 percent of the vote and garnered 326 of 550 available seats. The CHP placed second with 135 seats, followed by the Nationalist Action Party (MHP), with 53 and independents backed by the largely Kurdish Peace and Democracy Party (BDP) with 36. Erdogan was reconfirmed as prime minister, and he made writing a new constitution a top priority. In October 2011, a multiparty Constitution Reconciliation Commission was created to draft a new charter. However, tensions among the various parties on issues such as the Kurdish question, redefining secularism, and possibly adopting a presidential system of government, as well as stipulations that the proposed changes must be supported by all parties, dimmed hopes for progress on the document.

Meanwhile, arrests in the Ergenekon and other coup-related cases continued. By mid-2011, over 600 people had been charged. In July 2011, the arrest of 250 officers in the "Sledgehammer" case, involving an alleged 2003 coup plot, prompted the resignation of Turkey's military chief of staff and the heads of the army, navy, and air force. In the first half of 2012, several former military officials were indicted in connection with coup plots, including cases stretching back to 1980 and 1997. A special security court handed down prison sentences against 331 officers in the Sledgehammer case in September 2012. While some observers hailed the case as a breakthrough for civilian oversight of the military, others expressed concern about the rule of law and warned that the government was using the coup trials and KCK arrests to silence legitimate critics.

The civil war that had begun in Syria in 2011 continued throughout 2012, by which time over 100,000 refugees had entered Turkey, creating a humanitarian crisis. The Turkish government backs the Syrian rebels and is concerned about ties between Syrian Kurds and the PKK. A bout of cross-border shelling between Syrian and Turkish forces in September 2012 sparked fears of a wider regional conflict.

Political Rights and Civil Liberties: Turkey is an electoral democracy. Its 550-seat unicameral parliament, the Grand National Assembly, is elected every four years. Starting in 2014, the president will be elected by popular vote for a once-renewable, five-year term, replacing the existing system of election by parliament. The prime minister is head of government; the president has powers including a legislative veto and authority to appoint judges and prosecutors. The June 2011 parliamentary elections were widely judged to have been free and fair, although 12 candidates from the BDP were barred from running, and 8 winning candidates—6 from the BDP and 2 from the CHP—were in pretrial detention at the time of the elections. Both the BDP and CHP boycotted the opening of parliament. The 2011 elections were notable for featuring the first legal campaigning in Kurdish.

A party must win at least 10 percent of the nationwide vote to secure parliamentary representation. This is the highest electoral threshold in Europe. Political parties can be disbanded for endorsing policies not in agreement with constitutional parameters. The rule has frequently been applied to Islamist and pro-Kurdish parties. As of July 2012, more than 1,000 officials from the BDP, including over 300 elected mayors, remained jailed or in detention in the KCK cases for alleged links to the PKK. In May 2012, Leyla Zana, a BDP lawmaker who had previously spent 10 years in prison, was sentenced to another 10 years for ties to the PKK.

AKP-led reforms have increased civilian oversight of the military, but restrictions persist in areas such as supervision of defense expenditures. Constitutional amendments in 2010 limited the jurisdiction of military courts to military personnel and removed provisions that prevented the prosecution of leaders of the 1980 military coup. Trials against military officers continued throughout 2012. İlker Basbug, a former chief of the general staff, was put on trial in March; former president Kenan Evran, leader of the 1980 coup, went on trial in April; and in September a court handed down prison sentences against 325 officers allegedly connected to the Sledgehammer coup plot. Many observers expressed concern about the frequent use of lengthy pretrial detention and catch-all indictments and alleged that the trials and convictions rested on flimsy or doctored evidence.

Turkey struggles with corruption in government and in daily life. The AKP government has adopted some anticorruption measures, including a reform package in June 2012 that focuses on bribery and political financing. However, reports by international organizations still note only limited progress in this area. Prime Minister Recep Tayyip Erdogan has been accused of involvement in a number of scandals related to economic cronyism and nepotism. Turkey was ranked 54 out of 176 countries surveyed in Transparency International's 2012 Corruption Perceptions Index.

The right to free expression is guaranteed in the constitution, but legal impediments to press freedom remain. A 2006 antiterrorism law reintroduced jail sentences for journalists. A June 2012 reform package reduced prison sentences and pretrial detention for certain offenses, but observers noted that the changes failed to satisfy concerns expressed by the EU and the Council of Europe. Ahmet Sik and Nedim Sener, two journalists arrested in March 2011 in connection with the Ergenekon case, were released in March 2012. However, an October 2012 report from the Committee to Protect Journalists (CPJ) noted that more journalists were incarcerated in Turkey than in any other country. According to CPJ, by the end of 2012, 49 journalists were behind bars, compared to 8 a year earlier. Most were Kurdish and charged under antiterrorism laws in the KCK cases. The harsh legal environment has also encouraged self-censorship, and in 2012 some journalists who were critical of the government lost their jobs.

Nearly all media organizations are owned by giant holding companies with ties to political parties, contributing to self-censorship. Kurdish-language publications and television broadcasts are now permitted, but they can be temporarily shut down by authorities. Such was the case with the newspaper *Özgür Gündem* in March 2012 and *Demokratik Vatan* in May. The internet is subject to the same censorship policies that apply to other media. An internet filtration system was introduced in November 2011, with optional settings designed to protect minors. A September 2012 report from European Digital Rights noted an increase in prosecutions of people who share "illegal content" on social-networking sites. That month, a man was sentenced to a year in prison for insulting President Abdullah Gül on Facebook.

The constitution protects freedom of religion, but the state's official secularism has led to restrictions on the Muslim majority and others. Observant men may be dismissed from the military, and women are officially barred from wearing headscarves in public universities and government offices. The AKP has lobbied against the headscarf ban, and enforcement of this provision has become more lax in many universities. Three non-Muslim groups—Jews, Orthodox Christians, and Armenian Christians—are officially recognized. However, disputes over property, prohibitions on training of clergy, and interference in the internal governance of their religious organizations remain concerns. In an address to the parliament in February 2012, Ecumenical Patriarch Bartholomew I of the Orthodox Church advocated new constitutional protections for non-Muslims.

The Alevis, a non-Sunni Muslim group, lack protected status. Historically they have been targets of violence and discrimination, and their houses of worship—known as cemevis—do not receive state support, as mosques do. The government made overtures to the Alevi community in 2010, but in August 2012, Erdogan suggested that true Muslims only pray in mosques.

Academic freedom is limited by self-censorship and legal or political pressure regarding sensitive topics such as the Kurds, the definition of World War I–era massacres of Armenians as genocide, and the legacy of Atatürk. Scholars linked to the Kurdish issue have been subject to increased intimidation and in some cases detention. Notable examples include the October 2011 arrests of publisher and Nobel Peace Prize nominee Ragıp Zarakolu and political science professor Büra Ersanlı, a member of the constitutional commission of the BDP. Both were released on bail pending their trials, which began in July 2012. Separately, more than 3,000 students were reportedly in prison as of September, and several were convicted and sentenced; many had been charged with terrorism offenses after organizing to call for free higher education.

Freedoms of association and assembly are protected in the constitution, and Turkey has an active civil society. Many prior restrictions on public demonstrations have been relaxed, and in April 2012 activities related to the "Armenian Genocide Commemoration Day" proceeded peacefully. However, clashes with police still occur. Police used teargas and water cannons to disperse protests over a religious education bill in May. In October, the government banned celebrations of Republic Day, citing security concerns. Police subsequently clashed with secularists who went ahead with a rally in Ankara, and Erdogan labeled the protesters "terrorist hooligans." Members of human rights groups have received death threats and continue to face prosecution on various charges, including membership in the KCK.

Laws to protect labor unions are in place, but union activity remains limited in practice. Regulations for the recognition of legal strikes are onerous, and penalties for participating in illegal strikes are severe. Union officials were arrested on multiple occasions in 2012, including 69 leaders from the Confederation of Public Service Workers (KESK) who were rounded up in June in an anti-KCK operation. The constitution stipulates an independent judiciary, and in June 2012, the government passed a long-awaited measure to establish an ombudsman. In practice, however, the government can influence judges through appointments, promotions, and financing. Critics of the government are concerned about pressure put on judges, particularly in cases involving alleged coup plots and journalists. Defense lawyers in KCK cases have themselves been placed under investigation. The court system in general is undermined by procedural delays, with some trials lasting so long as to become a financial burden for the defense.

The government has enacted laws and introduced training to prevent torture, but reports of mistreatment are widespread. Prison conditions can be harsh. Overcrowding is common, access to medical care is uneven, and laws and oversight are inadequate. In March 2012, hundreds of minors reportedly had to be moved out of a prison in Adana after allegations of physical and sexual abuse.

In February 2011 the PKK ended a six-month unilateral ceasefire, and armed clashes between the group and the Turkish military in 2011 and 2012 killed hundreds of soldiers, police, militants, and civilians. An investigation continues into the December 2011 killing of 34 civilians by the Turkish military near the village of Uludere, along the border with Iraq.

The Kurdish question remains a key challenge for Turkey's democracy. Many past restrictions on the Kurdish language have been lifted, and in June 2012, the Ministry of Education approved a curriculum that would allow some teaching of Kurdish. However, use of Kurdish in the provision of public services remains prohibited. In the wake of renewed violence by the PKK, the government has stepped up anti-KCK operations, invoking antiterrorism laws to arrest large numbers of individuals who are critical of government policy. According to one estimate, in 2012, 7,748 people had been detained and 3,895 arrested in anti-KCK actions. Trials were ongoing at year's end.

Homosexual activity is not prohibited, but LGBT (lesbian, gay, bisexual, and transgender) people are subject to widespread discrimination, police harassment, and occasional violence. In September 2012, the AKP rejected a proposal to protect the rights of LGBT people in the constitution.

Property rights are generally respected in Turkey, with notable exceptions. Tens of thousands of Kurds were driven from their homes in the southeast during the 1990s, though some have returned or received financial compensation under a program set up in 2004. Non-Muslim religious communities that lack a corporate legal identity have difficulty owning property or regaining property previously seized by the state. Of the 117 judgments against Turkey by the European Court of Human Rights in 2012, 20 percent involved property rights.

The constitution grants women full equality before the law, but the World Economic Forum ranked Turkey 124 out of 135 countries surveyed in its 2012 Global Gender Gap Index. Only about a third of working-age women participate in the labor force, the lowest rate in Europe. Women hold just 78 seats in the parliament, up from 48 after the 2007 elections. Reports of domestic abuse have increased in recent years, and so-called honor crimes continue to occur. A March 2012 report found that 42 percent of Turkish women have been subjected to physical or sexual violence. That month the government passed a law forcing husbands who are deemed abusive by the courts to wear monitoring devices, and in August, the Ministry of Family and Social Policies announced its 2012–15 Action Plan to Combat Violence Against Women. However, critics complain that the government seems more committed to "family integrity" than women's rights. In May, Prime Minister Erdogan called for a ban on abortion and limits on caesarean births; the government backed away from formally introducing the controversial measures by year's end.

Turkmenistan

Political Rights: 7
Civil Liberties: 7
Status: Not Free

Population: 5,169,700
Capital: Ashgabat

Ten-Year Ratings Timeline For Year Under Review (Political Rights, Civil Liberties, Status)

2003	2004	2005	2006	2007	2008	2009	2010	2011	2012
7,7NF	7,7NF	7,7NF	7,7NF	7,7NF	7,7NF	7,7NF	7,7NF	7,7NF	7,7NF

Overview: President Gurbanguly Berdymukhammedov in February was reelected to a second five-year term, winning 97 percent of the vote, according to the election commission, against a field of candidates who were all associated with the ruling party. In March, Berdymukhammedov announced plans to form two new political parties, though both were organized by loyal members of the government and thus not expected to challenge the status quo.

Turkmenistan gained formal independence from the Soviet Union in 1991. Saparmurat Niyazov, head of the Communist Party of Turkmenistan, was the sole candidate in elections to the newly created post of president in October 1990. He won reelection in 1992, with a reported 99.5 percent of the vote. A 1994 referendum extended his term until 2002. In the December 1994 elections to the Mejlis (National Assembly), only Niyazov's Democratic Party of Turkmenistan (DPT), the former Communist Party, was permitted to field candidates.

In the 1999 Mejlis elections, every candidate was selected by the government, and all were members of the DPT. The Organization for Security and Cooperation in Europe (OSCE), citing numerous procedural inadequacies, refused to send even a limited assessment mission. The Mejlis unanimously voted in late December of that year to make Niyazov president for life.

In 2002, Niyazov survived an assassination attempt in the capital city of Ashgabat. The incident sparked a crackdown on the opposition and perceived critics of the regime, drawing condemnation from foreign governments and international organizations. Mejlis elections in 2004 followed the established pattern of executive control.

Niyazov's rule was marked by frequent government reshuffles, the gutting of formal institutions, the muzzling of media, and an elaborate personality cult. *The Ruhnama*, a rambling collection of quasi-historical and philosophical writings attributed to Niyazov, became the core of educational curriculums.

Niyazov's death in December 2006 from an apparent heart attack was followed by the rapid and seemingly well-orchestrated ascent of Deputy Prime Minister Gurbanguly Berdymukhammedov to the position of acting president. The succession appeared to circumvent constitutional norms, as criminal charges were brought against Mejlis Speaker Ovezgeldy Atayev, who would have become acting president upon Niyazov's death, according to the constitution. Berdymukhammedov cemented his formal status in a February 2007 presidential election, easily besting five obscure ruling-party candidates. The poll was not monitored by any international observers.

Berdymukhammedov gradually removed high-ranking Niyazov loyalists and took steps to replace Niyazov as the subject of the state's cult of personality. In August 2008, the Halk Maslahaty (People's Council), the country's supreme representative body, voted without public debate to approve a new constitution, effectively dissolving itself and dispersing its powers to the Mejlis and the president. Elections for a newly expanded Mejlis were held in December 2008, but as with previous votes, all of the nearly 300 candidates were preapproved by the presidential administration.

In February 2012, Turkmenistan held a scheduled presidential election. While Berdymukhammedov promised that the polls would include opposition parties and adhere to international norms, all seven of his challengers were minor figures associated with the ruling party. Berdymukhammedov was reelected to a second five-year term with 97 percent of the vote and 96 percent turnout, according to the country's election commission. Violating OSCE commitments, Turkmenistan did not invite external observers to monitor the election.

Turkmenistan's foreign relations continue to revolve around the country's energy exports, to the exclusion of most other issues. The government continued to take steps to limit freedom of movement to and from the country, including instituting random strip searches of female citizens returning from abroad in May 2-12. In August, students attempting to travel to Russia and Bulgaria to participate in U.S.-government sponsored higher education programs were denied the right to leave the country.

Political Rights and Civil Liberties: Turkmenistan is not an electoral democracy. None of the country's elections since independence in 1991 have been free or fair. President Gurbanguly Berdymukhammedov has maintained all the means and patterns of repression established by his predecessor, Saparmurat Niyazov, whose authoritarian rule lasted from 1985 to 2006. Local elections held in July 2009, December 2010, and August 2012 mimicked the country's previous stage-managed polls.

Under a new constitution approved in 2008, the Mejlis became the sole legislative body and the number of seats expanded to 125, from 50 previously, with members serving five-year terms. The new charter also gave citizens the right to form political parties, though the Mejlis remained a single party legislature through 2012. In January 2012, a new law on the formation of political parties further specified the legal basis for any citizen to form an independent party, barring parties formed on professional or religious lines. In March, Berdymukhammedov announced plans to form two new political parties—the Agrarian Party and the Party of Entrepreneurs and Industrialists. His announcement violated two sections of the new law, by creating profession-based parties and tasking a sitting member of the government with their creation; both parties were transparently organized by sitting members of the DPT.

Corruption is widespread, with public officials often forced to bribe their way into their positions. Allocation of state profits from gas exports remains opaque. According to a 2011 report by Crude Accountability, an environmental group that works in the Caspian Sea region, only 20 percent of revenues from the sale of hydrocarbons are transferred to the state budget. A 2011 amendment to the 2008 Law on Hydrocarbon Resources expanded the president's near-total control over the hydrocarbon sector and the revenue it produces; additional amendments in 2012 allowed the state agency for hydrocarbon resources to establish companies, buy a direct stake in foreign companies, and open branches abroad. The government's lack of transparency affects a variety of public services, including medical care. An April 2010 report by Doctors Without Borders found that Turkmen authorities were concealing "a dangerous public health situation, in which government officials actively deny the prevalence of infectious disease, medical data is systemically manipulated, and international standards and protocols are rarely applied in practice." Turkmenistan was ranked 170 out of 176 countries surveyed in Transparency International's 2012 Corruption Perceptions Index.

Freedom of the press is severely restricted by the government, which controls nearly all broadcast and print media. Turkmenistan's main internet service provider, run by the government, reportedly blocks undesirable websites and monitors users' activity. The authorities remained hostile to news reporting in 2012, and sought to suppress any independent sources of information.

The government restricts freedom of religion. Practicing an unregistered religion remains illegal, with violators subject to fines. Islamic cleric Shiri Geldimuradov reportedly died in prison under unclear circumstances in 2010.

The government places significant restrictions on academic freedom. Since 2009, students bound for university study abroad have routinely been denied exit visas.

The constitution guarantees freedoms of peaceful assembly and association, but in practice, these rights are severely restricted. Sporadic protests, usually focused on social issues, have taken place. A 2003 law on nongovernmental organizations (NGOs) deprived all such groups of their registration; the few groups that were subsequently reregistered are tightly controlled. Turkmenistan is still home to a few dedicated activists, but there is virtually no organized civil society sector. The government-controlled Association of Trade Unions of Turkmenistan is the only central trade union permitted. Workers are barred by law from bargaining collectively or staging strikes.

The judicial system is subservient to the president, who appoints and removes judges without legislative review. The authorities frequently deny rights of due process, including public trials and access to defense attorneys. A 2011 report by the UN Committee Against Torture expressed deep concern "over the numerous and consistent allegations about the widespread practice of torture and ill-treatment of detainees." Prisons suffer from overcrowding, and prisoners are poorly fed and denied access to adequate medical care. The Red Cross in April 2012 was permitted to visit a Turkmen prison, marking the first time a foreign NGO had been allowed access to one of the country's prisons since independence.

The government has released a number of political prisoners since Niyazov's death, but many others remain behind bars. Nothing is known about the condition of jailed former foreign ministers Boris Shikhmuradov and Batyr Berdyev. Rights activists Annakurban Amanklychev and Sapardurdy Khajiev, convicted on dubious espionage charges in 2006, remained in prison in 2012. Unanswered questions still surround the 2006 death in custody of Radio Free Europe/Radio Liberty correspondent Ogulsapar Muradova, whose family continued to face harassment in 2012.

Employment and educational opportunities for ethnic minorities are limited by the government's promotion of Turkmen national identity.

Freedom of movement is restricted, with a reported blacklist preventing some individuals from leaving the country. A few activists who hold dual citizenship and continue to reside in Turkmenistan are able to travel abroad using their Russian passports, but even this window is closing, as some activists were denied new Turkmen passports in recent years in a bid to make them choose either Russian or Turkmen citizenship.

A Soviet-style command economy and widespread corruption diminish equality of opportunity. The constitution establishes the right to private property, but the deeply flawed judiciary provides little protection to businesses and individuals. Arbitrary evictions and confiscation of property are common practices.

Traditional social and religious norms, inadequate education, and poor economic conditions limit professional opportunities for women, and NGO reports suggest that domestic violence is common.

Tuvalu

Political Rights: 1
Civil Liberties: 1
Status: Free

Population: 11,300
Capital: Funafuti

Ten-Year Ratings Timeline For Year Under Review (Political Rights, Civil Liberties, Status)

2003	2004	2005	2006	2007	2008	2009	2010	2011	2012
1,1F	1,1F	1,1F	1,1F	1,1F	1,1F	1,1F	1,1F	1,1F	1,1F

Overview: In 2012, Tuvalu continued to be threatened by rising sea levels and a shortage of safe drinking water. In March, Tuvalu signed a visa-free travel agreement with Abkhazia, a breakaway region of Georgia.

The Gilbert and Ellice Islands, situated in the central South Pacific Ocean, became a British protectorate in 1892 and a British colony in 1916. Polynesian Ellice Islanders voted to separate themselves from the Micronesian Gilbertese in 1974. In 1978, the Ellice Islands became independent under the name of Tuvalu, while the Gilbert Islands become part of Kiribati.

Politics in Tuvalu have been marked by intense personal and political rivalries and the use of no-confidence votes to unseat incumbents. In the September 2010 elections, 26 candidates—all independents—competed for 15 seats in Parliament. In December 2010, Prime Minister Maatia Toafa was ousted in a no-confidence vote and was replaced by Home Affairs Minister Willy Telavi.

The economy of Tuvalu—which has no known mineral resources and few exports—depends on the sale of fishing licenses, the lease of its internet suffix (.tv), and remittances from Tuvaluans abroad. About 10 percent of Tuvalu's annual budget is derived from the Tuvalu Trust Fund, a well-run overseas investment fund set up by Britain, Australia, and South Korea in 1987 to provide development assistance.

Global climate change and rising sea levels pose significant challenges for Tuvalu and other low-lying island states. Tuvalu's highest point is just five meters above sea level. Meanwhile, the weather pattern known as La Niña resulted in far less rainfall than usual in 2011 and 2012, causing a severe fresh water shortage for Tuvalu. In September 2011, the government declared a two-week state of emergency when about 50 percent of the population had only a two-day supply of fresh water; water usage was strictly monitored and rationed in some areas. New Zealand and the United States sent desalination equipment to alleviate the shortage, but lack of rainfall and basic water and sewage treatment facilities remain problems.

In March 2012, Tuvalu signed an agreement for visa-free travel with Abkhazia, a breakaway region of Georgia whose independence is recognized by only a handful of other countries, including Tuvalu and Russia.

Political Rights and Civil Liberties: Tuvalu is an electoral democracy. Britain's Queen Elizabeth II is the head of state and is represented by a governor general, who must be a citizen of Tuvalu. The prime minister, chosen by Parliament, leads the government. The unicameral, 15-member Parliament is elected to four-year terms. A six-person council administers each of the country's nine atolls. Council members are chosen by universal suffrage for four-year terms.

There are no formal political parties, though there are no laws against their formation. Political allegiances revolve around geography, tribal loyalties, and personalities, with elected representatives frequently changing sides and building new alliances.

Tuvalu is one of the few places in the Pacific Islands where corruption is not a serious problem, though international donors have called for improvements in governance.

The constitution provides for freedoms of speech and the press, and the government generally respects these rights in practice. The semi-public Tuvalu Media Corporation (TMC) operates the country's sole radio and television stations, as well as the biweekly newspaper *Tuvalu Echoes* and the government newsletter *Sikuelo o Tuvalu*. Human rights groups have criticized the TMC for its limited coverage of politics and human rights issues, but there have been no allegations of censorship or imbalances in reporting. Many residents use satellite dishes to access foreign programming. Internet use is largely limited to the capital because of cost and connectivity challenges, but authorities do not restrict access.

Religious freedom is upheld in this overwhelmingly Christian country, where religion is a major part of life. Academic freedom is generally respected.

The constitution provides for freedoms of association and assembly, and the government upholds these rights in practice. However, on January 13, 2011, the government for the first time invoked the Public Order Act for two weeks to ban public gatherings of three or more people on the main island of Funafuti. The decision was made after hundreds of protestors demanded the immediate resignation of Finance Minister Lotoala Metia for refusing to meet with traditional elders. The government cited a rumored arson threat against Metia as the reason for the ban.

Two weeks later, the ban was replaced by a regulation requiring protest organizers to obtain prior permission from police; this requirement was lifted after two weeks. Nongovernmental organizations (NGOs) provide a variety of health, education, and other services. A 2007 law allowing the incorporation of NGOs strengthened legal protection for civil society groups.

Workers have the right to strike, organize unions, and choose their own representatives for collective bargaining. Public sector employees, numbering fewer than 1,000, are members of professional associations that do not have union status. With two-thirds of the population engaged in subsistence farming and fishing, Tuvalu has only one registered trade union—the Tuvalu Overseas Seamen's Union—with about 600 members who work on foreign merchant vessels.

The judiciary is independent and provides fair trials. Tuvalu has a two-tier judicial system. The higher courts include the Privy Council in London, the Court of Appeal, and the High Court. The lower courts consist of senior and resident magistrates, the island courts, and the land courts. The chief justice, who is also the chief justice of Tonga, visits Tuvalu twice a year to preside over the High Court. A civilian-controlled constabulary force maintains internal order. There are no reports of abuse in the prison system.

Traditional customs and social norms condone discrimination against women and limit their role in society. Women enjoy equal access to education, but they remain underrepresented in positions of leadership in business and government. There are currently no women in Parliament. No law specifically addresses sexual harassment. There have been few reports of violence against women. Rape is illegal, but spousal rape is not included in the definition.

⬇ Uganda

Political Rights: 5
Civil Liberties: 4
Status: Partly Free

Population: 35,621,000
Capital: Kampala

Trend Arrow: Uganda received a downward trend arrow due to increased restriction and harassment of the opposition and a systematic campaign to obstruct and shut down civic groups that engage the government on sensitive issues such as gay rights, corruption, term limits, and land rights.

Ten-Year Ratings Timeline For Year Under Review (Political Rights, Civil Liberties, Status)

2003	2004	2005	2006	2007	2008	2009	2010	2011	2012
5,4PF	5,4PF	5,4PF	5,4PF	5,4PF	5,4PF	5,4PF	5,4PF	5,4PF	5,4PF

Overview:
Throughout 2012, the political opposition and civil society challenged President Yoweri Museveni on issues such as corruption, deteriorating economic conditions, transparency in the oil sector, and gay rights. Meanwhile, the government harassed and intimidated

opposition leaders and critical nongovernmental organizations. In December, parliament passed a bill regulating the oil sector that awarded significant power to the executive and threatened transparency.

Following independence from Britain in 1962, Uganda experienced considerable political instability. In 1971 authoritarian president Milton Obote was overthrown by Major General Idi Amin, who was responsible for hundreds of thousands of deaths. His 1978 invasion of Tanzania led to his ouster by Tanzanian forces and Ugandan exiles. After Obote returned to power in 1980 through fraudulent elections, opponents were savagely repressed.

Obote was overthrown again in a 1985 military coup, and in 1986 the rebel National Resistance Army, led by Yoweri Museveni, took power. Museveni introduced a "no party" system, under which only one supposedly nonpartisan political organization—the National Resistance Movement (NRM)—was allowed to operate unfettered. Museveni and the NRM won presidential and parliamentary elections in 2001, though a ban on most formal party activities restricted the opposition, which boycotted the legislative polls.

In 2005, voters approved a package of constitutional amendments in which the ban on political parties was lifted in exchange for an end to presidential term limits. A leading Museveni opponent, Kizza Besigye of the Forum for Democratic Change (FDC), returned from exile to contest the 2006 presidential election. However, he was arrested on charges including treason and rape, and was defeated at the polls by Museveni. The NRM won a large majority in concurrent parliamentary elections. In the following years, the government gradually stepped up intimidation and harassment of opposition officials and its use of questionable legal and extralegal measures to suppress opposition rallies.

Tensions between the government and the Buganda region increased in 2009, and in March 2010, a suspicious fire destroyed much of the Kasubi Tombs, the burial ground of the Baganda monarchs and a UNESCO World Heritage Site. Security forces fired into crowds that gathered following the fire, killing three. A government commission of inquiry produced a report in 2011, but it had yet to be made public by the end of 2012.

Separately, in July 2010, the Somalia-based Islamist militia group Al-Shabaab bombed two venues in Kampala, killing some 75 people. The attack was in retaliation for Uganda's leading role in the African Union (AU) peacekeeping mission in Somalia.

Museveni won the February 2011 presidential election, with 68 percent of the vote. Besigye, who had been cleared of treason, terrorism, murder, and firearms charges in October 2010, placed second with 26 percent. In concurrent parliamentary elections, the NRM took 263 of 375 elected seats, followed by the FDC with 34. International observers noted that the elections had been peaceful but marred by widespread administrative failings that led to mass disenfranchisement. Museveni and his party exploited the advantages of incumbency; observers criticized the passage of a $256 million supplementary budget shortly before the election, with much of the funds going to the president's office.

In April and May 2011, Besigye and his Activists for Change (A4C) pressure group led a "walk to work" campaign of marches against corruption and the rising cost of living. Police violence resulted in at least 10 deaths, and hundreds were arrested. Attempts to renew the protests in October led to 40 arrests and treason charges for three of the organizers.

Throughout 2012, Besigye and A4C continued to pressure the government through rallies and protests. In April, after a police officer was killed the previous month while trying to disperse an A4C rally, the group was declared an "unlawful society" and banned. Besigye and 14 others, including Kampala mayor Erias Lukwago, were charged with managing an unlawful assembly in connection with the officer's death. Besigye and his allies formed a new group, For God and My Country, and continued their campaign. The group's leaders were arrested twice in early October, in advance of celebrations of Uganda's 50th independence anniversary.

In November, Mugisha Muntu, Museveni's former army chief, was elected the new FDC president, replacing Besigye. Besigye said he would continue his campaign to pressure the government and "liberate Uganda."

Political Rights and Civil Liberties: Uganda is not an electoral democracy. According to observers from the European Union (EU) and the Commonwealth, the 2011 elections were undermined by flawed administration, extensive state media bias, and government spending on behalf of incumbents. The single-chamber National Assembly and the powerful president, who faces no term limits, are elected for five-year terms. Of the legislature's 386 members, 238 are directly elected and 137 are indirectly elected from special interest groups, including women, the military, youth, the disabled, and trade unions. Eleven ex-officio seats are held by cabinet ministers, who are not elected members and do not have voting rights.

NRM legislators have recently attempted to assert some independence from President Yoweri Museveni, censuring high-level executive officials, seeking to reestablish term limits, and exercising oversight to influence a number of government actions and policies. However, significant concerns remain over the ability of opposition parties to compete with the ruling NRM. The opposition is hindered by harassment of its leaders, restrictive party registration requirements, voter and candidate eligibility rules, the use of government resources to support NRM candidates, a lack of access to state media coverage, and paramilitary groups—such as the Kiboko Squad and the Black Mambas—that intimidate voters and government opponents. The military's representatives in the National Assembly have openly campaigned for Museveni. Despite questions over the independence of the electoral commission, Museveni renewed the panel and its chairman for a second seven-year term in 2009.

Although Uganda has a variety of laws and institutions tasked with combating corruption, enforcement is weak in practice. Uganda recently discovered large oil reserves. In October 2011, three ministers resigned pending an investigation into multimillion-dollar bribes allegedly paid by the British firm Tullow Oil, and the National Assembly voted to suspend all new oil deals until a new law regulating the sector was passed. Nevertheless, Museveni signed a deal with Tullow in February 2012. In December 2012, the National Assembly passed the Petroleum Bill, which regulated oil licensing, exploration, and development, in a 149–39 vote. The bill was passed in a roll call vote with nearly 200 legislators absent. NRM lawmakers forced through a clause that gave the energy minister regulatory and licensing powers, as well as the power to negotiate contracts and oversee transparency in the sector. The law was criticized by the opposition and international monitoring groups such as Global Witness for the lack of parliamentary or independent oversight of the energy minister's decisions.

In late 2012, the EU and several European nations froze aid to Uganda in response to a report by the auditor general's office revealing that $13 million in donor money had been embezzled by Prime Minister Amama Mbabazi's office. Uganda was ranked 130 out of 176 countries surveyed in Transparency International's 2012 Corruption Perceptions Index.

The constitution provides for freedom of speech, and the media sector has flourished in the last decade, with more than 275 radio stations and dozens of television stations and print outlets. Independent journalists are often critical of the government, but in recent years they have faced substantial, escalating government restrictions and intimidation, which encourage self-censorship. Continuing a pattern from the previous year, throughout 2012 journalists were prevented from covering opposition-related events or attacked while doing so, summoned for questioning about content they had produced, and verbally threatened by officials. Despite an apology in June 2012 by the head of the police force for numerous attacks on journalists by the police—as well as a pledge to create a unit to probe press freedom violations—police continue to be the main perpetrators of attacks on journalists. The authorities attempted to block the social-media sites Facebook and Twitter during the 2011 "walk to work" protests, but the services generally remained accessible, and continued to be used by activists in 2012 to organize rallies.

There is no state religion, and freedom of worship is constitutionally protected and respected in practice. Academic freedom is also generally respected.

Freedom of assembly is officially recognized but often restricted in practice, as illustrated by the continued police violence and criminal charges against opposition protesters during 2012. In early 2012, the executive renewed pressure on parliament to pass the Public Order Management Bill. The proposed bill would require that groups of three or more people receive prior police approval before holding a "public meeting" to discuss the "failure of any government, political party, or political organization," and would give police wide powers to allow or deny approval for such gatherings. The bill remained pending at the end of 2012.

Freedom of association is guaranteed in the constitution and the law but is often restricted in practice; nevertheless, civil society in Uganda remains vibrant. Several nongovernmental organizations (NGOs) address politically sensitive issues, but their existence and activities are vulnerable to legal restrictions, including the manipulation of burdensome registration requirements under the 2006 NGO Registration Amendment Act. In 2012, the government stepped up its campaign to harass and even shut down NGOs and civil society groups that advocate for sensitive issues, such as combating corruption, transparency in the oil sector, land rights, and LGBT (lesbian, gay, bisexual, and transgender) rights. For example, in February, Minister for Ethics and Integrity Simon Lokodo led a police raid on a capacity-building workshop run by LGBT activists in Entebbe. Meanwhile, other NGOs that focus on issues such as service delivery were largely allowed to operate freely.

Workers' rights to organize, bargain collectively, and strike are recognized by law, except for those providing essential government services, but legal protections often go unenforced. Many private firms refuse to recognize unions, and strikers are sometimes arrested.

Executive influence undermines judicial independence. Prolonged pretrial detention, inadequate resources, and poor judicial administration impede the fair exercise of justice. The country has also faced criticism over the military's repeated interference with court processes. The prison system is reportedly operating at nearly three times its intended capacity, with pretrial detainees constituting more than half of the prison population. Rape, vigilante justice, and torture and abuse of suspects and detainees by security forces remain problems. The Joint Anti-Terrorism Task Force, established under the 2002 Anti-Terrorism Act, has committed many of the worst rights abuses. It reportedly has stepped up its efforts in the wake of the 2010 Al-Shabaab bombings, illegally detaining and abusing terrorism suspects as well as expanding the scope of the law to crack down on the political opposition.

Northern Uganda is continuing to recover from 20 years of attacks by the Lord's Resistance Army (LRA), a cult-like rebel group led by Joseph Kony that is accused of killing, raping, and abducting tens of thousands of people in the region. Although the LRA continues to operate in neighboring countries, it has not staged attacks in Uganda itself since 2005. Many LRA fighters were given amnesty in 2000 in an effort to bring peace to the region; however, Kony and four other LRA leaders were charged with war crimes and crimes against humanity by the International Criminal Court in 2005. In October 2011, the United States dispatched 100 military advisers to Uganda to assist regional efforts to eliminate the LRA, and the AU in March 2012 set up a 5,000-member force to bolster those efforts. In May, Ugandan forces captured LRA leader Caesar Achellam in Central African Republic; his arrest sparked debate about whether he should be given amnesty or tried in Uganda.

Although the constitution enshrines the principle of gender equality, discrimination against women remains pronounced, particularly in rural areas. The law gives women the right to inherit land, but discriminatory customs often trump legal provisions in practice. Rape and domestic violence are widespread and underreported, and offenders are often not prosecuted. Cultural practices such as female genital mutilation persist. Women hold nearly 35 percent of the National Assembly seats, and one-third of local council seats are reserved for women. Sexual abuse of minors is a significant problem. Ritual sacrifice of abducted children has reportedly increased in recent years, with wealthier individuals paying for the killings to secure good fortune. Uganda continues to be a source and destination country for men, women, and children trafficked for the purposes of forced labor and prostitution.

Uganda's society and government remain exceptionally prejudiced against gays and lesbians, creating a climate of fear and insecurity. International controversy has surrounded the Anti-Homosexuality Bill, first introduced in 2009, that would make some sex acts capital crimes (under existing law, consensual sex between same-sex couples was already punishable by up to life in prison). It would also punish individuals for the "promotion" of homosexuality and for not reporting violations with 24 hours, potentially threatening health workers and advocates for LGBT rights. The bill was re-tabled in the National Assembly in February 2012, and passed a committee in November; there were some reports that the death penalty clause had been removed. The bill was not passed by the end of 2012.

⬇ Ukraine

Political Rights: 4　　　　　　　　　　　　　　　**Population:** 44,556,000
Civil Liberties: 3　　　　　　　　　　　　　　　　　　　　**Capital:** Kyiv
Status: Partly Free

Trend Arrow: Ukraine received a downward trend arrow due to a decline in the quality of its legislative elections, greater government pressure on the opposition, and a new language law that favored Russian speakers while neglecting smaller minorities.

Ten-Year Ratings Timeline For Year Under Review (Political Rights, Civil Liberties, Status)

2003	2004	2005	2006	2007	2008	2009	2010	2011	2012
4,4PF	4,3PF	3,2F	3,2F	3,2F	3,2F	3,2F	3,3PF	4,3PF	4,3PF

Overview:　　　　Ukraine's October 2012 parliamentary elections were deeply flawed, ending a string of national elections that had been considered free and fair. Former prime minister Yuliya Tymoshenko, who represented the most outspoken opposition to President Viktor Yanukovych's Party of Regions, remained in jail and was not allowed to compete. The new electoral law, revised at the end of 2011, delivered more seats to the ruling party than it would have won under the previous system. Monitors cited numerous abuses in the elections, which strengthened the position of antidemocratic factions in the parliament. Over the course of the year, the administration continued to exert pressure on the judiciary, media freedom declined, and corruption opportunities increased with the elimination of tendering requirements for state companies.

In December 1991, Ukraine's voters approved independence from the Soviet Union in a referendum and elected Leonid Kravchuk as president. Leonid Kuchma defeated Kravchuk in the 1994 presidential poll, and won reelection in 1999, amid media manipulation, intimidation, and the abuse of state resources. Kuchma faced growing criticism for high-level corruption and the erosion of political rights and civil liberties. Evidence implicating him in the 2000 murder of independent journalist Heorhiy Gongadze fueled mass demonstrations and calls for the president's ouster, but propresidential factions retained a majority in 2002 parliamentary elections.

In the significantly tainted first round of the October 2004 presidential election, reformist former prime minister Viktor Yushchenko led a field of 24 candidates, followed by Prime Minister Viktor Yanukovych, a representative of the eastern, Russian-speaking Donbas region, who enjoyed backing from Russian president Vladimir Putin. In the November runoff, the official results showed Yanukovych to be the winner by less than three percentage points, but voting irregularities in Yanukovych's home region led the domestic opposition and international monitors to declare his apparent victory "not legitimate."

In what became known as the Orange Revolution because of Yushchenko's ubiquitous campaign color, millions of people massed peacefully in Kyiv and other cities to protest fraud in the second-round vote. The Supreme Court on December

4 struck down the results and ordered a rerun on December 26. In the middle of the crisis, the parliament ratified constitutional reforms that shifted crucial powers from the president to the parliament, effective January 1, 2006. Although technically adopted in an unconstitutional manner, the compromise changes effectively lowered the stakes of the upcoming rerun, making it more palatable to Yushchenko's opponents. However, they also created an unclear division of power, which later led to constant conflict between the president and prime minister.

The repeat of the second round was held in a new political and social atmosphere. The growing independence of the media, the parliament, the judiciary, and local governments allowed for a fair and properly monitored ballot. Yushchenko won easily, and his chief ally, former deputy prime minister Yuliya Tymoshenko, became prime minister. However, their alliance quickly broke down, leading to a multilateral stalemate that prevented implementation of comprehensive political and economic reform. The unproductive wrangling continued during a short-lived Yanukovych premiership (2006–07) and another stint as prime minister for Tymoshenko (2007–10) after parliamentary elections in September 2007, seriously eroding public support for the Orange Revolution.

In the 2010 presidential election, which met most international standards, Yanukovych defeated Tymoshenko in the second round of voting in February, 49 percent to 46 percent. He quickly reversed many of the changes adopted in the wake of the Orange Revolution, securing Constitutional Court rulings that enabled him to oust Tymoshenko as prime minister and replace her with a loyalist, and to annul the 2004 constitutional compromise that had reduced the power of the presidency. He subsequently launched efforts that systematically reduced Ukrainian citizens' political and civil rights. The October 2010 local elections were widely viewed as less free and fair than elections held under Yushchenko.

In 2011, Yanukovych mounted a systematic campaign to eliminate any viable opposition to his ruling Party of Regions, most visibly by securing a seven-year prison sentence against Tymoshenko, his strongest opponent, in October. Her alleged offense was abusing her office as prime minister by signing an unfavorable gas deal with Russia without seeking cabinet approval, which was not viewed as a crime by most observers. At the end of 2011 Yanukovych introduced a new electoral system for the parliament, replacing the existing proportional-representation arrangement with a hybrid in which half of the lawmakers are elected in single-member districts. The nongovernmental group OPORA denounced this change as a bid to favor the Party of Regions, arguing that it was easier for the ruling party to manipulate the district elections.

Tymoshenko and her ally, Yuriy Lutsenko, remained behind bars in 2012, and neither was allowed to run in the October parliamentary elections. The European Court of Human Rights ruled in July that Lutsenko, a former interior minister, had been unlawfully detained. Over 400 other candidates were rejected ahead of the vote, with half turned away based on minor technical problems. In addition, the Organization for Security and Cooperation in Europe (OSCE) complained that the elections lacked a level playing field due to the abuse of administrative resources, opaque campaign and party financing, biased media coverage, and extensive influence wielded by powerful economic groups. Other abuses included the bribery of voters in single-member districts through the façade of charity organizations, and public-works projects designed to support progovernment candidates. Monitors also found that the tabulation process lacked transparency and that important parties were not granted fair representation on district- and precinct-level electoral commissions, often leaving progovernment individuals in control of the panels.

Despite such regime manipulation, the opposition was ultimately able to limit the ruling party's hold on the parliament and prevent it from securing a supermajority of 300 seats, which would have allowed it to change the constitution. However, prodemocracy parties captured only about a third of the seats. The Party of Regions retained a plurality with 185 seats, followed by Tymoshenko's Fatherland with 101, professional boxer Vitaliy Klychko's Ukrainian Democratic Alliance for Reform (UDAR) with 40, the radical Svoboda party with 37, and the Communist Party with 32. Independents won 43 seats, and four small parties divided the remainder. Five seats remained unfilled, because ballot tampering made it impossible to determine the winner, though the opposition claimed that they had won the seats. By year's end, the parliament approved the return of Prime Minister Mykola Azarov.

On November 27, Yanukovych signed a law that would allow the constitution to be amended by referendum if organizers are able to collect three million signatures from a variety of regions. Previously, constitutional amendments required a two-thirds vote in the parliament, a level of support the president would be unlikely to achieve under current conditions. The opposition fears that an increasingly unpopular Yanukovych may seek to amend the constitution to allow the parliament to elect the next president by a simple majority vote.

Political Rights and Civil Liberties: Ukraine remains an electoral democracy, although the numerous flaws in the 2012 parliamentary elections and the 2010 local elections have seriously threatened this status.

Citizens elect delegates to the Verkhovna Rada (Supreme Council), the 450-seat unicameral parliament, for four-year terms. The 2004 constitutional amendments, which were annulled in 2010, had extended this term to five years. Under the ruling Party of Regions, the parliament has largely become a rubber-stamp body. According to a new electoral law adopted in December 2011, Ukraine returned to a system in which half of the members are elected by proportional representation and half in single-member districts; blocs of parties are not allowed to participate. As expected, and in sharp contrast with the other major parties, the Party of Regions won most of its seats in the single-member districts during the October 2012 elections, giving it enough seats overall to forge working parliamentary majorities with the Communist Party and independents.

The president is elected to a maximum of two five-year terms. With the return to the 1996 constitution in October 2010, the president now dominates the political system. He issues decrees; exercises power over the courts, the military, and law enforcement agencies; appoints the prime minister with the Rada's approval and removes the prime minister at will; appoints and fires all other ministers without the Rada's approval; and appoints regional governors without consulting the prime minister. The Rada can dismiss the entire cabinet, but not individual ministers.

Political parties are typically little more than vehicles for their leaders and financial backers, and they generally lack coherent ideologies or policy platforms. President Viktor Yanukovych is systematically eliminating opposition to his party, either through repression (as with Yuliya Tymoshenko's Fatherland party) or coop-tation (as with former deputy prime minister Serhiy Tyhypko's Strong Ukraine party, which was absorbed by the Party of Regions in early 2012).

Corruption, one of the country's most serious problems, continues to worsen. Business magnates benefit financially from their close association with top politicians. For example, a Forbes study has shown that businessmen affiliated with the Party of Regions win a considerable portion of state tenders. In addition, a new law in 2012 established that state enterprises do not have to use tenders when buying goods, meaning tens of billions of dollars will be disbursed each year without transparency. Separately, Yanukovych has become the de facto owner of a huge estate outside of Kyiv, raising suspicions of illicit wealth, and his two sons have amassed both power and immense personal fortunes. The apparent corruption of the administration, and the precedent set by its politicized pursuit of charges against Tymoshenko and former members of her government, have increased Yanukovych's incentives to remain in power indefinitely. Small and medium-sized businesses continue to suffer at the hands of corrupt bureaucrats, tax collectors, and corporate raiders. Kickbacks in the build-up to the Euro 2012 soccer championship, which Ukraine cohosted, may have accounted for as much as one-third of the value of the related construction contracts.

The constitution guarantees freedoms of speech and expression. Libel is not a criminal offense, though the parliament in 2012 considered the restoration of prison terms as a punishment for libel before backing down in the face of protests. Conditions for the media have worsened since Yanukovych's election. The media do not provide the population with unbiased information, as business magnates with varying political interests own and influence many outlets, and the state controls a nationwide network and local television at the regional level. Some 69 percent of Ukrainians get their news from television, and the medium now features fewer alternative points of view, open discussions, and expert opinions. An analysis of 230 outlets in August 2012 showed that the ruling party received preferential coverage, and this was particularly true on state television during the parliamentary election campaign, though coverage of the opposition increased closer to election day. TVi, one of the last independent television channels with national reach, faces constant harassment from the authorities, including charges of tax evasion, fines, and denial of access to advertisers and cable networks. Ethical violations are a problem, and the number of paid articles in the media has been growing. Journalists continue to face the threat of violence in the course of their work. Vasyl Klymentyev, a journalist who investigated local corruption in Kharkiv, disappeared in August 2010 and is presumed dead.

Internet access is not restricted and is generally affordable; lack of foreign-language skills is the main barrier. While the Access to Public Information Act passed in January 2011, it did little to improve the overall environment.

The constitution and the 1991 Law on Freedom of Conscience and Religion define religious rights in Ukraine, and these are generally well respected. However, among other problems, Yanukovych publicly associates himself with one of the country's competing branches of the Orthodox Church (that associated with the Moscow patriarchate), and there have been some signs of anti-Semitism in political campaigns in recent years.

Academic freedom has come under pressure since Yanukovych took power. Education Minister Dmytro Tabachnyk has curtailed many programs designed to promote Ukrainian language and culture, and in 2010 he began a process aimed at bringing Ukrainian textbooks into line with those in Russia. Ministry budget cuts have focused heavily on schools with liberal reputations and universities in Kyiv and western Ukraine, while universities in the eastern Donetsk region have gained more funding.

The constitution guarantees the right to peaceful assembly but requires organizers to give the authorities advance notice of any demonstrations. Yanukovych's government has made it more difficult to assemble, and there has been a significant increase in the number of court rulings prohibiting peaceful assembly. The administration is also collecting extensive information on all protest organizers, including details about their professional activities, in order to exert pressure on them.

Although the vibrancy of Ukraine's civil society has declined since the height of the Orange Revolution, social, political, cultural, and economic movements of different sizes and with various agendas remain active. Civic activism is increasing, with a new language law driving many more protests in 2012 than occurred on other issues in recent years. Many Ukrainians also spoke out over the March murder of 18-year-old Mykolaiv resident Oksana Makar, who was brutally raped, set on fire, and left to die by three men with connections to local officials. Trade unions function, but strikes and worker protests are infrequent. Factory owners are still able to pressure their workers to vote according to the owners' preferences.

The judiciary is subject to intense political pressure and largely carries out the will of the executive branch, as the Tymoshenko case demonstrated in 2011. In a similar manner, in February 2012, the court sentenced former interior minister Yuriy Lutsenko to four years in prison and an additional three-year ban from public office. He had fought against ties between the Party of Regions and organized crime. Centralization of court administration in 2010 gave the authorities extensive control over the pay, promotion, and dismissal of judges. In 2011 Ukraine became the only state to ignore a pilot ruling of the European Court of Human Rights, having failed to implement a judgment designed to improve the enforcement of court decisions in the country.

Reports of police torture have grown in recent years. The number of raids by tax police and the security service against opposition-aligned businesses has also increased. Since 2010, Ukrainian authorities have misused psychiatry to intimidate civil society activists.

A language law adopted in August 2012 effectively favors Russian over Ukrainian by allowing regions to give Russian official status if it is spoken by more than 10 percent of the population. Genuine minorities—Crimean Tatars, Poles, Hungarians, and Ruthenians, among others—see no benefit from the law. While the country's Romany population suffers from discrimination, the government has generally interceded to protect the rights of most ethnic and religious minorities, including the Tatar community. Tatars continue to suffer discrimination at the hands of local authorities and communities in Crimea in terms of land ownership, access to employment, and educational opportunities.

In October 2012, the parliament began approval of a bill that would outlaw "pro-homosexual propaganda" and ban any positive depiction of gay people. It had not been adopted by year's end.

Gender discrimination is prohibited under the constitution, but women's rights have not been a priority for government officials. The cabinet in place until late 2012 did not include any women, making it the first of 14 Ukrainian governments to be exclusively male. However, the cabinet appointed on December 24 has three women. Human rights groups have complained that employers openly discriminate on the basis of gender, physical appearance, and age. The trafficking of women abroad for the purpose of prostitution remains a major problem.

⬇ United Arab Emirates

Political Rights: 6
Civil Liberties: 6
Status: Not Free

Population: 8,106,000
Capital: Abu Dhabi

Ratings Change: The United Arab Emirates received a downward trend arrow due to increased arrests of activists, lawyers, and judges calling for political reform; the passage of a highly restrictive internet law that punishes online activism and free expression; and the dismissal and deportation of academics who were critical of the government or its policies.

Ten-Year Ratings Timeline For Year Under Review (Political Rights, Civil Liberties, Status)

2003	2004	2005	2006	2007	2008	2009	2010	2011	2012
6,5NF	6,6NF	6,6NF	6,5NF	6,5NF	6,5NF	6,5NF	6,5NF	6,6NF	6,6NF

Overview: The United Arab Emirates increased its efforts to suppress political dissent throughout 2012, arresting scores of activists and imprisoning many without charge while deporting others. A highly restrictive cyber law was passed in November, giving authorities broader power to crack down on online criticism of the government and on activists using the internet or social media to organize demonstrations.

Attacks on shipping off the coast of what is now the United Arab Emirates (UAE) led the British to mount military expeditions against the local tribal rulers in the early 19th century. A series of treaties followed, including a long-term maritime truce in 1853 and an 1892 pact giving Britain control over foreign policy. The seven sheikhdoms of the area subsequently became known as the Trucial States. In 1971, Britain announced that it was ending its treaty relationships in the region, and six of the seven Trucial States formed the UAE federation. Ras al-Khaimah, the seventh state, joined in 1972. The provisional constitution, which was made permanent in 1996, left significant power in the hands of each emirate.

After the 2001 terrorist attacks on the United States, the government strengthened antiterrorism legislation, including introducing reforms in the financial services and banking sectors to block the financing of terrorism.

In 2006, Sheikh Mohammed bin Rashid al-Maktoum succeeded his late brother as ruler of the emirate of Dubai and prime minister of the UAE. The first-ever elections for 20 of the 40-seat, largely advisory Federal National Council (FNC) were held that year, with participation limited to a small electoral college appointed by the emirates' seven rulers. The UAE government appointed the remaining 20 members in February 2007.

In April 2009, *ABC News* publicized a video filmed in 2004 that showed Issa bin Zayed al-Nahyan, the UAE president's brother, torturing an Afghan grain dealer, and the Justice Department subsequently launched an investigation into the actions depicted in the video. In January 2010, a court acquitted al-Nahyan of charges of torture and rape stemming from the publication of the video; al-Nahyan's lawyer said the court had agreed with the defense's argument that al-Nahyan had been drugged and therefore committed the crime unknowingly.

While the UAE has not experienced the kinds of demonstrations that character-ized the Arab Spring elsewhere, activists began calling for greater political rights and a move toward a more democratic political system in early 2011. Authorities responded by arresting the most outspoken proreform voices. In March 2011, the UAE provided support to the military force that helped crush Bahrain's pro-democracy movement. In December, authorities cited security concerns in their decision to revoke the citizenship of seven men affiliated with the Islamist group the Association for Reform and Guidance, or al-Islah; the seven men had signed a petition earlier in the year calling for legislative reform and free elections.

Throughout 2012, the UAE's harsh response to prodemocracy activism contin-ued as authorities, citing vaguely defined security concerns as justification, arrested over 70 human rights activists, political reformers, bloggers, judges, and lawyers, holding many of them without charge or access to legal representation. Several nongovernmental organizations (NGOs) whose work focuses on empowering civil society were expelled from the country, as were academics critical of the regime's policies of suppression of free expression. The UAE also passed a restrictive cyber law in November.

Political Rights and Civil Liberties: The UAE is not an electoral democracy. All decisions about political leadership rest with the dynastic rulers of the seven emirates, who form the Federal Supreme Coun-cil, the highest executive and legislative body in the country. The seven leaders select a president and vice president, and the president appoints a prime minister and cabinet. The emirate of Abu Dhabi, the major oil producer in the UAE, has controlled the federation's presidency since its inception.

The 40-member FNC serves only as an advisory body, reviewing proposed laws and questioning federal government ministers. Half of the FNC's members were elected for the first time in 2006 by a 6,689-member electoral college chosen by the seven rulers. The other half of the council is directly appointed by the government for two-year terms. In September 2011, the UAE held elections to the FNC after having expanded the electoral college to just over 129,000 members; however, only about 36,000 voters participated.

Political parties are banned in the UAE. The allocation of positions in the gov-ernment is determined largely by tribal loyalties and economic power. Citizens have limited opportunities to express their interests through traditional consultative sessions.

The UAE is considered one of the least corrupt countries in the Middle East. It was ranked 27 out of 176 countries surveyed in Transparency International's 2012 Corruption Perceptions Index.

Although the UAE's constitution provides for some freedom of expression, the government restricts this right in practice. The 1980 Printing and Publishing Law applies to all media and prohibits criticism of the government, allies, and religion, and also bans pornography. Consequently, journalists commonly practice self-censorship, and the leading media outlets frequently publish government statements without criticism or comment. However, Dubai has a "Media Free Zone," where print and broadcast media is produced for audiences outside of the UAE with relatively few restrictions.

In November 2012, the UAE passed a cyber law giving authorities more latitude to crack down on activists using the internet or social media to criticize the government or to organize demonstrations. The law allows for the imprisonment of anyone who publishes material to the internet in which they insult the state, organize antigovernment protests, or publicize information deemed a threat to national security. Offenders can also be fined as mush as $272,000.

The constitution provides for freedom of religion. Islam is the official religion, and the majority of citizens are Sunni Muslims. The minority Shiite Muslim sect and non-Muslims are free to worship without interference. The government controls content in nearly all Sunni mosques. Academic freedom is limited, with the Ministry of Education censoring textbooks and curriculums in both public and private schools. In 2012, several academics critical of UAE government policies were dismissed from their positions and either arrested or expelled from the country. The RAND Corporation, a U.S.-based research institute, was forced to close its Abu Dhabi office in December 2012.

The government places restrictions on freedoms of assembly and association. Public meetings require government permits. NGOs must register with the Ministry of Labor and Social Affairs, and registered NGOs receive subsidies from the government. After members of two prominent teachers' and lawyers' associations publicly pledged support for democratic reforms in the UAE, authorities in April 2011 dissolved their elected boards of directors and replaced them with proregime sympathizers. In March 2011, over 130 intellectuals and activists signed a petition calling for political reforms, including the expansion of legislative powers for the FNC. Five of the country's most outspoken reform advocates were subsequently arrested and convicted of insulting the country's leaders, though they were pardoned by the president in November 2011. Seven signatories had their citizenship stripped in late 2011, leaving them stateless and without legal documentation. In March 2012, the UAE forced the closures of the offices of two NGOs: the National Democratic Institute in Dubai and Konrad-Adenauer-Stiftung in Abu Dhabi. In July, two prominent human rights lawyers, Mohamed al-Roken, who had previously defended UAE activists, and Mohamed al-Mansoori were arrested along with other activists under suspicion of "commiting crimes that harm state security." They remained in detention as of year's end.

The UAE's mostly foreign workers do not have the right to organize, bargain collectively, or strike. Workers occasionally protest against unpaid wages and poor working and living conditions, but such demonstrations are frequently broken up.

The judiciary is not independent, with court rulings subject to review by the political leadership. The legal system is divided into Sharia (Islamic law) courts, which address family and criminal matters, and secular courts, which cover civil law. Sharia courts sometimes impose flogging sentences for drug use, prostitution, and adultery. As part of its crackdown on dissent, the UAE arrested former judge Khamis Saeed al-Zyoudi in September 2012. In October, the UAE arrested Mohammed Saeed Ziab Abdouly, president of the penal circuit in the Appellate Court of Abu Dhabi. Both men were in detention at year's end. While the federal Interior Ministry oversees police forces in the country, each emirate's force enjoys considerable autonomy. Arbitrary arrests and detention have been reported, particularly of foreign residents. Prisons in the larger emirates are overcrowded.

Discrimination against noncitizens and foreign workers, who comprise more than 80 percent of the UAE's population, is common. Stateless residents, known as bidoon, are unable to secure regular employment and face systemic discrimination. While the Interior Ministry has established methods for stateless persons to apply for citizenship, the government uses unclear criteria in approving or rejecting such requests. Under UAE's kafala system, a migrant worker's legal status is tied to an employer's sponsorship; foreign workers are often exploited and subjected to harsh working conditions, physical abuse, and the withholding of passports with little to no access to legal recourse.

The constitution does not address gender equality. Muslim women are forbidden to marry non-Muslims and receive smaller inheritances than men. Women are underrepresented in government, though they have received government appointments at various levels in recent years, including to the cabinet, and there are several women in the FNC. Despite a 2006 anti-trafficking law and the opening of new shelters for female victims, the government has failed to adequately address human trafficking.

United Kingdom

Political Rights: 1
Civil Liberties: 1
Status: Free

Population: 63,212,800
Capital: London

Ten-Year Ratings Timeline For Year Under Review (Political Rights, Civil Liberties, Status)

2003	2004	2005	2006	2007	2008	2009	2010	2011	2012
1,1F	1,1F	1,1F	1,1F	1,1F	1,1F	1,1F	1,1F	1,1F	1,1F

Overview: A government report released in November 2012 recommended the formation of a new regulatory body to oversee the press, while a bill under discussion would allow authorities to access data retained by internet and phone companies on users' online communications—including e-mails, mobile phone calls, web browsing history, and details of messages sent on social media. In May local elections, the Labour Party had its best performance in 15 years. Controversial family migration rules introduced in June placed new restrictions on spouses, partners, and

dependents entering Britain. Meanwhile, in April, the United Kingdom fell into its first double-dip recession since the 1970s.

The English state emerged before the turn of the first millennium and was conquered by Norman French invaders in 1066. The Glorious Revolution of 1688–89 began a gradual—but eventually total—assertion of the powers of Parliament vis-à-vis the monarchy, as Britain became one of the modern world's first democracies. Wales, Scotland, and then Ireland were subdued or incorporated into the kingdom over the course of centuries, culminating in the creation of the United Kingdom of Great Britain and Ireland in 1801. A significant extension of voting rights was passed in 1832, and subsequent reforms led to universal adult suffrage.

Most of Ireland won independence after World War I, with Protestant-majority counties in the north remaining a restive part of what became the United Kingdom of Great Britain and Northern Ireland in 1921. Significant powers were devolved to a Scottish Parliament, and fewer to a Welsh Assembly, in 1997. The struggle between unionists and Irish nationalists over governance in Northern Ireland largely ended with the 1998 peace agreement, which established the Northern Ireland Assembly. However, the assembly was suspended a number of times before further peace talks, and the formal disarmament of the Irish Republican Army (IRA)—an outlawed Irish nationalist militant group—paved the way for fresh assembly elections in 2007. Those elections resulted in the formation of a power-sharing local government between Sinn Féin and the Democratic Unionist Party (DUP).

After nearly two decades of Conservative Party rule, the Labour Party won the 1997 general elections, and Prime Minister Tony Blair led Labour to another major victory in 2001, though he faced opposition within the party for his support of the U.S.-led war in Iraq beginning in 2003. Slow progress in improving public services and the continuation of the Iraq war led to a far less decisive Labour victory in 2005.

In June 2007, Blair resigned, and Chancellor of the Exchequer Gordon Brown became prime minister. Brown countered the international financial crisis in late 2008 and early 2009 by shoring up ailing banks with public money, and his approach was for a time hailed abroad. Nevertheless, in the June 2009 European Parliament elections, the Conservatives and the UK Independence Party (UKIP)—which strongly opposes British membership in the European Union—outperformed Labour, while the xenophobic British National Party (BNP) won its first two seats.

In the May 2010 Parliamentary elections, the Conservatives led with 306 seats. Labour placed second with 258, the Liberal Democrats took 57, and smaller parties divided the remainder. Conservative leader David Cameron, lacking a majority, formed a rare coalition government with the Liberal Democrats. The new government faced daunting economic challenges, including a ballooning budget deficit. Cameron introduced unpopular austerity measures in 2011, and economic growth remained just barely positive.

A March 2011 referendum increased the Welsh Assembly's autonomy, giving it authority to make laws in 20 subject areas without consulting Parliament. Sinn Féin and the DUP consolidated their control in May elections for the Northern Irish legislature, while the ruling Scottish National Party (SNP) made major gains in Scotland's election held the same day.

In July 2011, media mogul Rupert Murdoch's News Corporation closed the weekly tabloid *News of the World* amid mounting allegations that its reporters had hacked into the telephone messages of hundreds of public figures and crime victims. Cameron appointed Lord Justice Leveson that same month to lead an inquiry into the general operation of the UK press and suspected collusion between the police and reporters.

At an EU summit at the end of January 2012, the UK opted out of the EU fiscal compact—the Referendum on the Treaty on Stability, Coordination, and Governance in the Economic and Monetary Union—which restricts the borrowing and spending of EU member states. Cameron has discussed possibly offering a referendum on the treaty as part of the Conservative platform for the next general election in 2015. In preparation, the UK foreign secretary is currently performing an audit of the impact of EU legislation on the UK.

In April, the UK fell into its first double-dip recession since the 1970s. After three straight quarters of contraction, GDP rose by 1 percent in the third quarter of 2012, though analysts considered the improvement a "blip," with growth remaining largely unchanged.

After much debate between Westminster and the Scottish Parliament over the terms of a referendum on Scotland's independence from the United Kingdom, a compromise was reached in October between Cameron and Scottish first minister Alex Salmond. The agreement schedules the vote for the fall of 2014, with a single yes-or-no question on independence; those 16 years and older will be permitted to participate.

Developments during 2012 challenged the strength of the ruling coalition. In May local elections, the Labour Party' won 38 percent of the popular vote—its best performance since 1997. In July, a significant number of Conservatives voted against a bill that would have provided for an 80 percent directly elected House of Lords—instead of its current appointed and hereditary membership—fearing the change would threaten the primacy of the House of Commons. In response, the Liberal Democrats—who viewed the Conservatives' abandonment of the Upper House reform as violating the coalition agreement—said they would not support changes that would recast constituency boundaries.

Political Rights and Civil Liberties: The United Kingdom is an electoral democracy. Each of the members of the House of Commons, the dominant lower chamber of the bicameral Parliament, is elected in a single-member district. Parliamentary elections must be held at least every five years. Executive power rests with the prime minister and cabinet, who must have the support of the Commons.

The House of Lords, Parliament's upper chamber, can delay legislation initiated in the Commons. If it defeats a measure passed by the Commons, the Commons must reconsider, but it can ultimately overrule the Lords. The Lords' membership, currently around 800, consists mostly of "life peers" nominated by successive governments. There are also 92 hereditary peers (nobles) and 26 bishops and archbishops of the Church of England. The monarch, currently Queen Elizabeth II, plays a largely ceremonial role as head of state.

In addition to the Labour and Conservative parties and the left-leaning Liberal Democrats, other parties include the Welsh nationalist Plaid Cymru and the SNP.

In Northern Ireland, the main Catholic and republican parties are Sinn Féin and the Social Democratic and Labour Party, while the leading Protestant and unionist parties are the Ulster Unionist Party and the DUP. Parties that have never won seats in Parliament, such as the UKIP and BNP, fare better in races for the European Parliament, which feature proportional-representation voting.

Corruption is not pervasive in Britain, but high-profile scandals have damaged political reputations under both Labour and Conservative governments. The Bribery Act, which is considered one of the most sweeping anti-bribery legislation in the world, came into force in July 2011. In October 2012, a senior Scotland Yard official was charged with offering to illegally provide News of the World with information on a 2010 police inquiry into phone hacking.

Press freedom is legally protected, and the media are lively and competitive. Daily newspapers span the political spectrum, though the economic downturn and rising internet use have driven some smaller papers out of business. The state-owned British Broadcasting Corporation (BBC) is editorially independent and faces significant private competition. On rare occasions, the courts impose so-called superinjunctions, which forbid the media from reporting certain information or even the existence of the injunction itself. The government has faced criticism for rampant delays in fulfilling freedom of information requests. England's libel laws are among the most claimant-friendly in the world, leading wealthy foreign litigants—known as libel tourists—to use them to silence critics; a suit is possible as long as the allegedly libelous material was accessed in Britain, and the burden of proof falls on the defendant. Claimants win 90 percent of cases. A bill that would significantly overhaul the country's libel laws passed its third reading in the House of Commons in December 2012 and was pending in the House of Lords at year's end. UK newspaper and magazine publishers currently regulate themselves voluntarily under the Press Complaints Commission, which does not have any legal powers. On November 29, 2012, the Leveson Inquiry report recommended forming a new, independent regulatory body to oversee the press.

The BBC faced a series of scandals in 2012 that prompted the resignation of director general George Entwistle in November. In early October, ITV—BBC's main rival—released a documentary exposing allegations of sexual abuse against the late Jimmy Savile, a popular BBC television and radio presenter and philanthropist. The exposé led to a broad criminal investigation that implicated a number of police departments accused of mishandling abuse allegations and other government-funded institutions, such as the BBC, schools, and hospitals, where Savile is accused of having abused some 300 girls and young women. In late 2011, the BBC program *Newsnight* had canceled a segment on accusations against Savile of sexual abuse. An independent investigation, the Pollard Inquiry, was launched in late 2012 into the culture and practices at the BBC during Savile's era. The Pollard Inquiry's report, which was published in December, found that the BBC lacked adequate leadership and was highly disorganized, and stated that the decision to remove the *Newsnight* investigation into Savile was flawed but done in good faith by the program's editor. Separately, in early November, *Newsnight* wrongly linked Conservative Party politician Lord McAlpine to allegations of sexual abuse at a children's home in Wales.

The government does not restrict internet access. However, a draft communications data bill under consideration would require internet and phone companies to allow public authorities to see a year's worth of details about the identities, locations, and duration of online communications for users of social media, e-mails, mobile phone calls, and voice calls placed over the internet. However, in December 2012, the Joint Committee on the Communications Data Bill released a report criticizing the bill as too sweeping and calling for consultation with technical experts, public institutions, and civil rights groups, among others, before redrafting. The prime minister announced at year's end that the bill would be rewritten.

Although the Church of England and the Church of Scotland have official status, freedom of religion is protected in law and practice. Nevertheless, minority groups, particularly Muslims, report discrimination, harassment, and occasional assaults. A 2006 law banned incitement to religious hatred, with a maximum penalty of seven years in prison. Academic freedom is respected.

Freedoms of assembly and association are respected in law and in practice. Civic and nongovernmental organizations may operate freely. Workers have the right to organize trade unions, which have traditionally played a central role in the Labour Party.

A new Supreme Court began functioning in 2009, replacing an appellate body within the House of Lords. The police maintain high professional standards, and prisons generally adhere to international guidelines. A new Justice and Security Bill under consideration at the end of 2012 would allow civil courts to hear secret evidence in private in cases related to national security. Critics charged that defendants would not have access to evidence against them, and ministers, rather than judges, would decide which evidence would be withheld or presented in court. The new bill came after the government, unable to reveal sensitive intelligence information in court, had to settle millions of pounds in claims with terrorist suspects alleging abuse in November 2011. The bill was moving through Parliament at the end of 2012, having passed its second reading in the House of Commons in December.

Britain's strict antiterrorism laws have undergone several changes in recent years. In January 2011, the detention of terrorism suspects without charge was limited to 14 days. Britain's "control order" regime—including forcible relocation of terrorism suspects and restrictions on their internet usage—was replaced in January 2012 with new Terrorism Prevention and Investigation Measures (TPIMs). TPIMs limit restrictions on the movement of terrorist suspects, when evidence to prosecute or deport them is lacking, to two years and removes the possibility of their relocation.

The government has been accused of "outsourcing" torture by extraditing terrorism suspects to their home countries, where they could be abused in custody, but has consistently denied complicity in illegal rendition and torture. In January 2012, a criminal investigation was launched into MI6's role in delivering two Libyan opponents of Colonel Mu'ammar al-Qadhafi to Libya, where they were allegedly tortured for years by Qadhafi's secret police. A 1994 law protects MI6 agents who carry out decisions authorized by a cabinet minister from liability for criminal acts abroad, but the two Libyans are suing MI6, former Labour government ministers, and a number of other government institutions. A larger inquiry into the UK's involvement in improper treatment of detainees held by other countries was shelved in January due to the Libyan cases.

Violence in Northern Ireland has abated in recent years, and Queen Elizabeth II even shook hands with Martin McGuinness, deputy leader of Ireland's Sinn Féin party and former IRA commander, in June 2012. However, more than 20 Northern Irish police officers were injured in Belfast in July during rioting over the annual Protestant Orange Order parade in a nationalist area of northern Belfast. In November, an off-duty prison guard was shot and killed outside of the Maghaberry Prison, where protests from some 40 jailed members of various IRA splinter groups had occurred over the guards' policy of strip-searching inmates. A group claiming to be the successor of the IRA claimed responsibility for the shooting.

In July 2005, coordinated suicide bombings in London carried out by four British Muslims killed more than 50 people and wounded hundreds more. The attacks set off a public debate about the integration of immigrants and racial and religious minorities into British society. Riots in London and other UK cities in August 2011 sparked new debates in Parliament over policing, economic inequality, and the social integration of the children of immigrants. To improve immigrant integration, changes were proposed in July 2012 to the citizenship test given to foreign nationals to include more questions on Britain's history and culture. The government has also introduced a language test for spouses, allegedly to help immigrants assimilate.

Britain's large numbers of immigrants and their locally born offspring receive equal treatment under the law, but their living standards are lower than the national average, and they complain of having come under increased suspicion amid the recent terrorist attacks and plots. An immigration report released in November 2012 found that the UK has a large backlog of asylum cases, with some 147,000 asylum seekers who made a claim before March 2007 having waited an average of seven years for a decision. Conservatives pledged to reduce the number of immigrants significantly by 2015. In 2011, the government implemented a cap of 20,700 skilled migrants from outside the EU, which has been criticized as prohibiting growth. New family migration rules introduced in June 2012 set an annual income threshold for any British citizen wishing to bring a spouse, partner, or dependent into the UK from outside the European Economic Area, instituted a stricter language test, and increased the probationary period for partners.

A 2010 equality act consolidated previous antidiscrimination laws for age, disability, race, religion, sex, and sexual orientation. Since 2005, same-sex couples have been able to form civil partnerships with the same rights as married couples. In Northern Ireland, a judge in October 2012 rejected a 1987 law that prohibited unmarried and same-sex couples from adopting children, ruling that the law violated European human rights laws on privacy and discrimination.

While women receive equal treatment under the law, they remain underrepresented in top positions in politics and business. Women won 143 seats in the House of Commons in the 2010 elections. Abortion is legal in Great Britain but heavily restricted in Northern Ireland, where it is allowed only to protect the life or the long-term health of the mother. Ireland's first abortion clinic opened in Belfast in October 2012 and drew protests from about 400 people, who called for its shutdown. The clinic may provide abortions only in exceptional cases, and only to women who are less than nine weeks pregnant.

United States of America

Political Rights: 1
Civil Liberties: 1
Status: Free

Population: 313,858,000
Capital: Washington, D.C.

Note: The numerical ratings and status listed above do not reflect conditions in Puerto Rico, which is examined in a separate report.

Ten-Year Ratings Timeline For Year Under Review (Political Rights, Civil Liberties, Status)

2003	2004	2005	2006	2007	2008	2009	2010	2011	2012
1,1F	1,1F	1,1F	1,1F	1,1F	1,1F	1,1F	1,1F	1,1F	1,1F

Overview: President Barack Obama won a second term in November 2012, while his Democratic Party increased its majority in the Senate and narrowed the Republican Party's margin in the House of Representatives. Nevertheless, the Republicans maintained control of the House, meaning the United States faced at least two more years of divided government. Among other matters, Obama encountered mounting criticism during 2012 over military and intelligence agencies' extensive use of remotely piloted aircraft, or drones, to kill suspected terrorists in various foreign countries.

The United States declared independence in 1776, during a rebellion against British colonial rule. The current system of government began functioning in 1789, following ratification of the country's constitution. Because the founders of the United States distrusted concentrated government authority, they set up a system in which the federal government has three coequal branches—executive, legislative, and judicial—and left many powers with state governments and the citizenry.

For most of the country's history, power has alternated between the Democratic and Republican parties. In 2008, then senator Barack Obama, a Democrat, became the first black American to win a presidential election, taking 53 percent of the popular vote. Senator John McCain, the Republican nominee, took 46 percent. In concurrent legislative elections, the Democrats increased their majorities in both the House of Representatives and the Senate.

Obama entered the White House with an ambitious domestic agenda dictated in part by fears of economic collapse in the wake of the financial crisis of 2008. During his first two years in office, he pushed through measures to stimulate the economy, revive the automobile industry, and, after a lengthy and bitter struggle, overhaul the nation's health-care system. In response, Republicans accused the president of improperly expanding the government's involvement in economic affairs and increasing an already large budget deficit.

In the November 2010 congressional elections, Republicans recaptured control of the House and narrowed the Democratic majority in the Senate. Many of the successful Republican candidates aligned themselves with the Tea Party movement, a loose grouping of citizen and lobbying organizations that demanded reductions in the federal budget, a much smaller role for government in domestic affairs, and tax cuts.

The Republican electoral gains acted as a check on Obama's agenda. Indeed, the following year was notable for what most observers described as legislative gridlock. Several efforts to forge compromises aimed at reducing the budget deficit ended in failure, leading to a pattern of crises and grudging, temporary solutions. One rating agency downgraded the credit rating for U.S. bonds after a particularly damaging budget standoff in August 2011.

Obama won reelection in November 2012, though his margin of victory narrowed. He received 51 percent of the popular vote, while his Republican opponent, Mitt Romney, received 47 percent. In concurrent congressional elections, Democrats strengthened their hold on the Senate, with 53 seats plus 2 independents who generally vote with the party, versus 45 for the Republicans. In the House, Republicans retained control with 234 seats, versus 201 for the Democrats. Republicans also held the majority of state governorships and legislatures.

Although Romney won a solid majority among white voters, and won overwhelmingly among white men, Obama mobilized a winning coalition by scoring substantial majorities among black, Latino, and Asian voters, as well as young voters and women. The growing Latino population was regarded as particularly important to the future of American electoral politics, and a key issue for Latino voters was immigration reform. In the wake of the elections, some Republican leaders called on the party to adopt more immigrant-friendly policy positions, including support for long-stalled legislative proposals that would both offer legal status to the estimated 11 million undocumented immigrants in the country and strengthen controls at the U.S.-Mexico border.

Obama secured a second term despite the domestic economy's slow recovery since 2009 and an unemployment rate in excess of 7.5 percent—high by U.S. standards. During the campaign, the Republicans criticized Obama's stewardship of the economy, while the president accused Republicans of blocking legislation and refusing to agree to a compromise on reducing the federal budget deficit. While foreign policy was a secondary issue in the campaign, Obama focused on his having ended America's military role in Iraq, his promise to withdraw U.S. troops from Afghanistan by 2014, and a counterterrorism offensive punctuated by the 2011 killing of Osama bin Laden, leader of the international terrorist network al-Qaeda.

However, a major instrument of the administration's war on terrorism—targeted killings of suspected terrorists abroad by means of remotely piloted "drone" aircraft—drew criticism from a range of sources during 2012, including civil libertarians, members of Congress, elements of the press, and foreign governments. Some opponents argued that this use of drones constituted a violation of international law and the ethics of warfare. Others focused on the secretive and unaccountable nature of the administration's decision-making process regarding the selection of targets, urging more robust oversight and approval by Congress or a special court. The United States also continued to struggle with other aspects of counterterrorism policy. Early in his presidency, Obama had failed to persuade Congress to accept the closure of the prison facility at a U.S. military base in Guantanamo Bay, Cuba, where a number of terrorism suspects have been detained since al-Qaeda's 2001 attacks on the United States and the beginning of the war in Afghanistan. There were ongoing controversies and legal challenges involving the use of military tribunals to try key suspects at the base, as well as the indefinite detention of other Guantanamo inmates without charge or trial. Many had been cleared for repatriation, but remained at Guantanamo due to concerns about the security situations in their home countries.

Political Rights and Civil Liberties: The United States is an electoral democracy with a bicameral federal legislature. The upper chamber, the Senate, consists of 100 members—2 from each of the 50 states—serving six-year terms, with one-third coming up for election every two years. The lower chamber, the House of Representatives, consists of 435 members serving two-year terms. All national legislators are elected directly by voters in the districts or states they represent. The president and vice president are elected to four-year terms. Under a 1951 constitutional amendment, the president is limited to two terms in office.

Presidential elections are decided by an Electoral College, meaning it is possible for a candidate to win the presidency while losing the national popular vote. Electoral College votes are apportioned to each state based on the size of its congressional representation. In most cases, all of the electors in a particular state cast their ballots for the candidate who won the statewide popular vote, regardless of the margin. Two states, Maine and Nebraska, have chosen to divide their electoral votes between the candidates based on their popular-vote performance in each congressional district, and other states are now considering similar systems. In the 2012 election, President Barack Obama won the Electoral College tally by 332 to 206.

A great deal of government responsibility rests with the 50 states. Most criminal cases are dealt with at the state level, as are education, family matters, gun ownership policies, and many land-use decisions. States also have the power to raise revenues through taxation. In some states, citizens have a wide-ranging ability to influence legislation through referendums. Such direct-democracy mechanisms, often initiated by signature campaigns, have been hailed by some as a reflection of the openness of the U.S. system. However, they have also been criticized on the grounds that they can lead to incoherent governance, undermine representative democracy, and weaken the party system. Referendums in 2012 legalized same-sex marriage in three states and the recreational use of marijuana in two.

The intensely competitive U.S. political environment is dominated by two major parties, the right-leaning Republicans and the left-leaning Democrats. The country's "first past the post" or majoritarian electoral system discourages the emergence of additional parties, as do a number of specific legal and other hurdles. However, on occasion, independent or third-party candidates have significantly influenced politics at the presidential and state levels, and a number of newer parties, such as the Green Party or groups aligned with organized labor, have modestly affected politics in certain municipalities in recent years.

While the majoritarian system has discouraged the establishment of parties based on race, ethnicity, or religion, religious groups and minorities have been able to gain political influence through participation in the two main parties. A number of laws have been enacted to ensure the political rights of minorities. However, new laws in a number of states require voters to present driver's licenses, birth certificates, or other forms of identification before casting ballots. Sponsors claim that the intent is to combat voter fraud, but critics contend that such fraud is a minor problem at most, and accuse Republicans of adopting the laws to suppress voting by demographic groups that tend to support Democrats, particularly low-income blacks. While the courts have struck down some voter identity laws, others were in place for the 2012 elections. In the end, participation rates for minority voters were relatively high, especially for black Americans.

Election campaigns are long and expensive. The two parties and the constituency and interest groups that support them have used various methods to circumvent legal restrictions on campaign spending, and the Supreme Court on several occasions has struck down such restrictions, finding that they violated free speech rights. The cost of the 2012 presidential race alone reached at least $5.8 billion, with billions more spent on elections for Congress and state and local offices. In general, candidates with a financial advantage are more likely to prevail, though a number of Senate races were won by candidates who trailed in fund-raising.

American society has a tradition of intolerance toward corrupt acts by government officials, corporate executives, or labor leaders. In recent years, the most serious instances of political corruption have been uncovered among state-level officials. In New York State, a number of state legislators and municipal officials have been indicted on charges of bribery, theft, and other forms of graft. The media are aggressive in reporting on cases of corporate and official corruption; newspapers often publish investigative articles that delve into questions of private or public malfeasance. However, there are concerns that financial difficulties in the newspaper industry have reduced the press's willingness to devote resources to investigative journalism. Moreover, the expanding influence of interest groups and lobbyists on the legislative and policymaking processes, combined with their crucial role in campaign fund-raising, has given rise to public perceptions of enhanced corruption in Washington.

The federal government has a high degree of transparency. A substantial number of auditing and investigating agencies function independently of political influence. Such bodies are often spurred to action by the investigative work of journalists. Federal agencies regularly place information relevant to their mandates on websites to broaden public access. In an action widely praised by scholars and civil libertarians, Obama in 2009 ordered that millions of government documents from the Cold War era be declassified, and instructed federal agencies to adopt a cooperative attitude toward public information requests. But the administration has come under criticism for its lack of openness with the press and public and its determination to punish leaks by government officials.

The United States has a free, diverse, and constitutionally protected press. However, financially stressed newspapers have carried out major staff reductions over the past decade while instituting cost-cutting format changes, including dropping print editions altogether or limiting them to a few days a week. News websites now constitute a major source of political news, along with cable television networks and talk radio programs. News coverage has also grown more polarized, with particular outlets and their star commentators providing a consistently right- or left-leaning perspective.

Controversy has emerged in recent years over attempts by federal prosecutors and private attorneys to compel journalists to divulge their confidential sources or reporting materials, particularly in prosecutions of government employees accused of leaking information on national security issues. While laws that protect journalists' sources and materials have been adopted in 39 states, a similar measure at the federal level has yet to win congressional approval.

Congressional efforts in 2012 to adopt legislation to prevent copyright infringement on the internet were shelved in response to strong opposition from leading internet companies, websites, and ordinary users. The bills would have given the authorities sweeping powers to block entire sites containing allegedly unauthorized content, potentially affecting legal content and compelling host companies to police the activities of their users.

The United States has a long tradition of religious freedom. The constitution protects the free exercise of religion while barring any official endorsement of a religious faith, and there are no direct government subsidies to houses of worship. The debate over the role of religion in public life is ongoing, however, and religious groups often mobilize to influence political discussions on the diverse issues in which they take an interest. The academic sphere enjoys a healthy level of intellectual freedom.

In general, officials respect the right to public assembly. Demonstrations against government policies are frequently held in Washington, New York, and other major cities. Over the past decade, local authorities have often placed restrictions on the location or duration of large protests directed at meetings of international institutions, political party conventions, or targets in the financial sector. Police and protesters sometimes clashed during 2011 demonstrations by the Occupy movement against growing economic inequality, though similar demonstrations in 2012 generally took place without violence, as did protests at the national political conventions. The United States gives wide freedom to trade associations, nongovernmental organizations, and issue-oriented pressure groups to organize and argue their cases through the political process.

Federal law guarantees trade unions the right to organize and engage in collective bargaining. The right to strike is also guaranteed. Over the years, however, the strength of organized labor has declined, so that only about 7 percent of the private sector workforce is currently represented by unions. The country's labor code and decisions by the National Labor Relations Board (NLRB) during Republican presidencies have been regarded as impediments to organizing efforts. Union organizing is also hampered by strong resistance from private employers. In 2012 Michigan became the 24th state to adopt "right to work" legislation, which makes union organizing more difficult. Organized labor's political clout has diminished along with its membership, but unions provided significant support to Obama and other Democratic candidates during the 2012 election campaign.

Judicial independence is respected. Although the courts have occasionally been accused of intervening in areas that are best left to the political branches, most observers regard the judiciary as a linchpin of the American democratic system. In recent years, much attention has been paid to the ideological composition of the Supreme Court, which has issued a number of major decisions by a one-vote margin and is currently seen as having a conservative majority. Concern has also been raised about a trend toward the politicization of judicial elections in some states.

While the United States has a strong rule-of-law tradition, the criminal justice system's treatment of minority groups has long been a problem. Black and Latino inmates account for a disproportionately large percentage of the prison population. Civil liberties organizations and other groups have also advanced a broader critique of the justice system, arguing that there are too many Americans in prison, that prison sentences are often excessive, that too many prisoners are relegated to solitary confinement or other maximum-security arrangements, and that too many people are incarcerated for minor drug offenses. Over two million Americans are behind bars in federal and state prisons and local jails at any given time, producing the highest national incarceration rate in the world. The number of incarcerated Americans has continued to increase even as the national rate of violent crime has declined. There is also a large number of juveniles serving lengthy prison terms in adult penitentiaries. Concerns have been raised about prison conditions, especially the incidence of violence and rape.

The United States has the highest rate of legal executions in the democratic world, though the number has declined since a peak in the late 1990s. There were 43 executions in the United States in 2012. The death penalty has been formally abolished by 18 states, mostly recently Connecticut in April 2012, and 12 states where it remains on the books have not carried out executions for the past five years. Of particular importance in this trend has been the exoneration of some death-row inmates based on new DNA testing. The Supreme Court has ruled out the death penalty in cases where the perpetrator is a juvenile or mentally handicapped. In 2012 the Court further decided that juvenile offenders could not be sentenced to life imprisonment without the possibility of parole.

The United States is one of the world's most racially and ethnically diverse societies. In recent years, residents and citizens of Latin American ancestry have replaced black Americans as the largest minority group, and the majority held by the non-Latino white population has declined. An array of policies and programs are designed to protect the rights of minorities, including laws to prevent workplace discrimination, affirmative-action plans for university admissions, quotas to guarantee representation in the internal affairs of some political parties, and policies to ensure that minorities are not treated unfairly in the distribution of government assistance. The black population, however, continues to lag in overall economic standing, educational attainment, and other social indicators. Affirmative action in employment and university admissions remains a contentious issue. The Supreme Court has given approval to the use of race or ethnicity as a factor in university admissions under certain narrow conditions. However, affirmative action has been banned, in whole or in part, through referendums in five states.

The United States has generally maintained liberal immigration policies in recent decades. Most observers believe that the country has struck a balance that both encourages assimilation and permits new legal immigrants to maintain their religious and cultural customs. Many Americans remain troubled by the large number of illegal immigrants in the country, and the government has responded by strengthening border security and stepping up efforts to deport illegal immigrants, especially those found guilty of criminal offenses. Some states have enacted laws to restrict various economic and civil rights of undocumented immigrants, though the federal courts have struck down key sections of these laws, partly because of their potential side effects on the rights of U.S. citizens. During 2012, the Obama administration announced a reprieve from deportation for undocumented immigrants who arrived as children and meet certain other requirements.

Citizens of the United States enjoy a high level of personal autonomy. The right to own property is protected by law and is jealously guarded as part of the American way of life. Business entrepreneurship is encouraged as a matter of government policy.

The United States prides itself as a society that offers wide access to economic and social advancement and favors government policies that enhance equality of opportunity. Recently, however, studies have shown a widening inequality in wealth and a narrowing of access to upward mobility, trends that have been accentuated in the years since the 2008 financial crisis. Among the world's prosperous, stable democracies, the United States is unique in having a large underclass of poor people who have at best a marginal role in economic life.

Women have made important strides toward equality over the past several decades. They now constitute a majority of the American workforce and are well represented in professions like law, medicine, and journalism. Although the average compensation for female workers is roughly 80 percent of that for male workers, women with recent university degrees have effectively attained parity with men. Nonetheless, many female-headed families continue to live in conditions of chronic poverty. In recent years there has been a renewed effort in some states to restrict access to abortion; in the past, most such measures were ultimately struck down by the Supreme Court.

Federal antidiscrimination legislation does not include LGBT (lesbian, gay, bisexual, and transgender) people as a protected class, though many states have enacted such protections. Many states have passed laws or constitutional amendments explicitly banning same-sex marriage, but an increasing number have granted gay couples varying degrees of family rights, and by the end of 2012, same-sex marriage was legal in nine states and Washington, D.C. During the year, Obama reversed his previous opposition to same-sex marriage, which is now supported by a slight majority of Americans in many opinion polls.

Uruguay

Political Rights: 1
Civil Liberties: 1
Status: Free

Population: 3,381,000
Capital: Montevideo

Ten-Year Ratings Timeline For Year Under Review (Political Rights, Civil Liberties, Status)

2003	2004	2005	2006	2007	2008	2009	2010	2011	2012
1,1F	1,1F	1,1F	1,1F	1,1F	1,1F	1,1F	1,1F	1,1F	1,1F

Overview: Uruguay's President Mujica struggled with record low approval ratings in 2012, caused in part by increasing crime rates in the capital of Montevideo. Meanwhile, Venezuela's admittance into the trade bloc, Mercosur, increased tensions between Uruguay' government, which had supported the move, and the country's right-wing opposition, which had opposed it.

After gaining independence first from Spain and then later Brazil, the Republic of Uruguay was established in 1828. The ensuing decades brought a series of revolts, civil conflicts, and incursions by neighboring states, followed by a period of relative stability in the first half of the 20th century. The rival Colorado and Blanco parties vied for political power in the 1950s and 1960s, but economic troubles and an insurgency by the leftist Tupamaros National Liberation Front led to a military takeover in 1973. For the next 22 years, the country remained under the control of a military regime whose reputation for incarcerating the largest proportion of political prisoners per capita in the world earned Uruguay the nickname "the torture chamber of Latin America."

The military era came to an end after the 1984 elections, in which Julio María Sanguinetti of the Colorado Party won the presidency. Sanguinetti, the military's favored candidate, promoted a 1986 amnesty law—also known as the "Expiry Law"—which granted members of the armed forces immunity for human rights violations committed during the years of dictatorship. The military extracted the concession as its price for allowing the democratic transition the year before.

The 1990s were marked by relative economic stability and prosperity. Dr. Jorge Batlle of the Colorado party, who was elected president in 1999, immediately sought an honest accounting of the human rights situation under the former military regime, while showing equally firm determination to reduce spending and privatize state monopolies. In 2001, crises in the rural economy and an increase in violent crime, as well as growing labor unrest, set off alarms in what was still one of Latin America's safest countries.

In October 2004, Tabaré Vázquez of the Broad Front (FA) coalition was elected president in the first round of voting, dealing a crushing blow to the Colorado Party. Vázquez began his term by implementing a floating exchange rate, fiscal discipline, and an inflation-targeted monetary policy in a growing economy. His administration also introduced a personal income tax in 2007. Aided by increased commodity prices, Vázquez tripled foreign investment, maintained steady inflation, reduced poverty, and cut unemployment in half.

Aided by Vázquez's ongoing popularity, José Mujica of the FA coalition was elected president in November 2009. Mujica, a socialist senator who spent 14 years in prison for waging a guerrilla movement against the military regime, focused his first year on national reconciliation and maintaining moderate policies. Mujica's diverse FA coalition complicated reform efforts during his first three years in office, as the president aimed to appease the multiple elements of his coalition, as well as the right-leaning opposition. Public disagreement between Mujica and Vice President Danilo Astori delayed the administration's controversial proposal to tax large land holdings; the bill was finally passed in December 2011.

Uruguay's efforts to bring to justice those responsible for human rights violations committed during its military regime have been inconsistent and at times contradictory. A 1986 amnesty law gave the executive, rather than the judicial, branch final say over which cases could be tried. A majority of Uruguayans supported the amnesty and voted to maintain it in two separate referenda in 1989 and 2009. However, court rulings historically reinterpreted the law to allow for higher-level officers to be tried. Since the FA coalition took office in 2005, an estimated 20 former military officers have been tried and convicted. Former military dictator Gregorio

Álvarez was convicted in October 2009 of abducting political opponents and of 37 counts of murder during the period of military rule and was sentenced to 25 years in prison. In February 2010, former president Juan María Bordaberry received a 30-year prison sentence for the 1976 kidnapping and murder of two parliamentary leaders; he died in July 2011 while under house arrest.

Notwithstanding these convictions, lawmakers continued to push to eliminate the amnesty bill, especially in light of the February 2011 Inter-American Court ruling that Uruguay should investigate alleged crimes from its dirty war. Both houses of parliament voted to nullify the law in October 2011; despite going against popular opinion, Mujica signed the bill into law on November 1, 2011. His overall indecisive handling of the amnesty issue caused him to lose standing within the FA coalition.

Paraguay's June 2012 suspension from Mercosur and Venezuela's backdoor admittance to the customs union in July undermined cooperation between the Mujica administration and the opposition Congress. The latter had opposed Venezuela's membership, and felt sidelined when Mujica voted in favor of Venezuela's entry into the trade bloc. Moreover, the move prompted many members of the Colorado Party to resign from management positions in state companies and other state institutions they were offered after Mujica came to power in 2010.

While Uruguay is one of the safest countries in Latin America, homicides increased by 45 percent in 2012, compared to 2011. Officials attributed the rise in crime to warring drug gangs, as Uruguay becomes an increasingly important transit point for narcotics. The Mujica administration presented a package of 16 measures to Congress in June 2012, including increased police presence in Montevideo, as well as state regulation of the production and distribution of marijuana. The bill had not been voted on by year's end.

Political Rights and Civil Liberties: Uruguay is an electoral democracy. The 1967 constitution established a bicameral General Assembly consisting of the 99-member Chamber of Representatives and the 30-member Senate, with all members directly elected for five-year terms. The president is directly elected for a single five-year term.

The major political parties and groupings are the Colorado Party, the Independent Party, the Blanco Party, and the ruling FA coalition. The latter includes the Movement of Popular Participation, the New Space Party, the Socialist Party, and the Uruguayan Assembly, among other factions.

The Transparency Law criminalizes a broad range of potential abuses of power by officeholders, including the laundering of funds related to public corruption cases. Uruguay was ranked 20 out of 176 countries surveyed in Transparency International's 2012 Corruption Perceptions Index, making it one of the least corrupt countries in Latin America.

Constitutional guarantees regarding free expression are respected, and violations of press freedom are rare. The press is privately owned, and broadcasting includes both commercial and public outlets. There are numerous daily newspapers, many of which are associated with political parties. A June 2009 bill eliminated criminal penalties for the defamation of public officials. However, five government resolutions signed in July 2012 prevent disclosure of certain information regarding the police, such as information on disciplinary procedures and procedures for combatting crime. The government does not place restrictions on internet usage.

Freedom of religion is broadly respected. The government does not restrict academic freedom.

Rights to freedom of assembly and association are provided for by law, and the government generally observes these in practice. Civic organizations have proliferated since the return of civilian rule. Numerous women's rights groups focus on problems such as violence against women and societal discrimination. Workers exercise their right to join unions, bargain collectively, and hold strikes. Unions are well organized and politically powerful.

Uruguay's judiciary is relatively independent, but the court system remains severely backlogged. Pretrial detainees often spend more time in jail than they would if convicted of the offense in question and sentenced to the maximum prison term. Overcrowded prisons, poor conditions, and violence among inmates remain serious problems. Medical care for prisoners is substandard, and many rely on visitors for food.

The small Afro-Uruguayan minority, comprising an estimated 4 percent of the population, continues to face economic and social inequalities and is underrepresented in the government.

Women enjoy equal rights under the law but face traditional discriminatory attitudes and practices, including salaries averaging approximately two-thirds those of men. Violence against women remains a problem. Women hold only 12 percent of the seats in the Chamber of Representatives and 13 percent of the Senate. However, under a 2009 quota law, women must comprise one-third of a party's political candidate list beginning in 2014. The Uruguayan Congress approved ratification of the Domestic Workers Convention in April 2012, making Uruguay the first country worldwide to do so. Mandating core labor rights to domestic workers, the convention will become legal once it is ratified by at least two countries. Uruguay's Congress approved same-sex civil unions in 2007, making Uruguay the first South American country to approve these rights nationwide. Uruguay also became the second Latin American country, after Cuba, to allow abortion. The Senate passed a bill in October 2012 legalizing abortion for any reason during the first trimester; the law took effect in November.

Uzbekistan

Political Rights: 7
Civil Liberties: 7
Status: Not Free

Population: 29,779,600
Capital: Tashkent

Ten-Year Ratings Timeline For Year Under Review (Political Rights, Civil Liberties, Status)

2003	2004	2005	2006	2007	2008	2009	2010	2011	2012
7,6NF	7,6NF	7,7NF	7,7NF	7,7NF	7,7NF	7,7NF	7,7NF	7,7NF	7,7NF

Overview: As in previous years, Uzbekistan's government suppressed all political opposition in 2012. The few remaining civic activists and critical journalists in the country faced physical violence, prosecution, hefty fines, and arbitrary detention. Nevertheless, the regime further improved relations with the United States and Europe as it provided logistical support for NATO operations in Afghanistan.

Uzbekistan gained independence from the Soviet Union through a December 1991 referendum. In a parallel vote, Islam Karimov, the former Communist Party leader and chairman of the People's Democratic Party (PDP), the successor to the Communist Party, was elected president amid fraud claims by rival candidate Mohammed Solih of the Erk (Freedom) Party. Solih fled the country two years later, and his party was forced underground. Only progovernment parties were allowed to compete in elections to the first post-Soviet legislature in December 1994 and January 1995. A February 1995 referendum extended Karimov's first five-year term until 2000, allegedly with 99 percent voter support.

The government's repression of the political opposition and of Muslims not affiliated with state-sanctioned religious institutions intensified after a series of deadly bombings in Tashkent in February 1999. The authorities blamed the attacks on the Islamic Movement of Uzbekistan, an armed group seeking to overthrow the secular government and establish an Islamic state.

All of the five parties that competed in the December 1999 parliamentary elections, which were strongly criticized by international monitors, supported the president. In the January 2000 presidential poll, Karimov defeated his only opponent, allegedly winning 92 percent of the vote. The government refused to allow the participation of genuine opposition parties. A 2002 referendum extended presidential terms from five to seven years.

A series of suicide bomb attacks and related violent clashes in late March and early April 2004 killed some 50 people. Police appeared to be the main targets. Suicide bombers killed several people outside the U.S. and Israeli embassies in July 2004 amid conflicting claims of responsibility. In December, elections for the lower house of a new bicameral parliament were held, with only the five legal, propresidential parties allowed to participate.

In May 2005, a popular uprising in the Ferghana Valley city of Andijon triggered a violent government crackdown. The incident began on May 10 and 11, when family members and supporters of 23 local businessmen charged with involvement in a banned Islamic group staged a peaceful demonstration in anticipation of the trial verdict. The situation turned violent on the night of May 12, when armed men stormed a prison, freed the 23 businessmen and other inmates, and captured the local government administration building. Thousands of local residents subsequently gathered in the city center, where people began to speak out on political and economic issues, often making antigovernment statements.

Security forces responded by opening fire on the crowd, which included many women and children. Although the authorities maintained that the protesters were the first to open fire, eyewitnesses reported that the security forces began shooting indiscriminately. Official figures put the death toll at 187, but unofficial sources estimated the dead at nearly 800, most of them unarmed civilians.

Karimov repeatedly rejected calls from the European Union (EU), the Organization for Security and Cooperation in Europe (OSCE), and the United States for an independent international inquiry into the violence. In July 2005, Uzbekistan gave the United States six months to leave its military base at Karshi-Khanabad, which it had used to support operations in Afghanistan since late 2001. Russia and China endorsed the official Uzbek account of the violence.

The Uzbek authorities pursued a wide-ranging crackdown after the Andijon incident, targeting nongovernmental organizations (NGOs) with foreign funding, potential political opposition figures, human rights defenders, and even former officials.

Karimov's seven-year term ended in January 2007, and the constitution barred him from running for reelection. Nevertheless, he won a new term in December 2007 with an official 88 percent of the vote. Parliamentary elections in December 2009 offered voters no meaningful choice, though the four legal political parties, all of which supported the government, indulged in mild criticism of one another.

In June 2010, Uzbekistan briefly took in over 100,000 ethnic Uzbek refugees fleeing communal violence in neighboring Kyrgyzstan. However, the authorities quickly returned them to Kyrgyzstan amid some reports of coercion.

The legislature quietly altered the constitution in December 2011 to reduce future presidential terms to five years. In March 2012, another amendment moved up the next presidential election to early 2015, closing a loophole that would have added nearly a year to Karimov's current seven-year term.

Uzbekistan has largely repaired relations with the EU and United States in recent years, in part by agreeing to the overland transportation of NATO supplies to, and increasingly from, Afghanistan. The rapprochement continued in 2012, as the United States again approved waivers for Uzbekistan on some human rights–related sanctions, and high-level visits between U.S., European, and Uzbek officials increased. Nevertheless, Tashkent continued to resist public diplomacy efforts and educational exchanges, and to carefully restrict Uzbeks' access to the outside world.

Political Rights and Civil Liberties: Uzbekistan is not an electoral democracy. President Islam Karimov uses the dominant executive branch to suppress all political opposition, and his December 2007 reelection appeared to flout constitutional rules on term limits. Under electoral legislation adopted in 2008, the bicameral parliament's lower house now has 150 seats, with 135 members directly elected in single-member constituencies and 15 representing the newly formed Ecological Movement of Uzbekistan, which holds separate indirect elections. The 100-member upper house, or Senate, has 84 members elected by regional councils and 16 appointed by the president. All members of the parliament serve five-year terms.

Only four political parties, all progovernment, are currently registered, and no genuine opposition parties operate legally. Unregistered opposition groups function primarily in exile. In February 2012, exiled imam Obidkhon Nazarov, a prominent opposition supporter, was shot and seriously wounded outside his home in Sweden; Swedish prosecutors raised the possibility that Uzbek government agents were involved in the attack. In July, Free Farmers (Ozod Dehqonlar) party leader Nigora Hidoyateva fled the country after weeks of harassment and threats from the security services. Relatives of exiled opposition figures face persecution in Uzbekistan. In November, the 70-year-old father of Bahodyr Choriyev, the U.S.-based leader of the opposition Birdamlik movement, was fined $11,000 for supposedly slandering local authorities whom he accused of abuses.

Corruption is pervasive. Uzbekistan was ranked 170 out of 176 countries surveyed in Transparency International's 2012 Corruption Perceptions Index.

Despite constitutional guarantees, freedoms of speech and the press are severely restricted. The state controls major media outlets and related facilities, and state-run television has aired "documentaries" that smear perceived opponents of the government. Although official censorship was abolished in 2002, it has continued through semiofficial mechanisms that strongly encourage self-censorship. Foreign reporters are generally excluded from the country. In March 2012, independent journalist Viktor Krymzalov was convicted of slander for an anonymous article, despite a lack of evidence that he was the author. In April, independent journalist Elena Bondar was convicted and fined for "inciting ethnic, religious, or national hatred," similarly without evidence that she had written the articles in question. Under pressure from authorities, Bondar subsequently fled the country.

The government systematically blocks websites with content that is critical of the regime. Mainstream news, information, and social-media sites based outside the country are sometimes blocked as well. During 2012, for example, the government blocked access to the Russia-based blogging platform LiveJournal several times. In October, authorities expanded the list of banned proxy sites that allow users to access blocked content anonymously.

The government permits the existence of approved Muslim, Jewish, and Christian denominations, but treats unregistered religious activity as a criminal offense. The state exercises strict control over Islamic worship, including the content of sermons. Suspected members of banned Muslim organizations and their relatives have been subjected to arrest, interrogation, and torture. In February 2012, an ethnic Korean Protestant group was arrested for meeting in a home rather than in a church building. In June and August, several Orthodox Christian believers and a group of registered Protestants were arrested on charges of being Jehovah's Witnesses, who can meet legally only in one region of the country.

The government reportedly limits academic freedom. Bribes are commonly required to gain entrance to exclusive universities and obtain good grades. Open and free private discussion is limited by the mahalla committees, traditional neighborhood organizations that the government has turned into an official system for public surveillance and control.

Despite constitutional provisions for freedom of assembly, the authorities severely restrict this right in practice, breaking up virtually all unsanctioned gatherings and detaining participants. In March 2012, activists from a newly formed youth organization, Cholpon, distributed leaflets supporting opposition groups, leading to several arrests. In June, three Birdamlik members were arrested and given heavy fines for attempting to protest in front of the Kyrgyzstan embassy in Tashkent. In December, Birdamlik attempted to hold a Constitution Day rally in Tashkent, but many activists were prevented from leaving their homes or arrested on their way to the event.

Freedom of association is tightly constrained, and unregistered NGOs face extreme difficulties and harassment. After the 2005 unrest in Andijon, the government shut down virtually all foreign-funded organizations in Uzbekistan; Human Rights Watch, the last international monitoring group with a presence in the country, was forced to close its office in 2011. Throughout 2012, human rights activists continued to face harassment, prosecution, and travel restrictions, in addition to deadly violence, Gulshan Karayeva, head of the Human Rights Society of Uzbekistan branch in Kashkadarya, reported in May that she had refused a demand to serve as an informant for the security services. She was subsequently subjected to repeated attacks and threats on the street. Akromhoja Mukhitdinov, a member of the Human Rights Alliance of Uzbekistan and the Birdamlik movement, was stabbed to death in July in a suspected contract killing.

The Council of the Federation of Trade Unions is dependent on the state, and no genuinely independent union structures exist. Organized strikes are extremely rare.

The judiciary is subservient to the president, who appoints all judges and can remove them at any time. The creation in 2008 of a Lawyers' Chamber with compulsory membership increased state control over the legal profession. Law enforcement authorities routinely justify the arrest of suspected Islamic extremists or political opponents by planting contraband or filing dubious charges of financial wrongdoing. In 2012, the government released some high-profile political prisoners who had long been the subjects of human rights campaigns, including activist Alisher Karamatov, who had spent six years in prison before his release in April. In January, however, the courts extended the sentence of Muhammad Bekjonov, a former editor of the opposition newspaper *Erk* who had been behind bars since 1999, adding five years for alleged violations of prison regulations only days before his scheduled release.

Prisons suffer from severe overcrowding and shortages of food and medicine. As with detained suspects, prison inmates—particularly those sentenced for their religious beliefs—are often subjected to abuse or torture.

Although racial and ethnic discrimination is prohibited by law, the belief that senior positions in government and business are reserved for ethnic Uzbeks is widespread. Moreover, the government appears to be systematically closing schools for the Tajik-speaking minority. Under the penal code, sexual activity between men is punishable by up to three years in prison.

Permission is required to move to a new city, and bribes are commonly paid to obtain the necessary documents. A 2011 overhaul of the residency permit system for Tashkent reportedly resulted in increased denial of services to unregistered residents and their resettlement in less-developed provincial areas. Restrictions on foreign travel include the use of exit visas, which are often issued selectively. Despite such controls, millions of Uzbeks seek employment abroad, particularly in Russia and Kazakhstan.

Widespread corruption and the government's tight control over the economy limit equality of opportunity. In 2012, the government seized a local affiliate of the Russia-based MTS telecommunications company, taking more than $1 billion in assets and prosecuting several managers. TeliaSonera, a Sweden-based telecommunications firm, faced an inquiry by Swedish prosecutors over alleged bribery and money laundering linked to its 2007 purchase of an Uzbek operating license from a close associate of President Karimov's daughter.

Women's educational and professional prospects are limited by cultural and religious norms and by ongoing economic difficulties. Victims of domestic violence are discouraged from pressing charges against perpetrators, who rarely face prosecution. The trafficking of women abroad for prostitution remains a serious problem. A 2009 law imposed tougher penalties for child labor, and in August 2012, Uzbekistan's prime minister pledged to end the practice completely. However, while reports indicated that it may have been less pervasive than in the past, multiple organizations confirmed the ongoing use of child labor during the cotton harvest in 2012.

Vanuatu

Political Rights: 2
Civil Liberties: 2
Status: Free

Population: 258,000
Capital: Port Vila

Ten-Year Ratings Timeline For Year Under Review (Political Rights, Civil Liberties, Status)

2003	2004	2005	2006	2007	2008	2009	2010	2011	2012
2,2F	2,2F	2,2F	2,2F	2,2F	2,2F	2,2F	2,2F	2,2F	2,2F

Overview: The Vanuak'aku Party captured the most seats in the October 2012 parliamentary elections, followed by the People's Progress Party. Sato Kilman was reelected prime minister. Earlier in the year, a three-month suspension of the police commissioner led to confusion over who rightfully held the position. Vanuatu joined the World Trade Organization in July.

Vanuatu was governed as an Anglo-French "condominium" from 1906 until independence in 1980. The Anglo-French legacy continues to split society along linguistic lines in all spheres of life, including politics, religion, and economics.

Widespread corruption and persistent political fragmentation have caused governments to collapse or become dysfunctional. No-confidence votes have forced several changes of government in recent years, and parliamentary coalitions are frequently formed and dissolved. In the 2008 parliamentary elections, the Vanua'aku Party (VP) captured the most seats, while three other parties took the remaining seats. The role of prime minister changed hands several times in the first half 2011, with Sato Kilman of the People's Progressive Party (PPP) finally winning a June election to settle the dispute.

In June 2012, the Police Service Commission imposed a three-month paid suspension on police commissioner Joshua Bong to investigate allegations of incompetence. When the acting police chief Arthur Caulton refused to step down after Bong's suspension had ended, Bong ordered the arrest of Caulton and other officials, accusing them of mutiny. On September 30, the Police Service Commission appointed Bong to a five-year term as commissioner to reaffirm his position. Days later, however, President Iolu Johnson Abbil fired Bong and reappointed Caulton as the acting police commissioner. In December, Bong and several police officers were charged with mutiny, kidnapping, and false imprisonment, while Caulton was appointed the new police commissioner. The dispute stirred public concern about potential violence between competing parties and its effect on public order and safety.

In parliamentary elections held on October 30, 2012, the VP won 8 seats, the PPP took 6 seats, the Union of Moderate Parties (UMP) captured 5 seats, and the National United Party (NUP) took only 4 seats. The remainder of the 52 seats at stake went to 12 other parties and several independent candidates. Kilman retained the premiership.

The economy has suffered substantially from the global economic downtown. Like many other Pacific island states, Vanuatu has sought closer ties with China for investment and economic assistance. However, the rapid expansion of this Chinese presence has increased social tensions, especially with indigenous business owners. Vanuatu formally joined the World Trade Organization in July 2012, despite considerable opposition from churches and civil society groups. Australia's Seasonal Worker Scheme was launched in Vanuatu in October to provide new employment opportunities.

Political Rights and Civil Liberties: Vanuatu is an electoral democracy. The constitution provides for parliamentary elections every four years. The prime minister, who appoints his own cabinet, is chosen by the 52-seat unicameral Parliament from among its members. Members of Parliament and the heads of the six provincial governments form an electoral college to select the largely ceremonial president for a five-year term. The National Council of Chiefs works in parallel with Parliament, exercising authority mainly over language and cultural matters.

Many political parties are active, but politicians frequently switch affiliations. Politics is also driven by linguistic and tribal identity.

Corruption is a serious problem, and official abuse is serious and widespread. In March 2012, six provincial councils were suspended for irregularities in their financial operations. Seven senior officials at the National Provident Fund were suspended in August amid allegations of mismanagement and nepotism. The practice of politicians granting passports to foreign nationals in exchange for personal gain has long been a concern of local critics and international aid donors. In May, police arrested the chairman of the Citizenship Commission and several other officials for allegedly issuing illegal citizenship permits to Chinese migrants.

The government generally respects freedoms of speech and the press, though elected officials have been accused of threatening journalists for critical reporting. The state-owned Television Blong Vanuatu broadcasts in English and French. Newspapers include the state-owned *Vanuatu Weekly* and several privately owned daily and weekly papers. State monopoly of telecommunications services ended in 2008. Buzz FM, the first radio station not owned by the government or a politician, began broadcasting in the capital in October 2012. The number of internet users is growing, but access is limited by cost and lack of infrastructure.

The government generally respects freedom of religion in this predominantly Christian country. There were no reports of restrictions on academic freedom in 2012.

The law provides for freedoms of assembly and association, and the government typically upholds these rights. Public demonstrations are permitted by law and generally allowed in practice, though 24 people who were peacefully protesting the arrival of an Indonesian military aircraft were arrested in May 2012. Civil society groups are active on a variety of issues.

Workers can bargain collectively and strike. Five independent trade unions are organized under the umbrella Vanuatu Council of Trade Unions. In April 2012, public transportation workers went on strike to protest the poor condition of roads in Port Vila and Efate; the strike ended the next day when the government agreed to take action. In July, the government suspended a teacher for organizing a supposedly illegal assembly among teachers to discuss salary issues.

The judiciary is largely independent, but a lack of resources hinders the hiring and retention of qualified judges and prosecutors. Tribal chiefs often adjudicate local disputes, but their punishments are sometimes deemed excessive. Long pretrial detentions are common, and prisons fail to meet minimum international standards. Harsh treatment of prisoners and police brutality provoke frequent prison riots and breakouts. In July 2012, the Supreme Court ordered police to bring to justice those responsible for beating to death detainee John Bule in 2009; no progress had been reported in the investigation by year's end. In May, for the first time, the police arrested and charged nearly 40 people for harboring escapees.

Discrimination against women is widespread. No laws prohibit spousal rape, domestic abuse, or sexual harassment, which women's groups claim are common and increasing. Most cases go unreported due to victims' fear of reprisal or family pressure, and the police and courts rarely intervene or impose strong penalties.

Venezuela

Political Rights: 5
Civil Liberties: 5
Status: Partly Free

Population: 29,718,000
Capital: Caracas

Ten-Year Ratings Timeline For Year Under Review (Political Rights, Civil Liberties, Status)

2003	2004	2005	2006	2007	2008	2009	2010	2011	2012
3,4PF	3,4PF	4,4PF	4,4PF	4,4PF	4,4PF	4,4PF	5,5PF	5,5PF	5,5PF

Overview: President Hugo Chávez was reelected in October 2012 following a campaign in which economic growth, abuse of state resources, and public sympathy for the ailing incumbent trumped the opposition's increased level of unity and discipline. Chávez-linked candidates

also dominated state elections in December, winning 20 of 23 gubernatorial races. Nonetheless, the government's acknowledgment the same month that Chávez's undisclosed form of cancer had returned fueled uncertainty about the future of the president and his socialist revolution.

The Republic of Venezuela was founded in 1830, nine years after independence from Spain. Long periods of instability and military dictatorship ended with the establishment of civilian rule in 1958 and approval of a democratic constitution in 1961. Until 1993, the center-left Democratic Action (AD) party and the Social Christian Party (COPEI) dominated politics under an arrangement known as the Punto Fijo pact. President Carlos Andrés Pérez (1989–93) of AD, already weakened by the violent political fallout from his free-market reforms, was nearly overthrown in two 1992 coup attempts—one led by Lieutenant Colonel Hugo Chávez, and the other by a group of disgruntled military officers. Pérez was subsequently impeached as a result of corruption and his inability to stem the social consequences of economic decline, which had coincided with lower oil prices beginning in the 1980s. Rafael Caldera, a former president (1969–74) and founder of COPEI, was elected president in late 1993 as head of a 16-party coalition.

Chávez won the 1998 presidential contest on a populist, anticorruption platform, and immediately proceeded to draft a new constitution. The resulting document, approved by voters in 1999, strengthened the presidency and introduced a unicameral National Assembly. Although Chávez retained his post in elections held under the new charter in 2000, opposition parties won most governorships, about half of the mayoralties, and a significant share of the National Assembly seats.

Chávez's use of decrees to enact controversial laws in 2001 provoked the largest street protests ever recorded in Venezuela. In April 2002, following the deaths of 19 people in a massive antigovernment protest, dissident military officers attempted to oust Chávez, the vice president, and the National Assembly with backing from some of the country's leading business and labor groups. However, the coup was resisted by loyalist troops and protesters, who brought Chávez back to power. The country was racked by continued protests, and in December 2002, oil workers backed by opposition leaders called a general strike that lasted 62 days. With the help of the military, the president managed to survive the strike and place loyalists in charge of the national oil company. The opposition then sought to trigger a recall referendum through a signature campaign. Under strong international pressure, Chávez agreed to the referendum, which was scheduled for 2004. In preparation, he launched a series of bold social initiatives in 2003, including urban health and literacy projects, many of which were staffed by thousands of experts from Cuba. He also continued to increase the number of loyalists in the judiciary, electoral bodies, the media, and other institutions.

Chávez won the recall referendum, taking 58 percent of the vote amid high turnout. National Assembly elections in 2005 were boycotted by the opposition, which accused the National Electoral Council (CNE) of allowing violations of ballot secrecy. A mere 25 percent of eligible voters turned out, and all 167 deputies in the resulting National Assembly were government supporters.

In the 2006 presidential election, Chávez defeated Zulia state governor Manuel Rosales of the opposition A New Time party, 61 percent to 38 percent. The incumbent exploited state resources during the campaign and drew on enduring support among poorer Venezuelans who had benefited from his social programs. He was also aided by high abstention rates among opposition voters who were convinced that the balloting was futile or not entirely secret.

Soon after the vote, Chávez pressed forward with his program of radical institutional changes. Most progovernment parties merged into the Unified Socialist Party of Venezuela (PSUV), and the socialist "Bolivarian revolution" deepened economically with a series of nationalizations of private assets. Cuban advisers acquired increasing influence in the health and intelligence services, among other sectors.

Referendum voters in December 2007 narrowly defeated a package of constitutional amendments, among them the removal of presidential term limits. The vote reflected a new push for electoral participation among the opposition, public disappointment with rising inflation and crime rates, and a degree of disaffection among Chávez supporters. However, a set of 26 new laws decreed by Chávez in July 2008 appeared designed to institute measures that were rejected in the referendum.

State and local elections in November 2008 were preceded by the disqualification of over 300 candidates, including some opposition leaders, by the nominally independent but government-friendly comptroller. The opposition captured the mayoralty of greater Caracas as well as 5 of 22 states, including the 3 richest and most populous. Government candidates won 17 states and some 80 percent of the mayoralties.

A government-backed referendum in February 2009 abolished term limits. In March and April, the legislature passed laws allowing the national government to strip states of key governing functions and cut budget allocations; in practice, opposition-governed states and particularly the Caracas mayor's office were most affected.

In the run-up to National Assembly elections in September 2010, the PSUV benefited from significant exposure on state-run media and pressure on public employees and neighborhood groups. The opposition, grouped together as the Unity Roundtable (MUD), took more than 47 percent of the vote, the PSUV captured 48 percent, and the opposition-leaning Fatherland for All (PPT) party obtained over 3 percent. Due to electoral rules revised in 2009, however, PSUV candidates secured 98 of the 165 seats, MUD candidates took 65, and the PPT won the remaining 2.

With the PSUV facing the loss of its supermajority in the new legislature, Chávez urged the outgoing chamber to enact a raft of new legislation before dissolving. Over 20 laws were passed or modified in December, including highly controversial regulations related to the internet, funding for civil society groups, education, procedural issues within the National Assembly, territorial reorganization, and the distribution of resources to subnational governments and community groups. In addition, the legislature again voted to grant Chávez wide-ranging decree powers for 18 months.

In 2011 the opposition began its primary campaign for the 2012 presidential contest; Miranda state governor Henrique Capriles received a majority of the 3 million votes cast during the February 2012 primary. Also during 2011, after weeks of rumors surrounding an operation he underwent while visiting Cuba, Chávez revealed in late July that had been diagnosed with cancer, though he refused to divulge specifics and made clear his intention to run for reelection in 2012. Critics bemoaned the lack of transparency, particularly given Chávez's personalized style of rule and the absence of a clear line of succession within the PSUV. Meanwhile, unstable social and economic conditions continued to pose difficulties for the government, as moderate economic growth was paired with electrical blackouts in parts of the country, stagnant industrial production, escalating crime, and persistent shortages of some food items.

The economy regained strength in 2012, spurred by continued high oil prices and, typical of electoral years under Chávez, a boom in state spending. Real wages were increased substantially, especially for public employees. The largest disbursements went to a project known as the Great Venezuelan Housing Mission, which provided or promised new housing for over a million Venezuelans. Other spending included payments to senior citizens and the distribution of appliances to low-income households.

Capriles sought to project a centrist, positive image in his campaign, pledging to maintain popular social programs while improving the quality and efficiency of governance. The Chávez campaign was more negative, alleging that an opposition victory would signify the end of the Bolivarian revolution, a return to the "oligarchic" model of the Punto Fijo era, and the start of a new era of violence in politics. Campaigning was largely peaceful, although several violent episodes targeting Capriles supporters occurred. Capriles could not match the government's turnout machinery, due in part to the collection of detailed personal information from recipients of state support. Moreover, the Chávez campaign enjoyed a significant resource advantage, including the melding of official publicity and campaign propaganda, the use of state vehicles to transport supporters to rallies and voting sites, Chávez's legal ability to take over the airwaves to make speeches, and generally weak oversight provided by the CNE. The skewed media coverage was especially noticeable in nonurban areas, where most media are state controlled.

Turnout proved decisive on election day in October, and Chávez was reelected with over 55 percent of the vote, to Capriles's 44 percent, with some 80 percent of eligible voters participating.

Chavismo maintained its momentum in the December state elections, with PSUV candidates winning 20 of 23 contests, including in several populous states that had been governed by the opposition. However, Capriles was narrowly reelected as governor of Miranda, reaffirming his status as the opposition's standard bearer.

In early December, Chávez acknowledged the return of his cancer and departed for Cuba for an indefinite course of treatment. In a sign of the gravity of his condition, before leaving he anointed Vice President and Foreign Minister Nicolás Maduro as his preferred successor; in the event of the president's death, new elections would be required within 30 days. As the year ended, Chávez's ability to return for his inauguration on January 10, 2013, remained uncertain, and the constitutional implications of a failure to do so were the subject of heated debate.

Relations with the United States remained stable but tense, and the United States continued to lack an ambassador in Caracas in 2012. The bilateral friction was partly attributable to Chávez's creation of ostensible leftist alternatives to U.S.-backed regional trade pacts and political bodies; his weapons purchases from Russia; and his rhetorical support for and economic cooperation with Cuba, Iran, Syria, and other nondemocratic states. The Venezuelan government stirred regional controversy in September 2012 when it announced its withdrawal from the American Convention on Human Rights following a series of decisions against it by the Inter-American Court of Human Rights.

Political Rights and Civil Liberties: Venezuela is not an electoral democracy. While the act of voting is relatively free and the count has become fairer since 2006, the political playing field favors government-backed candidates, and the separation of powers is virtually nonexistent.

Ballot secrecy has been a source of controversy. After the failed 2004 presidential recall referendum, tens of thousands of people who had signed petitions in favor of the effort found that they could not get government jobs or contracts, or qualify for public assistance programs; they had apparently been placed on a blacklist of President Hugo Chávez's alleged political opponents. After a boycott of the 2005 National Assembly elections, the opposition decided to actively contest all subsequent elections, and the voting is generally considered free and fair, but the CNE has failed to limit the use of state resources by Chávez and the ruling PSUV. The promotion of social and infrastructure projects often blurs the line between PSUV candidates' official roles and their electoral campaigns. Public employees are subjected to heavy pressure to support the government.

The unicameral, 165-seat National Assembly is popularly elected for five-year terms. The ruling party's majority acts as a reliable rubber stamp for the executive, and Chávez's control of the 2006–10 assembly allowed him to further curb the independence of institutions including the judiciary, the intelligence services, and the Citizen Power branch of government, which was created by the 1999 constitution to fight corruption and protect citizens' rights. The December 2010 grant of decree powers to Chávez was the third time he received such authority. He used it to enact 54 laws before the period expired in June 2012. The president serves six-year terms, but due to the results of the 2009 referendum, he and other elected officials are no longer subject to term limits.

The merger of government-aligned parties into the PSUV is largely complete, though several groups retain nominal independence. PSUV leaders are generally selected by the president, rather than through internal elections.

In 2009, opposition parties established the MUD, which selected unity candidates—in part via primaries—for the 2010 and 2012 elections. Opposition leadership in some states and localities has been blunted in recent years by laws allowing the national government to strip important functions from subnational administrations.

The government plays a major role in the economy and has generated regulatory restrictions that increase opportunities for corruption. Several large development funds are controlled by the executive branch without independent oversight. The largest, the National Development Fund (FONDEN), has received over $100 billion since 2005 and provides half of Venezuela's public investment, with no legislative examination of its many large-scale, unproductive allocations. Anticorruption efforts are a low government priority, and the lack of state transparency makes citizen investigation and exposure of corruption difficult. Venezuela was ranked 165 out of 176 countries surveyed in Transparency International's 2012 Corruption Perceptions Index.

Although the constitution provides for freedom of the press, the media climate is permeated by intimidation, sometimes including physical attacks, and strong antimedia rhetoric by the government is common. The 2004 Law on Social Responsibility of Radio and Television gives the government the authority to control radio and television content. Opposition-oriented outlets make up a large portion of the print media, but their share of the broadcast media has declined in recent years, in part due to closures by regulators and other forms of official pressure such as selective exchange rate controls. Coverage of election campaigns by state media has been overwhelmingly biased in favor of the government; private outlets have also exhibited bias, though to a somewhat lesser degree. As of December 2012, the local press watchdog Institute for Press and Society had registered 194 press violations during the year.

The government does not restrict internet access, but in 2007 it nationalized the dominant telephone company, CANTV, giving the authorities a potential tool to hinder access. A law passed during the December 2010 lame-duck legislative session extended the 2004 broadcasting law's restrictions to the internet. In 2011 and 2012, dozens of prominent opposition activists and journalists found that their Twitter microblog accounts had been hacked and used to disseminate antiopposition messages.

Constitutional guarantees of religious freedom are generally respected, though government tensions with the Roman Catholic Church remain high. Government relations with the small Jewish community have also been strained at times. Academic freedom has come under mounting pressure since Chávez took office, and a school curriculum developed by his government emphasizes socialist concepts. A 2008 Organic Education Law included ambiguities that could lead to restrictions on private education and increased control by the government and communal councils. In universities, elections for student associations and administration positions have become more politicized, and rival groups of students have clashed repeatedly over both academic and political matters.

Freedom of peaceful assembly is guaranteed in the constitution. However, the right to protest has become a sensitive topic in recent years, and rights groups have criticized legal amendments that make it easier to charge protesters with serious crimes. According to the local rights group Provea, at least 10 protesters were subjected to unconstitutional trials within the military justice system in 2012. Workers, particularly employees of state-owned enterprises, are the most frequent demonstrators, followed by citizens protesting poor public-services deliveries and high crime rates.

Nongovernmental organizations (NGOs) are also frequent antagonists of the government, which has sought to undermine the legitimacy of human rights and other civil society organizations by questioning their ties to international groups. In December 2010, the lame-duck parliament passed the Law on Political Sovereignty and National Self-Determination, which threatens sanctions against any "political organization" that receives foreign funding or hosts foreign visitors who criticize the government. Dozens of civil society activists have been physically attacked in recent years, and other forms of harassment are common, including bureaucratic hurdles to registration.

Workers are legally entitled to form unions, bargain collectively, and strike, with some restrictions on public-sector workers' ability to strike. Control of unions has increasingly shifted from traditional opposition-allied labor leaders to new workers' organizations that are often aligned with the government. The growing competition has contributed to a substantial increase in labor violence as well as confusion during industry-wide collective bargaining. According to local rights monitors, labor violence caused the deaths of 65 workers between January and September 2012. Labor strife has also risen due to the addition of thousands of employees of nationalized companies to the state payroll, and the government's failure to implement new collective-bargaining agreements.

Politicization of the judicial branch has increased under Chávez, and high courts generally do not rule against the government. Conviction rates remain low, the public defender system is underfunded, and nearly half of all judges and prosecutors lack tenure, undermining their autonomy. The National Assembly has the authority to remove and appoint judges to the Supreme Tribunal of Justice (TSJ), which controls the rest of the judiciary. In December 2010 the outgoing legislature appointed nine new TSJ judges who are generally viewed as friendly to the government. In April 2012 a fired and exiled TSJ judge, Eladio Aponte, leveled accusations that administration officials instructed judges on decisions in sensitive cases. Judge María Lourdes Afiuni remained in confinement throughout 2012. She had been arrested on corruption charges in 2009 after ordering the release of a prominent banker who had been held without conviction for more than the maximum of two years. In November 2012, she alleged that she had been sexually assaulted while in custody; the minister of prisons responded by calling for a defamation investigation against her.

Venezuela's murder rate is among the world's highest. The nongovernmental Venezuelan Violence Observatory cited at least 21,692 murders in 2012, an unprecedented figure that represents a rate of approximately 73 homicides per 100,000 citizens. The police and military have been prone to corruption, widespread arbitrary detention and torture of suspects, and extrajudicial killings. In 2009, the justice minister admitted that police were involved in up to 20 percent of crimes; few officers are convicted, partly due to a shortage of prosecutors. Prison conditions in Venezuela remain among the worst in the Americas. The NGO Venezuelan Prison Observatory reported 523 violent deaths within prison walls between July 2011 and July 2012. In June 2012, the minister of prisons announced that 24 new prisons would be constructed over the following two years.

The increasingly politicized military has stepped up its participation in the delivery of public services. Foreign officials assert that the military has adopted a permissive attitude toward drug trafficking and Colombian rebel activity inside Venezuela, though improved relations with Colombia have led to increased cooperation, including the capture of Colombia's most wanted drug lord in Venezuela in September 2012. In recent years, the division of responsibility between the military and civilian militias has become less clear, and informal progovernment groups have been responsible for attacks on press outlets and, occasionally, individual journalists and opposition supporters.

Property rights are affected by the government's penchant for price controls and nationalizations. While the pace of nationalizations has declined from previous years—due in part to the state's dominant position in many strategic industries—the government continues to threaten to nationalize businesses deemed to lack commitment to revolutionary goals. Accusations of mismanagement, underinvestment, corruption, and politicized hiring practices within nationalized businesses are common. Declining productivity and other problems in the politically sensitive oil industry were highlighted by an August 2012 refinery explosion that killed 42 people.

The formal and constitutional rights of indigenous people, who make up about 2 percent of the population, have improved under Chávez, though such rights are seldom enforced by local authorities. The constitution reserves three seats in the National Assembly for indigenous people. Indigenous communities trying to defend their land rights are subject to abuses, particularly along the Colombian border. Afro-Venezuelans remain marginalized and underrepresented among the Venezuela elite.

Women enjoy progressive rights enshrined in the 1999 constitution, as well as benefits offered under a major 2007 law. However, despite some improvements on implementation, domestic violence and rape remain common and are rarely punished in practice. The problem of trafficking in women remains inadequately addressed by the authorities. Women are poorly represented in government, with just 17 percent of the seats in the National Assembly, but they hold a number of important offices in the executive branch.

Vietnam

Political Rights: 7
Civil Liberties: 5
Status: Not Free

Population: 88,983,600
Capital: Hanoi

Ten-Year Ratings Timeline For Year Under Review (Political Rights, Civil Liberties, Status)

2003	2004	2005	2006	20076	2008	2009	2010	2011	2012
7,6NF	7,6NF	7,5NF	7,5NF	7,5NF	7,5NF	7,5NF	7,5NF	7,5NF	7,5NF

Overview: **The government in 2012 continued its crackdown on dissent, particularly online, arresting and jailing additional bloggers and online columnists. Serious economic problems—including inflation and massive debts at state-owned enterprises—reportedly fueled turmoil within the ruling Communist Party and tighter controls on discussion of high-level party activities. Also during the year, the government drafted a decree that would expand the definition of speech crimes on the internet and force internet providers to block and filter content more thoroughly.**

Vietnam won full independence from France in 1954, but it was divided into a Western-backed state in the south and a Communist-ruled state in the north. Open warfare between the two sides erupted in the mid-1960s. A 1973 peace treaty officially ended the war, but fighting did not cease until 1975, when the north completed its conquest of the south. Vietnam was formally united in 1976.

War and unsound economic policies mired Vietnam in deep poverty, but economic reforms that began in 1986 drastically transformed the country over the next two decades. Tourism became a major source of revenue, as did the export of foodstuffs and manufactured products. However, the ruling Communist Party of Vietnam (CPV) rejected any parallel political reforms that would threaten the one-party system.

In 2005 and 2006, as it sought to join the World Trade Organization (WTO), the government worked to address international concerns about its human rights record as well as domestic frustration with rampant corruption. Controls on religious groups were eased, the media were given freer rein to report on cases of graft, and freedom of expression in general improved somewhat.

However, after Vietnam secured entry into the WTO in 2007, the government embarked on an extended crackdown on peaceful dissent, steadily though not completely reversing the previous years' gains. Dozens of dissidents were arrested, and many were sentenced to lengthy prison terms. The process continued over the next several years, with a growing emphasis on government critics who expressed themselves online.

At the 11th Communist Party Congress in January 2011, party members generally approved the current policies of gradual economic opening and rejection of political reform. The congress chose hard-liner Nguyen Phú Trong as CPV general secretary and picked officials with strong security and military ties for other top positions, sidelining some more moderate figures.

Tightly controlled elections for the one-party National Assembly were held in May 2011, with the CPV taking 454 seats, officially vetted nonparty members securing 42 seats, and self-nominated candidates garnering the remaining four. In July 2011, the legislature approved Nguyen Tan Dung, the prime minister since 2006, for another term, and elected Truong Tan Sang as the new state president.

In 2012 there were numerous reports of power struggles within the CPV over how to handle the country's growing economic problems, which included high inflation, capital flight, revelations of huge debts at state-owned enterprises, and the September arrest of prominent banking mogul Lý Xuân Hai for alleged financial crimes. Many analysts argued that the banker's arrest was itself part of the power struggle, with certain party factions using it to pressure his allies in government.

Also during the year, the authorities continued to punish dissidents. Among other cases, the government in May tried four Catholic activists for distributing prodemocracy material; by year's end, three had been convicted and sentenced to between 18 and 42 months in jail. Also in May, the courts rejected appeals by human rights activists Ho Thi Bích Khuong and Nguyen Trung Tôn, upholding prison sentences—five and two years, respectively—they received in December 2011 for "conducting propaganda against the Socialist Republic of Vietnam." Separately, in September, the courts sentenced three bloggers to between 4 and 12 years in prison; they belonged to the Free Journalists Club, a group of writers who focused on political reforms and civil liberties and posted their work online.

Vietnam's territorial dispute with China over the Spratly and Paracel Islands in the South China Sea escalated in 2012, with each side taking steps to solidify its claims. For its part, Vietnam passed legislation in June that reasserted its sovereignty over the islands, and the authorities allowed rare protests against China in July. Meanwhile, the United States continued to upgrade its defense ties with Vietnam despite concerns about the country's poor human rights record.

Political Rights and Civil Liberties: Vietnam is not an electoral democracy. The CPV, the sole legal political party, controls politics and the government, and its Central Committee is the top decision-making body. The National Assembly, whose 500 members are elected to five-year terms, generally follows CPV dictates. The Vietnam Fatherland Front, essentially an arm of the CPV, vets all candidates. The president, elected by the National Assembly for a five-year term, appoints the prime minister, who is confirmed by the legislature.

Corruption and abuse of office are serious problems. Although senior CPV and government officials have acknowledged growing public discontent, they have mainly responded with a few high-profile prosecutions of corrupt officials and private individuals rather than comprehensive reforms. Government decisions are made with little transparency, and revelations of contracts with Chinese and other foreign companies for major mining or development projects have generated considerable controversy. In 2012, according to many analysts, Prime Minister Nguyen Tan Dung came under intense criticism from fellow party leaders because of the expansion of corruption at state-owned enterprises since he took office in 2006.

The government tightly controls the media, silencing critics through the courts and other means of harassment. A 1999 law requires journalists to pay damages to groups or individuals found to have been harmed by press articles, even if the reports are accurate. A 2006 decree imposes fines on journalists for denying revolutionary achievements, spreading "harmful" information, or exhibiting "reactionary ideology." Foreign media representatives in theory cannot travel outside Hanoi without government approval, though they often do in practice. The CPV or state entities control all broadcast media. Although satellite television is officially restricted to senior officials, international hotels, and foreign businesses, many homes and businesses have satellite dishes. All print media outlets are owned by or are under the effective control of the CPV, government organs, or the army.

The government restricts internet use through legal and technical means. A 2003 law bans the receipt and distribution of antigovernment e-mail messages, websites considered "reactionary" are blocked, and owners of domestic websites must submit their content for official approval. Internet cafés must register the personal information of and record the sites visited by users. Internet-service providers face fines and closure for violating censorship rules. In 2012, the government drafted a new Decree on Management, Provision, and Use of Internet Services and Information on the Network that would tighten restrictions on online criticism of the party and government. Internet monitoring organizations expressed concern that the decree, if enacted, would force internet companies, both Vietnamese and foreign, to cooperate in identifying users who could then be prosecuted. Vietnamese bloggers and writers reported that the government's firewalls and other obstructions were becoming more sophisticated than in previous years, making them harder to evade through proxy servers.

Religious freedom remains restricted, having declined somewhat after a series of improvements in the mid-2000s. All religious groups and most individual clergy members must join a party-controlled supervisory body and obtain permission for most activities. The Roman Catholic Church can now select its own bishops and priests, but they must be approved by the government. Many restrictions on charitable activities have been lifted, and clergy enjoy greater freedom to travel domestically and internationally. However, harassment, arrests, and occasional attacks directed at religious minorities, activists, and Falun Gong practitioners continue to occur. Several Catholic organizations have been at the forefront of advocating for reform online and through leaflets, and in 2012 Catholic groups reported that authorities were still holding at least 17 Catholic activists who had been arrested in 2011 for advocating democracy; only fourteen apparently had come to trial by the end of 2012, but even that number was unclear because of the secretive nature of the trials.

Academic freedom is limited. University professors must refrain from criticizing government policies and adhere to party views when teaching or writing on political topics. Although citizens enjoy more freedom in private discussions than in the past, the authorities continue to punish open criticism of the state.

Freedoms of association and assembly are tightly restricted. Organizations must apply for official permission to obtain legal status and are closely regulated and monitored by the government. A small but active community of nongovernmental groups promotes environmental conservation, land rights, women's development, and public health. Human rights organizations and other private groups with rights-oriented agendas are banned.

The Vietnam General Conference of Labor (VGCL), closely tied to the CPV, is the only legal labor federation. All trade unions are required to join the VGCL. However, in recent years, the government has permitted hundreds of independent "labor associations" without formal union status to represent workers at individual firms and in some service industries. Farmer and worker protests against local government abuses, including land confiscations and unfair or harsh working conditions, have become more common. The central leadership often responds by pressuring local governments and businesses to comply with tax laws, environmental regulations, and wage agreements. Enforcement of labor laws covering child labor, workplace safety, and other issues remains poor. Critics allege that the government has intentionally kept minimum wages low to attract foreign investment, although wages have been rising in practice as multinational companies migrate to Vietnam due to labor unrest in China.

Vietnam's judiciary is subservient to the CPV, which controls courts at all levels. Defendants have a constitutional right to counsel, but lawyers are scarce, and many are reluctant to take on human rights and other sensitive cases for fear of harassment and retribution—including arrest—by the state. Defense attorneys cannot call or question witnesses and are rarely permitted to request leniency for their clients. Police can hold individuals in administrative detention for up to two years on suspicion of threatening national security. The police are known to abuse suspects and prisoners, and prison conditions are poor. Many political prisoners remain behind bars, and political detainees are often held incommunicado. In July 2012, Human Rights Watch reported that drug detention centers, which are supposed to offer noninvasive and voluntary treatment to drug users, have effectively become centers for torture and punishment in which users are beaten, subjected to forced labor, and shocked with electricity, among other abuses.

Ethnic minorities, who often adhere to minority religions as well, face discrimination in mainstream society, and some local officials restrict their access to schooling and jobs. Minorities generally have little input on development projects that affect their livelihoods and communities.

Land disputes have become more frequent as the government seizes property to lease to domestic and foreign investors. Affected residents and farmers rarely find redress in the courts, and their street protests often result in state harassment and arrests.

Women hold 122 seats in the National Assembly. Women generally have equal access to education and are treated similarly in the legal system as men. Although economic opportunities have grown for women, they continue to face discrimination in wages and promotion. Many women are victims of domestic violence, and thousands each year are trafficked internally and externally and forced into prostitution.

Yemen

Political Rights: 6
Civil Liberties: 6
Status: Not Free

Population: 25,569,300
Capital: Sanaa

Ten-Year Ratings Timeline For Year Under Review (Political Rights, Civil Liberties, Status)

2003	2004	2005	2006	2007	2008	2009	2010	2011	2012
5,5PF	5,5PF	5,5PF	5,5PF	5,5PF	5,5PF	6,5NF	6,5NF	6,6NF	6,6NF

Overview: **The 33-year reign of President Ali Abdullah Saleh ended in February 2012, and Vice President Abdu Rabu Mansur Hadi was chosen as his successor in uncontested presidential elections. A political transition agreement between Yemen's government and the opposition set the stage for a National Dialogue Conference in early 2013 and for elections in 2014. Sectarian clashes between Shiite Houthi rebels, the Yemeni military, and Sunni Islamists continued in northern Yemen, while a separatist movement and militant Islamic groups vied for control in the south. Both terrorism and a counterterrorism campaign marked by the use of American drone strikes against alleged al-Qaeda militants intensified throughout the year.**

For centuries after the advent of Islam, a series of dynastic imams controlled most of northern Yemen and parts of the south. The Ottoman Empire exercised some influence over Yemeni territory from the 16th to the early 20th century, and the British controlled the southern portion of the country, including the port of Aden, beginning in the 19th century.

After the reigning imam was ousted in a 1960s civil war and the British left the south in 1967, Yemen remained divided into two countries: the Yemen Arab Republic (North Yemen) and the People's Democratic Republic of Yemen (South Yemen). The two states ultimately unified in 1990, and northern forces put down a southern attempt to secede in 1994. In the face of widespread poverty and illiteracy, tribal influences that limited the central government's authority in certain parts of the country, a heavily armed citizenry, and the threat of Islamist terrorism, Yemen took limited steps to improve political rights and civil liberties.

In the 2003 parliamentary elections, the General People's Congress (GPC) party took 238 lower house seats. The two main opposition parties, the Islamist party Islah and the Yemeni Socialist Party, captured 46 and 8 seats, respectively.

In 2006, Yemen held its second presidential election since unification and the first in which a serious opposition candidate challenged the incumbent. President Ali Abdullah Saleh—who first came to power as president of North Yemen in 1978—was reelected with 77 percent of the vote, while his main opponent, Faisal Ben Shamlan, was supported by a coalition of Islamist and other opposition parties and received 22 percent of the vote. The GPC was victorious in concurrent provincial and local council elections.

In May 2008, Yemen held its first-ever elections for 20 governorships, which had previously been appointed. Opposition groups refused to participate, claiming electoral manipulation by the government. Progovernment candidates were elected in 17 of the 20 provinces that participated, and independents won in the remaining three. One province did not hold elections due to protests by unemployed Yemenis.

Tensions between the government and the opposition escalated in late 2008. The opposition Joint Meeting Parties (JMP)—a coalition that included the Yemeni Socialist Party and Islah—threatened to boycott parliamentary elections scheduled for April 2009. The two sides agreed in February 2009 to postpone the vote by two years pending the outcome of a national dialogue. Yemen's opposition grew increasingly frustrated in 2010, as Saleh ignored calls for electoral reform and appeared set on installing his son, Ahmed, as his successor.

Any possibility for elections in 2011 was upended after Yemenis launched a sustained protest campaign in January to call for Saleh's immediate ouster. The demonstrations started in the capital, Sanaa, and quickly spread to other parts of the country. In March, the parliament approved a set of emergency laws giving the president sweeping powers to imprison critics and censor speech. The laws suspended constitutional protections, outlawed protests, and gave security forces the power to arrest and detain without judicial review. Hundreds of thousands of Yemenis repeatedly took to the streets between February and June and in September in antigovernment demonstrations coordinated by young activists and eventually supported by the JMP.

In spite of high-profile defections from the government and military, the president retained some pillars of support. Pro-Saleh security services and military units used deadly violence in attempts to break up opposition protests, including sniper fire, shellings, and even airstrikes. Yemen's Ministry of Human Rights estimated that 2,000 people were killed as a result of the political crisis over the course of the year. Tribal groups, urban militias, and other anti-Saleh forces, including rogue army general Ali Mohsen al-Ahmar and his troops, also resorted to violence to oust Saleh and protect their own interests.

Under sustained pressure from the United States, the United Nations, and the Gulf Cooperation Council, Saleh signed a Saudi-brokered agreement in November 2011 that transferred his powers to Yemen's vice president, Abdu Rabu Mansur Hadi, in exchange for immunity from prosecution for his role in the violent crackdown during the 2011 demonstrations. A unity cabinet with both GPC and JMP ministers was formed in early December. In February 2012, Yemeni voters selected Hadi, who ran unopposed, as the country's new president.

As part of the transitional agreement, the Yemeni government and the opposition committed to holding a National Dialogue Conference in November 2012, which was subsequently postponed until early 2013. New presidential and parliamentary elections are tentatively scheduled for early 2014.

Throughout much of 2012, Hadi struggled to consolidate his political authority even as large-scale street protests and anti-demonstration violence ceased. Yemen's political stability was adversely affected by meddling by Saleh and his supporters within the military, unrest among autonomous tribal groups, a restive southern secessionist movement, a seven-year-old rebel movement rooted in the Zaidi Shiite Muslim community of the northern province of Saada, and Sunni Islamist militant groups affiliated with al-Qaeda. Hadi took steps to address Saleh's lingering influence within the military by restructuring the army and dismissing military leaders closely related to Saleh, including his son, brother, and one of his nephews.

The United States intensified its campaign of drone strikes against suspected al-Qaeda militants throughout the year, carrying out 25 confirmed attacks during 2012. The attacks, which killed a number of alleged terrorists along with an unknown number of civilians, proved ineffective at eroding al-Qaeda's presence and likely led to further radicalization.

Political Rights and Civil Liberties: Yemen is not an electoral democracy. Elections have been marred by flaws including vote-buying, the partisanship of public officials and the military, and exploitation of state control over key media platforms. The original six-year mandate of the current parliament expired in 2009, and elections were postponed again amid the turmoil of 2011. The political system has long been dominated by the ruling GPC party, and there are few limits on the authority of the executive branch. The president is elected for seven-year terms, and appoints the 111 members of the largely advisory upper house of parliament, the Majlis al-Shura (Consultative Council). The 301 members of the lower house, the House of Representatives, are elected to serve six-year terms. Provincial councils and governors are also elected.

Yemen's relatively well-developed and experienced opposition parties have historically been able to wring some concessions from the government.

Corruption is endemic. Despite recent efforts by the government to fight graft, Yemen lacks most legal safeguards against conflicts of interest. Auditing and investigative bodies are not sufficiently independent of executive authorities. Yemen was ranked 156 out of 176 countries surveyed in Transparency International's 2012 Corruption Perceptions Index.

The government does not respect freedoms of expression and the press. Article 103 of the Press and Publications Law bans direct personal criticism of the head of state and publication of material that "might spread a spirit of dissent and division among the people" or that "leads to the spread of ideas contrary to the principles of the Yemeni Revolution, [is] prejudicial to national unity or [distorts] the image of the Yemeni, Arab, or Islamic heritage." The state maintains a monopoly over terrestrial television and radio. Yemen's most popular newspaper, *Al-Ayyam*, was forcibly closed by the government in 2009 and remained closed in 2012. *Al-Ayyam* and other publications had been targeted for their reporting on the southern secessionist movement. The crisis of 2011 led to multiple raids or attacks by progovernment forces on various news outlets, including the bureaus of foreign satellite television broadcasters like Al-Jazeera. Copies of print media were frequently seized during distribution, and a number of journalists faced intimidation, arrest, and physical violence. Yemeni sources, including the Yemeni Journalist Syndicate and the Center for the Rehabilitation and Protection of Freedom of the Press, estimated nearly 500 cases of government harassment against local journalists during the first half of 2011. The Sanaa-based Freedom Foundation recorded accounts of dozens of attacks against journalists in the first half of 2012. In a controversial case, Abdulelah Haider Shaye, who was arrested and convicted in 2011 of allegedly having ties to al-Qaeda, remained imprisoned in 2012 despite having been pardoned by then-president Saleh shortly after his conviction. His continued imprisonment is the result of pressure from the U.S. government; Shaye had reported on American responsibility for military strikes that killed civilians. Access to the internet is not widespread, and the authorities block websites they deem offensive.

The constitution states that Islam is the official religion and declares Sharia (Islamic law) to be the source of all legislation. Yemen has few non-Muslim religious minorities, and their rights are generally respected in practice. The government has imposed some restrictions on religious activity in the context of the rebellion in the northern province of Saada. Mosques' hours of operation have been limited in the area, and imams suspected of extremism have been removed. Strong politicization of campus life, including tensions between supporters of the ruling GPC and the opposition Islah party, infringes on academic freedom at universities.

Yemenis have historically enjoyed some freedom of assembly, with periodic restrictions and sometimes deadly interventions by the government. The 2011 protest movement posed a serious challenge to the government's tolerance for public dissent. In spite of brutal violence, protesters persisted in taking to the streets, and continuously occupied certain locations in the capital and other major cities. Over the past four years, southern Yemenis have mounted growing protests to challenge the government's alleged corruption and abuse of power, the marginalization of southerners in the political system, and the government's inability to address pressing social and economic concerns. The protest movement has in the past called for secession by the south, although several of the movement's leaders agreed to participate in the National Dialogue Conference now set for 2013. Smaller protests continued in 2012 mostly against U.S. policy and influence in the country. In September, hundreds of protestors stormed the U.S. embassy in Sanaa in response to the Islamophobic film, *The Innocence of Muslims*.

Freedom of association is constitutionally guaranteed. Several thousand nongovernmental organizations work in the country, although their ability to operate is restricted in practice. The law acknowledges the right of workers to form and join trade unions, but some critics claim that the government and ruling party elements have increased efforts to control the affairs of these organizations. Virtually all unions belong to a single labor federation, and the government is empowered to veto collective bargaining agreements. In February 2012, employees at the state-owned oil company PetroMasila staged a short strike demanding pay owed to them by the government. The work stoppage temporarily interrupted the production of around 160,000 barrels of oil a day.

The judiciary is nominally independent, but it is susceptible to interference from the executive branch. Authorities have a poor record on enforcing judicial rulings, particularly those issued against prominent tribal or political leaders. Lacking an effective court system, citizens often resort to tribal forms of justice or direct appeals to executive authorities. Arbitrary detention is partly the result of inadequate training for law enforcement officers and a lack of political will on the part of senior government officials to eliminate the problem. Security forces affiliated with the Political Security Office (PSO) and the Ministry of the Interior torture and abuse detainees, and PSO prisons are not closely monitored. As part of the November 2011 agreement for him to step down from power, Ali Abdullah Saleh was granted immunity from prosecution for his role in the country's deadly crackdown in 2011.

Yemen is relatively ethnically and racially homogeneous. However, the Akhdam, a small minority group, live in poverty and face social discrimination. Several years of sectarian strife continued in 2012 with repeated clashes in northern Yemen throughout the year between Shiite Houthi rebels and Sunni Islamists, often backed by the state as well as by Saudi Arabia. Thousands of refugees seeking relief from war and poverty in the Horn of Africa are smuggled annually into Yemen, where they are routinely subjected to theft, abuse, and even murder.

Women continue to face discrimination in several aspects of life. A woman must obtain permission from her husband or father to receive a passport and travel abroad, cannot confer citizenship on a foreign-born spouse, and can transfer Yemeni citizenship to their children only in special circumstances. Women are vastly underrepresented in elected office; there is just one woman in the lower house of parliament. School enrollment and educational attainment rates for girls fall far behind those for boys. Yemen's penal code allows lenient sentences for those convicted of "honor crimes"—assaults or killings of women by family members for alleged immoral behavior. In April 2008, the parliament voted down legislation that would have banned female genital mutilation.

Zambia

Political Rights: 3
Civil Liberties: 4
Status: Partly Free

Population: 13,711,000
Capital: Lusaka

Ten-Year Ratings Timeline For Year Under Review (Political Rights, Civil Liberties, Status)

2003	2004	2005	2006	2007	2008	2009	2010	2011	2012
4,4PF	4,4PF	4,4PF	3,4PF	3,4PF	3,3PF	3,4PF	3,4PF	3,4PF	3,4PF

Overview: In its first full year in office, President Michael Sata's government began taking some outwardly positive steps to fight corruption, open up the media environment, and reform the constitution. However, it had not followed through with many concrete measures by the end of 2012. Meanwhile, Sata proved to be highly intolerant of dissenting viewpoints, using questionable legal tactics and politically motivated prosecutions against the opposition and critical journalists.

Zambia gained independence from Britain in 1964. President Kenneth Kaunda and his United National Independence Party subsequently ruled Zambia as a one-party state until free elections were held in October 1991, in which former labor leader Frederick Chiluba and his Movement for Multiparty Democracy (MMD) captured both the presidency and the National Assembly by wide margins. In the 1996 campaign, the MMD-led government manipulated the electoral process in favor of the incumbents, leading most opposition parties to boycott the polls and to an MMD victory. Dissent within the MMD, as well as protests by opposition parties and civil society, forced Chiluba to abandon an effort to change the constitution and seek a third term in 2001. Instead, the MMD nominated Levy Mwanawasa, who went on to win the 2001 elections. The MMD also captured a plurality of elected parliament seats amid charges of serious irregularities. In September 2006, Mwanawasa won a second term, and the MMD won concurrent legislative elections, with the opposition Patriotic Front (PF) placing second. The polls were deemed the freest and fairest in 15 years.

Mwanawasa died in August 2008 and was succeeded by Vice President Rupiah Banda, who went on to win an October special election. Banda's presidency was characterized by contentious politics, increasing infringements on civil liberties, and weakened anticorruption efforts. The government and MMD supporters took aggressive and violent actions against the political opposition and elements of civil society that they considered hostile to the president.

In the September 2011 presidential election, the PF's Michael Sata defeated Banda, 43 percent to 36 percent. Banda accepted the result, marking the second time in Zambian history that an incumbent peacefully surrendered the presidency after losing an election. In concurrent parliamentary elections, the PF won a plurality, taking 61 seats, to 55 for the MMD and 29 for the United Party for National Development (UPND). Although the elections were characterized by fierce campaigning, the misuse of state resources by the MMD, and isolated rioting that claimed at least two lives, the polls were deemed free and credible by international observers.

In 2012, the Sata administration made halting steps to fulfill campaign promises, including constitutional reform, anticorruption efforts, and press freedom initiatives. In April, a draft of the new constitution was unveiled, containing provisions including a requirement that a presidential candidate gain more than 50 percent of the vote to win. It would also make the electoral commission more independent and create a bill of rights. However, critics have asserted that the draft awards too much power to the president, especially regarding the appointment of key government officials. The charter's approval process has been criticized for delays and a lack of clarity in the way provincial and national consultations are conducted, as well as in the timeline for a national referendum. The final version of the constitution was scheduled to have been submitted by September; that date has been pushed back to 2013, and a referendum date has yet to be set. In September, Justice Minister Wynter Kabimba called for workshops being organized by civil society groups on the constitution-making process to be halted, on the grounds that only the government's technical committee should convene such meetings.

Under the Sata government, the climate of highly charged, polarized politics seen during the Banda administration continued. In a move condemned as politically motivated, the registrar of societies deregistered the MMD at a political party in

March because it had not paid its registration fees going back 20 years, and declared its parliamentary seats vacant. However, the MMD won a stay of the deregistration days later, and a high court judge overturned the suspension in June. Since taking office, Sata has filed a number of defamation lawsuits against his critics, including UPND leader Hakainde Hichilema and opposition news outlets.

Several by-elections were triggered during 2012 as a result of successful PF court challenges of seats it had lost in 2011, resulting in the PF gaining at least four more seats in the National Assembly at the expense of the MMD. The PF has also increased its power by encouraging MMD members to defect through offers of government posts.

Political Rights and Civil Liberties: Zambia is an electoral democracy. The long-ruling MMD relinquished control of both the presidency and the parliament in 2011, and local and international observers declared the voting to be generally free and credible. The president and the unicameral National Assembly are elected to serve concurrent five-year terms. The National Assembly includes 150 elected members, as well as 8 members appointed by the president.

The major political parties are the ruling PF, the MMD, and the UPND; the MMD was weakened considerably during 2012 due to infighting and a concerted effort by the PF to coopt its members.

Corruption is believed to be widespread, though the government of President Michael Sata has taken some steps to fight graft. In June 2010, the Global Fund to Fight AIDS, Malaria and Tuberculosis had suspended $300 million in funding, mainly out of concern over corruption in the Health Ministry, but it restored $100 million in June 2012, after several officials were fired. In April, the PF-controlled National Assembly reinserted an "abuse of office" clause into the Anti-Corruption Act, which had been removed by the MMD-dominated body in 2010. The clause allowed for the prosecution of public officials for violations such as abuse of authority or misuse of public funds, and was key to fighting government corruption. Meanwhile, Sata's administration launched corruption investigations against several former MMD ministers and officials, as well as Banda's family, and controversially reversed certain deals with foreign companies made by the MMD government on the grounds that they had been improperly awarded. However, the PF's own anticorruption credentials were called into question following cases in which party allies were acquitted of corruption. In one instance, Henry Kapoko, a distant relative of Sata, was acquitted in separate trials in November and December 2012 of engaging in theft and money laundering while he was a human resources officer at the Health Ministry; Kapoko had been involved in the scandal that triggered the Global Fund to Fight AIDS to suspend its funding. In October, however, the Anti-Corruption Commission opened ongoing corruption investigations of Justice Minister Wynter Kabimba and Defense Minister Geoffrey Mwamba, both leading members of the PF. Zambia was ranked 88 out of 176 countries surveyed in Transparency International's 2012 Corruption Perceptions Index.

Freedoms of speech and the press are constitutionally guaranteed, though the Banda government had restricted these rights in practice. Sata and the PF pledged to open up the media environment, but their accomplishments have been uneven.

One of those promises was to free the editorial boards at the public media—consisting of the widely circulated *Zambia Daily Mail* and *Times of Zambia*, as well as the Zambia National Broadcasting Corporation (ZNBC)—from government control. However, these outlets have generally continued to report along progovernment lines, and journalists practice self-censorship. The other main daily is the independent but pro-PF Post; as a result, all the major print publications now favor Sata's government. The ZNBC dominates the broadcast media, although several independent stations have the capacity to reach large portions of the population. The government has the authority to appoint the management boards of ZNBC and the Independent Broadcasting Authority, which regulates the industry and grants licenses to prospective broadcasters. Sata's government has made repeated promises to pass an access to information law, but had not done so by the end of 2012.

Independent and critical journalists continue to face intimidation from law enforcement officials and PF supporters, as well as the threat of legal action, and there have been numerous cases of attacks on journalists by opposition supporters. Sata and PF members have filed several criminal libel and defamation suits against journalists and opposition figures in response to critical stories and public statements. In one prominent case, Sata in May filed a defamation suit against UPND leader Hakainde Hichilema; Lloyd Himaambo, editor of the critical website *Zambian Watchdog*; and Richard Sakala, editor of the independent opposition *Daily Nation* newspaper, in connection with a May press release issued by Hichilema in which he accused Sata of corruption. The two media outlets—which were the subject of several other similar lawsuits in 2012—were targeted for publishing stories about the press release. The case was ongoing at year's end. Also in May, the *Zambian Watchdog* claimed to have suffered harassment and distributed-denial-of-service (DDoS) attacks in response to its reporting.

Constitutionally protected religious freedom is respected in practice. Sata became the country's first Catholic president in 2011. The government does not restrict academic freedom.

Under the Public Order Act, police must receive a week's notice before all demonstrations. While the law does not require permits, the police have frequently broken up "illegal" protests because the organizers lacked permits. The police can choose where and when rallies are held, as well as who can address them. The opposition has alleged that Sata's government often employs the Public Order Act to break up its protests. Nongovernmental organizations (NGOs) are required to register and reregister every five years. The law also established a board to provide guidelines and regulate NGO activity in the country.

The law provides for the right to join unions, strike, and bargain collectively. Zambia's trade unions are among Africa's strongest, and the Zambia Congress of Trade Unions operates democratically without state interference. However, there is significant labor exploitation in some sectors of the economy. Tensions between workers and management at Chinese-owned mines have been increasing. Labor abuses in Chinese-operated copper mines, including unsafe working conditions, resistance to unionization, and much lower pay than at other Zambian mines have been reported. In August 2012, a Chinese mine manager was killed during a protest at the Collum Coal Mine in which workers were demanding that their wages be increased to equal Zambia's new national minimum wage for laborers.

Judicial independence is guaranteed by law. However, Sata's critics charge that he has interfered in the judiciary. Upon taking office, Sata replaced most top judges and judicial officials, alleging that the system was corrupt and needed reform. In April 2012, Sata suspended three top judges for misconduct, a move that critics alleged was in retribution for a judgment they had issued against the president's allies. Legislation passed in 2009 allowed the executive to increase the number of judges serving on the High and Supreme Courts. However, the courts lack qualified personnel and significant trial delays are common. Pretrial detainees are sometimes held for years under harsh conditions, and many of the accused lack access to legal aid owing to limited resources. In rural areas, customary courts of variable quality and consistency—whose decisions often conflict with the constitution and national law—decide many civil matters.

Allegations of police corruption and brutality are widespread, and security forces have generally operated with impunity. There are reports of forced labor, abuse of inmates by authorities, and deplorable health conditions in Zambia's prisons. The death penalty was included in the new draft constitution, but a network of civil society organizations is lobbying for its removal.

Barotseland, a traditionally poor and marginalized region in western Zambia, has repeatedly demanded to secede from Zambia. Sata had pledged, if elected, to honor the 1964 Barotseland Agreement, which gave the region limited local self-governance and provided for future discussions of greater autonomy or independence. In March 2012, Sata reneged on his campaign promise, and Barotseland's governing council subsequently declared independence. In October, Barotseland's king inaugurated a caretaker government. Later that month, reports emerged that prison guards and paramilitary police severely beat jailed Barotse activists.

Societal discrimination remains a serious obstacle to women's rights. Women won just 17 of the 150 elected seats in the National Assembly in the September 2011 polls; 2 were later appointed to the 20-member cabinet, and 5 to the 11-member Supreme Court. Women are denied full economic participation, and rural, poor women often require male consent to obtain credit. Discrimination against women is especially prevalent in customary courts, where they are considered subordinate with respect to property, inheritance, and marriage. Domestic violence and rape are major problems, and traditional norms inhibit many women from reporting assaults. Consensual sexual activity between members of the same sex is illegal and punishable by prison sentences of up to 15 years. There are no registered civil society organizations that advocate for LGBT (lesbian, gay, bisexual, and transgender) rights. People living with HIV/AIDS routinely face discrimination in society and for employment.

Zimbabwe

Political Rights: 6
Civil Liberties: 6
Status: Not Free

Population: 12,620,000
Capital: Harare

Ten-Year Ratings Timeline For Year Under Review (Political Rights, Civil Liberties, Status)

2003	2004	2005	2006	2007	2008	2009	2010	2011	2012
6,6NF	7,6NF	7,6NF	7,6NF	7,6NF	7,6NF	6,6NF	6,6NF	6,6NF	6,6NF

Overview: Halting progress toward a new constitution continued in 2012, and the final draft was expected to reduce the power of the presidency and clear the way for elections in 2013. Low-level political violence persisted, as did the harassment of civic activists and journalists by both state and nonstate actors. Positive developments during the year included the issuance of two new radio licenses and the recovery of the domestic economy. In addition, the European Union suspended sanctions on aid to the government and on scores of individuals. The government moved ahead with efforts to achieve 51 percent indigenous ownership of mining assets, while accusations of graft and rights abuses continued to mar the country's diamond sector.

In 1965, a white-minority regime in what was then colonial Southern Rhodesia unilaterally declared independence from Britain. A guerrilla war led by black nationalist groups, as well as sanctions and diplomatic pressure from Britain and the United States, contributed to the end of white-minority rule in 1979 and the recognition of an independent Zimbabwe in 1980. Robert Mugabe and the Zimbabwe African National Union–Patriotic Front (ZANU-PF), first brought to power in relatively democratic elections, have since ruled the country.

Zimbabwe was relatively stable in its first years of independence, but from 1983 to 1987, the Shona-dominated government violently suppressed opposition among the Ndebele ethnic minority, and between 10,000 and 20,000 civilians were killed by government forces. Widespread political unrest in the 1990s, spurred by increased authoritarianism and economic decline, led to the creation in 1999 of the opposition Movement for Democratic Change (MDC), an alliance of trade unions and other civil society groups. However, President Mugabe and ZANU-PF claimed victory over the MDC in parliamentary elections in 2000 and 2005, as well as in a 2002 presidential poll. All three elections were seriously marred by political violence aimed at real or perceived MDC supporters, fraudulent electoral processes, and the ruling party's abuse of state resources and state-run media. Security forces violently crushed mass protests and labor actions called by the MDC and its leader, Morgan Tsvangirai during these years.

The 2005 parliamentary elections left ZANU-PF with a two-thirds majority and the ability to amend the constitution. It subsequently enacted amendments that nationalized all land, brought all schools under state control, and reintroduced an upper legislative house, the Senate. The MDC split over whether to participate in November 2005 elections for the upper chamber, allowing ZANU-PF to win an overwhelming majority amid voter turnout of less than 20 percent. That same year, the government implemented a slum-clearance effort known as Operation Murambatsvina, which means "drive out the trash" in the Shona language. It resulted in the destruction of thousands of informal businesses and dwellings as well as thousands of arrests. According to the United Nations, approximately 700,000 people were made homeless, and another 2.4 million were directly or indirectly affected. Initially moved into transit camps near cities, many displaced residents were forced to return to the rural areas designated on their national identity cards. Analysts maintain that the operation, billed as part of a law-and-order campaign, actually targeted urban MDC strongholds.

Violence before the concurrent parliamentary and presidential elections in March 2008, though serious, was less severe than during prior elections in the 2000s. In the parliamentary polls, the main, Tsvangirai-led faction of the MDC won 99 seats in the lower house, followed by ZANU-PF with 97 seats and a breakaway MDC faction, led by Arthur Mutambara, with 10. The results denied ZANU-PF a legislative majority for the first time in the country's 28-year history. In the Senate, ZANU-PF took half of the 60 elected seats, but it also controlled the chamber's 33 unelected seats. The MDC and its splinter faction won 24 and 6 Senate seats, respectively. Meanwhile, Tsvangirai outpolled Mugabe, 47.9 percent to 43.2 percent, in the presidential vote, requiring a runoff between the two. The MDC accused the Zimbabwe Electoral Commission (ZEC) of fraud and claimed Tsvangirai had won the election outright with 50.3 percent of the vote, citing a parallel vote count by a network of civic groups.

Between the March voting and the presidential runoff scheduled for June, ZANU-PF militias and state security forces carried out a brutal campaign of violence aimed at punishing and intimidating MDC members and their suspected supporters in civil society and the press. Tsvangirai ultimately withdrew from the runoff contest, allowing the unopposed Mugabe to win 85 percent of the vote amid low turnout and many spoiled ballots. Political violence continued after the election. According to international and domestic human rights organizations, some 200 MDC activists and supporters were killed over the course of 2008, about 5,000 were tortured, and more than 10,000 required medical treatment for injuries.

In September 2008, ZANU-PF and the MDC reached a power-sharing agreement brokered by the Southern African Development Community (SADC)—known as the Global Political Agreement, or GPA—that allowed Mugabe to remain president, created the post of prime minister for Tsvangirai, and distributed ministries to ZANU-PF (14, including defense, state security, and justice), Tsvangirai's MDC faction (13, including finance, health, and constitutional and parliamentary affairs), and Mutambara's faction (3). A constitutional amendment creating the post of prime minister was enacted in February 2009, and the new government was sworn in that month.

In practice, Mugabe retained control of the powerful executive branch, and in 2009 and 2010, he unilaterally appointed the central bank governor, the attorney general, and the police commissioner, as well as a number of senior judges and diplomats. Mugabe also refused to swear in some MDC ministers and all of its provincial governors, appointing ZANU-PF loyalists instead. Nevertheless, the economy began to recover after the government abandoned the Zimbabwean dollar—whose inflation rate had reached an astounding 13 billion percent in 2008—in favor of the South African and U.S. currencies in early 2009. Some international donors resumed their support under the power-sharing government, and schools and hospitals reopened.

The GPA set a February 2011 deadline for the adoption of a new constitution, but the draft had yet to be finalized by the end of 2012. ZANU-PF opposed the latest draft's provisions limiting the president's executive powers (including over security forces and the judiciary), diluting the authority of traditional leaders, and allowing Parliament to appoint provincial governors. It was also unclear how the ZEC would fund a constitutional referendum and subsequent parliamentary and presidential elections once a final draft was issued. Nevertheless, negotiations proceeded more peacefully in 2012 than previous years, and most parties predicted that an acceptable draft would be approved in early 2013.

Despite a 2011 decision by the Kimberley Process—an international mechanism designed to prevent the use of diamonds to fund armed conflicts—to lift a suspension of Zimbabwean diamond exports from a number of mines in the Marange diamond fields, allegations of graft and human rights abuses at mines continued to be reported in 2012. Some of the mines were controlled by security forces or powerful generals. A November report by Partnership Africa Canada (PAC) alleged that at least $2 billion in diamonds had been stolen from Marange by military and government officials, while Finance Minister Tendai Biti of the MDC claimed in July that the treasury had received only $46 million out of an expected $600 million in diamond revenues in 2011–12, an assertion that was denied by the state-owned Zimbabwe Mining Development Corporation.

Zimbabwe's economy continued to stabilize in 2012, though growth slowed significantly to 4.4 percent, from 9.3 percent in 2011, due to a decline in agricultural output. Citing political and economic progress, in February the European Union (EU) lifted sanctions on the assets and travel of 51 ZANU-PF officials and 20 government entities, though sanctions remained on Mugabe and over 100 other senior ZANU-PF members. In July, the EU suspended sanctions on providing aid to the Zimbabwean government.

Political Rights and Civil Liberties: Zimbabwe is not an electoral democracy. President Robert Mugabe and the ZANU-PF party have dominated the political landscape since independence in 1980, overseeing 18 amendments to the constitution that have expanded presidential power and decreased executive accountability. Presidential and legislative elections in March 2008 were marred by flawed voter registration and balloting, biased media coverage, and the use of state resources—including food aid—to bribe and threaten voters. The period leading up to the presidential runoff in June 2008 featured accelerated violence against the opposition, prompting a UN Security Council resolution declaring the impossibility of a fair poll. Mugabe ultimately ran unopposed, and the vote was declared illegitimate by observers from the African Union and the SADC. In keeping with the GPA, though much delayed, Parliament passed the Electoral Amendment Act in September 2012, reconstituting the ZEC with new, more independent commissioners. The ZEC's pre-GPA staff remained largely intact, however. The expectation of elections in the first half of 2013 left little time to reform Zimbabwe's voter rolls, which were allegedly riddled with millions of "ghost voters," including children and people aged over 100.

Since the restoration of the Senate in 2005, Zimbabwe has had a bicameral legislature. A 2007 constitutional amendment removed appointed seats from the House of Assembly, increased the size of the House of Assembly to 210 elected seats and the Senate to 60 elected seats, and redrew constituency boundaries. Commentators suggested that the new boundaries were intended to dilute the urban vote and reduce opposition representation in the House. In the Senate, at least 33 additional seats are still held by traditional chiefs, presidential appointees, and other unelected officials. The president and elected lawmakers serve five-year terms. A 2009 constitutional amendment stemming from the GPA created the posts of prime minister and two deputy prime ministers while retaining the presidency, leaving the country with a split executive branch. In practice, the Joint Operations Command, composed of the heads of the security services, continues to play a central role in decision-making.

In 2012, MDC-affiliated ministers and officials continued to face obstruction and harassment from state entities controlled by ZANU-PF. Most notably, in October 2012 Energy Minister Elton Mangoma was arrested and briefly detained for insulting Mugabe in a speech at a political rally. In December, 24 of 29 MDC members who had been detained for 19 months on charges of murdering a Harare policeman were released on bail.

State-sponsored political violence is a serious and chronic problem, though it declined somewhat in 2012. In general, MDC politicians, activists, and supporters are subject to harassment, assault, and arbitrary detention by security forces and militias allied with ZANU-PF. Some attacks have also been perpetrated by affiliates of the MDC. The Zimbabwe Elections Support Network continued to report in 2012 that ZANU-PF militants were setting up bases in disputed rural voting districts. In October, ZANU-PF-affiliated militias reportedly began attacking MDC-linked businesses as well as development projects and social-service providers in MDC-led municipalities. The Zimbabwe Human Rights Commission (ZHRC) Act, adopted that month, empowered the new ZHRC to investigate and recommend responses to human rights abuses committed only after February 2009; in December, commission chairman Reginald Austin resigned, citing inhibiting laws and a lack of resources.

Historically, Zimbabwe had a much more professional and less corrupt civil service than most other countries in sub-Saharan Africa. Since 2000, however, corruption has become endemic, including at the highest levels of government. The collapse in public-service delivery and the politicization of food and agricultural aid has made the problem ubiquitous at the local level. In 2011, the World Bank reported that almost half of Zimbabwe's civil servants were either not qualified for their positions or not working at all. The bulk of proceeds from the Marange diamond fields have bypassed the national treasury, fueling suspicions of official enrichment and patronage. Zimbabwe was ranked 163 out of 176 countries surveyed in Transparency International's 2012 Corruption Perceptions Index.

Freedom of the press is restricted. The country's draconian legal framework—including the Access to Information and Protection of Privacy Act (AIPPA), the Official Secrets Act, the Public Order and Security Act (POSA), and the Criminal

Law (Codification and Reform) Act—has yet to be reformed. In general, these laws restrict who may work as a journalist, require journalists to register with the state, severely limit what they may publish, and mandate harsh penalties, including long prison sentences, for violators. Journalists are routinely charged with defamation by government officials and powerful individuals, subjecting them to arrest, detention, and onerous lawsuits. Attacks and intimidation have also been common, although less so in 2012. In October, the editor and deputy editor of the *Daily News* were arrested and briefly detained after businessman and former Reserve Bank official Munyaradzi Kereke launched a $25 million defamation suit against them over an article suggesting that the disappearance of Kereke's family was a hoax.

As mandated by the GPA, in 2010 the newly formed and quasi-independent Zimbabwe Media Commission (ZMC) replaced the state-controlled Media and Information Commission (MIC). However, former MIC head Tafataona Mahoso was appointed chief executive of the new body. The ZMC has granted a number of new licenses, including to two news agencies and the long-shuttered *Daily News*, the country's most widely read independent daily until it was closed for violating AIPPA in 2003, but restrictions remain. ZMC chairman Godfrey Majonga warned in February that foreign newspapers would be banned if they failed to register with the ZMC, and began implementing this policy in July. In May, security forces began restricting the sale of *Newsday* and the *Daily News* in politically contested rural areas, especially Mashonaland East.

The government continues to dominate the broadcast sector via the state-controlled Zimbabwe Broadcasting Corporation (ZBC) and the NewZiana news agency. Access to international news via satellite television is prohibitively expensive for most Zimbabweans. In 2009, the government lifted a ban on foreign news organizations such as the British Broadcasting Corporation, but the MIC significantly raised the accreditation fees for these outlets. Accreditation and license fees for foreign outlets were raised again in 2011, though the Broadcasting Authority of Zimbabwe (BAZ) did issue a call for private radio applications in late 2011. BAZ issued two new radio licenses in 2012, one for Star FM and the other for ZiFM Stereo, both of which are affiliated with ZANU-PF. BAZ had yet to license a single private television broadcaster by year's end. Government jamming of domestic and foreign-based shortwave radio has decreased in recent years, but is still a problem. The 2007 Interception of Communications Act empowers the state to monitor telephonic and electronic communications.

While freedom of religion has generally been respected in Zimbabwe, church attendance has become increasingly politicized, and recent years featured stark restrictions on and harassment of religious groups—particularly the mainstream Anglican Church—that are not aligned with ZANU-PF. These restrictions declined significantly after a November 2012 Supreme Court ruling returned control of Anglican Church properties to Bishop Chad Gandiya of Harare, ending a six-year campaign by excommunicated pro-Mugabe bishop Nolbert Kunonga to seize the sites.

While academics rank among the regime's most vociferous critics, academic freedom is limited. Constitutional amendments in 2005 placed all schools under state control, and education aid has often been based on parents' political loyalties. Security forces and ZANU-PF thugs harass dissident university students, who have been arrested or expelled for protesting against government policy. Teachers, especially in rural areas, are often targets of political violence. In 2011, Amnesty International reported that thousands of children evicted during Operation Murambatsvina in 2005 were still attending makeshift schools in their new settlements. About one-third of Zimbabwean girls do not attend primary school and two-thirds do not attend secondary school due to poverty, abuse, and discriminatory cultural practices.

The 2002 POSA requires police permission for public meetings and demonstrations. Such meetings are often broken up, and participants are subject to arbitrary arrest as well as attacks by ZANU-PF militias. The POSA allows police to impose arbitrary curfews and forbids criticism of the president. In 2011, police raided a meeting of civil society activists inspired by the popular uprising in Egypt, arresting 46 people and charging them with treason, which can carry the death penalty. Those charges were subsequently dropped, and in March 2012 only six of the arrested individuals were punished for "inciting public violence." They received suspended two-year jail terms and were ordered to pay $500 fines and serve 420 hours of community service.

The nongovernmental sector is active and professional, but nongovernmental organizations (NGOs) continued to face legal restrictions and extralegal harassment in 2012. The 2004 Non-Governmental Organizations Act increased scrutiny of human rights groups and explicitly prohibited them from receiving foreign funds. In February, 29 social-service NGOs in Masvingo Province were banned by Governor Titus Maluleke following accusations that they colluded with the MDC and Western governments. In July, Abel Chikomo—the frequently targeted director of the Zimbabwe Human Rights NGO Forum—was summoned to stand trial on charges of running an illegal organization, for which he had been arrested in 2011. The following month police twice raided the Harare offices of Gay and Lesbian Zimbabwe (GALZ), confiscating equipment and briefly detaining 44 members of the organization following charges that the group's director had insulted the president. Similarly, in November security forces raided the offices of the Counseling Services Unit—a registered medical organization that counsels victims of political violence and torture—and arrested five people, three of whom were held for two days, though the others were released immediately.

The Labor Relations Act allows the government to veto collective-bargaining agreements that it deems harmful to the economy. Strikes are allowed except in "essential" industries. Because the Zimbabwe Congress of Trade Unions (ZCTU) has led resistance to Mugabe's rule, it has become a particular target for repression. In recent years, Gertrude Hambira, secretary general of the General Agriculture and Plantation Workers' Union (GAPWUZ), has also been subject to focused harassment by the authorities.

Pressure from the executive branch has substantially eroded judicial independence, though the situation has improved somewhat since the GPA. The accused are often denied access to counsel and a fair, timely trial, and the government has repeatedly refused to enforce court orders. It has also replaced senior judges or pressured them to resign by stating that it could not guarantee their security; judges have been subject to extensive physical harassment. Vacancies for scores of magistrate posts have caused a backlog of tens of thousands of cases.

Security forces abuse citizens with impunity, often ignoring basic rights regarding detention, searches, and seizures. The government has taken no clear action to halt the incidence of torture and mistreatment of suspects in custody. Formed in 2009 as part of the GPA, the Joint Monitoring and Implementation Committee has helped expose abuses of power by security forces, but the body has almost no enforcement powers. Security forces have also taken on major roles in crop collection and food distribution, and both the police and the military remain heavily politicized in favor of ZANU-PF despite the GPA. Meanwhile, ZANU-PF militias operate as de facto enforcers of government policy and have committed assault, torture, rape, extralegal evictions, and extralegal executions without fear of punishment. In September 2011, in a rare exception to the prevailing impunity, a court sentenced ZANU-PF militia commander Gilbert Mavhenyengwa to 20 years in prison for the 2008 rape of the wife of an MDC supporter.

Lengthy pretrial detention remains a problem, and despite some improvements in recent years, prison conditions remain harsh and sometimes life threatening. Overcrowding and funding shortages have contributed to HIV and tuberculosis infections among inmates and poor sanitation facilities.

People living in the two Matabeleland provinces continue to suffer political and economic discrimination, and security forces often target these areas as MDC strongholds. Restrictive citizenship laws discriminate against Zimbabweans born in neighboring African countries.

The state has extensive control over travel and residence. The government has seized the passports of its domestic opponents, and foreign critics are routinely expelled or denied entry. High passport fees inhibit legal travel. At the same time, badly underfunded immigration and border authorities lack the capacity to effectively enforce travel restrictions.

Property rights are not respected. Operation Murambatsvina in 2005 entailed the eviction of hundreds of thousands of city dwellers and the destruction of thousands of residential and commercial structures, many of which had been approved by the government. Despite a government resettlement program (Operation Garikai), by 2012 the majority of victims still lacked adequate housing and had no means of redressing the destruction of their property. Most victims have moved into existing, overcrowded urban housing stock or remained in rural areas. In rural areas, the nationalization of land has left both commercial farmers and smallholders with limited security of tenure, and the lack of title to land means that they have little collateral to use for bank loans.

The 2007 Indigenization Law, which stipulates that 51 percent of shares in all companies operating in Zimbabwe must be owned by black Zimbabweans, came into effect in 2010, with September 2011 the deadline for foreign companies to submit plans on share sales to the government. Although details concerning the implementation and enforcement of the law remained murky, by year's end nearly every foreign-owned mining company had submitted an indigenization plan to the government. In July 2012, the government announced that all banks operating in country must comply with the law before June 2013. Fewer than 400 white-owned farms remain out of the 4,500 that existed when land invasions started in 2000, and any avenues of legal recourse for expropriated farmers have been closed.

Women enjoy extensive legal protections, but societal discrimination and domestic violence persist. Women serve as ministers in national and local governments and hold 32 and 24 seats in the House of Assembly and Senate, respectively. The World Health Organization has reported that Zimbabwean women's "healthy life expectancy" of 34 years is the world's shortest, largely due to the country's HIV prevalence rate, which remains one of the highest in the world. Sexual abuse is widespread, and past election periods have seen rape used as a political weapon. Female members of the opposition often face particular brutality at the hands of security forces. The prevalence of customary laws in rural areas undermines women's civil rights and access to education.

Sex between men is a criminal offense and can be punished with a fine and up to a year in prison.

Abkhazia

Political Rights: 4*
Civil Liberties: 5
Status: Partly Free

Population: 216,000

Ratings Change: Abkhazia's political rights rating improved from 5 to 4 due to genuinely competitive parliamentary elections that allowed a shift toward independent candidates and away from either government or opposition parties.

Ten-Year Ratings Timeline For Year Under Review (Political Rights, Civil Liberties, Status)

2003	2004	2005	2006	2007	2008	2009	2010	2011	2012
6,5NF	6,5NF	5,5PF	5,5PF	5,5PF	5,5PF	5,5PF	5,5PF	5,5PF	4,5PF

Overview:

President Aleksandr Ankvab survived an assassination attempt in February 2012. Four suspects were arrested in April, and a former interior minister accused of masterminding the attack reportedly committed suicide before he could be detained. In March, Abkhazia held parliamentary elections that marked a shift toward independent candidates, with only three ruling party and four opposition party candidates winning seats in the 35-member People's Assembly.

Annexed by Russia in 1864, Abkhazia became an autonomous republic within Soviet Georgia in 1930. After the 1991 collapse of the Soviet Union, Abkhazia declared its independence from Georgia in 1992, leading to a year-long war that left thousands dead and displaced more than 200,000 residents, mainly ethnic Georgians. Abkhaz forces won de facto independence for the republic in 1993, and an internationally brokered ceasefire was signed in Moscow in 1994.

Incumbent Abkhaz president Vladislav Ardzinba ran unopposed for reelection in 1999, and a reported 98 percent of voters supported independence in a concurrent referendum. Deputies loyal to Ardzinba won all 35 seats in the 2002 parliamentary elections after the opposition withdrew to protest bias by the election commission and state-backed media.

Under pressure from a powerful opposition movement, Prime Minister Gennady Gagulia resigned in April 2003 and was succeeded by Defense Minister Raul Khadjimba, though Ardzinba refused to step down as president.

An opposition candidate, former prime minister Sergei Bagapsh, defeated Khadjimba in the December 2004 presidential election, but was pressured into a January 2005 rerun with Khadjimba—who was backed by Ardzinba and Moscow—as his vice-presidential running mate. The new ticket won the rerun with 91 percent of the vote.

Members of three pro-Bagapsh parties captured more than 20 seats in the 2007 parliamentary elections, and a number of opposition candidates also won seats, despite claims that Bagapsh interfered with the electoral process.

After years of rising tension, war broke out in August 2008 between Georgian forces on one side and Russian, South Ossetian, and Abkhaz forces on the other.

Although the brief conflict centered on South Ossetia, another Russian-backed Georgian territory that had won de facto independence in the early 1990s, Abkhaz troops succeeded in capturing the Kodori Gorge, the only portion of Abkhazia still under Georgian control, and additional territory on the Georgian-Abkhaz border.

In late August, following a French-brokered ceasefire, Russia formally recognized both Abkhazia and South Ossetia as independent states, though nearly all of the international community continued to view the territories as de jure parts of Georgia. Abkhaz authorities subsequently signed a series of new military and economic agreements with Russia.

Bagapsh won reelection in December 2009, capturing more than 59 percent of the vote. Khadjimba placed a distant second with just 15 percent. Though all five candidates reportedly endorsed Russia's preeminent role in the territory, Abkhaz opposition journalists and politicians, led by Khadjimba, accused the government of ceding undue control to Moscow.

In May 2011, Bagapsh died unexpectedly after surgery, leading to a snap presidential election in August between Vice President Aleksandr Ankvab, Prime Minister Sergei Shamba, and Khadjimba, running as an opposition candidate. Amid 70 percent turnout, Ankvab won with 55 percent of the vote, followed by Shamba with 21 percent and Khadjimba with 19.5 percent. The election was considered genuinely competitive, and Moscow did not publicly endorse a candidate, but all three promised to maintain strong ties with Russia.

Ankvab survived an assassination attempt in February 2012, though two of his bodyguards were killed. Four suspects were arrested in April, one of whom was later found hanged in his cell; the other three were in pretrial detention at year's end. The alleged mastermind of the attack, former interior minister Almazbei Kchach, reportedly commited suicide before he could be detained.

Also during the year, parliamentary elections were held in March. Amid a low 44 percent turnout, only 13 candidates won majorities in the first round on March 10, requiring runoff votes for the remaining 22 seats on March 24. Six of the nine incumbents seeking reelection were defeated, including the outgoing speaker of parliament. The voting marked a shift toward independents, who captured 28 seats, compared with only 3 for the ruling United Abkhazia party and 4 for opposition parties.

As of 2012, Abkhazia's independence was recognized only by Russia, Venezuela, Nicaragua, and three small Pacific Island states.

Political Rights and Civil Liberties: Residents of Abkhazia can elect government officials, but the more than 200,000 Georgians who fled the region during the war in the early 1990s cannot vote in the elections held by the separatist government. Most ethnic Georgians who remain in Abkhazia are unable to vote in local polls, as they lack Abkhaz passports, though 9,000 passports were issued to mostly ethnic Georgian residents of Gali for the 2011 presidential election, compared with 3,000 in 2009. None of the separatist government's elections have been recognized internationally.

The 1999 constitution established a presidential system, stating that only ethnic Abkhaz can be elected to the post. The president and vice president are elected for five-year terms. The parliament, or People's Assembly, consists of 35 members elected for five-year terms from single-seat constituencies.

Corruption is believed to be extensive, and government officials are not required to provide declarations of income. In January 2011, Russia's Audit Chamber accused Abkhaz leaders of misappropriating $12 million allocated by Moscow for infrastructure development. After taking office later that year, President Aleksandr Ankvab began a campaign against official corruption, which included the dismissal of the immigration bureau's entire staff.

Local broadcast media are largely controlled by the government, which operates the Abkhaz State Television and Radio Company (AGTRK). In November 2011, the authorities granted permission to Abaza, the sole independent television station, to expand its broadcast range and cover the entire territory. All the major Russian television stations also broadcast into Abkhazia. Facing persistent opposition complaints of progovernment bias at AGTRK, Ankvab in October 2011 fired its director, who had held his post for 15 years and was seen as an impediment to reform. Ankvab also established a working group to consider deeper changes at the broadcaster, but none had been implemented by year's end.

The print media are considered more influential, consisting of several weekly newspapers. The government publication *Respublika Abkhazii* competes with two main independent papers, *Chegemskaya Pravda* and *Novaya Gazeta*.

Internet access has increased since 2008, with an estimated 25 percent of the population online. Some legal restrictions apply to both traditional and online media, including criminal libel statutes.

Religious freedom in Abkhazia is affected by the political situation. The Abkhaz Orthodox Church declared its separation from the Georgian Orthodox Church in 2009, and a number of Georgian Orthodox clerics have been expelled for alleged spying or refusal to recognize separatist authorities. In 2011, the Abkhaz church split into two factions after a group of clerics objected to the leadership's more deferential stance toward the Russian Orthodox Church. Neither faction is internationally recognized as independent from the Georgian church. Abkhazia's Muslims, who make up about 30 percent of the population, are allowed to practice freely. Jehovah's Witnesses continue to practice openly, though they were banned by a 1995 decree and have recently reported increased pressure from local authorities. In March 2012, a Witness prayer building was attacked with a grenade, causing property damage.

The Abkhaz constitution offers some protection for education in minority languages. Armenian-language schools generally operate without interference, but many of Gali's Georgian-language schools have been converted to instruction in Russian, leaving the future status of the remaining Georgian-language schools uncertain. Some ethnic Georgian students regularly travel to Georgian-controlled territory to attend classes. Ethnic Georgian residents without Abkhaz passports are restricted from attending Sukhumi State University.

Although most nongovernmental organizations (NGOs) rely on funding from outside the territory, the NGO sector exerts significant influence on government policies. Freedom of assembly is somewhat limited, but the opposition and civil society groups have mounted protests in recent years. A new opposition civic union composed of NGOs and opposition parties was established in January 2012 to demand election law and media reforms ahead of the March elections.

The judicial code is based on Russia's, and the criminal justice system suffers from chronic problems, including limited defendant access to qualified legal counsel, violations of due process, and lengthy pretrial detentions. Local NGOs have petitioned for significant judicial reform.

Gali's ethnic Georgian residents continue to suffer from widespread poverty and undefined legal status within Abkhazia. In June 2012, Abkhaz authorities blamed Georgian agents for the recent kidnapping of several Gali residents and the May murder of two security officers and a civilian in the area.

Travel and choice of residence are limited by the ongoing separatist dispute. Most ethnic Georgians who fled Abkhazia during the early 1990s live in Tbilisi and western Georgia. As many as 47,000 former Gali residents have returned to Abkhazia since 1994, with an additional 5,000 who commute between Abkhazia and Georgia, though the process of obtaining travel permits remains expensive and burdensome. An Abkhaz campaign to repatriate ethnic Abkhaz living abroad resulted in a handful of returnees in 2012, mainly from Syria and Turkey.

Ethnic Georgians are eligible for Abkhaz passports—entitling them to vote, own property, run a business, and obtain Russian citizenship and pensions—on the condition that they give up their Georgian passports, which carry significant economic and legal benefits. About 90 percent of Abkhazia's residents hold Russian passports, as Abkhaz travel documents are not internationally recognized. However, since the 2008 war, ethnic Abkhaz have had greater difficulty receiving visas to travel abroad, including to the United States and European Union countries. The U.S. government announced in June 2012 that it would recognize so-called "status-neutral" travel documents issued by Georgia since mid-2011 to residents of Abkhazia and South Ossetia. The documents, meant to ease travel for participating individuals without explicitly asserting Georgian sovereignty, were lauded internationally but opposed by Russia and Abkhazia as an attempt to challenge Russian influence.

Under a law preventing foreigners from buying Abkhaz property, ethnic Russians have been barred from acquiring residences in the territory, and some have reported that their homes have been confiscated.

Equality of opportunity and normal business activities are limited by corruption, criminal organizations, and economic reliance on Russia, which pays for half the state budget and accounts for nearly all foreign investment.

A strong NGO sector has contributed to women's involvement in business and civil society. However, Abkhaz women complain of being underrepresented in government positions, holding only 1 of the 35 legislative seats and heading just 2 of 12 government ministries.

Gaza Strip

Political Rights: 6
Civil Liberties: 6
Status: Not Free

Population: 1,763,000

Note: Whereas past editions of *Freedom in the World* featured one report for Israeli-occupied portions of the West Bank and Gaza Strip and another for Palestinian-administered portions, the latest three editions divide the territories based on geography, with one report for the West Bank and another for the Gaza Strip. As in previous years, Israel is examined in a separate report.

Ten-Year Ratings Timeline For Year Under Review (Political Rights, Civil Liberties, Status)

2003	2004	2005	2006	2007	2008	2009	2010	2011	2012
--	--	--	--	--	--	--	6,6NF	6,6NF	6,6NF

Overview: Civil liberties remained severely curtailed in the Gaza Strip in 2012, despite some loosening of religious restrictions on women in particular. A May 2011 agreement between Hamas in Gaza and Fatah in the West Bank yielded no date for overdue Palestinian elections. In November 2012, Hamas and the Israel Defense Forces engaged in eight days of fighting, in which 160 Palestinians and 6 Israelis were killed. For the first time, Hamas rockets fired from Gaza reached the cities of Tel Aviv and Jerusalem. Under an Egyptian-brokered ceasefire, Israel eased its blockade on Gaza in return for commitments by Hamas to halt rocket attacks. At the end of November, the Fatah-led Palestine Liberation Organization won recognition for Palestine as a nonmember observer state at the UN General Assembly, a move that Hamas supported.

The Gaza Strip was demarcated as part of a 1949 armistice agreement between Israel and Egypt following the 1948 Arab-Israeli war. Populated mostly by Palestinian Arab refugees, the territory was occupied by Egypt until 1967. Israel conquered Gaza, along with the West Bank and other territories, in the 1967 Six-Day War, and ruled it thereafter through a military administration.

In 1968, Israel began establishing Jewish settlements in Gaza, a process regarded as illegal by most of the international community. Israel maintained that the settlements were legal since under international law Gaza was a disputed territory. In what became known as the first intifada (uprising), beginning in 1987, Palestinians living in the West Bank and Gaza staged massive demonstrations, acts of civil disobedience, and attacks against Israeli settlers and Israel Defense Forces (IDF) troops in the territories, as well as attacks within Israel proper. Israel and Yasser Arafat's Palestine Liberation Organization (PLO) reached an agreement in 1993 that provided for a PLO renunciation of terrorism and recognition of Israel, Israeli troop withdrawals, and phased Palestinian autonomy in Gaza and the West Bank. In 1994, the newly formed Palestinian Authority (PA) took control of most of the Gaza Strip; the PA also came to control about 40 percent of the West Bank.

As negotiations on a final settlement and the creation of a Palestinian state headed toward collapse, a second intifada began in September 2000, and the Israeli government responded by staging military raids into PA territory.

After Arafat died in November 2004, the PA in January 2005 held its second-ever presidential election, which had been repeatedly postponed; the first voting for president and the Palestinian Legislative Council (PLC) had taken place in 1996. Mahmoud Abbas of Arafat's Fatah faction won the 2005 contest with 62 percent of the vote. In subsequent municipal voting in Gaza, the Islamist group Hamas won 77 out of 118 seats in 10 districts, to Fatah's 26 seats. Each group accused the other of fraud, and there was some election-related violence.

In 2005, Israel unilaterally "disengaged" from Gaza, withdrawing all 7,500 settlers and military personnel. However, it retained control of the territory's airspace, its coastline, and most of its land border, including the passage of goods and people. Hamas won the 2006 elections for the PLC, securing 74 of 132 seats, while Fatah took 45. Hamas was particularly dominant in Gazan districts. The two factions formed a unity government headed by Prime Minister Ismail Haniya of Hamas. However, Israel, the United States, and the European Union (EU) refused to recognize the new government, citing Hamas's involvement in terrorism and its refusal to recognize Israel or past Israel-PA agreements. The United States and the EU, then the largest donors to the PA, cut off assistance to the government.

In June 2006, in response to the killing of eight Palestinian civilians by an artillery shell, (the source of which was disputed), Hamas declared an end to a 2005 truce with Israel and accelerated the firing of rockets at Israel from Gaza. Hamas and other militant groups subsequently carried out a raid near Gaza, killing two IDF soldiers and capturing a third, Corporal Gilad Shalit. Israel responded by invading Gaza, where the IDF destroyed rocket launchers and ammunition sites but failed to locate Shalit. The fighting killed dozens of civilians.

Armed clashes between Hamas and Fatah supporters in Gaza escalated in 2007, and in June, Hamas militants took over Fatah-controlled institutions in the territory. Some 600 Palestinians were killed in the fighting, and thousands of Gazans fled—along with most Fatah militants—to the West Bank. Abbas accused Hamas of staging a coup in Gaza, dismissed the Hamas-led government, and appointed an emergency cabinet led by former finance minister Salam Fayad. This resulted in a bifurcated PA, with Hamas governing Gaza and Abbas and Fayad governing the roughly 40 percent of the West Bank not directly administered by Israel. Hamas security forces and militants subsequently pursued a major crackdown on Fatah in Gaza, closing Fatah-affiliated civic organizations and media outlets, and allegedly torturing detainees.

Meanwhile, Israel declared the Gaza Strip a "hostile entity" in response to ongoing rocket attacks, and imposed an economic blockade, granting passage only to food and certain other humanitarian supplies. However, arms and goods were regularly smuggled through a developing tunnel network between Egypt and Gaza. The blockade was eased after Hamas and Israel declared a six-month truce in June 2008.

War erupted between Hamas and Israeli forces in December 2008 after the truce expired, and Hamas ramped up its rocket bombardment of Israeli towns near the Gaza border. The IDF launched near-daily air strikes and an almost three-week ground invasion of the Gaza Strip, an operation which the IDF dubbed Cast Lead. Israel declared a unilateral ceasefire in late January 2009, and Hamas soon did the same. During the conflict, Israeli forces damaged or destroyed large portions of Gaza's military, government, and civilian infrastructure. According to the United Nations, some 50,000 homes, 800 industrial properties, 200 schools, and 39 mosques or churches were damaged or destroyed. For its part, Hamas launched over 700 rockets and mortar shells into Israeli civilian areas, often from civilian areas in Gaza. While the Palestinian Centre for Human Rights reported that 1,434 Palestinians were killed, including 960 noncombatants, the IDF reported that 1,166 Palestinians were killed, including 295 to 460 noncombatants. Thirteen Israelis were killed, including three noncombatants.

Following the ceasefire, the blockade was eased somewhat to allow the transfer of a limited number of authorized goods, as well as international aid workers and individuals with specified medical and humanitarian needs. Gaza's Rafah border crossing with Egypt opened on an ad hoc basis.

In 2010 and 2011, a series of private ships carrying food and other goods attempted to break Israel's coastal blockade of Gaza. In May 2010, Israeli soldiers intercepted a six-ship flotilla from Turkey and killed nine activists on one of the ships—the *Mavi Marmara*—in an ensuing confrontation. The Israeli government was widely condemned internationally for the incident, but claimed its soldiers were acting in self-defense. Israel later eased the blockade, allowing in virtually all consumer goods while continuing to ban weapons, fertilizer, gas tanks, drilling equipment, and water disinfectant, as well as all exports and almost all travel; prohibitions on construction materials were also slightly loosened. In May 2011, Egypt opened the Rafah border crossing to women, children, and men over 40; Gazan men between 18 and 40 required a permit to cross the border, which officially remained closed to overland trade.

In August 2011, the British Broadcasting Corporation (BBC) reported that the opening of the Rafah border crossing and the development of more sophisticated smuggling tunnels between Egypt and Gaza had begun to relieve shortages of construction and other goods, leading to a significant increase in construction by the Hamas authorities. Separately, in October, Israel and Hamas negotiated a prisoner exchange, whereby Hamas freed IDF soldier Gilad Shalit in exchange for 1,027 Palestinian prisoners.

Fighting between Israel and Gazan militants broke out regularly during 2011 and 2012. In most cases, rocket and mortar fire into Israel from Gaza prompted Israeli air strikes and artillery bombardments, killing both combatants and civilians, including children. According to the Israeli human rights organization B'Tselem, in the first 10 months of 2012, Hamas and other militants fired 423 rockets and 90 mortar shells into Israel from Gaza.

In November 2012, fighting between Hamas and Israel intensified. Hamas launched hundreds of rockets into Israel, and Israeli forces assassinated Ahmed Jabari, the commander of Hamas's military wing. While 75,000 IDF reserve troops were called up, the eight-day operation—dubbed the Pillar of Defense by the IDF—stopped short of a ground invasion, and Egypt brokered a cease-fire between Israel and Hamas. During the conflict, the Palestinians fired 1,500 rockets into Israel, with some approaching Tel Aviv and Jerusalem. Six Israelis and more than 160 Palestinians were killed in the fighting. The ceasefire featured a loosening of the blockade, including the extension of fishing rights from three to six nautical miles from shore and more access to land near the border. The Kerem Shalom crossing between Israel and Gaza was also reopened to the transfer of goods. The ceasefire terms required Israel to refrain from extrajudicial killing, and for Hamas to cease rocket attacks. In December 2012, Egypt and Israel allowed building materials to pass through the Rafah border, crossing from Egypt into Gaza for the first time since 2007.

Political Rights and Civil Liberties: Residents of Gaza were never granted citizenship by either Egypt or Israel, and are mostly citizens of the Palestinian Authority (PA). The current Hamas-controlled government in the territory claims to be the legitimate leadership of the PA. However, the authority—a quasi-sovereign entity created by the 1993 Oslo Accords—is effectively fractured, and the Hamas government implements PA law selectively.

The PA president is elected to four-year terms, and international observers judged the 2005 presidential election to be generally free and fair. However, PA president Mahmoud Abbas lost control over Gaza after the 2007 Fatah-Hamas schism, and Prime Minister Ismail Haniya continues to lead the Hamas government despite being formally dismissed by Abbas. Other Hamas ministers remained in their posts in Gaza after almost all Fatah-affiliated officials were expelled or fled to the West Bank. When Abbas's elected term expired in 2009, Hamas argued that the PA Basic Law empowered the head of the Palestinian Legislative Council (PLC)—Aziz Dweik of Hamas—to serve as acting president.

The unicameral, 132-seat PLC serves four-year terms. Voting in Gaza during the 2006 PLC elections was deemed largely fair by international observers. However, the Hamas-Fatah rift, combined with Israel's detention of many (especially Hamas-affiliated) lawmakers, has prevented the PLC from meeting since 2007, and its term expired in 2010.

In May 2011, Hamas and Fatah agreed to form a national unity government that would organize presidential and parliamentary elections and increase security coordination. By the end of 2012, however, no unity government had been formed, and no election date had been set.In November 2012, the Fatah-led PLO won recognition for Palestine as a nonmember observer state at the UN General Assembly. Hamas supported the move.

Humanitarian organizations and donor countries allege that Hamas exerts almost total control over the distribution of funds and goods in Gaza, and allocates resources according to political criteria with little or no transparency, creating ample opportunities for corruption.

The media are not free in Gaza. In 2008, Hamas replaced the PA Ministry of Information with a government Media Office and banned all journalists not accredited by it; authorities also closed down all media outlets not affiliated with Hamas. In 2011, officials continued to ban the import of three West Bank newspapers—*Al-Ayyam, Al-Quds*, and *Al-Hayat al-Jadida*—that are generally associated with Fatah. According to the Palestinian Center for Development and Media Freedoms (MADA), a 2011 reconciliation deal promised to end the ban as of January 2012, but the ban had not been lifted by year's end. Blogging and other online media activity has reportedly increased in recent years.

According to MADA, there were a total of 100 media freedom violations in the Gaza Strip in 2012, an increase of 54 percent over the previous year. Of those violations, 63 were allegedly committed by Israeli forces. During Operation Pillar of Defense in November 2012, the Israeli air force reportedly attacked media offices in Gaza, injuring several journalists, and killed two news photographers in a car marked as a press vehicle. MADA noted that Palestinian broadcasting frequencies were seized by the IDF to urge Palestinian residents not to cooperate with Hamas during the fighting.

Freedom of religion is restricted in Gaza. The PA Basic Law declares Islam to be the official religion of Palestine and states that "respect and sanctity of all other heavenly religions (Judaism and Christianity) shall be maintained." Hamas authorities have enforced orthodox Sunni Islamic practices and conservative dress, and have regularly harassed worshippers at non-Hamas-affiliated mosques. However, restrictions on personal religious preferences reportedly eased somewhat during 2012. Christians, who make up less than 1 percent of the population, have also suffered routine harassment, though violent attacks have reportedly declined in recent years. There is one Christian member of the PLC based in Gaza.

The Israeli blockade has restricted access to school supplies. While university students are ostensibly allowed to leave Gaza, they must be escorted by foreign diplomats or contractors. In practice, Gazans are now mostly absent from West Bank universities. Hamas has taken over the formal education system, aside from schools run by the United Nations. A teachers' strike in 2009 led to the replacement of many strikers with new, Hamas-allied teachers. Hamas security officials have reportedly confiscated copies of "immoral" novels from (mostly university) bookstores, according to Human Rights Watch (HRW).

Since 2008, Hamas has significantly restricted freedoms of assembly and association, with security forces violently dispersing public gatherings of Fatah and other groups. A rare, 500-person demonstration took place in September 2012 in the Bureij refugee camp, calling for the overthrow of Hamas following the death of a three-year old boy from a fire during a power failure. The demonstration was quickly dispersed by Hamas forces. There is a broad range of Palestinian nongovernmental organizations (NGOs) and civic groups, and Hamas itself operates a large social-services network. However, following the 2009 conflict between Hamas and Israel, Hamas restricted the activities of aid organizations that would not submit to its regulations, and many civic associations have been shut down for political reasons since the 2007 PA split. In July 2011, Hamas began enforcing its 2010 demand to audit the accounts of some 80 international NGOs in Gaza.

Independent labor unions in Gaza continue to function, and PA workers have staged strikes against Hamas-led management. However, the Fatah-aligned Palestinian General Federation of Trade Unions, the largest union body in the territories, has seen its operations greatly curtailed. Its main Gaza offices were taken over by Hamas militants in 2007, and the building was severely damaged in a December 2008 Israeli air raid.

Laws governing Palestinians in the Gaza Strip derive from Ottoman, British Mandate, Jordanian, Egyptian, PA, and Islamic law (Sharia), as well as Israeli military orders. The judicial system is not independent, and Palestinian judges lack proper training and experience. In 2007, Abbas ordered judges to boycott judicial bodies in Gaza, and Hamas began appointing new prosecutors and judges in 2008. Hamas security forces and militants continued to carry out arbitrary arrests and detentions during 2012, and torture of detainees and criminal suspects is reportedly common.

The Palestinian human rights ombudsman agency—the Independent Commission for Human Rights—is banned from Hamas detention centers and Gaza's central prison.

According to B'Tselem, from February 2009 to the end of October 2012 (the period spanning two weeks after the end of Operation Cast Lead and two weeks prior to the start of Operation Pillar of Defense) 281 Palestinians in Gaza were killed by the IDF, and 56 were killed by other Palestinians. In 2012 Hamas executed 12 Palestinians in Gaza, double the number executed in 2011. Freedom of movement is severely restricted. Although Egypt opened the Rafah border crossing to women, children, and men over 40 in May 2011, with Gazan men between 18 and 40 requiring a permit to cross the border, the Israeli border remains sealed to the transfer of people, with exceptions for medical cases, students, and aid workers. The regular clashes between Israeli forces and Gaza-based militants greatly restrict freedom of movement within the Gaza Strip, as does the presence of unexploded ordnance.

Freedom of residence has been limited by the violent conflicts in and around Gaza. The conflict with Israel that ended in January 2009 was fought to a large extent in civilian neighborhoods, leading to the damage or destruction of some 50,000 homes. The November 2012 conflict resulted in the displacement of 3,000 Palestinians and the destruction of or severe damage to 450 homes, according to the United Nations.

The blockade has greatly reduced economic freedom and choice in the territory, though these conditions improved slightly in 2011 and 2012. A dense network of tunnels beneath Gaza's border with Egypt facilitates much economic activity and is used to transport weapons; they are routinely bombed by Israel. At the end of the 2012, Israel declared that it would allow the entry of raw construction materials, passenger buses, and trucks, and improve Gazan access to the Israeli electricity network, but the Palestinian Centre for Human Rights expressed doubt that the new rules would actually change conditions.

Under Hamas, personal status law is derived almost entirely from Sharia, which puts women at a stark disadvantage in matters of marriage, divorce, inheritance, and domestic abuse. Rape, domestic abuse, and so-called "honor killings" are common, and these crimes often go unpunished. The government has barred women from wearing trousers in public and declared that all women must wear hijab in public buildings, though these and other such controls on women's behavior were enforced less frequently in 2012.

Hong Kong

Political Rights: 5
Civil Liberties: 2
Status: Partly Free

Population: 7,129,600

Ten-Year Ratings Timeline For Year Under Review (Political Rights, Civil Liberties, Status)

2003	2004	2005	2006	2007	2008	2009	2010	2011	2012
5,3PF	5,2PF	5,2PF	5,2PF	5,2PF	5,2PF	5,2PF	5,2PF	5,2PF	5,2PF

Overview:

In March 2012, a limited election committee chose Leung Chun-ying as Hong Kong's new chief executive after an unusually turbulent race in which Beijing switched its support to Leung from another candidate. Pro-Beijing parties maintained their dominance following Legislative Council elections in September, though prodemocracy parties won a majority of the seats elected by popular vote. A series of large protests during the year reflected growing public frustration over the central authorities' meddling in the territory's politics, the unrepresentative nature of the electoral system, and government efforts to introduce a pro-Beijing school curriculum. Meanwhile, journalists faced increasing government restrictions on access to information and unusual violent attacks on media offices.

Hong Kong Island was ceded in perpetuity to Britain in 1842; adjacent territories were subsequently added, and the last section was leased to Britain in 1898 for a period of 99 years. In the 1984 Sino-British Joint Declaration, London agreed to restore the entire colony to China in 1997. In return, Beijing—under its "one country, two systems" formula—pledged to maintain the enclave's legal, political, and economic autonomy for 50 years.

Under the 1984 agreement, a constitution for the Hong Kong Special Administrative Region, known as the Basic Law, took effect in 1997. The Basic Law stated that universal suffrage was the "ultimate aim" for Hong Kong, but it initially allowed direct elections for only 18 of 60 seats in the Legislative Council (Legco), and provided for the gradual expansion of elected seats over the subsequent years. After China took control, it temporarily suspended the Legco and installed a provisional legislature that repealed or tightened several civil liberties laws during its 10-month tenure.

Tung Chee-hwa was chosen as Hong Kong's chief executive by a Beijing-organized election committee in 1997, and his popularity waned as the central government became increasingly involved in Hong Kong's affairs, raising fears that civic freedoms would be compromised. Officials were forced to withdraw a restrictive antisubversion bill after it sparked mass protests in July 2003.

In 2005, with two years left to serve, the deeply unpopular Tung resigned. He was replaced by career civil servant Donald Tsang, and China's National People's Congress (NPC) decided that Tsang would serve out the remainder of Tung's term before facing election. Tsang won a new term as chief executive in 2007, garnering 82 percent of the votes in the mostly pro-Beijing election committee. Meanwhile, pro-Beijing parties retained control of the Legco in elections held in 2004 and 2008, though few of their members were elected by popular vote. Most won seats determined by elite "functional constituency" voters.

In March 2012, the election committee chose Leung Chun-ying, a member of a mainland government advisory body, as the new chief executive. He won 689 of the 1,050 valid votes cast following an usually competitive race against two other candidates—Henry Tang, a high-ranking Hong Kong civil servant, who took 285 votes, and Democratic Party leader Albert Ho, who secured 76. Tang was initially Beijing's preferred candidate, but after his popularity fell due to a series of scandals, the central government switched its backing to Leung. Officials from China's Liaison Office reportedly lobbied members of the election committee to vote for Leung and castigated media outlets for critical coverage of him. Leung took office in July. During the Legco elections in September, which drew a high turnout of 53 percent, pro-Beijing parties won 43 seats, while prodemocracy parties took 27, enabling them to retain a veto on constitutional changes.

Hong Kong residents staged several large-scale demonstrations during the year, reflecting dissatisfaction with the government, concerns over Beijing's growing interference in Hong Kong affairs, and objections to a proposed school curriculum that allegedly promoted loyalty to the Chinese Communist Party (CCP). A series of corruption revelations involving Tsang and powerful tycoons contributed to public frustrations. In April, Tsang survived a vote of no confidence in the Legco—the first such vote brought against a leader since the handover to China in 1997.

Political Rights and Civil Liberties: Hong Kong's Basic Law calls for the election of a chief executive and a unicameral Legislative Council (Legco). Under electoral reforms adopted in 2010, the chief executive, who serves a five-year term, is chosen by a 1,200-member election committee: some 200,000 "functional constituency" voters—representatives of various elite business and social sectors, many with close ties to Beijing—elect 900 of the committee's members, and the remaining 300 consist of Legco members, Hong Kong delegates to the NPC, religious representatives, and members of the Chinese People's Political Consultative Conference (CPPCC), an advisory body to the NPC.

In keeping with the 2010 amendments to the Basic Law, the Legco added 10 seats in 2012. Thirty members are still chosen by the functional constituency voters, and 35—up from 30—are chosen through direct elections in five geographical constituencies. For the five remaining seats, members of Hong Kong's 18 district councils nominate candidates from among themselves, who then face a full popular vote. All 70 members serve four-year terms. The Basic Law restricts the Legco's lawmaking powers, prohibiting legislators from introducing bills that would affect Hong Kong's public spending, governmental operations, or political structure.

The NPC ruled in 2007 that universal suffrage might be adopted in 2017 for the chief executive election and 2020 for the Legco. The issue's omission from the 2010 electoral reforms heightened fears that the transition would be pushed further into the future.

In the territory's multiparty system, over a dozen factions won Legco seats in 2012. They included the prodemocracy Civic Party and Democratic Party and the pro-Beijing Democratic Alliance for the Betterment and Progress of Hong Kong. The CCP is not formally registered in Hong Kong but exercises considerable influence.

Pro-Beijing parties maintained their dominance by capturing 43 seats, though only 17 of those were directly elected. The prodemocracy camp took the remainder. Due to splits in the prodemocracy camp over the compromise behind the 2010 reform package, the long-established Democratic Party lost three seats, leading to the resignation of party chairman Albert Ho.

Hong Kong is generally regarded as having low rates of corruption, though business interests exercise a strong influence in the Legco and executive branch. A series of high-profile cases in 2012 contributed to growing public concerns about corruption. Outgoing chief executive Donald Tsang was placed under investigation by the territory's Independent Commission Against Corruption (ICAC) in February for allegedly accepting private trips and favors from Chinese businessmen; the probe was ongoing at year's end. Billionaire property developers Thomas and Raymond Kwok were arrested in March and charged in July with paying bribes in exchange for information on land sales. Rafael Hui, formerly Hong Kong's second-ranked executive official, was also charged in the case. Separately in July, the ICAC arrested development minister Mak Chai-kwong and assistant highways department director Tsang King-man for alleged abuse of government housing allowances.

Also during 2012, the ICAC continued to prosecute dozens of suspects in connection with vote rigging in the November 2011 district council elections, after prodemocracy legislators reported instances of voters registering under false or nonexistent addresses. In November 2012, the Court of Final Appeal defended the ICAC's strong investigative powers, ruling that it had the right to compel information during an investigation despite the potential for self-incrimination by witnesses. Hong Kong was ranked 14 out of 176 polities surveyed in Transparency International's 2012 Corruption Perceptions Index.

Under Article 27 of the Basic Law, Hong Kong residents enjoy freedoms of speech, press, and publication. These rights are generally respected in practice, and political debate is vigorous. There are dozens of daily newspapers, and residents have access to international radio broadcasts and satellite television. Foreign media operate without interference. However, political and economic pressures have narrowed the space for free expression. A 2012 poll conducted by the Hong Kong Journalists Association (HKJA) found that for the first time, journalists' concerns about tighter government control over access to information surpassed self-censorship as the most commonly cited threat to media freedom. Over the past two years, officials have increasingly used off-the-record briefings to announce policies and released official footage for news events rather than opening them to the press, while the police and fire departments have released less detailed and timely information about newsworthy incidents.

Direct or indirect efforts by Beijing to interfere in reporting on internal Hong Kong politics appeared to increase in 2012. During the run-up to the chief executive election in March, the central government's Liaison Office reportedly contacted newspapers and rebuked them for articles that were critical of Leung Chun-ying, its preferred candidate. Self-censorship by outlets aiming to please Beijing is also a problem. A political commentator with *Sing Pao Daily News* had his column discontinued after he complained that one of his articles had been altered to imply support for Leung and later submitted a column on the death of an exiled Chinese democracy advocate. Several media owners are current or former members of the NPC or CPPCC, and many have significant business interests in mainland China. In January, Wang Xiangwei, a mainlander who had once worked for the state-run *China Daily*, became the editor in chief of the popular local English-language paper *South China Morning Post*. He was accused of censoring the *Post*'s coverage of the suspicious death of Chinese dissident Li Wangyang in June, and of refusing to renew a contract with an award-winning reporter known for his articles about Beijing's poor human rights record.

Violence against journalists is rare in Hong Kong, though several cases were reported in 2012. In August, the office of a citizen journalism website was raided and vandalized by four masked men. Also that month, a stolen car was rammed into the headquarters of Sing Tao News Corporation. Several men wielding axes attacked the company's branch office in southern Kowloon in September. The motives for the attacks were unclear, though organized crime involvement was suspected in the Sing Tao incidents. Two journalists were assaulted by participants in a progovernment rally in December. During a visit by Chinese president Hu Jintao in June, a journalist from *Apple Daily* was briefly detained after yelling out a question regarding the 1989 Tiananmen Square massacre. Hong Kong journalists aiming to report from the mainland must obtain press cards from Beijing's Liaison Office, though even with accreditation, they are often subject to surveillance, threats, beatings, and occasional detention by mainland authorities.

The Basic Law provides for freedom of religion, which is generally respected in practice. Religious groups are excluded from the Societies Ordinance, which requires nongovernmental organizations (NGOs) to register with the government. Adherents of the Falun Gong spiritual movement, which is persecuted on the mainland, remain free to practice and hold occasional demonstrations, though government pressure on them to remove banners from public places has increased in recent years. In 2012, an apparently Beijing-linked association began mounting aggressive anti–Falun Gong banner campaigns that often involved verbal abuse, sparking complaints from activists and legislators that the Hong Kong authorities were not enforcing laws protecting religious freedom.

University professors can write and lecture freely, and political debate on campuses is lively, though a number of incidents in 2012 suggested growing threats to Hong Kong's academic freedom. The director of the University of Hong Kong's Public Opinion Programme, known for its politically sensitive polls, was criticized in more than 80 articles and commentaries in pro-Beijing newspapers early in the year. A political scientist at the Hong Kong University of Science and Technology was also singled out for criticism in the papers.

The Basic Law guarantees freedoms of assembly and association. Police permits for demonstrations are required but rarely denied, and protests on politically sensitive issues are held regularly. In 2012, the territory experienced especially large protests against the Chinese government. The annual June 4 vigil to commemorate the 1989 Tiananmen Square massacre drew at least 113,000 people, nearly double the 2011 attendance, with a fifth reportedly coming from mainland China, where such activities are banned. Other major demonstrations were held during the year to protest the suspicious death of mainland activist Li Wangyang; the inauguration of Leung as chief executive, which coincided with the July 1 anniversary of Hong Kong's handover to China; and a proposed school curriculum with pro-Beijing themes, which was subsequently shelved. At least three mainlanders were beaten or sentenced to labor camps after returning home from the July 1 protest in Hong Kong, the first such known cases of mainlanders punished for attending Hong Kong demonstrations.

In recent years, Hong Kong authorities have demonstrated reduced respect for freedom of assembly. Restrictions on protests near Beijing's Liaison Office, aggressive use of pepper spray, and the rate of arrests at demonstrations have all reportedly increased. Moreover, those arrested are more likely to face serious charges; 45 people were prosecuted under the Public Order Ordinance in 2011 alone, compared with a total of 39 from 1997 to 2010.

Hong Kong hosts a vibrant and largely unfettered NGO sector, and trade unions are independent. However, there is limited legal protection for basic labor rights. Collective-bargaining rights are not recognized, protections against antiunion discrimination are weak, and there are few regulations on working hours.

The judiciary is independent, and the trial process is generally fair. The NPC reserves the right to make final interpretations of the Basic Law, effectively limiting the power of Hong Kong's Court of Final Appeal, the territory's highest court. In October 2012, Kemal Bokhary stepped down as a permanent judge on the Court of Final Appeal after more than 15 years in office, having reached the mandatory retirement age. The government declined to extend his term of service, but gave his position to a judge nine months older. Amid a public outcry, Bokhary said he believed the extension was rejected because his judgments were too liberal.

Police are forbidden by law to employ torture and other forms of abuse. They generally respect this ban in practice, and complaints of abuse are investigated. Arbitrary arrest and detention are illegal; suspects must be charged within 48 hours of their arrest. Prison conditions generally meet international standards.

Citizens are treated equally under the law, though Hong Kong's 300,000 foreign household workers remain vulnerable to abuse, and South Asians routinely complain of discrimination in employment. Since foreign workers face deportation if dismissed, many are reluctant to bring complaints against employers. The independent Equal Opportunities Commission, tasked with enforcing a 2009 ordinance against racial discrimination, has been criticized for excluding discrimination through government actions and against immigrants. In March 2012, the Court of Appeal overturned a 2011 local court ruling that would have allowed foreign household workers, like other foreigners in Hong Kong, to apply for permanent residency after seven years of uninterrupted stay. Labor rights groups pledged to take the case to the Court of Final Appeal.

Hong Kong maintains its own immigration system, but periodic denials of entry to democracy activists, Falun Gong practitioners, and others have raised suspicions that the government enforces a Beijing-imposed political blacklist, particularly at sensitive times. The government does not control travel, choice of residence, or employment within Hong Kong, but documents are required to travel to the mainland, and employers must apply to bring in workers from China; direct applications from workers are not accepted. In 2012, the immigration department continued to delay a work visa for outspoken mainland journalist Chang Ping. Observers reported that while replies are typically obtained within four weeks, Chang had not received a response over a year after submitting his application.

Public resentment has increased regarding the growing trend of mainland women giving birth in Hong Kong, often with the aim of accessing its advanced welfare system or skirting China's one-child policy. Hundreds of such women were prosecuted for overstaying visas during 2012, and thousands were barred from entering, though tens of thousands of babies are reportedly born to mainland women in Hong Kong each year.

Women in Hong Kong are protected by law from discrimination and abuse, and they are entitled to equal access to schooling and to property in divorce settlements. However, they continue to face discrimination in employment opportunities, salary, inheritance, and welfare. Only 11 out of the 70 Legco members are women, and all of the judges on the Court of Final Appeal are men. Despite robust government efforts, Hong Kong remains a source, destination, and transit point for human trafficking linked to sexual exploitation and forced labor.

⬆ Indian Kashmir

Political Rights: 4   **Population:** 12,549,000
Civil Liberties: 4
Status: Partly Free

Trend Arrow: Indian Kashmir received an upward trend arrow due to the partial easing of draconian detention laws.

Ten-Year Ratings Timeline For Year Under Review (Political Rights, Civil Liberties, Status)

2003	2004	2005	2006	2007	2008	2009	2010	2011	2012
5,5PF	5,5PF	5,5PF	5,5PF	5,4PF	5,4PF	4,4PF	4,5PF	4,4PF	4,4PF

Overview: In April 2012, the government amended the Public Safety Act to prohibit the detention of minors and reduce periods of detention. The government has also signaled that it might phase out the Armed Forces Special Powers Act.

When British India was partitioned into India and Pakistan in 1947, the Hindu maharajah of Jammu and Kashmir tried to maintain his principality's independence, he eventually ceded it to India in return for autonomy and future self-determination. Within months, India and Pakistan went to war over the territory. As part of a UN-brokered ceasefire in 1949 that established the present boundaries, Pakistan gained control of roughly one-third of Jammu and Kashmir, leaving India with the remainder. The territory received substantial autonomy under Article 370 of India's constitution and a 1952 accord, but India annulled such guarantees in 1957 and formally annexed the portion of Jammu and Kashmir under its control. Since then, it has largely been governed as other Indian states, with an elected legislature and a chief minister. Under the 1972 Simla accord, New Delhi and Islamabad agreed to respect the Line of Control dividing the region and to resolve Kashmir's status through negotiations.

The pro-India National Conference (NC) party won state elections in 1987 that were marred by fraud, violence, and arrests of members of a new, Muslim-based opposition coalition, leading to widespread unrest. An armed insurgency against Indian rule gathered momentum after 1989, waged by the Jammu and Kashmir

Liberation Front (JKLF) and other proindependence groups that consisted largely of Kashmiris, as well as Pakistani-backed Islamist groups seeking to bring Kashmir under Islamabad's control.

New Delhi placed Jammu and Kashmir under federal rule in 1990 and attempted to quell the uprising. The Armed Forces Special Powers Act (AFSPA) was extended to the territory, allowing the army to make arrests and conduct searches without a warrant, and to use deadly force with virtual impunity. The JKLF abandoned its armed struggle in 1994, and Pakistani-backed extremist groups, which included fighters from elsewhere in the Muslim world, thereafter dominated the insurgency.

Although opposition parties joined together to form the All Parties Hurriyat Conference (APHC) in 1993, they boycotted the 1996 state elections, and the NC was able to form a government. The APHC also declined to participate in the 2002 elections, but the NC nevertheless lost more than half of its assembly seats, allowing the Congress Party and the People's Democratic Party (PDP) to form a coalition government.

Despite several setbacks, relations between the Indian government and moderate Kashmiri separatist groups generally improved after the 2002 elections. In 2004, talks were held for the first time between Kashmiri separatists and the highest levels of the Indian government. Moderate APHC leaders reiterated their renunciation of violence in 2005 and called for Kashmiris to become more deeply involved in the negotiating process. However, the talks were hampered by an emerging split within the APHC between those who favored a continuation of the insurgency and those who favored a political and diplomatic solution.

The coalition government collapsed in June 2008, when the PDP withdrew its support amid a high-profile dispute over land set aside for a Hindu pilgrimage site. State elections were held in November and December. Turnout was higher than expected, exceeding 60 percent on most polling dates, as voters largely ignored separatist groups' calls for a boycott. While early voting dates were generally peaceful, some violence pervaded later polling—particularly in early December—when antielection protesters clashed with security forces. The elections were considered mostly free and fair, however, with significantly reduced levels of voter intimidation, harassment, and violence compared with previous elections. The NC won a plurality of 28 seats, followed by the PDP with 21 seats and Congress with 17. The NC allied itself with Congress to form a governing coalition.

The security situation improved during 2009, with the number of militancy-related fatalities decreasing for the seventh consecutive year. In October, New Delhi announced plans to withdraw 15,000 troops from the Jammu region, granting local police more responsibility over the area.

In 2010, prompted by the police killing of a 17-year-old boy in June, opposition groups organized a protest movement called Quit Kashmir. They demanded that the Indian government recognize the Kashmir dispute as an international conflict, demilitarize the region, release all political prisoners, and revoke the AFSPA. For about three months, police and soldiers engaged in regular clashes with youthful, stone-throwing protesters, leaving more than 100 civilians dead. Tensions began to ease in September, when the central government announced plans to reduce the security presence in the territory, release jailed protesters, compensate the families of slain civilians, and reopen schools and universities. However, police arrested protest organizer Masrat Alam in October, and curfews and unrest continued sporadically for the rest of the year.

Calm was largely restored in 2011, and 2012 featured the lowest level of violence since 1989. This new stability has had economic benefits; the government reported that over 1.3 million tourists visited Kashmir in 2012, the highest number in years. From April to June 2011, panchayat (local council) elections were held across Kashmir for the first time since 2001; they represented the first truly open panchayat elections in Kashmir since 1978. Although separatist groups urged citizens to boycott the polls, turnout was reported at about 80 percent. However, problems remained; in November 2012, over 700 panchayat leaders resigned as a result of death threats after several were assassinated.

In April 2012, the Public Safety Act (PSA), which allows detention without charge or trial, for "the security of the State and public order," was amended; changes included the prohibition of the detention of minors and new rules that are expected to reduce the amount of time prisoners are held before trial. Chief Minister Omar Abdullah has also supported phasing out the AFSPA, though he has refused to commit to a timeline for doing so.

Political Rights and Civil Liberties: Jammu and Kashmir, like India's other states, is governed by an elected bicameral legislature and a chief minister entrusted with executive power. An appointed governor serves as symbolic head of state. Members of the 87-seat lower house, or state assembly, are directly elected, while the 46-seat upper house has a combination of members elected by the state assembly and nominated by the governor.

India has never held a referendum allowing Kashmiri self-determination as called for in a 1948 UN resolution. The state's residents can change the local administration through elections, which are supposed to be held at least once every five years. The Election Commission of India monitors the polls, but historically they have been marred by violence, coercion, and ballot tampering. Militants have enforced boycotts called for by separatist political parties, threatened election officials and candidates, and killed political activists and civilians during balloting. The 2002 campaign period was especially violent, but the 2008 legislative elections were considered generally free and fair, being largely peaceful despite some violence. Municipal elections originally slated for 2011 have been repeatedly delayed until 2013.

Corruption remains widespread, though the government has taken some steps to combat it. The legislature enacted the Jammu and Kashmir State Vigilance Commission Bill in February 2011, establishing an anticorruption commission with the power to investigate alleged offenses under the state's 2006 Prevention of Corruption Act.

India's 1971 Newspapers (Incitement to Offences) Act, which is in effect only in Jammu and Kashmir, gives district magistrates the authority to censor publications in certain circumstances, though it is rarely invoked. The protest-related violence in 2010 led some newspapers to suspend circulation, and curfews inhibited journalists from covering important stories, though conditions have improved. Foreign journalists are generally able to travel freely, meet with separatist leaders, and file reports on a range of issues, including government abuses. As in the rest of India, print media are thriving in Kashmir, and online media have proliferated, providing new platforms for public discussion. By the end of 2012, there were over 1,100 registered publications in Jammu and Kashmir, compared to 30 in 1989. Journalists remain subject to pressure from militants and the authorities. At times, the PSA has been used to arrest journalists and the government has withheld official advertising in disfavored media outlets. Journalists also face threats from militant groups.

Freedom of worship and academic freedom are generally respected by the authorities. Since 2003, the state government has permitted separatist groups to organize a procession marking the prophet Muhammad's birthday. However, militants at times attack Hindu and Sikh temples.

Freedoms of assembly and association are often restricted. Although local and national civil rights groups are permitted to operate, they sometimes encounter harassment by security forces. The separatist APHC is allowed to function, but its leaders are frequently subjected to short-term preventive detention, and its requests for permits for public gatherings are often denied. Protection of labor union rights in Kashmir is generally poor and has resulted in prolonged strikes by both public and informal sector workers.

The courts in Kashmir, already backlogged by thousands of pending cases, were further hampered in 2011 by intermittent lawyers' strikes triggered in part by the July 2010 arrest of Kashmir High Court Bar Association president Mian Abdul Qayoom under the PSA. Qayoom, who was accused of speaking out against Indian rule and fomenting protests, was released from detention in April 2011. Separately, in November 2011, members of the Jammu and Kashmir High Court Bar Association went on strike for 27 days to demand the revocation of a cabinet decision transferring the power to register land and property from judicial officers to the revenue department. In December, the High Court intervened in the matter with a stay order on the transfer of powers, and directed the lawyers to resume work.

The government and security forces frequently disregard court orders. Broadly written legislation, such as the AFSPA and the Disturbed Areas Act, allow security forces to search homes and arrest suspects without a warrant, shoot suspects on sight, and destroy buildings believed to house militants or arms. Under the AFSPA, prosecutions of security personnel cannot proceed without the approval of the central government, which is rarely granted. The government amended the PSA in 2012 after a particularly critical 2011 report by Amnesty International (AI). However, a follow-up report from AI indicated some continuing problems, including "revolving door" detentions in which detainees reaching the maximum detention threshold are released and rearrested shortly thereafter.

Indian security personnel based in Kashmir carry out arbitrary arrests and detentions, torture, forced disappearances, and custodial killings of suspected militants and their alleged civilian sympathizers. Meanwhile, militant groups based in Pakistan continue to kill pro-India politicians, public employees, suspected informers, members of rival factions, soldiers, and civilians. The militants also engage in kidnapping, extortion, and other forms of intimidation. However, violence associated with the struggle between security forces and militant groups continued a multiyear decline in 2012. According to the SATP, a total of 117 civilians, security personnel, and militants were killed during the year, down from 183 in 2011 and 375 in 2010.

Violence targeting Pandits, or Kashmiri Hindus, is part of a pattern dating to 1990 that has forced several hundred thousand Hindus to flee the region; many continue to reside in refugee camps near Jammu. Other religious and ethnic minorities such as Sikhs and Gujjars have also been targeted.

As in other parts of India, women face some societal discrimination as well as domestic violence and other forms of abuse. Female civilians continue to be subjected to harassment, intimidation, and violent attacks, including rape and murder, at the hands of both the security forces and militant groups.

Nagorno-Karabakh

Political Rights: 5*
Civil Liberties: 5
Status: Partly Free

Population: 141,400

Status Change: Nagorno-Karabakh's political rights rating improved from 6 to 5, and its status improved from Not Free to Partly Free, due to the participation of a genuine opposition in the July presidential election.

Ten-Year Ratings Timeline For Year Under Review (Political Rights, Civil Liberties, Status)

2003	2004	2005	2006	2007	2008	2009	2010	2011	2012
5,5PF	5,5PF	5,5PF	5,5PF	5,5PF	5,5PF	5,5PF	6,5NF	6,5NF	5,5PF

Overview: In July 2012, Bako Saakian was reelected president of Nagorno-Karabakh with 67 percent of the vote. Unlike the 2010 parliamentary elections, the presidential contest featured genuine competition, with opposition candidate Vitaly Balasanian receiving 32.5 percent of the ballots. An escalation in violence along the ceasefire line during the year peaked in June, killing about a dozen soldiers in total. Azerbaijan's August pardon of a man convicted of murdering an Armenian soldier further stymied progress on negotiations over Nagorno-Karabakh's status.

Nagorno-Karabakh, populated largely by ethnic Armenians, was established as an autonomous region inside Soviet Azerbaijan in 1923. In February 1988, the regional legislature adopted a resolution calling for union with Armenia. The announcement led to warfare over the next several years between Armenian, Azerbaijani, and local Nagorno-Karabakh forces.

In 1992, Nagorno-Karabakh's new legislature adopted a declaration of independence, which was not recognized by the international community. By the time a Russian-brokered ceasefire was signed in May 1994, Karabakh Armenians, assisted by Armenia, had captured essentially the entire territory and seven adjacent Azerbaijani districts. Virtually all ethnic Azeris had fled or been forced out of the region. The fighting resulted in thousands of deaths and created an estimated one million refugees and internally displaced persons (IDPs).

In December 1994, the head of Nagorno-Karabakh's state defense committee, Robert Kocharian, was selected as president by the territory's National Assembly. He won a popular vote for the presidency in 1996, but became prime minister of Armenia in March 1997. Foreign Minister Arkady Ghukassian was elected to replace him that September, and Kocharian went on to become Armenia's president in 1998.

Ghukassian easily secured a second term as president in 2002, and his ruling Democratic Party of Artsakh (AZhK) led the 2005 parliamentary elections, though the opposition accused the authorities of misusing state resources to influence the outcome. In 2006, a reported 98 percent of voters supported a referendum affirming Nagorno-Karabakh's independence. The referendum was not recognized by the international community.

Nagorno-Karabakh security chief Bako Saakian reportedly took more than 85 percent of the vote in the 2007 presidential election. His main opponent, Deputy Foreign Minister Masis Mailian, received 12 percent. The government subsequently absorbed or co-opted most of the political opposition.

Hope for progress on a peace agreement was shaken in 2008 by a series of external political developments with conflicting implications for Nagorno-Karabakh. These included a UN General Assembly resolution identifying Nagorno-Karabakh as part of Azerbaijan and calling on Armenia to withdraw its troops; Kosovo's declaration of independence from Serbia, which was opposed by Russia and some European Union countries; and Russia's recognition of the independence of the breakaway Georgian regions of Abkhazia and South Ossetia. In addition, skirmishes along the ceasefire line killed 16 soldiers on both sides.

Nagorno-Karabakh held parliamentary elections in May 2010. In contrast to the more competitive legislative polls of previous years, no genuine opposition candidates participated, and the balloting was swept by the three parties of the ruling coalition. Azat Hayrenik (Free Fatherland), the party of Prime Minister Ara Harutiunian, won 14 of the 33 seats, followed by AZhK with 10 and the Armenian Revolutionary Federation–Dashnaktsutiun party with 6. The remaining seats were captured by Hayrenik loyalists with no formal party affiliation.

The presidents of Armenia and Azerbaijan met with Russian president Dmitry Medvedev in June 2011 for highly anticipated talks on a peace agreement, but the summit ended in disappointment, when Baku refused to sign the proposed draft. With negotiations stalled and both sides engaged in a rapid military buildup, international observers expressed concerns about the threat of open warfare. Fears of open conflict intensified in 2012 amid an escalation of violence along the ceasefire line, with about a dozen soldiers from the two sides killed in June.

Saakian was reelected president in July 2012, with 66.7 percent of the vote. He faced a legitimate challenge from his main opponent, former Karabakh deputy defense minister Vitaly Balasanian, who received 32.5 percent. Balasanian claimed that administrative resources were misused to aid the incumbent. The two main candidates had nearly identical foreign-policy goals—achieving international recognition of Nagorno-Karabakh's independence—though Balasanian also called for social justice and accused the government of allowing corruption and fiscal mismanagement.

Azerbaijan's August pardon of Ramil Safarov, an Azerbaijani military officer who had murdered an Armenian soldier while both were training in Hungary in 2004, further strained relations between Armenia and Azerbaijan, effectively thwarting any immediate prospects for progress on peace talks.

Political Rights and Civil Liberties: Nagorno-Karabakh has enjoyed de facto independence from Azerbaijan since 1994 and retains close political, economic, and military ties with Armenia. The opposition has criticized recent elections for alleged fraud and other irregularities, including abuse of administrative resources. No opposition candidates participated in the 2010 parliamentary elections, but the 2012 presidential contest featured more competition. All Karabakh elections are considered invalid by the international community, which does not recognize the territory's independence.

The president, who is directly elected for up to two five-year terms, appoints the prime minister. Of the unicameral National Assembly's 33 members, 17 are elected by party list and 16 from single-mandate districts, all for five-year terms. The main political parties in Nagorno-Karabakh are Azat Hayrenik, the AZhK, and the Armenian Revolutionary Federation–Dashnaktsutiun, all of which currently support the government. Vitaly Balasanian, the defeated challenger in the 2012 presidential election, announced in August that he was forming a new opposition group.

Nagorno-Karabakh continues to suffer from significant corruption, particularly in the construction industry, as well as favoritism in filling civil service positions.

The territory officially remains under martial law, which imposes restrictions on civil liberties, including media censorship and the banning of public demonstrations. However, the authorities maintain that these provisions have not been enforced since 1995, a year after the ceasefire was signed.

The government controls many of Nagorno-Karabakh's media outlets, and the public television station has no local competition. The popular independent newspaper *Demo* and *Karabakh-Open.com*, the territory's only independent news website, were both closed by their publishers in 2008. The internet penetration rate is low but expanding. During the 2012 presidential election, the opposition campaigned heavily using social media.

Most residents belong to the Armenian Apostolic Church, and the religious freedom of other groups is limited. A 2009 law banned religious activity by unregistered groups and proselytism by minority faiths, and made it more difficult for minority groups to register. Although at least three were subsequently registered, a Protestant group and the Jehovah's Witnesses were reportedly denied registration. Unregistered groups have been fined for their religious activities, and conscientious objectors have been jailed for refusing to serve in the Karabakh army. In December 2011, a Jehovah's Witness received a 30-month jail term for refusing mandatory military service.

Freedoms of assembly and association are limited, but trade unions are allowed to organize. The handful of nongovernmental organizations (NGOs) that are active in the territory are virtually all progovernment, and they suffer from lack of funding and competition from government-organized groups.

The judiciary is not independent in practice. The courts are influenced by the executive branch as well as powerful political, economic, and criminal groups.

In August 2011, the legislature passed an amnesty law to release or commute the sentences of up to 20 percent of the prison population, on the condition that the inmates fought in the 1991–94 war or had family killed in the conflict. The amnesty also stipulated the closure of at least 60 percent of pending criminal cases and the release of suspects from pretrial detention.

The Karabakh army suffered from a series of noncombat deaths in 2011, including two shooting sprees that left 10 soldiers dead, and a number of soldiers faced criminal charges. One soldier who was found guilty of the killings was sentenced to life in prison in August 2011.

The majority of Azeris who fled the territory during the separatist conflict continue to live in poor conditions in IDP camps in Azerbaijan. Land mine explosions in the conflict zone cause deaths and injuries each year.

The continued control of major economic activity by powerful elites limits opportunities for most residents, though the government has instituted a number of economic rehabilitation projects in recent years.

Men and women have equal legal status, though women are underrepresented in government and the private sector. Women are not conscripted. The government administers a "birth-encouragement program," with the goal of repopulating the territory. Couples receive several hundred dollars when they marry and additional money for the birth of each child.

Northern Cyprus

Political Rights: 2
Civil Liberties: 2
Status: Free

Population: 339,000

Note: See also the country report for Cyprus.

Ten-Year Ratings Timeline For Year Under Review (Political Rights, Civil Liberties, Status)

2003	2004	2005	2006	2007	2008	2009	2010	2011	2012
2,2F	2,2F	2,2F	2,2F	2,2F	2,2F	2,2F	2,2F	2,2F	2,2F

Overview: **In April 2012, the United Nations cancelled a proposed international conference on the reunification of Cyprus, and Greek and Turkish Cypriot leaders continued to blame each other for lack of progress in negotiations. Meanwhile, conflicts over oil and gas drilling in disputed waters remained a source of tension between Cyprus and Turkey throughout the year.**

Cyprus, populated by ethnic Greeks and Turks, gained independence from Britain in 1960. Inter-ethnic relations were tense, and UN peacekeepers were sent to Cyprus in 1964. In July 1974, Greek Cypriot National Guard members staged an unsuccessful coup whose goal was to unite Cyprus with Greece. In response, Turkey, claiming it was protecting the ethnic Turkish minority, sent in troops, gaining control of 37 percent of the island and expelling 200,000 Greek Cypriots from the northern part. Cyprus has since been de facto divided by a UN-patrolled buffer zone known as the Green Line. In 1983, the Turkish-controlled area declared independence, calling itself the Turkish Republic of Northern Cyprus (TRNC). UN resolutions stipulate that Cyprus is a single country and that the Turkish occupation is illegal. Only Turkey recognizes the TRNC as an independent state.

For many years, Turkey and nationalist-oriented TRNC leaders resisted reunification of the island. The first opening of the Green Line occurred in April 2003, and December elections brought to power a pro-unification government led by Prime Minister Mehmet Ali Talat of the Republican Turkish Party (CTP). UN-sponsored talks on reunification progressed, culminating in a plan proposed by then-UN Secretary General Kofi Annan. At the same time, the Republic of Cyprus (RC, or Greek Cyprus) was poised to join the European Union (EU), and it was thought that the United Nations and EU could bring the two sides together. In April 2004, Turkish Cypriot voters approved the Annan Plan, but Greek Cypriots rejected it. With the island still divided, only the RC joined the EU in May 2004.

Rauf Denktas, who had been president of the TRNC since the declaration of independence, did not seek reelection in the April 2005 presidential election, which Talat won. Some progress was subsequently made in talks with the RC, including formation of a property commission and opening additional border crossings. However, Talat failed to achieve his stated goal of reunification, and the TRNC experienced a sharp economic downturn in 2008. In 2009 legislative elections, the anti-unification National Unity Party (UBP) prevailed, winning 26 of the 50 parliamentary seats. Its leader, Dervis Eroglu, became prime minister. Ero lu then defeated Talat in the April 2010 presidential election with just over 50 percent of the vote.

Since 2010, there has been little progress in reunification talks. In April 2012, the United Nations cancelled plans for an international conference on reunification, and Greek and Turkish Cypriot leaders blamed each other for the failure to reach an agreement; any progress awaits the election of a new RC president in February 2013. Greek Cypriot offshore gas drilling in November 2011 led to renewed tensions with Turkey, and Turkish drilling both offshore (supported by warships) and on TRNC-controlled territory has sparked protests from the RC. Turkey has also warned international companies against drilling in contested offshore waters. While some analysts have speculated that the discovery of oil and gas could generate incentives to reunify the island, Greek Cypriot officials maintained in 2012 that they would share resources only after the division of the island is resolved. Others, noting Israeli cooperation with the RC in developing offshore drilling sites, cite potential for broader regional conflict.

Meanwhile, continued economic problems and government austerity proposals in 2012 led to protests and strikes in the TRNC, with some protests critical of the Turkish government.

Political Rights and Civil Liberties: Elections in the TRNC are generally free and fair. The president and the 50-seat Assembly are elected to five-year terms. The prime minister is the head of the government. The main parties are the ruling anti-unification UBP and the pro-unification opposition CTP. Five parties are currently represented in the Assembly.

The Turkish military plays an important role in the TRNC, and the TRNC remains dependent on Turkey for security and economic support. In March 2012, a Turkish minister controversially suggested that Turkey might annex the TRNC if reunification talks fail. In September 2012, Özkan *Yorgancıo lu*, the CTP leader, expressed concern that Turkey was trying to exert excessive influence over government policies.

The results of a December 2011 census have been in dispute. The 2006 census showed that about half the population was composed of indigenous Turkish Cypriots, with most of the remainder consisting of immigrants from mainland Turkey. There were also a few hundred Greek Cypriots and Maronites who resided primarily in their ancestral villages and faced difficulties at Green Line checkpoints and alleged surveillance by TRNC authorities; they are RC citizens and do not vote in TRNC elections.

The government has made efforts to combat corruption in recent years, but graft, alleged vote-buying, and lack of transparency remain concerns. In May 2012, a group of British homeowners filed suit against the TRNC government for allegedly scheming to sell "stolen" property seized from Greek Cypriots and for which buyers could not obtain a clear legal title.

Freedom of the press is guaranteed by law, but problems persist. The government has been hostile to independent outlets. In 2011 there were several attacks on journalists, in particular on the editor of the newspaper *Afrika*, which is critical of the government and the Turkish military's presence on the island; nationalist groups were accused of orchestrating these actions. In September 2012, the government launched an investigation into *Afrika*'s publication of documents critical of the prime minister.

A 1975 agreement with Greek Cypriot authorities provides for freedom of worship, and the TRNC is officially a secular state. However, according to a March 2012 report from the U.S. Commission on International Religious Freedom, religious activities of non-Muslims are subject to some regulations, and there are still disputes over the condition of Christian churches and access to religious sites. In 2012, the CTP opposed the opening of an Islamic divinity school, which it claimed the Turkish government supported. Academic freedom is generally respected.

Freedoms of assembly and association are generally upheld, though police have been criticized for disrupting protests and allegedly using excessive force. Civic groups and nongovernmental organizations generally operate without restrictions. Workers may form independent unions, bargain collectively, and strike. However, in January 2012, a government decree blocked a strike of electrical workers in January 2012, and two dozen union members were arrested in August at a protest over government austerity measures.

The judiciary is independent, and trials generally meet international standards of fairness. Turkish Cypriot police, under the control of the Turkish military, sometimes fail to respect due process rights, and there have been allegations of abuse of detainees. Lawyers' associations and journalists have actively worked to remedy irregularities in the justice system.

The only direct flights from the TRNC are to Turkey. All EU citizens, including Greek Cypriots, can now travel to the north by presenting identity cards and no longer require passports or visas. Most governments do not recognize TRNC travel documents, so thousands of Turkish Cypriots have obtained RC passports since the option became available in 2004. However, in 2008, Turkey began forbidding Turkish Cypriots from leaving the TRNC through Turkey without TRNC passports.

A property commission formed by the TRNC in 2006 has resolved hundreds of restitution claims by Greek Cypriots who owned property in the north before the island's division. The European Court of Human Rights (ECHR) recognized the commission in 2010 as an "accessible and effective" mechanism. In July 2012, the RC government approved a controversial land swap involving property on both sides that was previously approved by the commission and the ECHR.

According to Articles 171 and 173 of the criminal code, male homosexuality is punishable with jail time. Two men were arrested in January 2012 for allegedly engaging in a homosexual act. In July 2012, a case was filed with the ECHR against Turkey—deemed responsible for administering the TRNC—to decriminalize homosexuality, though the law had not been repealed as of year's end.

Women have equal legal rights with men, but reports suggest that they face widespread discrimination. Women are underrepresented in politics, and only 4 of 50 members of parliament are women. Provisions for equal pay for women are not always enforced. In 2011, the government adopted the Council of Europe's Convention on Violence Against Women, but surveys suggest domestic violence is a major problem. The TRNC is a destination for trafficking in women, and local officials have done little to address this problem. Abortion is legal, but married women must receive permission from their husbands.

Pakistani Kashmir

Political Rights: 6   **Population:** 9,888,100
Civil Liberties: 5
Status: Not Free

Ten-Year Ratings Timeline For Year Under Review (Political Rights, Civil Liberties, Status)

2003	2004	2005	2006	2007	2008	2009	2010	2011	2012
7,5NF	7,5NF	7,5NF	7,5NF	7,5NF	6,5NF	6,5NF	6,5NF	6,5NF	6,5NF

Overview: Nationalist groups' demands for greater autonomy in Gilgit-Baltistan remained unfulfilled in 2012, and there was an increase in sectarian violence during the year. Ongoing talks between India and Pakistan yielded little substantive progress on the Kashmir dispute. Meanwhile, China continued to expand its military presence and involvement in development projects in the region.

When British India was partitioned into India and Pakistan in 1947, the Hindu maharajah of Jammu and Kashmir tried to maintain his principality's independence, but he eventually ceded it to India in return for autonomy and future self-determination. Within months, India and Pakistan went to war over the territory. Following a UN-brokered ceasefire in 1949, Pakistan refused to withdraw troops from the roughly one-third of Jammu and Kashmir that it had occupied, but unlike India, it never formally annexed its portion. The Karachi Agreement of April 1949 divided Pakistani-administered Kashmir into two distinct entities—Azad (Free) Kashmir and the Northern Areas. Pakistan retained direct administrative control over the Northern Areas, while Azad Kashmir was given a degree of nominal self-government.

A legislative assembly for Azad Kashmir was set up in 1970, and the 1974 interim constitution established a parliamentary system headed by a president and a prime minister. However, the political process was disrupted for long periods by military rule in Pakistan as a whole. Even when elections were held, Islamabad's influence over the voting and governance remained strong, and few observers considered the region's elections to be free or fair. The opposition Muslim Conference (MC) party won the 2001 elections, defeating the Azad Kashmir People's Party (AKPP), but within weeks Pakistani leader General Pervez Musharraf installed his own choice of president. In 2006, the MC again won a majority of the 41 directly elected seats in the legislature, and MC candidate Raja Zulqarnain Khan emerged as president. MC leader Sardar Attique Ahmed Khan became prime minister after receiving Musharraf's nomination, though he was eventually deposed in a 2009 no-confidence vote. Political instability and factional struggles led to a succession of several prime ministers in 2009 and 2010, with some alleging that the federal authorities had a hand in the turmoil.

In 2011 legislative elections, the AKPP won 20 of 41 seats, followed by the Pakistan Muslim League–Nawaz (PML-N) with 9 seats and the MC with 5. AKPP leader Chaudhry Abdul Majid became prime minister, and Sardar Muhammad Yaqoob Khan was installed as president.

Meanwhile, in the Northern Areas, the lack of political representation fueled demands for both formal inclusion within Pakistan and self-determination. In 1999, the Pakistani Supreme Court directed the administration to act within six months to give the Northern Areas an elected government with an independent judiciary, and to extend fundamental rights to the region's residents. The Pakistani government then announced a package that provided for an appellate court as well as an expanded and renamed Northern Areas Legislative Council (NALC). Elections to the NALC were held in 2004, but the body had few real fiscal or legislative powers. The court of appeals was established in 2005.

Faced with continued agitation for increased political rights in the Northern Areas, in August 2009 Islamabad issued the Gilgit-Baltistan Empowerment and Self-Governance Order (GBESGO), which renamed the region and replaced the Northern Areas Legal Framework Order (LFO) of 1994. It provided for a somewhat more powerful legislative body, the Gilgit-Baltistan Legislative Assembly (GBLA), with the authority to choose a chief minister and introduce legislation on 61 subjects. Nationalist groups argued that the arrangement still fell short of full internal autonomy, noting that ultimate authority rested with an appointed governor.

In November 2009 elections for the GBLA, the Pakistan People's Party (PPP), the ruling party at the federal level, won 12 of 24 directly elected seats; 10 of the remainder were divided among four other parties and four independents, and voting for two seats was postponed. Syed Mehdi Shah, head of the PPP's Gilgit-Baltistan chapter, became chief minister. Following the death of Governor Shama Khalid from cancer in September 2010, Pir Karam Ali Shah, a member of the GBLA, was appointed as governor in January 2011. In 2012, the chief minister announced that the region would be subdivided into three districts to improve administrative functions.

Despite periodic talks between India and Pakistan, little progress has been made toward a comprehensive resolution of the Kashmir dispute. Negotiations continued during 2012 without any significant breakthroughs. In recent years there has been an expanding Chinese military and economic presence in Gilgit-Baltistan, including troops involved in large-scale development and construction projects. Some locals have expressed concerns that the increasingly close relationship between Pakistan and China could pose a risk to peace and stability in the area.

Political Rights and Civil Liberties: The political rights of the residents of Pakistani-administered Kashmir remain severely limited, despite a number of improvements tied to the end of military rule and the election of a civilian government at the federal level in 2008, and elections for the new GBLA in 2009. Neither Gilgit-Baltistan nor Azad Kashmir has representation in Pakistan's Parliament.

Gilgit-Baltistan is still directly administered by the Pakistani government, meaning its status falls short of compliance with a 1999 Supreme Court ruling on the issue. Because the region is not included in the Pakistani constitution and has no constitution of its own, its people have no fundamental guarantee of civil rights, democratic representation, or separation of powers.

Under the 2009 GBESGO, Gilgit-Baltistan's political structure includes the 33-member GBLA and a chief minister, as well as a 15-member Gilgit-Baltistan Council (GBC) headed by the Pakistani prime minister and vice-chaired by the federally appointed governor. The GBC consists of six members of the GBLA and nine Pakistani Parliament members appointed by the governor. The GBLA in turn is composed of 24 directly elected members, 6 seats reserved for women, and 3 seats reserved for technocrats; the reserved seats are filled through a vote by the elected members. Ultimate authority rests with the governor, who has significant power over judicial appointments and whose decisions cannot be overruled by the GBLA. Many fiscal powers remain with the GBC rather than the elected assembly. A majority of high-level positions in the local administration are reserved under the GBESGO for Pakistani bureaucrats.

No proindependence candidates won seats in the 2009 GBLA elections. Local nationalist leaders accused the authorities of preventing their parties from holding public gatherings, and a number of nationalist leaders and candidates were arrested during the campaign period. Although violence erupted between supporters of rival candidates, the elections themselves were largely peaceful. Independent observer missions characterized the elections as competitive, despite flaws including an inaccurate voter list, allegations of rigging and interference, and misuse of state resources to benefit the ruling PPP.

Azad Kashmir has an interim constitution, an elected unicameral assembly, a prime minister, and a president who is elected by the assembly. Both the president and the legislature serve five-year terms. Of the 49 assembly seats, 41 are filled through direct elections: 29 with constituencies based in Azad Kashmir and 12 representing Kashmiri "refugees" throughout Pakistan. Another eight are reserved seats: five for women and one each for representatives of overseas Kashmiris, technocrats, and religious leaders. However, Pakistan exercises considerable control over the structures of government and electoral politics. Islamabad's approval is required to pass legislation, and the federal minister for Kashmir affairs handles daily administration and controls the budget. The Kashmir Council—chaired by the president of Pakistan and composed of federal officials, Kashmiri assembly members, and the Azad Kashmir president and prime minister—also holds a number of key executive, legislative, and judicial powers, such as the authority to appoint superior judges and the chief election commissioner. The Pakistani military retains a guiding role on issues of politics and governance.

Those who do not support Azad Kashmir's accession to Pakistan are barred from the political process, government employment, and educational institutions. They are also subject to surveillance, harassment, and sometimes imprisonment by Pakistani security services. The 2011 legislative elections in Azad Kashmir were marred by allegations of rigging and vote buying, as well as some violence and harassment, with at least three election-related killings reported.

Azad Kashmir receives a large amount of financial aid from Islamabad, but successive administrations have been tainted by corruption and incompetence. Aid agencies have also been accused of misusing funds. A lack of official accountability has been identified as a key factor in the poor socioeconomic condition of both Azad Kashmir and Gilgit-Baltistan. However, the region has benefited from improvements in accountability at the federal level and the transfer of some budgetary powers to the GBLA in 2009.

The Pakistani government uses the constitution and other laws to curb freedom of speech on a variety of subjects, including the status of Kashmir and sectarian violence. Media owners cannot publish in Azad Kashmir without permission from the Kashmir Council and the Ministry of Kashmir Affairs. Several dailies and weeklies operate in Gilgit-Baltistan, mostly under the auspices of the K-2 publishing house, and provide some scrutiny of official affairs. However, authorities have banned a number of local newspapers and detained or otherwise harassed journalists in recent years. In June 2012, Gilgit police arrested and briefly detained two journalists over an article alleging that a superior had addressed the law minister using foul language. Local journalists have also faced harassment and attacks from nonstate actors. In October 2012, PML-N supporters stormed a local press club meeting and assaulted at least two members. In the aftermath of a devastating 2005 earthquake, local press freedom organizations set up private radio stations that focus on news and humanitarian information, contributing to greater media diversity. Internet access is not usually restricted but remains rare outside urban centers. Both telephone and internet services in Gilgit-Baltistan are under the control of the Pakistani military, which has unfettered powers of surveillance. The government suspended cellular service in the region on multiple occasions during 2012.

Pakistan is an Islamic republic, and there are numerous official restrictions on religious freedom. Religious minorities also face unofficial discrimination and are occasionally subject to violent attack. Since 2009 there has been an upsurge in sectarian violence between Shiite Muslims, who form a majority in Gilgit-Baltistan, and Sunni Muslims who have migrated to the region with the tacit support of federal authorities. This trend continued in 2012. In February, men in Pakistani military uniforms stopped four buses en route to Gilgit near the region's border with Khyber Pakhtunkhwa and killed the 18 Shiite passengers. The authorities arrested five suspects in March. A similar massacre in August claimed the lives of 25 Shiites in the same border region. In April, assailants attacked a Sunni rally in Gilgit-Baltistan, killing 6 people and injuring 50. At least 10 Shiites were killed in retaliation. In May, the GBLA passed a law aimed at curbing Sunni-Shiite violence, forbidding clerics of one sect from issuing edicts or statements against the other.

Academic freedom and opportunities are limited. Local groups continue to call for the right to instruction on Shiite and Sufi Muslim teachings, as well as local languages and scripts, in government-run schools. Such practices are discouraged by the Pakistani authorities. Many areas do not have schools for girls, and hundreds of teachers receive below-minimum wages and are paid irregularly.

Freedoms of association and assembly are restricted. The constitution of Azad Kashmir forbids individuals and groups from engaging in activities that are prejudicial to the region's accession to Pakistan. Police in recent years have regularly suppressed antigovernment demonstrations and protests concerning economic hardship and displacement, sometimes violently. In May 2012, it was reported that five human rights activists had been tortured in custody, having been detained since August 2011 over their protests on behalf of displaced disaster victims. Political leaders in Gilgit-Baltistan have also faced arrest and detention.

Nongovernmental organizations (NGOs) that work on humanitarian issues are generally able to operate freely, while those focused on political or human rights issues face more scrutiny and occasional harassment. The situation for labor rights is similar to that in Pakistan, but with even fewer protections for workers. Unions and professional associations have routinely been banned by the authorities.

The chairman of the GBC appoints Gilgit-Baltistan's chief judge and other judges on the advice of the governor. All judicial appointments in Gilgit-Baltistan are based on three-year contracts subject to discretionary renewal by the bureaucracy, leaving the judiciary largely subservient to the executive. In addition, the judiciary is not empowered to hear cases concerning fundamental rights or cases against the executive. Meanwhile, as the 1999 Supreme Court ruling has not yet been fully implemented, cases concerning Gilgit-Baltistan are considered outside the jurisdiction of the Supreme Court of Pakistan.

Azad Kashmir has its own system of local magistrates and a High Court, with senior judges appointed by the president of Azad Kashmir in consultation with the Kashmir Council and the prime minister of Pakistan. Appeals are adjudicated by the Supreme Court of Pakistan. There are also Islamic judges who handle criminal cases concerning Islamic law (Sharia). Disputes over the politicization of judicial appointments remain a concern, and law professionals claim that favoritism and delays in appointments hinder the courts' ability to function effectively and independently. The High Court had been virtually nonfunctional due to unfilled vacancies, and over 9,000 cases are pending. In September 2012, the government increased the number of judges in both civil and Sharia courts in order to reduce case backlogs. Two Islamic judges were inducted in November, but four of seven High Court seats remained vacant.

Pakistan's Inter-Services Intelligence Directorate reportedly engages in extensive surveillance—particularly of proindependence groups and the press—as well as arbitrary arrests and detentions. In some instances, those detained by the security forces are tortured, and several cases of death in custody have been reported. Disappearances in Pakistani-held Kashmir have allegedly targeted individuals who refuse to cooperate with intelligence agencies or participate in militant actions on Indian-held territory. Impunity for such abuses remains the norm. In October 2012, Khushal Hussain Qazi, a former militant, was taken into custody in Azad Kashmir. His wife found him the following day in a hospital under the watch of military personnel, with visible signs of torture, before he was moved to an undisclosed location. His wife received threats after approaching the media regarding the disappearance. Under the colonial-era Frontier Crimes Regulations, residents are required to report to local police stations once a month. A large number of Pakistani military personnel are stationed in Gilgit-Baltistan, particularly at times of potential unrest.

Islamist militant groups that once focused on attacks in Indian-administered Kashmir are reportedly expanding their local influence and activities, including the establishment of religious schools. They have also increased cooperation with militants based in Pakistan's tribal areas. Tension between pro-Pakistan Islamist groups and proindependence Kashmiri groups—as well as some local residents—has reportedly grown in recent years, contributing to the rise in attacks against local Shiites.

Since the 1970s, the Pakistani government has encouraged the settlement of Pakistanis in Gilgit-Baltistan in an effort to shift the demographic and ethnic balance in the region. Under the GBESGO, many of these settlers were given formal citizenship rights in Gilgit-Baltistan. In response to outbreaks of sectarian violence in 2012, the city of Gilgit imposed a curfew in April that lasted 25 days. Authorities also discontinued cellular service and suspended traffic on the Karakoram Highway, leading to food shortages.

Several hundred families displaced by shelling between Indian and Pakistani forces prior to a 2003 ceasefire remain unable to return to their homes and have largely been excluded from assistance schemes launched after the 2005 earthquake. The Azad Kashmir government manages camps for refugees from Indian-administered Kashmir, the bulk of whom arrived after the situation on the Indian side worsened in 1989. Many more of the refugees (roughly 1.5 million) live elsewhere in Azad Kashmir and Pakistan. In January 2012, the Azad Kashmir government announced a $1.1 billion refugee resettlement plan that includes the eventual allocation of residential plots. Bus services linking Indian and Pakistani Kashmir have been established over the past decade, and limited trade across the Line of Control resumed in 2008 for the first time in over 60 years.

The status of women in Pakistani-administered Kashmir is similar to that of women in Pakistan. While honor killings and rape reportedly occur less frequently than in Pakistan, domestic violence, forced marriage, and other forms of abuse are issues of concern. Women are also at risk of molestation and attack by Pakistani troops, and such attacks often go unpunished. Women are not granted equal rights under the law, and their educational opportunities and choice of marriage partners remain circumscribed. As in some parts of Pakistan, suspected Islamists occasionally mount attacks against NGOs that employ women and on their female employees.

Puerto Rico

Political Rights: 1
Civil Liberties: 2
Status: Free

Population: 3,691,000

Ten-Year Ratings Timeline For Year Under Review (Political Rights, Civil Liberties, Status)

2003	2004	2005	2006	2007	2008	2009	2010	2011	2012
1,2F	1,2F	1,1F	1,1F	1,1F	1,1F	1,1F	1,1F	1,2F	1,2F

Overview: Accusations of police violations of civil rights, first reported by the U.S. Justice Department in 2011, were reinforced by similar findings from the American Civil Liberties Union in 2012. Alejandro García Padilla narrowly defeated incumbent Luis Fortuño in the November gubernatorial race. In a concurrent nonbinding resolution on Puerto Rico's territorial status, effectively fewer than half chose statehood.

Having been seized by U.S. forces during the Spanish-American War in 1898, Puerto Rico became a U.S. commonwealth following approval by plebiscite in 1952. As a commonwealth, Puerto Rico exercises approximately the same control over its internal affairs as do the 50 states.

Power has alternated between the pro-commonwealth Popular Democratic Party (PPD) and the pro-statehood New Progressive Party (PNP) for several decades. Aníbal Acevedo-Vilá of the PPD won the 2004 gubernatorial election, defeating his PNP opponent by a razor-thin margin. A U.S. grand jury indicted him on corruption charges in March 2008, but he refused to withdraw his candidacy before the November 2008 elections. The PNP gubernatorial candidate, Luis Fortuño, who had served as the island's representative in the U.S. Congress, thus soundly defeated the incumbent, while the PNP secured overwhelming majorities in both legislative chambers.

Fortuño raised taxes and cut 30,000 public jobs in order to combat a fiscal crisis exacerbated by the global economic downturn, triggering protests from trade unions in 2009. An additional 17,000 public jobs were cut in 2010, leading to further protests. From April to June 2010, University of Puerto Rico students went on strike, closing down 10 of the system's 11 campuses to protest tuition hikes and cuts in public spending for higher education. Police attempts to halt the protests resulted in some violence.

In September 2011, a U.S. Justice Department report accused the Puerto Rico Police Department (PRPD) of "profound" and "longstanding" patterns of civil rights violations and other illegal practices that have left it in a state of "institutional dysfunction." According to the report, police frequently attack nonviolent protesters and journalists in a manner that compromises their constitutionally protected rights to freedom of speech and assembly and use unnecessary or gratuitous force, especially in low-income and Dominican communities. The report also accused police of unwarranted searches and seizures. The police superintendent at the time, Emilio Díaz Colón, and the Puerto Rico Justice Department claimed the report was untrustworthy and lacked objectivity—a position that Héctor Pesquera, appointed superintendent in March 2012, apparently supported.

A June 2012 American Civil Liberties Union (ACLU) report on Puerto Rico's police force further corroborated the Justice Department findings. It charged that the PRPD's "use of excessive or lethal force is routine, and civil and human rights violations are rampant," and includes the targeting of poor, African-descent Puerto Ricans and Dominican immigrants.

In the November 6, 2012, gubernatorial election, Senator Alejandro García Padilla of the PPD received 47.7 percent of the vote, narrowly defeating incumbent Fortuño, who captured 47.1 percent. Four other candidates received less than 3 percent each.

A two-part, nonbinding referendum on Puerto Rico's territorial status was held on the same day as the election. The first question, which asked voters whether they wanted Puerto Rico to maintain its current territorial status, was supported by only 46 percent of the voters. A second question asked voters to choose whether they preferred statehood, independence, or a sovereign free associated state; the statehood option was selected by 61 percent of voters. However, with more than 470,000 voters choosing not to answer the question, in effect only 45 percent supported statehood.

Political Rights and Civil Liberties: The commonwealth constitution, modeled after that of the United States, provides for a governor elected for four-year terms and a bicameral legislature, consisting of a 27-member Senate and a 51-member House of Representatives elected for four-year terms. As U.S. citizens, Puerto Ricans are guaranteed all civil liberties granted in the United States, though they cannot vote in U.S. presidential elections. A single delegate represents Puerto Rico in the U.S. Congress and is allowed to vote on floor amendments to legislation, but not on the final passage of bills. For years, Puerto Ricans have been nearly equally divided between support for commonwealth status and full U.S. statehood, while a third option of independence enjoys little popular support.

Corruption is endemic in Puerto Rican politics. A number of leading political figures have been indicted in recent years on various corruption charges. Puerto Rico was ranked 33 out of 176 countries and territories surveyed in Transparency International's 2012 Corruption Perceptions Index.

Puerto Rico's tradition of varied and vigorous news media has been challenged by a decline in newspapers stemming from the economic crisis and other factors.

Freedom of religion is guaranteed in this largely Roman Catholic territory. A substantial number of Evangelical churches have also been established on the island in recent years. Academic freedom is guaranteed.

Freedom of assembly is protected by law, and Puerto Ricans frequently protest local or federal government policies. There is a robust civil society, with numerous nongovernmental organizations representing special interests. The government respects trade union rights, and unions are generally free to organize and strike.

The legal system is based on U.S. law, and the island's Supreme Court heads an independent judiciary. However, concerns about politicization at the Supreme Court emerged in 2010, when the four justices Governor Luis Fortuño appointed approved a congressional resolution expanding the court from seven to nine members, ostensibly to deal with a heavy caseload, over the objections of the three-justice minority. Fortuño appointed the two new justices in 2011, giving his appointees an overwhelming majority on the court, potentially for many years to come.

Crime is a serious problem in Puerto Rico. The center of the narcotics trade has shifted from San Juan to smaller communities, leaving housing projects in some towns under virtual siege by drug gangs. By October 2012, 759 people had been murdered, down 146 from the same date in 2011. Increasing numbers of homicides include hate violence against members of the LGBT (lesbian, gay, bisexual, and transgender) community, of which at least 30 have been documented since 2002.

In recent years, illegal immigration from various Caribbean countries to Puerto Rico has increased. There is evidence that police officers routinely discriminate against Dominicans living on the island.

Although women enjoy equal rights under the law, the 2011 U.S. Justice Department report cited evidence that police officers failed to investigate incidents of sexual assault and domestic violence, including spousal abuse by fellow officers.

Somaliland

Political Rights: 4
Civil Liberties: 5
Status: Partly Free

Population: 3,500,000

Ten-Year Ratings Timeline For Year Under Review (Political Rights, Civil Liberties, Status)

2003	2004	2005	2006	2007	2008	2009	2010	2011	2012
--	--	--	4,4PF	4,4PF	5,4PF	5,5PF	4,5PF	4,5PF	4,5PF

Overview: The Somaliland government employed a heavy-handed response to political criticism in 2012. More than 80 journalists were arrested and temporarily detained throughout the year. Postponed local elections were ultimately November, and opposition groups held protests over registration and vote count disputes throughout the year.

The modern state of Somalia was formed in 1960 when the newly independent protectorates of British Somaliland and Italian Somaliland agreed to unite. In 1969, General Siad Barre seized power, ushering in a violent era of clan rivalries and political repression. Barre was deposed in 1991. The current Somaliland, located in the northwestern corner of the country, took advantage of the resulting political chaos and declared independence later that year.

In a series of conferences, Somaliland's leaders formed a government system combining democratic elements, including a parliament, with traditional political structures, such as an upper house consisting of clan elders. Somaliland's first two presidents were appointed by clan elders. In 2003, Dahir Riyale Kahin became Somaliland's first elected president, and direct elections for members of the lower house of parliament were held for the first time in 2005, with no reports of widespread intimidation or fraud. The president's United People's Democratic Party (UDUB) captured the most seats, followed closely by the Peace, Unity, and Development Party (Kulmiye) and the Justice and Development Party (UCID).

In 2006, Riyale violated the constitution by postponing elections for the upper house and extending its term by four years. The presidential election was delayed until June 2010, eight months after Riyale's extended term officially expired. The leader of Kulmiye, Ahmed Mohamed Silanyo, captured almost 50 percent of the vote, comfortably ahead of Riyale, who received 33 percent. International monitors identified some irregularities, but declared the vote free and fair. While the presidential elections were a success, long overdue legislative elections were again postponed in 2010, until 2013 for the lower house and 2014 for the upper house.

Postponed local council elections eventually took place in November 2012. Though the elections were declared generally free and fair by international observers, large protests followed a recount in Hargeisa's city council elections. The UDUB had announced in September that it would not participate after alleged attempts by the Political Parties Registration and Verification Committee (PPR&VC) to discredit it by revoking the candidacy of two of the party's leading members on possibly dubious grounds. The PPR&VC had also been criticized in April after it refused to register nine political groups. That decision was met with protests in the cities of Hargeisa, Burao, and Berbera.

Somaliland has had difficult relations with the rest of Somalia, particularly the semiautonomous region of Puntland. The neighbors have rival claims to the Sool, Sanaag, and Cayn regions. Previously under the control of Somaliland, these three regions, now known as Khaatumo State, declared autonomy from Somaliland in January 2012 and stated their intention to remain part of greater Somalia. In February, 6,000 people were displaced in Buuhoodle, capital of the Cayn region, after clashes between Somaliland's military and clan militias loyal to Khaatumo. Clashes continued throughout 2012, including deadly demonstrations in Sool in November by members of the population who rejected the holding of the Somaliland local elections in that region.

The most devastating drought to hit the Horn of Africa in six decades had caused serious hardship in Somaliland in 2011, though the authorities responded fairly well to the crisis. Drought conditions persisted throughout 2012 due to erratic rainfall, with an estimated 20,000 affected families, and the Somaliland government appealed to the international community for support.

Political Rights and Civil Liberties: According to Somaliland's constitution, the president is directly elected for a maximum of two five-year terms and appoints the cabinet. The presidential election of 2010, originally scheduled for 2008, resulted in a smooth transfer of power from the UDUB party to the main opposition party, Kulmiye. Members of Somaliland's 82-seat lower house of parliament, the House of Representatives, are directly elected for five-year terms, while members of the 82-seat upper house, or Guurti, are indirectly elected for six-year terms. In 2010, the terms of the lower and upper house were extended until 2013 and 2014, respectively, on the grounds that Somaliland could not organize another election so soon after the presidential poll.

A constitutional restriction that allowed for a maximum of three political parties was relaxed in 2011 following a vote in parliament. In October 2011, a new party, Waddani, was formed by breakaway members of the UCID party. Although parties defined by region or clan are technically prohibited, party and clan affiliations often coincide.

Corruption in Somaliland was a serious problem under the government of President Dahir Riyale Kahin, but there have been signs of improvement under his successor, President Ahmed Mohamed Silanyo. In March 2012, three top officials charged with mismanaging food aid were fired. The three claimed that the government had pressured the judge to convict them. In June, Abdirashid Duraan, the judge who presided over the case, was wounded after being shot by unknown gunmen. A bill to strengthen the five-member Good Governance and Anti-Corruption Commission, an informal body established in 2010, passed the lower house in October and the upper house in November; this was the latest effort to crack down on the misuse of public funds.

While freedoms of expression and the press are guaranteed by the constitution, these rights are limited in practice. Journalists faced increased government interference and harassment in 2012. In August, the Somaliland Journalist Association characterized 2012 as "the worst time for freedom of expression in Somaliland," and in December cited the arrest and temporary detention of 81 journalists that year, compared to 51 cases in all of 2011. Demonstrations following a January 2012 police raid against Horn Cable TV, a private media outlet that Silanyo accused of "spreading propaganda against his administration," led to the arrest and temporary detention of more than 20 journalists. Somali 24 TV reporter Ahmed Ali Farah was arrested in late March for covering a conference announcing the independence of Khaatumo State. Somaliland National Television journalist Hodan Abokor Afi was beaten in August while covering a child custody case; her suspected attacker was a deputy police commander. Though she filed a complaint, it was reportedly dismissed. The government owns the only domestic radio station, Radio Hargeisa, and prohibits the establishment of private stations. There are seven private daily newspapers in addition to the state-owned *Mandeeq*, although they have limited circulations. The government does not restrict access to the internet.

Islam is the state religion, and nearly all Somaliland residents are Sunni Muslims. While the Somaliland constitution allows for freedom of belief, it prohibits conversion from Islam and proselytizing by members of other faiths. It also requires that candidates for the presidency, vice presidency, and House of Representatives be Muslim. Academic freedom is less restricted than in neighboring Somalia. The territory has at least 10 universities and colleges of higher learning, though none are adequately resourced.

Freedoms of assembly and association are constitutionally guaranteed. However, the government banned political demonstrations after the May 2012 arrests of three opposition leaders in Hargeisa, who were protesting the PPR&VC's decision to disqualify their groups from participating in the November local elections. The government mounted a crackdown on demonstrations held in support of the new government in Somalia. In August, dozens of men were arrested in Las Anod for organizing a demonstration to commemorate the new Somali parliament. In October, 15 elderly women and several journalists were arrested in the Sool region for rallying in support of the newly appointed Somali prime minister.

International and local nongovernmental organizations operate without serious interference. The constitution does not specifically mention the right to strike, though it does permit collective bargaining. The right to belong to a union is generally respected.

The judiciary is underfunded and lacks independence, while the Supreme Court is largely ineffective. Somaliland has approximately 100 judges, most of whom do not have formal legal training. Somaliland's constitution allows for three legal systems, based on Sharia (Islamic law), civil law, and customary law. Upon taking office, Silanyo pledged to strengthen the independence of the judiciary and release all prisoners who had not been charged with a crime, apart from those accused of terrorism or theft. In May 2011, he pardoned 751 prisoners to mark Somaliland's twentieth anniversary. Somaliland's police and security forces, while more professional than those in Somalia, have at times used excessive force.

Societal fault lines are largely clan based. Larger, wealthier clans have more political clout than the less-prominent groups, and clan elders often intervene to settle conflicts. There has been increased discrimination against foreigners. In January 2012, the government confirmed the forced return of 15 unregistered Ethiopian refugees and 5 asylum seekers who were squatting at an informal settlement in Hargeisa known as the Social Welfare Centre. Though condemned by Human Rights Watch, the deportations continued. In August, about 100 Ethiopian refugees, largely women and children, were deported.

While society in Somaliland is patriarchal, women have made modest advances in public life. Silanyo appointed 2 women to his 20-member cabinet. There is only one woman in the House of Representatives, one in the Guurti, and a woman was elected chairperson of the Somaliland Human Rights Commission. Female genital mutilation, while illegal, is practiced on the vast majority of women.

South Ossetia

Political Rights: 7
Civil Liberties: 6
Status: Not Free

Population: 70,000

Ten-Year Ratings Timeline For Year Under Review (Political Rights, Civil Liberties, Status)

2003	2004	2005	2006	2007	2008	2009	2010	2011	2012
--	--	--	--	--	7,6NF	7,6NF	7,6NF	7,6NF	7,6NF

Overview: Security forces prevented Alla Dzhioyeva, an opposition candidate who had led a November 2011 presidential election before the Supreme Court annulled the results, from proceeding with her unilateral inauguration in February 2012. A repeat election went forward in March with four new candidates, and former security chief Leonid Tibilov won the presidency with 54 percent of the vote in an April runoff. He pledged to root out his predecessor's alleged corruption and included Dzhioyeva and his runoff opponent in his cabinet. While the political crisis calmed somewhat during the year, further elite infighting and Russia's overriding influence continued to threaten the territory's stability.

South Ossetia first declared its independence from Georgia in 1920, igniting a war that left thousands dead. Both Georgia and South Ossetia were incorporated into the Soviet Union in 1922, with South Ossetia designated an autonomous oblast (region) within Georgia.

As Georgian nationalism grew toward the end of the Soviet era, South Ossetia declared independence from Georgia in 1990, and fighting broke out in January 1991, resulting in a thousand deaths and civilian displacement on both sides. In March 1991, a reported 99 percent of South Ossetian referendum voters endorsed independence, and 90 percent voted in favor of seeking to join Russia in a January 1992 referendum, after the final dissolution of the Soviet Union. Both plebiscites were rejected by Tbilisi.

In June 1992, a ceasefire agreement established a Russian-led peacekeeping force, and the Organization for Security and Cooperation in Europe was put in charge of monitoring the ceasefire and facilitating negotiations on a permanent resolution of the conflict.

Torez Kulumbegov led separatist South Ossetia from 1992 to 1993. He was succeeded by Lyudvig Chibirov, who went on to win the newly created post of president in 1996. After a period of relatively cordial relations with Tbilisi, the 2001 election of hard-liner Eduard Kokoity as president of South Ossetia renewed tensions. His Unity Party took the majority of seats in 2004 parliamentary elections; though four seats were reserved for the territory's ethnic Georgian population, only five Georgian villages were able to vote. All of the separatist regime's elections went unrecognized by Georgia and the international community.

In May 2004, recently elected Georgian president Mikheil Saakashvili ordered a campaign to dismantle the multimillion-dollar smuggling operation controlled by Kokoity's regime, triggering skirmishes and causing Ossetians to rally around Kokoity. The two sides agreed to a ceasefire in August, but the separatist government in Tskhinvali rejected Saakashvili's proposal for expanded South Ossetian autonomy within Georgia in September.

South Ossetia held a joint referendum and presidential election in November 2006, with 99.8 percent of voters on Ossetian-controlled territory reaffirming the bid for independence, according to Tskhinvali. Kokoity, who faced no genuine opposition, was reelected with a reported 98.1 percent of the vote. On the same day, Tbilisi organized a similarly lopsided election and referendum in South Ossetia's Georgian-controlled areas, but the resulting pro-Georgian government was never able to draw significant support away from separatist institutions.

Following weeks of skirmishes along the border, Tbilisi launched an attack on Tskhinvali on August 7, 2008. Russia immediately sent troops into South Ossetia, pushing back Georgian forces. Russia also invaded Georgia via Abkhazia, another breakaway Georgian territory in the northwest. Both sides signed a French-brokered ceasefire by August 16, and Russian troops eventually withdrew to the confines of South Ossetia and Abkhazia, though separatist forces retained some territory previously controlled by Tbilisi. Despite international criticism, Moscow recognized South Ossetia and Abkhazia as independent states on August 26 and subsequently concluded bilateral security agreements with the separatist governments, augmenting its long-term military presence.

In May 2009, South Ossetia held parliamentary elections that resulted in a legislature dominated by Kokoity supporters, amid accusations that the president had shut out and threatened opposition parties. Many Ossetians also accused Kokoity of embezzling Russian aid as the postwar reconstruction process dragged on in 2009 and 2010. A Russian report released in December 2009 found that only a fraction of the money had been used for its intended purposes, and Tskhinvali residents mounted several protests over the issue in 2010. Russia significantly expanded its control over the territory during 2011, and talk of annexation gained momentum.

In June 2011, the parliament rejected efforts by Kokoity supporters to lift term limits and allow him to participate in a presidential election set for November. Eleven candidates ultimately ran in the first round on November 13, including several Kokoity loyalists; six other candidates were forced or pressured to withdraw. Opposition candidate Alla Dzhioyeva, a former education minister who opposed Russian annexation, and Moscow-backed candidate Anatoly Bibilov, South Ossetia's emergency situations minister, each won about 25 percent of the vote and advanced to the November 27 runoff. Results showed Dzhioyeva as the second-round winner with nearly 57 percent, but amid questionable claims of electoral violations, the Supreme Court declared the election invalid and ordered a new vote for March 2012.

The ruling triggered protests by Dzhioyeva's supporters that continued until mid-December, when Russia brokered a compromise under which Dzhioyeva would accept the court's ruling if Kokoity stepped down immediately and the parliament fired the prosecutor general and the Supreme Court chairman. Kokoity stepped down, and Prime Minister Vadim Brovtsev became acting president. However, the parliament rejected the other conditions, prompting Dzhioyeva to announce that she would go ahead with her inauguration on February 10, 2012. On February 9, about 200 security personnel raided her headquarters and attempted to detain her. She was hospitalized after the confrontation, with some reports saying she was struck with a rifle and the authorities maintaining that she fainted due to high blood pressure.

Four new candidates, all reportedly favorable to Russia, ran in the repeat election on March 25. Dzhioyeva was barred from running, and neither her nor Kokoity's camp succeeded in fielding a candidate. Leonid Tibilov, who had led South Ossetia's Committee for State Security (KGB) in the 1990s, received 42 percent, followed by human rights ombudsman David Sanakoyev with about 25 percent. Tibilov won the April 8 runoff with 54 percent of the vote and was sworn in as president on April 19.

Having promised during the campaign to tackle corruption and foster stability, Tibilov initiated an investigation of Kokoity's alleged embezzlement and replaced a number of reputedly corrupt officials. He also left some officials in their posts, including Bibilov. In keeping with a pledge of national unity, he appointed Sanakoyev as foreign minister and Dzhioyeva as deputy prime minister.

Despite a period of relative calm after the election, violent attacks on public officials and ongoing political battles between the new leadership and Kokoity loyalists threatened to undermine the territory's fragile stability. In July, a former state security official was seriously injured by an unidentified gunman. A week later, a member of the prosecutor's office was abducted and killed. And in September, a bomb blast struck the home of the deputy defense minister.

Political Rights and Civil Liberties: Under the separatist constitution, the president and the 33-seat parliament are elected for five-year terms. South Ossetian elections are not monitored by independent observers or recognized by the international community. Most ethnic Georgians have either declined or been unable to participate in such elections.

During the May 2009 parliamentary elections, opposition parties reported significant violations, including substantial voter coercion. Opposition representation was also reduced as a result of 2008 election laws, which set a 7 percent vote threshold for parties to enter parliament and required all lawmakers to be elected by proportional representation.

The 2011 presidential election campaign featured violence and other abuses by the government of outgoing president Eduard Kokoity. The leading opposition candidates were prevented from registering due in part to a 10-year residency requirement that was added to the constitution earlier that year. Other opposition candidates were beaten or jailed, and one senior member of a disqualified candidate's party was murdered in North Ossetia in October.

Russia exerts an overriding influence on South Ossetian politics, and its degree of control increased substantially after the 2008 war. Officials reputedly endorsed by Moscow have held key government positions in recent years, and Russia was allegedly opposed to opposition candidate Alla Dzhioyeva taking office as president after the 2011 election. The parliament in 2011 signed a 49-year agreement allowing Russia to build and operate a new military base in Tskhinvali; there were already over 4,000 Russian troops stationed in the territory. In September 2012, the European Union Monitoring Mission in Georgia reported a buildup of Russian military forces along the administrative boundary separating South Ossetia from the rest of Georgia.

Corruption is believed to be extensive. Before the 2008 war, the territory reportedly hosted large-scale smuggling and black-market activities. Kokoity's alleged embezzlement of Russian funds earmarked for postwar reconstruction became a major issue in the 2011 and 2012 elections. After his inauguration in April 2012, President Leonid Tibilov ordered an investigation into Kokoity's alleged graft.

South Ossetia's local electronic and print media are almost entirely controlled by separatist authorities, and private broadcasts are prohibited. Foreign media, including broadcasts from Russia and Georgia, are accessible. Independent or opposition-oriented journalists in the territory face various forms of intimidation, including trumped-up criminal charges. According to opposition journalist Fatima Margiyeva, a brief period of relative press freedom during the 2012 presidential campaign was reversed under Tibilov.

Freedom of religion has sometimes been adversely affected by the political and military situation. While the majority of the population is Orthodox Christian, there is a sizeable Muslim community, many members of which migrated from the North Caucasus. The educational system reflects government views, and many South Ossetians receive higher education in Russia.

While antigovernment protests were extremely rare before the 2008 war, opposition groups mounted demonstrations following the flawed 2009 elections, and Tskhinvali residents have protested repeatedly in response to the slow postwar construction of new homes and alleged government corruption. In 2011, one human rights activist was beaten and another threatened after leading such demonstrations. Dzhioyeva's supporters held weeks of peaceful protests in November 2011 after the annulment of the presidential election, which Kokoity called unauthorized and threatened with violence. Civil society groups operate under the close scrutiny of the authorities, and activists are subject to intimidation.

South Ossetia's justice system has been manipulated to punish perceived opponents of the separatist leadership, while government allies allegedly violate the law with relative impunity. Russian prosecutors have attempted to curb malfeasance by local officials, but the Russian court system itself remains deeply flawed.

Indiscriminate attacks by both sides in the 2008 war killed and displaced civilians, and Ossetian forces seized or razed property in previously Georgian-controlled villages. Authorities in South Ossetia have barred ethnic Georgians from returning to the territory unless they renounce their Georgian citizenship and accept Russian passports. The de facto border with Georgia was tightened in 2011, with several Georgians subjected to detention by Ossetian and Russian border guards. Russian authorities have prevented ethnic Ossetians from entering Georgia, but travel to Russia is unimpeded.

Tibet

Political Rights: 7
Civil Liberties: 7
Status: Not Free

Population: 3,000,000 [Note: This figure from China's 2010 census covers only the Tibet Autonomous Region. Areas of eastern Tibet that were incorporated into neighboring Chinese provinces are also assessed in the report below.]

Ten-Year Ratings Timeline For Year Under Review (Political Rights, Civil Liberties, Status)

2003	2004	2005	2006	2007	2008	2009	20010	2010	2012
7,7NF	7,7NF	7,7NF	7,7NF	7,7NF	7,7NF	7,7NF	7,7NF	7,7NF	7,7NF

Overview: The security clampdown established after an uprising in 2008 was sustained during 2012 and increasingly extended to Tibetan areas outside the Tibet Autonomous Region. Over the course of the year, a total of 84 Tibetans set themselves on fire to protest Chinese Communist rule. The authorities responded with communications blackouts, "patriotic education" campaigns, travel restrictions, and intrusive new controls on monasteries. Despite the repressive atmosphere, many Tibetans expressed solidarity with self-immolators, protested language policies, and quietly maintained contact with the exile community.

The Tibetan plateau, or a substantial portion of it, was ruled by a Dalai Lama or his government from the mid-17th century onward. Chinese Communist forces entered Tibet in 1950 and defeated the Tibetan army. The region was formally incorporated into the People's Republic of China the following year. In 1959, Chinese troops suppressed a major uprising in Lhasa, reportedly killing tens of thousands of people. Tibet's spiritual and political leader—the 14th Dalai Lama, Tenzin Gyatso—was forced to flee to India with some 80,000 supporters.

During the next six years, China closed 97 percent of the region's Buddhist monasteries and defrocked about 100,000 monks and nuns. Most Tibetan territory was reorganized as the Tibet Autonomous Region (TAR) in 1965, but some eastern portions of the Tibetan plateau were included in separate Chinese provinces. During the Chinese Cultural Revolution (1966–76), nearly all of Tibet's estimated 6,200 monasteries were destroyed.

Under reforms introduced in 1980, limited religious practice was allowed again. Between 1987 and 1989, some 200 mostly peaceful demonstrations were mounted in Lhasa and surrounding areas. After the antigovernment protests escalated in March 1989, martial law was imposed until May 1990.

In the 1990s, Beijing reinvigorated its efforts to control religious affairs and undermine the exiled Dalai Lama's authority. Six-year-old Gendun Choekyi Nyima was detained by the authorities in 1995, and his selection by the Dalai Lama as the 11th Panchen Lama was rejected. He subsequently disappeared from public view, and Beijing orchestrated the selection of another six-year-old boy as the Panchen Lama. Since one of the roles of the Panchen Lama is to identify the reincarnated Dalai Lama, the move was widely seen as a bid to control the eventual selection of the 15th Dalai Lama.

China hosted envoys of the Dalai Lama in 2002, marking the first formal contact since 1993. The Tibetan government in exile sought genuine autonomy for Tibet, particularly to ensure the survival of its Buddhist culture, but the Chinese side said it would only discuss the return of the Dalai Lama and not broader conditions in Tibet. Meanwhile, other Tibetan exile groups increasingly demanded independence.

Under Zhang Qingli, who was appointed as Chinese Communist Party (CCP) secretary in the TAR in 2005, the authorities amplified their repressive policies. In addition, the party began extending harsher restrictions on Tibetan religion and language to the previously more open neighboring provinces, spurring growing resentment. In March 2008, after security agents suppressed a march by monks on the anniversary of the 1959 uprising, a riot erupted in Lhasa. Over 150 other protests, most of them reportedly peaceful, soon broke out in Tibetan-populated areas. The government responded with a massive deployment of armed forces. The authorities reported that 19 people were killed in Lhasa, primarily in fires, while overseas Tibetan groups claimed that between 100 and 218 Tibetans were killed as security forces suppressed the demonstrations.

The tight security conditions established in 2008 were generally maintained over the subsequent years, with especially restrictive measures imposed around politically sensitive dates. A young monk in Sichuan Province set himself on fire to protest CCP rule in 2009, and a series similar self-immolations gained momentum in 2011. In 2012, the incidents spread geographically and increasingly involved lay Tibetans rather than monks and nuns alone. A total of 84 Tibetans reportedly self-immolated during 2012. The vast majority of the incidents were in Sichuan, Qinghai, and Gansu Provinces, with only 8 of the 112 that had occurred since 2009 taking place in the TAR. Most of the self-immolators shouted slogans referring to political and religious freedom, and almost all died from their injuries.

The Chinese authorities responded with communications blackouts, invigorated political indoctrination campaigns, collective punishment, and arrests of those suspected of helping the immolators, sending information abroad, or strengthening Tibetan identity via cultural expression. State-run media and mass "patriotic education" campaigns sought to discredit the immolators and vilify the Dalai Lama as their instigator, fueling tensions between Tibetans and both the government and ethnic Chinese residents. The Dalai Lama declined to either condone or condemn the protests.

While the region had been periodically accessible to tourists and journalists under special conditions since 2008, travel restrictions on Tibetans and foreigners attempting to enter the TAR intensified in 2012, and access was extremely limited in the second half of the year. In November, the government rejected a request by the Office of the UN High Commissioner for Human Rights to allow a visit by independent monitors. The intermittent talks between the government and representatives of the Dalai Lama, last held in 2010, did not resume during 2012, marking the longest period without negotiations since 2002. Meanwhile, Beijing continued to press foreign leaders to refrain from meeting with the Dalai Lama and to endorse the official Chinese position on Tibet.

Political Rights and Civil Liberties: The Chinese government rules Tibet through administration of the TAR and 12 Tibetan autonomous prefectures or counties in the nearby provinces of Sichuan, Qinghai, Gansu, and Yunnan. Under the Chinese constitution, autonomous areas have the right to formulate their own regulations and implement national legislation in accordance with local conditions. In practice, decision-making power is concentrated in the hands of senior, ethnic Chinese CCP officials. In August 2011, Zhang Qingli was replaced as TAR party secretary by Chen Quanguo. The authorities' actions during 2012 dispelled speculation that Chen might not pursue repressive measures with as much zeal as Zhang. The few ethnic Tibetans who occupy senior positions serve mostly as figureheads and echo official doctrine on Tibet. Padma Thrinley (known as Pema Choling in the Chinese press), a Tibetan, has served as chairman of the TAR government since January 2010.

The Tibetan government in exile in Dharamsala, India, includes an elected parliament serving five-year terms, a Supreme Justice Commission that adjudicates civil disputes, and—since 2001—a directly elected prime minister, also serving five-year terms. The unelected Dalai Lama, who served as head of state, renounced his political role in March 2011. Lobsang Sangay was elected prime minister the following month, replacing a two-term incumbent and becoming the exile government's top political official.

Corruption is believed to be extensive in Tibet, as in the rest of China. Nevertheless, little information was available during the year on the scale of the problem or official measures to combat it.

Chinese authorities tightly restrict all media in Tibet. Such measures intensified in 2012 as the authorities sought to suppress information about self-immolations and related security crackdowns. International broadcasts are jammed and communications devices periodically confiscated. The online restrictions and monitoring in place across China are enforced even more stringently in the TAR. In July 2012, Human Rights Watch reported new media controls and invigorated state propaganda efforts, particularly in the TAR. These included distribution of satellite receivers fixed to government channels and a pilot project for broadcasting official messages via loudspeakers in 40 villages. A number of Tibetans who transmitted information abroad suffered repercussions including long prison sentences. Some internet and mobile-telephone users have been arrested solely for accessing banned information.

On several occasions in 2012, the authorities cut off the internet and mobile-phone text-messaging near the sites of self-immolations in Sichuan and Gansu Provinces. Also during the year, officials detained or imprisoned at least 10 cultural figures whose work—often circulated by hand within Tibet and shared with the outside world—emphasizes Tibetan identity. According to overseas Tibetan groups, more than 60 such writers, intellectuals, and musicians have been arrested since 2008, with some sentenced to lengthy prison terms.

Authorities continued to restrict access to the TAR for foreign journalists, human rights researchers, and even tourists in 2012. They were denied entry surrounding politically sensitive dates, such as the anniversary of the 2008 protests. During other periods, they were required to travel in groups and obtain official permission to visit the TAR, but even then, last minute travel bans were sometimes imposed. Foreign journalists were consistently prevented from entering Tibetan areas of Sichuan and other provinces, though no permission is technically required for travel there. Residents who assist foreign journalists are reportedly harassed.

The authorities regularly suppress religious activities, particularly those seen as forms of dissent or advocacy of Tibetan independence. Possession of Dalai Lama–related materials can lead to official harassment and punishment, though many Tibetans secretly possess such items. CCP members, government employees, and their family members are not allowed to practice Buddhism, at least within the TAR. The Religious Affairs Bureaus (RABs) control who can study in monasteries and nunneries. Officials allow only men and women over age 18 to become monks and nuns, and they are required to sign a declaration rejecting Tibetan independence, expressing loyalty to the government, and denouncing the Dalai Lama. In January 2012, the CCP announced that new committees of government officials were being set up within monasteries to manage their daily operations and enforce party indoctrination campaigns. Under the previous arrangement, managing committees comprised monks and nuns who had been deemed politically reliable. That system was reportedly retained in Tibetan regions outside the TAR, but with a government official appointed as deputy director. In addition, police posts are increasingly common even in smaller monasteries.

Ideological education campaigns that had been conducted sporadically since 1996 began to escalate in 2005, intensified again after 2008, and expanded further in 2012, reaching most monasteries and nunneries in the region. Such campaigns typically force participants to recognize the CCP claim that China "liberated" Tibet and to denounce the Dalai Lama. Some monks and nuns reportedly left their institutions to avoid the sessions, causing the closure of at least one monastery in the TAR. The effort was also extended to the lay population during the year, with students, civil servants, and farmers required to participate in discussions, singing sessions, and propaganda film screenings. In a new program initiated in 2011, 21,000 CCP cadres were sent to over 5,000 villages across the TAR to spread the government's message.

University professors cannot lecture on certain topics, and many must attend political indoctrination sessions. The government restricts course materials to prevent the circulation of unofficial versions of Tibetan history.

Freedoms of assembly and association are severely restricted in practice. Independent trade unions and human rights groups are illegal, and even nonviolent protests are often harshly punished. Nongovernmental organizations (NGOs) focused on development and public health operate under highly restrictive agreements. Despite the risks, Tibetans continue to seek avenues for expressing dissatisfaction with government policies. Most self-immolation protesters in 2012 were lay Tibetans, whereas in 2011 the majority were monks and nuns. Authorities responded with information blackouts, a heightened security presence, and increased surveillance. Late in the year, officials in some areas employed collective punishment tactics, canceling public benefits for the households of self-immolators, and ending state-funded projects in their villages. Notices offered rewards of up to 200,000 yuan ($31,500) for information on organizers.

In addition to the self-immolations, Tibetans staged periodic demonstrations or vigils to protest CCP rule or express solidarity with the immolators. Security forces sometimes responded violently. In January, police allegedly opened fire on unarmed protesters in Sichuan on three different occasions. At least 10 people were reportedly killed and scores injured; state media acknowledged at least one death. Later in the year, reports emerged of several Tibetans being sentenced to long prison terms for their alleged involvement in the protests. In other cases, such as two demonstrations with nearly 2,000 participants in Qinghai in February, security forces showed restraint and the protests proceeded without incident. Meanwhile, rural TAR residents continued to stage periodic protests against mining operations, while students in Qinghai protested efforts to replace Tibetan-language textbooks with Chinese editions.

The judicial system in Tibet remains abysmal, and torture is reportedly widespread. In March 2012, press watchdogs reported that public notices posted in eight counties in Gansu Province explicitly threatened "violent beating/torture" for those found distributing banned information. In June, a Tibetan monk in Sichuan died due to torture in custody after being detained the previous month for putting up proindependence posters. Defendants lack access to meaningful legal representation. Trials are closed if state security is invoked, and sometimes even when no political crime is listed. Chinese lawyers who offer to defend Tibetan suspects have been harassed or disbarred. Security forces routinely engage in arbitrary detention, and detainees' families are often left uninformed as to their whereabouts or well-being. In December 2012, the central authorities unveiled guidelines indicating that engaging in self-immolations and organizing, assisting, or gathering crowds related to such acts should be considered criminal offenses, including intentional homicide in some cases. A partial list of political prisoners published by the U.S. Congressional-Executive Commission on China included over 600 Tibetans as of September 2012; the commission's Political Prisoner Database included 267 cases of Tibetans detained in 2012.

Heightened restrictions on freedom of movement—including the use of troop deployments, roadblocks, and passport restrictions—were employed during 2012, particularly in areas where self-immolations took place. New travel restrictions introduced in March inhibited many Tibetans from entering the TAR. It was reported in May that Tibetans without permanent residency permits were being forced to leave Lhasa. Increased security efforts kept the number of Tibetans who successfully crossed the border into Nepal at between 300 and 600 in 2012, continuing a trend of annual declines from over 2,000 in 2007. In February, hundreds of Tibetans were interrogated and subjected to "reeducation" sessions upon returning from India, where they attended religious teachings by the Dalai Lama. According to Radio Free Asia, new regulations introduced in April led to almost no passports being issued to TAR Tibetans for the rest of 2012.

Tibetans receive preferential treatment in university admission examinations, but this is often not enough to secure entrance. The dominant role of the Chinese language in education and employment limits opportunities for many Tibetans. Private employers favor ethnic Chinese for many jobs, and Tibetans reportedly find it more difficult to obtain permits and loans to open businesses.

The government's extensive economic development programs in Tibet have disproportionately benefited ethnic Chinese residents and increased Chinese migration to the region, stoking Tibetan fears of marginalization and cultural assimilation.

Since 2003, the authorities have intensified efforts to resettle rural Tibetans—either by force or with inducements—in permanent-housing areas with little economic infrastructure. According to state-run media, by the end of 2011 a total of 1.85 million farmers and herders had been resettled within the TAR. Many have reportedly tried to return to their previous lands, risking conflict with officials.

China's restrictive family-planning policies are more leniently enforced for Tibetans and other ethnic minorities. As a result, the TAR is one of the few areas of China without a skewed sex ratio. Officials limit urban Tibetans to two children and encourage rural Tibetans to stop at three.

Transnistria

Political Rights: 6
Civil Liberties: 6
Status: Not Free

Population: 511,300

Ten-Year Ratings Timeline For Year Under Review (Political Rights, Civil Liberties, Status)

2003	2004	2005	2006	2007	2008	2009	2010	2011	2012
6,6NF	6,6NF	6,6NF	6,6NF	6,6NF	6,6NF	6,6NF	6,6NF	6,6NF	6,6NF

Overview: In a shift from the intransigence of his predecessor, newly elected president Yevgeny Shevchuk engaged in multilateral talks on Transnistria's status and took steps to ease trade and travel across the Dniester River during 2012. Nevertheless, the territory continued to rely heavily on Russian aid and patronage. In recognition of this relationship, the European Court of Human Rights in October held Russia legally responsible for human rights abuses by the separatist regime.

The Pridnestrovskaya Moldavskaya Respublika (PMR), bounded by the Dniester River to the west and the Ukrainian border to the east, is a breakaway region in eastern Moldova with a large population of ethnic Russians and ethnic Ukrainians. In the rest of Moldova, where the dominant language is essentially identical to Romanian, the separatist region is commonly known as Transnistria. It was attached to the territory that became Moldova when the area's borders were redrawn under Soviet leader Joseph Stalin in 1940. As the Soviet Union began to collapse in 1990, pro-Russian separatists in Transnistria, fearing that Moldova would unite with neighboring Romania, declared independence from Moldova and established the PMR under an authoritarian presidential system.

With weapons and other assistance from the Russian army, the PMR fought a military conflict with Moldova that ended with a 1992 ceasefire. A new Moldovan constitution in 1994 gave the territory substantial autonomy, but the conflict remained unresolved, and the separatist regime has since maintained a de facto independence that is not recognized internationally. Roughly 1,000 Russian troops are stationed in Transnistria to guard Soviet-era ammunition depots and uphold the ceasefire. The Organization for Security and Cooperation in Europe (OSCE), Russia, and Ukraine have attempted to mediate a final settlement between Moldova and the PMR. In 2005, the United States and the European Union (EU) were invited to join the negotiations as observers, creating the so-called 5+2 format.

The formal multilateral talks collapsed in early 2006 and remained dormant for the next several years. In the absence of active 5+2 negotiations, Moldovan president Vladimir Voronin pursued bilateral talks with Russia and took a number of steps to bring Moldova's foreign policy into line with the Kremlin's. However, an alliance of pro-European parties swept Voronin and his Communist Party from power in Moldova's July 2009 elections, and international pressure for renewed talks on Transnistria's status subsequently increased.

The pro-Russian Obnovleniye (Renewal) party maintained its majority in Transnistria's December 2010 legislative elections, winning 25 of 43 seats. Party leader Anatoly Kaminsky was reelected as speaker.

Founding PMR president Igor Smirnov, whom Moscow had urged not to seek a fifth term, was eliminated in the first round of the December 2011 presidential election, taking 24 percent of the vote in a field of six. Former parliament Speaker Yevgeny Shevchuk led with 39 percent, followed by Kaminsky, who had Russia's endorsement, with 26 percent. Shevchuk went on to win the runoff against Kaminsky, securing 74 percent of the vote.

Shevchuk had fallen out with Smirnov in 2009, was expelled from Obnovleniye in July 2011, and formed the Vozrozhdeniye (Revival) movement to back his presidential bid. Although he was committed to maintaining strong ties with Russia, he pledged to tackle corruption and laid out plans to reduce barriers to travel and trade with Moldova.

In January 2012, Shevchuk eliminated a 100 percent customs duty on goods from Moldova. He alleged in February that 90 percent of the PMR's foreign currency reserves had been transferred to foreign accounts in the weeks before Smirnov left office. PMR authorities in June accused Smirnov's longtime security chief, Vladimir Antiufeyev, of ordering the destruction of secret documents during the period surrounding the December 2011 election. In another sign of the shift in leadership, Shevchuk in October secured the resignation of incumbent prosecutor general Anatoly Guretsky, with whom he had reportedly clashed.

Meanwhile, in the wake of his defeat, Kaminsky resigned as parliament Speaker and head of Obnovleniye in June 2012. He was replaced in both posts by his deputy, Mikhail Burla.

Formal 5+2 negotiations, which had resumed in November 2011, continued during 2012, and Shevchuk also met regularly with Moldovan prime minister Vladimir Filat for bilateral discussions. The latter talks focused on restoring commercial, banking, and telecommunications links between Transnistria and the rest of Moldova, and yielded the reopening of freight rail routes across the Dniester in the spring.

Separately, Moldovan president Nicolae Timofti used his September 2012 speech at the UN General Assembly to reiterate calls for the withdrawal of Russian troops from Transnistria. The Council of Europe and the OSCE issued similar resolutions during the year, with the latter envisioning a multinational civilian observer mission to replace the Russian forces. Moscow has consistently rejected such proposals in recent years.

Political Rights and Civil Liberties: Residents of Transnistria cannot choose their leaders democratically, and they are unable to participate freely in Moldovan elections. While the PMR maintains its own legislative, executive, and judicial branches of government, no country recognizes its independence. Both the president and the 43-seat, unicameral Supreme Council are elected to five-year terms. In June 2011, the legislature approved constitutional amendments that created a relatively weak post of prime minister and set a two-term limit on the presidency. While the December 2011 presidential election was not recognized internationally, it featured increased competition and a somewhat broader choice for voters compared with previous polls.

The majority party in the legislature, Obnovleniye, is associated with Transnistria's monopolistic business conglomerate, Sheriff Enterprises, and maintains a close relationship with the ruling party in Russia. All of the PMR's political establishment, including nominal opposition parties, supports the separatist system and Russia's role as patron.

Native Moldovan speakers are not represented in government. While the authorities do not allow voting in Moldovan elections to take place in PMR-controlled territory, residents with Russian citizenship had access to two dozen polling stations for Russia's tightly controlled presidential election in March 2012. PMR president Yevgeny Shevchuk strongly endorsed the candidacy of Vladimir Putin.

Corruption and organized crime are serious problems in Transnistria. The authorities are entrenched in the territory's economic activities, which rely in large part on smuggling schemes. In October 2012, the deputy director of Moldova's Information and Security Service (SIS) alleged that criminal groups used the PMR's banking system to launder proceeds from trafficking in persons, drugs, and arms. PMR officials strongly denied the claims. The EU assists Ukraine and Moldova in efforts to maintain customs controls along their mutual border. Russia has a major stake in the Transnistrian economy and backs the PMR through loans, direct subsidies, and natural gas supplies. Transnistria has not paid the state-owned Russian energy giant Gazprom for gas imports since 2007, building up a debt of about $3.5 billion. Shevchuk said in September that the PMR's budget deficit of some 70 percent is largely supported by Russian assistance. Oleg Smirnov, son of the former president, remained under investigation in Russia in 2012 over his alleged embezzlement of Russian aid.

The media environment is restrictive. Nearly all media are state owned or controlled and refrain from criticizing the authorities. The few independent print outlets have small circulations. Critical reporting draws harassment by the government, which also uses tactics such as bureaucratic obstruction and the withholding of information to inhibit independent media. Sheriff Enterprises, which dominates the private broadcasting and cable television sectors, is the territory's only internet service provider. The government is not known to restrict internet access.

Religious freedom is limited. Orthodox Christianity is the dominant faith, and authorities have denied registration to several smaller religious groups. Unregistered groups face harassment by police and Orthodox opponents. There are no legal exemptions from military service for conscientious objectors, leading to criminal punishment of Jehovah's Witnesses and others.

Although a small minority of students study Moldovan using the Latin alphabet, this practice is restricted; the Moldovan language and Latin alphabet are associated with support for unity with Moldova, while Russian and the Cyrillic alphabet are associated with separatist goals. Parents who send their children to schools using Latin script, and the schools themselves, have faced harassment from the security services. An October 2012 ruling by the European Court of Human Rights found Russia liable for the PMR's restrictions on Moldovan-language education, ordering Moscow to pay about $1.4 million in damages to 170 Transnistria residents who had sued in 2004 and 2006.

The authorities severely restrict freedom of assembly and rarely issue required permits for public protests. Freedom of association is similarly circumscribed. All nongovernmental activities must be coordinated with local authorities, and groups that do not comply face harassment, including visits from security officials. The region's trade unions are holdovers from the Soviet era, and the United Council of Labor Collectives works closely with the government.

The judiciary is subservient to the executive and generally implements the will of the authorities. Defendants do not receive fair trials, and the legal framework falls short of international standards. Politically motivated arrests and detentions are common. Human rights groups have received accounts of torture in custody, and prison conditions are considered harsh and unsanitary. Suspicious deaths of military conscripts occur periodically amid reports of routine mistreatment.

Authorities discriminate against the ethnic Moldovan plurality. Ethnic Russians and ethnic Ukrainians together account for some 60 percent of the population. An estimated 150,000 residents hold Russian passports, and about 100,000 have Ukrainian passports, though many are believed to have multiple citizenship.

Travelers are frequently detained and questioned by the PMR authorities. In an incident that raised tensions along the de facto border, a Russian peacekeeper shot and killed a motorist in January 2012 as he returned home to Transnistria from Moldova and reportedly ignored commands to stop at a checkpoint. A Russian military court found the shooting lawful in July, but in December, Moldovan authorities said their investigation remained open.

Women are typically underrepresented in positions of authority, though Shevchuk's government included several female deputy premiers and ministers. Domestic violence against women is a problem. Transnistria is a significant source and transit point for trafficking in women for the purpose of prostitution. LGBT (lesbian, gay, bisexual, and transgender) people are reportedly subject to discrimination.

West Bank

Political Rights: 6
Civil Liberties: 5
Status: Not Free

Population: 2,677,000

Note: Whereas past editions of *Freedom in the World* featured one report for Israeli-occupied portions of the West Bank and Gaza Strip and another for Palestinian-administered portions, the latest three editions divide the territories based on geography, with one report for the West Bank and another for the Gaza Strip. As in previous years, Israel is examined in a separate report.

Ten-Year Ratings Timeline For Year Under Review (Political Rights, Civil Liberties, Status)

2003	2004	2005	2006	2007	2008	2009	2010	20011	2012
--	--	--	--	--	--	--	6,5NF	6,5NF	6,5NF

Overview:　　　　In 2012, the Palestinian Authority government in the West Bank continued to operate without an electoral mandate or a functioning legislature, despite ongoing state-building efforts by the administration. A May 2011 political agreement between the ruling Fatah faction and Gaza-based Hamas failed to produce a new caretaker government or a timetable for elections during the year. Meanwhile, Israel expanded its West Bank settlements, and attacks by Jewish settlers on Palestinian individuals and property continued. In November, the Fatah-led Palestine Liberation Organization won recognition for Palestine as a nonmember observer state at the UN General Assembly, a move which Hamas supported.

The West Bank was demarcated as part of the 1949 armistice agreement between Israel and Jordan. It consists of the land between the armistice line in the west and the Jordan River in the east. The territory was subsequently occupied and annexed by Jordan. During the 1967 Six-Day War, Israel conquered the West Bank along with the Gaza Strip and other territories, and later annexed East Jerusalem, leaving the rest of the West Bank and Gaza under a military administration.

After 1967, Israel began establishing Jewish settlements in the West Bank, a process that—along with the annexation of East Jerusalem—was regarded as illegal by most of the international community, according to Article 49 of the Fourth Geneva Convention. Israel maintained that the West Bank was a disputed territory under international law and that the settlements were consequently legal. In what became known as the first intifada (uprising), starting at the end of 1987, Palestinians in the West Bank and Gaza staged massive demonstrations, acts of civil disobedience, general strikes, stone throwing, and attacks against Israeli settlers and Israel Defense Forces (IDF) troops in the territories, as well as attacks within Israel proper. In 1993, Israel and Yasser Arafat's Palestine Liberation Organization (PLO) signed the Oslo Agreement, providing for a PLO renunciation of terrorism and recognition of Israel, Israeli troop withdrawals, and phased Palestinian autonomy in the West Bank and Gaza.

In subsequent years, the new Palestinian Authority (PA) took control of 40 percent of West Bank territory, including 98 percent of the Palestinian population outside of East Jerusalem. As negotiations stalled, a second and more violent intifada began in September 2000, and the IDF reentered most PA-administered areas.

After Arafat's death in 2004, the PA in January 2005 held its second-ever presidential election; the first voting for president and the Palestinian Legislative Council (PLC) had taken place in 1996. Mahmoud Abbas of Arafat's Fatah faction won with 62 percent of the vote. In municipal voting in the West Bank, Fatah won most municipalities, but the Islamist faction Hamas posted impressive gains. Each group accused the other of fraud, and there was some election-related violence.

Hamas won the January 2006 elections for the PLC with 74 of 132 seats, while Fatah took 45. The two then formed a unity government headed by Prime Minister Ismail Haniya of Hamas. Israel, the United States, and the European Union (EU) refused to recognize the new government, citing Hamas's involvement in terrorism and its refusal to recognize Israel or past Israel-PA agreements. The United States and the EU, then the largest donors to the PA, cut off assistance to the government.

Armed clashes between Hamas and Fatah supporters escalated in 2007, and in June Hamas militants seized Fatah-controlled facilities in Gaza, resulting in thousands fleeing to the West Bank. Abbas subsequently dismissed the Hamas-led government, declared a state of emergency, and appointed an emergency cabinet led by former finance minister Salam Fayyad. This resulted in a bifurcated PA, with Hamas governing Gaza and Abbas and Fayyad governing the roughly 40 percent of the West Bank not directly administered by Israel. Fatah later cracked down on Hamas in the West Bank, arresting its officials and supporters, shutting down its civic organizations and media outlets, and allegedly torturing some detainees.

In the years after the split, the Fatah-controlled PA in the West Bank benefited from renewed U.S. and EU aid as well as tax revenues released by Israeli authorities. So-called confidence-building measures between Israel and the PA in the West Bank included the release of hundreds of Palestinian prisoners held in Israel, the wider deployment of Palestinian security forces, and the removal of some Israeli checkpoints. Nevertheless, the IDF reportedly still controlled about 60 percent of the West Bank, and construction continued on a security barrier that ran roughly along the West Bank side of the 1949 armistice line and often jutted farther into the territory to place densely populated Jewish settlements on the Israeli side, frequently expropriating private Palestinian land and greatly reducing freedom of movement.

In April 2011, a UN report argued that recent improvements in governance, rule of law, social services, and infrastructure in the West Bank would allow the PA to effectively govern an independent state. The following month, Hamas and Fatah agreed to form a national unity government, but no such government had been formed by the end of 2012, despite ongoing attempts at reconciliation. In September 2011, PLO representatives unsuccessfully applied to the UN Security Council for recognition of a Palestinian state. In November 2011, Palestine won membership in the UN Education, Scientific, and Cultural Organization (UNESCO). To protest Fatah's agreement with Hamas and the PLO's moves at the United Nations, Israel withheld or threatened to withhold hundreds of millions of dollars in tax revenues from the PA. In November 2012, the PLO won recognition for Palestine as a nonmember observer state at the UN General Assembly, which voted 138–9 in favor of the move, with 41 abstentions.

After a construction freeze for most of 2010, Israel continued to expand Jewish settlements in the West Bank during 2012. Settlers also established a number of new "outposts" that were illegal under Israeli law, and although the government dismantled some such outposts during the year, it recognized 10 and failed to remove scores of others. Partly in reaction to the PA leadership's successful bid to upgrade Palestine's status at the United Nations, in early December 2012 the Israeli government announced that it would build 3,000 housing units in the controversial E1 corridor.

Political Rights and Civil Liberties: In 1988, Jordan rescinded citizenship for West Bank Palestinians, and Israel never granted them citizenship. Most Palestinian residents are citizens of the Palestinian Authority (PA), a quasi-sovereign entity created by the 1993 Oslo Accords. Jewish settlers in the West Bank are Israeli citizens.

The PA president is elected to four-year terms. The prime minister is nominated by the president but requires the support of the unicameral, 132-seat Palestinian Legislative Council (PLC), which also serves four-year terms. Voting in the West Bank during the 2005 presidential and 2006 PLC elections was deemed largely free and fair by international observers. However, after the bifurcation of the PA in 2007, elected officials on both sides were prevented from performing their duties. President Mahmoud Abbas appointed a new cabinet in the West Bank that lacked the PLC's approval. In 2008, PA security forces arrested hundreds of Hamas members and supporters. The rift, combined with Israel's detention of many Palestinian lawmakers, prevented the PLC from functioning, and its term expired in 2010.

Abbas's presidential term expired in 2009, and the PLO indefinitely extended his term. Moreover, Abbas issued a law permitting the Fatah-affiliated minister of local government to dissolve municipal councils, leading to the replacement of nearly all Hamas-affiliated municipal officials with Fatah loyalists. The May 2011 agreement between Hamas and Fatah envisioned a unity government that would organize presidential and parliamentary elections, but no such government had been formed by the end of 2012, nor had a timetable for elections been set.

After Israel annexed East Jerusalem in 1967, Arab residents were issued Israeli identity cards and given the option of obtaining Israeli citizenship. However, most have rejected this option. They can vote in municipal elections as well as PA elections, but are subject to restrictions imposed by the Israeli municipality of Jerusalem. In the 2006 PLC elections, Israel barred Hamas from campaigning in the city. By law, Israel strips Arabs of their Jerusalem residency if they remain outside the city for more than three months. East Jerusalem's Arab population does not receive a share of municipal services proportionate to its size.

Corruption remains a major problem in the West Bank, though Abbas has overseen some improvements. Prime Minister Salam Fayyad has been credited with significantly reducing corruption at the higher levels of the PA. An anticorruption commission has investigated over 80 cases, with one resulting in a conviction in June 2012. Critics have accused the commission of political bias.

The media are not free in the West Bank. Under a 1995 PA press law, journalists may be fined and jailed, and newspapers closed, for publishing "secret information" on PA security forces or news that might harm national unity or incite violence. Several small media outlets are routinely pressured to provide favorable coverage of the PA and Fatah. Journalists who criticize the PA or Fatah face arbitrary arrests, threats, and physical abuse. Since 2007, both the PA and Israeli forces have shut down most Hamas-affiliated radio and television stations in the West Bank. In 2011, Abbas ordered the closure of a television station affiliated with a Fatah rival, Mohammed Dahlan. According to a report by the Palestinian Center for Development and Media Freedoms (MADA), there were a total of 138 media freedom violations—ranging from physical violence to detentions, threats, and equipment confiscations—in the West Bank in 2012, a slight decrease from the previous year. Of those violations, some 73 percent were allegedly committed by Israeli forces. International press freedom groups regularly criticize Israel for blocking journalists' access to conflict zones, harming and sometimes killing reporters during armed clashes, and harassing Palestinian journalists. Israel insists that reporters risk getting caught in crossfire but are not targeted deliberately.

The Basic Law declares Islam to be the official religion of Palestine and states that "respect and sanctity of all other heavenly religions (Judaism and Christianity) shall be maintained." Blasphemy against Islam is a criminal offense. Synagogues are occasionally attacked by Palestinian militants. Some Palestinian Christians have experienced intimidation and harassment by radical Islamist groups and PA officials.

Israel generally recognizes freedom of religion in the West Bank, though recent years have featured a spike in mosque vandalism and other attacks by radical Israeli settlers. Citing the potential for violent clashes, Israel occasionally restricts Muslim men under age 50 from praying at the Temple Mount/Haram al-Sharif compound in Jerusalem.

The PA has authority over all levels of Palestinian education. Israeli military closures, curfews, and the security barrier restrict access to academic institutions, particularly those located between Israel and the barrier. Schools have sometimes been damaged during military actions, and student travel between the West Bank and the Gaza Strip has been limited. Israel accuses the PA of teaching incitement in public schools. Israeli academic institutions in the West Bank are increasingly subject to international and domestic boycotts. Primary and secondary education in West Bank settlements is administered by Israel, though religious schools have significant discretion over curriculum. According to the Association for Civil Rights in Israel (ACRI), East Jerusalem's schools are badly underfunded compared with schools in West Jerusalem.

The PA requires permits for demonstrations, and those against PA policies are generally forcibly dispersed. However, in December 2012, the authorities allowed the first Hamas rally in several years. Israel's Military Order 101 requires an IDF permit for all "political" demonstrations of more than 10 people, though demonstrations are routinely broken up with force, which occasionally results in fatalities. In 2012, Israeli forces continued to restrict and disperse frequent and sometimes violent demonstrations in opposition to the security barrier, especially those near the towns of Bil'in, Nil'in, Nabi Saleh, and Kufr Qaddum. The IDF declared many of these protest areas to be closed military zones every Friday, and regularly used rubber-coated bullets, stun grenades, and teargas to break up demonstrations. Protests also broke out in response to the Hamas-IDF conflict in Gaza in November, and the IDF used force to disperse them in some cases. In May, an Israeli military court sentenced Palestinian activist Bassem Tamimi to 13 months in prison for organizing illegal demonstrations in Nabi Saleh and urging children to throw stones. Human

Rights Watch (HRW) said the verdict violated his right to freedom of assembly, and noted that the second charge relied on coercively obtained testimony from a child.

A broad range of Palestinian nongovernmental organizations (NGOs) and civic groups operate in the West Bank, and their activities are generally unrestricted. Since 2007, however, many Hamas-affiliated civic associations have been shut down for political reasons. Researchers, lawyers, and activists are sometimes beaten by the PA security services, according to HRW. Workers may establish and join unions without government authorization. Palestinian workers seeking to strike must submit to arbitration by the PA Labor Ministry. There are no laws in the PA-ruled areas to protect the rights of striking workers. Palestinian workers in Jerusalem are subject to Israeli labor law.

The PA judicial system is only somewhat independent in practice, and Palestinian judges lack proper training and experience. Laws in effect in the West Bank derive from Ottoman, British Mandate, Jordanian, Israeli, and PA legislation, as well as Israeli military orders. The High Judicial Council handles most legal proceedings. Israel's Supreme Court hears petitions from non-Israeli residents of the West Bank regarding home demolitions, land confiscations, road closures, and IDF tactics. Decisions in favor of Palestinian petitioners, while rare, have increased in recent years. Though most applications have been rejected, the Israeli Supreme Court has repeatedly ordered changes to the route of the West Bank security barrier after hearing petitions from NGOs and Palestinians; for example, a section of the barrier near Bil'in was moved in June 2011, four years after the relevant ruling. As of November 2012, Israel's Ministry of Foreign Affairs reported that six petitions challenging particular sections of the barrier were pending before the Supreme Court.

The PA also has a military court system, which lacks almost all due process rights, including the right to appeal sentences, and can impose the death penalty. These courts handle cases on a range of security offenses, collaborating with Israel, and drug trafficking. There are reportedly hundreds of administrative detainees in Palestinian jails. Human rights groups regularly document torture complaints, but security officers rarely face punishment for such abuses. According to an August 2012 HRW report, the Independent Commission for Human Rights (ICHR), the Palestinian human rights ombudsman, received 584 torture complaints from 2009 to July 2012. Of the 120 cases reported by Amnesty International in 2012, more than 50 were allegedly perpetrated by police.

Palestinians accused of security offenses by Israel are tried in Israeli military courts, which grant some due process protections but limit rights to counsel, bail, and appeal. According to the Israeli human rights group B'Tselem, at the end of 2012 there were 4,517 Palestinians in Israeli jails: 3,089 serving sentences, 219 detainees, 1,031 being detained until the conclusion of legal proceedings, and 178 administrative detainees, held without charge or trial. A temporary order in effect since 2006 permits the detention of suspects accused of security offenses for 96 hours without judicial oversight, compared with 24 hours for other detainees. Most convictions in Israeli military courts are based on confessions, sometimes obtained through coercion. Israel outlawed the use of torture to extract security information in 2000, but milder forms of coercion are permissible when the prisoner is believed to have vital information about impending terrorist attacks. Human rights groups criticize Israel interrogation methods, including binding detainees to a chair in painful positions, slapping, kicking, and threatening violence against detainees and their relatives.

According to Defence for Children International (DCI), there were 178 Palestinian children being held in Israeli jails as of November 2012, and 21 Palestinian youths (ages 12–15). Most were serving sentences—handed down by a Special Court for Minors created in 2009—for throwing stones or other projectiles at Israeli troops in the West Bank; acquittals are rare. A 2012 report from DCI found that of 311 testimonies gathered between 2008 and 2012, 90 percent of the children reported being blindfolded, 95 percent had their hands tied, 75 percent experienced physical violence, and 60 percent were arrested between midnight and 5 a.m. East Jerusalem Palestinian minors are tried in Israeli civil juvenile courts.

Militant Jewish settlers continued to mount attacks on Palestinian individuals and property in 2012 as part of their "price tag" campaign, so named to imply retribution for Israeli policies aimed at limiting settlement. Following the November conflict between the IDF and Hamas in Gaza, the Israeli military conducted a wave of arrests across the West Bank, targeting suspected members of Hamas and Islamic Jihad.

Israeli soldiers accused of harassing or assaulting Palestinian civilians are subject to Israeli military law. A September 2012 report from B'Tselem stated that from September 2000 until the end of 2011, there were 473 alleged cases of IDF violence against Palestinians. Of the 241 cases sent to the Military Advocate General's Corps, investigations were opened in 200, though 134 were closed without any measures being taken and just seven led to indictments. Of 244 cases sent to the police, 113 were closed without measures being taken, and 12 led to indictments. Soldiers convicted of abuses typically receive relatively light sentences.

The easing of checkpoints and roadblocks and the wider deployment of PA security forces has improved economic conditions in the West Bank in recent years. The UN Office for the Coordination of Humanitarian Affairs (OCHA) reported that as of mid-2012, there were 542 obstacles to Palestinian freedom of movement within the West Bank, 436 of which were physical security features as opposed to staffed checkpoints. These obstacles stunt trade and restrict Palestinian access to jobs, hospitals, and schools.

Israel's West Bank security barrier, which was declared illegal by the International Court of Justice in 2004, has also cut off many Palestinians from their farms and other parts of the territory. It was 62 percent complete by mid-2012. Some 6,500 Palestinians currently live in the zone between the barrier and the 1949 armistice line, and if the planned route is completed, that number will rise to 25,000.

All West Bank residents must have identification cards to obtain entry permits to Israel, including East Jerusalem. While most roads are open to both Israelis and Palestinians, about 10 are open only to drivers with Israeli documents. A September 2012 report by OCHA noted easing measures put in place by the IDF from mid-2011 to mid-2012 that provided 100,000 Palestinian villagers with better access to six large West Bank cities and to East Jerusalem. However, 190,000 Palestinians are still required to use detour routes that extend their travel time by twice to five times the normal length.

According to the Israeli NGO Peace Now, 6,676 new housing units in Jewish settlements were approved in 2012, excluding East Jerusalem. Of these, only 7 percent were in settlements west of the security barrier; 25 percent were east of the planned route of the fence, and 69 percent were between the existing barrier and the approved route. Four new illegal outposts—meaning settlements that are illegal according to Israeli law—were established during the year, and 10 new settlements were established by approving existing illegal outposts, the first such approval in two decades. In July 2012, an Israeli-led commission tasked with identifying the legal status of Israeli outposts declared that Israel's rule over the West Bank is not occupation. As of the end of 2012, the Israeli cabinet had not decided which parts of the report to adopt.

In 2010, B'Tselem found that while settlements occupy 1 percent of the West Bank's land, 21 percent of that is private Palestinian land. Israel dismantled a number of settler outposts on private Palestinian land in 2012, but Peace Now reported that scores remained intact, and that Israeli authorities demolished unlicensed Palestinian buildings at a far greater rate than Jewish buildings in the IDF-controlled portion of the West Bank. The Israeli government maintains that Jewish and Palestinian residents in the area are subject to the same restrictions.

OCHA reported that two Palestinian families were forcibly evicted from their homes in the East Jerusalem neighborhood of Beit Hanina in April 2012. According to the United Nations, 35 percent of the land in East Jerusalem has been designated as state land by Israel. A 2010 UN Relief and Works Agency report stated that Palestinians can legally build in an area comprising about 13 percent of East Jerusalem, and that over 28 percent of Arab homes are built illegally.

While Palestinian women are underrepresented in most professions and encounter discrimination in employment, they have full access to universities and to many professions. Palestinian laws and societal norms, derived in part from Sharia (Islamic law), put women at a disadvantage in matters of marriage, divorce, and inheritance. For Christians, such personal status issues are governed by ecclesiastical courts. Rape, domestic abuse, and so-called "honor killings" are not uncommon. These murders often go unpunished.

Western Sahara

Political Rights: 7   **Population:** 567,000
Civil Liberties: 7
Status: Not Free

Ten-Year Ratings Timeline For Year Under Review (Political Rights, Civil Liberties, Status)

2003	2004	2005	2006	2007	2008	2009	2010	2011	2012
7,6NF	7,6NF	7,6NF	7,6NF	7,6NF	7,6NF	7,6NF	7,6NF	7,7NF	7,7NF

Overview: **UN envoy Christopher Ross continued efforts in 2012 to resolve the decades-long impasse over the status of Western Sahara, with no discernable progress. Two years after deadly clashes at the Gdeim Izik protest camp, two dozen people detained amid the incident remained incarcerated in a prison near Morocco's capital, with no trial scheduled.**

Western Sahara was ruled by Spain for nearly a century until Spanish troops withdrew in 1976, following a bloody guerrilla conflict with the proindependence Popular Front for the Liberation of Saguia el-Hamra and Rio de Oro (Polisario Front).

Mauritania and Morocco both claimed the resource-rich region, agreeing to a partition in which Morocco received the northern two-thirds of Western Sahara, and Mauritania received the rest. However, the Polisario Front proclaimed an independent Sahrawi Arab Democratic Republic (SADR) and continued its guerrilla campaign. Mauritania renounced its claim in 1979, and Morocco filled the vacuum by annexing the territory. During the 1980s, Moroccan forces built a 1,600-mile-long sand wall, or a "berm," that divides Moroccan-controlled territory in the west from a smaller region in the east controlled by the Polisario Front.

Moroccan and Polisario forces engaged in armed conflict until the United Nations brokered a ceasefire in 1991. The agreement called for residents of Western Sahara to vote in a referendum on independence the following year, to be supervised by the newly established UN Mission for the Referendum in Western Sahara (MINURSO). However, the vote never took place, with the two sides failing to agree on voter eligibility.

Morocco has tried to bolster its claim to Western Sahara over the years by offering financial incentives for Moroccans to move to Western Sahara, and for Sahrawis to move to Morocco. Morocco has also used coercive measures, engaging in forced resettlements of Sahrawis and long-term detention and "disappearances" of proindependence activists. Neighboring Algeria will not accept Moroccan control of the territory and hosts refugee camps in Tindouf, Algeria. According to the UNHCR, Tindouf is home to an estimated 90,000 Sahrawis, as well as the SADR government in exile.

In 2004, the Polisario Front accepted a UN Security Council plan calling for up to five years of autonomy, followed by a referendum on the territory's status. However, Morocco rejected the plan, fearing it could lead to Western Sahara's independence. In 2007, Morocco offered its own autonomy plan. The Polisario Front remains committed to an eventual referendum with self-determination and independence as options, with Morocco pushing for autonomy under Moroccan sovereignty.

The two sides have failed to make progress in a series of negotiations that started in 2007 and continued into 2012, with UN special envoy Christopher Ross brokering the talks. Algeria and Mauritania participate in the negotiations. Talks broke off abruptly after a November 8, 2010, confrontation in the Gdeim Izik protest camp outside Laayoune, in which Moroccan forces violently dispersed the camp's Sahrawi residents, who had been protesting the Moroccan occupation. Human Rights Watch reported that 11 police and two civilians were killed, with hundreds of civilians beaten and detained. Talks resumed in July 2011, but again sputtered.

In May 2012, Morocco criticized Ross for being biased following the release of a UN report suggesting that Morocco might have been spying on MINURSO. UN Secretary-General Ban Ki-moon refused calls by the Moroccan authorities to replace Ross. In August, Ross announced that he was temporarily retiring efforts to hold joint negotiations between Morocco and the Polisario Front, and would instead meet separately with the parties involved in an attempt to lay groundwork for renewed face-to-face talks.

Political Rights and Civil Liberties: As the occupying force in Western Sahara, Morocco holds authority over local elections and works to ensure that independence-minded leaders are excluded from both local political processes and the Moroccan legislature. The government in exile in Tindouf, Algeria, is formed from meetings held every four years of the General Popular Congress, which, in turn, is comprised of delegates from refugee camps.

Reports of corruption are widespread. Although the territory possesses extensive natural resources, including phosphate, iron ore deposits, hydrocarbon reserves, and fisheries, the local population remains largely impoverished.

The Moroccan constitution provides for freedom of the press, but this is severely limited in Western Sahara, and there is little independent Sahrawi media activity. Moroccan law bars the media and individuals from challenging Morocco's sovereignty over Western Sahara, leading to self-censorship. Moroccan authorities expel or detain Sahrawi, Moroccan, and foreign reporters who attempt to conduct firsthand reporting on the issue. On the 2012 anniversary of the clashes at Gdeim Izik, Morocco expelled 15 Spanish and 4 Norwegian journalists from Western Sahara. According to Morocco's interior ministry, they were planning to meet with "separatist" elements in Laayoune; Spanish media outlets, however, reported that most of the expelled foreigners were activists, rather than journalists. The internet and independent satellite broadcasts are largely unavailable due to economic constraints.

Nearly all Sahrawis are Sunni Muslims, as are most Moroccans, and Moroccan authorities generally do not interfere with their freedom of worship. There are no major universities or institutions of higher learning in Western Sahara.

Freedom of assembly is severely restricted, and Sahrawis are not permitted to form independent nongovernmental organizations. As in previous years, activists supporting independence and their suspected foreign sympathizers were subject to harassment. In November 2012, Sahwari human rights activist Aminatou Haidar was beaten by Moroccan police following a meeting with UN special envoy Christopher Ross.

Sahrawis are technically subject to Moroccan labor laws in Moroccan-controlled areas, but there is little organized labor activity in the territory.

Two years after the 2010 Gdeim Izik clashes, two dozen people detained amid the incident remain incarcerated in Salé prison near Rabat, Morocco's capital, with no trial scheduled.

Morocco and the Polisario Front both restrict free movement in potential conflict areas. Morocco has been accused of using force and financial incentives to alter the composition of Western Sahara's population.

The SADR government routinely signs contracts with firms for the exploration of oil and gas, but these contracts cannot be formally implemented given the territory's status, and no credible free market exists.

The significant reform in 2004 of the Moroccan Mudawwana—a law governing issues including marriage, divorce, inheritance, and child custody—does not appear to have been applied to the Moroccan-controlled areas of Western Sahara. Conditions are generally worse for women living in rural areas, where poverty and illiteracy rates are higher.

Freedom in the World 2013 Methodology

INTRODUCTION

The *Freedom in the World* survey provides an annual evaluation of the state of global freedom as experienced by individuals. The survey measures freedom—the opportunity to act spontaneously in a variety of fields outside the control of the government and other centers of potential domination—according to two broad categories: political rights and civil liberties. Political rights enable people to participate freely in the political process, including the right to vote freely for distinct alternatives in legitimate elections, compete for public office, join political parties and organizations, and elect representatives who have a decisive impact on public policies and are accountable to the electorate. Civil liberties allow for the freedoms of expression and belief, associational and organizational rights, rule of law, and personal autonomy without interference from the state.

The survey does not rate governments or government performance per se, but rather the real-world rights and freedoms enjoyed by individuals. Thus, while Freedom House considers the presence of legal rights, it places a greater emphasis on whether these rights are implemented in practice. Furthermore, freedoms can be affected by government officials, as well as by nonstate actors, including insurgents and other armed groups.

Freedom House does not maintain a culture-bound view of freedom. The methodology of the survey is grounded in basic standards of political rights and civil liberties, derived in large measure from relevant portions of the Universal Declaration of Human Rights. These standards apply to all countries and territories, irrespective of geographical location, ethnic or religious composition, or level of economic development. The survey operates from the assumption that freedom for all peoples is best achieved in liberal democratic societies.

The survey includes both analytical reports and numerical ratings for 195 countries and 14 select territories.[1] Each country and territory report includes an overview section, which provides historical background and a brief description of the year's major developments, as well as a section summarizing the current state of political rights and civil liberties. In addition, each country and territory is assigned a numeri-

---

1. These territories are selected based on their political significance and size. Freedom House divides territories into two categories: related territories and disputed territories. Related territories consist mostly of colonies, protectorates, and island dependencies of sovereign states that are in some relation of dependency to that state, and whose relationship is not currently in serious legal or political dispute. Disputed territories are areas within internationally recognized sovereign states whose status is in serious political or violent dispute, and whose conditions differ substantially from those of the relevant sovereign states. They are often outside of central government control and characterized by intense, longtime, and widespread insurgency or independence movements that enjoy popular support. Generally, the dispute faced by a territory is between independence for the territory or domination by an established state.

cal rating—on a scale of 1 to 7—for political rights and an analogous rating for civil liberties; a rating of 1 indicates the highest degree of freedom and 7 the lowest level of freedom. These ratings, which are calculated based on the methodological process described below, determine whether a country is classified as Free, Partly Free, or Not Free by the survey.

The survey findings are reached after a multilayered process of analysis and evaluation by a team of regional experts and scholars. Although there is an element of subjectivity inherent in the survey findings, the ratings process emphasizes intellectual rigor and balanced and unbiased judgments.

HISTORY OF THE SURVEY

Freedom House's first year-end reviews of freedom began in the 1950s as the *Balance Sheet of Freedom*. This modest report provided assessments of political trends and their implications for individual freedom. In 1972 Freedom House launched a new, more comprehensive annual study called The *Comparative Study of Freedom*. Raymond Gastil, a Harvard-trained specialist in regional studies from the University of Washington in Seattle, developed the survey's methodology, which assigned political rights and civil liberties ratings to 151 countries and 45 territories and—based on these ratings—categorized them as Free, Partly Free, or Not Free. The findings appeared each year in Freedom House's *Freedom at Issue* bimonthly journal (later titled *Freedom Review*). The survey first appeared in book form in 1978, under the title *Freedom in the World* and included short, explanatory narratives for each country and territory rated in the study, as well as a series of essays by leading scholars on related issues. *Freedom in the World* continued to be produced by Gastil until 1989, when a larger team of in-house survey analysts was established. In the mid-1990s, the expansion of *Freedom in the World*'s country and territory narratives demanded the hiring of outside analysts—a group of regional experts from the academic, media, and human rights communities. The survey has continued to grow in size and scope; the 2013 edition is the most exhaustive in its history.

RESEARCH AND RATINGS REVIEW PROCESS

This year's survey covers developments from January 1, 2012, through December 31, 2012, in 195 countries and 14 territories. The research and ratings process involved 64 analysts and 20 senior-level academic advisers—the largest number to date. The analysts used a broad range of sources of information—including foreign and domestic news reports, academic analyses, nongovernmental organizations, think tanks, individual professional contacts, and visits to the region—in preparing the country and territory reports and ratings.

The country and territory ratings were proposed by the analyst responsible for each related report. The ratings were reviewed individually and on a comparative basis in a series of six regional meetings—Asia-Pacific, Central and Eastern Europe and the Former Soviet Union, Latin America and the Caribbean, Middle East and North Africa, sub-Saharan Africa, and Western Europe—involving the analysts, academic advisers with expertise in each region, and Freedom House staff. The ratings were compared to the previous year's findings, and any major proposed numerical shifts or category changes were subjected to more intensive scrutiny. These reviews were followed by cross-regional assessments in which efforts were made to ensure comparability and consistency in the findings. Many of the key country reports were also reviewed by the academic advisors.

CHANGES TO THE 2013 EDITION OF FREEDOM IN THE WORLD

The survey's methodology is reviewed periodically by an advisory committee of political scientists with expertise in methodological issues. Over the years, the committee has made a number of modest methodological changes to adapt to evolving ideas about political rights and civil liberties. At the same time, the time series data are not revised retroactively, and any changes to the methodology are introduced incrementally in order to ensure the comparability of the ratings from year to year. No methodological changes were made to the 2013 edition of *Freedom in the World.*

RATINGS PROCESS

(NOTE: See the complete checklist questions and keys to political rights and civil liberties ratings and status at the end of the methodology essay.)

Scores – The ratings process is based on a checklist of 10 political rights questions and 15 civil liberties questions. The political rights questions are grouped into three subcategories: Electoral Process (3 questions), Political Pluralism and Participation (4), and Functioning of Government (3). The civil liberties questions·are grouped into four subcategories: Freedom of Expression and Belief (4 questions), Associational and Organizational Rights (3), Rule of Law (4), and Personal Autonomy and Individual Rights (4). Scores are awarded to each of these questions on a scale of 0 to 4, where a score of 0 represents the smallest degree and 4 the greatest degree of rights or liberties present. The political rights section also contains two additional discretionary questions: question A (For traditional monarchies that have no parties or electoral process, does the system provide for genuine, meaningful consultation with the people, encourage public discussion of policy choices, and allow the right to petition the ruler?) and question B (Is the government or occupying power deliberately changing the ethnic composition of a country or territory so as to destroy a culture or tip the political balance in favor of another group?). For additional discretionary question A, a score of 1 to 4 may be added, as applicable, while for discretionary question B, a score of 1 to 4 may be subtracted (the worse the situation, the more that may be subtracted). The highest score that can be awarded to the political rights checklist is 40 (or a total score of 4 for each of the 10 questions). The highest score that can be awarded to the civil liberties checklist is 60 (or a total score of 4 for each of the 15 questions).

The scores from the previous survey edition are used as a benchmark for the current year under review. In general, a score is changed only if there has been a real world development during the year that warrants a change (e.g., a crackdown on the media, the country's first free and fair elections) and is reflected accordingly in the narrative.

In answering both the political rights and civil liberties questions, Freedom House does not equate constitutional or other legal guarantees of rights with the on-the-ground fulfillment of these rights. While both laws and actual practices are factored into the ratings decisions, greater emphasis is placed on the latter.

For states and territories with small populations, the absence of pluralism in the political system or civil society is not necessarily viewed as a negative situation unless the government or other centers of domination are deliberately blocking its operation. For example, a small country without diverse political parties or media outlets or significant trade unions is not penalized if these limitations are determined to be a function of size and not overt restrictions.

Political Rights and Civil Liberties Ratings – The total score awarded to the political rights and civil liberties checklist determines the political rights and civil liberties rating. Each rating of 1 through 7, with 1 representing the highest and 7 the lowest level of freedom, corresponds to a range of total scores (see tables 1 and 2).

Status of Free, Partly Free, Not Free – Each pair of political rights and civil liberties ratings is averaged to determine an overall status of "Free," "Partly Free," or "Not Free." Those whose ratings average 1.0 to 2.5 are considered Free, 3.0 to 5.0 Partly Free, and 5.5 to 7.0 Not Free (see table 3). The designations of Free, Partly Free, and Not Free each cover a broad third of the available scores. Therefore, countries and territories within any one category, especially those at either end of the category, can have quite different human rights situations. In order to see the distinctions within each category, a country or territory's political rights and civil liberties ratings should be examined. For example, countries at the lowest end of the Free category (2 in political rights and 3 in civil liberties, or 3 in political rights and 2 in civil liberties) differ from those at the upper end of the Free group (1 for both political rights and civil liberties). Also, a designation of Free does not mean that a country enjoys perfect freedom or lacks serious problems, only that it enjoys comparably more freedom than Partly Free or Not Free (or some other Free) countries.

Indications of Ratings and/or Status Changes – Each country or territory's political rights rating, civil liberties rating, and status is included in a statistics section that precedes each country or territory report. A change in a political rights or civil liberties rating since the previous survey edition is indicated with a symbol next to the rating that has changed. A brief ratings change explanation is included in the statistics section.

Trend Arrows – Positive or negative developments in a country or territory may also be reflected in the use of upward or downward trend arrows. A trend arrow is based on a particular development (such as an improvement in a country's state of religious freedom), which must be linked to a score change in the corresponding checklist question (in this case, an increase in the score for checklist question D2, which covers religious freedom). However, not all score increases or decreases warrant trend arrows. Whether a positive or negative development is significant enough to warrant a trend arrow is determined through consultations among the report writer, the regional academic advisers, and Freedom House staff. Also, trend arrows are assigned only in cases where score increases or decreases are not sufficient to warrant a ratings change; thus, a country cannot receive both a ratings change and a trend arrow during the same year. A trend arrow is indicated with an arrow next to the name of the country or territory that appears before the statistics section at the top of each country or territory report. A brief trend arrow explanation is included in the statistics section.

GENERAL CHARACTERISTICS OF EACH POLITICAL RIGHTS AND CIVIL LIBERTIES RATING
POLITICAL RIGHTS

Rating of 1 - Countries and territories with a rating of 1 enjoy a wide range of political rights, including free and fair elections. Candidates who are elected actually rule, political parties are competitive, the opposition plays an important role and enjoys real power, and minority groups have reasonable self-government or can participate in the government through informal consensus.

Rating of 2 - Countries and territories with a rating of 2 have slightly weaker political rights than those with a rating of 1 because of such factors as some political corruption, limits on the functioning of political parties and opposition groups, and foreign or military influence on politics.

Ratings of 3, 4, 5 - Countries and territories with a rating of 3, 4, or 5 include those that moderately protect almost all political rights to those that more strongly protect some political rights while less strongly protecting others. The same factors that undermine freedom in countries with a rating of 2 may also weaken political rights in those with a rating of 3, 4, or 5, but to an increasingly greater extent at each successive rating.

Rating of 6 - Countries and territories with a rating of 6 have very restricted political rights. They are ruled by one-party or military dictatorships, religious hierarchies, or autocrats. They may allow a few political rights, such as some representation or autonomy for minority groups, and a few are traditional monarchies that tolerate political discussion and accept public petitions.

Rating of 7 - Countries and territories with a rating of 7 have few or no political rights because of severe government oppression, sometimes in combination with civil war. They may also lack an authoritative and functioning central government and suffer from extreme violence or warlord rule that dominates political power.

CIVIL LIBERTIES

Rating of 1 - Countries and territories with a rating of 1 enjoy a wide range of civil liberties, including freedom of expression, assembly, association, education, and religion. They have an established and generally fair system of the rule of law (including an independent judiciary), allow free economic activity, and tend to strive for equality of opportunity for everyone, including women and minority groups.

Rating of 2 - Countries and territories with a rating of 2 have slightly weaker civil liberties than those with a rating of 1 because of such factors as some limits on media independence, restrictions on trade union activities, and discrimination against minority groups and women.

Ratings of 3, 4, 5 - Countries and territories with a rating of 3, 4, or 5 include those that moderately protect almost all civil liberties to those that more strongly protect some civil liberties while less strongly protecting others. The same factors that undermine freedom in countries with a rating of 2 may also weaken civil liberties in those with a rating of 3, 4, or 5, but to an increasingly greater extent at each successive rating.

Rating of 6 – Countries and territories with a rating of 6 have very restricted civil liberties. They strongly limit the rights of expression and association and frequently hold political prisoners. They may allow a few civil liberties, such as some religious and social freedoms, some highly restricted private business activity, and some open and free private discussion.

Rating of 7 – Countries and territories with a rating of 7 have few or no civil liberties. They allow virtually no freedom of expression or association, do not protect the rights of detainees and prisoners, and often control or dominate most economic activity.

Countries and territories generally have ratings in political rights and civil liberties that are within two ratings numbers of each other. For example, without a well-developed civil society, it is difficult, if not impossible, to have an atmosphere supportive of political rights. Consequently, there is no country in the survey with a rating of 6 or 7 for civil liberties and, at the same time, a rating of 1 or 2 for political rights.

ELECTORAL DEMOCRACY DESIGNATION

In addition to providing numerical ratings, the survey assigns the designation "electoral democracy" to countries that have met certain minimum standards. In determining whether a country is an electoral democracy, Freedom House examines several key factors concerning the last major national election or elections.

To qualify as an electoral democracy, a state must have satisfied the following criteria:

1) A competitive, multiparty political system;

2) Universal adult suffrage for all citizens (with exceptions for restrictions that states may legitimately place on citizens as sanctions for criminal offenses);

3) Regularly contested elections conducted in conditions of ballot secrecy, reasonable ballot security, and in the absence of massive voter fraud, and that yield results that are representative of the public will;

4) Significant public access of major political parties to the electorate through the media and through generally open political campaigning.

The numerical benchmark for a country to be listed as an electoral democracy is a subtotal score of 7 or better (out of a possible total score of 12) for the political rights checklist subcategory A (the three questions on Electoral Process) and an overall political rights score of 20 or better (out of a possible total score of 40). In the case of presidential/parliamentary systems, both elections must have been free and fair on the basis of the above criteria; in parliamentary systems, the last nationwide elections for the national legislature must have been free and fair. The presence of certain irregularities during the electoral process does not automatically disqualify a country from being designated an electoral democracy. A country cannot be an electoral democracy if significant authority for national decisions resides in the hands of an unelected power, whether a monarch or a foreign international authority. A country is removed from the ranks of electoral democracies if its last national election failed to meet the criteria listed above, or if changes in law significantly eroded the public's possibility for electoral choice.

Freedom House's term "electoral democracy" differs from "liberal democracy" in that the latter also implies the presence of a substantial array of civil liberties. In the survey, all Free countries qualify as both electoral and liberal democracies. By contrast, some Partly Free countries qualify as electoral, but not liberal, democracies.

FREEDOM IN THE WORLD 2013
CHECKLIST QUESTIONS AND GUIDELINES

Each numbered checklist question is assigned a score of 0-4 (except for discretionary question A, for which a score of 1-4 may be added, and discretionary question B, for which a score of 1-4 may be subtracted), according to the survey methodology. The bulleted sub-questions are intended to provide guidance to the writers regarding what issues are meant to be considered in scoring each checklist question; the authors do not necessarily have to consider every sub-question when scoring their countries.

POLITICAL RIGHTS CHECKLIST
ELECTORAL PROCESS

1. Is the head of government or other chief national authority elected through free and fair elections?

- Did established and reputable national and/or international election monitoring organizations judge the most recent elections for head of government to be free and fair? (Note: Heads of government chosen through various electoral frameworks, including direct elections for president, indirect elections for prime minister by parliament, and the electoral college system for electing presidents, are covered under this and the following sub-questions. In cases of indirect elections for the head of government, the elections for the legislature that chose the head of government, as well as the selection process of the head of government himself, should be taken into consideration.)

- Have there been undue, politically motivated delays in holding the most recent election for head of government?

- Is the registration of voters and candidates conducted in an accurate, timely, transparent, and nondiscriminatory manner?

- Can candidates make speeches, hold public meetings, and enjoy media access throughout the campaign free of intimidation?

- Does voting take place by secret ballot or by equivalent free voting procedure?

- Are voters able to vote for the candidate or party of their choice without undue pressure or intimidation?

- Is the vote count transparent, and is it reported honestly with the official results made public? Can election monitors from independent groups and representing parties/candidates watch the counting of votes to ensure their honesty?

- Is each person's vote given equivalent weight to those of other voters in order to ensure equal representation?

- Has a democratically elected head of government who was chosen in the most recent election subsequently been overthrown in a violent coup? (Note: Although a peaceful, "velvet coup" may ultimately lead to a positive outcome—particularly if it replaces a head of government who was not freely and fairly elected—the new leader has not been freely and fairly elected and cannot be treated as such.)

- In cases where elections for regional, provincial, or state governors and/or other subnational officials differ significantly in conduct from national elections, does the conduct of the subnational elections reflect an opening toward improved political rights in the country, or, alternatively, a worsening of political rights?

2. Are the national legislative representatives elected through free and fair elections?

- Did established and reputable domestic and/or international election monitoring organizations judge the most recent national legislative elections to be free and fair?

- Have there been undue, politically motivated delays in holding the most recent national legislative election?

- Is the registration of voters and candidates conducted in an accurate, timely, transparent, and nondiscriminatory manner?

- Can candidates make speeches, hold public meetings, and enjoy media access throughout the campaign free of intimidation?

- Does voting take place by secret ballot or by equivalent free voting procedure?

- Are voters able to vote for the candidate or party of their choice without undue pressure or intimidation?

- Is the vote count transparent, and is it reported honestly with the official results made public? Can election monitors from independent groups and representing parties/candidates watch the counting of votes to ensure their honesty?

- Is each person's vote given equivalent weight to those of other voters in order to ensure equal representation?

- Have the representatives of a democratically elected national legislature who were chosen in the most recent election subsequently been overthrown in a violent coup? (Note: Although a peaceful, "velvet coup" may ultimately lead to a positive outcome—particularly if it replaces a national legislature whose representatives were not freely and fairly elected—members of the new legislature have not been freely and fairly elected and cannot be treated as such.)

- In cases where elections for subnational councils/parliaments differ significantly in conduct from national elections, does the conduct of the subnational elections reflect an opening toward improved political rights in the country, or, alternatively, a worsening of political rights?

3. Are the electoral laws and framework fair?

- Is there a clear, detailed, and fair legislative framework for conducting elections? (Note: Changes to electoral laws should not be made immediately preceding an election if the ability of voters, candidates, or parties to fulfill their roles in the election is infringed.)

- Are election commissions or other election authorities independent and free from government or other pressure and interference?

- Is the composition of election commissions fair and balanced?

- Do election commissions or other election authorities conduct their work in an effective and competent manner?

- Do adult citizens enjoy universal and equal suffrage? (Note: Suffrage can be suspended or withdrawn for reasons of legal incapacity, such as mental incapacity or conviction of a serious criminal offense.)

- Is the drawing of election districts conducted in a fair and nonpartisan manner, as opposed to gerrymandering for personal or partisan advantage?

- Has the selection of a system for choosing legislative representatives (such as proportional versus majoritarian) been manipulated to advance certain political interests or to influence the electoral results?

B. POLITICAL PLURALISM AND PARTICIPATION
1. Do the people have the right to organize in different political parties or other competitive political groupings of their choice, and is the system open to the rise and fall of these competing parties or groupings?

- Do political parties encounter undue legal or practical obstacles in their efforts to be formed and to operate, including onerous registration requirements, excessively large membership requirements, etc.?

- Do parties face discriminatory or onerous restrictions in holding meetings, rallies, or other peaceful activities?

- Are party members or leaders intimidated, harassed, arrested, imprisoned, or subjected to violent attacks as a result of their peaceful political activities?

2. Is there a significant opposition vote and a realistic possibility for the opposition to increase its support or gain power through elections?

- Are various legal/administrative restrictions selectively applied to opposition parties to prevent them from increasing their support base or successfully competing in elections?

- Are there legitimate opposition forces in positions of authority, such as in the national legislature or in subnational governments?

- Are opposition party members or leaders intimidated, harassed, arrested, imprisoned, or subjected to violent attacks as a result of their peaceful political activities?

3. Are the people's political choices free from domination by the military, foreign powers, totalitarian parties, religious hierarchies, economic oligarchies, or any other powerful group?

- Do such groups offer bribes to voters and/or political figures in order to influence their political choices?

- Do such groups intimidate, harass, or attack voters and/or political figures in order to influence their political choices?

- Does the military control or enjoy a preponderant influence over government policy and activities, including in countries that nominally are under civilian control?

- Do foreign governments control or enjoy a preponderant influence over government policy and activities by means including the presence of foreign military troops, the use of significant economic threats or sanctions, etc.?

4. Do cultural, ethnic, religious, or other minority groups have full political rights and electoral opportunities?

- Do political parties of various ideological persuasions address issues of specific concern to minority groups?

- Does the government inhibit the participation of minority groups in national or subnational political life through laws and/or practical obstacles?

- Are political parties based on ethnicity, culture, or religion that espouse peaceful, democratic values legally permitted and de facto allowed to operate?

C. FUNCTIONING OF GOVERNMENT
1. Do the freely elected head of government and national legislative representatives determine the policies of the government?

- Are the candidates who were elected freely and fairly duly installed in office?

- Do other appointed or non-freely elected state actors interfere with or prevent freely elected representatives from adopting and implementing legislation and making meaningful policy decisions?

- Do nonstate actors, including criminal gangs, the military, and foreign governments, interfere with or prevent elected representatives from adopting and implementing legislation and making meaningful policy decisions?

2. Is the government free from pervasive corruption?

- Has the government implemented effective anticorruption laws or programs to prevent, detect, and punish corruption among public officials, including conflict of interest?

- Is the government free from excessive bureaucratic regulations, registration requirements, or other controls that increase opportunities for corruption?

- Are there independent and effective auditing and investigative bodies that function without impediment or political pressure or influence?

- Are allegations of corruption by government officials thoroughly investigated and prosecuted without prejudice, particularly against political opponents?

- Are allegations of corruption given wide and extensive airing in the media?

- Do whistle-blowers, anticorruption activists, investigators, and journalists enjoy legal protections that make them feel secure about reporting cases of bribery and corruption?

- What was the latest Transparency International Corruption Perceptions Index score for this country?

3. Is the government accountable to the electorate between elections, and does it operate with openness and transparency?

- Are civil society groups, interest groups, journalists, and other citizens able to comment on and influence pending policies of legislation?

- Do citizens have the legal right and practical ability to obtain information about government operations and the means to petition government agencies for it?

- Is the budget-making process subject to meaningful legislative review and public scrutiny?

- Does the government publish detailed accounting expenditures in a timely fashion?

- Does the state ensure transparency and effective competition in the awarding of government contracts?

- Are the asset declarations of government officials open to public and media scrutiny and verification?

ADDITIONAL DISCRETIONARY POLITICAL RIGHTS QUESTIONS:

A. For traditional monarchies that have no parties or electoral process, does the system provide for genuine, meaningful consultation with the people, encourage public discussion of policy choices, and allow the right to petition the ruler?

- Is there a non-elected legislature that advises the monarch on policy issues?

- Are there formal mechanisms for individuals or civic groups to speak with or petition the monarch?

- Does the monarch take petitions from the public under serious consideration?

B. Is the government or occupying power deliberately changing the ethnic composition of a country or territory so as to destroy a culture or tip the political balance in favor of another group?

- Is the government providing economic or other incentives to certain people in order to change the ethnic composition of a region or regions?

- Is the government forcibly moving people in or out of certain areas in order to change the ethnic composition of those regions?

- Is the government arresting, imprisoning, or killing members of certain ethnic groups in order change the ethnic composition of a region or regions?

CIVIL LIBERTIES CHECKLIST
D. FREEDOM OF EXPRESSION AND BELIEF

1. Are there free and independent media and other forms of cultural expression? (Note: In cases where the media are state controlled but offer pluralistic points of view, the survey gives the system credit.)

- Does the government directly or indirectly censor print, broadcast, and/or internet-based media?

- Is self-censorship among journalists common, especially when reporting on politically sensitive issues, including corruption or the activities of senior officials?

- Does the government use libel and security laws to punish those who scrutinize government officials and policies through either onerous fines or imprisonment?

- Is it a crime to insult the honor and dignity of the president and/or other government officials? How broad is the range of such prohibitions, and how vigorously are they enforced?

- If media outlets are dependent on the government for their financial survival, does the government withhold funding in order to propagandize, primarily provide official points of view, and/or limit access by opposition parties and civic critics?

- Does the government attempt to influence media content and access through means including politically motivated awarding of broadcast frequencies and newspaper registrations, unfair control and influence over printing facilities and distribution networks, selective distribution of advertising, onerous registration requirements, prohibitive tariffs, and bribery?

- Are journalists threatened, arrested, imprisoned, beaten, or killed by government or nongovernmental actors for their legitimate journalistic activities, and if such cases occur, are they investigated and prosecuted fairly and expeditiously?

- Are works of literature, art, music, or other forms of cultural expression censored or banned for political purposes?

2. Are religious institutions and communities free to practice their faith and express themselves in public and private?

- Are registration requirements employed to impede the free functioning of religious institutions?

- Are members of religious groups, including minority faiths and movements, harassed, fined, arrested, or beaten by the authorities for engaging in their religious practices?

- Does the government appoint or otherwise influence the appointment of religious leaders?

- Does the government control the production and distribution of religious books and other materials and the content of sermons?

- Is the construction of religious buildings banned or restricted?

- Does the government place undue restrictions on religious education? Does the government require religious education?

3. Is there academic freedom, and is the educational system free of extensive political indoctrination?

- Are teachers and professors free to pursue academic activities of a political and quasi-political nature without fear of physical violence or intimidation by state or nonstate actors?

- Does the government pressure, strongly influence, or control the content of school curriculums for political purposes?

- Are student associations that address issues of a political nature allowed to function freely?

- Does the government, including through school administration or other officials, pressure students and/or teachers to support certain political figures or agendas, including pressuring them to attend political rallies or vote for certain candidates? Conversely, does the government, including through school administration or other officials, discourage or forbid students and/or teachers from supporting certain candidates and parties?

4. Is there open and free private discussion?

- Are people able to engage in private discussions, particularly of a political nature (in places including restaurants, public transportation, and their homes) without fear of harassment or arrest by the authorities?

- Does the government employ people or groups to engage in public surveillance and to report alleged antigovernment conversations to the authorities?

E. ASSOCIATIONAL AND ORGANIZATIONAL RIGHTS
1. Is there freedom of assembly, demonstration, and open public discussion?

- Are peaceful protests, particularly those of a political nature, banned or severely restricted?

- Are the legal requirements to obtain permission to hold peaceful demonstrations particularly cumbersome and time consuming?

- Are participants of peaceful demonstrations intimidated, arrested, or assaulted?

- Are peaceful protestors detained by police in order to prevent them from engaging in such actions?

2. Is there freedom for nongovernmental organizations? (Note: This includes civic organizations, interest groups, foundations, etc.)

- Are registration and other legal requirements for nongovernmental organizations particularly onerous and intended to prevent them from functioning freely?

- Are laws related to the financing of nongovernmental organizations unduly complicated and cumbersome?

- Are donors and funders of nongovernmental organizations free of government pressure?

- Are members of nongovernmental organizations intimidated, arrested, imprisoned, or assaulted because of their work?

3. Are there free trade unions and peasant organizations or equivalents, and is there effective collective bargaining? Are there free professional and other private organizations?

- Are trade unions allowed to be established and to operate free from government interference?

- Are workers pressured by the government or employers to join or not to join certain trade unions, and do they face harassment, violence, or dismissal from their jobs if they do?

- Are workers permitted to engage in strikes, and do members of unions face reprisals for engaging in peaceful strikes? (Note: This question may not apply to workers in essential government services or public safety jobs.)

- Are unions able to bargain collectively with employers and able to negotiate collective bargaining agreements that are honored in practice?

- For states with very small populations or primarily agriculturally based economies that do not necessarily support the formation of trade unions, does the government allow for the establishment of peasant organizations or their equivalents? Is there legislation expressively forbidding the formation of trade unions?

- Are professional organizations, including business associations, allowed to operate freely and without government interference?

F. RULE OF LAW
1. Is there an independent judiciary?

- Is the judiciary subject to interference from the executive branch of government or from other political, economic, or religious influences?

- Are judges appointed and dismissed in a fair and unbiased manner?

- Do judges rule fairly and impartially, or do they commonly render verdicts that favor the government or particular interests, whether in return for bribes or other reasons?

- Do executive, legislative, and other governmental authorities comply with judicial decisions, and are these decisions effectively enforced?

- Do powerful private concerns comply with judicial decisions, and are decisions that run counter to the interests of powerful actors effectively enforced?

2. Does the rule of law prevail in civil and criminal matters? Are police under direct civilian control?

- Are defendants' rights, including the presumption of innocence until proven guilty, protected?

- Are detainees provided access to independent, competent legal counsel?

- Are defendants given a fair, public, and timely hearing by a competent, independent, and impartial tribunal?

- Are prosecutors independent of political control and influence?

- Are prosecutors independent of powerful private interests, whether legal or illegal?

- Is there effective and democratic civilian state control of law enforcement officials through the judicial, legislative, and executive branches?

- Are law enforcement officials free from the influence of nonstate actors, including organized crime, powerful commercial interests, or other groups?

3. Is there protection from political terror, unjustified imprisonment, exile, or torture, whether by groups that support or oppose the system? Is there freedom from war and insurgencies?

- Do law enforcement officials make arbitrary arrests and detentions without warrants or fabricate or plant evidence on suspects?

- Do law enforcement officials beat detainees during arrest and interrogation or use excessive force or torture to extract confessions?

- Are conditions in pretrial facilities and prisons humane and respectful of the human dignity of inmates?

- Do citizens have the means of effective petition and redress when their rights are violated by state authorities?

- Is violent crime either against specific groups or within the general population widespread?

- Is the population subjected to physical harm, forced removal, or other acts of violence or terror due to civil conflict or war?

4. Do laws, policies, and practices guarantee equal treatment of various segments of the population?

- Are members of various distinct groups—including ethnic and religious minorities, homosexuals, and the disabled—able to exercise effectively their human rights with full equality before the law?

- Is violence against such groups widespread, and if so, are perpetrators brought to justice?

- Do members of such groups face legal and/or de facto discrimination in areas including employment, education, and housing because of their identification with a particular group?

- Do women enjoy full equality in law and in practice as compared to men?

- Do noncitizens—including migrant workers and noncitizen immigrants—enjoy basic internationally recognized human rights, including the right not to be subjected to torture or other forms of ill-treatment, the right to due process of law, and the rights of freedom of association, expression, and religion?

- Do the country's laws provide for the granting of asylum or refugee status in accordance with the 1951 UN Convention Relating to the Status of Refugees, its 1967 Protocol, and other regional treaties regarding refugees? Has the government established a system for providing protection to refugees, including against refoulement (the return of persons to a country where there is reason to believe they fear persecution)?

G. PERSONAL AUTONOMY AND INDIVIDUAL RIGHTS

1. Do citizens enjoy freedom of travel or choice of residence, employment, or institution of higher education?

- Are there restrictions on foreign travel, including the use of an exit visa system, which may be issued selectively?

- Is permission required from the authorities or nonstate actors to move within the country?

- Do state or nonstate actors determine or otherwise influence a person's type and place of employment?

- Are bribes or other inducements needed to obtain the necessary documents to travel, change one's place of residence or employment, enter institutions of higher education, or advance in school?

2. Do citizens have the right to own property and establish private businesses? Is private business activity unduly influenced by government officials, the security forces, political parties/organizations, or organized crime?

- Are people legally allowed to purchase and sell land and other property, and can they do so in practice without undue interference from the government or nonstate actors?

- Does the government provide adequate and timely compensation to people whose property is expropriated under eminent domain laws?

- Are people legally allowed to establish and operate private businesses with a reasonable minimum of registration, licensing, and other requirements?

- Are bribes or other inducements needed to obtain the necessary legal documents to operate private businesses?

- Do private/nonstate actors, including criminal groups, seriously impede private business activities through such measures as extortion?

3. Are there personal social freedoms, including gender equality, choice of marriage partners, and size of family?

- Is violence against women, including wife-beating and rape, widespread, and are perpetrators brought to justice?

- Is the trafficking of women and/or children abroad for prostitution widespread, and is the government taking adequate efforts to address the problem?

- Do women face de jure and de facto discrimination in economic and social matters, including property and inheritance rights, divorce proceedings, and child custody matters?

- Does the government directly or indirectly control choice of marriage partners through means such as requiring large payments to marry certain individuals (e.g., foreign citizens) or by not enforcing laws against child marriage or dowry payments?

- Does the government determine the number of children that a couple may have?

- Does the government engage in state-sponsored religious/cultural/ethnic indoctrination and related restrictions on personal freedoms?

- Do private institutions, including religious groups, unduly infringe on the rights of individuals, including choice of marriage partner, dress, etc.?

4. Is there equality of opportunity and the absence of economic exploitation?

- Does the government exert tight control over the economy, including through state ownership and the setting of prices and production quotas?

- Do the economic benefits from large state industries, including the energy sector, benefit the general population or only a privileged few?

- Do private interests exert undue influence on the economy through monopolistic practices, cartels, or illegal blacklists, boycotts, or discrimination?

- Is entrance to institutions of higher education or the ability to obtain employment limited by widespread nepotism and the payment of bribes?

- Are certain groups, including ethnic or religious minorities, less able to enjoy certain economic benefits than others? For example, are certain groups restricted from holding particular jobs, whether in the public or the private sector, because of de jure or de facto discrimination?

- Do state or private employers exploit their workers through activities including unfairly withholding wages and permitting or forcing employees to work under unacceptably dangerous conditions, as well as through adult slave labor and child labor?

KEY TO SCORES, PR AND CL RATINGS, AND STATUS

Table 1		Table 2	
Political Rights (PR)		**Civil Liberties (CL)**	
Total Scores	**PR Rating**	**Total Scores**	**CL Rating**
36–40	1	53–60	1
30–35	2	44–52	2
24–29	3	35–43	3
18–23	4	26–34	4
12–17	5	17–25	5
6–11	6	8–16	6
0–5*	7	0–7	7

Table 3	
Combined Average of the PR and CL Ratings	**Country Status**
1.0–2.5	Free
3.0–5.0	Partly Free
5.5–7.0	Not Free

* It is possible for a country's total political rights score to be less than zero (between -1 and -4) if it receives mostly or all zeros for each of the 10 political rights questions *and* it receives a sufficiently negative score for political rights discretionary question B. In such a case, a country would still receive a final political rights rating of 7.

Tables and Ratings

Table of Independent Countries

Country	PR	CL	Freedom Rating	Country	PR	CL	Freedom Rating
Afghanistan	6	6	Not Free	Djibouti	6	5	Not Free
Albania*	3	3	Partly Free	Dominica*	1	1	Free
Algeria	6	5	Not Free	Dominican Republic*	2	2	Free
Andorra*	1	1	Free	East Timor*	3	4	Partly Free
Angola	6	5	Not Free	⬇Ecuador*	3	3	Partly Free
Antigua and Barbuda*	2▲	2	Free	Egypt	5▲	5	Partly Free ▲
Argentina*	2	2	Free	El Salvador*	2	3	Free
Armenia	5▲	4	Partly Free	Equatorial Guinea	7	7	Not Free
Australia*	1	1	Free	Eritrea	7	7	Not Free
Austria*	1	1	Free	Estonia*	1	1	Free
Azerbaijan	6	5	Not Free	Ethiopia	6	6	Not Free
Bahamas*	1	1	Free	Fiji	6	4	Partly Free
Bahrain	6	6	Not Free	Finland*	1	1	Free
Bangladesh*	3	4	Partly Free	France*	1	1	Free
Barbados*	1	1	Free	Gabon	6	5	Not Free
Belarus	7	6	Not Free	The Gambia	6	6▼	Not Free
Belgium*	1	1	Free	Georgia*	3▲	3	Partly Free
Belize*	1	2	Free	Germany*	1	1	Free
Benin*	2	2	Free	Ghana*	1	2	Free
⬆Bhutan*	4	5	Partly Free	⬇Greece*	2	2	Free
Bolivia*	3	3	Partly Free	Grenada*	1	2	Free
Bosnia and Herzegovina*	3▲	3	Partly Free	Guatemala*	3	4	Partly Free
Botswana*	3	2	Free	⬆Guinea	5	5	Partly Free
Brazil*	2	2	Free	Guinea-Bissau	6▼	5▼	Not Free ▼
Brunei	6	5	Not Free	Guyana*	2	3	Free
Bulgaria*	2	2	Free	Haiti	4	5	Partly Free
Burkina Faso	5	3	Partly Free	Honduras	4	4	Partly Free
Burma	6▲	5▲	Not Free	Hungary*	1	2	Free
Burundi	5	5	Partly Free	Iceland*	1	1	Free
Cambodia	6	5	Not Free	India*	2	3	Free
Cameroon	6	6	Not Free	Indonesia*	2	3	Free
Canada*	1	1	Free	Iran	6	6	Not Free
Cape Verde*	1	1	Free	Iraq	6▼	6	Not Free
⬇Central African Republic	5	5	Partly Free	Ireland*	1	1	Free
Chad	7	6	Not Free	Israel*	1	2	Free
Chile*	1	1	Free	Italy*	2▼	1	Free
China	7	6	Not Free	Jamaica*	2	3	Free
Colombia*	3	4	Partly Free	Japan*	1	2	Free
Comoros*	3	4	Partly Free	⬇Jordan	6	5	Not Free
Congo (Brazzaville)	6	5	Not Free	⬇Kazakhstan	6	5	Not Free
Congo (Kinshasa)	6	6	Not Free	Kenya	4	4▼	Partly Free
Costa Rica*	1	1	Free	Kiribati*	1	1	Free
Côte d'Ivoire	5▲	5▲	Partly Free ▲	Kosovo	5	4	Partly Free
Croatia*	1	2	Free	Kuwait	5▼	5	Partly Free
Cuba	7	6	Not Free	Kyrgyzstan	5	5	Partly Free
Cyprus*	1	1	Free	Laos	7	6	Not Free
Czech Republic*	1	1	Free	Latvia*	2	2	Free
Denmark*	1	1	Free	⬇Lebanon	5	4	Partly Free
				Lesotho*	2▲	3	Free ▲
				Liberia*	3	4	Partly Free

Country	PR	CL	Freedom Rating	Country	PR	CL	Freedom Rating
Libya*	4▲	5▲	Partly Free ▲	Senegal*	2▲	3	Free ▲
Liechtenstein*	1	1	Free	Serbia*	2	2	Free
Lithuania*	1	1	Free	Seychelles*	3	3	Partly Free
Luxembourg*	1	1	Free	Sierra Leone*	2▲	3	Free ▲
Macedonia*	3	3	Partly Free	Singapore	4	4	Partly Free
⬇ Madagascar	6	4	Partly Free	Slovakia*	1	1	Free
⬆ Malawi*	3	4	Partly Free	Slovenia*	1	1	Free
Malaysia	4	4	Partly Free	Solomon Islands	4	3	Partly Free
Maldives	5▼	4	Partly Free	Somalia	7	7	Not Free
Mali	7▼	5▼	Not Free ▼	South Africa*	2	2	Free
Malta*	1	1	Free	South Korea*	1	2	Free
Marshall Islands*	1	1	Free	South Sudan	6	5	Not Free
Mauritania	6	5	Not Free	Spain*	1	1	Free
Mauritius*	1	2	Free	⬇ Sri Lanka	5	4	Partly Free
Mexico*	3	3	Partly Free	Sudan	7	7	Not Free
Micronesia*	1	1	Free	⬇ Suriname*	2	2	Free
Moldova*	3	3	Partly Free	Swaziland	7	5	Not Free
Monaco*	2	1	Free	Sweden*	1	1	Free
Mongolia*	1▲	2	Free	Switzerland*	1	1	Free
Montenegro*	3	2	Free	⬇ Syria	7	7	Not Free
Morocco	5	4	Partly Free	Taiwan*	1	2	Free
Mozambique	4	3	Partly Free	Tajikistan	6	6▼	Not Free
Namibia*	2	2	Free	Tanzania*	3	3	Partly Free
Nauru*	1	1	Free	Thailand*	4	4	Partly Free
Nepal	4	4	Partly Free	Togo	5	4	Partly Free
Netherlands*	1	1	Free	Tonga*	3	2▲	Free ▲
New Zealand*	1	1	Free	Trinidad and Tobago*	2	2	Free
Nicaragua	5	4	Partly Free				
Niger*	3	4	Partly Free	Tunisia*	3	4	Partly Free
⬇ Nigeria	4	4	Partly Free	Turkey*	3	4▼	Partly Free
North Korea	7	7	Not Free	Turkmenistan	7	7	Not Free
Norway*	1	1	Free	Tuvalu*	1	1	Free
⬇ Oman	6	5	Not Free	⬇ Uganda	5	4	Partly Free
Pakistan	4	5	Partly Free	⬇ Ukraine*	4	3	Partly Free
Palau*	1	1	Free	⬇ United Arab Emirates	6	6	Not Free
Panama*	1	2	Free				
Papua New Guinea*	4	3	Partly Free	United Kingdom*	1	1	Free
				United States*	1	1	Free
⬇ Paraguay*	3	3	Partly Free	Uruguay*	1	1	Free
Peru*	2	3	Free	Uzbekistan	7	7	Not Free
Philippines*	3	3	Partly Free	Vanuatu*	2	2	Free
Poland*	1	1	Free	Venezuela	5	5	Partly Free
Portugal*	1	1	Free	Vietnam	7	5	Not Free
Qatar	6	5	Not Free	Yemen	6	6	Not Free
Romania*	2	2	Free	Zambia*	3	4	Partly Free
⬇ Russia	6	5	Not Free	Zimbabwe	6	6	Not Free
Rwanda	6	6▼	Not Free				
St. Kitts and Nevis*	1	1	Free				
St. Lucia*	1	1	Free				
St. Vincent and the Grenadines*	1	1	Free				
Samoa*	2	2	Free				
San Marino*	1	1	Free				
São Tomé and Príncipe*	2	2	Free				
Saudi Arabia	7	7	Not Free				

PR and CL stand for Political Rights and Civil Liberties, respectively; 1 represents the most free and 7 the least free rating.

▼ ▲ up or down indicates an improvement or decline in ratings or status since the last survey.

⬆ ⬇ up or down indicates a trend of positive or negative changes that took place but were not sufficient to result in a change in political rights or civil liberties ratings.

* indicates a country's status as an electoral democracy.

Note: The ratings reflect global events from January 1, 2012, through December 31, 2012.

Table of Related Territories

Territory	PR	CL	Freedom Rating
Hong Kong	5	2	Partly Free
Puerto Rico	1	2	Free

Table of Disputed Territories

Country	PR	CL	Freedom Rating
Abkhazia	4▲	5	Partly Free
Gaza Strip	6	6	Not Free
⬆Indian Kashmir	4	4	Partly Free
Nagorno-Karabakh	5▲	5	Partly Free▲
Northern Cyprus	2	2	Free
Pakistani Kashmir	6	5	Not Free
Somaliland	4	5	Partly Free
South Ossetia	7	6	Not Free
Tibet	7	7	Not Free
Transnistria	6	6	Not Free
West Bank	6	5	Not Free
Western Sahara	7	7	Not Free

PR and CL stand for Political Rights and Civil Liberties, respectively; 1 represents the most free and 7 the least free rating.

▼ ▲ up or down indicates an improvement or decline in ratings or status since the last survey.

⬆ ⬇ up or down indicates a trend of positive or negative changes that took place but were not sufficient to result in a change in political rights or civil liberties ratings.

* indicates a country's status as an electoral democracy.

Note: The ratings reflect global events from January 1, 2012, through December 31, 2012.

Combined Average Ratings: Independent Countries

FREE

1.0
Andorra
Australia
Austria
Bahamas
Barbados
Belgium
Canada
Cape Verde
Chile
Costa Rica
Cyprus
Czech Republic
Denmark
Dominica
Estonia
Finland
France
Germany
Iceland
Ireland
Kiribati
Liechtenstein
Lithuania
Luxembourg
Malta
Marshall Islands
Micronesia
Nauru
Netherlands
New Zealand
Norway
Palau
Poland
Portugal
Saint Kitts and Nevis
Saint Lucia
Saint Vincent
and the Grenadines
San Marino
Slovakia
Slovenia
Spain
Sweden
Switzerland
Tuvalu
United Kingdom
United States
Uruguay

1.5
Belize
Croatia
Ghana
Grenada
Hungary
Israel

Italy
Japan
Mauritius
Monaco
Mongolia
Panama
South Korea
Taiwan

2.0
Antigua and Barbuda
Argentina
Benin
Brazil
Bulgaria
Dominican Republic
Greece
Latvia
Namibia
Romania
Samoa
Sao Tome and
Principe
Serbia
South Africa
Suriname
Trinidad and Tobago
Vanuatu

2.5
Botswana
El Salvador
Guyana
India
Indonesia
Jamaica
Lesotho
Montenegro
Peru
Senegal
Sierra Leone
Tonga

PARTLY FREE

3.0
Albania
Bolivia
Bosnia and Herzegovina
Ecuador
Georgia
Macedonia
Mexico
Moldova
Paraguay
Philippines
Seychelles
Tanzania

3.5
Bangladesh
Colombia
Comoros
East Timor
Guatemala
Liberia
Malawi
Mozambique
Niger
Papua New Guinea
Solomon Islands
Tunisia
Turkey
Ukraine
Zambia

4.0
Burkina Faso
Honduras
Kenya
Malaysia
Nepal
Nigeria
Singapore
Thailand

4.5
Armenia
Bhutan
Haiti
Kosovo
Lebanon
Libya
Maldives
Morocco
Nicaragua
Pakistan
Sri Lanka
Togo
Uganda

5.0
Burundi
Central African Republic
Côte d'Ivoire
Egypt
Fiji
Guinea
Kuwait
Kyrgyzstan
Madagascar
Venezuela

NOT FREE

5.5
Algeria

Angola
Azerbaijan
Brunei
Burma
Cambodia
Congo (Brazzaville)
Djibouti
Gabon
Guinea-Bissau
Jordan
Kazakhstan
Mauritania
Oman
Qatar
Russia
South Sudan

6.0
Afghanistan
Bahrain
Cameroon
Congo (Kinshasa)
Ethiopia
The Gambia
Iran
Iraq
Mali
Rwanda
Swaziland
Tajikistan
United Arab Emirates
Vietnam
Yemen
Zimbabwe

6.5
Belarus
Chad
China
Cuba
Laos

7.0
Equatorial Guinea
Eritrea
North Korea
Saudi Arabia
Somalia
Sudan
Syria
Turkmenistan
Uzbekistan

Combined Average Ratings: Related Territories

FREE
1.5
Puerto Rico

PARTLY FREE
3.5
Hong Kong

Combined Average Ratings: Disputed Territories

FREE
2.0
Northern Cyprus

PARTLY FREE
4.0
Indian Kashmir

4.5
Abkhazia
Somaliland

5.0
Nagorno-Karabakh

NOT FREE
5.5
Pakistani Kashmir
West Bank

6.0
Gaza Strip
Transnistria

6.5
South Ossetia

7.0
Tibet
Western Sahara

Electoral Democracies (118)

Albania	Iceland
Andorra	India
Antigua and Barbuda	Indonesia
Argentina	Ireland
Australia	Israel
Austria	Italy
Bahamas	Jamaica
Bangladesh	Japan
Barbados	Kiribati
Belgium	Latvia
Belize	Lesotho
Benin	Liberia
Bhutan	Libya
Bolivia	Liechtenstein
Bosnia-Herzegovina	Lithuania
Botswana	Luxembourg
Brazil	Macedonia
Bulgaria	Malawi
Canada	Malta
Cape Verde	Marshall Islands
Chile	Mauritius
Colombia	Mexico
Comoros	Micronesia
Costa Rica	Moldova
Croatia	Monaco
Cyprus	Mongolia
Czech Republic	Montenegro
Denmark	Namibia
Dominica	Nauru
Dominican Republic	Netherlands
East Timor	New Zealand
Ecuador	Niger
El Salvador	Norway
Estonia	Palau
Finland	Panama
France	Papua New Guinea
Georgia	Paraguay
Germany	Peru
Ghana	Philippines
Greece	Poland
Grenada	Portugal
Guatemala	Romania
Guyana	St. Kitts and Nevis
Hungary	St. Lucia

St. Vincent and the Grenadines	Switzerland
Samoa	Taiwan
San Marino	Tanzania
São Tomé and Príncipe	Thailand
Senegal	Tonga
Serbia	Trinidad and Tobago
Seychelles	Tunisia
Sierra Leone	Turkey
Slovakia	Tuvalu
Slovenia	Ukraine
South Africa	United Kingdom
South Korea	United States
Spain	Uruguay
Suriname	Vanuatu
Sweden	Zambia

The Survey Team

EDITORS

GENERAL EDITOR—Arch Puddington

MANAGING EDITOR—Aili Piano

ASSOCIATE EDITORS—Jennifer Dunham, Bret Nelson, Tyler Roylance

CONSULTANT EDITORS—Ronald Eniclerico, Alexandra Kendall, Lynn Messina, Shannon O'Toole

CONTRIBUTING AUTHORS

YASMIN ALEM is an expert on Iranian elections and domestic politics. She is the author of *Duality by Design: The Iranian Electoral System.* She has served as a consultant to international and nongovernmental organizations, including the Office of the UN High Commissioner for Human Rights, the Institute for War and Peace Reporting, the U.S. Institute of Peace, the Atlantic Council, and the International Foundation for Electoral Systems. She received a master of business administration degree in international organizations from the University of Geneva. She served as a Middle East and North Africa analyst for *Freedom in the World.*

MICHAEL E. ALLISON is an associate professor of political science at the University of Scranton in Pennsylvania. He received his master's degree and PhD in political science from Florida State University. His teaching and research interests include the comparative study of civil war and civil war resolution, particularly as it relates to the transformation of armed opposition groups into political parties in Latin America. His work has appeared in *Latin American Politics and Society, Conflict Management and Peace Science, and Studies in Comparative International Development.* He also blogs at Central American Politics. He served as an Americas analyst for *Freedom in the World.*

DAVID BAKER is an analyst and consultant for the U.S. Department of Defense and its Africa Command. He has researched and worked on sustainable development and conflict analysis in Africa and elsewhere for 15 years. He received a master's degree in cultural anthropology from Indiana University, Bloomington, with a concentration in African studies. He served as a sub-Saharan Africa analyst for *Freedom in the World.*

CAROLYN BARNETT is a research fellow in the Middle East Program at the Center for Strategic and International Studies. Her primary research interests are in the politics and society of North Africa. She also supports the Middle East Program's projects related to the Persian Gulf. She received master's degrees in Middle East politics and Islamic studies from the School of Oriental and African Studies in London, where she was a Marshall Scholar. She spent a year as a graduate fellow in the Center for Arabic Study Abroad program at the American University in Cairo on a Fulbright scholarship. She served as a Middle East and North Africa analyst for *Freedom in the World.*

ROBERT BLAIR is a PhD candidate in political science at Yale University. His research focuses on the dynamics of, and potential tradeoffs between, peacekeeping and state building in war-torn countries. He recently served as co-principal investigator on an evaluation of a large-scale alternative dispute resolution program in Liberia; an article based on that research is forthcoming in the *American Political Science Review.* Previously, he worked as a consultant for the Small Arms Survey and the UN Office of Rule of Law Security Institutions, among others. He served as a sub-Saharan Africa analyst for *Freedom in the World.*

S. ADAM CARDAIS is a contributing editor at *Transitions Online*, a Prague-based internet magazine covering politics, economics, and society in postcommunist Europe and the former Soviet Union. He received a master's degree in European studies, with a focus on postconflict peace building in the former Yugoslavia, from New York University. He served as a Central and Eastern Europe/Eurasia analyst for *Freedom in the World.*

FOTINI CHRISTIA is an associate professor of political science at the Massachusetts Institute of Technology. Her research interests deal with issues of conflict and co-operation in the Muslim world. She has done extensive ethnographic, survey, and experimental research on the effects of development aid in postconflict, multiethnic societies, with a focus on Afghanistan and Bosnia and Herzegovina. She is the author of *Alliance Formation in Civil Wars*, awarded the 2013 Gregory M. Luebbert Award for Best Book in Comparative Politics. Her research has also been published in *Science and in the American Political Science Review*, and she has written opinion pieces for *Foreign Affairs*, the *New York Times*, the *Washington Post*, and the *Boston Globe*. She received a PhD in public policy from Harvard University. She served as an Asia-Pacific analyst for *Freedom in the World.*

SARAH COOK is a senior research analyst for East Asia at Freedom House. She manages the team that produces the *China Media Bulletin*, a biweekly news digest of press freedom developments related to China. She previously served as assistant editor on three editions of Freedom House's *Freedom on the Net* index, which assesses internet and digital media freedom around the world. She coedited the English version of Chinese attorney Gao Zhisheng's memoir, *A China More Just,* and was a delegate to the UN Human Rights Commission for an organization working on religious freedom in China. She received a master's degree in politics and a master of laws degree in public international law from the School of Oriental and African Studies in London, where she was a Marshall Scholar. She served as an Asia-Pacific analyst for *Freedom in the World.*

BRITTA H. CRANDALL is an adjunct professor at Davidson College in North Carolina. She is the author of *Hemispheric Giants: The Misunderstood History of U.S.-Brazilian Relations.* Previously, she was associate director for Latin American sovereign risk analysis at Bank One and worked as a Latin American program examiner for the U.S. Office of Management and Budget. She received a PhD from the Johns

Hopkins University School of Advanced International Studies. She served as an Americas analyst for *Freedom in the World*.

CAROLINA CURVALE is a visiting researcher at the Latin American Faculty of Social Sciences (FLACSO) in Quito, Ecuador, where she focuses on understanding the determinants of political instability and long-term growth in Latin America. Previously, she served as senior political analyst for the U.S. State Department at the embassy in Quito and as a visiting professor at FLACSO. Her contributions have appeared in academic publications and opinion columns. She received a PhD in political science from New York University. She served as an Americas analyst for *Freedom in the World*.

JULIAN DIERKES is an associate professor and the Keidanren Chair in Japanese Research at the University of British Columbia's Institute of Asian Research, where he coordinates the Program on Inner Asia. His research has focused on history education and supplementary education in Japan, as well as contemporary Mongolia. He is the editor of *Change in Democratic Mongolia: Social Relations, Health, Mobile Pastoralism, and Mining*. He received a PhD in sociology from Princeton University. He served as an Asia-Pacific analyst for *Freedom in the World*.

JAKE DIZARD is a PhD candidate in political science at the University of Texas at Austin. He was previously the managing editor of *Countries at the Crossroads,* Freedom House's annual survey of democratic governance. His area of focus is Latin America, with a specific emphasis on the Andean region and Mexico. He received a master's degree from the Johns Hopkins University School of Advanced International Studies. He served as an Americas analyst for *Freedom in the World*.

RICHARD DOWNIE is deputy director and a fellow of the Africa Program at the Center for Strategic and International Studies. Previously, he was a journalist for the British Broadcasting Corporation (BBC). He received a master's degree in international public policy from the Johns Hopkins University School of Advanced International Studies. He served as a sub-Saharan Africa analyst for *Freedom in the World*.

JENNIFER DUNHAM is a senior research analyst for *Freedom in the World and Freedom of the Press* at Freedom House. Previously, she was the managing editor and Africa writer for *Facts On File World News Digest.* She received a master's degree in international relations from New York University, where she wrote her thesis on transitional justice in Rwanda and Sierra Leone. She served as a sub-Saharan Africa analyst for *Freedom in the World*.

NICHOLAS FARRELLY is a research fellow at the Australian National University's College of Asia and the Pacific. His academic interests are focused on the long-term study of Southeast Asian societies and politics. Since 2011, he has convened the university's undergraduate program in peace, conflict, and war studies. In 2012, he received an Australian Research Council fellowship for a three-year study of Burma's political cultures "in transition." He received a master's degree and PhD from Oxford University, where he was a Rhodes Scholar. He served as an Asia-Pacific analyst for *Freedom in the World*.

AMY FREEDMAN is a professor and the department chair of political science and international studies at Long Island University, C. W. Post Campus. Her research touches on various questions relating to democratization. She has a forthcoming book on the internationalization of domestic conflicts and is a coeditor of the journal *Asian Security.* She received a master's degree and PhD in political science from New York University. She served as an Asia-Pacific analyst for *Freedom in the World.*

THOMAS W. GOLD is the director of strategic initiatives and external affairs at the Research Alliance for New York City Schools at New York University. He is a former assistant professor of comparative politics at Sacred Heart University and the author of *The Lega Nord and Contemporary Politics* in Italy. He received a PhD in political science from the New School for Social Research and a Fulbright Fellowship to conduct research in Italy. He served as a Western Europe analyst for *Freedom in the World.*

EVA HOIER GREENE is a former research assistant at Freedom House. Previously, she covered nuclear disarmament, among other issues, at the Permanent Mission of Denmark to the United Nations. She received a bachelor's degree in international development in Denmark. She served as a Western Europe analyst for *Freedom in the World.*

NICOLE GREENE is a program associate with the Global Freedom of Expression Campaign at Freedom House. She received a master's degree in international relations from New York University's Center for Global Affairs, where she wrote her thesis on international attention and response in the Democratic Republic of the Congo and Sudan. She served as a sub-Saharan Africa analyst for *Freedom in the World.*

SHELBY GROSSMAN is a PhD candidate in government at Harvard University, focusing on the politics of informal trade in Nigeria. She has separate research projects on the politics of diversified business groups and on the determinants of illegal price discrimination in developing countries. She has research experience throughout Nigeria, and also in Liberia, Equatorial Guinea, and Cameroon. She served as a sub-Saharan Africa analyst for *Freedom in the World.*

HOLGER HENKE is assistant provost at York College, City University of New York, and a political scientist with a variety of research interests in international relations. He has authored and edited six books, including *Constructing Vernacular Culture in the Trans-Caribbean,* and has published numerous articles in journals such as *Cultural Critique and Latin American Perspectives.* He is the editor of *Wadabagei: A Journal of the Caribbean and its Diasporas.* He received a master's degree in political science from the Geschwister-Scholl-Institute of Political Science at the Ludwig Maximilians University of Munich and a PhD in government from the University of the West Indies at Mona, Jamaica. He served as an Americas analyst for *Freedom in the World.*

TED HENKEN is an associate professor in the Department of Sociology and Anthropology at Baruch College, City University of New York. He is a former chair of Baruch's Black and Latino Studies Department, where he holds a joint appointment. He is the current president of the Association for the Study of the Cuban Economy. He is the author of *Cuba: A Global Studies Handbook* and is coauthoring a book on the development of self-employment, microenterprise, and the underground economy in Cuba. He has published articles in journals including *Nueva Sociedad, Cuban Studies, and Latin American Research Review.* He writes about contemporary Cuba in his blog, *El Yuma,* and is frequently interviewed by major media outlets, including CNN, the *New York Times,* the BBC, and Univision. He received a PhD in Latin American studies from Tulane University. He served as an Americas analyst for *Freedom in the World.*

FRANKLIN HESS is the coordinator of the Modern Greek Program at Indiana University, a senior lecturer in West European studies, and codirector of a working group on the sovereign debt crisis. His scholarly work examines 20th- and 21st-century Greek popular culture, exploring the economic, geopolitical, and geocultural contexts of its production. He has published on topics including the role of popular culture in modern Greek studies, and his other scholarly interests include immigration and the cinematic representation of violence. He served as the secretary of the Modern Greek Studies Association from 2007 to 2009. He received a PhD in American studies from the University of Iowa, focusing on the influence of American television programming on Greek culture. He served as a Western Europe analyst for *Freedom in the World.*

DAN HOLODNIK is assistant general manager at Almona Inc., a Cairo-based firm facilitating new U.S. corporate investment in Egypt and the broader Middle East through in-country representation, marketing, and procurement support. Previously, he was a Middle East research associate at the Center for Strategic and International Studies. He received a master's degree in Islamic studies from Duke University. He served as a Middle East and North Africa analyst for *Freedom in the World.*

MAÏTÉ HOSTETTER is the program officer for West and Central Africa at Freedom House, where she focuses on human rights, transitional justice, and civil society engagement in the promotion of good governance and democratic reform. Previously, she worked as a West Africa program coordinator at the International Foundation for Electoral Systems. She received a master's degree in the social sciences from the University of Chicago with a concentration on human rights. She served as a sub-Saharan Africa analyst for Freedom in the World.

MORGAN HUSTON is a member of the research team at Freedom House, where she also contributes to the *Freedom of the Press* publication. She received a master's degree in international human rights from the Josef Korbel School of International Studies at the University of Denver. She served as a sub-Saharan Africa analyst for *Freedom in the World.*

RACHEL JACOBS is a PhD candidate in political science at the University of Wisconsin, Madison. Her research focuses on regime consolidation in Southeast Asia. Previously, she was a research analyst for *Countries at the Crossroads,* Freedom House's annual survey of democratic governance. She received a master's degree in international relations from the University of Chicago. She served as an Asia-Pacific analyst for *Freedom in the World.*

TOBY CRAIG JONES is an associate professor of history and the director of the Center for Middle Eastern Studies at Rutgers University, New Brunswick. From 2012 to 2014, he will serve as codirector of the Rutgers Center for Historical Analysis. He is also a nonresident scholar in the Middle East Program at the Carnegie Endowment for International Peace. Previously, he was the Persian Gulf analyst at the International Crisis Group. He is the author of *Desert Kingdom: How Oil and Water Forged Modern Saudi Arabia* and is currently writing a book entitled *America's Oil Wars.* He is an editor of *Middle East Report* and has published widely, including in the *International Journal of Middle East Studies,* the *New York Times,* and *Foreign Affairs.* He received a PhD from Stanford University. He served as a Middle East and North Africa analyst for *Freedom in the World.*

KARIN DEUTSCH KARLEKAR is the project director of *Freedom of the Press,* Freedom House's annual survey of global press freedom. A specialist on media freedom trends and measurement indicators, she also developed the methodology for and edited the pilot edition of *Freedom on the Net,* Freedom House's assessment of internet and digital media freedom. She has written South Asia reports for several Freedom House publications, and has been on research and advocacy missions to Afghanistan, Nigeria, Pakistan, Sri Lanka, South Africa, Uganda, Zambia, and Zimbabwe. She previously worked as a consultant for Human Rights Watch and as an editor at the Economist Intelligence Unit. She received a PhD in Indian history from Cambridge University. She served as an Asia-Pacific analyst for *Freedom in the World.*

SANJA KELLY is the project director of *Freedom on the Net,* Freedom House's assessment of internet and digital media freedom. An expert on internet freedom, democratic governance, and women's rights, she has also directed the research and production of Freedom House publications including *Women's Rights in the Middle East and North Africa* and *Countries at the Crossroads.* She is the author of numerous reports and articles on these topics, and has been on research assignments in the former Yugoslavia, the Caucasus, South and Southeast Asia, Africa, and the Middle East. She received a master's degree in international relations from Columbia University's School of International and Public Affairs. She served as a Central and Eastern Europe/Eurasia analyst for *Freedom in the World.*

ALEXANDRA KENDALL is a manager at Global Health Strategies (GHS), an international consulting company focused on global health issues. Prior to joining GHS, she spent two years at the Congressional Research Service, where she provided analysis on issues related to global health, gender-based violence, and postconflict and disaster reconstruction efforts for members of the U.S. House of Representatives and Senate. She has also worked in the field on programs related to women's health, HIV/AIDS, sexual violence, human trafficking, and youth education in Cambodia, Haiti, Rwanda, Senegal, and South Africa. She received a master's degree in international relations from Yale University. She served as a sub-Saharan Africa analyst for *Freedom in the World.*

SYLVANA HABDANK-KOŁACZKOWSKA is the project director of *Nations in Transit,* Freedom House's annual survey of democratic governance in Central and Eastern Europe and Eurasia. She also writes reports on Central Europe for the *Freedom of the Press* survey. Previously, she was the managing editor of the *Journal of Cold War Studies,* a peer-reviewed quarterly. She received a master's degree in Eastern European and Eurasian studies from Harvard University. She served as a Central and Eastern Europe/Eurasia analyst for *Freedom in the World.*

PAUL KUBICEK is a professor of political science and director of the International Studies Program at Oakland University. He is the author of numerous works on postcommunist and Turkish politics, which have appeared in journals including *Comparative Politics, Democratization,* and *Political Science Quarterly.* He is currently coeditor of *Turkish Studies* and is working on a book-length project examining the role of Islam in Muslim-majority democracies. He has taught in Ukraine, Turkey, and Austria, and was a Fulbright scholar in Slovenia. He received a PhD in political science from the University of Michigan. He served as a Western Europe analyst for *Freedom in the World.*

JOSHUA KURLANTZICK is a fellow for Southeast Asia at the Council on Foreign Relations. Previously, he was a scholar at the Carnegie Endowment for International Peace, where he focused on Southeast Asian politics and economics and China's relations with Southeast Asia. He is a longtime journalist whose articles have appeared in *Time,* the *New Republic,* the *Atlantic Monthly, Foreign Affairs,* and the *New Yorker,* among others. He is the author of the recently released book *Democracy in Decline.* He received a bachelor's degree in political science from Haverford College. He served as an Asia-Pacific analyst for *Freedom in the World.*

ASTRID LARSON is the language center administrative director for the French Institute Alliance Française. She has served as an analyst for Western Europe, sub-Saharan Africa, and the South Pacific for Freedom House's *Freedom of the Press* survey. She received a master's degree in international media and culture from the New School University. She served as a Western Europe analyst for *Freedom in the World.*

BEATRICE LINDSTROM is a human rights attorney with the Institute for Justice & Democracy in Haiti (IJDH) focusing on rule of law and access to justice. Prior to joining IJDH, she worked with the Bureau des Avocats Internationaux in Port-au-Prince, Haiti, where her activities included election monitoring, human rights reporting, and managing grassroots participation in the UN Universal Periodic Review. She received a juris doctor degree from New York University School of Law, where she was a Root Tilden Kern scholar. She served as an Americas analyst for *Freedom in the World.*

JOSHUA LUSTIG is managing editor of *Current History,* an international affairs journal based in Philadelphia. Previously, he was a senior editor at *Facts On File World News Digest,* covering Western Europe. He received a bachelor's degree in English literature from Columbia University. He served as a Western Europe analyst for *Freedom in the World.*

ELEANOR MARCHANT is a PhD student at the Annenberg School for Communications at the University of Pennsylvania, specializing in political communications and new technology in Africa. She is also a research associate at the Center for Global Communication Studies, where she advises on African and transnational media research projects. Previously, she worked at the Programme in Comparative Media Law and Policy at Oxford University, the Media Development Investment Fund, and the Media Institute in Nairobi. She also served as assistant editor for Freedom House's *Freedom of the Press* survey. She received a master's degree in international relations from New York University. She served as a sub-Saharan Africa analyst for *Freedom in the World.*

KATHERIN MACHALEK is a research analyst for *Nations in Transit,* Freedom House's annual survey of democratic governance from Central Europe to Eurasia. A specialist on Eastern Europe, the Caucasus, and Central Asia, she has authored several articles on political developments and corruption. Previously, she worked for the Geneva-based Human Rights Information and Documentation Systems (HURIDOCS), helping civil society organizations in Eurasia improve their use of information and communication technologies and digital advocacy. She received a master's degree in political science from the University of North Carolina, Chapel Hill. She served as a Central and Eastern Europe/Eurasia analyst for *Freedom in the World.*

SUSANA MOREIRA is a PhD candidate at the Johns Hopkins University School of Advanced International Studies, where her research focuses on Chinese national oil companies' investment strategies in Latin America and sub-Saharan Africa. She is involved in several other research projects, including the African Crisis Management in Comparative Perspective project sponsored by the U.S. military's Africa Command, and also works as a consultant for the World Bank's Gas, Oil, and Mining Division. She served as a sub-Saharan Africa analyst for *Freedom in the World.*

BRET NELSON is a research analyst for *Freedom in the World* and *Freedom of the Press* at Freedom House. He received master's degrees in political science from Fordham University and in Middle East studies from the Graduate Center, City University of New York. He served as a Middle East and North Africa analyst for *Freedom in the World.*

ALYSSON A. OAKLEY is a senior adviser at the International Republican Institute and an adjunct professor at Georgetown University. She has lived in Indonesia, with frequent postings to East Timor, for over 10 years, five of which were spent working on political development with a focus on political parties and local legislatures. She received a master's degree in international economics and Southeast Asian studies from Johns Hopkins University's School of Advanced International Studies. She served as an Asia-Pacific analyst for *Freedom in the World.*

ROBERT ORTTUNG is assistant director of the Institute for European, Russian, and Eurasian Studies at George Washington University's Elliott School of International Affairs, president of the Resource Security Institute, and a visiting scholar at the Center for Security Studies at the Swiss Federal Institute of Technology (ETH) in

Zurich. He is managing editor of *Demokratizatsiya: The Journal of Post-Soviet Democratization* and a coeditor of the *Russian Analytical Digest and the Caucasus Analytical Digest.* He received a PhD in political science from the University of California, Los Angeles. He served as a Central and Eastern Europe/Eurasia analyst for *Freedom in the World.*

SHANNON O'TOOLE is an editor and writer at *Facts On File World News Digest,* where she covers Eastern Europe, Russia, and the Balkans. She is a contributor to Freedom House's Freedom of the Press report, as well as to the blog for *Steppe,* a magazine focused on the culture, history, and people of Central Asia. She received a bachelor's degree in history and anthropology from the University of Missouri, Columbia. She served as a Central and Eastern Europe/Eurasia analyst for *Freedom in the World.*

TOM PERRAULT is an associate professor in the Geography Department at the Maxwell School of Syracuse University. He has published on issues including energy resource conflicts, peasant mobilization, and social justice in Bolivia. In 2012, he was a visiting professor in the History Department at Universidad de los Andes, Bogotá, Colombia. He received a PhD in geography from the University of Colorado at Boulder, where he focused on agrarian change, political mobilization, and identity construction among Quichua of the Alto Napo in Ecuadorian Amazonia. He served as an Americas analyst for *Freedom in the World.*

ARCH PUDDINGTON is vice president for research at Freedom House and coeditor of *Freedom in the World.* He has written widely on American foreign policy, race relations, organized labor, and the history of the Cold War. He is the author of *Broadcasting Freedom: The Cold War Triumph of Radio Free Europe and Radio Liberty* and *Lane Kirkland: Champion of American Labor.* He received a bachelor's degree in English literature from the University of Missouri, Columbia. He served as an Americas analyst for *Freedom in the World.*

MARK Y. ROSENBERG is a senior Africa analyst at Eurasia Group, focusing on the Southern Africa region. Previously, he worked as a researcher at Freedom House and assistant editor of *Freedom in the World.* His opinion articles have appeared in the *New York Times,* the *Jerusalem Post,* and *Business Day* (South Africa), and his research has been cited by publications including the *Economist* and the *Financial Times.* He received a master's degree and a PhD in political science from the University of California, Berkeley, where he was a National Science Foundation Graduate Fellow. He served as a sub-Saharan Africa analyst for *Freedom in the World.*

TYLER ROYLANCE is a staff editor at Freedom House and is involved in a number of its publications. Previously, he worked as a senior editor for *Facts On File World News Digest.* He received a master's degree in history from New York University. He served as a Central and Eastern Europe/Eurasia analyst for *Freedom in the World.*

YVONNE SHEN is an editor for the *China Media Bulletin,* Freedom House's biweekly news digest of press freedom developments related to China. Previously, she was a research fellow at the Taiwan Foundation for Democracy in Taipei. She received a master's degree from New York University's Wagner School of Public Service. She served as an Asia-Pacific analyst for *Freedom in the World.*

NEELANJAN SIRCAR is a PhD candidate in political science at Columbia University. His research interests include Indian political economy and voter behavior. He received a bachelor's degree in applied mathematics and economics from the University of California, Berkeley. Next year, he will join the Center for the Advanced Study of India at the University of Pennsylvania as a post-doctoral fellow. He served as an Asia-Pacific analyst for *Freedom in the World.*

MIRA SUCHAROV is an associate professor of political science at Carleton University in Ottawa, Canada. She is the author of *The International Self: Psychoanalysis and the Search for Israeli-Palestinian Peace*, and has had articles published in *International Studies Perspectives*, the *Journal of International Relations and Development*, the *International Journal*, and the *Journal of Political Science Education*. She blogs at *Haaretz* and the Daily Beast's *Open Zion*. She received a master's degree in political science from the University of Toronto and a PhD in government from Georgetown University. She served as a Middle East and North Africa analyst for *Freedom in the World.*

FARHA TAHIR is program coordinator and research associate for the Center for Strategic and International Studies (CSIS) Africa Program, where she conducts research related to U.S. strategic priorities throughout the continent. She previously worked for the CSIS Program on Crisis, Conflict, and Cooperation and the CSIS Commission on Smart Power. She also provides economic analysis for Pragnya Group. She cofounded EDGE Project (now Tawi UW), an organization that creates and implements community development projects in Lingira, Uganda. She received a master's degree in international public affairs from the University of Wisconsin, Madison. She served as a sub-Saharan Africa analyst for *Freedom in the World.*

LEIGH TOMPPERT is an independent researcher in the area of gender, human rights, and development. She currently works with the UN Entity for Gender Equality and the Empowerment of Women as a program specialist in the Leadership and Governance Section. She previously coedited Freedom House's *Women's Rights in the Middle East and North Africa* publication. She received master's degrees in comparative and cross-cultural research methods from the University of Sussex and in the social sciences from the University of Chicago. She served as an Americas analyst for *Freedom in the World.*

SILVANA TOSKA is a PhD candidate in political science at Cornell University, focusing on the causes and spread of revolutions. She received master's degrees in African studies from Oxford University, where she wrote on the effects of foreign aid on ethnic conflict, and in Arab studies from Georgetown University. She served as a sub-Saharan Africa analyst for *Freedom in the World.*

JENNY TOWN is the assistant director of the U.S.-Korea Institute at Johns Hopkins University's School of Advanced International Studies. Previously, she worked for the Human Rights in North Korea Project at Freedom House. She received a master's degree from Columbia University's School of International and Public Affairs, with a concentration in human rights. She served as an Asia-Pacific analyst for *Freedom in the World.*

MAI TRUONG is a staff editor and Africa analyst for *Freedom on the Net*, Freedom House's annual assessment of internet and digital media freedom. Prior to joining Freedom House, her work experiences focused on international development, food security, and women's rights issues in sub-Saharan Africa. She received a master's degree in international relations from Yale University's Jackson Institute for Global Affairs. She served as a sub-Saharan Africa analyst for *Freedom in the World.*

NOAH TUCKER has worked both in the nonprofit sector and as a researcher on Central Asian religion, human rights, security, and conflict. He served as a U.S. embassy policy specialist for Kyrgyzstan in 2011 and returned to Central Asia for fieldwork most recently in the summer of 2012. He received a master's degree from Harvard University's Davis Center for Russian and Eurasian Studies. He served as a Central and Eastern Europe/Eurasia analyst for *Freedom in the World.*

VANESSA TUCKER is the director for analysis at Freedom House. Previously, she was the project director of *Countries at the Crossroads*, Freedom House's annual survey of democratic governance. Prior to joining Freedom House, she worked at the Harvard University Kennedy School's Women and Public Policy Program, at the Kennedy School's Program on Intrastate Conflict, and with the Carter Center's Democracy Program. She received a master's degree in international relations from Yale University. She served as a Middle East and North Africa analyst for *Freedom in the World.*

DARIA VAISMAN is a New York–based writer and producer. Her first book, a narrative nonfiction account of U.S. foreign policy in the former Soviet Union, will be published in 2014. She is also codirector of a documentary film on diplomatic recognition and sovereignty, currently in production. Previously, she was an analyst at Transparency International and deputy director of Eurasia Foundation in Tbilisi, Georgia, and a journalist covering the Caucasus and Central Asia. She received a master's degree from Columbia University's School of International and Public Affairs and is a PhD student in criminal justice at the Graduate Center, City University of New York. She served as a Central and Eastern Europe/Eurasia analyst for *Freedom in the World.*

CHRISTINE WADE is an associate professor of political science and international studies at Washington College, where she is also the curator of the Louis L. Goldstein Program in Public Affairs. She has authored and coauthored numerous publications on Central American politics. She received a PhD in political science from Boston University. She served as an Americas analyst for *Freedom in the World.*

JASON WARNER is a PhD candidate in African studies and government at Harvard University. He has worked or consulted for the UN Development Programme, the Nigerian Mission to the United Nations, and the U.S. Army. He has published on African affairs in outlets including CNN, the Council on Foreign Relations, and UN Dispatch, as well as various academic journals. He received master's degrees in government from Harvard University and in African studies from Yale University. He served as a sub-Saharan Africa analyst for *Freedom in the World*.

GREG WHITE is a professor of government and the faculty director of the Global Studies Center at Smith College. He is the author of *Climate Change and Migration: Borders and Security in a Warming World* and the recipient of a Mellon Foundation New Directions Fellowship, as well as Fulbright-IIE and Fulbright-Hays scholarships to Tunisia and Morocco, respectively. He received a PhD from the University of Wisconsin, Madison. He served as a Middle East and North Africa analyst for *Freedom in the World*.

ANNY WONG is an adjunct political scientist with the RAND Corporation and a research fellow with the John G. Tower Center for Political Studies at Southern Methodist University in Dallas, Texas. Her research covers science and technology policy, international development, army manpower, and U.S. relations with states in the Asia-Pacific region. She received a PhD in political science from the University of Hawaii, Manoa. She served as an Asia-Pacific analyst for *Freedom in the World*.

ELIZA B. YOUNG is an analyst for the International Rescue Committee's Emergency Preparedness and Response Unit in New York City. She previously worked as a research analyst at Freedom House. She received a master's degree in international relations from King's College London. She served as a Central and Eastern Europe/Eurasia and Western Europe analyst for *Freedom in the World*.

ACADEMIC ADVISERS

JAVIER CORRALES is a professor of political science at Amherst College.

ROBERT LANE GREENE is a Berlin-based correspondent for the *Economist*, and a former adjunct assistant professor of global affairs at New York University.

ROB JENKINS is a professor of political science at Hunter College and the Graduate Center, City University of New York, and a human rights research fellow at the Roosevelt House Public Policy Institute at Hunter College.

THOMAS R. LANSNER is visiting professor at the Sciences Po Paris School of International Affairs.

ADRIENNE LEBAS is an assistant professor of government at American University's School of Public Affairs.

CARL LEVAN is an assistant professor at American University's School of International Service.

PETER LEWIS is an associate professor and director of the African Studies Program at Johns Hopkins University's School of Advanced International Studies.

HÉCTOR LINDO-FUENTES is a professor of history at Fordham University.

ELLEN LUST is an associate professor of political science at Yale University.

PETER MANDAVILLE is a professor of government and politics and director of the Ali Vural Ak Center for Islamic Studies at George Mason University.

RAJAN MENON is the Anne and Bernard Spitzer Professor of Political Science, Department of Political Science, City College of New York/City University of New York.

JOHN S. MICGIEL is an adjunct professor of international affairs and executive director of the East Central European Center at Columbia University.

CARL MINZNER is an associate professor at Fordham Law School.

ALEXANDER J. MOTYL is a professor of political science at Rutgers University, Newark.

TSVETA PETROVA is a fellow at the Harriman Institute, Columbia University.

MARTIN SCHAIN is a professor of politics at New York University.

PETER SINNOTT is an independent scholar working on Central Asia issues.

SCOTT TAYLOR is an associate professor in the School of Foreign Service and director of the African Studies Program at Georgetown University.

BRIDGET WELSH is an associate professor of political science at Singapore Management University.

COLETTA A. YOUNGERS is an independent consultant specializing in human rights and democracy issues in Latin America and a senior fellow at the Washington Office on Latin America.

PRODUCTION TEAM

IDA WALKER, Proofreader

MARK WOLKENFELD, Production Coordinator

Selected Sources for
Freedom in the World 2013

PUBLICATIONS/BROADCASTS/BLOGS

38 North [North Korea], www.38north.org

ABC Color [Paraguay], www.abc.com.py

Africa Confidential, www.africa-confidential.com

Africa Daily, www.africadaily.com

Africa Energy Intelligence,
www.africaintelligence.com

AFRICAHOME dotcom, www.africahome.com

Africa News, www.africanews.com

AfricaOnline.com, www.africaonline.com

African Elections Database,
http://africanelections.tripod.com

Afrol News, www.afrol.com

Aftenposten [Norway], www.aftenposten.no

Agence France-Presse (AFP), www.afp.com

Al-Arab al-Yawm [Jordan]: www.alarabalyawm.net

Al-Arabiya, www.alarabiya.net

Al-Ahram, www.ahram.org.eg/

Al-Ahram Weekly [Egypt], www.weekly.ahram.org.eg

Al-Akhbar [Beirut], www.al-akhbar.com

Al-Dustour [Egypt], www.addustour.com/

Al-Hayat, www.alhayat.com/

Al-Jazeera, http://english.aljazeera.net

allAfrica.com, www.allafrica.com

Al-Masry al-Youm [Egypt], www.almasryalyoum.com/

Al-Ray Al-'am [Kuwait], www.alraialaam.com

Al-Raya [Qatar], www.raya.com

Al-Sharq al-Awsat,
www.asharqalawsat.com/english/

Al-Quds al-Arabi, www.alquds.co.uk

Al-Thawra [Yemen], www.althawra.gov.ye

Al-Watan [Qatar], www.al-watan.com

American Broadcasting Corporation News (ABC),
www.abcnews.go.com

American RadioWorks, www.americanpublic
media.publicradio.org

The Analyst [Liberia], www.analystliberia.com

Andorra Times, www.andorratimes.com

An-Nahar [Lebanon], www.annahar.com/http://
web.naharnet.com/default.asp

Annual Review of Population Law (Harvard Law
School), annualreview.law.harvard.edu

Arab Advisors Group, www.arabadvisors.com/

Arabianbusiness.com, www.arabianbusiness.com

Arabic Network for Human Rights Information
(ANHRI), www.anhri.net

Arab Media, http://arab-media.blogspot.com/

Arab News [Saudi Arabia], www.arabnews.com

Arab Reform Bulletin,
www.carnegieendowment.org/

Asharq Alawsat, www.asharqalawsat.com

Asia Sentinel, www.asiasentinel.com/

Asia Times, www.atimes.com

Asia-Pacific Journal, www.japanfocus.org

As-Safir [Lebanon], www.assafir.com

Associated Press (AP), www.ap.org

The Atlantic Monthly, www.theatlantic.com

Austrian Times, www.austriantimes.at

Australia Broadcasting Corporation News Online,
www.abc.net.au/news

The Australian, www.theaustralian.news.com.au

Awareness Times [Sierra Leone], www.news.sl

Bahrain Post, www.bahrainpost.com

Bahrain Tribune, www.bahraintribune.com

Balkan Insight, www.balkaninsight.com

The Baltic Times, www.baltictimes.com

Bangkok Post, www.bangkokpost.co.th

The Boston Globe, www.boston.com

British Broadcasting Corporation (BBC),
www.bbc.co.uk

BruDirect.com [Brunei], www.brudirect.com/

The Budapest Sun, www.budapestsun.com

Budapest Times, www.budapesttimes.hu/

Business Day [South Africa], www.bday.co.za

Cabinda.net, www.cabinda.net

Cable News Network (CNN), www.cnn.com

Cameroon Tribune, www.cameroon-tribune.cm

The Caribbean & Central America Report
(Intelligence Research Ltd.)

CBS News, www.cbsnews.com

The Central Asia-Caucasus Analyst (Johns
Hopkins University), www.cacianalyst.org

Central News Agency [Taiwan],
http://focustaiwan.tw/

The China Post, www.chinapost.com.tw

Chosun Ilbo [South Korea],
http://english.chosun.com/

The Christian Science Monitor, www.csmonitor.com

CIA World Factbook, www.cia.gov/cia/
publications/factbook

Civil Georgia, www.civil.ge

Congo Siasa, http://congosiasa.blogspot.co.uk/

The Contemporary Pacific, http://pidp.eastwest
center.org/pireport/tcp.htm

The Copenhagen Post [Denmark],
www.cphpost.dk

Corriere della Sera [Italy], www.corriere.it

Czech News Agency, www.ceskenoviny.cz/news/

Daily Excelsior [India-Kashmir],
www.dailyexcelsior.com

Daily NK [South Korea], www.dailynk.com
Daily Star [Bangladesh], www.dailystar.net
Daily Star [Lebanon], www.dailystar.com.lb
The Daily Times, www.dailytimes.bppmw.com/
Danas [Serbia], www.danas.rs/danasrs/
   naslovna.1.html
Dani [Bosnia-Herzegovina], www.bhdani.com
Dawn [Pakistan], www.dawn.com
Der Spiegel [Germany], www.spiegel.de
Der Standard [Austria], www.derstandard.at
Die Zeit [Germany], www.zeit.de
Deutsche Presse-Agentur [Germany], www.dpa.de
Deutsche Welle [Germany], www.dwelle.de
The East Africa Standard [Kenya],
   www.eastandard.net
East European Constitutional Review (New York
University), www.law.nyu.edu/eedr
East Timor Law Journal [East Timor],
   www.eastimorlawjournal.org/
The Economist, www.economist.com
The Economist Intelligence Unit reports,
   www.eiu.com/
EFE News Service [Spain], www.efenews.com
Election Watch, www.electionwatch.org
Election World, www.electionworld.org
El Mercurio [Chile], www.elmercurio.cl
El Nuevo Herald [United States],
   www.miami.com/mld/elnuevo
El Pais [Uruguay], www.elpais.com.uy
El Tiempo [Colombia], www.eltiempo.com
El Universal [Venezuela], www.eluniversal.com.ve
Epoch Times, www.theepochtimes.com/
Eurasia Review, www.eurasiareview.com/
Expreso [Peru], www.expreso.co.pe
Far Eastern Economic Review, www.feer.com
Federal Bureau of Investigation Hate Crime
   Statistics, www.fbi.gov/
   ucr/2003/03semimaps.pdf
Federated States of Micronesia Congress press
releases www.fsmcongress.fm/
Federated States of Micronesia Information
   Services, www.fsmpio.fm/
Fijilive, www.fijilive.com
FijiSUN, www.sun.com.fj
Fiji Times Online, www.fijitimes.com
Fiji Village, www.FijiVillage.com
The Financial Times, www.ft.com
Finnish News Agency, http://virtual.finland.fi/stt
Folha de Sao Paulo, www.folha.com.br
Foreign Affairs, www.foreignaffairs.org
Foreign Policy, www.foreignpolicy.com
France 24, www.france24.com
Frankfurter Allgemeine Zeitung [Germany],
   www.faz.net
The Friday Times [Pakistan], www.thefridaytimes.com
The Frontier Post [Pakistan], www.frontierpost.com
FrontPageAfrica [Liberia],
   www.frontpageafrica.com

Gazeta.ru [Russia], www.gazeta.ru
Global Insight, www.globalinsight.com/
Global News Wire, www.lexis-nexis.com
Globus [Croatia], www.globus.com.hr
The Guardian [Nigeria],
   www.ngrguardiannews.com
The Guardian [United Kingdom],
   www.guardian.co.uk
Gulf Daily News [Bahrain],
   www.gulf-daily-news.com
Gulf News Online [United Arab Emirates],
   www.gulf-news.com
Gulf Times [Qatar], www.gulf-times.com
Haaretz [Israel], www.haaretz.com
Hankyoreh Shinmun [South Korea],
   http://english.hani.co.kr/kisa/
Harakah Daily [Malaysia], http://
bm.harakahdaily.net/
Harper's Magazine, www.harpers.org
Haveeru Daily [Maldives], www.haveeru.com.mv
The Hindustan Times [India],
   www.hindustantimes.com
Hurriyet [Turkey], www.hurriyetdailynews.com
Iceland Review, www.icelandreview.com
The Independent [United Kingdom],
   www.independent.co.uk
Index on Censorship, www.indexoncensorship.org
India Today, www.india-today.com
The Indian Express, www.indian-express.com
Info Matin [Mali], www.info-matin.com
Insight Magazine, www.insightmag.com
Insight Namibia Magazine, www.insight.com.na
Integrated Regional Information Networks (IRIN),
   www.irinnews.org
Inter Press Service, www.ips.org
Interfax News Agency, www.interfax-news.com
International Herald Tribune, www.iht.com
IRIN news, www.irinnews.org/
Irish Independent,
   www.unison.ie/irish_independent
Irish Times, www.ireland.com
Islands Business Magazine,
   www.islandsbusiness.com
Izvestia, www.izvestia.ru
The Jakarta Globe,
   www.thejakartaglobe.com/home/
The Jakarta Post, www.thejakartapost.com/
Jamaica Gleaner, www.jamaica-gleaner.com/
Jawa Pos [Indonesia],
   www.jawapos.co.id/utama/
Jeune Afrique [France], www.jeuneafrique.com/
Johnson's Russia List,
   www.cdi.org/russia/johnson/
Joongang Ilbo [South Korea], http://joongang
   daily.joins.com/?cloc=home|top|jdaily
The Jordan Times, www.jordantimes.com
Journal of Democracy,
   www.journalofdemocracy.org

Jyllands-Posten [Denmark], www.jp.dk
The Kaselehlie Press [Micronesia],
  www.bild-art.de/kpress/
Kashmir Times [India-Kashmir],
  www.kashmirtimes.com
Kathmandu Post [Nepal],
  www.nepalnews.com.np/ktmpost.htm
Kedaulatan Rakyat [Indonesia],
  www.kedaulatan-rakyat.com/
Khaleej Times [United Arab Emirates],
  www.khaleejtimes.com
The Kiribati Independent,
  www.thekiribatiindependent.co.nz/
Kommersant [Russia], www.kommersant.ru
Kompas [Indonesia], www.kompas.com/
Korea Central News Agency [North Korea],
  www.kcna.co.jp/index-e.htm
Korea Economic Daily [South Korea],
  http://english.hankyung.com/
Korea Herald [South Korea],
  www.koreaherald.com/index.jsp
The Korea Times [South Korea],
  http://times.hankooki.com
Kuensel [Bhutan], www.kuenselonline.com
Kurier [Austria], www.kurier.at
Kuwait Post, www.kuwaitpost.com
L'Informazione di San Marino, www.libertas.sm/
  News_informazione/news_frameset.htm
La Jornada [Mexico], www.jornada.uam.nx
La Nacion [Argentina], www.lanacion.com.ar
La Repubblica [Italy], www.repubblica.it
La Semaine Africaine [Congo-Brazzaville],
  www.lasemaineafricaine.com/
La Tercera [Chile], www.tercera.cl
Lanka Monthly Digest [Sri Lanka],
  www.lanka.net/LMD
Latin American Regional Reports,
  www.latinnews.com
Latin American Weekly Reports,
  www.latinnews.com
Le Faso [Burkina Faso], www.lefaso.net
Le Figaro [France], www.lefigaro.fr
Le Messager [Cameroon], www.lemessager.net
Le Monde [France], www.lemonde.fr
Le Quotidien [Senegal], www.lequotidien.sn/
Le Temps [Switzerland], www.letemps.ch
Le Togolais [Togo], www.letogolais.com/
Lexis-Nexis, www.lexis-nexis.com
Liberia Media Center, www.lmcliberia.com/
The Local [Sweden], www.thelocal.se
L'Orient-Le Jour [Lebanon], www.lorientlejour.com
The Los Angeles Times, www.latimes.com
Mail & Guardian [South Africa], www.mg.co.za
Malaysiakini [Malaysia], www.malaysiakini.com/
The Manila Times, www.manilatimes.net/
Marianas Business Journal, www.mbjguam.net/
Marianas Variety [Micronesia],
  www.mvariety.com

Marlborough Express [New Zealand],
  www.stuff.co.nz/marlborough-express
Marshall Islands government press releases,
  www.rmigovernment.org/index.jsp
Matangi Tonga Magazine, www.matangitonga.to
The Messenger [Georgia], www.messenger.com.ge
The Miami Herald,
  www.miami.com/mld/miamiherald
Middle East Desk, www.middleeastdesk.org
Middle East Online, www.middle-east-online.com
Middle East Report, www.merip.org
Minivan News [Maldives], www.minivannews.com
Mirianas Variety [Micronesia], www.mvariety.com
Misr Digital, http://misrdigital.blogspirit.com/
Moldova Azi, www.azi.md
Mongolia Focus, http://blogs.ubc.ca/mongolia/
The Mongolist, www.themongolist.com/
Mopheme News [Lesotho],
  www.lesoff.co.za/news
Mother Jones, www.motherjones.com
The Moscow Times, www.themoscowtimes.com
Munhwa Ilbo [South Korea], www.munhwa.com
Nacional [Croatia], www.nacional.hr
The Namibian, www.namibian.com.na/
The Nation, www.thenation.org
The Nation [Thailand],
  www.nationmultimedia.com
The Nation Online [Malawi],
  www.nationmalawi.com
The National [Papua New Guinea],
  www.thenational.com.pg
The National [UAE], www.thenational.ae
National Business Review [New Zealand],
  www.nbr.co.nz
National Public Radio (NPR), www.npr.org
National Review, www.nationalreview.com
Neue Zurcher Zeitung [Switzerland], www.nzz.ch
The New Dawn [Liberia],
  www.thenewdawnliberia.com/
The New Democrat Online [Liberia],
  www.newdemocratnews.com
New Mandala,
  http://asiapacific.anu.edu.au/newmandala/
The New York Times, www.nytimes.com
The New Yorker, www.newyorker.com
The New Zealand Herald, www.nzherald.co.nz
New Zealand government press releases,
  www.beehive.govt.nz/
News Agency of the Slovak Republic,
  www.tasr.sk/30.axd?lang=1033
Nezavisimaya Gazeta [Russia], www.ng.ru
NIN [Serbia], www.nin.co.rs/
Nine O'Clock [Romania], www.nineoclock.ro
NiuFM News [New Zealand], www.niufm.com/
North Korea Economy Watch,
  www.nkeconwatch.com
Noticias [Argentina],
  www.noticias.uolsinectis.com.ar

Notimex [Mexico], www.notimex.com
Novi Reporter [Bosnia-Herzegovina], www.novireporter.com
Nyasa Times [Malawi], www.nyasatimes.com
The Observer [Liberia], www.liberianobserver.com
O Estado de Sao Paulo, www.estado.com.br
O Globo [Brazil], www.oglobo.globo.com
OFFnews [Argentina], www.offnews.info
Oman Arabic Daily, www.omandaily.com
Oman Daily Observer, www.omanobserver.com
Oslobodjenje [Bosnia-Herzegovina], www.oslobodjenje.com.ba
Outlook [India], www.outlookindia.com
Pacific Business News, http://pacific.bizjournals.com/pacific/
Pacific Daily News, www.guampdn.com/
Pacific Islands Report, http://pidp.eastwestcenter.org/pireport
Pacific Magazine, www.pacificmagazine.net
Pacific Scoop [New Zealand], http://pacific.scoop.co.nz
Pagina/12 [Argentina], www.pagina12.com.ar
PANAPRESS, www.panapress.com
Papua New Guinea Post-Courier, www.postcourier.com.pg
The Perspective Newspaper [Liberia], www.perspective.org
The Philippine Daily Inquirer, www.inquirer.net/
Phnom Penh Post, www.phnompenhpost.com
The Pioneer [India], www.dailypioneer.com
Planet Tonga, www.planet-tonga.com
Political Handbook of the World, http://phw.binghamton.edu
Politics.hu [Hungary], www.politics.hu/
Politika [Serbia], www.politika.rs/
Port Vila Presse [Vanuatu], www.news.vu/en/
The Post [Zambia], www.zamnet.zm/zamnet/post/post.html
The Prague Post, www.praguepost.com
Radio and Television Hong Kong, www.rthk.org.hk
Radio Australia, www.abc.net.au/ra
Radio France Internationale, www.rfi.fr
Radio Free Europe-Radio Liberty, www.rferl.org
Radio Lesotho, www.lesotho.gov.ls/radio/radiolesotho
Radio Okapi [Congo-Kinshasa], www.radioOkapi.net
Radio New Zealand International, www.rnzi.com
Republika [Indonesia], www.republika.co.id/
Reuters, www.reuters.com
Ritzau [Denmark], www.ritzau.dk
Rodong Sinmun [North Korea], www.rodong.rep.kp
Royal African Society's African Arguments, http://africanarguments.org/
Sahel Blog, http://sahelblog.wordpress.com/

Saipan Tribune, www.saipantribune.com
The Samoa News, www.samoanews.com
Samoa Observer, www.samoaobserver.ws/
San Marino Notizie, www.sanmarinonotizie.com/
Savali Press [Samoa], www.savalipress.com
Semana [Colombia], www.semana.com
The Sierra Leone News, www.thesierraleonenews.com
Slobodna Bosna [Bosnia-Herzegovina], www.slobodna-bosna.ba
The Slovak Spectator, www.slovakspectator.sk
Slovak News Agency, www.sita.sk/eng/services/online/en/content.php
SME [Slovakia], www.sme.sk/
Sofia Echo, www.sofiaecho.com
Solomon Islands Broadcasting Corporation, www.sibconline.com.sb
Solomon Star, www.solomonstarnews.com
The Somaliland Times, www.somalilandtimes.net
South Asia Tribune [Pakistan], www.satribune.com
South China Morning Post [Hong Kong], www.scmp.com
Star Radio News [Liberia], www.starradio.org.lr
The Statesman [India], www.thestatesman.net
Straits Times [Singapore], www.straitstimes.asia1.com.sg
Sub-Saharan Informer, www.ssinformer.com/
Suddeutsche Zeitung [Germany], www.sueddeutsche.de
Tageblatt [Luxembourg], www.tageblatt.lu
Tahiti Presse, www.tahitipresse.pf
Taipei Times, www.taipeitimes.com
Talamua [Samoa], www.talamua.com
Tamilnet.com, www.tamilnet.com
Tax-News.com, www.tax-news.com
Téla Nón Diário de São Tomé e Príncipe, www.telanon.info/
The Telegraph [United Kingdom], www.telegraph.co.uk
Tempo [Indonesia], www.tempointeraktif.com/
Texas in Africa, http://texasinafrica.blogspot.co.uk/
This Day [Nigeria], www.thisdayonline.com
The Tico Times [Costa Rica], www.ticotimes.net
Time, www.time.com
The Times of Central Asia, www.times.kg
The Times of India, www.timesofindia.net
Times of Zambia, www.times.co.zm/
Today's Zaman [Turkey], www.todayszaman.com
TomPaine.com, www.TomPaine.com
Tonga USA Today, www.tongausatoday.com
Tongan Broadcasting Commission, http://tonga-broadcasting.com/
Transcaucasus: A Chronology, www.anca.org/resource_center/transcaucasus.php
Trinidad Express, www.trinidadexpress.com/

Tuvalu News, www.tuvalu-news.tv/
Union Patriótica de Cuba (UNPACU),
www.unpacu.org/acerca-de/sobre-unpacu/
University World News,
www.universityworldnews.com/
U.S. News and World Report, www.usnews.com
U.S. State Department Country Reports on Human
Rights Practices, www.state.gov/g/drl/rls/hrrpt
U.S. State Department Country Reports on Hu-
man Trafficking Reports, www.state.gov/g/tip
U.S. State Department International Religious
Freedom Reports, www.state.gov/g/drl/irf
The Vanguard [Nigeria], www.vanguardngr.com
Vanuatu Daily Post, www.vanuatudaily.com
Venpres [Venezuela], www.venpres.gov.ve
Voice of America, www.voa.gov
Waikato Times [New Zealand],
www.stuff.co.nz/waikato-times
The Wall Street Journal, www.wsj.com
The Washington Post, www.washingtonpost.com
The Washington Times,
www.washingtontimes.com
The Weekly Standard, www.weeklystandard.com
West African Democracy Radio, http://wadr.org/
World of Information Country Reports,
www.worldinformation.com
World News, www.wn.com
Xinhua News, www.xinhuanet.com
Yap State Government press release,
www.yapstategov.org/
Yedioth Ahronoth [Israel], www.ynetnews.com
Yemen Observer, www.yobserver.com
Yemen Times, www.yementimes.com
Yokwe Online [Marshall Islands], www.yokwe.net
Yonhap News Agency [South Korea],
www.yonhapnews.co.kr
Zawya, www.Zawya.com

ORGANIZATIONS

ActionAid Australia, www.actionaid.org.au/
Afghan Independent Human Rights Commission,
www.aihrc.org.af
Afghanistan Research and Evaluation Unit,
www.areu.org.pk
African Elections Project [Liberia],
www.africanelections.org/liberia/
African Health Observatory (WHO),
www.aho.afro.who.int/
Afrobarometer, www.afrobarometer.org
The Alliance of Independent Journalists
[Indonesia], www.ajiindonesia.org/index.php
Alternative ASEAN Network on Burma,
www.altsean.org/
American Bar Association Rule of Law Initiative,
www.abanet.org/rol/
American Committee for Peace in the Caucasus,
www.peaceinthecaucasus.org
American Civil Liberties Union, www.aclu.org

Amnesty International, www.amnesty.org
Annan Plan for Cyprus, www.cyprus-un-plan.org
Anti-Slavery International, www.antislavery.org
Asan Institute for Policy Studies,
www.asaninst.org/eng/
Asia Foundation, http://asiafoundation.org/
Asian Center for Human Rights [India],
www.achrweb.org
Asian Human Rights Commission [Hong Kong],
www.ahrchk.net
Asian Philanthropy Forum,
www.asianphilanthropyforum.org
Assistance Association for Political Prisoners
[Burma], www.aappb.org/
Australian Department of Education, Employment
and Workplace Relations, www.deewr.gov.au/
Pages/default.aspx
Balkan Human Rights Web, www.greekhelsinki.gr
Bangladesh Center for Development, Journalism,
and Communication, www.bcjdc.org
Belarusian Institute for Strategic Studies,
www.belinstitute.eu
British Helsinki Human Rights Group,
www.oscewatch.org/default.asp
Brookings Institution, www.brookings.edu
B'Tselem—The Israeli Information Center for
Human Rights in the Occupied Territories,
www.btselem.org
Cabindese Government in Exile, www.cabinda.org
Cairo Institute for Human Rights, www.cihrs.org
Cambridge International Reference on Current
Affairs, www.circaworld.com
Canadian Department of Foreign Affairs and
International Trade, www.dfait-maeci.gc.ca
Carnegie Endowment for International Peace,
www.carnegieendowment.org
The Carter Center, www.cartercenter.org
Center for Strategic and International Studies,
www.csis.org
The Centre for International Governance, http://
www.cigionline.org/
Centre for Monitoring Electoral Violence [Sri
Lanka], www.cpalanka.org/cmev.html
Centre for Policy Alternatives [Sri Lanka],
www.cpalanka.org
Centre for the Study of Violence and
Reconciliation, www.csvr.org.za
Chad/Cameroon Development Project,
www.essochad.com
Charter '97 [Belarus], www.charter97.org
Chatham House [United Kingdom],
www.chathamhouse.org.uk
Child Rights Information Network,
www.crin.org/resources/infodetailasp?ID=22188
The Committee for Human Rights in North Korea,
www.hrnk.org
Committee for the Prevention of Torture,
www.cpt.coe.int

Committee to Protect Journalists, www.cpj.org

Coordinating Ministry of Economic Affairs [Indonesia], www.ekon.go.id/

Council of Europe, www.coe.int

Council on Foreign Relations, www.cfr.org/index.html

The Danish Institute for Human Rights, www.humanrights.dk

Danish Ministry of Foreign Affairs, the Global Advice Network, www.business-anti-corruption.com

Ditshwanelo – The Botswana Centre for Human Rights, www.ditshwanelo.org.bw

Earth Institute Advisory Group for Sao Tome and Principe, www.earthinstitute.columbia.edu

East Asia Institute, www.eai.or.kr/english

Election Commission of India, www.eci.gov.in

Electoral Institute of Southern Africa, www.eisa.org.za

Electronic Iraq, www.electroniciraq.net

Eurasia Group, www.eurasiagroup.net

European Bank for Reconstruction and Development, www.ebrd.org

European Commission Against Racism and Intolerance, www.ecri.coe.int

European Institute for the Media, www.eim.org

European Roma Rights Center, www.errc.org/

European Union, www.europa.eu.int

European Union Agency for Fundamental Rights, http://fra.europa.eu

Executive Mansion of Liberia, www.emansion.gov.lr

Extractive Industries Transparency Initiative, www.eitransparency.org

Federal Chancellery of Austria, www.bka.gv.at

Forum 18, www.forum18.org

Forum for Human Dignity [Sri Lanka], www.fhd.8m.net

Forum of Federations/Forum des Federations, www.forumfed.org

Friends of Niger, www.friendsofniger.org

Global Integrity, www.globalintegrity.org

Global Policy Forum, www.globalpolicy.org

Global Rights, www.globalrights.org

Global Witness, www.globalwitness.org

Globe International [Mongolia], www.globeinter.org.mn/old/en/index.php

Government of Botswana Website, www.gov.bw

Government of Mauritania Website, www.mauritania.mr

Government of Sierra Leone State House, www.statehouse.gov.sl

Habitat International Coalition, http://home.mweb.co.za/hi/hic/

Heritage Foundation, www.heritage.org

Hong Kong Human Rights Monitor, www.hkhrm.org.hk

Human Rights Center of Azerbaijan, http://mitglied.lycos.de/hrca

Human Rights Commission of Pakistan, www.hrcp-web.org

Human Rights Commission of Sierra Leone, www.humanrightssl.org

Human Rights First, www.humanrightsfirst.org

Human Rights Watch, www.hrw.org

Hyundai Research Institute, www.hri.co.kr

Indolaw [Indonesia], www.indolaw.com.au/

Indonesian Institute of Sciences, www.lipi.go.id/

Indonesian Survey Institute, www.lsi.or.id/

INFORM (Sri Lanka Information Monitor)

Institute for Democracy in Eastern Europe, www.idee.org

Institute for Democracy in South Africa, www.idasa.org.za

Institute for Far Eastern Studies, www.isn.ethz.ch/Digital-Library/Organizations/Detail//?id=48861

Institute for Security Studies, www.iss.co.za

Institute for War and Peace Reporting, www.iwpr.net

Inter-American Dialogue, www.thedialogue.org

Inter-American Press Association, www.sipiapa.com

Internal Displacement Monitoring Center, www.internal-displacement.org/

International Alert, www.international-alert.org

International Bar Association, www.ibanet.org

International Campaign for Tibet, www.savetibet.org

International Centre for Ethnic Studies, www.icescolombo.org

The International Centre for Not-for-Profit Law: NGO Law Monitor, www.icnl.org/

International Commission of Jurists, www.icj.org

International Confederation of Free Trade Unions, www.icftu.org

International Crisis Group, www.crisisweb.org

International Federation of Journalists, www.ifj.org

International Foundation for Electoral Systems, www.ifes.org

International Freedom of Expression Exchange, www.ifex.org

International Helsinki Federation for Human Rights, www.ihf-hr.org

International Institute for Democracy and Electoral Assistance, www.idea.int

International Labour Organization, www.ilo.org

International Legal Assistance Consortium, www.ilacinternational.org

International Lesbian and Gay Association, www.ilga.org

International Monetary Fund, www.imf.org

International Network for Higher Education in Africa, www.bc.edu/bc_org/avp/soe/cihe/inhea/

International Organization for Migration, www.iom.int

International Press Institute, www.freemedia.at

International Republican Institute, www.iri.org

International Society For Fair Elections And Democracy [Georgia], www.isfed.ge

Jamestown Foundation, www.jamestown.org

Kashmir Study Group, www.kashmirstudygroup.net

Korea Development Institute, www.kdi.re.kr

Korea Institute for National Unification, www.kinu.or.kr

Kyrgyz Committee for Human Rights, www.kchr.elcat.kg

Legislature of Liberia, http://legislature.gov.lr/

Liberia Institute of Statistics and Geo-Information Services, www.lisgis.org/nada

Liberia Media Center, www.lmcliberia.com/

Macedonian Information Agency, www.mia.mk

MADA—Palestinian Center for Development and Media Freedoms, www.madacenter.org/index.php?lang=1

The Malawi Human Rights Commission, www.malawihumanrightscommission.org/

Malta Data, www.maltadata.com

Media Institute of Southern Africa, www.misa.org

Media Rights Agenda [Nigeria], www.mediarightsagenda.org

Migrant Assistance Programme Thailand, www.mapfoundationcm.org/eng/top/index.html

Millennium Challenge Corporation, www.mcc.gov MONUC, http://monuc.unmissions.org/

National Anti-Corruption Network [Burkina Faso], www.renlac.org

National Committee on North Korea, www.ncnk.org

National Democratic Institute for International Affairs, www.ndi.org

National Elections Commission of Liberia, www.necliberia.org

National Elections Commission of Sierra Leone, www.nec-sierraleone.org

National Endowment for Democracy, www.ned.org

National Human Rights Commission [India], www.nhrc.nic.in

National Human Rights Commission of Korea, www.humanrights.go.kr

National Organization for Human Rights in Syria, www.nohr-s.org

National Peace Council of Sri Lanka, www.peace-srilanka.org

National Society for Human Rights [Namibia], www.nshr.org.na

Nicaragua Network, www.nicanet.org

Observatory for the Protection of Human Rights Defenders, www.omct.org

Odhikar [Bangladesh], www.odhikar.org

Office of the High Representative in Bosnia and Herzegovina, www.ohr.int

Open Government Partnership, www.opengovpartnership.org/

Open Society Institute, www.soros.org

Organization for Economic Cooperation and Development, www.oecd.org

Organization for Security and Cooperation in Europe, www.osce.org

Oxford Analytica, www.oxan.com/

Pacific Islands Forum Secretariat, www.forumsec.org

Pacific Media Watch, www.pmw.c20.org

Parliament of Kiribati, www.tskl.net.ki/parliament/index.html

People's Forum for Human Rights [Bhutan]

Population Reference Bureau, www.prb.org

Portal for Parliamentary Development, www.agora-parl.org/

Publish What You Pay Campaign, www.publishwhatyoupay.org

Refugees International, www.refugeesinternational.org

Reliefweb, http://reliefweb.int/

Reporters Sans Frontieres, www.rsf.org

Republic of Angola, www.angola.org

Royal Institute of International Affairs, www.riia.org

Samsung Economic Research Institute, www.seriworld.org

Save the Children, www.savethechildren.org

Shan Women's Action Network, www.shanwomen.org

Sierra Leone Legal Information Institute, www.sierralii.org/

South African Human Rights Commission, www.sahrc.org.za

South African Press Association, www.sapa.org.za

South Asia Analysis Group [India], www.saag.org

South Asia Terrorism Portal [India], www.satp.org

South East Europe Media Organisation, http://seemo.org/

Southern African Development Community, www.sadc.int/

The Special Court for Sierra Leone, www.sc-sl.org

State House of Sierra Leone, www.statehouse.gov.sl/

Sweden.se, www.sweden.se

Syria Comment, www.joshualandis.com

Tibet Information Network, www.tibetinfo.net

Transitions Online, www.tol.cz

Transparency International, www.transparency.org

Truth and Reconciliation Commission of Liberia, www.trcofliberia.org

Turkish Ministry of Foreign Affairs, www.mfa.gov.tr

United Nations Development Program, www.undp.org

United Nations High Commissioner for Refugees, www.unhcr.org

United Nations High Commissioner on Human Rights, www.unhchr.ch

United Nations Integrated Peacebuilding Office in Sierra Leone (UNIPSIL), http://unipsil.unmissions.org/

United Nations Interim Mission in Kosovo, www.unmikonline.org

United Nations Mission in Liberia (UNMIL), www.unmil.org

United Nations Office for the Coordination of Humanitarian Affairs (OCHA), http://unocha.org/

United Nations Population Division, www.un.org/esa/population

United Nations Security Council, www.un.org

United States Agency for International Development, www.usaid.org

United States Department of the Interior, www.doi.gov/oia/index.cfm

United States Department of State, www.state.gov

University Teachers for Human Rights-Jaffna, www.uthr.org

The U.S.-Korea Institute at SAIS, www.uskoreainstitute.org

Washington Office on Latin America, www.wola.org

The World Bank, www.worldbank.org

World Markets Research Centre, www.wmrc.com

World Press Freedom Committee, www.wpfc.org